EUROPE

EYEWITNESS TRAVEL

EUROPE

LONDON, NEW YORK,
MELBOURNE, MUNICH AND DELHI
www.dk.com

Project Editor Ferdie McDonald, Claire Marsden

Art Editor Paul Jackson

Editors Sam Atkinson, Simon Hall, Andrew Szudek

Designers Anthony Limerick, Sue Metcalfe-Megginson, Rebecca Milner

Picture Researchers Katherine Mesquita, Alex Pepper, Lily Sellar

Map Coordinator Casper Morris

DTP Designer Maite Lantaron

Maps Ben Bowles, Rob Clynes, James Macdonald (Colourmap Scanning Ltd)

Photographers Max Alexander, Demetrio Carrasco, Kim Sayer, Linda Whitwam

Printed and bound by South China Printing Co. Ltd., China

First American Edition, 2001

14 15 16 17 10 9 8 7 6 5 4 3 2 1

Published in the United States by DK Publishing,
345 Hudson Street, New York, NY 10014

Reprinted with revisions 2002, 2003, 2004, 2006, 2008, 2010, 2012, 2015
Copyright © 2001, 2015 Dorling Kindersley Limited, London

Published in Great Britain by Dorling Kindersley Limited.
A Penguin Random House Company

A Catalog Record for this book is available
from the library of congress.

ISSN 1542-1554
ISBN 978-1-4654-1214-0

Floors are referred to throughout in accordance with European usage;
ie the "first floor" is the floor above ground level.

MIX
Paper from
responsible sources
FSC™ C018179
www.fsc.org

Front cover main image: Neuschwanstein Castle surrounded by glorious mountains and
overlooking the Alpsee, Bavaria, Germany *(see p527)*

 View of Santa Maddalena in Val di Funes at the foot of the Odle range, Italy

The tholos beside the Sanctuary of Athena
Pronaia at Ancient Delphi, Greece *(see p485)*

Contents

Statue of woman praying beside tomb of
Carlos I in Sao Vicente de Fora, Portugal

The historic center of Graz, overlooked by the thickly-wooded Schlossberg, Austria *(see p600)*

The Baroque church of Santa Maria della Salute, Venice, Italy *(see p440)*

The spectacular Mont-St-Michel, France *(see pp174–5)*

HOW TO USE THIS GUIDE

This Dorling Kindersley travel guide helps you to get the most from your visit to Europe. *Visiting Europe* maps the continent, and gives tips on practical considerations and travel. *Europe at a Glance* gives an overview of some of the main attractions and a brief history. The book is divided into seven sections, each covering a group of two, three, or four countries. The chapter on each country starts with a historical portrait and a map of the country. The main sightseeing section then follows, with maps of the major cities. For each country, there is a section of practical and travel information, followed by listings of recommended hotels and restaurants.

Europe Map

The colored areas shown on the map on the inside front cover indicate the 19 country chapters in this guide.

1 At a Glance
The map here highlights the most interesting cities, towns, and regions in the countries covered in the section (in this example Italy and Greece).

Each country chapter has color-coded thumb tabs.

2 Introduction to a Country
This section gives the reader an insight into the country's geography, historical background, politics, and the character of the people. A chart lists the key dates and events in the country's history.

3 Country Map
For easy reference, sights in each country are numbered and plotted on a map. The black bullet numbers (e.g. ❸) also indicate the order in which the sights are covered in the chapter.

Sights at a Glance lists the numbered sights in alphabetical order.

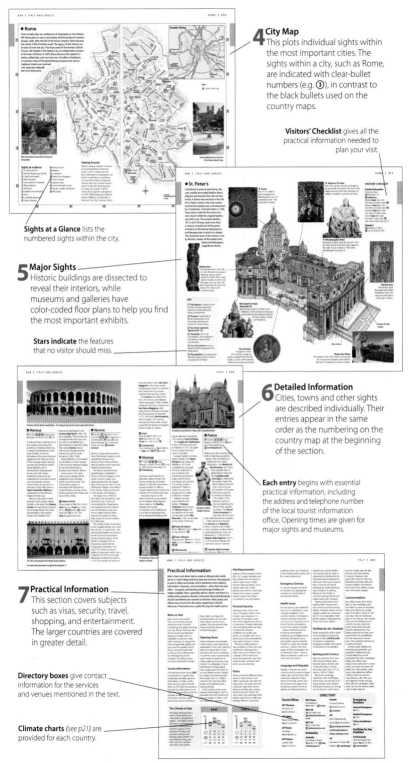

4 City Map
This plots individual sights within the most important cities. The sights within a city, such as Rome, are indicated with clear-bullet numbers (e.g. ③), in contrast to the black bullets used on the country maps.

Visitors' Checklist gives all the practical information needed to plan your visit.

Sights at a Glance lists the numbered sights within the city.

5 Major Sights
Historic buildings are dissected to reveal their interiors, while museums and galleries have color-coded floor plans to help you find the most important exhibits.

Stars indicate the features that no visitor should miss.

6 Detailed Information
Cities, towns and other sights are described individually. Their entries appear in the same order as the numbering on the country map at the beginning of the section.

Each entry begins with essential practical information, including the address and telephone number of the local tourist information office. Opening times are given for major sights and museums.

7 Practical Information
This section covers subjects such as visas, security, travel, shopping, and entertainment. The larger countries are covered in greater detail.

Directory boxes give contact information for the services and venues mentioned in the text.

Climate charts (see p21) are provided for each country.

VISITING
EUROPE

DISCOVERING EUROPE

The great cities of Europe are the key to discovering the countries in which they sit. In each, the visitor will get a real flavor of the history, culture, character, and, of course, cuisine of the nation – an ideal introduction for those on a short break. For visitors with more time available, these cities provide a perfect base for exploring farther afield. For anyone keen to tour more of the continent in a single trip, they are the hubs around which national and international travel revolves, with excellent rail, road, and air links. Each of the following 14 itineraries offers a two-day exploration of one of Europe's most beguiling cities, covering the must-visit sights. From vibrant Barcelona to elegant Stockholm, from romantic Paris to revitalized Berlin, there is something for everyone.

The Great Cities of Europe

- Enjoy delightful canalside walks in leafy **Amsterdam**.
- Reminders of seven millennia of history are all around **Athens**.
- **Barcelona** boasts Modernista buildings and medieval history.
- Modern **Berlin** is steeped in history, including relics of a tumultuous 20th century.
- **Dublin** provides art and culture, plus great Guinness.

- In **London**, royal heritage and history mingle with lively contemporary culture.
- Tapas, flamenco, and great museums: **Madrid** has the lot.
- Explore **Munich**'s architecture and art, and enjoy a stein or two.
- View the streets of **Paris** from on high, atop the Eiffel Tower.
- **Prague** is full of historic and cultural treasures waiting to be

discovered, as well as many architectural delights.
- **Rome** has ancient ruins, great art, and a lively café culture.
- **Stockholm** is a culture-packed city in a lovely lakeside setting.
- Exquisite **Venice** is a city that seems to rise out of the water.
- Get a bird's-eye view of the grand boulevards of **Vienna** from its iconic Ferris wheel.

Two days in Amsterdam

- Discover Amsterdam's distinguished history at the **Koninklijk Paleis**
- Stroll along the canals of the delightful **Grachtengordel**
- Be moved by the **Anne Frank House**

Day 1
Morning Start the day at the **Dam**, a busy square in the city center that is famous for its buildings and frequent events. Dodging the trams, proceed to the **Nieuwe Kerk** (p244), one of Amsterdam's most impressive Gothic buildings. Afterward, pop next door to explore the **Koninklijk Paleis** (p244). This royal palace was built in the 17th century, when the city was at its richest, as the town hall. Inside, the highlight is a magnificent marble chamber, the Citizens' Hall.

Afternoon Take a stroll along the Singel, the first of the four canals that make up the **Grachtengordel** (p246), or "girdle of canals". This is Amsterdam at its most beguiling, its olive-green canals spanned by hump-backed bridges. Don't miss the interesting exhibition at **Het Grachtenhuis** (p246) the **Westerkerk** (p246), with its mighty spire. Next, head for the **Anne Frank House** (p245), where the teenage Jewish diarist hid from the Nazis during World War II.

Day 2
Morning Spend a couple of hours at the **Rijksmuseum** (pp248–50), Amsterdam's principal art museum, admiring its fabulous collection of Dutch paintings, especially the Rembrandts. Afterward, visit the **Van Gogh Museum** (p251), which is devoted to arguably the greatest of all Dutch painters and contains a remarkable collection of his work.

Crowds of people in bustling Dam Square, Amsterdam

Afternoon After lunch, visit the city's third major museum, the **Stedelijk Museum** (p251), a gallery devoted to modern and contemporary art. Alternatively, if museum fatigue is setting in, venture out from the tourist zone to explore the maze-like streets of the **Jordaan** (p246) or rest your legs on a relaxing **canal tour** by boat (p259).

Two days in Athens

- Explore the **Parthenon** and other magnificent ruins of Ancient Greece
- Get lost among the flea markets and antiques stalls of **Monastiraki** and **Plaka**
- Admire exquisite works of art and craftsmanship at the **Museum of Cycladic Art** and the renowned **National Archaeological Museum**

Day 1
Morning Start early to beat the worst of the crowds. Wander through the ruins of the **Ancient Agora** (p453). Visit the museum in the **Stoa of Attalos**, which displays items unearthed during excavations, then make your way up to the **Acropolis** (pp454–6) and spend the rest of the morning admiring the **Parthenon** (p456) and visiting the **New Acropolis Museum** (p456).

Afternoon Make your way, via the **Tower of the Winds** (p453) in the Roman Agora, down to bustling **Plaka** (p453) for a late lunch of mezes. Spend the afternoon browsing Plaka's quirky crafts and antiques shops, then head over to the **Temple of Olympian Zeus** (p457) for dramatic sunset views of the Acropolis through Hadrian's Arch (entry is included in the price of your Acropolis ticket).

Day 2
Morning Devote part of the morning to the amazing flea market and stores of lively **Monastiraki** (p452). Pick up a selection of delicious freshly made savories and cakes from one of the many bakeries here, then pause for a picnic lunch in the shaded oasis of the National Gardens on your way to the **National Gallery of Art** (p457).

Afternoon Having admired the fine collection of Greek and other European art in the National Gallery, move on to the nearby **Museum of Cycladic Art** (p457), with its exquisite works of ancient art, and the fascinating **Benáki Museum** (p457), housed in a beautiful mansion. Alternatively, catch a bus across town to the vast **National Archaeological Museum** (p452), whose spectacular collections include many rare and unique exhibits.

Chimneys on the roof of the Gaudí-designed La Pedrera, Barcelona

Two days in Barcelona

- Admire Antoni Gaudí's unfinished masterpiece, the **Sagrada Família**
- Get lost in the medieval warren of the **Barri Gòtic** (Gothic Quarter)
- Tuck into authentic paella by the beach

Day 1
Morning Explore one of the largest and best-preserved medieval neighborhoods in Europe, the **Barri Gòtic** (pp298–9). Admire the stunning **Cathedral** (p299), particularly the enchanting cloister, and visit the remnants of the ancient Roman settlement in the **Museu d'Història de la Ciutat** (p299). Have lunch in one of the area's many restaurants and cafés.

Afternoon Stroll down **Las Ramblas** (p300), then make your way along the harbor to fascinating **Montjuïc** (p304) for spectacular city views and for the vibrant surrealist art on show at the **Fundació Joan Miró** (p304). Finish the day with paella on the seafront.

Day 2
Morning Head to the Eixample district, home to Antoni Gaudí's extraordinary **Sagrada Família** (pp302–3), its towers visible across the city, yet still awaiting completion. You'll want to

spend the whole morning discovering the basilica's many delights. This district has countless excellent restaurants and tapas bars to choose from for both lunch and dinner.

Afternoon Wander along the **Passeig de Gràcia** (p301), Barcelona's most fashionable street and the heart of the city's Quadrat d'Or ("golden square"), perhaps doing a bit of shopping at one of the chic boutiques here. This street is home to two of Gaudí's most spectacular domestic buildings: **La Pedrera** and **Casa Batlló** (p301). Both are open to visitors, or you could just admire their stunning facades.

Two days in Berlin

- Stroll down beautiful **Unter den Linden**, pausing for a spot of café culture on the way
- Reflect on Berlin's tumultuous recent past at **Checkpoint Charlie** and the **Kaiser-Wilhelm-Gedächtniskirche**
- Explore the **Kulturforum** or **Museum Island** for breathtaking art and other treasures

Day 1
Morning Start at the icons of a reunified Germany: climb up inside the glass dome of the **Reichstag** (p502), then circuit the mighty **Brandenburg Gate** (p502). Beyond it is **Unter den Linden** (p502), the leafy

promenade that reveals the swagger of 19th-century Prussia through monuments like the **Neue Wache** and the Baroque **Zeughaus** (p502). There are plenty of places here to pause for lunch, from charming cafés to jovial beer gardens.

Afternoon The handsome **Schlossbrücke** bridge hints at the cultural feast to be found on **Museum Island** (p500). With its remarkable collection of antiquities, the **Pergamon-museum** (p504) certainly deserves a visit. Afterward, stop in at the **Berliner Dom** (pp506–7), then take a quiet stroll into picturesque **Nikolaiviertel** (p505) to get a sense of Berlin's medieval roots.

Day 2
Morning After exploring Berlin's historic core, the focus shifts to more recent history. **Checkpoint Charlie** (p508), the East–West border immortalized by many Cold War thrillers, is an essential stop. The darkest period in German history is chillingly laid bare in the **Jüdisches Museum** (p508), while the wave-like **Holocaust Denkmal** (p503) represents the scale of the Jewish tragedy in stark sculptural form.

Afternoon After lunch in one of the several cafés in the **Tiergarten** (p503), enjoy a bucolic stroll there. Afterward, pore over the Old Masters in the **Gemäldegalerie** or the crafts in the **Kunstgewerbemuseum**, both part of the **Kulturforum** (p503). For more astonishing

The majestic cupola of the Berliner Dom, Berlin

craftsmanship, take the U-Bahn west from **Potsdamer Platz** (*p503*) to beautiful **Schloss Charlottenburg** (*p509*). Alternatively, admire the mosaics in the shattered **Kaiser-Wilhelm-Gedächtniskirche** (*p508*), the symbol of West Berlin, on the city's main shopping street, **Kurfürstendamm** (*p509*).

Two days in Dublin

- Marvel at the beautiful illuminated **Book of Kells**
- Explore lively **Temple Bar**
- Discover Dublin's past at **Dublinia and the Viking World**

Day 1
Morning Devote an hour to the magnificent **National Museum of Ireland – Archaeology** (*p119*). Afterward, visit **Trinity College** (*p118*) to see the breathtaking Book of Kells exhibition, and take a break in the college's lovely grounds. From here, it's a short walk to **Temple Bar** (*p120*), a good place to stop off for lunch.

Afternoon Venture a little way out of the center to visit the **Guinness Storehouse** (*p123*) and find out all there is to know about the nation's famous brew. If the weather allows, spend some time in **Phoenix Park** (*p123*), Europe's largest enclosed city park, which encompasses a zoo. In the evening, see a play at the wonderful **Gate Theatre** (*p123*).

Day 2
Morning Begin your day with a visit to the architecturally eclectic **Christ Church Cathedral** (*p121*). Just across the road is **Dublinia and the Viking World** (*p121*), where the history of Viking Dublin is on display. Take the excellent tour of **Dublin Castle** (*pp120–21*) and visit its **Chester Beatty Library** to see a range of beautiful historic manuscripts.

Afternoon Stroll down **Grafton Street** (*p119*), a pedestrianized

The Victorian Tower Bridge, spanning the River Thames in London

strip bustling with shoppers and street performers. Visit the **National Gallery of Ireland** (*p119*) to see the small but significant collection of Irish and international art. In the evening, enjoy the "craic" in one of the south side's lively pubs.

Two days in London

- Enjoy a spin on the **EDF Energy London Eye**
- Admire Wren's masterpiece, **St. Paul's Cathedral**
- Take a Beefeater tour of the **Tower of London**

Day 1
Morning Start off by examining the monuments to England's kings and queens on a self-guided tour of **Westminster Abbey** (*pp54–5*). Don't miss the intricate Lady Chapel and peaceful cloisters. Next, wander through Parliament Square into idyllic **St. James's Park** (*p56*), with its pelicans and black swans, reaching **Buckingham Palace** (*p56*) in time for some pomp and circumstance at the 11:30am Changing of the Guard ceremony. If it's fall or winter, try **Horse Guards Parade** (*p53*) instead. Walk through stately **Trafalgar Square** (*p58*) into the West End, and buy theatre tickets for the evening at bargain prices from the official cut-price booth on **Leicester Square** (*p58*).

Afternoon Head to **Chinatown** (*p58*) for dim sum, then spend an hour or two admiring works by Van Eyck, Van Gogh, and Constable at the **National Gallery** (*p57*). If there's time before the show, head to **Covent Garden**'s Piazza and Central Market (*p59*) to watch the street performers.

Day 2
Morning Begin the day at Sir Christopher Wren's glorious masterpiece, **St. Paul's Cathedral** (*p66*). Highlights here include the Whispering Gallery, the spectacular dome, and the crypt. Next, walk to the **Tower of London** (*pp68–9*), allowing two hours to join an entertaining Beefeater tour, and inspect the murderous-looking Tudor weaponry in the White Tower. Afterward, cross the iconic **Tower Bridge** (*p67*) to Bankside and admire the design and height of **The Shard** (*p67*), which dwarfs the surrounding buildings.

Afternoon Select something delicious for lunch from one of the artisan food stalls or cafés at **Borough Market** (*p99*), then stroll to **Shakespeare's Globe** (*p67*) for an enthralling auditorium tour. Next door is **Tate Modern** (*pp66–7*), housing paintings and art installations on a grand scale. End the day with a ride on the **EDF Energy London Eye** (*p53*), timing it to coincide with sunset.

Aerial view of the Gran Vía, Madrid's principal shopping street

Two days in Madrid

- Surround yourself with masterpieces at the **Prado**
- Enjoy the glamor and glitz of the **Gran Via**
- Feast on the mouth-watering morsels served in countless tapas bars

Day 1
Morning Start the day at **Plaza Mayor** (p274), the huge arcaded square in Madrid's historic heart, then take a relaxed stroll around the surrounding cobbled streets. Head into the pretty 19th-century Mercado de San Miguel, just off the square, for a gourmet lunch at one of its many chic tapas bars.

Afternoon Visit the magnificent **Prado** (pp278–80), Spain's biggest museum. Highlights here include the superlative *Las Meninas* by Velázquez, and a host of the artist's other works, created for the Spanish Habsburg monarchs. The charming gardens at the sumptuous **Ritz** (p277) next door are ideal for a post-museum cocktail.

Day 2
Morning Stroll along the **Gran Vía** (p275), Madrid's glittering answer to New York's Broadway, admiring the turn-of-the-20th-century theaters, as well as some of the city's first skyscrapers. The street is now a shopping mecca, packed with flagship stores.

Afternoon Head to the **Centro de Arte Reina Sofía** (p281) in time for lunch at the chic café-restaurant, then spend the rest of the day at this superb contemporary art museum. Admire Picasso's powerful *Guernica* and works by Gaudí, Miró, and Dalí, among others. In the evening, take a tour of the city's lively tapas bars.

Two days in Munich

- Admire the regal splendor and priceless treasures of the **Residenz**
- Enjoy a foaming tankard of beer and some hearty Bavarian cuisine
- Leave the city center for the pastoral delights of **Schloss Nymphenburg**

Day 1
Morning There's no finer introduction to Munich than the **Marienplatz** (p522), with its two monuments of civic pride: the **Neues Rathaus**, its facade a carnival of statues, and the **Altes Rathaus**. The soaring **Frauenkirche** (p522), unmissable because of its domed spires, is the image on almost every souvenir beer tankard; the other highlight of Munich's sacred architecture is the **Asamkirche** (pp522–3), an enchanting example of Bavarian Rococo. Stop for a *sauerbraten* and a stein at any of Munich's famous beer halls; for example, Hofbräuhaus, the site of Hitler's infamous Beer Hall Putsch.

Afternoon Suitably fortified, discover the head-spinning array of architecture, artworks, and treasures on display in the **Residenz** (pp520–21). This former palace of the Bavarian kings is so large it takes two tours just to see the half that is open to the public. Check if any seats are available for a night at its magical Cuvilliés-Theater.

Day 2
Morning The Bavarian kings reveal their impeccable taste again through their splendid art collection, hung in the **Alte Pinakothek** (p523). You can easily lose the morning among its Old Masters, which provides a comprehensive lesson in German art history. If your tastes veer more toward modern art, visit the neighboring **Neue Pinakothek** (p523) and the **Pinakothek der Moderne** (p524). Make time to walk to nearby Königsplatz, where the Neoclassical **Glyptothek** (p523) reveals why Munich was nicknamed "Athens on the Isar". The nearby **Staatliche Antiken-sammlungen** (p523) displays Ludwig I's antiquities.

Afternoon The **Deutsches Museum** (p524) is unbeatable for rainy days, with 20,000 arts and science exhibits spread over seven floors. Alternatively, head to **Schloss**

The iconic onion domes of the Frauenkirche in Munich

Prague Castle seen from a boat cruising on the Vltava River

Nymphenburg *(p525)*, as Electress Henriette-Adelaide did. Surprisingly, perhaps, her portrait is not one of those in the Gallery of Beauties, one of the highlights of this Italianate garden palace.

Two days in Paris

- Explore **Ile St-Louis** and visit majestic **Notre-Dame**
- Admire Old Masters and antiquities in the **Louvre**
- Ascend the **Eiffel Tower** at sunset for fabulous views across the city

Day 1
Morning Explore tranquil **Ile St-Louis** *(p152)* before crossing Pont St-Louis to take in the buttresses and gargoyles of glorious **Notre-Dame** *(pp154–5)*. Head west across **Ile de la Cité** *(p152)* to the Gothic jewel of **Sainte-Chapelle** *(p152)*. Alternatively, walk over to the Right Bank and spend your morning at the world-famous **Musée du Louvre** *(pp158–60)*, home to da Vinci's *Mona Lisa* and countless other treasures.

Afternoon Stroll through the charming **Jardin des Tuileries** *(p161)* to the architectural set piece of **Place de la Concorde** *(p161)*. Follow **Avenue des Champs-Elysées** *(p165)* to the **Arc de Triomphe** *(p165)*, which promises fabulous views from the top, before heading north

to arty **Montmartre** *(p166)*, where the **Sacré-Coeur** is splendidly illuminated at night.

Day 2
Morning Wander the ancient scholarly haunt of the **Latin Quarter** *(pp156–7)*, where bohemian **Rue Mouffetard** has a weekend market. There are also many great food stores from which to buy picnic supplies. Be sure to catch a glimpse of the bombastic **Panthéon** *(p157)* and the city's celebrated university, the **Sorbonne** *(p157)*. Pause for a picnic by the Seine.

Afternoon Make your way along the river to enjoy the dazzling Impressionist works in the **Musée d'Orsay** *(p162)*, then stroll past Louis XIV's imposing **Hôtel des Invalides** *(pp162–3)* to the legendary **Eiffel Tower** *(p163)*. At sunset, the views from the top are marvelous.

Two days in Prague

- Tour **Prague Castle**, a Gothic gem
- Watch the Town Hall Clock strike the hour in **Old Town Square**
- Visit the poignant sights of the **Jewish Quarter**

Day 1
Morning Start the day at the magnificent **Prague Castle** *(pp674–5)*. Take a tour of the

Gothic wonder that is **St. Vitus's Cathedral** *(p675)*, then visit the **Royal Palace** *(p676)*.

Afternoon After a picnic lunch and a wander through the stately **Royal Garden** *(p677)*, make your way down picturesque **Nerudova Street** *(p678)* to cross **Charles Bridge** *(p679)*, lined with statues of saints. Head to **Old Town Square** *(p682)* to watch the Town Hall Clock on the **Old Town Hall** *(pp682–3)* chime the hour. The pretty **Kinský Palace** *(p682)*, in the shadow of the spire-topped **Church of Our Lady Before Týn** *(p682)*, features ancient art. Take your choice from the square's many restaurants for dinner.

Day 2
Morning Begin by exploring the **Jewish Quarter** *(p681)*. Visit the **Old Jewish Cemetery** *(p681)*, with its tilting tombstones; the **Pinkas Synagogue** memorial to Holocaust victims; and the 13th-century **Old-New Synagogue** *(pp680–81)*.

Afternoon Cross the Vltava River to **Malá Strana** *(p678)*, which is lined with characterful shores as well as cafés and beer gardens that are perfect for a late lunch. On Little Quarter Square, the **Church of St. Nicholas** *(p678)* is the height of High Baroque and worthy of a peek inside. Afterward, go for a leisurely stroll amid bronze

The majestic iron structure of the Eiffel Tower, rising above the Champ de Mars, Paris

statues and peacocks in the grounds at **Wallenstein Palace** *(pp678–9)*.

Two days in Rome

- Marvel at the treasures in the **Vatican Museums**
- See the sites of the ancient city, including the spectacular **Colosseum**
- Watch the world go by from the **Spanish Steps**

The gardens of the Vatican Museums, Rome

Day 1

Morning Devote a full day to the Vatican and St. Peter's. The fast route through the **Vatican Museums** *(pp378–80)* takes in the **Sistine Chapel** *(p380)*. Don't miss Michelangelo's *Creation of Adam* on the ceiling and his dynamic altarpiece, *The Last Judgment*. The **Raphael Rooms** *(p380)* show another Renaissance master at his peak.

Afternoon Do not miss Michelangelo's *Pietà* inside the awe-inspiring **St. Peter's** *(pp376–7)*. Climb the dome for views, then descend to the papal tombs. Afterward, cross the Tiber to the *centro storico*. Admire the **Pantheon** *(p382)*, the only ancient Roman temple to survive intact, then spend the evening among the Baroque fountains and cafés of **Piazza Navona** *(p382)*.

The splendid Gothic interior of the Storkyrkan, Stockholm

◀ Tourists enjoying the sights of St Mark's Square in Venice, Italy

Day 2

Morning Wander through the evocative ruins of the **Roman Forum** *(p384)* and onward to the monumental **Colosseum** *(p385)*. Next, visit the **Palatine** *(p385)*, the leafy hill on which Rome's emperors once lived.

Afternoon For city views, head up to the **Capitoline Museums** *(p383)*. The Palazzo Nuovo has a selection of Greek and Roman statues. For some respite, visit the pretty 17th-century gardens of the **Museo e Galleria Borghese** *(p387)*. Climb the **Spanish Steps** *(p386)*, taking time for some people-watching at a café on Piazza di Spagna, and cast a coin into the Baroque **Trevi Fountain** *(p386)*.

Two days in Stockholm

- Explore **Gamla Stan**'s historic buildings and medieval cobbled streets
- Enjoy a restful afternoon walk in the **Kungsträd-gården**, the former royal kitchen gardens
- Hop on a ferry to enjoy the varied pleasures of the **Djurgården** peninsula

Day 1

Morning Spend the morning wandering around the city's historic hub, the Gamla Stan district. Here, you can admire the Gothic and Baroque interior of the **Storkyrkan** *(p605)*, then, at noon, catch

the Changing of the Guard at the **Royal Palace** *(p606)*, before heading indoors to visit some of its 608 grand rooms. Within the palace there are also two museums. Next, head west to tiny **Riddarholmen**, home to **Riddarholmskyrkan** *(p606)*, the final resting place of the Swedish sovereigns. Have lunch by the water here – it's less busy and more pleasant than Gamla Stan.

Afternoon Visit **Stadshuset** *(pp606–7)*, scene of the annual Nobel Prize festivities, built in National Romantic style. Take a break by enjoying the many delights of **Kungsträdgården** *(p607)*, the former royal kitchen gardens, before heading to the magnificent **Nationalmuseum** *(p607)*. Afterwards, enjoy the nightlife at **Stureplan** *(p607)*.

Day 2

Morning Take a ferry to the peninsula of **Djurgården** and spend a couple of hours at **Vasamuseet** *(p608)*. Housing the world's only preserved 17th-century warship, this is one of the city's must-see museums. Weather permitting, take a picnic lunch and eat alfresco in one of the peninsula's parks.

Afternoon Visit **Skansen** *(p608)*, the world's first open-air museum, home to 150 historic buildings from across Sweden. Here you can watch craftsmen and women demonstrate traditional skills. Round off the day with family favorite **Gröna Lund** (*p608*), Sweden's oldest amusement park.

Two days in Venice

- View Venice from the water – on a vaporetto or, better still, in a gondola
- Be dazzled by the riches of **St. Mark's Cathedral** and the **Doge's Palace**
- Watch Grand Canal boats go by from the famed **Rialto Bridge**

Day 1
Morning To start your exploration of Venice, travel by vaporetto or gondola along the **Grand Canal** (*p421*) to Piazza San Marco and **St. Mark's Cathedral** (*pp416–17*). The mosaics inside and out are ravishing, but so too are the Pala d'Oro (golden altarpiece), the jewels of the Treasury, and the four Horses of St. Mark on the balcony. Take the lift to the top of the adjacent Campanile to be rewarded with a view stretching all the way to the Alps.

Afternoon Join a pre-booked tour to get the most out of the **Doge's Palace** (*pp418–19*). The highlight here is the vast Sala del Maggior Consiglio, with a magnificent Tintoretto painting that takes up an entire wall. Then cross the Grand Canal to the **Accademia** (*p423*) for the best of the Venetian painters. For modern art, visit the **Peggy**

Guggenheim Collection (*p422*), in the 18th- century Palazzo Venier dei Leoni.

Day 2
Morning Head for the Grand Canal to watch the bustling canal traffic from the **Rialto Bridge**, and stock up for a picnic at the city's busiest market beside it. Also nearby is the church of **Santa Maria Gloriosa dei Frari** (*pp420–21*) with its exquisite altarpiece, a *Madonna and Child* by Bellini.

Afternoon Venture out into the lagoon, to the island of **Murano** (*p423*) for its glass museum and to watch the glassblowers at work. While some of their work can be very costly, small items such as bottle stoppers make attractive souvenirs and gifts. Back in Venice, be sure to sample some local snacks and drink an *aperitivo*.

Two days in Vienna

- Take a stroll around the streets of Old Vienna
- Watch the elegant horses of the **Spanish Riding School**
- Enjoy the panorama from Vienna's famous Ferris wheel in the **Prater**

Day 1
Morning Start at Vienna's cathedral, the **Stephansdom** (*p561*), then wander the pedestrianized medieval streets

A fountain in front of the Kunsthistorisches Museum (Museum of Fine Arts) in Vienna

of Old Vienna. Take a stroll along Kärntnerstrasse, the city's main shopping street, to the **Staatsoper** opera house (*p561*), for a tour and perhaps to buy tickets to the evening show. Enjoy a slice of Sachertorte at Café Sacher, just behind.

Afternoon Pick up the Ring Tram for a bargain 30-minute ride around **Ringstrasse** (*p556*), Vienna's grandest boulevard. Afterward, make your way to the **Belvedere** (*p564*) for some fine Austrian art and a stroll in its attractive gardens.

Day 2
Morning Head to the **Hofburg** (*pp558–60*), the imperial palace of the Habsburgs, where the main draws are the sumptuous State Apartments and Treasuries. But first, see whether there are any tickets available for a performance of the **Spanish Riding School** (*p560*), held most days at 11am.

Afternoon Walk a city block from the Hofburg to the **MuseumsQuartier Wien** (*p562*), a superb cultural complex next to the **Kunsthistorisches Museum** (*p562*). Choose carefully between the various museums here; it's easy to try to see too much. Afterward, get some fresh air in **Prater** park (*p564*), and take a spin on the famous giant Ferris wheel.

View of the Grand Canal, with the cupola of the church of La Salute, Venice

Putting Europe on the Map

The continent of Europe stretches as far east as
Russia's Ural Mountains, a total surface area of
10.4 million sq km (4 million sq miles). However, the
20 countries covered in this guide occupy a much
smaller area, being concentrated in the northwestern
and central parts of the continent and along the
Mediterranean coast in the south. These countries
are shown on this map in dark green. They include
18 of the nations that make up the European Union,
the political association of European states, based
in Brussels *(see p222)*. The map also shows the
principal international airports and the major
road links. Europe's rail network is shown on
the map on the inside back cover.

Key

— Highway
— Major road
--- Ferry route
▪▪▪ International boundary

Distance chart

Distance by road in kilometers
Distance by road in miles

Athens								
2564 1593	Berlin							
3023 1878	782 486	Brussels						
3227 2005	1057 657	327 203	London					
3883 2413	2342 1455	1568 974	1732 1076	Madrid				
2967 1844	1076 669	302 188	415 258	1267 787	Paris			
1902 1182	1520 945	1501 933	1802 1120	2093 1301	1460 907	Rome		
3650 2268	1035 643	1594 991	1820 1131	3222 2002	1861 1156	2622 1629	Stockholm	
2188 1360	589 366	1335 830	1838 1142	2932 1822	1623 1009	1834 1140	1601 995	Warsaw

PRACTICAL INFORMATION

Millions of visitors travel to Europe for reasons many Europeans take for granted – the rich diversity of history, architecture, art, and landscape. In Western Europe, tourist facilities are generally of a high standard, while in the former Communist countries of Eastern Europe their scope and quality have improved significantly over the past decade. As a result, the whole of Europe is more accessible. This section gives information on practical matters, such as passport formalities and how to get around. Many countries are members of the European Union, with certain laws in common, but there are also notable differences. In each country chapter a *Practical Information* section gives specific details for visitors.

When to Go

The best time to visit Europe depends on your itinerary, but most people prefer the summer months, between May and September. Due to the diverse geography of Europe, the weather has wide variations. Summers in northwestern Europe can be cool and rainy, while in the east they can be unbearably hot. The Mediterranean, with its hot, dry summers and relatively mild winters, has the balmiest climate, but crowds are a major drawback, particularly in July and August, making May and June better times to visit. August is the busiest month because this is when most French, Italian, and Spanish citizens take their vacations.

The climate of parts of Scandinavia is extreme: in winter in the north the sun rises only for a few hours and the roads can be blocked by snow, while summertime attracts many visitors, drawn by the prospect of enjoying the "midnight sun".

The mountainous areas of Europe have unique climates. The Pyrenees, Alps, and Apennines all have short summers and long winters with heavy snowfall. Consequently, these regions offer wonderful opportunities for skiing.

European Time Zones

The 20 countries covered in this guide fall across three time zones. Great Britain, Ireland, and Portugal are on GMT (Greenwich Mean Time), while the other European countries are one hour ahead (+1), except for Greece, which is two hours ahead (+2). In Europe the clocks go forward by one hour in March (Daylight Saving), and go back usually in October.

Passports and Visas

Most western European countries belong to the European Union. Based in Brussels, this European authority has the power to pass certain laws affecting all member states. There are currently 28 member states, with five more on the road to EU membership.

There are no passport controls between the following EU members: Germany, France, Spain, Portugal, Luxembourg, Belgium, the Netherlands, Italy, and Austria. In theory, it is sufficient to carry an identity card when traveling between these countries, but it is worth carrying your passport just in case. The other EU countries have yet to sign up to this agreement, and so passports are needed by everyone entering or leaving.

If you are arriving in Europe from a non-EU country, a passport is required. However, visitors from the United States, Canada, Japan, Australia, New Zealand, Norway, and Switzerland, amongst others, no longer require visas for visits under three months to countries in the EU. Check this with the embassy of the country you plan to visit. If you have a visa for one of the Schengen countries, you are permitted to visit all of the countries in the agreement. Some countries require a visa regardless of your length of stay; refer to the individual *Practical Information* sections in each chapter for full details.

Student Cards

As well as various bus and rail tickets that offer discounts on European travel *(see p26)*, students with a recognized student card may be eligible for a wider range of discounts. The best card is the International Student Identity Card (ISIC), which gives discounts on all kinds of goods and transport, as well as cheap admission to many museums, galleries, and other sights. Most students can obtain this card from their educational establishment at home, but it can also be obtained abroad from an ISIC-issuing office or from branches of STA Travel *(see p25)*. For US students, this card also includes some medical cover.

Customs and Duty-Free

Duty-free goods are not available for purchase when traveling between EU countries; these goods can only be bought on entry to, or exit from, the European Union as a whole. The allowances are as follows: tobacco (200 cigarettes, 50 cigars, or 250g of loose tobacco); alcohol (1 liter of strong spirits, 2 liters of alcohol under 22 percent proof, and 4 liters of wine); coffee (500g), and perfume (60ml).

When entering a country, you will be asked to declare certain items from abroad and pay duty on any amount that exceeds that country's allowance; the nature of these goods will vary from country to country. This process applies on returning to your home country with goods acquired in Europe.

Value Added Tax

In the EU, all goods and services (except certain items, such as food and children's clothes) are subject to a Value Added Tax, known as VAT in the UK, which is included in most prices. If you are not a European Union citizen, you may get a refund of this tax.

The easiest way to do this is to shop where you see the "Euro Free Tax" sign, although the stores that offer this service may be expensive or sell only luxury goods. After showing your passport to the shop assistant and completing a form, the VAT will be deducted from your bill.

In certain countries you need to keep your receipts and VAT forms and present them at the Tax Refund desk with your unopened purchases when you leave the country. These forms are processed and a refund will be sent to your home address.

Personal Security

Europe is one of the safest places to travel, but you should always take certain safety measures. If you are traveling alone and especially at night, it is best to avoid deserted and poorly lit buildings, parking lots, and back streets. If you should be a victim of crime, report it immediately to the police. Pickpockets are common throughout Europe, but certain crimes are worse in certain countries – specific information is given in the *Practical Information* section of each country chapter.

By far the safest way of carrying money is in the form of traveler's checks *(see p22)*, which allow you to keep your cash to a minimum. Never leave your belongings unattended, and make sure they are adequately insured before you leave home. Keep your valuables well concealed, especially in crowds. It is advisable to wear minimal jewelry when going out; leave it in your hotel safe instead.

Insurance and Medical Treatment

Travel insurance is essential to cover any loss or damage to your possessions and for unexpected medical and dental treatment. Many major credit cards offer some insurance if you purchase your flights or vacation package with them, so check this before buying a separate policy. If possible, buy one which pays for medical treatment on the spot, rather than a policy which reimburses you later. Most general insurance policies do not cover potentially dangerous activities, such as climbing, skiing, and scuba diving – these cost extra. If you plan to do any of these, check that you will be covered.

Recommended Hotels and Restaurants

The hotel and restaurant options in this guide have been selected across a wide range of prices and locations. The hotel listings have been chosen for their excellent facilities and good value, and vary from five-star luxury retreats to boutique hotels, humble B&Bs, and historic lodgings. Similarly, the selected restaurants adhere to a criterion of great food and atmosphere. These include no-frills seafood shacks, restaurants specialising in regional cuisine, and Michelin-starred fine dining. For the best of each country, look out for entries designated as DK Choices. Each of these has one or more exceptional features, such as a stunning location, a compelling history, or a special ambience.

Conversion Chart

Officially, the metric system is used throughout Europe, but in Britain imperial measures are also used. British pints and gallons are 20 percent larger than US measures.

Imperial to Metric
1 inch = 2.54 centimeters
1 foot = 30 centimeters
1 mile = 1.6 kilometers
1 ounce = 28 grams
1 pound = 454 grams
1 US pint = 0.47 liter
1 UK pint = 0.55 liter
1 US gallon = 3.8 liters
1 UK gallon = 4.6 liters

Metric to Imperial
1 millimeter = 0.04 inch
1 centimeter = 0.4 inch
1 meter = 3 feet 3 inches
1 kilometer = 0.6 mile
1 gram = 0.035 ounce
1 kilogram = 2.2 pounds
1 liter = 2.1 US pints
1 liter = 1.76 UK pints

The Climate of Europe

As a continent that ranges south from the Arctic Circle to just north of the tropics, Europe experiences a diversity of climates, yet because it is influenced by the warm Gulf Stream, its climate is, overall, much more temperate than other areas at the same latitudes. The *Practical Information* section for each country contains a panel, like the one below, giving details of average temperatures, rainfall, and sunshine for each season of the year.

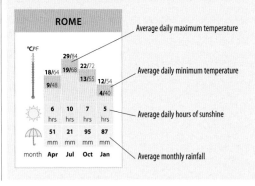

ROME

	Apr	Jul	Oct	Jan	
°C/°F	18/64	29/84 22/72	19/68 13/55	12/54	Average daily maximum temperature
	9/48			4/40	Average daily minimum temperature
☼	6 hrs	10 hrs	7 hrs	5 hrs	Average daily hours of sunshine
☂	51 mm	21 mm	95 mm	87 mm	Average monthly rainfall
month	Apr	Jul	Oct	Jan	

Communications and Money

In the 21st century, communications are developing quickly and evolving constantly. Cell phones and other mobile devices, social-media platforms, and the availability of Wi-Fi hotspots mean that communicating is now easier than ever, as well as being relatively cheap. Many hotels and restaurants readily accept most credit cards, so cash is normally only needed for smaller transactions or in remote spots. Having a common currency (the euro) in some countries has also made life much easier for travelers touring Europe.

Telephones

These days, when most people have a cell or mobile phone, the need for a public telephone is less urgent. Most US cell phones do not work in Europe and vice versa – but you can now buy phones that work in both continents. US companies will also rent cell phones for use while in Europe. If your network provider is either T-Mobile or AT&T, you will have a GSM phone that is compatible in Europe. In order to use it, simply ensure that it is unlocked, dual band (so that it uses European frequencies), and that it has been set up for roaming. If your home operator does not offer coverage in another country, your phone will usually roam into a host operator's network automatically. Be aware that roaming can be costly. A cheaper solution to stay in touch with family and friends back home is to turn off roaming and instead use Wi-Fi, which is usually free,

to communicate via social networks, email, or Skype. Alternatively, buy a SIM card in the country you are visiting and use it in your own phone.

Most European countries are in the process of phasing out public telephones.

Mail Services

Mail services are generally fast and efficient, with letters and cards typically taking five days to reach North America, or a week to get to Australasia. The mail service does vary across the continent, however, and in some areas, such as Eastern Europe and in remote parts of Greece, the service may be much slower.

Internet Access

Wi-Fi hotspots are widely available in every major city across Europe. Often hotels and restaurants offer wireless Internet access, too, so visitors with their own mobile device (smart phone, tablet, or laptop) should not have any trouble accessing email accounts or connecting to the web. Check in advance if there is a charge for using Wi-Fi. Although not as popular as they once were, Internet cafés can still be found in many towns and resorts. In Internet cafés, you normally pay a fee for a fixed amount of time, which varies according to local use and rates.

VoIP (Voice over Internet Protocol) is a way of communicating telephonically via your computer. In order to use it, you will need a Skype account (free to set up), a set of headphones and a microphone (these are often, but not always, provided by the café). Calls are free between Skype users, but there is a charge to land lines and cell phones.

Changing Money

Now that 23 countries take the euro, there is no need to change money so frequently. Check within each area chapter of this guide to see which countries participate.

Currency exchanges (bureaux de change) can be found in most towns – particularly within banks or post offices. Banks usually tend to offer the best rates. Most airports, central train stations, large hotels, and border posts also have currency exchanges.

Many visitors use traveler's checks when abroad because, unlike cash, they can be replaced by the bank if they are lost or stolen. However, if you have a plastic card with a pin number for your bank account or credit card, and as long as you belong to a global network such as Plus/Visa, or Cirrus/Mastercard, ATM machines can provide instant access to your funds. Be aware that credit cards charge interest if you take out cash. You can find ATM machines in banks, shopping malls, and stations. When paying by card, note that many European countries use "chip and pin" so swipe debit/credit cards may be refused.

International Dialing Codes

The list below gives the international dialing codes for the countries covered in this guide. When calling from the US and Canada prefix all numbers by "011;" from Australia by "0011;" from New Zealand by "00." When calling from within Europe, use the "00" prefix. If you are unsure, call international directory inquiries.

Country	Code		Country	Code
• Austria	43		• Luxembourg	352
• Belgium	32		• Netherlands	31
• Czech Republic	420		• Norway	47
• Denmark	45		• Poland	48
• Finland	358		• Portugal	351
• France	33		• Spain	34
• Germany	49		• Switzerland	41
• Greece	30		• Sweden	46
• Hungary	36		• United Kingdom	44
• Ireland (Republic)	353		(Great Britain and	
• Italy	39		Northern Ireland)	

The Euro

Entering circulation in 2002, the Euro (€) is the common currency of the European Union (EU). Countries that use the Euro as sole official currency are known as the Eurozone. Euro notes are identical throughout the Eurozone countries. The coins, however, have one side identical (the value side), and one side with an image unique to each country. Both notes and coins are exchangeable in each of the participating Euro countries. Several EU members have opted out of joining this common currency, such as the UK. For currency information for nations that are not part of the Eurozone nor EU members refer to the *Practical Information* sections found at near the end of each country's chapter.

Bank Notes

Euro bank notes have seven denominations. The €5 note (grey in color) is the smallest, followed by the €10 note (pink), €20 note (blue), €50 note (orange), €100 note (green), €200 note (yellow), and €500 note (purple). All notes show the stars of the European Union.

5 euros

10 euros

20 euros

50 euros

100 euros

200 euros

500 euros

2 euros

1 euro

50 cents

20 cents

10 cents

Coins

The euro has eight coin denominations: €1 and €2; 50 cents, 20 cents, 10 cents, 5 cents, 2 cents, and 1 cent. The €1 and €2 coins are both silver and gold in color. The 50-, 20-, and 10-cent coins are gold. The 5-, 2-, and 1-cent coins are bronze.

Europe by Air

With its network of international flights, Europe is one of the most accessible parts of the world to reach by air. Compared with North America and Australasia, European flights are a relatively cheap, quick and convenient way to get to and around Europe. In an industry previously dominated by state-run carriers and major private airlines, the recent rise of budget airlines offering "no-frills" flights has opened up many new destinations and made air travel more affordable.

Flying to Europe

If you are traveling from a major international airport, you will usually be able to find a direct flight to many European cities. Main destinations include London, Paris, Amsterdam, Rome, Milan, and Frankfurt. Most of the major North American airlines, such as Delta, Air Canada, American, and United Airlines, have frequent flights to all parts of Europe, as do Qantas and Emirates from Australia. For more details on flights to specific destinations, see the *Travel Information* sections for individual countries.

Although most major airports are based on the outskirts of European capitals and other big cities, all can be reached by efficient train, bus, taxi, and sometimes subway services. Many of the smaller airlines use less convenient airports, with a longer transfer time, but this is reflected in their cheaper fares.

European National Airlines

Most European countries have a national carrier which serves international destinations, and these usually offer frequent flights per day to their home countries at convenient times.

Scheduled flights on national airlines usually provide more legroom (essential on long flights) and a better quality of in-flight service than charter airlines, with complimentary items such as headphones and drinks. Fares can be more expensive, but it is worth shopping around for the best deals. The largest national carriers include **British Airways**, **Air France**, **Iberia** (Spain), **KLM** (the Netherlands), **Lufthansa** (Germany), **Alitalia** (Italy), and **SAS** (Scandinavia).

Flight Times

As a rough guide, flights from New York to London take about 6 hours 30 minutes, to Paris and Frankfurt 7 hours 30 minutes, and to Rome 8 hours 30 minutes. Flights from Sydney to London take around 23 hours via Bangkok, to Paris 23 hours via Singapore, to Frankfurt 22 hours via Singapore, and to Rome 25 hours via Bangkok. Flights from Auckland to London take about 24 hours, and to Frankfurt 23 hours.

Keeping Costs Down

As a rule, European air fares are cheaper between November and March (with the exception of Christmas and Easter weeks), while the high season is from June to mid-September. A "shoulder season" of moderate prices exists between these months. Try, if you can, to travel mid-week, because tickets are cheaper and airports are less busy.

Whatever season you travel, there are ways of saving money on air fares. A good way to start is to contact a travel agent that specializes in budget travel, such as **STA Travel** in the US. If you are young (under 25), a student, or a senior citizen, you will usually find special reduced-fare air tickets. Otherwise, you save money when you book in advance. If you can book 14 to 21 days ahead, APEX (Advanced Purchase Excursion) or Super APEX tickets are available direct from the airlines and are much cheaper. With these there is a minimum stay requirement of 7 days, but they can still be good value. It is cheaper still to buy air tickets through a travel agent. Be aware, however, that the cheaper the ticket, the more inflexible it usually is. You may not be able to alter, transfer, or cancel your flight, or if you do there may be stiff penalties, so check the conditions beforehand.

It is always cheaper to book a return (round-trip) ticket with fixed dates rather than an "open" return. You can also get an "open jaw" return, which allows you to enter via one city and exit via another (not necessarily in the same country). This is useful if you are doing a grand tour, but "open jaw" tickets are often more expensive than regular returns. Companies such as **Trailfinders** in the UK, and **STA Travel** in the US offer their own versions of these.

Depending on how far you have to travel, round-the-world (RTW) tickets can also work out cheaper than the standard long-haul returns. These enable you to fly around the world on specified stops, as long as you don't backtrack on yourself.

Look out for good deals from established travel agents and package operators that are advertised in newspapers and travel magazines. Airlines will quote you the regular price for a ticket, but they can often reduce this if they have unsold seats. Consolidators, or "bucket shops", buy unsold tickets in bulk (often for off-season travel) and sell them at cheaper rates.

Standby tickets are also economical, but you have to be flexible about your date and time of departure; be aware that you sometimes have to wait (possibly for days) for a cancellation.

Charter Flights

It is always worth investigating charter-flight fares. There are quite a few companies that book whole planes or blocks of seats in advance, then resell the tickets at more competitive rates. The main drawback with these tickets is that they are usually non-refundable. They also tend to land at remote airports and at wildly unsocial hours. The level of in-flight service and comfort is usually lower, too.

Package Deals

One of the easiest ways to arrange your visit to Europe is to book a package vacation. These are offered by all the major airlines, as well as various reputable independent companies, such as **Central Holidays** and **American Express**. They normally include flights, transfers, and accommodations, and sometimes side trips and food, and the cost can be far less than if you were to buy these separately. While an excellent way of reducing the strain of organizing your vacation, the downside with a package tour is that it usually involves traveling in large numbers on specific flights to a hotel which, because the price has been pared to the bone, may not offer a high standard of food or facilities. On the other hand, there are specialist package-tour operators that do offer top-quality hotels and use scheduled flights.

Fly-Drive

Many airlines, as well as numerous travel companies, offer fly-drive packages, which combine air fares and car rental. These deals are often worth considering, as they give you flexibility and offer a saving over arranging the two parts separately.

Internet Booking

The Internet is also a popular way of booking tickets. Two of the best sites for this are **Expedia** and **Opodo**. Expedia has a system called a "Fare Tracker" whereby you fill in a form online and they email you information when tickets become available. The US company **Europebyair** also provides excellent deals on flights to Europe. It offers a Flight Pass for non-European citizens, valid for 62 European cities and one-way flights between these destinations, for a very reasonable price.

Flights Within Europe

There is an extensive flight network serving most major cities, making it quick and easy to fly within Europe. If you are traveling some distance, and especially between Great Britain and other parts of Europe, flying can be the least expensive way to go. Indeed, if you want to get to destinations such as Portugal or Greece quickly, flying is almost the only option. However, between major cities, such as Berlin and Paris, you could go by train, which is almost as quick and cheap, and saves the trouble of getting to an airport (see p26).

It is best to avoid flying between major cities on Friday evenings and early Monday mornings because these flights can be crowded with European commuters.

As with transatlantic flights, you can get cheaper tickets by booking early. The best cities for finding good deals from "bucket shops" are London, Athens, and Amsterdam.

Low-Cost Airlines

Recent years have seen the emergence of so-called "no frills" airlines in Europe, such as **Ryanair**, **easyJet**, **Air Berlin**, and **Eurowings**, which offer very competitive prices. A return flight from London to Berlin, for example, can cost as little as £50 ($70). To keep prices down, there is usually less legroom, on-board catering, and checked luggage costs extra. Outlying airports may also be used. Unless you must have these benefits, the price justifies the inconvenience.

DIRECTORY

European National Airlines

Air France
Tel 800-237 2747 (US).
Tel 1-300 39 01 90 (Aus).
w airfrance.com

Alitalia
Tel 800-223 5730 (US).
w alitalia.com

British Airways
Tel 800-AIRWAYS (US).
Tel 1-300 767 177 (Aus).
w britishairways.com

Iberia
Tel 800-772 4642 (US).
w iberia.com

KLM
Tel 1-866 434 0320 (US).
Tel 01300 392 192 (Aus).
w klm.com

Lufthansa
Tel 800-645 3880 (US).
Tel 1-300 655 727 (Aus).
w lufthansa.com

SAS
Tel 800-221 2350 (US).
Tel 300 727 707 (Aus).
w flysas.com

Travel Agents

STA Travel
2871 Broadway,
New York, NY 10025, US.
Tel 212-865 2700.
w statravel.com

Trailfinders
194 Kensington High St,
London W8, UK.
Tel 020-7938 3939
(for long-haul travel).
Tel 020-7937 1234
(for European travel).
w trailfinders.com

Package Deals

American Express
Tel 1800-297 2977 (US).
w americanexpress.com/travel

Central Holidays
Tel 800-539 7098.
w centralholidays.com

Internet Booking

Europebyair
w europebyair.com

Expedia
w expedia.com

Opodo
w opodo.com

Low-Cost Airlines

Air Berlin
w airberlin.com

easyJet
w easyjet.com

Eurowings
w eurowings.com

Ryanair
w ryanair.com

Europe by Train

Trains are generally a popular, reliable, and comfortable means of travel, and also give visitors the chance to enjoy the passing countryside. With the Channel Tunnel in operation between Britain and France, it is now possible to travel all the way from Scotland to mainland Greece by rail, and the number of passes and discounts on offer ensure that costs need not be high.

Types of Train

All kinds of train serve the railroad network in Europe, from the slow local lines of remote regions to fast diesel-powered intercity expresses. For the latter, such as the French TGV (*Train à Grande Vitesse*), the Spanish AVE (*Alta Velocidad Española*), and the German ICE (InterCity Express), you usually need to reserve a seat in advance, and they are more expensive.

There is no such thing as a pan-European railroad system; however, the French operate TGV trains to Zürich, Bern, Turin, and Milan, where they link up with Italy's Pendolino trains; Brussels is connected to Paris, Amsterdam, Cologne, and Geneva by the high-speed Thalys network, while Germany's ICE system also runs to Bern, Switzerland.

Overnight trains are popular, offering couchettes, or bunks (usually four or six per compartment), or the more desirable sleepers (usually two or three beds per compartment). The price of a sleeper tends to be higher (three times the couchette price), but it is worth it if comfort is important.

Rail Passes for Non-Europeans

The cheapest way of seeing Europe by train is to buy one of the many passes available. For non-Europeans, the most popular of these is the Eurailpass from **Eurail**, or if you are under 26, the Eurail Youthpass. It is best to buy these tickets in the US or Australia before traveling because they can be 10 percent cheaper than if you wait and buy them in Europe. You can also buy these on the Internet through Eurail and **Voyages-SNCF**. These passes do not include the supplements payable on many of the faster trains: the EC (EuroCity), IC (InterCity), and EN (EuroNight) trains. You must pay these before boarding – if you don't and are caught by a conductor you will then have to pay the supplement plus a fine.

The Eurailpass offers unlimited travel in 27 European countries, including Austria, Belgium, Bulgaria, Croatia, Czech Republic, Denmark, Finland, France, Germany, Greece, Hungary, Ireland, Italy, the Netherlands, Norway, Portugal, Romania, Slovenia, Spain, Sweden, and Switzerland. It is available as a consecutive-day pass if you want to make frequent short hops by train, or as a flexipass if you are on a trip with extended stop-overs. It is also valid for some ferries.

Other variations on the Eurailpass include the Saver Flexipass, which gives at least a 15 percent reduction per person when two or more people are traveling together. The Youth Flexipass is an option for those under 26 years of age.

For further information on national train services and passes in individual countries see the *Travel Information* section for each country.

Passes for Europeans

For Europeans, the best pass is the Inter-Rail, which is available from Voyages-SNCF or from main train operators in individual countries. The Inter-Rail pass divides 30 countries in Europe into eight zones and is for anyone who has been resident in a European country for at least six months. There are special discounts for people under 26, the over-60s, and for families with children aged between four and 11. Children under four travel for free. What you pay depends on the number of zones you want to travel in and the length of your stay.

Eurostar/Eurotunnel

Connecting London's St. Pancras International Station to Lille and the Gare du Nord in Paris, the **Eurostar** foot-passenger train service provides the fastest link between the two capitals. It also operates to Brussels' Gare du Midi. These journeys take less than two and a half hours.

The **Eurotunnel** company operates a service between Folkestone in Great Britain and Calais in France that has drive-in compartments for vehicles. For a day trip, it costs a set price per car with passengers (the more passengers, the cheaper the cost per person). Daytime journeys are more expensive than those departing after 10pm.

DIRECTORY

Rail Passes

Eurail
w eurail.com
Official US website.
w railpass.com
Tel 877-RAILPASS (US).
Booking and information.

Voyages-SNCF
Travel Centre, 193 Piccadilly, London W1J 9EU.
Tel 0844-848 5848
(US: 1-800-622 8600).
Open 10am–6pm Mon–Fri, 10am–5pm Sat.
w voyages-sncf.com
For Eurailpasses.
w interrail.eu
For Inter-Rail passes.

Eurostar/Eurotunnel

Eurostar
Tel 08432-186 186 (UK).
Tel 01233-617 575 (outside UK).
w eurostar.com
For foot passengers.

Eurotunnel
Tel 08443-353 535 (UK).
Tel 0810-63 03 04 (France).
w eurotunnel.com
For cars & buses.

Europe by Road and Ferry

While many prefer the ease of traveling by train when they want to get somewhere fast, traveling by car gives you the chance to stop at will and explore many areas of Europe on the way. Car ferries and the Channel Tunnel have extended Europe's boundaries into the Scottish Hebrides and down to the Aegean.

Driving Permits

Many non-European licenses can be used in Europe, but an international driving permit is worth having, if only to make life easier when renting or leasing a vehicle (you have to be at least 21 years of age when renting). Be aware that it is mandatory to have an international permit in parts of Eastern Europe. The permit lasts for one year.

Driving In Europe

In Great Britain, Northern Ireland, the Republic of Ireland, Cyprus, Malta, and Gibraltar people drive on the left-hand side of the road. The rest of Europe drives on the right. Remember that in most of Europe, distances are measured in kilometers (1 km equals 0.6 miles). The exceptions are Great Britain and Ireland, which work in both metric and Imperial measurements. Most highways have a speed limit of around 100–135 km/h (60–80 mph). The fastest roads are in Germany, where the speed limit is 210 km/h (130 mph) on the *Autobahnen*. Roads are very congested during August, the vacation month, especially during the first and last weekends and on routes to the coast.

The cost of driving in Europe varies from country to country. Italian *autostrade*, French *autoroutes*, and Spanish *autopistas* are regularly punctuated by toll booths, while a one-time fee must be paid on entering Switzerland and Austria. However, the vast majority of roads are free in the Netherlands, Great Britain, and Germany, although tolls are charged on certain bridges.

Fuel prices vary enormously across Europe. Gibraltar, Andorra, and Luxembourg are by far the cheapest, while France, Italy, the Netherlands, and Great Britain are the most expensive, with Spain and Switzerland somewhere in between. The difference in price can be up to 30 percent. Unleaded gas is used almost exclusively in Scandinavia and Western Europe, but it is rarely available in the east.

Car Rental

Car rental is a competitive business in Europe, so prices are generally quite affordable. The biggest car rental companies in Europe are Europcar, Avis, Hertz, Sixt, and Budget, all of which offer an excellent level of service. Local contact details are given in the *Travel Information* section for each country. There are also US companies that specialize in European car rentals. These include firms such as **Europcar**, **Kemwel**, **Europe by Car**, and **Auto Europe**.

Traveling by Bus

Domestic bus services provide an alternative to the rail network throughout Europe, and while these are cheaper, they are also generally much slower and offer less in terms of comfort and amenities. The exceptions are Portugal, Greece, and parts of Spain, where buses have superseded trains, and Hungary, which has a bus system that is as good as the rail network. In most European countries, buses are best used as extensions of the railway, affording access to villages and remoter regions. Advance bookings for these are rarely needed.

International buses are also a second-best to express trains, but the tour options are worth considering. One example, **Eurolines**, offers passes that allow you to visit 43 European capitals over a 15- or 30-day period.

Traveling by Ferry

Once in Europe, you may need to go by boat to get to the more outlying areas. Many of the islands of Greece and Scotland, for example, are only accessible by sea. Or, if you start your trip to Europe by flying into Great Britain, it is possible to continue by ferry, catamaran, or hydrofoil to Ireland, France, Belgium, the Netherlands, and Spain. Companies operating regular ferries from Great Britain are **P&O** and **DFDS Seaways**.

It can also be easier and cheaper to travel by sea than by air from Spain to the Balearic Islands, from Italy to Sardinia and Sicily, and to Greece from Italy. For further details, see the *Travel Information* section of the individual countries.

DIRECTORY

Car Rental

Auto Europe
Tel 888-223 5555 (US).
W autoeurope.com

Europcar
Tel 877-940 6900 (US).
W europcar.com

Europe by Car
Tel 800-223 1516 (US).
W europebycarblog.com

Kemwel
Tel 877-820 0668 (US).
W kemwel.com

Traveling by Bus

Eurolines
Tel 08717-818 178 (UK).
W eurolines.co.uk

Ferry Services

DFDS Seaways
Tel 0871-574 7235 (UK).
W dfdsseaways.co.uk

P&O
Tel 08716-642 121 (UK).
W poferries.com

EUROPE AT A GLANCE

The Landscapes of Europe

A wide range of climatic and geological conditions has forged an impressive variety of landscapes in Europe. Although the appearance of much of the land has changed dramatically since mankind began to cultivate it around 7,000 years ago, there are still many remote and wild regions, such as the spectacular peaks of the Alps and the Pyrenees. As well as being simply beautiful in their own right, Europe's diverse landscapes offer endless opportunities for outdoor activities.

Norway
Indenting the country's west coast, the wild and rugged Norwegian fjords are a truly spectacular sight, offering some of the most breathtaking scenery in Scandinavia.

Great Britain
Dartmoor in southwest England is a wilderness of great natural beauty. The windswept open moorland at the area's bleak and isolated heart has inspired many romantic tales.

France
The wine-producing regions of France, such as Champagne, boast lush, fertile vegetation, with row upon row of neatly planted vines.

Portugal
The interior of southern Portugal is largely characterized by parched plains dotted with cork oaks and olive trees, and vast dusty wheat fields stretching uninterrupted to the horizon.

NC

North Sea

IRELAND

GREAT BRITAIN

NETHERLAND

BELGIUM & LUXEMBOURG

SWITZERLAN

Bay of Biscay

FRANCE

PORTUGAL

SPAIN

Mediterranea

0 km   250
0 miles   250

◄ Aerial view of St Peter's Square in the Vatican City, with Rome in the background, Italy

Hungary

North of the Hungarian capital, the Danube flows through a verdant landscape of vineyards, orchards, and thickly wooded hills. Known as the Danube Bend, this is one of the river's most beautiful stretches.

Switzerland

Switzerland's landscape is dominated by the Alps, Europe's highest mountain range. Dramatic, snow-covered peaks, stunning vistas, and a range of first-class winter sports facilities draw millions of visitors to this part of Europe every year.

Greece

The Greek mainland and islands have some of Europe's finest coastal scenery. There are thousands of beaches, ranging from small rocky coves backed by pine-clad cliffs to broad swathes of golden sand.

Great Museums and Galleries

The museums and galleries of Europe include national collections, the former collections of Europe's royal and noble families, and a whole host of smaller local institutions. The museums highlighted here are those with the largest and richest collections, which ought to be included in the itinerary of every visitor to Europe. Between them, they contain many of the world's best-known and best-loved artistic treasures. These range from archaeological finds from the early civilizations of the Middle East, through pieces from Egyptian, Greek, and Roman times, to masterpieces of the Renaissance and other great periods of European art.

Rijksmuseum, Amsterdam
The Rijksmuseum *(see pp248–50)* is known for its Rembrandts and other great Dutch paintings of the 17th century. Frans Hals' *Wedding Portrait* is a joyful celebration of Dutch life.

British Museum, London
A vast collection of antiquities and other artifacts from all over the world is housed inside Britain's national museum *(see pp60–61)*. There is a fascinating display of mummies and other exhibits from Ancient Egypt.

Louvre, Paris
The celebrated home of the *Mona Lisa* and the *Venus de Milo*, the Louvre also houses Jean Watteau's melancholy study *Gilles or Pierrot* (c.1717), one of many French works on display *(see pp158–60)*.

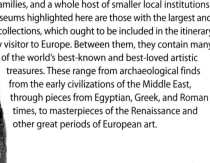

IRELAND

North Sea

GREAT BRITAIN

NETHERLAND

BELGIUM & LUXEMBOUR

Bay of Biscay

FRANCE

SPAIN

PORTUGAL

Mediterranea

Prado, Madrid
The former royal collection in Madrid *(see pp278–80)* contains the finest assembly of Spanish paintings in the world. Of many highly individual works, Goya's *Saturn Devouring His Son* is one of the most powerful.

0 km   250

0 miles   250

Pergamon Museum, Berlin
This fabulous collection of antiquities includes the famous blue-tiled Ishtar Gate from Babylon, dating from the 6th century BC *(see p504)*.

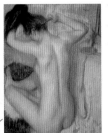

The Hermitage, St. Petersburg
The Hermitage *(see p658)* houses an impressive collection of Impressionist paintings, such as *Woman Combing her Hair* (c.1885) by Edgar Degas.

Kunsthistorisches Museum, Vienna
Based on the imperial collections of the Habsburgs, the museum *(see p562)* houses archaeology, paintings, and sculpture, such as this woodcarving of the Madonna (c.1495) by Tilman Riemenschneider.

Uffizi, Florence
The Uffizi *(see pp404–6)* was built originally as the "offices" of the Medici rulers of Florence. Transformed into a gallery in 1581, the building now displays such masterpieces as *The Annunciation* by da Vinci.

Vatican Museums, Rome
Classical and Early Christian statues excavated in Rome over the centuries include this charming *Good Shepherd* (4th century AD). The vast papal museum *(see pp378–80)* also holds great paintings by Michelangelo and Raphael, commissioned during the Renaissance.

The History of Europe

In this timeline of European history, important political and social events appear on the upper half of the page, while the lower half charts contemporary developments in art and architecture. In the art and architecture section, the emphasis is on structures and works of art that both illustrate major historical trends and can still be seen today. They are described in more detail in the main sightseeing section of the book.

451–429 BC The great general Perikles presides as uncrowned king of Athens. He establishes democracy in the city and commissions great buildings, such as the Parthenon *(see pp454–6)*. However, he also involves Athens in Peloponnesian Wars (431–404), in which Sparta and its allies defeat Athens

From Prehistory to the Early Middle Ages

From prehistoric times, Europe saw a succession of civilizations that flourished then collapsed. Much of our knowledge of the period comes only from archaeological remains, although the Mycenaeans did leave written inscriptions. Later periods are chronicled in Greek and Roman histories. However, many of these were written long after the events they describe and tend to be a blend of legend and fact.

c.1500 BC Mycenaean culture dominates mainland Greece. This gold death mask from Mycenae, known as the "Mask of Agamemnon," is on display at the National Museum of Archaeology in Athens *(see p452)*

750–600 BC Greek colonists spread to Sicily, southern Italy, Marseille, and Spain

509 BC Romans expel Etruscan kings and found republic

c.800 BC Rise of Etruscans in Italy

c.2300 BC Start of Bronze Age in Europe

2000–1100 BC Series of Minoan civilizations in Crete

c.1000 BC Iron-working reaches central Europe from the Near East

Prehistory				Classical Greece	
	2500 BC	2000 BC	1500 BC	1000 BC	500 BC
Minoan and Mycenanean				Greek and Etruscan	

447 BC Work begins on the Parthenon, the great temple dedicated to Athena on the Acropolis in Athens *(see pp454–6)*

c.1200 BC Collapse of Mycenaean culture

6th century BC Etruscan sarcophagi topped with lifelike terra-cotta sculptures of the deceased *(see p387)*

c.1450 BC Mycenaeans *(see p467)* take over palace of Knossos. Palaces in mainland Greece start to exhibit pillared, frescoed halls; ideas borrowed from the Minoans

4th century BC Magnificent Greek theater built at Epidaurus *(see p467)*

c.1700 BC First Minoan palace at Knossos on Crete destroyed. A new palace was immediately built to replace it. This colorful scene is one of many fine Minoan frescoes in the Irákleio Archaeological Museum in Crete *(see p476)*

6th century BC Greek vases of the red-figure type start to appear. The figures are left in the color of the clay, silhouetted against a black glaze. They often show scenes of myth and legend, such as the Trojan War

Art and Architecture

Artistic styles in prehistoric Minoan and Mycenaean cultures were strongly influenced by Egyptian and Middle Eastern models. However, during the Hellenistic period the trend was reversed. Following Alexander the Great's conquests, Greek styles of sculpture, temple architecture, and ceramics were exported to Egypt and as far east as Afghanistan. The Romans were great admirers of the Greeks and the growth of the Roman Empire helped spread the Greek aesthetic throughout western Europe.

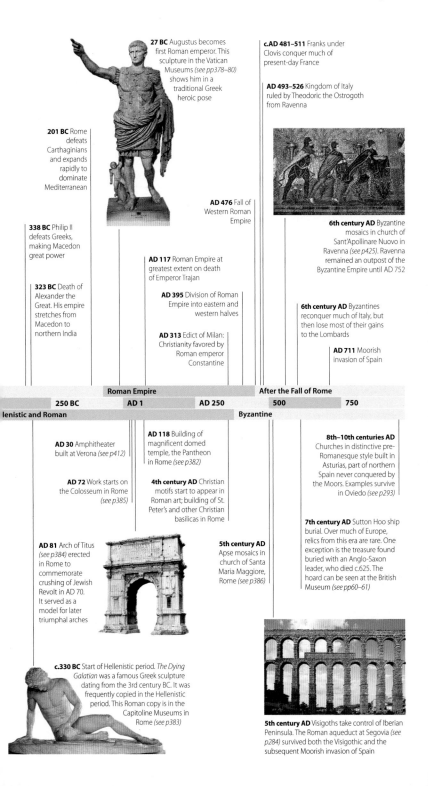

27 BC Augustus becomes first Roman emperor. This sculpture in the Vatican Museums (see pp378–80) shows him in a traditional Greek heroic pose

c.AD 481–511 Franks under Clovis conquer much of present-day France

AD 493–526 Kingdom of Italy ruled by Theodoric the Ostrogoth from Ravenna

201 BC Rome defeats Carthaginians and expands rapidly to dominate Mediterranean

AD 476 Fall of Western Roman Empire

338 BC Philip II defeats Greeks, making Macedon great power

6th century AD Byzantine mosaics in church of Sant'Apollinare Nuovo in Ravenna (see p425). Ravenna remained an outpost of the Byzantine Empire until AD 752

AD 117 Roman Empire at greatest extent on death of Emperor Trajan

323 BC Death of Alexander the Great. His empire stretches from Macedon to northern India

AD 395 Division of Roman Empire into eastern and western halves

6th century AD Byzantines reconquer much of Italy, but then lose most of their gains to the Lombards

AD 313 Edict of Milan: Christianity favored by Roman emperor Constantine

AD 711 Moorish invasion of Spain

Roman Empire		After the Fall of Rome	
250 BC	**AD 1**	**AD 250**	**500**	**750**

lenistic and Roman

Byzantine

AD 30 Amphitheater built at Verona (see p412)

AD 118 Building of magnificent domed temple, the Pantheon in Rome (see p382)

8th–10th centuries AD Churches in distinctive pre-Romanesque style built in Asturias, part of northern Spain never conquered by the Moors. Examples survive in Oviedo (see p293)

AD 72 Work starts on the Colosseum in Rome (see p385)

4th century AD Christian motifs start to appear in Roman art; building of St. Peter's and other Christian basilicas in Rome

7th century AD Sutton Hoo ship burial. Over much of Europe, relics from this era are rare. One exception is the treasure found buried with an Anglo-Saxon leader, who died c.625. The hoard can be seen at the British Museum (see pp60–61)

AD 81 Arch of Titus (see p384) erected in Rome to commemorate crushing of Jewish Revolt in AD 70. It served as a model for later triumphal arches

5th century AD Apse mosaics in church of Santa Maria Maggiore, Rome (see p386)

c.330 BC Start of Hellenistic period. *The Dying Galatian* was a famous Greek sculpture dating from the 3rd century BC. It was frequently copied in the Hellenistic period. This Roman copy is in the Capitoline Museums in Rome (see p383)

5th century AD Visigoths take control of Iberian Peninsula. The Roman aqueduct at Segovia (see p284) survived both the Visigothic and the subsequent Moorish invasion of Spain

From the Middle Ages to the 18th Century

During this period, many of the states of present-day Europe gradually took shape, with powerful centralized kingdoms, notably Spain, Portugal, France, and England, emerging from the medieval feudal system. The Middle Ages were marked by wars between kings and nobles and even between popes and emperors. The Catholic church owned extensive lands and was a powerful political force. However, its influence over much of northern Europe was lost in the Reformation of the 16th century, with the emergence of Protestantism.

9th century Vikings terrorize Europe, gaining control of much of England, Scotland, Ireland, and northern France. The Isle of Lewis chessmen (11th century) give a striking picture of the members of a Viking court. Carved of walrus ivory, they can be seen in the British Museum *(see pp60–61)*

1096–9 First Crusade; knights of northern Europe capture Jerusalem

1066 Norman conquest of England

896 Magyars reach eastern Europe, laying foundation of present-day Hungary

1054 East-West Schism: Roman Church splits definitively with Eastern Orthodox Church

955 Saxon king Otto defeats Magyars

800 The Frankish king, Charlemagne, is crowned Holy Roman Emperor

12th and 13th centuries Emperors and popes fight for control of Germany and Italy. Frederick I Barbarossa, Holy Roman Emperor, quarreled frequently with the pope but set off on the Third Crusade, only to drown in 1190 before he reached the Holy Land

12th and 13th centuries Gradual reconquest of Spain and Portugal from the Moors

12th century Venice grows rich supplying the crusades and trading with the east

Early Middle Ages			Middle Ages		
800	900	1000	1100	1200	
Byzantine and Romanesque				Gothic	

c.800 Book of Kells, the greatest of the Irish illuminated copies of the Bible created *(see p127)*

9th and 10th centuries Irish High Crosses *(see p126)*

c.785 Start of building of the Mezquita in Córdoba, capital of the Moorish Caliphate in Spain *(see pp316–17)*. The *mihrab* (prayer niche) is framed by a beautiful horseshoe arch. Spanish buildings retained Moorish features like this even after the completion of the reconquest of Spain in 1492

1064 Work begins on Pisa's Duomo *(see p393)*, a magnificent example of Italian Romanesque

1071 Completion of St. Mark's, Venice's great Byzantine basilica *(see pp416–17)*

10th century Beginnings of Romanesque architecture, characterized by rounded Roman arches, arcades, and tall bell towers

11th century Christianity reaches Norway – building of striking wooden "stave" churches *(see p618)*

Late 11th century Building of Durham Cathedral *(see p85)*, England's finest Norman (Romanesque) church

c.1194 Chartres Cathedral, France *(see pp180–81)* rebuilt in new Gothic style. Pointed arches and ribbed vaulting create possibility of soaring height in church design

c.1267–1336 Life of Giotto, who introduces a new realism to Italian painting. *St. Francis appears to the Monks at Arles* is one of a series of frescoes he painted for the Basilica di San Francesco in Assisi *(see pp388–9)*

Art and Architecture

The Middle Ages in Europe produced remarkable ecclesiastical architecture: first in the Romanesque style, then the even more spectacular Gothic. The Renaissance turned its back on the Gothic with the rediscovery of Classical principles, while Renaissance art was based on scientific understanding of perspective and anatomy, and also on the idealism of Classical sculpture.

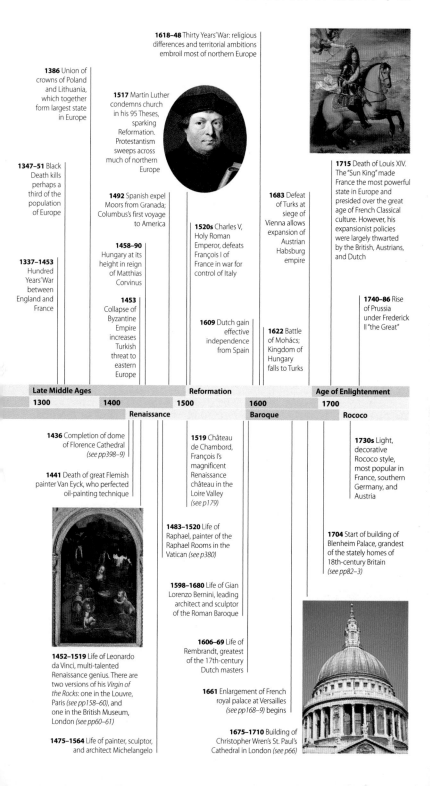

1618–48 Thirty Years' War: religious differences and territorial ambitions embroil most of northern Europe

1386 Union of crowns of Poland and Lithuania, which together form largest state in Europe

1517 Martin Luther condemns church in his 95 Theses, sparking Reformation. Protestantism sweeps across much of northern Europe

1715 Death of Louis XIV. The "Sun King" made France the most powerful state in Europe and presided over the great age of French Classical culture. However, his expansionist policies were largely thwarted by the British, Austrians, and Dutch

1347–51 Black Death kills perhaps a third of the population of Europe

1492 Spanish expel Moors from Granada; Columbus's first voyage to America

1683 Defeat of Turks at siege of Vienna allows expansion of Austrian Habsburg empire

1520s Charles V, Holy Roman Emperor, defeats François I of France in war for control of Italy

1458–90 Hungary at its height in reign of Matthias Corvinus

1337–1453 Hundred Years' War between England and France

1453 Collapse of Byzantine Empire increases Turkish threat to eastern Europe

1609 Dutch gain effective independence from Spain

1622 Battle of Mohács; Kingdom of Hungary falls to Turks

1740–86 Rise of Prussia under Frederick II "the Great"

Late Middle Ages		Reformation		Age of Enlightenment	
1300	**1400**	**1500**	**1600**	**1700**	
	Renaissance		Baroque	Rococo	

1436 Completion of dome of Florence Cathedral (see pp398–9)

1441 Death of great Flemish painter Van Eyck, who perfected oil-painting technique

1519 Château de Chambord, François I's magnificent Renaissance château in the Loire Valley (see p179)

1730s Light, decorative Rococo style, most popular in France, southern Germany, and Austria

1483–1520 Life of Raphael, painter of the Raphael Rooms in the Vatican (see p380)

1704 Start of building of Blenheim Palace, grandest of the stately homes of 18th-century Britain (see pp82–3)

1598–1680 Life of Gian Lorenzo Bernini, leading architect and sculptor of the Roman Baroque

1606–69 Life of Rembrandt, greatest of the 17th-century Dutch masters

1452–1519 Life of Leonardo da Vinci, multi-talented Renaissance genius. There are two versions of his *Virgin of the Rocks*: one in the Louvre, Paris (see pp158–60), and one in the British Museum, London (see pp60–61)

1661 Enlargement of French royal palace at Versailles (see pp168–9) begins

1675–1710 Building of Christopher Wren's St. Paul's Cathedral in London (see p66)

1475–1564 Life of painter, sculptor, and architect Michelangelo

From the French Revolution to the Present

The French Revolution established a supposedly democratic republic, but the need for a central authority allowed the brilliant general Napoleon to take power and proclaim himself Emperor. The Old Regime died hard and after Napoleon's defeat, many of the old rulers of Europe were restored to their thrones. In time, however, birthright and tradition had to give way to technological progress, the growth of capitalism, the rising power of the bourgeoisie, and the spread of workers' movements. Greater democracy gave the vote to more and more of the population, but wherever democracy broke down, there was the danger it would be replaced by a totalitarian regime, such as the Nazis in Germany and the Communist regimes of the old Soviet Bloc.

1901 First award of Nobel prizes in Sweden and Norway

1830–40 George Stephenson's *Rocket* becomes the prototype for steam locomotives. Following the success of the Liverpool–Manchester line, opened in 1930, the spread of railroads speeds the Industrial Revolution in Britain

1804 Napoleon crowns himself Emperor of the French

1805 Napoleon defeats Austrians at Austerlitz; by 1807, he controls most of western and central Europe

1789 French Revolution leads to execution by guillotine of Louis XVI and Reign of Terror in 1793

1812 Defeats in Peninsular War and Russia weaken French hold on Europe

1815 Napoleon defeated at Waterloo; Congress of Vienna more or less restores status quo in Europe

1831 Creation of Kingdom of Belgium

1838–1901 Reign of Queen Victoria: apogee of British Empire

1848 Year of revolutions throughout Europe

1852 Napoleon III becomes Emperor of France

1860 Unification of most of Italy

1870 Franco-Prussian War; German victory allows Bismarck to achieve unification of Germany

Age of Enlightenment		Industrial Revolution			Age of Imperialism	
1775	1800	1825		1850	1875	1900
Neoclassical	Empire	Regency	Realism		Impressionism	Art Nou

1785 *The Oath of the Horatii* by Jacques Louis David, French Neoclassical painter. This incident from early Roman history extols the republican spirit that would inspire the French Revolution

c.1814 Goya's paintings recording atrocities in the Peninsular War, *May 2, 1808* and *May 3, 1808*. They hang in the Prado, Madrid *(see pp278–80)*

c.1800 Empire style in fashion and furnishings. Many aspects of design in Europe influenced by Napoleon's Egyptian expedition

1874 Claude Monet uses the word "Impression" in title of a painting, giving rise to the term Impressionism

1883 Gaudí begins work on la Sagrada Família cathedral in Barcelona *(see pp302–3)*

1841–1919 Life of Pierre Auguste Renoir, one of the greatest of the artists associated with the Impressionist movement

1852–70 Second Empire style; rebuilding of Paris by Haussmann *(see p164)*

1857–65 The Ringstrasse built in Vienna, an example of grand 19th-century city planning

1890 Suicide of Dutch painter Van Gogh, unrecognized in his lifetime, now the most sought-after of Post-Impressionist painters *(see p251)*

Art and Architecture

Revivalist styles dominated 19th-century architecture, with imitations of Classical, Gothic, and Renaissance buildings. In contrast, painting evolved radically following the example of the French Impressionists. In the 20th century, new building materials – steel, concrete, and glass – were the inspiration of Modernism. Modern art, meanwhile, experimented with every conceivable form of expression, from Surrealism to Conceptual Art.

1890s Era of Art Nouveau. The posters of Czech-born Alfons Mucha typify the style, also known as Jugendstil or Secession. Many artists break away from the official academy of their country, notably in Vienna and Berlin

1907 First exhibition of Cubist works by Picasso and others

1914 Outbreak of World War I. Millions die as trench warfare along Western Front reaches stalemate

1989 Collapse of Communism in Eastern Europe. Poland, Hungary, Czechoslovakia, and other countries oust Communist rulers. Reopening of Berlin Wall leads to reunification of Germany in 1990

1939 Outbreak of World War II. Germany overruns Poland, then, in 1940, France

1918 Defeat of Germany, following American entry into war in 1917

1936–9 Spanish Civil War

1933 Hitler comes to power in Germany

1919 Treaty of Versailles (1919) creates new states, including Poland, Czechoslovakia, Hungary, and Finland

1944 Normandy Landings. Allied forces create second front, which leads to eventual defeat of Germany in 1945

1949 Berlin Air Lift stops Russian blockade of West Berlin

1956 Hungarian uprising against Communist rule crushed by Russian tanks

1957 Treaty of Rome: European Economic Community marks beginning of European Union

1968 Student protests in France and many other parts of Europe

1973 Carnation Revolution in Portugal

1995 Membership of European Union reaches 15, with entry of Sweden, Finland, and Austria

2002 Introduction of common currency, the euro, in 12 countries of the European Union

2004 Ten more countries join the European Union

2007 Bulgaria and Romania join the European Union

2013 Croatia joins the European Union

The European Union

| 1925 | 1950 | 1975 | 2000 | 2025 |

Art Deco and Modernism

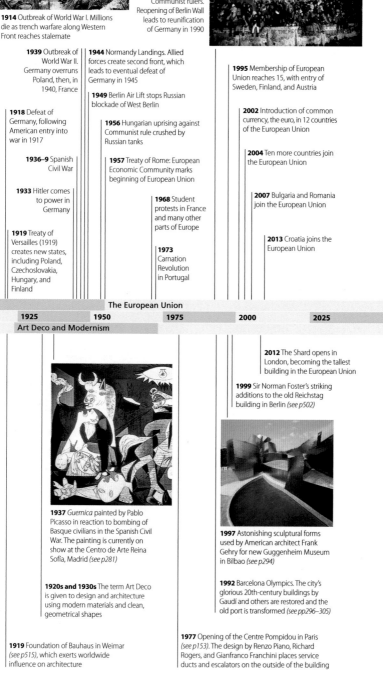

2012 The Shard opens in London, becoming the tallest building in the European Union

1999 Sir Norman Foster's striking additions to the old Reichstag building in Berlin *(see p502)*

1937 *Guernica* painted by Pablo Picasso in reaction to bombing of Basque civilians in the Spanish Civil War. The painting is currently on show at the Centro de Arte Reina Sofía, Madrid *(see p281)*

1920s and 1930s The term Art Deco is given to design and architecture using modern materials and clean, geometrical shapes

1919 Foundation of Bauhaus in Weimar *(see p515)*, which exerts worldwide influence on architecture

1997 Astonishing sculptural forms used by American architect Frank Gehry for new Guggenheim Museum in Bilbao *(see p294)*

1992 Barcelona Olympics. The city's glorious 20th-century buildings by Gaudí and others are restored and the old port is transformed *(see pp296–305)*

1977 Opening of the Centre Pompidou in Paris *(see p153)*. The design by Renzo Piano, Richard Rogers, and Gianfranco Franchini places service ducts and escalators on the outside of the building

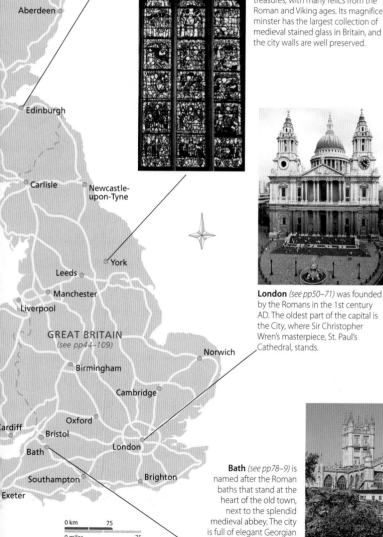

Edinburgh *(see pp90–94)* is the administrative and cultural capital of Scotland. Its castle, which dates back to the 12th century, gives spectacular views of the entire city.

Locator Map

York *(see pp86–7)* is a city of historical treasures, with many relics from the Roman and Viking ages. Its magnificent minster has the largest collection of medieval stained glass in Britain, and the city walls are well preserved.

Aberdeen

Edinburgh

Carlisle

Newcastle-upon-Tyne

Leeds

York

Manchester

Liverpool

GREAT BRITAIN
(see pp44–109)

Norwich

Birmingham

Cambridge

ardiff

Oxford

Bristol

London

Bath

Southampton

Brighton

Exeter

London *(see pp50–71)* was founded by the Romans in the 1st century AD. The oldest part of the capital is the City, where Sir Christopher Wren's masterpiece, St. Paul's Cathedral, stands.

0 km   75

0 miles   75

Bath *(see pp78–9)* is named after the Roman baths that stand at the heart of the old town, next to the splendid medieval abbey. The city is full of elegant Georgian terraces, built in local honey-colored limestone.

GREAT BRITAIN

Separated from the rest of Europe by the English Channel, Britain has been assiduous in preserving its traditions. However, the island can offer the visitor much more than stately castles and pretty villages. A diversity of landscape, culture, literature, art, and architecture, as well as a unique heritage, results in a nation balancing the needs of the present with those of the past.

Britain's character has been shaped by its geographical position as an island. Never successfully invaded again after 1066, the country has developed its own distinctive traditions, and although today a member of the European Union, Britain continues to delight in its nonconformity. Britain's heritage can be seen in its ancient castles, cathedrals, and stately homes, with their gardens and parklands. It is also evident in the many age-old customs played out across the nation throughout the year.

For a small island, Great Britain encompasses a surprising variety in its regions, whose inhabitants maintain distinct identities. Scotland and Wales are separate countries from England, with their own legislative assemblies. They also have their own surviving Gaelic languages and unique traditions.

The landscape is varied, too, from the mountains of Wales, Scotland, and the north, through the flat expanses of the Midlands and eastern England, to the soft, rolling hills of the south and west.

The long, broad beaches of East Anglia contrast with the rocky inlets along much of the west coast.

Despite the spread of towns and cities over the last two centuries, rural Britain still flourishes. The countryside is dotted with farms and charming villages with picturesque cottages and lovingly tended gardens. The most prosperous and densely populated part of the nation is the southeast, close to London, where modern office buildings bear witness to the growth of service and high-tech industries.

History

Britain began to assume a cohesive character as early as the 7th century AD, as Anglo-Saxon tribes migrating from the continent absorbed existing Celtic and Roman influences and finally achieved supremacy in England.

However, they suffered repeated Viking incursions and were overcome by the Normans at the Battle of Hastings in 1066, when William the Conqueror founded the

Punting on the River Cherwell, Oxford

 Fantastical gargoyles looking out from the Natural History Museum, London

royal lineage which still rules the country today. The disparate cultures of the Normans and Anglo-Saxons combined to form the English nation, a process nurtured by Britain's position as an island. Scotland's four divided kingdoms had also unified under one monarch by this time, with the crowning of Duncan I in 1034.

The next 400 years saw English kings extend their domain at home as well as abroad. Wales was conquered in 1282, and by 1296 control was also gained over Scotland. The Scots rose up again, however, winning back their independence under Robert the Bruce in 1314. The Tudor monarchs consolidated England's strength and laid the foundations for Britain's future commercial success. Henry VIII recognized the importance of sea power and, under his daughter, Elizabeth I,

Queen Elizabeth I (reigned 1558–1603)

English sailors ranged far across the world. The total defeat of the Spanish Armada in 1588 confirmed Britain's position as a major maritime power.

The Stuart period saw the English and Scottish crowns unite, but internal struggles eventually led to the Civil War in 1642. By the time of the Act of Union with Scotland in 1707, however, the whole island was united and the foundations for representative government had been laid. The combination of internal security and maritime strength allowed Britain to seek wealth overseas. By the end of the Napoleonic Wars in 1815, Britain was the world's leading trading nation. The opportunities offered by industrialization were seized, and by the reign of Queen Victoria (1837–1901), a colossal empire had been established across the globe. Challenged by Europe and the rise of the US, and drained by its role in two world wars, Britain's influence waned after 1945. By the 1970s, almost all its former colonies had become independent Commonwealth nations.

Society and Politics

British cities are melting-pots for people not just from different parts of the country, but also from overseas. Irish immigration has long ensured a flow of labor into the country, and since the 1950s, hundreds of thousands have come from countries in Africa, Asia, and the Caribbean, many of

KEY DATES IN BRITISH HISTORY

AD 43–410 Roman occupation of Britain

440–50 Start of Angle, Saxon, and Jute invasions

1034 Duncan I becomes first king of all Scotland

1066 William the Conqueror defeats King Harold and becomes the first Norman king of England

1256 First Parliament to include ordinary citizens

1533–4 Henry VIII forms Church of England

1535 Act of Union with Wales

1558–1603 Reign of Elizabeth I

1603 Union of English and Scottish crowns; James VI of Scotland becomes James I of England

1642 Civil War breaks out

1649 Charles I executed. Commonwealth declared by Parliament

1707 Act of Union with Scotland

1721 Robert Walpole becomes Britain's first Prime Minister

1837–1901 Reign of Queen Victoria. Industrial Revolution leads to growth of British Empire

1924 First Labour government

1948 National Health Service introduced

1973 Britain joins European Community

1999 Formation of Scottish Parliament and Welsh Assembly

2005 Terrorist attacks on public transport in London

2014 Referendum for Scottish Independence held

The colorful costumes of Notting Hill Carnival, an annual multicultural celebration held in London

The Eden Project, an entertaining educational center devoted to mankind's relationship with plants, Cornwall

which were former colonies are now members of the Commonwealth. Nearly five percent of Britain's 62 million inhabitants are from non-white ethnic groups – and about half of these were born in Britain. The result is a multicultural society that can boast a wide range of music, art, food, and religions.

Britain's class structure is based on a subtle mixture of heredity and wealth. Even though many of the great inherited fortunes no longer exist, some old landed families still live on their estates, and many now open them to the public. The monarchy's position highlights the dilemma of a people seeking to preserve its most potent symbol of national unity in an age when people are suspicious of inherited privilege. Without real political power, although still head of the Church of England, the Queen and her family are subject to increasing public scrutiny.

Democracy has deep foundations in Britain. With the exception of the 17th-century Civil War, power has passed gradually from the Crown to the people's elected representatives. During the 20th and 21st centuries, the Labour (left wing) and Conservative (right wing) parties have favored a mix of public and private ownership for industry and ample funding for the state health and welfare systems.

A cricketing pub sign showing the 18th-century version of the game

Culture and the Arts

Britain has a famous theatrical tradition stretching back to the 16th century and William Shakespeare. His plays have been performed on stage almost continuously since they were written, and the works of 17th- and 18th-century writers are also frequently revived. Modern British playwrights, such as Tom Stoppard, draw on this long tradition with their vivid language and use of comedy to illustrate serious themes.

In the visual arts, Britain has a strong tradition in portraiture, landscape, and watercolor. In modern times, artists David Hockney and Francis Bacon and sculptors Henry Moore and Barbara Hepworth have enjoyed worldwide recognition. Britain has also become famous for its innovative fashion designers, such as Vivienne Westwood and the late Alexander McQueen.

The national film industry produces occasional international hits, such as the *Harry Potter* saga and *The King's Speech*. British television is famous for the high quality of its news, current affairs, and nature programs, as well as for its drama.

The British are great sports fans. Soccer, rugby, cricket, and lawn tennis are popular. An instantly recognizable English image is that of the cricket match on a village green. The British also make use of their national parks as enthusiastic walkers and hikers.

Exploring Great Britain

Britain's main attraction is its capital, London, but there are many other noteworthy towns to explore throughout the country. Highlights include the university cities of Cambridge and Oxford, the historic centers of York and Bath, and Edinburgh, the capital of Scotland. In the sparsely populated regions of Northern England, Wales, and Scotland, the land itself becomes the center of attention – the Lake District, Snowdonia, and the Isle of Skye are all areas of outstanding natural beauty.

Sights at a Glance

1. London pp50–71
2. Canterbury
3. Brighton
4. Windsor Castle pp74–5
5. Winchester
6. Salisbury
7. Stonehenge
8. Devon and Cornwall
9. Bath pp78–9
10. Bristol
11. Cardiff
12. Snowdonia
13. Caernarfon
14. Oxford
15. Blenheim Palace pp82–3
16. Stratford-upon-Avon
17. Cambridge
18. Chester
19. Liverpool
20. Manchester
21. York pp86–7
22. Lake District
23. Durham
24. Edinburgh pp90–94
25. Glasgow
26. Stirling
27. St. Andrews
28. Aberdeen
29. Cairngorms
30. Inverness
31. Isle of Skye

Brighton's Palace Pier, viewed from the promenade

Key

— Highway

— Major road

— Railroad

···· Channel Tunnel

▬▪▬ International border

– – Administrative border

Distance chart

London

Distance by road in kilometers
Distance by road in miles

London								
179 111	Birmingham							
241 150	**164** 102	Cardiff						
599 372	**466** 290	**600** 373	Edinburgh					
626 389	**470** 292	**602** 374	**72** 45	Glasgow				
851 529	**721** 448	**853** 530	**254** 158	**269** 167	Inverness			
296 184	**130** 81	**278** 173	**343** 213	**344** 214	**597** 371	Manchester		
341 212	**332** 206	**261** 152	**784** 426	**785** 545	**1038** 250	**451**	Plymouth	
333 207	**208** 129	**381** 237	**301** 187	**344** 214	**550** 342	**106** 66	**532** 331	York

The haunting landscape of the Isle of Skye

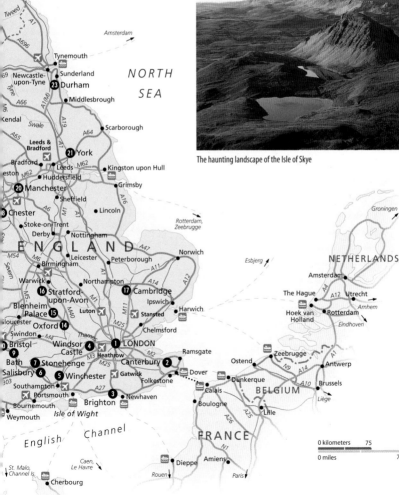

❶ London

The largest city in Europe, London is home to more than seven million people. Founded by the Romans in the first century AD as an administrative center and trading port, the capital is the principal residence of British monarchs, as well as the center of government and business, and is rich in historic buildings. In addition to its many museums and galleries, London is an exciting city, with a vast array of entertainments. In 2012, London hosted the Olympic Games. Developments completed for the event, such as the Aquatics Centre, designed by Zaha Hadid, have added to the city's attractions.

Millennium Foot Bridge, leading to Tate Modern on Bankside

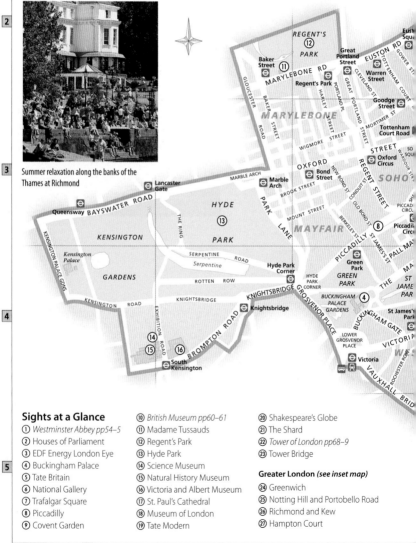

Summer relaxation along the banks of the Thames at Richmond

Sights at a Glance

① *Westminster Abbey pp54–5*
② Houses of Parliament
③ EDF Energy London Eye
④ Buckingham Palace
⑤ Tate Britain
⑥ National Gallery
⑦ Trafalgar Square
⑧ Piccadilly
⑨ Covent Garden

⑩ *British Museum pp60–61*
⑪ Madame Tussauds
⑫ Regent's Park
⑬ Hyde Park
⑭ Science Museum
⑮ Natural History Museum
⑯ Victoria and Albert Museum
⑰ St. Paul's Cathedral
⑱ Museum of London
⑲ Tate Modern

⑳ Shakespeare's Globe
㉑ The Shard
㉒ *Tower of London pp68–9*
㉓ Tower Bridge

Greater London *(see inset map)*

㉔ Greenwich
㉕ Notting Hill and Portobello Road
㉖ Richmond and Kew
㉗ Hampton Court

Getting Around

London's subway system – the "tube" or "underground" – runs from about 5:30am until just after midnight. Overground rail services are useful for trips farther afield. London's buses are now much quicker, since the introduction of the Congestion Charge (£10 a day) to enter central London with a car. The well-known black cabs are a safe and convenient way to travel from door to door.

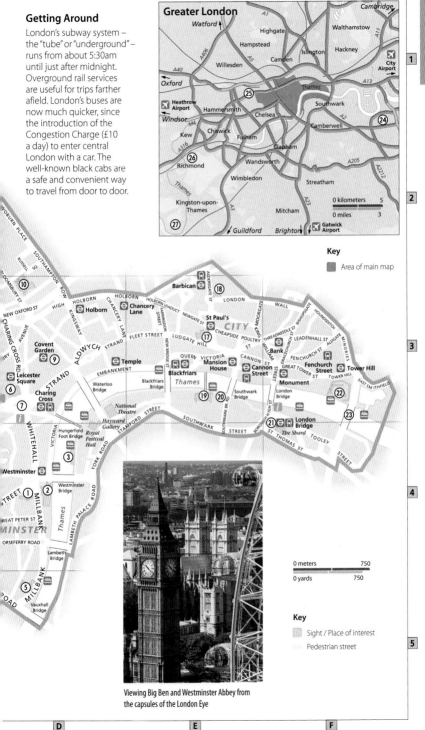

Viewing Big Ben and Westminster Abbey from the capsules of the London Eye

Key

Sight / Place of interest

Pedestrian street

Street by Street: Whitehall and Westminster

Westminster has been at the center of political and religious power in England since the 11th century, when King Canute built a palace here and Edward the Confessor founded Westminster Abbey. Whitehall is synonymous with the ministries concentrated around it. On weekdays, the streets are crowded with civil servants going about their business, replaced at weekends by a steady flow of tourists.

Downing Street
No. 10 has been the prime minister's official residence since 1732, when Sir Robert Walpole was given the house by George II.

The Cabinet War Rooms,
now open to the public, were Winston Churchill's World War II headquarters.

St. Margaret's Church
is a favorite venue for political and society weddings.

★ **Westminster Abbey**
The abbey (see pp54–5) is London's oldest and most important church. The north facade is a Victorian addition.

Central Hall was built in 1911 as a Methodist meeting hall. In 1946, it hosted the first General Assembly of the United Nations.

Dean's Yard
This secluded grassy square is surrounded by picturesque buildings from different periods, many used by Westminster School.

Statue of Richard the Lionheart (1860)

The Burghers of Calais is a cast of Auguste Rodin's 1886 original sculpture in France.

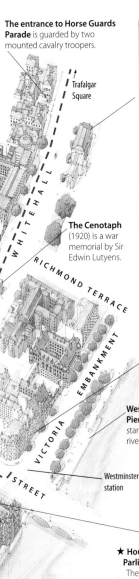

The entrance to **Horse Guards Parade** is guarded by two mounted cavalry troopers.

Trafalgar Square

WHITEHALL

RICHMOND TERRACE

EMBANKMENT

VICTORIA

STREET

The Cenotaph (1920) is a war memorial by Sir Edwin Lutyens.

The Norman Shaw Buidings were the site of the original Scotland Yard, headquarters of the Metropolitan Police.

Westminster Pier is the main starting point for river trips.

Westminster station

★ **Houses of Parliament**
The seat of government is dominated by the clock tower, holding the 14-ton bell Big Ben, hung in 1858. Its deep chimes are broadcast daily on BBC radio.

Banqueting House
Inigo Jones designed this elegant Palladian building in 1622. It is famous for this ceiling painted by Rubens for Charles I.

Key

— Suggested route

0 meters 100
0 yards 100

① **Westminster Abbey**

See pp54–5.

② **Houses of Parliament**

SW1. **Tel** 020-7219 3000.
🚇 Westminster. 🚌 3, 11, 12, 24, 53, 88, 148, 159, 211, 453. 📞 call 020-7219 4272 or email hcinfo@ parliament.uk for information. Tickets for guided tours are available through www.ticketmaster.co.uk 🌐 **parliament.uk**

Since the 16th century, this site has been the seat of the two Houses of Parliament: the House of Commons, made up of elected Members of Parliament (MPs), and the upper house, the House of Lords. The latter, formerly filled with hereditary peers, bishops, and life peers, was reformed in 2000.

The present Neo-Gothic building replaced the original palace, which was destroyed by fire in 1834.

To hear debates in either of the houses from the visitors' galleries, you can purchase a ticket on the day from next to the Jewel Tower in Abingdon Green. To attend Prime Minister's Question Time, apply for tickets to your local MP or to your embassy well ahead.

③ **EDF Energy London Eye**

South Bank SE1. **Tel** 0871-781 3000.
🚇 Waterloo, Westminster. 🚌 77, RV1, 381. **Open** daily. **Closed** Dec 25, Jan 8–21. 🌐 (pick up tickets at County Hall, next to the Eye, at least 30 mins before boarding time). 🌐 **londoneye.co.uk**

Reaching to a height of 135 m (443 ft) above the Thames River, this is the world's highest Ferris wheel, and was installed to mark the Millennium. Its capsules offer a gentle, 30-minute ride as the wheel makes a full turn, with breathtaking views over the city and for up to 42 km (26 miles) beyond. "Flights" are on the hour or half-hour, and need to be booked in advance.

① Westminster Abbey

Westminster Abbey has been the burial place of Britain's monarchs since the 11th century and the setting for many coronations and royal weddings, including the marriage of the Duke and Duchess of Cambridge in 2011. It has an exceptionally diverse array of architectural styles, ranging from the austere French Gothic of the nave to the astonishing complexity of Henry VII's chapel. Half national church, half national museum, the abbey is crammed with an extraordinary collection of tombs and monuments honoring some of Britain's greatest public figures, from politicians to poets.

★ Nave
Built under the direction of master mason Henry Yevele, the nave reaches to a height of 31 m (102 ft).

North/Main Entrance

The Coronation Chair has been used at every coronation since its construction in 1308.

KEY

① **Statesmen's Aisle** contains monuments to some of the country's greatest political leaders.

② **The Sanctuary**, built by Henry III, has been the scene of 38 coronations.

③ **The Pyx Chamber** is where the coinage was thoroughly tested in medieval times.

④ **The museum** has many of the abbey's treasures, including wood, plaster, and wax effigies of monarchs.

⑤ **The Cloisters**, built mainly in the 13th and 14th centuries, link the abbey church with the other buildings.

Coronation

The coronation ceremony is more than 1,000 years old and since 1066, with the crowning of William the Conqueror on Christmas Day, Westminster Abbey has been its sumptuous setting. The coronation of Queen Elizabeth II in 1953 was the first to be televised.

Flying Buttresses
The massive flying buttresses help transfer the great weight of the 31-m (102-ft) high nave.

★ Henry VII Chapel
The Chapel, built in 1503–19, has superb late Perpendicular vaultings and choir stalls dating from 1512.

VISITORS' CHECKLIST

Practical Information
Broad Sanctuary SW1. **Tel** 020-7222 5152. Cloisters: **Open** 8am–6pm daily. Royal Chapels, Poets' Corner, Chapter House, Choir, Statesmen's Aisle & Nave: **Open** 9:30am–4:30pm Mon–Fri (until 7pm Wed), 9:30am–2pm Sat. Museum: **Open** 10:30am–4pm Mon–Sat. 🚫 free to cloisters, College Garden and St. Margaret's Church; the rest has an admission charge. 📷 ♿ limited. ✝ Evensong: 5pm Mon–Fri, 3pm Sat & Sun. 📱 📷 **w westminster-abbey.org**

Transport
🚇 St. James's Park, Westminster. 🚌 3, 11, 12, 24, 53, 88, 148, 159, 211, 453. 🚢 Westminster Pier.

★ Chapter House
This beautiful octagonal room, remarkable for its 13th-century tiled floor, is lit by six huge stained-glass windows showing scenes from the abbey's history.

Historical Plan of the Abbey

The first abbey church was established as early as the 10th century, but the present French-influenced Gothic structure was begun in 1245 at the behest of Henry III. Because of its unique role as the coronation church, the abbey escaped Henry VIII's dissolution of Britain's monastic buildings (1536–9) during the Protestant Reformation.

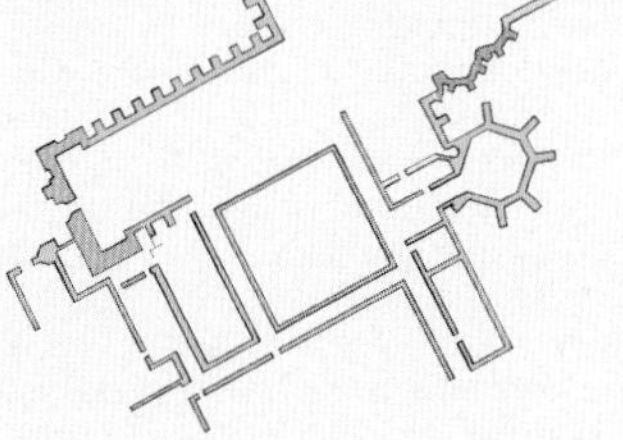

Key
- ▦ Built before 1400
- ▦ Built in 1503–19
- ▦ Completed by 1745
- ▢ Completed after 1850

Poets' Corner
Among the great poets honored here are Shakespeare *(above)*, Chaucer, and T.S. Eliot.

The Victoria Monument, Buckingham Palace

④ Buckingham Palace

SW1. **Tel** 020-7766 7300. 🚇 St. James's Park, Victoria, Green Park. 🚌 C1, C10, 11, 16, 36, 38, 52, 73, 211. State Rooms: **Open** Aug–end Sep: daily. 📷 🚫 ♿ phone first. Queen's Gallery: 📷 Changing of the Guard: 11:30am on alternate days (subject to change). **Tel** 020-7321 2233. 💳
w royalcollection.org.uk

The Queen's official London home is a very popular attraction. Conversion of the 18th-century Buckingham House was begun for George IV in 1826, but the first monarch to occupy the palace was Queen Victoria, in 1837. When the monarch is in residence, the Royal Standard flag is flown.

The palace tour takes visitors up the grand staircase and through the splendor of the state rooms. The royal family's private apartments are not open to the public.

In the Music Room, royal babies are christened and state guests presented. The Queen carries out many formal ceremonies in the richly gilded Throne Room, and the Ballroom is used for state banquets and investitures.

Valuable works of art, such as *The Music Lesson* (c.1660) by Dutch master Jan Vermeer, are on display in the Picture Gallery. A selection of works from the monarch's art collection, one of the finest and most valuable in the world, is displayed in the **Queen's Gallery**, a small building located to one side of the palace. The famous Changing of the Guard takes place on the palace forecourt. Crowds gather to watch the colorful half-hour parade of guards, dressed in red jackets and tall, furry hats called bearskins, exchanging the palace keys.

State coaches and other official vehicles may be viewed at the Royal Mews nearby. The star exhibit is the gold state coach built for George III in 1761, with fine panels by Giovanni Cipriani.

Overlooking the forecourt, the East Wing facade of the palace was redesigned by Aston Webb in 1913. He also created the spacious, tree-lined avenue known as the Mall, which leads from the palace to Trafalgar Square. Used for royal processions on special occasions, the Mall is closed to traffic on Sundays. The national flags of foreign heads of state fly from its flagpoles during official visits.

The avenue follows the edge of St. James's Park, a reserve for wildfowl and popular picnic spot in the heart of the city. Originally a marsh, the park was drained by Henry VIII and incorporated into his hunting grounds. Later, Charles II redesigned it as a fashionable promenade, with an aviary along its southern edge (from which Birdcage Walk takes its name). In summer, concerts are held on the park bandstand.

⑤ Tate Britain

Millbank SW1. **Tel** 020-7887 8888. 🚇 Pimlico. 🚌 77a, 88, 507, C10. 🚤 between Tate Britain and Tate Modern. **Open** 10am–6pm daily. **Closed** Dec 24–26. 📷 for major exhibitions. ♿ 🚫 📷 💳 📷
w tate.org.uk

Founded in 1897, the Tate Gallery, now called Tate Britain, focuses primarily on British art. Many of the modern works formerly kept here have been moved to the Tate Modern (see p67), further down the Thames River.

Tate Britain shows the world's largest display of British art, ranging from Tudor times to present day, in line with the original intention of the gallery's sponsor, sugar magnate Sir Henry Tate.

One of the most exquisite early works is a portrait of a bejeweled Elizabeth I (c.1575), by Nicholas Hilliard. The influence of the 17th-century Flemish artist Sir Anthony van Dyck on English painters can be seen in William Dobson's *Endymion Porter* (1642–5) and the works of Thomas Gainsborough (1727–88).

Among the collection are some fine examples of William Hogarth's sharply satirical pictures. The famed horse paintings of George Stubbs include *Mares and Foals in a Landscape* (1760).

Tate Britain holds a large number of paintings by the visionary poet and artist William

The portico of the Tate Britain building, dating from 1897

The Trafalgar Square facade of the National Gallery

Blake (1757–1827). His work was imbued with a mystical intensity, a typical example being *Satan Smiting Job with Sore Boils* (c.1826). England's great 19th-century landscape artists, Constable and Turner, are also well represented. John Constable's famous *Flatford Mill*, painted in 1816–17, is one of his many depictions of the Essex countryside. The Clore Galleries, open since 1987, house the works of J.M.W. Turner (1775–1851), whose paintings were left to the nation some years after his death on condition that they were kept together. His watercolor *A City on a River at Sunset* (1832) is a highlight.

The Tate also has on display many works by the 19th-century Pre-Raphaelites, including J.E. Millais' *Ophelia* (1851–2), as well as the works of several modern and contemporary artists, such as Henry Moore and David Hockney. The Tate's exhibitions change frequently to explore as much of the collection as possible.

⑥ National Gallery

Trafalgar Sq WC2. **Tel** 020-7747 2885. ⊖ Charing Cross, Leicester Sq, Piccadilly Circus. 🚌 3, 6, 9, 11 & many others. **Open** 10am–6pm daily (to 9pm Fri). **Closed** Jan 1, Dec 24–26. ♿ via Sainsbury Wing entrance. 🎫 📷 🖥 **nationalgallery.org.uk**

London's leading art museum, the National Gallery has more than 2,300 paintings, most on permanent display. The collection was started in 1824 when the House of Commons agreed to purchase 38 major paintings. These became the core of a national collection of European art that now ranges from Giotto in the 13th century to the 19th-century Impressionists. The gallery's particular strengths are in Dutch, Italian Renaissance, and 17th-century Spanish painting.

The gallery's paintings are hung in chronological order. In 1991, the modern Sainsbury Wing was added to the main Neoclassical building (1834–8) to house the impressive Early Renaissance collection (1260–1510). *The Leonardo Cartoon* (c.1500), a chalk drawing by Leonardo da Vinci of the Virgin and Child, St. Anne, and John the Baptist, has been moved from here to a more prominent position near the Trafalgar Square entrance. Other Italian painters represented include Masaccio, Piero della Francesca, and Botticelli. Perhaps the most famous of the Northern European works is *The Arnolfini Marriage* by Jan van Eyck (1434).

Most of the gallery's other exhibits are housed on the first floor of the main building. Among the 16th-century paintings, *The Adoration of the Kings* (1564) by Flemish artist Pieter Brueghel the Elder is notable. *Christ Mocked* (1490–1500) by Hieronymus Bosch is included in the Netherlandish and German section. The superb Dutch collection gives two rooms to Rembrandt. Annibale Carracci and Caravaggio are strongly represented among the Italian painters. Spanish artist Diego Velázquez's only surviving female nude, *The Rokeby Venus* (1647–51), is one of the most popular and well-known of the 17th-century works of art. The great age of 19th-century landscape painting is perhaps best represented by Constable's *The Hay Wain* (1821), a masterpiece of changing light and shadow.

In the Impressionist section, Renoir's *Boating on the Seine* (1879–80) demonstrates the free, flickering touch used by the movement's artists to capture the fleeting moment. Other 19th-century highlights include Van Gogh's *Sunflowers*, Monet's *Waterlilies*, Rousseau's *Tropical Storm with Tiger*, and Seurat's *Bathers at Asnières*.

Lesser paintings of all periods are displayed on the lower floor of the main building. The better of the gallery's two restaurants is located in the Sainsbury Wing.

Bathers at Asnières (1884), by Georges Seurat, in the National Gallery

The West End

The West End is the city's social and cultural center located right next to the London home of the royal family. Stretching from the edge of Hyde Park to Covent Garden, the district bustles all day and late into the night. Whether you are looking for art, history, or street- or café-life, it is the most rewarding area in which to begin an exploration of the city. Monuments, shops, cinemas, and restaurants radiate out from Trafalgar Square, and the entertainment scene is at its liveliest in the busy streets around Chinatown, Soho, and Leicester Square. From the garish lights of boisterous Piccadilly Circus to genteel St. James's Square, the West End embraces all aspects of London life, and caters to every budget.

Trafalgar Square by night, with Nelson's Column in the foreground

⑦ Trafalgar Square

WC2. ⊖ Charing Cross. 🚌 3, 6, 9, 11, 12, 13, 15, 23, 24, 29, 53, 88, 91, 139, 159, 176, 453.

London's main venue for rallies and outdoor public meetings, Trafalgar Square was conceived by John Nash and mostly constructed during the 1830s. The 50-m (165-ft) tall column commemorates Admiral Lord Nelson, Britain's most famous sea lord, and dates from 1842. Edwin Landseer's four lions were added 25 years later. Today the square is very popular with tourists.

Admiralty Arch, designed in 1911, separates courtly London from the hurly-burly of Trafalgar Square. The central gate is opened only for royal processions. The restored buildings on the square's south side were built in 1880 as the Grand Hotel. The north side is now taken up by the National Gallery and its Sainsbury Wing (see p57). In the northeast corner stands **St. Martin-in-the-Fields**. This 18th-century church by James Gibbs became a model for the Colonial style of church-building in the US.

Adjoining the National Gallery, the **National Portrait Gallery** depicts Britain's history through portraits, photographs, and sculptures. Subjects range from Elizabeth I to photographs of politicians, actors, and rock stars.

Further north, Leicester Square is at the heart of the West End's entertainment district, with the city's leading cinemas and lively nightclubs, while London's Chinatown attracts a steady throng of diners and shoppers. Bordering it, Shaftesbury Avenue is the main artery of London's theaterland.

🏛 National Portrait Gallery
2 St. Martin's Place WC2. **Tel** 020-7306 0055. **Open** daily. **Closed** Dec 24–26. 📷 for special exhibitions. 🚫 📱 🎞 🎧 audio guide. 🔗 **npg.org.uk**

⑧ Piccadilly

W1. ⊖ Piccadilly Circus, Green Park. 🚌 9, 14, 19, 22, 38.

The thoroughfare called Piccadilly links Hyde Park Corner with Piccadilly Circus, but the name also refers to the surrounding area. Today, Piccadilly has two contrasting faces: a bustling commercial district full of shopping arcades, eateries, and cinemas; and St. James's, to the south, which still focuses on a wealthy, glamorous clientele.

Piccadilly Circus, with its dazzling neon lights, is a focal point of the West End. It began as an early 19th-century crossroads between Piccadilly and John Nash's Regent Street. Briefly an elegant space, edged by curving stucco facades, by 1910 the first electric advertisements had been installed.

Crowds congregate beneath the delicately poised figure of Eros, the Greek god of love. Erected in 1892 as a memorial to the Earl of Shaftesbury, a Victorian philanthropist, the statue was originally intended to represent an angel of mercy.

Among the many notable sights along Piccadilly, the **Royal Academy**, founded in 1768, houses a permanent art collection, including a Michelangelo relief of the *Madonna and Child* (1505). Its annual summer exhibition is renowned for its clever juxtaposition of new and established works.

The tranquil **St. James's Church** was designed by Sir

Alfred Gilbert's 1892 statue of Eros in Piccadilly Circus

A street performer in front of crowds in Covent Garden's Piazza

Christopher Wren in 1684, and the 18th-century **Spencer House** contains fine period furniture and paintings. This Palladian palace was built for an ancestor of Princess Diana.

Shopping in and around Piccadilly is very expensive, especially in Bond Street, where many famous designer labels have stores, and in the Burlington Arcade, which is patroled by beadles. On Piccadilly itself, Fortnum and Mason, founded in 1707, is one of London's most prestigious food stores, while the grand Ritz hotel is a popular afternoon-tea venue for the suitably dressed. Jermyn Street is renowned for high-quality men's clothing.

South of Piccadilly is St. James's Square, laid out in the 1670s and dominated by a statue of William III. It has long been the most fashionable address in London. Pall Mall, named after the 17th-century game of *palle-maille* (a cross between croquet and golf) once played here, is lined with gentlemen's clubs, which admit only members and their guests. It leads to the 16th-century **St. James's Palace**, built for Henry VIII. The palace is still the official headquarters of the Court of St. James. Opposite is the **Queen's Chapel**, the first Classical church in England.

Royal Academy
Burlington House, Piccadilly W1.
Tel 020-7300 8000. **Open** daily.
Closed Good Fri, Dec 24 & 25. for exhibitions. reserve in advance.
royalacademy.org.uk

Spencer House
27 St. James's Pl SW1. **Tel** 020-7499 8620. **Open** Sun. **Closed** Jan & Aug.
compulsory (call 020-7514 1958). **spencerhouse.co.uk**

⑨ Covent Garden

WC2. Covent Garden. 1, 6, 9, 13, 15, 23, 59, 68, 87, 91, 168, 171, 176. daily.

Open-air cafés, street entertainers, stylish shops, and markets make Covent Garden a magnet for visitors. The name derives from a medieval convent garden which supplied Westminster Abbey with produce.

At its center is the Piazza, designed by 17th-century architect Inigo Jones as an elegant residential square, after an example from the Tuscan town of Livorno. For a time, houses around the Piazza were highly sought-after, but decline accelerated when a fruit and vegetable market developed. In 1973, the market moved to a new site and Covent Garden was revamped. Today, only **St. Paul's Church** remains of Inigo Jones's buildings. Samuel Pepys saw a Punch and Judy show under the portico in 1662, and street entertainment has been a tradition here ever since.

The **Royal Opera House** *(see p103)*, designed in 1858 by E.M. Barry, but totally renovated in 1997–9, is home to the Royal Opera and Royal Ballet Companies. Many of the world's greatest dance performers have appeared on its stage.

Covent Garden has many theatrical associations. The site of the **Theatre Royal**, completed in 1812, has been occupied by a theater since 1663. **St. Martin's Theatre** is home to the world's longest-running play, *The Mousetrap*.

Other attractions include the **London Transport Museum** and an area of "alternative" shops around Neal Street and Neal's Yard. The **Lamb and Flag** (1623) in Rose Street is one of London's oldest pubs.

London Transport Museum
Covent Garden WC2. **Tel** 020-7379 6344. **Open** daily. **Closed** Dec 24–26.
ltmuseum.co.uk

Statue of a resting ballerina facing the Royal Opera House

⑩ British Museum

The oldest public museum in the world, the British Museum was established in 1753 to house the collections of the physician Sir Hans Sloane (1660–1753). Sloane's artifacts have been added to by gifts and purchases from all over the world, and the museum now contains innumerable items stretching from the present day to prehistory. Robert Smirke designed the main part of the building (1823–50), but the architectural highlight is the modern Great Court, with its remarkable roof. The 94 galleries which run for more than 4 km (2 miles), cover civilizations from ancient Assyria to modern Japan.

Prehistoric and Roman Britain

Relics of prehistoric Britain are on display in this collection. The most impressive items include the Mold gold cape made from a sheet of decorated gold; an antlered headdress worn by hunter-gatherers some 9,000 years ago; and "Lindow Man," a 1st-century AD sacrificial victim who lay preserved in a bog until 1984. Some superb Celtic metalwork is also on show, alongside the silver Mildenhall Treasure and other notable Roman pieces. The Hinton St. Mary mosaic (4th century AD) features a roundel containing the earliest known British depiction of Christ.

Medieval, Renaissance, and Modern Objects

The spectacular Sutton Hoo ship treasure, the burial hoard of a 7th-century Anglo-Saxon king, is on display in Room 41. This superb find, unearthed in Woodbridge, near Suffolk, in 1939, revolutionized scholars' understanding of Anglo-Saxon life and ritual. The artifacts uncovered include a helmet and shield, Celtic hanging bowls, the remains of a lyre, and gold and garnet jewelry.

Adjacent galleries contain a collection of clocks and watches. Some exquisite timepieces are on view here, including an over 400-year-old clock from Prague, designed as a model galleon; in its day, it pitched, played music, and even fired a cannon. Also nearby are

Reconstruction of the ceremonial helmet found at Sutton Hoo

the famous 12th-century Lewis chessmen and a gold enameled reliquary of the Holy Thorn (Christ's Crown of Thorns), dating from the 15th century and said to have belonged to Jean, duc de Berry. Another highlight is a Byzantine icon painted on a wooden tablet.

The museum's modern collection includes Wedgwood pottery, glassware, and a series of Russian revolutionary plates.

Middle East

Numerous galleries at the museum are devoted to the Middle Eastern collections, covering 7,000 years of history. The most famous items are the 7th-century BC Assyrian reliefs from King Ashurbanipal's palace at Nineveh, but of equal interest are two large human-headed bulls from 7th-century BC Khorsabad, and an inscribed Black Obelisk of Assyrian King Shalmaneser III. Rooms 51–59, on the upper floor, contain pieces from ancient Sumeria, part of the Oxus Treasure (which lay buried for over 2,000 years), and the museum's collection of clay cuneiform tablets. The earliest of these are inscribed with the oldest known pictographs (c.3300 BC).

Ancient Egypt

Egyptian sculptures can be found in Room 4 on the main floor. These include a fine red granite head of a king, thought to be Amenophis III, and a colossal statue of king Ramses II. Also on show is the Rosetta Stone, which was used by Jean-François Champollion (1790–1832) as a primer for deciphering Egyptian hieroglyphs. An extraordinary array of mummies, jewelry, and Coptic art can also be found in rooms 61–66 upstairs, including a famous bronze cat with a gold nose-ring. The various instruments used by embalmers to preserve bodies before entombment are all displayed.

Ancient Egyptian tomb painting, *The Festival of Sekhet* (1410 BC)

The Portland Vase, depicting the betrothal of Peleus and Thetis

Greece and Rome

The Greek and Roman collections include the museum's most famous treasure, the Elgin Marbles. These 5th-century BC reliefs from the Parthenon once comprised a marble frieze which decorated Athena's temple at the Acropolis in Athens. Much of it was ruined in battle in 1687, and half of what survived was removed between 1801 and 1804 by the British diplomat Lord Elgin, and sold to the British nation. Other highlights include the Nereid Monument, and sculptures and friezes from the Mausoleum at Halicarnassus. The beautiful 1st-century BC cameo-glass Portland Vase is located in the Roman Empire section.

Oriental Art

Fine porcelain and ancient Shang bronzes (c.1500–1050 BC) are highlights of the museum's Chinese collection. Particularly impressive are the ceremonial ancient Chinese bronze vessels, with their enigmatic animal-head shapes. The fine Chinese ceramics range from delicate tea bowls to a model pond which is almost a thousand years old. Adjacent to these is one of the finest collections of Asian religious sculpture outside India. These include an assortment of sculpted reliefs which once covered the walls of the

The Young Prince with his Parents (c.1600), an Indian miniature

Buddhist temple at Amarati, and which recount stories from the life of the Buddha. A Korean section contains some gigantic works of Buddhist art.

Islamic art, including a stunning jade terrapin found in a water tank, can be found in Room 34. Rooms 90–94 house temporary exhibitions for prints and drawings from Asia.

Africa

An interesting collection of African sculptures, textiles, and graphic art can be found in Room 25, located in the basement. Famous bronzes from the Kingdom of Benin stand alongside modern African prints, paintings, and drawings, plus an array of colorful fabrics.

VISITORS' CHECKLIST

Practical Information
Great Russell St WC1.
Tel 020-7323 8299.
Open 10am–5:30pm daily
(to 8:30pm Fri). **Closed** Jan 1,
Dec 24–26. 🎫 🚻 🚹 📷 🏛
🖥 thebritishmuseum.ac.uk

Transport
🚌 7, 8, 10, 14, 19, 24, 25, 29, 30,
38, 55, 68, 134, 188.
🚇 Tottenham Court Road,
Holborn, Russell Square.

The Great Court and the Reading Room

Surrounding the Reading Room of the former British Library, the £100-million Great Court opened to coincide with the new millennium. Designed by Sir Norman Foster, the Court is covered by a wide-span, lightweight roof, creating London's first ever indoor public square. Originally completed in 1857, the Reading Room soon became a world-famous center of learning. From the outside, however, it is now scarcely recognizable as the space that was favored by the likes of Karl Marx, Mahatma Gandhi, and George Bernard Shaw. The Reading Room is housed in a multi-level construction which partly supports the roof, and which also contains a Center for Education, temporary exhibition galleries, bookstores, cafés, and restaurants. The Reading Room currently hosts major exhibitions, but its future use is under debate.

The Great Court and Reading Room of the British Museum

⑪ Madame Tussauds

Marylebone Rd NW1. **Tel** 0871-894 3000. ⊖ Baker St. **Open** from 9:30am daily; closing times vary. **Closed** Dec 24 (afternoon) & Dec 25. 🎨 🏛 💻 ♿ 🕸 **madame-tussauds.com**

Madame Tussaud began her wax-modeling career making death masks of victims of the French Revolution. In 1835, after moving to England, she set up an exhibition of her work in Baker Street, near the museum's present site.

Traditional techniques are still used to create the figures of royalty, politicians, actors, pop stars, and sporting heroes.

In the renowned Chamber of Horrors, some of the original French Revolution death masks are displayed, and vivid scenes of murders are staged: the murderer Dr. Crippen, Vlad the impaler, and the chilly gloom of an east London Victorian street during Jack the Ripper's time in the late 19th century.

In the final section – the Spirit of London – visitors travel in stylized taxi-cabs and participate in momentous events in the city's history, from the Great Fire of 1666 to the Swinging Sixties.

Making a model of singer Luciano Pavarotti at Madame Tussauds

⑫ Regent's Park

NW1. **Tel** 0300-061 2300. ⊖ Regent's Park, Great Portland St, Camden Town. **Open** daily. ♿ London Zoo: **Tel** 0844-225 1826. **Open** daily. **Closed** Dec 25. 🎨 🕸 **royalparks.org.uk**

This area of land was enclosed as a park in 1812. John Nash designed the scheme and originally envisaged a kind of garden suburb, dotted with

Wooden rowboats available to rent on Regent's Park boating lake

56 villas in a variety of Classical styles. Eight villas were eventually built inside the park (three survive round the edge of the Inner Circle).

The boating lake boasts many varieties of water birds. In summer, Queen Mary's Gardens are full of flowers and Shakespeare productions are staged at the Open Air Theatre nearby. Musical performances are also held at the bandstand on the weekend. Broad Walk provides a picturesque stroll north from Park Square towards Primrose Hill.

London Zoo, with its vast animal enclosures, borders the park, and is also an important center of wildlife research and conservation work.

⑬ Hyde Park

W2. **Tel** 0300-061 2000. ⊖ Hyde Park Corner, Knightsbridge, Lancaster Gate, Marble Arch. **Open** dawn–midnight daily. ♿ 🕸 **royalparks.org.uk**

The ancient manor of Hyde was part of the lands of Westminster Abbey seized by Henry VIII at the Dissolution of the Monasteries in 1536. James I opened the park to the public in the early 17th century, and it was soon one of the city's most fashionable public spaces. Unfortunately, it also became popular with duelists and highwaymen, prompting William III to have 300 lights hung along Rotten Row, the first street in England to be lit at night. Today, Rotten Row is used for horseback riding.

Statue of Peter Pan in Kensington Gardens

In 1730, the Westbourne River was dammed by Queen Caroline to create an artificial lake – the Serpentine. Today, cafés, restaurants, and the Serpentine Gallery, which has exhibitions of modern art, dot the fringes of the lake, which is a popular venue for boating and swimming.

At the southeast corner of Hyde Park stands Apsley House, the grand former home of the Duke of Wellington. Now a museum of memorabilia to the great politician and soldier, the lavish interiors designed by Robert Adam are also worth seeing.

A law passed in 1872 made it legal to assemble an audience and address it on whatever topic you chose. Since then, Speaker's Corner, at the northeast corner of the park, has been the established venue for budding orators. Crowds gather on Sundays to listen to lively speeches.

Adjoining Hyde Park are Kensington Gardens, the former grounds of Kensington Palace, which were opened to the public in 1841. A royal residence for centuries, the palace was Princess Diana's home until her untimely death.

Attractions in the gardens include the bronze statue of J. M. Barrie's fictional Peter Pan (1912), by George Frampton, and the Round Pond where model boats are sailed. The dignified Orangery (1704) is now an upscale café.

Street by Street: South Kensington

The numerous museums and colleges created in the wake of the Great Exhibition of 1851 *(see pp64–5)* continue to give this neighborhood its dignified character. Visited as much by Londoners as tourists, the museum area is liveliest on Sundays and on summer evenings during the Royal Albert Hall's famous season of classical "Prom" concerts *(see p102)*.

The Royal Albert Hall
Opened in 1870 and modeled on a Roman amphitheater, this magnificent concert hall hosts a range of events.

to Kensington Gardens

The Memorial to the Great Exhibition is surmounted by a bronze statue of its instigator, Prince Albert.

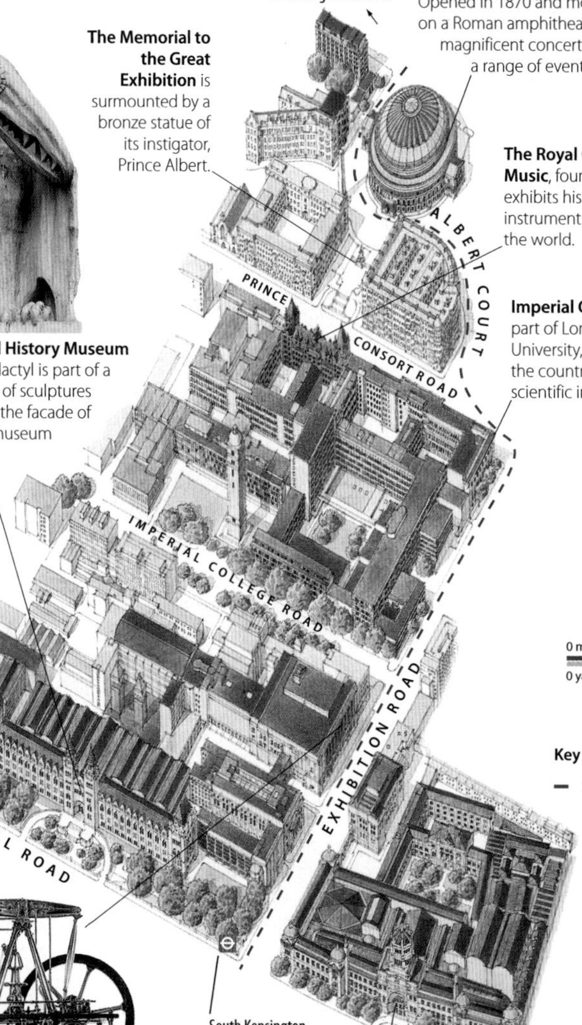

The Royal College of Music, founded in 1882, exhibits historic musical instruments from around the world.

Imperial College, part of London University, is one of the country's leading scientific institutions.

★ Natural History Museum
This pterodactyl is part of a menagerie of sculptures that adorn the facade of the great museum *(see p64)*.

ALBERT COURT

PRINCE CONSORT ROAD

IMPERIAL COLLEGE ROAD

EXHIBITION ROAD

CROMWELL ROAD

0 meters   100
0 yards   100

Key
— Suggested route

South Kensington station (two entrances on Exhibition Road)

★ Science Museum
Fascinating exhibits, such as this 18th-century steam engine, celebrate the history of science and technology *(see p64)*.

★ Victoria and Albert Museum
The museum has a fine collection of decorative arts from around the world *(see p65)*.

Children exploring the "Pattern Pod" at the Science Museum

⑭ Science Museum

Exhibition Rd SW7. ⊖ South Kensington. 🚌 14, 49, 70, 74, 345, 360, 414, 430, C1. **Tel** 0870-870 4868. **Open** daily. **Closed** Dec 24–26. 🅿 for special exhibitions only. 🛗
🖥 sciencemuseum.org.uk

Centuries of scientific and technological development are illustrated and explained at the Science Museum – from Ancient Greek and Roman medicine to space exploration and nuclear fission.

The massive and impressive collection, exhibited on five floors, includes steam engines, spacecraft, and early mechanical computers. The museum aims to bring entertainment to the process of learning, with numerous interactive displays for children and staff on hand to provide explanations. Of equal importance is the social context of science: how inventions have transformed day-to-day life, and the process of discovery itself.

The best of the displays are "Flight," which gives visitors the opportunity to experiment with aeronautical concepts, and "Launch Pad," designed to give 7- to 13-year-olds a knowledge of basic scientific principles.

"The Exploration of Space" exhibits the scarred Apollo 10 spacecraft which carried three astronauts to the moon and back in May 1969. There is also a video of the Apollo 11 moon landing a few weeks later.

The "Making the Modern World" gallery displays objects that have shaped the world as we know it. Among them are Stephenson's Rocket, the most advanced steam locomotive of its day, and Crick and Watson's DNA model.

Other popular sections include "Optics," which has holograms, lasers, and colormixing experiments, and "Power and Land Transport," which displays working steam engines, vintage trains, cars, and motorbikes.

The Wellcome Wing is devoted to contemporary science and technology. "Antenna" is a constantly updated exhibition devoted to the latest scientific breakthroughs. "Pattern Pod" introduces younger children to the patterns of science in a fun and colorful way. "In Future" is a multi-user game in which participants decide how current scientific research could affect the future. "Energy: Fuelling the Future" challenges kids to think about how mankind will meet its future energy needs through games and hands-on exhibits. Our understanding of human identity is the subject of "Who Am I?," where visitors can learn about genetics and current biomedical discoveries. The wing also contains an IMAX® cinema, a 4D motion-effects theater, and a café.

⑮ Natural History Museum

Cromwell Rd SW7. ⊖ South Kensington. 🚌 14, 49, 70, 74, 345, 360, 414, 430, C1. **Tel** 020-7942 5000. **Open** daily. **Closed** Dec 24–26. 🅿
🛗 🖥 nhm.ac.uk

This vast building, designed by Alfred Waterhouse, is the most architecturally flamboyant of the South Kensington museums. Its richly sculpted stonework conceals an iron and steel frame. This building technique was revolutionary when the museum first opened in 1881. The imaginative displays tackle fundamental issues, such as the ecology and evolution of the planet, the origin of species, and the development of human beings – all explained through a dynamic combination of the latest technology, interactive displays, and traditional exhibits.

Triceratops skull, Natural History Museum

The museum is divided into three sections: the Life and Earth Galleries and the Darwin Centre. In the Life Galleries, the Ecology exhibition begins its exploration of the complex web of the natural world, and man's role in it, through a convincing replica of a rain forest. The most popular exhibits are in the Dinosaur section, which has real dinosaur skeletons and life like animatronics. "Creepy Crawlies," with specimens from the insect and spider world, and the Mammals exhibition, enable visitors to see endangered and dangerous creatures.

The colorful "Antenna" section in the Science Museum Wellcome Wing

The Earth Galleries explore the history of Earth and its wealth of natural resources, and offer the opportunity to experience the rumblings of an earthquake. In the state-of-the-art Darwin Centre, housed in a steel-and-glass building, visitors can take an interactive journey inside a vast concrete cocoon that houses millions of specimens. It is also possible to observe how museum scientists work.

⑯ Victoria and Albert Museum

Cromwell Rd SW7. 🔵 South Kensington. 🚌 14, 74, C1. **Tel** 020-7942 2000. **Open** 10am–5:45pm daily (to 10pm Fri). **Closed** Dec 24–26. 🎟 for special exhibitions. 📷 ♿ 🌐 **vam.ac.uk**

Originally founded in 1852 as a Museum of Manufacturing – to inspire and raise standards among students of design – the V&A, as it is popularly known, has 11 km (7 miles) of galleries on four floors. The museum was renamed by Queen Victoria in 1899, in memory of her late husband, and contains one of the world's richest collections of fine and applied arts.

Since 1909, the museum has been housed in a building designed by Sir Aston Webb. The museum has undergone a dramatic restructuring of much of its collection and gallery spaces, alongside a grand development of the central John Madejski Garden.

Donatello's marble relief of *The Ascension* is included in the Sculpture collection, along with sculptures from India and the Middle and Far East. Craftsmanship in porcelain, glass, and pottery is displayed on levels 4 and 6, with rare pieces by Picasso and Bernard Leach, intricate Near Eastern tiles, and a wide selection of Chinese pieces.

The most celebrated item in the vast array of furniture is the *Great Bed of Ware*, made around

Facade of the Victoria and Albert Museum

18th-century wooden doll, Victoria and Albert Museum

1590. The Victorian designers who decorated the plush Morris, Gamble, and Poynter Rooms recreated historic styles with newer industrial materials. The fully furnished interiors offer a vivid picture of social life through their displays of furniture and other domestic objects. Among exhibits in the 20th-Century Gallery is Daniel Weil's painting *Radio in a Bag* (1983). The V&A has a wide collection of metalwork, including a 16th-century salt cellar, the *Burghley Nef*. The Silver Gallery also explores the history and techniques of silvermaking. Gallery III is devoted to the making of sculpture, ranging from medieval ivories to modern bronzes. Among the textiles, weapons, jewelry, metalwork, glass, and paintings of the South Asia Gallery is the automated *Tippoo's*

Tiger (c.1790), which mauls a European soldier when activated. Eight galleries devoted to the arts of the Far East display rare jade and ceramics, a giant Buddha's head from AD 700–900, and a Ming canopied bed. Among exhibits in the China Gallery is a watercolor on silk from the Qing Dynasty (1644–1912). The Toshiba Gallery focuses on Japanese art, including Samurai armor and woodblock prints. The world-renowned Fashion Court is displayed on level 1. Spanning more than four centuries, from the mid-1500s to the present day, it is the world's most comprehensive collection of clothing. Highlights include rare 17th-century gowns, 1930s eveningwear, and post-war couture, plus several key items from contemporary designers.

The museum also houses valuable illustrated documents in the National Art Library and the Photographs Gallery with images from 1856 to the present.

The City and Southwark

Dominated by gleaming office blocks, befitting its status as London's financial and business center, the City is also the oldest part of the capital. The Great Fire of 1666 obliterated many of its buildings, and much of the reconstruction was undertaken by Sir Christopher Wren. St. Paul's Cathedral is the most magnificent of his surviving works. Humming with activity in business hours, the City empties at night. Southwark, on the south bank of the Thames, was a refuge for prostitutes and gamblers in the Middle Ages. Theaters, including the Globe, where many of Shakespeare's plays were performed, and other places of entertainment were built along the waterfront in the second half of the 16th century.

Spacious interior of St. Paul's Cathedral, in the City

⑰ St. Paul's Cathedral

Ludgate Hill EC4. **Tel** 020-7246 8350.
🚇 City Thames Link. 🚇 St. Paul's,
Mansion House. 🚌 4, 11, 15, 17, 23,
25, 76 & 172. **Open** 8:30am–4pm
Mon–Sat; for services only Sun,
Dec 25 & Good Fri. Check website
for partial or full closures. 🎧 📷
🖥 stpauls.co.uk

Rebuilt on the site of a medieval cathedral after the Great Fire of 1666, this magnificent Baroque building, designed by Sir Christopher Wren, was completed in 1710.

St. Paul's has been the setting for great ceremonial events, including the funeral of Sir Winston Churchill in 1965 and the wedding of Prince Charles and Lady Diana in 1981.

At 110 m (360 ft) high, the dome is the second largest in the world, after that of St. Peter's in Rome. Supported by a brick cone, the lantern weighs a massive 850 tonnes. The dome's gallery affords a splendid view over London.

Modifications to Wren's original plan include the towers of the west front, the double colonnade of the west portico, and the balustrade – added against his wishes in 1718. Pediment carvings on the west portico show the Conversion of St. Paul.

Wren created a cool and majestic interior. The nave, transepts, and choir are arranged in the traditional shape of a cross. Its climax is in the great open space of the crossing, below the main dome, which is decorated with mono-chrome frescoes by Sir James Thornhill, a leading architectural painter of the time. From the south aisle, 259 steps ascend to the circular Whispering Gallery, so-called because of the unusual acoustics.

Much of the fine wrought ironwork was created by Jean Tijou, a Huguenot refugee. The intricate carvings of cherubs, fruits, and garlands on the choir stalls are the work of Grinling Gibbons.

Memorials to famous figures, such as Lawrence of Arabia and Lord Nelson, can be seen in the crypt. The inscription on Wren's tomb is fitting: "Reader, if you seek a monument, look all around you."

⑱ Museum of London

150 London Wall EC2. **Tel** 0207-0019
844. 🚇 Barbican, St. Paul's. **Open**
10am–6pm daily. **Closed** Dec 24–26.
♿ 🖥 museumoflondon.org.uk

This fascinating museum traces life in London from prehistoric times to the 20th century, through nine permanent galleries.

Objects from Roman London include a brightly colored 2nd-century fresco, while from the Tudor city, an example of an early English Delft plate, made in 1602 at Aldgate, bears an inscription praising Elizabeth I.

The 17th-century section contains the shirt Charles I wore on the scaffold, and an audio-visual display recreating the Great Fire of 1666. A dress in Spitalfields silk, dating from 1753, is among the many fine costumes on display.

One of the most popular exhibits is the lavishly gilded Lord Mayor's State Coach, built in 1757 and still used for the Lord Mayor's Show, held in November each year.

The Victorian Walk takes visitors back to the time of Charles Dickens, vividly recreating the atmosphere of 19th-century London with authentic shop interiors.

⑲ Tate Modern

Bankside SE1. **Tel** 020-7887 8888.
🚇 Southwark, Blackfriars, Waterloo.
🚌 45, 63, 100, 381, 344, RV1. 🚤 from
Tate Britain. **Open** 10am–6pm Sun–
Thu, 10am–10pm Fri & Sat. **Closed**
Dec 24–26. 🎟 special exhibitions.
♿ 📷 🖥 tate.org.uk/modern

One of the world's main collections of 20th-century art is housed in this imposing former power station, with its vast, cathedral-like spaces.

For hotels and restaurants see pp104–6 and pp107–9

Sculpture from the inaugural exhibition in the vast Turbine Hall, Tate Modern

Originally designed by Sir Giles Gilbert Scott, the architect of London's red telephone kiosks, the huge Bankside building was acquired by the Tate Gallery in 2000; it had been disused since 1981. Swiss architects were responsible for the building's redesign, which allows the works of art to be displayed in a dynamic style.

Unusually, the permanent collection is exhibited in four themed groups: poetry and dream, idea and object, states of flux and material gestures. The paintings and sculptures embrace Surrealism, Abstract Expressionism, Pop Art, and Minimal and Conceptual Art.

Major works include Picasso's *The Three Dancers*, Dalí's *The Metamorphosis of Narcissus*, and Andy Warhol's *Marilyn Diptych*. There are also temporary exhibitions of works by lesser-known artists, and by more controversial newcomers. At the top of the building are two floors enclosed in glass. One is a restaurant with superb views. Natural light filters down to the upper galleries.

⑳ Shakespeare's Globe

214 New Globe Walk SE1. **Tel** 020-7401 9919. ⊖ London Bridge, Mansion House, Southwark. **Open** daily. **Closed** Dec 24, 25. Performances: Apr–Oct. 🅿 ♿ 🅿 every 30 mins. 🆆 shakespearesglobe.com

A detailed reproduction of an Elizabethan theater has been built on the riverside close to the site of the original Globe, Shakespeare's "wooden O," where many of his plays were first performed. Open to the elements, the theater operates only in the summer. Seeing a play here can be a lively experience, with "groundlings" (those with cheap standing-room tickets) in front of the stage encouraged to cheer or jeer. An informative tour of the theater is offered by "resting" Globe actors, and visitors can enjoy being center stage among them. Beneath the theater is the Underglobe, where every aspect of Shakespeare's work is vividly brought to life through the use of modern technology and traditional crafts.

㉑ The Shard

London Bridge St, SE1. **Tel** 0844-499 7111 (bookings). ⊖ London Bridge. **Open** 9am–10pm daily. **Closed** Dec 25. 🅿 ♿ 🆆 theviewfromthe shard.com

Designed by the Italian architect Renzo Piano, The Shard is the tallest building in western Europe at 310 m (1,016 ft). Its iconic shape dominates the London skyline, its appearance changing with the weather thanks to the crystalline facade that reflects the sunlight and sky. The building's 95 floors are

home to offices, top restaurants, the five-star Shangri-La hotel, and apartments. There is also an observation gallery, The View, which allows visitors to enjoy 360-degree panoramas covering 64 km (40 miles). The top four floors of the building house a range of multimedia displays.

㉒ Tower of London

See pp68–9.

㉓ Tower Bridge

SE1. **Tel** 020-7403 3761. ⊖ Tower Hill, London Bridge. The Tower Bridge Exhibition: **Open** daily. **Closed** Dec 24–26. 🅿 ♿ 🅿 🆆 towerbridge. org.uk

This flamboyant piece of Victorian engineering, completed in 1894, soon became a symbol of London. Its two Gothic towers contain the mechanism for raising the roadway to permit large ships to pass through. The towers are made of a supporting steel framework clad in stone. When raised, the roadway creates a space 40 m (135 ft) high and 60 m (200 ft) wide. In its heyday, it was raised and lowered five times a day.

The bridge now houses **The Tower Bridge Exhibition**, with displays which bring its history to life. There are fine river views from the walkways between the towers, and the steam-engine room, which was in use until 1976, can be visited.

Tower Bridge, a symbol of London

㉒ Tower of London

Soon after he became king in 1066, William the Conqueror built a fortress here to guard the entrance to London from the Thames Estuary. In 1097, the White Tower, which today occupies the center of the complex, was completed in stone; other fine buildings have been added over the centuries. The Tower has served as a royal residence, armory, treasury, and most famously as a prison for enemies of the Crown. Some were tortured, and among those who met their death here were the "Princes in the Tower," the sons and heirs of Edward IV. Today, the Tower is a popular attraction, housing the Crown Jewels and other fine exhibits. Thirty seven Yeoman Warders, known as "Beefeaters," guard the complex and live here. Its most celebrated residents are seven ravens. Legend claims that the kingdom will fall if they desert the Tower.

Beauchamp Tower
Many high-ranking prisoners were held here, often with their own servants. The tower was built by Edward I around 1281.

Queen's House
This Tudor building is the sovereign's official residence at the Tower.

KEY

① **Tower Green** was the execution site for aristocratic prisoners, away from crowds on Tower Hill, where many had to submit to public execution. Seven people died here, including two of Henry VIII's six wives, Anne Boleyn and Catherine Howard.

② **Two 13th-century curtain walls** protect the tower.

Main entrance from Tower Hill
(Middle Tower)

The Crown Jewels

The world's best-known collection of precious objects, now displayed in a splendid exhibition room, includes the gorgeous regalia of crowns, scepters, orbs, and swords used at coronations and other state occasions. Most date from 1661, when Charles II commissioned replacements for regalia destroyed by Parliament after the execution of Charles I. Only a few older pieces survived, hidden by royalist clergymen until the Restoration. These included Edward the Confessor's sapphire ring, now incorporated into the Imperial State Crown. The crown was made for Queen Victoria in 1837 and has been used at the coronation of every monarch since.

The Sovereign's Ring (1831)

The Sovereign's Orb (1661), a hollow gold sphere encrusted with jewels

★ **Jewel House**
Among the magnificent Crown Jewels is the Scepter with the Cross (1660), which contains the world's largest diamond.

★ **White Tower**
When the tower was finished in 1097, it was London's tallest building at 27 m (90 ft) high.

VISITORS' CHECKLIST

Practical Information

Tower Hill EC3. **Tel** 0870-756 7070. **Open** 10am–5:30pm Sun & Mon; 9am–5:30pm Tue–Sat; closes 4:30pm in winter. Last adm: 30 mins before closing. **Closed** Jan 1, Dec 24–26. 🏵 🛗 limited, except Jewel House. Ceremony of the Keys: 9:30pm daily. 🅆 **hrp.org.uk**

Transport

🚇 Tower Hill; Docklands Light Railway to Tower Gateway; London Bridge; Fenchurch St. 🚌 15, 42, 78, 100. 🚢 from Westminster to Tower Pier.

★ **Chapel of St. John**
This austere yet beautiful Romanesque chapel is a particularly fine example of Norman architecture.

Thames

Traitors' Gate
The infamous entrance was used for prisoners brought from trial in Westminster Hall.

Bloody Tower
Explored in a display here, Edward IV's two sons were put in the Bloody Tower by their uncle, Richard of Gloucester, in 1483. The princes, depicted here by John Millais (1829–96), disappeared mysteriously and their uncle became King Richard III later that year. In 1674, the skeletons of two children were found nearby.

London: Farther Afield

Over the centuries, London has steadily expanded to embrace the scores of villages that once surrounded it. Although now linked in an almost unbroken urban sprawl, many of these areas have managed to retain a strong individual character. Portobello Road has hosted a market since 1837, while Notting Hill, once farmland, is now covered with townhouses. Greenwich and Richmond recall the days when the Thames was an important artery for transport and commerce. The riverside around Richmond and Kew, to the southwest of London, was a favorite site for the great country retreats of the aristocracy. Perhaps the grandest riverside residence of all is the royal palace of Hampton Court, set in elaborate, luxurious gardens.

View of the 17th-century Queen's House at Greenwich

㉔ Greenwich

SE10. 🚇 Greenwich, Maze Hill, & Docklands Light Railway to Cutty Sark, Greenwich. 🚢 from Westminster.

Best known as the place from which the world's time is measured, Greenwich also marks the historic eastern approach to London by land and water. The area is steeped in maritime and royal history.

The meridian line that divides the earth's eastern and western hemispheres passes through the **Royal Observatory Greenwich** (now housing a museum). Designed by Christopher Wren, the building is topped by a ball on a rod, dropped at 1pm every day since 1833 so that ships' chronometers could be set by it. The Observatory also boasts the **Peter Harrison Planetarium**, the only one of its kind in London.

Because of its links with time, Greenwich was chosen as the site for Britain's year 2000 exhibition. Formerly the Millennium Dome, the **O2 Arena** is now used as an entertainment complex.

The exquisite **Queen's House** has been restored to its late 17th-century glory. Highlights are the unusually shaped main hall and the intriguing spiral "tulip staircase."

The adjoining **National Maritime Museum** has exhibits ranging from primitive canoes through Elizabethan galleons to modern ships. Nearby, the **Old Royal Naval College** was designed in two halves so the Queen's House could retain its river view. The chapel and the Painted Hall are open to the public.

The **Cutty Sark** is the last surviving 19th-century clipper ship. It is possible to walk the decks and explore the hold, which houses several collections

A rare 24-hour clock at the Old Royal Observatory, Greenwich

of nautical objects, including a number of figureheads.

🏛 **Royal Observatory Greenwich**
Blackheath Ave. **Tel** 020-8858 4422.
Open daily. **Closed** Dec 24–26. ♿ 📷
w rmg.co.uk/royal-observatory

🏛 **Queen's House and National Maritime Museum**
Romney Rd SE10. **Tel** 020-8312 6608.
Open daily. **Closed** Dec 24–26. ♿
limited. 📷 **w** nmm.ac.uk

A colorful antique shop on London's Portobello Road

㉕ Notting Hill and Portobello Road

W11. 🚇 Notting Hill Gate, Ladbroke Grove. 🛍 Fri & Sat.

Notting Hill and Portobello Road have been a focus for the Caribbean community since the peak years of immigration in the 1950s and 1960s. Today, this is a trendy residential district, whose vibrant cosmopolitan spirit is captured in the 1999 film starring Julia Roberts and Hugh Grant.

The West Indian flavor is best experienced during Europe's largest street carnival. First held in 1966, it takes over the entire area on the August bank holiday weekend. For three days, costumed parades flood through the crowded streets.

Portobello Road market has a bustling atmosphere with hundreds of stands and shops selling a variety of collectables. The southern end consists almost exclusively of stands selling antiques, jewelry, and souvenirs popular with tourists.

For hotels and restaurants see pp104–6 and pp107–9

㉖ Richmond and Kew

SW15. 🚇 Kew Gardens, Richmond.
🚌 to Kew Bridge, Richmond.

The attractive village of Richmond took its name from a palace built in 1500 by Henry VII (formerly the Earl of Richmond), the remains of which can be seen off the green. The vast **Richmond Park** was once Charles I's royal hunting ground. In summer, boats sail from central London to Richmond and Kew.

The nobility continued to favor Richmond after royalty had left, and some of their mansions have survived. The Palladian villa, **Marble Hill House**, was completed in 1729 for the mistress of George II.

On the opposite side of the Thames, **Ham House**, built in 1610 for Sir Thomas Vavasour (Knight Marshal to James I), had its heyday later that century when the aristocratic Lauderdale family moved in. Ham was extended and refurbished as a palatial villa, reflecting the Duke of Lauderdale's status as one of Charles II's most powerful ministers. Much of this luxurious interior decor remains.

On the riverbank to the south, **Kew Gardens**, the most complete botanic gardens in the world, is flawlessly maintained, with examples of nearly every plant that can be grown in Britain. Highlights are the Palm House, with thousands of exotic tropical blooms, and the delicate plants of the Temperate House. The Gardens became a UNESCO World Heritage Site in 2003. Near the river, **Kew Bridge Steam Museum** is housed in an old water-pumping station.

An aerial view of the impressive Hampton Court Palace

🏠 **Ham House**
Ham St, Ham. **Tel** 020-940 1950.
Open Apr–Oct: Sat–Thu. Gardens, shop & café: **Open** daily. 🅿️ 🚻

🌷 **Kew Gardens**
Kew. **Tel** 020-8332 5655. 🚇 Kew Gardens. 🚌 65, 237, 267, 391, 419. **Open** daily. **Closed** Dec 24, 25. 🅿️ ♿ 🚻 🌐 kew.org

Deer grazing in Richmond Park, a former royal hunting ground

㉗ Hampton Court

East Molesey, Surrey. **Tel** 0844-482 7777. 🚉 🚂 Hampton Court. 🚌 111, 216, 411, 451, 461, R68. **Open** daily. **Closed** Dec 24–26. 🅿️ 🚻 ♿ 🌐 hrp.org.uk

Cardinal Wolsey, chief minister to Henry VIII, began building Hampton Court in 1514. A few years later, in the hope of retaining royal favor, he gave it to the king. The palace was

extended first by Henry, and again at the end of the 17th century by William III and Mary II, with the help of Christopher Wren.

From the outside, the palace is a harmonious blend of Tudor and English Baroque. A remarkable feature is the Astronomical Clock, created for Henry VIII in 1540.

Inside, Wren's Classical royal rooms, such as the King's Apartments, contrast with Tudor architecture, such as the Great Hall. The stained-glass window here shows Henry VIII flanked by the coats of arms of his six wives. Superb woodwork in the Chapel Royal, including the massive reredos by Grinling Gibbons, dates from a major refurbishment by Queen Anne (c.1711). In the Queen's Gallery, where entertainments were often staged, the marble chimneypiece is by John Nost. Many of the state apartments are decorated with furniture, paintings, and tapestries from the Royal Collection. The King's Staircase has wall paintings by Antonio Verrio. Nine canvases depicting the Triumph of Julius Caesar (1490) are housed in the Mantegna Gallery.

The restored Baroque privy garden, originally created for William and Mary, features radiating avenues of majestic limes and formal flowerbeds. The Fountain Garden still has a few yews planted during their reign. Other attractions are the maze and the Great Vine, planted in 1768.

The distinctive Palm House at London's famous Kew Gardens

② Canterbury

Kent. 🚗 50,000. 🚉 🚌 🚹 The Beaney House of Art & Knowledge, 18 High Street (01227-378 100). 🛒 Wed & Fri.

Canterbury was an important Roman town even before St. Augustine arrived in 597, sent by the pope to convert the Anglo-Saxons to Christianity. The town rose in importance, soon becoming the center of Christianity in England.

Under the Normans, the city maintained its position as the country's leading archbishopric. A new cathedral was built on the ruins of the Anglo-Saxon cathedral in 1070. It was enlarged and rebuilt many times; as a result, it embraces examples of all styles of medieval architecture.

The most poignant moment in the cathedral's history came in 1170 when Thomas Becket, the Archbishop of Canterbury and enemy of King Henry II, was murdered here. **Trinity Chapel** was built to house Becket's remains.

Until the Dissolution, the cathedral was one of the chief places of pilgrimage in all Christendom. The *Canterbury Tales* by Geoffrey Chaucer (c.1345–1400), one of the greatest works of early English literature, tells of a group of pilgrims who are traveling from London to Becket's shrine in 1387.

Adjacent to the ruins of **St. Augustine's Abbey** is **St. Martin's Church**, one of the oldest in

The domes and minarets of the Royal Pavilion, Brighton

England. Beneath Canterbury's streets lies the **Roman Museum**, highlights of which include the foundations of a Roman house.

🏛 Cathedral
Christ Church Gate. **Tel** 01227-762 862. **Open** daily. **Closed** during services & concerts, Good Fri, Dec 25. ♿ 🅿 🛒
🌐 **canterbury-cathedral.org**

③ Brighton

Sussex. 🚗 249,000. 🚉 🚌 🚹 5 Pavilion Bldgs (01273-290 337). 🛒 Mon–Sat. 🎭 International Arts Festival (May).

As the nearest south-coast city to London, Brighton is perennially popular.

The spirit of the Prince Regent (later George IV) lives on in the magnificence of the **Royal Pavilion**, where the prince resided with the Catholic widow Mrs. Fitzherbert after their secret marriage. As his parties became more lavish, George needed a suitably extravagant setting. In 1815, he employed architect John Nash to transform the house into the fantastic Oriental palace that we see today. Completed in 1822, the exterior remains largely unaltered.

Traditional seaside fun is focused on Brighton's pebble beach. **Brighton Pier**, a late-Victorian pleasure ground, is now filled with amusement arcades. Also worth visiting is the maze of shops and winding alleys from the original village of Brighthelmstone, called **The Lanes**.

🏛 Royal Pavilion
Old Steine. **Tel** 03000-290 900. **Open** daily. **Closed** Dec 25 & 26. ♿ 🅿 🖥 ♿ limited. 🌐 **royalpavilion.org.uk**

④ Windsor Castle

See pp74–5.

⑤ Winchester

Hampshire. 🚗 36,000. 🚉 🚌 🚹 Guildhall, High Street (01962-840 500). 🛒 Wed–Sat.

The capital of the ancient kingdom of Wessex, the city of Winchester was also the headquarters of England's Anglo-Saxon kings.

William the Conqueror built one of his first English castles here. The only surviving part is the **Great Hall**, erected in 1235 to replace the original. It is now home to the legendary Round Table of King Arthur, said to have been built by the wizard

Canterbury Cathedral, dominating the skyline

For hotels and restaurants see pp104–6 and pp107–9

Merlin, but actually made in the 13th century.

The **Westgate Museum** is one of two surviving 12th-century gatehouses in the city wall. The room (once a prison) above the gate has a glorious 16th-century painted ceiling.

Winchester has been an ecclesiastical center for centuries. Its fine **cathedral** was begun in 1079. Originally a Benedictine monastery, it has preserved much of its Norman architecture despite numerous alterations. The writer Jane Austen is buried here. Built around 1110, **Wolvesey Castle**, once home of the bishops of Winchester, now lies in ruins.

🏰 Great Hall
Castle Ave. **Tel** 01962-846 476.
Open 10am–5pm daily.
Closed Dec 25, 26. 🦽

The 13th-century Round Table in the Great Hall, Winchester

❻ Salisbury

Wiltshire. 🗺 40,000. 🚋 🚌
🛈 Fish Row (01722-342 860).
🛒 Tue & Sat. 🎪 Salisbury Festival (end May–mid-Jun).

Salisbury was founded in 1220, when the Norman hilltop settlement of Old Sarum was abandoned in favor of a site amid lush water meadows, where the Nadder, Bourne, Avon, Ebble, and Wylye meet.

A **cathedral** was built here in the early 13th century. It is a fine example of the Early English style of Gothic architecture, typified by tall, pointed lancet windows. The magnificent landmark spire is the tallest in England.

The spacious and tranquil **Close**, with its schools, alms-houses, and clergy housing,

The awe-inspiring megaliths of Stonehenge, Salisbury Plain

makes a fine setting for Salisbury's cathedral. In the medieval King's House, **the Salisbury and South Wiltshire Museum** has displays on early man, Stonehenge, and Old Sarum.

Beyond the walls of the Cathedral Close, Salisbury developed its chessboard layout, with areas devoted to different trades, perpetuated in street names such as Fish Row and Butcher Row.

The busy High Street leads to the 13th-century **Church of St. Thomas**, which has a lovely carved timber roof (1450). Nearby, on Silver Street, **Poultry Cross** was built in the 15th century as a covered poultry market. In the bustling **Market Place**, many of the brick and tile-hung Georgian facades conceal medieval houses.

🏛 Cathedral
The Close. **Tel** 01722-555 120.
Open daily. 🎟 donation. 📷 🦽
🌐 salisburycathedral.org.uk

🏛 Salisbury and South Wiltshire Museum
The Close. **Tel** 01722-332 151.
Open Mon–Sat (Jun–Sep: Sun pm).
Closed Dec 23–31. 📷 🦽 limited

❼ Stonehenge

Off A303, Wiltshire. **Tel** 0870-333 1181.
🚌 3 from Salisbury. **Open** daily.
Closed Dec 24 & 25. 📷 🛍 🦽

Built in several stages from about 3000 BC onward, Stonehenge is Europe's most famous prehistoric monument. We can only guess at the rituals that took place here, but the alignment of the stones leaves little doubt that the circle reflects the changing trajectory of the sun through the sky and the passing of the seasons.

Stonehenge's monumental scale is all the more impressive given that the only available tools were made of stone, wood, and bone. To quarry, transport, and erect the huge stones, its builders must have had the command of immense resources and pools of labor.

Stonehenge was completed in about 1250 BC; despite popular belief, it was not built by the Druids, who flourished in Britain 1,000 years later.

A collection of ceremonial bronze weapons, jewelry, and other finds excavated at Stonehenge can be seen in the museum in Salisbury.

Sculpture by Elisabeth Frink (1930–93) in Cathedral Close, Salisbury

❹ Windsor Castle

The oldest continuously inhabited royal residence in Britain, the castle, originally made of wood, was founded by William the Conqueror in the late 11th century to guard the western approaches to London. He chose the site because it was on high ground and just a day's journey from the Tower of London. Successive monarchs have made alterations that render it a remarkable monument to royalty's changing tastes. King George V's affection for it was shown when he chose Windsor for his family surname in 1917. The castle is an official residence of the present Queen, who often stays here at weekends.

Albert Memorial Chapel
First built in the 1240s, it was rebuilt in 1485 and finally converted into a memorial for Prince Albert in 1863.

King Henry VIII Gate

①

②

Castle Hill and main entrance

★ St. George's Chapel
The architectural highlight of the castle, this chapel was built between 1475 and 1528 and is an outstanding Late Gothic work. Ten monarchs are buried here.

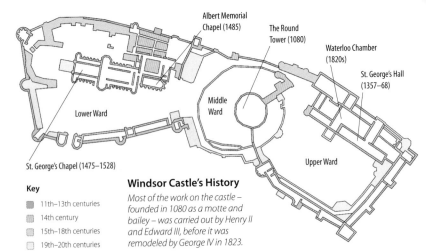

Albert Memorial Chapel (1485)

The Round Tower (1080)

Waterloo Chamber (1820s)

St. George's Hall (1357–68)

Middle Ward

Lower Ward

St. George's Chapel (1475–1528)

Upper Ward

Key

- 11th–13th centuries
- 14th century
- 15th–18th centuries
- 19th–20th centuries

Windsor Castle's History

Most of the work on the castle – founded in 1080 as a motte and bailey – was carried out by Henry II and Edward III, before it was remodeled by George IV in 1823.

Drawing Gallery
This chalk etching of Christ by Michelangelo is part of the *Resurrection Series*. It belongs to the Royal Collection, a small selection of which is shown here at any one time.

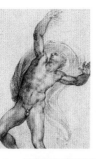

Waterloo Chamber
Created as part of Charles Long's brief for remodeling the castle in 1823, the Waterloo Chamber was previously a mere space between curtain walls.

VISITORS' CHECKLIST

Practical Information
Castle Hill. **Tel** 020-7766 7300. **Open** 9:45am–5:15pm (Nov–Feb: 4:15pm) daily (last adm: 1 hr 15 mins before closing). **Closed** Apr 8 & 18; Jun 16; Dec 25 & 26. St. George's Chapel: 5:15pm Mon–Sat; Sun (for worshippers).

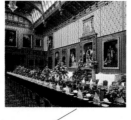

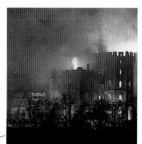

The Fire of 1992
A devastating blaze began during maintenance work on the State Apartments. St. George's Hall was damaged but has been rebuilt.

KEY

① **The Round Tower** was first built in wood by William the Conqueror. In 1170, it was rebuilt in stone by Henry II. It now houses the Royal Archives and Photographic Collection.

② **Statue of Charles II**

③ **The Audience Chamber** is where the Queen greets her guests.

④ **The Queen's Ballroom**

⑤ **Queen Mary's Dolls' House** was designed by Sir Edwin Lutyens in 1924. Nearly every item was built on a 1:12 ratio. The wine cellar contains genuine vintage wine.

⑥ **Brunswick Tower**

⑦ **The East Terrace Garden** was created by Sir Jeffry Wyatville for King George IV in the 1820s.

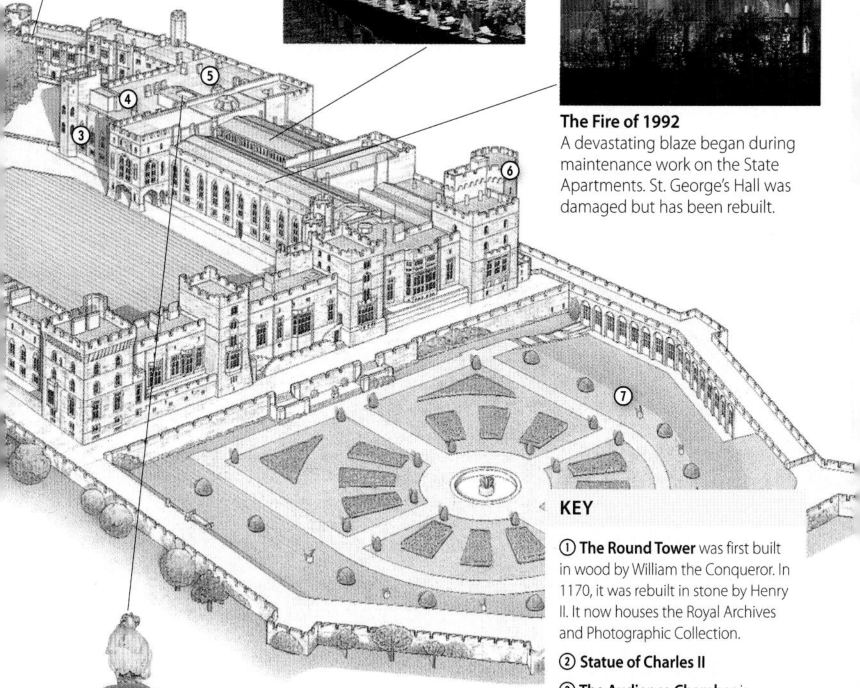

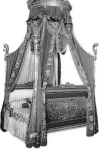

★ State Apartments
These rooms hold many treasures, including this late 18th-century state bed in the King's State Bedchamber, used for the visit in 1855 of Napoleon III.

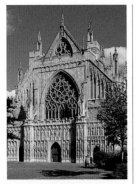

West front of the Cathedral Church of St. Peter in Exeter, Devon

❽ Devon and Cornwall

🚉 🚌 Truro (Cornwall), Exeter (Devon). 🛈 Boscawen Street, Truro (01872-274 555); Quay House, Quayside, Exeter (01392-271 611).

Miles of stunning coastline dominate this magical corner of Britain. Busy seaside resorts alternate with secluded coves and fishing villages rich in maritime history. Inland, lush pastures contrast with stark and treeless moorland.

Britain's most westerly point, **Land's End**, is noted for its remote and wild landscape. Nearby, the former Benedictine monastery of **St. Michael's Mount** rises dramatically from the waters of Mount Bay off Cornwall's southern coast. On the north coast, **St. Ives**, with its crescent of golden sands, is internationally renowned for its two art museums, the Barbara Hepworth Museum and the Tate Gallery St. Ives. The **Eden Project**

in St. Austell was built in 1998–2000 in an old Cornish china-clay pit. The aim of this vast educational and research center is to teach visitors about the vital relationship between plants, people, and resources in an informative and fun way. Two bulbous "greenhouses," huge segmented geodesic domes known as biomes, dominate the site, which holds some 4,500 species of plants.

The administrative capital of Cornwall is **Truro**, a city of gracious Georgian buildings and cobbled streets. Here, the Royal Cornwall Museum has displays on mining, smuggling, and Methodism.

Devon's capital is **Exeter**, a lively city with fine Roman and medieval relics. The mainly 14th-century Cathedral Church of St. Peter is one of the most superbly ornamented cathedrals in Britain.

Devon's most popular recreation area is **Dartmoor National Park**. At its heart is a bleak and windswept landscape, dotted with tors – out-crops of granite rock – and grazed by herds of wild ponies.

🟦 Eden Project
St. Austell. **Tel** 01726-811 911. 🚉 St. Austell, then local bus. **Open** daily. **Closed** Dec 24 & 25. 🅿 ♿
🌐 edenproject.com

🟦 Dartmoor National Park
Devon. 🚉 🚌 to Exeter, Plymouth, Totnes then local bus. 🛈 Visitor Centre, Princetown (01822-890414).

❾ Bath

See pp78–9.

A wild Dartmoor pony, a familiar sight in Devon's national park

❿ Bristol

Avon. 🏔 450,000. ✈ 🚆 🚌
🛈 E Shed, 1 Canon's Road (0906-711 2191). 🛥 daily. 🎪 Harbor Festival (Jul–Aug), International Balloon Fiesta (Aug).

The city of Bristol, at the mouth of the Avon, was once the main British port for transatlantic trade, pioneering the era of the steam liner. The city grew rich on the transportation of wine, tobacco, and, in the 17th century, slaves.

There is a covered market in the city center, part of which occupies the **Corn Exchange**, built by John Wood the Elder in 1743. **St. John's Gate** has colorful statues of Bristol's mythical founders, King Brennus and King Benilus.

Bristol's **cathedral** took an unusually long time to build. The choir was begun in 1298, the transepts and tower were finished in 1515, but the nave took another 350 years to build.

Designed by Isambard Kingdom Brunel, the **SS Great Britain** was the world's first large iron passenger ship. Launched in 1843, it traveled 32 times round the world. The ship is now in the dock where it was originally built, undergoing restoration.

The **British Empire and Commonwealth Museum**, in the 19th-century rail station at Temple Meads, is the first major museum to chart the 500-year history of the British Empire.

The **Arnolfini Gallery** is a showcase for contemporary art, dance, drama, and film. It is on the harborside, which is lined with cafés, bars, and galleries.

Cornwall's wild and rugged southern coastline

Wales

Wales is a country of outstanding natural beauty, with varied landscapes. Visitors come to climb dramatic mountain peaks, walk in the forests, fish in the broad rivers, and enjoy the miles of untainted coastline. The country's many seaside towns have long been popular with British vacationers. As well as outdoor pursuits, there is the vibrancy of Welsh culture, with its strong Celtic roots, to be experienced. The Welsh have their own language, which has survived despite the pervasive use of the English tongue.

Cardiff Castle's clock tower, a 19th-century addition by architect William Burges

⓫ Cardiff

Glamorgan. 🚋 310,000. ✈ 🚌 🚆
ℹ The Hayes (029-2087 3573). 🎨
Cardiff Festival (Jul/Aug).

Cardiff was first occupied by the Romans, who built a fort here in AD 75. In the 1830s, the town began to develop as a port, and by 1913 it was the world's leading coal exporter. Confirmed as the Welsh capital in 1955, it is now devoted to commerce and administration.

Cardiff Castle began as a Roman fort. It was renovated in the 19th century by William Burges, who created an ornate mansion rich in medieval images and romantic detail.

Cardiff's civic center is set around Alexandra Gardens. The Neoclassical **City Hall** (1905) is dominated by its huge dome and clock tower. The **Crown Building** now houses the Welsh Office, responsible for Welsh government affairs.

To the south of the center, the docklands have been transformed by the creation of a

marina and waterfront. Here, the **Pier Head Building**, constructed in 1896, is a reminder of the city's heyday.

🏛 **Cardiff Castle**
Castle St. **Tel** 029-2087 8100. **Open** daily. **Closed** Jan 1, Dec 25–26. 🅿 🅾
🖥 ♿ limited. 🌐 **cardiffcastle.com**

⓬ Snowdonia

Gwynedd. 🚉 Betws-y-Coed.
ℹ Station Road, Barmouth (01341-280 787).

The scenery of Snowdonia National Park ranges from rugged mountain country to moors and beaches. The area is well known as a destination for hikers, and villages such as **Betws-y-Coed** and **Llanberis** are busy hill-walking centers.

The main focus of this vast area is **Snowdon**, which at 1,085 m (3,560 ft) is the highest peak in Wales. Hikers wishing to explore Snowdonia's peaks should be wary of sudden weather changes. In summer, less intrepid visitors can take the Snowdon Mountain Railway from Llanberis to Snowdon's summit.

Snowdonia National Park, popular with climbers and hikers

⓭ Caernarfon

Gwynedd. 🚋 10,000. 🚌 ℹ Castle St (01286-672 232). 🅿 Sat.

One of the most famous castles in Wales looms over this busy town, created after Edward I's defeat of the last native Welsh prince, Llywelyn ap Gruffydd, in 1283. The town walls merge with modern streets that spread beyond the medieval center and open into a market square.

Caernarfon Castle was built as a seat of government for North Wales. A UNESCO World Heritage site, it contains several interesting displays, including the **Royal Welsh Fusiliers Museum** and an exhibition tracing the history of the Princes of Wales.

On the hill above the town are the ruins of **Segontium**, a Roman fort built around AD 78.

🏛 **Caernarfon Castle**
Y Maes. **Tel** 01286-677 617. **Open** daily. **Closed** Jan 1, Dec 24–26. 🅿 🅾

Caernarfon Castle, one of the forbidding fortresses built by Edward I

9 Street by Street: Bath

Bath owes its magnificent Georgian townscape to the bubbling pool of water at the heart of the Roman baths. The Romans transformed Bath into England's first spa resort and it regained fame as a spa town in the 18th century. At this time, the two brilliant John Woods (Elder and Younger) designed the city's fine Palladian-style buildings. Today, the traffic-free heart of this lively town is full of street musicians, museums, and enticing shops.

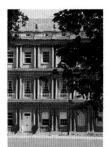

The Circus
This is a daring departure from the typical Georgian square, by John Wood the Elder (1704–54).

ROYAL CRESCENT
BROCK STREET
BENNETT STRE
THE CIRCUS
GAY STREET
GEOR
QUEEN
SQUARE
BARTON STRE
BEAUFORT SQ

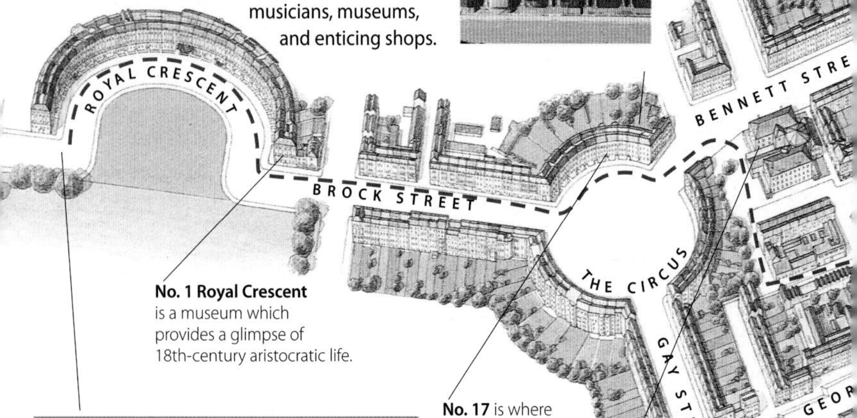

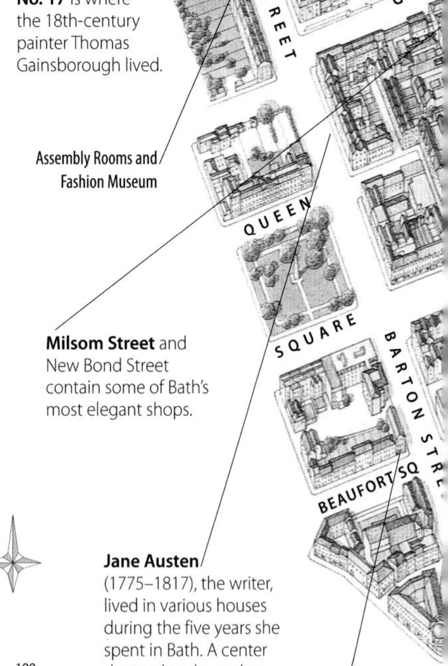

No. 1 Royal Crescent is a museum which provides a glimpse of 18th-century aristocratic life.

No. 17 is where the 18th-century painter Thomas Gainsborough lived.

Assembly Rooms and Fashion Museum

Milsom Street and New Bond Street contain some of Bath's most elegant shops.

Jane Austen (1775–1817), the writer, lived in various houses during the five years she spent in Bath. A center devoted to the author is located on Gay Street.

Theatre Royal (1805)

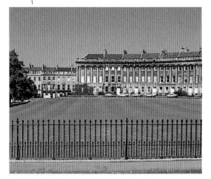

★ Royal Crescent
Hailed as the most majestic street in Britain, this graceful arc of 30 houses (1769–75) is the masterpiece of John Wood the Younger. West of the Royal Crescent, Royal Victoria Park (1830) is the city's largest open space.

Key

— Suggested route

0 meters 100
0 yards 100

For hotels and restaurants see pp104–6 and pp107–9

The Building of Bath Collection shows how, in the 18th century, the city was transformed from a medieval wool town into one of Europe's most elegant spas.

Pulteney Bridge
This charming bridge (1769–74), designed by Robert Adam, is lined with shops and links the center with the magnificent Great Pulteney Street.

VISITORS' CHECKLIST

Practical Information
Avon. ⓜ 85,000. ✈ Bristol Airport, 32 km (20 miles) W. ℹ Abbey Chambers, Abbey Church Yard (0906-711 2000). 🗓 daily. 🎵 International Music Festival (May–Jun). Roman Baths Museum: **Open** daily. **Closed** Dec 25 & 26. ♿ limited. 📷 📹

Transport
🚆 Dorchester St. 🚌 Manvers St.

★ Roman Baths
Built in the 1st century, this bathing complex is one of Britain's greatest memorials to the Roman era.

★ Bath Abbey
The splendid abbey stands at the heart of the old city in the Abbey Church Yard, a paved piazza enlivened by buskers. Its unique facade features stone angels climbing Jacob's Ladder to heaven.

Parade Gardens
Courting couples came to this pretty riverside park for secret liaisons in the 18th century.

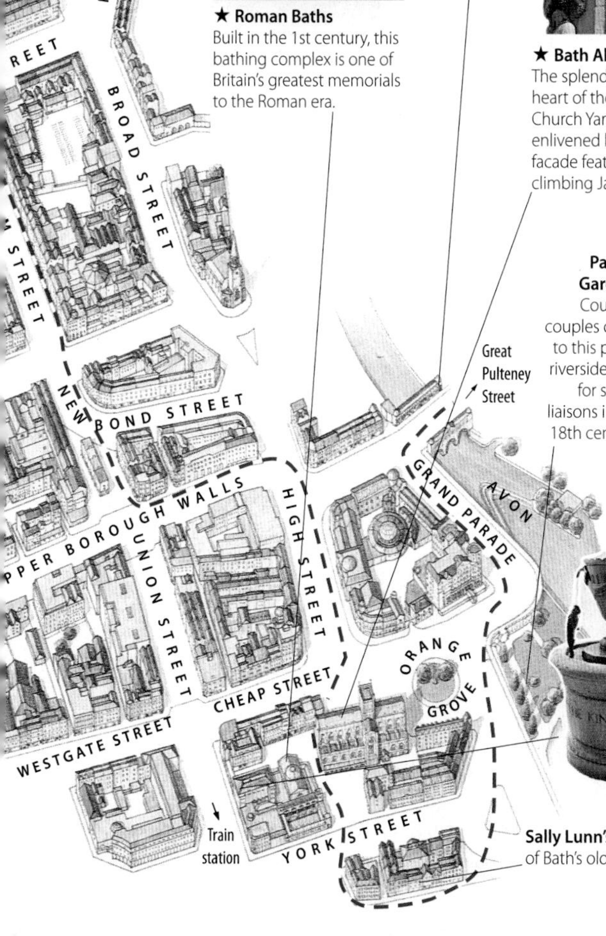

Great Pulteney Street

Pump Room
These tearooms once formed the social hub of the 18th-century spa community. They contain this decorative drinking fountain.

DOWN ROAD

PARAGON

REET

BROAD STREET

STREET

NEW

BOND STREET

UPPER BOROUGH WALLS

UNION STREET

HIGH STREET

GRAND PARADE

AVON

ORANGE GROVE

CHEAP STREET

WESTGATE STREET

→ Train station

YORK STREET

Sally Lunn's House (1482) is one of Bath's oldest houses.

The massive dining hall at Christ Church College, Oxford University

⑭ Oxford

Oxfordshire. 🗺 134,000. 🚉 🚌 ℹ️ 15–16 Broad St (01865-252 200). 🏪 Wed, Thu. 🎪 St. Giles Fair (Sep).

Oxford has long been a strategic point on the western routes into London – its name describes its position as a convenient spot for crossing the river (a ford for oxen).

English students expelled from Paris founded the university in 1167. The development of England's first university created the spectacular skyline of tall towers and "dreaming spires."

Many of the 38 colleges that make up **Oxford University** were founded between the 13th and 16th centuries and cluster around the city center. The colleges were designed along the lines of monastic buildings, but were surrounded by gardens.

Christ Church, the largest of the Oxford colleges, dates from 1525 when Cardinal Wolsey founded it as an ecclesiastical college. It has produced 13 British prime ministers in the last 200 years. Other colleges worth visiting are **All Souls**, **Magdalen**, **Merton**, **Lincoln**, and **Corpus Christi.**

The university's library, the **Bodleian**, was founded in 1320. One of its most famous rooms is the Divinity School (1488), which has a beautiful Gothic vaulted ceiling. The Baroque rotunda named the **Radcliffe Camera** (1748) is a reading room.

Oxford is more than just a university town and there is a wealth of interesting sights aside from the colleges.

One of the best British museums outside London, the **Ashmolean Museum** was opened in 1683. The museum's exceptional art collection includes works by Bellini, Raphael, Turner, Rembrandt, Michelangelo, Picasso, and a large group of Pre-Raphaelites. There is also the Alfred Jewel, an Anglo-Saxon artifact that is more than 1,000 years old.

Radcliffe Camera, Bodleian Library, Oxford

Carfax Tower is all that remains of the 14th-century Church of St. Martin, demolished in 1896. Watch the clock strike the quarter hours, and climb to the top for a panoramic view of the city.

The **Martyrs' Memorial** commemorates the three Protestants burned at the stake on Broad Street – Bishops Latimer and Ridley in 1555, and Archbishop Cranmer in 1556 – during the reign of Catholic Queen Mary.

St. Mary the Virgin Church is the official church of the university, and is said to be the most visited parish church in England. Two of Oxford's most interesting museums adjoin each other. The **University Museum of Natural History** contains fossils of dinosaurs as well as the remains of a dodo. The **Pitt Rivers Museum** has one of the world's most extensive ethnographic collections – including masks and tribal totems from Africa and the Far East – and archaeological displays.

Completed in 1669, the **Sheldonian Theatre** was the first building designed by Christopher Wren and was built as a place to hold university degree ceremonies. The ceiling depicts the triumph of religion, art, and science over envy, hatred, and malice.

🏛 **Ashmolean Museum**
Beaumont St. **Tel** 01865-278 002. **Open** 10am–5pm Tue–Sun & bank holiday Mon. **Closed** Dec 24–26. 🎟 Tue, Fri, Sat. ♿

🏛 **University Museum and Pitt Rivers Museum**
Parks Rd. **Tel** 01865-272 950/270 927. **Open** University: daily; Pitt Rivers: 10am–4:30pm daily. **Closed** Easter, Dec 24–26. ♿ limited.

⑮ Blenheim Palace

See pp82–3.

The Great Quadrangle of All Souls College, Oxford University

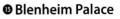

⑯ Stratford-upon-Avon

Warwickshire. 🚗 22,000. 🚉 🚌 ℹ️
Bridge Foot (0870-160 7930). 🛒 Fri.
🎭 Shakespeare's Birthday (late Apr).

Situated on the west bank of the River Avon, Stratford-upon-Avon attracts hordes of tourists eager to see buildings connected with William Shakespeare, born here in 1564. The town is also the provincial home of the Royal Shakespeare Company, whose performances are staged at the **Royal Shakespeare Theatre**.

The High Street turns into Chapel Street, the site of **New Place**. Shakespeare died here in 1616, and it is now a herb garden. The play-wright is buried at **Holy Trinity Church**. Bought for the nation in 1847, **Shakespeare's Birthplace** was restored to its Elizabethan style. It is regarded by many as a shrine to the great man, who lived here for many years, and offers a fascinating insight into his life.

Shakespeare monument at Holy Trinity Church, Stratford

Another Stratford native, John Harvard, emigrated to America and in 1638 left his estate to a new college, later renamed Harvard University. **Harvard House** displays family mementos.

No tour of Stratford would be complete without a visit to **Anne Hathaway's Cottage**. Before her marriage to Shakespeare, Anne lived here, 1.5 km (1 mile) from the town. Despite fire damage, the cottage is still impressive, with some original 16th-century furniture.

⑰ Cambridge

Cambridgeshire. 🚗 120,000. 🚉 🚌
ℹ️ Peas Hill (0871-226 8006). 🛒 daily.
🎭 Folk Festival (July).

Cambridge has been an important town since Roman times, being located at the first navigable point on the River Cam. When, in 1209, a group of religious scholars broke away from Oxford University after academic and religious disputes, they came here. Student life dominates the city, but it is also a thriving market center serving a rich agricultural region.

Cambridge University has 31 colleges, the oldest being **Peterhouse** (1284) and the newest **Robinson** (1979). Many of the older colleges have peaceful gardens backing onto the River Cam, which are known as "Backs." An enjoyable way to view these is to rent a punt (a long narrow boat propelled using a pole) from one of the boatyards along the river – with a "chauffeur," if required. The layout of the older colleges, as at Oxford, derives from their early connections with religious institutions, although few escaped heavy-handed alterations in the Victorian era.

Henry VI founded **King's College** in 1441. Work on the chapel – one of the most important examples of late-medieval English architecture – began five years later, and took 90 years to complete. Henry himself decided that the building should dominate the city and gave specific instructions about its dimensions. He also stipulated that a choir of six lay clerks and 16 boy choristers – educated at the College school – should sing daily at services. This still happens

The awe-inspiring choir of King's College Chapel, Cambridge

in term time, but today the choir also gives concerts all over the world.

St. John's College, whose alumni include the Romantic poet William Wordsworth, spans the Cam and boasts one of the town's most beautiful bridges. Known as the Bridge of Sighs, it was named after its Venetian counterpart.

One of Britain's oldest public museums, the **Fitzwilliam Museum** has works of exceptional quality and rarity, especially antiquities, ceramics, paintings, and manuscripts. These include paintings by Titian and the 17th-century Dutch masters, an impressive collection of works by the French Impressionists, and most of the important British artists of the past 300 years.

🏛️ **Fitzwilliam Museum**
Trumpington St. **Tel** 01223-332 900.
Open Tue–Sun & public hols.
Closed Jan 1, Good Fri, Dec 24–26, 31.
🎟️ donation. ♿ limited.

Bridge of Sighs, St. John's College, Cambridge University

⑮ Blenheim Palace

After John Churchill, the 1st Duke of Marlborough, defeated the French at the Battle of Blenheim in 1704, Queen Anne gave him the manor of Woodstock and had this palatial house built for him in gratitude. Designed by Nicholas Hawksmoor and Sir John Vanbrugh, it is one of the country's most outstanding examples of English Baroque. The magnificent palace grounds, at the center of which is a huge lake, owe their present appearance to the great 18th-century landscape designer, Lancelot (Capability) Brown. Blenheim Palace was the birthplace, in 1874, of the wartime British prime minister, Winston Churchill. Today, the palace is the home of the 11th Duke and Duchess of Marlborough.

★ **Long Library**
This 55-m (183-ft) long room was designed by Vanbrugh as a picture gallery. The stucco work on the ceiling is by Isaac Mansfield (1725).

★ **Water Terrace Gardens**
These splendid gardens were laid out in the 1920s by French architect Achille Duchêne in 17th-century style, with detailed patterned beds and fountains.

KEY

① **The Grand Bridge** was built in 1708. It has a 31-m (101-ft) main span and contains rooms within its structure.

② **The Chapel** holds a marble monument to the 1st Duke of Marlborough, sculpted in 1733.

③ **The lion sculptures** (1709), which overlook the Great Court, are by Grinling Gibbons.

④ **The Untold Story exhibition**

⑤ **East Gate**

⑥ **Red Drawing Room**

⑦ **The Green Drawing Room** has a full-length portrait of the 4th Duke of Marlborough by George Romney (1734–1802).

⑧ **The Italian Garden** contains the Mermaid Fountain, dating from the late 19th century.

Great Hall
The hall's magnificent ceiling, painted by Sir James Thornhill in 1716, shows Marlborough presenting his plan for the Battle of Blenheim to Britannia.

5 Entrance

4

8

6 **7**

★ **Saloon**
The murals and painted ceiling of the state dining room are by French artist Louis Laguerre (1663–1721). The room is used once a year on Christmas Day.

VISITORS' CHECKLIST

Practical Information
Woodstock, Oxfordshire.
Tel 0800-849 6500.
Palace & Gardens: **Open** Feb–Oct: 10:30am–5:30pm daily; Nov & Dec: Wed–Sun. 🗓 📷 ♿ limited. Park: **Open** 9am–5pm daily. 🅦 blenheimpalace.com

Transport
🚋 Oxford, then bus.

Other Notable Stately Homes

Burghley House:
Lincolnshire. **Tel** 01780-752 451.
Open Apr–Oct: daily. 🗓 📷 ♿ Built by Queen Elizabeth I's adviser, William Cecil, 1st Lord Burghley (1520–98).

Castle Howard:
Yorkshire. **Tel** 01653-648 333.
Open mid-Mar–Oct, end Nov–mid-Dec: daily. 🗓 📷 📷 ♿ Baroque mansion (1699–1712) by John Vanbrugh and Nicholas Hawksmoor.

Chatsworth House:
Derbyshire. **Tel** 01246-582 204.
Open mid-Mar–Dec: daily. 🗓 📷 📷 ♿ limited. Splendid Baroque palace built in 1687–1707 by the 4th Earl of Devonshire.

Hardwick Hall:
Derbyshire. **Tel** 01246-850 430.
Open Apr–Oct: Wed, Thu, Sat, Sun. 🗓 📷 📷 ♿ limited. Fine Tudor mansion begun in 1591 by Bess of Hardwick, Countess of Shrewsbury.

Transport
Burghley House: 🚋 Stamford
Castle Howard: 🚋 York, then bus
Chatsworth House and Hardwick Hall: 🚋 Chesterfield.

Eighteenth-century Gardens

Capability Brown (1715–83)

Styles of gardening in Britain expanded alongside architecture and other fashions. The 18th century brought a taste for large-scale "natural" landscapes, characterized by woods, lakes, and a seeming lack of boundaries. The pioneer of this new style was the famous landscape designer Lancelot (Capability) Brown (1715–83). His nickname came from his habit of telling clients that their land had "great capabilities." In 1764, he re-landscaped the grounds of Blenheim Palace, creating the magnificent, huge lake. Today, his reputation is controversial, because in creating his idyllic landscapes he swept away many of the beautiful formal gardens previously in vogue.

Detail of a carving on the facade of Bishop Lloyd's House, Chester

❶ Chester

Cheshire. 🚶 125,000. 🚌 🚃
ℹ️ Town Hall, Northgate St
(0845-647 7868). 🛍️ Mon–Sat.

First settled by the Romans in AD 79, the main streets of Chester are now lined with timber buildings, many dating from the 13th and 14th centuries. These are the **Chester Rows**, which, with their two tiers of stores and continuous upper gallery, anticipate today's multistory shops by several centuries. Their oriel windows and decorative timber-work are mostly 19th century. The facade of the 16th-century **Bishop Lloyd's House** on Watergate Street is the most richly carved in Chester. The Rows are at their most attractive where Eastgate Street meets Bridge Street.

A town crier calls the hour and announces news from the Cross – a reconstruction of a 15th-century stone crucifix. South of here, the **Grosvenor Museum** explains Chester's history. To the north is the **cathedral**. The choir stalls have splendid misericords and delicate spirelets on the canopies. The cathedral is surrounded on two sides by high city walls, originally Roman, but rebuilt at intervals. Also worth seeing is the **Roman amphitheater** just outside town, built in AD 100.

🏛 **Grosvenor Museum**
Grosvenor St. **Tel** 01244-972 197.
Open Mon–Sat, Sun pm.
Closed Jan 1, Good Fri, Dec 24–26.
♿ limited. 📷

❶ Liverpool

Liverpool. 🚶 450,000. ✈️ 11 km
(7 miles) SE. 🚌 🚃 ℹ️ Albert
Dock (0151-233 2008). 🛍️ Sun.
🌐 visitliverpool.com

During the 17th and 18th centuries, Liverpool's westerly seaboard gave it a leading role in the Caribbean slave trade. After the city's first ocean steamer set sail from here in 1840, would-be emigrants to the New World poured into the city, including a large number of Irish refugees of the potato famine.

Liverpool's waterfront is overlooked by the well-known **Royal Liver Building**. The 19th-century warehouses around Albert Dock have been redeveloped as museums, galleries, restaurants, and shops. Among these, the **Maritime Museum** and **Tate Liverpool**, which houses one of the best collections of contemporary art in England outside of London, are well worth visiting.

Liverpool is famous as the home town of the phenomenally successful Beatles. The **Beatles Story** is a walk-through exhibition which charts their meteoric rise to fame in the 1960s.

One of the most prestigious art galleries in the city is **The Walker**. Paintings range from

Clock tower of the Royal Liver Building, Liverpool

early Italian and Flemish works to 20th-century art.

Liverpool's Gothic-style **Anglican Cathedral**, completed in 1978 by Sir Giles Gilbert Scott, is the world's largest. The Roman Catholic **Metropolitan Cathedral of Christ the King** (1962–7) is a striking circular building surmounted by a stylized crown of thorns 88 m (290 ft) high.

🏛 **Tate Liverpool**
Albert Dock. **Tel** 0151-702 7400.
Open daily. **Closed** Good Friday,
Dec 24–26. 📷 ♿

🏛 **The Walker**
William Brown St. **Tel** 0151-478 4199.
Open daily. **Closed** Jan 1, Dec 24 (from 2pm), Dec 25 & 26. 📷 by appt. ♿

❷ Manchester

Manchester. 🚶 2.5 million. ✈️ 18 km
(11 miles) S. 🚌 🚃 ℹ️ Piccadilly
Plaza, Portland Street (0871-222 8223).
🛍️ daily.

Manchester is famous as a pioneer of the industrial age, with its cotton-spinning machines and early railways.

Among the city's many fine 19th-century buildings are the Neo-Gothic **cathedral**, the **Royal Exchange**, now a theater and restaurant, and the **Free Trade Hall**, now the Radisson Edwardian Hotel, with only the original facade remaining. The **Manchester Ship Canal**, opened in 1894, is a magnificent engineering feat.

The **Museum of Science and Industry in Manchester** captures the city's spirit of industrial might with a display of working steam

Modern city blocks on the banks of the Manchester Ship Canal

For hotels and restaurants see pp104–6 and pp107–9

Lush, green fields below the Skiddaw fells in the Lake District

engines and an exhibition on the Liverpool and Manchester Railway. Another museum of note is the **Whitworth Art Gallery**, with its splendid collection of contemporary art, textiles, and prints. The Turner watercolors are a highlight. Housed in a 19th-century porticoed building, the **City Art Galleries** contain an excellent selection of British art, as well as early Italian, Flemish, and French paintings.

📖 **Whitworth Art Gallery**
University of Manchester, Oxford Rd.
Tel 0161-275 7450. **Open** check websites for hours. ♿ 🔲
🔤 whitworth.manchester.ac.uk

㉑ York

See pp86–7.

㉒ Lake District

Cumbria. 🚃 Kendal; Windermere.
🚌 Kendal; Keswick; Windermere.
ℹ️ Made in Cumbria, 25 Stramongate, Kendal (01539-735 891); Moot Hall, Market Sq, Keswick (01768-772 645).

The Lake District boasts some of the country's most spectacular scenery, with high peaks, lonely fells, and beautiful lakes. The area constitutes Britain's largest national park and offers a range of outdoor activities, from hill walking to boating.

Kendal is the southern gateway to the Lake District. Of interest here is the Museum of Lakeland Life and Industry, housed in the stable block of the 18th-century Abbot Hall.

The nearest lake to Kendal is Windermere, which is more than 16 km (10 miles) long. A year-round car ferry connects the lake's east and west shores, and summer steamers link the main towns on the north-south axis. Among these, one of the most popular is **Bowness**, where the Windermere Steamboat Museum has a collection of superbly restored watercraft.

The Lakeland poet
William Wordsworth

Ambleside, another attractive lakeside town, is a good base for walkers and climbers. Nearby is Hill Top, the 17th-century farmhouse where the author Beatrix Potter wrote many of her famous children's stories.

The Lake District's most famous son, the Romantic poet William Wordsworth (1770–1850), lived for a while at **Grasmere**, on the shores of the lake of the same name, north of Ambleside. His home, Dove Cottage, contains a museum dedicated to his life.

To the west of Windermere lie Coniston Water and picturesque **Duddon Valley**, popular walking country.

In the northern part of the Lake District, **Keswick**, with its lake, Derwent Water, has been a busy vacation destination since Victorian days. The Keswick Museum and Art Gallery holds original manuscripts of Lakeland writers, such as Robert Southey

(1774–1843) and Wordsworth. To the east of the town lies the ancient stone circle of Castlerigg. North of Keswick is Skiddaw, England's fourth-highest peak and a straightforward climb for anyone reasonably fit.

㉓ Durham

County Durham. 🚃 🚌
ℹ️ 03000-26 26 26. 🚉 Sat.

Durham was built on a rocky peninsula in 995. The site was chosen as the last resting place for the remains of St. Cuthbert. The relics of the Venerable Bede were brought here 27 years later, adding to the town's attraction to pilgrims.

Durham's **cathedral**, built between 1093 and 1274, is a striking Norman structure. The vast dimensions of the ancient columns, piers, and vaults, and the lozenge, chevron, and dogtooth patterns carved into them, are its main innovative features. The exotic Galilee Chapel, begun in 1170, was inspired by the mosque at Córdoba, Spain (*see pp316–17*).

The Norman **castle**, begun in 1072, served as an Episcopal Palace until 1832, when Bishop William van Mildert gave it away to found Britain's third university here. In the castle grounds, Tunstal's Chapel was built around 1542 and has some particularly fine woodwork, including a unicorn misericord. The castle keep, sited on a mound, is now part of the university.

🏰 **Durham Castle**
Tel 0191-334 2932. **Open** for guided tours only. Term time: daily (pm); university hols: most days (am & pm); call ahead for special closures. 📷

Moorish-style arches in the 12th-century Galilee Chapel, Durham Cathedral

㉑ Street by Street: York

The city of York has retained so much of its medieval structure that walking into its center is like entering a living museum. Many of the ancient timbered houses, which overhang narrow, winding streets such as the Shambles, are protected by a conservation order. Cars are banned from the center, so there are always student bikes bouncing over cobbled streets. The chief glory of York is its cathedral, the Minster. The city also has 18 medieval churches, 5 km (3 miles) of medieval city walls, and many elegant Jacobean and Georgian buildings.

York's medieval city walls still encircle the old city. It is possible to walk round them, although there are large gaps. The gates are known as "bars."

At Monk Bar, the gatehouse retains a working portcullis.

★ York Minster
The 15th-century choir screen is lined with statues of the kings of England, from William I to Henry VI.

Thirsk →

St. Mary's Abbey

The Yorkshire Museum contains a fine collection of fossils, discovered at Whitby in the 19th century.

Lendal Bridge

↓
Train station, bus station, National Railway Museum, and Leeds

Ye Old Starre Inne is one of the oldest pubs in York.

In Coffee Yard, look out for the carved figure of a red devil, relic of a medieval print shop.

Guildhall
This two-headed medieval roof boss is on the 15th-century Guildhall, situated beside the River Ouse and restored after bomb damage during World War II.

St. Olave's Church
The 11th-century church, next to the gatehouse of St. Mary's Abbey, was founded by the Earl of Northumbria in memory of St. Olaf, King of Norway. To the left is the Chapel of St. Mary on the Walls.

For hotels and restaurants see pp104–6 and pp107–9

★ **Jorvik Viking Center**
The many artifacts on show here explore the time when York was a strategic Viking town.

VISITORS' CHECKLIST

Practical Information

120,000. 1 Museum St (01904-550 099). daily. Jorvik Festival (Feb); St. Nicholas Fair (Nov). York Minster: Deangate. **Tel** 01904-557 216. **Open** daily. Jorvik Viking Center: Coppergate Walk. **Tel** 01904-543 400. **Open** daily. **Closed** Dec 25. visityork.org

Transport

Station Rd.

Whip-Ma-Whop-Ma-Gate
is York's tiniest street. The name means "neither one thing nor the other street."

Merchant Adventurers' Hall

★ **York Castle Museum**
Converted from two 18th-century prisons, the museum features reconstructions of old York and the cell of the notorious highwayman Dick Turpin (1706–39).

St. Mary's Church

Clifford's Tower (c.1250)

Hull

Key

— Suggested route

0 meters 100
0 yards 100

Exploring York

To the Romans, the city of York was Eboracum, to the Saxons it was Eoforwic, and to the Vikings Jorvik. Danish street names are a reminder that from 867, York was a major Viking settlement. **Jorvik Viking Center**, the Viking museum, is built underground on an archaeological site excavated at Coppergate. The latest technology brings the sights and smells of 10th-century York dramatically to life.

Between 1100 and 1500, York was England's second city. **York Minster**, the largest Gothic church in northern Europe, was begun in 1220. It has a remarkable collection of medieval stained glass. The vast Great East Window (1405–8) depicts the Creation. In 1984, a disastrous fire in the south transept destroyed the roof and shattered its magnificent rose window. This has since been restored.

Much of York's wealth in the late Middle Ages came from the cloth trade. The **Merchant Adventurers' Hall**, the headquarters of a powerful guild of traders, is a beautifully preserved timber-framed building that dates from the mid-14th century.

In the 19th century, York's position on the route to Scotland made it a major rail center. Train enthusiasts should head for the **National Railway Museum**, the largest of its kind in the world, where the rolling stock on show includes Queen Victoria's royal carriage.

🏛 **National Railway Museum**
Leeman Rd. **Tel** 08448-153 139. **Open** daily. **Closed** Dec 24–26.

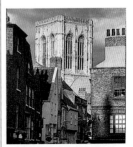

The square central tower of York Minster, rising above the city

For keys to symbols *see back flap*

Scotland

Scotland's landscape is breathtaking, with sparkling lochs, awesome mountains, and windswept isles. The ruggedness of its climate and natural environment has helped to forge a tough, self-reliant nation, whose history has been characterized by resistance to English domination. Castles, many in ruins, are found all over the country – a legacy of its turbulent past. Culturally, Edinburgh has always been the country's chief attraction, but the rival city of Glasgow has much to offer too, with many great free attractions.

The imposing City Chambers in George Square, Glasgow

㉔ Edinburgh

See pp90–94.

㉕ Glasgow

🏛 593,000. ✈ 🚌 🚊 ℹ 170 Buchanan Street (0845-859 1006). 🗓 Sat, Sun. 🎷 Jazz Festival (Jul). 🌐 **seeglasgow.com**

Glasgow's era of great prosperity was the industrial 19th century. Coal seams in Lanarkshire fueled the city's cotton mills and ironworks, belying its Celtic name, *Glas cu*, meaning "dear green place." Relics of this manufacturing past contrast starkly with the glossy image of modern Glasgow, renowned for its free galleries and museums. The deprived East End stands side by side with the restored 18th-century Merchant City and Victorian George Square.

Glasgow's **cathedral** was one of the few to escape destruction during the Scottish Reformation, and is a rare example of an almost complete 13th-century church. The crypt holds the tomb of St. Mungo. In the cathedral precinct, the **St. Mungo Museum of Religious Life and Art** is the first of its kind in the world, illustrating religious themes with a superb range of artifacts.

It is in the more affluent West End, where merchants used to retreat from industrial Clydeside, that Glasgow's most important galleries and museums can be found. The **Kelvingrove Art Gallery and Museum**, housed in a striking red sandstone building dating from 1901, is home to a splendid collection of art, with works by Botticelli, Giorgione, Rembrandt, Degas, Millet, and Monet, while the Scottish Gallery contains the famous *Massacre of Glencoe* by James Hamilton (1853–94). Other

Stained glass by Charles Rennie Mackintosh

highlights here include dinosaur skeletons, Egyptian artifacts and a real spitfire suspended in the main hall.

The **Hunterian Art Gallery** houses Scotland's largest print collection and paintings by major European artists from the 16th century to the present. A display of works by Glasgow's most celebrated designer, Charles Rennie Mackintosh (1868–1928), is supplemented by a reconstruction of No. 6 Florentine Terrace, where he lived from 1906 to 1914.

South of the river, Pollok Country Park is the site of the **Burrell Collection**, star of Glasgow's renaissance. Highlights include examples of 15th-century stained glass and tapestries, a bronze bull's head (7th century BC) from Turkey, Matthijs Maris' *The Sisters* (1875), and a self-portrait by Rembrandt (1632). On the same site, Pollok House is an attractive Georgian building. It holds one of Britain's best collections of 16th- to 19th-century Spanish paintings.

Other sights worth visiting are the **Tenement House**, a modest apartment in a tenement block preserved from Edwardian times, and **Provand's Lordship** (1471), the city's oldest-surviving house. The **House for an Art Lover** is a showcase for the work of Charles Rennie Mackintosh. For a social history of the city from the 12th to the 20th century, visit the **People's Palace**, a cultural museum located in the city's East End.

🏛 **Kelvingrove Art Gallery and Museum**
Argyle St, Kelvingrove. **Tel** 0141-276 9599. **Open** daily. **Closed** Jan 1–2, Dec 25–26. 🅿 ♿

🏛 **Hunterian Art Gallery**
82 Hillhead St. **Tel** 0141-330 5431. **Open** Mon–Sat. **Closed** Dec 24–Jan 5 & public hols. ♿ restricted.

🏛 **Burrell Collection**
Pollok Country Park. **Tel** 0141-287 2550. **Open** daily. **Closed** Jan 1–2, Dec 25–26 & 31. 🅿 ♿ 📷 📱

The Burrell Collection in Pollok Country Park on Glasgow's outskirts

The 15th-century Stirling Castle, atop its rocky crag

㉖ Stirling

🏙 90,000. 🚇 🚌 ℹ 1–5 Port St (01786-432 003).
🌐 **visitscotland.com**

Located between the Ochil Hills and the Campsie Fells, Stirling grew up around its **castle**, one of the finest examples of Renaissance architecture in the country. Dating from the 15th century, it was last defended – against the Jacobites – in 1746, and stands within sight of no fewer than seven battlefields. One of these – Bannockburn – was where Robert the Bruce defeated the English in 1314.

Stirling's Old Town is still protected by the original 16th-century walls, built to keep out Henry VIII. Two buildings stand out among a number of historic monuments in the town: the medieval **Church of the Holy Rude** and **Mar's Wark**, with its ornate facade.

🏰 **Stirling Castle**
Castle Wynd. **Tel** 01786-450 000.
Open daily. **Closed** Dec 25 & 26.
🎧 🎁 ♿ limited. 🍽 📷

㉗ St. Andrews

Fife. 🏙 17,000. 🚇 Leuchars. 🚌
ℹ 70 Market St (01224 269 180).
🌐 **standrews.co.uk**

Scotland's oldest university town and one-time ecclesiastical capital, St. Andrews is now a shrine for golfers from all over the world. Its main streets and cobbled alleys, lined with university buildings and medieval churches, converge on the ruined 12th-century **cathedral**. Once the largest in Scotland, it was later pillaged for stones to build the town.

St. Andrew's Castle was built for the bishops of the town in 1200.

The Royal and Ancient Golf Club, founded in 1754, has a magnificent links course and is the ruling arbiter of the game. The city has other golf courses, which are open to the public for a modest fee. These include the Old Course, which regularly hosts the British Open. St. Andrews is also home to the **British Golf Museum**.

🏛 **British Golf Museum**
Bruce Embankment. **Tel** 01334-460 046. **Open** 9:30am–5:30pm daily (Nov–Mar: 10am–4pm daily). 🎧 ♿ 📷

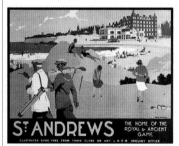

An old railroad poster illustrating the lure of St. Andrews for golfing enthusiasts

㉘ Aberdeen

🏙 220,000. ✈ 13 km (8 miles) NW.
🚇 🚌 ℹ 23 Union St (01224-288 828). 🍽 Thu, Fri, Sat.

Europe's offshore oil capital, Aberdeen is also one of Britain's most important fishing ports, and hosts Scotland's largest fish market.

Among its fine buildings is the 16th-century home of a former provost (mayor) of the city. Period rooms inside **Provost Skene's House** span 200 years of design and include the 17th-century Great Hall, a Regency Room, and a Georgian Dining Room. The Painted Gallery holds one of Scotland's most important cycles of religious art, dating from the 17th century.

Founded in 1495, **King's College** was the city's first university. The chapel has stained-glass windows by Douglas Strachan.

St. Andrew's Cathedral is the Mother Church of the Episcopal Communion in the United States. Coats of arms on the ceiling depict the American states.

Housed in a historic building overlooking the harbor, **Aberdeen Maritime Museum** traces the city's long seafaring tradition.

🚌 **Provost Skene's House**
Guestrow. **Tel** 01224-641 086. **Open** Mon–Sat. **Closed** Jan 1–2, Dec 25–31. 🌐 aagm.co.uk

Golf

Scotland's national game was pioneered on the sandy links around St. Andrews. The earliest record dates from 1457, when golf was banned by James II on the grounds that it was interfering with his subjects' archery practice. Mary, Queen of Scots enjoyed the game and was berated in 1568 for playing straight after the murder of her husband Darnley. Scotland has several other world-class golf courses, including Royal Troon, Gleneagles, and Carnoustie.

Victorian engraving of Mary, Queen of Scots at St. Andrews

㉔ Edinburgh

It was not until the reign of James IV (1488–1513) that Edinburgh gained its status as Scotland's capital. Overcrowding made the Old Town a difficult place to live, and led to the construction of a Georgian New Town in the late 1700s. Today, Edinburgh is second only to London as a financial center in the British Isles, and houses the new Scottish Parliament building, situated next to the old Palace of Holyroodhouse. Edinburgh hosts a celebrated annual International Festival every August. One of the world's premier arts jamborees, it features drama, dance, opera, music, and ballet. The more eclectic "Fringe" developed in parallel with the official event, but has now exceeded it in terms of size. It is estimated that the population of the city doubles from 400,000 to 800,000 every August.

View of Princes Street from the top of Calton Hill

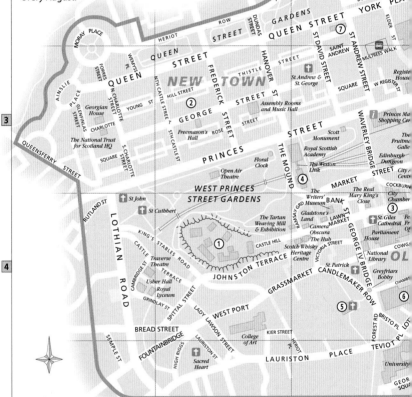

Getting Around

Central Edinburgh is compact, so walking or cycling is an excellent way to explore the city. Other options include a comprehensive bus service and a multitude of black taxis. Avoid exploring the center by car, because the streets tend to be congested with traffic, and parking may be difficult. Car use is actively discouraged.

Sights at a Glance

① Edinburgh Castle
② New Town
③ Royal Mile
④ National Gallery of Scotland
⑤ Greyfriars Kirk
⑥ National Museum of Scotland
⑦ Scottish National Portrait Gallery
⑧ Calton Hill
⑨ Palace of Holyroodhouse

An audience of thousands at the Military Tattoo at Edinburgh Castle, held during August each year

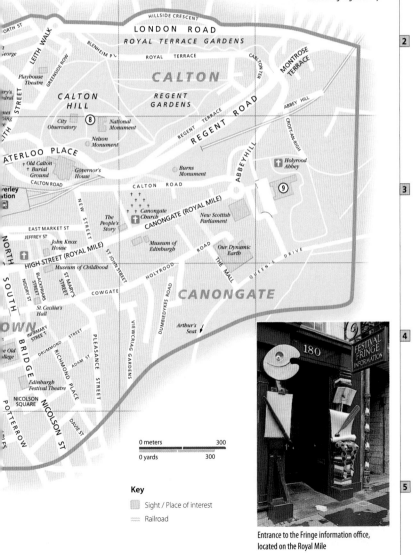

Key

▨ Sight / Place of interest

═ Railroad

Entrance to the Fringe information office, located on the Royal Mile

For keys to symbols *see back flap*

The battlements of Edinburgh Castle rising above Princes Street Gardens

① Edinburgh Castle

Castle Hill. **Tel** 0131-225 9846.
Open summer: 9:30am–6pm daily;
winter: 9:30am–5pm daily.
Closed Dec 25 & 26. 🅿 🗹 🔧
🆆 historic-scotland.gov.uk

Standing on the basalt core of
an extinct volcano, the castle is
an assemblage of buildings
dating from the 12th to the
20th centuries, reflecting its
changing role as fortress, palace,
military garrison, and state
prison. The castle was a favorite
royal residence until the Union
of 1603, after which monarchs
resided in England.

The Scottish regalia are
displayed in the 15th-century
palace where Mary, Queen of
Scots gave birth to James VI. The
castle also holds the Stone of
Destiny, a relic of ancient Scottish
kings seized by the English, and
returned in 1996. The castle's
oldest existing building is the
12th-century **St. Margaret's
Chapel**. A stained-glass window
depicts the queen of Malcolm III,
after whom it is named.

Other important buildings
include the 15th-century
Great Hall, meeting place of
the Scottish parliament until
1639, and the **Governor's
House** (1742). A 15th-century
Burgundian siege gun, known
as Mons Meg, is kept in the
vaults, where French graffiti
recall the prisoners held here
in the 18th- and 19th-century
wars. The One o'Clock Gun is
still fired at 1pm daily.

② New Town

The first phase of the "New
Town," to the north of Princes
Street, was built in the 18th
century to relieve the
congested and unsanitary
conditions of the Old Town.
Charlotte Square, with its l
avish town houses, was the
climax of this phase. On the
north side, the **Georgian
House**, owned by the National
Trust of Scotland, has been
furnished to show the lifestyle
of its 18th-century residents.

Charlotte Square in the New Town

The most magnificent of the
later developments is the **Moray
Estate** where a linked series of
large houses forms a crescent, an
oval, and a twelve-sided circus.

🏛 Georgian House
7 Charlotte Sq. **Tel** 0844-493 2117.
Open Mar–Dec: daily. 🅿 🔧 limited.

③ Royal Mile

Composed of four ancient
streets which formed the main
thoroughfare of medieval
Edinburgh, the Royal Mile linked
the castle to the Palace of
Holyroodhouse. A walk starting
from the castle takes you past
many of the city's oldest
buildings and a number of
interesting museums.

The lower floors of the **Tartan
Weaving Mill & Exhibition** date
from the early 1600s and were
once the home of the Laird of
Cockpen. The 19th-century
**Camera Obscura and World of
Illusions** is a popular attraction.
A little further on, **Gladstone's
Land** is a restored 17th-century
merchant's house. Another fine
mansion, built in 1622, has been
converted into a **Writers'
Museum**, housing memorabilia
of Robert Burns, Sir Walter Scott,
and Robert Louis Stevenson.

St. Giles Cathedral, properly
known as the High Kirk of
Edinburgh, was the base from
which Protestant minister John
Knox led the Scottish
Reformation. His house, also
on the Royal Mile, is open to
the public. The cathedral's
Thistle Chapel has impressive

rib-vaulting and carved heraldic canopies. It honors the knights of the Most Ancient and Most Noble Order of the Thistle. Just past St. Giles, the Italianate **Parliament House**, built in the 1630s, has housed the Scottish Courts since the 1707 Act of Union with England and Wales.

Thistle Chapel, St. Giles Cathedral, Royal Mile

Farther east, opposite **John Knox's House** (1450), is the excellent **Museum of Childhood**, while **The People's Story** (1591) tells the social history of Edinburgh.

🏠 **Gladstone's Land**

477B Lawnmarket. **Tel** 0844 493 2120. **Open** Apr–Oct: 10am–5pm daily (Jul–Aug: 10am–6:30pm daily). 🖼

④ National Gallery of Scotland

The Mound. **Tel** 0131-624 6200. **Open** daily. 📷 by appt. ♿ 🌐 nationalgalleries.org

One of Scotland's finest art galleries, the National Gallery of Scotland has an impressive collection of British and European paintings. Designed by William Henry Playfair, it was opened in 1859. Many of the works of art are still exhibited as they were in the 19th century. Serried ranks of paintings hang on deep red walls behind a profusion of statues and period furniture. Some of the highlights among the Scottish works are the society portraits by Allan Ramsay and Henry Raeburn, including the latter's *Reverend Robert Walker Skating on Duddingston Loch* (c.1800), an image reproduced annually on thousands of Christmas cards.

German works include Gerard David's almost comic-strip treatment of the *Three Legends of St. Nicholas*, dating from the early 16th century. Italian paintings include a fine *Madonna* by Raphael, as well as works by Titian and Tintoretto. From Spain there is a delightful genre painting of *An Old Woman Cooking Eggs* by Velázquez (c.1620).

An entire room is devoted to *The Seven Sacraments* by Nicholas Poussin, dating from around 1640. Dutch and Flemish painters represented include Rembrandt, Van Dyck, and Rubens, while among the British offerings are important works by Reynolds and Gainsborough.

An Old Woman Cooking Eggs by Velázquez, National Gallery of Scotland

⑤ Greyfriars Kirk

Greyfriars Place. **Tel** 0131-225 1900. **Open** Apr–Oct: Mon–Sat; Nov–Mar: Thu pm. 📷 ♿

Greyfriars Kirk played a key role in Scotland's history. In 1638, the National Covenant was signed here, marking the Protestant stand against Charles I's imposition of an episcopal church. Throughout the wars of the 17th century, the kirkyard was used as a mass grave for executed Covenanters. The Martyrs' Monument is a sobering reminder of the many Scots who lost their lives. Greyfriars is also known for its association with a faithful dog, Bobby, who lived beside his master's grave from 1858 to 1872. Greyfriars Bobby's statue stands outside Greyfriars Kirk.

Greyfriars Bobby

⑥ National Museum of Scotland

Chambers St. **Tel** 0300-123 6789. **Open** 10am–5pm daily. 📷 ♿ 🖼 🌐 nms.ac.uk

A great Victorian glass palace, completed in 1888, houses the National Museum of Scotland. It started life as an industrial museum, but over time acquired an eclectic array of more than 20,000 exhibits, ranging from stuffed animals to ethnographic artifacts.

In 1993, work began on a site next door, to display Scotland's impressive array of antiquities. The resulting collection, opened in 1998, tells the story of the country, starting with its geology and natural history, through to later industrial developments. Among its many stunning exhibits is St. Fillan's Crozier, said to have been carried at the head of the Scottish army at Bannockburn in 1314.

The view from the top of Calton Hill, Edinburgh

⑦ Scottish National Portrait Gallery

1 Queen St. **Tel** 0131-624 6200. **Open** 10am–5pm daily. **Closed** Dec 25 & 26. 🚻 ♿ 📷 ☗ **nationalgalleries.org**

The Portrait Gallery is housed in a red-sandstone, Gothic-revival building, which was restored between 2009 and 2011. It owns a wonderful collection of paintings that details the history of 12 generations of Stuarts, from the time of Robert the Bruce to Queen Anne. It also houses portraits of famous Scots, including one of the country's best-loved poet Robert Burns (1759–96) by Alexander Nasmyth. Others portrayed include Flora MacDonald, who helped Bonnie Prince Charlie escape after his defeat by the English in 1745, and Ramsay MacDonald, who became Britain's first Labour prime minister in 1924.

The building also holds the Scottish National Photography collection, which has over 30,000 images dating from the 1840s to the present day.

⑧ Calton Hill

City center east, via Waterloo Pl.

Calton Hill, at the east end of Princes Street, is a large open space dotted with Neoclassical monuments. It has one of Edinburgh's more memorable landmarks – a half-finished "Parthenon". Conceived as the National Monument to the dead of the Napoleonic Wars,

the structure was started in 1822, but funds soon ran out and it was never finished. Nearby, the **Nelson Monument** commemorates the British victory at Trafalgar. The Classical theme continues with Duncan's Monument and the old **City Observatory**, designed by William Playfair in 1818 and based on the Tower of the Winds in Athens. The Astronomical Society of Edinburgh arranges tours and free lectures here.

⑨ Palace of Holyroodhouse

East end of the Royal Mile. **Tel** 0131-556 5100. **Open** daily. **Closed** check for seasonal closures. 🅿 ♿ limited.

Queen Elizabeth II's official Scottish residence was built by James IV in the grounds of an abbey in 1498. It was later the home of James V and his wife, Mary of Guise, and was remodeled in the 1670s for

Charles II. The Royal Apartments (including the Throne Room and Royal Dining Room) are used for investitures and for banquets whenever the Queen visits. A chamber in the so-called James V tower is believed to have been the scene of David Rizzio's murder in 1566. He was the Italian secretary of Mary, Queen of Scots. She witnessed the grisly act, which was authorized by her jealous husband, Lord Darnley. Bonnie Prince Charlie, last of the Stuart pretenders to the English throne, also held court at Holyrood Palace, in 1745. The Queen's Gallery has an interesting program of art exhibitions.

The adjacent Holyrood Park, a former royal hunting ground, is home to three lochs, a large number of wildfowl, and the Salisbury Crags. Its high point is the hill known as Arthur's Seat, an extinct volcano and well-known Edinburgh landmark. The name is probably a corruption of Archer's Seat.

The grand 17th-century facade of Holyrood Palace

The Highlands

The Scotland of your imagination – filled with clans and tartans, whisky and porridge, bagpipes and heather – will come to life in the Highlands. Gaelic-speaking Celts arrived from Ireland before the 7th century, establishing small fishing and cattle-raising communities. Nowadays the region has oil and tourist industries. Inverness, the Highland capital, makes a good starting point for exploring Loch Ness and the Cairngorms. The Isle of Skye has some of Britain's most dramatic scenery.

Sea lochs on the Isle of Skye, dominated by the Cuillin peaks

Snow-covered peaks of the Cairngorms, viewed from Aviemore

㉙ Cairngorms

🚉 🚌 Aviemore. 🛈 Grampian Rd, Aviemore (01479-810 930).

Rising to a height of 1,309 m (4,296 ft), the Cairngorm mountains form the highest landmass in Britain.

Cairn Gorm itself is the site of one of Britain's first ski centers. Transportation to the 28 ski runs is provided daily from **Aviemore**. The chairlift that climbs Cairn Gorm affords superb views over the Spey Valley. **Rothiemurchus Estate** has a visitor center offering guided walks.

The **Cairngorm Reindeer Centre** organizes walks in the hills among Britain's only herd of reindeer, and ospreys can be observed at the **Loch Garten Nature Reserve**.

Drivers can see bison, bears, wolves, and boar in the **Kincraig Highland Wildlife Park**.

㉚ Inverness

🏙 60,000. 🚉 🚌 🛈 Castle Wynd (01463-252 401).
🔤 visithighlands.com

Inverness is the center of communication, commerce, and administration for the Highlands. Dominating the high ground above the town is

Inverness Castle, a Victorian building of red sandstone. Below the castle, the **Inverness Museum and Art Gallery** provides a good introduction to the region's history. Its exhibits include a fine collection of Inverness silver. The **Scottish Kiltmaker Visitor Centre** offers an insight into the history, culture, and tradition of the kilt.

In summer, **Jacobite Cruises** (call 01463-233 999 for information) runs regular boat trips along the Caledonian Canal and on famous **Loch Ness**, southwest of Inverness. The Loch is 39 km (24 miles) long and up to 305 m (1,000 ft) deep. On the western shore, the ruins of the 16th-century **Urquhart Castle** can be seen. The **Official Loch Ness Exhibition Centre**, in nearby Drumnadrochit, provides information about the Loch and its mythical monster.

🏛 Museum and Art Gallery

1 Castle Wynd. **Tel** 01463-237 114. **Open** Mon–Sat. **Closed** Jan 1–2, Dec 25–26. ♿

㉛ Isle of Skye

🏙 11,500. 🚢 from Mallaig or Glenelg. 🚌 🛈 Bayfield House, Portree (01478-614 906).

Skye, the largest of the Inner Hebrides, can be reached by the bridge linking Kyle of Lochalsh and Kyleakin. The coast is shaped by a series of dramatic sea lochs, while the landscape from the Quiraing – a plateau of volcanic towers and spikes in the north – to the Cuillins – one of Britain's most spectacular mountain ranges – is majestic. Bonnie Prince Charlie (1720–88) escaped here from the mainland disguised as a maidservant following the defeat of his army at Culloden.

Skye's main settlement is **Portree**, with its colorful harbor. **Dunvegan Castle**, on the island's northwest coast, has been the seat of the Clan MacLeod chiefs for over seven centuries. South of here, the **Talisker distillery** produces one of the best Highland malts.

The ruins of Urquhart Castle, on the western shore of Loch Ness

Practical Information

Colorful pageantry, ancient history, and a varied countryside attract millions of tourists to Britain each year. Facilities for visitors have improved considerably in recent years, with major urban centers offering a good variety of restaurants and hotels. The affluent southern region is more expensive than the rest of Britain. Telephone and postal systems are efficient, and violent crime is uncommon.

When To Visit

Britain's temperate maritime climate does not produce extremes of heat or cold, but weather patterns shift constantly, and the climate can differ widely in places only a short distance apart. The southeast is generally drier than elsewhere. Be sure to pack a mix of warm and light clothing, and an umbrella. Walkers can be surprised by bad weather.

Britain's towns and cities are all-year destinations, but some attractions open only between Easter and October. Some hotels are crammed at Christmas and New Year. The main family holiday months, July and August, and public holidays, are always busy. Spring and fall offer a good compromise: fewer crowds and relatively fine weather.

Tourist Information

The **British Tourist Authority (BTA)** has offices in a number of major cities worldwide. In Britain, tourist information is available in many towns and public places, including airports, main train and bus stations, and at some sites of historical interest. These bureaux offer general tourist advice and will also reserve accommodations.

Both the regional and national tourist boards have comprehensive lists of local attractions and registered accommodations. The monthly magazine of **VisitBritain**, *In Britain*, available in tourist offices, contains articles about worthwhile places to visit and also includes an events diary. A charge may be made for more detailed maps and books.

For route planning, road atlases and local maps and guidebooks are available in most bookstores.

Opening Hours

Many businesses and shops are closed on Sundays, though trading is now legal. Museums and galleries are generally open from 10am to 5 or 6pm, with many opening later in the day on Sundays. Those outside the capital are normally closed for one day or one afternoon a week. On public holidays, known as bank holidays in Britain, banks, offices, most shops, and some restaurants will be closed.

Visa Requirements and Customs

A valid passport is needed to enter Britain. Visitors from the European Union (EU), the United States, Canada, New Zealand, and Australia do not require a visa to enter the country. Anyone who arrives in Britain from a member country of the EU can pass through a special channel at customs, but random checks are still made to detect any prohibited goods.

When entering from outside the EU, go through the green customs channel if you have nothing to declare, and the red channel if you have goods which exceed allowances.

Personal Security

Britain is not a dangerous place for visitors, and it is most unlikely that your stay will be blighted by crime. Due to past terrorist attacks, there are occasional security alerts, notably on the underground, but these are mainly false alarms, often due to people accidentally leaving a bag or parcel lying around.

Police

The sight of a traditional British "bobby" patroling the streets in a tall hat is now less common than the police patrol car with flashing lights and sirens. However, police on foot can still be found, and are courteous and helpful. If you have anything stolen, you should report the theft at the nearest police station.

The Climate of Great Britain

The moderate British climate rarely sees winter nights colder than -15 °C (5 °F), even in the far north, or summer days warmer than 30 °C (86 °F) in the south. Despite the country's reputation, annual rainfall is quite low – less than 100 cm (40 in) – and heavy rain is rare. The Atlantic coast, warmed by the Gulf Stream, gives the west a warmer, wetter climate than the east.

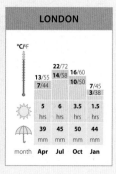

LONDON

°C/°F			
	22/72		
13/55	14/58	16/60	
7/44		10/50	7/45
			3/38
5 hrs	6 hrs	3.5 hrs	1.5 hrs
39 mm	45 mm	50 mm	44 mm
month Apr	Jul	Oct	Jan

EDINBURGH

°C/°F			
	18/62		
11/52	11/52	13/56	
4/39		7/44	16/61
			0/32
2.5 hrs	5.5 hrs	3 hrs	1.5 hrs
38 mm	70 mm	58 mm	47 mm
month Apr	Jul	Oct	Jan

Emergency Services

In an emergency, dial 999 to reach police, fire, and ambulance services, which are on call 24 hours a day. Calls are free. In coastal areas, this number also applies for calls to the voluntary coastguard-rescue service. You can also turn up at a hospital emergency room at any time. Emergency medical treatment in a British National Health Service (NHS) emergency room is free, but any kind of additional medical care could prove to be very expensive if you don't have insurance or your country does not have a reciprocal agreement.

Health Issues

You can buy a wide range of medicines from pharmacies, which in Britain are known as chemists. Boots is the best-known chain store. If you are likely to need prescription drugs, either bring your own or get your doctor to write out the generic name of the drug (as opposed to the brand name). Some pharmacies are open until midnight, while doctors' offices (known as surgeries) are normally open during the day only.

Facilities for the Disabled

The facilities on offer for disabled visitors to Britain are improving: new buildings offer elevators and ramps for wheelchair access, and adapted toilets. Many banks, theaters, and museums provide aids for the visually or hearing impaired. Given advance notice, rail, ferry, and bus personnel will help disabled passengers. The Disabled Person's Railcard provides discounted rail fares. Hertz offers hand-controled vehicles for rental at no extra cost. For more information, contact **RADAR**, **DisabledGo**, **Mobility International** or **Tourism For All**.

Banking and Currency

Britain's currency is the pound sterling (£), which is divided into 100 pence (p). Scottish banknotes are also legal tender in England and Wales, but not all stores take them.

Banking hours vary, but most are open from 9am to 5pm, Monday to Friday. Most banks cash traveler's checks, and have cash machines (ATMs) that accept most cards. You can also change money at private bureaux de change, which are located in tourist areas and operate longer hours than banks. Exchange rates and commission charges can vary.

Although credit cards are widely accepted in Britain, smaller stores, guesthouses, and cafés may not have the facilities for card transactions. Britain uses the "chip and PIN" system instead of a signature on a credit slip. You will need a four-digit PIN, so ask your bank for one before you leave.

Communications

Public telephone booths are available throughout Britain and may be card- or coin-operated. In major towns, some booths are able to accept credit cards and offer Internet access. It is cheaper to telephone in the evenings and at weekends.

Post offices are usually open from 9am to 5:30pm Monday to Friday, and until 12:30pm on Saturday. Sub-post offices are located in local stores. Stamps can be purchased from any outlet which displays the sign "Stamps sold here." Mail boxes are always painted red.

DIRECTORY

Tourist Information

Enjoy England
W enjoyengland.com

VisitBritain
W visitbritain.com

VisitBritain Australia
W visitbritain.com/au

Regional Tourist Boards

London
Opposite Platform 8,
Victoria Railway Station,
London SW1 1JU.
W visitlondon.com

Scotland
Tel 0845-859 1006.
W visitscotland.com

Wales
Tel 0870-830 0306.
W visitwales.com

Embassies

Australian High Commission
Australia House,
Strand, London WC2.
Tel 020-7379 4334.
W uk.embassy.gov.au/
lhlh/home.html

Canadian High Commission
MacDonald House,
1 Grosvenor Square,
London W1K.
Tel 020-7258 6600.
W canada.org.uk

New Zealand High Commission
80 Haymarket, London
SW1. Tel 020-7930 8422.
W nzembassy.com

US Embassy
24 Grosvenor Sq, London
W1. Tel 020-7499 9000.
W usembassy.org.uk

Emergencies Numbers

Police, Ambulance, Coastguard, and Fire services
Tel 999.

Facilities for the Disabled

DisabledGo
Ardent House, Gates Way,
Stevenage SG1 3HG.
Tel 0845-270 4627.
W disabledgo.com

Disabled Living Foundation
Tel 0300-999 0004.
W dlf.org.uk

Mobility International
North America
Tel 541-343 1284.
W miusa.org

RADAR
Tel 020-7250 3222.
W radar.org.uk

Tourism For All
7a Pixel Mill,
44 Appleby Road,
Kendal, Cumbria
LA9 6ES.
Tel 0845-124 9971.
W tourismforall.org.uk

Travel Information

Since it is an international gateway for air and sea traffic, Britain poses few problems for those arriving by air. Visitors have a large choice of carriers serving Australasia, Europe, and North America. Bus travel is an inexpensive form of transportation from Europe, while traveling by train is also easy, thanks to the Channel Tunnel. Traveling within Britain itself is fairly easy. There is an extensive road network reaching all parts of the country. The national rail road network is excellent and services to the smaller towns are good. Bus travel is the least-expensive option; buses serve most areas but can be slow.

Flying to Great Britain

London's Heathrow Airport is served by many of the world's leading airlines, with direct flights from most major cities. Other international airports include London Gatwick, London Stansted, Manchester, Newcastle, and Edinburgh.

British Airways has flights to destinations across the world. Other British airlines include **Virgin Atlantic**, with routes to the US and Far East, and **bmi regional**, which flies to the US and Western Europe. Several no-frills airlines, such as Ryanair and easyJet, offer low-cost flights to destinations all over Europe.

American airlines offering services to Britain include **Delta Air Lines**, **American Airlines**, and United; from Canada, the main carrier is **Air Canada**. From Australasia, **Qantas** and **Air New Zealand** vie for passengers with Far Eastern rivals, such as Emirates.

Charters and Package Deals

Charter flights are cheaper but have less-flexible departure times than standard scheduled flights. Packages are also worth considering, as airlines and tour operators can put together a great range of flexible deals to suit your needs. These can include car rental or rail travel.

Domestic Flights

Britain's size means that internal air travel only makes sense over long distances, such as from London to Scotland, or to one of the offshore islands.

The **British Airways** shuttle flights between London and cities such as Glasgow, Edinburgh, and Manchester are popular with business travelers. At peak times, flights leave every hour, while at other times there is usually a flight every two hours.

Traveling in London

In London, daily, weekly, and monthly tickets called Travel-cards are valid on all public transportation, as are pre-pay Oyster cards, which you can credit before your journey. Buses no longer accept cash payment, so if you are only using buses, buy a daily or weekly bus pass. Passes are available at most newsagents and train or underground stations.

Most travel services in London operate across six zones, with the tube, overground trains, and National Rail also operating in zones 7–9. There is a standard charge for travel within each zone and between zones, regardless of the distance traveled. The area covered by each zone varies slightly between buses and trains.

If you are in London for less than a week, buy a two-zone weekly Travelcard. Alternatively, choose a Visitor Oyster card, which can be topped up with credit at tube stations, Oyster Ticket Stops, and Travel Information Centres.

London also has express-train services to Britain's two busiest airports, Heathrow and Gatwick, which leave from Paddington and Victoria stations respectively at regular intervals. The journey time is 15 minutes to Heathrow, and 30 minutes to Gatwick.

When traveling by bus, you must purchase a ticket before boarding. The sightseeing buses that drive past many of London's historic sights are often run by private companies and will not accept bus passes or Travelcards.

All-night bus services are available in London from about 11pm until early morning. You can use Travelcards and bus passes on these. Night buses carry the letter N before the route number, and most pass through Trafalgar Square.

Taxis are available at major train stations, as well as at stands near hotels and all over central London. All licenced cabs must carry a "For Hire" sign, which is lit up whenever they are free. The famous black cabs are the safest taxis to use in London. Most cab drivers expect a tip.

Sometimes, the best way to see London is on foot, but however you choose to get around, try to avoid the rush hours from 8 to 9:30am, and 4:30 to 6:30pm.

London Underground

The underground in London, known as the tube, is one of the largest systems of its kind in the world. London tube trains run every day, except December 25, from about 5:30am until after midnight. Fewer trains run on Sundays. The 11 tube lines are color-coded and maps are available at every station, while maps of the central section are displayed on each train.

Rail Travel

Britain's privatized railroad network covers the whole of the country. It consists of several regional services, such as Great North Eastern Railways and Great Western Trains. **Virgin Trains**, which runs many cross-country routes, operates two other networks – West Coast Trains and Cross Country Trains. The system is generally quite reliable. The main stations in London all serve different areas of the country; Euston serves the

Midlands and northwest, King's Cross serves the northeast and Scotland, Liverpool Street serves East Anglia, Waterloo and Paddington serve the West Country and Wales, and Victoria and Charing Cross serve the South Coast.

First-class tickets for most journeys are available, and roundtrip fares are less costly than two one-way tickets. There are several types of fare for adults: Advance, purchased ahead of travel and to be used on a specific train; Off-Peak, if you can travel at less busy times; Anytime, which gives the most options, but is the most costly; and Rovers and Rangers, which offers unlimited travel within a specified area, with a few restrictions on when you travel.

If you plan to do much traveling by train around Britain, buy a rail pass. These can be bought from BR agents abroad, such as **CIE Tours International** and **Voyages-SNCF**. Passes are available for families and young people.

Long-distance Buses

In Britain, long-distance express buses and ones used for sightseeing excursions are usually referred to as coaches. Coach services are generally less expensive than rail travel. Journey times, however, are longer. Tickets can be purchased at major international airports, Victoria Coach Station – the main terminal for journeys into and out of London – and most large travel agents. The largest British coach operator is **National Express**. Another major operator is **Scottish Citylink**, with services between London, the North, and Scotland.

Traveling by Road

The most startling difference for many foreign motorists in Britain is that one drives on the left, with corresponding adjustments at traffic circles and junctions. Distances are measured in miles. Traffic density in towns and at busy holiday times can cause long delays. Parking is a big issue in towns and cities, so it is worth taking advantage of park-and-ride schemes.

Renting a car in Britain can be expensive. One of the most competitive national companies is **Autos Abroad**, but small local firms may undercut even these rates. International car rental companies such as **Avis**, **Budget**, and **Hertz** also operate in Britain. You need a valid driver's license and a passport when you rent.

Most companies will not rent to novice drivers, and set age limits (usually 21–70).

Ferry Services

About 20 car and passenger services travel regularly across the Channel and the North and Irish seas, the major ones including **DFDS Seaways** and **P&O**. Fares vary greatly according to the season, time of travel, and duration of stay.

Brittany Ferries run longer (often overnight) services between Plymouth, Poole, and Portsmouth to the west coast of France, as well as one 20-hour service outside the winter months between Plymouth and Santander in Spain.

Channel Tunnel

The Channel Tunnel offers a nonstop rail link between Britain and Europe. **Eurostar** services (for foot passengers) run from St. Pancras station in London to Lille and Paris in France, and Brussels in Belgium. Traveling from London direct to Brussels or Paris takes 2–2½ hours.

The **Eurotunnel** service (also known as the Shuttle) transports vehicles between Folkestone and Calais in about half an hour.

DIRECTORY

Airlines

Air Canada
Tel 0871-220 1111 (UK).
Tel 1888-247 2262 (US and Canada).

Air New Zealand
Tel 0800-028 4149 (UK).
Tel 0800-737 000 (NZ).

American Airlines
Tel 0844-499 7300 (UK).
Tel 800-433 7300 (US).

bmi regional
Tel 0844-417 2600 (UK).

British Airways
Tel 0844-493 0787 (UK).
Tel 1800-452 1201 (US).

Delta Air Lines
Tel 0871-221 1222 (UK).
Tel 1800-455 2720 (US).

Qantas
Tel 0845-774 7767 (UK).
Tel 13 13 13 (Australia).

Virgin Atlantic
Tel 0844-209 7777 (UK).
Tel 1800-862 8621 (US).

Rail Travel

CIE Tours International
Tel 020-8638 0715 (UK).

National Rail Inquiries
Tel 0845-748 49 50.

Virgin Trains
Tel 08719-774 222.

Voyages–SNCF
Tel 0844-848 5848.
W voyages-sncf.com

Bus Companies

National Express
Tel 08717-818 178.
W nationalexpress.com

Scottish Citylink
Tel 0871-266 3333.
W citylink.co.uk

Car Rental

Autos Abroad
Tel 0844-826 6536.
W autosabroad.com

Avis
Tel 0844-581 0147.
W avis.co.uk

Budget
Tel 0844-544 3470.
W budget.co.uk

Hertz
Tel 0843-309 3099.
W hertz.co.uk

Ferry Services

Brittany Ferries
Tel 0871-244 0744.

DFDS Seaways
Tel 0871-574 7235.

P&O
Tel 08716-642 121.

Channel Tunnel Services

Eurostar
Tel 08432-186 186.
W eurostar.com (for foot passengers).

Eurotunnel
Tel 0844-335 3535 (for cars & buses).

Shopping

While the West End of London is undeniably Britain's most exciting place to shop, many regional centers offer nearly as wide a range of goods. Moreover, regional shopping can be less stressful, less expensive, and remarkably varied, with craft studios, farm stores, street markets, and factory showrooms adding to the enjoyment of bargain-hunting. Britain is famous for its country clothing: wool, tartan, waxed cotton, and tweed are all popular, along with classic prints, such as those found at Liberty or Laura Ashley. Other particularly British goods include antiques, porcelain, glass, and local crafts.

Opening Hours

In general, you can assume most stores in Britain will open during the week from 9am or 10am until 5pm or 6pm. Hours on Saturdays may be longer, and stores may have late-night opening on Thursdays. Most large stores in town centers now open on Sundays; longer opening hours are more common as Christmas approaches. In villages, the stores may close at lunchtime for an hour, or for one afternoon each week. Market days vary from town to town; some markets are held on Sundays.

Out-of-town Shopping Centers

These large complexes, similar to American malls, are rapidly increasing around Britain. The advantages of car access and easy, cheap parking are undeniable, and most centers are accessible by public transportation. The centers usually feature clusters of popular upscale chain stores, with many facilities and services offered, such as nurseries, cafés, restaurants, and cinemas.

Department Stores

Certain big department stores are only found in London, but others have provincial branches. **John Lewis**, for example, has stores in 43 locations. It sells a huge range of fabrics, clothing, and household items, combining quality service with good value. **Marks & Spencer**, with branches throughout Britain, is even more

of a household name, famed for its good-value clothing and prepared food. The sizes of all chain stores, and the range of stock they carry, will differ from region to region.

The most famous of London's many department stores is **Harrods**, with 300 departments, 4,000 employees, and a spectacular Edwardian food hall. Nearby, **Harvey Nichols** stocks designer clothing and boasts the city's most stylish food hall. Gourmets should make a pilgrimage to **Fortnum and Mason**, which has stocked high-quality food for nearly 300 years. **Selfridges** sells virtually everything, from fine cashmeres to household gadgets. **Liberty**, the West End's last privately owned department store, still sells the hand-blocked silks and Oriental goods for which it was famous when it first opened in 1875.

Clothing Stores

Once again, London has the widest range, from haute couture to cheap and cheerful ready-made items. Shopping for clothing in the regions, however, can often be less tiring. Many towns that are popular with tourists – Oxford, Bath, and York, for instance – have independently owned clothing stores where you receive more personal service. Or you could try one of the chain stores found throughout the country for stylish, reasonably priced clothes, as well as younger and less-expensive fashions.

Traditional British clothing – waxed Barbour jackets and

Burberry trench coats – are found in outlets such as **Burberry** and **Gieves and Hawkes**, while **Laura Ashley** is renowned for its floral-print dresses. For kilts and tartans, the best place is **Hector Russell**, found in both Edinburgh and Glasgow.

London is the place for designer fashions, however, as many designers have specialized outlets here. **Vivienne Westwood**, doyenne of the punkish avant-garde, uses London as her British base.

Markets

Large towns and cities usually have a central covered market that operates most weekdays, selling everything from fresh produce to pots and pans. Many towns hold weekly markets in the main square.

The fashionable markets of London are **Covent Garden**, **Portobello Road**, and **Camden Lock**, where you can find an assortment of secondhand clothes, handmade crafts, and antiques. **Spitalfields** is a burgeoning East End market. Dating back to 1756, **Borough Market** sells quality fresh produce and gourmet foods.

Food and Drink

Supermarkets are a good place to shop for food. The range and quality of items in stock is usually excellent. Several large chains compete for market share and as a result, prices are generally lower than smaller stores. However, the smaller town-center stores, such as local bakeries, greengrocers, and markets, may give you a more interesting choice of fresh regional produce, and a more personal service.

Alcoholic beverages are available in a huge variety of stores around Britain, many of them wine merchants, such as the chain store **Oddbins**. For whisky, Scotland is the place to go; **Cadenheads** and **The Whisky Shop** both have a wide variety of rare scotches. Luxury chocolates can be purchased at **Hotel Chocolat**,

Montezuma's, and **Charbonnel et Walker**.

Books and Magazines

The capital is the hub of Britain's book trade, as many of the country's leading publishers are located within central London. Charing Cross Road is the focal point for those searching for new, antiquarian, and secondhand volumes, and it is the home of **Foyle's**, with its massive but notoriously badly organized stock. Large branches of such chains as **Waterstones** and **WH Smith** (which also sells magazines) are here, although they can also be found in most cities and major towns.

Gifts and Souvenirs

Most reputable large stores can arrange to ship expensive items back home for you. If you want to buy things that you can carry in a suitcase, the choice is wide.

For slightly more unusual presents, have a look in museum shops and at the range of items available in National Trust and English Heritage properties.

Some chain stores are very convenient places to pick up attractive gifts and souvenirs. **The Body Shop** sells natural cosmetics and toiletries in recyclable plastic packaging. For designer gifts, try the **Conran Shop** in London, which sells stylish accessories for the home.

Art and Antiques

Britain's long history means there are many interesting artifacts to be found. Many towns, such as Brighton, have dozens of antique shops. You might also like to visit a jumble or flea market in the hope of picking up a bargain.

The country's largest collection of original photographs for sale is at the **Photographers' Gallery** in London. For paintings and ceramics, the **Mayfair Gallery** excels in *belle epoque* masters. In Scotland, **The Scottish Gallery** has everything from jewelry to pieces by well-known Scottish artists, while the **Glasgow Antiques & Collectables Market** is a treasure trove of antiques.

DIRECTORY

Department Stores

Fortnum and Mason
181 Piccadilly, London W1. **Tel** 0845-300 1707.

Harrods
87–135 Brompton Rd, London SW1.
Tel 020-7730 1234.

Harvey Nichols
109–125 Knightsbridge, London SW1.
Tel 020-7235 5000.
One of many branches.

John Lewis
69 St. James Centre, Edinburgh EH1.
Tel 0844-693 1740.
One of many branches.

Liberty
210–220 Regent St, London W1.
Tel 020-7734 1234.

Marks & Spencer
173 & 458 Oxford St, London W1.
Tel 020-7935 7954.
Two of many branches.

Selfridges
400 Oxford St, London W1. **Tel** 0800-123 400.

Clothing Stores

Burberry
21–23 Bond Street, London W1.
Tel 020-7839 5222.

Gieves & Hawkes
1 Savile Row, London W1.
Tel 020-7432 6403.
One of several branches.

Hector Russell
110 Buchanan St, Glasgow G1.
Tel 0800 980 4010.

Laura Ashley
7–9 Harriet St, London SW1.
Tel 0871-223 1422.
One of many branches.

Vivienne Westwood
44 Conduit St, London W1.
Tel 020-7439 1109.

Markets

Borough Market
8 Southwark St, London SE1.
Open Mon–Sat.

Camden Lock
Chalk Farm Rd, London NW1.
Open 10am–6pm daily.

Covent Garden
The Piazza, London WC2.
Open 9am–5pm daily.

Portobello Road
Portobello Rd, London W10.
Open Mon–Sat; antiques 8am–5:30pm Sat.

Spitalfields
Commercial St, London E1.
Open 9am–5pm daily.

Food and Drink

Cadenheads
172 Canongate, Edinburgh EH8.
Tel 0131-556 5864.

Charbonnel et Walker
The Royal Arcade, 28 Old Bond Street, London W1.
Tel 020-7491 0939.

Hotel Chocolat
34 Coney St, York YO1.
Tel 01904-635 304.

Montezuma's
15 Duke St, Brighton BN1.
Tel 01273-324 979.

Oddbins
7 Borough High St, London SE1 9SU.
Tel 020-7407 5957.
One of many branches.

The Whisky Shop
Unit L2/O2, Buchanan Galleries, 220 Buchanan Street, Glasgow G1.
Tel 0141-331 0022.

Books and Magazines

Foyle's
113–119 Charing Cross Rd, London WC2.
Tel 020-7437 5660.

Waterstones
128 Princes St, Edinburgh. **Tel** 0131-226 2666.
One of many branches.

WH Smith
124 Holborn, London EC1.
Tel 020-7379 7313.
One of many branches.

Gifts and Souvenirs

The Body Shop
374 Oxford St, London W1.
Tel 020-7409 7868.
One of many branches.

Conran Shop
Michelin House, 81 Fulham Rd, London SW3.
Tel 020-7589 7401.

Art and Antiques

Finnie Antiques
The Red House, Croftamie, Lanarkshire G63.
Tel 01360-661 166.

Glasgow Antiques & Collectables Market
233 Gallowgate, Glasgow G40.
Tel 0141-552 6989.

Mayfair Gallery
39 South Audley St, London W1.
Tel 020-7491 3435.

Photographers' Gallery
16–18 Ramilies St, London W1F.
Tel 020-7087 9300.

The Scottish Gallery
16 Dundas St, Edinburgh EH3. **Tel** 0131-558 1200.

Entertainment

London is the entertainment capital of Britain, with an array of world-class cultural and sporting events. Around the country, theaters, opera houses, concert halls, and other venues host a wide range of performing- and dramatic-arts programs. The summer months also see numerous open-air arts festivals. Ticket prices are often less expensive outside the capital. Britain offers hundreds of special-interest holidays for those wanting to acquire a new skill or learn a new sport. Walking, sailing, skiing, pony-trekking, and golfing holidays are popular. Soccer, rugby, and cricket are favorite sports.

Entertainment Listings

For information about what's on in London, check the *Evening Standard* or the listings magazine *Time Out* (published every Wednesday). All the quality broadsheet newspapers have detailed arts reviews and listings of cultural events in London and throughout the country. Local newspapers, libraries, and tourist offices can supply details of regional events.

Tickets

Ticket availability varies from show to show. You may be able to buy a ticket at the door, especially for a mid-week matinee, but for the more popular West End shows, seats may have to be reserved weeks or even months in advance through agencies – ubiquitous in central London – or by telephone or in person at theater box offices. Half-price tickets for some same-day shows can be obtained from Leicester Square. Beware of counterfeit tickets offered by touts.

Theater

Britain has an enduring theatrical tradition dating back to Shakespeare. London is the place to enjoy theater at its most varied and glamorous. The West End alone has more than 50 theaters. The **Barbican** and the **National Theatre** stage a mixture of classics and challenging new productions. The major commercial theaters, showing more popular plays and musicals, are located along Shaftesbury Avenue and the Haymarket, and around Covent Garden and Charing Cross Road.

Outside the capital, at Stratford-upon-Avon, the **Royal Shakespeare Theatre** presents a year-round program of the great bard's works. The **Bristol Old Vic** is the oldest working theater in Britain. Good productions are staged at the Manchester **Royal Exchange**, and the **Traverse** in Edinburgh.

Open-air theater is a feature of city life in the summer, with street entertainers in London's Covent Garden and other urban centers. London's Globe theater *(see p66)* stages performances of Shakespeare's plays, and open-air theaters at Regent's Park and Holland Park also have a summer program.

Perhaps the liveliest theatrical festival in Britain is the two-week **Edinburgh Festival**, held in late summer. Many seaside resorts also have a summer theater season.

Music

A diverse musical repertoire can be found in a variety of venues across Great Britain. London, in particular, is one of the world's great centers for music, and home to several world-class orchestras and chamber groups. As well as classical concerts, there are dozens of rock, reggae, soul, folk, country, jazz, and Latin concerts taking place on every day of the week. There are also numerous nightclubs that play everything from 70s disco to the very latest house-music beats. Major pop-concert venues in the capital include **Wembley Arena** and the **Eventim Apollo**. The **Royal Albert Hall** hosts a range of concerts, including the popular classical Proms. The **Wigmore Hall**, the **Barbican Concert Hall**, and the **Royal Festival Hall** are also notable classical venues. The **Royal Opera House** is a world-class venue, and home to the Royal Opera. English National Opera performs at the **London Coliseum**. Classical open-air concerts are also held at Marble Hill House.

A wide range of musical events is staged in towns and cities across Great Britain. Liverpool and Manchester have excellent orchestras and are also centers for modern music, while **Glyndebourne** hosts an annual opera festival. Wales has a very strong choral tradition, while northern England is renowned for booming brass bands. Scotland, of course, is famous for its bagpipers.

Dance

Classical ballet is performed at the **Royal Opera House**, home of the Royal Ballet, and the **London Coliseum**, where the English National Ballet usually performs. **The Place** theater, **Sadler's Wells**, and the **Institute for Contemporary Art** (**ICA**) are major venues for contemporary dance.

Birmingham is home to the Birmingham Royal Ballet and is the best place to see performances outside London. Traditional English Morris dancing or the Scottish Highland fling and Celtic dancing *(ceilidhs)* can be enjoyed at local festivals.

Cinema

The latest movies can be seen in any large town. Premieres with international film stars are usually held at London's Leicester Square cinemas. The capital now has a 3D movie theater, the **BFI London IMAX**. Young children may see films graded U (universal) or PG (parental guidance). Cinema prices vary widely; some are less expensive at off-peak times, such as Mondays or afternoons. For first nights of new releases it is advisable to book in advance.

Special-Interest Vacations

Hundreds of options are available, from any kind of sport, to arts and crafts, such as painting, calligraphy, and jewelry-making, and a wide range of educational courses to suit all levels.

Reservations can be made with organizers or through a travel agent. The English and Scottish Tourist Boards have pamphlets on some of these activities.

Outdoor Activities

Britain has an extensive network of long-distance footpaths and shorter trail routes for walkers, together with designated cycle routes and bridle paths.

There are 2,000 golf courses in Britain and many clubs welcome visiting players (bring confirmation of your handicap). Green fees vary widely. Tennis courts can be found in every town and many hotels.

Sailing is popular in the Lake District, and the south-coast resorts have plenty of pleasure craft. Boating on the Thames and on Britain's network of canals is a common summer pursuit. Surfers and windsurfers head for the West Country and South Wales. The best game fishing (trout and salmon) is in the West Country, Wales, and Scotland. Soccer, rugby, cricket, and horse-racing are all popular sports in Britain. Details of matches and meetings can be found in national newspapers. During the last week of June and the first week of July, the Wimbledon tournament attracts many visitors to the **All England Lawn Tennis and Croquet Club.**

Among adventure-sport options are rock-climbing and mountaineering, aeronautical sports and gliding. Skiing and other winter sports are possible in Scotland. Ice-skating rinks are located in major cities and horse-riding centers are found throughout the country, with pony-trekking in tourist areas.

DIRECTORY

Theater

Barbican
Silk St, London EC2.
Tel 020-7638 4141.

Bristol Old Vic
King St Bristol BS1.
Tel 0117-987 7877.

Edinburgh Festival
The Hub, Castlehill,
Edinburgh EH1.
Tel 0131-473 2000.

National Theatre
Southbank Centre,
London SE1.
Tel 020-7452 3000.

Royal Exchange
St. Anne's Square,
Manchester M2.
Tel 0161-833 9833.

Royal Shakespeare Theatre
Stratford-upon-Avon
CV37. **Tel** 0844-800 1110.

Traverse
Cambridge St, Edinburgh
EH1. **Tel** 0131-228 1404.

Music

Eventim Apollo
Queen Caroline St,
London W6.
Tel 020-8563 3800.

Glyndebourne
Lewes, East Sussex BN8.
Tel 01273-812 321.

London Coliseum
St. Martin's Lane,
London WC2.
Tel 020-7845 9300.

Royal Albert Hall
Kensington Gore,
London SW7.
Tel 020-7589 8212
or 0845-401 5034.

Royal Festival Hall
Southbank Centre,
London SE1.
Tel 0844 875 0073.

Royal Opera House
Bow St, London WC2.
Tel 020-7304 4000.

Wembley Arena
Empire Way, Wembley,
Middlesex HA9.
Tel 0844-815 0815 or
0844-824 4824.

Wigmore Hall
36 Wigmore St, London
W1. **Tel** 020-7935 2141.

Dance

ICA
Nash House, Carlton
House Terrace, The Mall,
London SW1.
Tel 020-7930 3647.

Sadler's Wells
Rosebery Ave,
London EC1.
Tel 0844-412 4300.

The Place
17 Duke's Road,
London WC1.
Tel 020-7121 1100.

Cinema

BFI London IMAX
Waterloo Rd, London SE1.
Tel 0330-333 7878.

Outdoor Activities

**All England Lawn
Tennis and Croquet
Club**
Church Road, Wimbledon,
London SW19.
Tel 020-8944 1066.

**Association of
Pleasure Craft
Operators**
Marine House,
Thorpe Lea Rd,
Egham, Surrey.
Tel 01784-223603.

**British Activity
Providers Association**
Tel 01746-769 982.
W thebapa.org.uk

**British Mountain-
eering Council**
The Old Church, 177–179
Burton Rd, West Didsbury,
Manchester M20 2BB.
Tel 0161-445 6111.
W thebmc.co.uk

Canal & River Trust
First Floor North, Station
House, 500 Elder Gate,
Milton Keynes MK9 1BB.
Tel 0303-040 4040.
W canalrivertrust.
org.uk

English Golf Union
National Golf Centre,
The Broadway, Woodhall
Spa, Lincs LN10.
Tel 01526-354 500.
W englandgolf.org

Outward Bound
Hackthorpe Hall,
Hackthorpe,
Cumbria CA10 2HX.
Tel 01931-740 000.
W outwardbound.
org.uk

**Ski Club of Great
Britain**
57–63 Church Road,
London SW19.
Tel 0845-458 0780.
W skiclub.co.uk

Where to Stay

London

DK Choice

THE CITY AND SOUTHWARK:
Andaz Liverpool Street   ££
Boutique   **Map** F3
40 Liverpool Street, EC2M 7QN
Tel *020 7961 1234*
W london.liverpoolstreet.
andaz.com
Two characterful bars, three
excellent restaurants, and a
hidden Masonic temple await
in this refurbished palatial old
railroad hotel. Bedrooms are
minimalist but comfortable. The
lobby has a room for guests to
mingle over free refreshments.

REGENT'S PARK AND
BLOOMSBURY: The Arch   ££
Boutique
50 Great Cumberland Place, W1H 7FD
Tel *020 7724 4700*
W thearchlondon.com
Guests at these cleverly converted
townhouses can also enjoy The
Arch's bar and laid-back dining.

REGENT'S PARK AND
BLOOMSBURY: Hart House   ££
B&B   **Map** C2
51 Gloucester Place, W1U 8JF
Tel *020 7935 2288*
W harthouse.co.uk
Spotless rooms and excellent
breakfast can be found at this
award-winning townhouse B&B.

SOUTH KENSINGTON AND
HYDE PARK: The Ampersand   ££
Boutique   **Map** B4
10 Harrington Road, SW7 3ER
Tel *020 7589 5895*
W ampersandhotel.com
The whimsical interiors at this
hotel are inspired by music,
science, and nature.

WEST END AND WESTMINSTER:
The Goring   £££
Historic   **Map** C4
Beeston Place, SW1W 0JW
Tel *020 7396 9000*
W thegoring.com
A great English institution, with
liveried doormen, gardens, and
crackling fires on winter days.

WEST END AND WESTMINSTER:
The Ritz   £££
Luxury   **Map** C3
150 Piccadilly, W1J 9BR
Tel *020 7493 8181*
W theritzlondon.com
A treat, with stunning Louis XVI-
style bedrooms with all mod
cons and a gilded dining room.

Southern England

ARUNDEL: April Cottage   £
B&B
*Crossbush Lane, West Sussex,
BN18 9PQ*
Tel *01903 885 401*
W april-cottage.co.uk
This simple but charming
cottage located near the
wetlands serves good breakfasts.

BRIGHTON: Hotel Una   ££
Boutique
*55–56 Regency Square, East Sussex,
BN1 2FF*
Tel *01273 820 464*
W hotel-una.co.uk
Luxurious rooms, as well as
breakfast in bed at no extra cost.

CANTERBURY:
Cathedral Lodge   £
Boutique
The Precincts, Kent, CT1 2EH
Tel *01227 865 350*
W canterburycathedrallodge.org
Stylish rooms in the grounds
of Canterbury Cathedral.

Price Guide
Prices are based on one night's stay in
high season for a standard double room,
inclusive of service charges and taxes.

£	under £100
££	£100 to £200
£££	over £200

DK Choice

CHICHESTER:
Richmond House   £
B&B
*230 Oving Road, West Sussex,
PO19 7EJ*
Tel *01243 771 464*
W richmondhousechichester.
co.uk
This B&B offers a high level of
comfort and elegant rooms,
including one with French
windows opening onto the
garden. Large breakfast menu.
Chichester is a short walk away.

HEVER: Hever Castle B&B   ££
B&B
*The Astor Wing, Hever Castle, Kent,
TN8 7NG*
Tel *01732 865 224*
W hevercastle.co.uk
A luxury B&B with access to
the castle and a golf course.

LEWES: The Shelleys   ££
Historic
135–136 High St., East Sussex, BN7 1XS
Tel *01273 472 361*
W the-shelleys.co.uk
Family-run 17th-century country-
house hotel with luxurious rooms.

PORTSMOUTH:
Number 4 Hotel   £
Boutique
*69 Festing Road, Southsea,
Hampshire, PO4 0NQ*
Tel *02392 008 444*
W number4hotel.co.uk
Plush designer hotel close to
both the town and the seafront.

SALISBURY: St. Ann's House   £
B&B
33–34 St. Ann Street, Wiltshire, SP1 2DP
Tel *01722 335 657*
W stannshouse.co.uk
This four-star Georgian B&B offers
great views of Salisbury Cathedral.

SOUTHAMPTON:
Hotel Terravina   ££
Modern
*174 Woodlands Road, Woodlands,
Hampshire, SO40 7GL*
Tel *02380 293 784*
W hotelterravina.co.uk
On the edge of the New Forest.
Rooms feature rain showers.

Understated elegance at Richmond House, Chichester

The West Country and Wales

ABERYSTWYTH: Gwesty Cymru £
Boutique
19 Marine Terrace, Wales, SY23 2AZ
Tel *01970 612252*
W gwestycymru.com
Modern twist on traditional Welsh
seaside boarding house. Stylish
rooms with oak furniture, designer
bathrooms and sea views.

DK Choice

BATH: The Royal Crescent £££
Luxury
*16 Royal Crescent, Somerset,
BA1 2LS*
Tel *01225 823 333*
W royalcrescent.co.uk
Step into Georgian times while
enjoying modern amenities.
This opulent hotel has high-
ceilinged rooms, a candlelit spa,
and a gourmet restaurant.

**BEAUMARIS: Ye Olde Bull's Head
Inn and Townhouse** ££
Character
*Castle St, Isle of Anglesey, Wales,
LL58 8AP*
Tel *01248 810329*
W bullsheadinn.co.uk
A 15th-century inn with modern
facilities and a prized restaurant.

BRISTOL: Brooks Guesthouse £
B&B
St. Nicholas Street, BS1 1UB
Tel *01179 300 066*
W brooksguesthousebristol.com
This bright B&B behind St. Nick's
market offers doubles and triples.

**CARDIFF: St David's Hotel
& Spa** ££
Designer
Havannah St, Wales, CF10 5SD
Tel *02920 454045*
W thestdavidshotel.com
One of the most luxurious hotels
in Wales. State-of-the-art rooms
have private decks overlooking
the bay.

CLOVELLY: The Red Lion ££
Room with a view
The Quay, Devon, EX39 5TF
Tel *01237 431 237*
W clovelly.co.uk
There are fabulous views from this
hotel's nautically themed rooms.

**LYME REGIS:
1 Lyme Townhouse** £
B&B
1 Pound Street, Dorset, DT7 3HZ
Tel *01297 442 499*
W hotel1lyme.com

Luxurious touches include a
breakfast hamper of local produce.

**PENZANCE:
The Artist Residence** ££
B&B
20 Chapel Street, Cornwall, TR18 4AW
Tel *01736 365 664*
W arthotelcornwall.co.uk
Hip guesthouse in a mansion,
with bright art on the walls.

PORTMEIRION: Portmeirion £££
Character
Gwynedd, Wales, LL48 6ER
Tel *01766 770000*
W portmeirion-village.com
A fantasy village built by Clough
Williams-Ellis. Elegantly decorated
rooms, some with sea views.

Central England

CAMBRIDGE: Madingley Hall £
Historic
Madingley, Cambridgeshire, CB23 8AQ
Tel *01223 746 222*
W madingleyhall.co.uk
Grand 16th-century country
house offering functional and
modern rooms. Superb gardens.

**GREAT MILTON: Le Manoir
aux Quat'Saisons** £££
Luxury
Church Road, Oxfordshire, OX44 7PD
Tel *01844 278 881*
W manoir.com
Opulent rooms in a lush garden
setting, plus a Michelin-starred
restaurant and a cookery school.

LOWESTOFT: Britten House £
Room with a view
21 Kirkley Cliff Road, Suffolk, NR33 0DB
Tel *01502 573 950*
W brittenhouse.co.uk
This Victorian townhouse with
original features and sea views
was the family home of the
composer Benjamin Britten.

OXFORD: Old Bank Hotel ££
Luxury
92–94 High Street, Oxfordshire, OX1 4BJ
Tel *01865 799 599*
W oldbank-hotel.co.uk
Some rooms in this converted
bank have views of the Bodleian
Library and Radcliffe Camera.

ROSS ON WYE: Norton House £
B&B
*Old Monmouth Road, Whitchurch,
Herefordshire, HR9 6DJ*
Tel *01600 890 046*
W norton-house.com
Modern boutique option with
tasteful decor. The in-house
restaurant serves quality local
and seasonal food.

The luxurious Duke of York Master Suite at
The Royal Crescent, Bath

**SOUTHWOLD:
Sutherland House** ££
Historic
56 High Street, Suffolk, IP18 6DN
Tel *01502 724 544*
W sutherlandhouse.co.uk
Stay in an impressive house
dating back to 1455. Room
features include a sleigh bed
and a slipper bath. There is an
excellent fish restaurant on site.

**STRATFORD-UPON-AVON:
Twelfth Night Guesthouse** £
B&B
*13 Evesham Place, Warwickshire,
CV37 6HT*
Tel *01789 414 595*
W twelfthnight.co.uk
Stay in a refurbished Victorian
villa with bright and colorful
rooms. Not far from the Royal
Shakespeare Company theaters.

Northern England

**ARMATHWAITE:
Drybeck Farm** £
Boutique
*Drybeck Farm, Carlisle, Cumbria,
CA4 9ST*
Tel *07854 523 012*
W drybeckfarm.co.uk
Stay in a Mongolian yurt or a
gypsy caravan on a working farm.
Drybeck combines the comforts
of home with outdoor pleasures.

BLACKPOOL: The Kenley £
B&B
29 St. Chads Road, Lancashire, FY1 6BP
Tel *01253 346 447*
W kenleyhotel.co.uk
The Kenley is a boutique B&B
with contemporary kitsch styling.

HALIFAX: Holdsworth House ££
Boutique
*Holdsworth Road, Holmfield,
West Yorkshire, HX2 9TG*
Tel *01422 240 024*
w holdsworthhouse.co.uk
A Jacobean manor with some
period rooms. Breakfast is made
with locally sourced produce.

MANCHESTER: Didsbury House £
Luxury
*Didsbury Park, Didsbury Village,
M20 5LJ*
Tel *0161 448 2200*
w eclectichotels.co.uk
Renovated Victorian villa in
a leafy suburb. Rooms are
modern and individually styled.

**STRATFORD-UPON-AVON:
Twelfth Night Guesthouse** £
B&B
*13 Evesham Place, Warwickshire,
CV37 6HT*
Tel *01789 414595*
w twelfthnight.co.uk
Victorian villa with bright rooms.
A short walk from theatres.

DK Choice

**WINDERMERE:
Gilpin Lodge** £££
Luxury
Crook Road, Cumbria, LA23 3NE
Tel *01539 488 818*
w thegilpin.co.uk
This supremely stylish hotel
combines a warm welcome
with contemporary comforts
and haute cuisine. The garden
suites make the most of the
sylvan environs, while other
rooms are located in the
venerable old lodge itself.

YORK: Middlethorpe Hall £££
Luxury
*Bishopthorpe Road, Yorkshire,
YO23 2GB*
Tel *01904 641 241*
w middlethorpe.com
Superb mansion built in 1699
amid gardens and parkland.

Scotland

APPLECROSS: Applecross Inn £
Room with a view
Wester Ross, IV54 8LR
Tel *01520 744 262*
w applecross.uk.com
Lovely inn with views of the Isle
of Skye. Famous locally for the
quality of seafood and the large
portions served up in its eatery.

**ARISAIG: Old Library
Lodge & Restaurant** £
Historic
Inverness-shire, PH39 4NH
Tel *01687 450 651*
w oldlibrary.co.uk
Pleasant rooms in over 200-year-
old stables at a waterfront location.

**EDINBURGH:
Dalhousie Castle Hotel** £££
Historic
Bonnyrigg, EH19 3JB
Tel *01875 820 153*
w dalhousiecastle.co.uk
This retreat offers an excellent
spa and restaurant. It also has
grounds for falconry and archery.

FORT AUGUSTUS: The Lovat £
Modern
Inverness-shire, PH32 4DU
Tel *01456 490 000*
w thelovat.com
Relaxed accommodation on
the southern tip of Loch Ness.

DK Choice

**GLASGOW: Hotel du Vin at
One Devonshire Gardens** £££
Boutique
1 Devonshire Gardens, G12 0UX
Tel *08447 364 256*
w hotelduvin.com
Housed in a quintet of Victorian
townhouses, the Hotel du Vin is
Glasgow's most famous hotel.
The emphasis is on opulence –
from its spacious and unique
rooms, to the whiskey bar and
restaurant. Service is impeccable.

ISLE OF COLL: Coll Hotel ££
Room with a view
Ariangour, PA78 6SZ
Tel *01879 230 334*
w collhotel.com
Wonderfully appointed lochside
hotel with six comfortable
en-suite guest rooms and epic
views. Superb seafood restaurant.

**ISLE OF MULL: Highland
Cottage Hotel & Restaurant** ££
Luxury
*24 Breadalbane Street, Tobermory,
PA75 6PD*
Tel *01688 302 030*
w highlandcottage.co.uk
David Currie is the perfect host,
while his wife Jo cooks delicious
Scottish fare. Choose between
six individually styled and
luxuriously furnished rooms.

ORKNEY: The Foveran £
B&B
St. Ola, KW15 1SF
Tel *01856 872 389*
w foveranhotel.co.uk
Family-run hotel with wonderful
views over Scapa Flow. There are
eight en-suite guest rooms, plus
a lovely restaurant where locally
sourced seafood is the highlight.

SHETLAND: Skeoverick £
B&B
Brunatwatt, Walls, ZE2 9PJ
Tel *01595 809 349*
w visitscotland.com
Welcoming and spacious B&B in
a picturesque lochside location.
Immaculate en-suite rooms and
a lounge. Serves a great cooked
breakfast, with hen or duck eggs.

**ST. ANDREWS:
Old Course Hotel** £££
Luxury
Kingdom of Fife, KY16 9SP
Tel *01334 474 371*
w oldcoursehotel.kohler.com
One of the world's best golf-
resort hotels. Book a room
with an Old Course view,
and enjoy the treat of the
Kohler Waters Spa.

One of the delightful cottages at Middlethorpe Hall, York

Key to Price Guide *see page 104*

Where to Eat and Drink

The Art Nouveau surroundings of Bibendum, in South Kensington, London

London

THE CITY AND SOUTHWARK:
Lahore Kebab House   £
Pakistani
2–10 Umberston Street, E1 1PY
Tel *020 7481 9737*
Spiced curries and kababs will set
your taste buds tingling in this
warehouse-style space. Bring
your own bottle.

THE CITY AND SOUTHWARK:
Hawksmoor   £££
Steak House
157 Commercial Street, E1 6BJ
Tel *020 7426 4850*
Succulent steaks (prepared from
Longhorn cattle and dry-aged)
are cooked on a charcoal grill.
Hawksmoor is a carnivore's delight.

DK Choice

THE CITY AND SOUTHWARK:
Oxo Tower Restaurant,
Bar and Brasserie   £££
European   **Map** E3
Oxo Tower Wharf, Barge House
Street, SE1 9GY
Tel *020 7803 3888*
The delectable food and
international wine list at Oxo is
complemented by breathtaking
eighth-floor views: colorful by
day, glittering by night. Choose
between the relaxed brasserie
and sophisticated restaurant,
both superbly run by Harvey
Nichols. Picturesque terrace
seating in the summer.

REGENT'S PARK AND
BLOOMSBURY: Gem   £
Turkish
                     Map 4 F1
265 Upper St, N1 2UQ
Tel *020 7359 0405*

Serving fragrant meze in a
charming room decorated with
Kurdish farm implements.

DK Choice

REGENT'S PARK AND
BLOOMSBURY:
Golden Hind   £
British   **Map** C2
73 Marylebone Lane, W1U 2PN
Tel *020 7486 3644* **Closed** *Sun*
A welcoming no-frills place,
Golden Hind was established in
1914. The home-made fishcakes
with mushy peas are an enticing
alternative to their famous fish 'n'
chips. Bring your own bottle.

SOUTH KENSINGTON AND
HYDE PARK:
Buona Sera Jam   £
Italian
289 King's Road, SW3 5EW
Tel *020 7352 8827*
This lively trattoria is great for
families. Climb miniature ladders
to reach the top-tier tables and
enjoy terrific pizzas and pastas.

SOUTH KENSINGTON AND
HYDE PARK:
Café Mona Lisa   £
French
417 King's Road, SW10 0LR
Tel *020 7376 5447*
Popular café with friendly service
and warm interiors. Delicious
French fare, with daily specials.

SOUTH KENSINGTON AND
HYDE PARK: Jak's   £
Mediterranean
77 Walton Street, SW3 2HT
Tel *020 7584 3441*
Savor a range of healthy, organic
dishes and tempting desserts in
a country-style back room.

SOUTH KENSINGTON AND
HYDE PARK: The Abingdon   ££
International
54 Abingdon Road, W8 6AP
Tel *020 7937 3339*
A converted pub with a refined
feel and great brasserie-style food.
Opt for the comfortable booths.

SOUTH KENSINGTON AND
HYDE PARK: Assaggi   ££
Italian
39 Chepstow Place, W2 4TS
Tel *020 7792 5501* **Closed** *Sun*
A worthy addition to London's
foodie scene. The bright decor
reflects the vivid colors of chef's
native Sardinia. Choose from an
extensive menu of superb
regional specialties. Book ahead.

Price Guide
Prices include a three-course meal for
one, half a bottle of house wine, and all
charges, such as cover, service, and VAT.

£	under £35
££	£35 to £50
£££	over £50

SOUTH KENSINGTON AND
HYDE PARK: E&O   ££
Asian Fusion
14 Blenheim Crescent, W11 1NN
Tel *020 7229 5454*
Amid glossy decor, E&O serves
delicious tempura and sushi,
plus a few specials, such as
pad thai.

SOUTH KENSINGTON AND
HYDE PARK:
Hunan   ££
Chinese
51 Pimlico Road, SW1W 8NE
Tel *020 7730 5712* **Closed** *Sun*
Enjoy tapas-size portions of
Taiwanese-style Chinese food –
served fiery or mild, as preferred.

SOUTH KENSINGTON AND
HYDE PARK:
Kensington Place   ££
Fish 'n' chips
201 Kensington Church Street, W8 7LX
Tel *020 7727 3184*
This famous goldfish-bowl
brasserie serves fantastic beer-
battered fish 'n' chips.

SOUTH KENSINGTON AND
HYDE PARK: Le Metro
at the Levin Hotel   ££
British   **Map** B4
28 Basil Street, SW3 1AS
Tel *020 7589 6286*
Genteel basement brasserie
serving delectable fare and
featuring a good wine list.

SOUTH KENSINGTON
AND HYDE PARK:
Red House   ££
British
2 Elystan Street, SW3 3NS
Tel *020 7581 9139*
Enjoy a seasonal menu of
traditional British fare in a
great pub environment.

SOUTH KENSINGTON AND
HYDE PARK: Bibendum   £££
French   **Map** B4
Michelin House, 81 Fulham Road,
SW3 6RD
Tel *020 7581 5817*
Michelin House's Art Nouveau
stained glass makes for a
stunning backdrop to this airy
first-floor dining room. Come for
superb seasonal French cuisine
and excellent service.

SOUTH KENSINGTON AND HYDE PARK: Dinner by Heston Blumenthal £££
British   Map B4
Mandarin Oriental Hyde Park, 66 Knightsbridge, SW1X 7LA
Tel *020 7201 3833*
London's much hyped restaurant showcases this celebrity chef's inspired take on British cuisine.

SOUTH KENSINGTON AND HYDE PARK: Restaurant Gordon Ramsay £££
French   Map B4
68 Royal Hospital Road, SW3 4HP
Tel *020 7352 4441*   **Closed** *Sat & Sun*
Standards remain high at Gordon Ramsay's three-Michelin-starred shrine to haute cuisine. It is very expensive, but the menu is truly exciting.

WEST END AND WESTMINSTER: Food for Thought £
Vegetarian   Map 11 B1
31 Neal St, WC2H 9PR
Tel *020 7836 0239*
This vegetarian haven serves excellent fare, including perfectly cooked wild mushroom gnocchi.

WEST END AND WESTMINSTER: Hard Rock Café £££
American   Map C4
150 Old Park Lane, W1K 1QZ
Tel *020 7514 1700*
Savor American staples at this famous eatery with a fascinating collection of rock memorabilia.

WEST END AND WESTMINSTER: Murano £££
European   Map C4
20 Queen Street, W1J 5PP
Tel *020 7495 1127*   **Closed** *Sun*
The place for modern European cuisine with a bias toward Italian flavors. Indulge in the decadent five-course set menu.

WEST END AND WESTMINSTER: Nobu £££
Japanese   Map C4
Metropolitan Hotel, 19 Old Park Lane, W1K 1LB
Tel *020 7447 4747*
Enjoy beautifully prepared sashimi, tempura, and other contemporary Japanese dishes while spotting celebrities.

WEST END AND WESTMINSTER: Veeraswamy £££
Indian   Map C3
Victory House, 99 Regent Street, W1B 4RS
Tel *020 7734 1401*
This London institution, opened in 1926, offers contemporary and classic Indian dishes in lush interiors that evoke a royal palace.

Southern England

BRIGHTON: 24 St. Georges £££
British
25 St. George's Road, East Sussex, BN2 1ED
Tel *01273 626 060*   **Closed** *Sun & Mon*
Local and seasonal produce is used here to create a regularly changing menu of delicious food.

CANTERBURY: Kathton House £££
European
6 High Street, Sturry, Kent, CT2 0BD
Tel *01227 719 999*   **Closed** *Sun & Mon*
Upmarket modern restaurant. Try the crab ravioli and loin fillet of Godmersham venison.

EMSWORTH: 36 on the Quay £££
British/European
47 South Street, Hampshire, PO10 7EG
Tel *01243 375 592*   **Closed** *Sun & Mon*
Overlooking the bay in a fishing village, 36 on the Quay serves excellent Michelin-starred cuisine.

LEWES: Limetree Kitchen £££
European
14 Station Street, East Sussex, BN7 2DA
Tel *01273 478 636* **Closed** *Mon & Tue*
Open for breakfast through to evening meals, the fare ranges from eggs Benedict to sorbets.

WINCHESTER: Kyoto Kitchen £
Japanese
70 Parchment Street, Hampshire, SO23 8AT
Tel *01962 890 895*
Specializing in sushi and sashimi, Kyoto Kitchen provides a good introduction to Japanese cuisine. Great presentation and service.

The West Country and Wales

AVEBURY: The Circle Café £
Café
Near Marlborough, Wiltshire
Tel *01672 539 250*
Stop here for tea and homemade cakes after a visit to Stonehenge.

BATH: Demuths £££
Vegetarian
2 North Parade Passage, Somerset, BA1 1NX
Tel *01225 446 059*
Innovative and interesting small veggie dishes here include miso roast aubergine and shallot tart.

BRISTOL: Arnolfini £
Café
16 Narrow Quay, BS1 4QA
Tel *01179 172 300*
Italian-inspired café in the city's main modern art gallery. Ditch

the art, and concentrate on the fabulous food. Free snacks at 5:30pm on most Fridays.

FROME: Meadowside Farm £
Café
46 Vallis Way, Somerset, BA11 3BA
Tel *01373 472 555*
A local artisan food producer, Meadowside Farm has a café and deli serving breakfast, brunch, lunch, and takeout meals.

ST. IVES: Porthminster Beach Café £££
Café
Porthminster Beach, Cornwall, TR26 2EB
Tel *01736 795 352*
This award-winning beach café serves local specialties with an emphasis on seafood. Good kids' and vegetarian menus.

DK Choice

WRINGTON: The Ethicurean £££
Modern British
Barley Wood Walled Garden, Somerset, BS40 5SA
Tel *01934 863 713*   **Closed** *Mon*
The Ethicurean is an outstanding café-restaurant that serves dynamic and experimental organic food. Overlooking the Mendip Hills, it is worth the trek, especially in the fall. Delicious coffee and sticky-toffee apple cake.

Central England

BIRMINGHAM: Purnell's £££
British
55 Cornwall St., West Midlands, B3 2DH
Tel *01212 129 799*   **Closed** *Sun & Mon*
Michelin-starred traditional British fare, such as roast suckling pig.

Dinners enjoy freshly prepared Japanese cuisine at Nobu in Mayfair, London

CAMBRIDGE: The Oak Bistro ££
European
6 Lensfield Road, CB2 1EG
Tel *01223 323 361* **Closed** *Sun & bank hols*
This bistro has a beautiful walled garden to dine in when the weather allows. Try the filet of sea bream or the roasted lamb.

**SOUTHWOLD:
Sutherland House** £££
Seafood
56 High Street, Suffolk, IP18 6DN
Tel *01502 724 544* **Closed** *Oct–Mar: Mon*
Sutherland House's superb dining room is the ideal setting to enjoy dishes such as seared scallops and pan-fried wild sea bass. The menu also features excellent game dishes. Ingredients are sourced locally.

**STRATFORD-UPON-AVON:
The Opposition Bistro** £
International
13 Sheep Street, Warwickshire, CV37 6EF
Tel *01789 269 980* **Closed** *Sun except bank hols*
The Opposition Bistro's timber-framed interior creates a great atmosphere. Come here to enjoy traditional bistro standards, such as fish cakes and steak.

Northern England

AMBLESIDE: Fellini's £
Vegetarian
Church Street, Cumbria, LA22 0BT
Tel *01539 432 487*
This stylish modern vegetarian place is attached to a small but glamorous arthouse cinema.

**BOLTON ABBEY: Devonshire
Arms Brasserie** £
British/French
Skipton, North Yorkshire, BD23 6AJ
Tel *01756 710 441*
Enjoy British and French cuisine in a coaching inn dating back to 1753. Informal atmosphere.

DK Choice

CARTMEL: L'Enclume £££
British
Cavendish Street, Cumbria, LA11 6PZ
Tel *01539 536 362*
An ancient building with rough limewashed walls and low beams is the rustic setting for some extraordinary food. Savor local cuisine that is partly foraged and presented with close attention to detail.

The entrance to The Peat Inn, in Cupar, Scotland

LEEDS: Salvo's ££
Italian
107/115 Otley Rd., Headingley, LS6 3PX
Tel *01132 755 017*
This innovative Italian restaurant serves a contemporary menu in an informal ambience. It also has a well-stocked *salumeria* (deli).

MANCHESTER: The Pavilion 2 £
Bangladeshi
231 Spotland Rd., Rochdale, OL12 7AG
Tel *01706 526 666*
Excellent *balti* (bucket) curries and tandoori dishes. Banquet-style meals for big groups.

Scotland

CUPAR: The Peat Inn £££
Pubs
Near St. Andrews, Fife, KY15 5LH
Tel *01334 840 206* **Closed** *Sun & Mon*
The menu at this Michelin-starred rural retreat expertly utilizes local produce, such as salmon, langoustine, and beef. Diners get to savor dishes from the multicourse tasting menu.

DUNDEE: Jute Café Bar £
Café
Dundee Contemporary Arts, 152 Nethergate, DD1 4DY
Tel *01382 909 246*
This artistic café at the Dundee Contemporary Arts center serves light lunches, as well as a three-course evening meal. The menu includes dishes such as steak, as well as chocolate torte.

EDINBURGH: David Bann £
Vegetarian
56–58 St. Mary's Street, EH1 1SX
Tel *01315 565 888*
A stylish fine-dining restaurant with delicious vegetarian dishes,

such as leek, tarragon, and butternut-squash risotto. Try the tartlet made with creamy Scottish Dunsyre blue cheese and slow-dried tomatoes.

FINDHORN: The Bakehouse £
Café
91–92 Forres, IV36 3YG
Tel *01309 691 826*
The Bakehouse is renowned for its organic produce. Meat options include tasty pork and venison burgers. Mouthwatering home baking, too.

**FORT WILLIAM:
The Lime Tree** ££
Modern Scottish
The Old Manse, Achintore Road, PH33 6RQ
Tel *01397 701 806*
Highly praised hotel-restaurant famous for its warm service and excellent food. Specialties include pan-seared Glenfinnan venison, mackerel, West Coast crab, and smoked haddock.

GLASGOW: Café Gandolfi £
Café
64 Albion Street, G1 1NY
Tel *01415 526 813*
Café Gandolfi is a Glasgow institution and part of the Gandolfi mini-empire. Come here for great breakfasts, light lunches, or substantial dinners. A relaxed dining experience.

**TYNDRUM:
The Real Food Café** £
Café
Perthshire, FK20 8RY
Tel *01838 400 235*
The Real Food Café serves arguably the best fish 'n' chips in the whole of Scotland. Diners can enjoy a large or small fish supper and sample excellent coffee as well as cakes.

IRELAND

It is easy to see Ireland as a lush, green island dotted with quaint, thatched cottages and friendly pubs filled with music, wit, and poetry. Despite the contrasting reality of rapid economic growth and fundamental political change, the tourist industry helps sustain this image of rural bliss, and the genuine good humor of the people invariably makes Ireland a most welcoming place to visit.

History and religion have created two communities in Ireland, with the Protestant majority in the North determined to remain part of the United Kingdom. In the latter half of the 20th century, violent attacks in Northern Ireland tarnished the world's view of the country, but in 1998 the Good Friday Agreement brought new hopes for peace.

Despite the Troubles of the past, the Irish retain a positive attitude. The Republic of Ireland, formerly one of the poorer countries of the European Union, became one of its success stories during the economic boom known as the "Celtic Tiger" years. Between 1990 and 2007, the economy saw growth of between 7 and 11 percent annually. But in 2008, it became evident that the inflated economy was built on an unsustainable property bubble. The worldwide recession did not spare Ireland, but an €85 billion bailout provided by the EU and IMF in

2010 was paid off within three years. The economy is slowly recovering. Agriculture remains a mainstay, with dairy cattle feeding on rich meadowlands and sheep grazing on the poorer upland pastures. The traditional Irish talent for breeding and training racehorses is undiminished. Tourism also thrives, with more than 6.5 million visitors to the Republic each year. Dublin is one of Europe's hotspots for a weekend break, as well as being a tech hub, with many media companies having their headquarters there.

History

In the past, Ireland's isolation cut it off from many of the major events of European history. Roman legions never invaded, and the country's early history is shrouded in myths of warring gods and heroic High Kings.

Dingle, a picturesque fishing harbor in southwest Ireland

◀ O'Brien's Tower, on top of the majestic Cliffs of Moher, in County Clare, Ireland

O'Connell Street in Dublin just after the Easter Rising of 1916

The bellicose Celtic tribes were quick to embrace Christianity in the 5th century AD. Until the Viking invasions of the 9th century, Ireland enjoyed an era of relative peace. Huge monasteries were founded, where scholarship and the arts flourished. The Vikings never succeeded in gaining control of the island, but in 1169, the English arrived with greater ambitions. Many Irish chiefs submitted to Henry II of England, and his Anglo-Norman knights carved out large fiefdoms for themselves.

KEY DATES IN IRISH HISTORY

8th century BC Humans first inhabit Ireland

600 BC Arrival of Celts from Europe and Britain

AD 432 St. Patrick brings Christianity to Ireland

795 First Viking invasion

999 Viking king of Dublin defeated by Irish High King, Brian Boru

1169 Anglo-Norman invasion; Henry II of England proclaims himself overlord of Ireland

1541 Henry VIII declared King of Ireland

1690 William of Orange defeats James II at Battle of the Boyne

1695 Penal Laws restrict civil rights of Catholics

1801 Act of Union with Britain

1828 Catholic Emancipation Act

1845–8 Potato Famine leaves one million dead

1916 Easter Rising

1921 Anglo-Irish treaty divides Ireland into the Irish Free State and Northern Ireland

1937 The Irish Free State becomes entirely independent of Britain and is renamed Eire

1969 British troops sent to Northern Ireland

1998 Good Friday Agreement sets out framework for self-government in Northern Ireland

2005 Provisional IRA announces full ceasefire

2008 Crisis in the banking system ends boom

2013 An €85 bn bailout by the EU and IMF is paid off

Direct English control was usually limited to the "Pale," the well-defended area around Dublin. Matters changed when, in 1532, Henry VIII broke with the Catholic church. Ireland became a battleground between Irish Catholics and English armies dispatched to crush resistance. Irish lands were confiscated and granted to Protestants from England and Scotland. England's conquest was completed with William of Orange's victory over James II in 1690. During the English Ascendancy, repressive Penal Laws denied Irish Catholics the most basic freedoms, but opposition to English rule was never totally quashed.

The Famine of 1845–8 was the bleakest period of Irish history. More than two million either died or were forced to emigrate. A campaign for Home Rule gathered strength, but it took the war of 1919–21 to force the issue. The Treaty of 1921 divided the island in two. The South became the Irish Free State, gaining full independence in 1937. The Catholic minority in Northern Ireland suffered under Protestant rule, and in the late 1960s began to stage civil-rights protests. The situation quickly got out of hand. The British sent in troops and acts of terrorism and sectarian violence took the place of reasoned dialogue.

Language and Culture

Ireland was a Gaelic-speaking nation until the 16th century, when English rule sent the language into decline. The Republic today is officially bilingual, and 35 percent of adults claim to know some Gaelic. Many speak it fluently, but perhaps only 3 percent use it regularly. Some degree of knowledge is needed for careers in the public sector. Irish culture, on the other hand, is in no danger of being eroded. The people have a genuine love of legends, literature, and songs, and festivals play an important part in community life. Traditional and modern music flourishes, whether at well-attended concerts or impromptu sessions in the local pub.

Exploring Ireland

Dublin is Ireland's chief attraction, a small, friendly capital with most of its sights and lively nightlife concentrated in the center. Elsewhere the pace of life is less hectic and the country's great appeal is in its landscape: from the lush green pastures, bogs, and lakes of the center of the island to dramatic mountains and bleak, rocky headlands in the southwest. Touring by car is the most convenient way to explore Ireland, which has a good-quality road network on both sides of the border.

Jaunting car for hire in Killarney

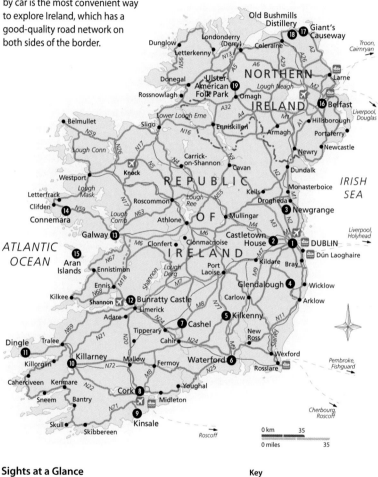

Sights at a Glance

1. Dublin pp114–23
2. Castletown House
3. Newgrange
4. Glendalough
5. Kilkenny
6. Waterford
7. Cashel
8. Cork
9. Kinsale
10. Killarney
11. Dingle
12. Bunratty Castle
13. Galway
14. Connemara
15. Aran Islands
16. Belfast
17. Giant's Causeway
18. Old Bushmills Distillery
19. Ulster-American Folk Park

Key

--- Highway
- - Highway under construction
--- Major road
— Railroad
•••• International border

For keys to symbols see back flap

● Dublin

Although it is a fairly small city, Ireland's capital is famous for its many pubs, and its rich cultural heritage attracts millions of visitors each year. The Liffey River runs through the middle of the city, and was the original source of its prosperity. The first harbor in Dublin was established in the early 9th century, when Vikings founded one of their largest settlements outside Scandinavia on the site of the present city. Since then, it has suffered wars and conflict over many centuries. In the 20th century, Dublin established its own identity and today it is a thriving, modern city, rich in history and proud of its past. Dublin and its surrounding county have a population of just over 1.1 million.

Sights at a Glance

① Trinity College
② Merrion Square
③ National Gallery of Ireland
④ National Museum of Ireland – Archaeology
⑤ Grafton Street
⑥ Temple Bar
⑦ Dublin Castle
⑧ St. Patrick's Cathedral
⑨ Christ Church Cathedral
⑩ Dublinia and the Viking World
⑪ The Liffey
⑫ O'Connell Street
⑬ Parnell Square

Greater Dublin *(see inset map)*

⑭ Guinness Storehouse
⑮ Phoenix Park

Key

▨ Sight / Place of interest
▨ Pedestrian street

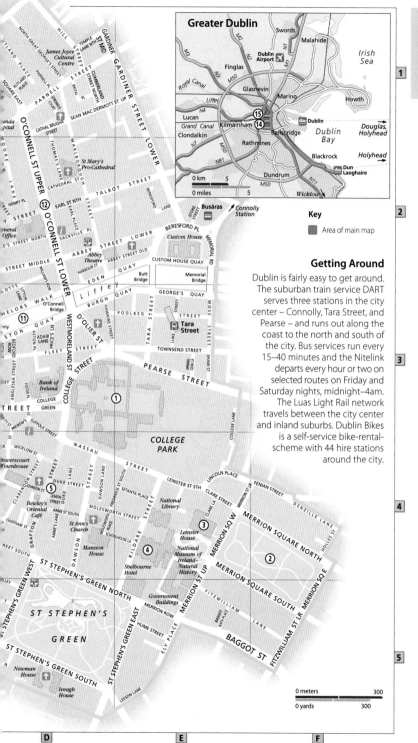

Greater Dublin

Swords
Malahide
M2
N1
M9
Dublin
Airport
Finglas
N2
M1
Irish
Sea
Royal Canal
N3
M50
Glasnevin
Marino
Howth
Liffey
Lucan
N4
Grand Canal
Kilmainham
⑮
⑭
Dublin
Douglas,
Holyhead
Clondalkin
Ballsbridge
Dublin
Bay
N7
M50
Rathmines
Holyhead
N81
Blackrock
Dun
Laoghaire
Dundrum
N11
0 km   5
M50
0 miles   5
Wicklow

Key

Area of main map

Getting Around

Dublin is fairly easy to get around. The suburban train service DART serves three stations in the city center – Connolly, Tara Street, and Pearse – and runs out along the coast to the north and south of the city. Bus services run every 15–40 minutes and the Nitelink departs every hour or two on selected routes on Friday and Saturday nights, midnight–4am. The Luas Light Rail network travels between the city center and inland suburbs. Dublin Bikes is a self-service bike-rental-scheme with 44 hire stations around the city.

0 meters   300
0 yards   300

Street by Street: Southeast Dublin

The area around College Green, dominated by the facades of the Bank of Ireland and Trinity College, is very much the heart of Dublin. The alleys and malls cutting across busy pedestrianized Grafton Street boast many of Dublin's better stores, hotels, and restaurants. Just off Kildare Street are the Irish Parliament, the National Library, and the National Museum of Ireland – Archaeology. To escape the city bustle, many head for sanctuary on St. Stephen's Green.

Dublin Castle ←

COLLEGE GREEN

SUFFOLK ST

GRAFTON

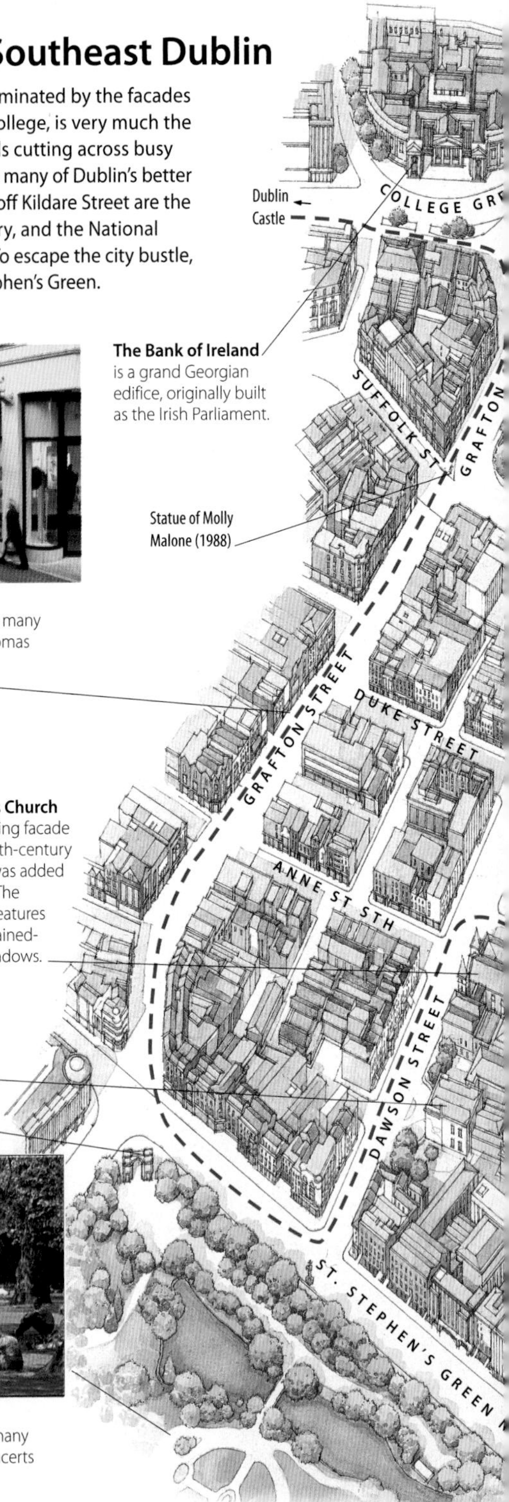

The Bank of Ireland
is a grand Georgian edifice, originally built as the Irish Parliament.

Statue of Molly Malone (1988)

Grafton Street
This popular pedestrian street is home to many of Dublin's best stores, such as Brown Thomas (see p119).

GRAFTON STREET

DUKE STREET

St. Ann's Church
This striking facade of the 18th-century church was added in 1868. The interior features lovely stained-glass windows.

ANNE ST STH

The Mansion House
has been the offical residence of Dublin's Lord Mayor since 1715.

DAWSON STREET

Fusiliers' Arch (1907)

ST. STEPHEN'S GREEN N

St. Stephen's Green
This relaxing city park is surrounded by many fine buildings. In summer, lunchtime concerts attract tourists and workers alike.

For hotels and restaurants see p138 and p139

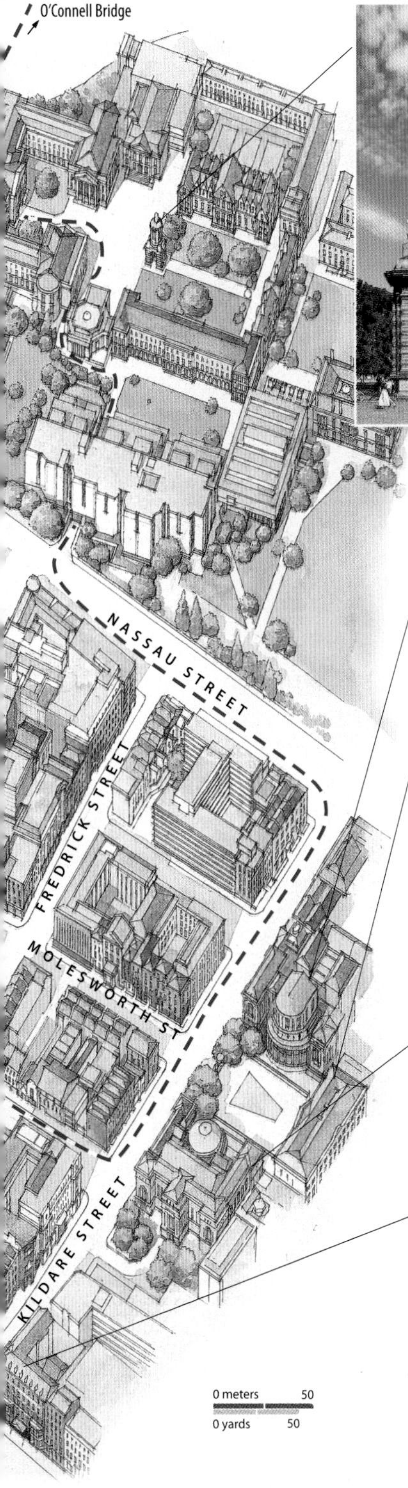

↗ O'Connell Bridge

★ Trinity College
The focal point of Parliament Square, the largest of Trinity's spacious quadrangles, is the elegant Italianate bell tower known as the "Campanile." Designed by Sir Charles Lanyon, it was erected in 1853 (see p118).

NASSAU STREET

FREDRICK STREET

MOLESWORTH ST.

KILDARE STREET

National Library
Saintly cherubs appear on the frieze around the library's magnificent old reading room, once a hangout of novelist James Joyce.

Leinster House
was taken over as the seat of the Irish Parliament in 1922.

★ National Museum of Ireland – Archaeology
The collection of Irish antiquities includes this bronze object from the 2nd century AD, known as the Petrie Crown (see p119).

The Shelbourne Hotel
Built in 1867, the hotel dominates the north side of St. Stephen's Green. It is popular with tourists and locals for afternoon tea.

| 0 meters | 50 |
| 0 yards | 50 |

Key

— Suggested route

View down the central aisle of Trinity College's Old Library

① Trinity College

College Green. **Tel** 01-896 2320. 🚊 DART to Pearse. 🚌 4, 7, 10, 14, 15, 46, 48 & many others. Old Library and Treasury: **Open** daily. **Closed** 10 days at Christmas. 🅿 🛗 🚾 **bookofkells.ie**

Trinity was founded in 1592 by Elizabeth I on the site of an Augustinian monastery as a bastion of Protestantism. It was not until the 1970s that Catholics started entering the university. Its cobbled quads and lawns still have a monastic feel, providing a pleasant haven in the heart of the city. In front of the main entrance, on College Green, are statues of two of Trinity's most famous 18th-century students, playwright Oliver Goldsmith and political writer Edmund Burke. Literary

alumni of more recent times include the playwrights Oscar Wilde (1854–1900) and Samuel Beckett (1906–89).

The oldest surviving part of the college is the red-brick building (the Rubrics) on the east side of Library Square, built around 1700. The Old Library itself dates from 1732. Its spectacular Long Room measures 64 m (210 ft) from end to end. It houses 200,000 antiquarian texts, marble busts of scholars and the oldest harp in Ireland. Below the Library is the Treasury, where the college's most precious volumes – the beautifully illuminated manuscripts produced in Ireland from the 7th to the 9th century – are kept. The most famous, the Book of Kells *(see p127)*, may have been created by monks from Iona, who fled to Kells in 806 after a Viking raid. The scribes embellished the text with intricate patterns as well as human figures and animals. Almost as fine is the *Book of Durrow*, which dates from the late 7th century.

Portrait of St. Matthew from the Book of Kells

② Merrion Square

🚊 DART to Pearse. 🚌 4, 7, 25, 44, 66 & many others.

Merrion Square is one of Dublin's largest and grandest Georgian squares. Covering about 5 ha (12 acres), the square was laid out by John Ensor around 1762.

On the west side are the impressive facades of the Natural History Museum, the National Gallery of Ireland, and the front garden of Leinster House, seat of the Dáil and the Seanad (the two houses of the Irish Parliament). The other three sides of the square are lined with lovely Georgian townhouses. Many have brightly painted doors and original features, such as wrought-iron balconies, ornate doorknockers, and fanlights. The oldest and finest houses are on the north side.

Many of the houses – now predominantly used as office space – have plaques detailing famous former occupants, such as Catholic emancipation leader Daniel O'Connell (No. 58), and poet

Facade of Trinity College, Dublin, the Republic's most prestigious university

For hotels and restaurants see p138 and p139

Georgian townhouses overlooking Merrion Square gardens

W.B. Yeats (No. 82). Oscar Wilde spent his childhood at No. 1.

The attractive central park has colorful flower and shrub beds. In the 1840s, it served a grim function as a soup kitchen, feeding the hungry during the Great Famine.

③ National Gallery of Ireland

Merrion Square West & Clare St. **Tel** 01-661 5133. 🚈 DART to Pearse. 🚌 4, 7, 25, 44 & many others. **Open** daily (pm only Sun). Parts of the gallery will close during extensive refurbishment until 2016. **Closed** Good Fri & Dec 24–26. 🎦 📷 🔗 📱 🖥 **nationalgallery.ie**

This purpose-built gallery was opened to the public in 1864. It houses more than 15,000 works of art from the 13th century to the present day, with a significant collection of works from the Italian, French, Flemish, and Dutch schools. The fine art collection is made up of celebrated masterpieces by the likes of Rembrandt, Vermeer, Gainsborough, Renoir, Picasso, and Van Gogh. The NGI also holds the most important collection of Irish painting, dating from the 17th century, plus a section dedicated to the works of Jack B. Yeats (1871–1957).

The gallery is currently undergoing a major program of refurbishment of its historic Dargan and Milltown wings, which date from the mid-19th century.

The work is scheduled for completion in 2016. Until then, entrance to the gallery is via the Millennium Wing on Clare Street.

④ National Museum of Ireland – Archaeology

Kildare St. **Tel** 01-677 7444. 🚈 DART to Pearse. 🚆 Luas green line to St. Stephen's Green. 🚌 15, 25, 38, 140 & many others. **Open** Tue–Sat & 2–5pm Sun. **Closed** Good Fri & Dec 25. 🎦 📷 📱 ♿ ground floor only. 🖥 **museum.ie**

The National Museum of Ireland – Archaeology was built in the 1880s to the design of Sir Thomas Deane. Its splendid domed rotunda features marble pillars and a zodiac mosaic floor. The ground floor holds *Ór – Ireland's Gold*, a collection of Bronze Age finds, including many beautiful pieces of jewelry. Objects from the later Iron Age Celtic period are on display in the Treasury. There are also many well-known treasures from the era of Irish Christianity *(see pp126–7)*. The first floor houses Viking artifacts and the Ancient Egypt gallery.

The Viking exhibition features coins, pottery, and swords excavated in the 1970s from the Viking settlement, discovered beside the Liffey at Wood Quay near Christ Church Cathedral *(see p121)*.

The Museum has another branch at Benburb Street, west of the city center. Housed in the vast Collins Barracks, established in 1700 by William III, is the National Museum of Ireland – Decorative Arts & History. The principal exhibits are the museum's collections of furniture, silver, weaponry, and scientific instruments, as well as an exhibition on the 1916 Easter Rising and events that occurred in the decade 1913–1923.

7th-century plaque depicting the Crucifixion, National Museum

⑤ Grafton Street

🚌 14, 15, 46 & many others.

The spine of Dublin's most stylish shopping district runs south from College Green to the glass St. Stephen's Green Shopping Centre. This busy pedestrianized strip, with its energetic buskers and talented street-theater artists, boasts one of Dublin's best department stores, Brown Thomas, and popular traditional pubs hidden along the side streets.

At the junction with Nassau Street is a statue by Jean Rynhart of *Molly Malone* (1988), the celebrated "cockles and mussels" street trader of the well-known Irish folk song.

Vermeer's *Woman Writing a Letter*, National Gallery of Ireland

Shoppers in Temple Bar

⑥ Temple Bar

🚌 11, 16A, 46A & many others.
ℹ️ Project Arts Centre: 39 East Essex Street. **Tel** 01-881 9613.
Open 11am–7pm Mon–Sat; shows nightly. 📷 ♿

The area of cobbled streets between Dame Street and the Liffey are named after Sir William Temple, who acquired the land in the early 1600s. The term "bar" meant a riverside path. In the 1800s, it was home to small businesses, but over the years went into decline. In the early 1960s, the land was bought up with plans for redevelopment. Artists and retailers took short-term leases, but stayed on when the plans were scrapped and Temple Bar prospered. Today, it is an exciting place, with restaurants, bars, clubs, shops, and galleries. Organizations based here include the **Irish Film Institute**, which has two screens, as well as a bookshop and café, **Project Arts Centre**, a contemporary-arts center for theater, dance, film, music, and visual art, and the **Gallery of Photography**, the only Irish art gallery devoted solely to photographs.

⑧ St. Patrick's Cathedral

St. Patrick's Close. **Tel** 01-453 9472.
🚌 49, 54A, 56A, 77A, 151. **Open** daily.
📷 ♿ 🌐 stpatrickscathedral.ie

Ireland's largest church was founded beside a sacred well where St. Patrick is said to have baptized converts around AD 450. It was originally just a wooden chapel, but in 1192, Archbishop John Comyn commissioned a magnificent new stone structure. The cathedral is 91 m (300 ft) long; at the western end is a 43-m (141-ft) tower, restored by Archbishop Minot in 1370 and now known as the Minot Tower. Much of the present building dates back to work completed between 1254 and 1270. Thanks to the generosity of Sir Benjamin Guinness, the

Jonathan Swift, Dean of St. Patrick's from 1713

⑦ **Dublin Castle**

For seven centuries, Dublin Castle was a symbol of English rule, ever since the Anglo-Normans built a fortress here in the 13th century. Remnants of the early structure include the Record Tower, the butt of the Powder Tower, and parts of the curtain wall. After a fire in 1684, the Surveyor-General, Sir William Robinson, laid down the plans for the Upper Castle Yard in its present form. On the first floor of the south side of the Upper Yard are the luxurious State Apartments. The Chester Beatty Library has artistic and religious treasures from around the world.

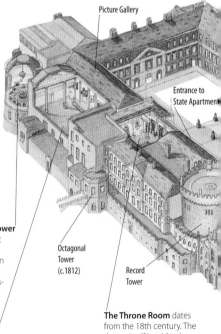

Picture Gallery

Entrance to State Apartment

Bermingham Tower can be viewed at Ship St Gate. It served as a prison and as a storage place for administration records.

Octagonal Tower (c.1812)

Record Tower

St. Patrick's Hall
This grand hall is hung with banners of the Knights of St. Patrick. The 18th-century ceiling paintings are allegories of the relationship between Britain and Ireland.

The Throne Room dates from the 18th century. The throne itself is said to have been built for King George IV in 1821.

cathedral underwent extensive restoration during the 1860s.

The interior is dotted with memorials. The most elaborate is the one erected in 1632 by Richard Boyle, Earl of Cork, in memory of his second wife Katherine. It is decorated with painted carvings of members of the Boyle family. Others remembered in the church include the harpist Turlough O'Carolan (1670–1738) and Douglas Hyde (1860–1949), Ireland's first President.

Many visitors come to see the memorials associated with Jonathan Swift (1667–1745), Dean of St. Patrick's and a scathing satirist best known as the author of *Gulliver's Travels*. In the south aisle is "Swift's Corner," which has various memorabilia, such as an altar table and a bookcase holding his death mask. On the southwest side of the nave, two brass plates mark his grave and that of his beloved "Stella," Ester Johnson.

⑨ Christ Church Cathedral

Christchurch Place. **Tel** 01-677 8099. 🚌 13, 49, 54A, 56A, 77A, 123. **Open** daily. **Closed** Dec 26 & 27. 🅿 ♿ limited. **W christchurchdublin.ie**

The cathedral was commissioned in 1172 by Richard de Clare, known as Strongbow, the Anglo-Norman conqueror of Dublin, and by Archbishop Laurence O'Toole. It replaced an earlier wooden church built by the Vikings. During the Reform-ation, the cathedral passed to the Protestant Church of Ireland. It was remodeled by architect George Street in the 1870s. Even so, the north wall, the one closest to the river, still leans out alarmingly as a result of subsidence. As part of the remodeling, the Old Synod Hall was built and linked to the cathedral by an attractive covered bridge.

Christ Church Cathedral viewed from the east, with the Old Synod Hall behind

In the atmospheric crypt are fragments removed from the cathedral during its restoration. There are also the mummified bodies of a cat and a rat found in an organ pipe in the 1860s. There is a permanent exhibition of the cathedral's treasures as well.

The nave has some fine early Gothic arches. At the west end is a memorial known as the Strongbow Monument. The large effigy in chain armor is probably not Strongbow, but the curious half-figure beside it may be part of his original tomb. The Chapel of St. Laud houses a casket containing the heart of St. Laurence O'Toole.

⑩ Dublinia and the Viking World

St. Michael's Hill. **Tel** 01-679 4611. 🚌 13, 49, 54A, 123. **Open** daily. **Closed** Dec 24–26. 🅿 ♿ **W dublinia.ie**

Housed in the Neo-Gothic Synod Hall, which is linked by a bridge to Christ Church Cathedral, this heritage center covers the period of Dublin's history from the arrival of the Anglo-Normans in 1170 to the closure of the monasteries in the 1540s. An audio tour takes visitors through lifesize reconstructions of the medieval city. There is also a Viking warship and an interactive archaeology exhibition.

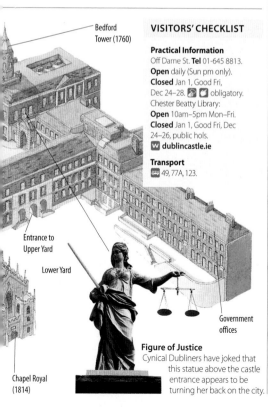

Bedford Tower (1760)

Entrance to Upper Yard

Lower Yard

Chapel Royal (1814)

Government offices

Figure of Justice
Cynical Dubliners have joked that this statue above the castle entrance appears to be turning her back on the city.

VISITORS' CHECKLIST

Practical Information
Off Dame St. **Tel** 01-645 8813.
Open daily (Sun pm only).
Closed Jan 1, Good Fri,
Dec 24–28. 🅿 📷 obligatory.
Chester Beatty Library:
Open 10am–5pm Mon–Fri.
Closed Jan 1, Good Fri, Dec 24–26, public hols.
W dublincastle.ie

Transport
🚌 49, 77A, 123.

James Gandon's Four Courts, overlooking the River Liffey

⑪ The Liffey

🚌 25, 25A, 51, 66, 66A, 67, 67A, 68, 69 and many others.

Though modest in size compared with the rivers of other capital cities, the Liffey features strongly in Dubliners' everyday lives and holds a special place in their affections. The handiest pedestrian link between Temple Bar *(see p120)* and the north of the city is **Ha'penny Bridge**. This attractive, cast-iron bridge, originally called Wellington Bridge, was opened in 1816. Its official name now is the Liffey Bridge. Its better-known nickname comes from the toll of a halfpenny levied on it up until 1919.

The two most impressive buildings on the Liffey are the **Custom House** and the **Four Courts**, both designed by James

Gandon at the end of the 18th century. In 1921, supporters of Sinn Féin celebrated their election victory by setting light to the Custom House, seen as a symbol of British imperialism. The building was not fully restored until 1991, when it reopened as government offices. A series of 14 magnificent heads by Edward Smyth, personifying Ireland's rivers and the Atlantic Ocean, form the keystones of arches and entrances.

The Four Courts suffered a similar fate during the Irish Civil War of 1921–2, when it was bombarded by government troops after being seized by anti-Treaty rebels. Here too, the buildings were restored to their original design. A copper-covered lantern dome rises above a Corinthian portico crowned with the figures of Moses, Justice, and Mercy.

⑫ O'Connell Street

🚌 2, 3, 11, 13, 16A, and many others.

Dublin's main thoroughfare, formerly called Sackville Street, was renamed in 1922 after Daniel O'Connell, who was known as the "Liberator" for his tireless campaigns for Catholic

rights in the 19th century. The street was laid out in the 18th century as an elegant residential parade, but the construction of Carlisle (now O'Connell) Bridge in 1790 turned it into the city's principal north-south route. As a result, little remains of its intended grandeur.

A few venerable buildings survive, including the **General Post Office**, which became a symbol of the 1916 Easter Rising. Members of the Irish Volunteers and Irish Citizen Army seized the building on Easter Monday, and Patrick Pearse read out the Proclamation of the Irish Republic from its steps. The rebels remained inside for a week, but shelling from the British eventually forced them out. During the following weeks, 14 of the leaders were caught and shot. Inside the building is a sculpture of the mythical Irish hero Cuchulainn, dedicated to those who died, and a small museum tells the history of the postal service.

A walk up the central mall is the best way to inspect the series of sculptures lining the route. At the south end stands a massive memorial to Daniel O'Connell, unveiled in 1882.

The monument to Daniel O'Connell

Carved head representing the River Liffey, Custom House

In the middle is an elegant spire and at the north end is the monument to Charles Stewart Parnell (1846–91).

⑬ Parnell Square

3, 11A, 13, 16A, 19A, 38 and many others. Dublin Writers Museum: 18 Parnell Sq North. **Tel** 01-872 2077. **Open** daily. **Closed** Dec 25 & 26. writersmuseum.com
Dublin City Gallery, The Hugh Lane: Charlemont House. **Tel** 01-222 5550. **Open** Tue–Sun. **Closed** Dec 24–27 & public hols. hughlane.ie

The square at the top of O'Connell Street looks sadly neglected. Even so, it contains a number of noteworthy sights, including the **Rotunda Hospital**, Europe's first purpose-built maternity hospital, opened in 1757. Its chapel has some fine Rococo stuccowork. The former grand supper room of the hospital is now the **Gate Theatre**, famous for producing new plays.

On the north side of the square, two grand 18th-century townhouses have been converted into museums: the **Dublin Writers Museum**, devoted to Irish literature, and the **Dublin City Gallery**, **The Hugh Lane**. The latter houses the Impressionist paintings bequeathed to Dublin Corporation by Sir Hugh Lane, who died on the torpedoed liner *Lusitania* in 1915. The square also has a **Garden of Remembrance**, opened in 1966, on the 50th anniversary of the Easter Rising.

Arthur Guinness

⑭ Guinness Storehouse

St. James's Gate, Dublin 8. **Tel** 01-408 4800. 51B, 78A, 123. **Open** daily. **Closed** Good Fri, Dec 24–26, Jan 1.
guinness-storehouse.com

Guinness is a black beer, known as "stout," renowned for its distinctive malty flavor and smooth creamy head. The Guinness brewery site at St. James's Gate is the largest brewery in Europe, and exports beers to more than 120 countries.

The World of Guinness exhibition is housed in a 19th-century warehouse, used for hop storage until the 1950s. It chronicles 200 years of brewing at St. James's Gate. The tour starts in a Victorian kieve (or mash filter), and goes on to examine all other stages of the brewing process. Displays show how production methods have changed over the years since 1759, when Arthur Guinness took over the backstreet brewery. Guinness started brewing ale, but was aware of a black beer called "porter," popular in London's markets. He developed a new recipe for porter (the word "stout" was not used until the 1920s). So successful was the switch that he made his first export shipment in 1769.

The tour ends with a complimentary pint of Guinness in the Granty Bar, where visitors can also enjoy 360-degree views of the city.

The Phoenix Column

⑮ Phoenix Park

Park Gate, Conyngham Rd, Dublin 8. 25, 66, 67, 68, 69. **Open** daily. Visitor Center: **Tel** 01-677 0095. **Open** daily (Jan–Mar: Wed–Sun only). limited. Zoo: **Tel** 01-474 8900. **Open** daily. dublinzoo.ie

Just to the west of the city center, ringed by an 11-km (7-mile) wall, is Europe's largest enclosed city park. The name "Phoenix" is said to be a corruption of the Gaelic Fionn Uisce, or "clear water." The Phoenix Column is crowned by a statue of the mythical bird. The park originated in 1662, when the Duke of Ormonde turned the land into a deer park. It was opened to the public in 1745.

Near Park Gate is the lakeside People's Garden. A little further on are the Zoological Gardens, which are renowned for the breeding of lions, including the one that introduces MGM movies.

The park has two very conspicuous monuments. The Wellington Testimonial is a 63-m (204-ft) obelisk, begun in 1817 and completed in 1861. Its bronze bas-reliefs were made from captured French cannons. The 27-m (90-ft) steel Papal Cross marks the spot where the pope said Mass in front of one million people in 1979. Buildings within the park include two 18th-century houses: Áras an Uachtaráin, the Irish President's official residence, for which 525 tickets are issued every Saturday for a free guided tour, and Deerfield, home of the US ambassador. Ashtown Castle is a restored 17th-century tower house, now the Phoenix Park Visitor Centre.

The Gallery of Writers at the Dublin Writers Museum, Parnell Square

Southeast Ireland

Enjoying the warmest climate in Ireland, the southeast has always presented an attractive prospect for invaders and settlers. Its highlights include the Neolithic tombs in the Valley of the Boyne, early Christian monastic sites, and towns such as Waterford that grew from Viking settlements. It is also the setting for many great 18th-century houses built by the ruling English aristocracy. The wildest landscapes of the region are to be found in the forested hills and desolate moorland of the Wicklow Mountains south of Dublin.

Elegant stuccoed hall and staircase at Castletown House

❷ Castletown House

Celbridge, Co. Kildare. **Tel** 01-628 8252. 🚌 67, 67A from Dublin. **Open** mid-Mar–Oct: 10am–6pm daily; Nov–mid-Mar: grounds only. 🔒 🎫 obligatory. 🅿 🛗 ♿ limited. 🌐 **castletown.ie**

Built in 1722–32 for William Conolly, Speaker of the Irish Parliament, Castletown was Ireland's first grand Palladian-style country house. Most of the interiors were commissioned by Lady Louisa Lennox, wife of Conolly's great-nephew, Tom, who lived here in the late 18th century. It was she who added the magnificent long gallery at the top of the house, with its Pompeiian-style friezes, cobalt-blue walls, and niches framing Classical statuary. From the long gallery, visitors can admire the curious obelisk-topped memorial to Speaker Conolly, erected by his widow in 1740.

A portrait of Lady Louisa is incorporated in the superb Rococo stuccowork by the Francini brothers in the staircase hall. Another personal reminder of Lady Louisa is the print room, the last surviving, intact example of its kind. In the 18th century, ladies pasted prints directly on to the wall and framed them with elaborate festoons.

❸ Newgrange

8 km (5 miles) E of Slane, Co. Meath. 🚆 to Drogheda. 🚌 to visitor center via Drogheda. Brú na Bóinne Interpretive Centre: **Tel** 041-988 0300. 🔒 **Open** daily. **Closed** Dec 24–27. 🎫 🎥 obligatory. 📷 in tomb. 🔲 🌐 **newgrange.com**

The origins of Newgrange, one of the most important passage graves in Europe, are steeped in mystery. Built around 3200 BC, it was rediscovered in 1699. When it was excavated in the 1960s, archaeologists realized that at dawn on the winter solstice (December 21), a beam of sunlight shines through the opening above the entrance to the tomb – a feature unique to Newgrange. The light travels along the 19-m (62-ft) passage and hits the central recess in the burial chamber. It is thus the world's oldest solar observatory.

Between 1962 and 1975, the grave and the mound, or cairn, covering it were restored. The retaining wall at the front of the cairn was rebuilt using white quartz and granite stones found scattered around the site. It is estimated that the original tomb, created by people who had neither the wheel nor metal tools, may have taken up to 70 years to build. About 200,000 tons of loose stones were transported to build the cairn. Larger slabs were used to make the circle around the cairn and the retaining kerb. Many of the kerbstones and the slabs lining the passage and chamber are decorated with zigzags, spirals, and other geometric motifs.

Each of the three recesses in the central chamber contained a chiseled "basin stone" that held funerary offerings and the bones of the dead. The chamber's corbeled ceiling has proved completely waterproof for 5,000 years.

Newgrange is very popular, especially in summer, so queues are likely and you have to wait your turn at the **Brú na Bóinne Interpretive Centre**. This has displays on the area's Stone Age heritage. The tour includes the nearby tomb at Knowth. The last one starts at 3:15pm in winter and at 5:15pm in midsummer.

Aerial view of Newgrange, showing the cairn and circle of standing stones

For hotels and restaurants see p138 and p139

Round tower at Glendalough

❹ Glendalough

Co. Wicklow. 🚌 St. Kevin's Bus from Dublin. Ruins: **Open** daily. 📷 in summer. Visitor Center: **Tel** 0404-45352. **Open** daily. **Closed** Dec 23–30. 🅿 ♿ limited. 🌐 **glendalough.ie**

The steep, wooded slopes of Glendalough, the "valley of the two lakes," harbor one of Ireland's most atmospheric ruined monasteries. Founded by St. Kevin in the 6th century, it functioned as a monastic center until the Dissolution of the Monasteries in 1539.

Most of the buildings date from the 10th to 12th centuries. The reconstruction (see pp126–7) shows how the monastery may have looked in its heyday. The main ruins lie near the smaller Lower Lake. You enter the monastery through the double stone arch of the gatehouse, from where a short walk leads to a graveyard with a restored round tower in one corner. Other ruins include the roofless cathedral, the tiny Priest's House and St. Kevin's Cross. Below, nestled in the lush valley, stands a small oratory. It is popularly known as St. Kevin's Kitchen, because its belfry resembles a chimney.

A path along the south bank of the river leads to the Upper Lake and some of the other buildings associated with St. Kevin. Here, the scenery is wilder and you are better able to enjoy the tranquility of Glendalough.

❺ Kilkenny

Co. Kilkenny. 🚶 26,000. 🚉 🚌 ℹ️ Shee Alms House, Rose Inn St (056-775 1500). 🎭 Kilkenny Arts Festival (Aug). 🌐 **kilkenny.ie**

In a lovely setting beside the River Nore, Kilkenny is Ireland's most attractive inland city. Many of its houses feature the local black limestone, known as Kilkenny marble. The city is proud of its heritage and hosts a major arts festival. It is also a brewery city, filled with atmospheric old pubs.

Kilkenny Castle is a 12th-century castle that was remodeled in Victorian times. It is set in extensive parkland, and was the seat of the Butler family for almost 600 years from around 1391 until 1967, when it was presented to the people of Kilkenny. Two wings of the castle have been restored to their 19th-century splendor, and include a library, a drawing room, and the magnificent Long Gallery. The River Wing houses the Butler Gallery of Contemporary Art.

The area known, in the days of segregation, as English Town boasts the city's grandest buildings, such as Rothe House, a fine Tudor merchant's house, built around two courtyards. The area of narrow alleyways, or "slips," is part of Kilkenny's medieval heritage.

The Irishtown district is dominated by **St. Canice's Cathedral** and a round tower that offers views of the city. The Gothic cathedral dates from the 13th century. It has a finely sculpted west door and an array of 16th-century tombs, with beautiful effigies of the Butler family, in the south transept.

🏰 **Kilkenny Castle**
The Parade. **Tel** 056-772 1450. **Open** Feb–Oct: daily; Nov–Jan: by appt. **Closed** Good Fri, Christmas (see website). 🚫 📷 obligatory. ♿ limited. 🌐 **kilkennycastle.ie**

❻ Waterford

Co. Waterford. 🚶 49,000. 🚉 🚌 🚌 ℹ️ The Granary, Merchant's Quay (051-875 823). 🛍 Sat. 🎭 International Festival of Light Opera (Sep). 🌐 **waterfordtourism.com**

Ireland's oldest city, Waterford was founded by the Vikings in 914, and later extended by the Anglo-Normans. Its commanding position on the Suir estuary made it southeast Ireland's main port. The 18th century saw the establishment of local industries, including the world-famous glassworks.

The remains of the city walls define the area fortified by the Normans. The largest surviving structure is **Reginald's Tower**, overlooking the river. Despite the city's medieval layout, most of its finest buildings are Georgian, including **Christchurch Cathedral**, designed in the 1770s by local architect John Roberts. From June to August, it is possible to take a pleasure cruise on the river.

Waterford Crystal decanter

The **Waterford Crystal Factory** lies 2.5 km (1.5 miles) south of the center. The original factory was founded in 1783, but closed in 1851. A new factory opened in 1947.

🏛 **Waterford Crystal Factory**
Kilbarry. **Tel** 051-317 0000. **Open** Apr–Oct: 9am–4:15pm daily; Nov–Mar: 9:30am–3:15pm Mon–Fri. 🚫 📷 ♿ 🌐 **waterfordvisitorcentre.com**

Tomb of 2nd Marquess of Ormonde in St. Canice's Cathedral, Kilkenny

Early-Celtic Christianity

Ireland became Christian in the 5th century, following the missions of St. Patrick and others. The situation was soon reversed, with many Irish missionaries, such as St. Columba and St. Columbanus, sailing to Great Britain, France, and beyond. The Irish church developed more or less free from the control of Rome, but nevertheless had strong links with the east. As in Egypt, the Christian faith inspired a proliferation of hermitages and remote monasteries. Decorative motifs in illuminated manuscripts reflect Egyptian Christian imagery, and materials used in making the inks came from the Middle East. The advent of the Vikings in the 9th century forced the monasteries to take defensive measures, but they continued to flourish despite frequent raids.

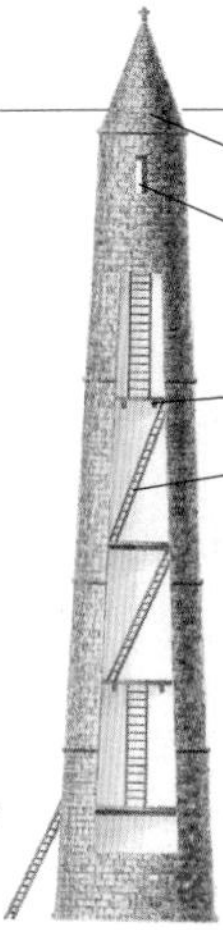

Conical roof

Lookout window

Wooden floor

Movable ladder

Round towers, first built in the 10th century, were bell houses, store houses, and landmarks for approaching visitors. The entrance could be 4 m (13 ft) above ground and was reached by a ladder.

Celtic Monastery

This reconstruction shows Glendalough (see p125) in about 1100. Monasteries were probably the largest centers of population in Ireland before the Vikings started to found towns.

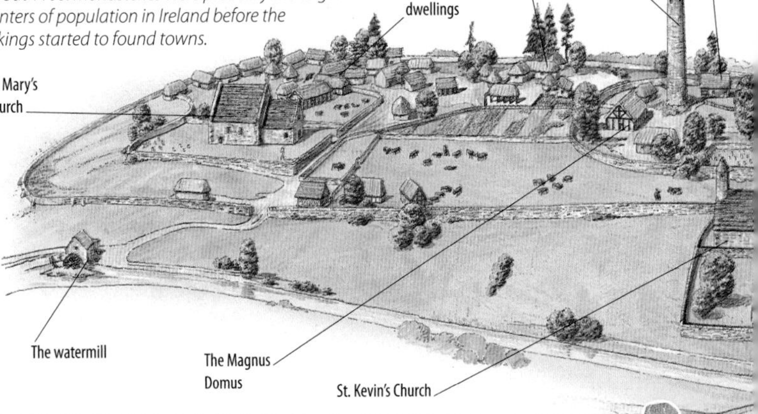

Refectory and kitchen

Abbot's house

Craftsmen's dwellings

St. Mary's Church

The watermill

The Magnus Domus

St. Kevin's Church

Ireland's High Crosses

High Crosses are found in parts of Britain as well as Ireland, yet in their profusion and craftsmanship, Irish crosses are exceptional. The ringed cross has become a symbol of Irish Christianity and is still imitated today. The medieval High Crosses were carved between the 8th and 12th centuries. Early ones, such as the 8th-century cross at Ahenny, bore spirals and interlacing patterns, but in the 9th and 10th centuries, a new style emerged with sculpted scenes from the Bible, "sermons in stone," aimed at educating a largely illiterate population.

Muiredach's Cross at Monasterboice is the finest surviving example of a cross carved with biblical scenes. This panel shows the Fall of Man: Eve offering Adam the apple in the Garden of Eden and Cain slaying Abel.

Ornamental High Cross at Ahenny

Cross of the Scriptures, Clonmacnoise

The Book of Kells

The most richly decorated of all the Irish illuminated manuscripts dating from the 8th–10th centuries, the Book of Kells contains the four gospels in Latin, copied onto leaves of high-quality vellum. It is remarkable both for the beauty of the script and for the inspired fantasy of the illumination. There is no record of its existence before the early 11th century, but it was probably created in about 800. It would have taken many years of work by the scriptorium of a monastery. It

Page of the Genealogy of Christ from the Book of Kells

may have been brought to Kells by monks from Iona who fled to Ireland after a Viking raid in 806. The manuscript was moved to Trinity College *(see p118)* in the 17th century for safe-keeping.

Where to see Early Christian Sites in Ireland

Important early Christian sites besides Glendalough include Clonmacnoise, the Rock of Cashel *(see p128)*, Ahenny, Clonfert, Kells, and Devenish Island. Though most of the monastic buildings are ruins, many have continued to be used as cemeteries right up to modern times. Monasteries were built on the Aran Islands *(see p131)* and even on the remote rocky Skellig Michael, off the Kerry Coast. Round towers and High Crosses are preserved all over Ireland, often standing beside churches of much more recent construction.

Clonmacnoise was founded in the 6th century. The monastery was noted for its piety and scholarship. Now it is an atmospheric collection of ruins in a remote spot on the Shannon. This carved Romanesque doorway is part of the Nun's Church.

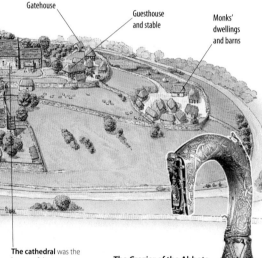

Gatehouse

Guesthouse and stable

Monks' dwellings and barns

The cathedral was the largest of the many churches built in and around the monastery.

The Crozier of the Abbots of Clonmacnoise dates from the 11th century. The incised patterns on the ornate silver casing show the strong influence of Viking designs.

The Voyage of St. Brendan is a fantastic legend of early-medieval Irish Christianity. The 6th-century saint and his followers set sail into the Atlantic in a small boat, sighting volcanic islands, ice floes, whales, and even, some say, America.

Devenish Island has a fine restored round tower and enjoys a peaceful setting on Lower Lough Erne. Lake islands were popular as monastic sites.

Southwest Ireland

Magnificent scenery has attracted visitors to this region since Victorian times. Killarney and its romantic lakes are a powerful magnet for tourists, as is the attractive coastline of Cork and Kerry, where rocky headlands jut out into the Atlantic and colorful fishing villages nestle in the bays. Yet much of the southwest remains unspoiled, with a friendly atmosphere and authentic culture still alive in Irish-speaking pockets.

The Rock of Cashel

❼ Cashel

Co. Tipperary. 🏠 11,400. 🚌
🛈 Heritage Centre, Main St
(062- 62511). Rock: **Tel** 062-61437.
Open daily. **Closed** Dec 24–26.
🅿️ 🎫 ♿ limited. 🌐 **cashel.ie**

The town's great attraction is the magnificent medieval Rock of Cashel. Many people stay overnight to enjoy eerie floodlit views of the rocky stronghold rising dramatically out of the Tipperary plain. The Rock was a symbol of royal and ecclesiastical power for more than a thousand years. From the 5th century AD, it was the seat of the Kings of Munster, rulers of southwest Ireland. In 1101, they handed Cashel over to the

Church, and it flourished as a religious center until a siege by a Cromwellian army in 1647 ended in the massacre of its 3,000 occupants.

A good proportion of the medieval complex still stands, though the main building, the Gothic cathedral, is roofless. The earlier Cormac's Chapel is an outstanding example of Romanesque architecture. Other prominent features of the Rock are a restored round tower and the weatherbeaten St. Patrick's Cross. The carved figure on the east face of the cross is said to be St. Patrick.

❽ Cork

Co. Cork. 🏠 123,000. ✈ 🚌
🛈 Tourist House, Grand Parade
(0214-255 100). 🎷 Jazz Festival (Oct);
Film Festival (Oct).

Cork city derives its name from the marshy banks of the Lee River – its Irish name, Corcaigh, means marsh – where St. Finbarr founded a monastery around AD 650. The center of Cork today occupies an island between two arms of the river. Its waterways, bridges, and narrow alleys,

combined with the Georgian architecture of the old Quays, give Cork a continental feel. In the 18th century, many of today's streets were waterways lined with warehouses and merchants' residences.

Noted for its chic bars, ethnic restaurants, bookstores, and boutiques, Paul Street is the hub of the liveliest district in town. The nearby **Crawford Art Gallery** has some fine Irish works of art.

A prominent landmark is the steeple of **St. Anne Shandon** on a hill in the north of the city. It is topped by a weather vane in the shape of a salmon. Visitors can climb up and ring the famous Shandon bells.

🏛 **Crawford Art Gallery**
Emmet Place. **Tel** 0214-805 042. **Open**
10am–5pm Mon–Sat. **Closed** public
hols, Dec 24–Jan 3. 🅿️ 🖥 📷 ♿
🌐 **crawfordartgallery.ie**

The battlemented keep and other ruined towers of Blarney Castle

Environs

Beautiful countryside surrounds Cork, especially along the valley of the Lee River. Outings include a tour of the whiskey distillery at the **Jameson Experience, Midleton,** and a trip to **Blarney Castle,** where a legendary stone bestows magical eloquence on all who kiss it. Walking and fishing are also popular.

🏛 **Jameson Experience, Midleton**
Midleton, Co. Cork. **Tel** 0214-613 594.
Open daily. **Closed** Jan 1, Good Fri,
Dec 24–27. 🅿️ 🎫 📷 🖥 ♿
🌐 **jamesonwhiskey.com**

🏠 **Blarney Castle**
Blarney, Co. Cork. **Tel** 0214-385252.
Open daily. **Closed** Dec 24 & 25. 📷
♿ grounds only. 🌐 **blarneycastle.ie**

South channel of the Lee River flowing through the city of Cork

For hotels and restaurants see p138 and p139

Newman's Mall in the quaint village of Kinsale

❾ Kinsale

Co. Cork. 🏔 3,400. 🚌 *i* Pier Road (0214-772 234). 🚣 Regatta (Aug); Festival of Fine Food (Oct). **W** kinsale.ie

One of the prettiest small towns in Ireland, Kinsale has had a long and checkered history. The defeat of the Irish forces and their Spanish allies at the Battle of Kinsale in 1601 signalled the end of the old Gaelic order.

An important naval base in the 17th and 18th centuries, Kinsale today is a popular yachting center. It is also famous for the quality of its cuisine and has a popular annual Festival of Fine Food.

Charles Fort, a fine example of a star-shaped bastion fort, was built by the English in the 1670s to protect Kinsale against foreign naval forces. To reach it, take the signposted coastal walk from the quayside.

🏰 Charles Fort

3 km (2 miles) E of Kinsale. **Tel** 0214-772 263. **Open** mid-Mar–Oct: 10am–6pm daily; Nov–mid-Mar: 10am–5pm daily. Last adm: 1 hr before closing. **Closed** Christmas week. 🚻 ♿ 🅿 🛒 limited.

❿ Killarney

Co. Kerry. 🏔 13,500. 🚌 🚂 *i* Beech Road (064-663 1633). **W** killarney.ie

Killarney is often derided as "a tourist town," but this does not detract from its cheerful atmosphere. The infectious Kerry humor is personified by the wise-cracking "jarveys," whose families have run jaunting cars (pony-and-trap rides) here for generations. The town does get very crowded in the summer, thanks to the lure of the **Lakes of Killarney**. The three lakes and many of the heather-covered hills surrounding them lie within **Killarney National Park**. Although the landscape is dotted with ruined castles and abbeys, the lakes are the focus of attention: the moody, watery scenery is subject to subtle shifts of light and color. Well-known beauty spots include the Meeting of the Waters, the Ladies' View, so called because it delighted Queen Victoria's ladies-in-waiting in 1861, and the Gap of Dunloe, a dramatic mountain pass. The largest of the lakes, Lough Leane, is dotted with uninhabited islands. Boat trips across the lake run from Ross Castle on the shore nearest Killarney.

Overlooking the lakes is **Muckross House**, an imposing mansion built in 1843 in Elizabethan style, set in beautiful gardens. It houses the Museum of Kerry Folklife. Next door is the Walled Garden Centre, which incorporates the garden, a restaurant, and a craft center.

The town is also the starting point for the popular **Ring of Kerry** tour around the Iveragh Peninsula. Allow a day's drive to enjoy its captivating scenery.

🏛 Muckross House

4 km (2.5 miles) S of Killarney. **Tel** 064-6670144. **Open** daily. **Closed** Jan 1, Dec 24–26. 🚻 ♿ 🅿 🛒 ♿ **W** muckross-house.ie

Gallarus Oratory, a tiny dry-stone Early Christian church

⓫ Dingle

Co. Kerry. 🏔 2,500. 🚌 *i* Strand St (06691-51188). 🚢 Fri.

This once remote Irish-speaking town is today a thriving fishing port and popular tourist center. Brightly painted – often fairly hippy – craft shops and cafés abound. Along the quayside are lively bars offering music and seafood. The harbor is home to Dingle's biggest star, Fungi the dolphin, who has been a permanent resident since 1983 and can be visited by boat or on swimming trips.

Environs

Dingle is a good base for exploring the scattered archaeological remains of the Dingle Peninsula. The most fascinating is the **Gallarus Oratory**, northwest of Dingle. This miniature dry-stone church, shaped like an upturned boat, was built from the 6th to the 9th centuries. West of Dingle, along the coast road, are the Iron Age fort of Dunbeg and Early Christian beehive huts.

The Upper Lake, smallest and most remote of the Lakes of Killarney

⑫ Bunratty Castle

This formidable 15th-century castle is one of Ireland's major tourist attractions. Its most important residents were the O'Briens, Earls of Thomond, who lived here from the early 16th century until the 1640s. The interior has been restored to look as it did under the so-called "Great Earl," who died in 1624. The adjacent Folk Park and the mock-medieval banquets held in the castle attract many visitors, but despite its commercialization, Bunratty is well worth a visit. The Folk Park recreates rural and urban life at the end of the 19th century, with a village, complete with stores, a school, and dwellings ranging from a laborer's cottage to an elegant Georgian house.

VISITORS' CHECKLIST

Practical Information
Bunratty, Co. Clare. **Tel** 061-360 788. **Open** 9am–5:30pm daily (Jun–Aug: 9am–6pm). Last entry to castle 4pm all year. **Closed** Good Fri, Dec 23–26. 🏛 ⬚ ♿ to Folk Park. 🔲 shannonheritage.com

Transport
🚌 from Limerick, Ennis & Shannon Airport. Castle & Folk Park

Great Hall
The castle's grandest room served as a banqueting hall and audience chamber. Among the furnishings bought by the owner, Lord Gort, when he set about restoring the castle in the 1950s, was this Tudor standard.

South Solar
The carved ceiling here is partly a reconstruction in late Tudor style.

The North Solar
was the Great Earl's private apartment.

The Murder Hole was designed for pouring boiling water or pitch onto the heads of attackers.

Entrance

The Earl's Robing Room
also served as a private audience chamber.

North Front
The entrance, raised well above ground level to deter invaders, is typical of castles of the period.

Main Guard
This was where the castle's soldiers ate, slept, and listened to music from the Minstrels' Gallery.

The imposing Kylemore Abbey, on the shores of Kylemore Lough, Connemara

⓭ Galway

Co. Galway. 🏙 60,000. 🚉 🚌
ℹ The Fairgreen, Foster St (091-537
700). 🛍 Sat & Sun. 🎭 Arts Festival
(mid-Jul); Galway Races (late Jul/Aug);
Oyster Festivals (early & late Sep).

Galway is the center for the Irish-speaking regions in the West of Ireland and a lively university city. In the 15th and 16th centuries, it was a prosperous trading port, controlled by 14 merchant families, or "tribes." Its allegiance to the English Crown cost the city dear when, in 1652, it was sacked by Cromwell's forces. In the 18th century, Galway fell into decline, but in recent years, its fortunes have revived through high-tech industries.

The city stands on the banks of the Corrib River. Many of the best stores, pubs, theaters, and historic sights are packed into the narrow lanes of the "Latin Quarter" around Quay Street.

Colorful storefronts lining Quay Street in Galway's "Latin Quarter"

Nearby is the Collegiate Church of St. Nicholas, the city's finest medieval building. To the south stands the 16th-century Spanish Arch, where ships from Spain unloaded their cargoes. Across the Corrib, facing the arch, is the Claddagh. The only remnants of this once close-knit, Gaelic-speaking community are its friendly pubs and Claddagh rings – betrothal rings that are traditionally handed down from mother to daughter.

⓮ Connemara

Co. Galway. 🚌 to Clifden or Letterfrack.
ℹ Mar–Oct: Galway Road, Clifden
(095-21163). National Park Visitors'
Center: **Tel** 095-41 054. **Open** Mar–Oct:
daily. 🖥 🚻 🌐 **connemaranational
park.ie** Kylemore Abbey: **Tel** 095-52
001. **Open** daily. 🅿 📷 compulsory.
🌐 **kylemoreabbeytourism.ie**

This wild region, to the west of Galway, encompasses bogs, mountains, and rugged Atlantic coastline. The small market town of Clifden is a convenient and popular base for exploring. Starting from Clifden, the **Sky Road** is an 11-km (7-mile) circular route with spectacular ocean views. South of Clifden, the coast road to Roundstone skirts a massive bog, impromptu landing site of the first transatlantic flight made by Alcock and Brown in 1919.

Connemara National Park, near Letterfrack, includes some spectacular scenery, dominated by the mountains known as the Twelve Bens. Here, visitors have a chance to spot red deer and the famous Connemara ponies.

Nearby **Kylemore Abbey** is a 19th-century romantic, battlemented fantasy. It became an abbey when Benedictine nuns, fleeing from Belgium during World War I, sought refuge here. A Victorian walled garden and nature trails through the woods and along the lake make the abbey a popular destination.

⓯ Aran Islands

Co. Galway. 🏙 900. ✈ from
Connemara (091-593 034).
⛴ from Rossaveal (091-568 903);
from Doolin (Easter–Sep: 065-707
4455). ℹ Kilronan, Inishmore (099-
61263). Heritage Center: **Open** daily.
🏛 📷 🚻

Inishmore, Inishmaan, and Inisheer, the three Aran Islands, are formed from a limestone ridge. The largest, Inishmore, is 13 km (8 miles) long and 3 km (2 miles) wide. The attractions of the islands include the austere landscape crisscrossed with dry-stone walls, stunning coastal views, and prehistoric stone forts. The islands are a bastion of traditional Irish culture, with most of the islanders engaged in fishing, farming, or tourism. Ferries sail at least once a day in winter and several times daily in summer. Cars cannot be taken to the islands.

At Kilronan on Inishmore, jaunting cars (ponies and traps) and minibuses wait by the pier to give tours; bicycles can also be hired. Nearby, the **Aran Heritage Centre** is dedicated to the disappearing Aran way of life. The islands are famous for their distinctive knitwear and traditional costumes.

Northern Ireland

The province of Northern Ireland was created after the partition of the island in 1921. Its six counties (plus Donegal, Monaghan, and Cavan, which became part of the Republic) were part of Ulster, one of Ireland's four traditional kingdoms. Though densely populated and industrialized around Belfast, away from the capital the region is primarily agricultural. It also has areas of outstanding natural beauty, notably the rugged Antrim coastline around the Giant's Causeway.

Mosaic of St. Patrick's journey to Ireland, Belfast Cathedral

⑯ Belfast

Co. Antrim. 🏔 500,000. ✈ 🚆 🚌
🛈 47 Donegall Place (028-9024 6609). 🎪 Royal Ulster Agricultural Show & Lord Mayor's Show (May); Belfast Festival at Queen's (late Oct–Nov). 🆆 visit-belfast.com

Belfast was the only city in Ireland to experience the full force of the Industrial Revolution. Its shipbuilding, linen, rope-making, and tobacco industries caused the population to rise to almost 400,000 by the end of World War I. The wealth it enjoyed is still evident in its imposing public buildings. The Troubles and the decline of traditional industries have damaged its economic life, but Belfast remains a handsome city. The cross-community desire for peace is palpable, with many new restaurants and clubs and a thriving arts scene.

Most of Belfast's main streets (and bus routes) radiate out from Donegall Square. In its center stands the Portland stone bulk of the 1906 **City Hall**, with its huge central copper dome. Statues around the building include Queen Victoria at the front and, on the east side, Sir Edward Harland, founder of the Harland and Wolff shipyard, which built the *Titanic*. A memorial to those who died when the ship sank in 1912

stands close by. Sights in and around the square include the **Linen Hall Library**, the late-Victorian **Grand Opera House** in Great Victoria Street, and Belfast's most famous pub, the **Crown Liquor Saloon**, which dates back to the 1880s.

The Neo-Romanesque **Belfast Cathedral**, in Donegall Street, is the Protestant cathedral, consecrated in 1904. The interior is remarkable for the vast mosaics added by the two Misses Martin in the 1920s. Lord Carson (1854–1935), implacable opponent of Home Rule, is buried in the south aisle. Across the water, **Titanic Belfast** tells the story of the famous ship.

Away from the center, Belfast has pleasant suburbs unaffected by the civil strife of the Troubles. The area around **Queen's**

University, to the south of the city, has two major attractions in the **Ulster Museum** and the **Botanic Gardens**. The museum covers all aspects of Ulster, from archaeology to technology. Its treasures include jewelry from the *Girona*, a Spanish Armada ship that sank off the Giant's Causeway in 1588.

🏛 **Titanic Belfast**
Queen's Rd. **Tel** 028-9076 6386.
Open daily. 🎫 🗐 🖳 🖥 📷
🆆 titanicbelfast.com

🏛 **Ulster Museum**
Botanic Gardens. **Tel** 0845-608 000.
Open 10am–5pm Tue–Sun. 📷 🖳
📷 🖳 🆆 ulstermuseum.org.uk

Detail of Titanic Memorial outside Belfast City Hall

⑰ Giant's Causeway

Co. Antrim. 🚆 to Portrush. 🚌 from Portrush, Bushmills, or Coleraine. Visitors' Center: (028-2073 1855). **Open** daily. 🖳 🗐 on request. 🚻 limited. 🆆 giantscausewaycentre.com

The bizarre regularity of the Giant's Causeway's basalt columns has made it the subject of numerous legends. The most popular tells how the giant, Finn MacCool, laid the causeway to provide a path across the sea to Scotland so that he could do battle with

The ornate Victorian interior of the Crown Liquor Saloon

IRELAND | 133

The extraordinarily regular columns of the Giant's Causeway, exposed at low tide

a rival Scottish giant. The geological explanation is that 61 million years ago, in a series of volcanic eruptions, molten lava poured from narrow fissures in the ground, filling in the valleys. The basalt lava cooled rapidly. In the process, it shrank and cracked evenly into polygonal blocks. Towards the end of the Ice Age, erosion by sea ice exposed the rocks and shaped the Causeway. Most of the columns are hexagonal, but some have four, five, eight, or even ten sides. They are generally about 30 cm (12 in) across. There are, in fact, three causeways: the Grand, Middle, and Little. Distinctive features have been given poetic names, such as the "Honeycomb" and the "Wishing Chair."

Tourists arrive by the busload from the visitors' center, but it is easy to escape the crowds by taking one of the coastal paths.

⑱ Old Bushmills Distillery

Bushmills, Co. Antrim. **Tel** 028-2073 3218. 🚌 from Giant's Causeway & Coleraine. **Open** daily (pm only Sun). **Closed** Good Fri pm, Jul 12, 2 weeks at Christmas. 🎫 📷 🚫 obligatory. 🚻 ♿ limited. 🌐 bushmills.com

Bushmills has an attractive square and an excellent river for salmon and trout fishing, but its

Whiskey barrel at Old Bushmills

main claim to fame is whiskey. The Old Bushmills plant prides itself on being the oldest distillery in the world, its "Grant to Distil" dating from 1608.

In 1974, Bushmills joined the Irish Distillers Group, based at the Midleton plant near Cork (see p128), but its brands have retained their distinctive character. "Old Bushmills" is unusual in that it is made from a blend of single malt and a single grain. The tour of the distillery, which features audio-visual displays, ends with a sampling session in the "1608 Bar," which is housed in the former malt kilns.

⑲ Ulster-American Folk Park

Co. Tyrone. **Tel** 028-8224 3292. 🚌 from Omagh. **Open** 10am–5pm Tue–Sun (Oct–Feb: to 4pm). 🎫 📷 🚫 ♿ 🌐 folkpark.com

One of the best open-air museums of its kind, the Folk Park grew up around the restored boyhood home of Judge Thomas Mellon (founder of the Pittsburgh banking dynasty). The park's permanent exhibition, called "Emigrants," examines why two million people left Ulster for America during the 18th and 19th

centuries. It also shows what became of them, following stories of both fortune and failure.

The park has more than 30 historic buildings, some of them original, some replicas. There are settler homesteads, a mass house, a post office, a schoolhouse, and a forge, some with craft displays, all with costumed interpretative guides. There's also an Ulster streetscape, a reconstructed emigrant ship, and a Pennsylvania farmstead, complete with log barn, corn crib, and smokehouse. The six-roomed farmhouse is based on one built by Thomas Mellon and his father in the early years of their new life in America.

The Centre for Migration Studies assists the descendants of emigrants in tracing their family roots. Popular American festivals, such as Halloween and Independence Day, are celebrated at the park.

Pennsylvania log farmhouse at the Ulster-American Folk Park

Practical & Travel Information

Ireland's capital cities compare favorably to any in Europe for ease of transportation and communications, but in remoter areas, the pace of life is slower. In the most isolated parts, public transportation can be infrequent. The division of Ireland into the Republic and Northern Ireland, with separate currencies and communication systems, complicates matters further.

Tourist Information

Before leaving for Ireland, you can get information from the **Fáilte Ireland** (Irish Tourist Board) or **Northern Ireland Tourist Board** (NITB) offices. Regional tourist offices provide more detailed information, including accommodations.

In summer, all the sights are open, but crowds are naturally at their biggest. In winter, many sights keep shorter hours or open only at the weekend and some close down completely.

Visa Requirements

Visitors from EU member states, the US, Canada, Australia, and New Zealand need a valid passport, but not a visa, for entry into the Republic or Northern Ireland. UK nationals do not need a passport to enter the Republic, but may find one useful as proof of identity.

Safety and Emergencies

Ireland is one of the safest places to travel in Europe. Petty theft, such as pickpocketing, is seldom a problem outside certain parts of Dublin and a few other large towns. Tourist offices and hoteliers will gladly point out the areas to be avoided. In Northern Ireland, the main security risk in the past was the threat of bombings, though even at the height of the Troubles, this hardly ever affected tourists. Since the Good Friday Agreement, security incidents are very rare. Visitors may find, on the rare occasion, they are confronted by a police checkpoint. If you see a sign indicating a checkpoint ahead, slow down and use low beams. Have your passport handy as proof of identity.

Travel insurance for the UK will not cover you for the Republic, so make sure you purchase an adequate insurance policy.

The police are called the Gardaí in the Republic and Police Service of Northern Ireland (PSNI) in the north.

Banking and Currency

The currency in the Republic is the euro (see p23). All euro notes and coins are exchangeable in each of the participating Eurozone countries. Northern Ireland uses British currency – pounds sterling (£). These currencies are not interchangeable. Alongside the Bank of England currency in the North, four provincial banks issue their own notes, for use only in the province.

Banking hours are from 10am to 4pm, although some banks close for lunch from 12:30 to 1:30pm.

Communications

Main post offices in the Republic and Northern Ireland are usually open from 9am to 5:30pm during the week and from 9am to 1pm on Saturdays. The postal service in Northern Ireland is much faster than in the Republic, where it can take at least five days for a letter to reach the United States.

Most phones in the Republic are operated by Eircom, and in Northern Ireland, by British Telecom. Both offer efficient, up-to-date card- and coin-operated public phones. Internet cafés are common, even in small towns, and most hotels and cafés will offer their customers complimentary Wi-Fi.

Flying to Ireland

Flights from most of the large European cities arrive at Dublin Airport. The major airlines operating between Britain and the Republic are **Aer Lingus** and budget rival **Ryanair**, which is based in Ireland. Aer Lingus and **Continental Airlines** fly direct from the US to Shannon Airport, 16 km (10 miles) outside Limerick, as well as to Dublin. Aeroflot flies from Shannon to Moscow via Amsterdam or Dublin.

There are flights for pilgrims to Knock International Airport from Dublin, London Stansted, Manchester Airport, and others.

Cork airport is served by flights from London (Heathrow and Stansted), Paris, Birmingham, Manchester, and Bristol airports amongst others.

bmi regional flies to Belfast International Airport from Cardiff, Manchester, and Birmingham. **easyjet** has flights to Britain, France, Spain, Portugal, Poland, Malta, the Netherlands, and Switzerland from Belfast.

The Climate of Ireland

Rain can be the scourge of a holiday in Ireland, especially on the west coast. However, strong winds off the Atlantic mean that the weather often changes with astonishing speed. Though the rainfall is heavy, winters are mild and there is little snowfall except on the higher mountains. Dublin and the sheltered east coast have the warmest climate and least rainfall.

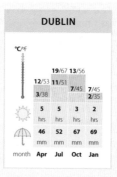

	DUBLIN			
°C/°F		19/67 **13/56**		
	12/53	11/51		
	3/38		7/45	7/45
				2/35
☼	5 hrs	5 hrs	3 hrs	2 hrs
☂	46 mm	52 mm	67 mm	69 mm
month	**Apr**	**Jul**	**Oct**	**Jan**

Arriving by Sea

Ferries from ports in Britain and France are a popular way of getting to Ireland, especially with groups or families intending to tour the country by car. There are large seasonal variations in fares, but discounts may be available on internet bookings. **Irish Ferries** and **Stena Line** operate regular crossings from Holyhead, Pembroke, and Fishguard in Wales to Dublin Port, Dun Laoghaire, and Rosslare. The fastest routes take about 1 hour 40 minutes. There are also Irish Ferries services from Holyhead to Dublin and to Rosslare from Cherbourg and Roscoff.

The fastest crossing to Belfast is the 1 hour 45 minute Stena Line service from Stranraer in Scotland. **P&O Irish Sea** crosses to Larne (north of Belfast) from Cairnryan in Scotland, and **Norfolkline** runs a regular service from Liverpool to Dublin and Belfast.

You can buy combined coach/ferry and train/ferry tickets from coach offices or train stations all over Britain.

Rail Travel

Although the more rural areas in the Republic are not served by rail, **Irish Rail** (Iarnród Éireann) operates a service to most large towns. Dublin has two main train stations: Connolly serves the north and the line south along the coast to Rosslare; Heuston serves Cork and the southwest, and Galway and the west. Dublin's local railroad service, the DART (Dublin Area Rapid Transit), links towns between Malahide (County Dublin) and Greystones (County Wicklow) with the center. The Luas tramline runs from Dublin city center to the inland suburbs.

There are two main routes out of Belfast: a line westward to Londonderry, and Ireland's only cross-border service, a high-speed service linking Belfast and Dublin.

Buses and Taxis

The Republic's national bus company, **Bus Éireann**, runs routes to all cities and most towns. **Ulsterbus** runs a service in Northern Ireland, with express links between all major towns. A "Rambler" ticket allows a period of unlimited bus travel in the Republic. In the North, a "Freedom of Northern Ireland" ticket offers the same benefits.

Taxis in Ireland range from saloon cars to people carriers. The most likely places to find taxis are at train and bus stations, hotels, and taxi stands.

Car Rental

Car-rental firms do good business, so in summer it is wise to book ahead. Car rental – particularly in the Republic – can be expensive and the best rates are often obtained by reserving in advance online. Broker companies, such as **Holiday Autos** in the UK, will shop around to get the best deal. If you intend to cross the border in either direction, you must inform the rental company, as there may be an additional insurance premium.

In both the Republic and Northern Ireland, motorists drive on the left, as in Great Britain (see p101).

DIRECTORY

Tourist Boards

Fáilte Ireland
Baggot St Bridge,
Dublin 2. **Tel** 01-602 4000.
US: 345 Park Avenue,
New York, NY 10154.
Tel 1800-223 6470.
W discoverireland.ie

Northern Ireland Tourist Board
St. Anne's Court, 59 North St, Belfast BT1 1NB.
Tel 028-9023 1221.
UK: 103 Wigmore St,
London W1U 1QS.
Tel 020-7518 0800.
W discovernorthern ireland.com

Embassies

Australia
7th Floor, Fitzwilton House, Wilton Terrace,
Dublin 2. **Tel** 01-664 5300.

Canada
7–8 Wilton Terrace,
Dublin 2.
Tel 01-234 4000.

UK
29 Merrion Rd,
Dublin 4.
Tel 01-234 4000.

US
42 Elgin Rd,
Ballsbridge, Dublin 4.
Tel 01-668 8777.

Emergency Services

Police, Ambulance, and Fire services
Tel 999.
(Republic and NI).

Airlines

Aer Lingus
Tel 0818 365 000.
Tel 0870-876 5000 (UK).
Tel 1800-474 7424 (US).
W aerlingus.com

bmi regional
Tel 01-283 0700.
Tel 0870-607 0555 (UK).
W flybmi.com

Continental Airlines
Tel 1890 925 252.
Tel 1800-523 3273 (US).
W continental.com

easyjet
Tel 0870-6000 000 (UK).
W easyjet.com

Ryanair
Tel 0818-303 030.
Tel 0871-246 000 (UK).
W ryanair.com

Ferry Companies

Irish Ferries
Tel 0818-300 400.
Tel 0870-517 1717 (UK).

Norfolkline
Tel 01-819 2999.
Tel 0844-499 0007 (UK).

P&O Irish Sea
Tel 0140-73434.
Tel 0871-664 4999 (UK).

Stena Line
Tel 01-204 7777.
Tel 0844-770 7070 (UK).

Rail Travel

Irish Rail (Iarnród Éireann)
Tel 01-836 6222.
W irishrail.ie

Northern Ireland Railways
Tel 028-9066 6630.
W translink.co.uk

Bus Companies

Bus Éireann
Tel 01-836 6111.
W buseireann.ie

Ulsterbus/Translink
Tel 028-9066 6630.
W translink.co.uk

Car Rental

Holiday Autos
Tel 0871-472 5229 (UK).
W holidayautos.ie

Shopping & Entertainment

Ireland offers a wide range of quality handmade goods, including Aran sweaters, Waterford crystal, fine Irish linen, and Donegal tweed. As with its produce, the best entertainment is local and highly individual. Ireland's cities are well served by theaters, movie theatres, and concert venues, but there are many other local events, including arts festivals with traditional music and dance. Not to be overlooked is the entertainment provided by a night in an Irish pub. Finally, the beautiful countryside offers the chance to unwind by walking, riding, fishing, or playing a round of golf.

Where to Shop

The choice of places to shop in Ireland ranges from tiny workshops to large factory outlets, and from chic boutiques to high-street chain stores.

In Dublin, the Temple Bar area contains a number of fashionable craft stores. One of the largest shopping centers in the city is St. Stephen's Green Shopping Centre, full of clothes and craft shops. Near Grafton Street is the Powerscourt Townhouse Shopping Centre.

Crafts

Crafts are a flourishing way of life in rural Ireland. The Crafts Council of Ireland, which has branches in Kilkenny and Dublin, can recommend good small-scale specialist stores. Outlets particularly worth visiting include the **Kilkenny Design Centre** and **Bricín**, which sell a wide selection of items.

Established in 19th-century Ulster, the **Belleek Pottery** produces creamy china with intricately worked decorative motifs, such as shamrocks and flowers. **Royal Tara China**, in Galway, is Ireland's leading fine-bone-china manufacturer, with designs inspired by Celtic themes.

Waterford Crystal is undoubtedly the most famous name in Irish glass-making, but there are many other names of similar quality. **Galway Irish Crystal** is an excellent make, available as elegant ornaments and gifts. Jerpoint Abbey in County Kilkenny inspires stylish local designs by **Jerpoint Glass**. With a tradition that dates back

to Celtic times, distinctive jewelry is produced all over Ireland. The Claddagh ring of Galway is the most famous. It is a symbol of friendship, love, and loyalty, and features two hands cradling a crowned heart.

Aran sweaters are sold all over Ireland, but particularly in County Galway and on the Aran Islands. A well-known outlet for these and other knitwear products is **Blarney Woollen Mills**. Donegal tweed is a byword for quality, noted for its texture and subtle colors. It can be bought at **Magee of Donegal**.

Damask linen was brought to Northern Ireland in the late 17th century by Huguenot refugees. The North is still the place for linen, with sheets and table linen on sale in Belfast at **Smyth's Irish Linen**.

Smoked salmon, farmhouse cheeses, handmade preserves, and, of course, Irish whiskey make perfect last-minute gifts.

Entertainment Listings and Tickets

The tourist board for the Republic, **Fáilte Ireland**, and the **Northern Ireland Tourist Board** (see p135) both publish a yearly *Calendar of Events* that lists major fixtures and events around the country. The regional tourist offices also provide local information.

Tickets are often available on the night, but it is safer to book in advance. Most venues will accept credit card bookings. Visit www. visitdublin.com for information about the city's nightlife.

Entertainment Venues

In many Irish cities, the main theaters host a wide range of concerts, events, and plays. In central Belfast, the **Grand Opera House** and **Lyric Theatre** put on an interesting program. Dublin's two most famous theaters, the **Abbey** and **Gate Theatre**, are renowned for their productions of Irish and international plays, as is the **Cork Opera House**.

Keep an eye out for smaller theater groups around the country. The **Druid Theatre** in Galway puts on an original repertoire, and Waterford boasts a resident drama company at the **Garter Lane Arts Centre**.

Other venues for classical music include Dublin's great auditorium, the **National Concert Hall**, the Crawford Art Gallery in Cork, and the **Ulster Hall** in Belfast.

The **Waterford Festival of Light Opera** and the **Wexford Festival of Opera** attract opera lovers from around the world. Wexford revives neglected operas while Waterford puts on more mainstream operas and musicals. Dublin's main opera venue is the 19th-century **Gaiety Theatre**, while the **Bord Gáis Energy Theatre** in the Docklands hosts mostly musicals.

Rock concerts are held in the **O2 Dublin** or at the many outdoor sites during the summer. Die-hard rock and jazz fans should search out the musical pubs for Irish bands.

Irish Music and Dance

The Irish pub has helped keep traditional music alive and provided the setting for the musical revival that began in the 1960s. Nights of Irish music and song are scheduled in pubs, such as Johnnie Fox's in Dublin, and The Laurels in Killarney. However, sessions of informal or impromptu music are commonplace. Wherever you are, the locals will advise you of the nearest musical pubs.

Popular dance spectaculars have raised the profile, if not the understanding, of real Irish country dance. Visit **Comhaltas Ceoltóirí Éireann**, in Monkstown near Dublin, or any of its branches around the country for genuine traditional music and dance nights all year.

Irish Festivals

The Irish are expert festival organizers, staging a week of street entertainment, theater, music, and dance to celebrate almost everything under the sun *(see Directory for listings)*.

Irish Pubs

The Irish pub is known for its convivial atmosphere and the "craic" – the Irish expression for fun. Wit is washed down with the national drinks of whiskey or Guinness.

City pubs often have grand interiors, a testament to the importance of the brewing and distilling industries in Victorian times. In the countryside, pubs provide an important focus for far-flung rural communities, and some even double as stores. Pubs vary greatly throughout the country, so be sure to try out a few wherever you visit. Dublin is famed for its literary pubs; the **Dublin Literary Pub Crawl** is an entertaining way to get a feel for the city's booze-fueled literary heritage. Music sessions are common in the pubs of Kilkenny and County Clare. Some of the most picturesque establishments are in Cork and Kerry. Galway's tourists and student population guarantee a lively pub atmosphere.

Outdoor Activities

No matter where you are in Ireland, the countryside is never far away. Horses thrive on the green turf and racing is a national passion. A day at the track during Galway Race Week in July is a great social event. Those who want to do more than just watch should try horseback riding through the unspoiled countryside.

Another way to experience the countryside is to take a river or canal cruise. **Emerald Star** has a fleet of cruisers for use on the waterways. Alternatively, you may want to play golf at one of Ireland's beautiful golf courses, or try some fishing. Maps and locations for fishing are available from the **Central Fisheries Board**. The **Golfing Union of Ireland** can advise on golf courses.

Detailed information on a wide range of outdoor activities is available from **Fáilte Ireland** *(see p135)*, and local tourist offices.

DIRECTORY

Crafts

Belleek Pottery
Belleek, Co. Fermanagh.
Tel 028-6865 8501.

Blarney Woollen Mills
Blarney, Co. Cork.
Tel 021-451 6111.

Brícín
26 High Street, Killarney,
Co. Kerry.
Tel 064-663 4902.

Galway Irish Crystal
Merlin Park, Galway.
Tel 091-757 311.

Jerpoint Glass
Stoneyford, Co. Kilkenny.
Tel 056-772 4350.

Kilkenny Design Centre
Castle Yard, Kilkenny.
Tel 056-22118.

Magee of Donegal
The Diamond, Donegal.
Tel 073-22660.

Royal Tara China
Tara Hall, Mervue, Galway.
Tel 091-705 602.

Smyth's Irish Linen
65 Royal Ave, Belfast.
Tel 028-9024 2232.

Waterford Crystal
Kilbarry, Waterford.
Tel 051-373 311.

Entertainment Venues

Abbey Theatre
Abbey St Lower,
Dublin 1.
Tel 01-878 7222.

Bord Gáis Energy Theatre
Grand Canal Square,
Docklands, Dublin 2.
Tel 01-677 7999.

Cork Opera House
Emmet Place, Cork.
Tel 021-427 0022.

Crawford Art Gallery
Emmet Place, Cork.
Tel 0214-805 024.

Druid Theatre
Flood St, Galway.
Tel 091-568 660.

Gaiety Theatre
South King St, Dublin 2.
Tel 01-677 1717.

Garter Lane Arts Centre
22A O'Connell St,
Waterford.
Tel 051-855 038.

Gate Theatre
Cavendish Row, Dublin 1.
Tel 01-874 4045.

Grand Opera House
Great Victoria St, Belfast.
Tel 028-9024 1919.

Lyric Theatre
Tel 028-9038 5685.
Ⓦ lyrictheatre.co.uk

National Concert Hall
Earlsfort Terrace, Dublin 2.
Tel 01-417 0000.

O2 Dublin
North Wall Quay, Dublin 1.
Tel 01-819 8888.

Ulster Hall
Bedford St, Belfast.
Tel 028-9032 3900.

Music, Dance, and Festivals

Comhaltas Ceoltóirí Éireann
32 Belgrave Sq,
Monkstown, Co. Dublin.
Tel 01-280 0295.

Dublin Theatre Festival
Assorted drama (Sep/Oct).
44 East Essex St, Dublin 2.
Tel 01-677 8439.

Galway Arts Festival
Theater, music, and dance
(Jul). Black Box Theatre,
Dyke Rd, Galway.
Tel 091-566 577.

Kilkenny Arts Festival
Visual art, literature,
theater, and dance (Aug).
9–10 Abbey Business
Centre, Kilkenny.
Tel 056-775 2175.

Waterford Festival of Light Opera
(late Sep–Oct). Theatre
Royal. **Tel** 051-874 402.

Wexford Festival of Opera
(Oct–Nov). Wexford
Opera House.
Tel 053-912 2144.

Irish Pubs

Dublin Literary Pub Crawl
1 Suffolk St.
Tel 01-670 5602.

Outdoor Activities

Central Fisheries Board
Tel 01-884 2600. Ⓦ cfb.ie

Emerald Star
The Marina, Carrick-on-Shannon, Co. Leitrim.
Tel 071-962 7633.

Golfing Union of Ireland
Ⓦ gui.ie

Where to Stay

Dublin

NORTH OF THE LIFFEY:
Gresham Hotel €€€
Modern **Map** D2
23 O'Connell St Upper, Dublin 1
Tel *01-874 6881*
🆆 gresham-hotels.com
One of Dublin's oldest and best-known hotels, the Gresham offers cheerful, well-equipped bedrooms with classic and contemporary furnishings.

NORTH OF THE LIFFEY:
The Morrison €€€
Boutique **Map** C3
Ormond Quay, Dublin 1
Tel *01-887 2400*
🆆 morrisonhotel.ie
This luxurious hotel overlooking the Liffey impresses with high ceilings, dark woods, and handcrafted Irish carpets.

SOUTHEAST DUBLIN:
Buswells €€€
Historic **Map** E4
25 Molesworth St, Dublin 2
Tel *01-614 6500*
🆆 buswells.ie
Open since 1882, Buswells is one of Dublin's oldest hotels. It is slightly old-fashioned, with a sophisticated interior.

SOUTHEAST DUBLIN:
The Merrion €€€
Luxury **Map** E5
Merrion St Upper, Dublin 2
Tel *01-603 0600*
🆆 merrionhotel.com
Georgian splendor in this luxurious, expansive hotel. Guests enjoy elegant interiors, roaring log fires, and the indulgent Tethra spa.

SOUTHWEST DUBLIN:
Avalon House €
Modern **Map** C4
55 Aungier St, Dublin 2
Tel *01-475 0001*
🆆 avalon-house.ie
Stay in well-priced and cheerful accommodations in a restored redbrick Victorian building. Clean dorms have pine floors and high ceilings.

SOUTHWEST DUBLIN:
Brooks Hotel €€
Luxury **Map** D4
59–62 Drury St, Dublin 2
Tel *01-670 4000*
🆆 brookshotel.ie
An immaculately maintained hotel with a great reputation. Contemporary flourishes and tasteful traditional decor.

Georgian elegance and grandeur at The Merrion, Dublin

DK Choice

FARTHER AFIELD:
Portmarnock Hotel and Golf Links €€
Modern
Portmarnock, Co. Dublin
Tel *01-846 0611*
🆆 portmarnock.com
A beautifully decorated grand old Victorian beachside house, with well-furnished rooms, an elegant, comfortable bar, and restaurants with epic views. There is also an 18-hole golf course and a luxury spa.

Rest of Ireland

ARDMORE: Cliff House Hotel €€€
Luxury
Middle Rd, Co. Waterford
Tel *024-87800*
🆆 thecliffhousehotel.com
Most rooms here have a balcony or terrace overlooking the sea. There is also a spa and two pools.

BELFAST: Europa Hotel €€
Modern
Great Victoria St, Co. Antrim, BT2 7AP
Tel *028-9027 1066*
🆆 hastingshotels.com
Classic hotel with an elegant bar, lounge, and two restaurants.

CASHEL: Cashel Palace Hotel €€
Historic
Main St, Co. Tipperary
Tel *062-62707*
🆆 cashel-palace.ie
Set in a Queen Anne-style house dating from 1730, with rooms overlooking tranquil gardens.

Price Guide
Prices are based on one night's stay in high season for a standard double room, inclusive of service charges and taxes.

€	up to €80
€€	€80 to €180
€€€	over €180

DINGLE: Greenmount House €€
Modern
Upper John St, Dingle, Co. Kerry
Tel *066-915 1414*
🆆 greenmounthouse.ie
Elegantly decorated rooms and suites overlooking the harbor, and an award-winning breakfast.

KILKENNY: Langton House Hotel €€
Boutique
69 John St
Tel *056-776 5133*
🆆 langtons.ie
A friendly hotel full of character. Excellent food and service.

LIMERICK: 1 Pery Square €€
Boutique
1 Pery Square, Georgian Quarter
Tel *061-402 402*
🆆 oneperysquare.com
A Georgian townhouse with modern and period-style rooms, plus a luxurious spa.

DK Choice

LOUGH ESKE:
Harvey's Point €€€
Luxury
Donegal Town, Co. Donegal
Tel *074-972 2208*
🆆 harveyspoint.com
This Swiss-style hotel offers palatial bedrooms overlooking the lake, some with four-poster beds. Renowned for its gourmet cuisine, the hotel's restaurant offers an international fine-dining experience.

NEWCASTLE: Hastings Slieve Donard €€
Modern
Downs Rd, Co. Down, BT33 0AH
Tel *028-4372 1066*
🆆 hastingshotels.com
A majestic redbrick hotel with spectacular views, all the comforts, and a golf course.

TRIM: Trim Castle Hotel €€€
Modern
Castle St, Co. Meath
Tel *046-948 3000*
🆆 trimcastlehotel.com
Bright, spacious rooms, some overlooking the ruins of Trim Castle. Friendly staff.

Where to Eat and Drink

Dublin

NORTH OF THE LIFFEY:
The Winding Stair €€
Irish **Map** C3
40 Lower Ormond Quay, Dublin 1
Tel 01-872 7320
Located above an iconic
bookstore, in a bright, high-
ceilinged room, this restaurant
offers imaginative Irish fare made
with artisanal ingredients.

NORTH OF THE LIFFEY:
Chapter One €€€
European **Map** C1
18–19 Parnell Square, Dublin 1
Tel 01-873 2266 **Closed** Sun & Mon;
first 2 wks Aug; Dec 24–Jan 8
A Michelin-starred restaurant
in a cellar of the Dublin Writers
Museum. Imaginative menu,
and a popular pre-theater deal.

DK Choice

SOUTHEAST DUBLIN:
Avoca Restaurant €€
Irish **Map** E4
11–13 Suffolk St, Dublin 2
Tel 01-672 6019
This bright restaurant, atop an
iconic Irish craft store is always
busy. From imaginative salad
offerings and sandwiches
to delicious hot dishes and
irresistible desserts, it is worth
the wait for a table. There is also
a deli. Open for lunch only.

SOUTHEAST DUBLIN:
Restaurant Patrick Guilbaud €€€
French **Map** E5
21 Upper Merrion St, Dublin 2
Tel 01-676 4192 **Closed** Sun & Mon;
bank hols; Dec 24–Jan 1
The jewel of Dublin dining,
boasting two Michelin stars.
Lunch is incredible value.

SOUTHWEST DUBLIN: Neon €
Asian **Map** C5
17 Camden St, Dublin 2
Tel 01-405 2222
Healthy and tasty Asian street
food is served in bright, lively,
and fun surroundings. Free ice-
cream cones for dessert.

SOUTHWEST DUBLIN:
Queen of Tarts €€
Café **Map** C3
4 Cork Hill, Dame St, Dublin 2
Tel 01-670 7499
This cozy French-style café
opposite Dublin Castle serves
soups, sandwiches, and an array
of sweet and savory tarts.

FARTHER AFIELD:
Johnnie Fox's €€
Irish
Glencullen, Co. Dublin
Tel 01-295 5647
One of the oldest pubs in Ireland,
Johnnie Fox's is a friendly place
with hearty Irish food and
traditional music.

Rest of Ireland

BELFAST: Mourne
Seafood Bar €€
Irish
34–36 Bank St, Co. Antrim, BT1 1HL
Tel 028-9024 8544 **Closed** Dec 24–26
A cozy bar-restaurant in the city
center. The food is terrific – fish
from the morning's catch and
shellfish from Mourne's own
beds in Carlingford Lough.

DK Choice

BLACKLION: MacNean
House & Bistro €€€
Irish
Main St, Co. Cavan
Tel 071-985 3022 **Closed** Mon &
Tue
Weekends tend to be booked
out months in advance at this
culinary gem. Run by
renowned chef Neven Maguire
and his wife Amelda, MacNean
House serves delicacies such as
wood pigeon with game
terrine and ballotine of rabbit. It
also has a full vegetarian menu.

CORK: Café Paradiso €€€
Vegetarian
16 Lancaster Quay
Tel 021-427 7939 **Closed** Sun & Mon;
Dec 24–Jan 1
Ireland's most famous vegetarian
restaurant serves many inventive
dishes. Even dedicated carnivores
will appreciate the food here.

DINGLE: Lord Baker's
Restaurant and Bar €€
Traditional
Main St, Co. Kerry
Tel 066-915 1277 **Closed** Thu
This ancient pub with stone walls
and open fires serves dishes such
as grilled sirloin in pepper sauce,
and poached salmon with a
lemon butter sauce.

GALWAY: Ard Bia at Nimmos €€
International
Spanish Arch, Co. Galway
Tel 091-561 114
A café by day and a restaurant
by night. This is the place for
hearty breakfasts and lunches.

KILKENNY: Campagne €€€
French
5 Gas House Ln.
Tel 056-777 2858 **Closed** Mon except
bank hols, Tue dinner after bank hols
Stylish restaurant serving French
dishes made with locally sourced
ingredients. Thoughtful wine list.

DK Choice

NEW QUAY: Linnane's
Lobster Bar €€
Traditional Seafood
The Pier, Co. Clare
Tel 065-707 8120 **Closed** Winter:
Mon–Thu; Good Friday, Dec 25
Set on the shoreline, Linnane's
enjoys stunning seascapes. On
the menu is simple Irish fare:
poached salmon with chive
cream sauce, steak in pepper
sauce. There is also a pub with
open fires in the winter and
outdoor seating for the summer.

The informal, relaxed interior of Café Paradiso, a vegetarian restaurant in Cork

FRANCE AND THE LOW COUNTRIES

France and the Low Countries at a Glance

France dominates the northwest of continental Europe. To the northeast of France lie Belgium and the Netherlands, known as the Low Countries because they occupy flat plains and land reclaimed from the sea. South of Belgium is the tiny state of Luxembourg. France has some of Europe's greatest attractions, notably the culture and nightlife of Paris. Visitors often choose to tour just one or two of the country's regions: the mountains of the Alps or the Pyrenees, one of the historic wine-growing areas, or the warm south. Belgium and the Netherlands have many historic cities full of fine museums and art galleries. Visiting these countries can be rewarding because all the major sights lie within easy reach of each other.

Paris *(see pp150–71)*, France's capital, is a city of distinctive districts. Montmartre, the hilltop artists' quarter, is dominated by the Sacré-Coeur.

Amiens

Cherbourg

Rouen

Paris

St. Malo

Chartres

Rennes

Orléans

The Loire Valley *(see pp176–9)* is one of France's most popular regions for touring. It is dotted with magnificent châteaux, built by kings and nobles during the Renaissance. One of the finest is Chenonceau.

Nantes

Poitiers

FRANC (see pp144–

Limoges

Southwest France *(see pp188–9)* has a huge variety of attractions, from the peaks of the Pyrenees to Atlantic seaside resorts, such as Biarritz, and the world-famous vineyards of Bordeaux *(see p186)*.

Bordeaux

Toulouse

Biarritz

Perpign

0 km 75
0 miles 75

◀ Avenue des Champs-Elysees from Arc de Triomphe at sunset, Paris

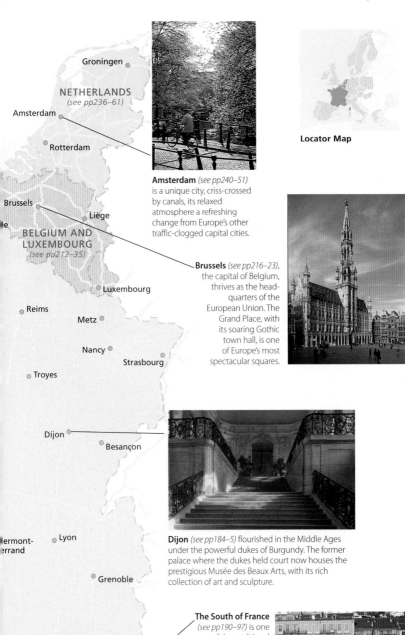

Locator Map

Amsterdam *(see pp240–51)* is a unique city, criss-crossed by canals, its relaxed atmosphere a refreshing change from Europe's other traffic-clogged capital cities.

NETHERLANDS *(see pp236–61)*

Groningen

Amsterdam

Rotterdam

Brussels

Liège

BELGIUM AND LUXEMBOURG *(see pp212–35)*

Luxembourg

Reims

Metz

Nancy

Strasbourg

Troyes

Dijon

Besançon

Lyon

Clermont-Ferrand

Grenoble

Avignon

Montpellier

Marseille

Nice

Brussels *(see pp216–23)*, the capital of Belgium, thrives as the head-quarters of the European Union. The Grand Place, with its soaring Gothic town hall, is one of Europe's most spectacular squares.

Dijon *(see pp184–5)* flourished in the Middle Ages under the powerful dukes of Burgundy. The former palace where the dukes held court now houses the prestigious Musée des Beaux Arts, with its rich collection of art and sculpture.

The South of France *(see pp190–97)* is one of the traditional playgrounds of Europe's rich and famous, where grand hotels, luxury yachts, and pristine beaches contrast with picturesque old fishing ports.

FRANCE

The best advocates for visiting France are the French themselves, convinced as they are that their way of life is best, and their country the most civilized on earth. The food and wine are justly celebrated, while French literature, art, cinema, and architecture can be both profound and provocative. France is a country that stimulates the intellect and gratifies the senses.

France belongs to both northern and southern Europe, encompassing regions ranging from Brittany, with its Celtic maritime heritage, and Germanic Alsace-Lorraine, to the Mediterranean sunbelt and the peaks of the Alps and Pyrenees. The capital, Paris, is the country's linchpin, with its intellectual excitement, intense tempo of life, and notoriously brusque citizens.

Strangely, as life in France becomes more city-based and industrialized, so the desire grows to safeguard the old, traditional ways and to value rural life. The idea of life in the country – *douceur de vivre* (the Good Life), long tables set in the sun for the wine and anecdotes to flow – is as seductive as ever for residents and visitors alike. Nevertheless, the rural way of life has been changing. Whereas in 1945 one person in three worked in farming, today it is only one in 20. France's main exports used to be luxury goods, such as perfumes, Champagne, and Cognac; today, these have been overtaken by chemicals, industrial machinery, telecommunications equipment, and fighter aircraft. The French remain firmly committed to their roots, however, and often keep a place in the country for vacations or their retirement.

History

Though famous for the rootedness of its peasant population, France has also been a European melting pot, from the arrival of the Celtic Gauls in the 1st millennium BC through to the Mediterranean immigrations of the 20th century. Roman conquest by Julius Caesar had an enduring impact but, from the 4th and 5th centuries AD, Germanic invaders destroyed much of the Roman legacy. The Franks provided political leadership in the following centuries, but when their line died out in the late 10th century, France was politically fragmented.

The traditional game of *boules* or *pétanque*, still a popular pastime – especially in the south

◄ The iconic monastery of Mont St-Michel in Normandy, northwestern France

The Capetian dynasty gradually pieced France together over the Middle Ages, a period of economic prosperity and cultural vitality. The Black Death and the Hundred Years' War brought setbacks, and French power was seriously threatened by the dukes of Burgundy and the English crown. In the Renaissance period, François I (reigned 1515–47) dreamt of making France a major power, but was thwarted by the Habsburg Emperor Charles V. The Reformation then plunged the country into religious conflict. However, the 17th century saw France, under Louis XIV, rise to dominate Europe militarily and intellectually.

Napoleon, the brilliant general who rose to be Emperor of France

In the Age of Enlightenment, French culture and institutions were the envy of Europe. The ideas of Voltaire and Rousseau undermined the authority of the Church and the state, nowhere more than in France itself. The Revolution of 1789 ended the absolute monarchy and introduced major social and institutional reforms, many of which were endorsed by Napoleon, whose empire dominated Europe at the start of the 19th century. Yet the Revolution also inaugurated the instability that has remained a hallmark of French politics: since 1789, France has seen three forms of monarchy, two empires, and five republics.

Throughout the political turmoil of the 19th century, France remained a leading source of literary and artistic movements. In painting, the French Impressionists were the inspiration for the development of modern art, and would-be painters began to flock to Paris instead of Rome. France also retained its position as the arbiter of taste in fashion, food, wine, and good manners.

Rivalry with Germany dominated French politics for most of the late 19th and early 20th centuries. The population losses in World War I were traumatic for France, while during 1940–44 the country was occupied by Germany. Yet since 1955, the two countries have proved the backbone of the developing European Union.

Modern Politics

For much of the 20th century, domestic politics was marked by confrontations

KEY DATES IN FRENCH HISTORY

1200–700 BC Arrival of the Celts during the Bronze and Iron Ages

51 BC Romans complete conquest of Gaul

AD 481 Frankish leader Clovis becomes first Merovingian king

800 Coronation of Charlemagne, greatest of the Carolingians, as Holy Roman Emperor

1180–1223 Reign of Philip Augustus

1337–1453 Hundred Years' War with England

1562–93 Wars of Religion

1660–1715 Reign of Louis XIV

1789 French Revolution

1804 Napoleon crowned emperor

1815 Defeat of Napoleon: monarchy restored

1848 Revolution; short-lived Second Republic

1852–70 Second Empire under Napoleon III

1919 Treaty of Versailles after World War I

1940 Germans overrun France

1958 Fifth Republic with president Charles de Gaulle

1968 Student uprising and de Gaulle's downfall

1994 Channel Tunnel opens

2002 Euro replaces Franc as legal tender

2010 Henry IV's skull found; burial ceremony at Basilica St. Denis in 2011

2012 New TGV line extends to Barcelona, Spain

The student uprising of May 1968, which challenged all the old assumptions of the French ruling elite

Relaxing in the sun at a traditional French café

between Left and Right. In 1958, the problems of governing the country led to the introduction of a new constitution – the Fifth Republic – with Charles de Gaulle as president. However, in 1968, protesting students and striking workers combined to paralyze the country and de Gaulle resigned the following year.

The old divide between Left and Right has given way to a more center-focused consensus fostered by François Mitterrand, Socialist President from 1981 to 1995, and forced on the Conservative Jacques Chirac, who succeeded him, by the election of Socialist Lionel Jospin as Prime Minister in 1997. In 2002, however, a land-slide victory for the center-right coalition ousted Jospin; the election of Nicolas Sarkozy as President in 2007 confirmed the center-right politics. However, in 2012, Sarkozy lost the presidency to the Socialist candidate François Holland.

Tempting display of *charcuterie* and cheeses on a Lyon market stall

Language and Culture

Culture is taken seriously in France: writers, intellectuals, artists, and fashion designers are held in high esteem. The French remain justly proud of their films, and are determined to defend it against pressures from Hollywood. Other activities – from the music industry to the French language itself – are subject to the same protectionist attitudes.

Avant-garde art and literature and modern architecture enjoy strong patronage in France. Exciting architectural projects range from new buildings in Paris – the Louvre pyramid and La Grande Arche at La Défense – to the post-modern housing projects of Nîmes and Marseille in the south.

Contemporary Society

Social change has resulted from the decline in the influence of the Catholic Church. Parental authoritarianism has waned and there is a much freer ambiance in schools – two trends resulting from the May 1968 uprising.

French social life, except between close friends, has always been marked by formality – handshaking, and the use of titles and the formal *vous* rather than the intimate *tu*. However, this is changing, especially among the young, who now call you by your first name, and use *tu* even in an office context. Standards of dress have become more informal too, though the French are still very keen to dress well.

France is a country where tradition and progress are found side by side. The Euro has taken over, yet some people still calculate in "new" Francs, introduced back in 1960. France's agri-business is one of the most modern in the world, but the peasant farmer is deeply revered. France has Europe's largest hyper-markets, which have been ousting local grocers. Although American in inspiration, they are French in what they sell, with wonderful displays of cheeses and a huge range of fresh vegetables, fruit, and herbs.

The TGV, France's impressive high-speed train

Exploring France

France is a large country and, although it has more than 60 million inhabitants, is less densely populated than most of its western European neighbors. Paris belongs to northern Europe, while the south is Mediterranean in climate and lifestyle. Distances limit the amount of the country you can visit, though train services are good and there is an extensive network of highways. Popular tourist destinations include the châteaux of the Loire, the mountains of the Alps and Pyrenees, historic wine-growing regions *(see pp186–7)*, and the resorts of the Côte d'Azur.

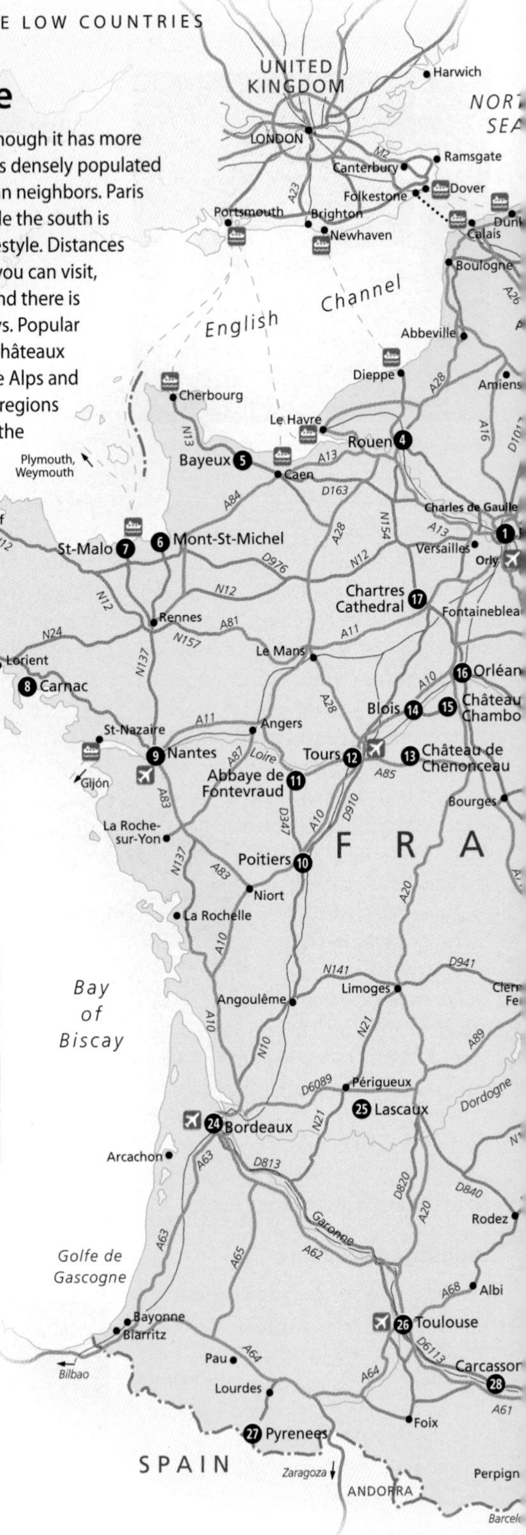

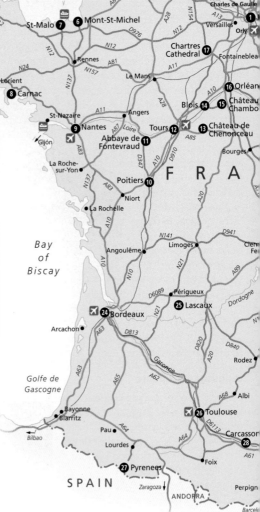

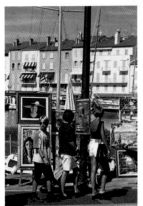

Admiring the work of local artists on the quayside at St-Tropez

Key

- Highway
- Major road
- Railroad
- Channel Tunnel
- International border

For keys to symbols *see back flap*

Distance chart

Paris									
579 360	**Bordeaux**								
221 137	**799** 496	**Lille**							
462 287	**538** 334	**682** 424	**Lyon**						
773 480	**648** 403	**992** 616	**313** 194	**Marseille**					
385 239	**325** 202	**604** 375	**653** 406	**973** 604	**Nantes**				
932 579	**808** 502	**1152** 716	**472** 293	**187** 116	**1132** 703	**Nice**			
490 304	**918** 570	**549** 341	**478** 297	**789** 490	**867** 539	**948** 589	**Strasbourg**		
744 462	**244** 152	**923** 574	**537** 334	**407** 254	**568** 353	**563** 349	**1013** 629	**Toulouse**	

Distance by road in kilometers
Distance by road in miles

Sights at a Glance

1. *PARIS pp150–71*
2. Strasbourg
3. Reims
4. Rouen
5. Bayeux
6. *Mont-St-Michel pp174–5*
7. St-Malo
8. Carnac
9. Nantes
10. Poitiers
11. Abbaye Royale de Fontevraud
12. Tours
13. *Château de Chenonceau pp178–9*
14. Blois
15. Château de Chambord
16. Orléans
17. *Chartres Cathedral pp180–81*
18. Vézelay
19. *Dijon pp184–5*
20. Beaune
21. Lyon
22. Annecy
23. Grenoble
24. Bordeaux
25. Lascaux
26. Toulouse
27. Pyrenees
28. Carcassonne
29. Nîmes
30. Avignon
31. *Arles pp192–3*
32. Camargue
33. Aix-en-Provence
34. Marseille
35. Cannes
36. Nice
37. Monaco

❶ Paris

Paris is a city of more than two million people, and has been the economic, political, and artistic hub of France since Roman times. During the medieval and Renaissance periods, Paris dominated northern Europe as a religious and cultural center. The city was rejuvenated in the mid-19th century, when its slums were replaced with the elegant avenues and boulevards that make modern Paris a delight to stroll around. Today, the city strives to be at the heart of a unified Europe. Chic cafés, gourmet restaurants, and fashionable shopping are the major attractions for many visitors.

Notre-Dame, viewed from the tranquil setting of Square Jean XXIII

Key

Sight / Place of interest

Sights at a Glance

① Ile de la Cité
② *Notre-Dame pp154–5*
③ Sainte-Chapelle
④ Centre Pompidou
⑤ Musée Picasso
⑥ Place des Vosges
⑦ Place de la Bastille
⑧ Panthéon
⑨ Jardin du Luxembourg
⑩ St-Germain-des-Prés
⑪ *Musée du Louvre pp158–60*

⑫ Jardin des Tuileries
⑬ Musée de l'Orangerie
⑭ Place de la Concorde
⑮ Musée d'Orsay
⑯ Musée Rodin
⑰ Les Invalides
⑱ Eiffel Tower
⑲ Musée du Quai Branly
⑳ Palais de Chaillot
㉑ Arc de Triomphe
㉒ Champs-Elysées

Greater Paris *(see inset map)*

㉓ Montmartre
㉔ Parc de la Villette
㉕ Cimetière du Père Lachaise
㉖ La Défense
㉗ Bois de Boulogne
㉘ *Château de Versailles pp168–9*
㉙ Basilique St-Denis
㉚ Disneyland Paris
㉛ Château de Vaux-le-Vicomte
㉜ Château de Fontainebleau

Getting Around

The Parisian subway consists of 16 metro lines, referred to by their number and terminus names. In central Paris, these lines overlap the routes of the RER commuter trains, which reach outlying areas. Buses are often the fastest way to travel short distances. The city's night buses are called Noctiliens. Taxis are expensive, but handy after the metro shuts down. A self-service bike system, Vélib, operates in central Paris.

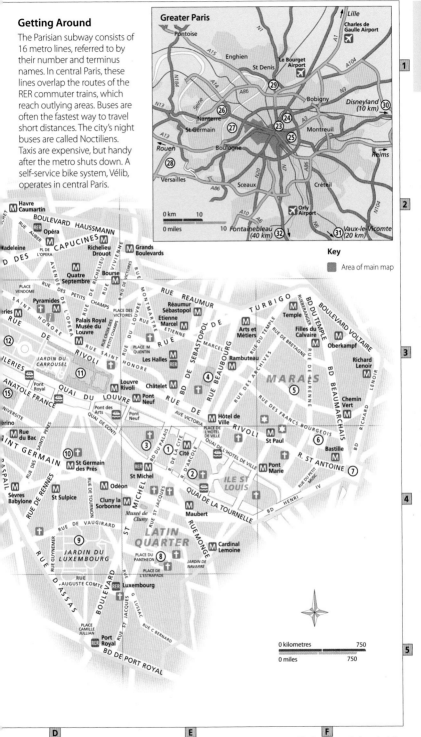

Greater Paris

Key

Area of main map

0 km 10
0 miles 10

0 kilometres 750
0 miles 750

Western end of the Ile de la Cité, where the island is crossed by the Pont Neuf

① Ile de la Cité

Ⓜ Châtelet, Cité. Conciergerie: 2 Blvd du Palais. **Tel** 01-53 40 60 80. **Open** daily. **Closed** Jan 1, May 1, Dec 25. 🏛 🖼 *(phone to check).* 🌐 **conciergerie. monuments-nationaux.fr**

This boat-shaped island on the Seine is the nucleus of Paris. The capital's name derives from the Parisii, one of the Celtic tribes who lived here in the 3rd century BC. The settlement was later expanded by the Romans, the Franks, and the Capetian kings.

Remains of the earliest buildings can be seen in the **Crypte Archéologique**, below the square in front of Notre-Dame cathedral, which stands at one end of the island. At the other end is another Gothic masterpiece: the Sainte-Chapelle church, surrounded by the huge complex of buildings forming the **Palais de Justice**. One of these, the sinister-looking **Conciergerie**, was a prison from 1391 until 1914. During the French Revolution, it filled to overflowing, and Marie-Antoinette was held in a tiny cell here until her execution in 1793. The Conciergerie has a superb Gothic Hall and a 14th-century clock tower. To the far east of the island, tiny Ile St Louis is a haven of riverside quays and quiet streets. There are many fine restaurants and chic shops here.

Crossing the western end of the Ile de la Cité is the oldest bridge in Paris, the **Pont Neuf** (new bridge), which dates back to 1578. The colorful Marché aux Fleurs et Oiseaux takes place daily in the Place Louis Lépine and is the city's most famous flower market. On Sundays, caged birds are also sold.

② Notre-Dame

See pp154–5.

③ Sainte-Chapelle

4 Boulevard du Palais. **Tel** 01-53 40 60 80. Ⓜ Cité. **Open** daily. **Closed** Jan 1, May 1, Dec 25. 🏛 🖼 🚻 ♿

Hailed as one of the great architectural masterpieces of the Western world, this church was likened to "a gateway to heaven" in the Middle Ages. Sainte-Chapelle was built in 1248 to house sacred relics, including Christ's Crown of Thorns, purchased from the Byzantine emperor at great expense by the devout King Louis IX.

The church consists of two chapels. The lower chapel was used by servants and minor officials, while the exquisite upper chapel, reached by means of a narrow, spiral staircase, was reserved for the royal family and courtiers. This chapel has many glorious stained-glass windows, separated by pencil-like columns soaring 15 m (50 ft) to the star-studded roof. More than 1,100 biblical scenes from the Old and New Testaments are depicted, as well as the story of how the relics were brought to Sainte-Chapelle. The 86 panels of the circular Rose Window, which are best seen at sunset, tell the story of the Apocalypse.

Badly damaged during the Revolution, and converted into a flour warehouse, the church was renovated a century later by architect Viollet-le-Duc. The spire, erected in 1853, rises 75 m (245 ft) into the air.

The Gothic Sainte-Chapelle church

For hotels and restaurants see pp206–8 and pp209–11

Pipes and ducts on the outside of the Centre Pompidou

④ Centre Pompidou

Pl G. Pompidou. **Tel** 01-44 78 12 33. **M** Rambuteau, Châtelet, Hôtel de Ville. **RER** Châtelet-Les-Halles. 21, 29, 38, 47 & many others. Musée National d'Art Moderne: **Open** 11am–9pm Wed–Mon. **Closed** May 1. **centrepompidou.fr**

With its skeleton of struts, ducts, and elevators scaling the outside of the building, and offering fine views of the city, this famous cultural center has room for a vast exhibition area inside.

Among the artists featured in the Musée National d'Art Moderne are Matisse, Picasso, Miró, and Pollock, representing such schools as Fauvism, Cubism, and Surrealism. Star attractions are *Sorrow of the King* (1952) by Matisse, and Georges Braque's *The Duo* (1937). A library is housed on the first, second, and third floors, while temporary exhibitions are held on the first and sixth floors.

Outside, the piazza is usually full of crowds watching the street performers. On one side of the square, the Atelier Brancusi is a reconstruction of the workshop of Romanian-born artist Constantin Brancusi (1876–1957), who left his entire oeuvre to the nation.

⑤ Musée Picasso

Hôtel Salé, 5 Rue de Thorigny. **Tel** 01-42 71 25 21. **M** St-Sébastien Froissart, St-Paul. **Open** Tue–Sun. **museepicassoparis.fr**

The Spanish-born artist Pablo Picasso (1881–1973) spent most of his life in France.

On his death, the French state inherited many of his works in lieu of death duties, opening a museum to display them in 1986. Housed in a 17th-century mansion originally built for a salt-tax collector, the collection comprises more than 200 paintings, 158 sculptures, 100 ceramic works, and some 3,000 sketches and engravings. The full extent of Picasso's artistic development is presented, from the somber Blue period *Self-Portrait* (1901) to Cubist collages and Neoclassical works, such as *Pipes of Pan*. Highlights include *The Two Brothers* (1906), *The Kiss* (1969), and *Two Women Running on the Beach* (1922). There is also a sculpture garden.

⑥ Place des Vosges

M Bastille, St-Paul.

This perfectly symmetrical square, laid out in 1605 by Henri IV, and known as Place Royale, was once the residence of the aristocracy. Considered among the most beautiful in the world by Parisians and visitors alike, the square is surrounded by 36 houses, nine on each side. Built of brick and stone, with dormer windows over arcades, they have survived intact for almost 400 years. Today, the historic houses accommodate antiques stores and fashionable cafés.

The square has been the scene of many historical events over the centuries, including a three-day tournament in celebration of the marriage of Louis XIII to Anne of Austria in 1615. Among the square's famous former residents are the literary hostess, Madame de Sévigné, born here in 1626, Cardinal Richelieu, pillar of the monarchy, and Victor Hugo, who lived in one of the houses for 16 years.

⑦ Place de la Bastille

M Bastille.

Nothing remains of the infamous prison stormed by the revolutionary mob on July 14, 1789, the event that sparked the French Revolution. A row of paving stones from No. 5 to No. 49 Boulevard Henri IV traces the line of former fortifications.

The 52-m (170-ft), hollow bronze Colonne de Juillet stands in the middle of the traffic-clogged square to honor the victims of the July Revolution of 1830. On the south side of the square (at 120 Rue de Lyon) is the 2,700-seat **Opéra Bastille**, completed in 1989, the bicentennial of the French Revolution.

Central fountain and fine Renaissance houses in the Place des Vosges

② Notre-Dame

No other building embodies the history of Paris more than Notre-Dame. It stands majestically on the Ile de la Cité, cradle of the city. Built on the site of a Roman temple, the cathedral was commissioned by Bishop de Sully in 1160. The first stone was laid in 1163, marking the start of two centuries of toil by armies of medieval architects and craftsmen. It has been witness to great events of French history ever since, including the coronation of Napoleon Bonaparte (1804) and the state funeral of Charles de Gaulle (1970). During the Revolution, the building was desecrated and rechristened the Temple of Reason. Extensive renovations (including the addition of the spire and gargoyles) were carried out in the 19th century by architect Viollet-le-Duc.

★ West Front
Three main portals with superb statuary, a central rose window, and an openwork gallery are the outstanding features of the cathedral's facade.

★ Galerie des Chimières
The cathedral's grotesque gargoyles (*chimières*) perch menacingly around ledges high on the facade.

KEY

① **The West Rose Window** depicts the Virgin in a medallion of rich reds and blues.

② **The Kings' Gallery** features 28 kings of Judah gazing down from above the main door.

③ **The South Tower** houses Emmanuel, the cathedral's most sonorous bell.

④ **The Spire**, designed by Viollet-le-Duc, soars to a height of 90 m (295 ft).

⑤ **The transept** was completed during the reign of Louis IX, in the 13th century.

⑥ **The Treasury** houses the cathedral's religious treasures, including ancient manuscripts and reliquaries.

★ Portal of the Virgin
A statue of the Virgin surrounded by kings decorates this massive 13th-century portal.

★ Flying Buttresses
Jean Ravy's spectacular flying buttresses at the east end of the cathedral have a span of 15 m (50 ft).

★ South Rose Window
The south facade window, with its central depiction of Christ, is an impressive 13 m (43 ft) in diameter.

Statue of Virgin and Child
Against the southeast pillar of the crossing stands the 14th-century statue of the Virgin and Child. It was brought to the cathedral from the chapel of St. Aignan and is known as Notre-Dame de Paris (Our Lady of Paris).

The Cathedral from the Left Bank
Notre-Dame's spectacular island setting is enhanced by the trees of Square Jean XXIII, a formal garden laid out at the eastern end of the Ile de la Cité.

Street by Street: Latin Quarter

Since the Middle Ages, this riverside quarter has been dominated by the Sorbonne – it acquired its name from early Latin-speaking students. The area is generally associated with artists, intellectuals, and a bohemian way of life, and has a history of political unrest. In 1871, the Place St-Michel became the center of the Paris Commune, and in May 1968, it was one of the sites of the student uprisings that briefly engulfed the city.

St-Séverin
Begun in the 13th century, this beautiful church took three centuries to build and is a fine example of the Flamboyant Gothic style.

★ Boulevard St-Michel
The northern end of the Boul'Mich, as it is affectionately known, is a lively mélange of cafés, bookstores, and clothes stores, with nightclubs and experimental film houses nearby.

St-Michel

Cluny- La Sorbonne

QUAI ST MICHEL

RUE DE LA HARPE

BLVD ST MICHEL

RUE DU PETIT PONT

BLVD ST GERMAIN

BLVD ST JACQUES

RUE THENARD

BLVD ST G

Little Athens
takes its name from the many Greek restaurants situated in its picturesque streets.

RUE DES ECOLES

★ Musée National du Moyen Age
The museum holds a fine collection of medieval art, with many beautiful tapestries. This detail is from the late 15th-century series of tapestries *The Lady with the Unicorn*.

0 meters		100
0 yards		100

La Sorbonne

Seat of the University of Paris until 1969, the Sorbonne was established in 1257 by Robert de Sorbon, confessor to Louis IX, to enable poor scholars to study theology. It achieved fame as a center of learning in the late Middle Ages. The first printing house in France was founded here in 1469. Suppressed during the Revolution for opposition to liberal 18th-century philosophical ideas, and re-established by Napoleon in 1806, the Sorbonne split into 13 separate universities in 1971. Lectures are still held on the original site.

View of the Panthéon from the Jardin du Luxembourg

⑧ Panthéon

Place du Panthéon. **Tel** 01-44 32 18 00 Ⓜ Place Monge, Cardinal-Lemoine. **Open** daily. **Closed** Jan 1, May 1, Jul 14, Dec 25. 🖼 🎫

Famous as the last resting place of some of France's greatest citizens, this magnificent church was built between 1764 and 1790 to honor Sainte Geneviève, patron saint of Paris. During the Revolution, it was turned into a pantheon to house the tombs of the illustrious.

Based on Rome's pantheon, the temple portico has 22 Corinthian columns, while the tall dome was inspired by that of St. Paul's in London *(see p66)*. Geneviève's life is celebrated in a series of 19th-century nave murals. Many French notables rest in the crypt, including Voltaire, Rousseau, and Victor Hugo. The ashes of Pierre and Marie Curie are also held here.

⑨ Jardin du Luxembourg

Ⓜ Odéon. 🚇 Luxembourg. **Open** daily.

This graceful and historic area offers a peaceful haven in the heart of Paris. The gardens, which cover 25 ha (60 acres), were opened to the public in the 19th century by their then owner, the Comte de Provence. They are centered on the Luxembourg Palace, which was built for Marie de Médicis, the widow of Henri IV, and is now the home of the French Senate. Dominating the gardens is an octagonal lake surrounded by formal terraces, where sunbathers gather on fine summer days.

⑩ St-Germain-des-Prés

3 Place St-Germain-des-Prés. **Tel** 01-55 42 81 33. Ⓜ St-Germain-des-Prés. **Open** daily. 🎫 (reserve in advance).

Originating in 558 as a basilica to house holy relics, this is the oldest church in Paris. St-Germain had become a powerful Benedictine abbey by the Middle Ages, but was largely destroyed by fire in 1794. Major restoration took place in the 19th century. A single tower survives from the original three, housing one of the most ancient belfries in France. Famous tombs include that of 17th-century philosopher, René Descartes.

After World War II, the area attracted writers and artists, including one of the leading figures of the Existentialist movement, Jean-Paul Sartre, and writer Simone de Beauvoir. Bars and cafés, such as *Les Deux Magots* and the *Café de Flore*, which were their daily haunts, are now popular with tourists.

St-Julien-le-Pauvre, one of the oldest churches in Paris, dates back to the 12th century.

Maubert-Mutualité

Key

— Suggested route

De Médicis fountain in the Jardin du Luxembourg

For keys to symbols *see back flap*

⑪ Musée du Louvre

The Musée du Louvre, containing one of the world's most important art collections, has a history dating back to medieval times. First built as a fortress in 1190 by King Philippe-Auguste, it lost its dungeon and keep in the reign of François I, who commissioned a Renaissance-style building. Thereafter, four centuries of kings and emperors improved and enlarged the palace. It was first opened as a museum in 1793 under the First Republic.

The Louvre's east facade, added in the 17th century

Building the Louvre

Over many centuries, the Louvre was enlarged by a succession of French rulers and, latterly, by the state, shown below with their dates.

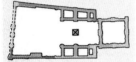

Major Alterations

- Reign of François I (1515–47)
- Catherine de' Médici (about 1560)
- Reign of Henri IV (1589–1610)
- Reign of Louis XIII (1610–43)
- Reign of Louis XIV (1643–1715)
- Reign of Napoleon I (1804–15)
- Reign of Napoleon III (1852–70)
- François Mitterrand (1981–95)

KEY

① **The Jardin du Carrousel** was once the grand approach to the Tuileries Palace, which was set ablaze in 1871 by insurgents of the Paris Commune.

② **The Carrousel du Louvre** underground visitors' complex (1993), with galleries, shops, restrooms, parking, and an information desk, lies beneath the Arc de Triomphe du Carrousel.

③ **The inverted glass pyramid** brings light to the subterranean complex, echoing the new main entrance to the museum in the Cour Napoléon.

④ **Cour Marly** is a glass-roofed courtyard that houses the famous *Marly Horses*, sculpted by Antoine Coysevox (1706) and Guillaume Coustou (1745) for the royal château at Marly.

⑤ **Richelieu Wing**

⑥ **The Hall Napoléon**, where temporary exhibitions are held, is situated under the pyramid.

⑦ **The Cour Napoléon** dates mostly from the 19th century.

⑧ **Sully Wing**

⑨ **Cour Carrée**

⑩ **Philippe-Auguste's old fortress**, with its distinctive tower and keep, was transformed into a royal residence by Charles V in about 1365.

⑪ **The Salle des Caryatides** is named after the four monumental statues created by Jean Goujon in 1550 to support the upper gallery. Built for Henri II, it is the oldest room in the palace.

⑫ **Cour Visconti–Islamic Art**

⑬ **Denon Wing**

★ **Arc de Triomphe du Carrousel**
This triumphal arch was built to celebrate Napoleon's military victories in 1806.

The Glass Pyramid

Plans for the modernization and expansion of the Louvre were first conceived in 1981. These included the transfer of the Ministry of Finance from the Richelieu Wing to offices elsewhere and a new main entrance. This took the form of a metal and glass pyramid designed by architect I.M. Pei. Opened in 1989, the pyramid enables the visitor to see the surrounding buildings, while allowing light down into the underground visitors' reception area.

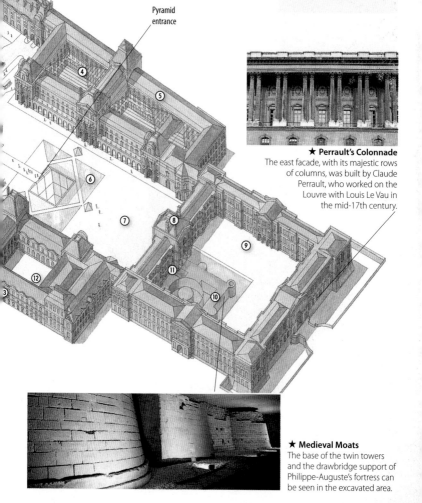

Pyramid entrance

★ **Perrault's Colonnade**
The east facade, with its majestic rows of columns, was built by Claude Perrault, who worked on the Louvre with Louis Le Vau in the mid-17th century.

★ **Medieval Moats**
The base of the twin towers and the drawbridge support of Philippe-Auguste's fortress can be seen in the excavated area.

Exploring the Louvre's Collection

Owing to the vast size of the Louvre's collection, it is useful to set a few viewing priorities before starting. The collection of European paintings (1400–1848) is comprehensive, with more than half the works by French artists. The extensively renovated departments of Oriental, Egyptian, Greek, Etruscan, and Roman antiquities are of world renown and feature numerous new acquisitions and rare treasures. The hugely varied display of *objets d'art* includes furniture, jewelry, scientific instruments, and armor.

The famously enigmatic *Mona Lisa* (c.1504), by Leonardo da Vinci

European Painting: 1400 to 1848

Notable Flemish paintings include Jan van Eyck's *Madonna of the Chancellor Rolin* (c.1435). The fine Dutch collection features *Self-portrait* and *Bathsheba* (1654), both by Rembrandt. Among important German works are a *Venus* (1529) by Lucas Cranach and a portrait of Erasmus by Hans Holbein.

Italian paintings are arranged chronologically, and include Fra Angelico's *Coronation of the Virgin* (1435) and the celebrated *Mona Lisa* (1504) by Leonardo da Vinci.

Outstanding French works are represented by Enguerrand Quarton's *Villeneuve-lès-Avignon Pietà* (1455) and the delightfully frivolous *The Bathers* (1770) by Fragonard.

Among English artists featured are Gainsborough, Reynolds, and Turner, while the Spanish collection has portraits by Goya and works by El Greco and Zurbarán.

European Sculpture: 1100 to 1848

The French section opens with a 12th-century figure of Christ and a head of St. Peter. Several works by French sculptor Pierre Puget (1620–94) are assembled in a glass-covered courtyard. Other masterpieces of French sculpture, including Jean-Antoine Houdon's busts of Diderot and Voltaire, stand in the Cour Marly. A notable Flemish sculpture is Adrian de Vries's long-limbed *Mercury and Psyche* (1593). Michelangelo's *Slaves* and Benvenuto Cellini's *Fontainebleau Nymph* are among the many splendid Italian works.

Oriental and Egyptian Antiquities

Important works of Mesopotamian art include one of the world's oldest documents, a basalt block, bearing a proclamation of laws by Babylonian King Hammurabi from about 1750 BC.

The warlike Assyrians are represented by delicate carvings, and a fine example of Persian art is the enameled brickwork depicting the king's archers (5th century BC).

Egyptian art on display, dating from between 2500 and 1400 BC, and mostly produced for the dead, includes lifelike funeral portraits, such as the *Squatting Scribe*, and several sculptures of married couples.

Greek, Etruscan, and Roman Antiquities

The famous Greek marble statues here, the *Winged Victory of Samothrace* and the *Venus de Milo*, both date from the Hellenistic period (late 3rd to 2nd century BC). A highlight of the Roman section is a 2nd-century AD bronze head of the Emperor Hadrian. Other fine pieces include a bust of Agrippa and a basalt head of Livia. The star of the Etruscan collection is the terra-cotta sarcophagus of a married couple. Among the vast array of earlier fragments, a geometric head from the Cyclades (2700 BC) and a swan-necked bowl hammered out of a gold sheet (2500 BC) are noteworthy.

Objets d'Art

More than 8,000 items feature in this collection, many of which came from the Abbey of St-Denis, where the kings of France were crowned. Treasures include a serpentine plate from the 1st century AD and a golden scepter made for King Charles V in about 1380. The French crown jewels include the splendid coronation crowns of Louis XV and Napoleon, scepters, and swords. The Regent, one of the purest diamonds in the world, worn by Louis XV at his coronation in 1722, is also on show. An entire room is taken up with a series of tapestries, the *Hunts of Maximilian*, executed for Emperor Charles V in 1530. The large collection of French furniture ranges from the 16th to the 19th centuries, and includes pieces by exceptional furniture-maker André Charles Boulle. He is particularly noted for his technique of inlaying copper and tortoiseshell. Among more unusual items is Marie-Antoinette's inlaid steel and bronze writing desk.

Venus de Milo

Neoclassical statues and urns in the Jardin des Tuileries

⑫ Jardin des Tuileries

Ⓜ Tuileries, Concorde. **Open** Apr–Sep: 7am–9pm daily; Oct–Mar: 7:30am–7pm daily.

These gardens once belonged to the Palais des Tuileries, a palace which was razed to the ground during the time of the Paris Commune in 1871.

The gardens were laid out in the 17th century by André Le Nôtre, royal gardener to Louis XIV. He created a Neoclassical garden with a broad central avenue, regularly spaced terraces, and topiary arranged in geometric designs. A project which started in 1998 created a garden with lime and chestnut trees and striking modern sculptures. Also in the gardens, two royal tennis courts built in 1851 and known as the *Jeu de Paume* – literally "game of the palm" – now host exhibitions of contemporary art.

⑬ Musée de l'Orangerie

Jardin des Tuileries, Place de la Concorde. **Tel** 01-44 77 80 07. Ⓜ Concorde. 🚌 24, 42, 52, 72, 73, 84, 94. **Open** 9am–6pm Wed–Mon. **Closed** May 1, Dec 25. 🖼 🗲 🏛 ♿ 🆆 musee-orangerie.fr

The museum reopened in 2006 following a long closure for restructuring. Claude Monet's crowning work, his celebrated water-lily series – known as the *Nymphéas* – still takes pride of place here. Most of the canvases were painted between 1899 and 1921 in the garden at Giverny, Normandy, where Monet lived from 1883 until his death at the age of 86.

This superb work is complemented by the Walter-Guillaume collection of artists of the Ecole de Paris, from the late Impressionist era to the inter-war period. Among a number of paintings by Cézanne are still lifes, portraits such as *Madame Cézanne*, and landscapes. The collection also features *The Red Rock*. There are 24 canvases by Renoir, one the most notable of which is *Les Jeunes Filles au Piano*. Picasso is represented by early works, such as *The Female Bathers*. Henri Rousseau has nine paintings, including *The Wedding and Le Carriole du Père Junier*. Among outstanding portraits is that of by Modigliano. Works by Sisley, Derain, and Utrillo are also featured. All the works are bathed in the natural light that filters through the windows of the museum.

Entrance to the great collection of Impressionist and other paintings at the Musée de l'Orangerie

⑭ Place de la Concorde

Ⓜ Concorde.

One of Europe's most magnificent and historic squares, covering more than 8 ha (20 acres), the Place de la Concorde was a swamp until the mid-18th century. It became Place Louis XV in 1763, when royal architect Jacques-Ange Gabriel was asked by the king to design a suitable setting for an equestrian statue of himself. He created an open octagon, with only the north side containing mansions.

The statue, which lasted here less than 20 years, was replaced by the guillotine (the Black Widow, as it came to be known), and the square was renamed Place de la Révolution. On January 21, 1793, Louis XVI was beheaded here, followed by more than 1,300 other victims, including Marie Antoinette, Madame du Barry, Charlotte Corday (Marat's assassin), and revolutionary leaders Danton and Robespierre. The blood-soaked square was optimistically renamed Place de la Concorde after the Reign of Terror finally came to an end in 1794.

The grandeur of the square was enhanced a few decades later when the 3,200-year-old Luxor obelisk was presented to King Louis-Philippe as a gift from the viceroy of Egypt (who also donated Cleopatra's Needle in London). Two fountains and eight statues personifying French cities were also installed.

Flanking the Rue Royale on the north side of the square are two of Gabriel's Neoclassical mansions, the Hôtel de la Marine and the exclusive Hôtel Crillon.

Obelisk in Place de la Concorde

Interior of the Musée d'Orsay, retaining its original station architecture

⑮ Musée d'Orsay

Rue de la Légion d'Honneur. **Tel** 01-40 49 49 78. **M** Solférino. **RER** Musée d'Orsay. 🚌 24, 68, 69, 84 & many others. **Open** Tue–Sun. **Closed** Jan 1, May 1, Dec 25. 🅿 🕐 ♿ **W musee–orsay.fr**

Originally built as a railroad terminus in the heart of Paris, Victor Laloux's superb building, completed in 1900, narrowly avoided demolition in the 1970s. In 1986, it reopened as the Musée d'Orsay, with much of the original architecture preserved. The majority of the exhibits are paintings and sculptures dating from between 1848 and 1914, but there are also displays of furniture, the decorative arts, and cinema. The social, political, and technological context in which these diverse visual arts were created is explained.

Paintings from before 1870 are on the ground floor, presided over by Thomas Couture's massive *Romans in the Age of Decadence* (1847). Neoclassical masterpieces, such as Ingres' *La Source*, hang near Romantic works like Delacroix's turbulent *Tiger Hunt* (1854), and canvases by Degas and Manet, including the latter's *Le Déjeuner sur l'Herbe* and *Olympia* (1863).

The museum's central aisle overflows with sculpture, from Daumier's satirical busts of members of parliament to Carpeaux's exuberant *The Dance* (1868). Decorative arts and architecture are on the middle level, where there is also a display of Art Nouveau, including Lalique glassware. Impressionist works on the upper level include Renoir's *Bal du Moulin de la Galette* (1876). Matisse's *Luxe, Calme et Volupté* is a highlight of the post-1900 collection.

⑯ Musée Rodin

79 Rue de Varenne. **Tel** 01-44 18 61 10. **M** Varenne. **RER** Invalides. 🚌 69, 82, 87, 92. **Open** Tue–Sun. **Closed** Jan 1, May 1, Dec 25. 🅿 ♿ restricted. **W musee-rodin.fr**

Auguste Rodin (1840–1917), widely regarded as one of France's greatest sculptors, lived and worked here in the Hôtel Biron, an elegant 18th-century mansion, from 1908 until his death. In return for a state-owned flat and studio, Rodin left his work to the nation, and it is now exhibited here. Some of his most celebrated sculptures are on display in the attractive garden and include *The Burghers of Calais, The Thinker, The Gates of Hell*, and *Balzac*.

The indoor exhibits are arranged in chronological order, spanning the whole of Rodin's career. Major works in the collection include *The Kiss* and *Eve*.

Rodin's *The Kiss* (1886) at the Musée Rodin

⑰ Les Invalides

M La Tour-Maubourg, Varenne. **RER** Invalides. 🚌 28, 63, 69 & many others. Hôtel des Invalides: **Tel** 08-10 11 33 99. **Open** daily. **Closed** Jan 1, May 1, Nov 1, Dec 25. St-Louis-des-Invalides, Museums & Dôme Church: **Open** daily (see website for times). **Closed** Jan 1, May 1, Jun 17, Nov 1, Dec 25, first Mon of each month (except Jul & Aug). 🅿 🕐 ♿ restricted. **W musee–armee.fr**

This vast ensemble of monumental buildings is one of the most impressive architectural sights in Paris. The imposing **Hôtel des Invalides**, from which the area takes its name, was commissioned by Louis XIV in 1671 for his wounded and homeless veterans. Designed by Libéral Bruand, it was completed in 1676 by Jules Hardouin-Mansart. Nearly 6,000 soldiers once resided here; today, there are fewer than 100. Behind the Hôtel's harmonious Classical facade – a masterpiece of French 17th-century architecture – are several museums.

The **Musée de l'Armée** is one of the most comprehensive museums of military history in the world, with exhibits covering all periods from the Stone Age to World War II. Among items on display are François I's ivory hunting horns and a selection of arms from China, Japan, and India.

The **Musée de l'Ordre de la Libération** (closed until mid-2015) was set up to honor feats of heroism during World War II, while the **Musée des Plans-Reliefs** has an extensive collection of detailed models of French forts and fortified towns, considered top secret until as late as the 1950s.

St-Louis-des-Invalides, the chapel of the Hôtel des Invalides, is also known as the "soldiers' church." It was built between 1679 and 1708 by Jules Hardouin-Mansart, to Bruand's design. The stark, Classical interior is designed in the shape of a Greek cross and has a fine 17th-century organ by Alexandre Thierry.

The **Dôme Church** was begun in 1676 to complement the existing buildings of Les Invalides, and to reflect the splendor of Louis XIV's reign. Reserved for the exclusive use of the Sun King himself, the resulting masterpiece is one of the greatest examples of *grand siècle* architecture and a monument to Bourbon glory. The crypt houses the tomb of Napoleon – six coffins with an enormous red sarcophagus on a pedestal of green granite. Marshal Foch, the World War I hero, is also buried here.

Facade of the Hôtel des Invalides, showing the splendid gilded dome

⑱ Eiffel Tower

Built for the Universal Exhibition of 1889, and to commemorate the centennial of the Revolution, the 324-m (1,063-ft) Eiffel Tower (Tour Eiffel) was meant to be a temporary addition to the Paris skyline. Designed by Gustave Eiffel, it was fiercely decried by 19th-century aesthetes. It was the world's tallest building until 1931, when New York's Empire State Building was completed. A number of crazy stunts have been attempted here. In 1912, a local tailor launched himself from the tower using a cape as wings. He plunged to his death.

Double-decker elevators take visitors to the top level, which can hold up to 400 people at a time.

The Jules Verne Restaurant is one of the best in Paris, offering excellent food and panoramic views.

The Eiffel Tower in Figures

• There are a total of 1,665 steps from bottom to top
• The tower is held together by a total of 2.5 million rivets
• It never sways more than 7 cm (2.5 in)
• The tower weighs 10,100 tons
• 50 tons of paint are used on the tower every seven years

VISITORS' CHECKLIST

Practical Information
Champ-de-Mars. **Tel** 08-92 70 12 39. **Open** daily. 🅿 ♿ limited. 🏠 ⁄ 🅦 tour-eiffel.fr

Transport
🚌 42, 69, 82, 87. Ⓜ Bir Hakeim. 🆁🅴🆁 Champ-de-Mars, Trocadéro.

The third level, 276 m (905 ft) above the ground, offers superb views. On a clear day, it is possible to see for 72 km (45 miles) – as far as Chartres Cathedral *(see pp180–81)*.

The second level, at 115 m (376 ft), is reached either by elevator or by 359 steps from the first level.

The Eiffel Tower at night

The first level, at 57 m (187 ft), can be reached by elevator or by 345 steps. This level is being entirely renovated.

Trocadéro fountains in front of the Palais de Chaillot

⑲ Musée du Quai Branly

37 Quai Branly. **Tel** 01-56 61 70 00.
Ⓜ Alma-Marceau. Ⓡ Pont de l'Alma.
Open Tue–Sun. ♿ 🚻 📷 ♿
Ⓦ quaibranly.fr

Built to give the arts of Africa, Asia, Oceania, and the Americas a platform as shining as that reserved for Western art, this museum boasts a collection of more than 3,000 objects. It is particularly strong on Africa, with stone, wooden, and ivory masks, as well as ceremonial tools. The Jean Nouvel-designed building, raised on stilts, is a sight in itself: the ingenious use of glass allows the surrounding greenery to act as a natural backdrop for the collection.

⑳ Palais de Chaillot

Place du Trocadéro 17. Ⓜ Trocadéro.
Ⓡ Trocadéro. 🚌 27, 30, 32, 63, 72, 82.
Museums: **Open** Wed–Mon. ♿ 📷
Aquarium: **Tel** 01-40 69 23 23. **Open**
daily. **Closed** Jul 14. 📷

With its curved colonnaded wings, each culminating in a vast pavilion, this palace was designed in Neoclassical style for the 1937 Paris Exhibition by Azéma, Louis-Hippolyte Boileau, and Jacques Carlu. It is adorned with sculptures and bas-reliefs, and the pavilion walls are inscribed in gold with words composed by the poet Paul Valéry. The square between the two pavilions is highly decorated with bronze sculptures, ornamental pools, and shooting fountains. Steps lead down from here to the **Théâtre National de Chaillot**, famous for its avant-garde productions.

The **Cité de l'Architecture et du Patrimoine** is a vast complex and information center incorporating Viollet-le-Duc's original Musée des Monuments Français (1882).

The **Musée de l'Homme**, in the west wing (closed until mid-2015), traces human evolution through a series of anthro-pological, archaeological, and ethnological displays. Next door is the **Musée National de la Marine**, devoted to French naval history.

The centerpiece of the lovely Jardins de Trocadéro is a long ornamental pool, bordered by statues. The gardens themselves are perfect for a quiet evening stroll. Also here is the **Aquarium de Paris – Cinéaqua**.

Baron Haussmann

A lawyer by training and civil servant by profession, Georges-Eugène Haussmann (1809–91) was appointed Prefect of the Seine in 1853 by Napoleon III. For 17 years Haussmann was responsible for the urban modernization of Paris. With a team of the best architects and engineers, he demolished the chaotic, insanitary streets of the medieval city and created a well-ventilated and ordered capital in a geometrical grid. He also increased the number of streetlights and sidewalks, giving rise to the cafés that enliven modern Parisian street life. The plan involved redesigning the area at one end of the Champs-Elysées and creating a star of 12 avenues centered around the new Arc de Triomphe.

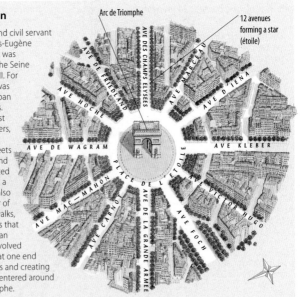

Arc de Triomphe

12 avenues forming a star (étoile)

The east side of the Arc de Triomphe

㉑ Arc de Triomphe

Place Charles de Gaulle. **Tel** 01-55 37 73 77. Ⓜ Ⓡⓔⓡ Charles de Gaulle–Etoile. 🚌 22, 30, 31, 73, 92. **Open** daily. **Closed** Jan 1, May 1, May 8 (am), Jul 14 (am), Nov 11 (am), Dec 25. 🅿️ 📷 🚻 limited. ⓦ arc-de-triomphe. monuments-nationaux.fr

After his greatest victory, the Battle of Austerlitz in 1805, Napoleon promised his men they would "go home beneath triumphal arches." The first stone of what was to become the world's most famous triumphal arch was laid the following year. But disruptions to architect Jean Chalgrin's plans – combined with the demise of Napoleonic power – delayed completion until 1836. Standing 50 m (164 ft) high, the Arc is encrusted with flamboyant reliefs, shields, and sculptures, depicting military scenes such as the Napoleonic battles of Austerlitz and Aboukir.

On Armistice Day, 1921, the body of the Unknown Soldier was placed beneath the arch to commemorate the dead of World War I. The flame of remembrance which burns above the tomb is rekindled by various veterans' organizations each evening. Today, the Arc de Triomphe is the customary rallying point for many victory celebrations and parades.

The viewing platform on top of the Arc overlooks the length of the Champs-Elysées. Inside the Arc, a museum documents its history and construction.

㉒ Champs-Elysées

Ⓜ Franklin D. Roosevelt, George V, Champs-Elysées Clemenceau. Grand Palais: Porte A, Ave Eisenhower. **Tel** 01-44 13 17 17. **Open** Wed–Mon (only for exhibitions). 📷 Palais de la Découverte: **Tel** 01-56 43 20 21. **Open** Tue–Sun. 📷 Petit Palais: Ave Winston Churchill. **Tel** 01-53 43 40 00. **Open** Tue–Sun. **Closed** public hols. 🚻 📷 for temporary exhibitions.

Paris's most famous and popular thoroughfare had its beginnings in about 1667, when landscape gardener André Le Nôtre exten-ded the royal view from the Tuileries by creating a tree-lined avenue. The Champs-Elysées (Elysian Fields) has also been known as the "triumphal way" since the homecoming of Napoleon's body from St. Helena in 1840. With the addition of cafés and restaurants in the late 19th century, it became the most fashionable boulevard in Paris.

The formal gardens that line the Champs-Elysées from Place de la Concorde to the Rond-Point have changed little since they were laid out by architect Jacques Hittorff in 1838, and were used as the setting for the 1855 World's Fair. The Grand Palais and the Petit Palais were also built here for the Universal Exhibition of 1900.

The exterior of the massive **Grand Palais** combines an imposing Neoclassical facade with Art Nouveau ironwork. A splendid glass roof is decorated with colossal bronze statues of flying horses and chariots at its four corners. Inside is a science exhibition (Le Palais de la Découverte) and the Galeries Nationales du Grand Palais, which holds frequent temporary exhibitions.

Facing the Grand Palais, the **Petit Palais** houses the Musée des Beaux-Arts de la Ville de Paris. Arranged around a semicircular courtyard and garden, the palace is similar in style to the Grand Palais, with Ionic columns, a grand porch, and a dome echoing that of the Invalides across the river. The exhibits are divided into medieval and Renaissance *objets d'art*, paintings, and drawings; 18th-century furniture and *objets d'art;* and works by the French artists Gustave Courbet, Jean Ingres, and Eugène Delacroix.

Musée des Beaux-Arts de la Ville de Paris, in the Petit Palais

The deceptively rustic exterior of Au Lapin Agile, one of the best-known nightspots in Paris

㉓ Montmartre

M Abbesses, Anvers. ☐ 30, 54, 80, 85. Sacré-Coeur: 35 Rue du Chevalier de la Barre. **Tel** 01-53 41 89 00. **Open** daily. ☐ for crypt and dome. ☐ restricted. **W** sacre-coeur-montmartre.com

The steep hill of Montmartre has been associated with artists for 200 years. Théodore Géricault and Camille Corot came here at the start of the 19th century, and in the early 20th century, Maurice Utrillo immortalized the streets in his works. Today, street artists of varying talents exhibit their work in the Place du Tertre, and thrive on the tourist trade. Exhibitions at the **Musée de Montmartre** usually feature works of artists associated with the area, while the **Musée d'Art Naïf Max Fourny** houses almost 600 examples of naive art. The **Espace Montmartre Salvador Dalí** displays more than 300 works by the Surrealist painter and sculptor. Much of the area still preserves its rather louche, prewar atmosphere. Former literary haunt **Au Lapin Agile**, or "Agile Rabbit," is now a club. The celebrated **Moulin Rouge** nightclub is also in the vicinity.

The name Montmartre, thought to derive from martyrs tortured and killed here in around AD 250, is also associated with the grandiose **Sacré-Coeur**. Dedicated to the Sacred Heart of Christ, the basilica was built as a result of a vow made at the outbreak of the Franco-Prussian War in 1870. Businessmen Alexandre Legentil and Hubert Rohault de Fleury

Approach to the Romano-Byzantine Sacré-Coeur basilica

promised to finance its construction should France be spared from the impending Prussian onslaught. Despite the war and the Siege of Paris, invasion was averted and work began in 1876 to Paul Abadie's designs. The basilica, completed in 1914, is one of France's most important Roman Catholic shrines. It contains many treasures, including a figure of the *Virgin Mary and Child* (1896) by Brunet.

Below the forecourt, Square Willette is laid out on the side of a hill in a series of descending terraces. A funicular railway takes visitors up from the bottom of the gardens to the foot of the steps of the basilica.

㉔ Parc de la Villette

30 Ave Corentin-Cariou. M Porte de la Villette. ☐ 75, 139, 150, 152, 250A. Cité des Sciences: **Tel** 01-40 05 80 00. **Open** Tue–Sun. ☐ ☐

The old slaughterhouses and livestock market of Paris have been transformed into this massive urban park, designed by Bernard Tschumi.

The major attraction of the site is the **Cité des Sciences et de l'Industrie**, a hugely popular science and technology museum. Architect Adrien

Fainsilber has created an imaginative interplay of light, vegetation, and water in the high-tech, five-floor building, which soars to a height of 40 m (133 ft). At the museum's heart is the Explora exhibit, a fascinating guide to the worlds of science and technology. The Géode, a giant entertainment sphere, houses a huge hemispherical cinema screen. In the auditorium of the Planetarium, special-effects projectors create exciting images of the stars and planets.

Also in the park, the **Grande Halle** was the old cattle hall, and has been turned into a huge exhibition space. The **Cité de la Musique** is a quirky but elegant complex that holds a music conservatory – home of the world-famous Paris *conservatoire* since 1990 – and a concert hall. There is also a museum covering the history of music from the Renaissance to the present day. Built as a venue for pop concerts, the **Zénith theater** seats more than 6,000 spectators.

㉕ Cimetière du Père Lachaise

16 Rue du Repos. Ⓜ Père-Lachaise, A Dumas. **Tel** 01-55 25 82 10. **Open** daily. Ⓦ pere-lachaise.com

Paris's most prestigious cemetery is set on a wooded hill overlooking the city. The land was once owned by Père de la Chaise, Louis XIV's confessor, but it was bought by order of Napoleon in 1803 to create a completely new cemetery. This became so popular with the Parisian bourgeoisie that its boundaries were extended six times during the 19th century. Here are buried celebrities such as the writer Honoré de Balzac, the famous playwright Molière, the composer Frédéric Chopin, singer Edith Piaf, and actors Simone Signoret and Yves Montand. Famous foreigners interred in the cemetery include Oscar Wilde and the singer Jim Morrison. The Columbarium, built at the end of the 19th century, houses the ashes of American dancer Isadora

Monument to Oscar Wilde in the Père Lachaise Cemetery

Duncan, among others. The equally charismatic Sarah Bernhardt, famous for her portrayal of Racine heroines, also reposes at Père Lachaise. Striking funerary sculpture and famous graves make this a pleasant place for a leisurely, nostalgic stroll.

㉖ La Défense

ⓇⒺⓇ La Défense. La Grande Arche **Tel** 01-47 74 84 24. **Open** Mon–Sat. Ⓑ Ⓒ Ⓦ ladefense.fr

This still-expanding skyscraper business city on the western edge of Paris is one of the largest office developments in Europe and covers 80 ha (198 acres). It was launched in 1957 to create a new home for leading French and foreign companies. **La Grande Arche** is an enormous hollow cube, spacious enough to contain Notre-Dame cathedral. Designed by Danish architect Otto von Spreckelsen, the arch houses an exhibition gallery and offers superb views over the city, though the rooftop is closed to the public.

㉗ Bois de Boulogne

Ⓜ Porte Maillot, Porte Dauphine, Porte d'Auteuil, Sablons. **Open** 24 hrs daily. 🎟 to specialist gardens and facilities. ♿

Located between the Seine River and the western edges of Paris, this 865-ha (2,137-acre) park offers a vast belt of greenery for strolling, cycling, riding, boating, picnicking, or spending a day at the races. The Bois de Boulogne was once part of the immense Forêt du Rouvre. In the mid-19th century, Napoleon III had the area redesigned and landscaped by Baron Haussmann along the lines of Hyde Park in London *(see p62)*. A number of self-contained parks include the Pré Catelan, which has the widest beech tree in Paris, and the Bagatelle gardens, with architectural follies and an 18th-century villa famous for its rose garden. The villa was built in just 64 days as the result of a bet between the Comte d'Artois and Marie-Antoinette.

By day, the Bois is busy with families, joggers, and walkers, but after dark it is notoriously seedy – and best avoided.

Kiosque de l'Empereur, on an island in the Grand Lac, Bois de Boulogne

㉘ Château de Versailles

Visitors passing through the dazzling state rooms of this colossal palace, or strolling in its vast gardens, will soon understand why it was the glory of the Sun King's reign. Started by Louis XIV in 1668, the palace grew from a modest hunting lodge built for his father, Louis XIII, to become the largest palace in Europe, housing some 20,000 people. Architect Louis Le Vau built the first section, which expanded into an enlarged courtyard. From 1678, Jules Hardouin-Mansart added the north and south wings and the superb Hall of Mirrors. He also designed the chapel, completed in 1710. The interiors were largely the work of Charles Le Brun, and the great landscape gardener André Le Nôtre redesigned the gardens with their monumental fountains.

★ Hall of Mirrors
This magnificent room, 70 m (233 ft) long, was the setting for great state occasions. It was here that the Treaty of Versailles was ratified at the end of World War I.

Marble Courtyard
The courtyard is decorated with marble paving, urns, and busts. Above the gilded central balcony, the figures of Hercules and Mars flank the clock on the pediment.

★ Chapelle Royale
Mansart's last great work, this Baroque chapel was Louis XIV's final addition to Versailles. The beautiful interior is decorated with Corinthian columns and superb Baroque murals.

The ornate main gate, designed by Mansart, is crowned by the royal coat of arms.

KEY

① **The South Wing** originally housed the apartments of great nobles. It is closed to the public.

② **Ministers' Courtyard**

③ **Royal Courtyard**

④ **The Opera House**, in the North Wing, was completed for the 1770 marriage of the future Louis XVI and Marie-Antoinette.

⑤ **Parterres (flowerbeds)**

VISITORS' CHECKLIST

Practical Information
Versailles, Yvelines. **Tel** 01-30 83 78 00. 🚇 Versailles Chantiers, Versailles Rive Droite.
🚆 Versailles Rive Gauche.
Open 9am–6:30pm Tue–Sun (5:30pm in winter). **Closed** some public hols. 🏛 Grand & Petit Trianon: **Open** pm daily.
Closed Jan 1, Dec 25. 🏛 🎫
♿ 🏛 Grands Eaux Nocturnes (Jul–Aug: Sat eve)
🌐 chateauversailles.fr

Transport
🚌 171 from Paris.

The 17th-century Fountain of Neptune, by Le Nôtre and Mansart

North Wing
The chapel, Opera House, and picture galleries occupy this wing, which originally housed royal apartments.

Exploring the Palace

The main rooms of the palace are on the first floor. Around the Marble Courtyard are the private apartments of the king and queen. Visitors can see the King's Bedroom, where Louis XIV died, aged 77, in 1715. The room next door, the Cabinet du Conseil, was where the monarch would receive ministers and family members.

On the garden side, the state apartments are richly decorated with colored marbles, carvings in stone and wood, murals, and gilded furniture. Each is dedicated to an Olympian deity. Louis XIV's throne room, the Salon d'Apollon, designed by Le Brun, is dedicated to the god Apollo. A copy of the famous portrait of Louis by Hyacinthe Rigaud hangs above the fireplace. The war theme of the Salon de la Guerre is reinforced by a stucco relief of Louis XIV riding to victory. The high point of the tour is the Hall of Mirrors, with its 17 great mirrors reflecting the light from tall arched windows.

Another major attraction is the beautiful Chapelle Royale.

The Gardens of Versailles

The gardens are a fitting counterpart to the colossal palace. Immediately in front of the palace is the Water Parterre, decorated with superb bronze statues. Paths lead through the formal gardens, with their regularly patterned flowerbeds and hedges, to groves, lakes, fountains, and architectural features, such as the Colonnade (1685), a circle of marble arches designed by Mansart. The largest stretch of water is the Grand Canal, where Louis XIV held spectacular boating parties.

The gardens contain two smaller palaces. The **Grand Trianon**, built of stone and pink marble, was designed by Mansart in 1687 as a discreet hideaway for Louis XIV and his mistress, Madame de Maintenon. The nearby **Petit Trianon** (1762) was built for Madame de Pompadour, Louis XV's mistress. It later became a favorite retreat of Marie-Antoinette. Behind it is the Hameau, a mini-village where the queen would dress up as a shepherdess and play with a flock of groomed and perfumed lambs.

Marie-Antoinette's beloved Petit Trianon

㉙ Basilique St-Denis

1 Rue de la Légion d'Honneur.
Ⓜ St-Denis-Basilique. ⓇⒺⓇ St-Denis.
Tel 01-48 09 83 54. **Open** daily.
Closed Jan 1, May 1, Dec 25. 🅿 to
the crypt. 📷 ♿ restricted.

Constructed between 1137 and
1281, the basilica is on the site of
the tomb of St. Denis, the first
bishop of Paris, who was beheaded in Montmartre in AD 250.
According to legend, his decap-
itated figure, clutching his head,
was seen here, and an abbey
was erected to commemorate
the martyred bishop. The basilica
was the first church to be built in
the Gothic style of architecture.

From as early as the 7th
century, St-Denis was a burial
place for French rulers, and all
the queens of France were
crowned here. During the
Revolution, many tombs were
desecrated and scattered, but
the best were stored, and now
represent a fine collection of
funerary art. Memorials include
those of Henri II (died 1559) and
Catherine de' Medici (died

1589), and Louis XVI and Marie-
Antoinette (died 1793).

Of the medieval effigies, the
most impressive are of Charles V
(1364) and a 12th-century
likeness of Blanche de France
with her dog. Their mask-like
serenity contrasts with the
realistic Renaissance portrayal
of agony in the sculptures of
the mausoleum of Louis XII
and Anne de Bretagne.

In 2011, the skull of Henry IV
was buried here, having been
in the possession of a private
collector since the 1950s.

㉚ Disneyland Paris

Marne-la-Vallée, Seine-et-Marne.
🚄 TGV from several major cities to
Marne la Vallée/Chessy; also Eurostar
from London St. Pancras, Ebbsfleet &
Ashford. ⓇⒺⓇ Marne-la-Vallée-Chessy.
🚌 from CDG & Orly airports.
Tel 08448 008 898. **Open** daily.
🅿 ♿ 🆆 **disneylandparis.com**

The theme park, which lies
32 km (20 miles) east of Paris,
covers 60 ha (150 acres). It is

divided into five themed areas.
Although these rely heavily on
Hollywood nostalgia,
Disneyland Paris has tried to
give the park a European touch.

"Frontierland," inspired by
the Wild West of 19th-century
America, can be explored on
paddlewheel steamboats.
A roller coaster trundles
through mountain scenery.

In "Adventureland," visitors
encounter characters and
tales from adventure fiction,
including Caribbean pirates and
the Swiss Family Robinson.

Small-town America at the
turn of the century is evoked in
"Main Street." Authentic details
include horse-drawn vehicles
and a traditional barber's shop.

Young children will enjoy
"Fantasyland," devoted to Disney
characters and tales, where they
can fly with Peter Pan or search
the Alice in Wonderland maze
for the Queen of Hearts' castle.

"Discoveryland" has futuristic
architecture and sophisticated
technology. Here, visitors can
choose to be miniaturized by a
hapless inventor or sent on a
thrilling space trip.

㉛ Château de Vaux-le-Vicomte

Maincy, Seine-et-Marne. 🚄 ⓇⒺⓇ Melun,
then taxi or shuttle bus (Apr–mid-Nov:
Sat & Sun). **Tel** 01-64 14 41 90. **Open**
mid-Mar–mid-Nov: daily. 🅿 ♿

Located 64 km (40 miles)
southeast of Paris, just north of
Melun, the château enjoys a
peaceful rural setting. Nicolas
Fouquet, a powerful court
financier to Louis XIV, challenged
architect Le Vau and decorator
Le Brun to create the most
sumptuous palace of the day.
The result was one of the
greatest 17th-century French
châteaux. However, it also led
to his downfall. Louis was so
enraged – because its luxury cast
the royal palaces into the shade
– that he had Fouquet arrested
and confiscated all his estates.

As befits Fouquet's grand tastes,
the interior is a gilded banquet of
frescoes, stucco, caryatids, and
giant busts. The Salon des Muses
boasts Le Brun's magnificent

The tomb of Louis XII and Anne de Bretagne in the Basilique St-Denis

Château de Vaux-le-Vicomte, designed by Le Nôtre, seen across the formal gardens

frescoed ceiling of dancing nymphs and poetic sphinxes. La Grande Chambre Carrée is decorated in Louis XIII style, with paneled walls and an impressive triumphal frieze, evoking Rome.

Much of Vaux-le-Vicomte's fame is due to landscape gardener André Le Nôtre (1613–1700). At Vaux he perfected the concept of the *jardin à la française*: avenues framed by statues and box hedges, water gardens with ornate pools, and geometrical parterres "embroidered" with floral motifs.

32 Château de Fontainebleau

Seine-et-Marne. **Tel** 01-60 71 50 70. **Open** Wed–Mon.
w musee-chateau-fontainebleau.fr

Fontainebleau was a favorite royal residence from the 12th to the mid-19th century. Its charm lies in its relative informality and its spectacular setting in a forest 65 km (40 miles) south of Paris. The present château dates back to François I. Drawn to the area by the local hunting, the Renaissance king created a decorative château modeled on Florentine and Roman styles. Subsequent rulers enlarged and embellished the château, creating a cluster of buildings in various styles from different

periods. During the Revolution, the apartments were looted by a mob, and remained bare until the 1800s, when Napoleon refurbished the whole interior.

The Cour du Cheval Blanc, once a simple enclosed courtyard, was transformed by Napoleon into the main approach to the château. At one end is the Escalier du Fer-à-Cheval (1634), an imposing horseshoe-shaped staircase.

The interior suites showcase the château's history as a royal residence. The Galerie François I has a superb collection of Renaissance art. The Salle de Bal, a Renaissance ballroom designed by Primaticcio (1552), features emblems of Henri II on the walnut-coffered ceiling and

reflected in the parquet floor. The apartments of Napoleon I house his grandiose throne, in the former Chambre du Roi. The complex of buildings also contains the Musée Napoléon, in which eight rooms recreate different scenes from the Emperor's life.

Nearby is the Chapelle de la Sainte Trinité, designed for Henri II in 1550. The chapel acquired its vaulted and frescoed ceiling under Henri IV, and was completed during the reign of Louis XIII.

The gardens are also worth exploring. The Jardin Anglais is a romantic "English" garden planted with cypresses and exotic species. The Jardin de Diana features a bronze fountain of Diana the huntress.

The Salle de Bal of Henri II, Château de Fontainebleau

Northern France

Northern France's main sights span thousands of years of history, from the awesome megaliths of Carnac, through the 18th-century grandeur of Nancy's town architecture, to Strasbourg's futuristic Palais de l'Europe, seat of the European Parliament. Its cities boast some of the country's greatest cathedrals, such as those of Reims and Rouen. The region's most famous religious monument is Mont-St-Michel, whose evocative silhouette has welcomed pilgrims since the 11th century.

Strasbourg's fine Gothic cathedral, surrounded by historic buildings

❷ Strasbourg

Bas Rhin. 🏙 450,000. ✈ 15 km (8 miles) SW. 🚉 🚌 ℹ 17 Place de la Cathédrale (03-88 52 28 28). 🎄 Christmas market (Dec). 🌐 otstrasbourg.fr

Located halfway between Paris and Prague, this cosmopolitan city is often known as "the crossroads of Europe." It is also home to the European Parliament.

A boat trip along the waterways that encircle Strasbourg's Old Town takes in the **Ponts-Couverts** – bridges with medieval watchtowers – and the old tanners' district, dotted with attractive half-timbered houses.

Dating from the late 11th century, the **Cathédrale Notre-Dame** dominates the city. There are wonderful views from the viewing platform on the rooftop.

The grand Classical **Palais Rohan** houses three museums: the Musée des Beaux Arts, the Musée Archéologique, and the Musée des Arts Décoratifs, which has one of the finest displays of ceramics in France. Also worth visiting is the **Musée d'Art Moderne et Contemporain**, **Le Vaisseau**, a scientific discovery center for children aged 3–15, and the **Musée Alsacien**, which overflows with exhibits on local traditions, arts, and crafts.

❸ Reims

Marne. 🏙 210,000. 🚉 🚌 ℹ 08-21 61 01 60. 🌐 reims-tourisme.com

Renowned throughout the world from countless champagne labels, Reims has a rich historical legacy.

The city's most famous monument is the magnificent Gothic **Cathédrale Notre-Dame**, begun in 1211. For several centuries, the cathedral was the setting for the coronation of French kings. Highlights are the 13th-century Great Rose Window and the west facade, decorated with over 2,300 statues.

On the eve of a coronation, the future king spent the night in the **Palais du Tau** (1690), the archbishops' palace, adjoining the cathedral.

Its 15th-century banqueting hall, the Salle du Tau, with its barrel-vaulted ceiling and Arras tapestries, is a star attraction.

Among other fine historic buildings are the 17th-century **Ancien Collège des Jésuites**, which is now a school, and the **Basilique St-Remi**, the oldest church in Reims.

Relics of the town's Roman past include the **Crypto-portique**, part of the former forum, and the **Porte Mars**, a triumphal Augustan arch.

The **Musée de la Reddition** occupies the building that served as Eisenhower's French headquarters during World War II. It was here, in 1945, that the general received the Germans' surrender, which ended the war.

🏛 **Cathédrale Notre-Dame**
Place du Cardinal Luçon. **Open** daily. 🎫 ♿

Environs
A short drive south of Reims is **Epernay**. Here, you can visit the cellars of a number of distinguished champagne "houses," including those of Moët et Chandon.

❹ Rouen

Seine Maritime. 🏙 138,000. ✈ 11 km (7 miles) SE. 🚉 🚌 ℹ 25 Place de la Cathédrale (02-32 08 32 40). 🌐 rouenvalleedeseine.com

Formerly a Celtic trading post, Roman garrison, and Viking colony, Rouen became the capital of the Norman Duchy in 911. Today, it is a rich and cultured city that boasts a wealth

Statuary on the west facade of the Cathédrale Notre-Dame, in Reims

Detail from the 11th-century Bayeux Tapestry

of splendid historical monuments. Rouen's Gothic cathedral, the **Cathédrale Notre-Dame**, has an impressive west facade, made famous by the great Impressionist painter Claude Monet (1840–1926), who made almost 30 paintings of it. A number of these can be seen in the city's excellent **Musée des Beaux Arts**.

From the cathedral, the Rue du Gros Horloge leads west, passing under the city's Great Clock, to the Place du Vieux Marché, where Joan of Arc was burnt at the stake in 1431.

The Flamboyant Gothic **Eglise St-Maclou** and **Eglise St-Ouen** are two of Rouen's finest churches. The Eglise St-Ouen is noted for its restored 14th-century stained-glass windows.

The **Musée de la Céramique** displays around 1,000 pieces of Rouen faïence – colorful glazed earthenware – as well as other pieces of French and foreign china.

The former family home of Gustave Flaubert (1821–80) has been converted into a museum containing memorabilia from this famous French novelist's life.

▥ Musée des Beaux Arts
Square Verdrel. **Tel** 02-35 71 28 40. **Open** Wed–Mon. **Closed** public hols. ▨ ♿

❺ Bayeux

Calvados. ▨ 15,000. ▤ ▤
ⓘ Pont-St-Jean (02-31 51 28).
ⓦ bayeux-bessin-tourisme.com

The main reason to visit this small town in Normandy is to see the world-renowned Bayeux Tapestry. This incredible work of art depicts William the Conqueror's invasion of England and the Battle of Hastings, which took place in the 11th century,

from the Norman perspective. It was probably commissioned by Bishop Odo of Bayeux, William's half-brother. The 70-m (230-ft) long embroidered hanging is displayed in a renovated seminary, the **Centre Guillaume-le-Conquérant**, which also gives a detailed audiovisual account of the events leading up to the Norman conquest.

As well as the tapestry, a cluster of 15th–19th-century buildings and the Gothic **Cathédrale Notre-Dame** are Bayeux's principal attractions.

Bayeux was the first town in Nazi-occupied France to be liberated by the Allies following the D-Day landings in 1944. On the southwest side of the town's ring road, the **Musée Mémorial de la Bataille de Normandie** traces the events of the Battle of Normandy in World War II.

▥ Centre Guillaume-le-Conquérant
Rue de Nesmond. **Tel** 02-31 51 25 50. **Open** daily. **Closed** 3 wks Jan, Dec 25 & 26. ▨ ♿

❻ Mont-St-Michel

See pp174–5.

❼ St-Malo

Ille-et-Vilaine. ▨ 53,000. ▤ ▦ ▤
ⓘ Esplanade St-Vincent (08-25 13 52 00). ◭ Tue, Fri (Old Town).
ⓦ saint-malo-tourisme.com

Once a fortified island, St-Malo stands in a commanding position at the mouth of the river Rance. In the 16th–19th centuries, the port won prosperity and power through the exploits of its sea-faring population. Intra-muros, the old walled city, is encircled by ramparts that provide fine

views of St-Malo and its offshore islands. Within the city walls is a web of narrow, cobbled streets with tall 18th-century buildings housing many souvenir stores, seafood restaurants, and creperies.

St-Malo's castle, the **Château de St-Malo** dates from the 14th and 15th centuries. The great keep today houses an interesting museum charting the city's history. In the three-towered fortification known as the **Tour Solidor**, to the west of St-Malo, is a museum devoted to the ships and sailors that rounded Cape Horn.

❽ Carnac

Morbihan. ▨ 4,600. ▤ ⓘ 74 Avenue des Druides (02-97 52 13 52). ⓦ ot-carnac.fr

This popular town is probably most famous as one of the world's great prehistoric sites. As long ago as 4000 BC, thousands of ancient granite rocks were arranged in mysterious lines and patterns in the countryside around Carnac by Megalithic tribes. Their original purpose is uncertain, though they are thought to have religious significance or to be related to an early astronomical calendar. Celts, Romans, and Christians have since adapted them to their own beliefs.

You can see some of the menhirs at the Kermario site, on the town outskirts, while in the center, the **Musée de Préhistoire** gives an insight into the area's ancient history.

Menhirs (prehistoric standing stones) in a field near Carnac

6 Mont-St-Michel

Shrouded by mist, the silhouette of Mont-St-Michel is one of the most enchanting sights in France. Now linked to the mainland by a causeway, the island of Mont-Tombe (Tomb on the Hill) stands at the mouth of the Couesnon River, crowned by a fortified abbey that almost doubles its height. Lying strategically on the frontier between Normandy and Brittany, Mont-St-Michel grew from a humble 8th-century oratory to become a Benedictine monastery that had its greatest influence in the 12th and 13th centuries. Pilgrims known as *miquelots* journeyed from afar to honor the cult of St. Michael, and the monastery was a renowned center of medieval learning. After the French Revolution, the abbey became a prison. It is now a national monument that draws some 850,000 visitors a year. Work on a footbridge to link the island to the mainland is due to finish in 2015.

★ **Abbey Church**
Four bays of the Romanesque nave in the abbey church survive. Three were pulled down in 1776, creating the West Terrace.

Gautier's Leap
Situated at the top of the Inner Staircase, this terrace is named after a prisoner who leaped to his death here.

Entrance

Visiting the Abbey

The abbey is built on three levels, which reflect the monastic hierarchy. The monks lived on the highest level *(shown here)*, in an enclosed world of church, cloister, and refectory. The abbot entertained his noble guests on the middle level. Soldiers and pilgrims further down on the social scale were received at the lowest level. Guided tours begin at the West Terrace at the church (highest) level and end on the lowest level in the almonry, where alms were distributed to the poor.

La Merveille is the name given to the buildings on the north side of the church.

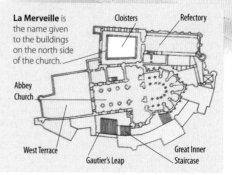

Cloisters

Refectory

Abbey Church

West Terrace

Gautier's Leap

Great Inner Staircase

★ **Cloisters**
With their elegant English Purbeck marble columns, the cloisters are a beautiful example of early 13th-century Anglo-Norman style.

VISITORS' CHECKLIST

Practical Information
ℹ️ Boulevard de l'Avancée
(02-33 60 14 30).
📧 ot-montsaintmichel.com
Abbey: **Tel** 02-33 89 80 00.
Open May–Aug: 9am–7pm; Sep–Apr: 9:30am– 6pm. Night visits during summer. **Closed** Jan 1, May 1, Dec 25. 🔲 🕇 12:15pm Tue–Sat; 11:30am Sun. 🕐 🕑
📧 **monuments-nationaux.fr**

Transport
🚉 to Pontorson, then bus.

★ **La Merveille**
The main three-story monastic complex, added to the church's north side in the early 13th century, is known as La Merveille (The Miracle). The Knights' Room, on the middle floor, has magnificent Gothic rib-vaulting and finely decorated capitals.

KEY

① **The ramparts** – a series of fortified walls with imposing towers – were built following attacks by the English during the Hundred Years' War.

② **Gabriel Tower**

③ **St. Aubert's Chapel**, built on an outcrop of rock, dates from the 15th-century and is dedicated to Aubert, the founder of Mont-St-Michel.

④ **Tour du Roy**

⑤ **The Arcade Tower** provided lodgings for the abbot's soldiers.

⑥ **Eglise St-Pierre**

⑦ **Liberty Tower**

★ **Grande Rue**
Now crowded with tourists and souvenir shops, the pilgrims' route, followed since the 12th century, climbs up past the Eglise St-Pierre to the abbey gates.

The Loire Valley

Renowned for its sumptuous châteaux, the relics of royal days gone by, the glorious valley of the Loire is rich in both history and architecture. As the Loire runs through the heart of France, so the region embodies the essence of the French way of life. Its sophisticated cities, luxuriant landscape, and magnificent food and wine add up to a modern paradise. The Loire has long been described as exemplifying *la douceur de vivre*: it combines a leisurely pace of life, a mild climate, and the gentle ways of its inhabitants. The overall impression is one of an unostentatious taste for the good things in life.

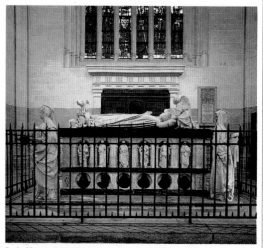

Tomb of François II in Cathédrale St-Pierre et St-Paul, Nantes

❾ Nantes

Loire-Atlantique. 🚈 270,000.
✈ 🚆 🚌 *i* 9 Rue des Etats
(08-92 46 40 44). 🕓 Tue–Sun.
🅆 nantes-tourisme.com

The ancient port of Nantes was the ducal capital of Brittany for 600 years, but is now considered a part of the Pays de la Loire. Many of its fine 18th- and 19th-century buildings were built on profits from maritime trade. Modern-day Nantes is a lively city, with good museums, chic bars and stores, and wide open spaces.

The **Cathédrale St-Pierre et St-Paul** was begun in 1434, but not completed until 1893. It is notable for its sculpted Gothic portals and Renaissance tomb of François II (1435–88), the last duke of Brittany.

The **Château des Ducs de Bretagne**, now with a museum documenting the town's history, was the birthplace of Anne of Brittany, who irrevocably joined her fiercely independent duchy to France by her successive marriages to Charles VIII and Louis XII. A smaller royal lodging lies to the west of it. It was here, in Brittany's Catholic bastion, that Henri IV signed the 1598 Edict of Nantes, which granted all Protestants freedom of worship.

The **Musée des Beaux-Arts** has a splendid array of paintings representing key movements from the 15th to the 20th century. Packed with mementos, books, and maps, the **Musée Jules Verne** is dedicated to the life and works of the famous writer (1828–1905).

🏛 **Musée des Beaux-Arts**
10 Rue Georges Clemenceau. **Tel** 02-51 17 45 00. **Closed** for restoration until 2016. 🛇 🔖 🖻 🖼

❿ Poitiers

Vienne. 🚈 85,000. ✈ 🚆 🚌 *i* 45 Place Charles de Gaulle (05-49 41 21 24). 🕓 Tue–Sun. 🅆 ot-poitiers.fr

Three of the greatest battles in French history were fought around Poitiers, the most famous in 732 when Charles Martel halted the Arab invasion. Today, the town is a dynamic regional capital with a rich architectural heritage.

Behind the Renaissance facade of the **Palais de Justice** is the 12th-century great hall of the palace of Henry II and Richard the Lionheart. This is thought to have been the scene of Joan of Arc's examination by a council of theologians in 1429.

Notre-Dame-la-Grande, whose west front is covered with superb 12th-century Poitevin sculpture, stands out among the city's churches, as does the 4th-century **Baptistère St-Jean**, one of the oldest Christian buildings in France. The latter contains Romanesque frescoes.

The **Musée Sainte-Croix** has archaeological exhibits, as well as paintings and sculpture.

Environs
Just 7 km (4.5 miles) north of Poitiers, **Futuroscope** is a theme park dedicated to state-of-the-art visual technology, including the largest cinema screen in Europe.

🏛 **Futuroscope**
Jaunay-Clan. **Tel** 05-49 49 11 12. **Open** check website. **Closed** Jan–mid-Feb. 🛇 🔖 🅆 futuroscope.com

The high-tech Kinémax cinema at Futuroscope, near Poitiers

⓫ Abbaye Royale de Fontevraud

Maine-et-Loire. 🚌 **Tel** 02-41 51 73 52. **Open** daily. **Closed** Jan, Nov–Feb: Mon, Dec 25. 🅿️ 📷 ♿ restricted. 🌐 abbaye-fontevraud.com

Fontevraud Royal Abbey, founded in 1101, was the largest of its kind in France. It now hosts concerts and exhibitions. The abbey's nuns lived around the Renaissance Grand Moûtier cloisters, and the leper colony's nurses were housed in the St-Lazare priory, now the abbey's hotel. Little remains of the monastic quarters, but the St-Benoît hospital survives. Most impressive is the octagonal kitchen in the Tour Evraud, a rare example of secular Romanesque architecture.

In the nave of the abbey church, the painted effigy of Henry Plantagenet (1133–1189), Count of Anjou and King of England, lies by those of his wife, Eleanor of Aquitaine, who died here in 1204, and their son, Richard the Lionheart (1157–1199).

⓬ Tours

Indre-et-Loire. 🚶 140,000. ✈️ 🚆 🚌 ℹ️ 78 Rue Bernard Palissy (02-47 70 37 37). 🛍️ Tue–Sun. 🌐 tours-tourisme.fr

The pleasant cathedral city of Tours is built on the site of a Roman town, and became an important center of Christianity in the 4th century under St. Martin. In 1461, Louis XI made the city the French capital. However, during Henri IV's reign, the city lost favor with the monarchy and the capital left Tours for Paris.

The medieval old town, Le Vieux Tours, is full of narrow streets lined with beautiful half-timbered houses. St. Martin's tomb lies in the crypt of the New Basilica, built on the site of the medieval Old Basilica. Two towers, the **Tour Charlemagne** and the **Tour de l'Horloge**, survive from the earlier building.

The foundation stone of the **Cathédrale St-Gatien** was laid in the early 13th century. Building work continued until the mid-16th century, and the cathedral provides an illustration of how the Gothic style developed over time. The Musée des Beaux Arts, housed in the nearby former archbishop's palace, overlooks beautiful gardens. The impressive collection features works by the likes of Rembrandt, Rubens, and Degas.

The **Château Royal de Tours**, a royal residence between the 13th and 15th centuries, houses modern art exhibitions and exhibits, which explain the history of Tours.

⓭ Château de Chenonceau

See pp178–9.

⓮ Blois

Loir-et-Cher. 🚶 60,000. 🚆 🚌 ℹ️ Place du Château (02-54 90 41 41). 🛍️ Sat.

A powerful feudal stronghold in the 12th century, Blois rose to glory under Louis XII, who established his court here in 1498. The town remained at the center of French royal and political life for much of the next century. Today, Blois is the quintessential Loire town. The partly pedestrianized old quarter is full of romantic courtyards and fine mansions. Home to kings Louis XII,

François I's staircase, Château de Blois

François I, and Henri III, **Château de Blois** has the most sensational history of all the Loire Châteaux. It was here, in 1588, that the ambitious Duc de Guise, leader of the Catholic Holy League, was murdered on the orders of Henri III. The building itself juxtaposes four distinct architectural styles, reflecting its varied history.

Among Blois' most impressive religious monuments are the beautiful three-spired **Eglise St-Nicolas**, formerly part of a 12th-century Benedictine abbey, and the **Cathédrale St-Louis**, which dominates the eastern half of the city. The cathedral is a 17th-century reconstruction of a Gothic church that was almost destroyed in 1678.

🏰 **Château de Blois**
Place du Château. **Tel** 02-54 90 33 33. **Open** daily. **Closed** Jan 1, Dec 25. 🅿️ 📷

The historic town of Blois, viewed from across the Loire

⑱ Château de Chenonceau

Chenonceau, stretching romantically across the Cher River, is considered by many to be the loveliest of the Loire châteaux. Surrounded by elegant formal gardens and wooded grounds, this pure Renaissance building began life as a modest manor and water mill. Over the centuries, it was transformed by the wives and mistresses of its successive owners into a palace designed solely for pleasure. On July and August evenings, the *Promenade Nocturne* allows visitors to stroll about the gardens accompanied by classical music.

Chambre de Catherine de' Medici
Henri II's wife, Catherine, made her own mark on Chenonceau's design with this sumptuous bedchamber.

Formal Gardens
The current designs of the formal gardens, created by Diane de Poitiers and Catherine de' Medici, date from the 19th century.

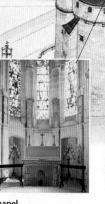

Chapel
The chapel has a vaulted ceiling and sculpted pilasters. The stained glass, destroyed by a bomb in 1944, was replaced in 1953.

Grande Galerie
The elegant gallery is Florentine in style. It was created by Catherine de' Medici in 1570–76 as an addition to the bridge built for Diane de Poitiers.

KEY

① **The Tour des Marques** survives from the 15th-century castle of the Marques family.

② **The Cabinet Vert** was originally covered with green velvet.

③ **Louise de Lorraine's room** was painted black and decorated with monograms, tears, and knots in white after the assassination of her husband, Henri III.

④ **The arched bridge** over the Cher was designed by Philibert de l'Orme in 1559 for Diane de Poitiers. It was built on the site of the old water mill.

Château de Chambord, on the banks of the Closson

⑮ Château de Chambord

Loir-et-Cher. to Blois, then taxi or
bus. **Tel** 02-54 50 40 00. **Open** daily.
Closed Jan 1, Feb 4, Dec 25.

The brainchild of the extravagant
François I, the château began as
a hunting lodge in the Forêt de
Boulogne. In 1519, the original
building was razed and
Chambord begun, to a design
probably initiated by Leonardo
da Vinci. By 1537, the keep, with
its towers and terraces, had been
completed by 1,800 men and
three master masons. The
following year, François I began
building a private royal pavilion
on the northeast corner, with a
connecting two-story gallery. His
son, Henri II, continued the west
wing with the chapel, and Louis
XIV completed the 440-roomed
edifice in 1685.

The innovative double-helix
Grand Staircase was supposedly
designed by Leonardo da Vinci.
The two flights of stairs ensure
that the person going up
and the person going down
cannot meet.

⑯ Orléans

Loiret. 113,000.
2 Place de l'Étape (02-38 24 05 05).
Tue–Sun. Fête Jeanne d'Arc (Apr
29–May 9). **tourisme-orleans.com**

Orléans was the capital of
medieval France, and it was
here that Joan of Arc battled
the English in 1429, during the

Hundred Years' War. Later
captured by the enemy and
accused of witchcraft, she was
burned at the stake in Rouen
at the age of 19. Since her
martyrdom, Joan has become a
pervasive presence in Orléans.

A faded grandeur lingers in
Vieil Orléans, the old quarter,
bounded by the imposing
Cathédrale Sainte-Croix, the
Loire, and the Place du Martroi.
The **Maison de Jeanne d'Arc**
was rebuilt in 1961 on the site
where Joan lodged in 1429.
Inside, audiovisual exhibits and
a short film recreate her life.

A selection of European
art from the 16th to the early
20th century is on display at the
Musée des Beaux-Arts.

Maison de Jeanne d'Arc
3 Place du Général de Gaulle. **Tel**
02-38 68 32 63. **Open** Tue–Sun (Oct–
Mar: pm only). **Closed** public hols.

The lofty interior of the Cathédrale
Sainte-Croix, Orléans

Diane de Poitiers

Diane de Poitiers was Henry II's
lifelong mistress, holding court
as queen of France in all but
name. Her beauty inspired
many French artists, who
often depicted her in the
role of Diana, the Classical
goddess of the hunt.

In 1547, Henry offered the
Château de Chenonceau to
Diane, who improved the
palace by creating stunning
formal gardens and an arched
bridge over the Cher River.

After Henry's accidental
death in 1559, Diane was
forced to leave Chenonceau
by his widow, Catherine de'
Medici, in exchange for the
fortress-like Château de
Chaumont. Diane retired to
Anet, and remained there
until her death in 1566.

⑰ Chartres Cathedral

According to art historian Emile Male, "Chartres is the mind of the Middle Ages manifest." Begun in 1020, the Romanesque cathedral was destroyed by a devastating fire in 1194. Only the north and south towers, south steeple, west portal, and crypt remained. Inside, the sacred *Veil of the Virgin* relic was the sole treasure to survive. Peasant and lord alike labored to rebuild the church in just 25 years. Few alterations were made after 1250 and, fortunately, Chartres was left unscathed by the Wars of Religion and the French Revolution. The result is an authentic Gothic cathedral with a true "Bible in stone and glass" reputation.

Elongated Statues
These statues on the Royal Portal represent Old Testament figures.

Gothic Nave
As wide as the Romanesque crypt below it – the largest in France – the Gothic nave reaches a lofty height of 37 m (121 ft).

KEY

① **The taller of the two spires** dates from the start of the 16th century. Flamboyant and Gothic in style, it contrasts sharply with the solemnity and relative simplicity of its Romanesque counterpart.

② **The stained-glass windows** on the west front, are 12th-century lancet windows. They are celebrated for their rare blue color, and are among the oldest of their kind in the world.

③ **The Royal Portal** (1145–55) and part of the west front survive from the original Romanesque church. The central tympanum has a carving of *Christ in Majesty.*

④ **The Labyrinth** is inlaid in the nave floor. Pilgrims used to follow the tortuous route by crawling on their knees, echoing the Way of the Cross.

⑤ **The vaulted ceiling** is supported by a network of ribs.

⑥ **The St. Piat Chapel** was built between 1324 and 1353.

Chartres' Stained Glass

More than 150 stained-glass windows in the cathedral illustrate biblical stories and daily life in the 13th century (bring binoculars if you can). During both World Wars, the windows were dismantled piece by piece and removed for safety. Some windows were restored and releaded in the 1970s, and in 2006 further restoration work commenced. Each window is divided into panels, which are usually read from left to right, bottom to top (earth to heaven). The number of figures or abstract shapes used is symbolic: three stands for the Church; squares and the number four symbolize the material world or the four elements; circles represent eternal life.

VISITORS' CHECKLIST

Practical Information
Place de la Cathédrale, Chartres, Eure-et-Loir. **Tel** 02-37 21 75 02.
Open 8:30am– 7:30pm daily.
🕐 11:45am (in the crypt) & 6pm Mon–Sat (9am Tue, Fri); 9:15 (Latin) & 11am Sun. ♿ 📷
🌐 **cathedrale-chartres.org**

Transport
🚌 🚃 from Paris.

Our Lady of the Pillar
Carved from dark pear wood, this 16th-century replica of a 13th-century statue is a striking shrine that is often surrounded by candles.

South Rose Window
The cathedral has three massive rose windows. The one on the south front (c.1225) illustrates the *Apocalypse*, with *Christ in Majesty*.

★ South Porch
Sculpture on the massive South Porch (1197–1209) reflects a selection of New Testament teaching.

Burgundy and the French Alps

Burgundy is France's richest province, historically, culturally, and gastronomically. The region's fine wines have inspired awe for centuries, and every year the historic town of Beaune hosts one of the most famous wine auctions in the world. Dijon is a splendid city, filled with the great palaces of the old Burgundian nobility. The majestic French Alps attract visitors for winter sports, and, in summer, walking and a host of watersports on the glittering mountain lakes.

Tympanum sculpture showing Christ and the apostles at Basilique Ste-Madeleine, Vézelay

⑱ Vézelay

Yonne. 🗺 400. 🚌 Basilique Ste-Madeleine: **Tel** 03-86 33 39 50. 🚉 Sermizelles, then bus. **Open** daily. 🎁

Tourists come to Vézelay to visit the picturesque **Basilique Ste-Madeleine**. In the 12th century, at the height of its glory, the abbey claimed to house the relics of Mary Magdalene, and it was a starting point for the pilgrimage to Santiago de Compostela in Spain *(see p292)*.

The star attractions of the Romanesque church are the tympanum sculpture (1120–35) above the central doorway, the exquisitely carved capitals in the nave and narthex, and the immense Gothic choir.

⑲ Dijon

See pp184–5.

⑳ Beaune

Côte D'Or. 🗺 23,000. 🚉 🚌 *i* Boulevard Pepreuil (03-80 26 21 30). 🎵 Baroque Music (Jul).

The indisputable highlight of the old center of Beaune is the **Hôtel-Dieu**. The hospice was founded in 1443 for the town's inhabitants, many of whom were left poverty-stricken

after the Hundred Years' War. Today, it is considered a medieval jewel, with its superb multicolored Burgundian roof tiles. It houses many treasures, including the religious masterpiece the *Last Judgement* polyptych, by Rogier van der Weyden.

The Hôtel des Ducs de Bourgogne, built in the 14th–16th centuries, houses the **Musée du Vin de Bourgogne**, with displays of traditional winemaking equipment.

Further to the north is the 12th-century Romanesque church the **Collégiale Notre-Dame**, which has a collection of fine 15th-century tapestries.

🏛 **Hôtel-Dieu**
Rue de l'Hôtel-Dieu. **Tel** 03-80 24 45 00. **Open** daily. **Closed** Dec–Mar: 11:30am–2pm daily. 🚭 🎁 ♿

㉑ Lyon

Rhône. 🗺 453,000. ✈ 25 km (16 miles) E. 🚉 🚌 *i* Place Bellecour (04-72 77 69 69). 🛥 daily. 🌐 lyon-france.com

Dramatically situated on the banks of the Rhône and Saône rivers, Lyon has been a vital gateway between the north and south since ancient times. Vieux Lyon, the oldest part of the city, is the site of the Roman settlement of Lugdunum, the commercial and military capital of Gau, I founded by Julius Caesar in 44 BC. Vestiges of this prosperous city can be seen in the superb **Musée de la Civilisation Gallo-Romaine**. There are also two excavated Roman amphitheaters: the **Grand Théâtre**, built in 15 BC to seat 30,000 spectators, and the smaller **Odéon**.

Other major sights are the 19th-century mock-Byzantine **Basilique Notre-Dame de Fourvière**, and the **Cathédrale St-Jean**, begun in the 12th century. Vieux Lyon's fine Renaissance mansions are the former homes of bankers and silk merchants.

The Dukes of Burgundy

In the 14th and 15th centuries, the dukes of Burgundy built up one of the most powerful states in Europe, which included Flanders and parts of Holland. From the time of Philip the Bold (1342–1404), the ducal court became a center of art, chivalry, and immense wealth. The duchy's demise came with the death of Charles the Bold in 1477.

Tomb of Philip the Bold in Dijon's Musée des Beaux Arts *(see p184)*

Cathédrale St-Jean, at the foot of the slopes of Vieux Lyon

The excellent **Musée des Beaux Arts** showcases the country's largest and most important collection of fine arts after the Louvre. The modern works, dating from after the mid-1900s, have found a new home in the **Musée d'Art Contemporain** in the north of the city. An exquisite display of silks and tapestries, some dating back to early Christian times, can be seen in the **Musée des Tissus**.

🏛 **Musée de la Civilisation Gallo-Romaine**
17 Rue Cléberg. **Tel** 04-72 38 49 30. **Open** Tue–Sun. **Closed** public hols. ♿

㉒ Annecy

Annecy. 🏔 51,000. 🚂 🚌 ℹ 1 Rue Jean Jaurès (04-50 45 00 33). 🕐 Tue, Fri–Sun. 🌐 **lac-annecy.com**

Annecy is one of the most beautiful towns in the Alps, set at the northern tip of Lac d'Annecy and surrounded by snowcapped mountains.

A stroll around the town's small medieval quarter, with its canals, flower-covered bridges, and arcaded streets, is one of the main attractions of a stay here. Look out for the formidable **Palais de l'Isle**, a 12th-century prison in the middle of the Thiou canal.

The turreted **Château d'Annecy**, perched high on a hill, affords fine panoramic views. The clear waters of the lake are perfect for swimming and watersports. Boat trips leave from the Quai Thiou.

Environs
One way to enjoy the area's spectacular scenery is to take a boat to **Talloires**, a tiny lakeside village noted for its hotels and restaurants.

Annecy's 12th-century Palais de l'Isle, on the Thiou canal

㉓ Grenoble

Isère. 🏔 165,000. ✈ 🚂 🚌 ℹ 14 Rue de la République (04-76 42 41 41). 🕐 Tue–Sun.

Ancient capital of Dauphiné, Grenoble is a busy and thriving city, attractively located at the confluence of the Drac and Isère rivers, in the shadow of the mighty Vercors and Chartreuse massifs.

A cable car from the Quai Stéphane-Jay, on the north bank of the Isère, takes you up to the 16th-century **Fort de la Bastille**, where you are rewarded with magnificent views of the city and surrounding mountains. From here, paths lead down through pretty gardens to the excellent **Musée Dauphinois** at the foot of the hill. Housed in a 17th-century convent, the museum contains displays on local history, arts, and crafts.

On the other side of the river, the focus of life is the Place Grenette, a lively square lined with sidewalk cafés. Nearby, the Place St-André is the heart of the medieval city, overlooked by Grenoble's oldest buildings, including the 13th-century **Eglise St-André** and the 15th-century **Palais de Justice**.

Also worth visiting is the **Musée de Grenoble**, the city's principal art museum. With works by Chagall, Picasso, and Matisse, the modern collection is especially good.

🏛 **Musée de Grenoble**
5 Place de Lavalette. **Tel** 04-76 63 44 44. **Open** Wed–Mon. **Closed** Jan 1, May 1, Dec 25. ♿

⓳ Street by Street: Dijon

The center of Dijon is noted for its architectural splendor – a legacy from the dukes of Burgundy (see p182). Wealthy parliament members also had elegant *hôtels particuliers* (private mansions) built in the 17th and 18th centuries. The capital of Burgundy, Dijon today has a rich cultural life and a renowned university. The city's great art treasures are housed in the Palais des Ducs. Dijon is also famous for its mustard and *pain d'épice* (gingerbread), a reminder of the town's position on the medieval spice route. A major railroad hub during the 19th century, it now has a TGV link to Paris.

Hôtel de Voguë
This elegant 17th-century mansion is decorated with Burgundian cabbages and fruit garlands by Hugues Sambin.

★ **Notre-Dame**
This magnificent 13th-century Gothic church is best known for its many gargoyles, the Jacquemart clock, and, on the north wall, the sculpted owl (*chouette*), said to bring good luck when touched.

Train and bus stations

RUE ODEBERT

RUE QUENTIN

RUE DE LA PREFECTURE

RUE MUSETTE

RUE DES FORGES

RUE DE LA LIBERTE

RUE DU BOURG

RUE J MERCIER

R VAUBAN

PL DE LA LIBERATION

Musée des Beaux Arts
The collection of Flemish masters here includes this 14th-century triptych by Jacques de Baerze and Melchior Broederlam.

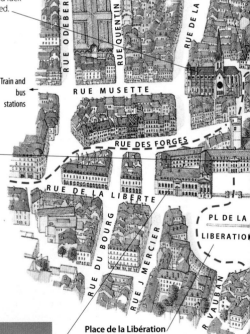

Place de la Libération
was created by Mansart in the 17th century.

★ **Palais des Ducs**
The dukes of Burgundy held court here, but the building seen today was mainly built in the 17th century for the parliament. It now houses the Musée des Beaux Arts.

Rue Verrerie
This cobbled street in the old merchants' quarter is lined with medieval half-timbered houses. Some, such as Nos. 8, 10, and 12, have fine wood carvings.

VISITORS' CHECKLIST

Practical Information
Côte d'Or. ⚑ 153,000.
ℹ 11 rue des Forges (08-92 70
05 58). ⊟ Tue, Fri, Sat. ⚘ Festival
de Musique (Jun); Fêtes de la
Vigne (Sep in odd-numbered
years). Musée des Beaux Arts: **Tel**
03-80 74 52 09. **Open** Wed–Mon.
Closed main public hols. ♿ ♿
Musée Magnin: **Tel** 03-80 67 11
10. **Open** Tue–Sun. **Closed** some
public hols. ♿ ♿ limited.

Transport
✈ 5 km (3 miles) SSE. 🚉
🚌 Cours de la Gare.

★ St-Michel
Begun in the 15th century and completed in the 17th century, St-Michel's facade combines Flamboyant Gothic with Renaissance details. On the richly carved porch, angels and biblical motifs mingle with mythological themes.

Musée Magnin
A collection of French and foreign 16th–19th-century paintings is displayed among period furniture in this 17th-century mansion.

The Eglise St-Etienne dates from the 11th century, but has been rebuilt many times. Its characteristic lantern was added in 1686.

0 meters 100
0 yards 100

Key
— Suggested route

The Wines of France

Winemaking in France dates back to pre-Roman times, although it was the Romans who disseminated the culture of the vine and the practise of wine-making throughout the country. The range, quality, and reputation of the fine wines of Bordeaux, Burgundy, and Champagne in particular have made them role models the world over. France's everyday wines can be highly enjoyable too, with plenty of good-value IGP *(Indication Géographique Protegée)* and *vins de France* now emerging from the southern regions. Many wine producers offer tours and have their own tasting rooms, where visitors can try a selection of wines without feeling pressurized to buy.

Château Cos d'Estournel, in the Bordeaux region, produces a rich and fruity Cabernet Sauvignon. The grandeur of its exotic design is typical of château architecture.

The Wine Regions of France

Each of the 10 main wine-producing regions has its own identity, based on grape varieties, climate, soil, and local culture. Around 40 percent of all French wines are included in the AOP (Appellation d'Origine Protégée) system, which guarantees their style and geographic origin, though not their quality.

Bordeaux Wines

Bordeaux is the world's largest fine wine region, and, for its red wines, certainly the most familiar outside France. The great wine-producing areas lie close to the banks of the Gironde, Garonne, and Dordogne rivers. Along with these, the river port of Bordeaux itself have been crucial to the region's wine trade; some of the prettiest châteaux line the river banks, enabling easy transportation. Grape varieties used include Cabernet Sauvignon, Merlot, and Petit Verdot (red); Sémillon and Sauvignon Blanc (white).

Château Pitray　**Château Thieuley**

How to Read a Wine Label

Even the simplest label will provide a key to the wine's flavor and quality. It will bear the name of the wine and its producer, its vintage (if there is one), and whether it comes from a strictly defined area *(Appellation d'Origine Protégée)* or is a more general IGP or *vin de France*. It may also have a regional grading, as with the *crus classés* in Bordeaux. The shape and color of the bottle is also a guide. Most good-quality wine is bottled in green glass, which helps to protect it from light.

The property or producer

Château-bottled, rather than a wine from a grower's cooperative or a merchant

Capacity of the bottle

The vintage, from the French word *vendange*, or harvest

The wine's *Appellation d'Origine Protégée*

Burgundy Wines

The tiny vineyards in each of Burgundy's wine-producing regions, from Chablis in the north to Beaujolais in the south, can produce wines that, at their best, are unequalled anywhere else. This is unmissable territory for the "serious" wine-lover, with its time-honored traditions and dazzling *grands crus*. Grape varieties used include Pinot Noir, Gamay, and César (red); Pinot Blanc and Chardonnay (white).

Domaine François Raveneau

Domaine Michel Lafarge

Tours of Major Wineries

Winemakers are usually happy to welcome tourists in summer, but try not to visit at harvest time (Sep–Oct), and be sure to make an appointment in advance.

Bordeaux
Château Figeac
Saint Emilion. **Tel** *05-57 24 72 26.*
W **chateau-figeac.com**

Château Haut-Brion
Pessac. **Tel** *05-56 00 29 30.*
W **haut-brion.com**

Château Margaux
Margaux. **Tel** *05-57 88 83 83.*
W **chateau-margaux.com**

Château Lafite Rothschild
Pauillac. **Tel** *05-56 73 18 18.*
W **lafite.com**

Burgundy
Domaine Brocard
Préhy, near Chablis. **Tel** *03-86 41 49 00.* W **brocard.fr**

Hameau Duboeuf
Romanèche-Thorins.
Tel *03-85 35 22 22.*
W **hameauduboeuf.com**

Maison Louis Latour
Beaune. **Tel** *03-80 24 81 00.*
W **louislatour.com**

Champagne
Moët & Chandon
Epernay. **Tel** *03-26 51 20 00.*
W **moet.com**

Piper Heidsieck
Reims. **Tel** *03-26 84 43 00.*
W **piper-heidsieck.com**

Tattinger
Reims. **Tel** *03-26 85 84 33.*
W **tattinger.com**

Reims
Épernay
A4
N71
NANCY
Metz
STRASBOURG
Chablis
A31
Mulhouse
Dijon
A36
Beaune
Meursault
Mâcon
A40
A6
Loire
LYON
A448
A43
ermont-
rrand
Etienne
GRENOBLE
N85
Rhône
Nîmes
A9
A8
NICE
Montpellier
MARSEILLE
ignan

Champagne is a region that is synonymous with the finest sparkling wines. The skill of the blenders, using reserves of older wines, creates consistency and excellence year on year. Champagne bubbles are produced by fermenting yeast inside the bottle – traditional methods are still used all over the region. In a process called *remuage*, bottles are gradually rotated in order to loosen the sediment, which is ultimately removed from the wine.

Key

▢ Alsace and Lorraine
▢ Bordeaux
▢ Burgundy
▢ Champagne
▣ Jura and Savoie
▢ Languedoc-Roussillon
▢ The Loire Valley
▢ Provence
▢ The Rhône Valley
▢ Southwest France

Chardonnay vines in the *grand cru* vineyard of Corton-Charlemagne produce some of the greatest white Burgundies of all. The Chardonnay grape is now cultivated not only in Burgundy and Champagne, but all over the world.

Southwest France

The southwest is farming France, a green and peaceful land where crops from sunflowers to walnuts thrive. Other key country products include forest timber, Bordeaux wines, and wild mushrooms. Major modern industries, including aerospace, are focused on the two chief cities, Bordeaux and Toulouse. Visitors are mainly drawn to the wine chateaux, the ski slopes of the Pyrenees, and the prehistoric caves of the Dordogne. The major sights of this favored region include some of France's most celebrated Romanesque buildings.

Monument aux Girondins, Place des Quinconces, Bordeaux

㉔ Bordeaux

Gironde. 220,000. ✈ 🚉 🚌
ℹ 12 Cours du 30 Juillet (05-56 00 66 00). 🛒 daily. 🎵 Fête du Vin (Jun, in even-numbered years). 🌐 bordeaux-tourisme.com

Built on a curve of the Garonne River, Bordeaux has been a major port since pre-Roman times and a focus and crossroads of European trade for centuries. The export of wine has always been the basis of the city's prosperity, and today the Bordeaux region produces more than 70 million cases of wine per year.

Along the waterfront, a long sweep of Classical facades is broken by the Esplanade des Quinconces, with its statues and fountains. At one end, the Monument aux Girondins (1804–1902) commemorates the Girondists sent to the guillotine by Robespierre during the Terror

(1793–5). Buildings of architectural interest include the massive **Basilique St-Michel**, begun in 1350, which took 200 years to complete, and the 18th-century **Grand Théâtre**, a magnificent example of the French Neoclassical style. The **Musée des Beaux Arts** holds an excellent collection of paintings, ranging from the Renaissance to our time.

🏛 **Musée des Beaux Arts**
20 Cours d'Albret. **Tel** 05-56 10 20 56.
Open Wed–Mon. **Closed** public hols.
🌐

Environs
The tourist office in Bordeaux organizes tours to various wine châteaux *(see pp186–7)*.

㉕ Lascaux

Montignac. **Tel** 05-53 51 95 03. **Open** mid-Feb–Mar & Nov–Dec: Tue–Sun; Easter–Oct: daily. **Closed** Jan–mid-Feb, Dec 25. 🌐 **semitour.com**

Lascaux is the most famous of the prehistoric sites in the Dordogne region. Four young boys and their dog came across

the caves and their astounding Palaeolithic paintings in 1940, and the importance of their discovery was swiftly recognized.

Lascaux has been closed to the public since 1963 because of deterioration due to carbon dioxide caused by breathing. An exact copy, Lascaux II, has been created a few minutes' walk down the hillside, using the same materials. The replica is beautiful and should not be spurned: high-antlered elk, bison, and plump horses cover the walls, moving in herds or files, surrounded by arrows and geometric symbols thought to have had ritual significance.

㉖ Toulouse

Haute-Garonne. 390,000. ✈ 🚉
🚌 ℹ Donjon du Capitole (08-92 18 01 80). 🛒 Tue–Sun. 🎵 Piano (Sep), Contemporary dance (end Jan–early Feb). 🌐 **toulouse-tourisme.com**

Toulouse, the most important town in southwest France, is the country's fourth-largest metropolis, and a major industrial and university city.

The area is also famous for its aerospace industry; Concorde, Airbus, and the Ariane space rocket all originated here. Airbus tours can be booked at www. taxiway.fr. **Cité de l'Espace** has a planetarium and interactive exhibits on space exploration.

The church known as **Les Jacobins** was begun in 1229 and took more over two centuries to finish. The Gothic masterpiece features a soaring, 22-branched palm tree vault in the apse. The

Palm vaulting in the apse of Les Jacobins, Toulouse

For hotels and restaurants see pp206–8 and pp209–11

A picturesque village set among the foothills of the Pyrenees mountains

bell tower (1294) is much imitated in southwest France. Toulouse became a center of Romanesque art in Europe due to its position on the route to Santiago de Compostela (see p292). The largest Romanesque basilica in Europe, the **Basilique de St-Sernin**, was built in the 11th–12th centuries to accommodate pilgrims. The **Musée des Augustins** has sculptures from the period, and incorporates cloisters from a 14th-century Augustinian priory. Also featured are French, Italian, and Flemish paintings.

The 16th-century palace known as the **Hôtel d'Assézat** now houses the Fondation Bemberg, named after local art-lover Georges Bemberg, with Renaissance art and 19th- and 20th-century French work.

🏛 Musée des Augustins
21 Rue de Metz. **Tel** 05-61 22 21 82.
Open daily. **Closed** Jan 1, May 1,
Dec 25. 🅿 📷 🏪 ♿ 🖥 **augustins.org**

❷ Pyrenees

✈ Pau. 🚌 🚏 Bayonne & Pau.
ℹ Place des Basques, Bayonne
(08-20 42 64 64); Place Royale,
Pau (05-59 27 27 08).

The mountains dominate life in the French Pyrenees. A region in many ways closer to Spain than France, over the centuries its remote terrain and tenacious people have given heretics a hiding place and refugees an escape route.

The **Parc National des Pyrénées** extends 100 km (62 miles) along the French–Spanish frontier. It boasts some of the most splendid alpine scenery in Europe, and is rich in flora and fauna. Within the park are 350 km (217 miles) of footpaths.

The region's oldest inhabitants, the Basque people, have maintained their own language and culture. **Bayonne**, on the Atlantic coast, is the capital of French Basque country, and has been an important town since Roman times. **Biarritz**, west of Bayonne, has two casinos and three good beaches, with the best surfing in Europe. A short distance south, **St-Jean-de-Luz** is a sleepy fishing village that explodes into life in summer. A main attraction is the Eglise St-Jean Baptiste, where Louis XIV married the Infanta Maria Teresa of Spain in 1660.

A lively university town with elegant architecture, **Pau** is the most interesting large town in the central Pyrenees. It has long been a favorite resort of affluent foreigners.

Other places of interest include the many mountain ski resorts, the shrine at **Lourdes**, and the pretty hilltop town of **St-Bertrand-de-Comminges**.

The Miracle of Lourdes

In 1858, a 14-year-old girl named Bernadette Soubirous experienced 18 visions of the Virgin at the Grotte Massabielle near the town of Lourdes. Despite being told to keep away from the cave by her mother – and the local magistrate – she was guided to a spring with miraculous healing powers. The church endorsed the miracles in the 1860s, and since then many people claim to have been cured by the holy water. A huge city of shrines, churches, and hospices has since grown up around the spring, with a dynamic tourist industry to match.

Pilgrims at an open-air mass in Lourdes

The South of France

The south is France's most popular holiday region, drawing millions of visitors each year to the resorts of the Riviera and the Côte d'Azur, and to the vivid landscape and historic villages of Provence. Painters such as Cézanne, van Gogh, and Picasso have been inspired by the luminous light and brilliant colors of the region. Agriculture is still a mainstay of the economy, but the high-tech industries of Nice also make a significant contribution to the region's prosperity.

Château Comtal, in the restored citadel of Carcassonne

㉘ Carcassonne

Aude. 🏛 46,000. 🚉 🚌 ✈ 🛈 28 Rue de Verdun (04-68 10 24 30). 🗓 Tue, Thu & Sat. 🎭 Festival de la Cité (mid-Jun–Jul), Medieval fête (Oct). **W** tourisme-carcassonne.fr

The citadel of Carcassonne is a perfectly restored medieval town. It crowns a steep bank above the Aude River, a fairy-tale vision of turrets and ramparts overlooking the Basse Ville below.

The strategic position of the citadel between the Atlantic and the Mediterranean led to its original settlement, consolidated by the Romans in the 2nd century BC.

At its zenith in the 12th century, the town was ruled by the Trencavels, who built the château and cathedral. The Cathars, a persecuted Christian sect, were given sanctuary here in 1209 but, after a two-week siege, the town fell to the Crusaders sent to eradicate them. The attentions of architectural historian Viollet-le-Duc led to Carcassonne's restoration in the 19th century.

Flanked by sandstone towers, the defenses of the **Porte Narbonnaise** included two portcullises, two iron doors, a moat, and a drawbridge. A fortress within a fortress, the **Château Comtal** has a surrounding moat and five defensive towers.

Within the Romanesque and Gothic **Basilique St-Nazaire** is the famous Siege Stone, inscribed with scenes said to depict the siege of 1209.

㉙ Nîmes

Gard. 🏛 145,000. ✈ 🚉 🚌 🛈 6 Rue Auguste (04-66 58 38 00). 🗓 daily. **W** ot-nimes.fr

An important crossroads in the ancient world, Nîmes is well known for its bullfights and Roman antiquities. The city has had a turbulent history, and suffered particularly in the 16th-century Wars of Religion, when the Romanesque **Cathédrale Notre-Dame et St-Castor** was badly damaged. In the 17th and 18th centuries, the town prospered from textile manufacturing, one of the most enduring products being denim, or *serge de Nîmes*.

All roads in the city lead to the amphitheater, **Les Arènes**. Built at the end of the 1st century AD, it is still in use today as a venue for concerts, sporting events, and bullfights.

The **Maison Carrée** is an elegant Roman temple, the pride of Nîmes. Built by Augustus' son-in-law Marcus Agrippa, it is one of the best preserved in the world, with finely fluted Corinthian columns and a sculpted frieze.

Set in the Roman wall is the **Porte d'Auguste**, a gateway built for travelers on the Domitian Way, which passed through the center of Nîmes. Nearby is the **Castellum**, a tower used for storing water brought in by aqueduct. The water was distributed around the town by a canal system. A display of Roman statues and mosaics can be seen at the **Musée Archéologique**.

Five floors of Nîmes' controversial arts complex, the **Carré d'Art**, which stands opposite the Maison Carrée, lie underground. The complex incorporates a library, a roof-terrace restaurant around a huge glass atrium, and the Musée d'Art Contemporain.

🏛 **Musée Archéologique**
13 bis Boulevard Amiral Courbet.
Tel 04-66 76 74 80. **Open** Tue–Sun.
Closed Jan 1, May 1, Nov 1, Dec 25.

Environs
To the northeast of the city lies the **Pont du Gard**, a 2,000-year-old aqueduct. The Romans considered this to be the best testimony to the greatness of their empire, and at 49 m (160 ft) it was the highest bridge they ever built.

The Pont du Gard, outside Nîmes, a major feat of Roman engineering

㉚ Avignon

Vaucluse. 🗺 100,000. ✈ 🚍 🚃
ℹ️ 41 Cours Jean Jaurès (04-32 74
32 74). 🏛 Tue–Sun. 🎭 Le Festival
d'Avignon (Jul). 🅦 **avignon-
tourisme.com**

Massive ramparts enclose
this fascinating town. The
huge **Palais des Papes** is
the dominant feature, but
Avignon contains other riches.
To the north of the Palais is the
13th-century **Musée du Petit
Palais**, once the Archbishop
of Avignon's residence. It has
received such notorious guests
as Cesare Borgia and Louis XIV.
Now a museum, it displays
Romanesque and Gothic
sculpture and paintings of
the Avignon and Italian
schools, with works by
Botticelli and Carpaccio.

Avignon boasts some fine
churches, such as the
12th-century **Cathédrale**

Open-air performance at the annual
Avignon Festival

de Notre-Dame-des-Doms,
with its Romanesque cupola
and papal tombs, and the
14th-century **Eglise St-Didier**.

The **Musée Lapidaire**
contains statues, mosaics, and
carvings from pre-Roman
Provence. The **Musée Calvet**
features a superb array of
exhibits, including Roman finds.
It also gives an overview of
French art during the past 500
years, with works by Rodin,
Manet, and Dufy. The Place de

l'Horloge is the center of
Avignon's social life. Under the
town hall's Gothic clock tower
stands a merry-go-round from
1900. Until the 19th century,
brightly patterned calicoes
called *indiennes* were printed
nearby. These inspired today's
Provençal patterns.

From early July for three
weeks, the Avignon Festival
takes place at the Palais des
Papes. France's largest festival,
it includes ballet, drama, and
classical concerts. The "Off"
festival has street theater and
music from folk to jazz.

The **Pont St-Bénézet**, built
from 1171–1185, once had
22 arches, but most were destroyed by floods in 1668. One
of the remaining arches bears
the tiny Chapelle St-Nicolas.

🏠 **Palais des Papes**
Place du Palais-des-Papes. **Tel** 04-32
74 32 74. **Open** daily. 🔲 📷

Palais des Papes

*Pope Clement V moved the papal court to Avignon in
1309. Here it remained until 1377, during which time his
successors transformed the modest episcopal building
into the present magnificent palace.*

The Consistory Hall
contains frescoes
(1340) by Simone
Martini.

Grand Tinel
This vast banqueting hall was used for
celebrating religious festivals.

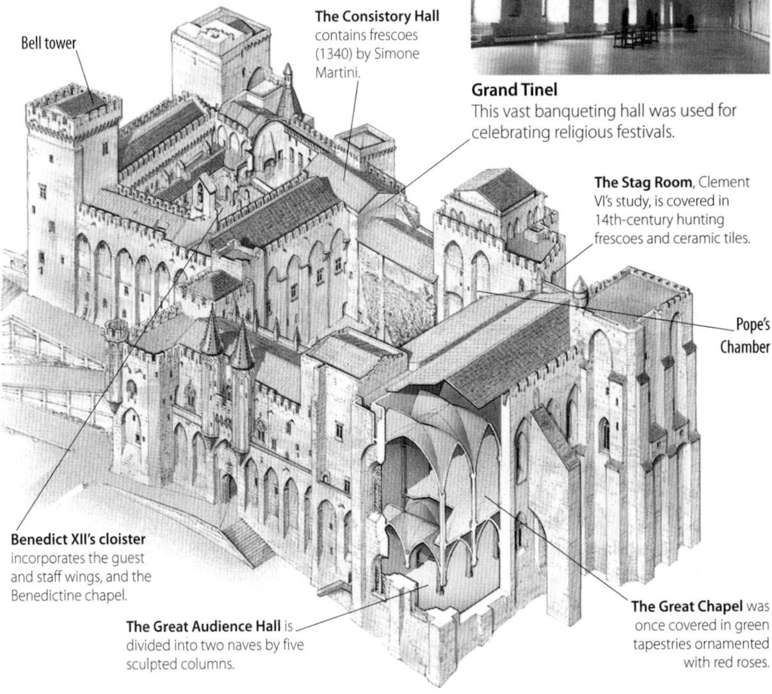

Bell tower

The Stag Room, Clement
VI's study, is covered in
14th-century hunting
frescoes and ceramic tiles.

Pope's
Chamber

Benedict XII's cloister
incorporates the guest
and staff wings, and the
Benedictine chapel.

The Great Audience Hall is
divided into two naves by five
sculpted columns.

The Great Chapel was
once covered in green
tapestries ornamented
with red roses.

③ Street by Street: Arles

Few other towns in Provence combine the region's many charms as well as Arles. Its position on the Rhône makes it a natural gateway to the Camargue (see p195). Its Roman remains, such as Constantine's baths and the amphitheater, are complemented by the ocher walls and Roman-tiled roofs of later buildings. Van Gogh spent time here in 1888–9, but Arles is no longer the industrial town he painted. Visitors are now its main business, and entertainment ranges from the Arles Festival to bullfights. A bastion of Provençal tradition and culture, its museums are among the best in the region. For enthusiasts, an inclusive ticket is available giving access to all museums and monuments. All the tourist sites in Arles are within walking distance of the central Place de la République.

The Musée Réattu houses 18th-century and modern art, including Picasso sketches, paintings by local artist Jacques Réattu (1760–1833), sculptures by Russian-born Ossip Zadkine (1890–1967), and photography.

View of Arles from the opposite bank of the Rhône

The Palais Constantine was once a grand imperial palace. Now only its vast Roman baths remain, dating from the 4th century AD.

RUE DU
RUE TRUCHET
RUE DE L'HOTEL DE VILLE
RUE
RU
RUE DU DR FANTON
PLACE DU
FORUM
RUE MISTRAL
RUE BAIZE
RUE DE LA REPUBLIQUE
PLAZA DE LA REPUBLIQUE
RUE JEAN JAURÈS
RUE MOLIERE
RUE DE LA ROTONDE
BOULEVARD GEORGES CLEMENCEAU

The Museon Arlaten was founded in 1904 by the Provençal poet Frédéric Mistral with his Nobel Prize money. It is currently closed for renovations, and due to reopen in 2016.

The Hôtel de Ville, the town hall, has an impressive vaulted ceiling.

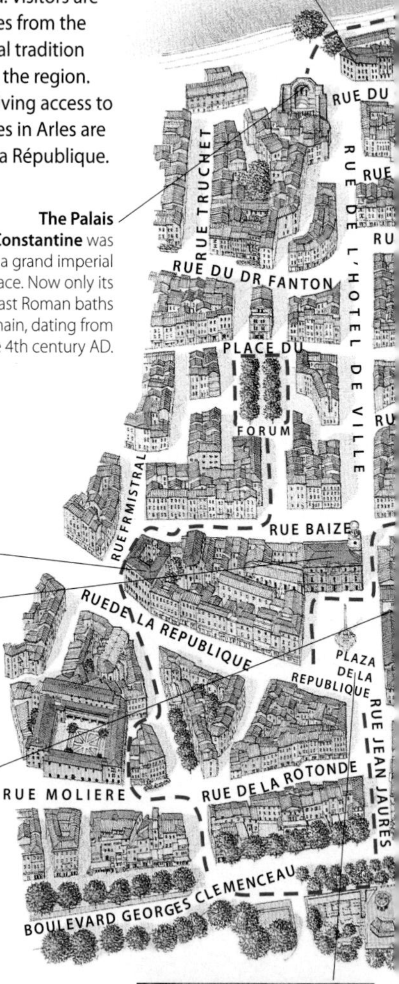

★ **Eglise St-Trophime**
This fine Romanesque church has an ornate 12th-century portal carved with saints and apostles.

Roman Obelisk
This ancient obelisk, with fountains at its base (one of which is shown here), came from the Roman circus across the Rhône.

Key

 Suggested route

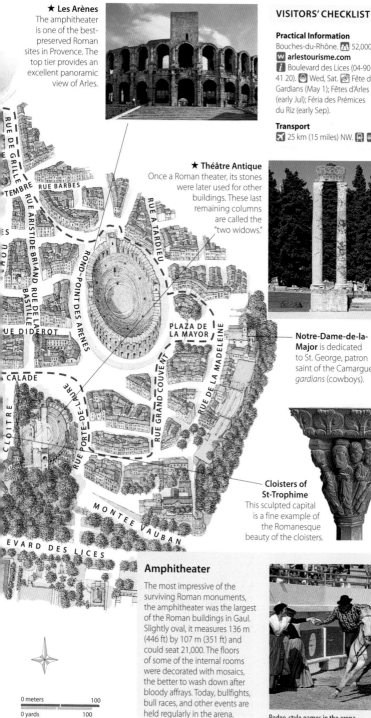

★ **Les Arènes**
The amphitheater is one of the best-preserved Roman sites in Provence. The top tier provides an excellent panoramic view of Arles.

★ **Théâtre Antique**
Once a Roman theater, its stones were later used for other buildings. These last remaining columns are called the "two widows."

Notre-Dame-de-la-Major is dedicated to St. George, patron saint of the Camargue *gardians* (cowboys).

Cloisters of St-Trophime
This sculpted capital is a fine example of the Romanesque beauty of the cloisters.

Map labels: RUE DE GRILLE, RUE BARBES, RUE ARISTIDE BRIAND, RUE DE LA BASTILLE, TEMBRE, RUE A TARDIEU, ROND-POINT DES ARENES, RUE DIDEROT, CALADE, PLAZA DE LA MAYOR, RUE GRAND COUVENT, RUE DE LA MADELEINE, CLOITRE, RUE PORTE-DE-LAURE, MONTEE VAUBAN, EVARD DES LICES

VISITORS' CHECKLIST

Practical Information
Bouches-du-Rhône. 52,000.
arlestourisme.com
Boulevard des Lices (04-90 18 41 20). Wed, Sat. Fête des Gardians (May 1); Fêtes d'Arles (early Jul); Féria des Prémices du Riz (early Sep).

Transport
25 km (15 miles) NW.

Amphitheater

The most impressive of the surviving Roman monuments, the amphitheater was the largest of the Roman buildings in Gaul. Slightly oval, it measures 136 m (446 ft) by 107 m (351 ft) and could seat 21,000. The floors of some of the internal rooms were decorated with mosaics, the better to wash down after bloody affrays. Today, bullfights, bull races, and other events are held regularly in the arena.

Rodeo-style games in the arena

0 meters   100
0 yards   100

⸹² Camargue

Bouches-du-Rhône. 🚉 🚌 **i** 5 Ave
Van Gogh, Stes-Maries-de-la-Mer
(04-90 97 82 55). 🎪 Pèlerinage des
Gitans (end May & end Oct).
w saintesmaries.com

This flat, sparsely populated
land is one of Europe's major
wetland regions and natural-
history sites. Extensive areas of
salt marshes, lakes, pastures,
and sand dunes cover a vast
140,000 ha (346,000 acres). The
native white horses and black
bulls are tended by the region's
cowboys, or *gardians*. Numerous
seabirds and wildfowl also
occupy the region.

Bullfights are advertised in
Saintes-Maries-de-la-Mer, the
region's main tourist center,
which has a sandy beach with
water sports and boat trips. A
few kilometers inland, the
information center at **Pont-
de-Gau** offers wonderful
views over the flat
lagoon. Photographs
and documents
chronicle the
history of the
Camargue and its
diverse flora and
fauna. Most of the
birds that live in, or
migrate within, the
region, including
thousands of
flamingoes which
come here to
breed, can be seen
at the nearby **Parc
Ornithologique
du Pont-de-Gau.**

Camargue
gardian

In the north of the region, a
traditional Provençal *mas*, or
farmhouse, Mas du Pont de
Rousty, has been converted to
accommodate the fascinating
Musée Camarguais. Displays
here provide an introduction to
the customs and traditions of
the Camargue.

🦜 **Parc Ornithologique
du Pont-de-Gau**
Pont-de-Gau. **Tel** 04-90 97 82 62.
Open daily. **Closed** Dec 25. 🌐 &

🏛 **Musée Camarguais**
Parc Naturel Régional de Camargue,
Mas du Pont de Rousty. **Tel** 04-90 97
10 82. **Open** Wed–Mon.
Closed public hols. 🌐 &

Impressionist painter Cézanne's studio in
Aix-en-Provence

⸹³ Aix-en-Provence

Bouches-du-Rhône. 🚗 140,000. 🚉
🚌 **i** 300 Ave Giuseppe Verdi, Les
Allées Provençales (04-42 16 11 61). 🏠
daily. **w** aixenprovencetourism.com

Provence's former capital is an
international students' town,
with a university that dates
back to 1409. The city was
transformed in the 17th century,
when ramparts, first raised by
the Romans in their town of
Aquae Sextiae, were pulled
down, and the mansion-lined
Cours Mirabeau was built.

North of the Cours Mirabeau
lies the town's old quarter.
Cathédrale St-Sauveur creaks
with history. The jewel of the
church is the triptych of *The
Burning Bush* (1476) by Nicolas
Froment. The modest **Atelier
Paul Cézanne**, a studio designed
by Cézanne himself, is much as
he left it when he died in 1906.

The main museum is the
Musée Granet. François Granet
(1775–1849) left his collection
of French, Italian, and Flemish

paintings to Aix. Work by
Provençal artists is also shown,
some by Granet.

🏛 **Musée Granet**
13 Rue Cardinale. **Tel** 04-42 52 88 32.
Open Tue–Sun. 🌐 &

⸹⁴ Marseille

Bouches-du-Rhône. 🚗 1,000,000.
✈ 25 km NW. 🚌 🚉 🚌 **i** 11 La
Canebière (08-26 50 05 00). 🏠 daily.
w marseille-tourisme.com

France's most important port and
oldest major city is centered on
the surprisingly attractive Vieux
Port. On the north side are the
commercial docks and the old
town, rebuilt after World War II.

The old town's finest building
is the **Vieille Charité**, a large
17th-century hospice that
houses the Musée d'Archéologie
Méditerranéenne and the
Musée d'Arts Africains,
Océaniens, Amérindiens.

The Neo-Byzantine **Notre-
Dame-de-la-Garde** dominates
the city, but Marseille's finest
piece of religious architecture is
the **Abbaye de St-Victor**, founded
in the 5th century, with crypts
containing catacombs, sarcophagi,
and the martyr St. Victor's cave.

During postwar rebuilding, the
Roman docks were uncovered.
The **Musée des Docks Romains**
mainly displays large storage
urns once used for wine, grain,
and oil. In the Centre Bourse
shopping center is the **Musée
d'Histoire de Marseille**. Reconstructions of the city at the height
of the Greek period make this a
good starting point for a tour.

Old harbor of Marseille, looking towards the Quai de Rive Neuve

Flavors of the South of France

It's a heady experience just to stand, look, and sniff in a Provençal market. Tables sag under piles of braided pink garlic, colorful fresh peppers, tomatoes, eggplants, zucchini, and asparagus. In the fall and winter, an earthy scent fills the air, with wild mushrooms, Swiss chard, walnuts, and quinces crowding the stalls. The waters of coastal Provence provide a bountiful sea harvest, including plump mussels, oysters, and *tellines* (tiny clams). The area is especially famous for its fish dishes, notably bouillabaisse. Lamb is the most common meat in Provence; the best comes from the Camargue, where lambs graze on herbs and salt-marsh grass. The South supplies France with the first of the season's peaches, cherries, and apricots.

Fish liquor

Red snapper

Conger eel

Monkfish

Red mullet

Bouillabaisse, a fish soup originating in Marseille, is a luxury today. It consists of an assortment of local seafood, including monkfish, mullet, snapper, scorpion fish, and conger eel, flavored with tomatoes, saffron, and olive oil. Traditionally, the fish liquor is served first with croutons spread with *rouille*, a spicy mayonnaise. The fish is eaten afterwards.

Croutons

Rouille (meaning "rust"), a mayonnaise with chillies and garlic

Olives and Olive Oil

Most of the olive crop is crushed for oil. Ripe olives are black and the unripe ones are green; both can be preserved in brine or oil. At the end of the olive harvest, tapenade is popular – a paste of black olives, capers, anchovies, and olive oil eaten with bread.

Fougasse is a flattish, lattice-like bread variously studded with black olives, anchovies, onions, and spices. The sweet version is flavored with almonds.

Black olives

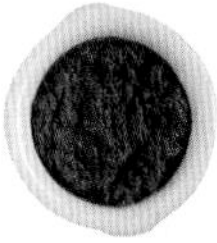

Tapenade

Olive oil

Aïoli is a sauce made of egg yolks, garlic, and olive oil. It is served with salt cod, boiled eggs, snails, or raw vegetables.

Ratatouille is a stew of onions, eggplants, zucchini, tomatoes, and peppers, cooked in olive oil and garlic.

Salade Niçoise comes in many versions, but always includes lettuce, green beans, tomatoes, black olives, eggs, and anchovies.

The Côte d'Azur

The Côte d'Azur is, without doubt, the most celebrated seaside in Europe. Almost everybody who has been anybody for the past 100 years has succumbed to its glittering allure. Today, the Côte d'Azur is busy all year round; expect heavy traffic around Cannes and St-Tropez in summer. Between Cannes and Menton, the coast forms the glamorous French Riviera, playground of the rich and famous. The bustling city of Nice lies at the area's heart, richly deserving the title "capital of the Côte d'Azur."

Beaches of the Côte d'Azur

The sun-drenched coastline of the Côte d'Azur is one of the busiest in Europe. To the east lie the Riviera's big, traditional resorts while to the west are smaller towns in coves and bays. Beaches are sandy west of Antibes, and more shingly to the east.

Menton
Monaco
Nice
Cap Ferrat
Cannes
Antibes
Juan-les-Pins
St-Raphaël
St-Tropez

0 kilometers 20
0 miles 20

Uma Thurman arriving at the Cannes Film Festival

㉟ Cannes

Alpes-Maritimes. 70,000. 📮 🚆 💻 ℹ Palais des Festivals, 1 La Croisette (04-92 99 84 22). 🗓 daily.

The first thing that most people associate with Cannes is its many festivals, especially the International Film Festival. held each May. The first Cannes Film Festival took place in 1946 and, for a while, it remained a small and exclusive affair. The mid-1950s marked the change from artistic event to media circus, but Cannes remains the international marketplace for moviemakers and distributors. The annual festival is held in the huge **Palais des Festivals**.

There is, however, more to the city than this glittering event. The Old Town is centered in the Le Suquet district, which is dominated by the church of **Notre-Dame de l'Espérance**, built in the 16th and 17th centuries in the Provençal Gothic style. The famed **Boulevard de la Croisette** is lined with palm trees. Luxury stores and hotels look out over fine sandy beaches.

Exploring the Côte d'Azur

The Côte d'Azur is the most popular destination in France for sun-worshipers, with its seaside vacation towns and long, golden beaches. **St-Tropez** is currently the trendiest resort; Tahini-Plage is the coast's showcase for fun, sun, fashion, and glamor. By contrast, the family resort of **St-Raphaël** is peaceful, with excellent tourist facilities.

East of **Cannes**, at the western edge of the Riviera, **Juan-les-Pins** is a lively resort. Its all-night bars, nightclubs, and cafés make it popular with teenagers and young adults. Founded by the Greeks, **Antibes** is one of the oldest towns along this stretch of coast, and home to a large museum of Picasso's work, donated by the artist himself.

Clifftop walks replace seafront promenades around the wooded peninsula of **Cap Ferrat**, where grand villas and private beaches can be glimpsed between the trees.

At the eastern edge of the Riviera, past the glitz of the casinos and hotels of **Monaco**, the beaches of **Menton** are the warmest along the coast; sunbathers enjoy a beach climate all year round.

㊱ Nice

Alpes-Maritimes. 346,000. ✈ 💻 🚆 💻 ℹ 5 Promenade des Anglais (08-92 70 74 07). 🗓 Tue–Sun. 🎭 Carnival (Feb). 🌐 **nicetourisme.com**

The largest resort on the Mediterranean coast, Nice has the second-busiest airport in France. Its temperate winter climate and verdant subtropical

St-Tropez harborside, on the Côte d'Azur

vegetation have long attracted visitors, and today it is also a center for business conferences and package travelers.

There are many art museums in Nice, two of which devote themselves to the works of particular artists. The **Musée Matisse** displays drawings, paintings, bronzes, fabrics, and artifacts. The **Musée Chagall** holds the largest collection of works by Marc Chagall, with paintings, drawings, sculpture, stained glass, and mosaics.

A strikingly original complex of four marble-faced towers linked by glass passageways houses the **Musée d'Art Contemporain**. The collection is particularly strong in Neorealism and Pop Art. The **Musée des Beaux Arts** displays works by Dufy, Monet, Renoir, and Sisley.

A 19th-century palace, the **Palais Masséna** is filled with paintings of the Nice school, works by the Impressionists, Provençal ceramics, folk art, and a gold cloak once worn by Napoleon's beloved Josephine.

The onion domes of the **Cathédrale Orthodoxe Russe St-Nicolas**, completed in 1912, make this building Nice's most distinctive landmark.

Musée Matisse
164 Ave des Arènes de Cimiez. **Tel** 04-93 81 08 08. **Open** Wed–Mon. **Closed** some public hols.

Musée Chagall
36 Ave du Docteur Ménard. **Tel** 04-93 53 87 20. **Open** Wed–Mon. **Closed** Jan 1, May 1, Dec 25.

A quiet stretch along Nice's 5 km (3 miles) of beachfront

Skyscrapers and apartment blocks of modern Monte Carlo in Monaco

37 **Monaco**

Monaco. 34,000. (Nice). 2a Boulevard des Moulins (092-16 61 16). daily. International Circus Festival (Jan–Feb).
visitmonaco.com

Arriving among the towering skyscrapers of Monaco today, it is hard to envisage the turbulence of its history. At first a Greek settlement, later taken by the Romans, it was bought from the Genoese in 1297 by the Grimaldis who, in spite of bitter family feuds, still rule as the world's oldest monarchy. Monaco covers 1.9 sq km (0.74 sq miles) and, although its size has increased by one-third in the form of landfills, it still occupies an area smaller than New York's Central Park.

The best-known section of Monaco is Monte Carlo. People flock to the annual car rally held here in January, but the area owes its renown mainly to its **Grand Casino**. Source of countless legends, it was instituted by Charles III to save himself from bankruptcy in 1856. So successful was this money-making venture that,

by 1870, he was able to abolish taxation for his people. Designed in 1878 and set in formal gardens, the casino gives a splendid view over Monaco. Even the most exclusive of the gaming rooms can be visited.

Across the harbor lies Monaco-Ville, the seat of government. The interior of the 13th-century **Palais Princier**, with its priceless furniture and magnificent frescoes, is open to the public from April to September.

The aquarium of the **Musée Océanographique** holds rare species of marine plants and animals. Marine explorer Jacques Cousteau established his research center here.

The lavish surroundings of the belle époque Grand Casino, Monaco

Practical Information

France is justifiably proud of its many attractions, for which it has good tourist information facilities. Both in France and abroad, French Government Tourist Offices are an invaluable source of reference for practical aspects of your stay, especially for those with special needs. If you are unfortunate enough to need medical or emergency assistance, France has excellent hospitals, ambulance, fire, and police services. The country also has a modern communications network, making it easy to keep in touch by telephone, post, or email.

Visa Requirements and Customs

Currently, there are no visa requirements for EU nationals or visitors from the United States, Canada, Australia, or New Zealand who plan to stay in France for under three months. Visitors from most other countries require a tourist visa. Non-EU visitors can, with some exceptions, reclaim the French sales tax (TVA) on goods if they spend more than a certain amount in one shop and get a *détaxe* receipt.

Tourist Information

All major cities and large towns have *offices de tourisme*. Small towns and even villages have *syndicats d'initiative*. Both will give you town plans, advice on accommodations, and information on regional recreational and cultural activities.

You can also get information before you leave for France from **French Government Tourist Offices**, or by contacting local tourist offices (see individual town headings in this guide) or the appropriate CRT (Comité Régional de Tourisme) – ask the FGTO for the address.

Personal Security

Violent crime is rare in France – even a major city such as Paris is surprisingly safe. However, muggings and brawls do occur, so avoid isolated or poorly lit places, especially at night. Women should take extra care, especially when traveling alone. Also beware of pickpockets, who are active in large cities.

Police

There are two types of police in France. The *Police Nationale* look after large towns and cities. If you need to contact them, find the Commissariat de Police (police headquarters). Small towns, villages, and country areas are policed by the Gendarmerie Nationale. If you need to report a crime in these places, go to the nearest local *gendarmerie*.

Opening Hours

Generally, opening hours for tourist sights are from 10am–5:40pm, with one late evening per week. Most close on public holidays.

National museums and sights are normally closed on Tuesdays, with a few exceptions which close on Mondays. Municipal museums normally close on Mondays. Churches are open every day, but sometimes shut at lunchtime.

Facilities for the Disabled

Facilities for the disabled vary in France. Details of services in most towns can be obtained from the **GIHP** (Groupement pour l'Insertion des Personnes Handicapées Physiques). The **Association des Paralysés de France** provides information on wheelchair access.

Medical Treatment

All EU nationals are entitled to French social-security coverage. However, treatment must be paid for at the time, and hospital rates vary widely. Reimbursements may be obtained if you have the correct documents before you travel, but the process is long and complicated.

All travelers, particularly non-EU nationals, should, therefore, consider purchasing travel insurance before they arrive. In the case of a medical emergency call **SAMU** *(Service d'Aide Médicale Urgence)*. However, it is often faster to

The Climate of France

Set on Europe's western edge, France has a varied, temperate climate. An Atlantic influence prevails in the northwest, with westerly sea winds bringing humidity and warm winters. The east experiences Continental temperature extremes with frosty, clear winters and often stormy summers. The south enjoys a Mediterranean climate, with hot, dry summers and mild winters.

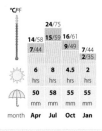

PARIS			
°C/°F			
	24/75		
14/58	15/59	16/61	
7/44		9/49	7/44
			2/35
6 hrs	8 hrs	4.5 hrs	2 hrs
50 mm	58 mm	55 mm	55 mm
month Apr	Jul	Oct	Jan

NICE			
°C/°F			
	27/80		
	19/67	21/70	
17/63		13/55	5/41
10/50			13/55
7.5 hrs	11 hrs	6.5 hrs	5 hrs
62 mm	16 mm	108 mm	83 mm
month Apr	Jul	Oct	Jan

call **Sapeurs Pompiers** (the fire department), which offers a first-aid and ambulance service. This is particularly true in rural areas.

Casualty departments *(service des urgences)* in public hospitals can deal with most medical problems. Your consulate should be able to provide you with details of an English-speaking doctor in the area. Pharmacists can also suggest treatments for many health problems. Look for the green-cross sign outside pharmacies.

Banking and Currency

The French unit of currency is the euro *(see p23)*.

Most credit cards are widely accepted in France, but, because of the high commissions charged, American Express is often not. The most commonly used credit card is Carte Bleue/Visa. Eurocard/MasterCard (Access in UK) is also often accepted. Credit cards issued in France contain a microchip and are called "smart cards," but some machines can also read cards with magnetic strips. If you find your conventional card cannot be read in the smart-card slot, get the cashier to swipe the card through the magnetic reader.

You will be asked to tap in your PIN code *(code confidentiel)* on a small keypad.

You can also use credit cards in most banks to withdraw cash; either from an ATM (automatic teller machine), which should have an English-language option, or from a cash desk. Most banks will cash traveler's checks. Opening hours are usually Mon–Fri, 9am–4:30 or 5:15pm, with some banks also open on Saturday morning. Many close for lunch, and many, especially in the south, are closed on Monday.

You can also exchange money at bureaux de change offices, which operate longer hours than banks. Exchange rates and commission charges can vary.

Communications

Payphones in France are being phased out, and they will likely be removed completely by 2016. Those that still remain take mainly plastic telephone cards *(télécartes)*– available from tobacconists *(tabacs)* and newsagents – and credit cards. For local calls, a unit lasts up to six minutes. Many phones also accept credit cards (with a PIN number). Some post offices have telephone booths *(cabines)* where you can call

first and pay afterwards. This is cheaper than making long-distance calls from hotels.

La Poste (the Post Office) used to be called the P.T.T. *(postes, télégraphes, téléphones)*, and some road signs still give directions to the P.T.T. The postal service in France is fast and reliable. However, it is not cheap, especially when sending a parcel abroad.

At La Poste, postage stamps *(timbres)* are sold singly or in *carnets* of seven or ten. They are also sold at *tabacs*, although you need to go to the post office for international stamps. At post offices, you can also use telephone directories *(annuaires)*, buy phonecards, cash or buy money orders *(mandats)*, and make international calls.

Post offices usually open from 9am–5pm Mon–Fri, often with a break for lunch, and 9am–noon on Saturdays. Mail boxes are yellow, and often have separate slots for the town you are in, the *département*, and other destinations *(autres destinations)*.

Although the Internet is widely used in France, Internet cafés have not proved to be successful. However, there are usually a few in the major cities and resorts. In Paris, there are free Wi-Fi spots in many metro stations.

DIRECTORY

Embassies

Australia
4 Rue Jean Rey, 75015 Paris. **Tel** 01-40 59 33 00.
🆆 france.embassy.gov.au

Canada
35 Ave Montaigne, 75008 Paris. **Tel** 01-44 43 29 00.
🆆 canadainternational.gc.ca/france

UK
Consulate: 18 bis Rue d'Anjou, 75008 Paris.
Tel 01-44 51 31 00. 🆆 amb-grandebretagne.fr

US
2 Ave Gabriel, 75008 Paris. **Tel** 01-43 12 22 22.
🆆 http://france.usembassy.gov

Tourist Information

Paris Convention & Visitors Bureau Headquarters
25–27 Rue des Pyramides, 75001 Paris.
Tel 01495-24263.
🆆 en.parisinfo.com

Australia
French Tourist Bureau, Level 22, 25 Bligh Street, Sydney, NSW 2000.
Tel 612-9321 5244.

Canada
1800 Ave McGill College, Suite 1010, Montréal, Québec H3A 3J6.
Tel 288-2026.

UK
Lincoln House, 300 High Holborn, London WC1V 7JH.
Tel 020-7061 6600.

US
825 Third Ave, New York, NY 10022.
Tel 212-838 7800.

Facilities for the Disabled

Association des Paralysés de France
17 Bld August Blanqui, 75013 Paris.
Tel 01-45 89 40 57.
🆆 apf.asso.fr

GIHP
61 fbg Poissonnière, 75009 Paris.
Tel 01-43 95 66 36.

Emergency Numbers

Ambulance (SAMU)
Tel 15 or 18 (Sapeurs Pompiers).

Fire (Sapeurs Pompiers)
Tel 18 or 112.

Police and Gendarmerie
Tel 17.

Banking

American Express
11 Rue Scribe, 75009 Paris.
Tel 01-47 77 70 00.

Travelex
Tel 0800 908 330.

Travel Information

France has highly advanced transportation systems, with Paris at the hub of its air, railroad, and road networks. Paris's two main airports have direct flights to North America, Africa, Japan, and the rest of Europe. The city's six major railroad stations connect it to some 6,000 destinations in France, and provide links to the whole of Europe. An extensive, well-developed road network makes it easy to reach all parts of the country by car or bus. France is also well connected by sea, with frequent ferry crossings from the UK to ports on the Channel.

Flying to France

France is served by nearly all international airlines. Paris is the major airline destination in France, but there are a number of other international airports across the country. Some airports near the border, such as Geneva, Basle, and Luxembourg, can also be used for destinations in France.

The main French airline is **Air France**, which has services to major cities across the world. The main British airline with regular flights to France is **British Airways**. Inexpensive flights from the UK to various French destinations are available from carriers such as **easyJet**, **Flybe**, and **Ryanair**. Major airlines including **American Airlines**, **Delta**, and **United** operate flights from the United States. **Air Canada** flies from several cities in Canada, and **Qantas** provides flights from Australia and New Zealand.

Air Fares

Airline fares are at their highest during the peak summer season in France, usually from July to September. Fierce competition between airlines, however, means there are often discounts on offer.

APEX fares are booked in advance. They cannot be changed or canceled without penalty and there are also minimum and maximum stay requirements. Packages are also worth considering, as airlines and tour operators can put together a great range of flexible deals to suit your needs. These can include car rental and train travel, enabling you to continue overland.

Domestic Flights

There are a number of domestic airlines that fly between the cities of France, some of which only operate within one region; others also fly to French-speaking countries, with Air France offering the largest number of routes. **Hop** is a French airline offering low-cost internal flights. However, unless you are eligible for discounts, you may find it cheaper and faster to travel on high-speed trains, given the time it can take to reach the airports.

Ferry Services

There are several crossings between the UK and French ports. **P&O Ferries** operates between Dover and Calais, with frequent crossings (75–90 mins). **Brittany Ferries** runs a 9-hour service from Portsmouth to St-Malo, a 6-hour service from Portsmouth to Caen, a 3-hour service from Poole or Portsmouth to Cherbourg, a 6-hour service from Plymouth to Roscoff, and a 4-hour crossing from Portsmouth to Le Havre. **LD Lines** runs an 8-hour overnight service from Portsmouth to Le Havre. **Transmanche Ferries'** route between Newhaven and Dieppe takes about 3 hours. **Norfolkline** has a 2-hour crossing from Dover to Dunkerque.

Channel Tunnel

The Channel Tunnel (*Tunnel sous La Manche*) was inaugurated in 1994. A car-carrying shuttle service, which is operated by **Eurotunnel**, runs between Folkestone and Calais. The passenger service, **Eurostar**, links London and Paris (2.5 hrs).

Getting Around Paris

Central Paris is compact, and the best way to get around is often to walk. Public transportation in the city is good, however, with an efficient metro (subway) system, frequent buses, and a commuter train service (RER). These are all operated by the Paris transportation company, RATP.

There are many types of ticket available, sold at metro and RER stations, and most can be used on any RATP service, including buses. Single bus tickets can also be bought from the driver when boarding. All tickets used on buses must be stamped in the machine on board.

Single RATP tickets are valid in metro/RER zones 1 or 2, or for any bus journey. *Carnets* (books of ten single tickets), are more economical if you plan to make a number of journeys. Various passes are also available, which entitle you to unlimited travel in certain zones for a set number of days.

Vélib is a self-service bike hire scheme in Paris. Users can hire a bike from one station and return it to another.

Rail Travel

France has always been known for the punctuality of its trains. The French state railroad, the **Société Nationale des Chemins de Fer (SNCF)**, provides an excellent railroad network which covers nearly all of France. The fastest services are provided by the high-speed TGV (Trains à Grande Vitesse) trains, which link most major cities.

Overnight services are popular in France, and most long-distance trains have *couchettes* (bunks), which you must reserve for a fee. Reservations are also compulsory for all TGV services, trains on public holidays, and for a *siège inclinable* (reclinable seat). Information on the various train services and fares is available from the **Voyages-SNCF** office in London. In France, leaflets are available at most stations. There are a number of special tickets available, including ones for over 60s, families, and under 26s. There are also special tickets for those doing a lot of train travel.

Automatic ticket and reservation machines (billetterie automatique) are found at main stations. They take credit cards or coins. You can also check train times, fares, and make reservations by phoning **SNCF**. Both reservations and tickets must be validated in one of the orange *composteur* machines near the platforms before boarding the train.

Traveling by Road

France has one of the densest road networks in Europe, with modern motorways which allow quick and easy access to all parts of the country. However, you can save money on tolls and explore France in a more leisurely way by using some of the other high-quality roads, such as RN (route nationale) and D (départementale) routes.

Most motorways in France have a toll system (autoroutes

à péage), which can be quite expensive, especially over long distances. There are some short sections which are free, however, usually close to major centers. Tolls can be paid with either credit cards or cash. Where only small sums are involved, you throw coins into a large receptacle and the change is given automatically.

Speed limits in France are shown in km/h. The limit in all towns, unless shown otherwise, is 50 km/h (30 mph). On major roads, higher limits are usually shown. On the *autoroutes*, the usual limit is 130 km/h (80 mph), but this is reduced to 110 km/h (70 mph) when it is raining. On-the-spot fines may be demanded for speeding offences, and there are severe penalties for drink-driving.

Sunday is usually a good time to travel in France, as there are very few trucks on the road. Try to avoid traveling at the French holiday-rush periods, known as the *grands départs*. The worst times are weekends in July, and at the beginning and end of August.

All the main international car-rental companies operate in France. It is worth ringing around before you leave for France as there are many special offers for rentals booked and prepaid in the UK or US. Good deals are often available from **Autos Abroad**, brokers who use cars owned by other car-rental companies. Booking in this way can be very cost effective.

Buses

Long-distance buses generally operate only where there is not a good train service in operation (for example, between Geneva and Nice). SNCF (the state railway) operates some bus routes and issues regional TER (Transports Express Régionaux) timetables and tickets. **Eurolines** serves a wider range of destinations within France, as well as providing services to hundreds of major cities across Europe. They also offer excursions and arrange accommodations.

There are also many local buses, which run from the town's Gare Routière.

DIRECTORY

Airlines

Air Canada
Tel 08-26 88 08 81.
Tel 888-247 2262 (Can).
W aircanada.com

Air France
Tel 3654.
Tel 0871-663 3777 (UK).
Tel 800-237 2747 (US).
W airfrance.com

American Airlines
Tel 08-26 46 09 50.
Tel 800-433 7300 (US).
W aa.com

British Airways
Tel 08-25 82 54 00.
Tel 0844-493 0787 (UK).
W britishairways.com

Delta Air Lines
Tel 08-92-70-26-09.
Tel 800-221 12 12 (US).
W delta.com

easyJet
Tel 0843-116 0021 (UK).
W easyjet.com

Flybe
Tel 0871-700 2000 (UK).
W flybe.com

Hop
Tel 08-25 30 22 22.
W hop.fr

Qantas
Tel 0845-774 7767 (UK).
Tel 13 13 13 (Aus).
W qantas.com.au

Ryanair
Tel 08-92-56-21-50.
W ryanair.com

United Airlines
Tel 0845-8444 777 (UK).
Tel 800-864 8331 (US).
W united.com

Ferry Services

Brittany Ferries
Tel 08-25 82 88 28.
Tel 0871-244 0744 (UK).
W brittanyferries.com

LD Lines
Tel 0844-576 8836 (UK).

Norfolkline
Tel 0871-574 7235 (UK).
W norfolkline.com

P&O Ferries
Tel 08716-64 21 21 (UK).
W poferries.com

Transmanche Ferries
Tel 0825 304 304.
Tel 0871-522 9955 (UK).
W transmache.co.uk

Channel Tunnel

Eurostar
Tel 01-70 70 60 88.
Tel 08432-186 186 (UK).
W eurostar.com

Eurotunnel
Tel 810-630 304.
Tel 0870-535 3535 (UK).
W eurotunnel.com

Rail Travel

SNCF, Paris
Tel 3635.
W voyages-sncf.com

Voyages-SNCF
193 Piccadilly,
London W1J 9EU.
Tel 0844-848 5848.

Car Rental

Autos Abroad
Tel 0844-826 6536 (UK).
W autosabroad.com

Avis
Tel 08-21 23 07 60.
Tel 0844-581 0147 (UK).
W avis.fr

Europcar
Tel 08-25 35 83 58.
Tel 0871-384 1087 (UK).
W europcar.com

Hertz
Tel 0825-86 18 61.
Tel 0843-309 3099 (UK).
W hertz.com

Buses

Eurolines
Tel 08-92 89 90 91.
W eurolines.fr

Shopping

Shopping in France is a delight. Whether you go to the hypermarkets and department stores, or seek out the many small specialist stores and markets, you will be tempted by the stylish presentation and high quality of the goods on offer. France is especially renowned for its wine, with a vast selection available, from cheap table wines to classic vintages. French food is also excellent, in particular the cheeses, cured meats, patés, cakes, and pastries. France also offers world-famous fashion, pottery, porcelain, crystal, and fine-quality antiques.

Opening Hours

Food stores open at about 7am and close around noon for lunch. After lunch most are open until 7pm or later. Bakeries often stay open until 1pm or later.

Shops that do not close at lunchtime include some supermarkets, department stores, and most hypermarkets.

General opening hours for non-food stores are around 9am–7pm Mon–Sat, often with a break for lunch. Many are closed on Mondays.

Food stores (and newsagents) are open on Sunday mornings. Virtually every shop in France is closed on Sunday afternoon, except for the last weeks before Christmas, when hypermarkets remain open all day. Smaller stores may be closed one day of the week, usually Monday. However, those in tourist regions are often open every day in the high season.

Larger Shops

Hypermarkets (*hypermarchés* or *grandes surfaces*) can be found on the outskirts of every sizeable town: look for signs indicating *centre commercial*. Among the biggest are Carrefour, Casino, Auchan, and Continent. Discount petrol is often sold, and most, but not all, now have pumps which take credit cards.

Department stores (*grands magasins*), such as the cheap-and-cheerful Monoprix, are often found in town centers. Others, like the more upscale **Printemps** and **Galeries Lafayette**, can be found both in town and out-of-town centers.

Specialist Shops

One of the pleasures of shopping in France is that specialist stores for food still flourish despite the new large supermarkets. The *boulangerie*, for bread, is frequently combined with a *pâtisserie* selling cakes and pastries. The *traiteur* sells prepared foods. Cheese shops (*fromagerie*) and other shops specializing in dairy products (*laiterie*) may also be combined, while the *boucherie* (butcher's) and *charcuterie* (pork butcher's/delicatessen) are often separate stores. For general groceries, go to an *épicerie*. An *épicerie fine* is a delicatessen.

Markets

Markets are found in towns and villages all over France. To find out where the market is, ask a passerby for *le marché*. Markets usually finish promptly at noon and do not reopen in the afternoon.

Look for local producers, including those with only one or two special items to sell, as their goods are often cheaper and of better quality.

By law, price tags include the origin of all produce: *pays* means local. Chickens from Bresse are marketed wearing a red, white, and blue badge, giving the name of the producer as proof of authenticity. If you are visiting markets over several weeks, look for items just coming into season, such as fresh walnuts, the first wild asparagus, truffles, early artichokes, or wild strawberries. The special seasonal markets held throughout France are the best places to find these

items, and there are often *foires artisanales* held at the same time, which sell local produce, arts, and crafts.

Regional Produce

French regional specialties can be bought outside their area of origin, although it is interesting to buy them locally. Provence, in the south, prides itself on the quality of its olive oil, while the southwest is notable for its patés. Central France is famous for snails, cured meats, and Epoisses cheese. Cheese is also an important product of the temperate north, the best-known varieties being Brie and Camembert.

Popular drinks are also associated with particular regions. Pastis, made from aniseed, is popular in the south, while Calvados, made from apples, is from the north.

Location also determines quality. Lyon's culinary importance stems from the many locally produced cheeses, the proximity of Bresse for chickens, Charolais for beef, and the Alsace region for sausages.

Wine

In wine-producing areas, follow the *dégustation* (tasting) signs to vineyards (*domaines*), where you can taste the wine. You will be expected to buy at least one bottle. Wine cooperatives sell the wine of small producers. Here, you can buy wine in five- and ten-liter containers (*en vrac*), as well as in bottles. The wine is often rated AOP, *appellation d'origine protégée*, selling at less than 2 euros a liter. As wine sold *en vrac* is "duty-free," customers receive a *laissez-passer* (permit) indicating their destination. Bottled wine sold by co-ops is duty-paid.

Clothing

France is famous for its fashion, and elegant clothes can be found even in quite small towns. Paris, however, is the home of haute couture. There are more than 100 fashion houses and designers listed with the Fédération Française de la

Couture, and most of these are concentrated on the Right Bank around Rue du Faubourg-St-Honoré and Avenue Montaigne. Famous names include **Yves Saint Laurent**, **Chanel**, **Guy Laroche**, **Gucci**, **Nina Ricci**, and **Christian Dior**. Other top designers include **Hermès** and **Giorgio Armani**.

Men don't have the luxury of *haute couture* dressing: their choice is limited to ready-to-wear, but most of the big-name womenswear designers also produce a range for men. A good example is **Gianni Versace**, with his classic Italian clothes for men. On the Right Bank, the household-name designers include **Giorgio Armani**, the stylish **Pierre Cardin**, **Yves Saint Laurent**, and **Lanvin**, who is particularly popular for his beautifully made leather accessories. If time is short and you want to make all your purchases under one roof, try the *grands magasins*. These stores offer a wide choice of fashions,

and prices will be more within most people's budgets. **Printemps**, for example, is huge, with separate buildings for menswear, household goods, and womens' and children's clothes. The beauty department, with its vast perfume selection, is definitely worth a visit. **Le Bon Marché**, on the Left Bank, was the first department store in Paris, and is the most chic, with an excellent food hall. **Galeries Lafayette** has a wide range of clothes at all price levels. There are also homewares, and the branch in Boulevard Haussmann has Paris's biggest souvenir shop.

Art and Antiques

You can buy fabulous art and antiques from stores, galleries, and flea-markets all over France. The best places to visit in Paris are **Le Louvre des Antiquaires**, a huge building containing around 250 antique dealers, and the famous **Marché aux Puces de St-Ouen** flea market (open

Saturday to Monday). To avoid paying duty, you will need a certificate of authenticity when exporting objets d'art over 20 years old and any goods over a century old that are worth more than €150,000. Seek professional advice and declare them at customs if in doubt.

Tax-Free Shopping

Visitors resident outside the European Union can reclaim the sales tax, TVA, on French goods if they spend more than €305 in one shop, get a *détaxe* receipt, and take the goods out of the country within six months. The form should be handed in at customs when leaving the country, and the reimbursement will be sent to you.

Exceptions for *détaxe* rebates are food and drink, medicines, tobacco, cars, and motorbikes. More information is available from the **Centre des Renseignements des Douanes**, but this is usually in French.

DIRECTORY

Clothing

Chanel
42 Ave Montaigne,
75008 Paris.
Tel 01-47 23 74 12.
5 Bld de la Croisette,
06400 Cannes.
Tel 04-93 38 55 05.

Christian Dior
30 Ave Montaigne,
75008 Paris.
Tel 01-40 73 73 73.
38 Bld de la Croisette,
06400 Cannes.
Tel 04-92 98 98 00.

Gianni Versace
45 Ave Montaigne,
75008 Paris.
Tel 01-47 42 88 02.

Giorgio Armani
2 Ave Montaigne,
75008 Paris.
Tel 01-56 89 01 19.

Gucci
60 Ave Montaigne,
75008 Paris.
Tel 01-56 69 80 80.

Guy Laroche
35 Rue François 1er,
75008 Paris.
Tel 01-40 69 68 00.

Hermès
24 Rue du Faubourg
St-Honoré, 75008 Paris.
Tel 01-40 17 47 17.

Lanvin
22 Rue de Faubourg
St-Honoré,
75008 Paris.
Tel 01-44 71 33 33.

Nina Ricci
39 Ave Montaigne,
75008 Paris.
Tel 01-83 97 72 12.

Pierre Cardin
9 Rue Duras,
75008 Paris.
Tel 01-42 66 14 92.

Yves Saint Laurent
6 Place St Sulpice,
75006 Paris
(women's fashion).
Tel 01-43 29 43 00.

32 Rue Faubourg
St. Honoré,
75008 Paris
(men's fashion).
Tel 01-53 05 80 80.
65 Bld Croisette,
06400 Cannes.
Tel 04-93 46 99 17.

Department Stores

Le Bon Marché
24 Rue de Sèvres,
75007 Paris.
Tel 01-44 39 80 00.

Galeries Lafayette
40 Bld Haussmann,
75009 Paris.
Tel 01-42 82 34 56.
11 Rue Ste Catherine,
33000 Bordeaux.
Tel 05-56 90 92 71.
6 Rue Maréchal Foch,
06400 Cannes.
Tel 04-97 06 25 00.

Printemps
64 Bld Haussman,
75009 Paris.
Tel 01-42 82 50 00.

Art and Antiques

Le Louvre des Antiquaires
2 Place du Palais-Royal,
75001 Paris.
Tel 01-42 97 27 27.

Marché aux Puces de St-Ouen
Av Porte de Clignancourt,
75018 Paris.
Tel 01-40 11 77 63.

Tax-free Shopping

Centre des Renseignements des Douanes
Direction Générale,
11 Rue des Deux
Communes,
93558 Montreuil.
Tel 08-11 20 44 44.
W douane-gouv.fr

Entertainment

The entertainment center of France is Paris. Whether your preference is for drama, ballet, opera, jazz, cinema, or dancing the night away, Paris has it all. Across the rest of the country the arts are also well represented, and there are a number of internationally renowned arts festivals throughout the year. With a varied physical, as well as cultural, landscape, there are also many possibilities for outdoor sports and activities, including golf, tennis, walking, and skiing. Specialist holidays cater to those interested in the language, food, and wine.

Entertainment Listings

Two of the best listings magazines in Paris are *Pariscope* and *L'Officiel des Spectacles*. Published every Wednesday, you can pick them up at any newsstand. Local newspapers and *offices de tourisme* are the best places to find entertainment listings for the regions.

Booking Tickets

Depending on the event, tickets can often be bought at the door, but for popular events it is wiser to purchase them in advance, at the box office or at **FNAC** chains. Theater box offices are usually open 11am–7pm daily. Most accept credit-card bookings by telephone. You can also buy tickets online (via www.ticketnet.fr), from **Kiosque Théâtre**, and from other commercial centers in large towns.

Theater

From the grandeur of the **Comédie Française** to slapstick farce and avant-garde drama, theater is flourishing in Paris. Founded in 1680 by royal decree, the Comédie Française is the bastion of French theater, aiming to keep classical drama in the public eye. In an underground auditorium in the Art Deco Palais de Chaillot, the **Théâtre National de Chaillot** stages lively productions of mainstream European classics. The **Théâtre National de la Colline** specializes in contemporary drama. Among the most important of the independents is the **Comédie des Champs-Elysées**, while for

more than 100 years, the **Palais Royal** has been the temple of risqué farce.

Excellent theaters and productions are also to be found in major cities across France, and there are big theater festivals held in Nancy (April) and Avignon (July; *see p191*).

Music

The music scene in Paris has never been so busy, especially with the emergence of many internationally successful contemporary French groups. There are numerous first-class venues in the city, with excellent jazz, opera, contemporary, and classical-music concerts.

Opened in 1989, the ultra-modern 2,700-seat **Opéra de Paris Bastille** stages classic and modern operas. Productions from outside France are staged at the **Opéra Comique**.

The **Salle Pleyel** is Paris's principal concert hall and home of the Orchestre de Paris. Paris's newest venue is the **Cité de la Musique** in the Parc de la Villette.

Top international and pop acts are usually to be found at huge arenas, such as the **Palais Omnisports de Paris-Bercy** or the **Zénith**. A more intimate atmosphere is found at the legendary **Olympia**.

Paris is, perhaps, most renowned for its jazz, and the best talent in the world can be heard here on any evening, especially throughout October during the jazz festival. All the great jazz musicians have performed at **New Morning**, which also hosts African, Brazilian, and other sounds. For Dixieland,

go to **Le Petit Journal St-Michel**. Jazz is also popular across France, and big international jazz festivals are held right through the year, in Cannes (February; *see p196*), Antibes and Juan-le-Pins (July), and Le Mans (April). Opera and classical music are also widely performed, notably at the Aix festival during July (*see p194*).

Clubs and Cabaret

Music in Paris nightclubs tends to follow the trends set in the US and Britain, although home-grown groups, especially those playing garage, are popular and influential both here and abroad.

Balajo, once frequented by Edith Piaf, and the ultra-hip **Le Social Club** are particularly up-to-the-minute with their music. For a more Latin touch, try **La Java**. The dance floor of this club, where Edith Piaf once performed, now sways to the sounds of Cuban and Brazilian music.

When it comes to picking a cabaret, the rule of thumb is simple: the better-known places are best. The **Folies-Bergère** is the oldest music hall in Paris and probably the most famous in the world. It is closely rivaled by the **Lido** and the **Moulin Rouge**, birthplace of the cancan.

Cinema

Paris is the world's capital of film appreciation. There are now more than 300 screens within the city limits, distributed among 100 movie theaters. Most are concentrated in clusters, which enjoy the added appeal of nearby restaurants and shops. The Champs-Elysées has the densest cinema strip in town, where you can see the latest Hollywood smash or French *auteur* triumph, as well as some classic re-issues.

The movie theaters on the Grands Boulevards include two notable architectural landmarks: the 2,800-seat **Le Grand Rex**, with its Baroque decor, and the **Max Linder Panorama**, which was refurbished in the 1980s. The largest screen in France is the **La Géode** flagship in the 19th *arrondissement*. On the Left

Bank, the area around Odéon-St-Germain-des-Prés has taken over from the Latin Quarter as the city's heartland for art and repertory movie theaters.

Outdoor Activities

A country as richly diverse in culture and geography as France offers an amazing variety of sport and leisure activities. Information on current activities in a particular region is available from the tourist offices listed for each town in this guide.

Golf is popular in France, especially along the north and south coasts and in Aquitaine. You will need to take your handicap certificate with you if you want to play. Tennis is also a favorite sport, and there are courts to rent in almost every town. More than 30,000 km (19,000 miles) of *Grandes Randonneés* (long-distance tracks)

and shorter *Petites Randonneés* cover France. The routes are clearly way marked, and vary in difficulty, including long pilgrim routes, alpine crossings, and tracks through national parks. Some routes are open to mountain bikes and horses.

The mountains offer excellent skiing and mountaineering. The Atlantic coast around Biarritz offers some of the best surfing and windsurfing in Europe. Sailing and waterskiing are popular across France, and swimming facilities are generally good, although beaches in the south can be crowded in August.

Specialist Vacations

French government Tourist Offices *(see p199)* have extensive information on travel companies offering special-interest vacations. Send off or download

from a selection of brochures. Vacations are based on subjects such as the French language, wine appreciation, and cooking, as well as craft activities and organized nature trips.

Spectator Sport

The main sporting action in France revolves largely around football, rugby, tennis, and horse racing. There are various stadia and circuits all over the country; the best are near major cities, particularly Paris. Here, the **Stade de France** and the **Palais Omni-sports de Paris-Bercy** host all the major events. **Parc des Princes** is home to the top Paris soccer team, Paris St-Germain.

Cycling is also a very popular sport in France, and there is racing action across the country. The most famous event is the annual Tour de France, held during July.

DIRECTORY

Booking Tickets

FNAC
Forum Les Halles,
1 Rue Pierre Lescot,
75001 Paris.
Tel 08-25 02 00 20.

Kiosque Théâtre
Place de la Madeleine,
75008 Paris.
W kiosquetheatre.com

Theater

**Comédie des
Champs-Elysées**
15 Ave Montaigne,
75008 Paris.
Tel 01-53 23 99 19.

Comédie Française
1 Pl Colette,
75001 Paris.
Tel 08-25 10 16 80.

Palais Royal
38 Rue Montpensier,
75001 Paris.
Tel 01-42 97 40 00.

**Théâtre National
de Chaillot**
Place du Trocadéro,
75016 Paris.
Tel 01-53 65 30 00.

**Théâtre National
de la Colline**
15 Rue Malte-Brun, 75020
Paris. **Tel** 01-44 62 52 52.

Music

Cité de la Musique
221 Ave Jean-Jaurès,
75019 Paris.
Tel 01-44 84 44 84.

New Morning
7–9 Rue des Petites-
Ecuries, 75010 Paris.
Tel 01-45 23 51 41.

Olympia
28 Bld des Capucines,
75009 Paris.
Tel 08-92 68 33 68.

Opéra Comique
(Salle Favart) 5 Rue Favart,
75002 Paris.
Tel 01-42 44 45 40.

**Opéra de Paris
Bastille**
120 Rue de Lyon,
75012 Paris.
Tel 01-40 01 17 89.

**Palais Omnisports
de Paris-Bercy**
8 Bld de Bercy 75012.
Tel 08-92-39 04 90.

**Le Petit Journal
St-Michel**
71 Bld St-Michel, 75005
Paris. **Tel** 01-43 26 28 59.

Salle Pleyel
252 Rue du Faubourg
St-Honoré, 75008 Paris.
Tel 01-42 56 13 13.

Zénith
211 Ave Jean-Jaurès,
75019 Paris.
W zenith-paris.com

Clubs and Cabaret

Balajo
9 Rue de Lappe, 75011
Paris. **Tel** 01-47 00 07 87.

Folies-Bergère
32 Rue Richer, 75009 Paris.
Tel 08-92 68 16 50.

La Java
105 Rue du Faubourg-
du-Temple, 75010 Paris.
Tel 01-42 02 20 52.

Lido
116 bis Ave Champs-
Elysées, 75008 Paris.
Tel 01-40 76 56 10.

Moulin Rouge
82 Bld de Clichy, 75018
Paris. **Tel** 01-53 09 82 82.

Le Social Club
142 Rue Montmartre,
75002 Paris.
Tel 01-40 28 05 55.

Cinema

La Géode
26 Ave Corentin-Cariou,
75019 Paris.
Tel 01-40 05 79 99.

Le Grand Rex
1 Bld Poissonnière,
75002 Paris.
Tel 01-45 08 93 89.

**Max Linder
Panorama**
24 Bld Poissonnière,
75009 Paris.
Tel 01-48 24 00 47.

Spectator Sport

**Palais Omnisports
de Paris-Bercy**
8 Bld de Bercy, 75012
Paris. **Tel** 01-40 02 60 60.

Parc des Princes
24 Rue du Commandant-
Guilbaud, 75016 Paris.
Tel 01-47 43 71 71.

Stade de France
La Plaine St-Denis, 93210
Paris. **Tel** 08-92 70 09 00.

Where to Stay

Paris

CHAMPS-ELYSEES & INVALIDES: Mayet €€
Boutique
3 Rue Mayet, 75006
Tel *01-47 83 21 35*
W mayet.com
Painted tables and abstract murals jazz up the interior of this hotel.

CHAMPS-ELYSEES & INVALIDES: Four Seasons George V €€€
Luxury **Map** B2
31 Avenue George V, 75008
Tel *01-49 52 71 00*
W fourseasons.com
This iconic establishment offers its guests modern comforts in an opulent setting.

ILE DE LA CITE, MARAIS & BEAUBOURG: Britannique €€
Boutique **Map** E3
20 Avenue Victoria, 75001
Tel *01-42 33 74 59*
W hotel-britannique.fr
Maritime details adorn this smart hotel with a British feel.

ILE DE LA CITE, MARAIS & BEAUBOURG: Caron de Beaumarchais €€
Boutique **Map** E3
12 Rue Vieille-du-Temple, 75004
Tel *01-42 72 34 12*
W carondebeaumarchais.com
This is a tastefully decorated hotel with 18th-century inspired decor as seen in the color schemes and elegant upholstered furniture.

ILE DE LA CITE, MARAIS & BEAUBOURG: Hospitel €€
Modern **Map** E4
1 Place du Parvis Notre-Dame, 75004
Tel *01-44 32 01 00*
W hotel-hospitel.fr

Modern French style at Le Pavillon de la Reine on Place des Vosges, Paris

Bright accommodations in a centrally located hotel. Free Wi-Fi.

ILE DE LA CITE, MARAIS & BEAUBOURG: Hôtel de la Bretonnerie €€
Boutique **Map** E3
22 Rue Ste-Croix de la Bretonnerie, 75004
Tel *01-48 87 77 63*
W hotelbretonnerie.com
Exposed beams, stone vaulting, and rich fabrics give this hotel a distinctly medieval flavor.

DK Choice

ILE DE LA CITE, MARAIS & BEAUBOURG: Le Petit Moulin €€
Romantic
29–31 Rue du Poitou, 75003
Tel *01-42 74 10 10*
W hotelpetitmoulinparis.com
The oldest *boulangerie* (bakery) in Paris now houses this wacky hotel. Rooms reflect the designer Christian Lacroix's love of opulence, and are romantic with audacious murals. There is free Wi-Fi, access for the disabled, and private parking.

DK Choice

ILE DE LA CITE, MARAIS & BEAUBOURG: Le Pavillon de la Reine €€€
Luxury **Map** F4
28 Place des Vosges, 75003
Tel *01-40 29 19 19*
W pavillon-de-la-reine.com
Overlooking the city's most beautiful square, Le Pavillon has an unrivaled setting. The 17th-century mansion has been refurbished in elegant country-house style, with romantic bedrooms and a lovely spa.

LEFT BANK: Les Degrés de Notre Dame €€
Boutique **Map** E4
10 Rue des Grands Degrés, 75005
Tel *01-55 42 88 88*
W lesdegreshotel.monsite-orange.fr
A vintage charmer with attractive beamed bedrooms.

LEFT BANK: Hôtel des Grands Hommes €€
Romantic
17 Place du Panthéon, 75005
Tel *01-46 34 19 60*
W hoteldesgrandshommes.com
Enjoy breathtaking views of the Panthéon from this elegant, glossy hotel.

LEFT BANK: Résidence Le Prince Regent €€€
Luxury
28 Rue Monsieur le Prince, 75006
Tel *01-56 24 19 21*
W leprinceregent.com
Here you'll find gracefully decorated rooms, spacious apartments, and a *hammam*.

TUILERIES & OPERA: Brighton €€
Boutique **Map** D3
218 Rue de Rivoli, 75001
Tel *01-47 03 61 61*
W paris-hotel-brighton.com
Enjoy breathtaking views of the Tuileries amid faux marble columns, antique furnishings, and glittering chandeliers.

TUILERIES & OPÉRA: Chopin €€
Modern
46 Passage Jouffroy, 75009
Tel *01-47 70 58 10*
W hotelchopin.fr
This simple hotel stands at the end of a 19th-century glass-roofed arcade, close to city attractions.

Northern France

MONT-ST-MICHEL: Terrasses Poulard €€€
Boutique
BP 18, 50170
Tel *02-33 89 02 02*
W terrasses-poulard.fr
This old stone building offers stunning views of the bay and the abbey. Small, clean rooms.

REIMS: Château Les Crayères €€€
Luxury
64 Boulevard Henry Vasnier, 51100
Tel *03-26 24 90 00*
W lescrayeres.com
Aristocratic luxury château in an English-style wooded park. Excellent on-site restaurant.

ROUEN: Hôtel de Bourgtheroulde €€
Luxury
15 Place de la Pucelle d'Orléans, 76000
Tel *02-35 14 50 50*
W hotelsparouen.com
The ornate Renaissance facade belies all the modern comforts of this boutique hotel. Great spa.

ST-MALO:
La Maison Armateurs €€
Boutique
6 Grand Rue, 35400
Tel 02-99 40 87 70
W maisondesarmateurs.com
An old ship-owners' house in the
old town is now a chic hotel with
bright and modern rooms.

STRASBOURG: Le Chut €
Budget
4 Rue du Bain aux Plantes, 67000
Tel 03-88 32 05 06
W hote-strasbourg.fr
Offers a classy Zen atmosphere
and sleek rooms. Great restaurant.

Exposed beams in one of the vast suites at the Domaine des Hauts de Loire, Onzain

The Loire Valley

CHARTRES:
Le Grand Monarque €€
Boutique
22 Place des Epars, 28005
Tel 02-37 18 15 15
W bw-grand-monarque.com
A converted 16th-century staging
post with spacious rooms, a bistro,
fine dining, and a luxury spa.

CHENONCEAUX:
Hôtel du Bon Laboureur €€
Luxury
6 Rue de Dr. Bretonneau, 37150
Tel 02-47 23 90 02
W bonlaboureur.com
Stay in neat rooms housed in
18th-century stone dwellings.

CHINON: Hôtel Diderot €
Budget
4 Rue Buffon, 37500
Tel 02-47 93 18 87
W hoteldiderot.com
Elegant creeper-clad hotel on a
quiet street near the city center.

DK Choice

ONZAIN: Domaine des
Hauts de Loire €€€
Luxury
79 Rue Gilbert Navard, 41150
Tel 02-54 20 72 57
W domainehautsloire.com
This ivy-clad hunting lodge
retains its grandeur with lavish
guest rooms. Those in the old
coach house are the most
opulent. The chef prepares
cutting-edge food, served
with superb local wines.

ORLEANS: Hôtel de l'Abeille €€
Boutique
64 Rue Alsace Lorraine, 45000
Tel 02-38 53 54 87
W hoteldelabeille.com
Grand Neoclassical building with
old-style rooms. Rooftop terrace.

TOURS: Hôtel l'Adresse €
Modern
12 Rue de la Rôtisserie, 37000
Tel 02-47 20 85 76
W hotel-ladresse.com
This modern hotel is concealed
behind the facade of an 18th-
century townhouse.

Burgundy and the French Alps

ANNECY:
Hôtel Palais de l'Isle €€
Historic
13 Rue Perrière, 74000
Tel 04-50 45 86 87
W palaisannecy.com
Renovated 18th-century house
on the Thouin Canal. Comfortable
rooms and modern decor.

CHAMBERY:
Hôtel des Princes €
Boutique
4 Rue de Boigne, 73000
Tel 04-79 33 45 36
W hoteldesprinces.eu
This quiet and comfortable hotel
near the Fontaine des Eléphants
offers friendly service.

DIJON: Le Jacquemart €
Historic
32 Rue Verrerie, 21000
Tel 03-80 60 09 60
W hotel-lejacquemart.fr
Rooms come in all shapes and
sizes at this hotel in a centrally
located 17th-century building.

GRENOBLE:
Splendid Hôtel €
Value
22 Rue Thiers, 38000
Tel 04-76 46 33 12
W splendid-hotel.com
Smart hotel with a walled garden.
Good amenities and rooms that
range from classic to modern.

LYON: Cour des Loges €€
Luxury
6 Rue du Boeuf, 69005
Tel 04-72 77 44 44
W courdesloges.com
The elegant rooms here blend
Renaissance-period features
and contemporary decor.

LYON: Hôtel des Artistes €€
Modern
8 Rue Gaspard-André, 69002
Tel 04-78 42 04 88
W hotel-des-artistes.fr
This delightful hotel, with
pleasant, bright, and airy rooms,
is a favorite haunt of actors.

POLIGNY: Hostellerie des
Monts de Vaux €€
Luxury
Monts Vaux, 39800
Tel 03-84 37 12 50
W hostellerie.com
A family-run hotel in a coaching
inn, with rooms decorated in a
classic bourgeois style.

Southwest France

BIARRITZ:
Hôtel du Palais €€€
Luxury
1 Ave de l'Impératrice, 64200
Tel 05-59 41 64 00
W hotel-du-palais.com
Famous palatial hotel in a superb
beach location, with an opulent
spa, pool, and other facilities.

BORDEAUX:
La Maison du Lierre €
Boutique
57 Rue Huguerie, 33000
Tel 05-56 51 92 71
W hotel-maisondulierre-
bordeaux.com
Charming hotel in a historic house
with a pretty garden. Breakfast is
served in the inner courtyard.

Abstract art and chocolate decor at the Hôtel Bristol, Pau

PAU: Hôtel Bristol €€
Room with a view
3 Rue Gambetta, 64000
Tel *05-59 27 72 98*
w hotelbristol-pau.com
Traditional, centrally located hotel with good facilities. Some rooms have balconies with fine views.

PAUILLAC:
Château Cordeillan-Bages €€
Luxury
Route des Châteaux, 33250
Tel *05-56 59 24 24*
w cordeillanbages.com
Magnificent 17th-century château with splendid gardens, set in the heart of the Médoc vineyards. Closed November to mid-March.

POITIERS: Les Cours du Clain €€
Historic
117 Chemin de la Grotte à Calvin, 86000
Tel *06-10 16 09 55*
w lescoursduclain-poitiers.com
A beautiful B&B set in a historic house with a garden and pool.

TOULOUSE:
Les Loges de Saint-Sernin €€
Boutique
12 Rue St-Bernard, 31000
Tel *05-61 24 44 44*
w leslogesdesaintsernin.com
Reserve well in advance for one of the four spacious rooms in this central Toulouse townhouse.

The South of France

AIX-EN-PROVENCE:
Hôtel Cézanne €€
Boutique
40 Avenue Victor Hugo, 13100
Tel *04-42 91 11 11*
w cezanne.hotelaix.com
Arty, vibrant decor by Charles Montemarco at this chic hotel.

ARLES:
Hôtel de l'Amphithéâtre €
Boutique
5–7 Rue Diderot, 13200
Tel *04-90 96 10 30*
w hotelamphitheatre.fr
Charming Provençal decor in the several family rooms at this gem.

DK Choice

ARLES: L'Hôtel
Particulier à Arles €€€
Historic
4 Rue de la Monnaie, 13200
Tel *04-90 52 51 40*
w hotel-particulier.com
Step into a world of rich elegance and opulent living at this historic hotel. The walled garden, swimming pool, and an ultra-sophisticated spa and *hammam* all make for a dreamy stay. Superb service.

AVIGNON: Hôtel Bristol €€
Modern
44 Cours Jean Jaurès, 84000
Tel *04-90 16 48 48*
w bristol-avignon.com
A classy hotel with refined rooms, including several for families. Pet-friendly. Convenient location.

AVIGNON: La Mirande €€€
Luxury
4 Place de la Mirande, 84000
Tel *04-90 14 20 20*
w la-mirande.fr
This cardinal's mansion by the Papal Palace has been sensitively renovated in 18th-century style.

CANNES: Carlton
InterContinental €€€
Luxury
58 la Croisette, 06400
Tel *04-93 06 40 06*
w intercontinental-carlton-cannes.com
Popular with celebrities, this Art Deco establishment has breath-taking suites and a private beach.

CARCASSONNE:
Hôtel de la Cité €€€
Luxury
Place August-Pierre Pont, 11000
Tel *04-68 71 98 71*
w hoteldelacite.com
Expect period rooms, a glorious pool, and gardens, plus three eateries with immaculate service.

MARSEILLE: Hotel
Résidence du Vieux Port €
Boutique
18 Quai du Port, 13002
Tel *04-91 91 91 22*
w hotel-residence-marseille.com
Enjoy color-drenched 1950s-style decor and fabulous views.

MONACO: Columbus €€€
Boutique
23 Avenue des Papalins, 98000
Tel *377-92 05 92 22*
w columbushotels.com
Sleek designer rooms feature dark stone and polished metal. Excellent restaurant and cigar bar.

MOUSTIERS-STE-MARIE:
La Bastide de Moustiers €€€
Historic
Chemin de Quinson, 04360
Tel *04-92 70 47 47*
w bastide-moustiers.com
This 17th-century building has gardens, mountain views, and a superb Alain Ducasse restaurant.

NICE: Hôtel Windsor €€
Boutique
11 Rue Dalpozzo, 06000
Tel *04-93 88 59 35*
w hotelwindsornice.com
Stay in individually decorated rooms. There is also a pool within an exotic garden.

NICE: Le Negresco €€€
Luxury
37 Promenade des Anglais 06000
Tel *04-93 16 64 00*
w hotel-negresco-nice.com
This renowned vintage hotel was designed by Henri Negrescu. It has superb works of art, flawless service, and top-notch facilities.

NIMES: Imperator-Concorde €€
Luxury
Quai de la Fontaine, 30000
Tel *04-66 21 90 30*
w hotel-imperator.com
Built in 1929, the Concorde is a favorite of celebrities, with a lovely garden featuring cedar and palm trees.

DK Choice

ST-TROPEZ: Pastis Hôtel
St-Tropez €€€
Boutique
6 Avenue du Général Leclerc, 83990
Tel *04-98 12 56 50*
w pastis-st-tropez.com
This ideal intimate hideaway is filled with 20th-century art. The heated garden pool is idyllic, surrounded by centuries-old palm trees – the perfect spot for breakfast or a nightcap.

VILLEFRANCHE SUR MER:
Hôtel Welcome €€
Boutique
1 Quai Amiral Courbet, 06230
Tel *04-93 76 27 62*
w welcomehotel.com
Artist Jean Cocteau's favorite hotel, the Welcome is full of period charm. Also has a great wine bar.

Key to Price Guide *see page 206*

Where to Eat and Drink

Paris

CHAMPS-ELYSEES & INVALIDES:
La Fontaine de Mars €€
Regional **Map** B3
129 Rue St-Dominique, 75007
Tel *01-47 05 46 44*
Duck *cassoulet* is the flagship dish
at this archetypal bistro. Beautiful
interiors and great service.

CHAMPS-ELYSEES & INVALIDES:
L'Arpège €€€
Traditional French **Map** C4
84 Rue de Varenne, 75007
Tel *01-47 05 09 06* **Closed** *Sat & Sun*
A mecca for vegetable-lovers, this
eatery is all about homegrown
produce and sophisticated dining.

CHAMPS-ELYSEES & INVALIDES:
Le Jules Verne €€€
Modern French **Map** B3
5 Avenue Gustave Eiffel, 75007
Tel *01-45 55 61 44*
Alain Ducasse's restaurant on
the Eiffel Tower's second platform
offers stylish dining to complement
the 360-degree views over Paris.

ILE DE LA CITE, MARAIS &
BEAUBOURG: L'Ambassade
d'Auvergne €€
Auvergnat **Map** 9 B2
22 Rue du Grenier St-Lazare, 75003
Tel *01 42 72 31 22*
This rustic inn serves Auvergne
dishes such as *aligot* (potatoes
with cheese and garlic).

ILE DE LA CITE, MARAIS &
BEAUBOURG: Frenchie €€
Modern French
5–6 Rue du Nil, 75002
Tel *01-40 39 96 19* **Closed** *Sat & Sun*
One of Paris's hottest bistros,
Frenchie serves exquisite dishes
on fixed-price menus. Book ahead.

DK Choice

ILE DE LA CITE, MARAIS &
BEAUBOURG: Spring €€€
Modern French **Map** D3
6 Rue Bailleul, 75001
Tel *01-45 96 05 72* **Closed** *Sun &*
Mon
Spring's chef Daniel Rose,
a magician in the kitchen,
produces a superlative
fixed-price tasting menu that
is dependent on the freshest
produce available. He cooks
unique versions of French
classics, which can be enjoyed
with great wines from a vast
selection. The sommeliers will
be able to advise on suitable
pairings. Open for dinner only.

LEFT BANK: L'Agrume €€
Modern French
15 Rue des Fossés St-Marcel, 75005
Tel *01-43 31 86 48* **Closed** *Mon*
& Sun
Foodies line up at L'Agrume to
sample the renowned chef's
five-course tasting menu.

LEFT BANK: El Loubnane €€
Lebanese **Map** E4
29 Rue Gallande, 75005
Tel *01-43 26 70 60* **Closed** *Mon*
Enjoy deliciously fragrant meze
at this family-run establishment.
Do not miss the pistachio-stuffed
crêpes and *katayef.*

LEFT BANK: Le Procope €€
Traditional French **Map** D4
13 Rue de l'Ancienne Comédie,
75006
Tel *01-40 46 79 00*
The city's oldest café, dating
from 1686, Le Procope still
retains its original atmosphere.
Great selection of desserts.

LEFT BANK:
La Tour d'Argent €€€
Traditional French **Map** E4
15 Quai de la Tournelle, 75005
Tel *01-43 54 23 31* **Closed** *Sun & Mon*
World-famous institution with a
romantic dining room boasting
panoramic views. The bar doubles
as a gastronomic museum.

TUILERIES & OPERA: Chartier €€
Traditional French
7 Rue du Faubourg Montmartre,
75009
Tel *01-47 70 86 29*
At this iconic brasserie,
traditionally dressed waiters serve
simple, good food in glorious
belle-époque surroundings.

TUILERIES & OPERA:
Chez Georges €€
Traditional French **Map** D2
1 Rue du Mail, 75002
Tel *01-42 60 07 11* **Closed** *Sat & Sun*
The bistro fare at this lovely
eatery is as old-fashioned as the
decor, but it remains sublime. It
was a favorite with famed cook
Julia Child.

TUILERIES & OPERA:
Le Grand Véfour €€€
Modern French **Map** D3
17 Rue de Beaujolais, 75001
Tel *01-42 96 56 27* **Closed** *Sat & Sun*
The highly acclaimed chef, Guy
Martin's innovative fare is served
in an 18th-century room where
Napoleon dined with Josephine.

FARTHER AFIELD: Bofinger €€
Regional **Map** F4
5–7 Rue de la Bastille, 75004
Tel *01-42 72 87 82*
One of the city's most beautiful
brasseries, with a perfectly
preserved *belle-époque* interior.
Excellent shellfish is served here.

Northern France

CARNAC: Le Calypso €€
Seafood
158 Rue du Pô, 56340
Tel *02-97 52 06 14* **Closed** *Sun*
dinner (except Jul & Aug); Mon
Le Calypso is a popular seafood
restaurant overlooking the oyster
beds of Anse du Pô.

Elegance and simplicity at L'Arpège, Paris

DK Choice

LILLE: A l'Huitrière €€€
Seafood
3 Rue des Chats Bossus, 59800
Tel *03-20 55 43 41* **Closed** *Sun dinner*
More than just a restaurant, A l'Huitrière is also an oyster bar and a seafood boutique where you can buy the day's catch. Try the vinaigrette salad of smoked eel with foie gras, pan-fried lobster with tarragon, crayfish, or the signature turbot.

DK Choice

REIMS: Café du Palais €€
Traditional French
14 Place Myron Herrick, 51100
Tel *03-26 47 52 54* **Closed** *Sun & Mon*
A much-loved family-run brasserie with excellent main dishes, great desserts, and a fine selection of champagnes. The decor consists of an Aladdin's cave of theatrical memorabilia under a stained-glass roof.

ROUEN: Le 37 €€
Bistro
37 Rue St-Etienne-des-Tonneliers, 76000
Tel *02-35 70 56 65* **Closed** *Sun & Mon*
Attractive city-center bistro serving modern cuisine. Find the daily specials on the blackboard.

ST-MALO: Le Chalut €€
Seafood
8 Rue de la Corne de Cerf, 35400
Tel *02-99 56 71 58* **Closed** *Mon & Tue*
Fishing nets, buoys, and an aquarium provide the perfect ambience to this seafood eatery.

STRASBOURG: Winstub Zuem Strissel €€
Regional
5 Place de la Grande Boucherie, 67000
Tel *03-88 32 14 73*
The oldest eatery in Alsace serves *baeckeoffe* (a mutton, beef, pork casserole) and *bibelekäse* (cream cheese and sautéed potatoes).

The Loire Valley

BLOIS: L'Orangerie du Château €€€
Fine Dining
1 Avenue Jean Laigret, 41000
Tel *02-54 78 05 36* **Closed** *Sun & Mon*
The fine setting, in a château's winter garden, is matched by the food and wine. The menu features innovative regional fare.

The dining room at the Café du Palais in Reims, featuring a stunning stained-glass roof

CHARTRES: Le Grand Monarque, Le Georges €€€
Fine Dining
22 Place des Epars, 28000
Tel *02-37 18 15 15* **Closed** *Sun dinner; Mon*
Sample excellent classic French cuisine at this gourmet restaurant, accompanied by grand cru wines.

DK Choice

NANTES: L'U.Ni €€
Modern French
36 Rue Fouré
Tel *02-40 75 53 05* **Closed** *Mon & Tue*
Savvy young chef Nicolas Guiet heads this restaurant, which has created ripples in gourmet circles. L'U.Ni's signature dishes include barely cooked brill with baby turnips and spinach, and desserts such as carrot and orange cake accompanied by a carrot and honey mousse.

ORLÉANS: La Dariole €€
Traditional French
25 Rue Etienne Dolet, 45000
Tel *02-38 77 26 67* **Closed** *Sat & Sun; Mon, Wed & Thu: dinner*
A 15th-century half-timbered building houses this little restaurant and tearoom.

SAUMUR: Auberge St-Pierre €€
Regional
6 Place St-Pierre, 49400
Tel *02-41 51 26 25*
On a square near the château, in a former 15th-century monastery, this convivial restaurant serves hearty Burgundy dishes.

TOURS: Les Saveurs €€
Bistro
1 Place Gaston Paillhou, 37000
Tel *02-47 37 03 13* **Closed** *Sun & Mon*
A chic and modern bistro serving tasty dishes. The kitchen uses seasonal produce sourced from the daily market.

TOURS: La Roche Le Roy €€€
Fine Dining
55 Rue de St-Avertin, 37000
Tel *02-47 27 22 00* **Closed** *Sun & Mon*
This Michelin-starred restaurant serves classic top-notch French cuisine and fine wines.

Burgundy and the French Alps

ANNECY: Le Belvédère €€€
Modern French
7 Chemin Belvédère, 74000
Tel *04-50 45 04 90* **Closed** *Sun dinner; Tue & Wed; Oct–May*
Lovely lake views and appetizing contemporary food. Try the vegetable and flower cheesecake served with a watercress coulis.

BEAUNE: Le Bistro de L'Hôtel €€
Bistro
3 Rue Samuel Legay, 21200
Tel *03-80 25 94 10* **Closed** *lunch; Sun*
This chic bistro uses high-quality ingredients sourced from local suppliers. It also boasts an excellent selection of wines.

CHABLIS: La Cuisine au Vin €€
Regional
16 Rue Auxerroise, 89800
Tel *03-86 18 98 52* **Closed** *Sun dinner; Mon & Tue; mid-Nov–Jan*
Expect innovative takes on classic dishes such as Burgundy snails and beef bourguignon. Friendly and efficient staff.

DIJON: Hostellerie du Chapeau Rouge €€€
Modern French
5 Rue Michelet, 21000
Tel *03-80 50 88 88* **Closed** *Sun & Mon*
One of Dijon's top restaurants, the Chapeau Rouge provides inventive modern fare. Expect dishes such as pigeon served with a beetroot and lychee sauce.

GRENOBLE: A Ma Table €€
Traditional
92 Cours Jean-Jaurès, 38000
Tel *04-76 96 77 04* **Closed** *dinner Tue, Wed & Fri; Sat–Mon*
This beautiful restaurant prepares dishes such as rabbit with mint served with zucchini tagliatelle.

LYON: La Gargotte €€
Modern French
15 Rue Royale, 69001
Tel *04-78 28 79 20* **Closed** *lunch Sun & Mon; Sat*
Classic dishes are reinterpreted with originality at this friendly restaurant, with retro decor and mirrored walls.

Southwest France

BIARRITZ: Chez Albert €€
Brasserie
51bis Allée Port des Pêcheurs, 64200
Tel *05-59 24 43 84* **Closed** *Wed*
This bright, bustling seafood brasserie in the port of Biarritz is blessed with great views. Try the mixed seafood platter.

BORDEAUX:
Le Bistrot d'Edouard €€
Bistro
16 Place du Parlement, 33000
Tel *05-56 81 48 87*
Come here for good-value brasserie-style dishes, such as prawns cooked in aniseed.

BORDEAUX: Le Chapon Fin €€€
Fine Dining
5 Rue Montesquieu, 33000
Tel *05-56 79 10 10* **Closed** *Sun & Mon*
Try Nicolas Frion's exquisite creative cuisine at this historic restaurant with *belle-époque* decor.

LA ROCHELLE:
Le Boute en Train €€
Bistro
7 Rue des Bonnes Femmes, 17000
Tel *05-46 41 73 74* **Closed** *Sun & Mon*
Enjoy hearty classic fare made with market-fresh ingredients. There is also a quality wine list.

ST-JEAN-DE-LUZ: Chez Pablo €
Regional
5 Rue Mlle Etcheto, 64500
Tel *05-59 26 37 81* **Closed** *Mon & Tue dinner (Nov–Easter); Wed*
Friendly eatery with bench seating and Basque seafood classics.

ST-JEAN-DE-LUZ: Le Kaïku €€€
Fine Dining
17 Rue de la République, 64500
Tel *05-59 26 13 20* **Closed** *Mon; Sep–Jun*
Inventive Basque cuisine by chef Nicolas Borombo is served in an old stone house. Superb fish.

TOULOUSE: Michel Sarran €€€
Fine Dining
21 Boulevard Armand Duportal, 31000
Tel *05-61 12 32 32* **Closed** *Sat & Sun; Aug*
This chic establishment is headed by one of France's finest chefs. A sublime gourmet experience.

The South of France

AIX-EN-PROVENCE:
Le Formal €€
Gastronomic
32 Rue Espariat, 13100
Tel *04-42 27 08 31* **Closed** *Sat lunch; Sun & Mon; late Aug–early Sep*
Le Formal is housed in a vaulted cellar with contemporary design. Good-value lunch menus, and plenty of truffle-based dishes.

ARLES: La Grignotte €
Regional **Map** B3
6 Rue Favorin, 13200
Tel *04-90 93 10 43* **Closed** *Sun*
Try the fish soup and beef stew with Camargue rice at this cheery eatery. Good house wines.

AVIGNON: La Fourchette €€
Regional
17 Rue Racine, 84000
Tel *04-90 85 20 93* **Closed** *Sat & Sun*
A quirky restaurant, offering its own innovative take on Provençal classics, with lots of seafood and delicious cheeses.

CANNES: Angolo Italiano €€
Italian
6 Rue des Batéguiers, 06400
Tel *04-93 68 42 36* **Closed** *Mon*
Neapolitan-run eatery with Italian *charcuterie* and cheeses, grilled meats, and seafood.

CANNES: La Palme d'Or €€€
Fine Dining
73 la Croisette, 06400
Tel *04-92 98 74 14* **Closed** *Sun–Tue*
This fashionable, two-Michelin-starred restaurant is part of the famous Hotel Martinez.

DK Choice

CARCASSONNE:
La Marquière €€
Regional
13 Rue St-Jean, 11000
Tel *04-68 71 52 00* **Closed** *Wed & Thu; Jan 10–Feb 10*
Located up in the Cité, La Marquière is a family-run local favorite. The food is authentic Southwestern – duck breasts and confits, foie gras, and *cassoulet*. Oysters and other seafood are also available.

DK Choice

MARSEILLE: Epuisette €€€
Seafood
Vallon des Auffes, 13007
Tel *04-91 52 17 82* **Closed** *Sun & Mon*
The gorgeous Epuisette boasts a spectacular dining room overlooking the sea. Enjoy heavenly *bouillabaisse*, lobster tagine, and other seafood dishes, all accompanied by excellent wines. Great desserts, too. A memorable experience.

NICE: Les Amoureux €
Italian
46 Boulevard Stalingrad, 06000
Tel *04-93 07 59 73* **Closed** *Sun & Mon*
Visit Les Amoureux for some of the best pizzas on the Riviera. The crusts alone are unparalleled.

NICE: Luc Salsedo €€
Fine Dining
14 Rue Maccarani, 06000
Tel *04-93 82 24 12* **Closed** *lunch*
Classics, such as ratatouille and lamb, are reinvented and served in style. Good vegetarian choices.

NIMES: Aux Plaisirs des Halles €€
Traditional French
4 Rue Littré, 30000
Tel *04-66 36 01 02* **Closed** *Sun & Mon*
Friendly eatery with tables indoors and outdoors. Chalkboard menu features foie gras, steaks, and duck.

Rustic accents and cozy dining at La Marquière, Carcassonne

BELGIUM AND LUXEMBOURG

Famed for its magnificent Flemish art and Gothic architecture, Belgium, like neighboring Luxembourg, is a melting pot of various influences, including Dutch, French, and German. The histories of the two countries have long been interlinked, but culturally and linguistically they are distinct. Luxembourg, a major financial center, is one of the smallest states in Europe.

In recent times, both Belgium and Luxembourg have largely avoided the limelight, but it was here, in the Middle Ages, that the first great towns of Northern Europe were born, and where the first experiments with oil paintings were made. Today, Brussels, as the center of government for the European Union, is theoretically the capital of Europe, but its reputation remains overshadowed by those of the larger European capitals.

Perhaps more than any other country in Europe, Belgium is most aptly defined by contrasts. The division between the Flemish inhabitants of the north and the French-speaking Walloons in the south is mirrored by a geographical divide; the estuarial plains of Brabant and Flanders give way to the rolling hill-country of the Ardennes, which stretches south and east through the castle-dotted woods of Luxembourg.

History

At the start of the 12th century, commerce became the guiding force in Europe, and the centers of trade quickly grew into powerful cities. Rivers and canals were keys to the growth of the area's towns; Brussels, Ghent, Ypres, Antwerp, and Bruges became the focus of a cloth trade between Belgium, France, Germany, Italy, and England.

In 1369 Philip, Duke of Burgundy, married the daughter of the Count of Flanders, and a few years later the Low Countries and eastern France came under the couple's Burgundian rule. A century later, the death of Mary of Burgundy left her husband, the Habsburg Emperor Maximilian, ruler of Belgium. In 1488, Brussels and the rest of Flanders rebelled against this new power, but the Austrians prevailed, largely because of a plague which decimated the population in 1490.

European Parliament building rising above the trees of Parc Léopold, Brussels

◀ One of the majestic gilt-edged buildings surrounding the Grand Place, Brussels

By 1555, the Low Countries had passed into the hands of the Spanish Habsburgs, whose Catholic repression of the Protestants sparked the Dutch Revolt. In the course of the wars that led to Dutch independence (1568–1648), the predominantly Catholic southern part of the Low Countries remained under Spanish rule. In 1700, the Spanish Habsburg dynasty died out, and England, Austria, and other powers united to oppose French designs on the region in the War of the Spanish Succession. When the war came to an end in 1713, the Treaty of Utrecht transferred Belgium and Luxembourg to the Austrian Habsburgs.

Belgium was again ruled by foreign powers between 1794 and 1830. First, by the French Republicans, and then, after

King Leopold I, the first king of the Belgians, crowned in 1830

Napoleon's defeat, by the Dutch. William I of Orange was appointed King of the Netherlands at the Congress of Vienna in 1815, and his autocratic style, together with a series of anti-Catholic measures, bred considerable discontent, especially among the French-speaking Walloons. An 1830 uprising ousted the Dutch and made Leopold I king of a newly independent Belgium. Nine years later, Luxembourg, a Grand-Duchy since 1815, also gained independence.

Both countries' economies flourished throughout the 19th century, but all was eclipsed with the start of World War I. In 1940, the Germans invaded again, this time under Hitler's command.

Belgium's history in the latter half of the 20th century was dominated by the ongoing language debate between the Flemings and the Walloons. The constitution was redrawn, creating a federal state with three separate regions: Flanders, Wallonia, and Brussels.

KEY DATES IN THE HISTORY OF BELGIUM AND LUXEMBOURG

56 BC Julius Caesar conquers the Low Countries

963 AD Count Siegfried establishes Luxembourg

1229 Brussels granted its first charter

1430 Under Burgundian rule, Brussels becomes the major administrative center of the region

1482 The region falls under Austrian sovereignty

1519 Charles V becomes Holy Roman Emperor

1555–1794 Spanish and Austrian rule

1794 French Republican armies take over

1815 Belgium and Luxembourg pass to William I of Orange, King of the Netherlands

1830 Belgium gains independence

1839 Luxembourg gains independence

1914 Both countries invaded by Germany

1940 Nazi troops occupy both countries

1958 EEC (now the EU) headquarters set up in Brussels

1962 Act of Parliament divides Belgium into Dutch-and French-speaking regions

1967 NATO headquarters move to Brussels

2000 Grand Duke of Luxembourg abdicates in favor of his eldest son, Henri

2013 King Albert II of Belgium abdicates in favor of his son Philippe

Language and Culture

In the north of Belgium, the Flemish have their roots in the Netherlands and Germany, while the Walloons of the south are related to the French. French is one of the official languages of Luxembourg, as is German, but the indigenous language is Letzeburgesch, a dialect of German spoken by all. Artistically, Belgium is best known for its 17th-century painters (including Rubens, van Dyck, and Jordaens) and more recently for its Art Nouveau style of architecture and Surrealist artists, such as Magritte. Today, the country is one of the world's most popular producers of chocolate and beer.

Exploring Belgium and Luxembourg

Brussels is not only the capital of Belgium, but also of Europe, as the center of government for the European Union. The city lies in the center of the country on the flat, fertile Brabant plain. Today, its excellent communications make it an ideal place from which to explore the historic towns of Antwerp, Ghent, and Bruges. Toll-free motorways compare favorably with any in France, train travel is swift and competitively priced, and there are good bus services in the areas not covered by trains. Transport in Luxembourg is equally good, with the hub of communications in Luxembourg City itself.

Sights at a Glance

1. Brussels pp216–23
2. Antwerp
3. Bruges pp226–8
4. Ghent
5. Waterloo
6. Luxembourg

The medieval market square, seen from the Belfort tower, Bruges

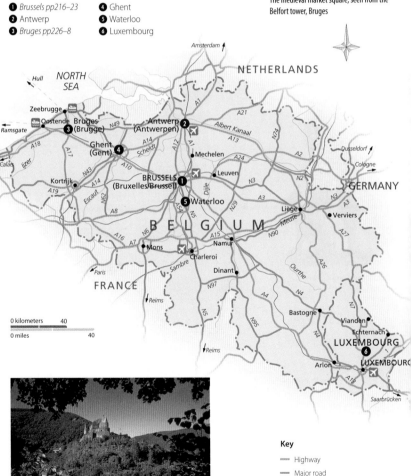

Picturesque Château de Vianden, Luxembourg

Key

- ▬▬▬ Highway
- ▬▬▬ Major road
- ▬▬▬ Railroad
- ▪▪▪ International border

For keys to symbols *see back flap*

● Brussels

With more than one million inhabitants, the Brussels-Capital Region is made up of nineteen districts. The actual city of Brussels is much smaller and divided into two main areas. Historically the poorer area, where workers and immigrants lived, the Lower Town is centered on the splendid 17th-century Grand Place. The Upper Town, traditional home of the aristocracy, is an elegant area that encircles the city's green oasis, the Parc de Bruxelles. Some of the most striking buildings in this part of the city are the shiny postmodern structures of European institutions.

Two famous Belgians: Tintin and Snowy

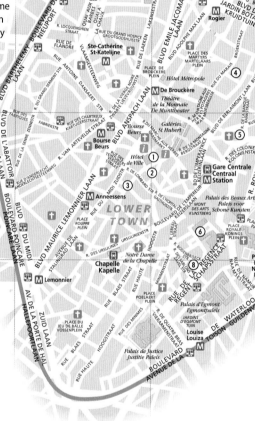

Sights at a Glance

① Grand Place
② Musée du Costume et de la Dentelle
③ Manneken Pis
④ Centre Belge de la Bande Dessinée
⑤ Cathédrale Sts-Michel et Gudule
⑥ Musées Royaux des Beaux-Arts
⑦ Palais Royal
⑧ Place du Grand Sablon
⑨ European Parliament Quarter
⑩ Parc du Cinquantenaire

Greater Brussels *(see inset map)*

⑪ Musée Horta
⑫ Bruparck

Getting Around

Brussels' Lower Town is well served by trams. However, many streets are pedestrianized, and usually the quickest way of getting around is on foot. In the Upper Town, the best option is to take one of the buses that run through the district. Brussels' metro stations are well placed for the main sights of interest, and the system offers a fast and efficient way of reaching the suburbs.

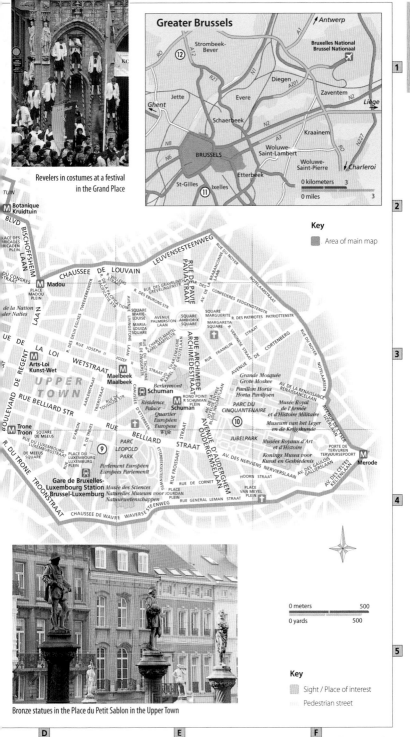

Revelers in costumes at a festival in the Grand Place

Greater Brussels

↗ Antwerp

Strombeek-
Bever

⑫

**Bruxelles National
Brussel Nationaal** ✈

Diegen

Jette

Evere

Zaventem

Ghent ←

Schaerbeek

Liège →

Kraainem

BRUSSELS

Woluwe-
Saint-Lambert

Etterbeek

Woluwe-
Saint-Pierre

↗ Charleroi

St-Gilles

⑪ Ixelles

0 kilometers   3

0 miles   3

Key

Area of main map

TUIN

Ⓜ Botanique
Kruidtuin

BLVD

BISCHOFFSHEIM
LAAN

LACE DES
RICADES
RICADEN
PLEIN

DU CONGRES
TRAAT

de la Nation
der Naties

CHAUSSÉE DE LOUVAIN

LEUVENSESTEENWEG

RUE DE PAVIE
PAVIASTRAAT

RUE DE LA BRABANÇONNE

RUE DU NOYER

Ⓜ Madou

PLACE
MADOU
PLEIN

AV. DES CONFEDERES EEDGENOTENSTR

NOTELAARSTRAAT

SQUARE
MARIE-
LOUISE
MARIA-
LOUIZA
LAAN

AVENUE
PALMERSTON
LAAN

SQUARE
AMBIORIX
SQUARE

SQUARE
MARGUERITE

MARGARETA
SQUARE

RUE DES PATRIOTES PATRIOTTENSTR

RUE DE CORTENBERG

LA
LOI
WETSTRAAT

Ⓜ Arts-Loi
Kunst-Wet

**U P P E R
T O W N**

RUE FRANKLIN

AVENUE

Ⓜ Maelbeek
Maalbeek

Berlaymont

Grande Mosquée
Grote Moskee

Pavillon Horta
Horta Paviljoen

AVENUE DE LA RENAISSANCE
RENAISSANCELAAN

Ⓜ Schuman

ROND POINT
R SCHUMAN
PLEIN

PARC DU
CINQUANTENAIRE

Musée Royal
de l'Armée
et d'Histoire Militaire

Ⓜ Trone
Troon

SQUARE
DE MEEUS

Résidence
Palace

Quartier
Européen
Europese
Wijk

⑩

Museum van het Leger
en de Krijgskunde

RUE
BELLIARD
STRAAT

AVENUE D'AUDERGHEM
OUDERGEMSELAAN

JUBELPARK

Musées Royaux d'Art
et d'Histoire

Konings Musea voor
Kunst en Geshiedenis

PORTE DE
TERVUREN
TERVUURSEPOORT

Ⓜ Merode

PLACE DU
LUXEMBOURG
LUXEMBURG

⑨

PARC
LEOPOLD
PARK

AV. DES NERVIENS
NERVIERSLAAN

AV. DE GAULOIS
GALLIERSLAAN

AV. DES CELTES
KELTENLAAN

PLACE
DE MEEUS
SQUARE

**Gare de Bruxelles-
Luxembourg Station
Brussel-Luxemburg**

Parlement Européen
Europees Parlement

Musée des Sciences
Naturelles Museum voor
Natuurwetenschappen

RUE DE CORNET

HOORN STRAAT

PLACE
VAN MEYEL
PLEIN

CHAUSSÉE DE WAVRE WAVERSESTEENWEG

PLACE
JOURDAN
PLEIN

RUE GENERAL LEMAN STRAAT

0 meters   500

0 yards   500

Ⓜ Bronze statues in the Place du Petit Sablon in the Upper Town

Key

Sight / Place of interest

Pedestrian street

D   E   F

For keys to symbols *see back flap*

Grand Place, Brussels's historic main square

① Grand Place

Ⓜ Bourse, Gare Centrale. 🚌 29, 38, 46, 47, 48, 66, 71. 🚊 3, 4, 31, 32. Musée de la Ville: Maison du Roi. **Tel** 02-279 4350. **Open** 10am–5pm Tue–Sun. **Closed** Jan 1, May 1, Nov 1 & 11, Dec 25. 🚫 📷 by prior arrangement.

The geographical, historical, and commercial heart of the city, the Grand Place is the first port of call for most visitors to Brussels. A market was held on this site as early as the 11th century. During the first half of the 15th century, Brussels' town hall, the Hôtel de Ville, was built, and city traders began to add individual guildhalls in a medley of styles. In 1695, however, two days of cannon fire by the French destroyed all but the town hall and two facades. Trade guilds were urged to rebuild their halls to designs approved by the town council,

La Maison du Roi, built on the site of old bread, meat, and cloth halls

resulting in the splendid Baroque ensemble that can be seen today.

Occupying the entire southwest side of the square, the Gothic **Hôtel de Ville** (see opposite) is the architectural masterpiece of the Grand Place. Opposite it stands **La Maison du Roi** (1536). Despite its name, no king ever lived here; the building was used as a temporary jail and a tax office. Redesigned in Gothic style in the late 19th century, it is now home to the Musée de la Ville, which contains 16th-century paintings and tapestries, and a collection of around 815 costumes created for the Manneken Pis.

On the square's eastern flank, the vast Neoclassical edifice known as **La Maison des Ducs de Brabant** was designed by Guillaume de Bruyn and consists of six former guildhalls. Facing it are **Le Renard**, built in the 1690s for the guild of haberdashers, and **Le Cornet** (1697), the boatmen's guild hall, whose gable resembles a 17th-century frigate's bow. **Le Roy d'Espagne**, also known as La Maison des Boulangers, was built in the late 17th century by the wealthy bakers' guild. The gilt bust over the entrance represents St. Aubert, patron saint of bakers. Today, the building houses one of the Grand Place's best-loved bars, whose first floor offers fine views of the bustling square.

② Musée du Costume et de la Dentelle

Rue de Violette 12. **Tel** 02-213 4450. Ⓜ Gare Centrale. 🚌 48, 95. **Open** 10am–5pm Thu–Tue. 🚫 📷 on request. ♿ restricted.

Located within two 18th-century gabled houses, this museum is dedicated to one of Brussels' most successful exports, Belgian lace, which has been made here since the 12th century. The ground floor has a display of costumes on mannequins showing how lace has adorned fashions of every era. Upstairs is a fine collection of antique lace from France, Flanders, and Italy.

③ Manneken Pis

Rues de l'Etuve & du Chêne. Ⓜ Gare Centrale. 🚌 48, 95. 🚊 3, 4, 31, 32.

The tiny statue of a young boy relieving himself is Brussels' most unusual sight. The original bronze statue by Jérôme Duquesnoy the Elder was first placed on the site in 1619. After it was stolen and damaged by a former convict in 1817, a replica was made and returned to its revered site. The inspiration for the statue is unknown, but the mystery only lends itself to rumor and fable and increases the little boy's charm. One theory claims that in the 12th century, the son of a duke was caught urinating against a tree in the midst of a battle, and was thus commemorated in bronze as a symbol of the country's military courage. When, in 1698, a city governor provided a set of clothes with which to dress the statue, he began a tradition that is still observed today. Visiting heads of state donate miniature versions of their national costume for the boy, and now a collection of 815 outfits, including an Elvis suit, can be seen in the Musée de la Ville.

Manneken Pis statue

Hôtel de Ville

The idea of erecting a town hall to reflect Brussels' growth as a major European trading center had been under consideration since the end of the 13th century, but it was not until 1401 that the first foundation stone was laid. Completed in 1459, the Hôtel de Ville emerged as the finest civic building in the country, a stature it still enjoys. Jacques van Thienen was commissioned to design the left wing, where he used ornate columns, sculptures, turrets, and arcades. Jan van Ruysbroeck's elegant spire helped seal the building's reputation. Tours of the interior are available, with its 15th-century tapestries and works of art.

VISITORS' CHECKLIST

Practical Information
Grand Place. **Tel** 02-279 2343.
Open for guided tours (in English: 3pm Wed, 10am & 2pm Sun; call 02-548 0447 for more details).
Closed public hols & election days.

Transport
Ⓜ Bourse, Gare Centrale.
🚌 many routes. 🚋 3, 4, 31, 32.

★ Maximilian Room
This lavish hall, used today by the city council, takes its name from the portrait of Maximilian I of Austria over the fireplace. It contains 18th-century tapestries depicting the history of 6th-century King Clovis.

★ Council Chamber
This room was where the ruling council of Brabant used to meet. Ancient tapestries and gilt mirrors line the walls above an inlaid floor.

The tower, begun in 1449, is 96 m (315 ft) high. It is topped by a statue of St. Michael, patron saint of Brussels.

The gabled roof, like much of the town hall, was fully restored in 1837 and cleaned in the 1990s.

Gothic Room

137 stone statues adorn the facades.

Wedding Room
A Neo-Gothic style dominates this civil marriage office. Its ornate carved timbers include mahogany inlaid with ebony.

Art Nouveau entrance hall of the Centre Belge de la Bande Dessinée

④ Centre Belge de la Bande Dessinée

20 Rue des Sables. **Tel** 02-219 1980.
🚌 29, 38, 63, 66, 71. 🚋 25, 55, 92, 93.
Ⓜ Botanique, Rogier, Centrale. **Open**
10am–6pm Tue–Sun. **Closed** Jan 1,
Dec 25. 🎫 📷 📎 🏠 ♿

This unique museum pays tribute to the Belgian passion for comic strips, or *bandes dessinées*, and to world-famous comic-strip artists from Belgium and abroad.

One of the exhibitions shows the great comic-strip heroes, from Hergé's Tintin – who made his debut in 1929 – to the Smurfs and the Flemish comic-strip characters Suske and Wiske. Other displays explain the stages of putting together a comic strip. There is also a series of life-size cartoon sets, of special appeal to children. The museum holds 6,000 original plates, and a valuable archive of photographs and artifacts.

The collection is housed in a beautiful building, built in 1903–6 to the design of the Belgian Art Nouveau architect Victor Horta (*see p223*).

⑤ Cathédrale Sts-Michel et Gudule

Parvis Ste-Gudule. **Tel** 02-217 8345.
🚌 29, 38, 63, 65, 66, 71. 🚋 92, 93.
Ⓜ Centrale. **Open** daily. 🎫 to crypt
and treasury. ♿ call in advance.
🌐 **cathedralestmichel.be**

Belgium's finest surviving example of Brabant Gothic architecture, the Cathédrale Sts-Michel et Gudule is the national church of Belgium. There has been a church on this site since

at least the 11th century. Work began on the Gothic cathedral in 1226 under Henry I, Duke of Brabant, and continued over a period of 300 years.

The cathedral interior is relatively bare, due to Protestant ransacking in 1579 and thefts during the French Revolution. Over the west door, however, is a magnificent 16th-century stained-glass window of the Last Judgment. Another splendid feature is the flamboyantly carved Baroque pulpit in the central aisle, by an Antwerp sculptor, Hendrik Frans Verbruggen. In the crypt are the remains of the original Romanesque church, which dates back to 1047.

⑥ Musées Royaux des Beaux-Arts

Rue de la Régence 3. **Tel** 02-508 3211.
🚌 27, 29, 38, 63, 65, 66, 71, 95.
🚋 92, 93. Ⓜ Parc, Centrale. **Open**
10am–5pm Tue–Sun. **Closed** public
hols. 🎫 📷 call in advance. 🏠 📱
📎 ♿ 🌐 **fine-arts-museum.be**

Six centuries of art, both Belgian and international, are displayed in the four museums that make up the Musées Royaux des Beaux-Arts: the Musée d'Art Ancien (15th–18th centuries), the Musée Fin-de-Siècle

The white limestone facade of the Cathédrale Sts-Michel et Gudule

(1868–1914), the Musée d'Art Moderne (19th century–present day), and the Magritte Museum.

The Musée d'Art Ancien holds one of the world's finest collections of works by the Flemish Primitive School. A work of particular note is *The Annunciation* (c.1415–25) by the Master of Flémalle. The trademarks of the Flemish Primitives are a lifelike vitality and a clarity of light. The greatest exponent of the style was Rogier van der Weyden (c.1400–64), the official city painter to Brussels, who has several splendid works on display at the museum.

Peter Brueghel the Elder (c.1525–69), one of the most outstanding Flemish artists, settled in Brussels in 1563. His earthy scenes of peasant life remain his best known works, and are represented here by paintings such as *The Bird Trap* (1565).

Another highlight of the Musée d'Art Ancien is the world-famous collection of works by Peter Paul Rubens (1577–1640). *The Assumption of the Virgin* stands out among his religious

The Assumption of the Virgin (c.1615) by Rubens at the Musées Royaux des Beaux-Arts

canvases. Other notable paintings include van Dyck's *Portrait of Porzia Imperial with her daughter Maria Francesca* (1620s) and *Three Children with Goatcart* by Frans Hals (c.1582–1666).

The Musée Fin-de-Siècle focuses on the years between 1868 and 1914, during which Brussels was the undisputed artistic capital of Europe, thanks to the efforts of James Ensor, Constantin Meunier, and Victor Horta, among others. In addition to visual arts, the museum explores the literature, poetry and music of the period. One of the highlights of this collection is a 3D reconstruction of six Art Nouveau buildings.

Works in the Musée d'Art Moderne vary greatly in style and subject matter, from Neoclassicism to Realism, Impressionism, and Symbolism. The museum is undergoing an extensive renovation program, and only part of its collection can be viewed at any one time.

The Magritte Museum is devoted to one of Belgium's most famous artists and a major exponent of Surrealism, René Magritte (1898–1967). Spread over five floors, it is the world's largest collection of his work and covers all periods of his life, from the dazzling early Cavernous period of the late 1920s to the renowned *Domain of Arnhem* (1962).

⑦ Palais Royal

Place des Palais. **Tel** 02-551 2020. 27, 29, 38, 63, 65, 66, 71, 95. 92, 93. Trône, Parc. **Open** 10:30am–5pm Tue–Sun. **Closed** mid-Sep–mid-Jul. **monarchie.be**

The official home of the Belgian monarchy, this is one of the finest 19th-century buildings in the Upper Town. Construction began in the 1820s on the site of the old Coudenberg Palace. Work continued under Léopold II (reigned 1865–1909), when much of the exterior was completed. The most lavish state reception rooms include the Throne Room, with 28 wall-mounted chandeliers, and the Hall of Mirrors. The latter, similar

The magnificent 19th-century Palais Royal in Upper Town

to the Hall of Mirrors at Versailles *(see pp168–9)*, is where ceremonial occasions are held, and guests presented to the king and queen.

⑧ Place du Grand Sablon

27, 48, 95. 92, 93. Louise, Parc.

Located on the slope of the escarpment that divides Brussels in two, the Place du Grand Sablon is like a stepping stone between the upper and lower towns. The name "sablon" derives from the French "sable" (sand), and the square is so called because this old route down to the city center once passed through sandy marshes.

Terrace café on the upscale Place du Grand Sablon

Today, this is an area of upscale antiques dealers, fashionable restaurants, and trendy bars, where you can stay drinking until the early hours of the morning.

At the far end of the square stands the lovely church of **Notre-Dame du Sablon**, built in the Brabant Gothic style, and boasting some glorious stained-glass windows. On the opposite side of the road to the church is the **Place du Petit Sablon**. In contrast to the busy café scene of the larger square, these pretty

Notre-Dame du Sablon window

formal gardens are a peaceful spot to stop for a rest. Sit and admire the 44 bronze statues by Art Nouveau artist Paul Hankar, each representing a different medieval guild of the city. At the back of the gardens is a fountain, built to commemorate Counts Egmont and Hoorn, the martyrs who led a Dutch uprising against the tyrannical rule of the Spanish under Philip II. On either side of the fountain are 12 further statues of prominent 15th- and 16th-century figures, including Gerhard Mercator, the Flemish geographer and mapmaker.

The triumphal central archway and surrounding colonnades of the Parc du Cinquantenaire

⑨ European Parliament Quarter

🚌 12, 21, 22, 27, 34, 36, 54, 64, 79, 80.
Ⓜ Maelbeek, Trône, Schuman.

The vast, modern steel-and-glass complex located just behind the Quartier Léopold train station is one of three homes of the European

Brussels's European Parliament building known as "Les Caprices des Dieux"

Parliament (the other two are in Strasbourg and Luxembourg). This gleaming building has its critics: the huge structure housing the hemicycle that seats the 700-plus MEPs has been dubbed "Les Caprices des Dieux" ("Whims of the Gods"), which refers both to the shape of the building, similar to a French cheese of the same name, and to its lofty aspirations. The Parc Léopold, next to the Parliament, has some notable Art Nouveau buildings and is a delightful spot for a walk or a picnic.

⑩ Parc du Cinquantenaire

Avenue de Tervuren. 🚌 27, 28, 36, 80.
🚋 81, 82. Ⓜ Schuman, Mérode.
Musées Royaux d'Art et d'Histoire:
Tel 02-741 7211. **Open** Tue–Sun.
Closed public hols. 🅿️ 📷
ⓦ **kmkg-mrah.be** Musée Royal de l'Armée et d'Histoire Militaire:
Tel 02-737 7811. **Open** Tue–Sun.
Closed Jan 1, Dec 25. 🅿️ ♿ ⓦ **klm-mra.be** Autoworld: **Tel** 02-736 4165.
Open 10am–6pm daily (5pm in winter). **Closed** Jan 1, Dec 25.

The finest of Léopold II's grand projects, the Parc and Palais du Cinquantenaire were built for the Golden Jubilee celebrations of Belgian independence in 1880. The park was laid out on unused marshland. The palace, at its entrance, was to comprise a triumphal arch, based on the Arc de Triomphe in Paris (see

Brussels and the European Union

In 1958, following the signing of the Treaty of Rome in the previous year, the European Economic Community (EEC), now the European Union (EU), was born, and Brussels became its headquarters. Today, the city remains home to most of the EU's institutions. The European Commission, the EU body that formulates policies, is based in the vast Berlaymont Building. The city is also one of the seats of the European Parliament, which currently has 751 members, known as MEPs (Members of the European Parliament). The most powerful institution is the Council of Ministers, composed of representatives of each member state. Each nation has a certain number of votes, according to its size. The Council must approve all legislation for the EU, often a difficult task to accomplish given that most Europe-wide legislation will not be to the liking of every state.

The signing of the Treaty of Rome, 1957

p165), and two large exhibition areas. By the time of the 1880 Art and Industry Exposition, however, only the two side exhibition areas had been completed. Further funds were found, and work continued for 50 years. The arch was completed in 1905. Until 1935, the large halls on either side of the central archway were used to hold trade fairs, before being converted into museums.

Also known as the Musée du Cinquantenaire, the excellent **Musées Royaux d'Art et d'Histoire** contain a vast array of exhibits. Sections on ancient civilizations cover Egypt, Greece, Persia, and the Near East. Other displays feature Byzantium and Islam, China and the Indian subcontinent, and the Pre-Columbian civilizations of the Americas. Decorative arts from all ages include glassware, silverware, porcelain, lace, and tapestries. There are also religious sculptures and stained glass.

The **Musée Royal de l'Armée et d'Histoire Militaire** deals with all aspects of Belgium's military history. There are new sections on both World Wars, as well as a separate hall containing historic aircraft.

Housed in the south wing of the Cinquantenaire Palace, **Autoworld** has one of the best collections of classic automobiles in the world.

Part formal gardens, part tree-lined walks, the park is popular with Brussels's Eurocrats and families at lunchtimes and weekends.

⑪ Musée Horta

Rue Américaine 23–25. **Tel** 02-543 0490. 🚌 54. 🚊 81, 82, 91. Ⓜ Albert, Louise. **Open** 2–5:30pm Tue–Sun. **Closed** public hols. 🌐 hortamuseum.be

Architect Victor Horta (1861–1947) is considered the father of Art Nouveau, and his impact on Brussels's architecture is unrivaled by any other designer of his time. A museum dedicated to his unique style is today housed in his restored family home, in the St. Gilles district. Horta

Historic aircraft display at Musée Royal de l'armée et d'Histoire Militaire

himself designed the house, between 1898 and 1901. The airy interior of the building displays trademarks of the architect's style – iron, glass, and curves – in every detail, while retaining a functional approach. Most impressive are the dining room, with its ornate ceiling featuring scrolled metalwork, and the central staircase. Decorated with curved wrought iron, the stairs are enhanced further by mirrors and glass, bringing natural light into the house.

⑫ Bruparck

Boulevard du Centenaire. **Tel** 02-474 8383. 🚌 84, 88. 🚊 7, 51. Ⓜ Heysel. Mini-Europe: **Tel** 02-474 1313. **Open** daily. **Closed** Jan–Mar. 🌊 Océade: **Tel** 02-478 4944. **Open** weekends, public hols & school hols. 🌊 ♿ Kinepolis: **Tel** 02-474 2603. **Open** for performances only. Atomium: **Tel** 02-475 4775. **Open** daily. 🌊 📷 🖥 🏠 🌐 bruparck.com

Located on the outskirts of the city, this theme park is popular with families. The most visited attraction is **Mini-Europe**, which has more than 300 miniature reconstructions (built at a scale of 1:25) of Europe's major sights, from Athens' Acropolis to London's Houses of Parliament.

For movie fans, **Kinepolis** has 27 cinemas, including an IMAX complex.

If warmth and relaxation are what you are looking for, **Océade** is a tropically heated water park that features giant slides, wave machines, and even artificial sandy beaches.

Towering over Bruparck is Brussels' most distinctive landmark, the **Atomium**. Designed by André Waterkeyn for the 1958 World's Fair, and representing an iron crystal magnified 165 billion times, the structure has a viewing platform and restaurant at the top.

The Atomium, rising 100 m (325 ft) over the Bruparck

Bronze statue of Silvius Brabo in Antwerp's Grote Markt

❷ Antwerp

🏛 500,000. ✈ 🚉 🚌 ℹ 13 Grote Markt (03-232 0103). 🌐 visit antwerpen.be

In the Middle Ages, Antwerp was a thriving hub of the European cloth trade, and the principal port of the Duchy of Brabant. Today, it is the main city of Flemish-speaking Belgium, and the center of the international diamond trade.

At the heart of the city's old medieval district is the Grote Markt. The Brabo Fountain, at its center, has a statue of the soldier Silvius Brabo, said to be the nephew of Julius Caesar. The square is overlooked by the ornately gabled **Stadhuis** (Town Hall), built in 1564, and the Gothic **Onze Lieve Vrouwe Kathedraal** (Cathedral of Our Lady), which dates back to 1352. Among the paintings inside the

cathedral are two triptychs by Antwerp's most famous son, Peter Paul Rubens (1577–1640).

The narrow, winding streets of the old town are lined with fine medieval guildhalls, such as the **Vleeshuis**, or Meat Hall, once occupied by the Butchers' Guild. Dating from the early 16th century, it is built in alternate stripes of stone and brick, giving it a streaky bacon-like appearance.

When Rubens died in 1640, he was buried in the family's chapel at the lovely sandstone **Sint Jacobskerk** (1491–1656), also located in the old town.

One of the most prestigious of Antwerp's many museums is the **Koninklijk Museum voor Schone Kunsten**, which houses an impressive collection of ancient and modern art. Works from the 17th century include masterpieces by the "Antwerp Trio" of van Dyck (1599–1641), Jordaens (1593–1678), and Rubens. More modern exhibits include works by the Surrealist René Magritte (1898–1967) and Rik Wouters (1882–1916). During renovations which will last until 2017, major works will be on display at various locations across the city.

Other museums of note are the **Diamond Museum** and the **Museum Plantin-Moretus**, which is devoted to the early years of printing and celebrates the achievements of Antwerp's most successful printer, Christopher Plantin.

Rubenshuis was Rubens' home and studio for the last 30 years of his life. A tour takes you around his living quarters,

equipped with period furniture, his studio, and the *kunst-kamer*, or art gallery, where he exhibited both his own and other artists' work and entertained friends and wealthy patrons.

🏛 **Koninklijk Museum voor Schone Kunsten**
Leopold de Waelplaats 1–9. **Tel** 03-224 9550. 🚌 8. **Closed** for renovations until 2017.

🏛 **Rubenshuis**
Wapper 9–11. **Tel** 03-201 1555. 🚌 22, 25, 26. 🚋 4, 7, 8, 10, 11. **Open** 10am–5pm Tue–Sun. **Closed** public hols. 🏪 ♿

❸ Bruges

See pp226–8.

Stone gatehouse of Ghent's medieval Het Gravensteen

❹ Ghent

🏛 240,000. 🚉 🚌 🚋 ℹ Sint-Veerleplein 5 (09-266 5660). 🌐 visitgent.be

The heart of Ghent's historic center was built in the 13th and 14th centuries, when the city prospered as a result of the cloth trade. The closure of vital canal links in 1648, however, led to a decline in the town's fortunes. In the 18th and 19th centuries Ghent flourished again as a major industrial center.

Dominating the old medieval quarter is the imposing **Het Gravensteen**, or Castle of the Counts. Parts of the castle, once the seat of the Counts of Flanders, date back to the

Jacob Jordaens's joyous *As the Old Sang, the Young Play Pipes* (1638), in the Koninklijk Museum voor Schone Kunsten, Antwerp

The Pacification Hall in Ghent's Stadhuis, with its impressive tiled floor

12th century, although most parts, including the gatehouse, were built later.

Many of Ghent's finest historic buildings are found on Graslei, a picturesque street that borders the Leie River. The street is lined with well-preserved guildhalls dating from the Middle Ages.

The magnificent **St Baafskathedraal** has features representing every phase of the Gothic style. In a small side chapel is one of Europe's most remarkable paintings, Jan van Eyck's *Adoration of the Mystic Lamb* (1432). Opposite the cathedral stands the huge 14th-century **Belfort** (belfry). From the top of the tower you can enjoy splendid views of the city. From here, it is a short walk to the **Stadhuis** (Town Hall), whose Pacification Hall was the site of the signing of the Pacification of Ghent (a declaration of the Low Countries' repudiation of Spanish rule) in 1576.

Ghent's largest collection of fine art, covering all periods up to the 20th century, is in the **Museum voor Schone Kunsten**, some 20 minutes' walk southeast of the center. There are works by Rubens and his contemporaries Jacob Jordaens and Anthony van Dyck. Occupying an elegant 18th-century townhouse, the **Design Museum Gent** is a decorative-arts museum, with lavishly furnished 17th-, 18th-, and 19th-century period rooms. An extension covers modern design, from Art Nouveau to contemporary works.

Het Gravensteen
Sint-Veerleplein. **Tel** 09-225 9306. **Open** 9am–5pm daily (Apr–Oct: 10am–6pm).

Museum voor Schone Kunsten
Citadelpark. **Tel** 09-240 0700. **Open** 10am–6pm Tue–Sun.

❺ Waterloo

30,000. Chaussée de Bruxelles 218 (02-352 0910).
waterloo-tourisme.com

This small town is most famous for its association with the Battle of Waterloo, which saw Napoleon and his French army defeated by the Duke of Wellington's troops on June 18, 1815. The best place to start a visit here is the **Musée Wellington**, which occupies the inn where Wellington stayed the night before the battle. Its narrow rooms are packed with curios alongside plans and models of the battlefield.

The **Musée de Cires** (Wax-work Museum) has models of soldiers dressed in period uniforms, while the **Eglise St-Joseph** contains dozens of memorial plaques to the British soldiers who died at Waterloo.

For an excellent view over the battlefield, head for the **Butte de Lion**, a 45-m (148-ft) high earthen mound, 3 km (2 miles) south of the town. Next to it is a gallery where Louis Demoulin's fascinating circular painting *Panorama de la Bataille* is displayed.

Musée Wellington
Chaussée de Bruxelles 147. **Tel** 02-357 2860. **Open** 10am–5pm daily.

The Butte de Lion, viewed from the battlefield of Waterloo

The Battlefields of Belgium

Belgium's strategic position between France and Germany has long made it the battleground, or "cockpit," of Europe. Napoleon's defeat at Waterloo was just one of many major conflicts resolved on Belgian soil. In the early 18th century, French expansion under Louis XIV was thwarted here, and more recently, Belgium witnessed some of the bloodiest trench warfare of World War I, including the introduction of poison gas at Ypres (Ieper). Today, there are several vast graveyards, where the tens of thousands of soldiers who died on the Western Front lie buried.

Aftermath of Passchendaele (Third Battle of Ypres), 1917

❸ Street by Street: Bruges

With good reason, Bruges is one of the most popular tourist destinations in Belgium. The city owes its pre-eminent position to the beauty of its historic center, where winding lanes and picturesque canals are lined with splendid medieval buildings. These are mostly the legacy of the town's heyday as a center of the international cloth trade, which flourished for 200 years from the 13th century. During this golden age, Bruges' merchants lavished their fortunes on fine mansions, churches, and a set of civic buildings of such extravagance that they were the wonder of northern Europe. Today, the streets are well maintained: there are no billboards or high-rises, and traffic is heavily regulated.

View of the Dijver River
A charming introduction to Bruges is provided by the boat trips along the city's canals.

Bus and train stations

Onze Lieve Vrouwekerk
Dating from 1220, the Church of Our Lady employs many styles of architecture and contains a Madonna and Child by Michelangelo.

Memling in Sint-Jan-Hospitaal Museum
This 12th-century hospital operated until 1976. It contains a well-preserved 15th-century dispensary.

★ The Markt

Medieval gabled houses line this 13th-century market square at the heart of Bruges, which still holds a market each Saturday.

Oude Griffie, or Old Recorder's House

VISITORS' CHECKLIST

Practical Information

117,000.

visitbruges.be

Markt 1 & t'Zand 34, inside Concertgebouw (050-44 46 46).

Transport

Stationsplein.

Stationsplein, Markt.

Blind Donkey Alley
This tiny alley leads from the Burg to the 18th-century Vismarkt (Fish Market).

BURG

WOLLESTRAAT

ROZENHOEDKAAI

Heilig Bloed Basiliek
(see p228)

DIJVER

Groeninge Museum
(see p228)

The Arentshuis Museum has paintings by Frank Brangwyn (1867–1956).

Gruuthuse Museum
(see p228)

★ Stadhuis

One of the oldest and finest town halls in Belgium, this was built between 1376 and 1420. Inside, the beautifully restored Gothic hall is noted for its 1385 vaulted ceiling.

Key

— Suggested route

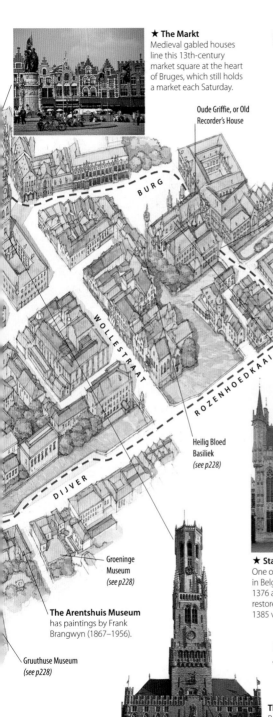

The Belfort

Built in the 13th century, the Belfort, or Belfry, is a stunning octagonal tower where the city's medieval charter of rights is held.

0 meters		100
0 yards		100

🏛 Groeninge Museum

Dijver 12. **Tel** 050-44 8711.
Open 9:30am–5pm Tue–Sun.
Closed Jan 1, Dec 25. 🖼

Bruges' premier fine-art museum holds a superb collection of early Flemish and Dutch masters. Artists featured include Rogier van der Weyden (c.1400–1464), Jan van Eyck (d.1441), and Hans Memling (c.1430–94). Van Eyck's *Virgin and Child with Canon* (1436), a richly detailed painting noted for its realism, and Memling's *Moreel* triptych (1484) are among the museum's most outstanding exhibits. Painted in the early 16th century, the *Last Judgment* triptych is one of a number of works at the museum by Hieronymus Bosch (c.1450–1516). Peter Brueghel the Younger (1564–1638) is also well represented. Later Belgian works include paintings by Surrealists Paul Delvaux (1897–1994) and René Magritte (1898–1967).

Fifteenth-century oak-paneled chapel in the Gruuthuse Museum

🏛 Gruuthuse Museum

Dijver 17. **Tel** 050-44 8762.
Open 9:30am–5pm Tue–Sun.
Closed Jan 1, Dec 25. 🖼

This museum occupies a large medieval mansion close to the Dijver Canal. In the 15th century, it was inhabited by a merchant (the Lord of the Gruuthuse), who had the right to levy a tax on "gruit," an imported mixture of herbs added to barley during the beer-brewing process. The mansion's labyrinthine rooms, with their ancient chimney-pieces and wooden beams, have survived intact, and today contain a collection of fine and applied arts. The exhibits range from wood carvings, tapestries,

Panel of Hans Memling's *Moreel* triptych in the Groeninge Museum

porcelain, and ceramics to medical instruments and weaponry. The authentic kitchen and beautiful oak-paneled chapel (1472) transport visitors back to medieval times.

🏛 Heilig Bloed Basiliek

Burg 13. **Tel** 050-33 6792. **Open** daily.
Museum: **Open** daily. **Closed** Wed
(Oct–Mar). 🖼 (for museum).

The Basilica of the Holy Blood is Bruges' holiest church, holding one of the most sacred relics in Europe. In the upper chapel, rebuilt after it was destroyed by the French in the 1790s, is a 17th-century tabernacle, which houses a phial said to contain a few drops of blood and water washed from the body of Christ by Joseph of Arimathea.

🏛 Begijnhof

Wijngaardplein 1. **Tel** 050-36 01 40.
Open daily. 🖼 (for Begijn House).

Béguines were members of a lay sisterhood founded in 1245, who did not take vows, but led a devout life. The *begijnhof*, or *béguinage*, is the walled complex in a town that housed the Béguines. In Bruges, this is an area of quiet tree-lined canals edged by white, gabled houses. Visitors can enjoy a stroll here and visit the simple church, built in 1602. One of the houses, now occupied by Benedictine nuns, is open to the public.

🏛 Houishbrouwerij de Halve Maan

Walplein 26. **Tel** 050-44 4222. **Open** 11am–4pm Sun–Fri, 11am–5pm Sat (Nov–Mar: to 3pm). 🖼 every hour, compulsory. 🖼 🌐 **halvemaan.be**

Before World War I, there were 31 breweries in Bruges. This one has been producing Straffe Hendrik since 1856. Here, you can follow the beer-making process, from the first hops to a taste of the finished product in the small bar. There are also good views of Bruges from the oast room at the top of the building.

🏛 Museum voor Volkskunde

Balstraat 43. **Tel** 050-44 8764.
Open 9:30am–5pm Tue–Sun.

This folk museum occupies an attractive row of 17th-century brick almshouses in the northeast of the town. Each of the houses is dedicated to a different aspect of traditional Flemish life. Several crafts are represented, and visitors are shown a series of typical historical domestic interiors.

Pretty 17th-century almshouses, home to the Museum voor Volkskunde

For hotels and restaurants see p234 and p235

❻ Luxembourg

One of Europe's smallest sovereign states, the Grand Duchy of Luxembourg is often overlooked by travelers in Europe. The capital, Luxembourg City, is well known as a world center of international finance, but behind the modern face of the city lies a rich history stretching back more than 1,000 years. The northern half of the country boasts some spectacular scenery, especially the Ardennes, a region of dense forests, deep valleys, and hilltop castles. Historic towns such as Vianden and Echternach are good bases for exploring the countryside and offer plenty of opportunities for outdoor activities.

View of Luxembourg City, with its aqueduct and hilltop historic center

Luxembourg City

🏙 92,000. ✈ 6 km (4 miles) E. 🚌
🚏 ℹ 30 Place Guillaume II (22 28
09). 🌐 **lcto.lu**

Luxembourg City enjoys a dramatic location, set atop hills and cliffs rising above the Alzette and Pétrusse valleys. The town grew up around a castle built on a rocky promontory, known as the Rocher du Bock, in AD 963. The castle was destroyed in the late 19th century by the city's inhabitants, but some of the fortifications have been preserved, most famously the Bock and Pétrusse **Casemates**. These huge networks of underground defensive galleries, which date back to the 17th century, not only provided shelter for thousands of soldiers, but also housed workshops, kitchens, bakeries, and slaughterhouses. The **Crypte Archéologique du Bock** has displays and an audiovisual presentation on the history of the city's fortifications. Luxembourg City's **Palais Grand**

Ducal has been the official royal residence since 1890. The oldest parts of the building, which used to be the town hall, date from the latter half of the 16th century. Nearby, the **Cathédrale Notre-Dame** was begun in 1613. Inside is a fine Baroque organ gallery by Daniel Muller.

Two museums worth visiting are the **Musée National d'Histoire et d'Art**, which has a good archaeological section and a collection of ancient and modern sculpture and paintings, and the **Musée de l'Histoire de la Ville de Luxembourg**, which focuses on the city's historical past.

🏰 **Casemates**
Bock Casemates: Montée de Clausen.
Open Mar–Oct: 10am–5pm. 🗺
Pétrusse Casemates: Place de la Constitution. **Open** Easter, Whitsun, & end May–mid-Sep: 11am–4pm. 🗺

🏛 **Musée National d'Histoire et d'Art**
Place Marché aux Poissons. **Tel** 47 93 301. **Open** 10am–6pm Tue–Sun. 🗺
🌐 🚻

Vianden

🏙 1,600. 🚌 ℹ 1a Rue du Vieux
Marché (83 42 571). Château de
Vianden: **Tel** 83 41 08. **Open** Apr–Sep:
10am–6pm; Oct, Mar: 10am–5pm;
Nov–Feb: 10am–4pm. **Closed** Jan 1,
Dec 25. 🗺 🌐

Surrounded by medieval ramparts, Vianden, in the Luxembourg Ardennes, is a popular tourist destination. The main attraction is the 11th-century **Château de Vianden**. Its rooms feature a range of architectural styles, from the Romanesque to the Renaissance. A cable car takes visitors to the top of a nearby hill, giving superb views of the castle.

Echternach

🏙 4,000. 🚌 ℹ 9–10 Parvis de la
Basilique (72 42 72). Abbey Basilica:
Open daily. Abbey Museum: **Open**
Apr, May & Oct: 10am–noon, 2–5pm
daily; Jun & Sep: 10am–noon, 2–6pm
daily; Jul & Aug: 10am–6pm daily. 🗺
🌐 **echternach-tourist.lu**

Located in Petite Suisse (Little Switzerland), a picturesque region of wooded hills north-east of the capital, Echternach is dotted with fine medieval buildings, including the 15th-century turreted town hall. The star sight, however, is the Benedictine abbey, founded by St. Willibrord in the 7th century. The crypt of the abbey basilica (c.900) contains some glorious frescoes. There are good walks and cycle routes in the surrounding countryside.

Medieval town hall in the Place du
Marché, Echternach

Practical & Travel Information

Visitors to Belgium and Luxembourg can expect high levels of service and comfort in all aspects of their stay. Public transportation is clean and efficient, and there are abundant tourist-information facilities, in addition to all the other modern conveniences one expects of a highly developed country. Brussels and Luxembourg City are among the safest capital cities in Europe, and can be easily explored on foot.

Tourist Information

In Belgium, the **Visit Brussels Information Office** publishes maps and guides, and also offers a Brussels Card. This "tourist passport" includes one-, two-, or three-day passes to all public transport in the Brussels region, combined with unlimited access to 30 museums. A similar scheme operates in Bruges, Antwerp, and Ghent.

Luxembourg's **National Tourist Office** offers the Luxembourg Card, which gives unlimited travel on public transport nationwide, as well as admission to more than 30 sites of interest, and reductions on many others. The card, valid for one, two, or three days between Easter and October, can be bought at the City Tourist Office as well as through the LNTO website and at hotels, campsites, youth hostels, and train and bus stations.

Local tourist information offices can be found in most towns and villages throughout Belgium and Luxembourg.

Opening Hours

Most stores and businesses in Belgium and Luxembourg are open from 10am until 5 or 6pm Monday to Saturday, with some local shops closing for an hour at lunch. Some stores open at noon on Mondays. In the major cities and towns, many stores are open on Sundays and until later in the evening.

In both countries, most museums are closed on Mondays. Outside the high season (April to September), be prepared to find many sights of interest closed.

Visa Requirements

Citizens of the EU, US, Australia, New Zealand, and Canada do not require a visa to enter either Belgium or Luxembourg, but must present a valid passport and hold proof of onward passage (EU citizens need a valid ID document). Bear in mind that in Belgium it is a legal requirement to carry ID on one's person at all times.

Safety and Emergencies

Belgium and Luxembourg are safe countries, with street crime against visitors a relatively rare occurrence. However, in Brussels, it is inadvisable to wander alone at night in the poorer areas to the west and north of the city center, or in the city's parks, especially Botanique.

In case of emergencies, the numbers to call are listed in the Directory opposite.

Language

The two principal languages of Belgium are Dutch, spoken in Flanders, and French, the language of the Wallonians. There is also a German-speaking enclave in the far east of the country. In the capital, both languages are used on all street signs and in place names.

Luxembourg has three official languages: French, German, and Letzeburgesch, or Luxembourgeois. In both Belgium and Luxembourg, especially in the capital cities, many people speak very good English.

Banking and Currency

The currency in Belgium and Luxembourg is the euro (see p23). All euro bills and coins are exchangeable in each of the participating Eurozone countries.

Banking hours are generally from 9am to 4pm Monday to Friday in Belgium and 9am to 4:30pm on weekdays in Luxembourg. In both countries, most of the banks close for an hour at lunchtime, and some of the city branches open on Saturday mornings.

Communications

Belgian post offices are open from 9am to 5pm Monday to Friday. In Luxembourg, the hours are 9am to noon and 1:30pm to 5pm Monday to Friday. Some larger branches open on Saturday mornings.

Many public payphones in Belgium and Luxembourg accept only phonecards, available at newsagents and post offices. In Brussels, you can use cash in the phone booths at metro stations. There are no local area codes in Luxembourg.

The Climate of Belgium and Luxembourg

Belgium and Luxembourg have a temperate climate, characterized by constant low rainfall throughout the year. Winters are usually chilly and damp, and rain may turn to snow or sleet. Summers are warmer and much brighter, but the evenings can still be cool. Spring is the driest season.

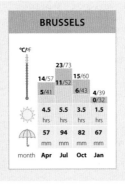

BRUSSELS

°C/°F	Apr	Jul	Oct	Jan
		23/73		
	14/57	11/52	15/60	
	5/41		6/43	4/39
				0/32
hrs	4.5	5.5	3.5	1.5
mm	57	94	82	67
month	Apr	Jul	Oct	Jan

Arriving by Air

Belgium's principal airport is Brussels National Airport, known locally as Zaventem. Flights into Luxembourg arrive at Findel Airport, which is 6 km (4 miles) east of Luxembourg City.

Airlines flying to Belgium and Luxembourg include **Brussels Airlines** (Belgium) and **Luxair** (Luxembourg), British Airways, bmi regional, KLM, and Lufthansa. Brussels is also served by Air Canada and Delta Air Lines. Most flights from Canada and the US go via another European city. Ryanair has low-cost flights between Brussels and various European cities.

Arriving by Sea

Belgium can be easily reached by ferry from Britain several times daily. **DFDS Seaways** has a number of crossings every day between Dover and Dunkirk. **P&O Ferries** also operates regular ferry crossings from Dover to Calais (France) and from Hull to Zeebrugge.

Rail Travel

Belgium is at the heart of Europe's high-speed train networks. **Eurostar** services between Brussels' Gare du Midi and London's St. Pancras station take just under 2 hours. The **Thalys** network links Brussels with Amsterdam, Paris, and Cologne.

Within Belgium, train services are operated by **Belgian National Railways** (Société Nationale de Chemins de Fer Belges/Belgische Spoorwegen). The network is modern and efficient, and usually the best way to travel between major cities and towns. Luxembourg's rail system is run by **Chemins de Fer Luxembourgeois (CFL)**. In both countries, a variety of train passes is available. The Benelux Tourrail pass allows unlimited travel on any three or five days within a month's period in Belgium, Luxembourg, and the Netherlands.

Traveling by Bus

In Belgium, the two main long-distance bus operators are **De Lijn**, which covers routes in Flanders, and **TEC**, which provides services in Wallonia. Bus terminuses are usually close to train stations.

Luxembourg benefits from an extensive bus network, which compensates for the more limited railroad system. One-day passes are available, and can be used on both long-distance and inner-city buses from the time of purchase until 8am the next day. Benelux Tourrail passes are valid on buses operated by Chemins de Fer Luxembourgeois.

Traveling by Car

Drivers from the UK can reach mainland Europe by the car train service offered by Eurotunnel. Within Belgium and Luxembourg, the freeways and main roads are well maintained and fast. Variations between the French and Flemish spellings of town names can be confusing for visitor drivers in Belgium; it is advisable to find out both names of your destination before beginning your journey. All the major car-rental firms are represented in Belgium and Luxembourg, but renting a vehicle is fairly expensive.

DIRECTORY

Tourist Offices

Belgium
Grand Place 1, 1000 Brussels. **Tel** 02-513 8940.
W visitbelgium.com

Luxembourg
City Office,
Place Guillaume II,
Luxembourg City.
Tel 42 82 82 20. W ont.lu

UK
Belgian Tourist Office
Tel 020-7537 1132.
Tel 0800-954 5245.
W belgiumtheplaceto.be
Luxembourg Tourist Office.
W luxembourg.com

US
Belgian Tourist Office
Tel 212-758 8130.
Luxembourg Tourist Office
W visitluxembourg.com

Embassies

UK (Belgium)
Ave d'Auderghem 10,
B-1040 Brussels.
Tel 02-287 6211.

UK (Luxembourg)
5 Blvd Joseph II, L-1840
Luxembourg City.
Tel 22 98 64.

US (Belgium)
Blvd du Régent 27,
B-1000 Brussels.
Tel 02-811 4000.

US (Luxembourg)
22 Blvd Emmanuel
Servais, L-2535
Luxembourg City.
Tel 46 01 23.

Emergency Numbers

Belgium
Police **Tel** 101.
Ambulance and fire
department **Tel** 100.

Luxembourg
Police **Tel** 113.
All other services **Tel** 112.

Airlines

Brussels Airlines
Tel 090-251 600 (Belgium).
Tel 0905-609 5609 (UK).
Tel 866-308 2230 (US).
W brusselsairlines.com

Luxair
Tel 0352-2456 4242
(Luxembourg). W luxair.lu

Ferry Companies

DFDS Seaways
Tel 0871-574 7235 (UK).
W dfdsseaways.co.uk

P&O Ferries
Tel 08716-642 121 (UK).
W poferries.com

Rail Travel

Belgian National Railways
Tel 02-528 2828.
W belgianrail.be

Chemins de Fer Luxembourgeois
Tel 24 89 24 89. W cfl.lu

Eurostar
Tel 070-79 79 79 (Belgium).
Tel 08432-186 186 (UK).
W eurostar.com

Thalys
Tel 070-79 79 79 (Belgium).
W thalys.com

Buses

De Lijn
Tel 070-220 200.
W delijn.be

TEC
Tel 01-023 5353.
W infotec.be

Shopping & Entertainment

Belgium is an ideal place to shop for luxury goods, from fine chocolates and cutting-edge fashion to mounted diamonds. As a virtually duty-free zone, Luxembourg attracts tourists in search of cheap cigarettes and alcohol. For relatively small cities, Brussels and Luxembourg City offer a wide range of cultural events. Those who prefer outdoor activities will find plenty to entertain them. The flat Flanders region in Belgium is ideal cycling country, while the hilly Ardennes and the Petite Suisse area of Luxembourg are popular with hikers.

Where to Shop

For luxury items and gifts, one of Brussels' best shopping arcades is the **Galéries Saint-Hubert**. It houses several jewelry stores, the Belgian leather-bag maker Delvaux, fine chocolate stores, and smart boutiques. The **Galéries d'Ixelles** is full of tiny ethnic shops and cafés, while the quaint **Galérie Bortier** is the place to shop for antiquarian books and maps.

Top fashion designers are well represented in Brussels. Their outlets can be found on Avenue Louise and Boulevard de Waterloo. For the original creations of the Antwerp Six and of new-wave designers, try Rue Antoine Dansaert.

Less expensive, mainstream stores, including Belgium's only department store, Inno, are located in the Rue Neuve. Inno is not spectacular by British or American standards.

The principal shopping areas in Luxembourg City are the Grand Rue and its side streets, and the Auchan shopping center, which is found on Kirchberg.

What to Buy

Belgian chocolate is considered by many to be the finest in the world. Among the internationally renowned "grandes maisons de chocolat," with stores in Brussels, are **Godiva** and **Wittamer**. The sweet-toothed will also be tempted by the edible chocolate sculptures produced by **Pierre Marcolini** and by the wares of fine-biscuit specialist **Dandoy**. Another famous Belgian export is lace, though

a fall in the number of people entering the trade in recent years has resulted in a shortage of authentic, handmade goods. Before purchasing an item, make sure it has not been manufactured in the Far East. Places to shop for authentic Belgian lace include **Maison F. Rubbrecht** in Brussels and the **Kant Centrum** in Bruges. The latter also has a museum of lace-making.

Specialty Belgian beers can be bought at Brussels' **Beer Mania**, while **Little Nemo** and **La Bande des Six Nez** specialize in comic-strip memorabilia. If you plan to invest in diamonds, or simply wish to gaze and admire, **Diamondland** in Antwerp is a good place to start.

Among the best buys in Luxembourg are fuel, tobacco, and alcohol, due to the low rate of duty imposed on such goods. One of the country's most famous manufacturing names is **Villeroy & Boch**, makers of fine porcelain and tableware. Their flagship store is in the Rue du Fossé in the capital. There is also a factory outlet northwest of the city center where you can buy seconds at a 20 percent discount.

Markets

From 9am on Saturdays and Sundays, Brussels' Place du Grand Sablon is the site of a fine antiques market. Also worth visiting is the huge, vibrant market around the Gare du Midi (Sundays, 6am to 1pm), with its mix of North African and home-grown delicacies, including oils, spices, and exotic herbs.

Brussels' famous Marché aux Puces is held daily on the Place du Jeu de Balle, though the biggest assortment of items can be found on Sundays.

Bookstores

In Brussels, **Waterstones** sells English-language magazines and books. For international newspapers, go to the **Librairie Louis d'Or** or **Sterling Books**.

English-language books and newspapers can be bought in Luxembourg City at **Chapter 1**.

Entertainment Listings

The principal sources of entertainment information in Belgium are The Bulletin, published weekly online, and the Agenda listings magazine.

Details of events in Luxembourg are available online via the www.visit luxembourg.com website.

Opera, Classical Music, and Dance

Brussels' Opera House, **La Monnaie**, is among Europe's finest venues for opera. The season runs from September through June, and most productions are sold out many months in advance.

Designed by Victor Horta in 1928, the **Palais des Beaux-Arts** is home to the Belgian National Orchestra and boasts the city's largest auditorium for classical music. The main concert season lasts from September to June.

Regular performances of contemporary dance take place at the Art Deco **Kaaitheater** and the **Halles de Schaerbeek**.

Luxembourg's Printemps Musical is a festival of classical music concerts and ballet that takes place in the capital throughout April and May. Principal venues include the **Conservatoire de Musique de la Ville de Luxembourg** and the **Théâtre Municipal**. The City Tourist Information Office on the Place d'Armes is able to provide more information and assist with ticket reservations.

Jazz, Rock, and Blues

One of the best places to catch good jazz acts in Brussels is **Sounds**, a large venue featuring some of Belgium's top artists. The club also has Blues nights. On Saturday and Sunday afternoons, it is worth stopping at **L'Archiduc**, a refurbished Art Deco bar in the center of town, where you can listen to jazz in a relaxed atmosphere. **Ancienne Belgique** hosts up-and-coming guitar bands, folk, Latin, and techno acts.

Cinema

At Brussels' Bruparck *(see p223),* the 27-screen Kinepolis cinema complex shows Hollywood blockbusters and major British and French releases. Real movie fans should not miss a visit to the Musée du Cinéma in the Palais des Beaux-Arts complex. The museum shows classic films, from Chaplin to Tarantino, with nightly programs of silent movies sometimes with a live-piano accompaniment.

Outdoor Activities

Belgium and Luxembourg have extensive networks of cycle tracks, and you can rent bicycles easily from a number of outlets, including many train stations. For route details, the best source of information is the local tourist information office. The US-based **Austin Adventures** organizes cycle tours in Belgium.

Tourist offices in Belgium and Luxembourg also offer walking guides and maps. To arrange hiking tours in the Ardennes area, contact Belgium-based **Europ'Aventure**.

In Luxembourg, the lake at Echternach offers plenty of opportunities for swimming, sailing, and windsurfing, while the rivers of the Ardennes region are fine territory for canoeing and kayaking. For further information on the latter, contact the **Fédération Luxembourgeoise de Canoë-Kayak**. For information on the whole range of sporting activities available, contact the **City Tourist Office**.

DIRECTORY

Shopping Arcades

Galérie Bortier
Rue de la Madeleine
17–19, Brussels.

Galéries d'Ixelles
Chaussée d'Ixelles,
Brussels.

Galéries Saint-Hubert
Rue des Bouchers,
Brussels.

Specialty Items

La Bande des Six Nez
Chaussée de Wavre 179,
Brussels.
Tel 02-513 7258.

Beer Mania
Chaussée de Wavre
174–176, Brussels.
Tel 02-512 1788.

Dandoy
Rue au Beurre 31,
Brussels.
Tel 02-511 0326.

Diamondland
Appelmansstraat 33A,
Antwerp.
Tel 03-229 2990.

Godiva
Grand Place 22,
Brussels.
Tel 02-511 2537.

Kant Centrum
Peperstraat 3A, Bruges.
Tel 050-33 00 72.

Little Nemo
Boulevard Lemmonier 25,
Brussels. **Tel** 02-514 6804.

Maison F. Rubbrecht
Grand Place 23, Brussels.
Tel 02-512 0218.

Pierre Marcolini
Rue des Minimes 1,
Brussels.
Tel 02-514 1206.

Villeroy & Boch
2 Rue du Fossé,
Luxembourg City.
Tel 46 33 43.

330 Rue Rollingergrund,
Luxembourg City.
Tel 46 82 12 78.

Wittamer
Place du Grand Sablon 6,
12–13 Brussels.
Tel 02-512 3742.
W wittamer.com

Bookstores

Chapter 1
42 Rue Astrid,
Luxembourg City.
Tel 44 07 09.

Librairie Louis d'Or
Rue du Bailli 54, Brussels.
Tel 02-640 6432.

Sterling Books
Rue du Fossé aux Loups
38, Brussels.
Tel 02-223 6223.

Waterstones
Boulevard Adolphe Max
71, Brussels.
Tel 02-219 2708.

Opera, Classical Music & Dance

Conservatoire de Musique de la Ville de Luxembourg
33 Rue Charles Martel,
Luxembourg City.
Tel 47 96 55 55.

Halles de Schaerbeek
Rue Royale Sainte-Marie
22a, Brussels.
Tel 02-218 2107.
W halles.be

Kaaitheater
Square Sainteclette 20,
Brussels.
Tel 01-201 5959.
W kaaitheater.be

La Monnaie
Place de la Monnaie,
Brussels.
Tel 02-229 1211.
W lamonnaie.be

Palais des Beaux-Arts
Rue Ravenstein 23,
Brussels.
Tel 02-507 8200.
W bozar.be

Théâtre Municipal
1 Rond-Point Robert
Schuman, Luxembourg
City. **Tel** 47 96 39 00.

Jazz, Rock & Blues

Ancienne Belgique
Boulevard Anspach 110,
Brussels.
Tel 02-548 2484.
W abconcerts.be

L'Archiduc
Rue Antoine Dansaert 6,
Brussels.
Tel 02-512 0652.
W archiduc.net

Sounds
Rue de la Tulipe 28,
Brussels.
Tel 02-512 9250.
W soundsjazzclub.be

Outdoor Activities

Austin Adventures
Tel 800-575 1540 (US).
W austinadventures.
com

Europ'Aventure
Tel 061-688 611 (Belgium).
W europaventure.be

Fédération Luxembourgeoise de Canoë-Kayak
3 Route d'Arlon,
L-8009, Strassen.
Tel 75 03 79.
W flck.lu

Luxembourg City Tourist Office
Tel 22 28 09. W lcto.lu

Where to Stay

A suite extending over two floors at Le Place d'Armes Hotel, in Luxembourg City

Brussels

LOWER TOWN:
Scandic Grand Place €
Budget **Map** C2
Rue d'Arenberg 18, 1000
Tel *02-548 1811*
[W] scandichotels.com
Centrally located and surprisingly well-appointed good-value hotel.

DK Choice

LOWER TOWN: Amigo €€€
Luxury **Map** C3
Rue de l'Amigo 23–27,1000
Tel *02-547 4747*
[W] hotelamigo.com
This five-star hotel provides supreme comfort, attention to detail, and polished service, where every client is treated as a cherished guest. Located close to the Grand Place, this is the hotel of choice for movie stars and presidents.

UPPER TOWN: Rembrandt
Hotel €
Budget
Rue de la Concorde 42, 1050
Tel *02-512 7139*
[W] hotelrembrandt.be
A small and friendly guesthouse with great charm and loads of individual character.

UPPER TOWN:
Odette en Ville €€€
Boutique
25 Rue du Châtelain, 1050
Tel *02-640 2626*
[W] chez-odette.com
Located in the trendy Châtelain area of Ixelles, Odette oozes retro style and has a fêted restaurant.

Rest of Belgium

ANTWERP: Hotel
Rubens – Grote Markt €€
Luxury
Oude Beurs 29, 2000
Tel *03-222 4848*
[W] hotelrubensantwerp.be
A well-presented four-star hotel, with a note of individuality owing to its medieval lookout tower.

BOUILLON: Panorama Hôtel €€
Modern
Rue au-dessus de la Ville 25, 6830
Tel *061-46 61 38*
[W] panoramahotel.be
Impeccably furnished family-run hotel-restaurant with lovely views over Bouillon and the castle.

DK Choice

BRUGES: Alegria €€
Modern
Sint-Jakobsstraat 34, 8000
Tel *050-33 09 37*
[W] alegria-hotel.com
Utterly charming family-run guesthouse, close to the Markt, the main square in Bruges. Each of the well-equipped rooms has been thematically styled; some overlook the garden to the rear. The owners offer excellent advice about what to do and where to eat. A good complimentary breakfast is served in the garden room.

GHENT: Sandton Grand
Hotel Reylof €€
Luxury
Hoogstraat 36, 9000
Tel *09-235 4070*
[W] sandton.eu
Affordable luxury at this centrally located hotel with well-appointed rooms, a spa, a good restaurant, and excellent service.

LEUVEN: Martin's Klooster €€
Boutique
Onze-Lieve-Vrouwstraat 18, 3000
Tel *01-621 3141*
[W] martins-hotels.com
Spacious suites and rooms with a stylish touch in a renovated 16th-century monastery.

LIÈGE: Crowne Plaza €€€
Luxury
Mont Saint-Martin 9–11, 4000
Tel *04-222 9494*
[W] crowneplaza.com
This stylish modern hotel is attached to the grand old palace of the Sélys Longchamps family.

Price Guide

Prices are based on one night's stay in high season for a standard double room, inclusive of service charges and taxes.

€	up to €100
€€	€100 to €260
€€€	over €260

Luxembourg

BERDORF: Le Bisdorff €€
Luxury
an der Heesbech 39, 6551
Tel *79 02 08*
[W] hotel-bisdorff.lu
Old-fashioned hotel-restaurant surrounded by a garden. Guests enjoy an indoor pool and sauna.

LUXEMBOURG CITY:
Belappart Studio Hotel €
Budget
Rue du Fort Neipperg 69, 2230
Tel *23 60 45 1*
[W] belappart.lu
Small, modern apartment accommodation, for both short and long stays.

DK Choice

LUXEMBOURG CITY:
Le Place d'Armes Hotel €€€
Boutique
Place d'Armes 18, 1136
Tel *27 47 37*
[W] hotel-leplacedarmes.com
Located on the central square, this five-star hotel is beautifully designed, blending the historic – original fireplaces and beamed ceilings – with the modern. The Cristallerie Restaurant and Le Café de Paris (a bristo with a wine bar), could dissuade guests from ever venturing out. Pampering luxury alongside impeccable service.

REMICH: Hôtel des Vignes €€
Modern
Route de Mondorf 29, 5552
Tel *23 69 91 49*
[W] hotel-vignes.lu
A polished hotel-restaurant set amid vineyards, with views out onto the Moselle river.

VIANDEN: Auberge
du Château €
Boutique
Grande-Rue 74–80, 9401
Tel *83 45 74*
[W] auberge-du-chateau.lu
Well-established hotel occupying a flower-decked townhouse. Rooms are comfortable and beautifully presented.

Where to Eat and Drink

Brussels

LOWER TOWN: Belga Queen €€
Belgian   Map C3
Rue Fossé aux Loups 32, 1000
Tel *02-217 2187*
A splendidly theatrical restaurant
in an imaginatively transformed
19th-century bank. The refined
cuisine has a Belgian slant. There
is also an oyster bar.

**UPPER TOWN: La
Canne en Ville** €€
French
Rue de la Réforme 22, 1050
Tel *02-347 2926* **Closed** *Sat lunch; Sat
& Sun (Jul & Aug)*
Delightful eatery in a converted
butcher's shop, with attractive
terrace seating in summer. A
good option before or after
visiting the nearby Musée Horta.

Rest of Belgium

ANTWERP: Het Pomphuis €€
Belgian/French
Droogdok, Siberiastraat 7, 2030
Tel *03-770 8625*
Housed in a 20th-century pump
house, this exhilarating eatery
retains much of the original
machinery. It serves French-
Belgian fare with an Asian twist.

ANTWERP: Zuiderterras €€
Belgian/French
Ernest van Dijckkaai 37, 2000
Tel *03-234 1275*
A pier leads out to this restaurant,
which boasts unparalleled views
of the Schelde river's estuary.
On the menu is a wide range
of French and Belgian classics.
Also open for breakfast.

BRUGES: Restaurant de Bühne €
Belgian/French
Sint-Salvatorskoorstraat 6, 8000
Tel *05-034 6649* **Closed** *Mon & Tue*
A charming restaurant serving
very good fish, fresh quiches and
pastries, and vegetarian options,
such as pumpkin soup. Try the
homemade fruit tarts for dessert.

GHENT: Brasserie Pakhuis €€
International
Schuurkenstraat 4, 9000
Tel *09-223 5555* **Closed** *Sun*
This converted warehouse full of
pizzazz is the place for French-
style brasserie fare, with twists
such as chicken cooked in hay,
and Japanese fusion dishes, plus
a few Belgian classics.

DK Choice
KNOKKE-HEIST: Sel Gris €€€
Belgian
Zeedijk 314, 8301
Tel *05-051 4937* **Closed** *Wed &
Thu*
This superb seafront restaurant,
a key player in the Belgian
culinary landscape, is run by
Frederik Deceuninck, who was
awarded his first Michelin star
in 2008. Plaice, mackerel, skate,
scallops, sole, lobster, and other
North Sea treasures all feature
in the exquisite dishes, which
are presented like edible
works of art.

**KRUISHOUTEM: Hof van
Cleve** €€€
Belgian
Riemegemstraat 1, 9770
Tel *09-383 5848* **Closed** *Sun &
Mon; Tue lunch*
Peter Goossens's celebrated
three-star Michelin restaurant is
housed in a pretty collection of
farm buildings, surrounded by
a tranquil countryside.

LEUVEN: Domus €
Brasserie
Tiensestraat 8, 3000
Tel *016-20 1449*
A traditional tavern supplied
by its own brewery next door.
Enjoy snacks and pub food, such
as pasta, salads, steaks, and
pancakes. Breakfast available, too.

TOURNAI: Giverny €€€
Belgian/French
Quai du Marché au Poisson 6, 7500
Tel *06-922 4464* **Closed** *Sun, Mon &
Tue dinner; Sat lunch*
High-quality French and Belgian
cuisine, with touches of fusion, is
beautifully presented in a 19th-
century baroque setting. Expect
to see sashimi and curry spices
alongside *waterzooi* of lobster.

Luxembourg

BOURGLINSTER: La Distillerie €€
French
Rue du Château 8, 6162
Tel *78 78 78 1* **Closed** *Mon & Tue;
Wed lunch; Sun dinner*
This renowned gourmet
restaurant benefits from its
magical setting in a medieval
castle. There is also a more down-
to-earth, but equally high-quality,
brasserie called Côté Cour.

DK Choice
**LUXEMBOURG CITY:
Clairefontaine** €€€
French
Place de Clairefontaine 9, 1341
Tel *46 22 11* **Closed** *Sat & Sun*
One of the top addresses in
the heart of Luxembourg City,
Clairefontaine is a culinary
experience that is not to be
missed. Arnaud and Edwige
Magnier offer exquisite French
cuisine for gourmands in classic
and sophisticated environs.
The seven-course menu is
an unforgettable treat for a
special occasion.

WORMELDANGE: Mathes €€
Belgian/French
Route du Vin 37, 5401
Tel *76 01 06* **Closed** *Mon & Tue*
Housed in a mansion by the
river, Mathes is famous for its
signature fish dish, *friture de la
Moselle*, along with other local
specialties and good-quality
French cuisine.

The magnificent interior of Belga Queen, housed in a former bank in Brussels

THE NETHERLANDS

Situated at the mouth of the Rhine River, the Netherlands is a man-made country that owes its life to the sea: much of the land once lay under water, and a maritime trading tradition was the principal source of the nation's wealth, most notably in the 17th century. The Netherlands is also one of the world's most liberal countries, with a long history of cultural and racial tolerance.

The shape of the Netherlands (or Holland, as it is also known) has changed dramatically over the last 2,000 years. Medieval maps show nearly half of the country under water, but since then, large areas have been reclaimed from the sea; the current shoreline is maintained by a drainage system of windmills, dykes, and canals.

With just under 17 million people in just 41,547 sq km (16,041 sq miles) of land, it is the third most densely populated country in Europe (after Monaco and Malta), but this is barely perceptible to the visitor. Only when arriving by plane do you see how much of the area is still covered with water, and how little precious land remains. The orderly Dutch cities and towns never seem overcrowded, but homes are often small, with steep, narrow staircases and modest gardens. Given the fragility of their environment, it is understandable that the Dutch are so good at preserving it.

The three biggest cities – Amsterdam, the capital, Rotterdam, the industrial hub, and the Hague, the seat of government –

are all in the west of the country and part of the urban conglomeration known as the Randstad.

History

Between the 4th and 8th centuries, after the collapse of the Roman Empire, the area corresponding to present-day Holland was conquered by the Franks. As with all the Low Countries, it was later ruled by the House of Burgundy, before passing into the hands of the Habsburgs. When the Habsburg Empire was divided in 1555, the region came under the control of the Spanish branch of the family, which caused the Dutch Revolt of 1568, led by William I of Orange. The Dutch Republic was finally established in 1579, with the Treaty of Utrecht, but it took until 1648 for the Spanish officially to recognize its sovereignty.

The battle for independence and the need for wealth to fight the Spanish armies stimulated trading success overseas. The Dutch colonized much of

Skating on a frozen Dutch river, flanked by drainage windmills

◀ A familiar sight of bicycles parked on the bridges that span the canal

Indonesia and established a profitable empire based on spice. The Dutch East India Company thrived, and in the New World, Holland briefly ruled over large parts of Brazil. Tulip bulbs were imported from Turkey and cultivated behind the dunes, thus beginning a lucrative flower industry that still flourishes today. However, war with England radically trimmed Dutch sea-power by the end of the 17th century, and from then on, the country's fortunes waned. In 1795, French troops ousted William V of Orange, and in 1813, with the retreat of Napoleon, the Netherlands united with Belgium, its neighbor, an arrangement which lasted for 17 years.

William I of Orange (1533–84), leader of the Dutch Revolt

The Netherlands remained neutral in both World Wars, and although it escaped occupation in 1914, the Nazi invasion of 1940 left lasting scars on the nation. In the 1960s, the country became a haven for the hippy counter-culture, an influence which is still visible today.

Language and Culture

Dutch, or Netherlandic, is a Germanic language which derives from the speech of the Western Franks. A number of dialects are spoken, and in Friesland the dialect (Fries) has Celtic influences. Nevertheless, as in so many European countries, the dialects are disappearing due to the popularity of national television stations on which a standardized version of Dutch is usually spoken.

Culturally, Holland has a huge amount to offer. Its rich history is reflected in countless old buildings and its large number of fine museum collections. The compact size of the city centers makes it easy to stroll along a canal admiring gabled houses, and step into a museum for an hour or two, before ending the day at a nearby café or pub. The Dutch also have much to boast in the realm of the performing arts, so visitors should find time to enjoy one of the world-famous orchestras or modern-dance companies, or attend an organ concert in an old church, or simply spend an evening in one of Amsterdam's jazz clubs or rock-and-pop venues.

A fiercely independent people, the Dutch have long been champions of freedom, and have a traditional tolerance of minorities. Jews have been welcome for centuries, and although Catholicism was banned after independence, the authorities turned a blind eye to its practise. Today, that tolerance is extended to asylum seekers, gays and lesbians, and people of different backgrounds. A respect for the right to live one's own life underlies the liberal laws on prostitution and drugs.

KEY DATES IN DUTCH HISTORY

300–700 Region ruled by the Franks

1419 Philip the Good of Burgundy begins to unify the Low Countries

1482 The Netherlands pass by marriage to the Austrian Habsburgs

1555 Philip II of Spain inherits the Netherlands

1568 The Dutch Revolt ends Spanish rule

1579 The northern districts unite, forming the Republic of the United Netherlands

1602 The Dutch East India Company founded

1606–69 Life of Rembrandt

1648 Spain recognizes Dutch independence

1794–1813 The Napoleonic era brings the Netherlands under French control

1914–18 Holland is neutral during World War I

1940–45 The country is occupied by Germany

1949 The Dutch East Indies gain independence, becoming Indonesia

1957 The Netherlands joins the European Community

1980 Princess Beatrix becomes Queen

2000 Parliament legalizes controlled euthanasia

2002 The euro replaces the Dutch guilder

2010 Rise of right-wing politician Geert Wilders

2013 Queen Beatrice abdicates; Willem-Alexander is crowned king

Exploring the Netherlands

Although the Netherlands' seat of government is at The Hague, Amsterdam is the nominal capital, and it is here that the main cultural attractions can be found. The folkloric villages of Marken and Volendam are only a short drive away, as are the towns of Alkmaar, famous for its traditional cheese market, Haarlem, with its nearby bulbfields, and Utrecht, with its medieval churches. The port of Rotterdam, the pottery center of Delft, and the university town of Leiden lie to the south and west.

The Netherlands

See main map

Sights at a Glance

1 Amsterdam pp240–51
2 Marken and Volendam
3 Alkmaar
4 Haarlem
5 Paleis Het Loo
6 Utrecht
7 Leiden
8 The Hague
9 Delft
10 Rotterdam

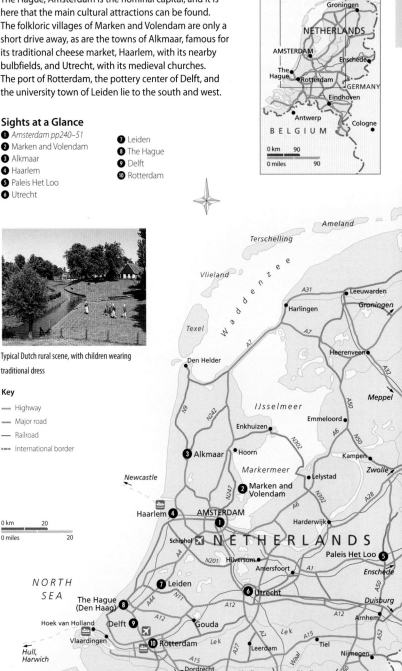

Typical Dutch rural scene, with children wearing traditional dress

Key

- Highway
- Major road
- Railroad
- International border

❶ Amsterdam

Amsterdam was founded in around 1200 as a small fishing village on marshland at the mouth of the Amstel River. The young township grew to become the chief trading city of northern Europe, and, in the 17th century, the center of a massive empire. With a population of around 770,000, Amsterdam is today a place where beauty and serenity coexist happily with a slightly seamy side. From the seedy nightspots of the Red Light District, to the grace and elegance of the city's 17th-century canal houses and the rich cultural heritage of its museums, Amsterdam boasts a variety of attractions.

Sights at a Glance

① Oude Kerk
② Museum Ons' Lieve Heer
   op Solder
③ Red Light District
④ Museum Het Rembrandthuis
⑤ Joods Historisch Museum
⑥ Nieuwe Kerk
⑦ Koninklijk Paleis
⑧ Amsterdam Museum
⑨ Begijnhof
⑩ Anne Frank House
⑪ Jordaan
⑫ Golden Bend
⑬ Nemo
⑭ Het Scheepvaartmuseum
⑮ Plantage
⑯ Hermitage Amsterdam
⑰ *Rijksmuseum pp248–50*
⑱ Van Gogh Museum
⑲ Stedelijk Museum

18th-century Torah mantle,
Joods Historisch Museum

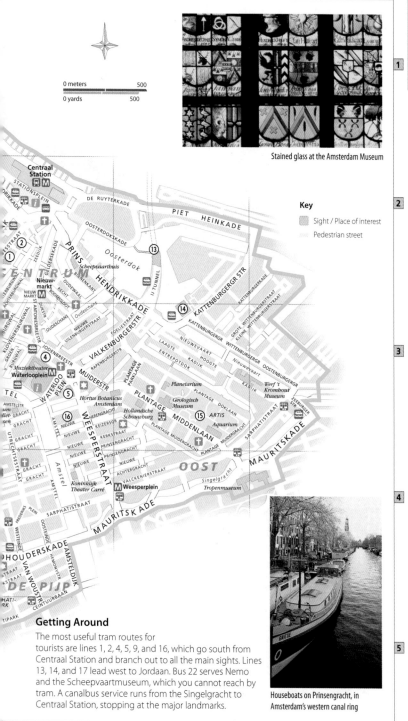

Stained glass at the Amsterdam Museum

Key

Sight / Place of interest

Pedestrian street

0 meters 500

0 yards 500

Getting Around

The most useful tram routes for tourists are lines 1, 2, 4, 5, 9, and 16, which go south from Centraal Station and branch out to all the main sights. Lines 13, 14, and 17 lead west to Jordaan. Bus 22 serves Nemo and the Scheepvaartmuseum, which cannot reach by tram. A canalbus service runs from the Singelgracht to Centraal Station, stopping at the major landmarks.

Houseboats on Prinsengracht, in Amsterdam's western canal ring

The Oude Kerk, a calm and peaceful haven at the heart of the Red Light District

① Oude Kerk

Oudekerksplein (entrance through tower). **Tel** 020-625 8284. 🚋 4, 9, 16, 24. **Open** daily (Sun: pm only). **Closed** Jan 1, Apr 27, Dec 25. 🕆 11am Sun. 🅿 ♿ 🌐 oudekerk.nl

The origins of the Oude Kerk (Old Church) go back to the early 13th century, when a wooden church was built on a burial ground on a sand bank. The present Gothic structure is 14th century, and has grown from a single-aisled church into a basilica. As it expanded, the building became a gathering place for traders and a refuge for the poor. Though many of its paintings and statues were destroyed following the Alteration in 1578, the delicate 15th-century vault paintings on the gilded ceiling escaped damage. In 1755, the paintings were hidden with layers of blue paint and were not revealed until 200 years later, in 1955. The Oude Kerk's beautiful stained-glass windows were also undamaged in the ransackings of the late 16th century. The Lady Chapel, which dates from 1552, contains some of the best stained glass. The magnificent oak-encased Great Organ, the work of Christian Vater, was added to the church in 1724.

② Museum Ons' Lieve Heer op Solder

Oudezijds Voorburgwal 38–40. **Tel** 020-624 6604. 🚋 4, 9, 16, 24. **Open** daily (Sun and public hols: pm only). **Closed** Apr 27. 🅿 📷 🌐 opsolder.nl

Tucked away on the edge of the Red Light District is a restored 17th-century canal house, with two smaller houses to the rear. The combined upper floors conceal a Catholic church,

The parlor in Ons' Lieve Heer op Solder

known as Ons' Lieve Heer op Solder (Our Lord in the Attic). After the Alteration, when Amsterdam officially became Protestant, many such hidden churches sprang up around the city. Built in 1663, the one here served the Catholic community until 1887, when the nearby St. Nicolaaskerk was completed. Above the mock-marble altar is Jacob de Wit's glorious painting *The Baptism of Christ* (1716). The tiny box bedroom where the resident priest slept is hidden off a bend in the stairs.

The building became a museum in 1888, and today contains elegantly refurbished rooms, as well as a fine collection of church silver, religious artifacts, and paintings. Restored to its former opulence, the parlor, with its magnificent fireplace, is a splendid example of a living room in the Dutch Classical style of the 17th century. The museum is expanding into the house next door, which will open in mid-2015.

③ Red Light District

🚋 4, 9, 14, 16, 24.

Prostitution in Amsterdam dates back to the city's emergence as a port in the 13th century. By 1478, it had become so widespread that attempts were made to contain it. Prostitutes straying outside their designated area were marched back to the sound of pipe and drum. A century later, the Calvinists tried

The Death of the Virgin Mary by Dirk Crabeth, one of three restored stained-glass windows in the Oude Kerk's Lady Chapel

to outlaw the practise, but their attempts were half-hearted, and by the mid-17th century, prostitution was openly tolerated. In 1850, Amsterdam had a population of 200,000 and a total of 200 brothels, most of which catered for rich clients.

Today, the Red Light District, known locally as de Walletjes (the little walls), is centered around the Oude Kerk. The area is crisscrossed by a network of tiny lanes lined with garish sex shops and seedy clubs. At night, the little alleys assume a sinister aspect, and it is not wise to wander around alone, but by day, hordes of visitors generate a festive atmosphere, and there are interesting museums, bars, and cafés, and beautiful canalside houses. The council is campaigning to make the area safer and culturally more attractive.

Interior of the Grote Synagoge, part of the Joods Historisch Museum

④ Museum Het Rembrandthuis

Jodenbreestraat 4. **Tel** 020-520 0400. Ⓜ Nieuwmarkt. 🚊 9, 14. **Open** daily. **Closed** Apr 27, Dec 25. 🅰 📷 💻 📷 Ⓦ rembrandthuis.nl

Born in Leiden, Rembrandt (1606–69) worked and taught in this house from 1639 until 1656. He lived in the ground-floor rooms with his wife, Saskia, who died here in 1642, leaving the artist with a baby son, Titus. Many of the artist's most famous paintings were created in the first-floor studio, which, along with the other rooms in the house, has been restored and refurbished to show exactly how it looked in the 17th century. On display is an excellent selection of Rembrandt's etchings and drawings, including various self-portraits showing the artist in different moods and guises. There are also landscapes, nude studies, and religious pieces, as well as temporary exhibitions of other artists' works.

⑤ Joods Historisch Museum

Nieuwe Amstelstraat 1. **Tel** 020-531 0310. Ⓜ Waterlooplein. 🚊 9, 14. 🎭 Muziektheater. **Open** daily. **Closed** Apr 27, Yom Kippur, Jewish New Year. 🅰 📷 on request. 🦽 Ⓦ jhm.nl

This complex of four synagogues was built in the 17th and 18th centuries by the Ashkenazi Jews, who arrived in Amsterdam from eastern Europe in the 1630s.

The house where Rembrandt lived and worked in the mid-17th century

At first restricted to working in certain trades, the Ashkenazi Jews were granted full civil equality in 1796. Their synagogues were central to Jewish life in Amsterdam until the devastation caused by the Nazi occupation of World War II, which left them empty. The buildings were restored in the 1980s and connected by internal walkways. In 1987, they opened as a museum dedicated to Jewish culture and the history of Judaism in the Netherlands.

The impressive Grote Synagoge, with its bright and airy interior, was designed by Elias Bouman and first opened in 1671. Next door is the Nieuwe Synagoge (New Synagogue), built in 1752. It is dominated by the wooden Holy Ark (1791), which came from a synagogue in Enkhuizen.

Religious art and artifacts on display include Hanukah lamps, Torah mantles, and scroll finials. The buildings were renovated in 2006; a print room was created in the basement and a children's museum on the upper floor in the former Obbene Shul.

18th-century Torah scroll finial

⑥ Nieuwe Kerk

Dam. **Tel** 020-638 6909. 🚋 1, 2, 4, 5 & many others. **Open** daily during exhibitions; see website for details. 🎨 ♿ 📷 🏛 🌐 nieuwekerk.nl

Dating from the late 14th century, Amsterdam's second parish church was built as the population outgrew the Oude Kerk *(see p242)*. During its turbulent history, the Nieuwe Kerk (New Church) has been destroyed by fire, rebuilt, and then stripped of its treasures after the Alteration of 1578, when the Calvinists took civil power. It eventually reached its present size in the 1650s.

Albert Vinckenbrinck's flamboyant carved pulpit (1664) is the focal point of the church interior, reflecting the Protestant belief that the sermon is central to worship. Other notable features include Jacob van Campen's ornate Great Organ (1645) and, in the apse, the tomb of the famous 17th-century commander-in-chief of the Dutch Navy, Admiral de Ruyter (1607–76), by Rombout Verhulst.

Rombout Verhulst's memorial to Michiel de Ruyter in the apse of the Nieuwe Kerk

⑦ Koninklijk Paleis

Dam. **Tel** 020-620 4060. 🚋 1, 2, 4, 5 & many others. **Open** for exhibitions during the summer & autumn; phone for details or consult website. **Closed** public hols and when King in residence. 🎨 📷 check website. ♿ 🌐 koninklijkhuis.nl

The Koninklijk Paleis, still used occasionally by the Dutch royal family for official functions, was built as the Stadhuis (Town Hall). Work began on this vast sandstone edifice in 1648, after the end of the 80 Years' War with Spain. It dominated its surroundings, and more than 13,600 piles were driven into the ground for the foundations.

The splendid Classical facade of the 17th-century Koninklijk Paleis

The Classical design by Jacob van Campen (1595–1657) reflects the city's mood of confidence after the Dutch victory. Civic pride is also shown in the allegorical sculptures by Artus Quellin (1609–68), which decorate the pediments, and in François Hemony's statues and carillon.

Inside, the full magnificence of the architecture is best appreciated in the huge Burgerzaal (Citizens' Hall). Based on the assembly halls of ancient Rome, this 29-m (95-ft) high room runs the length of the building, and boasts a superb marble floor, as well as epic sculptures by Quellien. Most of the furniture on display dates from 1808, when Louis Bonaparte took over the building as his royal palace.

⑧ Amsterdam Museum

Kalverstraat 92, St. Luciensteeg 27. **Tel** 020-523 1822. 🚋 1, 2, 4, 5, 9 & many others. **Open** daily. **Closed** Apr 27, Dec 25. 🎨 📷 ♿ 🏛 🌐 amsterdammuseum.nl

The convent of St. Lucien was turned into a civic orphanage in the latter half of the 16th century. The original red-brick convent was enlarged over the years, and in 1975 it opened as the city's historical museum. Today, some of the museum's exhibitions also focus on contemporary Amsterdam.

At the core of the collection is a 45-minute historical tour of the city called "Amsterdam DNA." This explores Amsterdam's four main characteristics: spirit of enterprise, freedom of thought, civic virtue, and creativity. Key moments from the city's history are explored chronologically, and there are displays featuring touch-sensitive multimedia screens showing animations and film footage.

Also contributing to the museum's detailed account of Amsterdam's history are such fascinating items as a globe belonging to the famous cartographer Willem Blaeu and a 1648 model of the Koninklijk Paleis, designed by Jacob van Campen (1595–1657).

Amsterdam's wealth from trade attracted many artists, who chronicled the era in great detail. There are paintings of the city and the port, as well as portraits of both prominent and ordinary citizens. The paintings of anatomy lessons include one by Rembrandt, *The Anatomy Lesson of Dr. Jan Deijman* (1656). This shows the dissection of "Black Jan," a convicted criminal who had been hanged.

In the Civic Guards' Gallery, contemporary group portraits hang between their 17th-century counterparts, emphasizing Amsterdam's cultural diversity.

Dominating the gallery is one of the museum's most extraordinary exhibits: a 17th-century 5.30-m (17-ft) statue of Goliath (c.1650). Children can experience life in a 17th-century orphanage in the "Little Orphanage" exhibition.

Statue of Goliath (c.1650) in the Amsterdam Museum

⑨ Begijnhof

Spui (entrance at Gedempte Begijnensloot). 1, 2, 5, 9, 14, 16, 24. **Tel** 020-623 3565. **Open** daily.
W begijnhofamsterdam.nl

The Begijnhof was built in 1346 as a sanctuary for the Begijntjes, a lay Catholic sisterhood who lived like nuns, although they took no monastic vows. In return for lodgings within the complex, these worthy women undertook to educate the poor and look after the sick. Although none of the earliest dwellings survives, the rows of beautiful houses that overlook the Begijnhof's well-kept green include Amsterdam's oldest surviving house, Het Houten Huis, at No. 34. Dating from around 1420, it is one of only two wooden-fronted houses in the city, since timber buildings were banned in 1521 after a series of catastrophic fires. On a wall directly behind No. 34 is a collection of fascinating stone plaques, illustrating biblical themes.

The southern side of the square is dominated by the Engelse Kerk (English Church), which dates from the 15th century and retains its original medieval tower. The church was confiscated after the Alteration and rented to a group of English and Scottish Presbyterians in 1607. Directly opposite is the Begijnhof Chapel (Nos. 29–30), a well-preserved hidden church, where the Begijntjes worshipped in secret until religious tolerance was restored in 1795. Tour groups are not permitted in the Begijnhof and the occupants request that noise should be kept to a minimum.

⑩ Anne Frank House

Prinsengracht 267. **Tel** 020-556 7105. 13, 14, 17. Prinsengracht. **Open** daily (Jan 1 & Dec 25: pm only). **Closed** Yom Kippur. **W** annefrank.org

For two years during World War II, the Frank and Van Pels families, both Jewish, hid here until their betrayal to the Nazis. The 13-year-old Anne began her famous diary in July 1942. First published in 1947 as *Het Achterhuis (The Annex)*, and since translated into dozens of languages, the journal gives a moving account of growing up under persecution, and of life in confinement. Anne made her last entry in August 1944, three days before her family was arrested.

Visitors climb to the second floor where an introductory video is shown. You then enter the annex where the families hid via the revolving bookcase that concealed its entrance. The rooms are now empty, except for the posters in Anne's room and Otto Frank's model of the annex as it was during the occupation. The house also has exhibitions on World War II and anti-Semitism. Try to arrive early or late in the day as the museum gets very crowded. Buy tickets via the Internet to avoid the queues.

Family photograph of Anne Frank (1929–45)

Attractive gabled houses and central green of Amsterdam's Begijnhof, which is still occupied by single women

The Westerkerk, designed by Hendrick de Keyser, overlooking the Prinsengracht in Jordaan

⑪ Jordaan

🚊 13, 14, 17.

The Jordaan grew up at the same time that Amsterdam's Grachtengordel (Canal Ring) was being developed in the first half of the 17th century. The marshy area to the west of the more fashionable canals was set aside as an area for workers whose industries were banned from the town center. Its network of narrow streets and waterways followed the course of old paths and drainage ditches. Immigrants fleeing religious persecution also settled here. It is thought that Huguenot refugees called the district *jardin* (garden), later corrupted to "Jordaan."

Flowing through the heart of the district are the tranquil tree-lined canals known as the Egelantiersgracht and the Bloemgracht. The canalside residences of the Egelantiersgracht were originally settled by artisans, while the Bloemgracht was a center for dye and paint manufacture. One of the most charming spots along the Egelantiersgracht is **St. Andrieshofje**, at Nos. 107–114. This *hofje* (almshouse) was built in 1617 and the passage that

leads to its courtyard is decorated with splendid blue and white tiles.

The 85-m (272-ft) high tower of the **Westerkerk** soars above Jordaan's streets, and gives panoramic views of the city. Begun in 1620, the church has the largest nave of any Dutch Protestant church.

Historically a poor area, the Jordaan now has a trendy and bohemian air, with quirky stores selling anything from designer clothes to old sinks, art galleries, and lively brown cafés and bars spilling onto the sidewalks during the summer.

⑫ Golden Bend

🚊 1, 2, 4, 5, 9, 14 & many others. Kattenkabinet: **Tel** 020-626 9040. **Open** 10am–4pm Mon–Fri; pm Sat & Sun. **Closed** public hols. Het Grachten-huis: 🌐 **hetgrachtenhuis.nl**

The most impressive canalside architecture in the city can be seen along the section of the Herengracht between Leidestraat and Vijzelstraat. This stretch of canal is known as the Golden Bend because of the great wealth of the shipbuilders,

merchants, and politicians who began building houses here in the 1660s. Most of the opulent mansions have been turned into offices or banks, but their elegance gives an insight into the lifestyle of the earliest residents.

Two of the finest and best-preserved buildings are No. 412, designed by Philips Vingboons in 1664, and No. 475, with its two sculpted female figures over the front door. Built in 1730, the latter is an example of the Louis XIV style, which became popular in the 18th century. The **Kattenkabinet** (Cat Museum), at No. 497, is one of the few houses on the Golden Bend accessible to the public. It is worth a visit for its unusual collection of feline artifacts. Also on view here are some splendid paintings by Jacob de Wit (1695–1754) and an attractive formal garden.

A multimedia exhibition at **Het Grachtenhuis**, a mansion on Herengracht, illustrates Hendrick Staets' plans for the Grachtengordel *(see below)*.

Ornate capital from the facade of a building on the Golden Bend

The Grachtengordel

Faced with a rapidly growing population at the beginning of the 17th century, Amsterdam's town planner, Hendrick Staets, formed an ambitious project to quadruple the size of the city. In 1614, work began on cutting three new residential canals, collectively known as the Grachtengordel (Canal Ring), to encircle the existing city. Built for the wealthiest citizens, the grand houses along the Keizersgracht (Emperor's Canal), Herengracht (Gentleman's Canal), and Prinsengracht (Prince's Canal) represent Amsterdam's finest architecture, and are a testimony to the city's Golden Age.

Seeing the world through a soap bubble at Nemo

⑬ Nemo

Oosterdok 2. **Tel** 020-531 3233. 🚌 22. **Open** 10am–5pm Tue–Sun. **Closed** Jan 1, Apr 27, Dec 25. 🅿 ♿ 🌐 e-nemo.nl

In June 1997, Holland's national science center moved to this curved building that protrudes 30 m (99 ft) over the water. Divided into five themed zones (Interactivity, Technology, Energy, Science, and Humanity), which are updated every three years, the center presents technological innovations in a way that allows visitors' creativity full expression. You can interact with virtual reality, operate the latest industrial equipment under expert supervision, harness science to produce a work of art, participate in countless games, experiments, demonstrations, and workshops, and take in a variety of lectures and films.

⑭ Het Scheep-vaartmuseum

Kattenburgerplein 1. **Tel** 020-523 2222. 🚌 22. 🚢 Oosterdok, Kattenburgergracht. **Open** daily. **Closed** Jan 1, Apr 27, Dec 25. 🅿 ♿ 🌐 scheepvaartmuseum.nl

Once the arsenal of the Dutch Navy, this vast Classical sandstone edifice was built in 1656. It is supported by 2,300 piles driven into the bed of the Oosterdok. The Navy stayed here until 1973, when the building was converted into the National Maritime Museum, holding the largest collection of boats in the world.

One of the museum's finest exhibits is a 17-m (54-ft) long gilded barge, made in 1818 for King William I. Another major attraction is a full-size model of a Dutch East Indiaman, the *Amsterdam*. During the 16th century, the Dutch East India Company used such vessels to sail as far as China, Japan, and Indonesia. The museum has a court with a magnificent high glass ceiling.

⑮ Plantage

🚊 9, 14. Artis: Plantage Kerklaan 30–40. **Tel** 0900-278 4796. **Open** daily. 🅿 🎫 ♿ Hortus Botanicus Amsterdam: Plantage Middenlaan 2. **Tel** 020-625 9021. **Open** daily. **Closed** Jan 1, Dec 25. 🅿 🎫 ♿ Hollandsche Schouwburg: Plantage Middenlaan 24. **Tel** 020-531 0310. **Open** daily. **Closed** Yom Kippur. ♿

The name Plantage dates from the time when it was an area

Seals basking in a pool at the Artis zoo complex in Plantage

of green parkland beyond the city wall, where 17th-century Amsterdammers spent their leisure time. Though much of the greenery has gone, there is still a lot to see and do here.

The area is dominated by **Artis**, a zoo complex founded in 1838, which has more than 5,000 animal species, a planetarium, and an excellent aquarium.

Nearby, the **Hortus Botanicus Amsterdam** has humble roots as it began as a small apothecaries' herb garden in 1682 and now contains one of the world's largest botanical collections.

Plantage has a strong Jewish tradition, and many monuments commemorate Jewish history in Amsterdam. The **Hollandsche Schouwburg** is a somber memorial to the 104,000 Dutch Jewish victims of World War II.

⑯ Hermitage Amsterdam

Amstel 51. **Tel** 020-530 8755. 🚊 4, 9, 14. **Open** daily. **Closed** Apr 27, Dec 25. 🅿 🎫 ♿ ♿ 🖥 🌐 hermitage.nl

This branch of the State Hermitage Museum in St. Petersburg is housed in the vast Amstelhof, a former old-people's home. Opened in 2004, this satellite museum displays temporary exhibitions drawn from the rich St. Petersburg collections. The venue is now one of Amsterdam's major museums.

The Dutch East Indiaman *Amsterdam*, moored in front of the Scheepvaartmuseum

⑰ Rijksmuseum

The Rijksmuseum is a familiar Amsterdam landmark. It possesses an unrivaled collection of about 1 million artworks, 8,000 of which are on display, arranged chronologically in 80 galleries. The museum opened in 1885 to criticism from Amsterdam's Protestant community for its Catholic Neo-Renaissance style. The main building, designed by P.J.H. Cuypers, underwent extensive renovation for ten years and reopened in 2013.

Second floor

Winter Landscape with Skaters (1618)
Mute painter Hendrick Avercamp specialized in intricate icy winter scenes.

★ **The Kitchen Maid** (1658)
The light falling through the window and the stillness of this domestic scene are typical of Jan Vermeer's style.

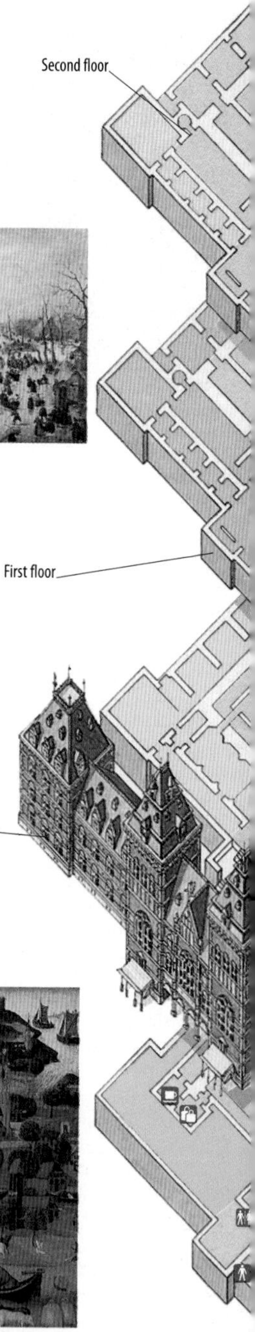

First floor

The Neo-Renaissance facade of Cuypers' building is red brick with elaborate decoration, including colored tiles.

Gallery Guide

The entrance to the main building is through the Atrium. The collection explores 800 years of Dutch history through paintings, sculpture, applied arts, and historical objects. Artworks are shown side by side, underlining contrasts and connections. A pavilion between the main building and the Philips Wing houses the Asiatic collection. The Philips Wing has a café and restaurant on the ground level, and a floor devoted to temporary exhibitions.

Key to Floorplan

- 1100–1600
- 1600–1700
- 1700–1800
- 1800–1900
- 1900–2000
- Asian Pavillion
- Special Collections
- Non-exhibition space

★ **St. Elizabeth's Day Flood** (1500)
An unknown artist painted this altarpiece, which shows a disastrous flood in 1421. The dykes protecting Dordrecht were breached, and 22 villages were swept away by the flood water.

★ **The Night Watch** (1642)
The showpiece of Dutch
17th-century art, this vast canvas by
Rembrandt was commissioned as
a group portrait of an
Amsterdam militia company.

VISITORS' CHECKLIST

Practical Information
Museumstraat 1.
Tel 020-674 7000.
[w] **rijksmuseum.nl**
Open 9am–5pm daily.

Transport
2, 3, 5, 7, 10, 12.
Stadhouderskade.

Gallery of
Honour

St. Catherine (c.1465)
This sculpture by the Master of
Koudewater shows the saint
stamping on Emperor
Maxentius, who allegedly
killed her with his sword.

Ground
floor

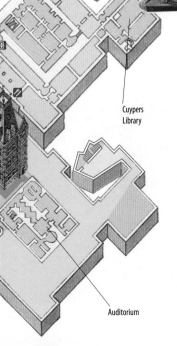

Cuypers
Library

Jan Steen's symbolic *Woman at her Toilet*, painted
around 1660

Genre Painting

For the contemporaries of Jan Steen
(1625–79), this cosy everyday scene
was full of symbols that are obscure to
the modern viewer. The dog on the
pillow may represent fidelity, and the
red stockings the woman's sexuality;
she is probably a prostitute. Such
genre paintings were often raunchy,
but nearly always had a moral twist –
domestic scenes by artists such as ter
Borch and Honthorst were symbolic of
brothels, while other works illustrated
proverbs. Symbols like candles or skulls
indicated mortality.

Auditorium

Exploring the Rijksmuseum

The Rijksmuseum is too vast to be seen in a single visit. If time is limited, start with the incomparable 17th-century Dutch paintings, taking in Rembrandt, Frans Hals, Vermeer, and many other Old Masters. The collection of Asiatic artifacts is equally wonderful, and a tour of the special-collections section also provides a rewarding experience. The gardens, redesigned according to Cuypers' original plans, are also well worth a look.

The heavily ornamented Neo-Gothic building, Rijksmuseum

1100–1600

Displayed alongside Flemish and Italian art are religious works by Netherlandish painters, such as *The Seven Works of Charity* (1504) by the Master of Alkmaar, Jan van Scorel's *Mary Magdalene* (1528), and Lucas van Leyden's triptych, *Adoration of the Golden Calf* (1530).

1650–1700

The 17th century was a golden age for Dutch art. By this time, religious themes in art had been replaced by secular subjects, such as realistic portraiture, landscapes, still lifes, seascapes, domestic interiors, and animal portraits.

The most famous artist of this era is Rembrandt, whose works here include *Portrait of Titus in a Monk's Habit* (1660), *Self-Portrait as the Apostle Paul* (1661), and *The Jewish Bride* (1663), as well as the brilliant *The Night Watch (see p249)*. Also not to be missed are Jan Vermeer's (1632–75) serenely light-filled interiors, such as *The Kitchen Maid (see p248)*

and *The Woman Reading a Letter* (1662). Of several portraits by Frans Hals (1580–1666), the best-known are *The Wedding Portrait* and *The Merry Drinker* (1630). *The Windmill at Wijk* by Jacob van Ruisdael (1628–82) is a great landscape by an artist at the height of his career. Other artists whose works contribute to this unforgettable collection include Pieter Saenredam (1597–1665), Jan van de Capelle (c.1624–79), and Jan Steen *(see p249)*.

1700–1800

Portraiture and still lifes continued to dominate 18th-century Dutch painting. The evocative *Still Life with Flowers and Fruit* by Jan van Huysum (1682–1749) stands out among works on display here. Other 18th-century artists represented are Adriaan van der Werff (1659–1722) and Cornelis Troost (1696–1750).

1800–1900

The 19th-century collection features works by the Hague School, a group of Dutch artists who came together in around 1870 in Den Haag. Their landscape work captures the atmospheric quality of subdued Dutch sunlight. Look out for Anton Mauve's *Morning Ride on the Beach* (1876) and the beautiful Polder landscape, *View near the Geestbrug*, by Hendrik Weissenbruch (1824–1903).

1900–2000

Below the rafters is a series of rooms devoted to 20th-century art and design. Highlights in this section include a white version of Gerrit Rietveld's iconic red-and-blue armchair (1923), Karel Appel's imposing oil painting *The Square Man* (1951), and an F.K.23 Bantam biplane from 1918.

Asiatic Art

Rewards of the Dutch imperial trading past are on show in this section. Some of the earliest artifacts are the most unusual: tiny bronze Tang-dynasty figurines from 7th-century China, and granite rock carvings from Java (c.8th century). Later exhibits include Chinese parchment paintings, inlaid Korean boxes, and decorative Vietnamese dishes.

The Jewish Bride by Rembrandt (1606–69)

The Bedroom, painted during Van Gogh's stay in Arles, France

⑱ Van Gogh Museum

Paulus Potterstraat 7. **Tel** 020-570 5200. 🚊 2, 3, 5, 12. **Open** daily. **Closed** Jan 1. 🎦 ♿ 📷 📧 📷
W vangoghmuseum.com

Vincent Van Gogh (1853–90), born in Zundert, began painting in 1880. He worked in the Netherlands for five years, before moving to Paris, and then settling at Arles *(see pp192–3)* in the south of France in February 1888. There he painted more than 200 canvases in 15 months. During his time in France, however, Van Gogh suffered recurrent nervous crises, hallucinations, and depression. After a fierce argument with the French artist Gauguin, he cut off part of his own ear and his mental instability forced him into an asylum. Van Gogh's final years were characterized by tremendous bursts of activity. During the last 70 days of his life he painted 70 canvases. In July 1890 he shot himself and died two days later. He was on the verge of being acclaimed.

Van Gogh's younger brother Theo, an art dealer, amassed a collection of 200 of his paintings and 500 drawings. These, together with around 850 letters written by the artist to Theo, form the core of the

Vincent Van Gogh in 1871

museum's collection. Famous works include *The Potato Eaters* (1885), from the artist's Dutch period, *The Bedroom* (1888), painted to celebrate his achievement of domestic stability in the Yellow House in Arles, and *Vase with Sunflowers* (1889). One of Van Gogh's last paintings is the dramatic *Wheatfield and Crows* (1890). The menacing crows and violence of the sky show the depth of the artist's mental anguish in the last few weeks before his death. In addition to Van Gogh's works, the museum displays paintings by artists who influenced, or were influenced by, him, as well as works by his friends and colleagues, such as Gauguin and Toulouse-Lautrec.

⑲ Stedelijk Museum

Museumplein 10. **Tel** 020-573 2911. 🚊 2, 3, 5, 12. **Open** 10am–6pm daily (to 10pm Thu). 🎦 ♿ 📷 📧 📷
W stedelijk.nl

The Stedelijk Museum was designed to hold a personal collection bequeathed to the city in 1890 by art connoisseur Sophia de Bruyn. It is housed in a late 19th-century Neoclassical building, adorned with statues of famous artists and architects. In 1938, the museum became

the national museum of modern art, showing works by well-known names such as Picasso, Matisse, Chagall, and Monet. Constantly changing exhibitions reflect the latest developments not only in painting and sculpture, but also in printing, drawing, photography, video, and industrial design.

Among the museum's best collections are works by the Dutch painter Mondriaan (1872–1944). One of the founding members of De Stijl (The Style) – an artistic movement which espoused clarity and simplicity – Mondriaan went on to produce many abstract geometrical compositions, such as *Composition in Red, Black, Blue, Yellow, and Grey*.

Other artists represented in the exhibitions include the American photographer Man Ray (1890–1977), the Russian Kazimir Malevich (1878–1935), founder of the abstract movement Suprematism, and the Swiss sculptor Jean Tinguely (1925–91), who created humorous sculptures from junk and recycled metal.

Reopened in 2012 after a renovation program, the museum now features a spectacular annexe (known as "the bathtub") for temporary exhibitions. The terrace offers great views of Museumplein.

Statue of 16th-century artist Pieter Aertsen on the Stedelijk's facade

A typical 17th-century gabled timber house in Marken

➋ Marken and Volendam

Marken: 🏘 2,000. 🚌 🚤 Volendam: 🏘 21,000. 🚌 ℹ Zeestraat 37 (0299-363747). 🎭 Sat. 🌐 vvv-volendam.nl

Located on the shores of the Marker Meer, and less than an hour's drive from Amsterdam, Marken and Volendam are extremely popular with tourists, who are drawn to their old-world character. In spite of the crowds, it is worth spending a few hours exploring their narrow streets and canals, lined, as they are, with attractive 17th-century gabled timber houses. You may even spot the local inhabitants wearing traditional dress.

Places to look out for include the **Marker Museum** in Marken, which consists of six historical houses. One of the houses is furnished as a traditional fisherman's dwelling. Volendam's **Spaander Hotel**, at No. 15 Haven, is also worth

a visit. The walls of the hotel's café are covered with works by late 19th-century artists who came here to paint the town.

➌ Alkmaar

🏘 94,000. 🚉 ℹ Waaggebouw, Waagplein 2–3 (072-5114 284). 🧀 cheese market: Apr–Sep: 10am–12:30pm Fri. 🌐 vvvhartvannoordholland.nl

Alkmaar is one of the few Dutch towns to maintain its traditional cheese market, which has been held here since medieval times. Every Friday morning in summer, local producers lay out Gouda and Edam cheeses in the Waagplein, and from here, porters sporting colorful straw hats take them off on sledges for weighing at the **Waaggebouw** (Weigh House). This imposing building, altered in 1582 from a 14th-century chapel, also houses the **Het Hollands Kaasmuseum**, where local cheese-making techniques are explained.

Alkmaar's massive Gothic church, the **Grote Kerk**, was completed in 1520 and contains the tomb of Floris V, Count of Holland. The nave is dominated by the 17th-century organ, designed by Jacob van Campen and painted by Cesar van Everdingen.

🏛 Het Hollands Kaasmuseum
Waaggebouw, Waagplein 2. **Tel** 072-5155 516. **Open** Easter–Oct: Mon–Sat. 🎫 ♿ 🌐 kaasmuseum.nl

The soaring pipes of the famous organ in Haarlem's Grote Kerk

➍ Haarlem

🏘 147,000. 🚉 ℹ Stationsplein 1 (0900-616 1600). 🎭 Mon, Fri & Sat. 🎷 Haarlem Jazz Festival (mid-Aug).

Haarlem is the center of the Dutch printing, pharma-ceutical, and bulb-growing industries. Most of the city's main attractions are within easy walking distance of the Grote Markt, a lively square overlooked by the Gothic **Grote Kerk**. Also known as Sint Bavo's, this huge church was built between 1400 and 1550. Its highly decorative organ (1735) has been played by both Handel and Mozart. Also on the Grote Markt, the **Stadhuis** (Town Hall) dates from 1250 and displays a mixture of architectural styles. The oldest part of the building is the beamed medieval banqueting hall of the counts of Holland.

The **Amsterdamse Poort**, the medieval gateway that once formed part of the city's defenses, was built in 1355.

Haarlem is well known for its *hofjes* (almshouses), which began to appear in the 16th century. Established in 1610, **St. Elisabeth's Gasthuis** now houses a historical museum. The **Frans Hals Museum** occupies the almshouse where the famous artist (1582–1666) supposedly lived out his last years. In addition to a superb collection of paintings by Hals himself, there is

Porters carrying cheeses at Alkmaar's traditional market

For hotels and restaurants see p260 and p261

a selection of Dutch paintings and applied art dating from the 16th and 17th centuries.

Frans Hals Museum
Groot Heiligland 62. **Tel** 023-5115 775.
Open Tue–Sat, pm Sun. **Closed** Jan 1, Dec 25.

❺ Paleis Het Loo

Koninklijk Park 1, Apeldoorn. **Tel** 055-577 2400. to Apeldoorn, then bus 102. **Open** Tue–Sun. **Closed** Jan 1. paleishetloo.nl

Stadholder William III built Het Loo in 1686 as a royal hunting lodge. Generations of the House of Orange used the lodge as a summer palace, which came to be regarded as the "Versailles of the Netherlands." The building's Classical facade belies the opulence of the interior. Among the most lavish apartments are the Royal Bedroom of William III (1713), with its wall coverings and draperies of rich orange damask and blue silk, and the Old Dining Room (1686). In the latter half of the 20th century, old prints, records, and plans were used to carefully recreate Het Loo's beautiful formal gardens.

The sumptuously decorated Royal Bedroom of Stadholder William III

❻ Utrecht

234,000. Domplein 9 (0900-236 000). Wed & Sat.

Utrecht was founded by the Romans in AD 47 to protect a strategic river crossing on the Rhine. The town was one of the first places in the Netherlands to

Bulbfields of the Netherlands

Bulb species cultivated in the Netherlands include lilies, gladioli, daffodils, hyacinths, irises, crocuses, and dahlias. The most famous

bulb of all, however, is the tulip. Originally from Turkey, it was first grown in Dutch soil by Carolus Clusius in 1593. Occupying a 30-km (19-mile) strip between Haarlem and Leiden, the Bloembollenstreek is the most important bulb-growing area in the country. From late January, the polders bloom with brightly colored bulbs, building to a climax in mid-April when the tulips flower. For a breathtaking showcase of flowering bulbs, visit the Keukenhof gardens, on the outskirts of Lisse and easily reached by bus from Leiden station or Schiphol Airport (Stationsweg Lisse; Tel: 0252-465 555; www.keukenhof.nl).

A blanket of color, formed by tulips in the Bloembollenstreek

embrace Christianity, and in the Middle Ages, it grew into an important religious center. The city retains many of its medieval churches and monasteries. The **Domkerk**, Utrecht's cathedral, was begun in 1254. Today, only the north and south transepts, two chapels, and the choir remain, along with the 15th-century cloisters and a chapterhouse. The **Domtoren**, which stands apart from the cathedral, is one of the tallest towers in the Netherlands, at 112 m (367 ft). Completed in 1382, on the site of the small 8th-century church of St. Willibrord, it affords magnificent views of the city.

Among Utrecht's many museums are the **Museum Catharijneconvent**, which deals with the troubled history of religion in the Netherlands and owns an award-winning collection of medieval art, and the **Nederlands Spoorwegmuseum**, a superb railroad museum, housed in the fully restored 19th-century Maliebaan station. At the heart of the collection at the **Centraal Museum** is a series of portraits by artist Jan van Scorel (1495–1562), known as the "Utrecht Caravaggisti." There is also an impressive collection of modern and contemporary art, with

works by Van Gogh, Courbet, and Damien Hirst, as well as sculpture, costume, and furniture collections.

Museum Catharijneconvent
Lange Nieuwstraat 38. **Tel** 030-2313 835. **Open** Tue–Sun. **Closed** Jan 1, Apr 27. catharijneconvent.nl

Centraal Museum
Nicolaaskerkhof 10. **Tel** 030-2362 362. **Open** Tue–Sun. **Closed** Jan 1, Apr 27, Dec 25. centraalmuseum.nl

Utrecht's massive Gothic Domtoren, which dominates the city

❼ Leiden

🗺 119,000. 🚉 🚌 ℹ Stationsweg 41 (071-516 600). 🛍 Wed, Sat. 🌐 leiden.nl

Leiden is a prosperous town that dates back to Roman times. Its famous university is the oldest in the Netherlands, founded in 1575 by William of Orange. Created in 1587, the university's botanical garden, the **Hortus Botanicus der Rijksuniversiteit Leiden**, is still open to the public.

One of Leiden's main attractions is the **Rijksmuseum van Oudheden** (National Museum of Antiquities). Established in 1818, the museum houses an outstanding collection of Egyptian artifacts, including the 1st-century AD Temple of Taffeh. There are also displays of textiles, musical instruments, Etruscan bronze-work, and fragments of Roman mosaics and frescoes.

The magnificent Gothic **Pieterskerk** was built in the 15th century. Its interior is rather austere, but there is a splendid organ (1642), enclosed in gilded woodwork.

Dating back to 1640, the old Lakenhal (Cloth Hall) now houses the **Stedelijk Museum De Lakenhal**, with exhibitions of art and furniture from the 16th century onward. The pride of the collection is Lucas van Leyden's Renaissance triptych, *The Last Judgment* (1526–7). Leiden also has an excellent ethnological museum, the **Museum Volkenkunde**, which has exhibits from many countries and hosts events on traditions, rituals, and practises of other cultures.

Hortus Botanicus, the tranquil botanical gardens of Leiden University

🏛 **Rijksmuseum van Oudheden**
Rapenburg 28. **Tel** 071-5163 163. **Open** Tue–Sun. **Closed** Jan 1, Apr 27, Oct 3, Dec 25. 🖼 ♿ 🏪 📷 🌐 rmo.nl

🏛 **Museum Volkenkunde**
Steenstraat 1. **Tel** 071-5168 800. **Open** Tue–Sun. **Closed** Jan 1, Apr 27, Oct 3, Dec 25. 🖼 📷 ♿ 🌐 mv.nl

❽ The Hague

🗺 497,000. 🚉 🚌 ℹ Spui 68 (070-361 8860). 🛍 Mon, Wed, Fri, Sat. 🌐 denhaag.com

The political capital of the Netherlands, The Hague (Den Haag or 's-Gravenhage) is home to prestigious institutions, such as the Dutch parliament and the International Court of Justice.

When The Hague became the seat of government in 1586, it was a small town built around the castle of the counts of Holland. That same castle, much rebuilt, stands at the heart of the city, and forms part of the Binnenhof, where today's parliament sits. The fairytale, double-turreted Gothic **Ridderzaal** (Hall of the Knights),

the 13th-century dining hall of Count Floris V, is open to the public when parliament is not in session.

An outstanding collection of works by Dutch Masters Rembrandt, Jan Vermeer, and Jan Steen is assembled in the Royal Picture Gallery at the **Mauritshuis**. More Dutch Golden Age paintings are on view at the **Museum Bredius** and the **Galerij Prins Willem V**.

The **Haags Gemeentemuseum** has an applied-arts section that includes the world's largest collection of paintings by De Stijl *(see p251)* artist Piet Mondrian.

Formerly called Het Oude Hof (the Old Court), the **Paleis Noordeinde** is a splendid 17th-century palace built in the Classical style. It is used as a temporary residence by Queen Beatrix.

🏛 **Ridderzaal**
Binnenhof 8a. **Tel** 070-364 6144. **Open** Mon–Fri (call in advance). **Closed** public hols. 🖼 📷 obligatory.

🏛 **Mauritshuis**
Korte Vijverberg 8. **Tel** 070-302 3456. **Open** Tue–Sun (daily Apr–Aug). **Closed** Jan 1, Dec 25. 🖼 📷 ♿

🏛 **Galerij Prins Willem V**
Buitenhof 35. **Tel** 070-302 3456. **Open** Tue–Sun (daily Apr–Aug). 🖼

Environs
Only a 15-minute tram ride from the center of Den Haag, **Scheveningen** has clean, sandy beaches and good seafood restaurants. The resort also has a Sea Life Center and Muzee, a small museum of marine-biology and local-history exhibits.

The Binnenhof, home of the Dutch parliament, The Hague

9 Delft

🏙 95,000. 🚍 🚌 ℹ Hippolytusbuurt 4 (0900-5151 555). 🛒 Thu, Sat.

The charming town of Delft is most famous for its blue-and-white pottery, known as Delftware, which was introduced to the Netherlands by immigrant Italian potters in the 16th century. **De Porceleyne Fles** is one of two Delftware potteries still in operation, and is open for guided tours.

Delft is also the resting place of William of Orange (1533–84), who commanded the Dutch Revolt against Spanish rule from his headquarters in the town. His richly decorated tomb lies in the **Nieuwe Kerk**, built between 1383 and 1510, but later restored following damage caused by fire and explosion. The former convent that William used as his military headquarters, and where he was assassinated by order of Philip II of Spain, is now home to the **Stedelijk Museum Het Prinsenhof**.

Hand-painted 17th-century Delft tiles

The museum contains a rare collection of antique Delftware, as well as tapestries, silverware, medieval sculpture, and portraits of the Dutch royal family.

Other sites of interest are the **Vermeer Centrum Delft**, which charts the life and works of Delft's most famous son, Jan Vermeer (1632–75), and the **Oude Kerk**, which dates from the 13th century. Vermeer is buried here, his grave marked by a simple stone tablet.

🏛 **Nieuwe Kerk**
Markt. **Tel** 015-2123 025. **Open** Mon–Sat. 🖼 🖥 **nieuwekerk-delft.nl**

🏛 **Stedelijk Museum Het Prinsenhof**
St. Agathaplein 1. **Tel** 015-2602 358. **Open** Tue–Sat, Sun pm. **Closed** Jan 1, Apr 27, Whitsun, Dec 25. 🖼 📷 🖥 **prinsenhof-delft.nl**

🏛 **Vermeer Centrum Delft**
Voldersgracht 21. **Tel** 015-213 8588. **Open** daily. **Closed** Jan 1, Dec 25. 🖼 🚻 🖥 📷 🖥 **vermeerdelft.nl**

Delft's Nieuwe Kerk, with its soaring 100-m (328-ft) high tower

10 Rotterdam

🏙 585,000. ✈ 6 km (4 miles) NW. 🚍 🚌 ℹ Coolsingel 195 (010-790 0185). 🛒 Tue, Fri, Sat, Sun.

Rotterdam occupies a strategic position where the Rhine meets the North Sea. Barges from the city transport goods deep into the continent, and ocean-going ships carry European exports around the world.

Following damage during World War II, the Oudehaven, Rotterdam's old harbor area, has been rebuilt in daring and avant-garde styles. The pencil-shaped **Gemeente Bibliotheek** (Public Library) is similar to the Pompidou Center in Paris (see p153), while Piet Blom's **Kijk-Kubus** (Cube Houses) of 1982 are extraordinary apartments set on a series of concrete stilts.

The excellent **Museum Boijmans-van Beuningen** holds Netherlandish and Dutch art, from the medieval paintings of Jan van Eyck to modern works using laser technology. Among its most famous exhibits are a number of paintings by Peter Brueghel and Rembrandt.

Other museums of note are the **Wereldmuseum Rotterdam**, with its superb ethnological collection, the **Kunsthal**, hosting eye-catching exhibitions of both high art and popular culture, and the **Maritiem Museum Rotterdam**, devoted to the history of shipping, whose highlight is an iron-clad warship, De Buffel, built in 1868.

For a spectacular view of the city, take the elevator up the 185-m (600-ft) high **Euromast**. Built in 1960, it is the tallest construction in the country, and has a restaurant and an exhibition area.

🏛 **Museum Boijmans-van Beuningen**
Museumpark 18–20. **Tel** 010-441 9400. **Open** Tue–Sun. **Closed** Jan 1, Apr 27, Dec 25. 🖼 ♿

🏛 **Wereldmuseum Rotterdam**
Willemskade 25. **Tel** 010-270 7172. **Open** Tue–Sun. **Closed** Jan 1, Apr 27, Dec 25. 🖼 🖥 📷 ♿

🏛 **Kunsthal**
Westzeedijk 341. **Tel** 010-440 0301. **Open** Tue–Sun. **Closed** Jan 1, Apr 27, Dec 25. 🖼 🖥 📷 🖥 **kunsthal.nl**

Peter Brueghel the Elder's The Tower of Babel (c.1553), in the Museum Boijmans-van Beuningen, Rotterdam

Practical & Travel Information

The Netherlands is a straightforward country to travel in, and visitors should find its citizens, who are often multilingual, helpful and friendly. One of the joys of a visit to Amsterdam is the relatively car-free environment. Trams, bicycles, and pedestrians are given a higher priority in the center than motor vehicles. Outside the capital, the Dutch public-transportation network is one of the most highly developed in Europe.

Tourist Information

The NBTC (**Netherlands Board of Tourism and Conventions**) has offices in many cities worldwide. Within the Netherlands, the state-run tourist-information organization is the Vereniging Voor Vreemdelingenverkeer, known as the **VVV**. They have around 450 offices throughout the country. Courteous and friendly staff provide information on sights, transportation, and events, and will also change money and reserve hotel rooms.

The Museum Card (*Museumkaart*), available from branches of the VVV, is valid for a year, and allows admission to more than 400 museums and galleries throughout the country.

Visa Requirements and Customs

Citizens of the EU, Australia, New Zealand, the US, and Canada need only a valid passport to enter the Netherlands. Those visitors coming from non-EU states can reclaim VAT on certain goods. Call the freephone customs-information line (0800-0143) for further details.

Safety and Emergencies

Amsterdam is much safer than many North American and European cities. Drugs-related crime is still a problem, but tourists should not be affected by this, as long as they act sensibly and avoid certain areas after dark, in particular the Zeedijk district.

In case of emergencies, the appropriate number to call is listed in the directory opposite.

Health Issues

Minor health problems can be dealt with by a chemist (*drogist*), who stocks non-prescription drugs. If you need prescription medicines, go to a pharmacy (*apotheek*), open from 8:30am to 5:30pm Monday to Friday.

Attracted by the canals, mosquitoes can be an irritant in Amsterdam, so bring plenty of repellent sprays and antihistamine creams with you.

Museum Opening Times

Many state-run museums are closed on Mondays, and open from 10am to 5pm Tuesday to Saturday, and from 1 to 5pm on Sunday. Most museums adopt Sunday hours for national holidays, apart from New Year's Day, when they are always closed.

Banking and Currency

The Dutch unit of currency is the euro (*see p23*). Banks open from 9 or 10am to 4 or 5pm Monday to Friday. Some city branches close at 7pm on Thursdays and open on Saturday mornings. Banks are usually the best place to change money, but official bureaux de change, the GWK (*grenswissel-kantoor-bureaus*), also have reasonable exchange rates. Credit cards are not as widely accepted in the Netherlands as in other European countries.

Communications

Most public telephones have been removed due to the use of cell phones, but you can still find some in stations and tourist areas. The majority of phone booths only accept cards, which can be bought at post offices, tobacconists, and train stations, but it might be easier and cheaper to buy a local SIM card for your phone.

Main post offices are open 9am–5pm Monday to Friday. Most small local post offices have been replaced by post-office agencies in supermarkets and bookstores. Stamps can be bought at post offices, tobacconists, or souvenir shops.

Flying to the Netherlands

Carriers operating non-stop flights from the US to the Netherlands include **American Airlines**, **Delta Air Lines**, **United Airlines**, and **KLM**. Seven airlines fly direct from the UK to the Netherlands, among them **British Airways** and low-cost airlines including **Ryanair**, **easyJet**, and **Transavia**. The least-expensive way to get from Amsterdam's Schiphol Airport to the city center is by the airport train service. Trains leave for Centraal Station seven times each hour between 5:40am and 1am, after which they run hourly. The journey takes 20

The Climate of the Netherlands

The Netherlands has a temperate climate. Winters are frequently freezing, and spring and autumn can be chilly. July and August are the warmest months, but North Sea winds often make it seem cooler. You should expect rainfall all year round, but spring is generally the driest season. The heaviest rainfall occurs in the autumn, especially in November.

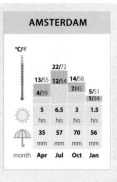

AMSTERDAM			
°C/°F			
	22/72		
13/55	12/54	14/58	
4/39		7/45	5/51
			1/34
5 hrs	6.5 hrs	3 hrs	1.5 hrs
35 mm	57 mm	70 mm	56 mm
month Apr	Jul	Oct	Jan

minutes. Schiphol Airport station is also connected to other cities in the Netherlands.

Arriving by Sea

Ferry companies offering car and passenger services from the UK to the Netherlands include **P&O North Sea Ferries**, with daily sailings from Hull to Rotterdam, and **Stena Line**, which sails from Harwich to Hook of Holland.

P&O also operates regular crossings from Hull to Zeebrugge in Belgium. **DFDS Seaways** runs an overnight service from Newcastle to Ijmuiden.

Rail Travel

International railroad routes provide a fast and efficient link between Amsterdam and many other European cities. From Centraal Station, high-speed **Thalys** trains run to Brussels in 2 hours 30 minutes, and to Paris in about 4 hours. In both Paris and Brussels, passengers can change to the **Eurostar** for an onward connection to London.

Stena Line offers a train and ferry combination ticket from London to Amsterdam.

The Dutch railroad system, operated by **NS (Nederlandse Spoorwegen)**, is one of the most modern and efficient in Europe, with an extensive route network. The NS website offers up-to-date information on train trips for tourists, plus details of special fares. It does not, however, issue tickets, which you buy at a ticket office; alternatively, use the *OV Chipkaart (see below)*. The info line **9292** provides details on all public transportation in the Netherlands. If you need to arrange train travel abroad, visit the offices of **NS Hispeed**, located in Amsterdam's Centraal Station.

Traveling by Bus

Long-distance bus travel is an inexpensive, if tiring, way to reach the Netherlands. **Eurolines** has at least two daily services from the UK to Amsterdam, via the Channel Tunnel.

Buses in the Netherlands are reliable and efficient, and they

accept the *OV Chipkaart*, a card the size of a credit card which can be loaded with credit at machines (found at bus and train stations, post offices, and supermarkets) and used on all means of public transport. The card is held against a card-reader upon entering and exiting the bus, train, or tram, and it is debited depending on the distance traveled. You can buy a *Chipkaart* at train and bus stations, tobacconists, post offices, and supermarkets.

Traveling by Car

An ever-expanding highway system makes it easy to travel to the Netherlands from anywhere in Europe. Major roads (marked N) and highways (labeled A or E) are generally well maintained. When driving in towns, especially in Amsterdam, be careful of cyclists, trams, taxis, and pedestrians.

Most of the principal international car-rental firms have offices in Amsterdam and at Schiphol Airport, but local companies are cheaper.

DIRECTORY

Netherland Board of Tourism and Conventions

UK
Tel 020-7539 7950.
[w] holland.com/uk

US
Tel 212-370 7360.
[w] holland.com/us

Tourist Offices in the Netherlands

VVV Centraal Station
Stationsplein, Amsterdam.
Tel 0900-400 4040.

Embassies

Australia
Carnegielaan 4, 2517 KH
Den Haag.
Tel 070-310 8200.

Canada
Sophialaan 7, 2514 JP Den
Haag.
Tel 070-311 1600.

Ireland
Scheveningseweg 12, Den
Haag. **Tel** 070-363 0993.

UK
Lange Voorhout 10,
2514 ED Den Haag.
Tel 070-427 0427.

US
Museumplein 19,
1071 DJ Amsterdam.
Tel 020-575 5309.

Emergencies

Ambulance/Fire/Police
Tel 112.

Airlines

American Airlines
Tel 800-433 7300 (US).
[w] aa.com

British Airways
Tel 0844-493 0787 (UK).
[w] britishairways.com

Delta Air Lines
Tel 800-241 4141 (US).
[w] delta.com

easyJet
Tel 0843-104 5000 (UK).
[w] easyjet.com

KLM
Tel 020-474 7747.
Tel 0871-231 0000 (UK).
[w] klm.com

Ryanair
Tel 0871-246 0000 (UK).
[w] ryanair.com

Transavia
Tel 352-2700 2728 (UK).
Tel 0900-0737.
[w] transavia.com

United Airlines
Tel 800-UNITED-1 (US).
[w] united.com

Ferry Companies

DFDS Seaways
Tel 0871-522 9955 (UK).
[w] dfdsseaways.co.uk

P&O European
Tel 08716-645 645 (UK).
[w] poferries.com

Stena Line
Tel 0844-770 7070 (UK).
[w] stenaline.co.uk

Rail Travel

9292
Tel 0900-9292.
[w] 9292.nl
[w] ov-chipkaart.nl

Eurostar
[w] eurostar.com

NS
[w] ns.nl

NS Hispeed
Tel 0900-9296.
[w] nshispeed.nl

Thalys
Tel 0900-9296.
[w] thalys.com

Buses

Eurolines UK Ltd
Tel 08717-818 178.
[w] eurolines.co.uk

Shopping & Entertainment

The Netherlands is justly famous for its cheeses, beers, and flowers, available at specialist stores and supermarkets across the country. Amsterdam is a cosmopolitan city, so it is also easy to find a selection of foreign and ethnic goods, from Indonesian beads to French designer wear. The famous brown cafés and coffee shops are an important part of Dutch social life, and visitors to the Netherlands should not miss the chance to try one.

Opening Hours

Stores in the Netherlands are usually open from 9 or 10am to 6pm Tuesday to Saturday, and from 1 to 6pm on Monday. In the larger cities, many shops stay open until 9pm on Thursdays and Sundays.

Where to Shop

Most of Amsterdam's large department and clothing stores are located in the Nieuwe Zijde, along Kalverstraat. The city's best-known department stores are **De Bijenkorf**, often described as the Dutch Harrods, and **Maison de Bonneterie**. Less expensive options include Vroom & Dreesman and Hema. For luxury fashion, PC Hooftstraat and Van Baerlestraat are lined with chic designer boutiques, such as Chanel, and Louis Vuitton.

The streets crossing Amsterdam's Canal Ring, such as Herenstraat and Hartenstraat, contain many specialist stores, selling everything from ethnic fabrics to handmade dolls.

What to Buy

One famous Dutch export is Delftware, the blue-and-white pottery from Delft (see p255). Only two factories still make it, though imitation pieces are found in tourist stores all over the country. A certification stamp indicates that an article is genuine. In Amsterdam, the **Galleria d'Arte Rinascimento** and **Jorrit Heinen** both stock authentic Delftware.

The Dutch are keen beer drinkers. As well as brand names like Heineken, Grolsch, and Amstel, there are many local specialties, such as Zatte, a rare, bottle-fermented beer, and Wieckse Witte, a white beer. Specialist store **De Bierkoning** offers the widest choice and best advice.

You can usually buy a good selection of Dutch cheeses at supermarkets, including any branch of **Albert Heijn**, street markets, or specialist food stores. Instead of buying the ubiquitous Edam, try one of the many varieties of Gouda. Mature Gouda has a rich, salty taste and crumbly texture, while young Gouda is fresh and curdy.

Other items for which the Netherlands is famous are flowers – which you can buy at street stalls, markets, and shores – and diamonds. For the latter, visit the diamond-cutting center **Gassan Diamonds**.

Markets

The Dutch love street trading and almost every town has at least one open-air market. In Amsterdam, the best-known are the Albert Cuypmarkt in Albert Cuypstraat, with a mix of Dutch and ethnic food, cheap clothes, and flowers and the Waterlooplein flea market, in Oude Zijde. The Looier Kunst en Antiekcentrum, at No. 109 Elandsgracht, is a covered market boasting the largest collection of art and antiques in the Netherlands. For flowers, visit the market along the Singel, between Konigsplein and Vizelstraat.

Entertainment Listings and Tickets

For up-to-date listings of events and concerts, the capital's official tourist website, www.iamsterdam.com, in English, is a good starting point. Time Out Amsterdam, a monthly magazine in English, carries extensive listings and restaurant reviews. The magazine is available from most newsagents in the city center.

The main reservations office for entertainment and cultural activities in Amsterdam is the **AUB** (Amsterdams Uitburo). The VVV and Dutch Tourist Information Office will also book tickets for some venues.

Entertainment Venues

Among Amsterdam's many theater venues are the **Theater Bellevue**, the **Stadsschouwburg**, and the **Felix Meritis**. For experimental theater, head for **De Brakke Grond** and other venues located along the street known as the Nes. The **Koninklijk Theater Carré** hosts long-running international musicals.

Dance is an important aspect of cultural life in the Netherlands. The Dutch National Ballet is housed in Amsterdam's large-capacity **Muziektheater**, while experimental dance can be enjoyed at **De Meervaart** and the **Stadsschouwburg**. The **Muziektheater** is also home to the Dutch National Opera.

The focus for Amsterdam's classical-music scene is the **Concertgebouw**, home to the celebrated Royal Concertgebouw Orchestra.

The Netherlands has a huge number of jazz venues. In Amsterdam, the internationally renowned **Bimhuis**, the **Muziekgebouw aan 't IJ**, and the **Alto Jazz Café** are worth visiting. The North Sea Jazz Festival, held in Rotterdam in July, attracts some of the biggest names in jazz.

Amsterdammers equate rock and pop with two venues, **De Melkweg** and **Paradiso**, which offer a varied program. Big-name bands also play at Rotterdam's Ahoy and Amsterdam's **Heineken Music Hall**.

Brown Cafés and Coffee Shops

The traditional Dutch "local pub," the brown café, is characterized by dark wooden furnishings, low ceilings, dim lights, and until the ban on smoking in public places was introduced in 2008, a fog of tobacco smoke. It is a friendly place, and often a social focus for the local neighborhood. There are hundreds in Amsterdam, but one of the best is the tiny and characterful **'t Doktertje**.

For many visitors, a stay in the Netherlands is incomplete without a trip to a smoking coffee shop, where cannabis is openly sold and, since the smoking ban was introduced, smoked in designated areas. Though technically illegal, the sale of soft drugs is tolerated by the authorities if it remains discreet. **Siberië** is one of the smaller, more relaxed places in Amsterdam, while **The Bulldog** is more tourist-filled.

Canal Tours

There are many operators in Amsterdam offering canal tours. In addition to the daytime sightseeing trips, there are night cruises, which often feature cheese-and-wine refreshments, a stop at a pub, or a romantic candlelit dinner. **Lovers** cruises are the most reasonably priced, while **P. Kooij** are more upscale.

Cycling

It is claimed that there are more bicycles in the Netherlands than inhabitants. The endlessly flat landscape and thousands of miles of well-maintained cycle tracks make cycling an extremely popular activity, even within cities. **Yellow Bike** organizes excursions in and around Amsterdam between April and October, while the US-based **Euro-Bike and Walking Tours** arranges week-long tours around the whole country. **Cycletours Holland** has a number of "bike-and-boat" itineraries covering the main regions of interest. For those who wish to do things independently, bicycles can be rented easily from many outlets across the country, and at more than 100 train stations. The VVV are able to supply detailed route maps.

DIRECTORY

Department Stores

De Bijenkorf
Dam 1, Amsterdam.
Tel 0900-0919.
Wagenstraat 32, Den Haag.
Tel 0900-0919.
Coolsingel 105,
Rotterdam. **Tel** 0900-0919.

Maison de Bonneterie
Rokin 140–142,
Amsterdam.
Tel 020-531 3400.
Gravenstraat 2, Den Haag.
Tel 070-330 5300.

Specialist Items

Albert Heijn
Jodenbreestraat 21,
Amsterdam.
Tel 020-624 1249.

De Bierkoning
Paleisstraat 125,
Amsterdam.
Tel 020-625 2336.

Galleria d'Arte Rinascimento
Prinsengracht 170,
Amsterdam.
Tel 020-622 7509.

Gassan Diamonds
Nieuwe Uilenburgerstraat 173, Amsterdam.
Tel 020-622 5333.

Jorrit Heinen
Muntplein 12,
Amsterdam.
Tel 020-623 2271.

Entertainment Tickets

AUB
Leidseplein 26, Amsterdam.
W amsterdamsuit buro.nl

Entertainment Venues

Alto Jazz Café
Korte Leidsedwarsstraat 115, Amsterdam.
Tel 020-626 3249.

Bimhuis
Piet Heinkade 3,
Amsterdam.
Tel 020-788 2188.
W bimhuis.nl

De Brakke Grond
Vlaams Cultureel Centrum,
Nes 45, Amsterdam.
Tel 020-622 9014.
W brakkegrond.nl

Concertgebouw
Concertgebouwplein 2–6,
Amsterdam.
Tel 020-671 8345.
W concertgebouw.nl

Felix Meritis
Keizersgracht 324,
Amsterdam.
Tel 020-623 1311.
W felix.meritis.nl

Heineken Music Hall
Blvd 590, Amsterdam Zuid
Oost. **Tel** 0900-6874 242.
W heineken-music-hall.nl

Koninklijk Theater Carré

Amstel 115–125,
Amsterdam.
Tel 0900-252 5255.
W carre.nl

De Meervaart
Meer en Vaart 300,
Amsterdam.
Tel 020-410 7700.
W meervaart.nl

De Melkweg
Lijnbaansgracht 234a,
Amsterdam.
Tel 020-531 8181.
W melkweg.nl

Muziekgebouw aan 't IJ
Piet Heinkade 1,
Amsterdam.
Tel 020-788 2000.
W muziekgebouw.nl

Het Muziektheater
Amstel 3, Amsterdam.
Tel 020-625 5455.
W het-muziektheater.nl

Paradiso
Weteringschans 6–8,
Amsterdam.
Tel 020-626 4521.
W paradiso.nl

Stadsschouwburg
Leidseplein 26, Amsterdam.
Tel 020-624 2311.
W ssba.nl

Theater Bellevue
Leidsekade 90, Amsterdam.
Tel 020-530 5301.
W theaterbellevue.nl

Brown Cafés & Coffee Shops

The Bulldog
Leidseplein 15,
Amsterdam.
Tel 020-627 1908.

't Doktertje
Rozenboomsteeg 4,
Amsterdam.
Tel 020-626 4427.

Siberië
Brouwersgracht 11,
Amsterdam.
Tel 020-623 5909.

Canal Tours

Lovers
Opposite Prins
Hendrikkade 26,
Amsterdam. **Tel** 020-530
1090. W lovers.nl

P. Kooij
Opposite Rokin 125,
Amsterdam. **Tel** 020-623
3810. W rederijkooij.nl

Cycling

Cycletours Holland
Buiksloterweg 7a,
Amsterdam. **Tel** 020-521
8400. W cycletours.nl

Euro-Bike and Walking Tours
Tel 1-800-575 1540.
W eurobike.com

Yellow Bike
Nieuwezijds Kolk 29,
Amsterdam. **Tel** 020-620
6940. W yellowbike.nl

Where to Stay

Amsterdam

CENTRAL CANAL RING:
The Golden Bear €
Historic **Map** C3
Kerkstraat 37, 1017 GB
Tel 020-624 4785
Ⓦ quentingoldenbear.com
Popular gay/lesbian hotel, with
two buildings dating back to 1731.
Breakfast is served until noon.

DK Choice

EASTERN CANAL RING:
Banks Mansion €€€
Canalside **Map** C3
Herengracht 519–525, 1017 BV
Tel 020-420 0055
Ⓦ carlton.nl
This former bank-cum-mansion
has been the winner of a
Travelers' Choice award. Rooms
have a Frank Lloyd Wright-
inspired decor and a choice of
pillows. Everything is included
in the price – movies, breakfast,
mini-bar, iPad loans, and more.

MUSEUM QUARTER: Stayokay
City Hostel Vondelpark €€
Family **Map** B4
Zandpad 5, 1054 GA
Tel 020-589 8996
Ⓦ stayokay.com
Hostel with double rooms and
dorms. Facilities include a TV
room and a bar/restaurant.

MUSEUM QUARTER: Conscious
Hotel Museum Square €€€
Boutique **Map** B5
de Lairessestraat 7, 1071 NR
Tel 020-671 9596
Ⓦ conscioushotels.com
An eco-friendly hotel with huge
plants and sustainable materials.
Guests enjoy organic breakfasts.

MUSEUM QUARTER:
Conservatorium €€€
Luxury **Map** B4
Van Baerlestraat 27, 1071 AN
Tel 020-570 0000
Ⓦ conservatoriumhotel.com
Housed within a former music
conservatory, this hotel has state-
of-the-art amenities and a spa.

OUDE ZIJDE: Droog
Luxury €€€
Map C3
Staalstraat 7B, 1011 JJ
Tel 020-523 5059
Ⓦ hoteldroog.com
Hotel with single apartment-style
rooms, an art gallery, a beauty
salon, a boutique, and an indoor
garden, as well as a tearoom.

PLANTAGE:
Amsterdam House €€
Family **Map** D3
's-Gravelandse Veer 3–4, 1011 KM
Tel 020-626 2577
Ⓦ amsterdamhouse.com
A houseboat with a well-equipped
kitchen and bathrooms. Ideal for
groups up of to eight people.

PLANTAGE: Hermitage
Canalside €€
Map D3
Nieuwe Keizersgracht 16, 1018 DR
Tel 020-623 8259
Ⓦ hotelhermitageamsterdam.com
A 1733 canal house with a garden.
Good for groups or families.

WESTERN CANAL RING:
Hotel Brouwer €€
Canalside **Map** C2
Singel 83, 1012 VE
Tel 020-624 6358
Ⓦ hotelbrouwer.nl
Unique rooms, named after Dutch
artists, with views. No credit cards.

WESTERN CANAL RING:
Sunhead of 1617 €€
Canalside **Map** C2
Herengracht 152, 1016 BN
Tel 020-626 1809
Ⓦ sunhead.com
A romantic hotel with superb
breakfasts and great views.

Rest of the Netherlands

DELFT: De Bieslandse
Heerlijkheid €
Value
Klein Delfgauw 61, 2616 LC
Tel 015-310 7126
Ⓦ bieslandseheerlijkheid.nl

Sumptuous furnishings at the Grand Hotel
Karel V, Utrecht

This rustic B&B in a converted
farmhouse is located close to
town. Two nights minimum stay.

HAARLEM: Stempels
Historic €€
Klokhuisplein 9, 2011 HK
Tel 023-512 3910
Ⓦ stempelsinhaarlem.nl
This boutique hotel is located
where the former royal stamps
and banknotes printing company
was housed.

THE HAGUE: Mozaic
Boutique €€
*Laan Copes van Cattenburgh 38–40,
2585 GB*
Tel 070-352 2335
Ⓦ mozaic.nl
This design hotel in an elegant
neighborhood has trendy, well-
appointed accommodations.

ROTTERDAM: Stayokay
Boutique €
Overblaak 85–87, 3011 MH
Tel 010-436 5763
Ⓦ stayokay.com
Located in the Cube Houses
built by Piet Blom in the 1980s.
Comfortable and distinctly quirky .

UTRECHT: Grand Hotel Karel V €€
Luxury
Geertebolwerk 1, 3511 XA
Tel 030-233 7555
Ⓦ karelv.nl
In the former monastery of the
German Knightly Order, this
hotel boasts five-star luxury,
stylishly decorated rooms, and
a Michelin-starred restaurant.

DK Choice

UTRECHT: Dom
Boutique €€€
Domstraat 4, 3512 JB
Tel 030-232 4242
Ⓦ hoteldom.nl
In the shadow of Utrecht's
landmark Dom tower, this
exclusive hotel is certainly
the hippest in town, with a
coveted restaurant, a cocktail
bar out of a Bond movie, and
rooms with Auping beds,
Nespresso machines, and
yoga mats. Two suites come
with private terraces.

Where to Eat and Drink

Amsterdam

CENTRAL CANAL RING:
Pancakes!　€
Dutch/Pancakes
38 Berenstraat, 1016 GH
Tel *020-528 9797*
Come here for delicious Dutch and international pancakes. The flour is sourced from the Dutch grain mill De Eersteling.

CENTRAL CANAL RING:
Restaurant Vinkeles　€€€
French
Keizersgracht 384, 1016 GB
Tel *020-530 2010*　**Closed** *Sun*
Dine among 18th-century bakery ovens or on a salon boat, and enjoy Michelin-starred dishes.

EASTERN CANAL RING:
de Waaghals　€€
Vegetarian　**Map** C4
Frans Halsstraat 29, 1072 BK
Tel *020-679 9609*　**Closed** *Mon*
The menu of dishes made with organic produce changes twice a month. Reserve a table in advance.

MUSEUM QUARTER:
Het Blauwe Theehuis　€
International　**Map** B4
Vondelpark 5, 1071 AA
Tel *020-662 0254*　**Closed** *Mon–Wed dinner*
Dine in a 1937 concrete, steel, and glass structure nestled in a park. The menu combines European and Mediterranean influences.

NIEUWE ZIJDE: Getto
Food & Drink　€
Café/Bar　**Map** D2
Warmoesstraat 51, 1012 HW
Tel *020-421 5151*　**Closed** *Mon*
This gay-friendly bar-restaurant offers home-style cooking. Its burgers are named after famous Amsterdam drag queens, like the "Jennifer Hopeless."

DK Choice
OUDE ZIJDE: Greetje　€€
Dutch　**Map** D3
Peperstraat 23, 1011 TJ
Tel *020-779 7450*
Hailed by the *New York Times* as the place where the Dutch go to eat Dutch – it does not get more authentic than Greetje. Locals love the *bloedworst* (blood sausage) with apple compote, and the *trekdrop* (liquorice) ice cream. The menu changes every two months.

PLANTAGE: Tempura
Japanese　€€
　Map E3
Plantage Kerklaan 26, 1018 TC
Tel *020-428 7132*　**Closed** *Mon*
Brasserie-style Japanese eatery offering sushi, *yakitori* (skewered chicken), and tempura dishes. The St. Jacques sashimi are wonderful.

WESTERN CANAL RING:
Greenwoods　€
Tearoom　**Map** C2
Singel 103, 1012 VG
Tel *020-623 7071*
Come to this tearoom for a full English breakfast, afternoon tea with clotted cream, or organic lamb burgers. A sister restaurant at Keizersgracht 465 does heartier fare, such as fish 'n' chips.

Rest of the Netherlands

DELFT: La Tasca
Mediterranean　€€
Voldersgracht 13B, 2611 ET
Tel *015-213 8535*　**Closed** *Sun*
Don't look for the menu – there isn't one. Guests are invited to tell the chef what they don't like, and he cooks up a three- to five-course surprise meal for them.

DK Choice
HAARLEM: De Jopenkerk　€€
Dutch
Gedempte Voldersgracht 2, 2011 WB
Tel *023-533 4114*
This century-old church has been transformed into a grand café, restaurant, and brewery. Most of the meat and fish dishes are cooked with beer, and every course comes with a beer recommendation. A favorite among the locals, this restaurant can get noisy, especially on weekend nights.

Price Guide
Prices are for a three-course meal for one, including half a bottle of house wine, and all extra charges.

€	under €35
€€	€35 to €50
€€€	over €50

THE HAGUE: HanTing Cuisine　€€
Fusion
Prinsestraat 33, 2513 CA
Tel *070-362 0828*　**Closed** *Mon*
Chinese chef Han expertly fuses French cooking with Oriental flavors, creating dishes that please the eye and the palate.

LEIDEN: Buddhas
Thai　€€
Botermarkt 20, 2311 EN
Tel *071-514 0047*　**Closed** *Mon*
Huge Buddha statues line the walls of this smart restaurant. It may be pricey, but the extensive menu, generous portions, and authentic food make up for that.

ROTTERDAM: FG Restaurant €€€
International
Lloydstraat 204, 3024 EA
Tel *010-425 0520*　**Closed** *Sun & Mon*
After cooking molecular cuisine at Heston Blumenthal's restaurant, François Geurds has become a Michelin-starred chef in his own right. Vegetarians get their own multi-course tasting menu, while the chef's table is a coveted spot. Affordable lunch menu.

UTRECHT: Badhu
Arabian　€
Willem van Noortplein 19, 3514 GK
Tel *030-272 0444*
As befits a restaurant in a 1920s bathhouse, Badhu's interior is inspired by a *hammam*. It serves an Arabian breakfast, meze for lunch and dinner, afternoon *chai*, and evening cocktails.

The brewing equipment behind the bar at De Jopenkerk, Haarlem

THE IBERIAN PENINSULA

The Iberian Peninsula at a Glance

A wonderful, warm climate and superb beaches have made the Iberian Peninsula a popular package-tour destination, drawing millions of visitors to well-known areas, such as the Algarve in Portugal and the Costa del Sol in Spain. But there are also tranquil fishing villages, first-class museums and galleries, and a wealth of splendid architecture, from the grand monuments left by the region's Moorish rulers to ultramodern, 20th-century designs. The Catholic faith has deep roots in Portugal and Spain. As well as spectacular cathedrals, there are many colorful religious festivals that take place all year round, making a visit all the more enjoyable.

0 km 100
0 miles 100

A Coruña
San
Oviedo
Lugo
Santiago de Compostela
León
Braganca
Valladolid
Oporto
Salamanca
Coimbra
To
PORTUGAL
(see pp336–63)
Lisbon
Merida
Ciudac
Evora
Córdoba
Seville
Faro

Toledo *(see pp286–8)* has one of the largest cathedrals in Christendom, a massive Gothic structure that soars above the rooftops of the perfectly preserved medieval town.

Lisbon *(see pp340–49)* rises above the estuary of the Tagus on a series of hills. The oldest part of the city is crowned by the restored battlements of the Castelo de São Jorge.

Seville *(see pp318–21)* is regarded as the soul of Andalusia. The city's famous bullring is arguably the finest in the whole of Spain, and a perfect venue for a first experience of the *corrida*, or bullfight.

◀ View of the Alhambra complex in Granada, Andalusia, Spain

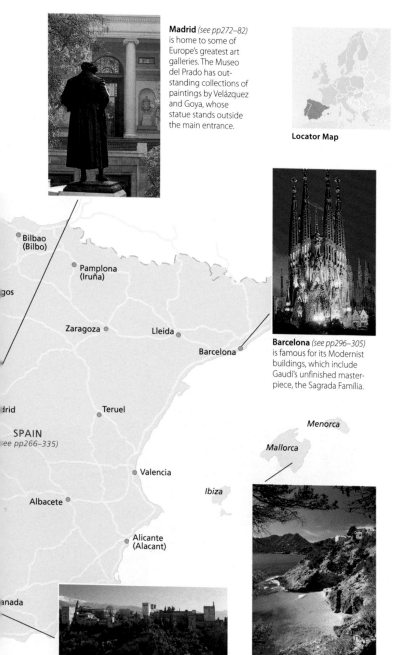

Madrid *(see pp272–82)* is home to some of Europe's greatest art galleries. The Museo del Prado has outstanding collections of paintings by Velázquez and Goya, whose statue stands outside the main entrance.

Locator Map

Bilbao (Bilbo)

Pamplona (Iruña)

gos

Zaragoza

Lleida

Barcelona

drid

Teruel

SPAIN *(see pp266–335)*

Valencia

Albacete

Alicante (Alacant)

Menorca

Mallorca

Ibiza

anada

Barcelona *(see pp296–305)* is famous for its Modernist buildings, which include Gaudí's unfinished masterpiece, the Sagrada Família.

The Balearic Islands *(see p309)* are often associated with mass tourism, but away from the busy resorts, there are hundreds of unspoiled coastal villages and beautiful coves to be discovered.

Granada *(see pp310 and 312–13)*, in the foothills of the snowcapped Sierra Nevada, is unmissable for its Moorish heritage. Its greatest monument is the stunning Alhambra palace.

SPAIN

The familiar images of Spain – flamenco dancing, bullfighting, tapas bars, and solemn Easter processions – do no more than hint at the diversity of this country. Spain has four official languages, two major cities, of almost equal importance, and a greater range of landscapes than any other European country. These contrasts make Spain an endlessly fascinating place to visit.

Separated from the rest of Europe by the Pyrenees, Spain reaches south to the coast of North Africa, and has both Atlantic and Mediterranean coastlines. The country's climate and scenery vary dramatically, from the snowcapped peaks of the Pyrenees, through the green meadows of Galicia and the orange groves of Valencia, to the dry, barren regions in the south.

Madrid, Spain's capital, lies geographically in the center of the country. The *madrileños* – as the city's inhabitants are known – have an individualistic spirit and a sardonic sense of humor that set them apart from other Spaniards. Madrid may be the nominal capital, but it is rivaled in commerce, sport, and the arts by Barcelona, the main city of Catalonia.

In the last 50 years, Spain has undergone more social change than anywhere else in western Europe. In the first half of the 20th century, it was largely a poor, rural country. Gradually people flooded into the cities, leaving the rural areas depopulated.

The 1960s saw the beginning of spectacular economic growth, partly due to a burgeoning tourist industry. Since then, Spain has become a major player in European and world affairs.

History

From the 11th century BC, the coastal regions of the Iberian Peninsula were colonized by sophisticated eastern Mediterranean civilizations, starting with the Phoenicians, then the Greeks and the Carthaginians. Celts mixed with native Iberian tribes, forming the Celtiberians. The Romans arrived in 218 BC to take possession of the peninsula's huge mineral wealth. The fall of the Roman Empire in the 5th century AD left Spain in the hands of the Visigoths, invaders from the north. Their poor political organization, however, meant they were easily conquered by the Moors, who arrived from North Africa in around 711.

Within a few years, the Moors controlled almost the entire peninsula. Europe's only

The art of bullfighting, still a strong tradition all over Spain

◄ View of Toledo, dominated by the fortress of the Alcázar

The Moor Boabdil surrendering Granada to the Catholic Monarchs

major Muslim territory, the civilization of Al Andalus excelled in mathematics, geography, astronomy, and poetry, and by the 9th century, Córdoba was Europe's leading city.

In the 11th century, northern Christian kingdoms initiated a military reconquest of Al Andalus. The marriage, in 1469, of Fernando of Aragón and Isabel of Castile – the so-called Catholic Monarchs – led to Spanish unity. They took Granada, the last Moorish stronghold, in 1492. In the same year, Columbus discovered the Americas, and the conquistadors began plundering the civilizations of the New World.

The 17th century was a golden age for Spain – a time of outstanding artistic and literary output. This brilliance occurred, however, against a backdrop of economic deterioration and ruinous wars with France and the Low Countries. Spain's misfortunes continued in the 19th century, with an invasion by Napoleon's troops, leading to the War of Independence (Peninsular War). In the course of this century, Spain also lost all her South and Central American colonies.

The late 19th century was a time of national decline, with anarchism developing as a response to rampant political corruption. Political instability led to dictatorship in the 1920s and, a decade later, the Spanish Civil War. The victor, the Nationalist General Franco, ruled by repression until his death in 1975. Since then, Spain has been a democratic state.

General Franco, Nationalist le
in the Spanish Civil War

KEY DATES IN SPANISH HISTORY

1100 BC Arrival of Phoenicians, first in a wave of settlers from across the Mediterranean

218–202 BC Romans oust Carthaginians from southeastern Spain

5th century AD Visigoths take control of Spain

711 Moors invade Spain and defeat Visigoths

756 Independent emirate established at Córdoba; Moorish civilization flourishes

11th century Christian kingdoms begin reconquest of Moorish territories

1492 Catholic Monarchs capture Granada, last Moorish stronghold. Columbus reaches America

1561 Madrid becomes capital of Spain

17th century Spain's Golden Age

1808–14 Spanish War of Independence

1898 Spain loses its last American colony, Cuba

1936–9 Spanish Civil War; Nationalist General Franco emerges victor

1975 Death of Franco; restoration of Bourbon monarchy as Juan Carlos I is proclaimed king

1986 Spain joins the EC (now EU)

1992 Barcelona hosts the Olympic Games

2000 Spain celebrates 25 years of democracy

2004 Nearly 200 people die in terrorist bomb attacks on trains in Madrid

2014 King Juan Carlos abdicates and his son ascends to the throne as King Felipe VI of Spain

Development and Diplomacy

After the death of the dictator General Franco in 1975, Spain became a constitutional monarchy under King Juan Carlos I. The post-Franco era, up until the mid-1990s, was dominated by the Socialist Prime Minister Felipe González, whose party, PSOE, was responsible for major improvements in roads, education, and health services. Spain's entry to the European Community in 1986 triggered a spectacular increase in the country's prosperity. Its international reputation was given a further boost in 1992, when

Barcelona hosted the Olympic Games and Seville was the site of Expo '92.

With the establishment of democracy, the 17 autonomous regions of Spain have acquired considerable powers. A significant number of Basques favor independence for the Basque Country. The Basque terrorist group ETA, and its campaign of violence, has been one of the major problems facing all governments; however, ETA declared a ceasefire in 2011.

Religion, Language, and Culture

Following the Christian Reconquest in the Middle Ages, a succession of rulers tried to impose a common culture, but today Spain remains a culturally diverse nation. Several regions have maintained a strong sense of their own identities. Catalonia, the Basque Country, Valencia, the Balearic Islands, and Galicia have their own languages, which are in everyday use, and, in some cases, have supplanted Castilian as the first language of the region.

During the Middle Ages, Spain gained a reputation for religious intolerance. The Inquisition, established by the Catholic Monarchs, saw thousands of non-Catholics tortured, executed, or expelled from the country. Today, Spain enjoys complete religious freedom. Catholicism is becoming a less powerful influence in society, but saints' days and other important events in the Christian calendar are still marked by many traditional ceremonies, enthusiastically maintained in towns and villages throughout modern Spain.

Religious procession in a Seville street during *Semana Santa* (Holy Week)

The Spanish Way of Life

The Spanish are known for their natural sociability and zest for living. They commonly put as much energy into enjoying life as they do into their work. The stereotypical "mañana" ("leave it until tomorrow") is a myth, but many people fit their work around the demands of their social life, rather than be ruled by the clock. The day is long in Spain, and the Spanish have a word, *madrugada*, for the time between midnight and dawn, when city streets are often still full of revelers enjoying themselves. Eating out is an important social activity, with friends and family often meeting up in a pavement café or restaurant for a chat and a meal.

Underpinning Spanish society is the extended family. In the past, a lack of efficient public services has forced the Spanish to rely on close relatives, rather than institutions, to find work or seek assistance in a crisis. It is not uncommon for three generations to live under one roof, and even lifelong city dwellers refer fondly to their *pueblo* – the town or village where their family comes from, and which they return to as often as they can.

Spaniards socializing over drinks and a meal at a sidewalk café

Exploring Spain

Although many visitors to Spain come for the beaches alone, increasingly tourists are drawn by the country's rich cultural heritage. The most popular destinations are Madrid and Barcelona, which boast world-class museums and a wealth of medieval and modern architecture. For those with time to travel further afield, Seville, Granada, and Córdoba in the far south are the best places to see relics of Spain's Moorish past. Spain is Europe's third-largest country, so getting around can be time-consuming. However, there is a reliable network of trains, as well as good highways and bus services.

Ciutadella harbor, on the island of Menorca, at twilight

Sights at a Glance

Distance chart

Madrid

Distance by road in kilometers
Distance by road in miles

Madrid	Barcelona	Bilbao	Córdoba	Malaga	Pontevedra	Seville	Valencia	Zaragoza
621 / 388	**Barcelona**							
397 / 248	**620** / 388	**Bilbao**						
400 / 250	**908** / 568	**795** / 497	**Córdoba**					
544 / 340	**997** / 623	**939** / 587	**187** / 117	**Malaga**				
623 / 389	**1129** / 706	**707** / 442	**977** / 611	**1153** / 721	**Pontevedra**			
538 / 336	**1046** / 654	**933** / 583	**138** / 86	**219** / 137	**922** / 576	**Seville**		
352 / 220	**349** / 218	**633** / 396	**545** / 341	**648** / 405	**975** / 609	**697** / 436	**Valencia**	
325 / 203	**296** / 185	**324** / 203	**725** / 453	**869** / 543	**833** / 521	**863** / 539	**326** / 204	**Zaragoza**

Key

— Highway

— Major road

— Railroad

-•- International border

The Giralda in Seville, a legacy of Spain's Moorish rulers

For keys to symbols see back flap

❶ Madrid

Spain's capital, a city of more than three million people, is situated close to the geographical center of the country, at the hub of both road and railroad networks. The origins of the city date back to AD 852, when the Moors built a fortress near the Manzanares River and a small community grew up around it. It was not until 1561, however, that the city became the capital of a newly formed nation-state. In the following centuries, under the Habsburgs and then the Bourbons, the city acquired some of its most notable landmarks, including the splendid Plaza Mayor and the Palacio Real. At the same time, the blossoming city attracted some of Spain's most outstanding artists, such as court painters Velázquez and Goya, whose works can be admired in the world-famous Museo del Prado.

19th-century *taberna* (taverna), one of the few left in Madrid today

Key

▨ Sight / Place of interest

⋯ Pedestrian street

0 meters   400

0 yards   400

Getting Around

The metro is the most efficient way of getting around. Lines 1, 2, 3, 5, and 10 serve the main sights; lines 1 and 2 are good for getting to the museums around the Paseo del Prado. Line 8 links Nuevos Ministerios and the airport. Useful buses include the 50, 51, 52, 53, and 150 to the Puerta del Sol, and 2, 9, 14, 15, 27, 74, and 146 to the Plaza de Cibeles. Buses to Barajas airport depart the terminal below Plaza de Colón.

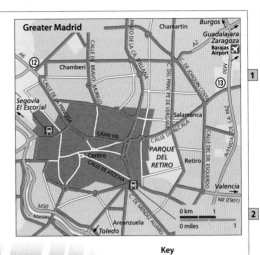

Greater Madrid

Key

Area of main map

Sights at a Glance

① Puerta del Sol
② Plaza Mayor
③ Monasterio de las Descalzas Reales
④ Gran Vía
⑤ Palacio Real
⑥ El Rastro
⑦ Museo Nacional del Prado *pp278–80*
⑧ Museo Thyssen-Bornemisza
⑨ Centro de Arte Reina Sofía
⑩ Parque del Retiro
⑪ Museo Arqueológico Nacional

Greater Madrid
(see inset map)

⑫ Museo de América
⑬ Plaza de Toros de las Ventas

The beautiful 17th-century Plaza Mayor, at the heart of Old Madrid

For keys to symbols *see back flap*

Old Madrid

When Felipe II chose Madrid as his capital in 1561, it was a small Castilian town of little importance. In the following years, it was to grow into the nerve center of a mighty empire. During the reign of the Habsburg dynasty, many royal monasteries, churches, and private palaces were built. In the 17th century, the Plaza Mayor was added, and the Puerta del Sol became the spiritual and geographical heart not only of Madrid, but of all Spain. Old Madrid's splendid Bourbon palace, the Palacio Real, was built under Felipe V in the first half of the 18th century.

Bear and strawberry tree, the symbol of Madrid, Puerta del Sol

① Puerta del Sol

Ⓜ Sol.

With its many shops and cafés, the Puerta del Sol ("Gateway of the Sun") is one of Madrid's liveliest areas, attracting huge crowds. The square marks the site of the original eastern entrance to the city, once occupied by a gatehouse and a castle.

A statue of Carlos III (reigned 1759–88) stands at the center of the square. On its southern edge is the austere Casa de Correos, dating from the 1760s. Originally the city's post office, it later became the headquarters of the Ministry of the Interior. During the Franco regime, the police cells below the building were the site of human-rights abuses. Outside the building, a symbol on the ground marks Kilometer Zero, considered the center of Spain's road network.

On the opposite side of the square is a bronze statue of the symbol of Madrid – a bear reaching for the fruit of a *madroño* (strawberry tree). The Puerta del Sol has witnessed many important

historical events. On May 2, 1808, the uprising against the occupying French forces began in the square, and in 1912, the liberal prime minister José Canalejas was assassinated here.

② Plaza Mayor

Ⓜ Sol.

For hundreds of years, this beautiful 17th-century square was a center of activity, with bullfights, executions, pageants, and trials by the Inquisition taking place here.

The first great public event was the beatification of the city's patron, St. Isidore, in 1621. Perhaps the greatest occasion, however, was the arrival from Italy of Carlos III (Carlos VII of Naples) in 1760. He became king of Spain after his half-brother, Fernando VI, died without an heir. Designed by architect Juan Gómez de Mora, the square was started in 1617

Facade of the Casa de la Panadería, on the Plaza Mayor

and built in just two years. At its center is an equestrian statue of Felipe III, who ordered the square's construction.

The elegant arcades that line the Plaza Mayor are today filled with cafés and craft stores. One of the more interesting buildings is the Casa de la Panadería, whose facade is decorated with splendid allegorical paintings.

On Sundays, the square is the venue for a collectors' market, with stalls selling coins, stamps, books, and other items.

Decorated chapel, Monasterio de las Descalzas Reales

③ Monasterio de las Descalzas Reales

Plaza de las Descalzas 3. **Tel** 91-454 88 00. Ⓜ Opera. **Open** 10am–2pm, 4–6:30pm Tue–Sat; 10am–3pm Sun & public hols. **Closed** Jan 1 & 6, 3 days after Easter, May 1, Dec 24, 25 & 31. 🎟 (except Wed & Thu pm for EU residents). 📷
🌐 patrimonionacional.es

This religious building is a rare surviving example of 16th-century architecture in Madrid. Around 1560, Felipe II's sister, Doña Juana, decided to convert a medieval palace on this site into a convent.

Doña Juana's rank accounts for the massive store of art amassed by the Descalzas Reales (Royal Barefoot Sisters), which includes a fresco of Felipe IV's family and, above the main staircase, a ceiling by Claudio Coello. The Sala de Tapices contains stunning tapestries,

The vast Palacio Real, Madrid's 18th-century Bourbon palace

while paintings on display include works by Brueghel the Elder, Titian, Zurbarán, Murillo, and Ribera.

④ Gran Vía

Ⓜ Plaza de España, Santo Domingo, Callao, Gran Vía.

A main traffic artery of the modern city, the Gran Vía was inaugurated in 1910.

Lined with movie theaters, tourist stores, hotels, and restaurants, this grand avenue also has many buildings of architectural interest. At the Alcalá end of the street, the French-inspired Edificio Metrópolis and the Edificio la Estrella (No. 10) are both worth seeing. The latter is a good example of the eclectic mix of Neoclassical design and ornamental detail that was fashionable when the street was first developed. Look out for

One of the many 1930s Art Deco buildings lining the Gran Vía

some interesting carved-stone decoration, such as the striking gargoyle-like caryatids at No. 12.

Further along the Gran Vía, around the Plaza del Callao, are a number of Art Deco buildings, including the well-known Capitol cinema and bingo hall, built in the 1930s.

⑤ Palacio Real

Calle de Bailén. **Tel** 91-454 88 00. Ⓜ Ópera, Plaza de España. 🚌 3, 25, 39, 148. **Open** 10am–8pm daily (Oct–Mar: to 6pm). **Closed** Jan 1 & 6, May 1 & 15, Sep 9, Dec 24, 25 & 31. 🅿 (except Mon–Thu from two hours before closing for EU residents). 🔲🔲🔲🔲 🌐 patrimonionacional.es

Madrid's vast and lavish Palacio Real (Royal Palace) was commissioned by Felipe V after the royal fortress that had occupied the site for centuries was ravaged by fire in 1734. The palace was the home of Spanish royalty until the abdication of Alfonso XIII in 1931. Today it is used by the present king for state occasions only.

The exuberant decor of the interior reflects the tastes of the Bourbon kings, Carlos III and Carlos IV. The walls and ceiling of the Porcelain Room, commissioned by the former, are covered in green and white royal porcelain, which is embossed with cherubs and wreaths. Named after its Neapolitan designer, the Gasparini Room is equally lavishly decorated. In the

adjacent antechamber hangs a portrait of Carlos IV by Goya. Other star attractions are the Dining Room, with its fine ceiling paintings and superb Flemish tapestries, and the 18th-century Throne Room.

Shoppers browsing around the Rastro flea market

⑥ El Rastro

Calle de la Ribera de Curtidores. Ⓜ La Latina, Embajadores. **Open** 10am–2pm Sun & public hols.

Madrid's famous flea market was established in the Middle Ages. Its heyday came in the 19th century, but today there are still plenty of locals, as well as tourists, who come to the Calle de la Ribera de Curtidores to browse around the many stalls selling a huge range of wares – from new furniture to second-hand clothes. The market's other main street is the Calle de Embajadores, which runs down past the dusty Baroque facade of the Iglesia de San Cayetano.

Street by Street: Paseo del Prado

In the late 18th century, before the museums and lavish hotels of Bourbon Madrid took shape, the Paseo del Prado was laid out and soon became a fashionable spot for strolling. Today, the Paseo's main attraction lies in its museums and art galleries. Most notable are the Museo del Prado (just south of the Plaza Cánovas del Castillo) and the Museo Thyssen-Bornemisza, both displaying world-famous collections of paintings. Among the monuments built under Carlos III are the Puerta de Alcalá, the Fuente de Neptuno, and the Fuente de Cibeles, which stand in the middle of busy roundabouts.

Paseo del Prado
Based on the Piazza Navona in Rome, the Paseo was built by Carlos III as a center for the arts and sciences in Madrid.

Banco de España
Spain's central reserve bank is housed in this massive building with three facades at the Plaza de Cibeles.

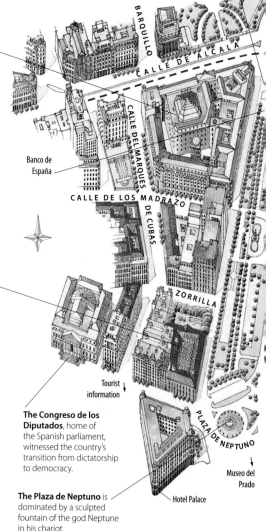

Banco de España

CALLE DE ALCALÁ

CALLE DEL MARQUES

CALLE DE LOS MADRAZO

DE CUBAS

BARQUILLO

ZORRILLA

Tourist information

PLAZA DE NEPTUNO

Museo del Prado

Hotel Palace

★ Museo Thyssen-Bornemisza
Petrus Christus's *Our Lady of the Dry Tree* (c.1450) is one of many early Flemish works in this excellent art collection (*see p281*).

The Congreso de los Diputados, home of the Spanish parliament, witnessed the country's transition from dictatorship to democracy.

The Plaza de Neptuno is dominated by a sculpted fountain of the god Neptune in his chariot.

| 0 meters | 100 |
| 0 yards | 100 |

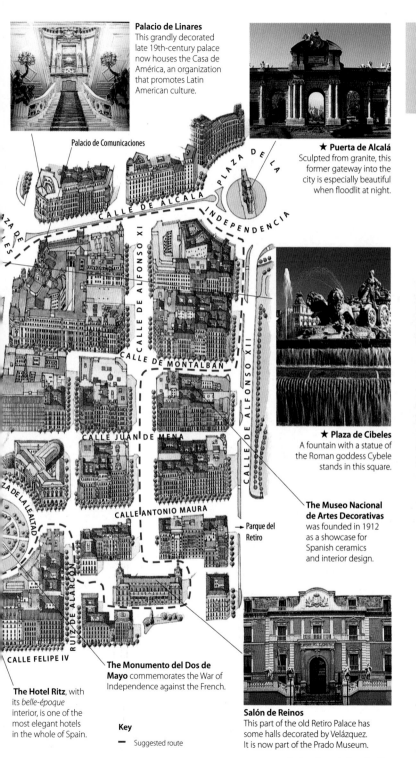

Palacio de Linares
This grandly decorated late 19th-century palace now houses the Casa de América, an organization that promotes Latin American culture.

Palacio de Comunicaciones

★ **Puerta de Alcalá**
Sculpted from granite, this former gateway into the city is especially beautiful when floodlit at night.

CALLE DE ALCALA

PLAZA DE LA INDEPENDENCIA

CALLE DE ALFONSO XI

CALLE DE MONTALBAN

CALLE DE ALFONSO XII

CALLE JUAN DE MENA

CALLE ANTONIO MAURA

→ Parque del Retiro

PLAZA DE LA LEALTAD

RUIZ DE ALARCON

CALLE FELIPE IV

★ **Plaza de Cibeles**
A fountain with a statue of the Roman goddess Cybele stands in this square.

The Museo Nacional de Artes Decorativas
was founded in 1912 as a showcase for Spanish ceramics and interior design.

The Monumento del Dos de Mayo commemorates the War of Independence against the French.

The Hotel Ritz, with its *belle-époque* interior, is one of the most elegant hotels in the whole of Spain.

Salón de Reinos
This part of the old Retiro Palace has some halls decorated by Velázquez. It is now part of the Prado Museum.

Key

— Suggested route

For keys to symbols *see back flap*

⑦ Museo Nacional del Prado

The Prado Museum houses the world's greatest assembly of Spanish paintings from the 12th to the 19th century, including major works by Velázquez and Goya. It also houses impressive foreign collections, particularly of Italian and Flemish works. The Neoclassical building was designed in 1785 by Juan de Villanueva on the orders of Carlos III. In 2006, a fully refurbished Casón del Buen Retiro and a new building in the cloisters on San Jéronimo's church opened to the public. In 2009, the former army museum (Salón de Reinos) also became part of the Prado.

★ **Velázquez Collection**
The Triumph of Bacchus (1629), Velázquez's first portrayal of a mythological subject, shows the god of wine (Bacchus) with a group of drunkards.

The Martyrdom of St. Philip (c.1639)
The Valencian José de Ribera moved to Naples as a young man. He was influenced by Caravaggio's use of light and shadow, known as *chiaroscuro*, as seen in this work.

Main entrance

The museum's facade, dating from the 18th century, illustrates the Neoclassical move toward dignity, away from the excesses of Baroque architecture.

The Garden of Delights (c.1505)
Hieronymus Bosch, known as El Bosco in Spanish, was one of Felipe II's favorite artists, and is especially well represented in the Prado. This enigmatic painting is part of a triptych depicting paradise and hell.

Ticket office

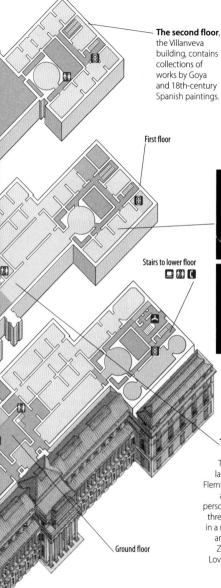

The second floor, the Villanveva building, contains collections of works by Goya and 18th-century Spanish paintings.

First floor

Stairs to lower floor

Ground floor

VISITORS' CHECKLIST

Practical Information
Paseo del Prado.
Tel 90-210 70 77.
🅦 **museodelprado.es**
Open 10am–8pm daily (to 7pm Sun). **Closed** Jan 1, May 1, Dec 25.
🎟 free from 6pm (5pm Sun). ♿

Transport
Ⓜ Atocha, Banco de España.
🚌 9, 10, 14, 19, 27, 34, 37, 45.

★ Goya Collection
In *The Clothed Maja* and *The Naked Maja* (both c.1800), Goya tackled the taboo subject of nudity, for which he was later accused of obscenity.

The Three Graces
(c.1635)
This was one of the last paintings by the Flemish master Rubens, and was part of his personal collection. The three women dancing in a ring – the Graces – are the daughters of Zeus, and represent Love, Joy, and Revelry.

Gallery Guide

The best way to enter the Prado is through the modern reception center situated between the main building and the church behind. The works are arranged in schools, with the oldest works displayed on the lowest floors. The magnificent Velázquez collection is located on the first floor, along with other 17th-century Spanish works.

Key to Floorplan

- 🔲 Spanish painting
- 🔲 Flemish and Dutch painting
- ⬛ Italian painting
- 🔲 French painting
- 🔲 German and British painting
- ⬛ Sculpture
- 🔲 Drawing
- ⬛ Non-exhibition space

Exploring the Prado's Collection

The importance of the Prado is founded on its royal collections. The wealth of foreign art, including many of Europe's finest works, reflects the historical power of the Spanish crown. The Low Countries and parts of Italy were under Spanish rule for hundreds of years. The 18th century was an era of French influence, following the Bourbon accession to the Spanish throne. The Prado is worthy of repeated visits, but if you go only once, see the Spanish works of the 17th century.

Spanish Painting

Right up to the 19th century, Spanish painting focused on religious and royal themes. There are a few examples of Spain's early-medieval art in the Prado, such as the anonymous mural paintings from the Holy Cross hermitage in Maderuelo. Spanish Gothic art can be seen in the works of Bartolomé Bermejo and Fernando Gallego.

Renaissance features began to emerge in the paintings of Pedro de Berruguete and Fernando Yáñez de la Almedina, whose work shows the influence of Leonardo da Vinci. Among examples of 16th-century Mannerism are paintings by Pedro Machuca and Luis de Morales "the Divine." One of the great masters of this period was the Cretan-born artist El Greco, who made his home in Toledo. The distortion of the human figure, typical of the Mannerist style, is carried to an extreme in his painting *The Adoration of the Shepherds* (1612–14).

The Golden Age of the 17th century produced such great artists as José de Ribera and Francisco de Zurbarán. Works by both are on display in the Prado. This period, however, is best represented by the work of Diego Velázquez, Spain's leading court painter. Examples of his royal portraits and religious and mythological paintings are displayed, including his masterpiece, *Las Meninas* (1656), a portrait of the Infanta Margarita surrounded by her courtiers.

Another great Spanish painter, Francisco de Goya, revived Spanish art in the 18th century. His later works embraces the horrors of war, as seen in *The 3rd of May* (1814), and culminated in a somber series known as *The Black Paintings*.

The Adoration of the Shepherds (1612–14), by El Greco

Flemish and Dutch Painting

Exceptional Flemish works of art include Rogier van der Weyden's masterpiece, *The Deposition* (c.1500), and some of Hieronymus Bosch's major paintings, such as the *Temptation of St. Anthony* (c.1500) and *The Haywain* (c.1485–90). Among the 16th-century paintings is the superb *Triumph of Death* (1562) by Brueghel the Elder. There are nearly 100 canvases by the 17th-century Flemish painter Peter Paul Rubens, of which the greatest is *The Adoration of the Magi*. The two most notable Dutch paintings on display are both by Rembrandt: *Artemisia* (c.1500) and a fine self-portrait.

Italian Painting

The most remarkable Italian paintings are Botticelli's dramatic wooden panels that depict *The Story of Nastagio degli Onesti*, Raphael's *Christ Falls on the Way to Calvary* (1516), and *Christ Washing the Disciples' Feet* (c.1547), by Tintoretto. Venetian masters Titian – Charles V's court painter – and Veronese are equally well represented. Also on display are works by Giordano, Fra Angelico, Caravaggio, and Tiepolo, master of Italian Rococo.

From the Early Renaissance, Fra Angelico's *The Annunciation* (c.1430)

French and German Painting

Marriages between French and Spanish royalty in the 17th century brought French art to Spain. This section contains a selection of works by Poussin, Jean Ranc, Claude Lorrain, and Antoine Watteau.

German art is represented by Albrecht Dürer's lively *Self-Portrait* (1498), as well as by the works of Lucas Cranach and the late 18th-century court painter Anton Raffael Mengs.

Casón del Buen Retiro

The Casón is a study center, housing restoration studios, a specialist school, and an art library. On weekends, there are guided visits of the dome painted by Luca Giordano. You will need to ask for permission to use the art library, as it is otherwise closed to the public.

Spacious interior of the Museo Thyssen-Bornemisza

⑧ Museo Thyssen-Bornemisza

Paseo del Prado 8. **Tel** 90-276 05 11.
Ⓜ Banco de España, Sevilla. 🚌 1, 2, 5, 9, 14, 15, 20. **Open** noon–4pm Mon, 10am–7pm Tue–Sun (to 9pm on Sat for temporary exhibitions). **Closed** Jan 1, May 1, Dec 25. (free Mon).
W **museothyssen.org**

This magnificent museum houses a collection of art assembled by Baron Heinrich Thyssen-Bornemisza and his son, Hans Heinrich. From its beginnings in the 1920s, the collection was intended to illustrate the history of Western art, from the 14th to the 20th century. Among the museum's exhibits are masterpieces by Titian, Goya, and Van Gogh.

The series of Dutch and Flemish works is a strong point of the collection. Highlights include Jan van Eyck's *The Annunciation* (c.1435–41), Petrus Christus's *Our Lady of the Dry Tree* (c.1450), and *The Toilet of Venus*

(c.1629), by Peter Paul Rubens. On the ground floor are two temporary exhibition galleries with free access.

An extension has joined the museum to two adjacent buildings in order to better display its collection of Impressionist works, mainly from the 19th century.

⑨ Centro de Arte Reina Sofía

Calle Santa Isabel 52. **Tel** 91-774 10 00.
Ⓜ Atocha. 🚌 6, 8, 10, 14, 19, 27, 45, 55, 60, 78. **Open** 10am–9pm Mon, Wed–Sat, 10am–2:30pm Sun (to 7:30pm for temporary exhibitions). **Closed** Tue, main public hols. (free from 7pm weekdays, from 3pm Sat & Sun).
W **museoreinasofia.es**

Housed in an 18th-century former general hospital, with three additional modern glass buildings, this superb museum traces art through the 20th century. It houses major works

by such influential artists as Picasso, Salvador Dalí, Joan Miró, and Eduardo Chillida. There is also space dedicated to post-World War II movements, such as Abstract, Pop, and Minimal Art.

The highlight of the collection is Picasso's *Guernica* (1937). This Civil War protest painting was inspired by the mass air attack in 1937 on the Basque village of Gernika by German pilots flying for the Nationalist air force.

⑩ Parque del Retiro

Ⓜ Retiro, Ibiza, Atocha. **Open** daily.
W **parquedelretiro.es**

The Retiro Park formed part of Felipe IV's royal-palace complex. All that remains of the palace is the Casón del Buen Retiro (now part of the Prado museum) and the Salón de Reinos (the former army museum). In 2008, the latter moved to the Alcázar in Toledo *(see p288)*.

First fully opened to the public in 1869, the Retiro remains a popular place for relaxing in Madrid. The park has a pleasure lake, where rowing boats can be hired. On one side of the lake, in front of a half-moon colonnade, stands an equestrian statue of Alfonso XII.

To the south of the lake are two attractive palaces. The Neoclassical Palacio de Velázquez and the Palacio de Cristal (Crystal Palace) were built by Velázquez Bosco in 1887 as exhibition venues.

Colonnade and statue of Alfonso XII (1901) overlooking the Parque del Retiro's boating lake

Roman floor mosaic in the Museo Arqueológico Nacional

⑪ Museo Arqueológico Nacional

Calle Serrano 13. **Tel** 91-577 79 12.
Ⓜ Serrano, Retiro. 🚌 1, 9, 19, 51, 74.
Open 9:30am–8pm (6:30pm Jul & Aug)
Tue–Sat, 9:30am–3pm Sun. **Closed**
main public hols. 🎫 (free from 2pm
Sat & Sun). 🌐 ♿ 🅦 **man.mcu.es**

Founded by Isabel II in 1867,
Madrid's National
Archaeological Museum has
hundreds of fascinating exhibits,
ranging from the prehistoric
era to the 19th century.

One of the highlights of
the prehistoric section is the
exhibition on the ancient
civilization of El Argar (1800–
1100 BC) – an advanced
agrarian society that flourished
in southeast Spain. There is also
a display of jewelry uncovered
at the Roman settlement of
Numantia, near Soria, and a
5th-century BC bust, *La Dama
de Elche*.

The museum's ground floor
is largely devoted to the period
between Roman and Mudéjar
Spain, and contains some
impressive Roman mosaics.

Outstanding pieces from
the Visigothic period include
a collection of 7th-century
gold votive crowns from Toledo
province, known as the Treasure
of Guarrazar.

Also on show are examples
of Andalusian pottery from
the Islamic era and various
Romanesque exhibits, among
them an ivory crucifix carved
in 1063 for King Fernando I.

Steps outside the museum's
entrance lead underground to
an exact replica of the Altamira
caves in Cantabria – complete
with their Paleolithic paintings.
The earliest engravings and
drawings date back to around
18000 BC. The boldly colored
bison paintings date from
around 13000 BC.

⑫ Museo de América

Avde los Reyes Católicos 6. **Tel** 91-549
26 41. Ⓜ Moncloa. **Open**
10am–8:30pm Tue–Sat (Nov–Apr: to
6:30pm), 10am–3pm Sun. **Closed**
some public hols. 🎫 (free on Sun).
♿ 🅦 **museodeamerica.mcu.es**

This fine museum houses a
collection of artifacts relating
to Spain's colonization of the
Americas. Many of the exhibits,
which date back to prehistoric
times, were brought to Europe
by the early explorers of the
New World. The collection is
arranged thematically, with
individual rooms on, for

example, society, religion, and
communication. One of the
highlights of the museum is
the rare Mayan *Códice Tro-
cortesiano* (AD 1250–1500)
from Mexico – a hieroglyphic
parchment illustrated with
scenes of everyday life. Also
worth seeing are the Treasure
of the Quimbayas, pre-
Columbian gold and silver
items dating from AD 500–
1000, and the display of
contemporary folk art from
some of Spain's former
American colonies.

⑬ Plaza de Toros de las Ventas

Calle Alcalá 237. **Tel** 91-356 22 00.
Ⓜ Ventas. **Open** for bullfights &
guided visits only. Museo Taurino:
Tel 91-725 18 57. **Open** 9:30am–
2:30pm Tue–Fri, 10am–1pm Sun
(Nov–Feb: 9:30am–2:30pm Mon–Fri).
🎫 daily (687-739 032). ♿
🅦 **las-ventas.com**

Las Ventas is undoubtedly one
of the most beautiful bullrings
in Spain. Built in 1929 in Neo-
Mudéjar style, it replaced the
city's original bullring, which
stood near the Puerta de
Alcalá. Outside the bullring are
monuments to two famous
bullfighters: Antonio
Bienvenida and José Cubero.

Adjoining the building,
the Museo Taurino contains
bullfighting memorabilia, such
as portraits and sculptures of
famous matadors. There is also
a display of the tools of the
bullfighter's trade, including
capes and *banderillas* – sharp
darts used to wound the bull.

Plaza de Toros de Las Ventas, Madrid's magnificent bullring

For hotels and restaurants see pp330–32 and pp333–5

The Art of Bullfighting

Bullfighting is a sacrificial ritual in which men (and a few women) pit themselves against an animal bred for the ring. In this "authentic religious drama," as the poet Federico García Lorca described it, the spectator experiences the same intensity of fear and exaltation as the matador. There are three stages, or *tercios*, in the *corrida* (bullfight). The first two, which involve a team of men both on horseback and on foot, are aimed at progressively weakening the bull. In the third, the matador moves in for the kill. Despite opposition on the grounds of cruelty, bullfighting is still very popular. For many Spaniards, the *toreo*, the art of bullfighting, is a noble part of their heritage. However, fights today are often debased by practices designed to disadvantage the bull, in particular shaving its horns to make them blunt.

The *toro bravo* (fighting bull), bred for courage and aggression, enjoys a full life prior to its time in the ring. Bulls must be at least four years old before they can fight.

Manolete is regarded by most followers of bullfighting as one of Spain's greatest matadors. He was finally gored to death by the bull Islero at Linares, Jaén, in 1947.

The matador wears a *traje de luces* (suit of lights), a colorful silk outfit embroidered with gold sequins.

Banderillas, barbed darts, are thrust into the bull's back muscles to weaken them.

Joselito was a leading matador, famous for his purist style. He displayed superb skill with the *capote* (red cape) and the *muleta* (matador's stick). Following a short retirement, he has returned to the *ruedos* (bullring).

The Bullring

The audience at a bullfight is seated in the *tendidos* (stalls) or in the *palcos* (balcony), where the *presidencia* (president's box) is situated. Opposite are the *puerta de cuadrillas*, through which the matador and team arrive, and the *arrastre de toros* (exit for bulls). Before entering the ring, the matadors wait in a *callejón* (corridor) behind *barreras* and *burladeros* (barriers). Horses are kept in the *patio de caballos* and the bulls in the *corrales*.

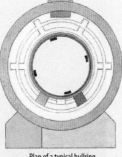

Key

- ☐ Tendidos
- ▨ Palcos
- ▨ Presidencia
- ▨ Puerta de cuadrillas
- ▨ Arrastre de toros
- ▨ Callejón
- ▨ Barreras
- ▨ Burladeros
- ☐ Patio de caballos
- ☐ Corrales

Plan of a typical bullring

Central Spain

Much of Spain's vast central plateau, the *meseta*, is covered with wheat fields or dry, dusty plains, but there are many attractive places to explore. Spain's largest region, Castilla y León, has a rich history. It boasts some of the country's most splendid architecture, from Segovia's famous Roman aqueduct, to the Gothic cathedrals of Burgos and Léon, and the Renaissance grandeur of Salamanca's monuments. Avila's medieval city walls are a legacy of the long struggles between the Christians and the Moors. Dotted with windmills and medieval castles, Castilla-La Mancha is home to the historic town of Toledo, another popular destination.

The Library at El Escorial, with its 16th-century frescoed ceiling

❷ El Escorial

El Escorial. **Tel** 91-890 59 03. 🚇 from Atocha or Chamartín, Madrid. 🚌 661, 664 from Moncloa, Madrid. **Open** 10am–7pm Tue–Sun (to 6pm Oct–Mar). **Closed** public hols. 🎟 (except Wed & Thu pm for EU residents). 📷

Felipe II's imposing palace of San Lorenzo de El Escorial was built in 1563–84 in honor of St. Lawrence. The austere, unornamented building set a new architectural style – known as "Herreriano," after the palace's architect, Juan de Herrera. Its interior was conceived as a mausoleum and contemplative retreat rather than a splendid residence.

Among the most impressive parts is the **Library**, with a collection of more than 40,000 books and manuscripts. Its ceiling is decorated with 16th-century frescoes by Tibaldi. The **Royal Pantheon**, a mausoleum made in marble, contains the funerary urns of

Spanish monarchs. Some of the most important works of the royal Habsburg collections, including Flemish, Italian, and Spanish paintings, are housed in the **Museum of Art**, located on the first floor. Other fine works of art can be found in the chapter houses, with their fresco-adorned ceilings, and in the basilica.

In contrast to the artistic wealth of other parts of the palace, the royal apartments are remarkably humble.

❸ Toledo

See pp286–8.

❹ Segovia

Segovia. 🗺 56,000. 🚇 🚌 ℹ️ Plaza Mayor 10 (921-46 03 34).

Segovia is one of the most spectacularly sited cities in Spain. The old town is set high on a rocky spur, surrounded by the Eresma and Clamores rivers. With its cathedral, aqueduct,

and castle dominating the skyline, the view of the town from the valley below at sunset is magical.

Perched on a rocky outcrop at the city's western end is the **Alcázar**, a fairytale castle with gabled roofs, turrets, and crenellations. Begun in the 12th century, the castle assumed its present form between 1410 and 1455, though it had to be largely rebuilt following a fire in 1862. The castle contains a museum of weaponry and several sumptuous apartments.

Dating from 1525, Segovia's **cathedral** was the last great Gothic church to be built in Spain. It replaced the old cathedral, destroyed in 1520 when the Castilian towns revolted against King Carlos I. Other churches in the old town include the Romanesque **San Juan de los Caballeros**, which has an outstanding sculpted portico, **San Esteban**, and **San Martín**.

Segovia's Roman **aqueduct** was built in the 1st century AD and remained in use until the late 19th century.

🏰 **Alcázar**
Plaza de la Reina Victoria Eugenia.
Tel 921-46 07 59. **Open** daily.
Closed Jan 1 & 6, Dec 25. 🎟 📷
(by appt and for fee). ♿

Environs
The palace of **Riofrío**, 11 km (7 miles) southwest of the city, was built as a hunting lodge for Felipe V's widow, Isabel Farnese, in 1752. Today, it houses a hunting museum.

Segovia's distinctive Alcázar, perched high above the city

Section of Avila's 12th-century city walls

❺ Avila

Avila. 🏔 58,000. 🚉 🚌 ℹ️ Calle San Segundo 17 (920-21 13 87).

The perfectly preserved medieval walls that encircle this historic city were built in the 12th century by Christian forces as a defense against the Moors. Of the nine gateways in the walls, the most impressive is the **Puerta de San Vicente**. Avila's **cathedral**, whose unusual exterior is carved with beasts and scaly wild men, also forms part of the city walls.

Avila is the birthplace of St. Teresa (1515–82), one of the Catholic Church's greatest mystics and reformers. The **Convento de Santa Teresa** occupies the site of the home of this saint, who also lived for many years in the **Monasterio de la Encarnación**.

Among the city's finest churches are the 12th-century **Iglesia de San Vicente** and the Romanesque-Gothic **Iglesia de San Pedro.**

Beyond the town center, the beautiful **Real Monasterio de Santo Tomás** contains the tomb of Tomás de Torquemada (1420–98), the notorious head of the Spanish Inquisition.

❻ Salamanca

Salamanca. 🏔 155,000. ✈️ 15 km (9 miles) E. 🚉 🚌 ℹ️ Plaza Mayor 32 (923-21 83 42). 🌐 **salamanca.es**

Home to one of the oldest universities in Europe, Salamanca is also Spain's best showcase of Renaissance and Plateresque architecture. The city's famous **university** was founded by Alfonso IX of León in 1218. The 16th-century facade of the main building on the Patio de las Escuelas is a splendid example of the Plateresque style. This form of early Spanish Renaissance architecture is so called because of its fine detail, which resembles ornate silverwork – *platero* in Spanish means silversmith.

The 16th-century, mainly Gothic **new cathedral** and the 12th- to 13th-century Romanesque **old cathedral** stand side by side. A highlight of the old cathedral is the richly colored altarpiece (1445) by Nicolás Florentino. The magnificent **Plaza Mayor** was built by Felipe V in the 18th century to thank the city for its support during the War of the Spanish Succession. Among the arcaded buildings lining the square are the Baroque town hall and the Royal Pavilion, from where the royal family used to watch events in the square.

Other fine monuments located in the heart of the city include the 16th-century **Iglesia-Convento de San Esteban**, with its lovely ornamented facade, and the **Convento de las Dueñas**, which preserves Moorish and Renaissance features.

The **Museo Art Nouveau y Art Deco** holds an important collection of 19th- and 20th-century paintings, jewelry, ceramics, and stained glass.

On the city outskirts, the 1st-century AD Roman bridge, the **Puente Romano**, offers a good view over the entire city.

🏛 **Universidad**
Calle Libreros. **Tel** 923-29 44 00.
Open daily. **Closed** Dec 25.
🎫 (except Mon am).

🏛 **Museo Art Nouveau y Art Deco**
Calle Gibraltar 14. **Tel** 923-12 14 25.
Open Tue–Sun. 🎫 (free Thu am).
♿ 📷

View of Salamanca's twin cathedrals, from the Puente Romano

❸ Street by Street: Toledo

Picturesquely sited on a hill above the Tagus River is the historic center of Toledo. Behind the old walls lies much evidence of the city's rich history. The Romans built a fortress on the site of the present-day Alcázar. In the 6th century AD, the Visigoths made Toledo their capital, and left behind many churches. After it was captured from the Moors by Alfonso VI in 1085, the city became the capital of the Christian kingdom of Castile. During the Middle Ages, Toledo was a melting pot of Christian, Muslim, and Jewish cultures, and it was during this period that the city's most outstanding monument – its cathedral – was built. In the 16th century, the painter El Greco came to live in Toledo, and today the city is home to many of his works.

Iglesia de San Román
This church contains a museum relating the city's past under the Visigoths.

Puerta de Valmardón

★ Iglesia de Santo Tomé
This church, with a beautiful Mudéjar tower, houses El Greco's masterpiece, *The Burial of the Count of Orgaz.*

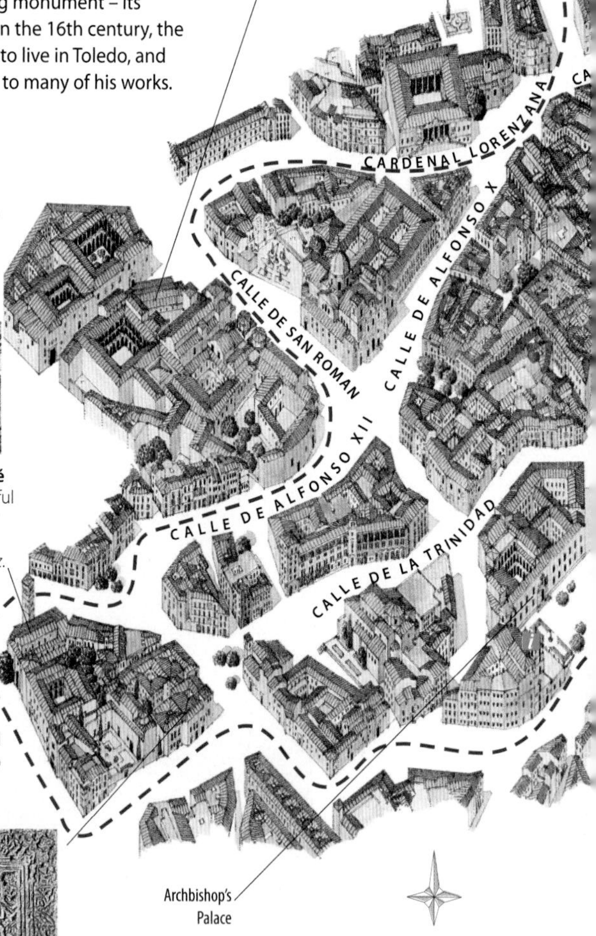

CARDENAL LORENZANA

CALLE DE SAN ROMAN

CALLE DE ALFONSO X

CALLE DE ALFONSO XII

CALLE DE LA TRINIDAD

Sinagoga del Tránsito and Casa-Museo de El Greco

Archbishop's Palace

Taller del Moro
This Mudéjar palace houses a museum of Mudéjar ceramics and tiles. It is, however, closed for renovation with no confirmation of an end date.

0 meters   100
0 yards   100

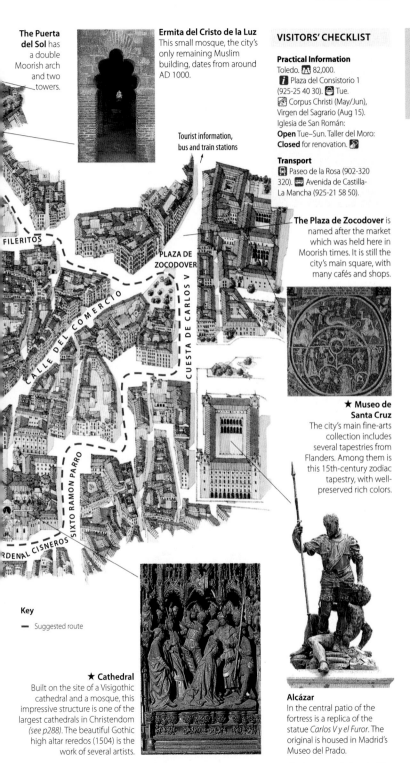

The Puerta del Sol has a double Moorish arch and two towers.

Ermita del Cristo de la Luz
This small mosque, the city's only remaining Muslim building, dates from around AD 1000.

Tourist information, bus and train stations

FILERITOS

PLAZA DE ZOCODOVER

CALLE DEL COMERCIO

CUESTA DE CARLOS V

SIXTO RAMON PARRO

RDENAL CISNEROS

The Plaza de Zocodover is named after the market which was held here in Moorish times. It is still the city's main square, with many cafés and shops.

★ Museo de Santa Cruz
The city's main fine-arts collection includes several tapestries from Flanders. Among them is this 15th-century zodiac tapestry, with well-preserved rich colors.

Alcázar
In the central patio of the fortress is a replica of the statue *Carlos V y el Furor*. The original is housed in Madrid's Museo del Prado.

Key
— Suggested route

★ Cathedral
Built on the site of a Visigothic cathedral and a mosque, this impressive structure is one of the largest cathedrals in Christendom (*see p288*). The beautiful Gothic high altar reredos (1504) is the work of several artists.

For keys to symbols *see back flap*

Exploring Toledo

Easily reached from Madrid by train, bus, or car, Toledo is best explored on foot. To visit all the main sights you need at least two days, but it is possible to walk around the medieval and Jewish quarters in a long morning. To avoid the heavy crowds, go midweek and stay for a night, when the city is at its most atmospheric.

Toledo cathedral, rising above the rooftops of the medieval quarter

🏛 Cathedral

Calle Cardenal Cisneros 1. **Tel** 925-22 22 41. Choir, Treasury, Chapterhouse, and Sacristy **Open** Mon–Sat, Sun pm.
🏛 📷 ♿

The splendor of Toledo's cathedral reflects its history as the spiritual heart of the Spanish church and the seat of the Primate of all Spain. The present cathedral stands on the site of a 7th-century church. Work began in 1226, but the last vaults were not completed until 1493. This long period of construction explains the cathedral's mixture of styles: the exterior is pure French Gothic, while inside, Spanish decorative styles, such as Mudéjar – a hybrid Christian-Islamic style – and Plateresque, are used.

Among the cathedral's most outstanding features are the polychrome reredos of the high altar (1504) and the choir. In the treasury is a 16th-century Gothic silver monstrance, over 3 m (10 ft) high. The monstrance is carried through the streets of Toledo during the Corpus Christi celebrations. Standing out from the mainly Gothic interior, the Transparente is a stunning Baroque altarpiece of marble, jasper, and bronze, sculpted by Narciso Tomé.

🏛 Museo de Santa Cruz

Calle Cervantes 3. **Tel** 925-22 10 36. **Open** daily. **Closed** Jan 1, May 1, Dec 25. This museum of fine arts has a superb collection of medieval and Renaissance tapestries, paintings, and sculptures. There are also works by the Cretan artist El Greco, as well as examples of two typical Toledan crafts: armor and damascened swords, the latter made by inlaying blackened steel with gold wire. The museum is housed in a fine renovated Renaissance building and has an elegant courtyard.

🏛 Iglesia de Santo Tomé

Calle Santo Tomé s/n. **Tel** 925-25 60 98. **Open** daily. 📷 (except Wed pm for EU residents).

Visitors come to this church mainly to admire El Greco's masterpiece, *The Burial of the Count of Orgaz*. The church is thought to date back to the

The Assumption (1613) by El Greco, in the Museo de Santa Cruz

12th century, and its tower is one of the best examples of Mudéjar architecture in Toledo.

🏛 Alcázar

Cuesta de Carlos V. **Tel** 925-23 88 00. **Open** 11am–5pm Thu–Tue. 📷 (free Sun).

Charles V's fortified palace stands on the site of former Roman, Visigothic, and Muslim fortresses. In 1936, it was almost completely destroyed during a 70-day siege by the Republicans. The restored building houses the Museo del Ejército (National Army Museum) and a private library, which holds a valuable collection of books and manuscripts dating back to the 11th century.

🏛 Sinagoga del Tránsito

Calle Samuel Leví. **Tel** 925-22 36 65. **Open** Tue–Sun. 📷 (free Sat pm & Sun).

A wonderfully elaborate Mudéjar interior is hidden behind the humble facade of this 14th-century former synagogue. Next door is a museum dedicated to the Sephardic (Spanish Jewish) culture.

🏛 Casa-Museo de El Greco

Paseo del Tránsito. **Tel** 925-216 967. **Open** Tue–Sun. 📷 (free from 2pm Sat & all day Sun).

It is uncertain whether El Greco actually lived in or simply near to this house, now a museum containing a collection of his works. Canvases include the superb series *Christ and the Apostles*. On the ground floor is a chapel with a fine Mudéjar ceiling and works of art by painters of the Toledan School, such as Luis Tristán, a student of El Greco.

🏛 Puerta Antigua de Bisagra

When Alfonso VI of Castile conquered Toledo in 1085, he entered it through this gateway – the only one in the city to have kept its original 10th-century military architecture. The towers are topped by a 12th-century Arab gatehouse.

The Arco de Santa María in Burgos, adorned with statues and turrets

❼ Burgos

Burgos. 🔼 178,000. 🚆 🚌 **ℹ** Plaza de Alonso Martínez 7 (947-20 31 25).

Founded in 884, Burgos was the capital of the united kingdoms of Castile and León from 1073 until 1492. A few hundred years later, Franco chose Burgos as his headquarters during the Civil War.

Approaching the city via the bridge called the Puente de Santa María, you enter the old town through the grand **Arco de Santa María**. The other main route into Burgos is the Puente de San Pablo, where a statue commemorates local hero El Cid (1043–99). Born Rodrigo Díaz de Vivar, this great warrior fought for both the Moors and the Christians in the Reconquest, and for his heroism was named El Cid, from the Arabic *Sidi* (Lord). He is immortalized in the anonymous poem, *El Cantar del Mío Cid* (1180).

Not far from the statue of El Cid stands the **Casa del Cordón**, a 15th-century former palace (now a bank). It was here that the Catholic Monarchs welcomed Columbus on his return, in 1497, from the second of his voyages to the Americas.

Burgos's **cathedral** *(see pp290–91)* is a UNESCO World Heritage site and the city's most prominent landmark. Nearby, the **Iglesia de San Nicolás** boasts a fine 16th-century altarpiece, while the **Iglesia de San Lorenzo** has a splendid Baroque ceiling. The **Museo de Burgos** contains archaeological and fine-art collections.

West of the city is the 12th-century **Real Monasterio de Huelgas**, a former convent that houses a textile museum.

🏛 Museo de Burgos
Calle Miranda 13. **Tel** 947-26 58 75. **Open** Tue–Sun. 🖼 (except Sat & Sun). ♿

🏛 Real Monasterio de Huelgas
Calle de los Compases. **Tel** 947-20 16 30. **Open** 10am–2pm, 3:45–6:30pm Tue–Sat; 10:30am–3pm Sun & public hols. **Closed** Jan 1 & 6, Good Fri, May 1, May 30, Dec 24, 25, & 31. 🖼 ♿ 🖼 (except Wed & Thu pm for EU residents).

❽ León

León. 🔼 134,000. 🚆 🚌 **ℹ** Plaza de la Regla 4 (987-23 70 82).

Founded as a camp for the Romans' Seventh Legion, León became the capital of the kingdom of León in the Middle Ages and played a

Statue of El Cid, Burgos's most famous son

central role in the early years of the Reconquest.

The city's Gothic **cathedral**, on Plaza de la Regla, dates from the mid-13th century. As well as some glorious stained glass, it has a splendid west front, decorated with a series of 13th-century carvings.

The **Colegiata de San Isidoro** is built into the Roman walls encircling the city. The Romanesque **Panteón Real** (Royal Pantheon) is decorated with carved capitals and 12th-century frescoes. León's old quarter is a maze of narrow alleyways, lined with bars, cafés, churches, and old mansions. The **Hostal de San Marcos** was founded in the 12th century as a monastery for pilgrims on route to Santiago *(see p292)*. A gem of Spanish Renaissance architecture, the present building was begun in 1513 for the Knights of Santiago. Today, it houses a luxurious hotel and the **Museo de León**.

🏛 Museo de León
Plaza Santo Domingo. **Tel** 987-23 64 05. **Open** Tue–Sun. **Closed** main public hols. 🖼 (free Sat & Sun).

Environs
To the east of León, the 10th-century **Iglesia de San Miguel de Escalada** is one of the finest surviving churches built by the Mozarabs – Christians influenced by the Moors.

Detail from a 13th-century carving decorating the west front of León's cathedral

Burgos Cathedral

Spain's third-largest cathedral was founded in 1221 under Fernando III and was named a UNESCO World Heritage site in 1984. The groundplan – a Latin cross – measures 84 m (276 ft) by 59 m (194 ft). Its construction was carried out in several stages over three centuries, involving artists and architects from across Europe. The style is almost entirely Gothic, with influences from Germany, France, and the Low Countries. In the Middle Ages, the cathedral was a main stopping point for pilgrims on the road to Santiago *(see p292)*. Burgos's most celebrated son, the medieval hero of the Reconquest, El Cid, is buried in the cathedral, as is his wife.

West Front
The lacy, steel-grey spires soar above a sculpted balustrade depicting Castile's early kings.

★ Golden Staircase
Diego de Siloé's elegant Renaissance staircase (1519–22) links the nave with the Gothic Coronería Gate (kept locked) at street level.

KEY

① **The Capilla de la Presentación** (1519–24) is a funerary chapel with a star-shaped, traceried vault.

② **Capilla de Santa Tecla**

③ **Tomb of El Cid**

④ **Capilla de Santa Ana** is a chapel with a beautiful altarpiece (1490) by the sculptor Gil de Siloé. The central panel shows the Virgin with St. Joachim.

⑤ **The Lantern** is a 59 m (194 ft) octagonal tower positioned over the nave and crowned with eight spires.

⑥ **Capilla de San Juan Bautista and museum**

⑦ **Capilla de la Visitación**

⑧ **Capilla del Santísimo Cristo**

Puerta de Santa María (main entrance)

Ambulatory
Several of the reliefs around the chancel were carved by Philippe de Bigarny. This expressive scene, which was completed in 1499, depicts the road to Calvary.

VISITORS' CHECKLIST

Practical Information
Plaza de Santa María.
Tel 947-27 39 50.
Open mid-Mar–Oct: 9:30am–7:30pm daily; Nov–mid-Mar: 10am–7pm. ⛪ 9am, 10am, 11am, 7:30pm daily; Sun also: noon (sung), 1pm, 2pm.

★ **Constable's Chapel**
The tomb of the High Constable of Castile and his wife lies beneath the openwork vault of this chapel of 1496.

Sacristy (1765)
The sacristy was rebuilt in Baroque style, with an exuberant plasterwork vault and Rococo altars.

Puerta de la Coronería
The tympanum of this portal of 1240 shows Christ flanked by the Evangelists. Statues of the apostles sit below.

★ **Crossing**
The star-ribbed central dome, begun in 1539, is supported by four huge pillars. It is decorated with effigies of prophets and saints. Beneath it is the tomb of El Cid and his wife.

Northern Spain

Northern Spain encompasses a variety of landscapes and cultures. In the far northwest of the peninsula, the Galicians are fiercely proud of their customs and language. Spain's greenest region, Galicia boasts some of the most attractive stretches of Atlantic coast, as well as the beautiful city of Santiago de Compostela. Popular with hikers and naturalists, the spectacular Picos de Europa massif sits astride the border between Asturias and Cantabria. The Basque Country is a unique part of Spain, whose main attractions include superb cuisine, fashionable seaside resorts, and the cultural center of Bilbao, with its famous Guggenheim Museum.

Santiago de Compostela's grand cathedral, towering over the city

❾ Santiago de Compostela

A Coruña. 🚆 95,000. ✈ 10 km (6 miles) N. 🚌 🚐 ⓘ Calle Rúa do Villar 63 (981-55 51 29). 🎉 Fiesta (Jul 25). 🅦 santiagoturismo.com

In the Middle Ages, this fine city was Christendom's third most important place of pilgrimage after Jerusalem and Rome. In 813, the body of Christ's apostle James was supposedly discovered here, and in the following centuries, pilgrims from all over Europe flocked to the city.

On the Praza do Obradoiro stands the city's **cathedral**, built in honor of St. James. The present structure dates from the 11th–13th centuries, but the Baroque west facade was added in the 18th century. The square's northern edge is flanked by the grand **Hostal de los Reyes Católicos**, built by the Catholic Monarchs (*see p268*) as a resting

place for sick pilgrims. It is now a parador hotel. Nearby are the 9th-century **Convento de San Paio de Antealtares**, one of the city's oldest monasteries, and the **Convento de San Martiño Pinario**, whose Baroque church has a wonderfully ornate Plateresque facade.

The **Convento de Santo Domingo de Bonaval**, east of the center, is also worth visiting. Part of the monastery now houses a Galician folk museum.

There is also the **Centro Gallego de Arte Contemporáneo**, with works by leading Galician artists.

🏛 **Centro Gallego de Arte Contemporáneo**
Calle Valle Inclán s/n. **Tel** 981-54 66 19. **Open** Tue–Sun. ◧ by prior appointment (call 981-54 66 23). ♿

❿ Rías Baixas

Pontevedra. 🚆 🚐 Pontevedra. ⓘ Praza da Verdura s/n, Pontevedra (986-09 08 90).

The southern part of Galicia's west coast consists of four large *rías*, or inlets, between pine-covered hills. Known as the Rías Baixas (Rías Bajas), they offer fine beaches, safe bathing, and lovely scenery.

The main town on the coast is lively **Pontevedra**, which has many historic monuments, such as the Gothic Convento de Santo Domingo, and an excellent provincial museum.

Many areas along the coast have become popular holiday resorts, such as **Sanxenxo**, west of Pontevedra. To the south, **Baiona** and **Panxón** both have good beaches, as well as sailing and a variety of water sports. In spite of tourism, much of the coastline, particularly the quieter northernmost part, remains unspoiled. Here you can visit many small fishing ports and watch the locals harvesting mussels and clams.

While in Rías Baixas, look out for *hórreos* – traditional stone-built granaries raised on stilts. The waterfront of picturesque **Combarro** is lined with these buildings, typical of the whole of Galicia.

The tranquil fishing village of Combarro in the Rías Baixas

Santa María del Naranco, a Pre-Romanesque church in Oviedo

⓫ Oviedo

Asturias. 🅰 225,000. 🚋 🚌
ℹ Marqués de Santa Cruz 1 (985-22 75 86). 🅦 turismoviedo.es

Oviedo, the cultural and commercial capital of Asturias, is best known for its Pre-Romanesque buildings. This style flourished in the 8th–10th centuries and was confined to a small area of the kingdom of Asturias, one of the few areas of Spain that escaped invasion by the Moors.

With its huge barrel-vaulted hall and arcaded galleries, the church of **Santa María del Naranco**, in the north of the city, was built as a summer palace for Ramiro I in the 9th century. Equally impressive are the church of **San Miguel de Lillo** and the 9th-century church of **San Julián de los Prados**, with its frescoes.

In the center of Oviedo, the Flamboyant Gothic **cathedral** and the 9th-century **Iglesia de San Tirso** are both worth taking some time to see.

The city has two museums of note: the **Museo Arqueológico**, which contains local prehistoric, Roman, and Romanesque treasures, and the **Museo de Bellas Artes** (Museum of Fine Arts).

🏛 **Museo Arqueológico**
Calle San Vicente 5. **Tel** 985-20 89 77.
Open Wed–Sun. ♿

🏛 **Museo de Bellas Artes**
Calle Santa Ana 1. **Tel** 985-21 30 61.
Open Tue–Sun. ♿

⓬ Picos de Europa

Asturias, Cantabria, and Castilla y León.
🚌 Oviedo to Cangas de Onís. ℹ
Cangas de Onís (985-84 86 14). Fuente Dé cable car: **Tel** 942-73 66 10. **Open** daily. **Closed** Jan 1 & 6; Dec 24, 25 & 31.

This beautiful mountain range – christened "Peaks of Europe" by returning sailors, as this was often the first sight of their homeland – offers superb upland hiking and supports a diversity of wildlife.

The two main gateways to the Picos are **Cangas de Onís**, northwest of the park, and **Potes**, on the eastern side. About 8 km (5 miles) southeast of the former, **Covadonga** is where, in 722, the Visigoth Pelayo is said to have defeated a Moorish army, inspiring Christians to reconquer the peninsula. The road south from Cangas de Onís follows the spectacular gorge known as the Desfiladero de los Beyes.

The Fuente Dé cable car, in the heart of the park, climbs 900 m (2,950 ft) to a rocky plateau, offering magnificent panoramic views.

⓭ Santander

Cantabria. 🅰 182,000. ✈ 🚢 🚋 🚌
ℹ Jardines de Pereda (942-203 000).
🎭 International Festival (Jul–Aug).

Cantabria's capital, Santander, is a busy port that enjoys a splendid site on a deep bay on Spain's north Atlantic coast. The **cathedral** was rebuilt in Gothic

The early 20th-century Palacio de la Magdalena in Santander

style, following a fire in 1941 that destroyed the entire town. The 12th-century crypt has been preserved. Nearby, the **Museo de Bellas Artes** has works by Goya and Zurbarán, while the **Museo de Prehistoria y Arqueología** displays local finds, including Neolithic axe heads, Roman coins, pottery, and figurines.

On the Península de la Magdalena stands the **Palacio de la Magdalena**, built for Alfonso XIII in 1912. The upscale seaside resort of **El Sardinero**, to the north, has a long beach, chic cafés, and a majestic white casino.

🏛 **Museo de Bellas Artes**
Calle Rubio 6. **Tel** 942-20 31 20.
Open Tue–Sun. 🅿

🏛 **Museo de Prehistoria y Arqueología**
Calle Hernán Cortés 4. **Tel** 942-20 71 09. **Open** Wed–Sun. 🅿 ♿ 🅿

19th-century Neo-Romanesque basilica in Covadonga, Picos de Europa

Frank Gehry's ultramodern Museo Guggenheim building in Bilbao

⑭ Bilbao

Vizcaya. 🖭 354,000. ✈ 🚢 🚆 🚌
ⓘ Plaza Circular 1 (944-79 57 60).
🎪 Fiesta (third week Aug).

Bilbao (Bilbo) is the center of Basque industry and Spain's leading commercial port, yet it has many cultural attractions worth visiting. In the city's medieval quarter – the *Casco Viejo* – the **Museo Arqueológico, Etnográfico e Histórico Vasco** displays Basque art and folk artifacts, while in the newer town, the **Museo de Bellas Artes** is one of Spain's best art museums.

The jewel in Bilbao's cultural crown, however, is the **Museo Guggenheim Bilbao**, which has a superb collection of Modern and contemporary art. It is just one of the city's many pieces of modern architecture, which also include the striking **Palacio de la Música y Congresos Euskalduna**.

🏛 Museo Guggenheim
Av Abandoibarra. **Tel** 944-35 90 00.
Open 10am–8pm. **Closed** Sep–Jun:
Mon; public hols. 🎨 ⬛ ⬛
🅿 🚹 🔲 guggenheim-bilbao.es

⑮ San Sebastián

Guipúzcoa. 🖭 185,000. 🚆 🚌
ⓘ Boulevard 8 (943-48 11 66).
🎪 International Film Festival (late Sep).

Popular with the aristocracy, San Sebastián (Donostia) became a fashionable seaside resort in the late 19th century. At the heart of the old town

are the handsome Plaza de la Constitución and the church of **Santa María del Coro**, with its Baroque portal. Behind the old town, Monte Urgull is worth climbing for the superb views from its summit. At the foot of the hill, the **Museo de San Telmo** holds exhibits ranging from Basque funerary columns to works by El Greco.

A short bus ride from the Calle Oquendo takes you to **Chillida-Leku**, a display of works by renowned Basque sculptor, Eduardo Chillida.

Between the city's two main beaches – the Playa de la Concha and the Playa de Ondarreta – is the **Palacio Miramar** (1889), built for Queen María Cristina.

🏛 Museo de San Telmo
Plaza Zuloaga. **Tel** 943-48 15 80.
Open 10am–8pm Tue–Sun.
🎨 (free Tue). 🚹 🔲

Mural by Josep Maria Sert in the Museo de San Telmo, San Sebastián

Bulls scattering the runners during Sanfermines in Pamplona

⑯ Pamplona

Navarra. 🖭 198,000. ✈ 🚆 🚌
ⓘ Av Roncesvalles 4 (848-420 420).
🎪 Sanfermines (Jul 6–14).

Supposedly founded by the Roman general, Pompey, Pamplona is most famous for the fiesta of Los Sanfermines, with its daredevil bull running.

West of the city's mainly Gothic **cathedral** lies the old Jewish quarter, with the Neoclassic **Palacio del Gobierno de Navarra** and the medieval **Iglesia de San Saturnino**.

The **Museo de Navarra** is a museum of regional history, archaeology, and art.

Southeast of the center is Felipe II's massive **citadel**, erected in the 16th century.

🏛 Museo de Navarra
Calle Santo Domingo. **Tel** 848-42 64 92. **Open** Tue–Sun. 🎨 free Sat pm, Sun. 🚹 🔲 by appointment.

Basque Culture

The Basques are one of the oldest people in Europe. Long isolated in their mountain villages, they have preserved their unique language (Euskera), myths, and art – almost untouched by outside influences – for millennia. Many families still live in the stone *caseríos*, or farmhouses, built by their forebears. Among the most popular exponents of Basque cultural life are the *bertsolaris*, oral poets, originally from rural areas, who improvise verses and who are still very popular among the younger generations. Though the Basque region has had its own parliament since 1975 (as all other Spanish regions), there has always been a strong separatist movement seeking to sever links with the government in Madrid.

The Ikurriña, the flag of the Basque region

Catalonia

A nation-within-a-nation, Catalonia has its own semi-autonomous regional government, and its own language. Spoken by more than eight million people, Catalan has supplanted Castilian Spanish as the first language of the region, and is used on road signs and in place names everywhere. Barcelona is the region's capital, rivaling Madrid in economic and cultural importance. Catalonia offers a variety of attractions. The flower-filled valleys of the Pyrenees offer a paradise for naturalists and walkers, while inland are medieval towns, Roman ruins, and spectacular monasteries, such as Montserrat.

⓱ Parc Nacional d'Aigüestortes

Lleida. 🚉 La Pobla de Segur. 🚌 El Pont de Suert, La Pobla de Segur. 🛈 Boí (973-69 61 89).

The pristine mountain scenery of Catalonia's only national park is among the most spectacular in the Pyrenees. The main village in the area is the mountain settlement of Espot, on the park's eastern edge. Dotted around the park are waterfalls and more than a hundred lakes and tarns.

The most beautiful scenery is around Sant Maurici lake, from where several walks lead north to the towering peaks of Agulles d'Amitges. The park is home to an impressive variety of wildlife: chamois, beavers, otters, and golden eagles have all found a habitat here.

⓲ Barcelona

See pp296–305.

⓳ Monestir de Montserrat

See pp306–7.

⓴ Poblet

Off N240, 10 km (6 miles) from Montblanc. **Tel** 977-87 00 89. 🚉 to L'Espluga de Francolí, then taxi. 🚌 **Open** 10am–12:45pm, 3–5:30pm daily. **Closed** Jan 1, Dec 25 & 26. 🈲

Santa Maria de Poblet was the first and most important of three medieval monasteries, known as the "Cistercian triangle." In 1835, during the

The superb altarpiece at Santa Maria de Poblet

Carlist upheavals, the abbey sustained serious damage. Restoration began in 1930, and monks returned a decade later.

Poblet is enclosed by fortified walls that have hardly changed since the Middle Ages. Its evocative, vaulted cloisters were built in the 12th and 13th centuries. Beautiful, carved scrollwork decorates the capitals. Behind the stone altar, an impressive alabaster reredos, carved by Damià Forment in 1527, fills the apse. Other highlights include the Royal Tombs, where many Spanish monarchs are buried. Begun in 1359, they were reconstructed by Marès in 1950.

㉑ Tarragona

Tarragona. 🚗 140,000. 🚆 🚌 🛈 Carrer Major 39 (977-25 07 95).

Now a major industrial port, Tarragona preserves many remnants of its Roman past, when it was the capital of the Roman province, Tarraconensis.

Among the extensive ruins are the **Anfiteatro Romano** (Roman Amphitheater) and the Praetorium, a Roman tower that was later converted into a medieval palace. Also known as the Castell de Pilato (after Pontius Pilate), the tower houses the **Museu de la Romanitat**, which contains Roman and medieval finds and gives access to the cavernous passageways of the 1st-century AD Roman circus. In the adjacent building is the **Museu Nacional Arqueològic**, which holds the most important collection of Roman artifacts in Catalonia, including some beautiful frescoes. An archaeological walk follows part of the Roman city wall.

Tarragona's 12th-century **cathedral** was built on the site of a Roman temple and an Arab mosque, and exhibits a harmonious blend of styles.

🏛 Museu Nacional Arqueològic de Tarragona

Plaça del Rei 5. **Tel** 977-23 62 09. **Open** Jun–Sep: 9:30am–8:30pm Tue–Sat; Oct–May: 9:30am–6pm Tue–Sat, 10am–2pm Sun all year. 🈲 (Oct–Jun: free Tue). 🈳

View across the Roman amphitheater at Tarragona

⑱ Barcelona

Barcelona, one of the Mediterranean's busiest ports, is more than the capital of Catalonia. In culture, commerce, and sport, it rivals not only Madrid, but also many of Europe's greatest cities. The success of the 1992 Olympic Games, staged in the Parc de Montjuïc, confirmed this to the world. Although there are many historical monuments in the Old Town, the city is best known for the scores of superb buildings left behind by the artistic explosion of Modernisme in the decades around 1900. Today, Barcelona still sizzles with creativity; its bars and public parks speak more of bold contemporary design than of tradition.

Greater Barcelona

0 km 2
0 miles

Key

Area of main map

Sights at a Glance

① Barcelona Cathedral
② Museu d'Història de la Ciutat – Conjunt Monumental de la Plaça del Rei
③ La Ramblas
④ Basílica de Santa Maria del Mar
⑤ Museu Picasso
⑥ Vila Olímpica
⑦ *Sagrada Família pp302–3*
⑧ Quadrat d'Or
⑨ Montjuïc
⑩ Fundació Joan Miró
⑪ Museu Nacional d'Art de Catalunya

Greater Barcelona
(see inset map)

⑫ Parc Güell
⑬ Tibidabo

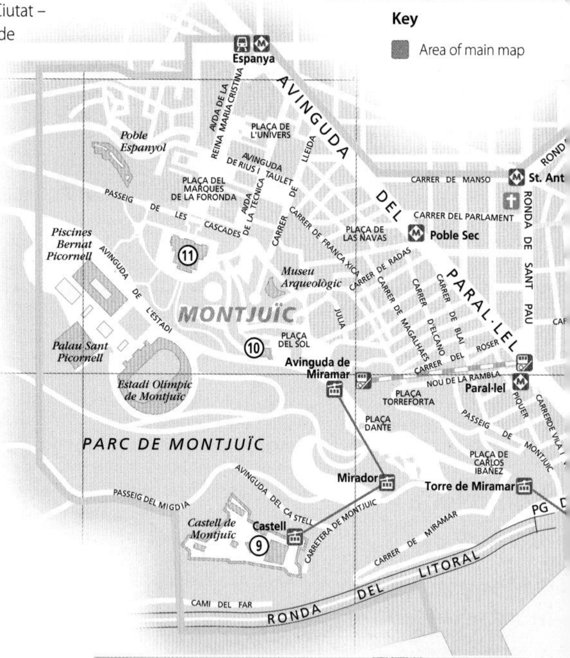

Key

▮ Sight / Place of interest
▰▰ Pedestrian street
— Cable car line
▱ Motorway
▱▱ Funicular railway

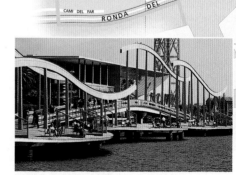

Pedestrian swing bridge in Port Vell, at the end of La Ramblas

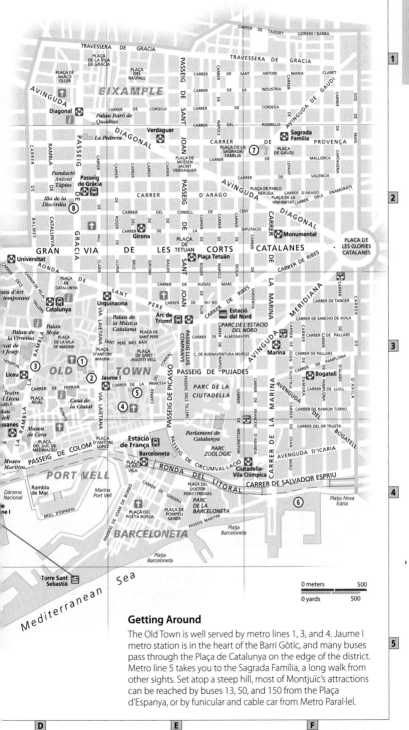

Getting Around

The Old Town is well served by metro lines 1, 3, and 4. Jaume I metro station is in the heart of the Barri Gòtic, and many buses pass through the Plaça de Catalunya on the edge of the district. Metro line 5 takes you to the Sagrada Família, a long walk from other sights. Set atop a steep hill, most of Montjuïc's attractions can be reached by buses 13, 50, and 150 from the Plaça d'Espanya, or by funicular and cable car from Metro Paral·lel.

Street by Street: Barri Gòtic

The Barri Gòtic (Gothic Quarter) is the true heart of Barcelona. This site was chosen by the Romans in the reign of Augustus (27 BC–AD 14) to found a new *colonia* (town), and has been the location of the city's administrative buildings ever since. The Roman forum was on the Plaça de Sant Jaume, where the medieval Palau de la Generalitat, Catalonia's parliament, and the Casa de la Ciutat, the town hall, now stand. Nearby are the Gothic cathedral and royal palace, where Columbus was received by the Catholic Monarchs on his return from the New World in 1492.

The Casa de l'Ardiaca (Archdeacon's House), a Gothic-Renaissance building on the Roman city wall, now houses Barcelona's historical archives.

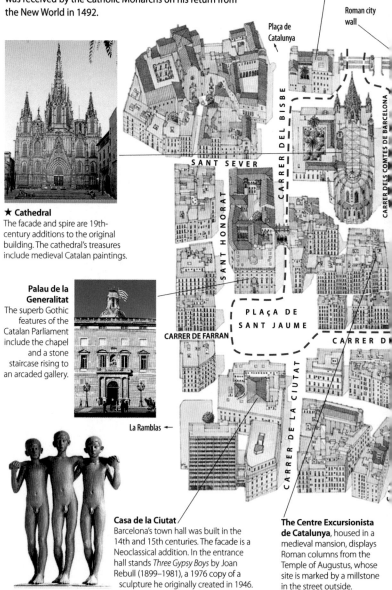

Roman city wall

Plaça de Catalunya

CARRER DEL BISBE

CARRER DELS COMTES DE BARCELONA

SANT SEVER

SANT HONORAT

PLAÇA DE SANT JAUME

CARRER DE FARRAN

CARRER D

CARRER DE LA CIUTAT

★ **Cathedral**
The facade and spire are 19th-century additions to the original building. The cathedral's treasures include medieval Catalan paintings.

Palau de la Generalitat
The superb Gothic features of the Catalan Parliament include the chapel and a stone staircase rising to an arcaded gallery.

La Ramblas ←

Casa de la Ciutat
Barcelona's town hall was built in the 14th and 15th centuries. The facade is a Neoclassical addition. In the entrance hall stands *Three Gypsy Boys* by Joan Rebull (1899–1981), a 1976 copy of a sculpture he originally created in 1946.

The Centre Excursionista de Catalunya, housed in a medieval mansion, displays Roman columns from the Temple of Augustus, whose site is marked by a millstone in the street outside.

Museu Frederic Marès

This medieval doorway is from an extensive display of Spanish sculpture – the mainstay of this museum's extraordinarily eclectic and high-quality collections.

★ **Conjunt Monumental de la Plaça del Rei**

The 14th-century Capella Reial de Santa Àgata, with its 1466 altarpiece, is one of the best-preserved sections of the palace.

Capella Reial de Santa Àgata

Plaça del Rei

Palau del Lloctinent

VIA LAIETANA

M
Jaume I

Museu d'Història de la Ciutat – Conjunt Monumental de la Plaça del Rei

Housed in a 14th-century mansion are the most extensive subterranean Roman ruins in the world. Visitors can see the streets of Roman Barcelona and an exhibition on the city's 13th- and 14th-century growth.

SOTS – TINENT NAVARRO

Key

— Suggested route

| 0 meters | 100 |
| 0 yards | 100 |

① Barcelona Cathedral

Plaça de la Seu. **Tel** 93-342 82 62. Ⓜ Jaume I. 🚌 17, V17, 45. **Open** 8am–7:30pm daily. 🎵 (lunchtime). 📷 ♿

Begun in 1298 under Jaime II on the foundations of a site dating back to Visigothic times, this compact Gothic cathedral was not finished until the late 19th century. The interior has beautiful Gothic cloisters and carved 15th-century choir stalls with painted coats of arms. Beneath the main altar, the crypt houses the sarcophagus of St. Eulalia, martyred in the 4th century AD. The nave has 28 side chapels, and a vaulted ceiling that rises to 26 m (85 ft).

The wide Catalan Gothic nave of Barcelona Cathedral

② Museu d'Història de la Ciutat – Conjunt Monumental de la Plaça del Rei

Plaça del Rei. **Tel** 93-256 21 00. Ⓜ Jaume I. **Open** 10am–7pm Tue–Sat, 10am–8pm Sun. **Closed** Jan 1, May 1, Jun 24, Dec 25. 🎵 (free first Sun of month & from 3pm every Sun). 📷 by appt.

The Royal Palace, founded in the 13th century, was the residence of the count-kings of Barcelona. The complex includes the Gothic Saló del Tinell and the Capella de Santa Àgata, with a painted-wood ceiling by Jaume Huguet. Entire streets of old Barcino are accessible via walkways suspended over the ruins.

For keys to symbols *see back flap*

③ Las Ramblas

Ⓜ Drassanes, Liceu, Catalunya.

Busy around the clock, this is one of the most famous streets in Spain. A stroll down its tree-shaded, central walkway to the seafront, taking in the mansions, shops, and cafés, makes a perfect introduction to Barcelona life.

The name (Les Rambles in Catalan) comes from the Arabic *ramla*, meaning the dried-up bed of a seasonal river. Barcelona's 13th-century city wall followed the left bank of one such river. During the 16th century, convents, monasteries, and a university were built on the opposite bank. Later demolished, they have left their legacy in the names of the five sections of the street. Today, Las Ramblas is thronged by street vendors, tarot readers, musicians, and mime artists.

Among its many famous buildings is the **Palau Güell**, a Neo-Gothic mansion that established the international reputation of Catalan architect Antoni Gaudí for outstanding, original architecture. Built in

The Gothic interior of the Basílica de Santa Maria del Mar

1889, this fascinating work of art is located on a narrow street just off Las Ramblas. Nearby, the **Gran Teatre del Liceu**, the city's fine opera house, has been restored twice after fires in 1861 and 1994. Further along is the huge **Mercat de Sant Josep**, a colorful food market popularly known as "La Boqueria."

On the opposite side of Las Ramblas, midway between the Drassanes and Liceu metro stations, the **Plaça Reial** is

Barcelona's liveliest square and dates from the 1850s. Also worth visiting, the **Museu de Cera** (wax-work museum) is housed in an atmospheric 19th-century building, and holds around 300 exhibits.

🏛 **Palau Güell**
Carrer Nou de la Rambla 3–5.
Tel 93-472 57 75. Ⓜ Drassanes, Liceu.
Open 10am–8pm Tue–Sun (Nov–Mar: to 5:30pm). 🎟 (free from 5pm Sun; Nov–Mar: 1st Sun of month). 🎫 ♿

④ Basílica de Santa Maria del Mar

Plaza Sta. Maria 1. **Tel** 93-310 23 90.
Ⓜ Jaume I. **Open** 9am–1:30pm, 4:30–8pm daily (from 10am Sun).

This beautiful building, the city's favorite church, has superb acoustics for concerts. It is also the only surviving example of an entirely Catalan Gothic-style church.

The church took just 55 years to build. The speed of its construction – unrivaled in the Middle Ages – gave it a unity of style both inside and out. The west front has a 15th-century rose window of the Coronation of the Virgin. More stained glass, dating from the 15th to the 18th centuries, lights the wide nave and high aisles.

The choir and furnishings were destroyed during the Spanish Civil War (1936–9), which only serves to enhance the sense of space and simplicity.

Monument to Columbus at the southern end of the tree-lined Ramblas

⑤ Museu Picasso

Carrer Montcada 15–23. **Tel** 93-256 30 00. Ⓜ Jaume I. **Open** 9am–7pm Tue–Sun (to 9:30pm Thu). **Closed** Jan 1, May 1, Jun 24, Dec 25 & 26. 🎟 (free Sun pm & first Sun of month). 🛍 ♿
Ⓦ **museupicasso.bcn.es**

One of Barcelona's most popular attractions, the Picasso Museum is housed in five adjoining palaces on the Carrer Montcada. It was founded in 1963, displaying works donated by Jaime Sabartes, a great friend of Picasso. Later, Picasso himself donated paintings, including some graphic works left in his will. Several ceramic pieces were given to the museum by his widow, Jacqueline.

The strength of the 3,000-piece collection is Picasso's early drawings and paintings, such as *The First Communion* (1896), produced when he was still an adolescent. The most famous work on show is the series *Las Meninas*, based on Velázquez's 1656 masterpiece *(see p280)*.

Yachts in the marina at the Port Olímpic, overlooked by skyscrapers

⑥ Vila Olímpica

Ⓜ Ciutadella-Vila Olímpica.

The most dramatic rebuilding for the 1992 Olympics was the demolition of the old industrial waterfront and the laying out of 4 km (2 miles) of promenade and pristine sandy beaches. Suddenly Barcelona seemed

The rippled facade of Gaudí's Casa Milà "La Pedrera" in the Quadrat d'Or

like a seaside resort, with a new estate of 2,000 apartments and parks called Nova Icària. The area is still popularly known as the Vila Olímpica because the buildings once housed Olympic athletes.

On the seafront there are twin 44-floor towers – Spain's tallest skyscrapers. They stand beside the Port Olímpic, also built for the Olympics. Two levels of restaurants, stores, and nightclubs around the marina attract business people at lunchtimes and pleasure seekers at weekends.

⑦ Sagrada Família

See pp302–3.

⑧ Quadrat d'Or

Ⓜ Diagonal, Passeig de Gracia.

Called the "Golden Square" because it contains so many of the city's best Modernista buildings, the Quadrat d'Or is made up of around a hundred city blocks centering on the Passeig de Gràcia. The wealthy bourgeoisie, who favored this area of the Eixample, embraced the new artistic and architectural style, both

for their homes and offices. Many interiors are open to the public, revealing a feast of stained glass, ceramics, and ironwork.

The most remarkable single block is the **Illa de la Discòrdia**, where four of Barcelona's most famous Modernista houses – all built between 1900 and 1910 – vie for attention. Nearby, the late 19th-century **Fundació Tàpies**, by Domènech i Montaner, houses paintings, sculptures, and graphics, and is topped by Tàpies' wire sculpture, *Cloud and Chair*.

Gaudí's famous **Casa Milà "La Pedrera"** has a wave-like facade and a roofscape of chimneys and vents resembling abstract sculptures. The Palau Baró de Quadras, designed by Puig i Cadalfalch in 1904, now houses offices and is closed to the public.

Carving of a coiled beast on the doorway of the Casa Asia, Quadrat d'Or

⑦ Sagrada Família

Europe's most unconventional church, the Temple Expiatori de la Sagrada Família is an emblem of a city that likes to think of itself as individualistic. Full of symbolism inspired by nature and striving for originality, it is the greatest work of Catalan architect Antoni Gaudí (1852–1926). In 1883, a year after work began on a Neo-Gothic church on the site, he was given the task of completing it. Gaudí changed everything, extemporizing as he went along. It became his life's work and he lived like a recluse on the site for the last few years of his life. He is buried in the crypt. By the time of his death, only one tower on the Nativity facade had been completed, but several more have since been finished to his original plans. After the Civil War, work resumed and continues today, financed by public subscription.

Bell Towers
Eight of the 12 spires, one for each apostle, have been built. Each is topped by Venetian mosaics.

The Finished Church

Gaudí's initial ambitions have been scaled down over the years, but the design for the building's completion remains impressive. Still to come is the central tower, which is to be encircled by four large towers representing the Evangelists. Four towers on the Glory (south) facade will match the existing four on the Passion (west) and four on the Nativity (east) facades. An ambulatory – like an inside-out cloister – will run round the outside of the building.

Entrance to Crypt

Main entrance

★ Passion Facade
This bleak facade was completed from 1986 to 2000 by artist Josep Maria Subirachs. A controversial work, its sculpted figures are angular and often sinister.

Spiral Staircases
The stone steps pictured are not open to the public, but there is an elevator instead. There are majestic views from the towers and upper galleries.

VISITORS' CHECKLIST

Practical Information
Calle Mallorca 401.
Tel 93-208 04 14.
w sagradafamilia.org
Open 9am–8pm (Oct–Mar: to 6pm). **Closed** Jan 1 & 6, Dec 25 & 26 (from 2pm). ✝ 9am, 8:15pm Mon–Sat, 9am, 10:30am, 11:45am, 1pm, 8:15pm Sun. 🔊 📷 ♿ to ground floor.

Transport
Ⓜ Sagrada Família. 🚌 19, 33, 34, 50, 51, 54.

★ Nativity Facade
The most complete part of Gaudí's church has doorways representing Faith, Hope, and Charity. Scenes of the Nativity and Christ's childhood contain imagery, such as doves, which symbolize the congregation.

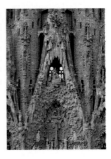

★ Crypt
The crypt, where Gaudí is buried and services are currently held, was begun by the original architect, Francesc de Paula Villar i Lozano, in 1882. A small museum traces the careers of both architects and the church's complicated history.

Nave
In the nave, a forest of fluted pillars support five galleries above the side aisles, while skylights let in natural light.

KEY

① **The apse** was the first part of the church Gaudí completed. Stairs lead down from here to the crypt below.

② **The altar canopy**, designed by Gaudí, is still waiting for the altar.

③ ④ **Tower with elevator**

Pretty whitewashed houses in Poble Espanyol, Montjuïc

⑨ Montjuïc

Ⓜ Espanya, Poble Sec, Paral·lel.
🚌 13, 50, 150 from Plaça Espanya.

The hill of Montjuic, rising to 213 m (699 ft) above the commercial port on the south side of the city, is Barcelona's biggest recreation area. Its museums, art galleries, amusement park, and nightclubs make it popular night and day. The hill is also a spectacular vantage point from which to view the city.

There was probably a Celt-Iberian settlement here before the Romans built a temple to Jupiter on their Mons Jovis, which may have given Montjuïc its name. Another theory suggests that a Jewish cemetery on the hill inspired the name Mount of the Jews. Many buildings were erected in 1929, for an International Exhibition, and later for the 1992 Olympics. On the western edge is the **Poble Espanyol** – a "village" of streets and squares, created in 1929 to showcase Spanish architectural styles. The **Museu Arqueològic** holds finds from prehistoric cultures in Catalonia and the Balearic Islands. The **Museu Etnològic** houses artifacts from Oceania, Africa, Asia, and Latin America.

The summit of Montjuïc is occupied by the huge 18th-century **Castell de Montjuïc**, built for the Bourbon family. The castle is being converted into an International Peace Center, with exhibitions on the history of the castle and the Montjuïc Mountain. Renovations will last until 2016.

🏰 Castell de Montjuïc
Parc de Montjuïc. **Tel** 93-256 44 45.
Ⓜ Paral·lel, then funicular & cable car.
Open daily. **Closed** Jan 1, Good Fri, May 1, Dec 25 & 26.

🏛 Museu Arqueològic
Passeig Santa Madrona 39. **Tel** 93-423 21 49. Ⓜ Espanya, Poble Sec. **Open** Tue–Sat, Sun am & public hols. **Closed** Jan 1, Dec 25 & 26. 🎟 ♿ 🖥 mac.es

⑩ Fundació Joan Miró

Parc de Montjuïc. **Tel** 93-443 94 70.
Ⓜ Espanya or Paral·lel, then bus 55 or 150. **Open** Tue–Sat, Sun am & public hols. **Closed** Jan 1, Dec 25 & 26. 🎟 ♿ 🖥 fundaciomiro-bcn.org

Housed in a boldly modern building designed in 1975 by Josep Lluís Sert, this collection of paintings, sculptures, and tapestries by Catalan artist Joan Miró (1893–1983) is lit by natural light.

An admirer of primitive Catalan art and Gaudí's Modernism, Miró developed a Surrealistic style, with vivid colors and fantastical forms that suggested dreamlike situations. Miró himself donated the works displayed here. Some of the best pieces at the museum include his *Barcelona Series* (1939–44), a set of 50 black-and-white lithographs. Temporary exhibitions of other artists' work are also held here.

The Palau Nacional, home of the Museu Nacional d'Art de Catalunya

⑪ Museu Nacional d'Art de Catalunya

Palau Nacional, Parc de Montjuïc. **Tel** 93-622 03 76. Ⓜ Espanya. **Open** Tue–Sat, Sun am & public hols. **Closed** Jan 1, May 1, Dec 25. 🎟 📷 call 93-622 03 75 in advance. ♿

Originally built for the 1929 International Exhibition, since 1934 the austere Palau Nacional (National Palace) has been used to house the city's most important art collection.

The museum contains one of the greatest displays of Romanesque art in the world, its centerpiece being a series of magnificent 12th-century frescoes. These have been peeled from Catalan Pyrenean churches (to save them from the ravages of pollution and time) and pasted on to replicas of the original vaulted ceilings and apses they adorned.

A section of the 18th-century castle on the summit of Montjuïc

The most remarkable are the wall paintings from the churches of Santa Maria de Taüll and Sant Climent de Taüll in Vall de Boí.

The museum's superb Gothic collection covers the whole of Spain, but is particularly good on Catalonia. Several outstanding works by El Greco, Velázquez, and Zurbarán are on display in the Renaissance and Baroque section.

⑫ Parc Güell

Carrer d'Olot. **Tel** 902-200 302.
Ⓜ Lesseps. **Open** daily. 🅿 🚻 ♿
Casa-Museu Gaudí: **Tel** 93-219 38 11.
Open daily. **Closed** Jan 1 & 6, Dec 25 & 26 (am). 🅿

Designated a World Heritage site by UNESCO, the Parc Güell is Gaudí's most colorful creation. He was commissioned in the 1890s by Count Eusebi Güell to design a garden city on 20 hectares (50 acres) of family estate. Little of Gaudí's grand plan for decorative buildings among landscaped gardens became reality. What we see today was completed between 1910 and 1914.

Most atmospheric is the Room of a Hundred Columns, a cavernous covered hall of 84 crooked pillars, which is brightened by glass and ceramic mosaics. Above it, reached by a flight of steps flanked by ceramic animals, is the Gran Plaça Circular –

Mosaic-encrusted chimney by Gaudí at the entrance of Parc Güell

an open space with a snaking balcony of colored mosaics, said to have the longest bench in the world. It was executed by Josep Jujol, one of Gaudí's chief collaborators.

The two mosaic-decorated pavilions at the entrance are by Gaudí, but the **Casa-Museu Gaudí**, a gingerbread-style house where he lived from 1906–26, was built by Francesc Berenguer. The drawings and furniture inside are all by Gaudí.

⑬ Tibidabo

Plaça del Tibidabo 3–4. **Tel** 93-211 79 42. Ⓜ Av Tibidabo, then Tramvia Blau & funicular, or TibiBus from Plaça Catalunya. Amusement Park: **Open** call to check. **Closed** Oct–Apr: Mon–Fri. ♿ Temple del Sagrat Cor: **Tel** 93-417 56 86. **Open** daily.
ⓦ tibidabo.cat

The heights of Tibidabo are reached by Barcelona's last surviving tram, the Tramvia Blau,

and a funicular railway. The name, inspired by Tibidabo's views of the city, comes from the Latin *tibi dabo* (I shall give you) – a reference to the Temptation of Christ, who was taken up a mountain by Satan and offered the world.

The popular amusement park at **Parc d'Atraccions** first opened in 1908. The rides were completely renovated in the 1980s. While the old ones retain their charm, the newer ones provide the latest in vertiginous experiences. Their hilltop location at 517 m (1,696 ft) adds to the thrill. Also in the park is the **Museu d'Automates**, which displays automated toys, jukeboxes, and gaming machines.

Tibidabo is crowned by the **Temple Expiatori del Sagrat Cor** (Church of the Sacred Heart), built with religious zeal but little taste by Enric Sagnier between 1902 and 1911. Inside, an elevator takes you up to an enormous statue of Christ.

An ornate merry-go-round at the Parc d'Atraccions, Tibidabo

⑲ Monestir de Montserrat

Its highest peak rising to 1,236 m (4,055 ft), the "Serrated Mountain" *(mont serrat)* is a magnificent setting for Catalonia's holiest place, the Monastery of Montserrat, which is surrounded by chapels and hermits' caves. The earliest record of a chapel on this site is from the 9th century. The monastery was founded in the 11th century. In 1811, when the French attacked Catalonia in the War of Independence, the monastery was destroyed and the monks killed. Rebuilt and repopulated in 1844, it was a beacon of Catalan culture in the Franco years. Today, Benedictine monks live here. Visitors can hear the famous male choir singing the *Salve Regina* and the *Virolai* (the Montserrat hymn) at 1pm Monday to Saturday, noon and 6:45pm Sunday (except in July and August), and from December 26 to January 8.

Plaça de Santa Maria
The focal points of the square are two wings of the Gothic cloister built in 1476. The modern monastery facade is by Françesc Folguera.

The Way of the Cross
This path passes 11 statues representing the Stations of the Cross. It begins near the Plaça de l'Abat Oliba.

View of Montserrat
The complex includes cafés and a hotel. A second funicular railway takes visitors to nature trails above the monastery.

★ **Basilica Facade**
Agapit Vallmitjana sculpted Christ and the apostles on the basilica's Neo-Renaissance facade. It was built in 1900 to replace the Renaissance facade of the original church, consecrated in 1592.

★ **Black Virgin**
La Moreneta looks down from behind the altar, protected behind glass. Her wooden orb protrudes for pilgrims to touch.

VISITORS' CHECKLIST

Practical Information
Montserrat (Barcelona province).
Tel 93-877 77 77.
🌐 **abadiamontserrat.net**
Basilica: **Open** 7am–8pm Mon–Thu; 7am–8:15pm Sat, Sun & Aug. 🕆 from 9am Mon–Sat, from 9:30am Sun & religious hols. 📷 Museum: **Open** 10am–5:45pm Mon–Fri, 10am–6:45pm Sat & Sun. 📷 📷 ♿

Transport
🚆 to Aeri de Montserrat (from Barcelona via Monistrol), then cable car. 🚌 from Barcelona.

Basilica Interior
The sanctuary in the domed basilica is adorned by a richly enameled altar and paintings by Catalan artists.

KEY

① **Funicular to the holy site of Santa Cova**

② **Information Office**

③ **The Museum** holds 19th- and 20th-century Catalan paintings and many archaeological exhibits from West Asia.

④ **Gothic cloister**

⑤ **The Inner Courtyard** has a baptistry (1958), with sculptures by Charles Collet. Pilgrims may approach the Virgin through a door to the right.

⑥ **The rack railroad** follows the course of a historic railroad line built in 1880.

⑦ **Terminal for cable car from Aeri de Montserrat train station**

The Virgin of Montserrat

The small wooden statue of La Moreneta ("the dark one") is the soul of Montserrat. It is said to have been made by St. Luke and brought here by St. Peter in AD 50. Centuries later, the statue is believed to have been hidden from the Moors in the nearby Santa Cova (Holy Cave). Carbon dating suggests, however, that the statue was carved around the 12th century. In 1881, Montserrat's Black Virgin became patroness of Catalonia.

The Black Virgin of Montserrat

Eastern Spain and the Balearic Islands

Eastern Spain covers an extraordinary range of climates and landscapes, from the snowbound peaks of the Pyrenees in Aragón to the beaches of the Costa Blanca. The region has many historical sights, including the striking Mudéjar churches of Zaragoza and the great cathedral of Valencia. The coastal resorts of Eastern Spain are a popular destination, as are the Balearic Islands. Mallorca is the most culturally rich of the islands, while Menorca is dotted with prehistoric sites. Ibiza is chiefly known for its exuberant nightlife, but Formentera remains largely unspoiled. A dialect of the Catalan language, brought by 13th-century settlers, is still widely spoken on the islands.

Cupolas of the Basílica de Nuestra Señora del Pilar in Zaragoza

❷ Zaragoza

Zaragoza. 🚹 675,000. ✈ 🚊 🚌
ℹ Plaza del Pilar (902-14 20 08).
🛒 Wed, Sun.

The Roman settlement of Caesaraugusta gave Zaragoza its name. Located on the fertile banks of the Río Ebro, it grew to become Spain's fifth-largest city, and the capital of Aragón.

Badly damaged during the early 19th-century War of Independence, the old center nevertheless retains several fine monuments. Overlooking the vast Plaza del Pilar is the **Basílica de Nuestra Señora del Pilar**. With its 11 brightly tiled cupolas, it is one of the city's most impressive sights.

Also on the square are the Gothic-Plateresque **Lonja** (commodities exchange), the **Palacio Episcopal**, and Zaragoza's cathedral, **La Seo**, which displays a great mix of styles. Part of the exterior is faced with typical Mudéjar brick and ceramic decoration, while inside are a fine Gothic reredos and splendid Flemish tapestries. Nearby is the flamboyant Mudéjar bell tower of the **Iglesia de la Magdalena**, and remains of the Roman forum.

Parts of the Roman walls can be seen on the opposite side of the Plaza del Pilar near the **Mercado de Lanuza**, a market with sinuous iron-work in Art Nouveau style. The **Museo Camón Aznar** houses the eclectic collection of an art historian, whose special interest was the locally born artist Goya.

The **Alfajería**, a beautiful 11th-century Moorish palace with gardens and a mosque, lies on the main road to Bilbao.

🏛 **Museo Camón Aznar**
Calle Espoz y Mina 23. **Tel** 976-39 73 87. **Open** Tue–Sun. ♿

❷ Valencia

Valencia. 🚹 810,000. ✈ 8 km (5 miles) SW. 🚊 🚌 🚌 ℹ Plaza de la Reina 19 (963-15 39 31). 🎉 Las Fallas (Mar 15–19). 🌐 **turisvalencia.es**

Valencia, Spain's third-largest city, is famous for its ceramics, and for the spectacular fiesta of Las Fallas, marked by the erection and burning of elaborate papier-mâché monuments (*fallas*).

Among the city's finest buildings are **La Lonja**, an exquisite Late Gothic hall built between 1482 and 1498, and the **cathedral** (1262) on Plaza de la Reina. Other monuments worth visiting include the Gothic **Palau de la Generalitat**, with its splendidly decorated first-floor chambers, and the 17th-century **Basílica de la Virgen de los Desamparados**.

Beyond the city center is the **Torres de Serranos** gateway, erected in 1391.

Valencia has a number of fine museums. The **Museo de Bellas Artes** holds 2,000 paintings and statues dating from antiquity to the 19th century, including six paintings by Goya, while the **Museo Domingo Fletcher** has a unique collection of local Stone Age engravings. Valencia's metro system takes tourists to the extensive beaches of El Cabañal and La Malvarrosa, east of the city.

🏛 **La Lonja**
Plaza del Mercado s/n. **Tel** 96-352 54 78 (ext. 4153). **Open** daily. ♿

Effigy burning in Valencia during the annual fiesta of Las Fallas

The mountain village of Castell de Guadalest, Costa Blanca

🏛 Palau de la Generalitat
Calle Caballeros 2. **Tel** 96-386 34 61.
Open by prior appointment only.

🏛 Museo de Bellas Artes
Calle San Pio V 9. **Tel** 96-387 03 00.
Open 11am–5pm Mon, 10am–7pm Tue–Sun. **Closed** Jan 1, Good Friday, Dec 25. 🎫 ♿

㉔ Costa Blanca

✈ 🚢 🚗 🚌 Alicante. ℹ Calle Portugal 17, Alicante (96-592 98 02).
🌐 comunidadvalenciana.com

The Costa Blanca occupies a prime stretch of Mediterranean coastline. The main city, **Alicante** (Alacant), has an 18th-century Baroque town hall and a 16th-century castle, the Castillo de Santa Bárbara. The nearest beach to the city center is the popular Postiguet; slightly farther afield are the vast beaches of La Albufereta and Sant Joan.

The massive, rocky outcrop of the **Penyal d'Ifach** towers over Calp harbor, and is one of the Costa Blanca's most dramatic sights. Its summit offers spectacular views. A short drive inland, **Castell de Guadalest** is a pretty mountain village with castle ruins and a distinctive belfry perched precariously on top of a rock.

Also worth visiting are the whitewashed hilltop town of **Altea**, **Denia**, which has good snorkeling, and the cliffs and coves around **Xabia**. South of Alicante, **Guardamar del Segura** has a quiet beach bordered by pine woods, while **Torrevieja** is a highly developed resort with sweeping, sandy shores.

㉕ Mallorca and the Balearic Islands

✈ 🚢 🚌 Palma, Mallorca; Maó, Menorca. ℹ Passeig des Born 27, Palma, Mallorca (902-10 23 65).

The largest of the Balearic islands, Mallorca has a varied landscape and a rich cultural heritage. A massive Gothic cathedral is poised high on the sea wall of **Palma**, its capital. Completed in 1587 and known locally as Sa Seu, the cathedral is one of Spain's most breathtaking buildings. The interior was remodeled by Antoni Gaudí and a highlight is the Baldachino, his bizarre wrought-iron canopy above the altar.

Also worth visiting in Palma are the Basílica de Sant Francesc, the Moorish Palau de l'Almudaina, and the Fundació Pilar i Joan Miró – a stunning modern building housing Miró's studio and a collection of the artist's work.

Around the island, **Andratx** is a chic and affluent town with yachts moored along its harbor, while **Pollença** is a popular tourist resort which has remained relatively unspoiled. The 18th-century family home

La Granja, and **Alfàbia**, which exudes a Moorish atmosphere, are aristocratic estates open to the public. The **Monasteri de Lluc**, in the remote mountain village of the same name, incorporates a guesthouse, a museum, and a church.

Menorca
Menorca's capital, **Maó**, has one of the finest harbors in the Mediterranean, an 18th-century Carmelite church, and a museum – the Collecció Hernández Mora – housing Menorcan art and antiques. The town of **Ciutadella** boasts an impressive main square and a delightful Art Nouveau market. Menorca's many Bronze Age villages – to which there is usually free access – are mostly the work of the "talaiotic" people, who lived from 2000–1000 BC.

Ibiza and Formentera
A popular package-tour destination, Ibiza has some of the wildest nightclubs in Europe. An hour's boat ride from Ibiza harbor are the tranquil shores of Formentera. The capital, **Sant Francesc**, has a pretty 18th-century church and a folk museum.

View across the marina to the spectacular cathedral, Palma, Mallorca,

Southern Spain

One large region – Andalusia – extends across the south of Spain. It was here that the Moors lingered longest and left their greatest monuments in the cities of Granada, Córdoba, Málaga, and Seville. The eight southern provinces span a wide range of landscapes, with deserts in the east, sandy beaches along the Costa del Sol, and sherry-producing vineyards around Jerez. From flamingoes in the wetland Doñana National Park to flamenco – the uniquely Andalusian art form – the region has something to interest every visitor.

Antonio Palamino's cupola in the Monasterio de la Cartuja, Granada

🏛 Granada

Granada. 🏙 239,000. ✈ 12 km (7 miles) SW. 🚉 🚌 ℹ Plaza Mariana Pineda (958-24 71 28). 🎭 Corpus Christi (May–Jun). 🌐 turismodegranada.org

The ancient city of Granada, founded by the Iberians, was for 250 years the capital of a Moorish kingdom. The Nasrid dynasty, who ruled from 1238 until 1492, when Granada fell to the Catholic Monarchs, left some outstanding examples of Moorish architecture here. The greatest legacy of their rule is the spectacular palace complex of the Alhambra *(see pp312–13)*. Under the Nasrids, the city enjoyed a golden age, acquiring an international reputation as a major cultural center. Later, under Christian rule, the city became a focus for the Renaissance.

Granada's 16th-century Gothic **cathedral** has a Renaissance facade and a Baroque west front. Nearby, the **Capilla Real** (Royal Chapel), built between 1505 and 1507,

houses Carrara marble figures of the Catholic Monarchs, whose bodies lie in the crypt. Equally impressive are the **Museo Casa de los Tiros**, a fortress-like palace built in Mudéjar style, and the **Monasterio de la Cartuja**, both dating from the 16th century. Founded by a Christian warrior, the latter has a dazzling cupola by Antonio Palomino.

Relics of the Moorish era in the old town include the **Corral del Carbón**, a former storehouse and inn for merchants, and the **Palacio de la Madraza**. Originally an Arab university, the palace has a splendid Moorish hall with a finely decorated *mihrab* (prayer niche). The palace holds temporary art exhibitions.

Granada's Moorish ancestry is most evident in the hillside Albaicín district, which faces the Alhambra. Along its cobbled alleys stand *cármenes* – villas with Moorish decor and gardens – and **El Bañuelo**, the 11th-century brick-vaulted Arab baths. The churches here were mostly built on the sites of mosques. The most beautiful

of these, the **Iglesia de Santa Ana**, has an elegant Plateresque portal. The **Real Chancillería**, or Royal Chancery (1530), boasts a beautiful Renaissance facade.

Also worth visiting in the Albaicín district is the **Museo Arqueológico**, with Iberian, Phoenician, and Roman finds.

From one end of the district, a road leads up to **Sacromonte**. Granada's gypsies once lived in the caves lining this hillside. Their legacy lives on in the flamenco shows performed here in the evenings.

From the northern side of the Alhambra, a footpath leads to the **Generalife** *(see pp312–13)*, the country estate of the Nasrid kings. The gardens, begun in the 13th century, originally contained orchards and pastures. Today, their lush greenery, pools, and graceful water fountains provide a magical setting for the many events staged each year between mid-June and early July on the occasion of the city's international music and dance festival.

🏛 **Museo Casa de los Tiros**
Calle Pavaneras 19. **Tel** 958-57 54 66. **Open** Tue–Sun. **Closed** main public hols. 🔖 ♿

🏛 **Palacio de la Madraza**
Calle Oficios 14. **Tel** 958-24 34 84. **Open** 10:30am–1pm & 3:30–6:30pm Mon–Sat, 11am–1pm Sun.

🏛 **Museo Arqueológico**
Carrera del Darro 43. **Tel** 958-57 54 08. **Closed** for renovations.

Entrance to the Moorish *mihrab* in the Palacio de la Madraza, Granada

The main facade of Málaga's unusual cathedral, consecrated in 1588

㉗ Málaga

Málaga. 🚹 570,000. ✈ 🚢 🚍 🚏 🚌
ℹ Avda. Cervantes 1 (95-220 96 03).

Málaga, the second-largest city in Andalusia, was a thriving port under Phoenician, Roman, and Moorish rule. It also flourished during the 19th century, when sweet Málaga wine was one of Europe's most popular drinks. At the heart of the old town is the **cathedral**, begun in 1528 by Diego de Siloé. The half-built second tower, abandoned in 1765 when funds ran out, gave the cathedral its nickname: La Manquita ("the one-armed one").

The **Casa Natal de Picasso**, where the painter spent his early years, is now the headquarters of the international Picasso Foundation, while Málaga's **Museo de Bellas Artes** is housed in the Palacio de la Aduana.

The city's vast fortress – the **Alcazaba** – was built between the 8th and 11th centuries. Its major attractions are the display of Phoenician, Roman, and Moorish artifacts, as well as a Roman theater. The ruined **Castillo de Gibralfaro**, a 14th-century Moorish castle, lies behind the Alcazaba.

🏛 Museo de Bellas Artes
Plaza Aduana. **Tel** 95-222 47 31.
Open call in advance of your visit.
🌐 museosdeandalucia.es

🏰 Alcazaba
Calle Alcazabilla. **Tel** 95-222 72 30.
Open 9am–8pm daily.

㉘ Costa del Sol

✈ 🚢 🚍 🚌 Málaga. ℹ Avda
Cervantes 1, Málaga (95-220 96 03).

With its year-round sunshine and varied coastline, the Costa del Sol attracts crowds of vacationers every year and also has half a million foreign residents.

Its most stylish resort is **Marbella**, frequented by royalty and film stars, who spend their summers here in the smart villas or luxury hotels overlooking the area's 28 beaches. Puerto Banús is its ostentatious marina. In winter, the major attraction is golf: 30 of Europe's finest golf courses lie just inland.

Among the highlights of Marbella's old town is the Museo de Grabado Contemporáneo, which displays some of Picasso's least-known work, the peaceful Iglesia de Nuestra Señora de la Encarnación, and the town hall, with its exquisite, panelled Mudéjar ceiling.

Sotogrande, to the west of Marbella, is an exclusive resort of luxury villas. The marina is fronted by good seafood restaurants. In spite of tourism, **Estepona** preserves its Spanish character, with pretty tree-filled squares and inexpensive tapas bars.

To the east are the package-holiday resorts of **Fuengirola** and **Torremolinos**. Once the brash haunt of young northern European tourists, they are now more family-oriented.

Player on a green at one of Marbella's high-profile golf courses

Moorish Spain

Typical Moorish *alcazaba*, dating from the 10th century

In the 8th century, the Iberian Peninsula came almost entirely under Moorish rule. The Muslim settlers called Spain "Al Andalus." A powerful caliphate was established in Córdoba, which became the center of one of the most brilliant civilizations of early-medieval Europe. The Moors erected *alcazabas* (castles built into city ramparts) and palaces surrounded by patios, pools, and gardens, making lavish use of arches, stucco work, glazed wall tiles (*azulejos*), and ornamental calligraphy. They also introduced new crops to Spain, such as oranges and rice. By the 11th century, the caliphate had collapsed into 30 *taifas* (splinter states) and the northern Christian kingdoms were reconquering parts of Moorish Spain. In 1492, the Catholic Monarchs took Granada, its last stronghold. Though many Muslims were expelled from Spain following the Reconquest, some were employed to build new churches and palaces for the Christian rulers. Known as Mudéjares (the name literally means "those permitted to stay"), these craftsmen developed a hybrid Christian-Islamic style that survived into the 18th century.

Granada: the Alhambra

A magical use of space, light, water, and decoration characterizes this most sensual piece of architecture. It was built under Ismail I, Yusuf I, and Muhammad V, caliphs when the Nasrid dynasty (1238– 1492) ruled Granada. Seeking to belie an image of waning power, they created their idea of paradise on earth. Modest materials were used (plaster, timber, and tiles), but they were superbly worked. Although the Alhambra suffered decay and pillage, including an attempt by Napoleon's troops to blow it up, it has been restored and its delicate craftsmanship still dazzles the eye.

★ **Salón de Embajadores**
The ceiling of this sumptuous throne room, built between 1334 and 1354, represents the seven heavens of the Muslim cosmos.

★ **Patio de Arrayanes**
This pool, set amid myrtle hedges and graceful arcades, reflects light into the surrounding halls.

Entrance

KEY

① **Patio de Machuca**

② **Patio del Mexuar** council chamber, was completed in 1365, and is where the reigning sultan listened to the petitions of his subjects and met with his ministers.

③ **Sala de la Barca**

④ **Washington Irving's apartments**

⑤ **Jardín de Lindaraja**

⑥ **Baños Reales**

⑦ **Sala de las Dos Hermanas**, with its spectacular honeycomb dome, is regarded as the ultimate example of Spanish Islamic architecture.

⑧ **Sala de los Reyes** is a great banqueting hall was used to hold extravagant parties and

sumptuous feasts. Beautiful ceiling paintings on leather, from the 14th century, depict tales of hunting and chivalry.

⑨ **Puerta de la Rawda**

⑩ **The Palace of Charles V** (1526) houses a collection of Spanish Islamic art, whose highlight is the Alhambra vase.

Palacio del Partal
A pavilion with an arched portico and a tower is all that remains of this palace, the oldest building in the Alhambra.

VISITORS' CHECKLIST

Practical Information
For the Alhambra and Generalife.
Tel 902-88 80 01. **Open** 8:30am–8pm daily (mid-Oct–mid-Mar: to 6pm). Night visits: mid-Mar–mid-Oct: 9–10:30pm Tue, Thu & Fri; 10–11:30pm Wed & Sat; mid-Oct–mid-Mar: 8–9:30pm Fri & Sat.
(reservations are essential).
alhambra-patronato.es or **alhambra-tickets.es**

Transport
2.

★ Sala de los Abencerrajes
This hall takes its name from a noble family – rivals of the last Nasrid ruler, Boabdil. Legend claims he had the family massacred while they attended a banquet here. The geometrical ceiling was inspired by Pythagoras' theorem.

★ Patio de los Leones
Built by Muhammad V, this patio is lined with arcades supported by 124 slender marble columns. At its center, a fountain rests on 12 stocky marble lions.

Plan of the Alhambra

To the Generalife

Main gate

The Alhambra complex includes the Casas Reales, the 13th-century Alcazaba, the 16th-century Palace of Charles V, and the Generalife *(see p310)*, which is located just off the map.

Key

■ Palacios Nazaríes (shown above)
■ Palace of Charles V
■ Alcazaba
■ Gardens
■ Iglesia de Santa María
■ Other buildings

The Puente Nuevo, spanning the deep Tajo gorge at Ronda

㉙ Ronda

Málaga. 🏘 37,000. 🚉 🚌 ℹ️ Plaza de España 9 (95-287 12 72).

Ronda sits on a massive rocky outcrop, straddling a precipitous limestone cleft. Because of its impregnable position, it was one of the last Moorish bastions, finally falling to the Christians in 1485.

On the south side perches a classic *pueblo blanco* – a white town – so-called because the houses are whitewashed in the Moorish tradition.

Among Ronda's historic buildings is the **Palacio Mondragón**, adorned with original Moorish mosaics. The facade of the 18th-century **Palacio del Marqués de Salvatierra** is decorated with images of South American Indians. From the **Casa del Rey Moro**, built on the site of a Moorish palace, 365 steps lead down to the river.

Across the **Puente Nuevo,** or "New Bridge," which spans the deep Tajo gorge, is the modern town, and the site of one of Spain's oldest bullrings. Inaugurated in 1785, the **Plaza**

de Toros and its bullfighting museum, the **Museo Taurino**, attract aficionados from all over the country.

🎭 Plaza de Toros & Museo Taurino
Calle Virgen de la Paz. **Tel** 952-87 41 32. **Open** daily. 🎟️ 🚻

㉚ Córdoba

Córdoba. 🏘 328,000. 🚉 🚌
ℹ️ Calle Campo Santo de los Mártires (in front of Alcázar (902-20 17 74).

With its glorious mosque and pretty Moorish patios, Córdoba is northern Andalusia's star attraction. In the 10th century, the city enjoyed a golden age as the western capital of the Islamic empire.

Córdoba's most impressive Moorish monument is the mighty Mezquita *(see pp316–17)*. To the west of its towering walls, the **Alcázar de los Reyes Cristianos**, in the old Jewish quarter, is a stunning 14th-century palace-fortress built by Alfonso XI. The Catholic Monarchs stayed here during

their campaign to wrest Granada from Moorish rule.

The small Mudéjar-style **synagogue** (c.1315) has decorative plasterwork with Hebrew script. Nearby, the **Museo Taurino**, a bullfighting museum, contains a replica of the tomb of Manolete, a famous matador, and the hide of the bull that killed him.

A Roman bridge spanning the Río Guadalquivir links the old town to the 14th-century **Torre de la Calahorra**. This defensive tower houses a small museum depicting life in 10th-century Córdoba.

In the newer part of the city, the **Museo Arqueológico** displays Roman and Moorish artifacts. The **Museo de Bellas Artes** contains sculptures by local artist Mateo Inurria (1867–1924) and paintings by Murillo and Zurbarán. Other notable buildings are the beautiful 17th-century **Palacio de Viana**, filled with works of art, and the handsome arcades of the **Plaza de la Corredera**.

🏰 Alcázar de los Reyes Cristianos
Calle Caballerizas Reales s/n. **Tel** 957-42 01 51. **Open** 8:30am–8pm Mon, 8:30am–8:45pm Tue–Fri, 8:30am–4:30pm Sat. **Closed** Jan 1, Dec 25. 🎟️ (free 8:30–9:30am Tue–Fri).

㉛ Seville

See pp318–21.

Water gardens at the Alcázar de los Reyes Cristianos, Córdoba

Marshes and sand dunes of the Parque Nacional de Doñana

㉜ Parque Nacional de Doñana

Huelva & Sevilla. 🛈 959-43 96 27. Park interior: **Open** summer: Mon–Sat; winter: Tue–Sun. **Tel** 959-43 04 32 for reservations.

Doñana National Park is ranked among Europe's greatest wetlands, comprising more than 74 hectares (185,000 acres) of marshes and sand dunes. The area, officially protected since 1969, was once a ducal hunting ground (coto).

A road runs through part of the park, with information points located along it. There are also several self-guided walks on the park outskirts, but the interior can be visited on official guided day tours only.

Doñana is home to wild cattle, fallow and red deer, and the lynx – one of Europe's rarest mammals. The greater flamingo and the rare imperial eagle can also be seen. It is also a stopping place for thousands of migratory birds.

㉝ Jerez de la Frontera

Cádiz. 🛉 209,000. ✈ 🚆 🚌
🛈 Alameda Cristina 7 (956-33 88 74).
🌐 turismojerez.com

Jerez is the capital of sherry production and many bodegas (cellars) can be visited here including **González Byass** and **Pedro Domecq**.

The city is also famous for its **Real Escuela Andaluza de Arte Ecuestre**, a school of equestrian skills. Public-dressage displays

are held on Thursdays. On the Plaza de San Juan, the 18th-century **Palacio de Penmartín** houses the Centro Andaluz de Flamenco, with exhibitions on this music and dance tradition. The 11th-century **Alcázar** encompasses a well-preserved mosque, now a church. Just to the north is the **cathedral**. Its most famous treasure is, *The Sleeping Girl* by Zurbarán.

🍷 Sherry Bodegas

González Byass: Calle Manuel María González 12, Jerez. **Tel** 956-35 70 00. 🅿 🛉 Pedro Domecq: Calle San Ildefonso 3, Jerez. **Tel** 956-15 15 00. **Open** Mon–Sat.

㉞ Cádiz

Cádiz. 🛉 126,000. 🚆 🚌 🛈 Paseo de Canalejas (956-24 10 01) or Avda Ramón de Carranza (956-28 56 01).

Surrounded almost entirely by water, Cádiz lays claim to being Europe's oldest city. After the Catholic reconquest, the city prospered on wealth brought from the New World.

Modern Cádiz is a busy port, with a pleasant waterfront, while the old town has narrow alleys and lively markets. The Baroque and Neoclassical **cathedral**, with its dome of golden-yellow tiles, is one of Spain's largest.

The **Museo de Cádiz** has one of the largest art collections in Andalusia, and arch-aeological exhibits chart the history of the city. The 18th-century **Oratorio de San Felipe Neri** has been a shrine to liberalism since 1812, when a provisional government assembled in the church to try to establish Spain's first constitutional monarchy. The **Torre Tavira**, an 18th-century watchtower, offers spectacular views of the city.

Golden chalice from the treasury of Cádiz cathedral

🏛 Museo de Cádiz

Plaza de Mina. **Tel** 956-20 33 68. **Open** Tue–Sun. **Closed** public hols.

Tapas

The light snacks known as tapas – and sometimes as *pinchos* – originated in Andalusia in the 19th century as an accompaniment to sherry. The name derives from a bartender's practice of covering a glass with a saucer, or *tapa* (cover), to keep out flies. The custom progressed to a chunk of cheese or a few olives placed on a platter to serve with a drink. Today tapas range from cold snacks to elaborately prepared hot dishes, generally eaten standing at the bar rather than sitting at a table. Almost every village in Spain has a tapas bar. In the larger towns, it is customary to move from bar to bar, sampling the specialties of each.

Olives

Jamón serrano (salt-cured ham)

Patatas bravas (potatoes in spicy tomato sauce)

Córdoba: the Mezquita

Córdoba's great mosque, dating back 12 centuries, embodied the power of Islam on the Iberian Peninsula. Abd al Rahman I built the original mosque between 785 and 787. The building evolved over the centuries, blending many architectural forms. In the 10th century, al Hakam II made some of the most lavish additions, including the elaborate *mihrab* (prayer niche) and the *maqsura* (caliph's enclosure). During the 16th century, a cathedral was built in the heart of the mosque, part of which was destroyed.

Patio de los Naranjos
Orange trees grow in the courtyard where the faithful washed before prayer.

KEY

① **The Puerta de San Esteban** is set in a section of wall from an earlier Visigothic church.

② **The Puerta del Perdón** is a Mudéjar-style entrance gate, built during Christian rule in 1377. Penitents were pardoned here.

③ **Torre del Alminar** is a bell tower, 93 m (305 ft) high, built on the site of the original minaret. Steep steps lead to the top for a fine view of the city.

④ **Capilla Mayor**

⑤ **The cathedral choir** has Churrigueresque – excessive Baroque-style – stalls carved by Pedro Duque Cornejo in 1758.

⑥ **Capilla Real**

Expansion of the Mezquita

Abd al Rahman I built the original mosque. Extensions were added by Abd al Rahman II, al Hakam II, and al Mansur.

Key to Additions

☐ Original mosque (785–787)

▦ Added by Abd al Rahman II (833)

▦ Added by al Hakam II (c.961)

☐ Added by al Mansur (c.987–90)

☐ Patio de los Naranjos

Cathedral
Part of the mosque was destroyed to accommodate the cathedral, begun in 1523. Featuring an Italianate dome, it was designed chiefly by members of the Hernán Ruiz family.

VISITORS' CHECKLIST

Practical Information
C/Cardenal Herrero 1. **Tel** 957 47 05 12. **Open** 10am–7pm Mon–Sat, 8:30–11:30am, 3–7pm Sun (winter: 8:30am–6pm Mon–Sat, 8:30–11:30am & 3–6pm Sun). 🚻 (free 8:30–9:30am Mon–Sat). 🛐 9:30am Mon–Sat, noon & 1:30pm Sun. ♿

★ Arches and Pillars
More than 850 columns of granite, jasper, and marble support the roof, creating a dazzling visual effect. Many were taken from Roman and Visigothic buildings.

★ Mihrab
This prayer niche, richly ornamented, held a gilded copy of the Koran. The worn flagstones indicate where pilgrims circled it seven times on their knees.

★ Capilla de Villaviciosa
The first Christian chapel was built in the mosque in 1371 by Mudéjar craftsmen (see p311). Its multi-lobed arches are stunning.

③ Street by Street: Seville

The maze of narrow streets that makes up the Barrio de Santa Cruz represents Seville at its most romantic and compact. This is a good place to begin an exploration of the city, since many of the best-known sights are located here. As well as the expected souvenir shops, tapas bars, and strolling guitarists, there are plenty of picturesque alleys, hidden plazas, and flower-decked patios to reward the casual wanderer. Once a Jewish ghetto, this area boasts many restored buildings, with characteristic window grilles that are now a harmonious mix of upscale residences and tourist accommodations. Good restaurants and bars make the area well worth an evening visit.

Plaza Virgen de los Reyes
This delightful square, which is often lined with horse-drawn carriages, has an early 20th-century fountain by José Lafita.

Palacio Arzobispal, the 18th-century Archbishop's Palace, is still used by Seville's clergy.

Bus station

★ Cathedral and La Giralda
This huge Gothic cathedral and its Moorish bell tower are Seville's most popular sights *(see p320).*

Convento de la Encarnación (1591)

Archivo de Indias
Built in the 16th century as a merchants' exchange, the Archive of the Indies now houses documents and maps relating to the Spanish colonization of the Americas.

Plaza del Triunfo
The square was built to celebrate the city's survival of the great earthquake of 1755. In the center is a modern statue of the Virgin Mary.

Calle Mateos Gago
This street is filled with souvenir stores and tapas bars. Bar Giralda at No.2, whose vaults are the remains of a Moorish bath, is popular for its wide variety of tapas.

VISITORS' CHECKLIST

Practical Information
Sevilla. 🚃 704,000.
ℹ️ Avda de la Constitución 21 (95-478 75 78), Plaza del Triunfo (95-421 00 05). **Archivo de Indias Tel** 95-450 05 28.

Transport
✈️ 4 km (2.5 miles) NE. 🚆 Santa Justa, Avda de Kansas City. 🚌 Plaza de Armas, Calle de Arjona.

Train station

MESON DEL MORO

XIMENEZ ENCISO

SANTA TERESA

LOPE DE RUEDA

The Plaza Santa Cruz is adorned by an ornate iron cross from 1692.

PLAZA STA CRUZ

RODRIGO CARO

JAMERDANA

REINOSO

GLORIA

JUSTINO DE NEVE

CALLEJON DEL AGUA

PL DONA ELVIRA

SUSONA

PIMIENTA

VIDA

Hospital de los Venerables
The 17th-century home for elderly priests has a splendidly restored Baroque church (see p320).

Callejón del Agua
This whitewashed alleyway offers glimpses of enchanting plant-filled patios, such as the one pictured here.

★ Real Alcázar
Seville's Royal Palace is a rewarding combination of exquisite Mudéjar (see p311) craftsmanship, regal grandeur, and landscaped gardens (see p320).

| 0 meters | | 50 |
| 0 yards | | 50 |

Key

— Suggested route

The mighty Giralda bell tower, rising above the Gothic cathedral

⬆ Cathedral and La Giralda

Avda de la Constitución. **Tel** 954-21 49 71. **Open** 11am–5pm Mon–Sat (Jul & Aug: 9:30am–4pm), 2:30–6pm Sun. 🅿 🔥 except Giralda tower.

Seville's cathedral occupies the site of a great mosque, built by the Almohads in the late 12th century. La Giralda, its huge bell tower, and the beautiful Patio de los Naranjos, which is filled with orange trees, are a legacy of this Moorish structure. Work on the Christian cathedral began in 1401. The bronze spheres on the original Moorish minaret were replaced by Christian symbols, though the Giralda did not assume its present appearance until 1568. Today, it is crowned by a bronze sculpture portraying Faith. This weathervane *(giraldillo)* has given the tower its name. Visitors can climb La Giralda for superb views of the city.

The cathedral houses many fine works of art, including the stunning high-altar reredos, with its 44 gilded reliefs, carved by Spanish and Flemish sculptors in 1482–1564.

🏛 Real Alcázar

Patio de Banderas. **Tel** 95-450 23 24. **Open** 9:30am–7pm daily (Oct–Mar: to 5pm); Jul & Aug: also open at night for concerts, tel 902-45 99 54 for details. 🅿 🌐 alcazarsevilla.org

In 1364, Pedro I of Castile ordered the construction of a royal residence within the palaces that had been built in the 12th century by the Moors. Craftsmen from Granada and Toledo created a stunning complex of Mudéjar patios and halls, the Palacio Pedro I, now at the heart of Seville's Real Alcázar. Successive monarchs added their own distinguishing marks: Isabel I dispatched navigators to explore the New World from her Casa de Contratación, while Carlos I (the Holy Roman Emperor Charles V) had grandiose, richly decorated apartments built.

A star feature of the palace is the Salón de Embajadores (Ambassadors' Hall), with its dazzling dome of carved and gilded, interlaced wood. The hall overlooks the Patio de las Doncellas (Patio of the Maidens), which boasts some exquisite plasterwork and has been restored to its function as a "floating garden," as it was during Pedro I's reign.

Laid out with terraces, fountains, and pavilions, the gardens of the Real Alcázar provide a delightful refuge from the bustle of Seville.

🏛 Hospital de los Venerables

Plaza de los Venerables 8. **Tel** 95-456 26 96. **Open** 10am–2pm, 4–8pm daily. **Closed** Jan 1, Good Friday, Dec 25. 🅿 (free Sun pm). 🔥

This late 17th-century home for elderly priests has been restored as a cultural center, its upper floors, cellar, and infirmary serving as exhibition galleries. The Hospital church is a showcase of Baroque splendors, with frescoes by both Juan de Valdés Leal and his son Lucas Valdés. There are also fine sculptures by Pedro Roldán.

🏛 Torre del Oro

Paseo de Cristóbal Colón. **Tel** 95-422 24 19. **Open** 10am–2pm Tue–Fri, 11am–2pm Sat & Sun. **Closed** Aug. 🅿 except Tue.

The Moors built the Torre del Oro (Tower of Gold) as a defensive lookout in 1220. Its turret was not

Fresco by Juan de Valdés Leal in the Hospital de los Venerables

Arcaded arena of the Plaza de Toros de la Maestranza

added until 1760. The gold in the tower's name may refer to the gilded *azulejos* (ceramic tiles) that once clad its walls, or to treasures from the Americas unloaded here. It now houses the **Museo Marítimo**, which exhibits maritime maps and antiques.

🏛 Plaza de Toros de la Maestranza

Paseo de Cristóbal Colón 12.
Tel 95-421 03 15. **Open** daily.
Closed for bullfights. 🅿 📷

Built between 1761 and 1881, Seville's famous bullring seats up to 14,000 spectators.

Visitors who take a guided tour of this enormous building are shown many interesting features, including a chapel where the matadors pray for success, and the stables where the horses of the *picadores* (lance-carrying horsemen) are kept. There is also a small museum.

Between Easter Sunday and October, *corridas* (bullfights) take place every Sunday evening. Tickets can be bought from the *taquilla* (ticket office) at the bullring or online at www. plazadetoroslamaestranza.com.

🏛 Museo de Bellas Artes

Plaza del Museo 9. **Tel** 955-54 29 42.
Open 10am–8:30pm Tue–Sat,
10am–5pm Sun. 📷 ♿

The magnificent Convento de la Merced Calzada houses one of Spain's best art museums. Delightful tree-filled patios, colorful *azulejos*, and a church with a beautiful Baroque painted ceiling make this a wonderful setting for the fine works of art.

The museum's collection of Spanish art and sculpture – which covers all periods from the medieval to the modern – focuses on the work of the Seville School artists. Among the star attractions are masterpieces by Murillo, Juan de Valdés Leal, and Zurbarán.

🏛 Parque María Luisa

In 1893, Princess María Luisa donated part of the grounds of the Palacio San Telmo to the city for this park. Its most extravagant feature is the semicircular Plaza de España, designed by Aníbal González for the 1929 Ibero-American Exposition. At the center of the park, the Pabellón Mudéjar houses the **Museo de Artes y Costumbres Populares**, with displays of traditional Andalusian folk arts. Nearby, located in the grand Neo-Renaissance Pabellón de Bellas Artes, is the provincial **Museo Arqueológico** (Archaeological Museum).

🏛 Monasterio de Santa María de las Cuevas

Calle Americo Vespucio 2, Isla de la Cartuja. **Tel** 95-503 70 70. **Open** 11am–9pm Tue–Sat, Sun am. 📷 (free Sat). 📷 by prior appt only. ♿

This 15th-century Carthusian monastery was inhabited by monks until 1836. Columbus lay

Flamenco

More than just a dance, flamenco is an artistic expression of the joys and sorrows of life. A uniquely Andalusian art, its origins are hard to trace. Gypsies may have been the main creators of the art, mixing their own Indian-influenced culture with existing Moorish and Andalusian folklore, and with Jewish and Christian music. Gypsies were already living in Andalusia by the early Middle Ages, but only in the 18th century did flamenco begin to develop into its present form. There are many styles of *cante* (song) from different parts of Andalusia, but no strict choreography – dancers (*bailaores*) improvise from basic movements, following the rhythm of the guitar and their feelings.

Flamenco dancer
(*bailaora*)

buried in the crypt of its church between 1507 and 1542. The monastery stands at the heart of the Isla de Cartuja, the site of Expo '92, and also houses the **Museo de Arte Contemporáneo**, with its collection of Spanish and international art. The **Isla Mágica** theme park is also nearby.

Seville's dazzling Plaza de España in the Parque María Luisa

Practical Information

Spain's tourist-information service is efficient and extensive, with offices in most towns providing advice on lodgings, restaurants, and local events. In August, many businesses close and roads are busy. It is worth finding out whether local fiestas will coincide with your visit, as while these are enjoyable, they may also cause closures. Public telephones are widely available, but international call charges are high. When changing money, credit cards often offer the best exchange rate and can be used in cash dispensers. The Spanish lunch hour extends from 2pm to 5pm.

When to Visit

August is Spain's busiest vacation month. Spanish locals on holiday and millions of foreign tourists flock to the coast. Easter is a good time to visit: temperatures are more bearable, especially in the south, the countryside is in bloom, and some of the country's most important fiestas take place. In the mountains the ski season is from mid-December until March/April.

Tourist Information

All major cities and towns have a tourist information office (oficina de turismo), which will provide town plans, lists of hotels and restaurants, and details of local activities. There is a **Spanish National Tourist Office** in several large cities worldwide.

Opening Hours

Most monuments and museums in Spain close on Mondays. On other days, they are generally open from 10am to 2pm, and, usually, reopen from 5pm to 8pm. The main museums stay open through lunch. Most charge for entry. Some churches may only be opened for services.

In smaller towns, churches, castles, and other sights are often kept locked. The key, available on request, will be lodged in a neighboring house, in the town hall, or perhaps with the local bar owners.

Visa Requirements and Customs

Citizens of the EU, Switzerland, Iceland, and Norway do not require a visa for entry to Spain. A list of entry requirements – available from Spanish embassies – specifies other countries, including the US, Canada, Australia, and New Zealand, whose nationals do not need a visa for visits of less than 90 days.

Non-EU residents can reclaim IVA (sales tax) on some single items. You pay the full price and ask the sales assistant for a formulario (tax-exemption form). On leaving Spain, you must ask customs to stamp your formulario (this must be within six months of the purchase). You receive the refund by mail or on your credit card account.

Personal Security

Violent crime is rare in Spain. Petty theft is the main problem in the cities, especially Madrid, Barcelona, and Seville, where visitors should be extra vigilant. Men may make complimentary remarks (piropos) to women in the street. This is customary and not intended to be intimidating.

Police

There are essentially three types of police force in Spain. The Guardia Civil (National Guard) mainly police rural areas and impose fines for traffic offenses. The Policía Nacional operate in larger towns. They are replaced by a regional force, the Ertzaintza, in the Basque country, and by the Mossos d'Esquadra in Catalonia. The Policía Local, also called Policía Municipal or Guardia Urbana, operate independently in each town and have a branch for city traffic control.

All three services will direct you to the relevant authority in the event of an incident requiring police help.

Emergency Services

Only the Policía Nacional operates a nationwide

The Climate of Spain

Spain's large landmass, with its mountain ranges and the influences of the Atlantic and Mediterranean, accounts for a varied climate. The eastern and southern coasts and islands have mild winters; however, winter temperatures in the interior often fall below freezing. Summers everywhere are hot, except in upland areas. Northern Spain is the wettest area all year round.

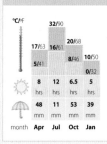

MADRID			
°C/°F	32/90		
	17/63 16/61	20/68	
	5/41	8/46	10/50
			0/32
8 hrs	12 hrs	6.5 hrs	5 hrs
48 mm	11 mm	53 mm	39 mm
month	Apr	Jul	Oct	Jan

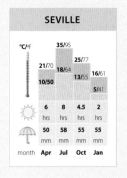

SEVILLE			
°C/°F	35/95		
	21/70 18/64	25/77	
	10/50	13/55	16/61
			5/41
6 hrs	8 hrs	4.5 hrs	2 hrs
50 mm	58 mm	55 mm	55 mm
month	Apr	Jul	Oct	Jan

emergency phone number *(see Directory)*. Telephone directories list local emergency numbers under *Servicios de Urgencia*. For emergency medical treatment, call the Cruz Roja (Red Cross), look under *Ambulancias* in the phone book, or go to a hospital emergency room *(Urgencias)*.

Health Issues

Spanish pharmacists have wide responsibilities. They can advise and, in certain cases, prescribe without consulting a doctor (antibiotics not included). In a non-emergency, a *farmacéutico* is a good person to see first. It is usually easy to find one who speaks English.

The pharmacy *(farmacia)* sign is a green or red illuminated cross. Those open at night are listed in the windows of all the local pharmacies.

Facilities for the Disabled

Spain's national association for the disabled, the Confederación Coordinadora Estatal de Minusválidos Físicos de España (**COCEMFE**), has a tour company, Servi-COCEMFE,

which publishes guides to facilities in Spain and will help plan a vacation to individual requirements. A Spanish travel agency, **Viajes 2000**, specializes in vacations for disabled people.

Language and Etiquette

The Spanish commonly greet and say goodbye to strangers at bus stops and in stores and other public places. People shake hands when introduced and whenever they meet. In Catalonia and the Basque country, regional languages are as much in use as the national tongue, which is Castilian Spanish.

Banking and Currency

The Spanish unit of currency is the euro *(see p23)*. Generally, banks are open from 8am to 2pm Monday to Friday. Some branches are also open on Thursday afternoon. Some have a foreign exchange desk with the sign *Cambio* or *Extranjero*. Take some form of ID when changing money. Bureaux de change charge higher rates of commission,

but are open longer hours. The best rate is to be found by withdrawing cash from an ATM or paying by credit card. Visa and Mastercard are accepted in most places.

Communications

Most public telephone booths *(cabinas)* take coins, but some take tokens. Phonecards can be bought at newsstands and *estancos* (tobacconists). At public telephone offices, which are called *locutorios*, you can make a call and pay for it afterwards. Telefónica run the official ones, which are less expensive than private offices.

The Spanish postal service, Correos, is rather slow: a national or international delivery may take more than a week. Send important mail by *urgente* (express) or *certificado* (registered) mail. The main Correos offices open from 8:30am to 8:30pm Monday to Friday and from 9am to 2pm Saturday. Conveniently, you will find that stamps for letters and postcards can also be bought from an *estanco*.

DIRECTORY

Travel Information

Spain has an increasingly efficient transportation system. All the major cities and islands have airports, and flights from around the globe arrive at those of Madrid and Barcelona. Both the road and rail networks were greatly improved during the 1980s and in the run-up to the Barcelona Olympics in 1992. Intercity rail services are reliable, but buses are a faster and more frequent option between smaller towns. In much of rural Spain, however, public transportation is limited and a car is the most practical solution for getting around. Ferries connect mainland Spain with the Balearic Islands, Morocco, and ports in the UK.

Flying to Spain

Of the several US airlines serving Spain, **American Airlines** flies to Madrid, while **United Airlines** and **Delta Air Lines** fly to both Madrid and Barcelona. **Iberia**, the Spanish national airline, has direct flights to Madrid from New York, Miami, and Los Angeles.

Iberia also offers scheduled flights daily to Madrid and Barcelona from all Western European capitals, including Dublin, which is served by the affiliated Air Nostrum. Its partner **British Airways** has scheduled flights to Madrid and Barcelona and several other cities daily from London Heathrow or Gatwick.

From Australasia, the best connections to Spain are via Dubai, Doha, Bangkok, Frankfurt, and London.

Charters and Package Deals

Charter flights from the UK serve airports such as Málaga, Alicante, and Girona. These can be inexpensive, but are less reliable and have limited schedules. Make sure your agent is ABTA bonded before booking. Special deals are often offered in the winter and may include accommodations. Low-cost airline **easyJet** serves Madrid, Barcelona, Mallorca, Málaga, Alicante, and Ibiza from London Luton, Stansted, and Gatwick airports, Liverpool, and Bristol, while **bmibaby** and **Ryanair** fly from London Stansted and other UK regional airports to mainland and island Spain.

Domestic Flights

Most of Spain's domestic flights have traditionally been operated by **Iberia**, however, this monopoly has been broken to encourage competition. The two main alternative Spanish carriers are **Air Europa** and **Vueling**.

The most frequent shuttle service is the Puente Aéreo, run between Barcelona and Madrid by Iberia. Flights leave every 15 minutes at peak business times. A ticket machine allows passengers to buy tickets up to 15 minutes before departure. The journey usually takes 50 minutes.

Air Europa services between Madrid and the regional capitals are not as frequent as the Puente Aéreo. Air services within the Canary Islands are run by **Binter**, which is affiliated to Iberia Airlines. The low-cost company **Ryanair** also serves many destinations in Spain.

Getting Around Madrid and Barcelona

The metro is the quickest and least expensive way to travel around Madrid. It is open from 6am to 1:30am and consists of 11 color-coded lines, plus the Ópera-Príncipe Pío link and a service to the airport. Day buses run from 6am until midnight; night buses continue operating until 6am and leave from the Plaza de Cibeles. A *Metrobus* ticket, valid for ten trips on the buses and metro, can be bought at any metro station, as well as from newsstands and *estancos* (tobacconists). Sightseeing bus tours are run by **Madrid City Tour**.

Barcelona's metro system generally runs from 5am to midnight; on Fridays it stays open until 2am, and all night on Saturdays. There are various types of travelcard available, valid for bus, metro, and the FGC *(Ferrocarrils de la Generalitat de Catalunya)* suburban train network. The city buses in Barcelona are usually colored white and red. The *Nitbus* (night bus) runs from around 10pm to 5am; and the *Aerobús* provides an excellent service between the Plaça de Catalunya and the two terminals of the airport.

Sightseeing tours in Barcelona are operated by Bus Turístic on three routes from Plaça de Catalunya.

Rail Travel

Spain offers many options for users of the state railroad **RENFE**. The high-speed services are the intercity TALGO trains and the AVE service between Madrid, Seville, and Málaga via Córdoba; from Madrid to Barcelona via Zaragoza and Lleida; and from Barcelona to Seville or Málaga. Tickets for these are the most expensive and may be bought at train stations from the *taquilla* (ticket office), obtained from travel agents, or ordered via the Renfe website or telephone booking line.

The *largo recorrido* (long-distance trains) and *regionales y cercanías* (regional and local) services are frequent, inexpensive, but slower. Tickets for local travel may be purchased from machines at the station.

In Madrid the major stations for long-distance trains are Atocha and Chamartín. Barcelona's two principal train stations are Sants and Francia.

Regional rail companies operate in three areas of Spain. Catalonia and Valencia each has its own *Ferrocarrils de la Generalitat*, known respectively as the **FGC** and the **FGV**. The Basque country has the **ET** *(Eusko Trenbideale)*. **Iberrail** holidays offer rail-plus-hotel deals for traveling between

Spanish cities. Two services similar to the Orient Express are also operated by Iberrail. The El Expreso de la Robla has two routes, one around Bilbao and the other from Gijon to Galicia. The Transcantábrico, run by **FEVE** (*Ferrocarriles de Vía Estrecha*), leaves San Sebastián to travel the length of Spain's north coast, ending its journey in Santiago de Compostela. Passengers travel in style in 14 restored period carriages that date from 1900–30.

Long-distance Buses

Spain has no national long-distance bus company. The largest private company, **Alsa**, offers a variety of bus tours and sightseeing trips throughout Spain. Other companies operate in particular regions. Tickets and information for long-distance travel are available at main bus stations and from travel agents.

Traveling by Road

Spain's fastest roads are its *autopistas*. They are normally dual carriageways subject to *peajes* (tolls). *Autovías* are similar, but have no tolls. Smaller roads are less well kept but are a more relaxed way to see rural Spain.

As well as the international car rental companies, a few Spanish companies, such as **Atesa**, operate nationwide. The best deals with international companies are accessed through the companies' websites. There are also fly-drive package deals, which include car rental. *Gasolina* (gas) is priced by the liter. Spanish law requires drivers to carry at all times valid insurance and registration documents, a driver's license, and ID.

Ferry Services

Two car ferry routes link the Spanish mainland with the UK. **Brittany Ferries** sails from Plymouth and Portsmouth in the UK to Santander in Cantabria, and from Portsmouth to Bilbao. The crossings take more than 24 hours. Advance reservations are essential in the summer.

Trasmediterránea runs car ferry services from Barcelona and Valencia on the Spanish mainland to the Balearic Islands. The crossing takes about eight hours. The same company also operates frequent inter-island services.

DIRECTORY

Iberia and Affiliates

International and domestic flights
Tel 902-400 500.
Tel 0870-609 0500 (UK).
Tel 800-772 4642 (US).
w **iberia.com**

Other Airlines

Air Europa
Tel 902-401 501.
w **aireuropa.com**

American Airlines
Tel 902-115 570.
Tel 800-433 7300 (US).
w **aa.com**

bmibaby
w **bmibaby.com**

British Airways
Tel 902-111 333.
Tel 08444-930 787 (UK).
Tel 800-247 92 97 (US).
w **britishairways.com**

Delta Air Lines
Tel 902-81 08 72.
Tel 800-241 41 41 (US).
w **delta.com**

easyJet
w **easyjet.com**

Ryanair
w **ryanair.com**

United Airlines
w **united.com**

Vueling
Tel 807-001 717.
w **vueling.com**

Madrid Tours

Madrid City Tour
w **madridcitytour.es**

Rail Travel

ET
Tel 902-54 32 10.
w **euskotren.es**

FEVE
Tel 985-98 23 81.
w **feve.es**

FGC
Tel 93-205 15 15.
w **fgc.cat**

FGV
Tel 96-526 27 31.
w **fgv.es**

Iberrail
Tel 902-10 80 23.
w **iberrail.es**

RENFE
Tel 902-32 03 20.
w **renfe.es**

Bus Companies

Alsa
Tel 90-242 22 42.
w **alsa.es**

Eurolines
Tel 90-240 50 40.
Tel 0871-781 81 81 (UK).
w **eurolines.es**
w **eurolines.com**

Bus Stations

Madrid
Estación Sur (for whole of Spain).
Tel 91-468 42 00.

Intercambiador des Autobuses (for northern Spain).
Tel 902-42 22 42.

Terminal Auto Res (for Valencia, Extremadura, Andalusia).
Tel 90-202 09 99.

Barcelona
Estació del Nord.
Tel 90-226 06 06.

Seville
Estación Plaza de Armas.
Tel 90-245 05 50.

Car Rental

Atesa
Tel 902-10 01 01.
w **atesa.com**

Avis
Tel 90-218 08 54.
Tel 0844-54 45 566 (UK).
w **avis.com**

Europcar
Tel 902-10 50 30.
Tel 08457-222 525 (UK).
w **europcar.com**

Hertz
Tel 901-10 10 01.
Tel 0870-844 8844 (UK).
w **hertz.es**
w **hertz.co.uk**

Ferry Services

Brittany Ferries
Tel 942-36 06 11.
Tel 0871-244 0744 (UK).
w **brittany-ferries.com**

Trasmediterránea
Tel 90-245 46 45.
Tel 0870-499 1305 (UK).
w **trasmediterranea.es**

Shopping

Shopping in Spain is a pleasurable activity, particularly if you approach it in a leisurely way, punctuating it with frequent breaks for coffee. In small, family-run shops especially, people will go out of their way to fulfill your smallest request. Markets sell the freshest of produce and quality wines can be found at almost any grocer. Leatherwork is still highly regarded among Spain's many traditional crafts. Spanish design has come to the forefront in both fashion and decor.

Opening Hours

Stores usually open at 10am, close at 2pm, and reopen from 5pm to 8pm. Bakeries generally open early, at around 8am. Supermarkets and department stores stay open over lunchtime.

Rural markets are held in the morning only. In some regions, Sunday trading is just limited to the bakeries, *pastelerías* (pastry stores), and newspaper kiosks, but in many tourist resorts stores open on Sunday.

Larger Stores

The *hipermercados* (super-stores) are sited outside towns and can often be found by following signs to the *centro comercial*. The best known are Carrefour, Alcampo, and Hipercor.

Spain's leading department store is **El Corte Inglés**. It has branches in all cities and in the larger regional towns.

Major seasonal sales are advertised by the word *Rebajas*, displayed in store windows.

Clothing Stores

The larger cities naturally offer the widest selection of clothing stores, but Spanish designer labels can be found even in the smaller towns.

The Calle de Serrano and Calle de José Ortega y Gasset are the main streets for fashionwear in Madrid, while the work of young designers is mostly located in the Chueca district. **Adolfo Domínguez** is the doyen of Madrid's minimalist look. The adventurous will appreciate the designs of **Agatha Ruiz de la Prada**. In Barcelona, international fashion labels and clothes by young designers can be found in and around the Passeig de Gràcia, including **Armand Basi**, vendors of quality leisure and sportswear.

Victorio & Lucchino in Seville sells clothes with a distinctly Andalusian style.

Leather Goods

Leather accessories and shoes are a popular purchase and there is a wide range in terms of quality and price. It is the practise in mid-range stores for customers to choose from the selection in the window and give the sales assistant the code number indicated and the *talla* (size) required. If you want an all-leather shoe, look for *cuero*, the hide label mark. **Calçats Sole** in Barcelona is well known for its classic hand-made shoes and boots.

Leather clothes and bags of all kinds are usually of good quality and well designed. The prestigious **Loewe** hand-bags are sold in retail outlets in Madrid and other major Spanish cities. Madrid's **Piamonte** also offers stylish bags at affordable prices.

Specialty Stores

Specialty stores are often run by generations of the same family. *Panaderías* (also called *hornos*) are bakeries selling bread and *bollos* (sweet buns). Cakes and pastries are sold in *pastelerías*.

Fresh meat can be bought in a *carnicería*, but a *charcutería* will have the best selection of cold, cooked meats, and also sells a wide selection of cheeses. *Pescaderías* sell fish and shellfish, although the best fish is often to be found on the local market stands.

For fruit and vegetables, a *frutería* or *verdulería* will have better produce, because they stock only what is in season.

Hardware stores are called *ferreterías*. *Librerías* are in fact bookshops, not libraries, and *papelerías* are stationers. Anything you buy as a *regalo* (gift) will be gift-wrapped on request. When you buy flowers from a *floristería*, the assistant will expect to arrange them.

Markets

Every large town has a daily market *(mercado)*, open from 9am to 2pm, and from 5pm to 8pm. Small towns have one or more market days a week.

Markets usually have the best fresh produce, but they sell all types of food, including *frutos secos* (dried fruits) and seasonal produce, such as mushrooms, soft fruit, and game. There are also usually other types of goods on sale, such as flowers, hardware, and clothes.

Flea markets *(rastros)* are held everywhere in Spain, but the largest – known as **El Rastro** – is in Madrid, and is held on Sundays and public holidays. Prices on the clothes, records, antiques, and other items sold here can be bargained down. Madrid also has a coin, stamp, and postcard market held on Sundays in the Plaza Mayor.

The **Encants Vells**, the flea market in Barcelona, is held on Mondays, Wednesdays, Fridays, and Saturdays. The food market, **La Boqueria**, is open daily on La Ramblas.

Food and Drink

Spanish regional specialties are often better value when bought where they are made. Each region produces its own type of sausage. In Burgos, for example, *morcilla* (blood sausage) is made, while a fiery red *chorizo* comes from Guijuelo, Extremadura. Andalusia is renowned for olives and olive oil, and Galicia for its cheeses. Among the preserves and sweets of Spain, Seville marmalade is famous. The delicious almond-based nougat, called *turrón*, is eaten at Christmas, but can be bought all year from food stores around the country.

Wine can be bought by the liter at a *bodega* (local wine store). It can also be purchased directly from vineyards (also called *bodegas*), but you may need an appointment.

Spain's most famous vine-growing regions are La Rioja and Navarra, Penedés, home of *cava* (sparkling wine), Valdepeñas, Ribera del Duero, and Jerez, the sherry region.

Traditional Crafts

Authentic items, such as guitars, fans, castanets, and flamenco shoes, are sold in major cities. Madrid's **Flomi Detalles** has a good selection of hand-painted fans. **Guitarras de Luthier** sells handmade guitars. Some traditional crafts originated with the Moors, such as Toledo's filigree metalwork and the *azulejos* (ceramic tiles) of Andalusia. **Cántaro**, near the Plaza de España in Madrid, **La Caixa de Fang** in Barcelona, and **Azulejos Santa Isabel** in Seville all sell ceramics.

Catalan-style espadrilles are another popular buy. **La Manual Alpargatera** in Barcelona makes them by hand on the premises and sells them in a wide range of colors.

Lace from the villages of the Sierra de Gata in Extremadura and Galicia's Costa da Morte is prized. Spanish linen and silk shawls can be purchased from **Borca**, off the Puerta del Sol in Madrid. In Barcelona, **L'Arca de l'Avia** sells antique silk and lace. One of the most celebrated traditional hat makers in Spain is the **Sombrerería Herederos de J. Russi** in Córdoba.

Household and Kitchen Goods

Department stores have a good selection of household goods, but the *ferreterías* (small hardware shops) often have the more authentic selection. Traditional pottery, such as red clay *cazuelas* (dishes) that can be used in the oven and on the hob are inexpensive. Paella pans have always been made of iron or enamel, but now come in stainless steel or with non-stick finishes. Table linen is often a bargain on market stands. Spanish lighting design is widely admired and sold in *lampisterías*. Traditional wrought-iron goods, such as candlesticks and door hardware, are always popular.

DIRECTORY

Department Stores

El Corte Inglés
Calle de Preciados 1–3,
Madrid.
Tel 90-112 21 22.
🔲 elcorteingles.es

Plaça Catalunya 14,
Barcelona.
Tel 93-306 38 00.

Plaza Duque de la Victoria
10, Seville.
Tel 95-459 70 00.

Clothing Stores

Adolfo Domínguez
Calle de Serrano 5,
Madrid.
Tel 91-577 47 44.
Passeig de Gràcia 32,
Barcelona.
Tel 93-487 41 70.

Armand Basi
Passeig de Gràcia 49,
Barcelona.
Tel 93-215 14 21.
🔲 armandbasi.com

Agatha Ruiz de la Prada
Calle de Serrano 27,
Madrid.
Tel 91-319 05 01.

Victorio & Lucchino
Calle de las Sierpes 87,
Seville.
Tel 95-422 79 51.

Leather Goods

Calçats Sole
Carrer Ample 7,
Barcelona.
Tel 93-301
69 84.

Loewe
Calle de Serrano 26,
Madrid.
Tel 91-577 60 56.
Plaza Nueva 12, Seville.
Tel 95-422 52 53.

Piamonte
Calle del Marqués de
Monasterio 5, Madrid.
Tel 91-575 55 20.

Markets

La Boqueria
Las Ramblas 100,
Barcelona.

Encants Vells
Plaça de les Glòries
Catalanes, Barcelona.

El Rastro
Calle de la Ribera de
Curtidores, Madrid.

Traditional Crafts

L'Arca de l'Avia
Carrer dels Banys Nous 20,
Barcelona.
Tel 93-302 15 98.

Azulejos Santa Isabel
Calle Alfarería 12,
Triana, Seville.
Tel 95-434 46 08.

Borca
Calle del Marqués Viudo
de Pontejos 2, Madrid.
Tel 91-532 61 53.

La Caixa de Fang
Calle Freneria 1,
Barcelona.
Tel 93-315 17 04.

Cántaro
Calle de la Flor
Baja 8, Madrid.
Tel 91-547 95 14.

Flomi Detalles
Calle Encomienda 3,
Madrid.
Tel 91-467 31 58.

Guitarras de Luthier
Calle Doctor Mata 1,
Madrid.
Tel 91-468 19 54.

La Manual Alpargatera
Calle d'Avinyó 7,
Barcelona.
Tel 93-301 01 72.

Sombrerería Herederos de J. Russi
Cde Cardenas 1, Córdoba.
Tel 957-47 79 53.

Entertainment

The Spanish take particular pride in their cultural heritage. As well as the traditional art form of flamenco dance and the three-act drama of the bullfight (corrida), the theaters and opera houses of Spanish cities provide one of the best ways of sharing the experience of Spain. Many activities begin well after midnight, and taking full advantage of the afternoon siesta is a good way to prepare for the evening ahead. Spain's mountain ranges, woodlands, and extensive coast offer great potential for scenic tours and sports vacations as alternatives to lounging on the beach.

Entertainment Listings

For Spanish speakers, the most complete guide to what's going on in Madrid and Barcelona can be found in the weekly Guía del Ocio (published on Fridays). Daily newspapers such as El País, El Mundo, and ABC have weekly entertainment supplements. The free monthly English-language publication, In Madrid, can be found in bookstores and Irish bars.

Seasons and Tickets

The main concert and theater season in Spain runs from September to June.

In Madrid and Barcelona, the easiest ways to acquire tickets for the theater, concerts, and opera are by telephone or online. **Entradas.com** and **Telentrada** both accept credit card payment. Other agencies are **El Corte Inglés** and **FNAC**.

In Barcelona, theater tickets can also be bought from ATMs at branches of the Catalunya Caixa and from **Ticket Rambles** at the Palau de la Virreina, which also has last-minute reduced price tickets and a good website. Tickets for special events can be bought from tourist offices.

In other parts of Spain, your hotel or local tourist office will provide details of events and where to purchase tickets.

Tickets for bullfights, generally held between mid-March and mid-October, are sold at the reservations office (taquilla) of the bullring. The **TEYCI** agency sells tickets for bullfights, but charges up to 20 percent commission.

Opera and Zarzuela

A visit to the Spanish capital would not be complete without spending a night at the zarzuela, Madrid's own variety of comic opera. The best productions are those staged at the **Teatro de la Zarzuela**. Other venues include **Los Teatros del Canal** and the **Teatro Príncipe – Palacio de las Variedades**. Several other theaters offer zarzuela productions throughout the summer.

The best place to see national and international opera, including Madrid's own opera company, is the **Teatro Real de Madrid**. The Teatro Calderón also hosts excellent classical and modern opera productions. Barcelona's opera house, the **Gran Teatre del Liceu**, is now fully operational following a fire in 1994.

Theater

Madrid's most prestigious theaters are the **Teatro de la Comedia** (closed for renovations until 2016) and the **Teatro María Guerrero**. The former stages classic works by Spanish playwrights, while the latter hosts foreign productions and modern Spanish drama. The **Teatro Muñoz Seca** and **Teatro Reina Victoria** put on comedy productions. Madrid's autumn festival of classical and modern drama (Festival de Otoño) takes place between mid-September and mid-November.

In Barcelona, the **Teatre Nacional de Catalunya** is a fine showcase for Catalan drama.

Classical Music

In Madrid, the two concert halls of the **Auditorio Nacional de Música** host international classical music performances, and the Orquesta Nacional de España plays here regularly. The **Teatro Real de Madrid** also hosts important classical music concerts.

Barcelona's Modernista **Palau de la Música Catalana** is one of the world's most beautiful concert halls, with world-renowned acoustics.

Bullfighting

Bullfighting continues to be a popular spectacle throughout the country, but it is not for the squeamish. The **Plaza de Toros de Las Ventas** in Madrid is the most famous bullring in the world. It holds corridas every Sunday during the bullfighting season. During the May Fiestas de San Isidro, fights are held every day. Some of Spain's most important fights are held at the **Maestranza** bullring in Seville during the Feria de Abril (a spring fair held during the fortnight after Easter). Since 2012, bullfights have been banned in Catalonia. Most towns in Andalusia have their own bullrings: Ronda, Córdoba, and Granada are among the best-known venues.

Flamenco

A spontaneous musical art form, flamenco has its roots in the gypsy culture of Andalusia. However, many of the best exponents are now based in the capital.

In Madrid, **Casa Patas** is still the best place to catch the raw power of genuine flamenco guitar and cante singing. Both music and dance can be enjoyed at **Café de Chinitas**.

Flamenco is performed late at night with most venues offering dinner and a show. In Andalusia, visitors can enjoy top-quality performances in the tablaos (flamenco bars) of the Barrio de Santa Cruz in Seville, and listen to soul-stirring songs in the bars of another of the city's districts, Triana. One of the best-known flamenco venues in Granada is in the gypsy caves of Sacromonte (see p310).

Special Interest Vacations

All tourist offices in Spain can provide details of special interest vacations. Cookery, wine, and painting courses, as well as history and archaeology tours, are popular. Nature lovers and hikers head for Spain's many national parks.

Information about Spanish language courses is provided by **Canning House** in London and the **Instituto Cervantes**.

Outdoor Activities

For information on horseback riding and pony trekking in most regions, contact the **Real Federación Hípica Española** or local Spanish tourist offices.

Picturesque minor roads in many parts of Spain are excellent for cycle-touring. Walking tours are also popular. The **Federación Española de Montaña y Escalada** can provide information about climbing and many other mountain sports.

Spain's most popular resorts for downhill skiing are the Vall d'Aran in Catalonia and the Sierra Nevada, near Granada. As well as white-water rafting

and canoeing, a wide variety of watersports is possible in Spain. Jet skis and windsurfing equipment are available to rent in many coastal resorts. Information about sailing can be obtained from the **Real Federación Española de Vela**.

Spain has an abundance of top-quality golf courses. The **Real Federación Española de Golf** will give locations and more detailed information. In most tourist areas, there are tennis courts for rental by the hour. Travel agents arrange tennis holidays for enthusiasts. More information is available from the **Real Federación Española de Tenis**.

DIRECTORY

Tickets

Entradas.com
Tel 902-48 84 88 (Madrid).

El Corte Inglés
Tel 902-40 02 22 (Madrid).
w elcorteingles.es

Telentrada
Tel 902-10 12 12.
w telentrada.com

TEYCI
Madrid.
w ticketstoros.com

Ticket Rambles
La Rambla 99, Barcelona.
w tiquetrambles.
bcn.cat

Opera and Zarzuela

Gran Teatre del Liceu
La Rambla 51, Barcelona.
Tel 93-485 99 00.

Los Teatros del Canal
Calle Cea Bermúdez 1, Madrid. Tel 902-48 84 88.

Teatro Príncipe – Palacio de las Variedades
Calle de las Tres Cruces 8, Madrid. Tel 91-521 83 81.

Teatro Real de Madrid
Plaza de Oriente, Madrid.
Tel 90-224 48 48.

Teatro de la Zarzuela
Calle de Jovellanos 4, Madrid. Tel 91-524 54 00.

Theater

Teatre Nacional de Catalunya
Plaça de les Arts 1, Barcelona.
Tel 93-306 57 00.

Teatro de la Comedia
Calle del Príncipe 14, Madrid. Tel 91-532 79 28.

Teatro María Guerrero
Calle de Tamayo y Baus 4, Madrid. Tel 91-310 29 49.

Teatro Muñoz Seca
Plaza del Carmen 1, Madrid. Tel 91-523 21 28.

Teatro Reina Victoria
Carrera de San Jerónimo 24, Madrid.
Tel 91-369 22 88.

Classical Music

Auditorio Nacional de Música
Calle del Príncipe de Vergara 146, Madrid.
Tel 91-337 01 40.

Palau de la Música Catalana
Carrer de Palau de la Musica 4–6, Barcelona.
Tel 90-244 28 82.

Bullfighting

Plaza de Toros de la Maestranza
Paseo de Cristóbal Cólon 12, Seville.
Tel 95-450 13 82.

Plaza de Toros de las Ventas
Calle de Alcalá 237, Madrid. Tel 91-356 22 00.

Flamenco

Café de Chinitas
Calle de Torija 7, Madrid.
Tel 91-547 15 02.

Casa Patas
Calle de Cañizares 10, Madrid. Tel 91-369 04 96.

Special Interest Vacations

Canning House
2 Belgrave Square, London SW1X 8PJ.
Tel 020-7811 5600.

Instituto Cervantes
Calle Libreros 23, 28801 Alcalá de Henares, Madrid. Tel 91-436 75 70.
UK: 102 Eaton Square, London SW1W 9AN.
Tel 020-7235 0353.

Outdoor Activities

Federación Española de Montaña y Escalada
Calle Floridablanca 84, 08015 Barcelona.
Tel 93-426 42 67.
w fedme.es

Real Federación Española de Golf
Paseo Joaquin Rodrigo 4, letra 1, 28224 Pozuelo de Alarcón, Madrid.
Tel 90-220 00 52.
w golfspain federacion.com

Real Federación Española de Tenis
Passeig Olimpic 17, 08038 Barcelona.
Tel 93-200 53 55.
w rfet.es

Real Federación Española de Vela
Calle Luis Salazar 9, 28002 Madrid.
Tel 91-519 50 08.
w rfev.es

Real Federación Hípica Española
Calle Monte Esquinza 28 3, 28010 Madrid.
Tel 91-436 42 00.

Where to Stay

Madrid

BOURBON MADRID:
Hotel Liabeny €€
Boutique **Map** C4
C/de la Salud 3, 28013
Tel 915-31 90 00
W liabeny.es
Classically decorated rooms and
a surprisingly long list of facilities
– including a sauna, restaurant,
and gym – for the price.

BOURBON MADRID:
De Las Letras €€
Boutique **Map** D3
Gran Vía 11, 28013
Tel 915-23 79 80
W hoteldelasletras.com
An elegant hotel with rooms
dedicated to famous writers, and
a stunning rooftop bar and terrace
that offers tremendous views.

DK Choice

BOURBON MADRID: Ritz €€€
Luxury **Map** E4
Plaza de la Lealtad 5, 28014
Tel 917-01 67 67
W ritzmadrid.com
A belle époque-style gem
located right next to the Prado,
the Ritz boasts an opulent
interior and the air of another
century; it even imposes a dress
code after 11am. The superb
bar is where luminaries such as
Dalí and Lorca once held court.
Excellent service.

OLD MADRID: Abracadabra €
B&B
C/Bailen 39, 28005
Tel 656-85 97 84
W abracadabrabandb.com
Friendly B&B near the Royal Palace.
Rooms are furnished with esoteric
objects from around the world.
Delicious, generous breakfasts.

OLD MADRID: Las Meninas €
Boutique **Map** B4
C/Campomanes 7, 28013
Tel 915-41 28 05
W hotelmeninas.es
This small but delightful hotel on
a tranquil street boasts rooms
with polished wooden floors and
charming contemporary decor.

OLD MADRID: Hotel Petit
Palace Ducal €€
Historic **Map** D3
C/Hortaleza 3, 28004
Tel 915-21 10 43
W hthoteles.com
Set in a handsomely converted
19th-century mansion, this is a
smart, modern hotel in the heart
of the fashionable Chueca district.

Barcelona

EIXAMPLE: Hotel Actual €€
Boutique **Map** D3
Rosselló 238, 08008
Tel 935-52 05 50
W hotelactual.com
This chic hotel in the center has
minimalist rooms decorated in
monochromatic tones. Free Wi-Fi.

DK Choice

EIXAMPLE: Alma €€€
Boutique **Map** F2
Mallorca 271, 08008
Tel 932-16 44 90
W almabarcelona.com
Housed in a fashionable
townhouse, this hotel oozes
elegance and is famed for its
service. Some of the original
19th-century details have
been preserved, but the rooms
are chic and minimalist. The
glorious secret courtyard
and stylish roof terrace are
ideal spots for relaxing.

Price Guide
Prices are based on one night's stay in
high season for a standard double room,
inclusive of service charges and taxes.

€	up to €130
€€	€130 to €240
€€€	over €240

OLD TOWN: Bonic Barcelona €
B&B **Map** D4
Josep Anselm Clavé 9, 08002
Tel 626-05 34 34
W bonic-barcelona.com
A little charmer of a B&B in the
Gothic Quarter, with individually
designed rooms, delightful staff,
and lots of thoughtful extras.

DK Choice

OLD TOWN: Hotel Espanya €€
Historic **Map** D3
Sant Pau 9–11, 08001
Tel 935-50 00 00
W hotelespanya.com.
This beautifully restored
Modernista gem dates back
to 1859, and combines
contemporary furnishings with
beautiful details, including
superb frescoes by Montaner.
There is a fabulous restaurant,
a bar with a fireplace, and a
gorgeous roof terrace.

OLD TOWN: Hotel Mercer €€€
Luxury **Map** D3
Lledó 7, 08002
Tel 933-10 74 80
W mercerbarcelona.com
Chic and intimate, this ravishing
hotel occupies a restored historic
mansion. Roof terrace with a
plunge pool, and a shaded patio.

OLD TOWN: Hotel Neri €€€
Boutique **Map** D3
Sant Sever 5, 08002
Tel 933-04 06 55
W hotelneri.com
Enchanting hideaway, with a
superb restaurant, in an 18th-
century palace located in the
Gothic Quarter.

Northern Spain

BILBAO: Miróhotel €€
Boutique
Alameda Mazarredo, 77, 48009
Tel 946-61 18 80
W mirohotelbilbao.com
Designed by Antonio Miró, this
minimalist luxury hotel overlooks
the famous Guggenheim
Museum. There is a wellness
center and a library on site.

The regal interiors at the Ritz, Madrid

CANGAS DE ONIS: Parador de Cangas de Onis €€
Historic
Villanueva de Cangas, 33550 (Asturias)
Tel *985-84 94 02*
W parador.es
A spectacular 8th-century monastery on the banks of the Sella with a backdrop of the Picos.

DK Choice

ELCIEGO: Hotel Marqués de Riscal €€€
Boutique
Calle Torrea, 1 Elciego 01340
Tel *945-18 08 80*
W hotel-marquesderiscal.com
Designed by Frank Gehry, this hotel combines avant-garde design with an unbeatable location in the heart of the Basque wine country. Indulge in grape-based spa treatments, a rooftop lounge and wine bar, and organized wine tours through the adjacent vineyards.

FUENTE DÉ: Parador de Fuente Dé €
Historic
Ctra de Espinama s/n, 39588
Tel *911-77 61 42*
W parador.es
A modern *parador*, surrounded by majestic mountains, with high standards and amenities.

LAGUARDIA: Hospedería Los Parajes €€
Spa
Mayor 46-48, 01300
Tel *945-62 11 30*
W hospederiadelosparajes.com
This stylish 15th-century hotel features a spa with a *hammam* and wine therapy.

Catalonia & Eastern Spain

ALICANTE: Eurostars Mediterranea Plaza €€
Luxury
Plaza del Ayuntamiento 6, 03002
Tel *965-21 01 88*
W eurostarsmediterraneaplaza.com
Close to a beach, this magnificently refurbished hotel offers great views from the roof terrace.

BORREDÀ: Masia Jaume Coll €
Historic
Carretera C-26, km 169, 08619
Tel *938-23 90 95*
W masiajaumecoll.com
There are just a handful of rooms at this stone *masia* (farmhouse), set in the stunning countryside.

CARTAGENA: La Manga Club Principe Felipe €€
Luxury
La Manga Club, 30385 (Murcia)
Tel *968-33 12 34*
W lamangaclub.com
Enjoy world-class facilities at this exclusive Spanish village-style hotel, popular with celebrities.

DELTEBRE: Delta Hotel €
B&B
Avda del Canal, Camí de la Illeta s/n, 43580
Tel *977-48 00 46*
W deltahotel.net
The charming, family-run Delta Hotel makes a great base for exploring the Ebro delta.

DK Choice

FORTUNA: Balneario Leana €
Historic
Calle Balneario, 30630 (Murcia)
Tel *902-44 44 10*
W balneariodeleanafortuna.com
Renowned as Murcia's oldest hotel – it was founded in 1860 – this atmospheric health spa conjures up a unique aura of the past. Modernist details include the original woodwork.

MURCIA: Arco de San Juan €
Historic
Plaza de Ceballos 10, 30003
Tel *968-21 04 55*
W arcosanjuan.com.
A converted palace, with a blend of old and new furnishings.

VILAFAMÉS: El Jardin Vertical €
Historic
Calle Nou 15, 12192 (Castellón)
Tel *964-32 99 38*
W eljardinvertical.com.
A refurbished 17th-century red-stone house set amid olive and almond groves.

XÁTIVA: Hostería Mont Sant €
Historic
Subida al Castillo, 46800
Tel *962-27 50 81*
W mont-sant.com
Beautiful mansion with citrus-filled gardens, spa, and restaurant.

Central Spain

ALMAGRO: Casa Grande Almagro €
Historic
C/Federico Relimpio 10, 13270
Tel *671-49 62 88*
W casagrandealmagro.com
A 16th-century property, close to Plaza Mayor and the famous medieval theater.

Elegant neutral tones set the scene at the Hotel Rector, Salamanca

BURGOS: Posada Torre-Palacio de los Alvarado €
Historic
Calle Palacio 16, El Ribero Merindad de Montija, 09514
Tel *947-61 70 33*
W palacioalvarado.com
Good-value accommodations at this renovated former palace.

DK Choice

SALAMANCA: Hotel Rector €€
Boutique
Paseo Rector Esperabé 10, 37008
Tel *923-21 84 82*
W hotelrector.com
Formerly the mansion of one of Salamanca's most distinguished families, this refined hotel oozes elegance, but it also has a personal touch. Considered to be one of Spain's most celebrated boutique hotels.

SEGOVIA: Hotel Don Felipe €
Historic
Calle de Daoiz 7, 40001
Tel *921-46 60 95*
W hoteldonfelipe.es
A converted mansion with modern facilities and a garden.

SIGÜENZA: Molino de Alcuneza €€
Spa
Carretera Alboreca, km 0.5, 19264
Tel *949-39 15 01*
W molinodealcuneza.com
This idyllic hotel is well placed for exploring the medieval city. The modern spa includes a *hammam*.

TOLEDO: Hotel Sercotel San Juan de Los Reyes €€
Luxury
C/Reyes Católicos 5, 45002
Tel *925-28 35 35*
W hotelsanjuandelosreyes.com
A four-star hotel in a converted mill. Located in the historic center.

The stylish Portixol, perched at the water's edge, Mallorca

TRUJILLO: NH Palacio de Santa Marta €€
Historic
Ballesteros, 6, 10200
Tel 927-65 91 90
w nh-hotels.com
This 16th-century palace blends traditional features with modern-day comforts.

Southern Spain

ARCOS DE LA FRONTERA: Casa Grande €
Historic
C/Maldonaldo 10, 11630
Tel 956-70 39 30
w lacasagrande.net
A gleaming 18th-century mansion with splendid views of the countryside. Good breakfasts.

CÁDIZ: Hotel Playa Victoria €€
Boutique
Glorieta Ingeniero La Cierva 4, 11010
Tel 956-20 51 00
w palafoxhoteles.com
This eco-friendly seafront hotel features avant-garde interior furnishings and decor.

CÓRDOBA: Hotel Maestre €
Inn
Calle Romero Barros 4–6, 14003
Tel 957-47 24 10
w hotelmaestre.com
A classic hotel with a flower-filled patio. Simple rooms and self-catering apartments available.

CORTES DE LA FRONTERA : Casa Rural €
Inn
Bda El Colmenar, 29490
Tel 952-15 30 46
w ahoraya.es
Chic, rural hideaway nestled in a valley. Health facilities include Turkish massages, a spa, and clay treatments.

GRANADA: Posada del Toro €
Inn
C/Elviria 25, 18010
Tel 958-22 73 33
w posadadeltoro.com
Renovated 19th-century inn blending old charm and modern comforts. Wi-Fi in all rooms.

GRANADA: Casa 1800 €€
Boutique
C/Benalua 11, 18010
Tel 958-21 07 00
w hotelcasa1800granada.com
Romantic hotel in a 17th-century mansion. Suites have king- or queen-sized beds and great vistas. Wi-Fi available.

MÁLAGA: Salles Hotel €
Luxury
C/Marmoles 6, 29007
Tel 952-07 02 16
w salleshotels.com
Well-appointed hotel with modern and classically decorated rooms. The rooftop pool and terrace offer superb views.

SEVILLE: Cervantes €€
Boutique
C/Cervantes 10, 41003
Tel 954-90 02 80
w hotel-cervantes.com
Set in a lovely 16th-century property, with colored-glass ceilings and a tiled patio. Rooms are individually decorated.

DK Choice

SEVILLE: Casa Numero Siete €€€
Boutique
C/Virgenes 7, 41004
Tel 954-22 15 81
w casanumero7.com.
Discover luxury in a historic 19th-century mansion right in the heart of Seville's evocative old quarter. The decor at this guesthouse includes antiques and family heirlooms. Relax in the elegant lounge, and enjoy the discreet but friendly service.

The Balearic Islands

FORMENTERA: Hotel Entre Pinos €€
B&B
Ctra La Mola, km 12.3, Es Calo, 07820
Tel 971-32 70 19
w hostalentrepinos.com
A family-run hotel enclosed in pine woods and close to the beaches of Es Caló and Arenal. There is also a terrace bar, garden, and pool – where BBQs are held.

IBIZA: Mirador de Dalt Vila €€€
Historic
Plaza España 4, Ibiza City, 07800
Tel 971-30 30 45
w hotelmiradoribiza.com
In Ibiza town's upper village, this sumptuous 19th-century palace offers elegant rooms and suites, plus top-notch services.

DK Choice

MALLORCA: Portixol €€€
Boutique
C/Sirena, Portixol, 07006
Tel 971-27 18 00
w portixol.com
Located on a small fishing port, Portixol has been made over into one of the island's most stylish and best-loved hotels. A smooth Scandinavian vibe reigns throughout, with impeccable service and a variety of rooms – from spacious suites to cool little overnighters.

MENORCA: Agroturisme Biniatram €
Boutique
Ctra Cala Morell s/n, Cala Morell, 07760
Tel 971-38 31 13
w biniatram.com
This rustic finca has eight suites, all with self-catering facilities. Rooms are airy, and there is a large pool in the grounds.

An antique-filled room at Casa Rural, in Cortes de la Frontera

Where to Eat and Drink

Colorful artworks in the dining room at Delic, Madrid

Madrid

BOURBON MADRID:
Bar Tomate €€
Mediterranean **Map** D2
C/Fernando el Santo 26, 28046
Tel 917-02 38 70
A fashionable spot for market-
fresh dishes like tuna tartare
with guacamole or hake with
olives and tomatoes. The airy,
loft-style interior has big wooden
tables, perfect for groups.

BOURBON MADRID:
Café Gijón €€
Café **Map** D3
C/Paseo de Recoletos 21, 28004
Tel 915-21 54 25
One of Madrid's famous literary
cafés, established in 1887. Gijón
serves classic dishes in a dining
room or on the large terrace.

BOURBON MADRID:
La Casa del Abuelo €€
Tapas **Map** C4
C/Victoria 12, 28012
Tel 910-00 01 33
La Casa del Abuelo (grandfather's
house) specializes in delicious
prawns served with a local sweet
wine, plus a range of tasty tapas.

BOURBON MADRID:
Estado Puro €€
Gourmet tapas **Map** C4
Hotel NH Palacio de Tepa, Plaza del
Angel 9, 28012
Tel 914-29 98 17
Super-stylish spot with gourmet
tapas by celebrated chef Paco
Roncero, who brilliantly reinvents
classic recipes, such as buñuelos
de bacalao (cod puffs).

BOURBON MADRID:
Paradis de Madrid €€
Mediterranean **Map** D4
C/Marqués de Cubas 14, 28014
Tel 914-29 73 03
At Paradis de Madrid, guests dine
on delicious Mediterranean rice

dishes, fresh seafood, and
Catalan specialties, such as
calçots (leek-like vegetables).

OLD MADRID:
Bodegas La Ardosa €
Tapas **Map** C3
C/Colón 13, 28004
Tel 915-21 49 79
An old-fashioned tapas bar to
enjoy salmorejo cordobés – a
chilled tomato and almond soup
– and other traditional staples.

DK Choice

OLD MADRID: Delic €
Café **Map** B4
Plaza de la Paja s/n, 28005
Tel 913-64 54 50 **Closed** Mon &
Tue (for events)
A hip favorite on a charming
square, Delic is perfect for a lazy
breakfast or a tasty light lunch –
try the leek tart or the Japanese
dumplings. With wonderful
tarts, muffins, and brownies, it
is also a great stop for tea and
cake in the afternoon. Later in
the evening, come for cocktails
and occasional live music.

OLD MADRID: Naïa €€
Modern Spanish **Map** B4
Plaza de la Paja 3, 28005
Tel 913-66 27 83 **Closed** Mon
This chic bistro is popular with
actors and artists. Dishes on offer
might include a spicy monkfish
and scallop stew, or cod with
oranges and black olives.

Barcelona

OLD TOWN: Can Culleretes €
Traditional Regional **Map** D3
Quintana 5, 08002
Tel 933-17 30 22 **Closed** Sun dinner;
Mon; mid-Jul–mid-Aug
Barcelona's oldest restaurant, Can
Culleretes is great for classics

such as botifarra amb seques
(country sausage with beans)
and seafood stews.

DK Choice

OLD TOWN: Kaiku €
Mediterranean **Map** D4
Plaça del Mar 1, 08003
Tel 932-21 90 82 **Closed** Sun
dinner; Mon; Aug
This deceptively simple-looking
restaurant serves fantastic
dishes prepared with smoked
rice and homegrown
vegetables. The excellent
desserts are served on a platter.

OLD TOWN: Lo de Flor €
Mediterranean
Carretes 18, 08001
Tel 934-42 38 53 **Closed** Tue; 2 wks
Aug
A romantic, rustic restaurant with
minimalist decor and a short but
well-chosen wine list. Dinner only.

OLD TOWN: Senyor Parellada €
Mediterranean **Map** E3
Argenteria 37, 08003
Tel 933-10 50 94
Enjoy modern Mediterranean
fare in this elegant restaurant
in a 19th-century townhouse.

OLD TOWN: Pla €€
Fusion **Map** D3
Bellafila 5, 08002
Tel 934-12 65 52 **Closed** lunch
This reliably good dinner spot
offers deftly prepared fusion
food in stylish surroundings.

OLD TOWN: Dos Palillos €€€
Fusion **Map** D3
Elisabets 9, 08001
Tel 933-04 05 13 **Closed** Tue & Wed
lunch; Sun & Mon; late Dec–early
Jan, 3 wks Aug
Ultra-chic yet relaxed, this eatery
with a Michelin star serves up
spectacular Asian fusion tapas.

OLD TOWN: Koy Shunka €€€
Japanese **Map** D3
C/Copons 7, 08002
Tel 934-12 79 39 **Closed** Sun dinner;
Mon; Aug
Arguably the best Japanese
restaurant in the city, Koy Shunka
boasts an adventurous menu.

Northern Spain

LAREDO: La Marina Company €
Seafood
Calle Zamanillo, 39770
Tel *942-60 63 35*
The place for well-executed, simple traditional fare. Excellent-value set-menu options.

NOJA: Restaurante Sambal €€
Fine Dining
Calle el Arenal, 39180
Tel *942-63 15 31*   **Closed** *Oct–May: dinner Sun–Thu*
Gourmet dining accompanied by fine views. Terrace seating in good weather and an excellent wine list.

PAMPLONA: Café Bar Gaucho €
Regional
Calle de Espoz y Mina 7, 31002
Tel *948-22 50 73*
This small, buzzing place is one of Pamplona's best *pintxo* (small snack) bars, with a huge variety of flavorsome dishes. Cash only.

SAN SEBASTIAN: Arzak €€€
Modern Regional
Alcalde José Elosegui 273, 20015
Tel *943-28 55 93*   **Closed** *Sun & Mon; Jun 15–Jul 2 & Nov 2–26*
The iconic eatery of living legend Juan Mari Arzak and his daughter Elena, who was voted the World's Best Female Chef in 2012.

Catalonia & Eastern Spain

DK Choice

GIRONA: El Celler de Can Roca €€€
Modern Catalan
C/de Can Sunyer 48, 17007
Tel *972-22 21 57*   **Closed** *Sun & Mon; Apr 13–21, Aug, Dec 22–Jan 8*
This temple to molecular gastronomy boasts three Michelin stars. It is run by the Roca brothers: Joan is head chef, Jordi is the dessert chef, and Josep is the sommelier. Expect unique dishes, such as caramelized olives served on a bonsai tree, and oysters with champagne. Reserve at least a year in advance.

TARRAGONA: Sol-Ric €€
Mediterranean
Avda Via Augusta 227, 43007
Tel *977-23 20 32*
Divine seafood and regional fare in an elegant setting, with a great terrace for alfresco dining.

A much-coveted table at the Michelin-starred Celler de Can Roca, Girona

VALENCIA: L'Estimat €€
Seafood
Avda de Neptuno 16, 46011
Tel *963-71 10 18*   **Closed** *Mon & Sun dinner; Tue*
One of the best seafood spots on the entire Valencia beachfront, L'Estimat has a wide selection of set menus, plus excellent à la carte choices.

ZARAGOZA: Palomeque €
Spanish
C/ Agustín Palomeque 11, 50004
Tel *976-21 40 82*   **Closed** *Sun*
Come here for tapas in the morning and more substantial meals for lunch and dinner – all presented with sheer artistry.

Central Spain

CHINCHON: Mesón Cuevas del Vino €
Traditional
C/Benito Hortelano 13, 28370
Tel *918-94 02 06*   **Closed** *Sun dinner*
This rustically decorated restaurant in a 17th-century mill is a good bet for classic dishes, such as lamb chops.

NAVACERRADA: El Rumba €
Modern Spanish
Plaza del Doctor Gereda, 28491
Tel *918-56 04 05*   **Closed** *Mon & Tue in winter*
Wonderful charcoal-grilled meats, and a sprinkling of modern dishes like scallops with citrus and *sal-morejo* (tomato and bread purée).

SAN LORENZO DE EL ESCORIAL: Casa Zaca €€
Traditional
C/Embajadores 6, San Ildefonso, 40100
Tel *921-47 00 87*
The town's most elegant restaurant features classic fare, such as *cocido* (chickpea-based stew).

SEGOVIA: Restaurante José María €€
Regional
C/Cronista Lecea 11, 40001
Tel *921-46 11 11*
Come here to savor chef José María's unique take on Segovian staples. Try the roast suckling pig.

DK Choice

ZAFRA: El Acebuche €
Regional
Santa Marina, 3, 06300
Tel *924-55 33 20*
Housed in a historic building with modern decor, this restaurant offers traditional food with contemporary influences. The adjoining tapas bar serves lighter fare.

Southern Spain

ALGECIRAS: La Cabaña €
Traditional
Avda Agua Marina 5, 11203
Tel *956-66 73 79*   **Closed** *Mon*
Traditional restaurant with indoor and terrace dining. Offerings include Galician-style octopus and charcoal-grilled sirloin steaks.

CÁDIZ: Ventorillo del Chato €€€
Seafood
Via Augusta Julia, 11011
Tel *956-25 00 25*   **Closed** *Sun dinner (except Aug)*
This 18th-century seaside inn specializes in fish. Try the *corvino al vapor* (steamed sea bass).

CÓRDOBA: San Miguel €€
Traditional
Plaza San Miguel 1, 14002
Tel *957-47 01 66*   **Closed** *Sun*
The regional specialties served here include Iberian cured meats, *pisto* (ratatouille), and *manitas de cerdo* (pig's trotters).

DK Choice

GRANADA: Mirador de Morayma €€
Traditional
C/Pianista Gracia Carrillo 2, 18010
Tel *958-22 82 90*   **Closed** *Sun dinner*
Located beside the patio of a private house, Mirador enjoys marvelous city views. Few restaurants offer such a winning combination of idyllic setting and quality cuisine. Try the *fresh remojón* (salad with salt cod, olives, and orange) and *salmorejo* (a thicker version of gazpacho).

LA LINEA: La Marina €€
Seafood
Paseo Maritimo, La Atunara s/n, 11300
Tel *956-17 15 31* **Closed** *Sun dinner; Mon (Oct–Mar)*
A large seaside eating spot with nautical decor and great views. Delicious clams and *revuelto de gambas y hortiguillas* (scrambled eggs with prawns and nettles).

PUERTO DE SANTA MARIA: Casa Flores €€€
Traditional
Ribera del Rio 9, 11500
Tel *956-54 35 12*
This stalwart has traditional tiles and a bullfight motif decor to go with its menu of staple dishes, such as *langostinos* (king prawns) and *percebes* (goose barnacles). Good lamb and pork dishes, too.

RONDA: Tragabuches €€€
Traditional
C/Jose Aparicio 1, 29400
Tel *952-19 02 91* **Closed** *Mon & Sun dinner; Jan*
Try the chef's supreme *ajo blanco* (cold summer almond and garlic soup) at this Michelin-starred restaurant. Scintillating **menu de degustación**. Impeccable service.

SEVILLE: Bodeguita Casablanca €
Traditional
C/Adolfo Rodriguez Jurado 12, 41002
Tel *954-22 47 14* **Closed** *Sat dinner; Sun; Aug*
Very popular with locals, this is a traditional tapas bar with a no-frills decor of tiles and barrel tables. First-rate mini menu.

SEVILLE: Casa Robles €€
Seafood
C/Alvarez Quintero 58, 41001
Tel *954-21 31 50*
A prize-winning spot with stunning decor and great fish and shellfish dishes. Cathedral views from the terrace, plus one of the best wine lists in Seville.

SEVILLE: Don Raimundo €€
Traditional
C/Argote del Molino 26, 41004
Tel *954-22 33 55*
A sumptuously converted 17th-century convent adorned with stone walls, vivid tiles, ceiling beams, and huge chandeliers. It serves splendid *langostinos* (giant prawns) and *jabali al horno* (oven-cooked wild boar).

The Balearic Islands

FORMENTERA: Pequeña Isla €€
Regional
Avda El Pilar, 101 El Pilar de la Mola
Tel *971-32 70 68*
This unpretentious, reliable restaurant in the hilltop village of La Mola serves all the local dishes, such as fish stew and dorado baked in salt.

DK Choice

IBIZA: La Paloma €
Mediterranean
C/Can Pou 4, San Lorenzo, 07812
Tel *971-32 55 43* **Closed** *dinner; Mon (Mar, Apr & Oct); Nov–Feb*
A labor of love undertaken by two families, La Paloma is a postcard-pretty garden restaurant in a renovated finca, surrounded by fruit orchards. On the menu are Italian-inspired homemade dishes created with organic, local ingredients. Pleasant service.

IBIZA: Las Dos Lunas €€€
Italian/Mediterranean
Ctra Ibiza–San Antonio, km 5, 07840
Tel *971-19 81 02* **Closed** *Nov–Apr*
One of Ibiza's most exclusive restaurants, Las Dos Lunas is often frequented by celebrities. Dishes are made with produce from its own vegetable garden.

MALLORCA: La Taberna de la Bóveda €
Tapas
Paseo Sagrera 3, Palma, 07012
Tel *971-72 00 26* **Closed** *Sun*
A perennially popular tapas bar that also serves more substantial dishes hailing from Galicia and Castilla. Pretty period setting.

DK Choice

MALLORCA: Santi Taura €€
Regional
C/Joan Carles I 48, Lloseta, 07360
Tel *971-51 46 22* **Closed** *Mon lunch, Sun dinner; Tue*
Local chef Santi Taura is a sort of food anthropologist – unearthing old recipes of the islands, which he reinterprets in this restaurant. Three weekly tasting menus are presented, and with each course, the waiter, or Santi himself, will explain the history and culture of the food.

MENORCA: Es Tast de na Silvia €€
Market Cuisine
Avda Portixol 21–22, Cala 'N Bosch, 07760
Tel *971-38 78 95* **Closed** *Wed; Nov–Mar*
The best option among the crowd of touristy restaurants. It serves top-notch cuisine based on local and organic produce.

DK Choice

MENORCA: La Minerva €€€
Regional
Moll de Llevant 87, Mahón, 07701
Tel *971-35 19 95* **Closed** *Mon; Jan*
This classic hangout for the island's yacht set is the place to be seen, particularly for those lucky enough to get a table on the floating terrace on the harbor. The menu (the longest in Menorca) features both meat and fish dishes. Do not miss the seafood *zarzuela* (stew).

Murals and delicious banquettes add to the cozy feel at La Paloma, Ibiza

PORTUGAL

Most visitors to Portugal head for the sandy coves, pretty fishing villages, and manicured golf courses of the Algarve. But beyond the south-coast resorts lies the least-explored corner of Western Europe: a country of rugged landscapes, ancient cities with proud traditions, and quiet rural backwaters.

Portugal appears to have no obvious geographical claim to nationhood, yet the country has existed within borders virtually unchanged for nearly 800 years, making it one of the oldest nation states in Europe. Its ten million people are proudly independent from, and distrustful of, neighboring Spain.

For a small country, the regions of Portugal are immensely varied. The rural Minho and Trás-os-Montes in the north are the most traditional. Over the last few decades, many inhabitants of these neglected regions have been forced to emigrate in search of work. At the same time, the Algarve, with its beautiful sandy beaches and warm Mediterranean climate, has become a vacation playground for Northern Europeans, as well as the Portuguese themselves. Lisbon, the capital, at the mouth of the Tagus, is a cosmopolitan metropolis with a rich cultural life. Oporto is a serious rival, especially in terms of commerce and industry, and is the center for the production and export of Portugal's

most famous product – port wine, grown on steeply terraced vineyards hewn out of mountainsides in the wild upper reaches of the Douro valley.

History

The Romans, who arrived in 216 BC, called the whole peninsula Hispania, but the region between the Douro and Tagus rivers was named Lusitania after the Celtiberian tribe that lived there. After the collapse of the Roman Empire in the 5th century, Hispania was overrun first by Germanic tribes, then by Moors from North Africa in 711.

Reconquest by the Christian kingdoms of the north began in earnest in the 11th century. In the process, Portucale, a small county of the kingdom of León and Castile, was declared an independent kingdom by its ruler, Afonso Henriques, in 1139. With the aid of English crusaders, he succeeded in recapturing Lisbon in 1147.

The kingdom expanded south to the Algarve, and Portuguese sailors began to explore the African coast and the Atlantic.

Fishing boats on the beach at the popular Algarve resort of Albufeira

◄ The picturesque white village of Azenhas do Mar, clinging to a clifftop overlooking the Atlanic Ocean

Portugal's golden age reached its zenith in the reign of Manuel I, with Vasco da Gama's voyage to India in 1498 and the discovery of Brazil in 1500. The era also produced the one uniquely Portuguese style of architecture: the Manueline. Trade with the East brought great wealth, but military defeat in Morocco meant that the prosperity was short-lived. Spain invaded in 1580 and ruled Portugal for the next 60 years.

After Portugal regained independence, its fortunes were restored by gold from Brazil. In the late 18th century, the chief minister, the Marquês de Pombal, famous for rebuilding Lisbon after the 1755 earthquake, began to modernize the country. However, Napoleon's invasion in 1807 and the loss of Brazil in 1825 left Portugal impoverished and divided.

Manuel I (reigned 1495–1521), who made vast profits from Portugal's spice trade

Absolutists and Constitutionalists struggled for power, until, in 1910, a republican revolution overthrew the monarchy.

The weakness of the economy led to a military coup in 1926 and a long period of dictatorship. António Salazar, who held power from 1932 to 1968, rid the country of its debts, but poverty was widespread and all opposition banned. The country was a virtual recluse in the world community, the prime concern of foreign policy being the defense of its African and Asian colonies. The bloodless Carnation Revolution ended the dictatorship in 1974, and full democracy was restored in 1976. Since its entry into the European Community in 1986, Portugal has enjoyed rapid economic growth and assumed the self-confident attitude of a modern Western European state.

Language and Culture

The family is the hub of Portuguese daily life and Catholicism remains a powerful force in rural communities. But the country has come a long way since the repression and self-censorship of the Salazar era. Urban Portugal, in particular, presents a fairly emancipated and eagerly consumerist face to the world.

The national psyche encapsulates this dualism in its struggle between a forward-looking, realistic approach to life and the dreamy, inward-looking side that finds expression in the Portuguese notion of *saudade*, a melancholy yearning for something lost or unattainable.

The Portuguese language is a source of national pride, and visitors should not assume that it is interchangeable with Spanish. Portuguese people are also often eager to speak English. Pride, too, is taken in *fado*, the native musical tradition that expresses *saudade*.

KEY DATES IN PORTUGUESE HISTORY

139 BC Romans subdue the Lusitani

415 AD Visigoths invade Iberian Peninsula

711 Muslim army conquers Visigothic kingdom

1139 Afonso Henriques declares himself king

1147 Afonso Henriques takes Lisbon

1249 Conquest of Algarve complete

1385 João I defeats Castilians at Aljubarrota

1418 Prince Henry the Navigator made governor of Algarve; sponsors expeditions to Africa

1578 King Sebastião killed on ill-fated expedition to Morocco

1580 Philip II of Spain becomes king of Portugal

1640 Restoration; Duke of Bragança crowned João IV; start of war of independence

1668 Spain recognizes Portugal's independence

1807 French invade; royal family flees to Brazil

1910 Revolution; Manuel II abdicates and flees to England; republic proclaimed

1932 António Salazar becomes prime minister

1974 Carnation Revolution

2000 Portugal joins European single currency

2011 The economic crisis forces Portugal in to a €78 billion bailout agreement with the EU and IMF

2013 Government approves further austerity measures to avoid a second international bailout

Exploring Portugal

Portugal is a small country and there are fast road and train links between the country's four great cities: Lisbon, Coimbra, Oporto, and Faro. Many of the most famous sights, such as the royal palaces at Sintra and the monastery of Alcobaça, make a good day's outing from Lisbon. In the south, the great attractions are the sandy beaches of the Algarve. Arriving from the north is quite easy on the Lisbon-Algarve motorway, but most visitors fly direct to Faro airport and once there, traveling between the various resorts is no problem.

Sintra, dominated by the conical chimneys of the old royal palace

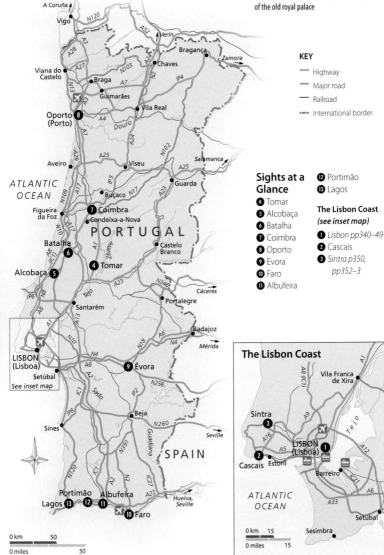

KEY

— Highway

— Major road

— Railroad

▪▪▪ International border

Sights at a Glance

④ Tomar
⑤ Alcobaça
⑥ Batalha
⑦ Coimbra
⑧ Oporto
⑨ Evora
⑩ Faro
⑪ Albufeira
⑫ Portimão
⑬ Lagos

The Lisbon Coast
(see inset map)

① *Lisbon pp340–49*
② *Cascais*
③ *Sintra p350, pp352–3*

The Lisbon Coast

Vila Franca de Xira

Sintra ③

LISBON (Lisboa) ①

Cascais ② Estoril

Barreiro

ATLANTIC OCEAN

Sesimbra

Setúbal

0 km   15
0 miles   15

For keys to symbols see back flap

❶ Lisbon

The capital of Portugal occupies a hilly site on the estuary of the Tagus. Over the centuries, the city expanded along the coast to Belém, the starting point for the voyages of discovery in the 15th century, and to the other side of the river, known as the Margem Sul. It has now spread far inland, making the population of Greater Lisbon nearly two million. The historic center (the Baixa) is a small, low-lying area, pinned between the heights of the Alfama to the east and the Bairro Alto to the west. The city underwent a great cleanup for the Expo '98 exhibition, especially in the old docks and industrial areas along the waterfront.

Portugal's coat of arms in the treasury of the Sé (cathedral)

Sights at a Glance

③ São Vicente de Fora
④ Alfama
⑤ Castelo de São Jorge
⑥ Sé
⑦ Praça do Comércio
⑧ Baixa
⑨ Bairro Alto
⑪ Museu Nacional de Arte Antiga

Greater Lisbon
(see inset map)

① Oceanário de Lisboa
② Museu Nacional do Azulejo
⑩ Museu Calouste Gulbenkian

Belém *(see inset map)*

⑫ Museu Nacional dos Coches
⑬ Monument to the Discoveries
⑭ *Mosteiro dos Jerónimos pp348–9*
⑮ Museu da Marinha
⑯ Torre de Belém

Getting Around

Lisbon's limited metro system links the north of the city with sights in the center around Rossio square. Buses cover the whole city and are the most common form of public transportation. Take the Santa Justa lift to reach the Bairro Alto district and the 28 tram to climb the steep hill up to the Alfama. Belém is served by tram, train, and bus. Taxis are inexpensive, but a taxi ride can be alarming, as can any experience of driving in Lisbon.

Mosteiro dos Jerónimos, overlooking Praça do Império

Greater Lisbon

Vila Franca

Lisbon Airport
Olivais
Oriente
①
Amadora
Pontinha
Campo Grande
Xabregas
②
Benfica
⑩
Estefânia
PARQUE FLORESTAL DE MONSANTO
Carnaxide
Graça
Cascais
Alcântara
Montijo
Belém
Tejo
Barreiro
Cacilhas
Almada
Porto Brandão Trafaria
Seixal
Setúbal

0 meters 500
0 yards 500

0 km 2
0 miles 2

Key

Area of main map

R. S. A. DOS CAPUCHOS

GRAÇA

Martim Moniz

Restauradores
Rossio
ROSSIO (PRAÇA DOM PEDRO IV)
Rossio

São Roque

ALFAMA
⑤
④
③
Santa Engrácia

Santa Apolónia

Museu Militar

Santa Apolónia

Igreja do Carmo
⑧
BAIXA

CHIADO
RUA GARRETT

Baixa-Chiado
Teatro de São Carlos
Museu do Chiado
⑥
RUA SÃO

AVENIDA INFANTE DOM HENRIQUE

⑦
RUA DO ARSENAL
Tejo

AVENIDA DA RIBEIRA DAS NAUS

Estação Fluvial Terreiro do Paço

Terreiro do Paço

Belém

ESTÁDIO MUNICIPAL DO RESTELO
BELÉM
AJUDA
D. MÉMORIA

⑮
⑭
⑫
Belém

Centro Cultural de Belém
PRAÇA DO IMPÉRIO

Estação Fluvial de Belém

AVENIDA DA ÍNDIA

AVENIDA DE BRASÍLIA
⑬

0 meters 250
0 yards 250

⑯
Tejo

Key

Sight / Place of interest
Pedestrian street
Funicular railway

D
E
F

For keys to symbols *see back flap*

① Oceanário de Lisboa

Esplanada Dom Carlos I, Parque das Nações. **Tel** 218-917 002.
Ⓜ Oriente. ▭ 705, 728, 744, 750.
🚃 Gare do Oriente. **Open** daily.
▨ ♿ Ⓦ oceanario.pt

This huge oceanarium, on the banks of the Tagus, is the second largest in the world. It was designed for Expo '98 by the American architect Peter Chermayeff to illustrate the environmental theme of "The Oceans: A Heritage for the Future."

The central feature is a gigantic aquarium, the "Open Tank," with enough water to fill four Olympic swimming pools. Representing the open ocean, this contains fauna of the high seas, from sea bream to sharks. Around the main tank four smaller aquariums reconstruct the ecosystems of the Atlantic, Antarctic, Pacific, and Indian oceans.

② Museu Nacional do Azulejo

Rua da Madre de Deus 4. **Tel** 218-100 340. ▭ 28, 718, 742, 759, 794.
Open Tue–Sun. **Closed** Jan 1, Easter, May 1, Dec 25. 🖥 ⊘ ▨
Ⓦ museudoazulejo.pt

The idea of decorative tiles was a legacy of the Moors. From the 16th century onward, Portugal started producing its own painted ceramic tiles *(azulejos)*. The blue-and-white tiles of the Baroque era are considered by many to be the finest.

The National Tile Museum is housed in the Convento da Madre de Deus, founded by Dona Leonor (widow of João II) in 1509. The interior of the church has striking Baroque decoration, added by João V.

An important surviving feature of the original convent is the Manueline cloister. Along with the larger Renaissance cloister, it provides a stunning setting for the museum. Decorative panels, individual tiles, and photographs trace tile-making from its introduction, through Spanish influence and the development of Portugal's own styles, to today.

Statue of woman praying beside tomb of Carlos I in São Vicente de Fora

Panels from churches, monasteries, and other sites around Portugal have been reassembled here. Highlights include a blue-and-white, 18th-century panorama showing Lisbon before the earthquake, and colorful 17th-century carpet tiles (so-called because they imitated the patterns of Moorish rugs).

Detail from 16th-century altarpiece in the Museu Nacional do Azulejo

③ São Vicente de Fora

Largo de São Vicente. **Tel** 218-810 500.
🚋 28. ▭ 712, 734. **Open** Tue–Sun.
Closed public hols. ▨ to cloisters.

St. Vincent was proclaimed Lisbon's patron saint in 1173, when his relics were brought to a church on this site. The present church was completed in 1627. The Italianate facade has statues of Saints Vincent, Augustine, and Sebastian over the entrance. The church has reopened after extensive renovation.

Behind the church is the old refectory, transformed into the Bragança Pantheon in 1885. The tombs of almost every Bragança king and queen are here, from João IV, who died in 1656, to Manuel II, last king of Portugal. Only Maria I and Pedro IV are not buried here. A stone mourner kneels at the tomb of Carlos I and his son Luís Felipe, assassinated in Praça do Comércio *(see p344)* in 1908.

④ Alfama

▭ 737. 🚋 12, 28.

A fascinating quarter at any time of day, the Alfama comes to life in the late afternoon and early evening, when the small restaurants and bars start to fill and music, often *fado*, can be heard in the alleyways. It is hard to believe that this, the oldest part of Lisbon, was once the most desirable quarter of the city. In the Middle Ages, wealthy residents started to move away, fearing earthquakes, leaving the quarter to fishermen and paupers. Ironically, the Alfama was spared by the earthquake of 1755. Today, the area is a warren of narrow streets and small, picturesque houses clinging to the hillside below the Castelo de São Jorge.

The least strenuous way to see this area is to start at the castle at the top and work your way down. Attractions on the way include the **Museu de Artes Decorativas** (Museum of Decorative Arts), which has its own workshops, and the sweeping views from the terrace of the **Miradouro de Santa Luzia**. You could also visit, on a Tuesday or Saturday, the colorful **Feira da Ladra** (Thieves' Market) in Campo de Santa Clara, to the east of the castle, or the early morning fish market in Rua de São Pedro.

⑤ Castelo de São Jorge

Porta de S. Jorge, Rua do Chão da Feira. **Tel** 218-800 620. 🚌 737. 🚋 28. **Open** daily. 📷 🌐 castelodesaojorge.pt

Following the recapture of Lisbon from the Moors in 1147, King Afonso Henriques transformed their citadel – which crowned Lisbon's eastern hill – into the residence of the Portuguese kings. In 1511, Manuel I built a more lavish palace beside the river *(see p344)*. In the centuries that followed, the Castelo de São Jorge was used variously as a theater, a prison, and an arms depot. After the 1755 earthquake, the ramparts lay in ruins until 1938, when the castle was completely rebuilt. It was restored again, along with parts of the Santa Cruz district, in 2006.

The castle gardens and narrow streets of the old Santa Cruz district, which lies within the walls, are a pleasant place for a stroll, and the views are the finest in Lisbon. Visitors can climb the towers, one of which has a camera obscura, walk along the reconstructed ramparts, or stand on the shaded observation terrace. Within the castle's outer walls there is also a museum and an archaeological site.

The Sé, Lisbon's austere 12th-century cathedral

⑥ Sé

Largo da Sé. **Tel** 218-866 752. 🚌 737. 🚋 12, 28. **Open** daily. Cloister & treasury: **Open** daily. 📷

In 1150, Afonso Henriques built a cathedral for the first bishop of Lisbon (Gilbert of Hastings) on the site of the Moorish mosque. Sé denotes the seat of a bishop.

Though much renovated over the centuries, the Sé has kept its solid Romanesque facade. The Capela de Santo Ildefonso, one of nine Gothic chapels in the ambulatory behind the altar, contains two fine 14th-century tombs and in the Franciscan chapel by the entrance stands the font where St. Antony of Padua was baptized in 1195. In the Gothic cloister behind the Sé, excavations have unearthed Roman and other remains.

The treasury, located in one of the towers, has a splendid collection of exhibits, including the relics of St. Vincent. Legend has it that his remains were watched over by two ravens on their journey to Lisbon in 1173, hence the raven on the city's coat of arms.

View of the Castelo de São Jorge across the Baixa, Lisbon's lower town

Panorama of the charming Bairro Alto district, located high on a hill

⑦ Praça do Comércio

🚌 711, 714, 732, 759, 794 & many others. 🚋 15, 18.

More commonly known as Terreiro do Paço (Palace Square), this was the site of the royal palace for 400 years. Manuel I transferred the royal residence here, from the Castelo de São Jorge, in 1511. The first palace, along with its library and 70,000 books, was destroyed in the 1755 earthquake. Its replacement was built around three sides of the square. After the 1910 revolution, it became government administrative offices.

The south side looks across the Tagus and was once the finest gateway to Lisbon – used by royalty and ambassadors – with marble steps up from the river. In the center of the square is an equestrian statue of José I (1775) by Machado de Castro, leading Portuguese sculptor of the 18th century. The impressive

triumphal arch on the north side, decorated with statues of historical figures, leads into Rua Augusta and the Baixa. Take the elevator to the top of the arch for sweeping views of the city.

On February 1, 1908, King Carlos and his son, Luís Felipe, were assassinated in the square. In 1974, it witnessed the first uprising of the Armed Forces Movement, which overthrew the Caetano regime in a bloodless coup that became known as the Carnation Revolution.

⑧ Baixa

🚌 711, 714, 732, 736, 759, 794 & many others. 🚋 15, 18. Ⓜ Rossio, Restauradores, Terreiro do Paço.

Following the 1755 earthquake, the Marquês de Pombal created an entirely new city center, one of Europe's first examples of town planning. Using a grid layout of streets, the Praça do

Comércio was linked with the busy central square of Rossio. The streets were flanked by splendid Neoclassical buildings.

The Baixa (lower town) is still the commercial hub of the city, housing banks, offices, and stores. The streets are crowded by day, especially the central Rua Augusta, but less so after dark.

By the Restauradores metro station is the **Palácio Foz**, an 18th-century palace. Tourists are naturally drawn to Rossio, an elegant square and social focal point with cafés and *pastelarias*. The **National Theater** stands on the north side. Just to the east of Rossio is the less attractive Praça da Figueira, the city's main marketplace in Pombal's time. Rua das Portas de Santo Antão, north of the two squares, is a lively pedestrian street full of restaurants.

⑨ Bairro Alto

🚌 732, 758. 🚋 28 (also Elevador da Glória & Elevador da Santa Justa). Ⓜ Baixa-Chiado.

The hilltop Bairro Alto quarter, dating from the 16th century, is one of Lisbon's most picturesque districts. Its narrow, cobbled streets house a traditional, close-knit community, with small workshops and family-run *tascas* (cheap restaurants). This predominantly residential area has become fashionable at night for its bars, nightclubs, and *fado* houses *(see p361)*. Very different in character is the neighboring, elegant, commercial district, known as the Chiado, where

Rossio Square and the Neoclassical National Theater in the Baixa

For hotels and restaurants see p362 and p363

The Earthquake of 1755

The first tremor of the devastating earthquake was felt at 9:30am on November 1. It was followed by a second, far more violent, shock a few minutes later, which reduced over half the city to rubble. A third shock was followed by fires, which quickly spread. An hour later, huge waves came rolling in from the Tagus, flooding the lower part of the city. Most of Portugal suffered damage, but Lisbon was the worst affected: an estimated 15,000 people died in the city. Sebastião José de Carvalho e Melo, chief minister to King José I, later Marquês de Pombal, restored order and began a progressive town-planning scheme. His cool efficiency gained him almost total political control.

Marquês de Pombal

artists exhibited include Ghirlandaio, Rubens, Guardi, Gainsborough, Turner, Manet, and Renoir. The collection also includes sculpture, jewelry, textiles, manuscripts, porcelain, and a variety of decorative arts.

⑪ Museu Nacional de Arte Antiga

Rua das Janelas Verdes. **Tel** 213-912 800. 🚌 713, 714, 727. 🚊 15, 18. **Open** Tue–Sun (Tue: pm only). **Closed** public hols. 🅿️ 🎫 📷 ♿ 🚫 **W** museudearteantiga.pt

The national art collection, housed in a 17th-century palace, was inaugurated in 1770. In 1940 a modern annex (including the main facade) was added. This was built on the site of a monastery, largely destroyed in the 1755 earthquake. Its only surviving feature, the chapel, has been integrated into the museum.

The first floor houses 14th–19th-century European paintings, decorative arts, and furniture. Artists exhibited include Piero della Francesca, Hans Holbein the Elder, Raphael, Lucas Cranach the Elder, Hieronymus Bosch, and Albrecht Dürer. Oriental and African art, Chinese ceramics, and the gold, silver, and jewelry collection are on the second floor. The top floor houses Portuguese works.

The pride of the Portuguese collection is the *Panels of St. Vincent* (c.1467–70), attributed to Nuno Gonçalves. It is an altarpiece painted on six panels, featuring portraits of a wide range of contemporary figures, from beggars and sailors to bishops and princes, including Henry the Navigator and the future João II, all paying homage to the saint. Another fascinating aspect of the Age of Exploration is recorded in the 16th-century Japanese screens, which show Portuguese traders arriving in Japan.

The Elevador de Santa Justa, which links the Baixa to the Chiado district

affluent Lisboetas shop. On the main street, Rua Garrett, the Café Brasileira – once frequented by writers and intellectuals – remains popular. The Chiado was devastated by fire in 1988, but has been painstakingly renovated.

The best way to reach the Bairro Alto from the Baixa is via the Chiado district and the **Elevador de Santa Justa**, a Neo-Gothic elevator dating from 1901–2. Tourist attractions include the richly decorated **São Roque** church, the ruined **Igreja do Carmo**, once the largest church in Lisbon, and the **Museu Nacional de Arte Contemporânea (MNAC)**, which houses art from 1850–1950.

⑩ Museu Calouste Gulbenkian

Avda de Berna 45. **Tel** 217-823 000. Ⓜ Praça de Espanha, São Sebastião. 🚌 716, 756, 726, 746. **Open** Tue–Sun. **Closed** Mon & public hols. 📷 (free Sun). 🚫 📷 ♿ **W** museu.gulbenkian.pt

Thanks to wealthy Armenian oil magnate Calouste Gulbenkian, Portugal owns one of the finest personal art collections assembled during the 20th century. Gulbenkian moved to Portugal in World War II, because of the country's neutral status. This museum was inaugurated in 1969, as part of the charitable institution bequeathed to the nation. The building was devised to create the best layout for the founder's varied collection: the exhibits span 4,000 years, from ancient Egypt and China, through an extensive collection of Islamic ceramics and carpets, to Art Nouveau. Gulbenkian was a friend of René Lalique, the great glassware and jewelry maker, and one room is filled with his work.

Highlights of the European art collection include Van der Weyden's *St. Catherine* and Rembrandt's *Portrait of an Old Man*. Other major

Statue of the founder at the Gulbenkian Museum

Belém

At the mouth of the Tagus, where the Portuguese mariners set sail on their voyages of discovery, Manuel I commissioned two grand monuments in the exuberant Manueline style of architecture: the Mosteiro dos Jerónimos and the Torre de Belém. Today, Belém is a spacious, relatively green suburb with museums and gardens, including the vast Praça do Império, a formal square with a central fountain in front of the monastery. The area enjoys an attractive riverside setting, with cafés and a promenade; on sunny days, it has a distinct seaside feel. In Rua de Belém is the Antiga Confeitaria de Belém, a 19th-century café that sells the local specialty: *pastéis de Belém*, rich flaky-pastry custard tarts.

There is also a 19th-century Lisbon cab, painted black and green, the colors of taxis right up to the 1990s. The 18th-century Eyeglass Chaise has a black leather hood pierced with sinister eyelike windows. It dates from the era of Pombal *(see p345)*, when lavish decoration was discouraged.

⑫ Museu Nacional dos Coches

Praça Afonso de Albuquerque. **Tel** 213-610 850. 🚌 714, 727, 728, 729, 751. 🚋 15. 🚊 Belém. **Open** Tue–Sun. **Closed** Jan 1, Easter, May 1, Dec 25. 🎫 (free 10am–2pm Sun). ♿ 🌐 museudoscoches.pt

The National Coach Museum was established in 1905 by King Carlos's wife, Dona Amélia, whose pink riding cloak can be seen on display. It occupies the former riding school of the Palace of Belém. The rest of the elegant pink palace is now the residence of the president of Portugal. The coaches on display span three centuries and range from the practical to the

preposterous. The main gallery, in Louis XVI style with a splendid painted ceiling, is the setting for two rows of coaches created for Portuguese royalty. The oldest is the comparatively plain 16th-century red leather and wood coach of Philip II of Spain. The coaches become increasingly sumptuous, interiors lined with red velvet and gold, exteriors carved with allegorical figures. The most extravagant of all are three Baroque coaches made in Rome for the Portuguese ambassador to the Vatican in the early 18th century.

The neighboring gallery includes pony-drawn chaises.

Baroque coach in the Museu Nacional dos Coches

⑬ Monument to the Discoveries

Padrão dos Descobrimentos, Avda de Brasília. **Tel** 213-031 950. 🚌 727, 728, 729, 751. 🚋 15. **Open** Tue–Sun. **Closed** public hols. 🎫 🌐 padrao dosdescobrimentos.pt

Standing prominently on the Belém waterfront, the Padrão dos Descobrimentos was built in 1960 to mark the 500th anniversary of the death of Henry the Navigator *(see p338)*. The 52-m (170-ft) high monument resembles a caravel – the small, lateen-rigged ship used by Portuguese sailors to explore the coast of Africa –

Eastern Face of the Monument to the Discoveries

Afonso V (1432–81)

Henry the Navigator (1394–1460), patron of the first explorers

Pedro Álvares Cabral (1467–1520), discoverer of Brazil

Vasco da Gama (1460–1524)

Fernão Magalhães (Magellan), who crossed the Pacific in 1520–21

Padrão erected by Diogo Cão in the Congo in 1482

with Portugal's coat of arms on the sides. Henry the Navigator stands at the prow with a caravel in hand. In two sloping lines either side of the monument are heroes linked with the Discoveries.

In front of the monument is a huge mariner's compass cut into the paving. The central map, dotted with galleons and mermaids, shows the routes of the discoverers in the 15th and 16th centuries. Inside the monument, an elevator whisks you to the sixth floor, where steps lead to the top for a splendid panorama.

⑭ Mosteiro dos Jerónimos

See pp348–9.

⑮ Museu de Marinha

Praça do Império. **Tel** 213-620 019. 🚌 727, 728, 729, 751. 🚋 15. **Open** Tue–Sun. **Closed** public hols. 🎟 (free on Sun). ♿ 🌐 **museu.marinha.pt**

The Maritime Museum was inaugurated in 1962 in the west wing of the Jerónimos monastery. A hall devoted to the Discoveries illustrates the rapid progress in ship design from the mid-15th century. Small replicas show the transition from the bark to the lateen-rigged caravel, through the faster square-rigged caravel, to the Portuguese *nau,* or great ship. There is also a display of astrolabes and navigational instruments, and replicas of 16th-century maps. The pillars carved with the Cross of the Order of Christ are replicas of various kinds of *padrão,* a stone marker set up to denote sovereignty over the new lands discovered.

Beyond the Hall of Discoveries are models of modern Portuguese ships and the Royal Quarters, housing the exquisitely furnished wood-paneled cabin of King Carlos and Queen Amélia from the royal yacht *Amélia,* built in Scotland in 1900. The modern pavilion opposite houses original royal barges and a display of seaplanes.

The Torre de Belém, a landmark for sailors returning to Lisbon

⑯ Torre de Belém

Avenida da India. **Tel** 213-620 034. 🚌 727, 728, 729, 751. 🚋 15. 🚉 Belém. **Open** Tue–Sun. **Closed** Jan 1, Easter Sun, May 1, Dec 25. 🎟 (free 10am–2pm Sun; public hols). ♿ ground floor only. 🌐 **torrebelem.pt**

Commissioned by Manuel I, the tower was built as a fortress in the middle of the Tagus in 1515–21. Before nearby land was reclaimed in the 19th century, the tower stood much further from the shore than it does today. As the starting point for the navigators who set out to discover the trade routes to the east, this Manueline gem became a symbol of Portugal's great era of expansion. On the terrace, facing the sea, stands a

Royal coat of arms on the Torre de Belém

statue of Our Lady of Safe Homecoming, watching over the lives of Portugal's sailors.

The beauty of the tower lies in the exterior decoration: Manueline ropework carved in stone, openwork balconies, and Moorish-style watchtowers. The distinctive battlements are in the shape of shields, decorated with the squared cross of the Order of Christ, the emblem that also adorned the sails of Portuguese ships.

The space below the terrace, which served as a storeroom and a prison, is very austere, but the private quarters in the tower are worth visiting for the elegant arcaded Renaissance loggia and the wonderful panorama.

Vasco da Gama (c.1460–1524)

In 1498 Vasco da Gama sailed around the Cape of Good Hope and opened the sea route to India. Although the Hindu ruler of Calicut, who received him wearing diamond and ruby rings, was not impressed by his humble offerings of cloth and wash basins, da Gama returned to Portugal with a valuable cargo of spices. In 1502 he sailed again to India, establishing Portuguese trade routes in the Indian Ocean. João III nominated him Viceroy of India in 1524, but he died of a fever soon after.

Portrait of Vasco da Gama, painted in India

⑭ Mosteiro dos Jerónimos

A monument to the wealth of Portugal's Age of Discovery, the monastery is the culmination of the Manueline style of architecture. Commissioned by Manuel I in around 1501, soon after Vasco da Gama's return from his historic voyage, it was funded largely by "pepper money", taxes on spices, precious stones, and gold. Various masterbuilders worked on the building, the most notable being Diogo Boitac, replaced by João de Castilho in 1517. The monastery was entrusted to the Order of St. Jerome (Hieronymites) until 1834, when all religious orders were disbanded.

Tomb of Vasco da Gama
The 19th-century tomb of the explorer *(see p347)* is carved with ropes, armillary spheres, and other seafaring symbols.

View of the Monastery
The facade of the monastery church is dominated by the magnificent South Portal. This makes dramatic use of the Manueline style of architecture, essentially a Portuguese variant of Late Gothic.

Entrance to church and cloister

KEY

① **Gallery**

② **The West Portal** was designed by the French sculptor Nicolau Chanterène. One of the niches holds a sculpture of the kneeling figure of King Manuel I.

③ **The modern wing**, built in 1850 in Neo-Manueline style, houses the National Museum of Archaeology and part of the Maritime Museum *(see p347)*.

④ **Refectory** walls are tiled with 18th-century *azulejos*. The panel at the northern end depicts the Feeding of the Five Thousand.

⑤ **The fountain** is in the shape of a lion, the heraldic animal of St. Jerome.

⑥ **The chapter house** holds the tomb of Alexandre Herculano (1810–77), historian and first mayor of Belém.

⑦ **The chancel** was commissioned in 1572 by Dona Catarina, wife of João III.

⑧ **The tombs** of Manuel I, his wife Dona Maria, João III, and Catarina are supported by elephants.

★ **Cloister**
João de Castilho's pure Manueline creation was completed in 1544. Delicate tracery and richly carved images decorate the arches and balustrades.

VISITORS' CHECKLIST

Practical Information
Praça do Império.
Tel 213-620 034.
🅦 **mosteirojeronimos.pt**
Open 10am–6pm (6:30pm May–Sep) Tue–Sun (last adm: 30 mins before closing).
Closed public hols. 🎫 (free am Sun). ♿ cloister.

Transport
🚌 714, 727, 728, 729, 751. 🚊 15.

Nave
The spectacular vaulting in the church of Santa Maria is held aloft by slender octagonal pillars. These rise like palm trees to the roof creating a feeling of space and harmony.

Tomb of King Sebastião
The tomb of the "longed for" Dom Sebastião stands empty. The young king never returned from battle in 1578 *(see p338)*.

★ **South Portal**
The strict geometrical architecture of the portal is almost obscured by the exuberant decoration. João de Castilho unites religious themes, such as this image of St. Jerome, with the secular, exalting the kings of Portugal.

Beach at Estoril, east of Cascais

❷ Cascais

🏠 33,000. 🚉 🚌 *i* Rua Visconde
da Luz 14 (214-822 327). 🗓 first and
third Sundays in month.

A harbor since prehistoric times,
Cascais became a fashionable
resort in the 1870s, when
Luís I's summer palace was
sited here. Today, it is a bustling
cosmopolitan resort, with
many upscale stores in the
pedestrian streets of the old
town and a new marina
complex. Fishing is still an
important activity, and the
day's catch is auctioned near
the harbor in the afternoon.

Environs
Along the coast, 3 km (2 miles)
to the east, the resort of **Estoril**
has been home to exiled
European royalty. It has retained
its sense of place with grand
villas and hotels lining the coast.

   Guincho, 10 km (6 miles) west
of Cascais, has a magnificent
sandy beach. Its Atlantic
breakers make it popular with
surfers. Further north is **Cabo
da Roca**, the most westerly
point of mainland Europe.

❸ Sintra

🏠 25,000. 🚉 🚌 *i* Praça da
República 23 (219-231 157). 🗓 2nd
and 4th Sun of month in São Pedro.
🎪 Sintra Festival (Jun–Jul).

Sintra's setting among wooded
ravines and fresh-water springs
made it a favorite summer
retreat for the kings of Portugal,
who built the fabulous
Palácio Nacional de Sintra
(see pp352–3) here.

   Designated a UNESCO World
Heritage site in 1995, the town
draws thousands of visitors, yet
there are many tranquil walks
in the surrounding hills.

   Present-day Sintra is a maze
of winding roads, and exploring
the town on foot involves much
walking and climbing; for a
more leisurely tour,
take a horse-and-
carriage ride. The
Miradouro da Vigia
in São Pedro offers
impressive views, as
does the cozy **Casa
de Sapa** café, where
you can sample
queijadas, cheese
tarts spiced
with cinnamon.

   High above the
town is the **Castelo
dos Mouros**, an
8th-century Moorish
castle. On a nearby
hilltop stands the
Palácio da Pena, built in the
19th century for Ferdinand, King
Consort of Maria II, in a bizarre
medley of architectural styles.
A magnificent park surrounds
the fairy-tale castle.

Manueline window at
Tomar's monastery

🏰 Castelo dos Mouros
Estrada da Pena, 5 km (3 miles) S. **Tel**
219-237 300. 🚌 434 or taxi from Sintra.
Open daily. **Closed** Jan 1, Dec 25.

🏛 Palácio da Pena
Estrada da Pena, 5 km (3 miles) S.
Tel 219-237 300. 🚌 434 or taxi
from Sintra. **Open** daily. **Closed** Jan 1,
May 1, Jun 29, Dec 25. 🎫
W parquesdesintra.pt

❹ Tomar

🏠 43,000. 🚉 🚌 *i* Avda Dr.
Cândido Madureira (249-329 823).
🗓 Fri. 🎪 Festa dos Tabuleiros (Jul,
every 4 years, next one will be 2015).

Founded in 1157 by Gualdim
Pais, the first Grand Master
of the Order of the Templars in
Portugal, Tomar is dominated
by the castle containing
the **Convento
de Cristo**. It was
begun in 1162, built
on land given to the
Templars for services
in battle, and
preserves many
traces of its founders
and the inheritors of
their mantle, the
Order of Christ. The
nucleus of the castle
is the 12th-century
Charola, the Templars'
octagonal oratory. In
1356, Tomar became
the headquarters of
the Order of Christ.

   Cloisters were built in the
time of Henry the Navigator,
but it was in the reigns of
Manuel I (1495–1521) and his
successor, João III (1521–57),
that the greatest changes were
made, with the addition of the
Manueline church and
Renaissance cloisters. The
church window (c.1510),
commissioned by Manuel I,
is probably the best-known
single example of the
Manueline style of architecture.

   Other fascinating features
include the Terrace of Wax,
where honeycombs were left
to dry, and the "bread" cloister,
where loaves were handed
out to the poor.

   The town of Tomar is the
site of the curious Festa dos
Tabuleiros, in which young girls

Palácio da Pena in Sintra, the hilltop retreat of the last kings of Portugal

For hotels and restaurants see p362 and p363

carry towering structures made of 30 loaves of bread on their heads. They parade through the main square, Praça da República. The square's focal point is the 15th-century Gothic church of **São João Baptista**. Tomar is also home to one of Portugal's oldest synagogues, now the **Museu Luso-Hebraico de Abraham Zacuto**, a Jewish museum.

⌂ Convento de Cristo
Tel 249-313 481. **Open** daily. **Closed** Jan 1, Easter, May 1, Dec 25. 🖼

The Convento de Cristo, Tomar

❺ Alcobaça

Praça 25 de Abril, Alcobaça. **Tel** 262-505 120. 🚌 from Lisbon or Coimbra. **Open** daily. **Closed** Jan 1, Easter, May 1, Dec 25. 🖼

The Mosteiro de Santa Maria de Alcobaça is Portugal's largest church and a UNESCO World Heritage site. Founded in 1153, the abbey is closely linked to the arrival of the Cistercian order in Portugal in 1138, as well as to the birth of the nation. In March 1147, Afonso Henriques conquered the Moorish

stronghold of Santarém. To commemorate the victory, he gave land and money to build a church to the Cistercians. Completed in 1223, the church is a beautiful building of austere simplicity. Portugal's rulers continued to endow the monastery, notably King Dinis (1279–1325), who added the main cloister, known as the Cloister of Silence. In the Sala dos Reis, 18th-century tiles depict the founding of the abbey, and statues of Portuguese kings adorn the walls.

Among those buried here are the tragic lovers King Pedro (1357–67) and his murdered mistress, Inês de Castro (d.1355), whose tombs face each other across the transept of the abbey church. Inês' death was ordered by Pedro's father, Afonso IV (1325–57). After Afonso's death, Pedro had two of Inês' murderers killed brutally. He then had her body exhumed and reburied.

One of Alcobaça's most popular features is the vast kitchen. Here whole oxen could be roasted on a spit inside the fireplace and a specially diverted stream provided a constant water supply.

❻ Batalha

Mosteiro de Santa Maria da Vitória, Batalha. **Tel** 244-765 497. 🚌 from Lisbon, Leiria, Porto de Mós & Fátima. **Open** daily. **Closed** Jan 1, Easter, May 1, Dec 25. 🖼 (free 9am–2pm Sun).

The Dominican Abbey of Santa Maria da Vitória at Batalha is a masterpiece of Portuguese Gothic architecture and a

Manueline portal leading to the Unfinished Chapels at Batalha

UNESCO World Heritage site. The pale limestone monastery was built to celebrate João I's historic victory at Aljubarrota in 1385. Today, the abbey still has military significance: two unknown soldiers from World War I lie in the chapter house. João I, his English wife, Philippa of Lancaster, and their son, Henry the Navigator, are also buried here, in the Founder's Chapel.

The abbey was begun in 1388 and work continued for the next two centuries. King Duarte, João's son, began an octagonal mausoleum for the royal house of Avis. The project was taken up again, but then abandoned by Manuel I. It is now known as the Unfinished Chapels. Much of the decoration of the abbey is in the Manueline style.

The magnificent Gothic tomb of Pedro I in the transept of the monastery church at Alcobaça

Palácio Nacional de Sintra

At the heart of the old town of Sintra (Sintra Vila), a pair of unusual conical chimneys rises high above the Royal Palace. The main part of the palace, including the central block with its plain Gothic facade and the large kitchens beneath the chimneys, was built by João I in the late 14th century, on a site once occupied by the Moorish rulers. The Paço Real, as it is also known, became the favorite summer retreat for the court and continued as a residence for Portuguese royalty until the 1880s. Additions to the building by the wealthy Manuel I in the early 16th century, echo the Moorish style. Gradual rebuilding of the palace has resulted in a fascinating amalgamation of various different styles.

★ **Sala dos Brasões**
The domed ceiling of this majestic room is decorated with stags holding the coats of arms (brasões) of 72 noble Portuguese families. The lower walls are lined with 18th-century Delft-like tiled panels.

★ **Sala das Pegas**
The 15th-century painted ceiling features 136 magpies (pegas) holding ribbons with King João I's motto, "Por bem" (In honour), and roses to represent Queen Filipa's House of Lancaster.

Azulejos – Painted Ceramic Tiles

The Palácio Nacional de Sintra contains azulejos from the 16th–18th centuries, many painted with Moorish-influenced designs. In the early 16th century, tiles were produced by compartmental techniques, using raised and depressed areas to prevent the tin-glaze colors from running. The maiolica technique appeared in the mid-16th century. This allowed artists to paint directly onto prepared flat tiles using several colors, as these did not run in the firing process. By the 18th century, no other European country was producing as many decorative tiles as Portugal, and there are many examples of 18th-century blue-and-white azulejos in the palace at Sintra, notably in the Sala dos Brasões.

Spanish-made, Moorish-style tiles from the palace chapel (1510)

For hotels and restaurants see p362 and p363

★ Sala dos Cisnes
The magnificent ceiling of the former banqueting hall, painted in the 16th century, is divided into octagonal panels decorated with swans (*cisnes*).

VISITORS' CHECKLIST

Practical Information
Largo Rainha Dona Amélia.
Tel 219-106 840. **Open** Mar 23–Oct 25: 9:30am–7pm daily; Oct 26–Mar 22: 9:30am–6pm daily (last adm: 30 mins before closing).
Closed Jan 1, Dec 25. 🎫 🚫 (free 9:30am–1pm Sun).

Chapel
Symmetrical Moorish patterns decorate the original 15th-century chestnut and oak ceiling and the mosaic floor of the private chapel.

Sala das Sereias
Intricate Arabesque designs on 16th-century tiles frame the door of the Room of the Sirens.

KEY

① **Dom Sebastião's bedroom**

② **Jardim da Preta, a beautiful walled garden**

③ **The Sala das Galés** (galleons) houses a varied program of temporary exhibitions.

④ **The Torre da Meca** has dovecotes below the cornice decorated with armillary spheres and nautical rope.

⑤ **The Sala dos Árabes** is decorated with fine *azulejos*.

⑥ **The kitchens**, beneath the huge conical chimneys, have spits and utensils once used for preparing royal banquets.

⑦ **Manuel I** added the *ajimene* windows, a distinctive Moorish design with a slender column dividing two arches.

⑧ **Sala dos Archeiros, the entrance hall**

18th-century library of Coimbra University

❼ Coimbra

🗺 144,000. 🚍 🚌 ℹ Edifício da Biblioteca Geral da Universidade de Coimbra (239-834 158); Largo da Portajem (239-488 120). 🛒 Mon–Sat. 🎭 Queima das Fitas (early May).

Afonso Henriques chose Coimbra as his capital in 1139, an honor it retained until 1256. Today, the city on the Mondego is famous as the home of Portugal's oldest university. Most sights are within walking distance of each other, so Coimbra is best explored on foot, despite the steep hill on which it is built.

Coimbra's two cathedrals, the **Sé Velha** ("old") and **Sé Nova** ("new"), lie in the shadow of the hilltop University. The Sé Velha, begun in 1064, is seen as the finest Romanesque building in Portugal. The Sé Nova was founded in 1598 by the Jesuits.

The **University**, a short walk away, was founded in 1290 by King Dinis. Originally its location alternated between Lisbon and Coimbra, but it was finally installed in Coimbra's royal palace in 1537. Its oldest buildings are grouped around the Pátio das Escolas. The **belltower** (1733) can be seen from all over the city. The **Library** was a gift from João V (1706–50). Its rooms, of gilt and exotic wood, are lined with

300,000 books. Nearby is the similarly ornate **Capela de São Miguel**. Each May, at the end of the academic year, the Queima das Fitas takes place, at which students hold a ceremonial burning of their faculty ribbons, a tradition that dates back 700 years.

Another fascinating site is the **Museu Nacional Machado de Castro**, which holds some of Portugal's finest 15th- to 20th-century paintings and sculpture set among the elegant 16th-century loggias and courtyards of the former bishops' palace.

After visiting this area (the "upper town"), head to the "lower town." Largo da Portagem is a useful starting point, and river trips depart from nearby. In the Praça do Comércio, alongside coffee shops and bars, is the restored 12th-century church of **São Tiago**. North of this is **Santa Cruz**, founded in 1131, where Portugal's first two kings are buried.

In the southeast of the city is the **Jardim Botânico**. The gardens, which are Portugal's largest, were created in 1772 and house 1,200 plant species.

On the opposite bank of the Mondego are the two convents of **Santa Clara**; these have ties with Santa Isabel, the widow of

King Dinis (1279–1325), and Inês de Castro, stabbed to death here in 1355 *(see p351)*. Nearby is a fun place for those with children: the **Portugal dos Pequenitos** theme park.

🏛 **University**
Paço das Escolas. **Tel** 239-859 884. **Open** daily. **Closed** Dec 25. 🚫 ♿ Library only. 🌐 **visit.uc.pt**

🏛 **Museu Nacional Machado de Castro**
Largo Dr. José Rodrigues. **Tel** 239-853 070. **Open** Tue–Sun. 🚫

Portugal dos Pequenitos
Santa Clara. **Tel** 239-801 170. **Open** daily. **Closed** Dec 25. 🚫 ♿

Environs
Buçaco National Forest, 16 km (10 miles) north of Coimbra, was once the retreat of Carmelite monks. Part ancient woodland and part arboretum, it is dotted with chapels and fountains. It also houses the splendid Palace Hotel Bussaco, built in Neo-Manueline style as a royal hunting lodge in 1907. Buçaco was also the site of a crucial battle (1810) in the Peninsular War. The Roman town of **Conímbriga** lay south of modern Coimbra. Portugal's largest Roman site, it has some opulent villas with fine floor mosaics, and an excellent museum.

Student, May celebrations

🏛 **Conímbriga**
2 km (1 mile) S of Condeixa-a-Nova. 🚌 from Coimbra. Site: **Open** daily. **Closed** public hols. Museum: **Tel** 239-941 177. **Open** daily. 🚫 ♿ museum.

The Palace Hotel Bussaco, in its enchanting woodland setting

The Douro River and old city of Oporto, with the Ponte de Dom Luís I and modern metro line in the foreground

❽ Oporto

🏙 245,000. ✈ 10 km (6 miles) N.
🚉 🚌 ℹ Rua Clube dos Fenianos 25
(223-393 472); Praça Dom João I 43
(222-057 514); Terreiro de Sé (223-325
174). 🎉 São João do Porto (Jun
23–24). 🌐 **portoturismo.pt**

Ever since the Romans built a fort here, at the mouth of the Douro, Oporto (Porto in Portuguese) has prospered from commerce. Today it is Portugal's second city and a thriving industrial center.

The commercial center of the city and the Baixa ("lower") district attract fashionable shoppers. Also in the Baixa is the colorful Bolhão market. Most of the tourist sights, however, are to be found in the older riverside quarters.

High above the river, on Penaventosa Hill, stands Oporto's cathedral, or **Sé**, originally a fortress church. A noteworthy 13th-century feature is the rose window, while the upper level of the beautiful 14th-century cloister affords splendid views.

Nearby are the Renaissance church of **Santa Clara**, and **São Bento Station**, completed in 1916, decorated with spectacular *azulejo* panels.

Below the Sé is the hillside **Barredo** quarter, seemingly unchanged since medieval days. This leads down to the riverside quarter, the **Ribeira**, its houses decorated with tiled or pastel-painted facades. The district is being restored, attracting restaurants and clubs.

Sights close to the river include the **Palácio da Bolsa**, the city's stock exchange, built in 1842. Its highlight is the Arabian Room decorated in the style of the Alhambra. Close by is the 14th-century **São Francisco** church. Its interior is richly covered in carved and gilded wood.

In the Cordoaria district, west of the Sé, stands the 18th-century **Igreja dos Clérigos**. The church tower, at 75 m (246 ft), offers superb views.

Situated in the lovely Serralves park, the **Fundação de Serralves** is dedicated to contemporary art. It presents temporary exhibitions in the Art Deco Casa de Serralves, and its art collection, from the 1960s to the present, in the Modernist Museu de Arte Contemporânea, designed by Alvaro Siza Vieira.

The oldest of the five bridges spanning the Douro are the Dona Maria Pia railroad bridge (1877), designed by Gustave Eiffel, and the two-tiered Ponte de Dom Luís I (1886), by one of Eiffel's assistants.

Across the river is the town of **Vila Nova de Gaia**, the center of port production, housing the lodges (*armazéns*) of over 50 companies. Many offer guided tours.

🏛 **Fundação de Serralves**
Rua Dom João de Castro 210. **Tel** 226-156 500. **Open** 10am–5pm Tue–Fri, 10am–7pm Sat, Sun, & public hols (to 8pm in summer). **Closed** Jan 1, Dec 25. 🎫 (free 10am–2pm Sun).
♿ 💻 📷 🌐 serralves.pt

The Story of Port

Port comes only from a demarcated region of the upper Douro valley. Its "discovery" dates from the 17th century, when British merchants added brandy to Douro wine to stop it turning sour in transit. Over the years, methods of maturing and blending were refined and continue today in the port lodges of Vila Nova de Gaia. Much of the trade is still in British control.

A classic after-dinner drink, port is rich and usually full-bodied. The tawnies are lighter in color than ruby or vintage, but can be more complex. All ports are blended from several wines, selected from scores of samples. White port, unlike the other styles, is drunk chilled as an aperitif.

Traditionally, the wine was shipped

Tiled panel of a *barco rabelo* on the Douro

down the Douro from the wine-growing estates (*quintas*) to the port lodges on narrow sailing barges called *barcos rabelos*. Some of these can still be seen moored along the quay at Vila Nova de Gaia.

Southern Portugal

Southern Portugal encompasses the Alentejo and the Algarve, which are separated by ranges of hills. The Alentejo, nearly one-third of Portugal, stretches south from the Tagus. It is typified by vast rolling plains of olive trees, cork oaks, or wheat, as well as whitewashed villages, castles, and a sense of space and tranquility. The Algarve is very different from the rest of Portugal in climate, culture, and scenery. Its stunning coastline and year-round mild weather make it a popular vacation resort.

Renaissance fountain in Evora's main square, Praça do Giraldo

Carved figures of the Apostles on the portal of the Sé, Evora

❾ Evora

🏙 55,000. 🚉 🚌 *ℹ* Praça do Giraldo (266-777 071). 🛒 Sat & 2nd Tue of month. 🎎 Festa de São João (Jun).

Rising dramatically out of the Alentejo plain, the enchanting city of Evora is set in Roman, medieval, and 17th-century walls. In 1986, UNESCO declared it a World Heritage site.

The fortresslike cathedral, the **Sé**, on the Largo do Marquês de Marialva, was begun in 1186. The portal is flanked by a pair of unmatched towers. Inside, a glittering treasury houses sacred art. Beside it stands a 16th-century palace that houses the newly renovated **Museu de Evora**, which has exhibits on the history of the city from Roman columns to modern sculpture. Opposite the museum is a **Roman temple** – erected in the 2nd or 3rd century AD – believed to have been dedicated to Diana.

Walk from the Sé past the craft stores of Rua 5 de Outubro to reach Praça do Giraldo, the main square, with its Moorish arcades and central fountain (1571). In 1573, the square was the site of an Inquisitional burning. Just outside the city's Roman walls stands the

University, founded by the Jesuits in 1559. It was closed in 1759 by the Marquês de Pombal (*see p345*). The building, with its graceful cloister and notable *azulejos*, forms part of the present-day university, and the 18th-century Baroque chapel is used for graduation ceremonies.

Evora has more than 20 churches and monasteries, including the 15th-century **São Francisco**. The church's gruesome 17th-century **Capela dos Ossos** was created from the bones of 5,000 monks.

Northwest of the city stands the remaining 9 km (5 miles) of Evora's aqueduct, the **Aqueduto da Água de Prata**, (1531–37), which was damaged in the 17th century, during the War.

🏛 Museu de Evora

Largo do Conde de Vila Flor. **Tel** 266-702 604. **Open** Tue–Sun. **Closed** some public hols. 🔲

🏛 University

Largo dos Colegiais. **Tel** 266-740 875. **Open** Mon–Sat am. **Closed** public hols.

❿ Faro

🏙 55,000. ✈ 🚉 🚌 *ℹ* Rua da Misericórdia 8 (289-803 604). 🛒 daily. 🎎 Dia da Cidade (Sep 7).

Faro has been the capital of the Algarve since 1756. It was damaged by the 1755 earthquake and, although some parts of the ancient city walls remain, most of the buildings date from the 18th or 19th centuries.

The old city is easy to explore on foot. At its heart is the Largo da Sé, lined with orange trees and flanked by the 18th-century bishops' palace, the **Paço Episcopal**, which is still in use today.

The **Sé** itself is a mixture of Baroque and Renaissance styles and has a fine 18th-century organ. Next to the Sé is the **Museu Municipal**, which contains Roman, medieval, and Manueline archaeological finds from all over the region.

On the other side of the old city wall is the impressive 18th-century church of **São Francisco**.

Orange trees in front of the Bishops' Palace in the old city of Faro

The lively center of modern Faro, along the Rua de Santo António, is stylish and pedestrianized, full of stores, bars, and restaurants. A little to the north is Faro's parish church, the Baroque and Italianate **São Pedro**. In the nearby Largo do Carmo is the impressive **Igreja do Carmo**. Its magnificent facade and richly decorated interior are in sharp contrast to its somber **Capela dos Ossos** (Chapel of Bones), built in 1816.

At the far northeast corner of the town is the **Cemitério dos Judeus**. The Jewish cemetery served from 1838 until 1932; there is no Jewish community in Faro today.

Museu Municipal
Largo Dom Afonso III. **Tel** 289-870 827. **Open** Tue–Sun. **Closed** public hols.

Yachts and powerboats at the Vilamoura marina, east of Albufeira

⓫ Albufeira

31,000. Rua 5 de Outubro (289-585 279). 1st & 3rd Tue of month.

This charming fishing port has become the tourist capital of the Algarve. The Romans built a castle here and under the Arabs the town prospered from trade with North Africa. The oldest part of the town, around Rua da Igreja Velha, retains some original Moorish arches.

Environs
From **Praia de São Rafael**, 1 mile (2 km) west of Albufeira, to **Praia da Oura** due east, the area is punctuated by small sandy coves set between

Ocher sandstone rocks sheltering the Praia de Dona Ana beach, Lagos

eroded ocher rocks. East of Albufeira, **Vilamoura** is set to become Europe's largest leisure complex. It has a large marina with lively cafés, stores, and restaurants.

⓬ Portimão

40,000. Avda Tomás Cabreira, Praia da Rocha (282-419 132). first Mon of month.

The Romans were attracted to Portimão by its natural harbor. It is still a flourishing fishing port and one of the largest towns in the Algarve.

The town center, around the pedestrianized Rua Vasco da Gama, dates mainly from the 18th century, since it was rebuilt after the 1755 earthquake. The 14th-century origins of the church of Nossa Senhora da Conceição are revealed in its portico. The interior contains 17th- and 18th-century *azulejo* panels.

Environs
Just 3 km (2 miles) south of Portimão is **Praia da Rocha**, a series of fabulous sandy coves. At its east end is the 16th-century castle, Fortaleza de Santa Catarina, with a superb view of the beach and cliffs – and a swathe of high-rise hotels. Inland from Portimão is the town of **Silves**, once the Moorish capital, Xelb. It has an impressive castle and picturesque groves of orange and lemon trees.

⓭ Lagos

16,000. Praça Gil Eanes (282-763 031). first Sat of month.

Lagos is set on one of the Algarve's largest bays; it was the region's capital from 1576–1756. The town suffered badly in the 1755 earthquake, so as a result, most of the buildings date from the late 18th and 19th centuries.

In the 15th century, Lagos became an important naval center, unfortunately also becoming the site of the first slave market in Europe.

Lagos's parish church is the 16th-century **Santa Maria**. The 18th-century **Santo António** is worth a visit for its Baroque *azulejos* and carving. The statue of St. Anthony, kept in the church, accompanied the local regiment during the Peninsular War (1807–11).

Environs
The promontory, **Ponta da Piedade**, shelters the bay of Lagos and should not be missed. **Praia de Dona Ana** beach is 25 minutes' walk from the town center, but **Praia do Camilo** may be less crowded. **Meia Praia**, east of Lagos, stretches for 4 km (2 miles).

Lying 10 km (6 miles) north is the peaceful **Barragem de Bravura** reservoir. Another popular excursion is south-west to **Sagres** and the rocky headland of **Cabo de São Vicente**.

Practical & Travel Information

The Portuguese are a hospitable people, and in Lisbon, Oporto, and the Algarve the choice of hotels, restaurants and entertainment is vast, and English is widely spoken. Elsewhere, visitors will usually find help easily available, with locals keen to show off their region.

Travel and communication networks in Portugal have improved greatly in recent years. For national travel there are efficient rail and bus services. Cities have buses and trams, and Lisbon has a metro as well.

Tourist Information

The country is divided into tourist regions, separate from its administrative districts. All cities and large towns have a *posto de turismo* (tourist office), where you can obtain information about the region, lists of hotels, and details of regional events. Visitors can also consult Portuguese tourist offices abroad.

Most state museums open from 10am to 5pm and are usually closed on Mondays. Many museums and sights also close for lunch for one or two hours.

In Lisbon, the convenient Lisboa Card entitles visitors to free public transportation, and free or reduced entry to museums. It can be bought at the airport, the city's tourist offices, and some hotels, travel agents, and major sights. It is valid for up to three days.

Visa Requirements

There are currently no visa requirements for American, Canadian, Australian, and New Zealand nationals for stays up to 90 days. It is worth checking with the nearest Portuguese embassy or consulate as this may change. Citizens of the EU need only a valid passport to enter Portugal.

Personal Security

Violent crime is rare, but visitors should take sensible precautions after dark, especially in Lisbon, Oporto, and the Algarve. To report a crime, contact the nearest police station. Ask for an interpreter if necessary. Theft of documents, such as a passport, should also be reported to your consulate or embassy. Many travel insurance companies insist on policy holders reporting thefts within 24 hours to substantiate any subsequent claim.

Emergency Services

The number to call in an emergency is 112. Ask for either *polícia* (the police), *ambulância* (an ambulance), or *bombeiros* (the fire brigade). For emergency medical treatment, you should go to the emergency room (*serviço de urgência*) of the nearest main hospital.

Health Issues

For non-emergency medical treatment, details of how to contact an English-speaking doctor can be found in English-language newspapers, such as *Algarve Resident*.

Pharmacies (*farmácias*) can dispense a range of drugs that would require a prescription in many other countries. They open from 9am to 1pm and 3pm to 7pm (not Sat), and carry a sign with a green illuminated cross. No vaccinations are needed for Portugal, although a typhoid shot and polio booster are recommended.

Facilities for the Disabled

These are limited, although the situation is improving. Wheelchairs and adapted restrooms are available at airports and major stations, and ramps, reserved parking, and elevators are becoming more common. Lisbon has a special taxi service, but you have to book well in advance.

Language and Etiquette

Written Portuguese looks similar to Spanish, but its pronunciation is very different. The Portuguese do not take kindly to being spoken to in Spanish, so it is useful to learn a few basic phrases before you go. It is polite to address strangers as *senhor* or *senhora* and, when introduced to someone, to shake their hand.

Although dress is generally relaxed, especially in the more tourist-oriented areas, when visiting religious buildings, arms and knees should be kept covered.

Banking and Currency

The currency in Portugal is the euro (see p23). Money can be changed at most banks, hotels, and bureaux de change (*câmbio*). Banks tend to offer a good rate of exchange. Traveler's checks can often be expensive to cash, although they are a safe way of carrying money. Most major credit cards can be used to make withdrawals from ATMs.

The Climate of Portugal

In the south of the country, especially along the sheltered coast of the Algarve, winters are very mild, but July and August can be extremely hot. Between April and October, the north is pleasantly warm, though rain is not unusual. Winters in the north can be very cold, especially in the mountainous inland regions. The best times to visit are spring and fall.

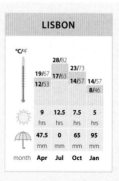

LISBON				
°C/°F		28/82	23/73	
	19/67	17/63	14/57	14/57
	12/53			8/46
	9 hrs	12.5 hrs	7.5 hrs	5 hrs
	47.5 mm	0 mm	65 mm	95 mm
month	Apr	Jul	Oct	Jan

Communications

The Portuguese postal service is known as *Correios*. First-class mail *(correio azul)* and overseas letters are posted in blue mailboxes; second-class mail *(normal)* is posted in red mailboxes.

Public payphones take either coins or cards (including credit cards), although there are fewer payphones now due to widespread use of cell phones. It is also possible to make calls from post offices.

Flying to Portugal

The only direct flight from New York (Newark) to Lisbon is operated by **TAP Air Portugal**. Once in Lisbon, passengers can change for Faro or Oporto. Internal flights to Madeira and the Azores are operated by **SATA**.

Many US airlines operate flights from the United States to several European hubs, such as London, Paris, or Madrid, where passengers can change for Lisbon.

There are no direct flights to Portugal from Australia or New Zealand; visitors from these countries should fly via London or Madrid. Regular flights go from many European cities direct to Lisbon, Faro, and Oporto in Portugal.

Rail Travel

Direct trains to Portugal go from Paris and Madrid. Once in Portugal, you can reach many places by rail, but services vary enormously. The high-speed Alfa service from Lisbon to Oporto via Coimbra and to the Algarve is good, but local trains can be slow and infrequent. Fares are cheap compared to other parts of Europe and tourist tickets are available, including the InterRail/Eurail One Country Pass, valid for three, four, six, or eight days. It is best to book in advance.

Lisbon can be confusing for visitors as there are five main stations. **Santa Apolónia** and **Oriente** (on the same line) serve international routes and the north; for the Alentejo, you must take a ferry to Barreiro on the south bank of the Tagus. Trains to the Algarve depart from Oriente. Trains from Rossio go to Sintra and a few destinations on the coast; trains from Cais do Sodré serve Estoril and Cascais.

Long-distance Buses

Some long-distance bus services – Lisbon to Evora for example – are quicker and more comfortable than going by train. Lisbon's coach station is located at Sete Rios. Tourist offices and travel agencies offer information.

Traveling by Car

Portugal's highway network is expanding, but many older roads are in need of repair and minor roads can be treacherous. Driving can be a hair-raising experience – the country has one of the highest accident rates in Europe and traffic jams are a problem in and near cities. Beware of reckless drivers and do not drive in the rush hour if you can possibly avoid it.

If renting a car, check its condition and insurance very carefully. Always carry your passport, car insurance, license, and rental contract with you (or you may incur a fine).

Traffic drives on the right hand side and Continental European regulations apply. Seat belts must be worn. Speed limits are 50 kph (31 mph) in towns, 90 kph (55 mph) on other roads, and 120 kph (74 mph) on highways. Tolls are payable on highways and some bridges. Do not use the *Via Verde* (green lane) at tolls; this is for drivers who have paid automatically. If you are involved in a car accident on a highway or a main road, use one of the orange SOS telephones to call for help.

Gas stations can be scarce in remote areas, so always fill up your car before leaving a town.

DIRECTORY

Tourist Offices

Lisbon
Lisboa Welcome Center, Praça do Comércio.
Tel 210-312 810.

Oporto
Rua Clube dos Fenianos 25. **Tel** 223-393 472.
W visitporto.travel

UK
11 Belgrave Square, London SW1X 8PP.
Tel 020-7201 6666.

US
866 Second Ave, 8th floor, New York, NY 10017.
Tel 646-723 0200.
W visitportugal.com

Embassies

Australia
Av. da Liberdade 196–200, 2nd floor (Edifício Victoria), 1269-121 Lisbon.
Tel 213-101 500.

Canada
Av. da Liberdade 196–200, 3rd floor (Edifício Victoria), 1269-121 Lisbon.
Tel 213-164 600.

Ireland
Av. da Liberdade 200, 4th Floor, 1250-147 Lisbon.
Tel 213-308 200.

UK
Rua de São Bernardo 33, 1249-082 Lisbon.
Tel 213-924 000.

US
Avenida das Forças Armadas, 1600-081 Lisbon. **Tel** 217-273 300.

Emergencies

Ambulance, Police, and Fire services
Tel 112.

Airlines

SATA
Tel 707-227 282.

TAP Air Portugal
Tel 707-205 700.
Tel 0845-601 0932 (UK).
Tel 800-221 73 70 (US).
W flytap.com

Train Information

Tel 707-210 220.
W cp.pt

Car Rental

Auto Jardim, Faro
Tel 289-818 491.
W auto-jardim.com

Budget, Oporto
Tel 808-25 26 27.
W budget.pt

Europcar, Faro
Tel 289-818 726.

Hertz, Lisbon
Tel 219-426 300.
W hertz.pt

Sixt, Lisbon
Tel 217-998 701.

Shopping & Entertainment

Traditional arts and crafts flourish in Portugal. A wide range of interesting pottery can be found in all parts of the country, while in the north-embroidery, lace, and gold-filigree jewelry from the Minho region make unusual presents. Many visitors come to Portugal for the sporting facilities, principally the golf courses of the Algarve. Watersports, both in the Algarve and on the wilder west coast, are another great attraction. Tourists are usually encouraged to sample *fado*, Lisbon's native folk music, and there are also classical cultural events to be enjoyed in the big cities and at annual festivals.

Where to Shop

Although it is not difficult to find stores that seem a little behind the times when compared with other European countries, modern shopping malls are now a common feature of most cities. In Lisbon, **Amoreiras** shopping center led the way, with 247 shops, underground parking, movie theaters, and restaurants. **Colombo** followed, and is Portugal's largest mall. **Cascaishopping**, between Sintra and Estoril, is similar in style. Opening times for shopping centers are usually from 10am until 11pm daily (including Sunday). Ordinary stores open at 9am or 10am and close at 7pm, though smaller stores and those in quieter areas usually close for lunch between 1pm and 3pm.

Reclaiming Tax

Value Added Tax (IVA) can be reclaimed by non-EU residents who stay for less than 180 days. Ask for an *Isenção de IVA* form or invoice in triplicate, describing the goods, quantity, value, and buyer's identity (best done where you see the "Global Blue" signs). Present the forms at customs on departure.

What to Buy

Portugal is not expensive when compared with the rest of Europe, and prices are very reasonable for traditional crafts, especially away from the big cities and tourist centers. The Portuguese are well known for their delicate embroidery and fine lace. Some of the finest examples come from towns in the Minho such as Viana do Castelo, also famous for its brightly printed shawls. Embroidered bedspreads are made in Castelo Branco in the Beira Baixa, and colorful carpets are sold in the Alentejo.

Filigree jewelry *(filigrana)* from the Minho is typically worn at local festivals. Gold and silver threads are worked into intricate brooches, earrings, and pendants.

Woven baskets, produced throughout the country, make delightful souvenirs. Cork from the Alentejo is used to make articles such as mats and ice buckets.

Ceramics

In most cities, you can buy as well as commission ceramic tiles and panels. Portugal has a long-standing tradition of ceramics, both for decorative purposes and for home use. Styles range from elegant Vista Alegre porcelain to simple glazed brown earthenware, plain or painted with simple patterns. Antique *azulejos* are highly sought after and very expensive, but you can buy reproductions of well-known historic designs at places such as Lisbon's Museu Nacional do Azulejo *(see p342)*.

Markets

A social and commercial occasion, the street market is integral to Portuguese life. It is usually held in the town's main square. Most markets sell a wide range of goods, from food to household items and clothes, but you will also see sites devoted to antiques, pottery, lace, rugs, clothes, and local crafts. Most markets are held in the morning only, but in tourist areas they may go on until late afternoon.

Food and Drink

Some visitors may want to buy regional produce, such as Serra cheese from the Serra da Estrela mountains. However, more are likely to bring back a bottle as a souvenir – most probably of port. It is not especially cheap, but you will never have the opportunity to sample so many styles and vintages as you will on a tour of the port lodges of Vila Nova de Gaia *(see p355)*. When it comes to table wines you might enjoy the young, slightly sparkling *vinho verde* from Douro in the north, an aged red Dão, or one of the southern wines from Alentejo.

Entertainment Listings and Tickets

Tickets for almost all events in Lisbon can be bought in **FNAC** stores, or be reserved by visiting or phoning the Agência de Bilhetes para Espectáculos **(ABEP)**. Pay in cash when you collect them from the kiosk. Some movie theaters and theaters take phone or credit-card reservations.

Previews of forthcoming events and listings of bars and clubs appear in several magazines in Lisbon. English-language publications include the monthly *Follow Me Lisboa*, which is available free from tourist offices.

Classical Music, Opera, and Dance

Lisbon's top cultural centers are the **Fundação Calouste Gulbenkian** and the vast **Centro Cultural de Belém**. These host national and international events, including ballet, opera, and concerts. The Portuguese national opera house is the **Teatro Nacional de São Carlos**.

One of the best Classical music festival is the summer festival in Sintra *(see p350)*.

Theater and Cinema

In Lisbon, theater-lovers can enjoy performances of Portuguese and foreign-language plays at the **Teatro Nacional Dona Maria II**.

Cult movies and international arthouse films can be seen at the **Cinemateca Portuguesa**, which has a comprehensive monthly film calendar.

In Portugal, movies are almost always shown in the original language version with Portuguese subtitles.

Fado

Fado is an expression of longing and sorrow. Literally meaning "fate," the term may be applied to an individual song as well as the genre itself. The dominant emotion is *saudade* – a longing for what has been lost or has never been attained. It is sung as often by women as men, accompanied by the *guitarra* (a flat-backed instrument shaped like a mandolin, with paired strings) and the *viola* (acoustic Spanish guitar).

The traditional way to enjoy *fado* is with a meal at a *fado* house. It can be an expensive night out, so make sure you like *fado* before you go. The best establishments are run by the *fadistas* themselves, for example the **Parreirinha de Alfama**, which is now run by the legendary performer, Argentina Santos.

Outdoor Activities

Although a small country, Portugal offers a great variety of terrain, with sports and activities to match. Water-sports are extremely popular along its 500 miles (800 km) of coast. The best beach for surfing is the world-famous Guincho, near Cascais *(see p350)*. However, the ocean breakers there are only suitable for experienced surfers. In fact, all along the Atlantic coast conditions can be dangerous for swimming and watersports, hence the appeal of the sheltered bays of the Algarve. These are well-equipped for all kinds of activities. Windsurfing boards and small sailboats can be rented at most resorts and lessons are easily arranged. The marinas at Lagos and the giant vacation complex of Vilamoura are the most important yachting centers.

Many parts of Portugal's rugged interior are excellent for hiking, cycling, and horseback riding.

Golf and Tennis

Most of Portugal's best golf courses are concentrated in the Algarve, which has gained a reputation as one of Europe's prime destinations for golfing vacations. The mild climate ensures that a game can be enjoyed all year round, and many courses have been designed by top professionals. Some of the best courses insist that players show a reasonable degree of proficiency, while others welcome golfers of any ability and provide excellent coaching. Serious golfers might consider booking a specialist golf vacation. For information on golfing activities and vacations, contact the **Federação Portuguesa de Golfe**.

Tennis courts are found virtually all over Portugal, especially alongside tourist facilities. Some of the larger Algarve resorts offer tennis-coaching vacations. Based in London, **Jonathan Markson Tennis** organizes special vacation packages at resorts in Portugal for tennis enthusiasts.

Bullfighting

Portuguese bullfighting differs from the Spanish version in many ways. The bull is not killed in the ring and the star of the show is the horseman *(cavaleiro)*. An added attraction is the *pega*, in which a team of men, the *forcados*, attempts to topple the bull and immobilize it with their bare hands.

The traditional center for bullfighting is the Ribatejo, but Lisbon has a splendid Neo-Moorish arena at Campo Pequeno, which now has a modern retractable ceiling.

DIRECTORY

Shopping Malls

Amoreiras
Avenida Eng. Duarte Pacheco. **Tel** 213-810 240.

Cascaishopping
Estrada Nacional 9, Alcabideche - Estoril.
Tel 210-121 628.

Colombo
Avenida Lusíada, Lisbon.
Tel 217-113 600.

Entertainment Tickets

ABEP
Praça dos Restauradores, Lisbon. **Tel** 213-461 189.

Classical Music, Opera & Dance

Centro Cultural de Belém
Praça do Império, Belém, Lisbon.
Tel 217-941 400.

Fundação Calouste Gulbenkian
Avenida de Berna 45, Lisbon.
Tel 217-823 700.

Teatro Nacional de São Carlos
Rua Serpa Pinto 9, Lisbon.
Tel 213-253 000.

Theater and Cinema

Cinemateca Portuguesa
Rua Barata Salgueiro 39, Lisbon.
Tel 213-596 200.

Teatro Nacional Dona Maria II
Praça Dom Pedro IV, Lisbon.
Tel 213-250 800.

Fado

Parreirinha de Alfama
Beco do Espírito Santo 1, Lisbon. **Tel** 218-868 209.

Golf and Tennis

Federação Portuguesa de Golfe
Tel 214-123 780.

Jonathan Markson Tennis
Mulberry House, 583 Fulham Road, London SW6 5UA, UK.
Tel 020-7603 2422.

Where to Stay

Modern decor and 18th-century architecture feature at Solar do Castelo, Alfama

Lisbon

ALFAMA: Solar do Castelo €€€
Historic   Map E3
Rua das Cozinhas 2, 1100-181
Tel 218-806 050
W solardocastelo.com
Housed in a splendid 18th-century mansion, Solar do Castelo has both modern and classic decor.

BAIRRO ALTO: Lisbon Dreams Guesthouse €€
Modern   Map C3
Rua Rodrigo Da Fonseca 29, 1250-189
Tel 213-872 393
W lisbondreamsguesthouse.com
Rooms at this bright and cheerful hotel have shared bathrooms. There is also an apartment for longer stays.

BAIRRO ALTO: Bairro Alto Hotel €€€
Boutique   Map D3
Praça Luis De Camões, Nº 2, 1200-243
Tel 213-408 288
W bairroaltohotel.com
Stay in this luxurious boutique hotel featuring a gourmet restaurant and a massage room.

BAIXA AND AVENIDA: Shiado Hostel €
Boutique   Map D3
Rua Anchieta, 5, 3rd floor, 1200-023
Tel 213-429 227
W shiadohostel.com
A designer "superhostel" offering private rooms. Colorful and bright, with a shared kitchen and bathrooms. Buffet breakfast.

BAIXA AND AVENIDA: Métropole €€
Historic   Map D3
Praça Dom Pedro IV 30, 1100-200
Tel 213-219 030
W themahotels.pt
This hotel retains an elegant retro vibe, with authentic Art Deco furnishings.

DK Choice

BAIXA AND AVENIDA: Internacional Design Hotel €€€
Boutique   Map E3
Rua da Betesga 3, 1100-090
Tel 213-240 990
W idesignhotel.com
Each floor of this hotel is based around a different theme: urban chic, Zen philosophy, tribal, and pop culture. The delicious breakfasts, choice of pillows, and butler service make for a great stay.

BELÉM: Pestana Palace Hotel €€€
Historic
Rua Jau 54, 1300-314
Tel 213-615 600
W pestana.com
A 19th-century palace featuring lavish rooms and suites.

Rest of Portugal

ALBUFEIRA: Grande Real Santa Eulália Resort & Hotel Spa €€€
Modern
Praia Santa Eulália, 8200-916
Tel 289-598 000
W realhotelsgroup.com
Modern, well-equipped five-star beach resort with a Thalasso spa.

DK Choice

CASCAIS: Pérgola Guest House €€
Historic
Avenida Valbom 13, 2750-508
Tel 214-840 040
W pergolahouse.com
A beautiful 19th-century mansion with marble floors, stucco ceilings, and ornate furnishings. The friendly owners serve guests a complimentary glass of port, and dinners are available on request.

COIMBRA: Vintage Lofts €€
Historic
Rua Simão de Évora, 11, 3000-386
Tel 964-326 556
W coimbravintagelofts.com
Studios and apartments in a tastefully renovated 18th-century building. Daily housekeeping.

COIMBRA: Quinta das Lágrimas €€€
Historic
Rua António Augusto Gonçalves, 3041-901
Tel 239-802 380
W quintadaslagrimas.pt
A luxurious palace with a spa and gorgeous botanical gardens.

OPORTO: Grande Hotel de Paris €€
Historic
Rua da Fábrica, 27/29, 4050-247
Tel 222-073 140
W hotelparis.pt
Rooms have antique furnishings and balconies at this Art Deco hotel with a lovely garden.

DK Choice

OPORTO: The Yeatman €€€
Modern
Rua do Choupelo, 4400-088
Tel 220-133 100
W the-yeatman-hotel.com
An award-winning hotel, The Yeatman has a stylish decor. Famous for its attentive service and exquisite gourmet food, it also offers a pool, spa, and an indoor hot tub with great views.

SINTRA: Sintra Bliss Hotel €€
Boutique
Rua Dr. Alfredo Costa, Nº.15–17, 2710-524
Tel 219-244 541
W sintra-b-hotels.com
Stay in rooms with contemporary interiors and private balconies. Two-room apartment available.

SINTRA: Tivoli Palácio de Seteais €€€
Historic
Rua Barbosa do Bocage 10, 2710-517
Tel 219-233 200
W tivolihotels.com
This romantic hotel is housed in an 18th-century mansion.

Where to Eat and Drink

Lisbon

ALFAMA: Tentações de Goa €
Goan **Map** E3
Rua São Pedro Mártir 23, 1100-555
Tel *218-875 824* **Closed** *Mon lunch; Sun; public holidays*
Brightly painted walls and a friendly welcome make this a cheerful dining option. The chef cooks outstanding Goan cuisine and will adapt the level of spice to individual tastes. Cash only.

DK Choice

BAIRRO ALTO:
Taberna Ideal €€
Modern Portuguese **Map** C4
Rua Esperança 112, 1120-114
Tel *213-962 744* **Closed** *lunch (except Sun); Mon & Tue*
This warm taverna serves traditional Portuguese cuisine with a modern twist. Expect great explanations and advice on the inventive menu, which is designed to be shared. Perfect for all – solo travelers, couples, and groups. Reservations highly recommended. Cash only.

BAIXA AND AVENIDA:
Os Tibetanos €
Vegetarian **Map** D3
Rua do Salitre 117, 1250-198
Tel *213-142 038* **Closed** *Sun*
This informal restaurant with a garden terrace serves a healthy selection of Tibetan dishes, plus international options like tofu with pesto. Cash only.

BAIXA AND AVENIDA:
Fábulas €€
International **Map** D3
Calçada Nova de São Francisco, 14, 1200-300
Tel *216-018 472* **Closed** *Sun*
Exposed brickwork offset by an eclectic collection of furniture sets the tone at this café. A number of seating areas accommodate both mood and the weather. The menu offers organic fare, and the wine list is great.

BAIXA AND AVENIDA:
Bistro 100 Maneiras €€€
International **Map** D3
Largo Trindade 9, 1200-466
Tel *210-990 475* **Closed** *lunch; Sun*
Bistro 100 Maneiras is a glamorous place favored by a fashionable clientele. The upstairs dining area is quite charming, and the creative menu features world cuisine.

BELÉM: Vela Latina €€€
Modern Portuguese
Doca do Bom Sucesso, 1400-038
Tel *213-017 118* **Closed** *Sun*
Peaceful, stylish restaurant set in lush gardens with views of the river and the marina. Popular dishes include lobster-filled crêpes and hake fillet with rice.

CHIADO:
Café Buenos Aires €€
Steak House **Map** D3
Calçada do Duque 31, 1200-155
Tel *213-420 739* **Closed** *Sun*
Enjoy succulent and cooked-to-perfection Argentinian steaks in a cozy, unpretentious setting. Also try the flower salad. Book ahead.

LAPA: Restaurante Lapa €€€
Portuguese/Italian **Map** B4
Olissippo Lapa Palace, Rua do Pau da Bandeira 4, 1249-021
Tel *213-949 494*
Housed in a 19th-century palace, this refined restaurant serves gourmet dishes, such as *leitão de Bairrada* (Bairrada-style suckling pig). Exemplary wine list.

Rest of Portugal

DK Choice

AMARANTE:
Largo do Paço €€€
International
Casa da Calçada, Largo do Paço 6, 4600-017
Tel *255-410 830*
The elegant Largo do Paço boasts a Michelin star and offers a culinary experience that would satisfy the most refined and demanding taste buds. Chef Vítor Matos changes the various degustation menus seasonally to incorporate the freshest ingredients.

CASCAIS: Casa Velha €€
Seafood
Avenida Valbom 1, 2750-508
Tel *214-832 586*
Casa Velha features a rustic ambience with stone walls. Menu favorites include *caldeirada de peixe* (fish stew), *cherne grelhado* (grilled halibut), and *paella*.

DK Choice

COIMBRA: A Taberna €€
Traditional Portuguese **Map** C3
Rua dos Combatentes da Grande Guerra 86, 3030-181
Tel *239-716 265* **Closed** *Sun dinner; Mon*
This lovely eatery with a warm interior offers local delicacies prepared in an open kitchen. The veal is tender and delicious, as is the octopus. The homemade bread with *requeijão* (ricotta cheese) is divine.

OPORTO: Cometa €€
International
Rua Tomás Gonzaga 87, 4050-607
Tel *222-008 774* **Closed** *lunch; Sun*
The menu at Cometa features dishes from countries as far apart as Vietnam and Poland. Cash only; reservations recommended.

OPORTO: The Yeatman €€€
International
Rua do Choupelo, 4400-088
Tel *220-133 100*
This luxurious Michelin-starred restaurant is bound to impress. Fantastic views accompany an inspired gourmet menu and a well-chosen wine list.

Alfresco dining under large parasols at Fábulas, Lisbon

ITALY AND GREECE

Italy and Greece at a Glance

The appeal of Italy and Greece is both cultural and hedonistic. As the cradles of Europe's two great Classical civilizations, both countries are famous for their ancient temples and monuments, concentrated principally in the cities of Rome and Athens. Located in the southern half of Europe, Italy and Greece share a sunny Mediterranean climate and a correspondingly laid-back way of life. Away from the main cultural sights, the peaceful countryside, beautiful beaches, and warm seas guarantee a relaxed vacation.

Venice *(see pp414–23)* is a city quite unlike any other: a fabulous treasure house of art and architecture, built on a series of islands, where there are no cars and the streets are canals.

Florence *(see pp394–407)* embodies the Renaisssance of art and learning in the 15th century. Familiar masterpieces of the period, such as this copy of Michelangelo's *David*, adorn the streets.

Rome *(see pp374–87)* owes its grandest monuments to the era of papal rule. The vast colonnaded square in front of St. Peter's and the Vatican was created by Bernini in the 17th century.

◀ Aerial view of Florence from Fiesole hill on a foggy morning, Italy

Trieste

Milan
Venice

Turin

Parma
Genoa

Bologna

Florence
Ancona

Siena

ITALY
(see pp368–443)
Pescara

Rome

Foggia

Naples

Sardinia

Cagliari

Reggio di Calabria

Palermo

Sicily

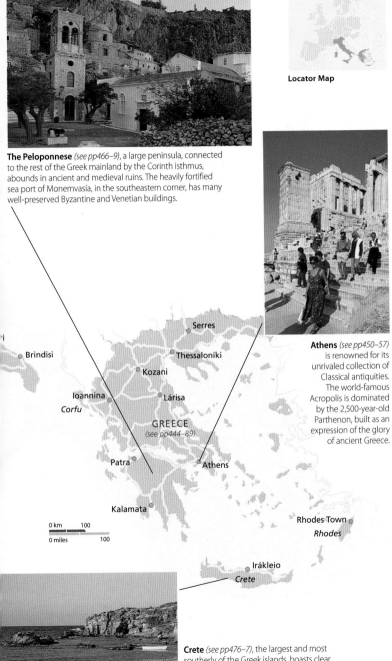

Locator Map

The Peloponnese *(see pp466–9)*, a large peninsula, connected to the rest of the Greek mainland by the Corinth isthmus, abounds in ancient and medieval ruins. The heavily fortified sea port of Monemvasía, in the southeastern corner, has many well-preserved Byzantine and Venetian buildings.

Athens *(see pp450–57)* is renowned for its unrivaled collection of Classical antiquities. The world-famous Acropolis is dominated by the 2,500-year-old Parthenon, built as an expression of the glory of ancient Greece.

Serres

Brindisi

Thessaloníki

Kozani

Ioannina

Lárisa

Corfu

GREECE
(see pp444–89)

Patra

Athens

Kalamata

0 km   100

0 miles   100

Rhodes Town

Rhodes

Irákleio

Crete

Crete *(see pp476–7)*, the largest and most southerly of the Greek islands, boasts clear blue seas and fine sandy beaches. Inland, there are ancient Minoan palaces and dramatic mountainous landscapes.

ITALY

Italy has drawn people in search of culture and romance for centuries. Few countries can compete with its Classical origins, its art, architecture, musical, and literary traditions, its scenery, or its food and wine. Since World War II, Italy has climbed into the top ten world economies, yet at its heart it retains many of the customs, traditions, and regional allegiances of its agricultural heritage.

Italy has no single cultural identity. Between the snowy peaks of the Alps and the rugged shores of Sicily lies a whole series of regions, each with its own distinctive dialect, architecture, and cuisine. There is also a larger regional division. People speak of two Italies: the rich industrial north and the poorer agricultural south, known as *Il Mezzogiorno* (Land of the Midday Sun).

The north is directly responsible for Italy's place among the world's top industrial nations, a success achieved by names such as Fiat, Pirelli, Olivetti, Zanussi, Alessi, and Armani. The south, in contrast, has high unemployment, many areas in the grip of organized crime, and regions that rank among the most depressed in Europe.

History and geography have both contributed to the division. The north is closer both in location and spirit to Germany and France, while the south has suffered a succession of invasions from foreign powers: Carthaginians and Greeks in ancient times, Saracens and Normans in the Middle Ages, and until the middle of the last century, the Bourbons from Spain held sway.

History

Italy is a young country; it did not exist as a unified nation state until 1861. The idea of Italy as a geographic entity goes back to the time of the Etruscans, but prior to the 19th century, the only time the peninsula was united was under the Romans, who by the 2nd century BC had subdued the other Italian tribes and the Greek colonies around the coast. Rome became the capital of a huge empire, introducing its language, laws, and calendar to most of Europe before falling to Germanic invaders in the 5th century AD.

A timeless view and way of life amid the hills of Tuscany

◄ The awe inspiring ruins of the Roman Forum, Rome

The ostentatious Victor Emmanuel Monument in Rome, built to commemorate the completion of the unification of Italy in 1870

Another important legacy of the Roman Empire was Christianity, with the pope as head of the Catholic church throughout western Europe. The medieval papacy summoned the Franks to drive out the Lombards from Italy and, in AD 800, crowned the Frankish king Charlemagne Holy Roman Emperor. Unfortunately, for five centuries, popes and emperors fought to decide which of them should be in charge of their nebulous empire.

Meanwhile, a succession of foreign invaders – Normans, Angevins, and Aragonese – conquered Sicily and the south. The north, in contrast, saw a growth of independent city states, the most powerful being Venice, fabulously wealthy from trade with the East. Northern Italy became the most prosperous and cultured region in western Europe, and it was the artists and scholars of 15th-century Florence who inspired the Renaissance. Small, fragmented states, however, could not compete with great powers. In the 16th century, Italy's petty kingdoms fell prey to a foreign invader, this time to Spain. The north subsequently came under the control of Austria, while the papacy ruled a small region in the center.

One small kingdom that remained independent was Piedmont, and in the 19th century it became the focus for a movement towards a united Italy, a goal that was achieved in 1870, thanks largely to the heroic military exploits of Garibaldi. In the 1920s, the Fascists seized power and, in 1946, the monarchy was abandoned for today's republic.

Governments in the postwar era have consistently been short-lived coalitions, dominated by the Christian Democrats. Investigations in Milan in 1992 revealed an organized network of corruption which exposed a huge number of politicians and businessmen. Silvio Berlusconi, Prime Minister from 2001–2006, was succeeded by Romano Prodi, but then re-elected in 2008.

KEY DATES IN ITALIAN HISTORY

c.800 BC First Greek colonists reach Italy

c.700 BC Rise of the Etruscans

509 BC Foundation of Roman Republic

202 BC Victory over Carthaginians makes Rome dominant power in the Mediterranean

27 BC Augustus establishes Roman Empire

AD 476 Collapse of Western Roman Empire

564 Lombards invade northern Italy

878 Saracens gain control of Sicily

1061 Start of Norman conquest of Sicily

1321 Dante writes *The Divine Comedy*

15th century Medici rule Florence; Renaissance

1527 Sack of Rome by Emperor's troops puts end to political ambitions of the papacy

1713 Much of the north passes to Austria

1735 Bourbon dynasty become rulers of Naples and Sicily (Kingdom of the Two Sicilies)

1860 Garibaldi and the Thousand capture Kingdom of the Two Sicilies

1861 Unification of most of Italy under House of Savoy, rulers of Piedmont and Sardinia

1870 Rome becomes capital of modern Italy

1922 Fascists come to power under Mussolini

1946 Foundation of modern Italian republic

2002 Italy joins European single currency

2005 Pope John Paul II dies

2006 Italy wins World Cup in Germany

2013 Former president Silvio Berlusconi expelled from parliament due to tax fraud conviction

Tradition and Progress

Variations between Italy's regions have much to do with the mountainous landscape and inaccessible valleys. Throughout the country, ancient techniques of husbandry endure and many livelihoods are linked to the land and the seasons. Main crops include wheat, olives, and grapes. Although some of the north's postwar economic prosperity can be attributed to industry (especially car production in Turin), much of it has grown from the expansion of family-owned artisan businesses exporting handmade goods abroad. The clothes chain, Benetton, is a typical example of Italian design flair capturing a large slice of the global market.

Language and Culture

A tradition of literary Italian was established back in the 14th century by the poets Dante and Petrarch, who wrote in a cultured Florentine dialect. Yet, even today, with national television and radio stations, Italy's regional dialects show an astonishing resilience and northerners have great difficulty understanding a Neapolitan or Sicilian.

The arts in Italy have enjoyed a long and glorious history and Italians are very proud of this. Given the fact that Italy has some 100,000 monuments of major historical significance, it is not surprising that there is a shortage of funds to keep them in good repair. However, with tourism accounting for 3 percent of Italy's GDP, efforts are being made to put as many great buildings and art collections on show as possible.

The performing arts are also underfunded, yet there are spectacular cultural festivals. In the land of Verdi and Rossini, opera is well supported, with almost every town having its own opera house. Cinema is another art form that flourishes, with great directors of the second half of the 20th century, such as Federico Fellini, and Vittorio de Sica.

The Italian soccer team celebrates its 2006 FIFA World Cup victory

Children on their way to take First Communion in the Basilica di Monte Berico, Vicenza

Modern Life

The number of practising Catholics in Italy is in decline. In spite of this, Italian society is still highly traditional, and Italians can be very formal. Italian chic decrees that your clothes should give the impression of wealth. If people wear similar outfits, it is because Italians are conformists in fashion as in many other aspects of daily life.

The emphasis on conformity and a commitment to the family remain key factors in Italian society despite the country's low, and falling, birth rate. Grandparents, children and grandchildren still live in family units, although this is becoming less common. All children are pampered but the most cherished ones are, usually, male. Attitudes to women in the workplace have changed, particularly in the cities. However, the idea that men should help with housework is still a fairly foreign notion to the older generation.

Food and football are the great constants; Italians live for both. Much time is spent on preparing food and eating. The Italian diet, particularly in the south, is among the healthiest in the world. Football is a national passion and inspires massive public interest.

Despite the political upheaval and corruption scandals of the 1990s, Italy appears little changed to foreign visitors, maintaining its regional identities and traditional values. The cost of living has soared, however, since the introduction of the euro in 2002, leading to increased poverty for some. The global economic crisis has also had a serious impact on Italy.

Exploring Italy

Italy's elongated shape means travel can take up a fair proportion of your visit. Rome, Florence, and Venice are naturally the main tourist destinations, but there are many other attractive historic towns and cities that merit a detour of a couple of days or more. Visitors with time to explore often choose to tour a particular region, such as Tuscany, the Veneto, or the island of Sicily. Road and rail connections are generally better in the north, where Milan, Bologna, and Verona are the key transport hubs.

Sights at a Glance

1. *ROME pp374–87*
2. *Assisi pp388–9*
3. Perugia
4. *Siena pp390–92*
5. San Gimignano
6. *Florence pp394–407*
7. Pisa
8. Lucca
9. Portofino Peninsula
10. Genoa
11. Turin
12. Milan
13. Lake Maggiore
14. Lake Como
15. Lake Garda
16. Mantua
17. Verona
18. Vicenza
19. Padua
20. *Venice pp414–23*
21. Ferrara
22. Bologna
23. Ravenna
24. Urbino
25. Naples
26. Pompeii
27. Amalfi Coast
28. Palermo
29. Taormina
30. Mount Etna
31. Syracuse
32. Agrigento

0 km 80
0 miles 80

Distance chart

Rome

Distance by road in kilometers
Distance by road in miles

383	**Bologna**						
238							
562	**783**	**Brindisi**					
349	487						
278	**106**	**832**	**Florence**				
173	66	517					
510	**291**	**1064**	**225**	**Genoa**			
317	181	661	140				
575	**210**	**990**	**299**	**145**	**Milan**		
357	130	615	186	90			
219	**594**	**354**	**489**	**714**	**786**	**Naples**	
136	369	220	304	444	488		
673	**332**	**1111**	**395**	**170**	**138**	**884**	**Turin**
418	206	691	245	106	86	549	
530	**154**	**928**	**255**	**397**	**273**	**741**	**402**	**Venice**
329	96	577	158	247	170	460	250	

Key

— Highway
— Major road
— Railroad
▪▪▪ International border
---- Ferry route

For keys to symbols *see back flap*

➊ Rome

From its early days as a settlement of shepherds on the Palatine hill, Rome grew to rule a vast empire stretching beyond western Europe. Later, after the fall of the Roman empire, Rome became the center of the Christian world. The legacy of this history can be seen all over the city. The Pope, head of the Roman Catholic Church, still resides in the Vatican City, an independent enclave at the heart of Rome. In 1870, Rome became the capital of a newly unified Italy, and now has over 2.8 million inhabitants. In summer, many of the grand Baroque piazzas and narrow medieval streets are crammed with attractive sidewalk bars and restaurants.

View of the Roman Forum with the Colosseum rising behind

Sights at a Glance

① St. Peter's pp376–7
② Vatican Museums pp378–80
③ Castel Sant'Angelo
④ Villa Farnesina
⑤ Santa Maria in Trastevere
⑥ Piazza Navona
⑦ Pantheon
⑧ Galleria Doria Pamphilj
⑨ Gesù
⑩ Capitoline Museums
⑪ Trajan's Markets
⑫ Roman Forum
⑬ Palatine
⑭ Colosseum
⑮ Santa Maria Maggiore
⑯ Trevi Fountain
⑰ Spanish Steps
⑱ Santa Maria del Popolo
⑲ Museo e Galleria Borghese
⑳ Villa Giulia

Getting Around

Rome's subway system is known as la metropolitana (metro for short). Line A crosses the city from northwest to southeast, Line B from southwest to northeast. The two lines meet at Stazione Termini, the city's central station, which is also the starting point for many bus routes. A third metro line is due for completion in 2018. Official taxis are white or yellow. Walking is preferable to driving in the city's narrow streets.

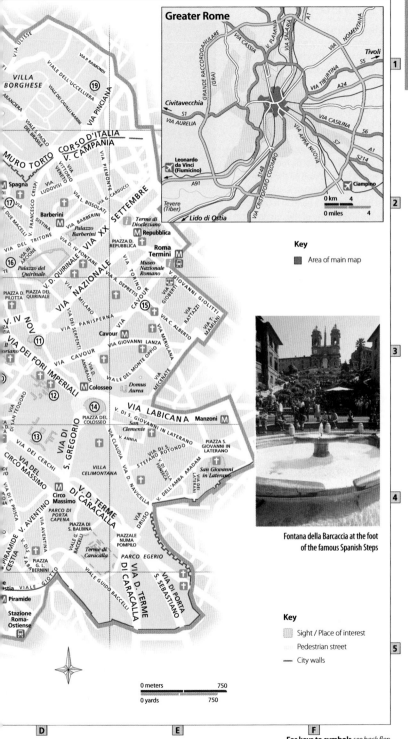

Greater Rome

Tivoli

Civitavecchia

Leonardo
da Vinci
(Fiumicino)

Ciampino

Tevere
(Tiber)

Lido di Ostia

Key

Area of main map

0 km 4
0 miles 4

Fontana della Barcaccia at the foot
of the famous Spanish Steps

Key

Sight / Place of interest

Pedestrian street

City walls

0 meters 750
0 yards 750

① St. Peter's

Catholicism's most sacred shrine, the vast, marble-encrusted basilica draws pilgrims and tourists from all over the world. A shrine was erected on the site of St. Peter's tomb in the 2nd century and the first basilica was commissioned by Constantine. Centuries later, in 1506, Pope Julius II laid the first stone of a new church while the original basilica was still in use. The present basilica, 187 m (615 ft) long, took more than a century to build and all the great architects of the Roman Renaissance and Baroque had a hand in its design. The dominant tone of the interior is set by Bernini, creator of the *baldacchino* below Michelangelo's magnificent dome.

★ Dome
The 137-m- (448-ft-) dome, designed by Michelangelo, was not completed until 1590, long after his death.

Baldacchino
Commissioned by Urban VIII in 1624, Bernini's extravagant Baroque canopy stands above the Papal Altar, a plain slab of marble, at which only the pope may say mass. The altar is sited directly above the tomb of St. Peter in the Grottoes below.

KEY

① **The Treasury** is reached via the Sacristy. It houses ecclesiastical treasures, including reliquaries, tombs, and vestments.

② **The apse** is dominated by Bernini's spectacular bronze monument containing the Throne of St. Peter in Glory.

③ **Two minor cupolas by Vignola (1507–73)**

④ **The facade** (1614) is by Carlo Maderno, who lengthened the basilica to create its Latin-cross floorplan.

⑤ **From this window**, the pope blesses the faithful gathered in the piazza below.

⑥ **The nave floor** has markings that show the lengths of other churches compared with St. Peter's.

Monument to Pope Alexander VII
Bernini's last work in St. Peter's was finished in 1678 and shows the pope surrounded by the allegorical figures of Truth, Justice, Charity, and Prudence.

The Grottoes
A fragment of this 13th-century mosaic by Giotto, salvaged from the old basilica, is now in the Grottoes, where many popes are buried.

★ Statue of St. Peter
This 13th-century bronze is thought to be by Arnolfo di Cambio. The foot of the statue has worn thin from the kisses of millions of pilgrims over the centuries.

VISITORS' CHECKLIST

Practical Information
Piazza San Pietro.
Tel 06-69 88 37 31.
🅦 vatican.va
Basilica: **Open** 7am–7pm
(Oct–Mar: to 6:30pm) daily. ♿
Treasury: **Open** 8am–7pm
(Oct–Mar: to 6:15pm) daily. 🚻
Grottoes: **Open** 8am–6pm
(Oct–Mar: to 5:30pm) daily.
Dome: **Open** 8am–6pm
(Oct–Mar: to 5pm) daily. 🚻
Strict dress code inside church.

Transport
Ⓜ Ottaviano S. Pietro.
🚌 23, 40, 49, 64, 81, 492.

★ Michelangelo's Pietà
Protected by glass since an attack in 1972, the *Pietà* stands in the first side chapel on the right. It was created in 1499 when Michelangelo was only 25.

Filarete Door
This bronze door, decorated with reliefs by Filarete (1439–45), was one of the doors of the old St. Peter's.

Entrance for stairs to dome

Main entrance

Piazza San Pietro
The piazza in front of St. Peter's is enclosed by a vast pincer-shaped colonnade by Bernini. It is topped by statues of saints.

② **Vatican Museums**

Four centuries of papal patronage and connoisseurship have resulted in one of the world's great collections of Classical and Renaissance art. The Vatican houses many of the great archaeological finds of central Italy, including the *Laocoön* group and the *Apollo del Belvedere*. The museums are housed in palaces originally built for wealthy Renaissance popes such as Innocent VIII, Sixtus IV, and Julius II. Parts of these were decorated with wonderful frescoes by the finest painters of the age – most notably the Borgia Apartment, the Raphael Rooms and the Sistine Chapel *(see p380)*.

Gallery of the Candelabra
Once an open loggia, this gallery of Greek and Roman sculpture has a fine view of the Vatican Gardens.

Room of the Biga (a two-horse chariot)

Gallery of Tapestries

Gallery of Maps
The gallery is an important record of 16th-century cartography and history. This painting shows the Turkish siege of Malta in 1565.

Etruscan Museum

The Raphael Loggia
contains Raphael frescoes, but special permission is needed to visit it.

Upper floor

Sistine Chapel

Raphael Rooms
This detail from the *Expulsion of Heliodorus from the Temple* contains a portrait of Julius II. It is one of a series of frescoes painted by Raphael for the pope's private apartments *(see p380)*.

The Cortile del Belvedere was designed by Bramante in 1506.

The Borgia Apartment, frescoed by Pinturicchio in a highly decorative style in the 1490s, also houses a collection of modern religious art.

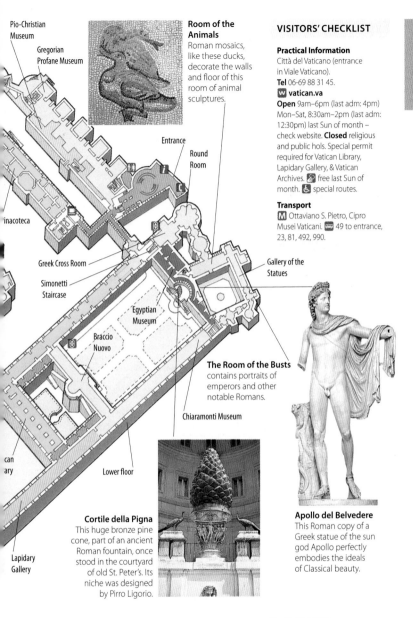

Pio-Christian Museum

Gregorian Profane Museum

Room of the Animals
Roman mosaics, like these ducks, decorate the walls and floor of this room of animal sculptures.

Entrance

Round Room

inacoteca

Greek Cross Room

Simonetti Staircase

Egyptian Museum

Braccio Nuovo

Gallery of the Statues

The Room of the Busts contains portraits of emperors and other notable Romans.

Chiaramonti Museum

can ary

Lower floor

Lapidary Gallery

Cortile della Pigna
This huge bronze pine cone, part of an ancient Roman fountain, once stood in the courtyard of old St. Peter's. Its niche was designed by Pirro Ligorio.

Apollo del Belvedere
This Roman copy of a Greek statue of the sun god Apollo perfectly embodies the ideals of Classical beauty.

Gallery Guide

Visitors have to follow a one-way system. It is best to concentrate on a single collection or to choose one of the suggested itineraries. These are color-coded so that you can follow them throughout the museums. They vary in length from 90 minutes to five hours. If you are planning a long visit, make sure you allow plenty of time for resting. Conserve your stamina for the Sistine Chapel and the Raphael Rooms; they are 20–30 minutes' walk from the entrance, without allowing for any viewing time along the way.

Key to Floorplan

- Egyptian and Assyrian art
- Greek and Roman art
- Etruscan and Italic art
- Early Christian and medieval art
- 15th- to 19th-century art
- Modern religious art
- Non-exhibition space
- Open by special permit only

Exploring the Vatican's Collections

The Vatican's greatest treasures are its Greek and Roman antiquities, which have been on display since the 18th century. The 19th century saw the addition of exciting discoveries from Etruscan tombs and excavations in Egypt. Then there are works by many of Italy's greatest Renaissance artists housed in the Pinacoteca (art gallery) and decorating the walls of chapels and papal apartments.

The *Laocoön*, a Roman copy of a Greek original, excavated in Rome in 1506

Ancient Art

The Egyptian collection contains finds from 19th- and 20th-century excavations, as well as items brought to Rome in Imperial times. There are also Roman imitations of Egyptian art. Genuine Egyptian works include the tomb of Iri, guardian of the Pyramid of Cheops (22nd century BC).

Prize Greek and Roman art in the Pio-Clementine Museum includes Roman copies of the 4th-century BC Greek statues *Apoxyomenos* and the *Apollo del Belvedere*, and a splendid *Laocoön* from the 1st century AD.

The Chiaramonti Museum is lined with ancient busts, and its extension, the Braccio Nuovo, has a 1st-century BC statue of Emperor Augustus.

The Etruscan Museum houses a superb collection, including the bronze throne, bed, and funeral cart, found in the 650 BC Regolini-Galassi tomb in Cerveteri.

In the Vatican Library is the *Aldobrandini Wedding*, a beautiful Roman fresco from the 1st century AD.

Christian Art

The Pio-Christian Museum has Early Christian art, such as inscriptions and sculpture from catacombs and basilicas. The first two rooms of the Pinacoteca house medieval art, including Giotto's *Stefaneschi Triptych* (c.1300), which decorated the main altar of the old St. Peter's. Other rooms in the Pinacoteca contain Renaissance works. 15th-century highlights are a *Pietà* by Giovanni Bellini and Leonardo da Vinci's unfinished *St. Jerome*. Exceptional 16th-century pieces include an altarpiece by Titian, a *Deposition* by Caravaggio, *St. Helen* by Paolo Veronese, and a whole room devoted to Raphael.

The Sistine Chapel

The Sistine Chapel takes its name from Pope Sixtus IV; it was built in 1473 at his request. The walls were frescoed by some of the finest artists of the age, including Signorelli, Botticelli, Roselli, Ghirlandaio, and Perugino (who is credited with having overseen the project). There are 12 frescoes on the side walls, painted between 1481 and 1483. Their subjects are parallel episodes in the lives of Moses and Christ.

In 1508–12, at the request of Pope Julius II, Michelangelo created what has become his most famous work, the chapel ceiling. The main panels chart the *Creation of the World* and *Fall of Man*. They are surrounded by subjects from the Old and New Testaments.

In 1534–41 Michelangelo completed the chapel walls, painting *The Last Judgment* on the altar wall. It depicts the souls of the dead rising up to face the wrath of God and the damned being hurled down to hell. The artist's own tormented attitude to his faith is seen in his self-portrait, painted on the skin held by the martyr, St. Bartholomew.

Raphael Rooms

Pope Julius II chose Raphael (1483–1520) to redecorate four rooms *(stanze)* of his apartments. The frescoes in the Room of the Segnatura (1508–11) include the famous *School of Athens*, which centers on a debate between Plato and Aristotle. Raphael depicted Leonardo da Vinci and Michelangelo as philosophers. The decoration of the Room of Heliodorus (1512–4) incorporates a famous portrait of Julius II, whereas the Room of the Fire in the Borgo (1514–7) was painted during the reign of Pope Leo X, Julius II's successor. All the frescoes here exalt the new pope or his earlier namesakes.

The Hall of Constantine (1517–25) was largely the work of Raphael's pupils.

Original Sin, from Michelangelo's fresco on the Sistine Chapel ceiling

View across the Tiber to Castel Sant'Angelo, crowned by the figure of the angel that gave it its name

③ Castel Sant'Angelo

Lungotevere Castello 50. **Tel** 06-681 91 11. 23, 34, 40, 280. **Open** Tue–Sun. **Closed** public hols. 🅿 ♿ 🆆 **castel santangelo.beniculturali.it**

This massive cylindrical fortress takes its name from the vision of the Archangel Michael, experienced by Pope Gregory the Great in the 6th century, as he led a procession across the bridge, fervently praying for the end of the plague.

The castle began life in AD 139 as the Emperor Hadrian's mausoleum. Since then it has been a bridgehead in the Emperor Aurelian's city wall, a medieval citadel and prison, and a place of safety for popes during times of war or political unrest.

Visitors are given a glimpse into all aspects of the castle's history – from its dank prison cells to the lavish apartments of Renaissance popes.

④ Villa Farnesina

Via della Lungara 230. **Tel** 06-68 02 73 97. H, 280, 780. **Open** Mon–Sat. **Closed** public hols. 🅿

The fabulously wealthy Sienese banker, Agostino Chigi, commissioned this villa in 1508 from his fellow Sienese, Baldassare Peruzzi. Chigi's main home was across the Tiber – the villa was just for extravagant banquets. Chigi

also used it for sojourns with the courtesan Imperia, who allegedly inspired one of the *Three Graces* painted by Raphael in the Loggia of Cupid and Psyche.

The simple, harmonious design of the Farnesina, with a central block and projecting wings, made it one of the first true villas of the Renaissance. Peruzzi decorated some of the interiors himself, such as the Sala della Prospettiva upstairs, in which illusionistic frescoes create the impression of looking out over Rome through a marble colonnade.

The painted vault of the main hall, the Sala di Galatea, shows the position of the stars at the time of Chigi's birth. After his death the banking business collapsed, and in 1577 the villa was sold to the Farnese family.

Trompe l'oeil view in the Sala della Prospettiva, Villa Farnesina

⑤ Santa Maria in Trastevere

Piazza Santa Maria in Trastevere. **Tel** 06-581 94 43. H, 23, 280, 630, 780. **Open** daily. ♿

Trastevere, the area "across the Tiber," is one of the city's most attractive quarters: a maze of narrow, cobbled alleys. Once home to the city's poor, it has witnessed a proliferation of fashionable clubs, restaurants, and boutiques.

At the heart of Trastevere, overlooking an attractive traffic-free square stands the Basilica of Santa Maria – probably the first official place of Christian worship in Rome. It was founded by Pope Callixtus I in the 3rd century, when Christianity was still a minority cult. According to legend, it was built on the site where a fountain of oil had sprung up miraculously on the day that Christ was born.

The basilica became the focus of devotion to the Madonna. Mary and Christ are among the figures depicted in the facade mosaics (c.12th century). In the apse is a stylized 12th-century mosaic *Coronation of the Virgin*, and below it, a series of realistic mosaic scenes from the life of Mary by the 13th-century artist Pietro Cavallini. The oldest image of the Virgin is a 7th-century icon, which depicts her as a Byzantine empress flanked by a guard of angels.

For hotels and restaurants see pp438–40 and pp441–3

⑥ Piazza Navona

🚌 40, 46, 62, 64, 81, 87, 116, 492, 628.

Rome's most spectacular Baroque piazza follows the shape of a 1st-century AD stadium, built by Domitian and used for athletic contests *(agones),* chariot races, and other sports. The foundations of the surrounding buildings come from the ruined stadium, traces of which are visible below the church of Sant' Agnese in Agone. The church, created by the architects Girolamo and Carlo Rainaldi and Francesco Borromini, is dedicated to the virgin martyr, St. Agnes. When she was stripped naked to force her to renounce her faith, her hair grew miraculously long, concealing her body.

The piazza began to take on its present appearance in the 17th century, when Pope Innocent X commissioned a new church, palace, and fountain. The fountain, the Fontana dei Quattro Fiumi, is Bernini's most magnificent, with statues of four gods

The Pantheon, a place of worship since the 2nd century AD

personifying the world's greatest known rivers at the time – the Nile, the Plate, the Ganges, and the Danube – sitting on rocks below an obelisk. Bernini also sculpted the muscle-bound Moor in the Fontana del Moro, though the present statue is a copy.

⑦ Pantheon

Piazza della Rotonda. **Tel** 06-68 30 02 30. 🚌 116 & many others. **Open** daily. **Closed** Jan 1, May 1, Dec 25. ♿

The Pantheon, the Roman "temple of all the gods," is the most extraordinary and best preserved ancient building in Rome. The first temple on the site is thought to have been a conventional rectangular affair erected by Agrippa between 27 and 25 BC. The present structure was built, and possibly designed, by Emperor Hadrian in AD 118. The temple is

fronted by a massive pedimented portico, screening what appears to be a cylinder fused to a shallow dome. Only from the inside can the true scale and beauty of the temple be appreciated; a vast hemispherical dome equal in radius to the height of the cylinder gives perfectly harmonious proportions to the building. A circular opening in the center of the coffered dome, the *oculus,* lets in the only light.

In the 7th century, Christians claimed that they were being plagued by demons as they passed by, and permission was given to turn the Pantheon into a church. Today it is lined with tombs, ranging from the restrained monument to Raphael to the huge marble and porphyry sarcophagi holding the bodies of Italian monarchs.

⑧ Galleria Doria Pamphilj

Via del Corso 305. **Tel** 06-678 09 39. 🚌 64, 70, 81, 85, 117, 119, 492. **Open** daily. **Closed** Jan 1, Easter Sun, May 1, Aug 15, Dec 25. 📷 ♿ 🆆 dopart.it/roma

Galleria Doria Pamphilj is a vast stone edifice, whose oldest parts date from 1435. It was owned by the della Rovere family and then by the Aldobrandini family, before the Pamphilj family took possession of it in 1647. The Pamphilj added a new wing, a splendid

Personification of the Ganges, Fontana dei Quattro Fiumi, Piazza Navona

For hotels and restaurants see pp438–40 and pp441–3

chapel, and a theater. The family art collection has over 400 paintings dating from the 15th to the 18th century, including a portrait of Pope Innocent X by Velázquez and works by Caravaggio, Titian, Guercino, and Claude Lorrain. The opulent rooms of the private apartments retain many of their original furnishings, including Brussels and Gobelins tapestries, Murano chandeliers, and a gilded crib.

In the first half of the 18th century, Gabriele Valvassori created the gallery above the courtyard and a new facade along the Corso, using the highly decorative style of the period, known as the *barocchetto*, which now dominates the building.

Triumph of Faith over Heresy by Pierre Legros in the Gesù

⑨ Gesù

Piazza del Gesù. **Tel** 06-69 70 01. many routes. **Open** daily.

The Gesù, built between 1568 and 1584, was Rome's first Jesuit church. The Jesuit order was founded in Rome in 1537 by a Basque soldier, Ignatius Loyola, who became a Christian after he was wounded in battle. The order was intellectual, austere, and heavily engaged in teaching and missionary activities.

The much-imitated design of the Gesù typifies Counter Reformation architecture: a large nave with side pulpits for preaching to crowds, and a main altar as the centerpiece for the mass. The illusionistic decoration that covers the nave ceiling and the dome was

added by Il Baciccia during the 17th century. The painting in the nave depicts the *Triumph of the Name of Jesus* and its message is clear: faithful, Catholic worshippers will be joyfully uplifted to heaven while Protestants and heretics are flung into the fires of hell. The message is reiterated in the Cappella di Sant'Ignazio, a rich display of lapis lazuli, serpentine, silver, and gold. The Baroque marble by Pierre Legros, *Triumph of Faith over Idolatry*, shows a female "Religion" trampling on the head of the serpent "Idolatry."

⑩ Capitoline Museums

Musei Capitolini, Piazza del Campidoglio. **Tel** 06-06 08. 63, 64, 70, 75 & many others. **Open** Tue–Sun. **Closed** Jan 1, May 1, Dec 25. **museicapitolini.org**

When Emperor Charles V announced he was to visit Rome in 1536, Pope Paul III asked Michelangelo to give the Capitol, formerly the citadel of Ancient Rome, a facelift. He redesigned the piazza, renovated the facades of its palaces and built a new staircase, the Cordonata. This gently rising ramp is now crowned with the massive Classical statues of Castor and Pollux.

The Capitoline Museums, the Palazzo Nuovo, and the Palazzo dei Conservatori stand on opposite sides of the impressive Piazza del Campidoglio. Since 2000, they have been connected via a subterranean passage. In the center of the piazza is an equestrian statue of Marcus Aurelius (it is a copy; the original bronze is in the Palazzo Nuovo).

The facade of the Palazzo Nuovo was designed by Michelangelo, but the work was finished in 1655 by the brothers Carlo and Girolamo Rainaldi.

Statue of Marcus Aurelius in the center of Piazza del Campidoglio

The Palazzo dei Conservatori had been the seat of the city's magistrates during the late Middle Ages. Its frescoed halls are still used occasionally for political meetings and the ground floor houses the municipal registry office. The current building was begun in 1536, built by Giacomo della Porta, who also carried out Michelangelo's other designs for Piazza del Campidoglio.

A collection of Classical statues has been kept on the Capitoline Hill since the Renaissance. When the Palazzo Nuovo was completed, some of the statues were transferred there. In 1734, Pope Clement XII decreed that the building be turned into the world's first public museum.

The museum is still devoted chiefly to sculpture. Most of its finest works, such as *The Dying Galatian*, are Roman copies of Greek masterpieces. There are also two collections of busts, assembled in the 18th century, of the philosophers and poets of ancient Greece and the rulers of ancient Rome.

Although much of the museum is given over to sculpture, it also houses a collection of porcelain, and its art galleries contain various works by Veronese, Titian, Caravaggio, Rubens, van Dyck, and Tintoretto.

Esquiline Venus, Capitoline Museums

Ancient Rome

Traces of ancient Rome are visible all over the city, occasionally a whole building, often just a column from a temple or an arch of an aqueduct recycled in a later construction. The major archaeological sites are to be found along Via dei Fori Imperiali, which runs from Piazza Venezia to the Colosseum. On the north side lie Trajan's Markets and the forums of various emperors; on the south side are the Roman Forum and the Palatine Hill. Many museums hold extensive collections of antiquities excavated in the city.

Romans fortifying a town in a detail from Trajan's Column

⑪ Trajan's Markets

Via IV Novembre 94. **Tel** 06-06 08. 📠 40, 60, 171. **Open** Tue–Sun. **Closed** public hols. 📷
W mercatiditraiano.it

Originally considered among the wonders of the Classical world, Trajan's Markets now show only a hint of their former splendor.

Emperor Trajan and his architect, Apollodorus of Damascus, built this visionary complex of 150 shops and offices in the early 2nd century AD. The Markets sold everything from Middle Eastern silks and spices to fresh fish, fruit, and flowers. It was also the place where the corn dole was administered; a free ration for Roman men.

Shops opened early and closed about noon. Almost all the shopping was done by men and the traders were almost exclusively male.

The **Forum of Trajan** (AD 107–13) was built in front of the market complex. It was a vast colonnaded open space with a huge basilica, and included two

libraries. Dominating the ruins today is **Trajan's Column**. Spiralling up its 30-m- (98-ft-) high stem are minutely detailed scenes showing episodes from Trajan's successful campaigns in Dacia (present-day Romania).

⑫ Roman Forum

Entrances: Via di San Gregorio and Via della Salara Vecchia 56. **Tel** 06-39 96 77 00. 🅼 Colosseo. 📠 60, 75, 85, 87, 117, 175, 186, 810, 850. **Open** daily. **Closed** Jan 1, May 1, Dec 25. 📷 (includes entry to the Colosseum and Palatine). **W** coopculture.it

The Forum was the center of political, commercial, and judicial life in ancient Rome. As Rome's population grew, however, this ancient Forum became too small, so Julius Caesar built a new one (46 BC). This move was emulated by successive emperors. The newer forums are known as the "Imperial Fora."

The ruins of the Roman Forum date from many eras and the layout is confusing. It is a good idea to view them from the vantage point of the Capitoline

Hill, before walking around. From there you can make out the Via Sacra, the route of religious and triumphal processions.

The best preserved monuments are two triumphal arches. The **Arch of Titus** commemorates the crushing of the Jewish Revolt by Titus in AD 70. The later **Arch of Septimius Severus** (AD 203) records the emperor's victories over the Parthians.

Most of the other ruins are temples or basilicas. The latter were huge public buildings, which served as law courts and places of business. At the western end of the forum are the scant remains of the **Basilica Julia**, named after Julius Caesar, and the earlier **Basilica Aemilia**. Close to the latter stands the reconstructed **Curia**, where the Roman Senate once met.

The eastern end of the Forum is dominated by the shell of the **Basilica of Constantine and Maxentius** (4th century AD). The adjacent **Temple of Romulus** is now part of a church. Cross the Via Sacra from here to see the partly reconstructed **Temple of Vesta** and the **House of the Vestal Virgins**.

Further east past the Arch of Titus are the extensive ruins of the **Temple of Venus and Rome**, built in AD 121 by Hadrian. Attached to the ruined temple is the church of **Santa Francesca Romana** – patron saint of motorists. On March 9, drivers bring their cars here to have them blessed.

Central garden of the House of the Vestal Virgins in the Roman Forum

Ruins of oval fountain in the Domus Flavia on the Palatine

⑬ **Palatine**

Entrances: Via di San Gregorio and near the Arch of Titus on Via Sacra. **Tel** 06-39 96 77 00. Ⓜ Colosseo. 🚌 60, 75, 81, 160, 175 & many others. 🚃 3. **Open** daily. **Closed** public hols. (includes entry to the Colosseum and Forum). 🖼 🌐 coopculture.it

The Palatine, the hill where the Roman aristocracy lived and emperors built their palaces, is the most pleasant and relaxing of the city's ancient sites. Shaded by pines and carpeted with wild flowers in the spring, it is dominated by the imposing ruins of the **Domus Augustana** and the **Domus Flavia**, two parts of Domitian's huge palace (1st century AD).

Other remains here include the **House of Augustus** and the **House of Livia**, where the Emperor Augustus lived with his wife Livia; and the **Cryptoporticus**, a long underground gallery built by Nero.

The **Huts of Romulus**, not far from the House of Augustus, are Iron Age huts (10th century BC), which provide archaeological support for the area's legendary links with the founding of Rome. According to legend, Romulus and Remus grew up on this hill in the 8th century BC.

After admiring the ancient sights, visit the **Farnese Gardens**, created in the mid-16th century by Cardinal Alessandro Farnese, with tree-lined avenues, rose gardens, and glorious views.

⑭ **Colosseum**

Piazza del Colosseo. **Tel** 06-3996 77 00. Ⓜ Colosseo. 🚌 75, 81, 85, 87, 117, 175, 673, 810. 🚃 3. **Open** daily. **Closed** Jan 1, May 1, Dec 25. 🖼 (includes entry to the Palatine and Forum). 🖼 ♿ limited. 🌐 coopculture.it

Rome's great amphitheater, commissioned by the Emperor Vespasian in AD 72, was built on the marshy site of a lake in the grounds of Nero's palace.

It is likely that the arena took its name, not from its own size, but from that of an enormous statue, the Colossus of Nero, that stood nearby.

The Colosseum was the site of deadly gladiatorial combats and wild animal fights, staged free of charge by the emperor and wealthy citizens. It was built to a very practical design, its 80 entrances allowing easy access for 55,000 spectators. Excavations in the 19th century exposed a network of rooms under the arena, from which animals could be released.

The four tiers of the outside walls were built in differing styles. The lower three are arched; the bottom with Doric columns, the next with Ionic, and the third with Corinthian. The top level supported a huge awning, used to shade spectators from the sun.

Beside the Colosseum stands the **Arch of Constantine**, commemorating Constantine's victory in AD 312 over his co-emperor Maxentius. Most of the medallions, reliefs, and statues were scavenged from earlier monuments. Inside the arch are reliefs showing one of Trajan's victories.

Ancient Roman Sites and Museums

Practical Information
Baths of Caracalla:
Viale delle Terme di Caracalla 52. **Tel** 06-39 96 77 00. **Open** Tue–Sun & Mon am. 🖼 🖼
Extensive ruins of bath complex built in AD 217.
Theatre of Marcellus:
Via del Teatro di Marcello. **Open** daily. An Imperial theater, which later housed a number of medieval shops.
Museo Nazionale Romano:
Palazzo Massimo, Largo di Villa Peretti 1. **Tel** 06-39 36 77 00. **Open** Tue–Sun. 🖼 ♿
Sculpture, mosaics, wall-paintings, and a Roman mummy. Another branch of the museum is at the Baths of Diocletian across the road.
Palazzo Altemps:
Piazza Sant'Apollinare 44. **Tel** 06-39 36 77 00. **Open** Tue–Sun. 🖼 ♿
Fine collection of Classical statuary set in a beautiful Renaissance palazzo.
Temples of the Forum Boarium:
Piazza della Bocca della Verità. Two miraculously preserved Republican-era temples.

Transport
Baths of Caracalla: Ⓜ Circo Massimo. 🚌 160, 628. 🚃 3.
Theatre of Marcellus 🚌 30, 44, 63, 81, 95, 130, 160, 170, 271, 628, 630, 715, 716, 780, 781.
Museo Nazionale Romano:
Ⓜ Repubblica, Termini. 🚌 36, 38, 64, 86, 110, 170, 175, H, and many others to Piazza dei Cinquecento.
Palazzo Altemps: 🚌 70, 81, 115, 116, 280, 492, 628.
Temples of the Forum Boarium: 🚌 44, 81, 95, 160, 170, 280, 628, 715, 716.

The Colosseum, a majestic sight despite centuries of damage and neglect

⑮ Santa Maria Maggiore

Piazza di Santa Maria Maggiore. **Tel** 06-69 88 68 00. Ⓜ Termini, Cavour. 🚌 16, 70, 71, 714. 🚋 14. **Open** daily. 📷

Of all the great Roman basilicas, Santa Maria has the most successful blend of different architectural styles. Its colonnaded triple nave is part of the original 5th-century building; the marble floor and Romanesque bell tower, with its blue ceramic roundels, are medieval; the Renaissance saw a new coffered ceiling; and the Baroque gave the church twin domes and its imposing front and rear facades.

Santa Maria is most famous for its mosaics. Those in the nave and on the triumphal arch date from the 5th century. Medieval mosaics include a 13th-century enthroned Christ in the loggia and Jacopo Torriti's *Coronation of the Virgin* (1295) in the apse.

The gilded ceiling was a gift of Alexander VI, the Borgia pope. The gold used is said to be the first brought back from America by Columbus.

⑯ Trevi Fountain

Piazza di Trevi. 🚌 52, 53, 61, 62, 63, 71, 80, 95, 116, 119 & many others.

Most visitors gathering around the coin-filled fountain assume that it has always been there, but by the standards of the Eternal City, the Trevi is a fairly recent creation. Nicola Salvi's theatrical design for Rome's

The Spanish Steps, with the church of Trinità dei Monti above

largest and most famous fountain was completed only in 1762. The central figure is Neptune, flanked by two Tritons. One Triton struggles to master a very unruly "sea-horse," the other leads a far more docile animal. These symbolize the two contrasting moods of the sea.

The site was originally the terminal of the Aqua Virgo aqueduct (19 BC). A relief shows the legendary virgin, after whom the aqueduct was named, pointing to the spring from which the water flows.

⑰ Spanish Steps

Scalinata della Trinità dei Monti, Piazza di Spagna. Ⓜ Spagna. 🚌 116, 117, 119, 590.

The steps, which link the church of Trinità dei Monti with Piazza di Spagna below, were completed in 1726. They combine straight sections, curves, and terraces to create one of the city's most dramatic and distinctive landmarks. To the right as you look at the steps from the square is the **Keats-Shelley Memorial House**, a small museum in the house where the poet John Keats died of consumption in 1821.

In the 19th century the steps were a meeting place for artists' models; today they are filled with people sitting, writing postcards, taking photos, flirting, busking, or just watching the passers-by. Eating here is not allowed.

The steps overlook Via Condotti and the surrounding streets. In the 18th century this area was full of hotels for foreigners doing the Grand Tour. It now contains the smartest shops in Rome.

Trevi Fountain, the most famous of Rome's Baroque landmarks

For hotels and restaurants see pp438–40 and pp441–3

⑱ Santa Maria del Popolo

Piazza del Popolo 12. **Tel** 06-361 08 36. Ⓜ Flaminio. 🚌 95, 117, 119, 120, 150, 491. **Open** daily.

Santa Maria del Popolo was commissioned by Sixtus IV in 1472. After his death in 1484, the pope's family chapel, the Della Rovere Chapel (first on the right), was frescoed by Pinturicchio.

In 1503, Sixtus IV's nephew Giuliano became Pope Julius II and had Bramante build a new apse. Pinturicchio was called in again to paint its vaults with Sibyls and Apostles framed by freakish beasts.

In 1513, Raphael created the Chigi Chapel (second on the left) – a Renaissance fusion of the sacred and profane – for the banker Agostino Chigi. Bernini later added the statues of Daniel and Habakkuk. In the Cerasi Chapel, left of the altar, are two Caravaggios: *The Crucifixion of St Peter* and *The Conversion of St Paul*.

The Chigi Chapel in Santa Maria del Popolo, designed by Raphael

⑲ Museo e Galleria Borghese

Piazzale Scipione Borghese 5. **Tel** 06-328 10 (reservations). 🚌 52, 53, 910. 🚋 3, 19. **Open** Tue–Sun (reservations obligatory). **Closed** Jan 1, May 1, Dec 25. 📷 🆆 **galleria borghese.beniculturali.it**

The Villa Borghese and its park were designed in 1605 for Cardinal Scipione Borghese,

Detail from Bernini's *Rape of Proserpine* in the Museo Borghese

nephew of Pope Paul V. The park was the first of its kind in Rome. It was laid out with 400 pine trees, sculpture by Bernini, and dramatic water features.

The villa was used for entertaining and displaying the cardinal's impressive collection of paintings and sculpture. Unfortunately, between 1801 and 1809, Prince Camillo Borghese, husband to Napoleon's sister Pauline, sold many of these to his brother-in-law, and swapped 200 of Scipione's Classical statues for an estate in Piedmont. The statues are still in the Louvre. However, some Classical treasures remain, including fragments of a 3rd-century AD mosaic of gladiators fighting wild animals.

The highlights of the remaining collection are the sculptures by the young Bernini. *Apollo and Daphne* (1624), shows the nymph Daphne being transformed into a laurel tree to escape being abducted by Apollo. Other striking works are *The Rape of Proserpine* and a *David*, whose face is said to be a self-portrait of Bernini. The most

notorious work is a sculpture by Canova of Pauline Borghese as *Venus Victrix* (1805), in which the semi-naked Pauline reclines on a chaise longue.

The Galleria Borghese, on the upper floor, houses some fine Renaissance and Baroque paintings. These include Raphael's *Deposition*, along with works by Pinturicchio, Correggio, Caravaggio, Rubens, and Titian.

Within the Villa Borghese park are other museums and galleries, foreign academies, a zoo, schools of archaeology, an artificial lake, and an array of fountains and follies.

⑳ Villa Giulia

Piazzale di Villa Giulia 9. **Tel** 06-322 65 71. 🚌 52, 88, 95, 490, 495 926, 🚋 3, 19. **Open** Tue–Sun. **Closed** Jan 1, May 1, Dec 25. 📷 🎧 audio. ♿

Villa Giulia was built as a country retreat for Pope Julius III. Today, it houses a world-famous collection of Etruscan and other pre-Roman remains. There are fascinating pieces of jewelry, bronzes, mirrors, and a marvelous terra-cotta sarcophagus of a husband and wife from Cerveteri.

The delightful villa was the work of architects Vasari and Vignola, and the sculptor Ammannati. Michelangelo also contributed. At the center of the garden is a *nympheum* – a sunken courtyard decorated with mosaics, statues, and fountains, built in imitation of ancient Roman models.

The cheerful figures of an Etruscan married couple on their sarcophagus, Villa Giulia

Assisi: Basilica di San Francesco

The burial place of St. Francis, this basilica was begun in 1228, two years after the saint's death. Over the next century, its Upper and Lower Churches were decorated by the foremost artists of their day, among them Cimabue, Simone Martini, Pietro Lorenzetti, and Giotto, whose frescoes of the *Life of St. Francis* are some of the most renowned in Italy. Many of the basilica's frescoes were badly damaged in the earthquake that hit Assisi in 1997, but all have been restored. The basilica, which dominates Assisi, is one of the great Christian shrines and receives vast numbers of pilgrims throughout the year.

★ Cappella di San Martino
The frescoes in this chapel on the life of St. Martin (1315) are by the Sienese painter Simone Martini. This panel shows the death of the Saint. Martini was also responsible for the fine stained glass in the chapel.

★ Frescoes by Lorenzetti
The bold composition of Pietro Lorenzetti's fresco, entitled *The Deposition* (1323), is based around the truncated Cross, focusing attention on the twisted figure of Christ.

★ Frescoes by Giotto
The Ecstasy of St. Francis is one of 28 panels that make up Giotto's cycle on the *Life of St. Francis* (c.1290–95).

KEY

① **A Renaissance portico** shelters the original Gothic portal of the Lower Church.

② **The crypt** contains the tomb of St. Francis.

③ **Steps to the Treasury**

④ **The vaulting** of the Lower Church is covered almost entirely in frescoes.

⑤ **St. Francis**, Cimabue's simple painting (c.1280), captures the humility of the revered saint, who stood for poverty, chastity, and obedience.

⑥ **The choir** (1501) features a 13th-century stone papal throne.

⑦ **Faded paintings** by Roman artists line the walls above Giotto's *Life of St. Francis.*

⑧ **The Upper Church** has soaring Gothic vaulting painted with a starry sky, symbolizing the heavenly glory of St. Francis. Its style influenced that of many later Franciscan churches.

⑨ **The facade** and its rose window are early examples of Italian Gothic.

VISITORS' CHECKLIST

Practical Information
Piazza San Francesco, Assisi.
Tel 075-819 001.
w sanfrancescoassisi.org
Open daily.

Transport

The ancient Tempio di Minerva in the Piazza del Comune, Assisi

❷ Assisi

👥 25,000. 🚌 🚍 ℹ️ Piazza del Comune 22 (075-813 86 80). 🛍 Sat.
w assisi.regioneumbria.eu

This beautiful medieval town, with its geranium-hung streets, lovely views, and fountain-splashed piazzas, is heir to the legacy of St. Francis (c.1181–1226), who is buried in the **Basilica di San Francesco**.

Piazza del Comune, Assisi's main square, is dominated by the columns of the **Tempio di Minerva**, a Roman temple-front from the Augustan age. The Palazzo Comunale, opposite, houses an art gallery, the **Pinacoteca Comunale**.

The town has many other interesting churches. On Corso Mazzini is the **Basilica di Santa Chiara**. Here, St. Clare – Francis's companion and the founder of the Poor Clares (an order of nuns) – is buried. The **Duomo** has a superb Romanesque facade. **San Pietro** is a simple, well-restored Romanesque church, while the nearby **Oratorio dei Pellegrini**, a 15th-century pilgrims' hospice, contains well-preserved frescoes by Matteo da Gualdo.

❸ Perugia

👥 160,000. 🚌 🚍 ℹ️ Piazza Matteotti 19, Loggia dei Lanari (075-572 64 58). 🛍 Tue, Thu, Sat.

Perugia's old center hinges around Corso Vannucci, named after the local painter Pietro Vannucci (Perugino). It is dominated by Umbria's finest building and former town hall, the monumental **Palazzo dei Priori**. Among its richly decorated rooms is the Sala dei Notari or Lawyers' Hall (c.1295), vividly frescoed with scenes from the Old Testament. Superlative frescoes (1498–1500) by Perugino cover the walls of the Collegio del Cambio, Perugia's medieval money exchange. The **Galleria Nazionale dell'Umbria** on the third floor displays a fine collection of paintings.

The Cappella del Santo Anello in Perugia's 15th-century **Duomo** houses the Virgin's agate "wedding ring," said to change color according to the character of its wearer. The Renaissance *Madonna delle Grazie* by Gian Nicola di Paolo hangs in the nave.

On Piazza San Francesco, the **Oratorio di San Bernardino** (1457–61), has a colorful façade by Agostino di Duccio. Beyond the old city walls, the 10th-century **San Pietro** is Perugia's most extravagantly decorated church. **San Domenico** (1305–1632), on Piazza Giordano Bruno, is Umbria's largest church. It houses the tomb of Pope Benedict XI (c.1304) and the **Museo Archeologico Nazionale dell'Umbria**, a collection of prehistoric, Etruscan, and Roman artifacts.

🏛 **Galleria Nazionale dell'Umbria**
Corso Vannucci 19. **Tel** 075-572 10 09.
Open Tue–Sun. **Closed** Jan 1, May 1, Dec 25.

Palazzo dei Priori, Perugia's imposing medieval town hall

Entrance to Upper Church

⑧

⑨

The rose window is framed by the carved symbols of the four Evangelists.

❹ Street by Street: Siena

Siena's principal sights cluster in the maze of narrow streets and alleys around the fan-shaped Piazza del Campo. One of Europe's greatest medieval squares, the piazza sits at the heart of the city's 17 *contrade*, the historic districts whose ancient rivalries are still acted out in the twice-yearly Palio *(see p392)*. Loyalty to the *contrada* of one's birth is fierce, and as you wander the streets you will see the parishes' animal symbols repeated on flags, plaques, and carvings.

The Duomo dominating Siena's skyline

Via della Galluzza
leads to the house of
St. Catherine, Siena's
patron saint *(see p392)*.

The Baptistry has
fine frescoes and
a font with reliefs
by Donatello,
Jacopo della
Quercia, and
Ghiberti.

★ Duomo
Striped black and white
marble pillars, surmounted
by a carved frieze of the
popes, support the Duomo's
vaulted ceiling, painted blue
with gold stars to resemble
the night sky *(see p392)*.

Each tier of the Duomo's bell
tower has one more window
than the floor below.

Cafés and shops fill
the streets around
Piazza del Duomo.

Bus station
Train station
VIA D. GALLUZZA
PIAZZA INDIPENDENZA
VIA DI FONTEBRANDA
VIA DI DIACCETO
VIA DEI PELLEGRINI
VIA FRANCIOSA
PIAZZA SAN GIOVANNI
VIA DEL FUSARI
PIAZZA DEL DUOMO
VIA DEL POGGIO
VIA DI CITTÀ
VIA DEL CAPITANO

**Museo dell'Opera
del Duomo**
The museum *(see p392)* houses weathered sculptures
from the cathedral, including this battered she-wolf
suckling Romulus and Remus.

Key
— Suggested route

0 meters   300
0 yards   300

Loggia della Mercanzia
This graceful arcade (1417) was used by Siena's medieval merchants and money dealers.

Palazzo Piccolomini,
built in 1460, now holds the Sienese state archives. Many of the original painted wooden bindings are on display.

Tourist information

A BANCHI DI SOTTO

VIA RINALDINA

VIA DI PANTANETO

VIA DEL PORRIONE

ZZA EL MPO

VIA DI SALICOTTO

DEL MERCATO

VIA DUPRE

Fonte Gaia
The reliefs on the fountain are 19th-century copies of the 15th-century originals by Jacopo della Quercia.

★ **Palazzo Pubblico**
The graceful Gothic town hall was completed in 1342. At 102 m (330 ft), the bell tower, the Torre del Mangia, is the second highest medieval tower ever built in Italy.

VISITORS' CHECKLIST

Practical Information
🗺 60,000.
ℹ Piazza del Campo 56 (0577-28 05 51). 🛒 Wed. 🎭 Palio (Jul 2, Aug 16); Estate Musicale Chigiana – classical music concerts (Jul–Sep). 🌐 terresiena.it

Transport
🚉 Piazzale Rosselli. 🚌 Piazza San Domenico.

🏛 Palazzo Pubblico
Piazza del Campo 1. **Tel** 0577-29 21 11. **Museo Civico & Torre del Mangia Tel** 0577-29 22 32. **Open** daily. **Closed** Dec 25. 📷

Although the Palazzo Pubblico (1297–1342) continues in its ancient role as Siena's town hall, the **Museo Civico** is also housed here. Many of the rooms, some decorated with paintings of the Sienese School, are open to the public. They include the main council chamber, or Sala del Mappamondo, named after a map of the world painted here by Ambrogio Lorenzetti in the early 14th century. One wall is covered by Simone Martini's fresco *Maestà* (1315), which depicts the Virgin in Majesty. The Sala della Pace houses the famous *Allegory of Good and Bad Government*, a pair of frescoes by Lorenzetti finished in 1338.

In the palace courtyard is the magnificent **Torre del Mangia** bell tower, which offers superb views of the city.

🏛 Piazza del Campo
Italy's loveliest piazza occupies the site of the old Roman forum, and for much of Siena's early history was the city's principal marketplace. The Council of Nine, Siena's ruling body, gave the order for work to start on the piazza in 1293. The red-brick paving was finished in 1349. It is divided into nine sections, representing not only the authority of the council, but also the protective folds of the Madonna's cloak. The piazza has been the focus of city life ever since, a setting for executions, bullfights, and the drama of the Palio. Cafés, restaurants, and fine medieval palazzi now line the square, which is dominated by the Palazzo Pubblico and the Torre del Mangia.

Piazza del Campo, viewed from the top of the Torre del Mangia

Exploring Siena

Once a capital to rival Florence, Siena is still unspoiled and endowed with the grandeur of the age in which it was at its peak (1260–1348). The magnificent Duomo is one of Italy's greatest cathedrals. The best place to begin an exploration of the historic city center is Piazza del Campo and the surrounding maze of medieval streets. Siena's hilly position means that walks through the city are rewarded with countless sudden views of the surrounding countryside.

Richly decorated facade of Siena's Duomo

🏛 Duomo

Piazza del Duomo. **Tel** 0577-28 30 48. **Open** daily. **Closed** Sun am. Museo dell'Opera del Duomo: **Tel** 0577-28 30 48. **Open** Mar–May: 10am–7:30pm daily; Jun–Aug: 10am–8pm daily; Sep & Oct: 10:30am–7:30pm daily; Nov–Feb: 10:30am–6:30pm daily. **Closed** Jan 1, Dec 25. 🅿

Siena's cathedral (1136–1382) is a spectacular example of Pisan-influenced Romanesque-Gothic architecture. Had the 14th-century plan to create a new nave come to fruition, it would have become the largest church in Christendom, but the idea was abandoned when the Black Death of 1348 virtually halved the city's population. Among the Duomo's treasures are sculptural masterpieces by Nicola Pisano, Donatello, and Michelangelo, a fine inlaid marble floor, and a magnificent fresco cycle by Pinturicchio.

In the side aisle of the unfinished nave, which has been roofed over, is the **Museo dell'Opera del Duomo**. The museum is devoted mainly to sculpture removed from the exterior of the Duomo, including a *tondo* (circular relief) of a Madonna and Child, probably by Donatello. The highlight is Duccio's huge altarpiece, *Maestà* (1308–11), which depicts the *Madonna and Child* on one side, and *Scenes from the Life of Christ* on the other.

🖼 Pinacoteca Nazionale

Via San Pietro 29. **Tel** 0577-28 61 43. **Open** daily. **Closed** Sun & Mon pm, Jan 1, May 1, Dec 25. 🅿 🅶

Housed in the Palazzo Buonsignori, this gallery contains an unsurpassed collection of paintings by artists of the Sienese School. Highlights include Duccio's *Madonna dei Francescani* (1285) and Simone Martini's *The Blessed Agostino Novello and Four of his Miracles* (c.1330).

🏛 San Domenico

Piazza San Domenico. **Open** daily. The preserved head of the city's patroness, St. Catherine of Siena (1347–80), can be seen in a gilded tabernacle on the altar

Massacre of the Innocents, a detail from the Duomo's marble floor

of a chapel dedicated to her in this huge, barn-like Gothic church. Built in 1460, the chapel is dominated by Sodoma's frescoes (1526), which show Catherine in states of religious fervor. The church has the only portrait of St. Catherine considered authentic, painted by her friend Andrea Vanni.

St. Catherine's house, the **Casa di Santa Caterina**, is also a popular shrine for visitors to Siena.

🏰 Fortezza Medicea

Viale Maccari. Fortezza: **Open** daily. Enoteca Italiana: Piazza Libertà 1. **Tel** 0577-22 88 11. **Open** noon–1am Mon–Sat. 🅿

This huge red-brick fortress was built by Cosimo I in 1560, following Siena's defeat by Florence in the 1554–5 war. After an 18-month siege, during which more than 8,000 Sienese died, the town's banking and wool industries were suppressed by the Florentines.

The fortress now houses the **Enoteca Italiana**, where you can taste and buy Italian wines.

The Palio

The Palio is Tuscany's most celebrated festival and it occurs in the Campo each year on July 2 and August 16. This bareback horse race was first recorded in 1283, but it may have had its origins in Roman military training. The jockeys represent Siena's 17 *contrade* (districts) and the horses are chosen by the drawing of lots. Preceded by days of colorful pageantry and heavy betting, the races themselves last only 90 seconds each, the winner being rewarded with a silk *palio* (banner).

Drummer taking part in the Palio's noisy pre-race pageant

The skyline of San Gimignano, bristling with medieval towers

❺ San Gimignano

Siena. 🚐 7,000. 🚌 𝒊 Piazza del Duomo 1 (0577-94 00 08). 🚢 Thu. 🎪 San Gimignano (Jan 31).

The thirteen towers that dominate San Gimignano's skyline were built by rival noble families in the 12th and 13th centuries, when the town's position on the main pilgrim route to Rome brought it great prosperity. The plague of 1348, and later the diversion of the pilgrim route, led to its economic decline and its miraculous preservation.

Full of good restaurants and shops, the town is also home to many fine works of art. The **Museo Civico** holds works by Pinturicchio, Benozzo Gozzoli, and Filippino Lippi, while the church of **Sant'Agostino** has a Baroque interior by Vanvitelli (c.1740) and a fresco cycle on *The Life of St. Augustine* by Benozzo Gozzoli (1465).

❻ Florence

See pp394–407.

❼ Pisa

🚐 90,000. ✈ Galileo Galilei, 5 km (3 miles) S. 🚉 🚌 𝒊 Piazza Vittorio Emanuele 16 (050-42 291). 🚢 Wed & Sat. 🖥 pisaunicaterra.it

In the Middle Ages, Pisa's navy dominated the western Mediterranean. Trade with Spain and North Africa brought vast wealth, reflected in the city's splendid buildings. The **Duomo**, begun in 1064, is a magnificent example of Pisan-Romanesque

architecture, its four-tiered facade an intricate medley of creamy colonnades and blind arcades. Inside, highlights include a pulpit (1302–11) by Giovanni Pisano and a mosaic of *Christ in Majesty* by Cimabue (1302).

Begun in 1173 on sandy silt subsoil, the famous **Leaning Tower** (Torre Pendente) was completed in 1350. The tower has attracted many visitors over the centuries, including Galileo, who came here to conduct experiments on falling objects. Recent engineering work has reduced the tower's tilt to approximately 4.12 m (13.5 ft).

The graceful **Baptistry** was begun in 1152 and finished a century later by Nicola and Giovanni Pisano.

The **Museo Nazionale di San Matteo** holds Pisan and Florentine art from the 12th to the 17th centuries. Major 15th-century works include Masaccio's *St. Paul*, Gentile da Fabriano's radiant *Madonna of Humility*, and Donatello's reliquary bust of *San Rossore*.

🏛 Museo Nazionale di San Matteo
Piazza San Matteo 1. **Tel** 050-54 18 65. **Open** Tue–Sun. **Closed** Sun pm. 🅿

❽ Lucca

🚐 85,000. 🚉 🚌 𝒊 Piazza Santa Maria 35 (0583-91 99 31). 🚢 Wed, Sat, 3rd Sun of month (antiques).

The city of Lucca is still enclosed within its 17th-century walls, and visitors can stroll along the ramparts, which were converted into a public park in the early 19th century. Within the walls, narrow lanes wind among dark medieval buildings, opening suddenly to reveal stunning churches and piazzas, including the vast Piazza del Anfiteatro, which traces the outline of the old Roman amphitheater. The finest of the churches are all Romanesque: **San Martino**, the 11th-century cathedral, **San Michele in Foro**, built on the sight of the old Roman forum, and **San Frediano**.

The Baptistry in front of Pisa's Duomo, with the Leaning Tower behind

❻ Florence

Florence is a monument to the Renaissance, the artistic and cultural reawakening of the 15th century. The buildings of Brunelleschi and the paintings and sculptures of artists such as Botticelli and Michelangelo turned the city into one of the world's greatest artistic capitals. During this time Florence was at the cultural and intellectual heart of Europe, its cosmopolitan atmosphere and wealthy patrons, such as the Medici, providing the impetus for a period of unparalleled artistic growth. The legacy of the Renaissance draws many visitors to the city today, with its numerous museums, galleries, churches, and monuments the major attractions. Florence's best sights are encompassed within such a compact area that the city seems to reveal its treasures at every step.

Sights at a Glance

① Duomo pp398–9
② San Lorenzo
③ Santa Maria Novella
④ Galleria dell'Accademia
⑤ San Marco
⑥ Bargello
⑦ Santa Croce
⑧ Piazza della Signoria
⑨ Palazzo Vecchio
⑩ Museo di Storia della Scienza
⑪ Uffizi pp404–6
⑫ Ponte Vecchio
⑬ Palazzo Pitti
⑭ Boboli Gardens

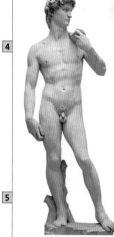

Michelangelo's *David* in the
Galleria dell'Accademia

The dome of the cathedral, or Duomo, Florence's greatest landmark

Key

- ▦ Sight / Place of interest
- ▫▫▫ Pedestrian street
- — City walls

Getting Around

Buses in Florence are bright orange; most can be picked up at Santa Maria Novella station. Lines run until at least 9:30pm, the most popular until midnight or 1am. Information about routes can be found on www.ataf.net. Official taxis are white, and are generally costly. What with one-way systems, erratic drivers, and limited traffic zones – where only authorized vehicles are permitted to go – driving is not recommended. Walking is easily the most enjoyable way to get around and explore the city.

0 meters 300
0 yards 300

① **Duomo**

See pp398–9.

② **San Lorenzo**

Piazza di San Lorenzo. 🚌 many routes.
Basilica: **Tel** 055-21 40 42. **Open** daily.
Closed Sun (Nov–Feb), religious hols.
🖼 Biblioteca: **Tel** 055-21 07 60. **Open**
daily. **Closed** Sun (Nov–Feb), public
hols. Cappelle Medicee: Piazza di
Madonna degli Aldobrandini 6. **Tel**
055-238 86 02. **Open** daily (to 4:20pm).
Closed alternate Mon & Sun of
month, Jan 1, May 1 & Dec 25. 🖼 ♿

San Lorenzo was the parish
church of the Medici family,
who lavished their wealth
on its adornment. Rebuilt in
Renaissance Classical style in
1419, the outer facade was
never completed.

The inner facade of the
Basilica was designed by
Michelangelo. Cosimo il Vecchio,
founder of the Medici dynasty, is
buried under a stone slab before
the High Altar. The bronze pulpits
in the nave are Donatello's last
works. Opposite is Bronzino's
vast fresco of the human form
in various poses (1659).

The **Biblioteca Mediceo-
Laurenzia**, which housed the
family's manuscripts, has an
elaborate sandstone staircase,
desks, and ceilings designed
by Michelangelo in 1524.

The **Cappelle Medicee**
incorporate three sacristies
which epitomize different
periods of art. Donatello's
decoration of the
Old Sacristy
contrasts with
the design

Detail from Donatello pulpit, San Lorenzo

Facade of Santa Maria Novella, redesigned by Alberti in 1456–70

of the New Sacristy by
Michelangelo. The latter's
funerary figures (1520–34)
around its walls are among his
greatest works. The Chapel of
the Princes (1604) is opulently
decorated with inlaid semi-
precious stones and bright
frescoes. Six Grand Dukes of the
Medici family are buried here.

③ **Santa Maria Novella**

Piazza di Santa Maria Novella. 🚌 many
routes. ♿ Church: **Tel** 055-21 92 57.
Open daily *(pm only Fri–Sun & religious
hols)*. 🖼 Museum: **Tel** 055-28 21 87.
Open 9am–5:30pm Mon–Thu, Sat.
Closed Jan 1, Easter Sun, May 1. 🖼 ♿

The Gothic church of Santa
Maria Novella, built by the
Dominicans between 1279 and
1357, contains some of the
most important works of art in
Florence. The interior displays a
number of superb
frescoes, including
Masaccio's *Trinity* (c.1428),
which is renowned
as a masterpiece of
perspective and
portraiture. The close
spacing of the nave
piers at the east end
accentuates the illusion
of length. The Tornabuoni
Chapel contains
Ghirlandaio's famous
fresco cycle, *The Life of
John the Baptist* (1485).
In the Filippo Strozzi
Chapel, Lippi's dramatic

frescoes show St. John raising
Drusiana from the dead and
St. Philip slaying a dragon.
Boccaccio set the beginning
of *The Decameron* in this
chapel. The Strozzi Tomb (1493)
is by Florentine sculptor
Benedetto da Maiano.

The 14th-century frescoes
in the Strozzi Chapel are by
two brothers (Nardo di Cione
and Andrea Orcagna) and
were inspired by Dante's
Divine Comedy.

Beside the church is a walled
cemetery with grave niches. The
cloisters on the other side of the
church form a museum. The
Green Cloister's name derives
from the green tinge to Uccello's
Noah and the Flood frescoes,
damaged by the 1966 floods.
The adjoining Spanish Chapel
contains frescoes on the theme
of salvation and damnation.

④ **Galleria dell'Accademia**

Via Ricasoli 60. 🚌 many routes.
Tel 055-29 48 83 (bookings). **Open**
Tue–Sun. **Closed** Mon & public hols.
🖼 ♿ 🌐 polomuseale.firenze.it

The Academy of Fine Arts in
Florence, founded in 1563,
was the first school in Europe
set up to teach drawing,
painting, and sculpture.

Since 1873, many of Michelangelo's most important works
have been in the Accademia.
Perhaps the most famous of
all dominates the collection:

Michelangelo's *David* (1504). This colossal nude depicts the biblical hero who killed the giant Goliath; it established Michelangelo, then aged 29, as the foremost sculptor of his time. The statue was moved here from the Palazzo Vecchio in 1873 to protect it from the elements.

Michelangelo's other masterpieces include a statue of St. Matthew finished in 1508, and the *Quattro Prigioni* (four prisons), sculpted between 1521 and 1523. The muscular figures struggling to free themselves from the stone are among the most dramatic of his works.

The gallery contains an important collection of paintings by 15th- and 16th-century Florentine artists, and many major works including the *Madonna del Mare* attributed to Botticelli (1445–1510), Pacino di Bonaguida's *Tree of Life* (1310), and *Venus and Cupid* by Jacopo Pontormo (1494–1556). Also on display is an elaborately painted wooden chest, the *Cassone Adimari* (c.1440) by Lo Scheggia. It was originally used as part of a bride's trousseau, and is covered with details of Florentine daily life, clothing, and architecture.

The Salone della Toscana (Tuscany Room) exhibits more modest 19th-century sculpture and paintings by members of the Accademia.

Fra Angelico's *Annunciation*, in the monastery of San Marco

⑤ San Marco

Piazza di San Marco. 🚌 many routes.
🚻 partial. Church: **Open** daily.
Museum: **Tel** 055-29 48 83 (bookings).
Open Mon–Fri: am only, Sat: am & pm.
Closed Jan 1, May 1, Dec 25, 2nd & 4th Mon and 1st, 3rd, & 5th Sun each month. 📷 🚻

The church of San Marco, and the monastery built around it, date from the 13th century. Following the transfer of the site to the Dominicans of Fiesole by Pope Eugene IV in 1436, Cosimo il Vecchio paid a considerable sum for its reconstruction, overseen by his favorite architect, Michelozzo. The single-naved church holds valuable works of art, and the funerary chapel of St. Anthony is considered Giambologna's main work of architecture. To the right of the church, the oldest part of

the monastery is now a museum. It contains a remarkable series of devotional frescoes by Fra Angelico. The former Pilgrims' Hospice houses *The Deposition* (1435–40), a poignant scene of the dead Christ; his *Crucifixion* (1441–2) can be seen in the Chapter House.

There are over 40 cells adorned with frescoes by Fra Angelico. *The Annunciation* (c.1445) demonstrates his mastery of perspective. Relics of the fiery orator Savonarola (1452–98), dragged from here and executed in Piazza della Signoria, are also on display.

The monastery houses Europe's first public library, designed by Michelozzo in a light and airy colonnaded hall. Valuable manuscripts and bibles are held here.

A scene from Lo Scheggia's *Cassone Adimari* in the Galleria dell'Accademia

① **Duomo**

Set in the heart of Florence, Santa Maria del Fiore – the Duomo, or cathedral, of Florence – dominates the city with its enormous dome. Its sheer size was typical of Florentine determination to lead in all things, and to this day, no other building stands taller in the city. The Baptistry, with its celebrated doors, is one of Florence's oldest buildings, dating perhaps from the 4th century. In his capacity as city architect, Giotto designed the Campanile in 1334; it was completed in 1359, 22 years after his death.

★ Campanile
At 85 m (276 ft), the Campanile is 6 m (20 ft) shorter than the dome. It is clad in white, green and pink Tuscan marble. The first-floor reliefs are by Andrea Pisano.

★ Baptistry
Colorful 13th-century mosaics illustrating *The Last Judgment* decorate the ceiling above the large octagonal font where many famous Florentines, including Dante, were baptized.

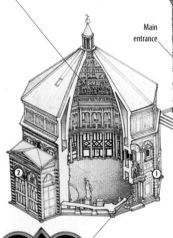

Main entrance

South Door Panels
This scene from the south doors of the Baptistry, completed by the sculptor Andrea Pisano in 1336, depicts *The Baptism of St. John the Baptist.*

Steps to Santa Reparata
The crypt contains the remains of the church of Santa Reparata, built in the 4th century, and demolished in 1296 to make way for a cathedral which would more fittingly represent Florence and rival those of Siena and Pisa.

For hotels and restaurants see pp438–40 and pp441–3

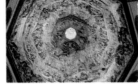

★ Dome
Brunelleschi's revolutionary achievement was to build the largest dome of its time without scaffolding. As you climb the 463 steps to the top, you can see how an inner shell provides a platform for the timbers that support the outer shell.

Chapels at the East End
The three apses each house five chapels and are crowned by a miniature copy of the dome. The 15th-century stained glass is by Lorenzo Ghiberti and other artists.

Entrance to steps to the dome

Marble Pavement
As you climb up to the dome, you can see that the 16th-century marble pavement, designed in part by Baccio d'Agnelo, is laid out as a maze.

KEY

① **The east doors**, known as the "Gate of Paradise" (1424–52), were made by Ghiberti. While replicas adorn the Baptistry, the originals can be found in the Duomo museum.

② **The Baptistry doors** demonstrate the artistic ideas that led to the Renaissance.

③ **The Neo-Gothic marble facade** echoes the style of Giotto's camp-anile, but was added in 1871–87.

④ **Gothic windows**

⑤ **The top of the dome** offers spectacular views over the city.

⑥ **Last Judgment frescoes by Vasari**

⑦ **Bricks of varying size** were set in a self- supporting herring-bone pattern – a technique Brunelleschi copied from the Pantheon in Rome.

⑧ **The octagonal marble sanctuary** around the High Altar was skilfully decorated by Baccio Bandinelli.

⑥ Bargello

Via del Proconsolo 4. **Tel** 055-238 86 06. 🚌 A, 14. **Open** 8:15am–1:50pm daily. **Closed** 1st, 3rd & 5th Sun and 2nd & 4th Mon of each month, Jan 1, May 1, Dec 25. 📷 ♿

Florence's second-ranking museum after the Uffizi, the Bargello houses Italy's finest collection of Renaissance sculpture and some superb Mannerist bronzes. Begun in 1255, the fortress-like building was initially the town hall but later home to the chief of police (the *Bargello*). The renovated building opened as one of Italy's first national museums in 1865.

The key exhibits range over three floors, beginning with the Michelangelo Room. Here visitors can admire *Bacchus* (1497), the sculptor's first large free-standing work, a delicate circular relief depicting the *Madonna and Child* (1503–5), and *Brutus* (1539–40), his only known portrait bust. Among other sculptors' works in the same room is *Mercury* (1564), Giambologna's famous bronze. Across the courtyard, two more rooms contain exterior sculptures removed from sites around the city and an external staircase leads

Donatello's statue of *David* in the Bargello

to a first-floor collection of bronze birds by Giambologna. To the right, the Salone del Consiglio Generale contains the cream of the museum's Early Renaissance sculpture, including Donatello's heroic *St George* (1416) and his androgynous *David* (c.1430). Restored in 2008, it is famous as the first free-standing nude by a Western artist since antiquity.

Beyond the Salone, the Bargello's emphasis shifts to the applied arts, with room after room devoted to rugs,

Gaddi's night scene fresco in the Baroncelli Chapel, Santa Croce

ceramics, silverware, and other *objets d'art*. The Salone del Camino on the second floor holds the finest collection of small bronzes in Italy. Benvenuto Cellini (1500–71) is among the artists featured.

⑦ Santa Croce

Piazza di Santa Croce. **Tel** 055-246 61 05. 🚌 C, 14, 23. **Open** daily (Sun: pm only). 📷 ♿

The Gothic church of Santa Croce (1294) contains the tombs and monuments of many famous Florentines, among them Galileo, Michelangelo, and Machiavelli, as well as radiant early 14th-century frescoes by Giotto and his gifted pupil, Taddeo Gaddi. In 1842 the Neo-Gothic campanile of Santa Croce was added, and the facade in 1863.

In the Basilica, Rossellino's effigy (1447) of Leonardo Bruni, the great Humanist depicted in serene old age, is a triumph of realistic portraiture. Close by it is the 15th-century *Annunciation* by Donatello. The remainder of the monastic buildings scattered around the cloister form a museum of religious painting and sculpture. The museum houses Cimabue's *Crucifixion*, a 13th-century masterpiece damaged in the flood of 1966, and Gaddi's magnificent *Last Supper* (c.1355–60).

Of the church's many chapels, the most famous is the Bardi Chapel, decorated by Giotto with frescoes of the life of St. Francis (1315–23). The Peruzzi Chapel houses further Giotto frescoes. Gaddi's 1338 fresco in the Baroncelli Chapel of an angel appearing to sleeping shepherds is notable as the first true night scene in Western art.

In the cloister alongside the church is Brunelleschi's Cappella de' Pazzi (Pazzi Chapel), a masterpiece of Renaissance architecture. The delicate gray stonework of the domed chapel is set off by white plaster, which is inset with terra-cotta roundels of the Evangelists by Luca della Robbia.

⑧ Piazza della Signoria

🚌 A, B.

Piazza della Signoria has been at the heart of Florence's political and social life for centuries. Citizens were once summoned to public meetings here, and the square's statues celebrate events in the city's history. That of Grand Duke Cosimo I (1595) by Giambologna commemorates

Statue of Cosimo I in Piazza della Signoria

the man who subjugated all Tuscany, while Ammannati's *Neptune Fountain* honors Tuscan naval victories. Michelangelo's original *David* stood here until 1873, when it was replaced by a copy. Donatello's original statue of the heraldic lion of Florence, known as the *Marzocco*, is now in the Bargello.

Other notable statues include Cellini's bronze *Perseus*, and *The Rape of the Sabine Women* by Giambologna, carved from a single block of marble.

Painting of Penelope in Eleonora's rooms in the Palazzo Vecchio

The *Putto* fountain in Vasari's courtyard, at the Palazzo Vecchio

⑨ Palazzo Vecchio

Piazza della Signoria. **Tel** 055-276 83 25. ⓦ A, B. **Open** daily (Thu: am only). 📷 ♿

Palazzo Vecchio, completed in 1322, has retained its external medieval appearance, and its imposing bell tower dominates the square. The "Old Palace" still fulfils its original role as Florence's town hall. Much of the interior was remodeled for Duke Cosimo I in the mid-16th century by Vasari, whose work includes several frescoes that laud the Duke's achievements.

The palazzo is entered via a courtyard, in which stands Verrochio's *Putto* fountain. A staircase leads to the Salone dei Cinquecento, which is graced by Michelangelo's *Victory* statue (1525), and to the tiny Studiolo decorated by 30 of Florence's leading Mannerist painters.

Eleonora of Toledo, wife of Cosimo I, had a suite of rooms in the palace, decorated with scenes of virtuous women. Highlights of the palace include the paintings by Il Bronzino in the Cappella di Eleonora and the loggia, which has wonderful views over the city. The Sala dei Gigli (Room of Lilies), contains frescoes of Roman heroes and Donatello's *Judith and Holofernes*.

There is also a Children's Museum, with story-telling sessions and tours in various languages. One tour takes in formerly secret stairways, hidden passages, and attics.

⑩ Museo di Storia della Scienza

Piazza de'Giudici 1. **Tel** 055-26 53 11. **Open** 9:30am–6pm Mon–Sat (to 1pm Tue). **Closed** public hols. 📷 ⓦ museogalileo.it

This lively museum devotes numerous rooms on two floors to different scientific themes, illustrating each with fine displays and beautifully made early scientific instruments. It is also something of a shrine to the Pisa-born scientist, Galileo Galilei (1564–1642), and features two of his telescopes as well as large-scale reconstructions of his experiments into motion, weight, velocity, and acceleration. These are sometimes demonstrated by the attendants. Other exhibits come from the Accademia del Cimento (Academy for Experimentation), founded in memory of Galileo by Grand Duke Ferdinand II in 1657.

Some of the finest exhibits include early maps, antique microscopes, astrolabes, and barometers. Of equal interest are the huge 16th- and 17th-century globes illustrating the motion of the planets and stars. Be sure to see Lopo Homem's 16th-century map of the world, showing the newly charted coasts of the Americas, and the nautical instruments invented by Sir Robert Dudley, an Elizabethan marine engineer employed by the Medicis.

The second-floor rooms display fine old clocks, calculators, a horrifying collection of 19th-century surgical instruments, weights and measures, and graphic anatomical models.

Armillary sphere, Museo di Storia della Scienza

The Florentine Renaissance

Fifteenth-century Italy saw a flowering of the arts and scholarship unmatched in Europe since Ancient Greek and Roman times. It was in wealthy Florence that this artistic and intellectual activity, later dubbed the Renaissance, was at its most intense. The patronage of the rich banking dynasty, the Medici, rulers of Florence from 1434, was lavished on the city, especially under Lorenzo the Magnificent (1469–92), and the city aspired to become the new Rome. Architects turned to Classical models for inspiration, while the art world, with a new understanding of perspective and anatomy, produced a series of painters and sculptors that included such giants as Donatello, Botticelli, Leonardo da Vinci, and Michelangelo.

Italy in 1492
- Republic of Florence
- Papal States
- Aragonese possessions

The Procession of the Magi

Benozzo Gozzoli's fresco (1459) in the Palazzo Medici-Riccardi, Florence, depicts members of the Medici family and other contemporary notables. It contains references to the church council held in Florence in 1439, which, it was hoped, would effect a reconciliation between the Church of Rome and the Eastern Church.

Giuliano was the younger son of Piero de' Medici.

Piero de' Medici, Lorenzo's father, was given the nickname "the Gouty."

Pope Leo X
There were two Medici popes: Giovanni, who reigned as Leo X (1513–21), and Giulio, who took his place as Clement VII (1521–34). Corruption in the church under Leo inspired Luther and the growth of Protestantism.

1420 Martin V re-establishes papacy in Rome

1434 Cosimo de' Medici comes to power in Florence

Cosimo de' Medici

1435 Publication of *On Painting* by Alberti, which contains the first system for the use of linear perspective

1436 Brunelleschi completes dome of Florence cathedral

1425

1450

1452 Birth of Leonardo da Vinci

1453 Fall of Constantinople

1464 Death of Cosimo il Vecchio

1469 Lorenzo the Magnificent becomes ruler of Florence

Filippo Brunelleschi
In order to realize his design for the dome of Florence's cathedral, Brunelleschi devised engineering techniques decades ahead of their time.

Michelangelo's Sculpture
The *Quattro Prigioni* (see p397), unfinished works intended for the tomb of Pope Julius II, illustrate Michelangelo's ideal of liberating "the figure imprisoned in the marble."

Renaissance Architecture

In place of the spectacular Gothic style, Renaissance architects favored the rational, orderly, human scale of Greek and Roman buildings. The various stories of a palazzo were designed according to Classical proportions and there was a widespread revival in the use of Roman arches and the Doric, Ionic, and Corinthian orders of columns.

Palazzo Strozzi
(1489–1536) is a typical Florentine building of the period. Rusticated stonework gives an impression of great strength. Decorative detail is largely on the upper stories above the fortress-like ground floor.

Lorenzo de' Medici (the Magnificent) is depicted as one of the three kings traveling to Bethlehem.

The Medici emblem of seven balls appears on the trappings of Lorenzo's horse.

The Spedale degli Innocenti, an orphanage, was one of Brunelleschi's first buildings in Florence. Slender Corinthian columns support a delicate arcade.

Humanism
Carpaccio's painting *St. Augustine in his Study* (1502) is thought to show Cardinal Bessarion (c.1395–1472), one of the scholars who revived interest in Classical philosophy, especially Plato.

1498 Savonarola executed; Machiavelli secretary to ruling Council in Florence

1513 Giovanni de' Medici crowned Pope Leo X

1532 Machiavelli's book *The Prince* is published, five years after his death

1530 Medici restored as rulers of Florence

75 | **1500** | **1525**

75 Birth of helangelo

1483 Birth of Raphael

1494 Italy invaded by Charles VIII of France. Florence declared republic under leadership of the religious fanatic Savonarola

1512 Michelangelo completes Sistine Chapel ceiling

Niccolò Machiavelli

⑪ Uffizi

The Uffizi was built in 1560–80 as a suite of offices (uffici) for Duke Cosimo I's new Tuscan administration. The architect, Vasari, used iron reinforcement to create an almost continuous wall of glass on the upper story. From 1581 Cosimo's heirs, beginning with Francesco I, used this well-lit space to display the Medici family art treasures, thus creating what is now the oldest art gallery in the world.

The Vasari Corridor leads to the Palazzo Vecchio.

Main staircase

Entrance Hall

Entrance

The café terrace merits a visit for its unusual views of Piazza della Signoria (see pp400–1).

Bar

Corridor ceilings are frescoed in the "grotesque" style of the 1580s, inspired by Roman grottoes.

Gallery Guide

The Uffizi art collection is housed on the top floor. Ancient Greek and Roman sculptures are displayed in the corridor running round the inner side of the building. The paintings are hung in a series of rooms off the main corridor, in chronological order, to reveal the development of Florentine art from Gothic to High Renaissance and beyond. Most of the best-known paintings are grouped in rooms 7–18. To avoid the long queues, book your visiting time in advance.

The Ognissanti Madonna
Giotto's grasp of spatial depth in this altarpiece (1310) was a milestone in the mastery of perspective.

Buontalenti staircase

Entrance to the Vasari Corridor

Key

- ☐ East Corridor
- ☐ West Corridor
- ☐ Arno Corridor
- ☐ Gallery Rooms 1–45
- ☐ Non-exhibition space

★ **The Venus of Urbino** (1538)
Titian's sensuous nude was condemned for portraying the goddess in such an immodest pose.

★ **The Duke and Duchess of Urbino** (1460)
Piero della Francesca's panels are among the first true
Renaissance portraits. He even recorded the Duke's
hooked nose – broken by a sword blow.

VISITORS' CHECKLIST

Practical Information
Piazzale degli Uffizi 6.
Tel 055-29 48 83 (bookings).
Open 8:15am–6:50pm Tue–Sun
(last adm: 45 mins before closing).
Closed Jan 1, May 1, Dec 25.
🅿️ ♿ (partial). 📷 📱
🆆 polomuseale.firenze.it

Transport
🚌 B, 23.

The Tribune,
decorated in
red and gold,
contains the
works that
the Medici
valued most.

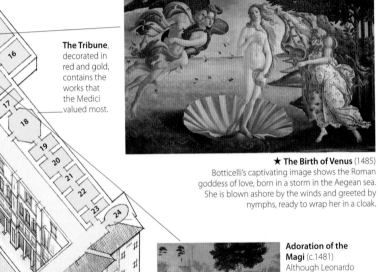

★ **The Birth of Venus** (1485)
Botticelli's captivating image shows the Roman
goddess of love, born in a storm in the Aegean sea.
She is blown ashore by the winds and greeted by
nymphs, ready to wrap her in a cloak.

**Adoration of the
Magi** (c.1481)
Although Leonardo
da Vinci did not finish
this painting of the
wise men worshipping
the baby Jesus, it is
considered to be one
of his most important
early works.

Vasari's
Classical
Arno facade

★ **The Holy Family** (1507)
Michelangelo's painting, the first to break with the
convention of showing Christ on the Virgin's lap,
inspired subsequent Mannerist artists through its
expressive handling of color and posture.

Exploring the Uffizi's Collection

The Uffizi houses some of the greatest art of the Renaissance. Accumulated over the centuries by the Medici, the collection was first housed in the Uffizi in 1581, and eventually bequeathed to the people of Florence by Anna Maria Lodovica, the last of the Medici (1667–1743). Roman statues collected by the Medici are on display in the Arno Corridor, but the pride of the gallery is its matchless collection of paintings.

Gothic Art

Following the collection of statues and antiquities in room 1, the gallery's next six rooms are devoted to Tuscan art from the 12th to the 14th centuries, notably works by Cimabue, Duccio, and Giotto, the three greatest artists of this period. Giotto (1266–1337) introduced a degree of naturalism new to Tuscan art. This is apparent in the range of emotions expressed by the angels and saints in his *Ognissanti Madonna* (1310). There are also fine works by Ambrogio and Pietro Lorenzetti, and Simone Martini of the Sienese School.

Early Renaissance

A better understanding of geometry and perspective allowed Renaissance artists to create an illusion of space and depth in their works. No artist was more obsessed with

Madonna of the Goldfinch (1506) by Raphael

perspective than Paolo Uccello (1397–1475), whose *Battle of San Romano* is displayed in room 7. Portraits include two panels by Piero della Francesca (1410–92), depicting the Duke and Duchess of Urbino, while Fra Filippo Lippi's *Madonna and Child with Angels* (1455–66) is a work of great warmth and humanity.

For most visitors, however, the famous Botticellis in rooms 10–14 are the highlight of the gallery. In *The Birth of Venus*, Botticelli replaces the Virgin with the Classical goddess of love, while in *Primavera* (1480), he breaks with Christian religious painting to depict the pagan rite of spring.

High Renaissance and Mannerism

Room 15 contains works attributed to the young Leonardo da Vinci. The evolution of his masterly style can be traced in *The Annunciation* (1472–5) and his unfinished *Adoration of the Magi* (1481). The octagonal Tribune (room 18) displays some of the best-loved pieces of the Medici collection, including the 1st century BC *Medici Venus*, considered the most erotic of ancient statues. There are also paintings of family members, including Bronzino's fine portrait of Eleonora of Toledo, Cosimo I's wife (1545).

Rooms 19 to 23 illustrate the spread of Renaissance ideas and techniques beyond Florence to other parts of Italy and beyond. The Umbrian artist Perugino (1446–1523) and northern

Madonna of the Long Neck by Parmigianino (c.1534)

European painters such as Dürer (1471–1528) are well represented.

Michelangelo's *Holy Family* (1507), in Room 25, is striking for its vibrant colors and the curious twisted pose of the Virgin. This painting had great influence on the next generation of Tuscan painters, notably Bronzino (1503–72), Pontormo (1494–1556), and Parmigianino (1503–40), whose *Madonna of the Long Neck* with its contorted anatomy and unusual colors is a classic example of what came to be known as Mannerism.

Sublime examples of High Renaissance art located nearby include Raphael's *Madonna of the Goldfinch* and Titian's notorious *Venus of Urbino* (1538), considered by many to be the most beautiful nude ever painted.

Later Paintings

Rooms 41–45 of the Uffizi hold paintings acquired by the Medici in the 17th and 18th centuries. These include works by Rubens (1577–1640). Three paintings by Caravaggio – *Bacchus* (c.1589), *The Sacrifice of Isaac* (c.1590), and *Medusa* (1596–8) – are in the Sala del Caravaggio. Room 44 is dedicated to northern European painting, and features *Portrait of an Old Man* (1665) by Rembrandt.

⑫ Ponte Vecchio

🚌 many routes.

The Ponte Vecchio, the oldest surviving bridge in the city, was designed by Taddeo Gaddi, and built in 1345. The three-arched bridge rests on two stout piers with boat-shaped cutwaters. Its picturesque shops were originally occupied by blacksmiths, butchers, and tanners (who used the river as a convenient garbage dump). They were evicted in 1593 by Duke Ferdinando I and replaced by jewelers and goldsmiths who were able to pay higher rents. A bust of the most famous of Florence's goldsmiths, Benvenuto Cellini (1500–71), is located in the middle of the bridge.

The elevated Vasari Corridor runs along the eastern side of the bridge, above the shops. It was designed in 1565 to allow the Medici to move from the Palazzo Vecchio to Palazzo Pitti via the Uffizi, without having to mix with the public. The Mannelli family refused to demolish their tower to make way for the corridor, and it stands there defiantly to this day. The corridor passes around it, supported on brackets.

The "Old Bridge," at its most attractive when viewed at sunset, was the only one to escape destruction during World War II. Visitors today come to admire the views and to browse among the antiques and specialized jewelry shops.

The massive Renaissance Palazzo Pitti, home to several museums

⑬ Palazzo Pitti

Piazza de' Pitti. 🚌 D, 11, 36, 37. **Tel** 055-29 48 83. **Open** 8:15am–6:50pm Tue–Sun. **Closed** public hols. ♿ &
W polomuseale.firenze.it

Palazzo Pitti was originally built for the banker Luca Pitti, but his attempt to outrival the Medici backfired when costs of the building, begun in 1457, bank-rupted his heirs. The Medici moved in and subsequent rulers of the city lived here. Today, the richly decorated rooms exhibit many treasures from the Medici collections.

The Palatine Gallery contains numerous works of art and ceiling frescoes glorifying the Medici. Raphael's *Madonna della Seggiola* (c.1515) and Titian's *Portrait of a Gentleman* (1540) are among the exhibits.

On the first floor of the south wing, the royal apartments – Appartamenti Reali – are opulently decorated with gold and white stuccoed ceilings. The rooms are hung with portraits of the Medici family and decorated with beautiful frescoes and Gobelins tapestries.

Other collections at the Palazzo include the Galleria d'Arte Moderna, with mainly 19th-century works of art, the Galleria del Costume, opened in 1983, which reflects changing taste in courtly fashions, and the Museo degli Argenti which displays the family's lavish tastes in silverware and furniture.

L'Isolotto with Giambologna's *Oceanus Fountain*, Boboli Gardens

⑭ Boboli Gardens

Piazza de' Pitti. 🚌 D, 11, 36, 37. **Tel** 055-29 48 83 (bookings). **Open** daily. **Closed** 1st & last Mon of month, Jan 1, May 1, Dec 25. ♿ &

Laid out behind Palazzo Pitti, the Boboli Gardens are a great example of stylized Renaissance gardening. Formal box hedges lead to peaceful groves of holly and cypress trees, interspersed with Classical statues.

Highlights include the stone amphitheater where early opera performances were staged and L'Isolotto (Little Island), with its statues of dancing peasants around a moated garden. The Grotta Grande is a Mannerist folly, which houses several statues including *Venus Bathing* (1565) by Giambologna and Vincenzo de' Rossi's *Paris with Helen of Troy* (1560).

View of the Ponte Vecchio and the Arno at sunset

🟠 Portofino Peninsula

🚌 🚤 *i* Via Roma 35,
Portofino (0185-26 90 24).
ⓦ terrediportofino.eu

Portofino is the most exclusive harbor and resort town in Italy, crammed with the yachts of the wealthy. Cars are not allowed in the village but boats run regularly between here and the resort of **Santa Margherita Ligure**. Boats also run to the **Abbazia di San Fruttuoso**, an 11th-century abbey situated on the other side of the peninsula.

Further west along the coast is **Punta Chiappa**, a rocky promontory famous for the changing colors of the sea. Other attractive resorts along the Ligurian coast include the fishing village of **Camogli**, **Rapallo** and its patrician villas, and romantic **Portovenere**.

🔟 Genoa

🏔 660,000. ✈ Cristoforo Colombo 6 km (4 miles) W. 🚌 🚊 🚤 *i* Via Garibaldi (010-557 29 03). 🏛 Mon, Wed, & Thu. 🎭 International Ballet Festival (Jul); Fiera Nautica (Oct). ⓦ visitgenoa.it

The most important commercial port in Italy, Genoa (Genova in Italian) also possesses palaces, paintings, and sculptures dotted

Gothic facade of San Lorenzo, Genoa

around the city, which are among the finest in northwestern Italy.

The austere-looking **Palazzo Reale**, one-time residence of the Kings of Savoy, has a highly ornate Rococo interior, a collection of paintings including works by Parodi and van Dyck, and an attractive garden. Opposite the palace is the old **University** (1634), built on four levels and designed by the architect Bartolomeo Bianco.

Palazzo Bianco, on the **Via Garibaldi**, contains the city's prime collection of paintings, including works by Lippi, van Dyck, and Rubens. Across the street, **Palazzo Rosso** houses works by Dürer and Caravaggio,

and 17th-century frescoes by local artists.

Once the seat of the doges of Genoa and now an arts and cultural center, the **Palazzo Ducale** is located between **San Lorenzo** cathedral with its attached museum, and **Il Gesù**, a Baroque church. All that remains of the Gothic church of **Sant' Agostino**, bombed in World War II, is the bell tower, which is decorated with colored tiles. Two surviving cloisters of its surrounding monastery have been turned into the **Museo di Sant'Agostino**, which contains the city's collection of sculptural and architectural fragments.

🏛 **Palazzo Reale**
Via Balbi 10. **Tel** 010-271 02 36.
Open Tue–Sun (Tue & Wed am only).
Closed Jan 1, Apr 25, May 1, Dec 25.
🚫 ♿ ⓦ palazzorealegenova.it

🏛 **Palazzo Bianco**
Via Garibaldi 11. **Tel** 010-557 21 93.
Open Tue–Sun. 🚫 Palazzo Rosso:
Tel 010-557 49 72. **Open** Tue–Sun. 🚫

🏛 **Museo di Sant'Agostino**
Piazza Sarzano 35R. **Tel** 010-251 12 63.
Open Tue–Sun. **Closed** public hols.
🚫 ♿ ⓦ museosantagostino.it

Portofino's famous harbor, lined with colourful terraces

The Dome of San Lorenzo in Turin

⓫ Turin

🏙 940,000. ✈ Caselle 15 km (9 miles) N. 🚖 🚌 ℹ Piazza Castello (011-53 51 81). 🛍 Sat. 🎉 Festa di San Giovanni (Jun 24). 🌐 **turismotorino.org**

Home of the Fiat car company, the famous Shroud, and the Juventus football team, Turin (Torino to the Italians) is also a town of grace and charm, with superb Baroque architecture.

Many of Turin's monuments were erected by the House of Savoy (rulers of Piedmont and Sardinia) from their capital here, before Italian unification in 1861 made the head of the House of Savoy King of Italy.

The **Museo Egizio** – one of the world's great collections of Egyptian artifacts – was amassed by Bernardo Drovetti, Napoleon's Consul General in Egypt. Wall and tomb paintings, papyri, sculptures, and a reconstruction of the 15th-century BC **Rock Temple of Ellessya** are among its marvels.

The **Galleria Sabauda**, in the same building, was the House of Savoy's main painting collection, and houses a stunning array of works by Italian, French, Flemish, and Dutch masters.

Other notable buildings include **San Lorenzo**, the former Royal Chapel designed by Guarino Guarini (1624–83), which boasts an extraordinary geometric dome. The **Palazzo Reale**, seat of the Savoys, holds a vast arms collection.

The **Duomo** (1497–8), Turin's cathedral dedicated to St. John the Baptist, is the only example of Renaissance architecture in the city. Inside, the **Cappella della Sacra Sindone**, also designed by Guarini, houses the famous Turin Shroud.

Inside the **Palazzo Madama**, the **Museo Civico d'Arte Antica** contains a variety of Classical and antique treasures. Turin's symbol, the 167-m (547-ft) Mole Antonelliana, hosts the excellent **Museo Nazionale del Cinema**.

🏛 Museo Egizio
Via Accademia delle Scienze 6. **Tel** 011-561 77 76. **Open** Tue–Sun. **Closed** Jan 1, Dec 25. 🚫 ♿ 📷 🌐 **museoegizio.it**

🏛 Palazzo Reale
Piazzetta Reale 1. **Tel** 011-436 14 55. **Open** Tue–Sun. **Closed** Jan 1, May 1, Dec 25. 🚫 🎧 ♿ 🖥 📷 🌐 **ilpalazzorealeditorino.it**

🏛 Museo Nazionale del Cinema
Via Montebello 20. **Tel** 011-813 85 60. **Open** Tue–Sun. **Closed** Jan 1, Dec 25. 🚫 🖥 📷 🌐 **museocinema.it**

The imposing portico of the Baroque Basilica di Superga

Environs
In the countryside near Turin, two superb monuments to the House of Savoy are worth visiting. About 9 km (5 miles) southwest of Turin, **Stupinigi** is a magnificent hunting lodge, sumptuously decorated with frescoes and paintings. It has a vast collection of 17th- and 18th-century furniture.

The Baroque **Basilica di Superga**, on a hill to the east of Turin, offers good views of the city. Its mausoleum commemorates kings of Sardinia and other royals.

🏛 Stupinigi
Piazza Principe Amedeo 7. **Tel** 011-013 30 73. 🚌 41. **Open** Tue–Sun. 🚫 ♿

⛪ Basilica di Superga
Strada Basilica di Superga 75. **Tel** 011-899 74 56. 🚃 Historic tram from Sassi. **Open** daily. Tombs: 🚫 🌐 **basilicadisuperga.com**

The Turin Shroud

The most famous – and most dubious – holy relic of them all is kept in Turin's Duomo. The shroud, said to be the sheet in which the body of Christ was wrapped after the Crucifixion, bears the imprint of a man with a side wound, and bruises, possibly from a crown of thorns.

The shroud's early history is unclear, but the House of Savoy was in possession of it around 1450, and displayed it in Guarini's chapel in the Duomo from 1694. The shroud sits in a silver casket inside an iron box within a marble coffer. This been placed inside an urn on the chapel altar. A replica shroud is on view. Tests done in 1988 claiming the shroud to be only a 12th-century relic were discredited by a US scientist in 2005. The shroud may be 1,300–3,000 years old, pending further tests.

The supposed face of Christ imprinted on the Turin Shroud

The giant Gothic Duomo in central Milan, crowned with spires

⑫ Milan

🏙 1,350,000. ✈ Malpensa 55 km (34 miles) NW; Linate 8 km (5 miles) E. 🚉 🚌 ℹ️ Piazza Duomo 19A (02-77 40 43 43). 🛍 daily, major market Sat. 🎭 Sant'Ambrogio (Dec 7). 🌐 **turismomilano.it**

Center of fashion and business, Milan (Milano in Italian) also has a wealth of impressive sights reflecting its long and checkered history.

An important trading center since it was founded by the Romans in 222 BC, Milan's central position made it a favored location for the empire's rulers. It was here that Emperor Constantine declared that Christianity was officially recognized, following his own conversion (known as the Edict of Milan, AD 313).

By the Middle Ages Milan was one of many cities in Lombardy which opposed the power of the Holy Roman Emperor. A period of local dynastic rule followed the fall of the region to the Visconti family in 1277. They were succeeded by the Sforzas during the Renaissance.

These dynasties became great patrons of the arts, with the result that Milan has acquired a host of artistic treasures. Today this chic, bustling, and prosperous metropolis also offers opportunities for designer shopping and gastronomic pleasures.

Situated at the very heart of Milan, the giant **Duomo** is one of the largest Gothic churches in the world. The roof is extraordinary with 135 spires and innumerable statues and gargoyles. Inside, there are remarkable stained-glass windows, bas-reliefs, and a medieval treasury. More religious artifacts can be seen in the **Museo del Duomo** located in the Palazzo Reale.

An ornate shopping arcade completed in 1878, the **Galleria Vittorio Emanuele II** links the Piazza del Duomo with the Piazza della Scala. It boasts a superb metal and glass roof crowned with a central dome, has mosaic floors, and houses stylish shops and restaurants.

The Neo-Classical **Teatro alla Scala** opened in 1778 and is among the most prestigious opera houses in the world. Its stage is one of the largest in Europe. The adjoining **Museo Teatrale** displays past sets and costumes and offers a glimpse of the auditorium.

The **Castello Sforzesco**, a symbol of Milan, was initially the palace of the Visconti family. Francesco Sforza, who became lord of Milan in 1450, embellished it, turning it into a magnificent Renaissance residence. The building has a forbidding exterior, a delightful interior, and contains an impressive collection of furniture, antiquities, and paintings. Michelangelo's unfinished sculpture, known as the *Rondanini Pietà*, can also be seen here.

Milan's finest art collection is held in the imposing 17th-century Palazzo di Brera. Major works of Italian Renaissance and Baroque painters including *The Marriage of the Virgin* by Raphael, and Mantegna's *Dead Christ*, hang in

The glass dome of the Galleria Vittorio Emanuele II in Milan

For hotels and restaurants see pp438–40 and pp441–3

the 38 rooms of the **Pinacoteca di Brera**. Works by some of Italy's 20th-century artists are also on display.

The beautiful 15th-century Renaissance convent of **Santa Maria delle Grazie**, in the southwest of the city, is a must-see because it contains one of the key images of western civilization: the *Last Supper* (or *Cenacolo*) of Leonardo da Vinci. The large wall painting has deteriorated badly but remains an iconic work of great subtlety.

Sant'Ambrogio is a mainly 10th-century Romanesque basilica dedicated to the patron saint of Milan whose tomb lies in the crypt. The 4th-century church of **San Lorenzo** holds an important collection of Roman and early Christian remains.

🏛 Duomo
Piazza del Duomo. 🏛 roof, baptistry and treasury. 🏛 Museo del Duomo: **Tel** 02-86 03 58. **Open** Tue–Sun.

🏛 Castello Sforzesco
Piazza Castello. **Tel** 02-88 46 37 00. **Open** Tue–Sun. **Closed** public hols. 🏛 limited.

🏛 Pinacoteca di Brera
Via Brera 28. **Tel** 02-72 26 31. **Open** Tue–Sun. **Closed** Jan 1, May 1, Dec 25. 🏛🏛🏛🏛

🏛 Santa Maria delle Grazie
Piazza Santa Maria delle Grazie 2. Cenacolo: **Tel** 02-46 76 11 25. **Open** daily (booking compulsory). **Closed** public hols. 🏛🏛

🔟 Lake Maggiore

🚆 to Stresa and Laveno. 🚌 🚢 Navigazione Lago Maggiore (800 55 18 01). 🚹 Piazza Marconi 16, Stresa (0323-301 50).

Lake Maggiore is a long expanse of water that nestles right against the mountains and stretches away into Alpine Switzerland. In the center lie the exquisite Borromean islands named after the chief patron of the lake, St. Carlo Borromeo, of whom there is a giant statue in **Arona**.

Further up the western coast of the lake is **Stresa**, the chief resort and main jumping-off point for visits to the islands.

Statue of Carlo Borromeo, patron saint of Lake Maggiore, in Arona

From here **Monte Mottarone**, a snow-capped peak offering spectacular panoramic views, can be reached by cable car.

🔟 Lake Como

🚆 to Como and Lecco. 🚌 🚢 Navigazione Lago di Como (800 55 18 01). 🚹 Piazza Cavour 17, Como (031-26 97 12). 🌐 **turismocomo.it**

Set in an idyllic landscape, Como has long attracted visitors who come to walk in the hills or to go boating. The long, narrow lake, also known as Lario, is shaped like an upside-down Y, and offers fine views of the Alps.

In the heart of the town of **Como** lies the elegant Piazza Cavour. The beautiful 14th-century **Duomo** nearby has 15th- and 16th-century reliefs and paintings, and fine tombs.

Bellagio, at the junction of the "Y," has spectacular views, and is one of the most popular spots on Lake Como.

In the lakeside town of **Tremezzo**, the 18th-century **Villa Carlotta** is adorned with sculptures and celebrated for its terraced gardens.

🔟 Lake Garda

🚆 to Desenzano and Orta San Giulio. 🚌 🚢 Navigazione Lago di Garda (800-55 18 01). 🚹 Piazza Virgilio 52, Colombare di Sirmione (030-990 91 84).

Garda, the largest of the northern lakes, borders the three regions of Trentino, Lombardy, and Veneto.

Hydrofoils and catamarans ply the lake, offering stops at **Sirmione**, site of a medieval castle, **Gardone** with the curiosity-filled **Villa il Vittoriale**, and **Salò** where Mussolini established a short-lived Republic in 1943.

Lake Como, one of the most attractive summer resorts of northern Italy

The Arena, Verona's Roman amphitheater – the setting for spectacular summer opera performances

⑯ Mantua

🏙 55,000. 🚉 🚌 ℹ️ Piazza Andrea Mantegna 6 (0376-43 24 32). 🛒 Thu.

A striking if stern-looking city of fine squares and aristocratic architecture, Mantua (Mantova in Italian) is bordered on three sides by lakes. It was the birthplace of the poet Virgil and playground for three centuries of the Gonzaga dukes. Mantua was also the setting for Verdi's opera *Rigoletto*, and is mentioned in Shakespeare's *Romeo and Juliet*. These theatrical connections are celebrated in local street names and monuments, and are reinforced by the presence in the town of the 18th-century **Teatro Scientifico Bibiena**, a masterpiece of late Baroque theater architecture.

Mantua is focused on three attractive main squares. Piazza Sordello is the site of the **Palazzo Ducale**, the vast former home of the Gonzaga family which also incorporates a 14th-century fortress and a basilica. The frescoes by Mantegna in the **Camera degli Sposi** (1465–74), are a highlight. They portray the Gonzaga family and court, and the room is completed by a light-hearted *trompe l'oeil* ceiling. The nearby **Duomo** has an 18th-century façade and fine interior stuccoes by Giulio Romano (c.1492–1546).

Piazza dell'Erbe is dominated by the Basilica di Sant' Andrea (15th century), designed largely by the early Renaissance architect and theorist, Alberti.

Across town is the early 16th-century Palazzo del Tè, designed as the Gonzaga family's summer retreat. This extraordinary palace is decorated with frescoes by Giulio Romano and has rooms lavishly painted with horses and signs of the zodiac.

🏛 Palazzo Ducale

Piazza Sordello 40. **Tel** 0376-22 48 32. **Open** Tue–Sun. **Closed** Jan 1, May 1, Dec 25. 🎟 🎧 (audio). ♿ Camera degli Sposi: **Tel** 041-241 18 97. **Open** by appointment only.

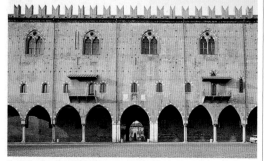

The 13th-century facade of the Palazzo Ducale in Mantua

⑰ Verona

🏙 261,000. ✈️ Villafranca 12 km (7 miles) SW. 🚉 🚌 ℹ️ Via degli Alpini 9 (045-806 86 80). 🛒 daily. 🎭 Estate Teatrale Veronese (Jun–Aug); Opera Festival (Jul–Sep). 🌐 **tourism. verona.it**

Verona, a large and prosperous city of the Veneto region, boasts magnificent Roman ruins, second only to those of Rome itself, as well as some important medieval monuments.

The Arena, Verona's Roman amphitheater completed in AD 30, is the third largest in the world. Concerts, plays, and opera productions are staged here. Other Roman sites include the Roman Theater, and artifacts from Roman times can be seen in the Museo Archeologico.

The tragic story of Romeo and Juliet, first set here by Luigi da Porto in the 1520s and immortalized by Shakespeare, has inspired local monuments such as Romeo's House and the so-called Tomb of Juliet. Verona's focal point is Piazza Erbe, scene of colorful markets for 2,000 years.

The ornate tombs of members of the Scaglieri family, who ruled the city for 127 years from 1263, are situated beside the entrance to the church of Santa Maria Antica. Another legacy of the family is Castelvecchio, an impressive castle built by Cangrande II between 1355 and 1375. There is a fine art gallery in the castle, which has a collection of 15th-century late Renaissance Madonnas. Built in 1125–35 to house the shrine of

Verona's patron saint, **San Zeno Maggiore** is the most ornate Romanesque church in northern Italy, famous for its unusual medieval bronze door panels.

The **Duomo** also dates from the 12th century and displays Titian's *Assumption*. Other notable medieval churches in Verona are **San Fermo Maggiore**, with many interior frescoes including the *Annunciation* by Pisanello (1377–1455), and **Sant'Anastasia**, which houses 15th-century frescoes and holy water stoups supported by figures of beggars known locally as *i gobbi*.

Arena
Piazza Brà. **Tel** 045-800 32 04.
Open daily (Mon: pm only).
Closed Jan 1, Dec 25–26.

Castelvecchio
Corso Castelvecchio 2. **Tel** 045-806 26 11. **Open** daily. (audio).

Vicenza
116,000. Piazza Matteotti 12 (0444-32 08 54). Tue & Thu. Concert season (May–Jun).
vicenzae.org

Vicenza is celebrated for its splendid, varied architecture. Known as the city of Andrea Palladio (1508–80), stonemason turned architect, it offers a unique opportunity to study the evolution of his distinctive style.

Piazza dei Signori at the heart of Vicenza is dominated by the Palazzo della Ragione, known also as the **Basilica**. Palladio's first public commission, this building has a roof like an upturned boat, and a balustrade bristling with

The illusionistic stage set of the Teatro Olimpico in Vicenza

statues. Beside it stands the 12th-century **Torre di Piazza**.

The **Loggia del Capitaniato**, to the northwest, was built by Palladio in 1571. Its upper rooms contain the city's council chamber.

Europe's oldest surviving indoor theater, the **Teatro Olimpico** was begun by Palladio in 1579 and completed by his pupil, Vincenzo Scamozzi. It was Scamozzi who created the permanent stage, built of wood and plaster and painted to look like marble. It represents Thebes, a Greek city, and uses perspective to create an illusion of depth.

Palladio was also responsible for the design of **Palazzo Chiericati** which houses the **Museo Civico**, but the epitome of his work can be seen in the **Villa Rotonda**, in the countryside to the south of Vicenza.

Memorial to Andrea Palladio in Vicenza

Piazza dei Signori
Basilica: **Tel** 0444-22 28 11. **Open** daily during exhibitions.

Teatro Olimpico
Piazza Matteotti. **Tel** 0444-271 90 44.
Open Tue–Sun. **Closed** Jan 1, Dec 25.

Villa Rotonda
Via della Rotonda 45. **Tel** 0498-79 13 80. Villa: **Open** Mar–Nov: Wed.
Garden: **Open** Tue–Sun.
villalarotonda.it

The Basilica di Sant'Antonio in Padua, with its Byzantine domes

Padua
220,000. Vicolo Pedrocchi (049-876 79 27). Mon–Sat at Piazza delle Erbe.
turismopadova.it

Padua is an old university town with an illustrious academic history. The city (Padova in Italian) has two major attractions – the **Basilica di Sant'Antonio**, one of the most popular sites of pilgrimage in Italy, and the **Cappella degli Scrovegni**, a beautifully decorated chapel. The exotic Basilica was built from 1232 to house the remains of the great Franciscan preacher, St. Anthony of Padua.

The chapel (1303) features a series of frescoes depicting the life of Christ, painted by Giotto. The **Museo Civico Eremitani** on the same site has a rich coin collection and an art gallery.

Other attractions include the **Duomo** and **Baptistry**, which contains one of Italy's most complete medieval fresco cycles (painted by Giusto de' Menabuoi in 1378), and the **Palazzo della Ragione**, built in 1218 to serve as Padua's law court and council chamber.

Cappella degli Scrovegni
Piazza Eremitani. **Tel** 049-201 00 20.
Open daily (advance booking necessary). **Closed** public hols.

⑳ Venice

Created on a series of mud banks in a lagoon, with canals in place of roads, Venice can truly claim to be unique. Originally a province of the Byzantine Empire, by the 12th century Venice was an independent city-state and, through its control of the spice and silk trade from the East, the richest trading nation in Europe. The banks of its canals are lined with magnificent palaces dating from this period up until the 18th century. By then, Venice's power and influence were waning. It finally lost its independence in 1797, since when this astonishing city has remained more or less frozen in time.

Ponte della Paglia beside the Doge's Palace

Sights at a Glance

① St. Mark's pp416–17
② Doge's Palace pp418–19
③ Museo Correr
④ Scuola Grande di San Rocco
⑤ Santa Maria Gloriosa dei Frari
⑥ Grand Canal
⑦ Santi Giovanni e Paolo
⑧ Scuola di San Giorgio degli Schiavoni
⑨ Santa Maria della Salute
⑩ Peggy Guggenheim Collection
⑪ Accademia

The Lagoon (see inset map)
⑫ Murano

Key

▨ Sight / Place of interest

0 meters   300
0 yards   300

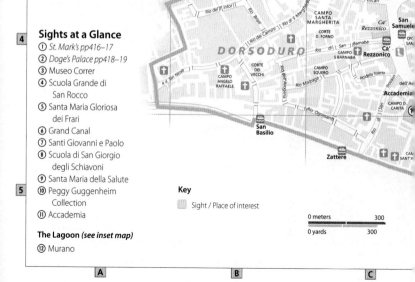

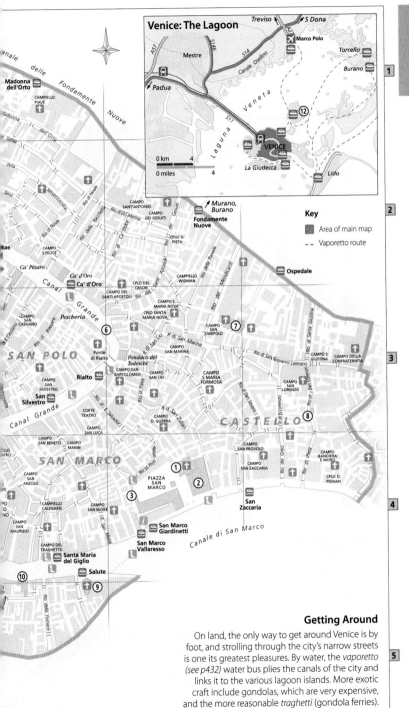

Getting Around

On land, the only way to get around Venice is by foot, and strolling through the city's narrow streets is one its greatest pleasures. By water, the *vaporetto* (see p432) water bus plies the canals of the city and links it to the various lagoon islands. More exotic craft include gondolas, which are very expensive, and the more reasonable *traghetti* (gondola ferries). The speediest means of travel is water taxi.

① St. Mark's

The basilica blends architectural and decorative styles from East and West to create one of Europe's greatest buildings. Built on a Greek-cross plan and crowned with five huge domes, it is the third church to stand on this site. The first, built to enshrine the body of St. Mark in the 9th century, was destroyed by fire. The second was pulled down in the 11th century to make way for a truly spectacular edifice, reflecting the growing power of the Republic and its links with Byzantium. The dark interior is clad in wonderful mosaics, gleaming with gold. Many treasures – statues, icons, and the famous horses – were brought to St. Mark's after the 4th Crusade had plundered Constantinople in 1204.

★ Pentecost Mosaic
The interior of the dome above the nave is decorated with a 12th-century mosaic of the Holy Spirit descending on the Apostles in tongues of fire.

St. Mark flanked by Angels
The statues crowning the central arch were added in the early 15th century.

★ Horses of St. Mark
The four horses are replicas of the gilded bronze originals, kept in the Museo Marciano, reached from the atrium.

Main entrance

★ Facade Mosaics
These are either heavily restored or replacements of the originals. This 17th-century work shows the body of St. Mark being smuggled out of Alexandria.

★ Pala d'Oro
The greatest treasure of St. Mark's is kept behind the high altar. The magnificent altarpiece, created originally in the 10th century, is made up of 250 gold panels, adorned with enamels and precious stones.

★ Treasury
This contains many treasures looted from Constantinople by the Venetians in 1204. This 11th-century silver-gilt reliquary is in the shape of a domed basilica.

KEY

① **The central arch** features 13th-century carvings of the Labours of the Months.

② **The atrium**, or narthex, contains many fine mosaics, notably those of the Genesis Cupola showing the Creation.

③ **The Ascension Dome** features a magnificent 13th-century mosaic of Christ surrounded by angels, the 12 Apostles, and the Virgin Mary.

④ **The altar canopy**, or *baldacchino*, has alabaster columns carved with New Testament scenes.

⑤ **St. Mark's body**, thought to have been lost in the fire of 976, reappeared when the new church was consecrated in 1094. The remains are housed below the altar.

⑥ **Allegorical mosaics** decorate the floor of the south transept.

⑦ **Baptistry**

The Tetrarchs
This porphyry sculptural group (4th-century Egyptian) may represent Diocletian, Maximian, Constantius, and Valerian – the four joint rulers of the Roman Empire c.AD 300, known as the tetrarchs.

② Doge's Palace

The official residence of the Venetian ruler (Doge) was founded in the 9th century. The present palace owes its external appearance to the building work of the 14th and early 15th centuries. To create their airy Gothic masterpiece, the Venetians broke with tradition by perching the bulk of the palace (built of pink Veronese marble) on top of an apparent fretwork of loggias and arcades (built of white Istrian stone). A tour of the palace leads through a succession of richly decorated chambers and halls, ending with the Bridge of Sighs and the prisons.

★ Giants' Staircase
Statues by Sansovino of Neptune and Mars at the top of this late 15th-century staircase symbolize Venice's power at sea and on land. Doges were crowned with the glittering *zogia* or ducal cap on the landing.

★ Porta della Carta
This 15th-century Gothic gate was the principal entrance to the palace. From it, a vaulted passageway leads to the Arco Foscari and the internal courtyard.

Exit

KEY

① **The balcony** on the west facade was added in 1536 to mirror the early 15th-century balcony looking onto the quay.

② **Arco Foscari**

③ In the **Sala del Collegio** the doge would receive ambassadors. The ceiling is decorated with 11 paintings by Veronese.

④ **The Sala del Senato** was the home of the senate, which had some 200 members.

⑤ **Anticollegio**

⑥ **The Sala del Consiglio dei Dieci** was once the meeting place of the powerful Council of Ten.

⑦ **Sala della Bussola (Compass Room)**

⑧ **Ponte della Paglia**

Torture Chamber
Suspects under interrogation were hung on the walls of this room by cords tied around their wrists.

VISITORS' CHECKLIST

Practical Information
Piazza San Marco 1.
Tel 041-271 59 42.
Open Apr–Oct: 8:30am–7pm daily; Nov–Mar: 8:30am–5:30pm daily. **Closed** Jan 1, Dec 25. 🎫 🎒 💻 🎧 (audio). ♿ limited.

Transport
🚏 San Marco.

Bridge of Sighs
The bridge was built in 1600 to link the palace with the state prisons. It reputedly acquired its name from the sighs of prisoners being led across it to face trial.

Drunkenness of Noah
This early 15th-century sculpture, symbolic of the frailty of man, is set on the corner of the palace.

⑥ ⑦

⑧

Main entrance

★ Sala del Maggior Consiglio
This vast chamber was the meeting hall of Venice's Great Council. By the 16th century this had over 2,000 members. The entire end wall is taken up by Tintoretto's *Paradise* (1588–92).

Portrait of a Young Man in a Red Hat
(anonymous), Museo Correr

③ Museo Correr

Piazza San Marco (entrance in Ala Napoleonica). **Tel** 041-240 52 11. 🚇 San Marco. **Open** daily.
Closed Jan 1, Dec 25. 🖼️ 🏛️ 🎧 💻 ♿
🌐 correr.visitmuve.it

Teodoro Correr bequeathed his extensive collection of works of art to Venice in 1830, thus forming the core of the city's fine civic museum.

Its first rooms form a suitably Neo-Classical backdrop for early statues by Antonio Canova (1757–1822). The rest of the floor covers the history of the Venetian Republic, with maps, coins, armor, and a host of doge-related exhibits.

The second floor contains the picture gallery. Works are hung chronologically, enabling one to trace the evolution of Venetian painting. The most famous include the *Portrait of a Young Man in a Red Hat* (c.1490), once attributed to Carpaccio, now thought to be by an artist from the Ferrara/Bologna area, and Carpaccio's *Two Venetian Ladies* (c.1507).

④ Scuola Grande di San Rocco

Campo San Rocco. **Tel** 041-523 48 64. 🚇 San Tomà. **Open** daily. **Closed** Jan 1, Easter, Dec 25. 🖼️ ♿ 🏛️ 📷 (audio).

Founded in honor of San Rocco (St. Roch), a saint who dedicated his life to helping the sick, the Scuola started out as a charitable confraternity. Construction began in 1515. The work was financed by donations from Venetians keen to invoke San Rocco's protection, and the Scuola quickly became one of the wealthiest in Venice. In 1564, its members decided to commission Tintoretto to decorate its walls and ceilings. His earliest paintings, the first of over 50 works he eventually created for the Scuola, fill the small Sala dell'Albergo off the Upper Hall. His later paintings are in the Ground Floor Hall, just inside the entrance.

The ground floor cycle was executed in 1583–7, when Tintoretto was in his sixties, and consists of eight episodes from the life of Mary. They are remarkable for the tranquil serenity of paintings such as *The Flight into Egypt* and *St. Mary of Egypt*.

Scarpagnino's great staircase (1544–6), leads to the Upper Hall, which was decorated by Tintoretto in 1575–81. The ceiling is painted with scenes from the Old Testament. The three large square paintings in the center show episodes from the Book of Exodus, all alluding to the charitable aims of the Scuola in alleviating thirst, sickness, and hunger. The vast wall paintings feature episodes from the New Testament, linking with the ceiling paintings. Two of the most striking are *The Temptation of Christ*, which shows a handsome young Satan offering Christ two loaves of bread, and

The Adoration of the Shepherds. The carvings below the paintings were added in the 17th century by sculptor Francesco Pianta. They include (near the altar) a caricature of Tintoretto with his palette and brushes.

The Sala dell'Albergo contains perhaps the most breathtaking of all Tintoretto's masterpieces – the *Crucifixion* (1565). Henry James once remarked of this painting: "no single picture contains more of human life; there is everything in it, including the most exquisite beauty."

⑤ Santa Maria Gloriosa dei Frari

Campo dei Frari. **Tel** 041-272 86 11. 🚇 San Tomà. **Open** Mon–Sat & Sun pm. **Closed** Jan 1, Jan 6, Easter, Dec 25. 🖼️ unless attending mass. 📷

More commonly known as the Frari (a corruption of Frati, meaning brothers), this vast Gothic church dwarfs the eastern area of San Polo. Its 83-m (272-ft) campanile is the tallest in the city after that of San Marco. The first church on the site was built by the Franciscans in 1250–1338, but was replaced by a larger building completed in the mid-15th century. The airy interior is striking for its sheer size and for the quality of its works of art, including masterpieces by Titian and Giovanni Bellini, a statue by Donatello, and several grandiose tombs.

Detail from Tintoretto's *Flight into Egypt*, Scuola Grande di San Rocco

For hotels and restaurants see pp438–40 and pp441–3

The sacristy alterpiece, *The Madonna and Child* (1488) by Bellini, with its sublime use of color, is one of Venice's most beautiful Renaissance paintings. The main altarpiece is *The Assumption of the Virgin*, a spectacular, glowing work by Titian (1518), which draws the eye through the Renaissance rood screen to the altar. Between the altar and the screen is the Monks' Choir (1468), its three-tiered stalls lavishly carved with saints and Venetian city scenes.

The Tomb of Canova, a marble, pyramid-shaped tomb, was built after Canova's death in 1822 by his pupils. It is similar to a design Canova himself had planned for a memorial for Titian. The Titian monument in the shape of a triumphal arch that stands opposite was built by two of Canova's pupils in 1853.

High altar of the Frari church with Titian's *Assumption of the Virgin*

⑥ Grand Canal

🚌 1 from Ferrovia and many others.

The best way to view the Grand Canal as it winds through the heart of the city is from a *vaporetto*, or water bus. Several lines travel the length of the canal. The palaces lining the waterway were built over a span of five centuries and present a panoramic survey of the city's history, almost all bearing the name of some once-great Venetian family.

Nearly 4 km (2.5 miles) long, the canal varies in width from 30 to 70 m (100 to 230 ft) and is spanned by three bridges, the Scalzi, the Rialto, and the

View across the Grand Canal to the Pescheria (fish market)

Accademia. After passing the Rialto, the canal doubles back on itself along a stretch known as La Volta (the bend). It then widens out and the views become more spectacular approaching San Marco. Facades may have faded and foundations rotted, yet the canal remains, in the words of the French ambassador in 1495, "the most beautiful street in the world."

⑦ Santi Giovanni e Paolo

Campo Santi Giovanni e Paolo (also signposted San Zanipolo). **Tel** 041-523 59 13. 🚌 Fondamenta Nuove or Ospedale Civile. **Open** daily. **Closed** Sun am for mass. 🚻 📷

Known colloquially as San Zanipolo, Santi Giovanni e Paolo vies with the Frari as the city's greatest Gothic church. Built by the Dominicans in the 14th century, it is striking for its vast scale and architectural austerity. Known as the Pantheon of Venice, it houses monuments to no fewer than 25 doges. Among these are several fine works of art, executed by the Lombardi family and other leading sculptors. Pietro Lombardo created the magnificent tombs of the doges Nicolò Marcello (died 1474) and Pietro Mocenigo (died 1476). His masterpiece, the Tomb of Andrea Vendramin (died 1478), takes the form of a Roman triumphal arch.

The main doorway, which is decorated with Byzantine reliefs and carvings, is one of Venice's earliest Renaissance architectural works. On the right as you enter the church is a polyptych by Giovanni Bellini (c.1465) showing St. Vincent Ferrer, a Spanish cleric, flanked by St. Sebastian and St. Christopher.

The Gondolas of Venice

The gondola has been a part of Venice since the 11th century. With its slim hull and flat underside, the craft is perfectly adapted to negotiating narrow, shallow canals. There is a slight leftward curve to the prow, which counteracts the force of the oar, preventing the gondola from going around in circles.

In 1562, it was decreed that all gondolas should be black to stop people making an ostentatious show of their wealth. For special occasions they were decorated with flowers. Today, gondola rides are expensive and usually taken by tourists.

Gondolas moored in a Venice canal

⑧ Scuola di San Giorgio degli Schiavoni

Calle Furlani. **Tel** 041-522 88 28. 🚤 San Zaccaria. **Open** daily. **Closed** Mon am, Sun pm. 🅿️

Within this small Scuola, established in 1451 and rebuilt in 1551, are some of the finest paintings of Vittore Carpaccio (c.1460–1525). Commissioned by the Schiavoni, or Dalmatian Slav trading community in Venice, Carpaccio's exquisite frieze (1502–08) shows scenes from the lives of three saints: St. George, St. Tryphon, and St. Jerome. Each episode of the narrative cycle is remarkable for its vivid coloring and minutely observed detail of Venetian life. *St. George Slaying the Dragon* and *The Vision of St. Jerome* are both outstanding.

⑨ Santa Maria della Salute

Campo della Salute. **Tel** 041-241 00 18. 🚤 Salute. **Open** daily. 🅿️ to sacristy.

The great Baroque church of Santa Maria della Salute, standing at the entrance of the Grand Canal, is an imposing architectural landmark of Venice.

The Baroque church of Santa Maria della Salute, viewed from the other side of the Grand Canal

The single-story palazzo housing the Peggy Guggenheim Collection

Construction of the church, begun in 1630 by Baldassare Longhena, was not completed until 1687, five years after his death.

The comparatively sober interior of Santa Maria della Salute consists of a large octagonal space below the cupola and six chapels radiating from the ambulatory. The sculptural group around the grandiose high altar is by Giusto Le Corte and represents the Virgin and Child protecting the city of Venice from the plague.

In the sacristy to the left of the altar, Titian's early altarpiece *St. Mark Enthroned with St. Cosmas, St. Damian, St. Roch and St. Sebastian* (1511–12) and his dramatic ceiling paintings of *David and Goliath, Cain and Abel*, and *The Sacrifice of Isaac* (1540–9) are considered the finest paintings in the church.

The Wedding at Cana (1551) on the wall opposite the entrance, is a major work by Jacopo Tintoretto.

The church was named *Salute*, which means both "health" and "salvation," in thanksgiving for the deliverance of the city from the plague epidemic of 1630. Each November, in a moving ceremony of remembrance, worshipers light candles and approach the church across a bridge of boats which spans the mouth of the Grand Canal.

⑩ Peggy Guggenheim Collection

Palazzo Venier dei Leoni. **Tel** 041-240 54 11. 🚤 Accademia. **Open** Wed– Mon. **Closed** Dec 25. 🅿️ 📷 (audio). 📷 🖥️ 🌐 **guggenheim-venice.it**

Intended as a four-story palace, the 18th-century, Palazzo Venier dei Leoni in fact never rose beyond the ground floor – hence its nickname "The Unfinished Palace." In 1949, the building was bought by Peggy Guggenheim (1898–1979), an American collector, dealer, and patron of the arts. One of the most visited sights of Venice, the palace is the best place in the city to see modern art. The light-filled rooms and modern canvases are in striking contrast to the majority of the art on display in Venice.

Her collection consists of 200 fine paintings and sculptures, representing the 20th century's most influential modern art movements. The dining room has notable Cubist works of art, including *The Poet* by Pablo Picasso, and an entire room is devoted to Jackson Pollock, who was "discovered" by Guggenheim. There are also works by Braque, Chagall, Dalí, Klee, Mondrian, and Magritte, whose Surreal *Empire of Light* (1953–4) shows a night scene of a darkened house with bright daylight above.

The sculpture collection, which includes Constantin Brancusi's elegant *Bird in Space* (c.1923), is laid out in the house and the garden.

Perhaps the most provocative piece, on the canal terrace, is Marino Marini's *Angelo della Città* (1948). It shows a man sitting on a horse, erect in all respects.

⑪ **Accademia**

Campo della Carità. **Tel** 041-520 03 45 (bookings). 🚤 Accademia. **Open** daily (Mon: am only). **Closed** Jan 1, May 1, Dec 25. 🔲 📷 (audio). 📷
W gallerieaccademia.org

Spanning five centuries, the matchless collection of paintings in the Accademia provides a complete spectrum of the Venetian school, from the Byzantine period through the Renaissance to the Baroque and later.

Housed in three former religious buildings, the basis of the collection was the Accademia di Belle Arti, founded in 1750 by the painter Giovanni Battista Piazzetta. In 1807, Napoleon moved the academy to its present premises, greatly enlarging the collection with artworks from churches and monasteries he suppressed.

The gallery is currently being enlarged and some rooms may be closed.

A highlight of the Byzantine and Gothic section is Paolo Veneziano's *Coronation of the Virgin* (1325), which contrasts with the delicate naturalism of Giambono's painting of the same name (1448).

The Bellini family played a dominant role in the early Venetian Renaissance, and outstanding examples of their work include Giovanni Bellini's *Madonna and Child between St. John the Baptist and a Saint* (c.1504), and other paintings of his Madonna collection in room 13. One of Bellini's students, Giorgione, painted

The colonnaded apse of Murano's Basilica dei Santi Maria e Donato

the atmospheric *Tempest* (c.1507). Among Renaissance works on display are *Feast in the House of Levi* (1573) by Veronese, and *The Miracle of the Slave* (1548), which made the reputation of Jacopo Tintoretto.

The long gallery of Baroque, genre, and landscape paintings alongside Palladio's inner courtyard (1561) features works by Giambattista Tiepolo, the greatest Venetian painter of the 18th century, and a view of Venice (1763) by Canaletto.

Rooms 20 and 21 contain two cycles of paintings portraying Venetian settings: *The Stories of the Cross*, and *Scenes from the Legend of St. Ursula*, painted by Carpaccio (1490s).

⑫ **Murano**

🚤 LN, 41 and 42 from Fondamenta Nuove; DM from Ferrovia and Piazzale Roma.

Like the city of Venice, Murano consists of a cluster of small islands, connected by bridges. In the 15th and 16th centuries,

Murano was the principal glass-producing center in Europe, and today most tourists visit to tour the furnaces and buy traditionally designed glass from the manufacturers' showrooms.

The **Museo del Vetro** in the Palazzo Giustinian houses a fine collection of antique pieces. The prize exhibit is the dark blue wedding cup (1470–80) with enamel work by Angelo Barovier.

The architectural highlight of the island is the 12th-century **Basilica dei Santi Maria e Donato** with its lovely colonnaded apse. Of particular note are the Gothic ship's-keel roof, the mosaic Madonna in the apse, and the beautiful medieval mosaic floor, which dates from 1140.

🏛 **Museo del Vetro**
Fondamenta Giustinian 8. **Tel** 041-73 95 86. **Open** daily (partially closed for renovation until 2015). **Closed** Jan 1, May 1, Dec 25. 🔲 📷

⛪ **Basilica dei Santi Maria e Donato**
Campo San Donato. **Tel** 041-73 90 56. **Open** daily (Sun: pm only).

Veronese's painting of Christ's Last Supper, retitled *The Feast in the House of Levi* (1573), in the Accademia

❹ Ferrara

🏛 140,000. 🚆 🚌 ℹ️ Castello Estense, Piazza Castello (0532-20 93 70). 🛍 Mon & Fri.

The d'Este dynasty has left an indelible mark on Ferrara, one of the Emilia-Romagna region's greatest walled towns. The noble family took control of the town under Nicolò II in the late 13th century, holding power until 1598. **Castello Estense**, the family's dynastic seat, with its moats, towers, and battlements, looms over the town center.

Bronze statues of Nicolò III and Borso d'Este, one of Nicolò's reputed 27 children, adorn the medieval **Palazzo del Comune**. The d'Este summer retreat was the **Palazzo Schifanoia**. Begun in 1385, it is famous for its Salone dei Mesi, whose walls are covered with murals by Cosmè Tura and other Ferrarese painters. Access is limited due to damage from the 2012 earthquake.

Ferrara's **cathedral** has an excellent museum, which contains marble reliefs of the *Labours of the Months* (late 12th century), two painted organ shutters (1469) of *St. George* and the *Annunciation* by Tura, and the *Madonna of the Pomegranate* (1408) by Sienese sculptor Jacopo della Quercia (c.1374–1438).

🏰 Castello Estense
Piazza Castello. **Tel** 0532-29 92 33. **Open** Tue–Sun (Mar–Jun & Sep: daily). **Closed** Dec 25. 🈲 ♿

🏛 Palazzo Schifanoia
Via Scandiana 23. **Tel** 0532-24 49 49. **Open** Tue–Sun. **Closed** public hols. 🈲

The medieval Castello Estense and surrounding moat in Ferrara

Flagged medieval street with shady, arcaded buildings, typical of central Bologna

❷ Bologna

🏛 385,000. ✈️ Marconi 9 km (5 miles) NW. 🚆 🚌 ℹ️ Piazza Maggiore 1/e (051-23 96 60). 🛍 Fri & Sat. 🎪 Bologna Estate (Jun–Sep).

Capital of Emilia-Romagna and one of Italy's most prosperous cities, Bologna has a rich cultural heritage, ranging from medieval palaces and churches to leaning towers.

Celebrated in the Middle Ages for its university – believed to be the oldest in Europe – Bologna came under papal rule in 1506 and a large part of the city was given over to monasteries and convents. After the arrival of Napoleon's occupying force in 1797, the university was moved from its Catholic cradle in the **Archiginnasio** to a science building where Marconi later studied. After unification the old city walls were demolished and an era of prosperity was ushered in.

The two central squares of the city, Piazza Maggiore and Piazza del Nettuno, are bordered to the south by the churches of **San Petronio** and **San Domenico**. The former ranks among the greatest of Italy's brick-built medieval buildings. Founded in 1390, its construction was halted halfway due to financial constraints, and the planned central row of columns became the eastern flank. Twenty-two

chapels open off the nave of the Gothic interior, many with fine works of art.

San Domenico is the most important of Italy's many Dominican churches, housing, as it does, the tomb of St. Dominic himself. A magnificent composite work, the tomb features statues and reliefs by Nicola Pisano, while the figures of angels and saints are early works by Michelangelo. The **Torri degli Asinelli e Garisenda** are among the few surviving towers of the 200 that once formed the skyline of Bologna. Both were begun in the 12th century. The Garisenda tower (closed to the public) leans some 3 m (10 ft), while the Asinelli tower has a 500-step ascent and offers fine views.

The Romanesque-Gothic church of **San Giacomo Maggiore**, begun in 1267 but altered substantially since, is visited mainly for the superb Bentivoglio family chapel, decorated with frescoes by Lorenzo Costa (1460–1535). The Bentivoglio tomb is among the last works of Jacopo della Quercia.

Bologna's main art gallery, the **Pinacoteca Nazionale**, stands on the edge of the university district. Its two highlights are Perugino's *Madonna in Glory* (c.1491) and Raphael's famous *Ecstasy of St. Cecilia*, painted around 1515.

The cuisine of Bologna is among the finest in Italy. To try the famous Bolognese meat sauce you should order *tagliatelle al ragù*.

🗼 Torri degli Asinelli e Garisenda
Piazza di Porta Ravegnana. **Open** daily. 🈲

🏛 Pinacoteca Nazionale
Via delle Belle Arti 56. **Tel** 051-420 94 11. **Open** Tue–Sun. **Closed** May 1, Aug 16. 🈲 ♿ 🌐 pinacoteca bologna.beniculturali.it

㉓ Ravenna

🏠 140,000. ☷ ☷ ℹ️ Via Salara 8–12 (0544-357 55). ☷ Wed & Sat.

Ravenna rose to power in the 1st century BC when Emperor Augustus built a port and naval base nearby, but gained further prominence after becoming the administrative capital of the Byzantine Empire in AD 402.

Most people visit the city for its superb early Christian mosaics. Spanning the years of Roman and Byzantine rule, they can be seen in many of Ravenna's 5th- and 6th-century buildings. In the church of **San Vitale**, apse mosaics (526–547) show the saint being handed a martyr's crown. Another mosaic depicts Emperor Justinian, who ruled from 527 to 565, and members of his court. Next door, the tiny **Mausoleo di Galla Placidia** is adorned with a mosaic of *The Good Shepherd*. Galla Placidia ran the Western Empire for

Byzantine Italy

By the 5th century AD, the Roman Empire was split into two. Rome and the Western Empire could not stem the tide of Germanic invaders as they migrated southwards and Italy fell to the Goths. In the years after 535 AD, however, the Eastern Empire reconquered most of Italy. Its stronghold, Ravenna, became the richest, most powerful Italian city. Most of the peninsula was subsequently lost to the Lombards who invaded in 564, but Ravenna, protected by marshes and lagoons, was able to hold out until 752 when the Lombard King Aistulf finally recaptured the city.

Byzantine Emperor Justinian

Apse of San Vitale, Ravenna, showing 6th-century mosaics

20 years after the death of her husband, the Visigothic King Altauf. The 6th-century church of **Sant'Apollinare Nuovo** is dominated by two rows of mosaics which depict pro- cessions of martyrs and virgins bearing gifts.

Travelers in Ravenna can also visit **Dante's Tomb** – the great writer died here in 1321 – and the **Museo Nazionale**, which houses icons, paintings, and archaeological displays. The best place to relax and take a break from sightseeing is among the lovely ensemble of medieval buildings in the Piazza del Popolo.

🏛 **San Vitale & Mausoleo di Galla Placidia**
Via Fiandrini. **Tel** 800-30 39 99. **Open** daily. **Closed** Jan 1, Dec 25. 🗓 🛇

🏛 **Sant'Apollinare Nuovo**
Via di Roma. **Tel** 0544-54 16 88. **Open** daily. **Closed** Jan 1, Dec 25. 🗓 🛇

㉔ Urbino

🏠 16,000. ☷ ℹ️ Piazza Rinascimento 1 (0722-26 13). ☷ Sat.

Urbino traces its origins to the Umbrians, centuries before Christ, and became a Roman municipality in the 3rd century BC. The city's zenith, however, came in the 15th century under the rule of the philosopher- warrior Federico da Montefeltro, who commissioned the building of the **Palazzo Ducale** in 1444. This beautiful Renaissance palace has an extensive library, hanging gardens, and numerous fine paintings. Two great 15th-century works, *The Flagellation* by Piero della Francesca, and *Ideal City* attributed to Luciano Laurana, are notable for their use of perspective.

Of special interest in the Neo-Classical **Duomo**, built in 1789, is the painting of the *Last Supper* by Federico Barocci (c.1535–1612). The **Museo Diocesano** contains a collection of ceramics, glass, and religious artifacts.

The **Casa Natale di Raffaello**, home of Urbino's famous son, the painter Raphael (1483– 1520), is also open to visitors.

🏛 **Palazzo Ducale**
Piazza Duca Federico 13. **Tel** 0722-32 26 25. **Open** 8:30am–7:15pm Tue– Sun, 8:30am–2pm Mon. **Closed** Jan 1, Dec 25. 🗓 🏠 🛇

🏛 **Casa Natale di Raffaello**
Via di Raffaello 57. **Tel** 0722-32 01 05. **Open** daily (Nov–Feb: am only). **Closed** Jan 1, Dec 25. 🗓

The Palazzo Ducale, rising above the rooftops of Urbino

View across the Bay of Naples to the slopes of Mount Vesuvius

㉕ Naples

🏠 1,100,000. ✈ Capodichino
4 km (2.5 miles) NW. 🚢 🚉 🚌
ℹ Piazza del Gesù (081-551 27 01).
🏛 daily. 🎭 Maggio dei Monumenti
(May), San Gennaro (Sep 19).

The chaotic yet spectacular city of Naples (Napoli) sprawls around the edge of a beautiful bay in the shadow of Mount Vesuvius.

Originally a Greek city named Neapolis, founded in 600 BC, Naples became an "allied city" of Rome two centuries later. It has since had many foreign rulers. The French House of Anjou controled Naples between 1266 and 1421, when power passed to Alfonso V of Aragón. A colony of Spain by 1503, in 1707 Naples was ceded to Austria, and in 1734 Charles III of Bourbon took over. In 1860, Naples became part of the new kingdom of Italy. The centuries of occupation

Tomb of King Ladislas of Naples in San Giovanni a Carbonara

have left Naples with a rich store of ancient ruins, churches, and palaces, many of which can be seen in the compact center of the old city. The **Museo Archeologico Nazionale** holds treasures from Pompeii and Herculaneum, including a bust of Seneca, fine glassware, frescoes, mosaics, and the fabulous Farnese Classical sculptures. Nearby, the church of **San Giovanni a Carbonara** houses some glorious medieval works of art, such as the tomb of King Ladislas of Naples (1386–1414). The French Gothic **Duomo** holds the relics of San Gennaro, martyred in 305 AD. Next to it is one of Italy's finest Renaissance gateways, the **Porta Capuana**, completed in 1490.

Also worth visiting, the **Monte della Misericordia**, a 17th-century octagonal church, houses Caravaggio's huge *Seven Acts of Mercy* (1607).

Central Naples is particularly rich in 14th- and 15th-century churches. **San Domenico Maggiore** contains some fine Renaissance sculpture while **Santa Chiara** houses the tombs of the Angevin monarchs and a museum whose exhibits include the ruins of a Roman bathhouse. Southeast Naples is home to the city's castles and the royal

palace of **Castel Nuovo**, built for Charles of Anjou in 1279–82. Another star sight, the **Palazzo Reale** was designed for the viceroy Ruiz de Castro, and has a superb library, richly adorned royal apartments, and a court theater. Begun in 1600, the palace was not completed until 1843.

The Palazzo Reale di Capodimonte, once a hunting lodge, now houses the **Museo di Capodimonte**, with its magnificent collection of Italian paintings, including works by Titian, Botticelli, and Raphael. This part of Naples is also known for its "Spanish Quarter," or **Quartieri Spagnoli**, a neighborhood of narrow, cobbled alleys often used to represent the archetypal Neapolitan street scene.

Environs

A trip by funicular railway up **Vomero** hill brings you to the **Certosa di San Martino**. This 14th-century charterhouse has been lavishly redecorated over the centuries. The Church and the Prior's Residence are particularly impressive. Just behind the Certosa lies the **Castel Sant Elmo**, which offers fine views.

Farnese Hercules, Museo Archeologico Nazionale

Boat excursions can be taken along the Posillipo coast, and to the islands of **Capri, Ischia**, and **Procida**. Inland, **Caserta** has its own **Palazzo Reale**, which boasts over 1,000 sumptuously decorated rooms. The town of **Santa Maria Capua Vetere** has a Roman amphitheater and a Mithraeum.

🏛 **Museo Archeologico Nazionale**
Piazza Museo Nazionale 19. **Tel** 081-44 22 149. Ⓜ Museo. **Open** Thu–Wed. **Closed** May 1, Dec 25. 📷

🏛 **Museo di Capodimonte**
Parco di Capodimonte. **Tel** 081-749 91 11. **Open** Thu–Tue. 📷 ♿

A breathtaking view of the steep village of Positano on the Amalfi Coast

㉖ Pompeii

Porta Marina. **Tel** 081-857 53 47.
Open daily. **Closed** Jan 1, May 1,
Dec 25.

Ancient Pompeii, destroyed
in AD 79 by an eruption of
Vesuvius, lay buried under rock
and ash until the 18th century.
When excavations began in
1748, a city frozen in time was
revealed. Many buildings
survived, some complete with
paintings and sculptures. The
villa of the wealthy patrician
Casii is known as House of the
Faun after its bronze statuette.
The House of the Vettii, named
after its owners, contains rich
wall decorations.

The original layout of the
city can be clearly seen. The
Forum was the center of public
life, with administrative and
religious institutions grouped
around it. Theaters, the
marketplace, temples, stores,
and even brothels can be
visited. Around 2,000 people
died at Pompeii and casts of
numerous recumbent figures
have been made.

Much of our knowledge of
the daily lives of the ancient
Romans has been derived from
the excavations at Pompeii and
nearby Herculaneum. The baths
were divided into separate
sections for men and women,
but the citizens of Pompeii were
not prudish – graphic frescoes
reveal the services offered by
male and female prostitutes in
the *lupanares*, or brothels.

Many works of art, domestic
items, and other artifacts were
preserved by the mud and ash
are on permanent display in
the Museo Archeologico
Nazionale in Naples.

㉗ Amalfi Coast

Amalfi. *i* Via delle
Repubbliche Marinare 19–21,
Amalfi (089-87 11 07).

The most enchanting and most
visited route in Campania skirts
the southern flank of Sorrento's
peninsula: the Amalfi Coast
(Costiera Amalfitana). Among
the popular pleasures here
are dining on locally caught
grilled fish and sipping icy
Lacrima Christi from Vesuvian
vineyards, interspersed with
beach-hopping.

From **Sorrento**, a well-
developed holiday resort, the
road winds down to **Positano**,
a village clambering down a
vertiginous slope to the sea.
Further on, **Praiano** is another
fashionable resort.

Amalfi – the coast's largest
town – was a maritime power
before it was subdued in 1131
by King Roger of Naples. Its
most illustrious citizens were
buried in the 13th-century
Chiostro del Paradiso, flanking
the 9th-century Duomo.
Above Amalfi, **Ravello** offers
peace and quiet and superb
views of the coast.

Sacrarium of the Lares, shrine of Pompeii's guardian deities

Sicily

Located at a crossroads in the Mediterranean, Sicily was a magnet for colonists and invaders from half the ancient civilized world. As Greek, Arab, and Norman conquerors came and went, they left behind a rich and varied cultural heritage. This has evolved into a colorful mixture of language, customs, and cuisine, and is reflected in the diverse art and architecture of the island. Sicily has magnificent beaches, remote hilltowns, flower-covered mountain ranges, and an active volcano whose lava flows over the centuries have created a fertile land of walnut trees, citrus groves, and vineyards.

Front facade of the Norman Duomo in Palermo

㉘ Palermo

700,000. Punta Raisi 32 km (20 miles) W. Via Maqueda 81 (091-662 82 91). Mon–Sat. U Festinu for Santa Rosalia (Jul 10–15).

Capital of Sicily and situated along the bay at the foot of Monte Pellegrino, Palermo was originally called Panormos, or "port" by the Phoenicians. A prosperous Roman town, Palermo's golden age came later, while under Arab domination. The Baroque period (17th–18th centuries) has also left a lasting mark on the city's civic and religious buildings.

Palermo suffered heavy bombardment by the Allies in World War II, but, despite chaotic rebuilding, the city remains an exotic mix of the oriental and the European.

The old Arab quarter can be found in North Palermo, typified by **Vucciria**, one of the city's lively markets. On Piazza Marina, the focal point of North Palermo, the Palazzo Abatellis houses the **Galleria Regionale di Sicilia**, which has a fine collection of sculptures, medieval crucifixes, frescoes, and paintings.

On the Piazza della Vittoria in South Palermo, the **Palazzo Reale** – a focus of power since Byzantine rule – is now home to Sicily's regional government. Its splendid **Cappella Palatina** is adorned with mosaics. The **Duomo**, founded in 1184, has a Catalan Gothic portico (1430) and a cupola in Baroque style.

The **Museo Regionale Salinas** is considered one of Italy's most important archaeology museums.

Galleria Regionale di Sicilia
Via Alloro 4. **Tel** 091-623 00 11. **Open** am daily, pm Tue–Thu.

Palazzo Reale & Cappella Palatina
Piazza Indipendenza. **Tel** 091-626 28 33. **Open** daily.

Museo Regionale Salinas
Piazza Olivella 24. **Tel** 091-611 68 05. **Open** Tue–Sun (am only Sat, Sun & hols).

Environs

A few miles inland from Palermo, the cathedral at **Monreale**, founded in 1172, is one of the great sights of Norman Sicily. The glittering mosaics and Saracenic-style cloisters, represent Norman artistry at its peak.

Monreale
Piazza Vittorio Emanuele. Cloister: **Tel** 091-640 44 13. **Open** daily (am only Sun & hols). for treasury & terrace.

㉙ Taormina

Messina. 10,000. Palazzo Corvaja, Piazza Santa Caterina (0942 232 43). Wed.

Sicily's most popular tourist resort has sandy beaches and numerous restaurants.

The most illustrious relic of the past is the 3rd-century BC **Theater**, begun by the Greeks, and rebuilt by the Romans. Among other Classical ruins are the **Odeon** (a musical theater) and the **Naumachia** (a man-made lake for mock battles).

The 14th-century **Palazzo Corvaia** and the 13th-century **Duomo**, renovated in 1636, are also worth visiting.

Taormina's Classical theater with Mount Etna in the background

Fishing boats moored in the picturesque harbor of Syracuse

⑩ Mount Etna

Catania. 🚃 to Linguaglossa or Randazzo; Circumetnea (095-541 250). 🚌 to Nicolosi. 🛈 Via G Garibaldi 63, Nicolosi (095-91 44 88).

One of the world's largest active volcanoes, Mount Etna was thought by the Romans to have been the forge of Vulcan, the god of fire. To view it in comfort, take the Circumetnea railway, which runs around the base from Catania to Riposto.

Now a protected area, about 58 sq km (22 sq miles) in size, Etna offers numerous opportunities for excursions. One of the most popular is from Zafferana to the Valle del Bove. Guided hikes can also be taken up to the large craters at the summit.

⑪ Syracuse

🏔 118,000. 🚢 🚍 🚃 🛈 Via Maestranza 33 (0931-464 255). 🛒 Wed.

The most important and powerful Greek city from 400 to 211 BC when it fell to the Romans, Syracuse (Siracusa in Italian) was also regarded as the most beautiful.

The peninsula of Ortigia is the hub of the old city. A highlight is the 18th-century **Duomo**. Its Baroque facade masks the **Temple of Athena** (5th century BC), which has been absorbed into it. Nearby is the **Palazzo Beneventano del Bosco** (1778–88) where

Admiral Nelson once stayed. At Ortigia's farthest point is the **Castello Maniace**, built by Frederick II around 1239, and the **Galleria Regionale di Palazzo Bellomo**, where Caravaggio's *Burial of St. Lucy* (1608) may be seen.

One of the most important examples of ancient theater architecture, the 5th-century BC **Greek Theater** has a 67-tier auditorium or *cavea*. The great Greek playwrights staged their works here.

At Tyche, north of Syracuse, the **Museo Archeologico Regionale Paolo Orsi** houses an important collection of artifacts excavated from local digs, which date from the Paleolithic to the Byzantine era.

🏛 Galleria Regionale di Palazzo Bellomo
Palazzo Bellomo, Via Capodieci 16. **Tel** 0931-695 11. **Open** Tue–Sat, Sun am.

🏛 Museo Archeologico Regionale Paolo Orsi
Viale Teocrito 66. **Tel** 0931-46 40 22. **Open** Tue–Sat, Sun am.

⑫ Agrigento

🏔 57,000. 🚢 🚍 🚃 🛈 Via Empedocle 73 (0922-203 91). 🛒 Fri.

Modern Agrigento occupies the site of Akragas, an important city of the ancient Greeks. Following the Roman conquest of 210 BC, Agrigento was renamed and successively occupied by Byzantines, Arabs,

and Normans. The historic medieval core of the city focuses on the Via Atenea. The 13th-century abbey complex of **Santo Spirito** houses stuccoes by Giacomo Serpotta (1695).

Environs
South of Agrigento, the **Valley of Temples** is the principal sacred site of ancient Akragas. The mainly 5th- and 6th-century ruins rank among the most impressive complexes of ancient Greek buildings outside Greece. **Museo Regionale Archeologico** houses outstanding artifacts from the temples and the city.

🏛 Museo Regionale Archeologico
Contrada San Nicola, Viale Panoramica. **Tel** 0922-62 16 11. **Open** daily. 🚶

The Temple of Concord (c.430 BC) in the Valley of Temples, Agrigento

Practical Information

Italy's charm and allure help to mask an idiosyncratic infrastructure in which delays and long lines are common. Be prepared to wait in offices and banks, and to persevere when seeking information. However, communications – other than the post office – are good, and banking and exchange facilities are widely available. Italy is generally safe for visitors and there is a visible police presence should a crisis arise. Personal belongings should nevertheless be watched at all times. Many shops and offices close at lunch for the siesta, reopening in the late afternoon. Pharmacies are a useful first stop for health advice.

When to Visit

Italy's towns and historic sites are extremely popular attractions and it is worth considering this when planning your trip. Rome, Florence, and Venice are all crowded from spring to October and it is advisable to reserve a hotel well in advance. In August the cities are generally slightly less busy, and the seaside resorts fill up. June and September can be as hot as midsummer, but the beaches are less crowded. The skiing season runs from December to Easter.

Tourist Information

The national tourist board, **ENIT**, has branches in capital cities worldwide and offers general information on Italy. Locally, there are two types of tourist office: an EPT *(Ente Provinciale di Turismo)* has information on its town and surrounding province, whereas an **APT** *(Azienda di Promozione Turistica)* deals exclusively with an individual town. Both can help with practical issues such as hotel reservations and local tour guides. They also provide free maps and guide-books in several languages.

Opening Hours

Italian museums are gradually conforming to new regulations, particularly in the north, opening daily from about 9am to 7pm, but some still close on Mondays. In summer, many museums stay open longer at weekends. In winter, opening times are more limited. It is advisable to check beforehand. Archaeological sites usually open from 9am to an hour before sunset, Tuesday to Sunday. Churches are open from about 7am to 12:30pm and 4 to 7pm, but they often prefer not to admit tourists during services.

Visits to some of the more popular tourist sights, such as Leonardo da Vinci's painting of *The Last Supper* in Milan, must be organized in advance.

Visa Requirements

Citizens of the European Union (EU), US, Canada, Australia, and New Zealand do not require a visa for stays of up to three months. Most European Union visitors need only a valid identity document to enter Italy. Citizens from other countries should contact their Italian consulate for visa information.

Personal Security

Although petty crime in the cities is frequent, violent crime in Italy is rare. However, it is common for people to raise their voices aggressively during an argument. Usually, remaining calm and being polite will help to defuse the situation. Unofficial tour guides, taxi drivers, or strangers who try to advise you on accommodations may expect money in return.

Women traveling alone in Italy are likely to meet with a lot of attention, although this is often more of an irritation than a danger. Staff at hotels and restaurants generally treat their single female customers with extra care and attention.

Police

There are several different police forces in Italy and each one fulfills a particular role. Both the state police, the *polizia* and the *carabinieri*, deal with crime in general and they also conduct random security checks. The *vigili urbani*, the municipal traffic police, issue fines for traffic and parking offences. If you have

The Climate of Italy

The Italian peninsula has a varied climate falling into three distinct geographical regions. Cold Alpine winters and warm, increasingly wet summers characterize the northern regions. In the extensive Po Valley, arid summers contrast with freezing, damp winters. The rest of Italy has long, and often very hot, summers and mild, sunny winters.

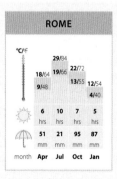

ROME			
°C/°F			
	29/84		
18/64	19/66	22/72	
9/48		13/55	12/54
			4/40
6 hrs	10 hrs	7 hrs	5 hrs
51 mm	21 mm	95 mm	87 mm
month Apr	Jul	Oct	Jan

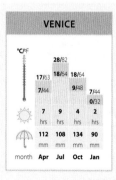

VENICE			
°C/°F			
	28/82		
17/63	18/64	18/64	
7/44		9/48	7/44
			0/32
7 hrs	9 hrs	4 hrs	2 hrs
112 mm	108 mm	134 mm	90 mm
month Apr	Jul	Oct	Jan

anything stolen, you should go to the nearest police station and file a report (denuncia).

Emergency Services

In case of emergencies while on vacation, the appropriate numbers to call are listed in the directory below.

Health Issues

No inoculations are needed for Italy, but it is advisable to carry mosquito repellent in the summer months. If emergency medical treatment becomes necessary, you should go to the Pronto Soccorso (emergency room) of the nearest hospital.

Various medical products, including homeopathic medicines, are available in any pharmacy (farmacia), but a prescription may be required. Thanks to a night rota (servizio notturno) – listed in the local pages of daily newspapers and on pharmacy doors – there is always a pharmacy open in all cities and most towns.

Language and Etiquette

People in Italy are very dress-conscious and unusual or risqué clothes get noticed. Strict dress codes are enforced in many places of worship, where your torso, knees, and upper arms should be covered. Forms of address are still governed by traditional social formalities. Ciao should only be used as a greeting for familiar friends, otherwise piacere (pleased to meet you), buon giorno (good day), or buona sera (good evening) are polite greetings. Say arrivederci on parting. Kissing on the cheeks is common among friends, but shake hands with strangers.

Tipping of taxi drivers and waiting staff in restaurants is not common practice among Italians. However, when a service charge is added to a restaurant bill, it is non-negotiable. Hotel porters expect a reasonable tip if they have been helpful.

Facilities for the Disabled

Public awareness of the needs of the disabled is improving quickly in Italy. CO.IN.Sociale (Consorzio Cooperative Integrate) provides information on facilities for the disabled.

Banking and Currency

Italy has used the euro since 2002 (see p23). Banks open between about 8:30am and 1:30pm Monday to Friday. Most also open from 2:15 to 3pm or 2:30 to 3:30pm.

Electronic exchange machines, with multilingual instructions, are located at all major airports, train stations, and banks. Bureaux de change can be found in main towns, and are usually open all day, and also into the evening in resorts. However, they quite often tend to have less favorable exchange rates and charge a higher commission than banks. Post offices usually have the lowest charges.

Communications

Post offices open from about 8am to 2pm weekdays, and from 8am to noon on Saturday. Main post offices are usually open from 8am to 6pm or 7pm non-stop. The red mailboxes (blue in the Vatican City) usually have two slots labeled per la città (for the city only) and tutte le altre destinazioni (for all other destinations). The Italian postal service was once renowned for its unreliability, but has improved in recent years. The standard mail service is called prioritaria.

The few public telephones remaining are generally card-operated. A telephone card (scheda telefonica) can be purchased from bars, newspaper kiosks, post offices, and tobacconists (tabacchi). A corner of the card must be broken off before use. Alternatively, many towns have telephone offices (Telefoni) with low rates for long-distance calls. Here, you are assigned a booth and pay after calls are completed. Credit cards can only be used to make calls at major airports.

DIRECTORY

Tourist Offices

APT Florence
Via Cavour 1R.
Tel 055-29 08 32.

APT Milan
Piazza Duomo 19A.
Tel 02-77 40 43 43.

APT Rome
Via Parigi 5.
Tel 06-488 992 12.

APT Venice
Castello 5050.
Tel 041-529 87 11.

ENIT Rome
Via Marghera 2.
Tel 06-497 11. **W** enit.it

ENIT UK
Tel 020-7408 1254.
W italiantouristboard.
co.uk

ENIT US
Tel 212-245 5618.
W italiantourism.com

Embassies

Australia
Via A. Bosio 5, Rome.
Tel 06-85 27 21.
W italy.embassy.gov.au

Canada
Via Zara 30, Rome.
Tel 06-854 44 39 37.
W canada.it

UK
Via XX Settembre 80,
Rome. **Tel** 06-42 20 00 01.
W gov.uk/government/
world/organisations/
british-embassy-rome

US
Via Veneto 121, Rome. **Tel** 06-467 41. **W** usembassy.it

Emergency Numbers

General Emergency
Tel 113.

Medical Emergency
Tel 118.

Police (Carabinieri)
Tel 112.

Facilities for the Disabled

CO.IN.Sociale
Via Enrico Giglioli 54A,
Rome. **Tel** 06-712 9011.
W coinsociale.it

Travel Information

Italy has transportation systems of varying efficiency, from the modern road, bus, and rail networks of the north to the slower and more antiquated systems of the south. Numerous airlines operate flights to the country's major airports. Highways are good, but busy at weekends and peak periods, and delays are common at Alpine passes. Train travel is inexpensive and services generally frequent, although they can be overcrowded during local holidays. The major Italian cities have a number of transportation options and that most suited to the tourist varies from place to place: the bus is more practical in Rome and the metro in Milan.

Flying to Italy

Flight destinations and routes change frequently, but **United Airlines**, **Delta**, and **American Airlines** all operate regular flights to Italy from the United States. **Air Canada** flies from several Canadian airports, and **Qantas** has flights from various Australian airports to Rome.

Alitalia offers regular services to the United States and Europe. It may be more convenient and less expensive for long-haul passengers to take a budget flight to London, Frankfurt, Paris, or Amsterdam before continuing their journey to Italy from there. **Meridiana** also has direct flights to Italy from New York.

Low-cost airlines **easyJet** and **Ryanair** offer flights from various UK airports to numerous Italian destinations according to the season.

Rome's Leonardo da Vinci (Fiumicino) and Milan's Malpensa are the key airports for long-haul flights into Italy. Milan's Linate airport handles European flights.

Charters and Package Deals

Package holidays to Italy are usually less costly than traveling independently, unless you are on a tight budget and are prepared to make use of youth hostels and campsites. Rome, Florence, and Venice are often offered as separate or linked package deals, and many operators have packages to Tuscany and Umbria, the Lakes, the Riviera, Naples,

Sicily, and the Amalfi Coast. Several firms organize fly-drive packages. In winter, ski packages to many Alpine resorts are available. Specialty walking, gastronomy, and art tours are increasingly common.

Domestic Flights

Alitalia, **Air One**, and Ryanair run regular services between many Italian cities. Long-haul passengers can transfer to domestic flights in Rome and Milan.

As internal flights can be expensive, and busy at peak periods, trains are a good alternative. Flights to airports in the north can be disrupted by fog in the winter.

Traveling in Cities

Milan and Rome both have a metro system known as *la metropolitana* (*metro* for short). Rome's network amounts to just two lines – A and B – which converge at Stazione Termini, the city's central train station. Several stations are useful for key sights, but the system is designed for commuters and carriages are usually stiflingly hot in summer. A third metro line is under construction, with the first stretch open in 2014.

Milan has three principal lines – MM1 (the red line), MM2 (green), and MM3 (yellow) – that give easy access to the city's main sights.

Cars are a liability in all city centers and many have a large limited-traffic zone. Walking is

usually the easiest and most enjoyable way to negotiate the narrow streets of historic town centers. Trams still run in some cities such as Milan and Rome. Taxis must be met at official taxi stands or reserved by telephone; in theory, you cannot hail a taxi in the street.

Most Italian cities and towns have a bus system which is inexpensive, comprehensive, and as efficient as traffic will allow. Bus stops are known as *fermate*, and buses *(autobus)* usually run from about 6am to midnight. Train stations are invariably linked to the city centers by shuttle buses. Tickets *(biglietti)* must usually be bought before boarding the bus, and are available from kiosks, bars, and *tabacchi* (tobacconists). Buses are boarded via the front and rear doors and exited via the central doors. Tickets are validated by being punched in machines on board.

Getting around Venice

The water buses *(vaporetti)* are an entertaining form of public transportation in Venice, although most journeys within the city can easily be covered on foot. The main route for the water buses is the Grand Canal. They also link the city to the islands in the lagoon. Tickets can be purchased from kiosks at each stop, and the main routes run every 10 to 20 minutes until early evening. For general inquiries, contact the **ACTV Information Office**.

Gondolas are a luxury form of transportation. Sharing can make it cheaper. Before boarding, agree on a price with the gondolier. *Traghetti* (gondola ferries), on the other hand, are an inexpensive, convenient way of crossing the Grand Canal.

For those with sufficient funds, the most practical means of traveling around Venice is by water taxi. These motorboats run from 16 water taxi ranks and can reach the airport in 20 minutes. Extra charges are made for luggage, waiting, night service, and calling out a taxi.

Rail Travel

The bulk of Italy's rail network is an integrated partially privatized system operated by the **Ferrovie dello Stato** (FS). In addition, the railway company **Italo** operates fast trains on the Milan–Rome–Naples line. Train journeys into Italy from other parts of Europe wind through the Alps and are an exciting way to travel. **Alta Velocità** (high-speed trains) and **Eurostar** require pre-booking of seats. These and intercity (IC) trains only stop at main stations and require the payment of a supplement (*supplemento*). *Regionale* trains make more stops and require no supplement.

The most useful pass for visitors is the Interrail One Country, which gives unlimited travel for 3–8 consecutive or non-consecutive days over a one-month period, with special rates for those under 26. This pass can be purchased at most mainline stations and various agencies outside Italy. It is available only to non-residents.

Before traveling, all tickets need to be validated in one of the yellow machines found on the platform.

Traveling by Bus

Long-distance buses (*pullman* or *corriere*) operate between towns and can be less expensive and more frequent than the trains. Tickets can be purchased on board, and services usually depart from a town's train station or main square. Buses in some areas may be run by several companies (*see Directory below*).

Traveling by Road

A car is invaluable for touring the Italian countryside. Drivers should take into account high gas (*benzina*) prices, the difficulty of parking in towns, and the Italians' often erratic approach to driving. Italy has a good network of highways, but most have tollbooths, often leading to congestion. Care should be taken at night when many traffic lights switch to flashing amber. Car theft is rife in Italy and valuables should not be left unattended.

Car rental (*autonoleggio*) is expensive in Italy, and should be organized beforehand through fly-drive deals or pre-booked with firms that have branches in Italy. Local firms may be less expensive than the international firms. Most airports have rental offices on site (*see Directory below*). Visitors from outside the EU need an international license, but in practice not all rental firms insist on this.

Ferry Services

Italy's large number of off-shore islands means that it has a well-developed network of ferries. Boats of various kinds also operate on the Italian Lakes.

Ferries depart for Sicily from Naples and Reggio di Calabria. They also run from the mainland and from Sicily to surrounding islands and archipelagoes, for example from Naples to Capri and Ischia. Boats for Sardinia leave from Civitavecchia near Rome, Livorno, and Genoa. There are car ferry services from Brindisi to Corfu and Patras in Greece. In summer, these ferries can get very crowded, so make sure you reserve well in advance.

DIRECTORY

Airlines

Air Canada
Tel 1-888 247 2262 (Canada).
[w] aircanada.com

Air One
Tel 89-24 44.
Tel +39 (091) 255 10 47 (from abroad).
[w] flyairone.it

Alitalia
Tel 06-22 22.
Tel 800-223 5730 (US).
Tel 08714 241 424 (UK).
[w] alitalia.com

American Airlines
Tel 199-257 300.
Tel 800-433 7300 (US).
[w] aa.com

British Airways
Tel 02-69 63 36 02.
Tel 0844-493 0787 (UK).
[w] ba.com

Delta
Tel 02-38 59 10 87.
Tel 800-221 1212 (US).
[w] delta.com

easyJet
[w] easyjet.com

Meridiana
Tel 89 29 28.
[w] meridiana.it

Qantas
Tel 02-91 29 48 01.
Tel 13 13 13 (Australia).
[w] qantas.com

Ryanair
[w] ryanair.com

United Airlines
Tel 02-69 63 37 07.
Tel 1-800-864 83 31 (US).
[w] united.com

Getting around Venice

ACTV Information Office
Piazzale Roma, Venice.

Tel 041-24 24.
[w] actv.it

Consorzio Motoscafi Rialto (Water Taxis)
Tel 041-522 23 03.

Rail Travel

Alta Velocità
See Ferrovie dello Stato.

Eurostar
[w] raileurope.com (US).
[w] eurostar.com (UK).

Ferrovie dello Stato
Tel 89-20 21.
[w] trenitalia.com

Italo
Tel 06-0708.
[w] italotreno.it

Bus Companies

Cotral
Tel 800-17 44 71 (Rome).
[w] cotralspa.it

Lazzi
Tel 0573-193 79 00 (Florence). [w] lazzi.it

Sita
Tel 055-47 821.
[w] sitabus.it

Car Rental

Avis
Tel 199-10 01 33.
[w] avisautonoleggio.it

Europcar
Tel 199-30 70 30.
[w] europcar.it

Hertz
Tel 199-11 22 11.
[w] hertz.it

Maggiore
Tel 199-15 11 20 (Rome).
[w] maggiore.it

Sixt
Tel 06-65 21 11.
[w] sixt.it

Shopping

Italy is known for its quality designer goods, ranging from chic clothing and sleek cars to stylish household items. There is a strong tradition of craftsmanship, often from family-run businesses, and there are numerous markets selling regional specialties. Apart from the town markets, it is not a country for bargains, but the joys of window-shopping will offer plenty of compensation.

Opening Hours

Opening times for shops are usually 9:30am–1pm, and 3:30 or 5–8pm. In many places, stores are traditionally closed on Monday mornings, but shopkeepers are increasingly working more flexible hours.

Department Stores

Department stores are often open without a lunchbreak (*orario continuato*) from 9am until 8pm Monday to Saturday. **La Rinascente** stores are good for ready-to-wear clothes, haberdashery, and perfumes.

Designer Fashion

Italy is famous worldwide for its fashion industry. Milan, its designer capital, is stormed each year by Italians and foreigners alike in search of the latest catwalk novelty. **Giò Moretti**, in Via della Spiga, features articles by the top names, as well as pieces by up-and-coming designers.

Retail outlets of famous designers can be found in most Italian city centers. In Venice, **Armani** and others have stylish shops just off the Piazza San Marco. Rome's most famous designer is **Valentino**. His and other top fashion names dominate Rome's Via Condotti, Via de'Tornabuoni in Florence, and the Chiaia district of Naples.

Clothing Stores

Less expensive clothes are available in high-street stores, where the styles tend to be more conventional and classical. Sales (*saldi*), are held during summer and winter. The rare secondhand shops may seem expensive, but the quality of the clothes is good.

Jewelry

Glitzy gold jewelry is very popular in Italy and every *gioielleria* (jewelry shop) will offer a wide selection of items. Elegant, classic jewelry can be purchased at **Cusi** in Milan, while Venice's smartest jewelers are **Missiaglia** and **Nardi** in Piazza San Marco. **Bulgari**, known for its beautiful jewelry and watches, has a number of retail outlets, as does **Buccellati**, famous for its delicately engraved designs inspired by the Italian Renaissance. For reasonably priced jewelry try **Gioie** in Rome. Naples has several jewelers', and goldsmiths' shops where traditional engraving and cameo work can still be seen. Unusual and original items can often be found in artisan shops (*oreficeria*).

Accessories

Stylish Italian leather shoes and handbags have an international market, and are a popular purchase of visitors to all parts of the country. **Ferragamo**, the well-known Italian designer, has stores in most Italian cities, offering elegant, classic shoes. Leather bags and luggage are available at **Gatti Francesco**, and **Mandarina Duck** bags are sold in boutiques throughout Italy. **Ottica Nuova di Malizia Michela** sells trendy sunglasses, and **Borsalino** is the place for top-quality classic hats.

One-off pieces by local designers can also be found. In Naples, **Marinella** has a store selling her famous ties worn by many celebrities.

Household Items

Household stores in cities and towns throughout the country sell the well-designed utensils for which Italy is famous. Stainless steel and copper kitchenware is a favorite buy with visitors.

Regional Crafts

Traditional crafts are still practised in Italy and range from delicate lacework and glassware in Venice to leatherwork, jewelry, and marbled paper in Florence. Elaborate Tuscan pottery, hand-painted dishes from around Amalfi, and De Simone's stylized designer plates from Sicily are among many ceramic styles available.

Among the best craft workshops in Rome is **Spazio Artigiano**, which specializes in original, handmade wood, glass, and terra-cotta items. Naples' **Il Cantuccio della Ceramica** is the place to go for ceramics.

In Venice, the best place to buy local blue- and claret-colored glass is the island of Murano. Here, **Barovier e Toso** produces original designs. Some of the most expensive glass in Venice can be bought from **Venini**. Carnival masks, available from **Tragicomica**, and traditional Burano lace are also popular buys.

The Etruscan art of working alabaster is best seen in Volterra. Handmade perfumes and toiletries, and hand-painted majolica are favorite purchases in Tuscany. Sicily is well known for its ceramics, and for traditional puppets. The latter, now rare, can still be found in antique shops.

Gourmet Foods

Many of Italy's regional food specialties are world-famous: Parma ham, Chianti wine, olive oil, and grappa. Regional sweets, including Sienese *panforte* and Sicilian marzipan, are also well-known, as are cheeses such as Gorgonzola from Lombardy and Parmesan from Emilia-Romagna. Other delicacies include truffles from Piedmont and Umbria. The Lombardy region produces the famous *panettone* cake, and *amaretto* biscuits are made in the Veneto. *Vesuvio* chocolate with rum from Naples is also delicious. To make the most of Italian food, try to buy what is in season. Mushrooms and grapes are best in the fall, whereas spring is the season for asparagus, strawberries, and artichokes. In winter, cauliflower and broccoli are at their best, as are lemons from Amalfi and Sicilian blood oranges. Summer is the time for plums, pears, and cherries, as well as zucchini, eggplant, tomatoes, and melon.

Food Stores

Specialty stores are the most interesting way to shop for food in Italy. A *fornaio* has the best bread and a *macellaio* has the finest meat (go to a *norcineria* for pork products). Vegetables are freshest from market stands or the *fruttivendolo*. You can buy cakes at the *pasticceria*, milk at the *latteria*, and pasta, ham, and cheese at the well-stocked *alimentari* and delicatessens.

To buy wine, head for the *enoteca, vineria,* or *vinaio*, where you can sometimes taste the products first. Italy is a major wine producer and stores stock a wide range of labels, from the prized Barolo and Barbaresco vintages to the inexpensive but palatable local *vino da tavola*.

Markets

All Italian towns have at least one market a week. Large towns have small, daily markets in addition to a weekly flea market, usually held on a Sunday. Traders set up early and usually start to clear away at about 1:30pm. Bargaining is not usual when buying food, but it is worth asking for a discount *(sconto)* for clothes and other items.

Larger markets have stands piled high with secondhand clothes, and many markets sell fake Ray-Ban sunglasses, Lacoste T-shirts, and Levi's jeans. Popular gifts from Italy include the ceramics and wooden kitchen items sold in most markets.

Specialty markets can be found in many cities. Milan's antique market, the Mercatone dell'Antiquariato, is held on the last Sunday of the month, and the Via Sannio and Porta Portese markets of Rome are a mecca for secondhand clothes. The fish market by the Rialto Bridge in Venice is an interesting place to visit.

DIRECTORY

Department Stores

La Rinascente
Galleria Alberto Sordi,
Piazza Colonna, Rome.
Tel 06-678 42 09.
Piazza Fiume, Rome.
Tel 06-884 12 31.
Piazza della Repubblica 1,
Florence.
Tel 055-21 91 13.
Piazza Duomo, Milan.
Tel 02-885 21.

Designer Fashion

Armani
Via Condotti 77, Rome.
Tel 06-699 14 60.
Via de Tornabuoni 48r,
Florence.
Tel 055-21 96 90.
Via Manzoni 31, Milan.
Tel 02-7231 86 00.
Piazza Martiri 61, Naples.
Tel 081-42 58 16.

Giò Moretti
Via della Spiga 4, Milan.
Tel 02-76 00 31 86.

Valentino
Via Montenapoleone 20,
Milan. **Tel** 02-276 006 182.
Via dei Tosinghi 52r,
Florence.
Tel 055-29 31 42.

Jewelry

Buccellati
Mercerie dell'Orologio
214, Venice.
Tel 041-522 65 40.
Ponte Vecchio 20,
Florence.
Tel 055-21 55 02.
Via Montenapoleone 23,
Milan. **Tel** 02-79 50 59.

Bulgari
Via Condotti 10, Rome.
Tel 06-679 38 76.
Via della Spiga 6, Milan.
Tel 02-76 01 34 48.

Cusi
Corso Monforte 23, Milan.
Tel 02-76 28 12 93.

Gioie
Via di Grotta Rossa 126,
Rome. **Tel** 06-33 26 03 51.

Missiaglia
Procuratie Vecchie, Piazza
San Marco 125, Venice.
Tel 041-522 44 64.

Nardi
Procuratie Nuove, Piazza
San Marco 69, Venice.
Tel 041-522 57 33.

Accessories

Borsalino
Piazza del Popolo 20,
Rome. **Tel** 06-32 65 08 38.
Galleria Vittorio Emanuele
II 92, Milan.
Tel 02-890 15 436.

Ferragamo
Via Condotti 65, Rome.
Tel 06-678 11 30.
Via de' Tornabuoni 16r,
Florence.
Tel 055-29 21 23.
Via Montenapoleone 3,
Milan. **Tel** 02-76 00 66 60.

Gatti Francesco
Via di Propaganda 19,
Rome. **Tel** 06-679 39 58.

Mandarina Duck
Via dei due Macelli 59,
Rome. **Tel** 06-67 86 414.

Marinella
Riviera di Chiaia 287A,
Naples. **Tel** 081-245 11 82.

Ottica Nuova di Malizia Michela
Via P. Rossi 38, Milan.
Tel 02-648 03 10.

Regional Crafts

Barovier e Toso
Fondamenta Vetrai 28,
Murano. **Tel** 041-73 90 49.

Il Cantuccio della Ceramica
Via Benedetto Croce 38,
Naples. **Tel** 081-552 58 57.

Spazio Artigiano
Vicolo dei Serpenti 13,
Rome. **Tel** 06-47 82 48 60.

Tragicomica
Calle dei Nomboli,
San Polo 2800, Venice.
Tel 041-72 11 02.

Venini
Piazzetta dei Leoncini,
San Marco 314, Venice.
Tel 041-522 40 45.

Entertainment

With world-class sporting and a host of cultural events, Italy has something to offer everyone. The cities boast a varied and lively nightlife, while its Riviera resorts, hill villages, and classical sites are ideal for the avid sightseer or walker. Skiing in the Alps, water sports of all kinds on the coast, and pony trekking in the countryside, are tourist favorites. The open-air theater and music performances in summer are world-famous. Or simply join the Italians in their traditional evening stroll, the *passeggiata*, followed by a drink at a bar or café in a picturesque piazza.

Entertainment Listings

Information about what's on in Rome can be found in *Trovaroma*, the weekly Thursday supplement to the *La Repubblica* newspaper. *Where Rome* magazine, available for free in hotels, has up-to-date entertainment listings.

In Florence, the monthly magazine *Firenze Spettacolo* has restaurant and café guides, as well as details of concerts, exhibitions, and sporting events. *Milano Mese* is a free brochure listing concerts and other cultural events held in and around the city.

Un Ospite di Venezia (A Guest in Venice), produced by the Hotels' Association, comes out fortnightly in summer and monthly in winter and is free.

If you can read Italian, regional newspapers are also a good source of information about current events. Local tourist offices display posters advertising forthcoming events.

Tickets

Making advance reservations for concerts is not the custom in Italy, where decisions are often made on the spur of the moment. To guarantee a seat you may have to visit the box office in person, although online agencies such as **Ticketone** (www.ticketone.it) and **Listicket** (www.listicket.it) sell tickets for many events. You may have to pay an advance booking supplement, or *prevendita*, which is generally about 10 percent of the ticket price.

Tickets for popular music concerts are normally sold through record and music shops, whose names are displayed on the publicity material distributed.

Whereas tickets for classical concerts are sold on the spot for same-day performances, opera tickets are purchased months in advance. Prices vary significantly according to the artists scheduled to perform and the type of venue.

Entertainment Venues

Rome's city churches and the **Parco della Musica** are favorite venues for classical music lovers. Venice also makes good use of its most magnificent churches as concert halls. **La Pietà** was Vivaldi's own church and is still used for classical music performances. In Milan, by contrast, the **San Siro** football stadium is often used as a concert venue along with the 5,400-capacity **Pala AJ**.

Open-Air Venues

During the summer, Italy's historic buildings and classical ruins become dramatic settings for open-air events. Concerts are held in the grounds of Rome's Villa Celimontana and Villa Ada, while Greek and Roman plays are staged in the restored theater of **Ostia Antica**, southwest of Rome.

In Venice the gardens of the Baroque palace, **Ca'Rezzonico**, and the ornate, enclosed courtyard of the Doge's Palace *(see pp418–19)* are used as outdoor concert venues. The 1st-century Teatro Romano *(see pp412–13)* in Verona also stages open-air concerts.

Opera

Opera is one of the great cultural delights of Italy, whether experienced in the magnificent opera houses of **La Scala** in Milan or Venice's **Teatro La Fenice**, or in a spectacular open-air venue like Verona's superb **Arena**. The opera house of Naples, **San Carlo**, also boasts world-class performers. Rome's **Teatro dell'Opera** has a late winter season and an open-air summer festival in the Terme di Caracalla archaeological park.

The opera season at the Verona Arena runs from the first week in July until the beginning of September, and every year features a lavish production of Verdi's *Aida*.

Clubs and Discos

Cities and resorts in Italy are packed with trendy discos, and upscale night-clubs. **Gilda**, with its two elegant restaurants and large dancefloor, is a favorite with Rome's jet set. A younger crowd frequents **Goa**. In the summer months, the nightlife shifts to the Roman seaside resort of Fregene.

Currently attracting the fashion crowd of Milan is the **Hollywood** club. Venice's historic casino **Casinò di Venezia** draws well-dressed gamblers from far and wide. There are a number of discos at Mestre on the mainland.

Italian Festivals

The distinctive regionalism which has survived in modern Italy is marked by the diverse local festivals celebrated each year. For example, on April 25, Venetians commemorate St. Mark with a gondola race, and on June 24, Florence relives its past with a procession of people in 16th-century costumes. The Sienese celebrate the Palio – a bareback horse race dating from 1283 – on July 2 and August 16 each year. Traditional dress is worn in the processions and pre-race pageants. Other *festas* celebrate the harvesting of local produce: the wine festivals held in September and October in Chianti, Tuscany, and the Castelli Romani south of Rome, are popular with visitors.

Many events have an international flavor, such as the film festivals held in Venice (Aug–Sep), Taormina, (Jul–Aug), and Rome (Oct). From May to June, Florence hosts an arts festival and Syracuse celebrates Greek drama. Ravello, near Naples, hosts an international festival of music each May.

Masked Venetians spill onto the streets during Carnival in February, and on summer evenings throughout Italy, tourists can join in street dancing at local *festas*.

Special Interest Vacations

Culinary holidays run by English-speaking experts in Italian cooking are very popular.

Tasting Places, for example, organizes wine tours and week-long courses in Italian cuisine. The course locations include the Veneto, Sicily, Tuscany, and Umbria.

The **Società Dante Alighieri** provides courses in the Italian language, literature, history of art, and culture. There are both full- and part-time courses available, for every level of ability.

The **Gruppo Archeologico Romano** runs digs in various regions. There are summer and winter trips for both adults and children.

For those with an interest in more energetic activities, the **Federazione Arrampicata Sportiva Italiana** has a list of mountain-climbing schools that organize climbs for people of all abilities. Ski holidays are best arranged with agents offering package deals. Trekking excursions can be organized with **Club Alpino Italiano (CAI)**. Nature walks and bird-watching

trips are run by the **Italian Birds Protection League (LIPU)**. Cyclists will find miles of flat and scenic cycling routes in the Po Delta.

Water Sports

Most lakeside towns and many seaside resorts in Italy rent out sailboats, canoes, and windsurfing equipment and lessons are often available. Longer courses in a variety of water sports are organized by clubs, which usually require membership.

The **Federazione Italiana Attività Subacquee** runs underwater diving courses. Most travel agents have a selection of sailing vacations.

Swimming pools are expensive in Italy, but it is cheaper if you pay for a certain number of sessions or for a short membership. Water parks are popular and provide pools, slides, wave machines, and games.

DIRECTORY

Entertainment Venues

Ca'Rezzonico
Fondamenta Rezzonico 3136, Venice.
Tel 041-241 01 00.

La Pietà
Calle della Pietà, Venice.
Tel 041-522 21 71.

Ostia Antica
Viale dei Romagnoli 717, Rome. **Tel** 06-56 35 02 15.

Pala AJ
Piazza Stuparich 1, Milan.

Parco della Musica
Viale de Coubertin, Rome.
Tel 06-80 24 11.

San Siro
Piazzale Angelo Moratti, Milan. **Tel** 02-48 79 82 01.

Opera

Teatro alla Scala
Via Filodrammatici 2, Milan. **Tel** 02-86 07 75.
W teatroallascala.org

Teatro dell'Opera
Piazza Beniamino Gigli 7, Rome. **Tel** 06-48 16 01.
W operaroma.it

Teatro La Fenice
San Marco Campo, San Fantin 1965, Venice.
Tel 041-78 65 11.

Teatro San Carlo
Via San Carlo 98/f, Naples.
Tel 081-797 21 11.

Verona Arena
Via Dietro Anfiteatro 6/b, Verona. **Tel** 045-800 51 51.

Clubs and Discos

Casinò di Venezia
Calle Vendramin, Cannaregio 2040.
Tel 041-529 71 11.

Gilda
Via Mario de' Fiori 97, Rome. **Tel** 06-67 84 838.

Goa
Via Libetta 13, Rome.
Tel 06-574 82 77.

Hollywood
Corso Como 15, Milan.
Tel 02-659 89 96.

Pala AJ
Piazza Carlo Stuparich 1, Milan.

Special Interest Vacations

Club Alpino Italiano
Via Galvani 10, 00153 Rome.
Tel 06-57 28 71 43.
W cairoma.it

Federazione Arrampicata Sportiva Italiana
Via del Terrapieno 27, Bologna.
Tel 051-601 48 90.
W federclimb.it

Gruppo Archeologico Romano
Via Baldo degli Ubaldi 168, Rome.
Tel 06-638 52 56.
W gruppo archeologico.it

Italian Birds Protection League
Via Trento 49, 43100 Parma.
Tel 0521-27 30 43.
W lipu.it

Società Dante Alighieri
Piazza Firenze 27, 00186 Rome.
Tel 06-687 36 94.
W ladante.it

Tasting Places
PO Box 38174, London W10 5ZP, England.
Tel 0208-964 5333.
W tastingplaces.com

Water Sports

Federazione Italiana Attività Subacquee
Via A. Dona 8, 20124 Milan.
Tel 02-670 50 05.
W fias.it

Where to Stay

Rome

Around Piazza Navona

Sole al Biscione   €
Historic
Via del Biscione 76, 00186
Tel 06-688 068 73
🆆 solealbiscione.it
This basic but charming hotel
claims to be the oldest in Rome.
It also allows pets. Free Wi-Fi.

Teatro di Pompeo   €€
Historic   **Map** C3
Largo del Pallaro 8, 00186
Tel 06-683 001 70
🆆 hotelteatrodipompeo.it
Built on the ruins of Pompeii's
ancient theater, this hotel has
simple rooms and friendly staff.

Grand Hotel de La Minerve €€€
Luxury   **Map** C3
Piazza della Minerva 69, 00186
Tel 06-695 201
🆆 grandhoteldelaminerve.com
Excellent views from nearly every
room. The decor is luxurious, and
the service is excellent.

Northeast Rome

DK Choice

Hassler   €€€
Luxury   **Map** D2
Piazza Trinità dei Monti 6, 00187
Tel 06-699 340
🆆 hotelhasslerroma.com
The discreet service, plush
furnishings, and stunning
rooms make the Hassler a
favorite with celebrities. Guests
can dine at the Michelin-starred
Imàgora restaurant or enjoy a
cocktail in the Hassler Bar.

The Vatican and Trastevere

Hotel Ottaviano   €
Budget
Via Ottaviano 6, 00192
Tel 06-397 381 38
🆆 pensioneottaviano.com
Located close to the Vatican
Museums, this affordable hotel
is a backpacker's paradise.

Hotel Trastevere   €
Budget   **Map** C3
Via Luciano Manara 24, 00153
Tel 06-581 47 13
🆆 hoteltrastevere.net
Simple, clean, and large rooms are
available at this hotel, which also
offers a good breakfast spread.

Arco del Lauro   €€
B&B
Via dell'Arco de' Tolomei 27, 00153
Tel 06-978 403 50
🆆 arcodellauro.it
This tiny hotel in a picturesque
medieval location offers simple
but lovely rooms.

Aventine and Lateran

Domus Aventina   €€
Modern   **Map** D4
Via di Santa Prisca 11b, 00153
Tel 06-574 61 35
🆆 hoteldomusaventina.com
A well-located hotel, with many
attractions within walking
distance. Quiet and simple rooms
open onto a lush courtyard.

San Anselmo   €€
Boutique   **Map** D4
Piazza San Anselmo 2, 00153
Tel 06-570 057
🆆 aventinohotels.com
Four-poster beds and clawfoot
tubs are available at this tasteful
hotel that is close to many sights.

Florence

Residenza Johanna   €
Pensione
Via Bonifacio Lupo 14, 50129
Tel 055-481 896
🆆 johanna.it
This tiny and charming hotel is
fantastic value. Free parking.

Antica Dimora Firenze   €€
B&B
Via San Gallo 72/r, 50129
Tel 055-462 72 96
🆆 johanna.it
Canopy beds, antique furniture,
and terracotta floors set this B&B
apart. Laptops and free Wi-Fi.

Relais Il Campanile   €€
B&B
Via Ricasoli 10, 50125
Tel 055-211 688
🆆 relaiscampanile.it
Quaint rooms with wrought-iron
features in a 17th-century palazzo.

DK Choice

Relais Uffizi   €€
Historic
Chiasso del Buco 16, 50122
Tel 055-267 62 39
🆆 relaisuffizi.it
Situated behind the Piazza
della Signoria, the Relais Uffizi
is housed in a restored 16th-
century palace. The rooms are
large, bright, and charmingly
decorated. A buffet breakfast is
served in a room overlooking
the piazza. Pets are welcome.

Brunelleschi   €€€
Historic
Piazza Sant'Elisabetta 3, 50122
Tel 055-273 70
🆆 hotelbrunelleschi.it
Housed in a Byzantine tower, the
Brunelleschi has opulent rooms.

Grand Hotel Minerva   €€€
Historic
Piazza di Santa Maria Novella 16,
50123
Tel 055-272 30
🆆 grandhotelminerva.com
A panoramic terrace with a pool
gives a modern touch to one of
the city's oldest hotels.

Plush furnishings in the Grand Hotel de La Minerve, Rome

Antiques and gilt mirrors adorn the rooms at Palazzo Abadessa, Venice

Venice

CANNAREGIO:
Palazzo Abadessa €€
Historic **Map** C2
Calle Priuli 4011, 30131
Tel 041-241 37 84
🅦 abadessa.com
A charming 16th-century palace
with antiques in its large rooms.

CASTELLO: Pensione Wildner €€
Pensione **Map** F4
Riva degli Schiavoni 4161, 30122
Tel 041-522 74 63
🅦 hotelwildner.com
Family-run establishment with
wonderful views from the terrace.

CASTELLO: Londra Palace €€€
Boutique **Map** F4
Riva degli Schiavoni 4171, 30122
Tel 041-520 05 33
🅦 londrapalace.com
Spacious and luxurious rooms,
plus splendid views of the city
and the lagoon. Excellent service.

DORSODURO:
Agli Alboretti €€
Pensione **Map** C5
Rio Terrà Foscarini 884, 30123
Tel 041-523 00 58
🅦 aglialboretti.com
Simple, comfortable rooms are
equipped with a free minibar.

LIDO DI VENEZIA:
Villa Mabapa €€
Room with a view
Riviera San Nicolò 16, 30126
Tel 041-526 05 90
🅦 villamabapa.com
Stay in attractive period villas that
look onto the lagoon.

SAN MARCO: Saturnia
and International €€
Luxury **Map** D4
Via XXII Marzo 2398, 30124
Tel 041-520 83 77
🅦 hotelsaturnia.it
Opulence in a warm setting. This
hotel features antique furnishings
and a pretty courtyard.

SAN MARCO: Gritti Palace €€€
Boutique **Map** D4
Santa Maria del Giglio 2467, 30124
Tel 041-79 46 11
🅦 thegrittipalace.com
Stay in an iconic palazzo dating
back to 1475 but featuring most
modern comforts.

DK Choice

SANTA CROCE: Al Sole €€
Historic **Map** C4
Santa Croce 136, 30124
Tel 041-244 03 28
🅦 alsolehotels.com
Housed in Palazzo Marcello,
a 15th-century palace with a
beautiful façade and marble-
floored reception area, Al Sole
offers well-appointed rooms.
Enjoy the rich breakfast spread
served in a patio garden.

Northern Italy

GENOA: Hotel Villa Pagoda €€
Room with a view
Via Capolungo 15, 16167
Tel 010-372 61 61
🅦 villapagoda.it
A luxurious 19th-century villa
with antique furniture. Located
just steps away from the coast.

LAKE GARDA: Locanda
San Vigilio €€
Room with a view
Località San Vigilio 17, 37016
Tel 045-725 66 88
🅦 locanda-sanvigilio.it
Exuding old-world charm, this
is one of the loveliest, most
exclusive hotels on Lake Garda.

MANTUA: Casa Poli €€
Boutique
Corso Giuseppe Garibaldi 32, 46100
Tel 0376-28 81 70
🅦 hotelcasapoli.it
Located near the harbor, Casa
Poli offers cozy rooms and
minimalist decor.

DK Choice

MILAN: Antica Locanda
Leonardo €€
Boutique
Corso Magenta 78, 20123
Tel 02-48 01 41 97
🅦 anticalocandaleonardo.com
Peacefully located in an elegant
19th-century palazzo, this
family-run hotel has well-
decorated rooms overlooking
a charming and picturesque
inner garden. The staff are
helpful and friendly.

MILAN: Antica Locanda
Solferino €€
Boutique
Via Castelfidardo 2, 20121
Tel 02-657 01 29
🅦 anticalocandasolferino.it
A welcoming guesthouse
with eclectic old-world charm.
Small pets are allowed.

PADUA: Augustus Terme €€
Luxury
Viale Stazione 150, 35036
Tel 049-79 32 00
🅦 hotelaugustus.com
Comfortable hotel with opulent
rooms, thermal swimming pools,
and a reputable restaurant.

PORTOFINO: Splendido €€€
Luxury
Salita Baratta 16, 16034
Tel 0185-26 78 01
🅦 hotelsplendido.com
Housed in a former monastery,
this hotel has elegantly furnished
rooms, many with private terraces.

TURIN: Hotel Conte
Biancamano €
Pensione
Corso Vittorio Emanuele 73, 10128
Tel 011-562 32 81
🅦 hotelcontebiancamano.it
An intimate hotel with elegant
decor, located on the third floor
of a 19th-century palazzo.

VERONA: Il Torcolo €€
Modern
Vicolo Listone 3, 37121
Tel 045-800 75 12
🅦 hoteltorcolo.it
Small, family-run property with
simple rooms and a pleasant
terrace where breakfast is served.

VICENZA: Glam
Boutique Hotel €€
Boutique
Via A. Giuriolo 10, 36100
Tel 0444-32 64 58
🅦 gboutiquehotel.com
Stylish space with a perfect blend
of traditional and modern decor.
Room service and free Wi-Fi.

Central Italy

ASSISI: Subasio €€
Modern
Via Elia Frate 2c, 06081
Tel *075-81 22 06*
Ⓦ hotelsubasio.com
Atmospheric and spacious rooms, some with terraces. Located beside the famous basilica.

DK Choice

BOLOGNA: Grand Hotel Majestic €€€
Luxury
Via Indipendenza 8, 40121
Tel *051-225 445*
Ⓦ grandhotelmajestic. hotelsbologna.it
This legendary hotel expertly combines opulent old-world elegance with modern comfort and hospitality. Each room is individually decorated with lush fabrics and antique furniture. Breakfast is served on the romantic rooftop terrace with sweeping views of the city. The dining room boasts beautiful frescoes.

FERRARA: Principessa Leonora €€
Boutique
Via Mascheraio 39, 44121
Tel *0532-20 60 20*
Ⓦ principessaleonora.it
This 16th-century residence is exquisitely decorated with antique French tapestries and traditional furniture.

PISA: Guerrazzi €
B&B
Via Francesco da Buti 4, 56125
Tel *338-932 81 69*
Ⓦ bbguerrazzi.hostel.com
Simple but quaint, with comfortable and clean rooms. Conveniently located close to the airport and train station.

PISA: Royal Victoria Hotel €
Historic
Lungarno Antonio Pacinotti 12, 56126
Tel *050-94 01 11*
Ⓦ royalvictoria.it
Set in a 10th-century tower, the Royal Victoria has stately decor and spacious rooms.

SIENA: Antica Residenza Cicogna €
Pensione
Via Termini 67, 53100
Tel *0577-28 56 13*
Ⓦ anticaresidenzacicogna.it
Housed in a medieval building, this is a charming, refurbished hotel with modern amenities.

Naples and The South

AMALFI: Antica Repubblica €
Boutique
Vico dei Pastai 2, 84011
Tel *089-873 63 10*
Ⓦ anticarepubblica.it
A charming hotel with a terrace and elegantly furnished rooms featuring modern comforts.

AMALFI: Hotel Desirée €
Room with a view
Via Capo 31, 80067
Tel *081-878 15 63*
Ⓦ desireehotelsorrento.com
This simple cliffside hotel offers excellent value. There is also an elevator to a small private beach.

AMALFI: Bellevue Syrene €€€
Luxury
Piazza della Vittoria 5, 80067
Tel *081-878 10 24*
Ⓦ bellevue.it
Housed in a dreamy 18th-century villa with a flowering terrace and private beach access.

CAPRI: Bellavista €€
Boutique
Via Giuseppe Orlandi 10, 80071
Tel *081-837 14 63*
Ⓦ bellavistacapri.com
At this 1960s-style hotel, all rooms have private balconies with sea or garden views.

CAPRI: Grand Hotel Quisisana €€€
Luxury
Via Camerelle 2, 80073
Tel *081-837 07 88*
Ⓦ quisisana.com
The Quisisana features deluxe accommodations oozing Mediterranean elegance. Spa treatments and a Turkish bath.

NAPLES: Decumani €€
Historic
Via del Grande Archivio 8, 80100
Tel *081-420 13 79*
Ⓦ palazzodecumani.com
A 20th-century Baroque palace with tasteful, contemporary furnishings. Free Wi-Fi.

NAPLES: Grand Hotel Vesuvio €€
Room with a view
Via Partenope 45, 80121
Tel *081-764 00 44*
Ⓦ vesuvio.it
Sumptuous lodgings with views of the iconic Gulf of Naples. The two on-site restaurants also offer panoramic views.

Sicily

AGRIGENTO: Camere del Sud €
B&B
Via Ficani, 92100
Tel *349-638 44 24*
Ⓦ camereasud.it
Stay in a warm, simple room at this sunny B&B with friendly and helpful owners.

ERICE: Elimo €
Room with a view
Via Vittorio Emanuele 73, 91016
Tel *0923-86 93 77*
Ⓦ hotelelimo.it
Small but lovely rooms – some with balconies that afford views of the countryside.

PALERMO: Principe di Villafranca €
Luxury
Via Giuseppina Turrisi Colonna 4, 90141
Tel *091-611 85 23*
Ⓦ principedivillafranca.it
Elegant hotel full of intricate and colorful design details, including antique art and furnishings.

Richly decorated suite at Grand Hotel Vesuvio, Naples

Where to Eat and Drink

Rome

Around Piazza Navona

Acchiappafantasmi   €
Pizzeria   Map C3
Via dei Cappellari 66, 00186
Tel *06-687 34 62*   **Closed** *Mon*
With a bright and inviting interior,
Acchiappafantasmi, or "Ghost-
busters," serves ghost-shaped
pizzas – amusing and delicious.

Camponeschi   €€
Fine Dining   Map C3
Piazza Farnese, 50/50a, 00186
Tel *06-687 49 27*
World-class dining in the heart of
town. Try the *tagliolini* pasta with
lobster and black truffles. Wild
game is the house specialty.

Roscioli   €€
Enoteca   Map 9 C4
Via dei Giubbonari 21, 00186
Tel *06-687 52 87*   **Closed** *Sun*
Part wine bar, part *salumeria*
(deli), with drool-worthy meats
and cheeses, and a dizzying
selection of wine labels.

Hostaria dell'Orso   €€€
Fine Dining   Map C3
Via dei Soldati 25c, 00186
Tel *06-683 011 92*   **Closed** *Aug*
This legendary restaurant and
nightclub, located in a beautiful
house, has been welcoming
guests since the 16th century.

Northeast Rome

San Marco   €
Pizzeria   Map D2
Via Sardegna 38, 00187
Tel *06-420 126 20* **Closed** *1 wk Aug;
Dec 24*
A wine bar and grill noted for its
delicious pizzas and gracious
service. The blackboard-covered
walls list the day's specials.

Trimani il Wine Bar   €
Enoteca   Map E2
Via Cernaia 37b, 00185
Tel *06-446 96 30* **Closed** *Sun; Jan 1;
2 wks Aug; Dec 25 & 26*
Modern wine bar with labels that
pair perfectly with cold and hot
dishes, as well as Italian cheeses.

Hamasei   €€
Japanese   Map D2
Via della Mercede 35/36, 00187
Tel *06-679 21 34*   **Closed** *Mon; Aug*
Inventive sushi and sashimi
dishes are served in a minimalist
setting, with low tables for
authentic Oriental-style dining.

The enticing window of Roscioli, a deli and
wine bar in the heart of Rome

La Campana   €€
Regional Italian   Map C2
Vicolo della Campana 18, 00186
Tel *06-687 52 73*   **Closed** *Mon; Aug*
The oldest restaurant in Rome,
dating back to 1518, La Campana
serves traditional favorites and
plenty of fish dishes.

The Vatican and
Trastevere

Arian   €
Persian
Via Tacito 54, 00193
Tel *06-454 411 22*   **Closed** *Sun &
Mon lunch; 1 wk Aug*
Savor authentic Iranian cuisine
in a vibrant atmosphere. Belly-
dancing performances liven up
the atmosphere on Friday and
Saturday nights.

DK Choice

Isole di Sicilia   €€
Regional Italian
Via Garibaldi 68, 00153
Tel *06-583 342 12*   **Closed** *Wed*
The elaborate dishes at this
cheerful restaurant are inspired
by the cuisine of the islands
around Sicily. A vast *antipasto*
spread of cold meats and
vegetables kicks off a lovely
meal. In good weather, you can
dine on the tree-lined street.

Antico Arco   €€€
Fine Dining   Map C3
Piazzale Aurelio 7, 00152
Tel *06-581 52 74*   **Closed** *Jan 1*
Truffles, wild strawberries, gluten-
free bread and pastas, and other
such delights are on offer here.
The vast wine list is tantalizing.

Price Guide
Prices are based on a three-course meal
per person, with a half-bottle of house
wine, and all extra charges.

€	up to €40
€€	€40 to €75
€€€	over €75

Florence

Il Vegetariano   €
Vegetarian
Via delle Ruote 30, 50129
Tel *055-47 50 30*   **Closed** *Sat & Sun
lunch; Mon; 3 wks Aug, Christmas*
Enjoy excellent-value fare at this
long-established restaurant
where the menu changes daily.

Ruth's   €
Kosher/Vegetarian
Via Luigi Carlo Farini 2, 50121
Tel *055-248 08 88*   **Closed** *Fri dinner
& Sat lunch; Jewish festivities*
Located beside the synagogue,
this kosher restaurant serves
Jewish-inspired recipes, plus a
wide range of vegetarian and
seafood options.

Alle Murate   €€
Regional Italian
Via del Proconsolo 16/r, 50122
Tel *055-24 06 18*   **Closed** *Sun lunch;
Mon*
This unique restaurant offers an
opportunity to combine art and
food. Housed in a 14th-century
palace, it boasts original frescoes
on the walls and vaulted ceilings.

Da Kou   €€
Japanese
Via del Melarancio 19/r, 50123
Tel *055-28 29 22*   **Closed** *Mon*
Fresh and authentic sushi is
prepared with skill and served
in generous portions here. The
decor is modern and informal.

Dei Frescobaldi   €€
Enoteca
Via dei Magazzini 2–4/r, 50122
Tel *055-28 47 24*   **Closed** *Mon
lunch; 1 wk Jan, 3 wks Aug*
Sample fine wines and
meticulously matched dishes
in a setting of frescoed walls
and exposed stonework.

Bistrò Del Mare   €€€
Fine Dining
Lungarno Corsini 4/r, 50123
Tel *055-239 92 24*   **Closed** *Mon;
1 wk Aug*
Steps away from Ponte Vecchio,
this refined restaurant serves
dishes inspired by old Tuscan
recipes but with a modern twist.

The outdoor eating area at Osteria da Rioba, Venice

Venice

DK Choice

BURAN0-MAZZORBO:
Venissa €€€
Modern Italian
*Fondamenta Santa Caterina 3,
30170*
Tel *041-527 22 81* **Closed** *Tue;
Oct–May*
Venissa guarantees a special
gastronomic experience. The
menu features seafood, meat,
and vegetarian options made
using home-grown produce.

CANNAREGIO:
Osteria da Rioba €€
Seafood **Map** C2
*Fondamenta della Misericordia 2553,
30121*
Tel *041-524 43 79* **Closed** *Mon*
A charming canal-side restaurant
decorated with a seafood mosaic.
Reserve in advance.

CASTELLO: Ristorante Wildner €€
Regional Italian **Map** F4
Riva degli Schiavoni 4161, 30122
Tel *041-522 74 63* **Closed** *Tue;
3 wks Jan*
Diners can feast on fresh fish and
locally grown organic vegetables
at this restaurant. There is also an
interesting wine list.

SAN MARCO: Acqua Pazza €€
Seafood **Map** D4
Campo Sant'Angelo 3808, 30124
Tel *041-277 06 88* **Closed** *Mon;
Jan–Feb*
This is where the Amalfi Coast
meets Venice. A different take
on fish, with wines to match.

SAN MARCO:
Trattoria Do Forni €€€
Fine Dining **Map** D4
Calle dei Specchieri 468, 30124
Tel *041-523 21 48*
Two dining areas with different
decor serve careful interpreta-
tions of classic Venetian cuisine.

SAN POLO: Da Fiore €€€
Fine Dining **Map** C3
Calle del Scaleter 2202, 30125
Tel *041-72 13 08* **Closed** *Sun & Mon;
Jan 8–22; 3 wks Aug*
Seasonal produce is the rule at
this restaurant said to be the best
in the city. Leave room for dessert.

Northern Italy

GENOA: Cantine Squarciafico €€
Regional Italian
Piazza Invrea 3r, 16123
Tel *010-247 08 23* **Closed** *Mon
lunch; 1 wk Jan, 2 wks Aug*
This wine bar serves up a range
of Ligurian specialties, including
great *stracci* (a type of lasagne).

DK Choice

LAKE COMO:
L'Angolo del Silenzio €
Regional Italian
Viale Lecco 25, 22100
Tel *031-377 21 57* **Closed** *Mon &
Tue lunch; 2 wks Aug*
This *osteria* (wine bar) offers
pasta, meat, game, and fish
dishes in a friendly atmosphere.
Try the wild boar with red-
currant sauce and Roquefort.
An inexpensive one-dish lunch
is available on weekdays, and
gluten-free dishes are prepared
upon request. Book ahead.

MILAN: Pasta Madre €
Modern Italian
Via Bernardino Corio 8, 20135
Tel *02-55 19 00 20* **Closed** *Sun; Aug*
Contemporary decor and a
relaxed ambience. Pasta Madre
serves creative Italian fare, as
well as gluten-free desserts.

MILAN: U Barba €
Regional Italian
Via Decembrio 33, 20137
Tel *02-45 48 70 32* **Closed** *Mon; Tue–
Fri; lunch*
A friendly Genoese *osteria* with
a bocce ball court. On the menu

are great fish and game dishes.
Try the freshly made gnocchi.

DK Choice

MILAN:
Nobile Bistrò de Milan €€
Regional Italian
Corso Venezia 45, 20121
Tel *02-49 52 65 92* **Closed** *2 wks
Aug*
Well-known Milanese chef
Claudio Sadler prepares
traditional meat and fish dishes
with a modern twist at this
reasonably priced restaurant.
Breakfast, lunch, afternoon tea,
aperitivo (aperitif), and dinner
are all served in an informal
atmosphere. Sit indoors or
in the private courtyard.

PADUA: Trattoria San Pietro €
Regional Italian
Via San Pietro 95, 35139
Tel *049-876 03 30* **Closed** *Sun; Jul*
The perfect place for regional
dishes cooked with fresh local
ingredients. Informal ambience.

PORTOFINO: Da O Batti €€
Seafood
Vico Nuovo 17, 16034
Tel *0185-26 93 79* **Closed** *Mon;
Nov–mid-Jan*
A chic, intimate restaurant in one
of Liguria's most elegant towns.
Exceptional fish cuisine.

VERONA: Il Desco €€€
Fine Dining
Via Dietro San Sebastiano 5-7, 37121
Tel *045-595 358* **Closed** *Sun & Mon
(except Mon dinner Jul, Aug & Dec);
2 wks Jun & Dec*
Housed in an old patrician house,
this elegant Michelin-starred
restaurant offers a creative take
on traditional Italian cuisine.

Central Italy

ASSISI: La Fortezza €
Regional Italian
Vicolo della Fortezza 2b, 06081
Tel *075-81 29 93* **Closed** *Thu; Jul*
Mostly traditional cuisine, with
some creative touches. Friendly
but professional service and a
good price–quality ratio.

BOLOGNA:
Antica Trattoria della Gigina €
Regional Italian
Via Stendhal 1, 40128
Tel *051-32 23 00*
This eatery delivers a modern
take on regional cuisine without
compromising on the flavors.
Extensive wine list.

BOLOGNA: Pappagallo €€
Fine Dining
Piazza della Mercanzia 3, 40125
Tel *051-232 807* **Closed** *2 wks Aug*
Excellent traditional cuisine is served under dramatically high ceilings. The desserts are delicious, and the wine cellar is well stocked.

PISA: La Taverna di Emma €
Modern Italian
Via Carlo Salomone Cammeo 50, 56122
Tel *050-555 003* **Closed** *Sun; 1 wk Feb; last 2 wks Aug*
A talented chef whips up creative yet traditional recipes at this simple eatery. Delicious desserts.

PISA: V. Beni €€
Seafood
Piazza Chiara Gambacorti 22, 56125
Tel *050-250 67* **Closed** *Sun; 2 wks Aug*
Located slightly off the tourist track, this local favorite is housed in a rustic 15th-century building.

DK Choice

SIENA: 53 Cento €
Enoteca
Viale Pietro Toselli 19, 53100
Tel *0577-050 169* **Closed** *Sat lunch; Sun; 2 wks Aug*
An eclectic wine bar open from breakfast until late into the night, 53 Cento serves pan-Mediterranean cuisine, with imaginative takes on Italian staples, including many vegetarian options. There is an oyster bar, as well as a well-stocked cellar. The staff are happy to make suggestions.

URBINO:
Antica Osteria da la Stella €€
Regional Italian
Via Santa Margherita 1, 61029
Tel *0722-320 228* **Closed** *Mon; 2 wks Jul*
Famous painters such as Raphael and Piero della Francesca have dined at this historic restaurant. Elegant interiors with a fireplace.

Naples and The South

AMALFI: La Caravella €€€
Fine Dining
Via Matteo Camera 12, 84011
Tel *089-87 10 29* **Closed** *Tue; Jan & Nov*
The award-winning chef at La Caravella uses local flavors to exalt the regional cuisine.

CAPRI: Da Paolino €€
Regional Italian
Via Palazzo a Mare 11, 80073
Tel *081-837 61 02* **Closed** *Oct–Apr*
A rustic country restaurant with rich regional cuisine. Guests dine amid lemon trees.

CAPRI: L'Olivo €€
Fine Dining
Via Capodimonte 14, 80071
Tel *081-978 01 11* **Closed** *mid-Oct– mid-Apr*
The chefs here use ingredients such as saffron, bergamot, fava beans, and asparagus to create gorgeous flavor combinations.

DK Choice

NAPLES: Da Michele €
Pizzeria
Via Cesare Sersale 1, 80139
Tel *081-553 92 04* **Closed** *Sun; 2 wks Aug*
A trip to Naples would not be complete without tasting a pizza here, probably the most famous pizzeria in the world. Only two types of pizza are available: margherita and marinara.

NAPLES: La Cantinella €€
Fine Dining
Via Cuma 42, 80132
Tel *081-764 86 84* **Closed** *Sun*
This award-winning restaurant with a bamboo-forest decor boasts an imaginative chef.

NAPLES: Il Comandante €€€
Fine Dining
Via Cristoforo Colombo, 80133
Tel *081-017 50 01* **Closed** *Tue*
The chef here creates exquisite dishes from a handful of basic ingredients. Sunny patio seating.

POSITANO: Le Terrazze €€
Enoteca
Via Grotte dell'Incanto 51, 84017
Tel *089-875 874* **Closed** *Oct–Apr*
Wine bar with a cellar that is carved right into the hillside rock. Panoramic sea views.

Sicily

AGRIGENTO: Kokalos €€
Regional Italian
Via Cavaleri Magazzeni 3
Tel *0922-60 64 27*
Sample traditional Sicilian fare prepared using local ingredients, including oranges, almonds, and sun-dried tomatoes.

PALERMO:
Antico Caffè Spinnato €
Enoteca
Via Principe di Belmonte 111, 90139
Tel *091-749 51 04* **Closed** *Christmas*
Come for the wines, liqueurs, and espresso coffee, but stay for traditional desserts such as cannoli and gelato.

PALERMO: Bye Bye Blues €€
Fine Dining
Via del Garofalo 23, 90149
Tel *091-684 14 15* **Closed** *Mon; 2 wks Jan*
At this Michelin-starred restaurant, diners can watch their dishes being prepared. Fantastic value.

SIRACUSA: Oinos €€
Modern Italian
Via della Giudecca 69/75, 96100
Tel *0931-464 900*
Dine in an intimate setting and enjoy a variety of dishes based on recipes from all over Italy.

DK Choice

TAORMINA: Al Duomo €€
Seafood
Vico Ebrei (Piazza Duomo), 98039
Tel *0942-625 656* **Closed** *winter: Mon*
This restaurant is set on a terrace in Taormina's most beautiful piazza, with the backdrop of a 12th-century cathedral. Classic and modern fish dishes are whipped up with enthusiasm by the chefs. The kitchen is open well past midnight.

Dine amid a lemon orchard at Da Paolino, on the island of Capri

GREECE

Greece is one of the most visited countries in Europe, yet remains one of the least known. Although most visitors will be familiar with the images of Ancient Greece, the modern Greek state dates only from 1830. Situated at a geographical crossroads, Greece combines cultural elements of the Balkans, the Middle East, and the Mediterranean.

For a small country, Greece possesses marked regional differences. Nearly three-quarters of the land is mountainous, uninhabited, or uncultivated. On the mainland, fertile agricultural land supports tobacco farming in the northeast, with orchard fruits and vegetables grown farther south. A third of the population lives in the capital, Athens, the cultural, financial, and political center, where ancient and modern stand side by side. Of the myriad islands, only about a hundred are today inhabited.

For centuries, a large number of Greeks have lived abroad. Currently, there are over half as many Greeks outside the country as in, although recent years have seen reverse immigration, with expatriates returning home, especially to the islands.

Rural and urban life in contemporary Greece has been transformed since the start of the 20th century, despite foreign occupation and civil war. Until the 1960s, the country remained underdeveloped, with many rural areas lacking basic amenities. A number of improvements, including the growth of tourism, helped Greece develop into a relatively wealthy, modern state. However, the financial crisis of 2009 has led to a rise in unemployment, a series of unpopular austerity bills, and political instability.

History

Early Greek history is marked by a series of internal struggles, from the Mycenaean and Minoan cultures of the Bronze Age to the competing city-states of the 1st millennium BC. In spite of warfare, the 4th and 5th centuries BC were the high point of ancient Greek civilization, a golden age of exceptional creativity in philosophy and the arts.

In 338 BC, the Greeks were conquered by Philip II of Macedonia at Chaironeia, and Greece soon became absorbed into Alexander the Great's vast empire. With the defeat of the Macedonians by the Romans in 168 BC, Greece was made a

The idyllic Myrtos Bay as seen from the clifftops of Kefalonia, one of the Ionian islands

◄ Dusk falls over picturesque Oia village, on the island of Santorini, in the Cyclades province of Rome. As part of the Eastern Empire, it was ruled from Constantinople and became a powerful element within the Orthodox Christian, Byzantine world.

Following the Ottomans' momentous capture of Constantinople in 1453, the Greek mainland was ruled by the Turks for the next 350 years. Crete and the Ionian islands were seized for long periods by the Venetians. Eventually, the Greeks rebelled and, in 1821, the Greek War of Independence began. In 1832, the Great Powers that dominated Europe established a protectorate over Greece, marking the end of Ottoman rule. During the 19th century, the Greeks expanded their national territory, reasserting Greek sovereignty over many of the islands. Almost a century of significant territorial gains came to a disastrous end in 1922, when millions of Greeks were expelled from Smyrna in Turkish Anatolia, bringing to a close thousands of years of Greek

19th-century lithograph celebrating the Greek War of Independence

presence in Asia Minor. The ensuing years were a time of hardship and instability. The Metaxás dictatorship was followed by Italian, German, and Bulgarian occupation during World War II, and then a bitter civil war. The present boundaries of the Greek state date from 1948, when the Dodecanese were finally returned by the Italians. Today, Greece is a stable democracy and has been a member of the European Union since 1981.

KEY DATES IN GREEK HISTORY

3000–1200 BC Bronze Age; Cycladic, Minoan, and Mycenaean cultures flourish

800 Emergence of city-states

5th century Classical period; high point of Athenian culture under Perikles

431–404 Peloponnesian Wars; defeat of the Athenians by the city-state of Sparta

338 Greek army conquered by Philip II of Macedonia

333 Alexander the Great declares himself king of Asia; Greece absorbed into his vast empire

168 Greece becomes province of Rome

AD 49–54 St. Paul preaches Christianity in Greece

395 Greece becomes part of the new Eastern Roman Empire, ruled from Constantinople

1453 Constantinople falls to the Ottoman Turks

1821 Start of the Greek War of Independence

1832 Great Powers establish protectorate over Greece, and appoint Otto of Bavaria king

1922 Greeks fail to capture Smyrna from Turks

1946–9 Civil war leaves thousands dead or homeless

1981 Admission to the European Union

2002 Euro becomes legal currency

2004 Greece hosts Olympic Games and wins the football European Cup

2010 Greece narrowly avoids bankruptcy after taking a €110 billion loan from the EU and IMF

Religion, Language and Culture

During Venetian and Ottoman domination, the Greek Orthodox church succeeded in preserving the Greek language and identity. Today, the Orthodox church is still a powerful force. Great importance is placed on baptisms and church weddings, although civil marriages are valid in law. Sunday mass is very popular with women, for whom church is a meeting place for socializing, just as the *kafeneía* (cafés) are for men.

The Greek language was for a long time a field of conflict between *katharévousa*, an artificial form devised around the time of independence, and the slowly evolved everyday speech, or *dimotikí*. Today's prevalence of *dimotikí* was perhaps a foregone conclusion in an oral culture. The art of storytelling is as prized now as it was in Homer's time, with conversation pursued for its own sake in *kafeneía* and at dinner tables. Singers, writers, and poet-lyricists have all kept *dimotikí* alive until the present day.

Development and Diplomacy

Greece remains one of the poorer members of the European Union. It still bears the hallmarks of a developing economy, with agriculture and the service sector accounting for two-thirds of the GNP. Tourism has compensated for the decline in other industries, such as world shipping, but unemployment remains high.

The fact that the Greek state is less than 200 years old, combined with recent periods of political instability, means that there is little faith in government institutions. Life operates on networks of personal friendships and official contacts. In the political sphere, the years following World War II were largely shaped by the influence of two men: Andréas Papandréou of the Panhellenic Socialist Movement (PASOK) and Conservative Konstantínos Karamanlís, who between them held office for the most part of the 1980s and 1990s.

The conservative New Democracy Party led by Costas Karamanlís (nephew of Konstantínos) took over from PASOK after a convincing election win in 2004. PASOK were back in power by autumn

Typical scene at a Greek taverna, a popular place for friends and family to socialize

2009. In 2010, it was revealed that the Greek state was close to bankruptcy and a €110 billion loan from the EU and IMF was agreed. In 2012, New Democracy won the election and Antonis Samaras became Prime Minister.

Home Life

The late Andréas Papandréou, three times Greek premier

The family is still the basic Greek social unit. Traditionally, one family would farm its own land independently, and today, family-run businesses are common in urban settings. Family life and social life are usually one and the same, and tend to revolve around eating out. Arranged marriages and dowries, though officially banned, persist. Most single young adults live with their parents and outside the largest cities, few unmarried couples dare to cohabit. Despite the previous generations' love of children, Greece has one of the lowest birth rates in Europe. Recently, the status of urban Greek women has greatly improved. They are now better represented in medicine and law, and many women run their own firms. However, in the country, macho attitudes still exist, women often sacrificing a career to look after the house and children. New imported attitudes have crept in, but generally the Greek traditional way of life remains resolutely strong.

Fishermen mending their nets on one of the Greek islands

Exploring Greece

From beaches to ancient archaeological sites, Greece boasts a wide range of attractions. The nation's greatest ancient monuments are located in the capital, Athens, but relics of the Mycenaean, Minoan, Classical, and Byzantine civilizations can be found all over. The Greek islands attract thousands of tourists, many of whom come simply to enjoy the sun and sand and the relaxed pace of life. Ferries link the different island groups to the mainland, and "island-hopping" is a popular way to explore the many archipelagos.

Key

— Highway

— Major road

— Railroad

··· International boundary

Sights at a Glance

1. ATHENS pp450–57
2. Soúnio
3. Monastery of Dafní
4. Monastery of Osios Loukás
5. Ancient Delphi
6. Pílio
7. Metéora pp462–3
8. Thessaloníki
9. Ancient Pélla
10. Mount Athos
11. Mount Olympos
12. Ancient Corinth
13. Mycenae
14. Epidaurus

15. Náfplio
16. Monemvasía
17. Máni Peninsula
18. Mystrás
19. Loúsios Gorge
20. Ancient Olympia
21. Corfu and the Ionian Islands

Islands South of the Mainland
(see inset map)

22. Cyclades
23. Rhodes and the Dodecanese
24. Crete

BULGARIA

Néstos

Kastaniés

Orestiáda

Istanbul

idirókastro

Dráma

14

Xánthi

Komotiní

Souflí

51

Sérres

Néa
Zíchni

12

Angítis

Kavála

Keramotí

Istanbul

Amfípoli

2

2

2

Alexandroúpoli

a Moudaniá

16

Thásos

Thracian Sea

Ouranoúpoli

10 Mount
Athos

Samothráki

Imvros

Límnos

Tēnedos

Agios
Efstrátios

T U R K E Y

kiáthos

Gioúra

Alónnisos

Kyrá Panagiá

Peristerá

Skópelos

Lésvos

Skýros

A e g e a n

S e a

Psará

Oinoússes

Kými

Chíos

Chalkída

44

7

stery
Dafní

3

Marathónas

Marmari

Kárystos

1 ATHENS

aeus

Andros

Aígina

Makrónisos

2

Soúnio

Kéa

éthana

Póros

Gyáros

Tinos

ýdra

Kýthnos

Sýros

Sámos

Sérifos

Antiparos

Páros

Sifnos

Mílos

Kímolos

Polýaigos

Sikinos

Folegándros

Islands South of the Mainland

TURKEY

ATHENS

Chios

Andros

Sámos

Kéa

Tinos

Ikaria

Kýthnos

Syros

Mýkonos

Pátmos

Delos

Sérifos

Páros

Náxos

Kálymnos

The Cyclades **22**

Sifnos

Amorgós

Kos

Milos

Ios

Astypálaia

Rhodes
Town

Santorini

Anáfi

Rhodes and
the Dodecanese **23**

Lindos

Rhodes

Kárpathos

MEDITERRANEAN
SEA

Chaniá

Irákleio

0 km   50

Kásos

Crete **24**

Agios
Nikólaos

0 miles   50

For keys to symbols *see back flap*

● Athens

Athens has been inhabited for 7,000 years. The city's greatest glory was during the Classical period (4th and 5th centuries BC) of ancient Greece, from which so many buildings and artifacts survive. The city is dominated by the world-famous Acropolis and its theaters and temples, including the Parthenon, erected by Perikles as part of his grand building plan in the mid-5th century BC. Within the Byzantine Empire and under Ottoman rule, Athens played only a minor role. It returned to prominence in 1834, when King Otto made it capital of Greece. When the king's architects planned the new, European-style city, they included many splendid Neoclassical public buildings, which today provide elegant homes for some of Athens' best museums and galleries.

Marble figurine from the
Museum of Cycladic Art

Sights at a Glance

① National Archaeological Museum
② Monastiráki
③ Ancient Agora
④ *Acropolis pp454–6*
⑤ Plaka
⑥ Temple of Olympian Zeus
⑦ Benáki Museum
⑧ Museum of Cycladic Art
⑨ National Gallery of Art

The 1st-century BC Tower of the Winds in Monastiráki, central Athens

Getting Around

The sights of Athens' city center are closely packed, and often the best way of getting around is on foot, especially with the appalling traffic. There are about 20 bus and trolley bus routes that crisscross the city. The metro system is most useful for crossing the city, getting to the port of Piraeus and to the airport.

Key

▨ Sight / Place of interest
▨ Pedestrian street
━ City walls

0 meters 300
0 yards 300

For keys to symbols *see back flap*

Neoclassical entrance to the National Archaeological Museum

① National Archaeological Museum

Patissión 44. **Tel** 213-214 4890. Ⓜ Omónoia. **Open** summer: 9am–8pm daily (from 1pm Mon); winter: 1–8pm Mon, 9am–4pm Tue–Sun. 🄳 🄲 ♿
Ⓦ **namuseum.gr**

When it was opened in 1891, this museum brought together antiquities that had previously been stored in different places all over the city. New wings were added in 1939, but during World War II, the museum's priceless exhibits were dispersed and buried underground to protect them from possible damage. The museum reopened in 1946, but it has taken another 50 or so years of renovation and reorganization to finally do justice to its formidable collection. With the combination of such unique exhibits as the Mycenaean gold, and an unrivaled assembly of sculpture, pottery, and jewelry, it can definitely be claimed as one of the finest museums in the world. It is a good idea to plan ahead and be selective when visiting the museum and not attempt to cover everything in one visit.

The museum's exhibits can be divided into seven main collections: Neolithic and Cycladic, Mycenaean, Geometric and Archaic sculpture, Classical sculpture, Roman and Hellenistic sculpture, the pottery collections, and the Thíra frescoes. There are also other smaller collections that are well

worth seeing. These include the stunning Eléni Stathátou jewelry collection and the Egyptian rooms.

High points of the museum include the unique finds from the grave circle at Mycenae (see p467), in particular the gold Mask of Agamemnon. Also not to be missed are the Archaic *kouroi* statues and the unrivaled collection of Classical and Hellenistic statues. Two of the most important and finest of the bronzes are the *Horse with the Little Jockey* and *Poseidon*. One of the world's largest collections of ancient ceramics can also be found here, comprising a vast array of elegant red- and black-figure vases from the 6th and 5th centuries BC and some Geometric funerary vases that date back as far as 1000 BC.

② Monastiráki

Ⓜ Monastiráki. Market: **Open** daily.

This lively and atmospheric area, which is named after the little monastery in Plateía Monastirakíou, is synonymous with Athens' famous flea market. Located next to the ancient Agora, it is bounded by Sari in the west and Aiólou in the east. The streets of Pandrósou, Ifaístou, and Areos leading off Plateía Monastirakíou are full of shops, selling a range of goods from expensive antiques, leather, and silver to tourist trinkets.

The heart of the flea market is in Plateía Avyssinías, west of Plateía Monastirakíou, where every morning junk dealers arrive with pieces of furniture and various odds and ends. During the week, the shops and stalls are filled with antiques, second-hand books, rugs, leatherware, taverna chairs, army surplus gear, and tools.

On Sunday mornings, when the shops are closed, the market itself still flourishes along Adrianoú and in Plateía Agíou Filíppou. There are always numerous bargains to be had. Items particularly worth investing in include some of the brightly colored woven and embroidered cloths and an abundance of good silver jewelry.

Shoppers browsing in Athens's lively Monastiráki market

View across the Agora, showing the reconstructed Stoa of Attalos on the right

③ Ancient Agora

Main entrance at Adrianoú,
Monastiráki. **Tel** 210-321 0185.
Ⓜ Thiseío, Monastiráki. Museum
and site: **Open** 8am–7:30pm daily
(winter: to 3pm). **Closed** main public
hols. 🚻 ♿ limited.

The American School of
Archaeology commenced
excavations of the Ancient
Agora in the 1930s, and since
then a complex array of public
buildings and temples has been
revealed. The democratically
governed Agora was the
political and religious heart
of ancient Athens. Also the
center of commercial and daily
life, it abounded with schools
and elegant stoas, or roofed
arcades, filled with shops. The
state prison was here, as was
the city's mint. Even the
remains of an olive oil mill
have been found.

The main building standing
today is the impressive two-
story Stoa of Attalos. This was
rebuilt in the 1950s on the
original foundations and using
ancient building materials.
Founded by King Attalos of
Pergamon (ruled 159–138 BC),
it dominated the eastern
quarter of the Agora until it
was destroyed in AD 267. It
is used today as a museum,
exhibiting the finds from the
Agora. These include a *klepsydra*
(a water clock that was used
for timing plaintiffs' speeches),
bronze ballots, and items from
everyday life such as some
terra-cotta toys and leather
sandals. The best-preserved
ruins on the site are the Odeion
of Agríppa, a covered theater,
and the Hephaisteion, a temple
to Hephaistos, also known as
the Theseion.

④ Acropolis

See pp454–6.

⑤ Plaka

Ⓜ Monastiráki, Acropolis. 🚌 1, 2, 4,
5, and many others.

The area of Plaka is the historic
heart of Athens. Even though
only a few buildings date back
farther than the Ottoman
period, it remains the oldest
continually inhabited area in the
city. One probable explanation
of its name comes from the
word used by Albanian soldiers
in the service of the Turks who
settled here in the 16th century
– *pliaka* (old) was how they
used to describe the area.
Despite the constant swarm of
tourists and Athenians, who
come to eat in old-fashioned
tavernas or browse in the
antique and icon shops, Pláka
still retains the atmosphere of a
traditional neighborhood. The
Lysikrates Monument in Plateía
Lysikrátous is one of a number
of monuments that were built
to commemorate the victors at
the annual choral and dramatic
festival at the Theater of
Dionysos. Taking its name from
the sponsor of the winning
team, it is the only such
monument still intact in Athens.

Many churches are worth a
visit: the 11th-century **Agios
Nikólaos Ragavás** has ancient
columns built into the walls.

The **Tower of the Winds**, in
the far west of Pláka, lies in the
grounds of the Roman Agora. It
was built by a Syrian astronomer
in the 2nd century BC as a
weather vane and water clock.
The name comes from external
friezes depicting the eight
mythological winds.

The Byzantine church of Agios Nikólaos Ragavás in Plaka

④ Acropolis

In the mid-5th century BC, Perikles persuaded the Athenians to begin a grand program of new building work. The resulting transformation has come to embody the political and cultural achievements of ancient Greece. Three contrasting temples were built on the Acropolis, together with a monumental gateway. The Theater of Dionysos and the Theater of Herodes Atticus were added later, in the 4th century BC and the 2nd century AD respectively.

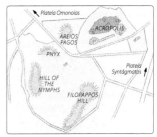

Locator Map

★ **Porch of the Caryatids**
These statues of women were used in place of columns on the south porch of the Erechtheion. The originals, four of which can be seen in the Acropolis Museum, have been replaced by casts.

★ **Temple of Athena Nike**
This temple to Athena of Victory is on the west side of the Propylaia. It was built in 426–421 BC.

KEY

① **Theater of Herodes Atticus**, was originally built in AD 161. Restored in 1955, it is now used for outdoor concerts.

② **Pathway to Acropolis from ticket office**

③ **The Beulé Gate** was the first entrance to the Acropolis.

④ **The Propylaia** was built in 437–432 BC to form a new entrance to the Acropolis.

⑤ **An olive tree** now grows where Athena first planted her tree in a competition against Poseidon.

⑥ **Two Corinthian columns** are the remains of choregic monuments erected by sponsors of successful dramatic performances.

⑦ **Panagía Spiliótissa** is a chapel set up in a cave in the Acropolis rock.

⑧ **Shrine of Asklepios**

⑨ **Stoa of Eumenes**

⑩ **The Acropolis rock** was an easily defended site. It has been in use for nearly 5,000 years.

★ Parthenon
Although few sculptures are left on this famous temple to Athena, some can still be admired, such as this one from the east pediment *(see p456)*.

VISITORS' CHECKLIST

Practical Information
Dionysíou Areopagítou (main entrance), Pláka. **Tel** 210-321 0219. **W** **acropolisofathens.gr**
Open Apr–Oct: 8am–8pm daily; Nov–Mar: 8am–4:30pm daily.
Closed Jan 1, Mar 25, Easter Sun, May 1, Dec 25 & 26. New Acropolis Museum: **Tel** 210-321 4172. **Open** 8am–8pm daily (Nov–Mar: to 5pm). **Closed** Jan 1, Mar 25, Easter Sun, May 1, Dec 25 & 26.

Transport
Acropolis. 230, 231.

Theater of Dionysos
This figure of the comic satyr, Silenus, can be seen here. The theater visible today was built by Lykourgos in 342–326 BC.

The newly arrived Elgin Marbles at the British Museum, in a painting by A. Archer

The Elgin Marbles

These famous sculptures, also called the Parthenon Marbles, are held in the British Museum in London. They were acquired from the occupying Turkish authorities by Lord Elgin in 1801–3. He sold them to the British nation for £35,000 in 1816. There is great controversy surrounding the Marbles. While some argue that they are more carefully preserved in the British Museum, the Greek government does not accept the legality of the sale and believes they belong in Athens.

Exploring the Acropolis

Once you are through the Propylaia, the grand entrance to the site, the Parthenon exerts an overwhelming fascination. The other fine temples on "the Rock" include the Erechtheion and the Temple of Athena Nike. Since 1975, access to all the temple precincts has been banned. However, it is a miracle that anything remains at all. The ravages of war, the removal of treasures, and pollution have all taken their irrevocable toll on the Acropolis.

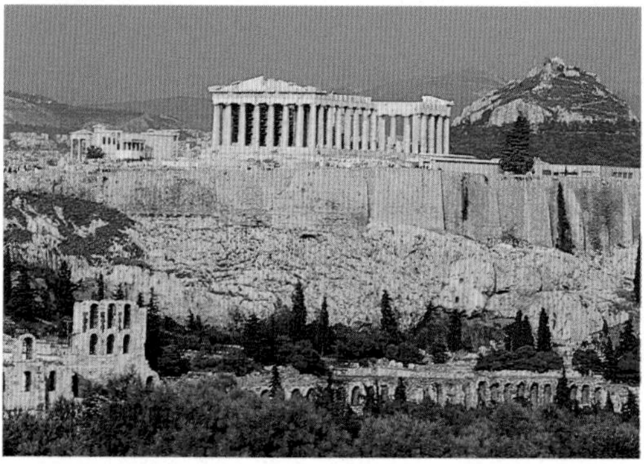

View of the Parthenon from the southwest at sunrise

The Parthenon

One of the world's most famous monuments, the Parthenon was commissioned by Perikles as part of his rebuilding plan. Work began in 447 BC, when the sculptor Pheidias was entrusted with supervising the building of a new Doric temple to Athena, the patron goddess of the city. Built on the site of earlier temples, it was designed primarily to house the *Parthenos*, Pheidias's cult statue of Athena.

Taking just nine years to complete, the temple was dedicated to the goddess in the course of the Great Panathenaia festival of 438 BC. Designed and constructed in Pentelic marble by the architects Kallikrates and Iktinos, the Parthenon replaces straight lines with slight curves. It is thought that this complex architectural style was used to create an illusion of perfection *(see pp458–9)*.

For the pediments and the friezes that ran all the way around the temple, an army of sculptors and painters was employed. Agorakritos and Alkamenes, both pupils of Pheidias, are two of the sculptors who worked on the frieze, which depicted the people and horses in the Panathenaic procession.

Despite much damage and alterations made to adapt it to various uses, which have included a church, a mosque, and even an arsenal, the Parthenon remains a majestic sight today.

New Acropolis Museum

Dionysiou Areopagitou 15, Makrygianni. **Tel** 210-900 0900. **Open** summer: 8am–8pm Tue–Sun (to 10pm Fri); winter: 9am–5pm Tue–Sun (to 10pm Fri, to 8pm Sat & Sun). **Closed** Jan 1, Easter Sun, May 1, Dec 25 & 26. **W theacropolismuseum.gr**

Located a short walk from the Acropolis, this ultra-modern glass, steel, and concrete building, built by the Swiss architect Bernard Tschumi, exhibits finds from the Acropolis site.

The ground floor is made of partially reinforced glass, which exposes 4th century BC archaeological excavations below the building. Cases set in the walls display finds from early sanctuaries on the Acropolis, including votive offerings such as jewelry, figurines, and female *protomes* (busts) symbolizing fertility.

The Archaic Gallery showcases statues of young men, women, and horses, while the entire top floor is devoted to a reconstruction of a marble frieze that once ran around the top of the Parthenon. The original bas-reliefs are combined with crude white plaster copies of the so-called Elgin Marbles, removed by Lord Elgin in 1801 and now displayed in the British Museum in London *(see p455)*.

Around the Acropolis

The area around the Acropolis was the center of public life in Athens. In addition to the Agora in the north *(see p453)*, there were two theaters on the southern slope, the Theater of Herodes Atticus and the Theater of Dionysos. Political life was largely centered on the Areopagos and the Pynx Hills to the west of the Acropolis; the Ekklesia (citizens' assembly) met on the latter, while the former was the seat of the Supreme Judicial Court. Filopáppos Hill has always played an important defensive role in the city's history – a fort was built here overlooking the strategic Piraeus road in 294 BC. On the tree-clad Hill of the Nymphs, the 19th-century Danish-built Asteroskopeíon (Observatory) occupies the site of an old sanctuary dedicated to nymphs associated with childbirth.

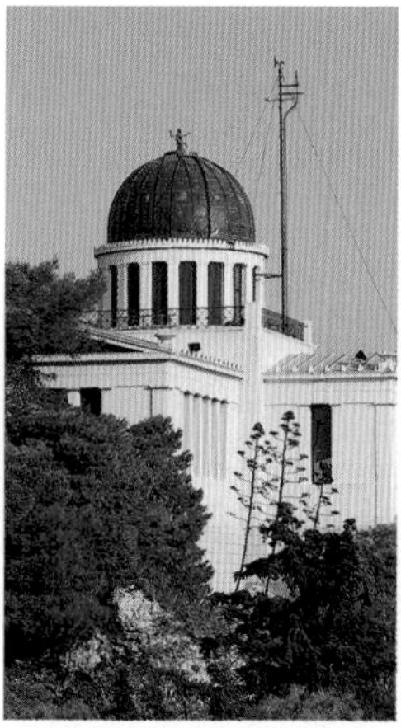

The Asteroskopeíon (Observatory) on the Hill of the Nymphs

⑥ Temple of Olympian Zeus

Corner of Amalías & Vasilíssis Olgas, Pláka. **Tel** 210-922 6330. 🚎 2, 4, 11. **Open** summer: 8am–7:30pm daily; winter: 8am–3pm daily. **Closed** main public hols. 🦽 ♿ limited.

This vast temple is the largest in Greece, exceeding even the Parthenon in size. The tyrant Peisistratos allegedly initiated the building of the temple in the 6th century BC to gain public favor. It was not completed until 650 years later.

In AD 132, the Roman Emperor Hadrian dedicated the temple to Zeus Olympios and set up a statue of the god inside, a copy of the original by Pheidias at Olympia *(see p469)*. Next to it he placed a huge statue of himself. Both statues have since been lost.

Only 15 of the original 104 columns remain, but enough to give a sense of the once enormous size of this temple – approximately 96 m (315 ft) long and 40 m (130 ft) wide. Roman-style Corinthian capitals were added to the original Doric columns in 174 BC.

The temple lies next to Hadrian's Arch, built in AD 131 and marking the boundary between the ancient city and the new Athens of Hadrian.

⑦ Benáki Museum

Corner of Koumpári & Vasilíssis Sofías, Kolonáki. **Tel** 210-367 1000. 🚎 3, 7, 8, 13. **Open** 9am–5pm Wed–Sun (to midnight Thu & Sat, to 3pm Sun). **Closed** public hols. 🦽 except Thu. ♿ limited. 🌐 **benaki.gr**

This museum contains a superb collection of Greek art and crafts, jewelry, regional costumes, and political memorabilia from the Neolithic era to the 20th century. It was founded by Antónios Benákis (1873–1954), who was interested in Greek, Persian, Egyptian, and Ottoman art from an early age and started collecting while living in Alexandria. On moving to Athens in 1926, he donated his collection to the Greek state. The family home, an elegant 19th-century

The remains of the Temple of Olympian Zeus

Neoclassical mansion, was used as a museum and opened to the public in 1931.

A major part of the Benáki collection consists of gold jewelry dating from as far back as 3000 BC. Also on display are icons, liturgical silverware, Egyptian artifacts, and Greek embroideries.

⑧ Museum of Cycladic Art

Neofýtou Doúka 4 (new wing at Irodótou 1), Kolonáki. **Tel** 210-722 8321. 🚎 3, 7, 8, 13. **Open** 10am–5pm Wed–Mon (to 8pm Thu, from 11am Sun). **Closed** main public hols. 🦽 ♿ 🌐 **cycladic.gr**

A magnificent selection of ancient Greek art, including the world's most important collection of Cycladic figurines, is on view at this modern museum.

The displays start on the first floor, with the Cycladic collection. Dating back to the 3rd millennium BC, the Cycladic figurines were found mostly in graves, although their exact usage remains a mystery. Ancient Greek art is exhibited on the second floor and the Charles Polítis collection of Classical and Prehistoric art on the fourth floor. The third floor displays some excellent ancient Cypriot art. Another wing in the adjoining Stathátos Mansion contains the Greek Art Collection of the Athens Academy.

⑨ National Gallery of Art

Vasiléos Konstantínou 50, Ilísia. **Tel** 210-723 5937. 🚎 3, 13. **Closed** for restoration until late 2015. 🦽 ♿

This modern building holds a permanent collection of European and Greek art. European exhibits include various works by van Dyck, Cézanne, Dürer, Rembrandt, Picasso, and Caravaggio. The majority of the collection, however, is made up of Greek art from the 18th to 20th centuries and includes paintings of the Greek War of Independence, seascapes, and some excellent portraits.

Modern sculpture outside the National Gallery of Art

Temple Architecture

Temples were the most important public buildings in ancient Greece, largely because religion was a central part of everyday life. Often placed in prominent positions, temples were also statements about political and divine power. The earliest temples, in the 8th century BC, were built of wood and sun-dried bricks. Many of their features were copied in marble buildings from the 6th century BC onward.

The Parthenon on the Acropolis in Athens

Temple Construction

This drawing is of an idealized Doric temple, showing how it was both built and used.

The cella, or inner sanctum, housed the cult statue.

The pediment, triangular in shape, often held sculpture.

The cult statue was of the god or goddess to whom the temple was dedicated.

Fluting on the columns was carved *in situ*, guided by that on the top and bottom drums.

The column drums were initially carved with bosses for lifting them into place.

A ramp led up to the temple entrance.

The stepped platform was built on a stone foundation.

The Illusion of Perfection

Every aspect of the Parthenon was built on a 9:4 ratio to make the temple completely symmetrical. The sculptors also used visual trickery to counteract the laws of perspective. The illustration *(right)* is exaggerated to show the techniques they employed.

The base of the temple is higher in the middle than at the edges.

Entasis (a bulge in the middle) makes each column look straight.

Each column leans slightly inward.

The gable ends of the roof were surmounted by statues, known as *akroteria*, in this case of a Nike or "Winged Victory". Almost no upper portions of Greek temples survive.

The roof was supported on wooden beams and covered in rows of terra-cotta tiles, each ending in an upright antefix.

Stone blocks were smoothly fitted together and held by metal clamps and dowels: no mortar was used in the temple's construction.

The ground plan was derived from the megaron of the Mycenaean house: a rectangular hall with a front porch that was supported by columns.

Caryatids, or figures of women, were used instead of columns in the Erechtheion at Athens' Acropolis. In Athens' Agora *(see p453)*, tritons (half-fish, half-human creatures) were used.

The Development of Temple Architecture

Greek temple architecture is divided into three styles, which evolved chronologically, and are most easily distinguished by the column capitals.

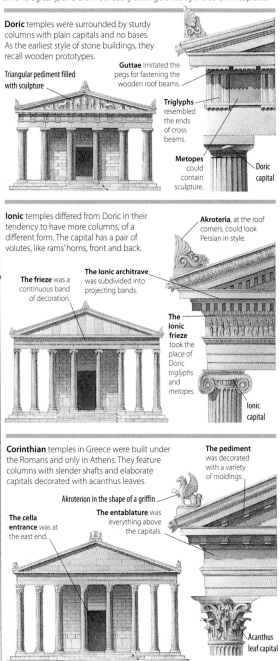

Doric temples were surrounded by sturdy columns with plain capitals and no bases. As the earliest style of stone buildings, they recall wooden prototypes.

Triangular pediment filled with sculpture

Guttae imitated the pegs for fastening the wooden roof beams.

Triglyphs resembled the ends of cross beams.

Metopes could contain sculpture.

Doric capital

Ionic temples differed from Doric in their tendency to have more columns, of a different form. The capital has a pair of volutes, like rams' horns, front and back.

Akroteria, at the roof corners, could look Persian in style.

The frieze was a continuous band of decoration.

The Ionic architrave was subdivided into projecting bands.

The Ionic frieze took the place of Doric *triglyphs* and *metopes*.

Ionic capital

Corinthian temples in Greece were built under the Romans and only in Athens. They feature columns with slender shafts and elaborate capitals decorated with acanthus leaves.

The pediment was decorated with a variety of moldings.

Akroterion in the shape of a griffin

The cella entrance was at the east end.

The entablature was everything above the capitals.

Acanthus leaf capital

Central Greece

Beyond the endless urban sprawl of Athens, the vast expanse of central Greece has a little of everything for the visitor, from sandy beaches and fishing ports, to one of the country's most important archaeological sites, Ancient Delphi. Not to be missed is the Byzantine splendor of the monasteries of Dafní and Osios Loúkas, while the extraordinary mountain-top monasteries of Metéora are another of the region's principal attractions. The beautiful wooded mountain slopes of the Pílio offer some of the best scenery on the mainland.

The Temple of Poseidon on the cape at Soúnio

❷ Soúnio

9 km (5.5 miles) S of Lávrio, Attica. **Tel** 22920-39363. 🚌 to Lávrio. **Open** 9:30am–sunset daily. 🏛

The temple of Poseidon, situated at the top of sheer cliffs tumbling into the Aegean Sea at Soúnio (Cape Sounion), was ideally located as a place to worship the powerful god of the sea. Its brilliant white marble columns have been a landmark for ancient and modern mariners alike.

The present temple, built in 444 BC, stands on the site of older ruins. An Ionic frieze, made from 13 slabs of Parian marble, is located on the east side of the temple's main approach path. It is very eroded, but is known to have depicted scenes from mythological battles, as well as the adventures of the hero Theseus, said in some legends to be the son of Poseidon.

Local marble from the quarries at Agriléza was used for the temple's 34 slender Doric columns, of which 15 survive today. In 1810 the British Romantic poet, Lord Byron,

carved his name on one of the columns, setting an unfortunate precedent of vandalism at the temple.

❸ Monastery of Dafní

10 km (6 miles) NW of Athens, Attica. **Tel** 210-581 1558. 🚌 **Open** 9am–2pm Tue & Fri. 🚹 limited.

Founded in the 5th century AD, the Monastery of Dafní is named after the laurels (dáfnes) that once grew here. It was built with the remains of an ancient

The 5th-century Byzantine Monastery of Dafní, near Athens

sanctuary of Apollo, which had occupied the site until it was destroyed in AD 395. In the early 13th century, Otto de la Roche, the first Frankish Duke of Athens, bequeathed it to Cistercian monks in Burgundy. Greek Orthodox monks took the site in the 16th century, erecting the elegant cloisters just south of the church. The monastery is presently closed for restoration, due to an earthquake which hit in the year 2000.

Among the monastery's principal attractions are the beautiful gold-leaf Byzantine mosaics in the katholikón (main church). Byzantine church architecture was concerned almost exclusively with decoration. Mosaics and frescoes portraying the whole body of the Church, from Christ downward, had a dual purpose: they gave inspiration to worshipers and represented windows to the spiritual world. The most impressive mosaics at Dafní are the Esonarthex Mosaics, which include the *Last Supper*, the *Washing of the Feet*, and the *Betrayal of Judas*. Equally magnificent, the *Christ Pantokrátor* is a mosaic of Christ in judgment that fills the church's huge dome.

❹ Monastery of Osios Loúkas

8 km (5 miles) E of Dístomo, Stereá Elláda. **Tel** 22670-22228. 🚌 **Open** 8am–6pm daily. 🏛

Dedicated to a local hermit and healer, Osios Loúkas ("Holy Luke"), who lived in the 10th century, this splendid monastery was one of medieval Greece's most important buildings architecturally. It was built around AD 1011 by the Emperor Romanós, who extended an earlier church dating from 944. The octagonal style of the main church, the katholikón, became a hallmark of late Byzantine church design, while the mosaics inside lifted Byzantine art into its final great period.

Among the most impressive features of the monastery are the 10th-century crypt, which is

Detail from an 11th-century mosaic in the Monastery of Osios Loúkas

from the original church and contains the sarcophagus of Holy Luke, and a mosaic entitled *Washing of the Apostles' Feet*. This 11th-century work, based on a style dating back to the 6th century, is the finest of a number of mosaics found in the narthex, the western entrance hall. The monastery's main dome is decorated with an imposing mural of Christ, painted in the 16th century to replace fallen mosaics.

❺ Ancient Delphi

Mount Parnassus, Stereá Elláda. **Tel** 22650-82312. 🚌 **Open** 8:30am–7:30pm daily (winter: to 3pm). **Closed** main public hols. 🚻 ♿

In ancient times, Delphi was believed to be the center of the earth. The site was renowned as a dwelling place of Apollo, and from the late 8th century BC people came here to worship and seek advice from the god. With the political rise of Delphi in the 6th century BC, and the establishment of the Pythian Games – a cultural, religious, and athletic festival – the site entered a golden age that lasted until the arrival of the Romans in 191 BC. The Delphic Oracle was abolished in AD 393 after Christianity was introduced as the state religion.

The Sanctuary of Apollo, also known as the Sacred Precinct, forms the heart of the complex, and one of its most impressive sights is the **Temple of Apollo**. A temple has stood on this spot since the 6th century BC, but

the remains visible today date from the 4th century BC. Leading from the sanctuary entrance to the Temple of Apollo is the **Sacred Way**, once lined with some 3,000 statues and treasuries. Also worth seeing is the well-preserved **Stadium**. The present structure dates from Roman times, and most of the seating is still intact.

The Marmaria Precinct, or marble quarry, is where the **Sanctuary of Athena Pronaia** is found. Here, the most remarkable monument is the *tholos*, which dates from the 4th century BC. The purpose of this circular structure, originally surrounded by 20 columns, remains a mystery.

The museum at Ancient Delphi houses an impressive collection of sculptures and architectural remains.

❻ Pílio

Thessaly. 🚌 Vólos. 🚊 🛈 Plateía Riga Feraíou, Vólos (24210-23500).

The Pilio Peninsula is one of the most beautiful areas of the mainland. The mountain air is sweet with the scent of herbs, which in ancient times were renowned for their healing properties. The area became populated in the 13th century by Greeks retreating from the

Traditional-style guesthouses in the Pílio village of Vyzítsa

Ottomans. After centuries of protecting its culture, the Pílio is known for its strong local cuisine.

The main town on the peninsula is **Vólos**, which has an excellent Archaeological Museum. From here you can make a tour of the many traditional hillside villages and fishing ports. Worth visiting are **Miliés**, with its Folk Museum and fresco-adorned church, and picturesque **Vyzítsa**. **Argalastí** has a busy market, though its tavernas and cafés retain a peaceful atmosphere. For fine sandy beaches and excellent seafood, visit the popular coastal resorts of **Plataniá** or **Agios Ioánnis**.

The *tholos* beside the Sanctuary of Athena Pronaia at Ancient Delphi

❼ Metéora

The extraordinary sandstone towers of Metéora (or "suspended rocks") were formed by the action of the sea that covered the plain of Thessaly around 30 million years ago. The huge columns of rock were first used as a religious retreat in AD 985, when a hermit named Barnabas occupied a cave here. In the mid-14th century, Neílos, the Prior of Stagai convent, built a small church. A few years later, in 1382, the monk Athanásios, from Mount Athos, founded the huge monastery of Megálo Metéoro on one of the many pinnacles. A further 23 monasteries were built, though most had fallen into ruin by the 19th century. In the 1920s, stairs were cut in the rock faces to make the remaining six monasteries more accessible, and today a religious revival has seen the return of a number of monks and nuns.

Location of Monasteries of Metéora

Rousánou
Moní Rousánou, perched precariously on the very tip of a narrow spire of rock, is the most spectacularly located of all the monasteries. Its church of the Metamórfosis (1545) is renowned for its harrowing frescoes, painted in 1560 by the iconographers of the Cretan school.

KEY

① **Outer walls**

② **Monastic cells**

③ **The refectory** contains a small icon museum.

④ **Net descending from tower**.

Megálo Metéoro
Also known as the Great Meteoron, this was the first and, at 623 m (2,045 ft), highest monastery to be founded. By the entrance is a cave in which Athanásios first lived. His body is buried in the main church.

Katholikón
Dedicated to Agioi Pántes (All Saints), the church is adorned with frescoes, including one of Theofánis (right) and Nektários, its founders.

VISITORS' CHECKLIST

Practical Information
Thessaly. 🚹 Pindou & Ioannina Street (24320-78000). Megálo Metéoro: **Tel** 24320-75398. **Open** summer: Wed–Mon; winter: Thu–Mon. Varlaám: **Tel** 24320-22277. **Open** summer: Sat–Thu; winter: Sat–Wed. Agíou Nikoláou: **Open** Sat–Thu. Rousánou: **Tel** 24320-22649. **Open** Thu–Tue. Agías Triádas: **Tel** 24320-22220. **Open** summer: Fri–Wed; winter: Fri–Tue. Agíou Stefánou: **Tel** 24320-22279. **Open** Tue–Sun. All monasteries: **Closed** 1–3pm. 🚫 🚻 Agías Triádas & Agíou Stefánou.

Transport
🚌

Ascent Tower
Goods and people were brought to the top of the rock in a net that was pulled up by a winch mechanism, made in 1536.

Entrance

④

Varlaam
Founded in 1518, the monastery of Varlaám is named after the first hermit to live on this rock in 1350. The katholikón (main church) was built in 1542 and contains frescoes by the Theban iconographer Frágkos Katelános.

The Building of the Monasteries

Though it is unknown how the first hermits at Metéora reached the tops of these often vertical rock faces, it is likely that they hammered pegs into tiny gaps in the rock and hauled building materials to the summits. Another theory is that kites were flown over the tops, carrying strings attached to thicker ropes, which were made into the first rope ladders. How the ladders were anchored to the rock is uncertain.

Northern Greece

Northern Greece offers an appealing combination of comparatively unexplored natural beauty and a rich cultural heritage. The stunning scenery of places like Mount Olympos holds special appeal to walking enthusiasts, while of historical interest in the region are several ancient archaeological sites, including Pélla, the birthplace of Alexander the Great. Many of northern Greece's finest examples of Byzantine architecture and art are to be found on the Athos Peninsula and in the bustling city of Thessaloníki.

The 15th-century White Tower on the waterfront in Thessaloníki

❽ Thessaloníki

👥 1,000,000. ✈ 25 km (15 miles) SE. 🚌 🚆 🚢 ℹ 136 Tsimiski (2310-221100).

Thessaloníki, also known as Salonica, is Greece's second city, and was founded by King Kassandros in 315 BC. The capital of the Roman province of Macedonia Prima from 146 BC, it later became part of the Byzantine Empire. In 1430 it was captured by the Turks, who held it until 1912. Today Thessaloníki is a bustling cosmopolitan city and a major religious center.

On the *paralía*, the city's attractive waterfront, stands one of Thessaloníki's most famous sights, the **White Tower**. Built in 1430, this is one of three towers that were added to the city walls by the Turks. Today it houses a permanent exhibition tracing the city's history. The **Arch of Galerius** was built in

AD 303 by the Emperor Galerius to celebrate victory over the Persians, and is the principal architectural legacy of Roman rule. Standing north of the arch is the **Rotónda**, believed to have been constructed as a mausoleum for Galerius. Now closed, it has been used in the past as both a church and a mosque.

Thessaloníki has a number of museums, including the **Museum of Byzantine Culture** and the **Museum of the Macedonian Struggle**, which focuses on the centuries of Turkish domination. The star attractions at the city's **Archaeological Museum** are the Roman floor mosaics, and the splendid Dervéni Krater, a

4th-century BC bronze wine-mixing bowl. You should also make time to see the museum's stunning collection of Macedonian gold.

Visitors should not miss the city's rich array of UNESCO-listed Byzantine churches, which include the 5th-century **Agios Dimítrios** – the largest church in Greece. Dating from the mid-8th century, **Agía Sofía** is an important building, both for its mosaics and for its role in influencing future architectural development, while the 14th-century **Agios Nikólaos Orfanós** contains the best-preserved collection of late Byzantine frescoes in the city.

🏛 **Archaeological Museum**
Manóli Andrónikou & Leof Stratoú. **Tel** 2310-830538. 🚌 3. **Open** daily. **Closed** main public hols. 🅿 ♿ 🌐 amth.gr

❾ Ancient Pélla

38 km (24 miles) NW of Thessaloníki. **Tel** 23820-33094. **Open** daily. **Closed** main public hols. 🅿 ♿

This small site was once the flourishing capital of Macedonia. The court was moved here from Aigai (near modern Vergína) in 410 BC by King Archelaos, who ruled from

The Macedonian Royal Family

The gold burial casket found at Vergína is emblazoned with the Macedonian Sun, the symbol of the king. Philip II was from a long line of Macedonian kings that began in about 640 BC with Perdiccas I. Philip was the first ruler to unite the whole of Greece as it existed at that time. Much of Greece's pride in the symbol lies in the fact that Alexander the Great used it throughout his empire. He was just 20 when his father was assassinated in 336 BC. He inherited his father's already large empire and also his ambition to conquer the Persians. In 334 BC, Alexander crossed the Dardanelles with 40,000 men and defeated the Persians in three different battles, advancing as far as the Indus Valley before he died at the age of 33. With his death, the Macedonian empire divided.

Gold burial casket from the Royal Tombs at Vergína

For hotels and restaurants see pp484–6 and pp487–9

The Russian Orthodox monastery Agíou Panteleímonos, on Mount Athos

413 to 399 BC. It is here that Alexander the Great was born in 356 BC, and was later tutored by the philosopher Aristotle. Some sense of the existence of a city can be gained from a plan of the site, which shows where the main street and stores were located. The palace, believed to have been north of the main site, is still being excavated.

At the site, and in the museum, are some of the best-preserved pebble mosaics in Greece. Dating from about 300 BC, the mosaics depict vivid hunting scenes. One of the most famous is of Dionysos riding a panther; it is housed in the now-covered, 4th-century BC House of the Lion Hunt. Originally comprising 12 rooms around three open courtyards, this building was constructed at the end of the 4th century BC.

⑩ Mount Athos

Athos Peninsula. 🚢 Dáfni (boat trips from Ouranoúpoli & Thessaloníki for the west coast, or from Ierissós for the east coast). 🚌 to Karyés. 🎫 donation.

Also known as the Holy Mountain, Mount Athos is the highest point on the Athos Peninsula – an autonomous republic, ruled by the 1,700 monks who live in its 20 monasteries. Only adult males may visit the peninsula, but it is possible to see many of the monasteries from a boat trip along the coast. They include some fine examples of Byzantine architecture and provide a fascinating insight into Orthodox monastic life.

For the monks who live here, the day begins at 3 or 4am with morning services and prayers. They eat two meals a day, which consist mainly of food they grow themselves. There are 159 fasting days in the year. Between meals, the monks spend their time working, resting, and praying.

Ouranoúpoli is the main town on Athos and where the boat trips for the peninsula's west coast start. Among the monasteries that can be viewed are the 10th-century **Docheiaríou, Agíou Panteleímonos**, an 11th-century Russian Orthodox monastery, and **Moní Agíou Pávlou**. On the east coast, **Megístis Lávras** was the first monastery to be founded on Athos, while 10th-century **Moní Vatopedíou**, farther north, is one of the largest and best-preserved buildings. Adult males wishing to visit any of the monasteries must obtain a letter of recommendation from the Greek consul in their country. The Ministry of Foreign Affairs in Athens, or Ministry of Macedonia and Thrace in Thessaloníki, will then issue a permit allowing a stay of up to four nights. Accommodations are free, though donations are expected.

⑪ Mount Olympos

17 km (10 miles) W of Litóchoro. 🚌 Litóchoro. ℹ️ EOS: Evángelou Karavákou 20, Litóchoro (23520-83000). 🌐 **olympusfd.gr**

The name Mount Olympos refers to a whole range of mountains, 20 km (12 miles) across. The highest peak in the range is Mytikas, at 2,917 m (9,570 ft). The entire area constitutes the Olympos National Park, an area of outstanding natural beauty that attracts naturalists and walkers alike. The park's rich flora and fauna include 1,700 plant species, in addition to chamois, boars, and roe deer. From **Litóchoro**, which has several hotels and tavernas, walkers can follow a series of trails.

A short distance from Litóchoro is **Ancient Díon**, considered a holy city by the ancient Macedonians. The flat plains were used as a military camp by King Philip II of Macedon in the 4th century BC. The ruins visible today – which include mosaics, baths, and a theater – date mainly from the Roman era. A museum shows finds from the site.

The peaks of the Mount Olympos range rising above Litóchoro

The Peloponnese

One of the primary strongholds and battlefields of the 1821–31 Revolution, the Peloponnese is the kernel from which the modern Greek state grew. The region boasts a wealth of ancient and medieval ruins, from Bronze Age Mycenae to the Byzantine town of Mystrás. As popular as its vast array of historical sites is the Peloponnese's spectacularly varied landscape. The breathtaking scenery of places like the Loúsios Gorge attracts walkers and naturalists in their thousands.

The ruins of Acrocorinth, south of Ancient Corinth

⑫ Ancient Corinth

7 km (4 miles) SW of modern Corinth. **Tel** 27410-31207. **Open** 8am–8pm daily (winter: to 3pm). **Closed** main public hols. limited.

A settlement since Neolithic times, Ancient Corinth was razed in 146 BC by the Romans, who rebuilt it a century later. Attaining a population of 750,000 under the patronage of the Roman emperors, the town gained a reputation for licentious living, which St. Paul attacked when he came here in AD 52. Excavations have revealed the vast extent of the ancient city, which was destroyed by earthquakes in Byzantine times. The ruins constitute the largest Roman township in Greece.

Among the most impressive remains are the **Lechaion Way**, the marble-paved road that linked the nearby port of Lechaion with the city, and the **Temple of Apollo**, with its striking Doric columns. The temple was one of the few buildings preserved by the Romans when they rebuilt the city in 44 BC. Of the **Temple of Octavia**, once dedicated to the sister of Emperor Augustus, three ornate Corinthian columns, overarched by a restored architrave, are all that remain. The **Odeion** is one of several buildings endowed to the city by Herodes Atticus, the wealthy Athenian and friend of the Emperor Hadrian.

Close to the Odeion, the **Museum** houses a collection of exhibits representing all periods of the town's history. The Roman gallery is particularly rich, containing some spectacular 2nd-century AD mosaics lifted from the floors of nearby villas.

Just 4 km (2 miles) south of Ancient Corinth is the bastion of **Acrocorinth**, to which there is access between 8:30am and 3pm each day. Held and refortified by every occupying power in Greece from Roman times onward, it was one of the country's most important fortresses in medieval times. The ruins show evidence of Byzantine, Turkish, Frankish, and Venetian occupation. The summit of Acrocorinth affords one of the most sweeping views in the whole of Greece.

Reconstruction of Ancient Corinth (c.AD 100)

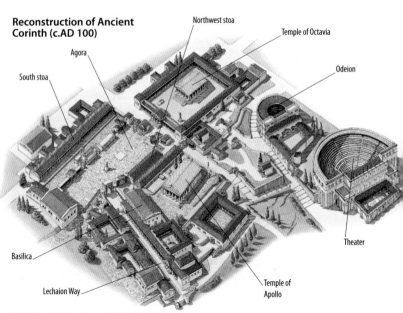

- Northwest stoa
- Temple of Octavia
- Agora
- Odeion
- South stoa
- Basilica
- Lechaion Way
- Temple of Apollo
- Theater

Interior of the tomb known as the Treasury of Atreus, at Mycenae

⓭ Mycenae

2 km (1 mile) N of Mykínes. **Tel** 27510-76585. 🚌 to Mykínes. **Open** daily. **Closed** main public hols. ♿ 🏛 Treasury of Atreus and museum only.

Discovered in 1874, the fortified palace complex of Mycenae is an early example of sophisticated citadel architecture. The Mycenaeans were a Bronze Age culture that existed between 1700 and 1100 BC. Only the ruling class inhabited the palace, with artisans and merchants living outside the city walls. The citadel was abandoned in 1100 BC after much disruption in the region.

The tombs at Mycenae are one of the most famous attractions of the site. The city's nobles were entombed in shaft graves, such as those at **Grave Circle A**, or, later, in *tholos* ("beehive") tombs, so-called because of their shape. The *tholos* tombs, found outside the palace walls, were buried under an earth mound, the only entrance being via a *dromos*, or open-air corridor. The 14th-century BC **Treasury of Atreus** is the most outstanding of the *tholos* tombs. Here a Mycenaean king was buried with his weapons and enough food and drink for his journey to the underworld. The so-called **Tomb of Klytemnestra** is equally well preserved. Also

of interest at the site are the remains of the **Royal Palace**, the **Secret Stairway**, which leads down to a cistern deep beneath the citadel, and the 13th-century BC **Lion Gate**, the grand entrance to Mycenae.

⓮ Epidaurus

30 km (19 miles) E of Náfplio. **Tel** 27530-22009. 🚌 **Open** daily. **Closed** main public hols. ♿ 🏛 limited. 🎧

Active from the 6th century BC until at least the 2nd century AD, the Sanctuary of Epidaurus was an extensive therapeutic and religious center, dedicated to the healing god Asklepios.

The site is most renowned for its magnificent **Theater**, whose *cavea* (cavity) is 114 m (374 ft) across and surrounds a 20-m- (66-ft-) diameter *orchestra* (stage). Designed in the late 4th century BC, the theater is well known for near-perfect acoustics, and has the only circular *orchestra* to have survived from antiquity. Today, it is the venue for an annual summer festival of ancient drama.

Most of the **Asklepieion**, or Sanctuary of Asklepios, is currently being re-excavated. Accessible remains include the *propylaia*, or monumental gateway, a late Classical stadium, and the *tholos* – a circular building, thought to have been used either as a pit for sacred serpents, or as the setting for religious rites. Of Asklepios's temple, to the east of the *tholos*, only the foundations have survived.

⓯ Náfplio

🏠 12,000. 🚗 🚌 🛈 Ikosíspémptis Martíou 24 (27520-24444).

One of the most elegant towns in mainland Greece, Náfplio emerged in the 13th century and later endured many sieges during the struggles between the Turks and the Venetians for the ports of the Peloponnese. From 1829 to 1834, it was the first capital of liberated Greece.

A number of fortifications testify to the town's checkered history. The island fortress of **Boúrtzi** is a legacy of the second Venetian occupation (1686–1715). **Akronafplía**, also known as Its Kale ("Inner Castle" in Turkish), was the site of the Byzantine and early medieval town, while the Venetian citadel of **Palamídi** was built between 1711 and 1714.

The Plateía Syntágmatos, the hub of public life, looks much as it did three centuries ago, when two mosques were built by the victorious Ottomans. These are now the cathedral, **Agios Geórgios**, and the **Catholic church**.

The town has two museums of note: the award-winning **Folk Art Museum**, and the **Archaeological Museum**, which houses mainly local pre-Mycenaean artifacts.

Located 4 km (2 miles) outside Náfplio, the 12th-century convent of **Agía Moní** is worth visiting.

🏛 **Archaeological Museum**
Plateía Syntágmatos. **Tel** 27520-27502. **Open** summer: 8am–8pm Tue–Sun (Mon pm only); winter: 8am–3pm Tue–Sun. **Closed** main public hols.

The fortified isle of Boúrtzi, north of Náfplio harbor

The cliff-top church of Agía Sofía, Monemvasía upper town

16 Monemvasía

🗺 800. 🚌 🚈 ℹ 27320-61210.

This fortified town is built on two levels on a rock rising 350 m (1,150 ft) above the sea. A town of 50,000 in its 15th-century halcyon days, Monemvasía was for centuries a semi-autonomous city-state, which prospered thanks to its strategic position astride the sea lanes from Italy to the Black Sea. After a long and protracted siege, the town was finally surrendered by the Turks in 1821 during the War of Independence.

In the restored lower town, enclosed by the formidable 16th-century walls, are a number of mosques and churches. They include the 18th-century **Panagía Myrtidióssa** and the 13th-century cathedral, **Christós Elkómenos**, with its Venetian belfry. Also found in the lower town is **Giánnis Rítsos's House**, where this prominent 20th-century Greek poet and communist was born.

The upper town, which lies largely in ruins, has been uninhabited since 1911. It was first fortified in the 6th century, and is the oldest part of Monemvasía. Here, the most impressive sight is the still-intact, cliff-top church of **Agía Sofía**, founded by Emperor Andronikos II (1282–1328) and modeled on the Monastery of Dafní *(see p460)*. Visitors can also see the remains of a 13th-century fortress.

17 Máni Peninsula

🚌 Gýtheio. 🚈 Kalamáta (Outer Máni), Areópoli (Inner Máni). ℹ Vasiléos Georgiou 20, Gýtheio (27330-24484).

The harsh and remote Máni Peninsula is divided into two areas, Outer Máni and Inner Máni, separated by a ravine at Oítylo. The area is most famous for its history of internal feuding, which led to the building of many fine tower houses. From the 15th century, rival clansmen, fighting over the inadequate land, used the towers to shoot at their opponents. After years of bloodshed, the clans finally united, instigating the Greek Independence uprising in 1821.

The main places of interest in more fertile Outer Máni are **Oítylo**, with its elegant 19th-century mansions, and **Kardamýli**, the lair of the Troupákis family, one of the most important Maniot clans. In the environs of Kardamýli are the stunning **Vyrós Gorge**, and **Stoúpa**, popular for its two sandy bays. **Mount Taÿgetos** is one of the area's beauty spots, and can offer several days of wilderness trekking to experienced, well-equipped mountaineers.

In Inner Máni, bustling **Gýtheio** is one of the most attractive coastal towns in the southern Peloponnese. Its 18th-century fortress houses the Museum of the Máni. **Areópoli**, "the city of Ares" (god of war), was where the Maniot uprising against the Turks was proclaimed by Pétros Mavromichális. Nearby

Fishing boats moored in Gýtheio harbor in Inner Máni

is the 17th-century Ottoman **Kelefá Castle**. Visitors to Inner Máni should also see the **Pýrgos Diroú** cave system, and the many Byzantine churches scattered along the west coast. Built between the 10th and 14th centuries, the finest churches include **Taxiarchón**, at Charoúda, **Agios Theódoros**, at Vámvaka, and, near Ano Mpoulárioi village, **Agios Panteleímon** contains 10th-century frescoes. Overlooking the sea and Cape Taínaro, **Vátheia** is one of the most dramatically located of the villages in the Máni. It is worth visiting just to see its collection of tower houses.

Ruins of the Despots' Palace in the Byzantine town of Mystrás

18 Mystrás

5 km (3 miles) W of Spárti. **Tel** 27310-83377. 🚌 to Néos Mystrás. **Open** daily. **Closed** main public hols. 🚫

Majestic Mystrás occupies a panoramic site on a spur of the severe Taÿgetos range. Founded by the Franks in 1249, the town soon passed to the Byzantines, under whom it attained a population of 20,000 and, after 1348, became the seat of the Despots of Morea. The despotate acted semi-independently and, by the 15th century, Mystrás had become the last major Byzantine cultural center, attracting scholars and artists from Italy, Constantinople, and Serbia. One result was the uniquely cosmopolitan decoration of Mystrás's churches, whose pastel-colored frescoes, crowded with detail, reflect Italian Renaissance influence.

Now in ruins, Mystrás consists of an upper and lower town, with a wealth of churches, monasteries, palaces, and houses lining its narrow, winding streets. Among the churches and monasteries worth visiting are **Mitrópoli** – the oldest church in Mystrás, dating from 1291 – **Moní Perivléptou**, and **Moní Pantánassas**. The **Vrontóchion**, a 13th-century monastic complex, was the cultural heart of medieval Mystrás. Visitors can also explore the ruins of the **Despots' Palace**, and the **Kástro**, an impressive fortification that crowns the summit of the upper town, and affords magnificent views of the entire site.

⑲ Loúsios Gorge

🚌 Dimitsána. All monasteries **Open** dawn to dusk daily. Moní Aimyalón **Closed** 2–5pm.

Although merely a tributary of the Alfeiós River, the Loúsios stream boasts one of the most impressive canyons in Greece. Scarcely 5 km (3 miles) long, the Loúsios Gorge is nearly 300 m (985 ft) deep at its narrowest section. A number of hiking trails

Moní Agíou Ioánnou Prodrómou in the Loúsios Gorge

Remains of the Palaestra, or training center, at Ancient Olympia

connect the area's highlights, which include several churches and monasteries clinging to the steep cliffs of the gorge. Of these, the most impressive are **Moní Aimyalón**, founded in 1605 and containing some magnificent frescoes, the 17th-century **Néa Moní Filosófou**, and the 10th-century **Moní Agíou Ioánnou Prodrómou**, wedged into the canyon's east flank. Occupying a sunken excavation on the stream's west bank is the Asklepieíon, or therapeutic center, of **Ancient Gortys**. On this site lie the foundations of a 4th-century BC temple to Asklepios, the god of healing.

Overlooking the gorge, the beautiful hillside towns of **Dimitsána** and **Stemnítsa** make a good base from which to explore the area.

🏛 **Ancient Gortys**
Open daily. **Closed** main public hols.

⑳ Ancient Olympia

Tel 26240-22517. 🚌 🚐 **Open** daily. **Closed** main public hols. 🎫

The sanctuary of Olympia enjoyed over 1,000 years of renown as a religious and athletics center. Though it flourished in Mycenaean times, its historic importance dates to the coming of the Dorians, at the beginning of the first

millennium BC. They brought the worship of Zeus, after whose abode on Mount Olympos the site was named. Olympia reached its zenith in the 5th century BC, but by the end of the reign of Roman Emperor Hadrian (AD 117–38), it had begun to have less religious and political significance. The first Olympian Games, the forerunner of the Olympic Games, took place here in 776 BC, but were banned in AD 393 by Emperor Theodosius I, who took a dim view of the pagan festival.

The most important ruins include the 5th-century BC Doric **Temple of Zeus**, of which only column bases and tumbled sections remain, and the partly reconstructed **Palaestra**, which was a training center for athletes. In **Pheidias's Workshop**, a huge statue of Zeus was sculpted in the 5th century BC.

Also not to be missed is the **Archaeological Museum**, one of the richest museums in Greece, with exhibits from prehistory, through to the Classical period and the Roman era. The central hall houses the pediment and metope sculpture from the Temple of Zeus. There is also a small museum dedicated to the Olympic Games.

🏛 **Archaeological Museum**
Tel 26240-22742. **Open** daily. **Closed** main public hols, May–mid-Oct. 🎫 📷 ♿

㉑ Corfu and the Ionian Islands

The Ionian Islands are the greenest and most fertile of all the island groups. Lying off the west coast of mainland Greece, they have been greatly influenced by Western Europe. Periods of rule by the Venetians, French, and British have left their mark on many of the islands, especially in the mixed architecture of places like Corfu town. The Ionians first became a holiday destination during the Roman era, and today their beaches remain one of their most popular attractions.

Locator Map

The elegant parade of cafés known as the Liston in Corfu town

Corfu

🏙 100,000. ✈ 3 km (1.5 miles) S of Corfu town. ⛴ Xenofóntos Stratigoú, Corfu town. 🚌 ℹ Evangelistrias 4 (26610-37520).

Corfu offers the diverse attractions of secluded coves, bustling resorts, and traditional hill villages. Between 229 BC and AD 337 it was part of the Roman empire. It remained under Byzantine rule until the 14th century, when the Venetians took control. French and British occupation followed, before unification with Greece in 1864. Though the island is most popular for its beaches, inland there are many places where you can still observe the traditional lifestyle of the Corfiot people.

Corfu Town

The checkered history of the island is reflected in Corfu town's varied architecture. With its grand French-style colonnades, elegant Italianate buildings, and famous cricket pitch, the town is a delightful blend of European influences.

The **Palace of St. Michael and St. George** was built by the British between 1819 and 1824 to serve as the residence of a high commissioner. Used for a short time by the Greek royal family after the British left the island, the palace is now home to the **Museum of Asiatic Art**.

The palace overlooks the Esplanade, or Spianáda, a mixture of park and town square, and the site of the cricket ground. Once a Venetian firing range, the cricket pitch was developed by the British, and local teams play here regularly. Nearby, the Enosis Monument commemorates the 1864 union of the Ionian Islands with the rest of Greece. The **Liston**, a parade of cafés that was built in 1807 as a copy of the Rue de Rivoli in Paris, lines one side of the square.

Another of the town's most famous sights, the distinctive red-domed belfry of **Agios Spyrídon** is the tallest belfry on Corfu. The church was built in 1589 and dedicated to the island's patron saint.

Also worth seeing are the **Town Hall** – a grand Venetian building located in the Plateía Dimarcheíou – the **Byzantine Museum**, and the fascinating **Archaeological Museum**. The latter's centerpiece is a stunning Gorgon frieze.

On the town's eastern side stands the 16th-century Venetian-built **Old Fortress**, which affords magnificent views of the town and along the island's east coast. The **New Fortress** was built shortly after the old one to strengthen the town's defenses.

🏛 **Palace of St. Michael and St. George**
Palaia Anaktora. **Tel** 26610-30443. **Open** Tue–Sun. **Closed** main public hols.

Northern Corfu

Northern Corfu, in particular the northeast coast, is a busy vacation destination, which boasts a whole host of popular resorts and beaches. Set around a fishing harbor, **Kassiópi** has retained its character in spite

The multiple picturesque bays of Palaiokastrítsa in northern Corfu

Vacation apartments at Fiskárdo on the island of Kefalloniá

of the influx of tourists. Nearby are the ruins of a 13th-century castle, and the church of Kassiopítissa, which occupies the site of a former temple of Jupiter.

The bustling vacation center of **Sidári** is famous for its sandy beaches and unusual rock formations, while picturesque **Palaiokastrítsa** has safe swimming and water sports, as well as boat trips to nearby grottoes. Vacationers wanting a diversion from the busy resort atmosphere can visit the 17th-century monastery, **Moní Theotókou**.

Mount Pantokrátor, a short drive north of Corfu town, is popular with walkers and naturalists. The highest point on Corfu, it offers fine views of the whole island.

Southern Corfu

More varied than the north, southern Corfu offers other attractions apart from beaches. Tranquil hillside villages, such as **Vátos** and **Pélekas**, contrast with noisy resorts like **Benítses**, offering a more traditional image of Greece.

Among the more peaceful spots in the south is the **Korisíon Lagoon**, a 5-km- (3-mile-) stretch of water, separated from the sea by some of the most beautiful dunes and beaches on Corfu. The area provides a habitat for many species of birds and wild flowers.

A popular day trip from any of Corfu's resorts is to the **Achílleion Palace**, built between 1890 and 1891 as a personal retreat for the Empress

Elizabeth of Austria (1837–98). After a tour of the palace and its gardens, visit the Vasilákis Tastery opposite, and sample this local distiller's products.

🏛 Achílleion Palace
19 km (12 miles) SW of Corfu town. 📞 **Tel** 26610-56210. **Open** daily.

Kefalloniá

🏛 31,000. ✈ 9 km (6 miles) S of Argostóli. ⛴ Argostóli, Fiskárdo. 🚌 Ioánnou Metaxá, Argostóli. 🛈 Waterfront, Argostóli (26710-22248).

The largest island in the Ionians, Kefalloniá has a range of attractions, from busy beach resorts to areas of outstanding natural beauty.

The capital, **Argostóli**, is a busy town located by a bay. Of interest are the Historical and Folk Museum and the Archaeological Museum.

Around the island, the liveliest places are **Lássi** and the south-coast resorts, but elsewhere there are quiet villages and

stunning scenery. **Mount Aínos** and the **Mount Aínos National Park**, in the south, and the haunting, subterranean **Melissaní Cave-Lake** are sights not to be missed. **Fiskárdo**, with its 18th-century Venetian houses clustered by the harbor, is Kefallonia's prettiest village. From here ferry services are available to the islands of **Ithaca** and **Lefkáda**.

Zákynthos

🏛 30,000. ✈ 4 km (2.5 miles) S of Zákynthos town. ⛴ Zákynthos town, Agios Nikólaos. 🚌 Zákynthos town. 🛈 Molos Ag Dionysios, Zákynthos town (26953-61300).

Zákynthos is an attractive and green island, with good beaches and beautiful scenery to be enjoyed.

Zákynthos town is the point of arrival on the island. Here, the impressive church of Agios Dionysios, and the Byzantine Museum, which houses a breathtaking array of frescoes, both deserve a visit.

The growth of tourism on Zákynthos has been heavily concentrated in **Laganás** and its 14-km- (9-mile-) sweep of soft sand. The town's hectic nightlife continues until dawn. Alternatively, visitors can head to the island's north coast for the beach resorts of **Tsiliví** and **Alykés**, the latter being especially good for windsurfing. At the northernmost tip of the island are the unusual and spectacular **Blue Caves**. The caves can be visited by boat from the resort of **Agios Nikólaos**.

The Blue Caves of Zákynthos at the northern tip of the island

㉒ Cyclades

The most visited island group, the Cyclades are everyone's Greek island ideal, with their whitewashed, cliff-top villages, blue-domed churches, and stunning beaches. The islands vary greatly, from the quiet and traditional to the more nightlife-oriented. The cradle of the Cycladic civilization (3000–1000 BC), they also offer a rich ancient history. Important archaeological sites, such as those on Delos and Santoríni, provide a fascinating insight into the past.

Locator Map

Working 16th-century windmill, part of the Folk Museum in Mýkonos town

Mýkonos

🏛 4,500. ✈ 3 km (1.5 miles) SE of Mýkonos town. ⛴ Mýkonos town. 🚌 Polykandrióti, Mýkonos town (for north of island); on road to Ornós, Mýkonos town (for south of island). 🛈 Harborfront, Mýkonos town (22890-23261).

Sandy beaches and dynamic nightlife combine to make Mýkonos one of the most popular islands in the Cyclades. Visited by intellectuals in the early days of tourism, today it thrives on its reputation as the glitziest island in Greece. In addition to offering sun, sea, and sand, the island is a good base from which to visit the ancient archaeological site on Delos.

Mýkonos Town

The supreme example of a Cycladic town, Mýkonos town (or Chóra) is a tangle of dazzling white alleys and cube-shaped houses. It has a bustling port, from where taxi boats for the island of **Delos** leave. To the south, the **Archaeological Museum** has a fine collection of exhibits, including finds from the excavations of the ruins on Delos.

In the Kástro, the oldest part of town, is the excellent **Folk Museum**. The 16th-century Vonís Windmill, still in working order, is part of the museum. Nearby, the most famous church on the island is **Panagía Paraportianí**, which dates back to 1425. From Kástro, the lanes run down into picturesque Venetía, or Little Venice, the artists' quarter. Also worth visiting are the **Maritime Museum of the Aegean** and the **Municipal Art Gallery**.

🏛 Archaeological Museum
Harborfront. **Tel** 22890-22325. **Open** Tue–Sun. **Closed** main public hols. 🐾

Around the Island
Mýkonos is popular primarily for its beaches and one of the best is stylish **Platýs Gialós**, 3.5 km (2 miles) south of Mýkonos town. There are also several nudist beaches, including quiet **Parága** and the more lively **Paradise**, **Super Paradise**, and **Eliá**.

Inland, the traditional village of **Ano Merá** remains largely unspoiled by tourism. The main attraction here is the 16th-century monastery **Panagía i Tourlianí**.

🏛 Delos
2.5 km (1 mile) SW of Mýkonos town. **Tel** 22890-22259. ⛴ 8–10am daily from Mýkonos town returning noon–2pm. **Open** Tue–Sun. **Closed** main public hols. 🐾 🎫

The tiny, uninhabited island of Delos is one of the most important archaeological sites in Greece. The legendary birthplace of Artemis and Apollo, from 1000 BC it was home to the annual Delian Festival, held in honor of the god Apollo. By 700 BC, it had become a major religious center and place of pilgrimage. In addition to some impressive 2nd-century BC mosaics and temple ruins, the most important remains on Delos are the magnificent 7th-century BC **Lion Terrace**, the **Theater**, built in 300 BC to hold 5,500 people, and the **Theater Quarter**.

Lions carved from Naxian marble along the Lion Terrace on Delos

Terraces of whitewashed buildings in Firá, Santoríni

Santoríni

🏔 12,500. ✈ 5 km (3 miles) SE of Firá. ⛴ Skála Firón. 🚌 50 m (160 ft) S of main square, Firá. ℹ Firá (22860-27199).

Colonized by the Minoans in 3000 BC, this volcanic island erupted in 1450 BC, forming Santoríni's distinct crescent shape. A popular tourist destination, it is a stunning island, as famous for its ancient archaeological sites as for its whitewashed villages, volcanic cliffs, and black sand beaches.

Firá

Founded in the late 18th century, Firá was destroyed by an earthquake in 1956 and rebuilt along terraces in the volcanic cliffs. Packed with hotels, bars, and restaurants, its streets enjoy magnificent views out to sea. The tiny port of Skála Firón, 270 m (890 ft) below, is connected to the town by cable car or by mule up 580 steps.

Among Firá's most interesting sights are the **Archaeological Museum**, with finds from Ancient Thíra and Minoan Akrotíri, and the 18th-century church of **Agíos Minás**. The pretty ocher chapel of **Agios Stylianós** is also worth a visit on the way to the Frangika, or Frankish quarter, with its maze of arcaded streets.

A donkey ride in Firá, Santoríni

🏛 **Archaeological Museum**
Opposite cable car station. **Tel** 22860-22217. **Open** 8am–3pm Tue–Sun. **Closed** main public hols. 📷

Around the Island

Within easy reach of Firá, on the headland of Mésa Vounó, the ruins of the Dorian town of **Ancient Thíra** are not to be missed. Most of the ruins date from the Ptolemies, who built temples to the Egyptian gods in the 4th and 3rd centuries BC. There are also Hellenistic and Roman remains. Below the site are the popular beaches of **Aperíssa** and **Kamári**. Another of the Cyclades' most inspiring archaeological sites, the Minoan settlement of **Akrotíri** was unearthed in 1967, still wonderfully preserved after some 3,500 years of burial under volcanic ash. Some of the frescoes discovered here are now on display in the National Archaeological Museum in Athens *(see p452)*.

🏛 **Ancient Thira**
11 km (7 miles) SW of Firá. **Tel** 22860-23217. 🚌 to Kamári. **Open** Tue–Sun. **Closed** main public hols.

Náxos

🏔 20,000. ✈ 2 km (1 mile) S of Náxos town. ⛴ Harborfront, Náxos town. ℹ Harborfront, Náxos town (22853-60401).

The largest of the Cyclades, Náxos was a major center of the Cycladic civilization. The Venetians, who arrived in the 13th century, built many fortifications that still stand on the island today. History and superb beaches make Náxos an ideal vacation destination.

Náxos Town

Overlooking Náxos town's bustling harbor is the huge, marble, 6th-century BC Portára gateway, built as the entrance to the unfinished Temple of Apollo. To the south, **Agios Geórgios** is the main tourist center, with a wealth of hotels, apartments, and restaurants. The old town divides into the Kástro – the 13th-century Venetian fortifications – and the medieval Bourg. The fine 18th-century Orthodox cathedral, the **Mitrópoli Zoödóchou Pigís**, stands in the Bourg, which also has a busy market area. In the Kástro, the **Archaeological Museum**, in the Palace of Sanoúdo, has one of the best collections of Cycladic marble figurines in the Greek islands.

🏛 **Archaeological Museum**
Palace of Sanoúdo. **Tel** 22850-22725. **Open** Tue–Sun. **Closed** main public hols. 📷

Around the Island

South of Náxos town are many fine beaches, including **Agía Anna** and **Kastráki** – both good for water sports – and tranquil **Pláka**. Inland, the Tragaía Valley is a walkers' paradise. It is dotted with picturesque villages, such as **Chalkí**, with its Byzantine and Venetian architecture, and **Filóti**, which sits on the slopes of 1,000-m- (3,300-ft-) Mount Zas.

The Portára gateway that overlooks Náxos town's harbor

㉓ Rhodes and the Dodecanese

The Dodecanese offer a wide range of landscapes and activities. Their hot climate and fine beaches attract many visitors, but the islands also boast lush, fertile valleys and wooded mountains. The Dodecanese have been subject to several invasions, with periods of occupation by the medieval Knights of St. John, the Ottomans, and the Italians. This checkered history is still apparent in the islands' impressively varied architecture and wealth of historical sites.

Locator Map

The Palace of the Grand Masters in Rhodes town

Rhodes

🏙 100,000. ✈ 25 km (15 miles) SW of Rhodes town. 🚢 Commercial harbor, Rhodes town. 🚌 Mandráki, Rhodes town. 🛈 Archiepiskopou Makariou 1, Rhodes town (22410-44335).

An important center from the 5th to 3rd centuries BC, Rhodes was later part of both the Roman and Byzantine empires before being conquered by the Knights of St. John, the order founded in the 11th century to tend Christian pilgrims in Jerusalem. They occupied the island from 1306 to 1522, and their medieval walled city still dominates Rhodes town. Ottoman and Italian rulers followed, leaving their own traces of occupation. Rhodes' rich and varied history, sandy beaches, and lively nightlife attract tens of thousands of tourists each year.

Rhodes Old Town

The town of Rhodes has been inhabited for over 2,400 years. A city was first built here in 408 BC, and when the Knights of St. John arrived in 1306, they built their citadel over these ancient remains. Surrounded by moats and 3-km- (2-miles-) of walls, the Knights' medieval citadel forms the center of the Old Town, which is divided into the Collachium and the Bourg. The Collachium was the Knights' quarter, while the Bourg was home to the rest of the population.

Dominating the Old Town is the 14th-century **Palace of the Grand Masters**, the seat of 19 Grand Masters of the Knights during two centuries of occupation. The palace houses several priceless mosaics from sites in Kos, as well as two permanent exhibitions about ancient and medieval Rhodes.

The medieval **Street of the Knights** is lined by the Inns of the Tongues of the Order of St. John. The Inns – there was one for each of the seven Tongues, or nationalities, into which the Order was

divided – were used as meeting places for the Knights. Begun in the 14th century in Gothic style, they were restored by the Italians in the early 20th century.

The **Archaeological Museum** and the **Byzantine Museum**, both located in the Collachium, contain many fine exhibits from different periods in Rhodes' history.

In the Bourg area, the **Mosque of Suleiman the Magnificent** was built to commemorate the Sultan's victory over the Knights in 1522. The **Library of Ahmet Havuz**, which houses the chronicle of the Turks' siege of Rhodes, and the **Hammam**, the public baths, provide further reminders of the town's Turkish past.

🏛 **Palace of the Grand Masters**
Ippotón. **Tel** 22413-65270. **Open** Tue–Sun. **Closed** main public hols. 🛂 ♿ limited.

Rhodes New Town

Beyond the original citadel walls, the new town of Rhodes is made up of a number of areas. These include **Néa Agora**, with its Moorish domes and lively market, and **Mandráki harbor** in the eastern half of town. Close to the harbor are the mock Venetian Gothic **Government House** – a legacy of the Italian occupation of the 1920s – and the **Mosque of Murad Reis**, with its graceful minaret. The west side of town is a busy tourist center, with lively streets and a packed beach.

The minaret of the Mosque of Murad Reis

The acropolis overlooking Líndos town on Rhodes

Western Rhodes

A short distance southwest of Rhodes town, set on the beautiful green and wooded hillsides of Filérimos, is **Moní Filerímou**. A place of worship for 2,000 years, this monastery has layers of history and tradition, from Phoenician to Byzantine, Orthodox, and Catholic.

A few kilometers farther southwest, **Ancient Kámeiros** is one of the best-preserved Classical Greek cities. Its remains include a 3rd-century BC Doric temple.

Also worth visiting are the wine-making village of **Emponas**, and **Petaloúdes**, or Butterfly Valley. Popular with walkers, this valley teems with Jersey tiger moths from June to September.

🏛 Ancient Kámeiros
36 km (22 miles) SW of Rhodes town. **Open** Tue–Sun. **Closed** main public hols. 🚫 🚶 to lower sections only.

Eastern Rhodes

Halfway along Rhodes' sheltered east coast, **Líndos** is one of the island's most popular resorts. A magnet for tourists seeking sun, sea, and sand, it is also famous for its cliff-top acropolis overlooking the bay. This temple site, crowned by the 4th-century BC Temple of Lindian Athena, was one of the most sacred spots in the ancient world.

Located in the Valley of Aíthona, between Líndos and Rhodes town, **Archángelos** is famous for its pottery, hand-woven rugs and leather boots.

Above the town are the ruins of the Crusader Castle, built in 1467 by the Knights of St. John as a defense against the Turks.

🏛 Acropolis at Líndos
1 km (0.5 miles) E of Líndos village. **Tel** 22440-31258. **Open** Jul–Sep: daily; Oct–Jun: Tue–Sun. **Closed** main public hols. 🚫

Kos

🏛 27,000. ✈ 27 km (16 miles) W of Kos town. 🚌 🚍 Aktí Koudouriótou, Kos town. ℹ Vasiléos Georgíou 1, Kos town (22420-29910).

Mainly flat and fertile, Kos is known as the "Floating Garden." It has a wealth of archaeological sites, Hellenistic and Roman ruins, and Byzantine and Venetian castles, many of which can be found in **Kos town**. Here, the 16th-century Castle of the Knights, the Ancient Agora, and the Roman remains should not be missed. Most visitors to Kos come for the sandy beaches. The best of these are easily reached from the resort of **Kamári** on the island's southwest coast. **Kardámaina** is Kos's biggest and noisiest resort, while the northwest bays, such as **Tigkáki**, are ideal for water sports. In spite of tourist development, inland you can still see remnants of Kos's traditional lifestyle.

Kos is a good base from which to explore the more northerly islands of the Dodecanese, including **Pátmos**, home to the 11th-century Monastery of St. John.

Kárpathos

🏛 5,000. ✈ 17 km (11 miles) S of Kárpathos town. 🚌 corner of 28 Oktovríou & Dimokratías, Kárpathos town. ⛴ Kárpathos town, Diáfani. ℹ Kárpathos town (22450-22222).

Despite an increase in tourism from the late 1990s onwards, wild and rugged Kárpathos remains largely unspoiled. Its capital, **Kárpathos town**, is a busy center, with hotels, cafés, and restaurants around its bay. Nearby is the main resort of **Amoopí**, with its sweep of sandy shore. In addition to some magnificent beaches on the west coast, including **Lefkós** and **Apélla**, the island has places of archaeological and historical interest. **Vroukoúnda** is the site of a 6th-century BC city, while in the village of **Olympos**. traditional Greek life and customs can still be observed.

Windmills in the traditional village of Olympos on Kárpathos

㉔ Crete

Rugged mountains, sparkling seas, and ancient history combine with the Cretans' relaxed nature to make this island an idyllic vacation destination. The center of the Minoan civilization over 3,000 years ago, Crete has also been occupied by Romans, Byzantines, Venetians, and Turks. Historic towns such as Irákleio, Chaniá, and Réthymno, and the famous Minoan palaces at Knossos and Phaestos, give a fascinating insight into some of the most important periods in Cretan history.

Locator Map

Irákleio's harbor, dominated by the vast Venetian fortress

Irákleio

116,000. ✈ 5 km (3 miles) E. 🚢 🚌 ℹ Xanthoudídou 1 (2810-246299).

A busy, sprawling town of concrete buildings, Irákleio nevertheless has much of interest to the visitor. Four centuries of Venetian rule have left a rich architectural legacy, evident in the imposing 16th-century **fortress** overlooking the harbor, and the elegantly-restored 17th-century **Loggia**, a former meeting place for the island's nobility. Among Irákleio's many churches, **Agios Márkos**, built by the Venetians in 1239, and 16th-century **Agios Títos** deserve a visit. Also not to be missed are the Archaeological Museum *(see below)* and the **Historical Museum**, which traces the history of Crete from early Christian times. The heart of the town is the Plateía Eleftheríou Venizélou, a bustling pedestrianized zone of cafés and shops.

Those interested in the beaches should head to the package-tour resorts of **Mália** and **Chersónisos**, just a short drive east of the town.

🏛 Irákleio Archaeological Museum

Corner of Xanthoudídou & Mpofór, Plateía Eleftherías.
Tel 2810-279086/279000.
Open Tue–Sun. 🏛

This impressive museum displays Minoan artifacts from all over Crete. Its most magnificent exhibits include the famous Minoan frescoes from Knossos, and the Phaestos Disk, which was discovered at the site of the palace of Phaestos in 1903. Inscribed with pictorial symbols, the disk's meaning and origin remain a mystery. Among the museum's many other treasures are the Snake Goddesses, two figurines dating from around 1600 BC.

🏛 Palace of Knossos

5 km (3 miles) S of Irákleio.
Tel 2810-231 940. 🚌 **Open** daily.
Closed main public hols. 🏛 🖼

The capital of Minoan Crete, Knossos was the largest and most sophisticated of the Minoan palaces on the island. Built around 1900 BC, the first palace of Knossos was destroyed by an earthquake in about 1700 BC and was soon completely rebuilt. The ruins visible today are almost entirely from this second palace. They were restored by Sir Arthur Evans in the early 20th century; although the subject of academic controversy, his reconstructions give one of the best impressions of life in Minoan Crete to be found anywhere on the island.

Highlights of a tour of the site – the focal point of which is the vast Central Court – include the replica of the Priest-King Fresco, the Giant Pithoi, one of over 100 *pithoi* (storage jars) unearthed at Knossos, the Throne Room, believed to have served as a shrine, and the Royal Apartments. The original frescoes from the palace are now housed in Irákleio's Archaeological Museum.

The South Propylon (entrance) of the Palace of Knossos

Phaestos

65 km (40 miles) SW of Irákleio.
Tel 28920-42315. 🚌 **Open** 8am–
8pm daily (winter: 8:30am–3pm).
Closed main public hols. 🅿️

Phaestos was one of the most
important Minoan palaces
on Crete. In 1900 Italian-led
excavations unearthed two
palaces. Remains of the first
palace, constructed around
1900 BC and destroyed by an
earthquake in 1700 BC, are still
visible. Most of the present
ruins, however, are of the
second palace. Phaestos was
finally destroyed in the 2nd
century BC by the ancient
city-state of Górtys.
   The most impressive remains
are the Grand Staircase, which
was the main entrance to the
palace, and the Central Court.
   A few kilometers northeast
of Phaestos, the archaeological
remains of ancient **Górtys** date
from about 1000 BC to the late
7th century AD.

Agios Nikólaos

🏙️ 10,000. 🚌🚌 ℹ️ Koundoúrou 21
(28410-22357). 🚤 Wed.

The main transport hub
for the east of the island,
delightful Agios Nikólaos is
a thriving vacation center
with an attractive harbor and
fine beaches, as well as an
interesting **Folk Museum** and
an **Archaeological Museum**.
   A few kilometers north is
the well-established resort of
Eloúnda, boasting attractive
sandy coves and a good range
of accommodations.

Chaniá

🏙️ 50,000. ✈️ 16 km (10 miles) E.
🚌🚌 ℹ️ Kriári 40 (28310-92943).

One of Crete's most appealing
cities, Chaniá was ruled by the
Venetians from 1204 to 1669,
and is dotted with elegant
houses, churches, and
fortifications dating from this
period. Many of these can be
found in the Venetian quarter
around the harbor, and in the
picturesque Splántzia district.

The **Mosque of the Janissaries**,
on one side of the harbor, dates
back to the arrival of the Turks in
1645, and is the oldest Ottoman
building on Crete. The lively
covered market, with its many
shops and fresh produce stalls, is
an area worth exploring. Nearby
the **Archaeological Museum** is
housed in the Venetian church
of San Francesco.
   A short walk west of Chaniá
is the relatively undisturbed
beach of **Agioi Apóstoloi**.

Samariá Gorge

44 km (27 miles) S of Chaniá. 🚌 to
Xylóskalo. 🚤 Agía Rouméli to Sfakiá
or Palaiochóra (via Soúgia); last boat
back leaves at 5pm. **Open** May–mid-
Oct: 6am–4pm daily; Apr 10–30 & Oct
16–31: if weather permits.

Crete's most spectacular
scenery lies along the Samariá
Gorge, the longest ravine in
Europe. When it became a
national park, the inhabitants of
the village of Samariá moved
elsewhere, leaving behind the
ruined buildings and chapels
seen here today. Starting from
the Xylóskalo (Wooden Stairs),
an 18-km- (11-mile-) trail leads
to the seaside village of Agía
Rouméli. A truly impressive
sight along the route is the
Sideróportes, or Iron Gates,
where the path squeezes
between two towering walls
of rock, only 3 m (9 ft) apart.
Upon reaching Agía Rouméli,
walkers can take a boat to
Sfakiá, Soúgia, or Palaiochóra
to join the road and buses
back to Chaniá.

The narrow defile known as the Iron Gates
in the Samariá Gorge

Réthymno

🏙️ 24,000. 🚌🚌 ℹ️ Sofokli
Venizélou (28310-29148). 🍷 Wine
Festival (mid-Jul).

Despite tourism and modern
development, Réthymno has
retained much of its charm.
The old quarter is rich in well-
preserved Venetian and
Ottoman architecture, including
the elegant 16th-century
Venetian **Lótzia** (Loggia) and
the **Nerantzés Mosque**,
converted from a church by
the Turks in 1675. The huge
Fortétsa was built by the
Venetians in the 16th century
to defend the port against
both pirates and the Turks.
Below it is a pretty harbor, lined
with cafés and restaurants. Also
worth visiting in the town is the
Archaeological Museum.
   East of Réthymno, there are
several resorts, while to the
west lies a 20-km- (12-mile-)
stretch of uncrowded beach.

Tavernas and bars along Réthymno's waterfront

Practical Information

Tourism is one of Greece's most important industries, and as a consequence, visitors to the country are well catered for: transportation networks are relatively efficient, there are banks and exchange facilities in all the major resorts, and telecommunications have improved dramatically in recent years. The country's hot climate, together with the easy-going outlook of its people, are conducive to a relaxed vacation, and it is usually best to adopt the philosophy *sigá, sigá* (slowly, slowly). In summer, almost everything closes for a few hours after lunch, reopening later in the day when the air cools and Greece comes to life again.

When to Visit

Tourist season in Greece – late June to early September – is the hottest and most expensive time to visit, as well as being very crowded. December to March are the coldest and wettest months, with reduced public transportation facilities, and many hotels and restaurants closed for the winter. Spring is a good time to visit; there are fewer tourists, and the weather and the countryside are at their best.

Tourist Information

Tourist information is available in many towns and villages throughout Greece, from government-run **EOT** offices (Ellinikós Organismós Tourismoú), municipally run tourist offices, the local tourist police, or privately owned travel agencies. However, visitors should be aware that not all of the information published by the EOT is reliable or up-to-date.

Opening Hours

Opening hours tend to be vague in Greece, varying from day to day, season to season, and place to place. To avoid disappointment, visitors are advised to confirm the opening times of sites covered in this chapter once they arrive in the country.

All post offices and banks, and most stores, offices, state-run museums, and archaeological sites close on public holidays. Some facilities may also be closed on local festival days.

The main public holidays in Greece are January 1, March 25, Good Friday, Easter Sunday, May 1, December 25 and 26.

Visa Requirements and Customs

Visitors from EU countries, the US, Canada, Australia, and New Zealand need only a valid passport for entry to Greece (no visa is required), and can stay for up to 90 days. The unauthorized export of antiquities and archaeological artifacts from Greece is treated as a serious offence, incurring hefty fines or even a prison sentence.

Prescription drugs brought into the country should be accompanied by a prescription note for the purposes of the customs authorities.

Personal Security

The crime rate in Greece is low compared with other European countries, but it is worth taking a few sensible precautions, such as keeping all personal possessions secure. Parts of Athens, such as Omonia, can be dangerous after midnight. If you have anything stolen, you should contact either the police or the tourist police.

Foreign women traveling alone in Greece are usually treated with respect, especially if they are dressed modestly. However, hitch-hiking alone is not advisable.

Police

Greece's police are split into three forces: the regular police, the port police, and the tourist police. The tourist police provide advice to vacationers in addition to carrying out normal police duties. Should you suffer a theft, lose your passport, or have cause to complain about shops, restaurants, tour guides, or taxi drivers, you should contact them first. Every tourist police office claims to have at least one English speaker. Their offices also offer maps, brochures, and useful advice on finding accommodations in Greece.

Emergency Services

In the event of an emergency while on vacation, the appropriate numbers to call are listed in the Directory opposite.

Health Issues

No inoculations are required for visitors to Greece, though tetanus and typhoid boosters may be recommended by your doctor. Tap water in Greece is generally safe to drink, but in

The Climate of Greece

On the mainland, summers are very hot, while spring and autumn generally bring milder but wetter weather. In winter, rainfall is at its greatest everywhere. Mountainous regions usually get heavy snow, but around Athens, temperatures rarely drop below freezing. Throughout the islands, the tendency is for long, dry summers and mild but rainy winters.

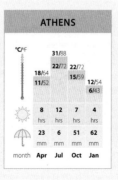

ATHENS			
°C/°F	31/88		
	22/72	22/72	
18/64		15/59	12/54
11/52			6/43
8 hrs	12 hrs	7 hrs	4 hrs
23 mm	6 mm	51 mm	62 mm
month Apr	Jul	Oct	Jan

remote communities it is a good precaution to check with the locals.

Jellyfish, sea urchins, and weaver fish are potential hazards on beach holidays.

Pharmacies

Greek pharmacies, *farma-keía*, are open from 8:30am to 2pm Monday to Friday, but are usually closed in the afternoon and all day on Saturdays. In larger towns, there is often a rota system to maintain a service from 7:30am to 2pm and from 5:30 to 10pm. Details are posted in pharmacy windows, in both Greek and English.

Facilities for the Disabled

There are few facilities in Greece for assisting the disabled, so careful, advance planning is essential.

Etiquette

Though formal attire is rarely needed, modest clothing (trousers for men and skirts and covered shoulders for women) should be worn when visiting churches and monasteries. In restaurants, the service charge is always included in the check, but tips are still appreciated – the custom is to leave between 10 and 15 percent. Public restroom attendants should also be tipped. Taxi drivers, hotel porters, and chambermaids do not expect a tip, but are not averse to them either.

Photography

Taking photographs inside churches and monasteries is officially forbidden in Greece. Inside museums, photography is usually permitted, although flashes and tripods are often not. Wherever you go, it is best to gain permission before using a camera, as rules vary.

Banking and Currency

The Greek unit of currency was the drachma, but since January 2002 it has been replaced by the euro (see p23).

Greek banks open from 8am to 2pm Monday to Thursday, and 8am to 1:30pm on Friday. In major cities and resorts, at least one bank usually opens its exchange desk for a few hours on weekday evenings and on Saturday mornings in summer. Exchange facilities are also available at post offices, travel agents, hotels, tourist offices, and car rental agencies. Take your passport with you when cashing traveler's checks. Cash point machines (ATMs) operate 24 hours a day.

Communications

Public telephones can be found in hotel lobbies and street kiosks, although they are becoming less and less easy to find with the advent of the mobile phone. Before you leave your home country, make sure your phone has international roaming, although this can prove to be very expensive. A better option is to buy a pay-as-you-go SIM card, particularly as the first €10 of calls are free with Vodafone (Greece), which will cover a few calls and texts.

Greek post offices (*tachydromeía*) are generally open from 7:30am to 2pm Monday to Friday; some main branches close as late as 8pm and occasionally open for a few hours at weekends. All post offices are closed on public holidays. Those displaying an "Exchange" sign will change money in addition to offering the usual services.

DIRECTORY

Tourist Information

Greek National Tourist Board
w visitgreece.gr

EOT in Greece:
Tsoha 24, 10564 Athens.
Tel 210-870 7000.

Australia
37–49 Pitt St,
Sydney, NSW 2000.
Tel 2-9241 1663.

Canada
1500 Don Mills Road Suite 102, Toronto, Ontario M3B 3K4. Tel 416-968-2220.

UK
4 Conduit St, London W15 2DJ. Tel 020-7495 9300.

US
Olympic Tower, 645 Fifth Ave, New York, NY 10022. Tel 212-421-5777.

Embassies

Australia
Thon Building, Kifisias & Alexandras, Ambelopiki, 11521 Athens.
Tel 210-870 4000.

Canada
Gennadíou 4, 11521 Athens. Tel 210-727 3400.

New Zealand
76 Kifisias, Ambelopiki 11526 Athens.
Tel 210-692 4821.
w nzembassy.com

Ireland
Vassiléos Konstantínou 7, 10674 Athens.
Tel 210-723 2771.

UK
Ploutárchou 1,
10675 Athens.
Tel 210-727 2600.

US
Vasilíssis Sofías 91,
10160 Athens.
Tel 210-721 2951.

Emergency Numbers (Nationwide)

Police
Tel 100.

Ambulance
Tel 166.

Fire
Tel 199.

Road assistance
Tel 10400.

Coastguard patrol
Tel 108.

Emergency Numbers (Athens)

Tourist police
Tel 171.

Doctors
Tel 1016.

Pharmacies
For information on 24-hour pharmacies:
Tel 14944.

Travel Information

During the tourist season (late June–early September), there are countless international flights bringing millions of vacationers to the shores of Greece, especially from the colder parts of northern Europe and North America. Traveling within Greece is easy enough. While many of the larger islands can be reached from the mainland by plane, there are ferry routes to even the remotest destinations. Greece's extensive bus network serves virtually everywhere, from the largest city to the tiniest community. Renting a car or motorcycle is another popular way of exploring the country.

Flying to Greece

There are around 20 international airports in Greece that can be reached directly from Europe. Only Crete, Rhodes, and Corfu among the islands, and Athens and Thessaloníki on the mainland, handle both charter and scheduled flights. The other international airports can only be reached directly by charter flights.

Direct scheduled flights from London to Athens and Thessaloníki are operated by **Aegean Airlines**, British Airways, Ryanair, and easyJet (Athens only). From outside Europe, all scheduled flights to Greece arrive in Athens, and only a few airlines offer direct flights. Continental Airlines and Delta Air Lines operate direct flights daily from New York.

Flights from Southeast Asia with connections to Australia are run by Singapore Airlines and Thai Airways.

Athens' international airport, Eléfthérios Venizélos, is located 27 km (17 miles) northeast of the center. There are four 24-hour bus services from the city to the airport: the X93 from Kifisos intercity bus station (65 mins); the X95 from Plateía Syntágmatos (1 hour); the X96 from Piraeus (90 mins); and the X97 from Elliniko metro station (45 mins). Metro line 3 now runs from Syntagma to the airport.

Charters and Package Deals

Charter flights to Greece are nearly all from within Europe, and mostly operate between May and October. Tickets are sold by travel agencies either as part of an all-inclusive package tour or as a flight-only deal.

Domestic Flights

Most internal flights in Greece and the Greek Islands are operated by **Olympic Air**. Olympic Air operates direct flights from Athens and Thessaloníki to many of the islands. In addition, there are a number of inter-island services available throughout the year. Private companies, such as **Aegean Airlines** and **Athens Airways** also provide services between Athens and some of the major mainland and island destinations. Fares for domestic flights are at least double the equivalent bus journey or deck-class ferry trip.

Getting around Athens

Athens has a network of buses, trolley buses, and trams, in addition to a metro system. Buses are inexpensive, but can be very slow, as well as crowded. Tickets for buses and trams must be purchased in advance from a *períptero* (street kiosk), a transport booth, or a metro station. A brown, red, and white logo, with the words *eisitíria edó*, indicates where you can buy them. Each ticket is valid for one journey only, regardless of the distance traveled.

Since most of the major sights in the city center are within walking distance of one another, you can avoid using public transportation.

Rail Travel

Greece's rail network is operated by the state-owned **OSE** (Organismós Sidirodrómon Elládos). Limited to the mainland, it is fairly skeletal by European standards. First- and second-class tickets are less expensive than the equivalent bus journey, but services tend to be slower. Though more costly, tickets for intercity express trains are worth it for the time they save. A Greek Rail Pass allows the user three or five days of unlimited rail travel in one month on first- and second-class services, anywhere in Greece.

Traveling by Bus

International buses connect Greece with eastern Europe, though during the tourist season fares are more expensive than charter flights.

Within Greece, the long-distance bus network is extensive, with buses stopping at least once a day at even the remotest destinations, and frequent express services on all the major routes.

From Athens there are regular departures to all the larger mainland towns, apart from those in Thrace, which are served by buses from Thessaloníki. Athens' Terminal A serves Epirus, Macedonia, the Peloponnese, and the Ionian islands of Corfu, Kefalloniá, Lefkáda, and Zákynthos. Terminal B serves most destinations in central Greece, including Delphi.

Traveling by Car

On the mainland there are express highways between Athens, Thessaloníki, Vólos, and Pátra. These roads are very fast, but tolls are charged for their use. There has been much upgrading of the roads on the islands, but they are still often poorly surfaced, particularly in more remote areas.

Car rental agencies are found in every tourist resort and major town. International companies such as **Budget**, **Avis**, **Hertz**, and **Europcar** tend to be more expensive than their local counterparts. The car rental agency should have an agreement with an emergency recovery company, such as Express, Hellas, or the InterAmerican Towing Company, in the event of a vehicle breakdown. Mopeds and motorcycles are also available for rent in many tourist resorts.

Greece has one of the highest road traffic accident rates in Europe; take extra care when driving around.

Ferry Services

There are regular, year-round ferry crossings from Italy, Israel, and Turkey to the Greek mainland and islands.

Piraeus, the port of Athens, is Greece's busiest port, with ferry routes to international destinations, as well as to scores of locations on the mainland and islands. A number of companies run the ferry services, each with their own ticket agency on the dockside. All fares except first class are set by the Ministry of Transport, so a journey should cost you the same, regardless of which shipping company you choose.

Ferry tickets can be purchased from the shipping line office on the dockside, or any authorized travel agency. Advance reservations are essential in peak season, which runs from June to August. In off-season, services may be reduced or suspended altogether. Check local sources – such as the Greek tourist office or a travel agency – for the latest information before you travel. The port police, who have an office at Piraeus, are also a good source of reliable, up-to-date information.

In addition to the large ferries, there are smaller vessels that make inter-island crossings in summer.

Hydrofoils and Catamarans

The main operator of hydrofoil and catamaran services between the mainland and the islands is **Flying Dolphin** (run by Hellenic Seaways). However, all hydrofoils, regardless of which company they are operated by, are known locally as "Flying Dolphins." They are twice as fast as ferries, but twice as expensive. Most vessels function only in the summer months and are often cancelled in bad weather.

DIRECTORY

Olympic Air

Tel 210-355 0500.
w olympicair.com

Domestic Airlines

Aegean Airlines
Viltanoti 31, 14561
Athens. **Tel** 80-11 12 00
00. **Tel** 30-210-626 1000
(aboard).
w aegeanair.com

Athens Airways
Tel 210-669 6600.
w athensairways.com

Travel Agencies in Greece

National Travel
Information.
Tel 14541 (boat, train, coach times).

American Express Travel Services
Messogion Ave 318,
15341 Athens.
Tel 210-659 0700.

Sunisle Travel

Eslin 4, Athens.
Tel 210-641 0881.
w sunisle.gr

Superfast Ferries
Syngrou 123-4,
11745 Athens.
Tel 210-891 9130.
w superfast.com

Rail Travel

OSE (Information & Reservations)
Sína 6, Athens.
Tel 1110.
w trainose.gr

Rail Europe
Tel 08708-371 371 (UK).
w raileurope.co.uk

Train Stations in Athens
Laríssis station (for northern Greece).
Tel 210-529 7777.

Buses

Bus Terminals in Athens
Terminal A: Kifisoú 100.
Tel 210-512 4910.
Terminal B: Liosíon 260.
Tel 210-832 9585.

Car Rental Agencies

Avis
Leofóros Amalías 48,
10558 Athens.
Tel 210-322 4951.
w avis.com

Budget
Syngroú 8,
11742 Athens.
Tel 210-921 4771.
w budget.com

Europcar
Syngroú 25,
11742 Athens.
Tel 210-921 1444.
w europcar.com

Hertz

Syngroú 12,
11742 Athens.
Tel 210-922 0102.
w hertz.gr

Piraeus Port

Tel 210-422 6000
(port police).
Tel 14541 (ferry timetable).

Hydrofoil and Catamaran Services

Flying Dolphin
Hellenic Seaways.
Tel 210-419 9000.
w hellenicseaways.gr

Shopping & Entertainment

The choice of places to shop in Greece ranges from colorful, bustling street markets, found in almost every town and village, through traditional arts and crafts shops, to the designer fashion boutiques of Athens. Entertainment is as varied; visitors can try an open-air concert in the atmospheric setting of an ancient theater, or enjoy some late-night dining in a local taverna before heading for a bar or disco. With its dry, sunny climate and clear, warm seas, Greece offers countless opportunities for outdoor activities, from snorkeling to windsurfing, sailing, and hiking.

What to Buy

Traditional handicrafts, though often expensive, are the most genuinely Greek souvenirs. In Athens, Monastiráki and Pláka are the best places to purchase such items. There are also many unusual shops offering unique services, such as that of self-styled poet, **Stávros Melissinós**, who makes a wide variety of sturdy sandals and leather items. An excellent selection of goods, including tapestries and rugs, is available at **Oikotexnia**, while at the fascinating **Center of Hellenic Tradition** you can buy, among other things, finely crafted ceramics.

Some of the country's best ceramics can be found in the markets and shops of Athens' northern suburb Maroúsi, and on the island of Crete.

Brightly colored embroidery and wall-hangings are produced in many Greek villages. Colorful *flokáti* rugs, which are handwoven from sheep or goat's wool, are made mainly in the Píndos mountains, but can also be found in other parts of the mainland and on the islands.

Sold throughout Greece, leather goods are particularly noted on Crete, where the town of Chaniá hosts a huge leather market.

Well-crafted copies of ancient and Byzantine Greek art can be found in museum shops in many of the major cities. In Pláka in Athens, **Orféas** offers good quality marble and pottery copies of Classical Greek works, in addition to glittering Byzantine icons. For jewelry, Athens is the best place to shop. Exclusive names include **Vourákis** and **Anagnostópoulos**, on Voukourestíou. The **Ilías Lalaoúnis Jewelry Museum** has over 3,000 designs, inspired by Classical and other archaeological sources.

Markets

Most towns in Greece have a weekly street market (*laïkí agorá*), where fresh produce is sold alongside shoes, fabrics, and sundry household items. In Athens, the one on Xenokrátous in centrally located Kolonáki takes place every Friday. The busy Central Market is excellent for food, while the famous Sunday-morning flea market in Monastiráki should not be missed.

Food and Drink

Culinary delights to look for in Greece include honey, olives, olive oil, pistachios, and cheeses, such as the salty feta. Also worth trying are *ouzo* (an anise-flavored liquor), *retsina* (wine flavored with pine resin), and the firewater *tsípouro*.

Entertainment Listings and Tickets

For detailed information on entertainment in Athens, try the weekly *Athinorama*, (in Greek only), the English-language *Athens News*, or *This is Athens* (www.thisisathens.org).

Most theaters and music clubs in the capital sell tickets at the door on the day of the performance. However, tickets for the summer Athens Festival and for concerts at the Mégaron – The Athens Concert Hall should be purchased in advance; there is a central ticket office, open daily from 10am to 4pm, located near the Plateía Syntágmatos.

Elsewhere, your nearest tourist office should be able to provide information on what is happening locally.

Entertainment Venues

The main entertainment venues in Athens host a wide variety of events. As well as excellent productions of 19th-century Greek and European plays, the **National Theater** puts on opera, ballet, and contemporary dance. The **Mégaron – The Athens Concert Hall** is a first-class classical concert venue, while the Olympia Theater is home to the **Lyrikí Skiní** (National Opera). At the **Dóra Strátou Dance Theater**, there is traditional regional Greek dancing nightly between May and September.

Open-Air Cinemas and Theaters

Found in towns and cities all over Greece, the outdoor cinema is extremely popular with Greeks and an experience not to be missed by anyone visiting the country in summer. Most movies are in English with Greek subtitles.

Open-air performances of Classical and modern drama, held at famous ancient archaeological sites, are an equally popular form of entertainment. The **Herodes Atticus Theater** hosts plays, as well as opera, ballet, and classical music concerts, during the annual Athens Festival (mid-June to mid-September). The theater at **Epidaurus** in the Peloponnese is another well-known venue.

Traditional Greek Music

To hear traditional Greek music in Athens, head for

Diogénis Studio or Rex. At Taksími and Rempétiki Istoría, you can hear genuine *bouzouki* (Greek mandolin) music. In smaller towns and resorts around the country, the local taverna is often a good place to see traditional musicians perform while you dine.

Special Interest Vacations

Companies offering special interest vacations include Inntravel and Ramblers Holidays, which organize archaeological tours, and Andante Travels. Inntravel also runs courses on creative writing, drawing, and painting in Greece.

For specialist wildlife tours, contact Naturetrek, Limosa Holidays, or the Hellenic Ornithological Society.

Outdoor Activities

With miles of coastline, and crystal clear seas, Greece is the perfect place to pursue water sports. Windsurfing, water-skiing, jet-skiing, and parasailing are all available in the larger resorts. Snorkeling and scuba diving are also popular, although the latter is restricted. A list of places where it is permissible to dive with oxygen equipment can be obtained from the EOT (Greek Tourist Office; *see p478*).

For information on sailing vacations and chartering yachts, contact the Hellenic Sailing Federation. Cruises on luxury liners can be booked through Swan Hellenic Cruises, while inexpensive mini-cruises and boat trips are best arranged at a local travel agent on the spot.

Those wishing to relax on the beach should look for one with a Blue Flag; this indicates that the water is regularly tested for purity, and that the beach meets the environmental criteria for both cleanliness and safety.

Inland, the range of leisure opportunities includes kayaking, white-water rafting, canoeing, and hiking. Trekking Hellas organizes activity vacations.

DIRECTORY

Art and Crafts

Center of Hellenic Tradition
Mitropóleos 59 (Arcade) – Pandrósou 36, Monastiráki, Athens.
Tel 210-321 3023.

Oikotexnia
Filenninon 14, Pláka, Athens. Tel 210-325 0240.

Stávros Melissinós
Ag. Theklas 2, Psyrri, Athens.
Tel 210-321 9247.

Museum Copies

Orféas
Pandrósou 28, Pláka, Athens.
Tel 210-324 5034.

Jewelry

Anagnostópoulos
Voukourestíou 3, Kolonáki, Athens.
Tel 210-360 4426.

Ilías Lalaoúnis Jewelry Museum
Karyatidon 4a, Pláka, Athens.
Tel 210-922 1044.

Vourákis
Voukourestíou 4, Kolonáki, Athens.
Tel 210-322 1600.

Theaters

Dóra Strátou Dance Theater
Filopáppou Hill, Filopáppou, Athens.
Tel 210-324 4395.

National Theater
Agíou Konstantínou 22, Omónoia, Athens.
Tel 210-528 8100.

Classical Music and Opera

Lyrikí Skiní, Olympia Theater
Akadimías 59, Omónoia, Athens.
Tel 210-366 2100.

Mégaron – The Athens Concert Hall
V Sofías & Kókkali, Stégi Patrídos, Athens.
Tel 210-728 2000.

Open-Air Theaters

Herodes Atticus Theater
Dionysíou Areopagítou, Acropolis, Athens.
Tel 210-327 2000.

Traditional Greek Music

Diogénis Studio
Leof A Syngroú 259, N. Smyrni, Athens.
Tel 210-942 5754.

Rempétiki Istoría
Ippokrátous 181, Neápoli, Athens. Tel 210-642 4937.

Rex
Panepistimíou 48, Omonoia, Athens.
Tel 210-381 4591.

Taksími
C Trikoúpi & Isávron 29, Neápoli, Athens.
Tel 210-363 9919.

Special Interest Vacations

Andante Travels
The Old Barn, Old Road, Alderbury, Salisbury, SP5 3AR, England.
Tel 01722-713 800.
W andantetravels. co.uk

Hellenic Ornithological Society
Vasileos Irakleion 24, 10682 Athens.
Tel 210-822 7937.

Inntravel
Castle Howard, York, YO60 7JU, England.
Tel 01653-617 755.
W inntravel.co.uk

Limosa Holidays
West End Farmhouse, Chapel Field, Stalham, Norfolk, NR12 9EJ, UK.
Tel 01692-580 623.
W limosaholidays. co.uk

Naturetrek
Cheriton Mill, Cheriton, Alresford, Hants, SO24 0NG, England.
Tel 01962-733 051.
W naturetrek.co.uk

Ramblers Holidays
Box 43, Welwyn Garden City, Herts, AL8 6PQ, England.
Tel 01707-331 133.
W ramblersholidays. co.uk

Outdoor Activities

Hellenic Sailing Federation
Akti Possidónas 51, Moschato, Athens.
Tel 210-940 4825.
W eio.gr

Swan Hellenic Cruises
Compass House, Rockingham Road, Market Harborough, Leicestershire, LE16 7QD, UK. Tel 0844-871 4603.
W swanhellenic.com

Trekking Hellas
Saripoulou 10, 10682 Athens.
Tel 210-331 0323.
W trekking.gr

Where to Stay

Athens

EXARCHEIA: Exarchion Hotel €€
Modern   **Map** D1
Themistokleous 55, 106 83
Tel *210-38 00731*
W exarchion.com
Simple but good-value
accommodations in the heart
of the district's nightlife scene.

EXARCHEIA: Melia Athens €€
Luxury   **Map** C1
Chalkokondyli 14, 106 77
Tel *210-33 20100*
W melia.com
A superb central hotel with
fantastic views from its rooftop
pool and restaurant. Located
close to the city's main sights.

KOLONAKI:
St. George Lycabettus €€
Boutique   **Map** E3
Kleomenous 2, 106 75
Tel *210-74 16000*
W sglycabettus.gr
The rooms at the St. George
are a mix of retro and modern
minimalist. Rooftop pool and
two well-regarded restaurants.

KOUKAKI: Marble House €
Boutique   **Map** B5
An. Zinni 35, Acropolis, 117 41
Tel *210-92 28294*
W marblehouse.gr
Quiet family-run pension with
simple but tidy rooms that have
pine furniture and white tiles.

**MAKRYGIANNI: Divani
Palace Acropolis** €€
Modern   **Map** B5
Parthenonos 19–25, 117 42
Tel *210-92 80100*
W divanis.com
Popular business hotel with a
rooftop restaurant that affords
great views of the Acropolis.

MAKRYGIANNI: Hera Hotel €€
Boutique
Falirou 9, Koukaki, 117 42
Tel *210-92 36682*
W herahotel.gr
Well-located near the city's main
sights, the Hera has rooms with
lovely decor, plus a rooftop bar
and restaurant with great views.

MONASTIRAKI: Cecil Hotel €
Historic   **Map** B3
Athinas 39, 105 54
Tel *210-32 17079*
W cecilhotel.gr
Housed in a restored 19th-
century building, this good-value
hotel has tasteful en-suite rooms.

MONASTIRAKI:
Arion Athens Hotel €€
Boutique   **Map** B3
Ag. Dimitrou 18, Psiri, 105 54
Tel *210-32 40415*
W arionhotel.gr
A modern hotel with designer
furnishings. The best rooms
have balconies with views of
the Acropolis.

OMONOIA: Athens Art Hotel €
Boutique   **Map** B1
Marni 27, 104 32
Tel *210-52 40501*
W arthotelathens.gr
One of the best boutique hotels
in Athens, in a converted Neo-
Classical mansion with striking
artworks on the walls.

DK Choice

PLAKA: Sweet Home Hotel €€
Luxury   **Map** C4
Patrou 5, 105 57
Tel *210-32 29029*
W sweethomehotelathens.com
At the Sweet Home Hotel,
the affable owner, Afrodite,
has achieved a great
combination of old and new,
with spiral wooden staircases,
flat-screen TVs, and shabby-
chic furniture. Exceptionally
high levels of service.

PLAKA: New Hotel €€€
Boutique   **Map** C5
Fillelinon 16, 105 57
Tel *210-32 73000*
W yeshotels.gr
The design features at this
incredible hotel include tree-like
wooden structures emerging
from the restaurant floor.
Consistently good service.

Neutral tones and fresh flowers in a double
room at the Hera Hotel, Athens

**PSYRRI: Athens Center
Square Hotel** €€
Modern   **Map** B3
Aristogitonos 15 & Athinas, 105 52
Tel *210-32 22706*
W athenscentersquarehotel.gr
Located close to the main sights,
this hotel has a terrace with
panoramic city views. Free Wi-Fi.

PSYRRI: Fresh Hotel €€
Boutique   **Map** B3
Sofokleous 26, 105 52
Tel *210-52 48511*
W freshhotel.gr
Fresh Hotel combines minimalist
chic with bright colors. Rooms
are small but cleverly designed.
Stylish rooftop pool and bar.

DK Choice

SYNTAGMA:
Grande Bretagne €€€
Luxury   **Map** D4
Syntagma Square, 105 64
Tel *210-33 30000*
W grandebretagne.gr
Originally built in 1842 for King
Otto, the Grande Bretagne has
always been Athens' most
exclusive hotel. The rooms are
lavishly furnished, and guests
have an overwhelming choice
of facilities, including indoor
and outdoor pools, a spa center,
and a superb rooftop restaurant.

Rest of Mainland
Greece

ÁGIOS IOANNIS: Anesis Hotel €€
Modern
Agios Ioannis Pelio, 370 12
Tel *24260 31123*
W hotelanesis.gr
A pleasant seaside place with
comfortable rooms and a lovely
terrace overlooking the sea.

ANCIENT CORINTH:
Jo Marinis Rooms €
Modern
Archaia Korinthos, Kórinthos, 200 07
Tel *27410 31481*
W jorooms.com.gr
Enjoy spacious rooms at this
centrally located guesthouse.
The service is superb.

Most rooms at the Hotel Pelops in Olympia have balconies with views over the hills

DK Choice

AREOPOLI: Ktima Karageorgou €€
Luxury
Main St, 230 62
Tel *27330 51368*
🌐 mani.ktimakarageorgou.gr
A superb complex of beautifully decorated rooms and apartments that are built in a traditional style yet offer all the modern comforts for a relaxing stay. Excellent service.

DELPHI: Acropole Delphi Hotel €
Modern
Filellinon 13, 330 54
Tel *22650 82675*
🌐 delphi.com.gr
Pleasant hilltop guesthouse with great views and comfortable accommodations. Free Wi-Fi.

DIMITSANA: En Dimitsani €€
Boutique
Arcadia, 220 07
Tel *27950 31748*
🌐 en-dimitsani.gr
This atmospheric place has an interior featuring exposed stone walls. Rooms offer lovely views.

GYTHEIO: Gythion €
Modern
Vasileos Pavlou 33 Peloponnese, 232 00
Tel *27330 23452*
🌐 gythionhotel.gr
Once a gentleman's club, this Neo-Classical building is now a stylish hotel. Gythion overlooks the seafront and harbor.

KALAMPAKA: Mythos Guesthouse €
Modern
Vlachava 20 (Platanos Square), 422 00
Tel *24320 23952*
🌐 mythos-guesthouse.com
Centrally located guesthouse with large rooms featuring four-poster beds and exposed brick walls.

KARDAMYLI: Katikies Manis €€
Luxury
Main St, 240 22
Tel *21057 89320*
🌐 katikiesmanis.com
This gloriously isolated hotel is a short walk away from an idyllic bay. Large, airy rooms.

MONEMVASIA: Malvasia €€
Historic
Kastro Monemvasias, 230 70
Tel *2732 063007*
🌐 malvasia-hotel.gr
Each room here is different, with traditional furniture, a terrace, and sea views.

MYKINES: Belle Helene €
Historic
Tsounta 15
Tel *27510 76225*
This hotel has hosted famous guests such as Virginia Woolf. The lack of en-suite bathrooms adds to the Victorian ambience.

NAFPLIO: King Othon €
Historic
Farmakopoulou 4, Nafplio Argolida 211 00
Tel *27520 27585*
🌐 kingothon.gr
Named for Greece's first king, this is a beautifully restored mansion near the old town center.

NAFPLIO: Amphitryon Hotel €€€
Luxury
Spiliadou 3–5, 211 00
Tel *27520 70700*
🌐 amphitryon.gr
This is a luxury hotel with every conceivable facility and rooms overlooking the bay.

NEOS MYSTRAS: Pyrgos Of Mystra €€€
Historic
Manousaki 3, 231 00
Tel *27310 20770*
🌐 pyrgosmystra.gr
An imposing 19th-century mansion featuring period

furniture, high ceilings, and tasteful decor. Located beneath the cliffs of Mount Taygetos.

OLYMPIA: Hotel Pelops €
Modern
Varela 2, 270 65
Tel *26240 22543*
🌐 hotelpelops.gr
A stylish hotel within walking distance of the archaeological sites, the Pelops offers fully equipped rooms with balconies.

THESSALONIKI: Tourist €
Historic
Mitropoleos 21, 546 24
Tel *2310 270501*
🌐 touristhotel.gr
With its parquet-floored lounges and irregularly shaped rooms, this is a popular historic hotel.

Corfu and Ionian Islands

CORFU: Glyfada Beach Hotel €
Modern
Glyfada Beach, Pélekas, 491 00
Tel *26610 94257*
🌐 glyfadabeachhotel.com
Excellent-value, clean hotel just a short walk from the beach. Enjoy local specialties at the taverna.

CORFU: Bella Venezia €€
Historic
N. Zampeli 4, 491 00
Tel *26610 46500*
🌐 bellaveneziahotel.com
Bella Venezia is housed in a restored Neo-Classical mansion. Rooms have garden or city views.

KEFALLONIA: Emelisse Hotel €€€
Luxury
Emplisis Bay, Fiskárdhon, 280 84
Tel *26740 41200*
🌐 emelissehotel.com
Traditional stone houses with rooms boasting four-poster beds and stunning sea views.

DK Choice

ZAKYNTHOS: Villas Cavo Marathia €€
Luxury **Map** yes
Keri-Marathias 336, Keríon, 290 92
Tel *26950 22120*
🌐 villas-cavo-marathia.com
Occupying superb vantage points above the sea, the hotel's secluded bungalows are amply furnished and come with kitchenettes; some even have private pools. Extras such as bed linen, towels, and room service are provided. Fabulous service.

The Cyclades

MYKONOS:
Rocabella Art Hotel　€€
Boutique
Agios Stefanos, 846 00
Tel *22890 28930*
W rocabellamykonos.com
A splendid hotel with a modern
and stylish interior, state-of-the-
art spa facilities, and sweeping
sea views.

MYKONOS: Cavo Tagoo　€€€
Luxury
Aegean Coasts S.A., 846 00
Tel *22890 20100*
W cavotagoo.gr
Located on a hillside, Cavo Tagoo
stands in splendid isolation
amid shady eucalyptus trees.
Picturesque sea views.

NAXOS: Summer Memories
Studios & Apartments　€€
Family
Naxos Town, Water Sports Area, 843 00
Tel *22850 24380*
W naxos-summer.com
Great-value hotel featuring large,
tastefully decorated rooms with
kitchenettes and balconies. Enjoy
fruit from the owner's garden.

SANTORINI: Atrium Villa　€€
Family
P.O. Box 5, Fira, 847 00
Tel *22860 23781*
W atriumvilla.gr
This small guesthouse has just
four rooms, but each is comfort-
ably furnished and has a large
balcony with views of the sea.

SANTORINI: Katikies Hotel　€€€
Luxury
Main St, Oía, 847 02
Tel *22860 71401*
W katikieshotelsantorini.com
Each of the elegant cave-rooms
here has a private terrace; some
also have whirlpools. Stunning
views from the infinity pool.

Rhodes and the Dodecanese

DK Choice

KOS: Grecotel
Kos Royal Park　€€€
Luxury
Agios Geórgios, Marmári, 853 00
Tel *22420 41488*
W grecotel.gr
This well-appointed resort on
the sandy Marmári beach offers
all-inclusive packages as well
as standard rates. Facilities
and activities include pools for
adults and children, windsurfing,
pedaloes, canoes, beach sports,
and live entertainment.

LAKHANIÁ: Atrium Prestige
Thalasso Spa Resort & Villas　€€€
Luxury
Main St., 851 09
Tel *22440 46222*
W atriumprestige.gr
Facilities at this vast spa resort
beside the sea, on the southern
tip of Rhodes, include two pools,
four restaurants, and a chapel.

RHODES: Apollo Guest House　€
Family
Omirou 28c, Old Town
Tel *22410 32003*
W apollo-touristhouse.com
This restored old house within
the citadel has a pretty inner
courtyard and bright, breezy
rooms with four-poster beds.

RHODES: San Nikolis Hotel　€€
Historic
*Hippodamou 61, Medieval Town,
851 00*
Tel *22410 34561*
W s-nikolis.gr
A small but charming hotel in
an old townhouse. The rooms
have antique furnishings and
exposed stone walls.

RHODES:
Rodos Park Suites & Spa　€€€
Luxury
Riga Fereou 12, 851 00
Tel *22410 89700*
W rodospark.gr
Spa hotel offering ultra-modern
styling and exceptionally high
standards of service.

Crete

DK Choice

AGIOS NIKOLAOS: St. Nicolas
Bay Resort Hotel & Villas　€€€
Luxury
Thessi Nissi, P.O. Box 47, 721 00
Tel *28410 90200*
W stnicolasbay.gr
This magnificent complex of
bungalows and luxury suites
enjoys a gorgeous seaside
location. Landscaped gardens
full of citrus and olive trees
surround the buildings, and
the hotel even has its own,
virtually private, beach.

CHANIA: Hotel Amfora　€€
Family
*2nd Passage of Theotokopoulou St,
Old Venetian Harbor, 731 31*
Tel *28210 93224*
W amphora.gr
This 13th-century mansion has
tasteful rooms and a charming
terrace overlooking the harbor.

ELOUNDA: Corali Studios
& Portobello Apartments　€
Family
Akti Posidonos, 720 53
Tel *28410 41712*
W coralistudios.com
Close to the beach, this excellent
budget option has self-catering
rooms and apartments.

IRAKLEIO: Lato Boutique　€€
Boutique
Epimenidou 15, 712 02
Tel *28102 28103*
W lato.gr
Stay in stylish rooms with
balconies, terraces, or glassed-in
mini-conservatories.

RETHYMNO: Palazzo Vecchio
Exclusive Residence　€€
Historic
*Heroon Politechniou & Melissinou,
741 00*
Tel *28310 35351*
W palazzovecchio.gr
New meets old in this 15th-
century townhouse converted
into a stylish hotel. Rooms have
kitchenettes.

The blue-and-white color scheme at the Rocabella Art Hotel, Mykonos

Where to Eat and Drink

Athens

EXARCHEIA:
Mparmpa Giannis   €
Traditional Greek   **Map** C2
Emmanouíl Mpenáki 94, 106 81
Tel *210-38 24138*
A favorite that hasn't changed much in decades, Mparmpa Giannis dishes up consistently good *mageireftá* (baked dishes) and a handful of grills.

DK Choice

KERAMIKOS:
Funky Gourmet   €€€
Traditional Greek
Paramithias 13 and Salaminos, 104 35
Tel *210-52 42727*
The highly acclaimed and award winning Funky Gourmet is a favourite among restaurant critics, so diners will need to book a table weeks ahead. The head chefs have created a magnificent menu that artfully twists traditional Greek themes to produce delicacies such as lamb *giouvetsi* (meat with orzo pasta and tomato sauce) and mustard ice cream, each of which are paired with handpicked wines.

KOLONAKI: Ouzadiko
Modern Greek   **Map** E3
Karneádou 25–29, 106 76
Tel *210-72 95484*   **Closed** *Sun & Mon*
This *ouzerí* (tavern) claims to offer more varieties of *ouzo* (liquor) and *tsípouro* (wine spirit) than anywhere else in town. Always crowded and convivial, Ouzadiko is a popular hangout.

KOLONAKI:
Orizontes Lykavittou   €€€
International   **Map** E3
Lycabettus Hill, 106 75
Tel *210-72 27065*
The views are sky-high, and so are some of the prices at this restaurant near the summit of the hill, accessible only by cable car or a long hike.

MAKRYGIANNI: Strofi
Traditional Greek   €€€
Rovertou Galli 25, 117 42
Tel *210-92 14130*   **Closed** *Mon*
Strofi has long been one of Athens' best restaurants. The impeccable service is matched by the superb selection of simple Greek favorites on the menu. Reserve a table in advance.

Views over downtown Athens from the first-floor dining room at Funky Gourmet

MONASTIRAKI: Thanasis
Traditional Greek   **Map** B4
Mitropóleos 69, 105 55
Tel *210-32 44705*
A perennial candidate for the best purveyor of *souvláki* (kebab) in town, Thanasis is always packed. No prior bookings, so be prepared to join the crowds of Athenians waiting in line for takeout or a table.

MONASTIRAKI:
Café Avissynia   €€
Macedonian   **Map** B4
Kynéttou 7, off Plateía Avissynías, 105 55
Tel *210-32 1704*   **Closed** *Mon*
Come here for delicious Macedonian staples such as mussel pilaf and baked feta. Always packed at weekend lunchtimes and Friday evenings, when an accordionist and a singer entertain diners.

OMONOIA: Ideal
Greek/International   **Map** C2
Panepistimíou 46, 106 78
Tel *210-33 03000*   **Closed** *Sun*
A city-center institution since 1922. At Ideal, guests may dine on schnitzel and chops or on a range of more Hellenic dishes, such as milk-fed veal with eggplant and stuffed zucchini.

PLAKA: O Platanos
Traditional Greek   €
Diogénous 4, 105 56   **Map** C4
Tel *210-32 20666*   **Closed** *Sun*
Taking its name from the *plátanos* (plane) tree outside, this taverna serves meat-based stews and *laderá* (cooked vegetables). It also has exceptionally good barreled *retsina*.

PLAKA: Apollonia Lyra
Traditional Greek   **Map** C4
Lysiou 12, 105 56
Tel *210-32 29727*
Apollonia is an enchanting little restaurant within a restored old building that oozes period charm. Greek standards fill the menu, and the moussaka is an absolute must-try.

SYNTAGMA: Avocado
Vegetarian   **Map** D3
Nikis 30, 105 57
Tel *210-32 37878*
Perfect for those who are tired of meat-heavy Greek cuisine, Avocado offers a tantalizing range of vegan and vegetarian fare. Dishes are served with fantastic home-made bread, and there is a good choice of organic wines and fresh juices.

SYNTAGMA:
Grande Bretagne Hotel Roof Garden Restaurant   €€€
Modern Mediterranean   **Map** D4
Syntagma Square, 105 64
Tel *210-33 30766*
Perched atop the luxury Grande Bretagne Hotel, this stylish rooftop restaurant boasts both fabulous food and glorious views of Athens and the Acropolis.

THISEIO: Kuzina
Mediterranean   **Map** A4
Adrianou 9, 105 55
Tel *210-32 40133*
This increasingly popular restaurant serves quirky interpretations of traditional Greek cuisine, such as risotto with feta cheese and Cretan smoked pork. There is also an art gallery and a rooftop terrace with stunning views of the Acropolis.

TSOKRI: Smile
Traditional Greek   €
Syngrou 24, Tsokri Square, 117 42
Tel *210-92 18911*
A fantastic budget eatery that is considered one of the best in Athens. Smile is a great place to sample Greek staples such as kebabs, moussaka, spinach pies, and gyros. Enjoy the shaded outdoor seating and friendly service.

Rest of Mainland Greece

GYTHEIO: Saga   €€
Seafood
Odós Tzanetáki, opposite
Marathonísi, 232 00
Tel 27330-23220
This pleasant restaurant is a great place for sampling fresh fish, with a wide selection, including several types of sea bream. Also try the fish soup and charcoal-grilled octopus.

DK Choice

KALAMPAKA: Meteora   €€
Traditional Greek
Ikonomou 4, 422 00
Tel 24320 22316
Over a century old, this family-run restaurant is considered one of the town's best. The home-cooked Greek dishes are delicious and great value. Sit at a shaded outdoor table and enjoy the lovely views of Meteora's famous rocks.

MONEMVASIA: Skorpiós   €
Traditional Greek
South coast rd, Géfyra district, 230 70
Tel 27320 62090
Head to Skorpiós for tasty meze like *tzatzíki* and *tyrokafterí* (spicy cheese dip), and simple small fish like marinated *gávros* and *atherína*. Also serves good wine.

NAFPLIO: Ta Fanária   €€
Traditional Greek
Staïkopoulou 13, 211 00
Tel 27520 27141
The best bet is for lunch, when *maghireftá* (baked dishes) such as moussaka and *soutzoukákia* (a minced lamb and tomato dish) are served fresh from the oven.

NAFPLIO: 3Sixty   €€€
International
Papanikolaou 26, Palaio Nafplio
Tel 27520 28068
Extraordinarily stylish spot within a restored Neo-Classical building. It serves a lovely selection of international dishes and local wines, and it transforms into a hip club at night.

THESSALONIKI:
Nea Diagonios   €€
Traditional Greek
89 Plastira Nikolaou, 551 32
Tel 2310 029085
One of Thessaloniki's best eateries, this is the place to try *soutzoukakia* (meat balls) and *gyros*. The outdoor tables have sea views and the service is great.

Delicious surf-and-turf skewer at El Correo Cocina Argentina, Thessaloniki

THESSALONIKI:
El Correo Cocina Argentina   €€€
Argentinian
Katouni 6, 546 25
Tel 23105 06506
Steak lovers should look no further: El Correo serves the best steaks in the city, as well as mouthwatering desserts. Vintage decor and attentive service.

THESSALONIKI: The
Excelsior Restaurant   €€€
Fusion
Komninon 10 & Mitropoleos 23,
546 24
Tel 23100 21000
This classy restaurant within the luxury Excelsior Hotel serves an intriguing fusion of Greek, Italian, and French cuisine that is truly Mediterranean. Live music and wine tastings on Friday nights.

Corfu and the Ionian Islands

CORFU: Rouvas   €
Greek/International
Stamatiou Desila 13, 491 00
Tel 26610 31182   **Closed** *Sun*
One of the most affordable places in town, Rouvas has a reputation for offering some of the best Corfiot, international, and traditional Greek dishes – all made with fresh local ingredients.

CORFU: Rex   €€
Traditional Greek
Kapodistriou 66, 491 00
Tel 26610 39649
Housed in a mid-19th-century building, Rex is a Corfu institution – a truly traditional restaurant serving authentic Corfiot food. Specialties include swordfish *bourtheto* (a spicy stew).

CORFU: Sapori e Vini   €€
Italian/Mediterranean
Solomou 1 (New Fortress), 491 00
Tel 26610 81785   **Closed** *Mon*
Widely considered one of Corfu's best restaurants, Sapori e Vini is tucked away down a side street. It is a tranquil spot with a laid-back atmosphere. Great value.

KEFALLONIA: Patsouras   €
Traditional Greek
Vergoti Kalipsous 1, Argostóli
Tel 26714 00302
Patsouras is a surprisingly affordable family-run taverna. The menu includes all the traditional Greek favorites, plus a few Kefallonián specialties.

DK Choice

KEFALLONIA: Tassia   €€
Traditional Greek
Limáni Fiskardou
Tel 26740 41205 **Closed** *Nov–Apr*
This internationally acclaimed restaurant features a wine list that emphasizes some of Kefallonia's own vintages, recognized as among the best in Greece. The menu includes fine seafood as well as pasta dishes, plus sublime desserts. Located right on the harbor.

ZAKYNTHOS:
Essence Restaurant   €€€
Traditional Greek
Kalamaki, back road to Zante Town
Tel 69785 65232   **Closed** *Mon & Tue*
Serving five-star cuisine prepared by its owner, a former head chef on a cruise ship, Essence is considered one of Kalamaki's best restaurants. The themed menus change through the year.

The Cyclades

MYKONOS: Bakalo   €€
Traditional Greek
Lakka, 846 00
Tel 22890 78121
A lovely eatery within a restored 18th-century house. Bakalo serves scrumptious home-made dishes that include stuffed vine leaves and aubergine moussaka.

MYKONOS: Katerina's Bar
& Restaurant   €€€
Traditional Greek
Agion Anargiron 8, Little Venice, 846 00
Tel 22890 23084
Gloriously positioned, with tables on platforms jutting right out into the sea, this restaurant is not to be missed. Dine on typical Greek dishes at reasonable prices.

MYKONOS: M-eating €€€
Mediterranean
Kalogera 10, 846 00
Tel *22890 78550*
Simple fare in an eatery that is
a refreshing alternative to the
tourist traps along the harbor.
Consistently high standards of
cuisine and service.

**NAXOS: Ippokampos
Beach Restaurant** €€
Mediterranean
St. George Beach, Naxos City
Tel *22850 24648*
A supremely laid-back place with
deckchairs on the beach and
seating with lovely sea views. The
cuisine is a modern take on Greek
fare, with plenty of fish options.

SANTORINI: Volcano Blue €€
Seafood
Caldera Fira, 847 00
Tel *22860 22850*
Tricky to find, but well worth the
effort, Volcano Blue has glorious
views from its hillside position. It
serves a great range of fresh fish
dishes, including fried squid and
baked snapper, alongside the
usual Greek favorites.

SANTORINI: 1800 €€€
Greek/Mediterranean
Main St, Oía, 847 02
Tel *22860 71485*
The menu at this swanky
restaurant blends European and
Greek influences. There is also
an extensive wine list featuring
Santorini's more interesting
vintages and labels. Book ahead.

Rhodes and the Dodecanese

**KARPATHOS:
The Olive Garden** €€
Traditional Greek
Kira Beach, Kira Panagia
Tel *22450 23663*
A delightful restaurant
surrounded by lush greenery on

a rocky hillside. It serves delicious
home-cooked food prepared
using fresh local ingredients.

KOS: O Makis €
Seafood
Mastichári, 853 02
Tel *22420 59061*
One of the best tavernas on the
island, O Makis is located next to
a harbor from which it sources
its seafood. Expect fresh *tsipoura*
(bream), as well as prawns, squid,
and octopus.

KOS: Agkyra Restaurant €€
Seafood
Averof 14, 853 00
Tel *22420 26861*
Highly regarded fish restaurant
with outdoor tables overlooking
the harbor. This is a good place to
sample roasted shrimp or grilled
octopus, washed down with
Agkyra's home-made brandy.

RHODES: Marco Polo Café €€
Traditional Greek
*Ag. Fanuriu 42, Old Town,
851 00*
Tel *22410 25562*
A truly entrancing place within
an old building that has been
furnished to resemble an
Ottoman-era mansion. Marco
Polo serves delicious light Greek
dishes in a shaded courtyard.

RHODES: To Meltemi €€
Seafood
Plateia Kountourioti, 851 07
Tel *22410 30480*
The simple menu at this
unpretentious restaurant on the
beach has a good choice of hot
and cold appetizers, grills, and
fish dishes. A basket of fresh hot
bread is served with every meal.

**RHODES: Melenos
Lindos Restaurant** €€€
Traditional Greek
Lindos, 851 07
Tel *22440 32222*
Popular with wedding parties,
this exquisite restaurant has a

hilltop vantage point that offers
diners dramatic views of the bay.
It serves excellent food.

Crete

**AGIOS NIKOLAOS:
The Ferryman** €€
Seafood
Akti, Elounda, 720 53
Tel *28410 41230*
Family-run restaurant with tables
right at the water's edge. Large
portions of top-quality Greek
food and an excellent wine list.

DK Choice

CHANIA: Dounias €€
Traditional Greek
Main Rd, Drakona, 731 00
Tel *28210 65083*
A trip to this very special
restaurant, hidden away high
up in the hills, is worth the
effort. The owner spent years
revitalizing the local village
economy, and all the dishes
are made from organic, local
ingredients using traditional
recipes and cooking techniques.

CHANIA: Cosmos €€€
Mediterranean
Upper Platanias Old Village, Platanias
Tel *28210 68558*
The views from the terrace of this
restaurant, the highest in the
village, warrant the climb. High-
quality Greek fare is accompanied
by a choice of over 300 wines.

**IRAKLEIO:
Ippokambos Ouzeri** €€
Traditional Greek
Sofokli Venizelou 3, 713 02
Tel *28102 80240*
At this surprisingly good *ouzerie*,
diners are expected to share a
number of small dishes rather
than order only for themselves.

IRAKLEIO: Loukoulos €€€
Mediterranean
Korai 5
Tel *28102 24435*
Enjoy a menu of mainly Italian
dishes in upmarket surroundings
– with white linen tablecloths
and candles in the evening.

RETHYMNO: Avlí €€€
Greek Fusion
Xanthoudidou 22, 741 00
Tel *28310 58250*
Dine in the vaulted rooms or the
courtyard of an old mansion. The
menu consists mainly of grilled
and roast meats, and there is also
an extensive Greek wine list.

Dining with a view over the Aegean Sea at Volcano Blue, Santorini

GERMANY, AUSTRIA, AND SWITZERLAND

Germany, Austria, and Switzerland at a Glance

Europe's three main German-speaking countries occupy a broad swathe of Europe stretching from the Alps to the North Sea and the Baltic. Germany has many great cities, the former capitals of the small states that made up Germany under the Holy Roman Empire. It also has beautiful countryside, rivers, and forests. Austria's main attractions are the former imperial capital Vienna, the river Danube, and its mountains. More than half of Switzerland, which also has important French- and Italian-speaking regions, is mountainous, dominated by its permanently snow-capped Alpine peaks.

Kiel

Lübeck

Hamburg

Bremen

Hanover

Münster

Essen · Dortmund

Kassel

Düsseldorf

Cologne

GERMANY
(see pp494–551)

Koblenz

Frankfurt
am Main

Trier   Mainz

Würzburg

Stuttgart

Ulm

Freiburg
im Breisgau

Basel

Zürich

Bern

SWITZERLAND
(see pp576–95)

Lausanne

Geneva

The Rhine Valley *(see pp530–31)* attracts hordes of visitors in summer, drawn by the beautiful scenery, medieval and mock-medieval castles, and Germany's finest white wines. You can either tour by car or take a river cruise from cities such as Mainz and Koblenz.

The Swiss Alps *(see pp583–8)* are a popular destination all year round: in winter for the skiing and other winter sports, in summer for the excellent walking or simply for the crisp, clean air and unrivaled scenery.

| 0 km | 100 | |
| 0 miles | | 100 |

◄ The Schreckhorn looming large over a valley in the Bernese Alps, Switzerland

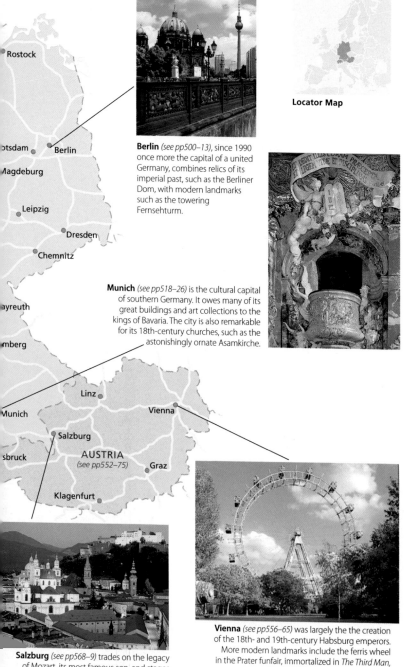

Locator Map

Berlin *(see pp500–13)*, since 1990 once more the capital of a united Germany, combines relics of its imperial past, such as the Berliner Dom, with modern landmarks such as the towering Fernsehturm.

Munich *(see pp518–26)* is the cultural capital of southern Germany. It owes many of its great buildings and art collections to the kings of Bavaria. The city is also remarkable for its 18th-century churches, such as the astonishingly ornate Asamkirche.

Salzburg *(see pp568–9)* trades on the legacy of Mozart, its most famous son, and stages one of the world's great music festivals. It also boasts a rich architectural heritage from the prince-archbishops who ruled the city from 1278 to 1816.

Vienna *(see pp556–65)* was largely the the creation of the 18th- and 19th-century Habsburg emperors. More modern landmarks include the ferris wheel in the Prater funfair, immortalized in *The Third Man*, the 1949 film starring Orson Welles.

GERMANY

By reputation the Germans are a hard-working, efficient, competitive people and this is borne out by their recent economic success. However, Germany's turbulent, divided past and the centuries when it was a patchwork of many tiny states mean that there are profound regional differences, apparent in a wealth of fascinating historical sights and colorful local traditions.

Thanks initially to American aid, industry and commerce boomed in West Germany following World War II. This so-called *Wirtschaftswunder* (economic miracle) made West Germany a dominant member of the European Economic Community (now the European Union). Demand for labor led to reliance on migrant workers or *Gastarbeiter* (guest workers). As a result, over 7 million immigrants now live in Germany, the largest number coming from Turkey, but many too from Italy, Greece, and increasingly the former Yugoslavia. In the manufacturing city of Stuttgart, one inhabitant in three is an immigrant.

Despite its many industrial cities and a population of over 80 million, Germany is large enough to also possess a great variety of attractive rural landscapes. For many, the Rhine epitomizes Germany, especially the romantic stretch between Mainz and Cologne. However, the country has much more to offer in the way of scenery, especially its forests, heaths, and mountains. In the far south, the Alps are the major attraction, especially around Lake Constance (the Bodensee), the large lake that borders Austria and Switzerland.

History

Germanic tribes became established in the region sometime during the 1st millennium BC. They clashed with the Romans, defeating them in AD 9 at the Teutoburger forest. Thereafter, the Romans fixed their frontier along the Rhine and the Danube. Although relations were often hostile, the Goths and other Germanic tribes traded and made alliances with Rome, and as the Roman Empire collapsed, these peoples carved out kingdoms of their own.

The dome of Berlin's Reichstag – home to the Bundestag (Federal Parliament)

◀ The Frauenkirche Lutheran church illuminated in the early evening in Dresden, Germany

The people who eventually inherited the largest kingdom were the Franks, who conquered France and in the early 9th century, under Charlemagne, subdued most of the German tribes, including the Saxons, Swabians, and Bavarians. The pope gave his blessing to Charlemagne's overlord-ship, thus creating the Holy Roman Empire.

After Charlemagne, the German kingdom became separated from the rest of the empire. The next strong German ruler was the Saxon Otto I, who increased his power further after his defeat of the Magyars in 955.

Frederick II (the Great), King of Prussia (1740–86)

The Middle Ages saw the development of a complicated feudal system with hundreds of dukedoms, counties, and ecclesiastical estates owing allegiance to the German emperor, as well as free "imperial cities." In the 11th and 12th centuries, popes and emperors joined in a fierce struggle over

who should grant lands, appoint bishops, and collect revenues. Each would try to bribe the Electors (Kurfürsten) – princes and bishops who chose the emperor.

The role of the Electors was clarified in the Golden Bull issued by Emperor Charles IV in 1356, but by the 16th century, the position had become the more or less hereditary right of the Austrian Habsburgs.

The power of the church created many problems and it was no surprise that the Reformation began in Germany in 1517 with Martin Luther's *95 Theses* pointing out the abuses of the clergy. In the ensuing wars of religion, princes saw a chance to increase their lands at the expense of the Church. The Peace of Augsburg in 1555 established the principle *cuius regio eius religio* – each state followed the religion of its ruler. In the 17th century, religious differences were again a major factor in the Thirty Years' War. Other countries, such as France and Sweden, joined the conflict, which laid waste most of Germany.

In the 17th and 18th centuries Germany remained a patchwork of small states, theoretically still part of the Habsburg Empire. However, Prussia gradually became a power to rival the Habsburgs. During the Enlightenment and Romantic periods, German literature found its voice, especially in the dramas of Goethe and Schiller, and Napoleon's invasion of Germany sparked ideas of nationalism. In the mid-19th century, it was Prussia that assumed the leadership of Germany through the skilful politics of Otto von Bismarck, the Prussian chancellor. After the Prussians had defeated the Austrians in 1866 and the French in 1870, the Second German Reich was declared with the Prussian King as Kaiser Wilhelm I.

Wilhelm's grandson Wilhelm II had great ambitions for the new empire, and rivalry with Britain, France, and Russia plunged Europe into World War I. The humiliation

KEY DATES IN GERMAN HISTORY

5th century AD Germanic peoples overrun large parts of Roman Empire

c.750 Mission of St. Boniface to Germany

843 Charlemagne's empire divided

962 Otto I crowned emperor

1077 Pope Gregory VII and Emperor Heinrich IV clash over investiture of bishops

13th century North German Hanseatic League starts to dominate trade in Baltic region

1356 Golden Bull establishes role of Electors

1517 Martin Luther attaches his *95 Theses* to the door of a church in Wittenberg

1555 Peace of Augsburg ends religious wars

1618–48 Germany ravaged by Thirty Years' War

1740–86 Reign of Frederick the Great

1806 Napoleon abolishes Holy Roman Empire

1871 German Empire proclaimed

1914–18 World War I

1933 End of Weimar Republic; Hitler comes to power

1939–45 World War II: after Germany's defeat, country divided into West and East

1990 Reunification of Germany

2002 Germany joins single European currency

2005 First female chancellor, Angela Merkel, is elected

2014 Minimum wage is set for the first time in Germany

of defeat and the terms of the Treaty of Versailles (1919) left Germany in economic chaos. The Weimar Republic struggled on until 1933 when Hitler seized power. His nationalist policies appealed to a demoralized people, but his territorial ambitions led the country into World War II and a second defeat.

Despite the atrocities committed by the Nazis, the Germans were soon forgiven by both America and Russia as they divided the country in such a way that it became the theater for the Cold War between East and West. The Berlin Wall, erected in 1961 to stop East Germans fleeing to the West, became the symbol of an era. Its fall in 1989 was the start of the process of reunification.

Modern Germany is a federal country, with each *Land* (state) electing its own parliament. Regional differences due to Germany's checkered history are still much in evidence, the Catholic south being much more conservative than the north. Differences between the former West Germany and the old DDR (East Germany) are also very visible. The East suffers from high unemployment and its people tend to be suspicious of the motives of the West Germans, despite all the money poured into the region to equalize living standards.

Culture and the Arts

Germany is rich in legends and sagas, such as the tale of Siegfried told in the epic poem the *Nibelungenlied*, written down around 1200. It has been reworked many times, notably in Richard Wagner's great *Ring* opera cycle.

Celebrating the fall of the Berlin Wall in 1989

Of all the arts, it is to classical music that Germany has made the greatest contribution, Johann Sebastian Bach from the Baroque period and Ludwig van Beethoven from the Classical period being perhaps the two most influential figures. In the 19th century, poems by Goethe, Schiller, and others were set to music by composers Robert Schumann, Johannes Brahms, and Hugo Wolf.

Germany has also produced many of the world's most influential philosophers: from Immanuel Kant (1724–1804), father of modern philosophy, to Karl Marx (1818–83), founder of the 20th century's most potent political ideology.

Modern Life

The German economy tends to be dominated by long-established giants such as Siemens in the electrical and electronic sectors, Volkswagen and BMW in cars, and BASF in chemicals. Despite the continuing success of German industry and banking, and the people's reputation for hard work, the Germans actually enjoy longer annual holidays and spend more money on foreign travel than any other European nation. When at home, they are enthusiastic participants in many sports, and have enjoyed great success in recent years at football, motor racing, and tennis. They also enjoy gregarious public merrymaking, for example at *Fasching* (carnival) and the Oktoberfest, Munich's annual beer festival.

Munich's Olympic Stadium, built for the 1972 Olympic Games

Exploring Germany

Visitors in search of classical German landscapes flock to the Black
Forest, the Rhine Valley, and the Bavarian Alps. The attractive
German countryside is easily accessed thanks to the best road
network in Europe. Of the cities, the most popular destinations
are the capital Berlin, a vibrant metropolis in a state of
transition since reunification in 1990, and Munich, the
historic former capital of the Kingdom of Bavaria. East
Germany, now open for tourism, has many attractions
to draw visitors – particularly the city of Dresden,
rebuilt after World War II.

Sights at a Glance

1. Berlin pp500–13
2. Dresden
3. Leipzig
4. Weimar
5. Bayreuth
6. Bamberg
7. Würzburg
8. Rothenburg ob der Tauber
9. Nuremberg
10. Munich pp518–25
11. Passau
12. Neuschwanstein
13. Lake Constance
14. Freiburg im Breisgau
15. Black Forest
16. Stuttgart
17. Heidelberg
18. Trier
19. Mosel Valley
20. Mainz
21. Rhine Valley
22. Koblenz
23. Frankfurt am Main
24. Bonn
25. Cologne pp533–5
26. Münster
27. Hanover
28. Bremen
29. Hamburg
30. Lübeck

Wooded landscape of the Black Forest region

Distance chart

Berlin					Distance by road in kilometers				
574 356	Cologne				Distance by road in miles				
198 123	**629** 390	Dresden							
540 335	**189** 117	**511** 317	Frankfurt						
285 117	**431** 268	**483** 300	**495** 307	Hamburg					
288 179	**294** 183	**376** 233	**354** 220	**156** 97	Hanover				
585 363	**590** 366	**474** 294	**400** 248	**781** 485	**616** 382	Munich			
415 258	**415** 258	**304** 189	**231** 143	**585** 363	**441** 274	**170** 105	Nuremberg		
629 397	**374** 232	**522** 324	**208** 129	**652** 405	**508** 315	**231** 143	**218** 135	Stuttgart	

Kaiser-Wilhelm-Gedächtniskirche with its octagonal extension and bell tower, Berlin

Key

- Highway
- Major road
- Railroad
- International border
- Ferry route

For keys to symbols *see back flap*

❶ Berlin

Since becoming the capital of the Federal Republic of Germany following reunification in 1990, Berlin has become an ever popular destination for visitors. The historic heart of the city is located around the wide avenue Unter den Linden and on Museum Island, which takes its name from the fine museums built there in the 19th and early 20th centuries. South of Unter den Linden is Checkpoint Charlie, a legacy of Berlin's status as a divided city during the Cold War. To the west are the green open spaces of Tiergarten and Kurfürstendamm, the center of the former West Berlin. Farther afield, the splendid palaces of Potsdam, now almost a suburb of Berlin, are not to be missed.

The grand approach to the 18th-century Rococo Schloss Sanssouci in Potsdam

Sights at a Glance

① Brandenburg Gate
② Reichstag
③ Unter den Linden
④ Potsdamer Platz
⑤ Kulturforum
⑥ Tiergarten
⑦ Altes Museum
⑧ Pergamonmuseum
⑨ Humboldt-Box

⑩ *Berliner Dom pp506–7*
⑪ Centrum Judaicum & Neue Synagoge
⑫ Fernsehturm
⑬ Nikolaiviertel
⑭ Kreuzberg
⑮ Zoologischer Garten
⑯ Kaiser-Wilhelm-Gedächtniskirche

⑰ Kurfürstendamm
⑱ Sammlung Berggruen
⑲ Schloss Charlottenburg

Greater Berlin *(see inset map)*

⑳ Grunewald
㉑ Dahlem
㉒ Potsdam and Park Sanssouci

Getting Around

Berlin's U- and S-Bahn train systems provide the quickest way of getting around the city. They also serve outlying areas, such as Grunewald, Dahlem, and Potsdam. Buses are reliable, but slow, especially during rush hour, owing to congestion. Trams are another option in the east of the city, and accept the same tickets as the buses and S-Bahn lines.

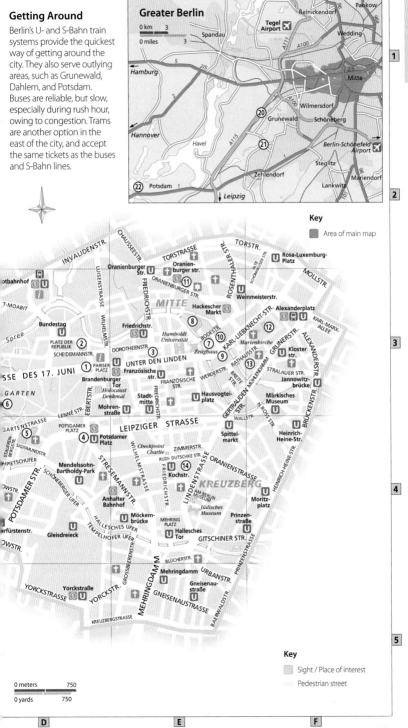

Key

Area of main map

Key

Sight / Place of interest
Pedestrian street

0 meters 750
0 yards 750

D E F

For keys to symbols *see back flap*

The imposing Brandenburg Gate at Pariser Platz, at the western end of Unter den Linden

① Brandenburg Gate

Pariser Platz. Ⓢ Unter den Linden. 🚌 100, TXL.

The Brandenburg Gate is the quintessential symbol of Berlin. This magnificent Neoclassical structure was designed by Carl Gotthard Langhans and modeled on the Propylaia of the Acropolis in Athens *(see p4)*. It was erected between 1788 and 1791, although the sculptural decorations were not completed until 1795. Pavilions frame its simple Doric colonnade, and bas-reliefs on the entablature above the columns depict scenes from Greek myth. The structure is crowned by the famous sculpture of a *quadriga* – a chariot drawn by four horses – designed by Johann Gottfried Schadow.

The Brandenburg Gate has witnessed many important historical events. Military parades and demonstrating workers have marched under its arches, and it was the site of celebrations marking the birth of the Deutsches Reich in 1871. It was here, too, that the Soviet flag was raised in 1945.

Restored between 1956 and 1958, for the next 30 years the gate stood watch over the divided city, until the fall of the Berlin Wall in 1989. It was renovated once again in 2002.

② Reichstag

Platz der Republik. Ⓢ Unter den Linden. 🚌 U55, 100. **Tel** 030-2273 2152. Dome & Assembly Hall: **Open** daily. **Closed** Dec 24 & Dec 31. 🛇

Built to house the German Parliament, the Reichstag was intended as a symbol of national unity and to showcase the aspirations of the new German Empire, declared in 1871. Constructed between 1884 and 1894, the Neo-Renaissance building by Paul Wallot captured the prevailing spirit of German optimism. On the night of February 27, 1933,

a fire destroyed the main hall. Rebuilding work undertaken between 1957 and 1972 removed the dome and most of the ornamentation on the façades. On December 2, 1990, the Reichstag was the first meeting place of a newly-elected Bundestag following German reunification.

The latest rebuilding project, completed in 1999 to a design by Sir Norman Foster, transformed the Reichstag into a modern meeting hall crowned by an elliptical glass dome.

③ Unter den Linden

🚆 Unter den Linden. 🚌 100, TXL.

One of the most famous streets in Berlin, Unter den Linden was once the route to the royal hunting grounds that were transformed into the Tiergarten. In the 17th century, it was planted with lime trees, to which it owes its name.

In the 18th century, Unter den Linden became the main street of the westward-growing city. It gradually filled with prestigious buildings, such as the Baroque **Zeughaus**, home of the Deutsches Historisches Museum, and the **Humboldt Universität** (1753). Next door, the **Neue Wache** (1816–18) commemorates the victims of war and dictatorship.

Since reunification, many buildings have been restored and Unter den Linden has acquired several cafés and restaurants, as well as smart new shops. The street is also the venue for outdoor events.

The Reichstag, crowned by a dome designed by Sir Norman Foster

④ **Potsdamer Platz**

Ⓤ Ⓢ Potsdamer Platz.

Before the onset of World War II, Potsdamer Platz was one of the busiest and most densely built-up areas of Berlin. Most of the area's landmarks ceased to exist after the bombing of 1945, and the destruction was completed when the burned-out ruins were finally pulled down to build the Berlin Wall.

Since the mid-1990s, a new financial and business district has sprung up on this empty wasteland, which once divided East and West Berlin. The huge complex comprises not only office buildings, but also a concert hall, a multi-screen cinema, and the Arkaden shopping mall. The first finished structure was the Daimler-Benz-Areal office block, designed by Renzo Piano and Christoph Kohlbecker. To the north lies the impressive Sony-Center complex, by Helmut Jahn.

Silver and ivory tankard from the Kunstgewerbemuseum

⑤ **Kulturforum**

Ⓤ Ⓢ Potsdamer Platz. **Tel** 030-266 3666. Kunstgewerbemuseum: **Open** Tue–Sun. **Closed** first Tue after Easter, Whitsun, Oct 1, Dec 24, 25 & 31. ♿ ♿ Gemäldegalerie: **Open** Tue–Sun. **Closed** first Tue after Easter, Whitsun, May 1, Dec 24, 25 & 31. ♿ ♿ Neue Nationalgalerie: **Open** Tue–Sun. ♿ ♿

The idea of creating a new cultural center in West Berlin was first mooted in 1956.

The first building to go up was the **Philharmonie** (Berlin Philharmonic concert hall), built to an innovative design by Hans Scharoun in 1961. Most of the other plans for the Kulturforum were realized between 1961 and 1987. With many museums and galleries, the area attracts millions of visitors every year.

The **Kunstgewerbemuseum** (Museum of Arts and Crafts) holds a rich collection of decorative art and crafts dating from the early Middle Ages to the modern day. Goldwork is very well represented, and the museum takes great pride in its late Gothic and Renaissance silver.

The **Gemäldegalerie** fine art collection is in a modern building designed by Heinz Hilmer and Christopher Sattler. Works by German Renaissance artists, including Albrecht Dürer and Hans Holbein, dominate the exhibition space, but there are also pieces by van Dyck, Rembrandt, Raphael, Velázquez, and Caravaggio.

Housed in a striking building with a flat steel roof over a glass hall, the **Neue Nationalgalerie** contains mainly 20th-century art, but begins with artists of the late 19th century, such as Edvard Munch and Ferdinand Hodler. Paintings from the *Die Brücke* movement include pieces by Ernst Ludwig Kirchner and Karl Schmidt-Rottluff. The museum is shut until 2017 for a revamp; key works will be shown elsewhere.

A tranquil stretch of water in Berlin's 19th-century Tiergarten

⑥ **Tiergarten**

Ⓢ Tiergarten, Bellevue. 🚌 100, 200.

Situated at the center of the city, the Tiergarten is the largest park in Berlin occupying a 210-ha (520-acre) area. Once a hunting reserve, the forest was transformed into a landscaped park in the 1830s. A triumphal avenue was built at the end of the 19th century, lined with statues of the nation's rulers and statesmen.

World War II inflicted huge damage on the Tiergarten, including the destruction of the triumphal avenue. Replanting has restored the garden, and many of its avenues are now lined with statues of national celebrities, including Goethe.

To the east of the Tiergarten is the **Holocaust Denkmal**. Designed by architect Peter Eisenman, this wave-like monument represents the overwhelming scale of the Holocaust.

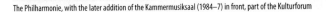

The Philharmonie, with the later addition of the Kammermusiksaal (1984–7) in front, part of the Kulturforum

Mosaic from Hadrian's Villa (2nd century AD), at the Altes Museum

⑦ Altes Museum

Am Lustgarten. **Tel** 030-266 3660. ⓢ Hackescher Markt. 🚊 M1, M4, M5, M6. 🚌 100, 200. **Open** daily. 🅿️

The Altes Museum, designed by Karl Friedrich Schinkel, is one of the world's finest Neoclassical structures, with an impressive 87-m- (285-ft-) high portico supported by Ionic columns. The stately rotunda is decorated with sculptures and ringed by a colonnade.

Officially opened in 1830, this was one of the first purpose-built museums in Europe, designed to house the royal collection of paintings and antiquities. Following World War II, the building was used to display temporary exhibitions. Since 1998 the Altes Museum has housed a portion of the Antikensammlung, a magnificent collection of Greek and Roman antiquities. Among the highlights are a colorful floor mosaic from Hadrian's Villa near Tivoli, and Perikles' Head, a Roman copy of the sculpture by Kresilas that stood at the entrance to the Acropolis in Athens.

⑧ Pergamon-museum

Bodestraße 1–3 (entrance from Am Kupfergraben). **Tel** 030-266 3666. ⓢ Hackescher Markt, Friedrichstrasse. 🚌 100, 200, TXL. **Open** daily. **Closed** Jan 1, first Tue after Easter and Pentecost, Dec 24, 25 & 31. 🅿️ ♿

Built between 1912 and 1930 to a design by Alfred Messel and Ludwig Hoffmann, the Pergamonmuseum is one of Berlin's major attractions. Its three large independent collections form one of Europe's most famous archives of antiquities.

A highlight of the Greek and Roman antiquities collection (Antikensammlung) is the huge Pergamon Altar from the acropolis of ancient Pergamon in Asia Minor (closed for restoration until 2019). Also impressive is the 2nd-century market gate from the Roman city of Miletus.

Major excavations begun in the 1820s form the basis of the Museum of Near Eastern Antiquities (Vorderasiatisches Museum). One striking exhibit is the splendid Ishtar Gate, built during Nebuchadnezzar II's reign (604–562 BC) in ancient Babylon. There are also pieces from neighboring Persia, Syria, and Palestine, including a basalt sculpture of a bird from Tel Halaf and a glazed wall relief from Artaxerxes II's palace in Susa, capital of the Persian Empire. In 1904, the history of the Museum of Islamic Art (Museum für Islamische Kunst) began with a large collection of carpets donated by Wilhelm von Bode, who also brought a 45-m (150-ft) section of the facade of a Jordanian desert palace. Another fascinating exhibit is a beautiful 13th-century *mihrab* (Islamic prayer niche).

Persian relief, Pergamon-museum

⑨ Humboldt-Box

Humboldt-Box Schloßplatz 5. **Tel** 01805-030 707. ⓢ Alexanderplatz. 🚊 M4, M6, M8. 🚌 100, 200. **Open** daily.

This information center overlooks Berlin's largest building site, the Humboldt-Forum, where the Berliner Stadtschloss, a palatial 18th-century residence of the Hohenzollerns that was pulled down after World War II, is being reconstructed. It will house the Dahlem museums *(see p510)*, a library, and part of Humboldt University. Highlights of the info center include a model of early 20th-century Berlin and displays on the city's turbulent past.

⑩ Berliner Dom

See pp506–7.

Relief carving of Athena from the Pergamon Altar, Pergamonmuseum

The splendidly reconstructed gilded domes of the Neue Synagoge

⑪ Centrum Judaicum & Neue Synagoge

Oranienburger Straße 28 & 30. **Tel** 030-8802 8316 (Centrum Judaicum). Ⓢ Oranienburger Straße. 1, M1, M6. **Open** Sun–Thu, Fri am. **Open** Jewish festivals.

Occupying the former premises of the Jewish community council, the Centrum Judaicum contains an extensive library, archives, and a research center all devoted to the history and cultural heritage of Berlin's Jews. Next door, the restored rooms of the Neue Synagoge are used as a museum, exhibiting material relating to the local Jewish community.

The building of the New Synagogue was started in 1859 and completed in 1866, when it was opened in the presence of Chancellor Otto von Bismarck. The narrow facade is flanked by a pair of towers and crowned with a dome that sparkles with gold and contains a round vestibule.

This fascinating structure was Berlin's largest synagogue. However, on November 9, 1938, it was partially destroyed during the infamous "*Kristallnacht*" ("Night of the Broken Glass"), when thousands of synagogues, cemeteries, and Jewish homes and shops all over Germany were looted and burned. The building was damaged further by Allied bombing in 1943, and was finally demolished in 1958. Reconstruction began in 1988 and was completed in 1995.

⑫ Fernsehturm

Panoramastraße. Ⓤ Ⓢ Alexanderplatz. M4, M6, M8. 100, 200, 248. **Open** daily.

Known as the *Telespargel*, or toothpick, by the locals, this 368-m- (1,206-ft-) high television mast soars above the massive Alexanderplatz. It is the tallest structure in Germany and one of the tallest in Europe.

The concrete shaft contains elevators that carry passengers to the viewing platform. Situated inside a steel-clad giant sphere, this platform is 203 m (666 ft) above the ground. Visitors can also enjoy a bird's-eye view of the whole city while sipping a cup of coffee in the revolving café. Visibility can reach up to 40 km (25 miles).

⑬ Nikolaiviertel

Ⓤ Alexanderplatz, Klosterstraße. Ⓢ Alexanderplatz. M48. 100, 143, 200, 248, TXL.

This small area on the bank of the Spree, known as the Nikolaiviertel (St. Nicholas Quarter), is a favorite strolling ground for both Berliners and tourists. Some of Berlin's oldest houses stood here until they were destroyed in World War II. The redevelopment of the area, carried out between 1979 and 1987, proved to be an interesting, if somewhat

Berlin's massive Fernsehturm, towering over the city

controversial, attempt at recreating a medieval village. Today, the area consists mostly of newly built replicas of historic buildings. The narrow streets are filled with small shops, cafés, bars, and restaurants, among them the popular Zum Nussbaum, a historical inn that was once located on Fischer Island. Dating from 1507, the original building was destroyed, and subsequently reconstructed at the junction of Am Nussbaum and Propststraße.

Riverside buildings of the Nikolaiviertel

⑩ Berliner Dom

This Protestant cathedral was built by Jan Boumann between 1747 and 1750 on the site of a Dominican church. It incorporated the crypt of the Hohenzollern dynasty, which ruled the city for nearly 500 years, and is one of the largest of its kind in Europe. The present Neo-Baroque structure is the work of Julius Raschdorff and dates from 1894–1905. The central copper dome reaches 98 m (322 ft), with an inner cupola which is 70 m (230 ft) high. Following severe damage sustained in World War II, the building has been restored in a simplified form, including the dismantling of the Hohenzollern memorial chapel, which originally adjoined the northern wall.

Philipp der Großmütige
At the base of the arcade stand statues of church reformers and princes who supported the Reformation. The statue of Philip the Magnanimous, Landgrave of Hesse (1509–67) is the work of Walter Schott.

★ Church Interior
The impressive, richly-decorated interior was designed by Julius Raschdorff at the turn of the 20th century.

Sauer's Organ
The organ, the work of Wilhelm Sauer, has an exquisitely carved case. The instrument contains some 7,200 pipes.

Main entrance

★ Hohenzollern Sarcophagi
The imperial Hohenzollern family crypt, hidden beneath the floor of the cathedral, contains 100 richly decorated sarcophagi, including that of Prince Friedrich Ludwig.

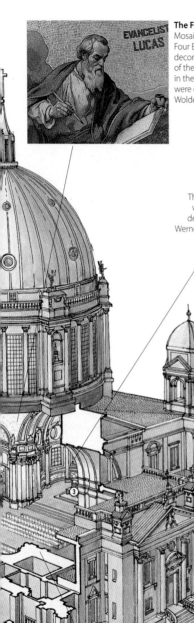

The Four Evangelists
Mosaics depicting the Four Evangelists decorate the ceilings of the smaller niches in the cathedral. They were designed by Woldemar Friedrich.

VISITORS' CHECKLIST

Practical Information
Am Lustgarten.
Tel 030-20 26 91 19.
🆆 **berlinerdom.de**
Open 9am–8pm Mon–Sat, noon–8pm Sun (Oct–Mar: until 7pm). 🈂 🛈 10am & 6pm Sun.

Transport
Ⓢ Hackescher Markt.
🚌 100, 200.

The Resurrection
The stained glass in the windows of the apses, designed by Anton von Werner, shows scenes from the life of Jesus.

KEY

① **Figures of the Apostles**

② **The Pulpit**, an example of elaborate Neo-Baroque design, is part of the cathedral's ornate decor dating from the early 20th century.

③ **The main altar**, saved from the previous cathedral, is the work of Friedrich August Stüler and dates from 1850.

★ Sarcophagi of Friedrich I and his Wife
Both of these were designed by Andreas Schlüter. The sculpture on Sophie Charlotte's sarcophagus depicts death.

⑭ Kreuzberg

Checkpoint Charlie: Friedrichstraße 43–45. **Tel** 030-253 7250. **U** Kochstraße. 🚌 M29. **Open** 9am–10pm daily. 🏛 Jüdisches Museum: Lindenstraße 14. **U** Hallesches Tor, Kochstraße. 🚌 248. **Tel** 030-2599 3300. **Open** 10am–10pm Mon, 10am–8pm Tue–Sun.

Kreuzberg is an area of contrasts, with luxury apartments next to dilapidated buildings. The district's attractions are its wealth of restaurants and Turkish bazaars, as well as a wide selection of theaters, cinemas, and galleries.

Checkpoint Charlie was once the notorious border crossing between the Soviet and American sectors, and witness to a number of dramatic events during the Cold War. The museum close by, Haus am Checkpoint Charlie, houses exhibits connected with the ingenious attempts by East Germans to escape to the West.

The imaginative architecture of the **Jüdisches Museum**, dedicated to Jewish history and art, conveys something of the tragic history of the millions of Jews who lost their lives in the Holocaust. The zigzag layout recalls a torn Star of David, while the interior arrangement is dominated by a long empty area, which symbolizes the void left in Europe by the exile and murder of countless thousands of Jews.

Berlin Wall sculpture at entrance to Haus am Checkpoint Charlie

Zoologischer Garten, home to over 1,400 animal species

⑮ Zoologischer Garten

Hardenbergplatz 8 or Budapester Straße 34. **Tel** 030-254 010. **U** **S** Zoologischer Garten. 🚌 100, 204, 249 & many others. **Open** daily. 🏛

The Zoological Garden forms part of the Tiergarten and dates from 1844, making it the oldest zoo in Germany. It offers a number of attractions, including the monkey house, which contains a family of gorillas, and a specially darkened pavilion for observing nocturnal animals. The hippopotamus pool has a glazed wall that enables visitors to watch these enormous creatures moving through the water. The aquarium, one of the largest in Europe, contains sharks, piranhas, and unusual animals from coral reefs. There is also a huge terrarium with an overgrown jungle that is home to a group of crocodiles.

⑯ Kaiser-Wilhelm-Gedächtniskirche

Breitscheidplatz. **Tel** 030-218 5023. **U** Zoologischer Garten, Kurfürstenstraße. **S** Zoologischer Garten. 🚌 100, 200, X9. Gedenkhalle: **Open** Mon–Sat, Sun pm. 🏛

The damaged roof of this former church has become one of the best-known symbols of postwar Berlin. The vast Neo-Romanesque building was consecrated in 1895, but was destroyed by bombs in 1943.

After World War II, the ruins were removed, leaving only the massive front tower, at the base of which the Gedenkhalle (Memorial Hall) is situated. This hall documents the history of the church and contains some of the original ceiling mosaics, marble reliefs, and liturgical objects. The latter include the Coventry Crucifix, a modest cross fashioned from nails found in the ashes of Coventry Cathedral, England, which was destroyed in the bombing raids of the 1940s.

In 1963, Egon Eiermann designed a new octagonal church in blue glass. His hexagonal bell tower stands on the site of the former nave of the destroyed church.

New and old bell towers of the Kaiser-Wilhelm-Gedächtniskirche

A bustling outdoor café on the Kurfürstendamm

⑰ Kurfürstendamm

Ⓤ Kurfürstendamm. 🚌 204, 249, M0, M19, M29, M46, X10.

This wide avenue was established in the 1880s on the site of a former track that led to the Grunewald forest *(see p510)*. It quickly acquired many imposing buildings and grand hotels. In the 20 years between World Wars I and II, the Ku'damm, as it is popularly called, was renowned for its cafés, visited by famous film directors, writers, and painters.

After World War II, new buildings replaced the damaged houses, but this did not change the character of the street. Elegant shops and pretty cafés still attract a chic crowd. Not far from here is the city's newest photography museum, the **Museum für Fotografie**.

⑱ Sammlung Berggruen

Schlossstraße 1. **Tel** 030-326 9580. Ⓤ Richard-Wagner-Platz, Sophie-Charlotte-Platz. Ⓢ Westend. 🚌 109, 309, M45. **Open** 10am–6pm Tue–Sun. 🖼 ♿

Heinz Berggruen assembled this art collection dating from the late 19th and first half of the 20th centuries. The museum is known for its large array of paintings, drawings, and gouaches by Pablo Picasso. There is also a display of more than 20 works by Paul Klee and paintings by Van Gogh, Braque, and Cézanne. The Sammlung Scharf-Gerstenberg opposite covers the Surrealists and their predecessors.

⑲ Schloss Charlottenburg

Spandauer Damm. **Tel** 030-3209 1440. Ⓤ Richard-Wagner-Platz, Sophie-Charlotte-Platz. Ⓢ Westend. 🚌 109, 309, M45. **Open** Tue–Sun. 🖼 compulsory on ground floor. 📷

The palace in Charlottenburg was intended as a summer residence for Sophie Charlotte, Elector Friedrich III's wife. Construction began in 1695 to a design by Johann Arnold Nering. Between 1701 and 1713, the palace was enlarged, and a Baroque cupola and an orangery were added. Subsequent extensions were undertaken by Frederick the Great (King Friedrich II), who added the Neuer Flügel (New Wing) between 1740 and 1746.

Restored to its former elegance after World War II, the palace's richly decorated interior is unequalled in Berlin. In the central section of the palace, the mirrored gallery of the Porzellankabinett has walls lined with fine Japanese and Chinese porcelain.

The Neuer Flügel, the new wing of the palace, used to house the Galerie der Romantik. The former private apartment of Friedrik the Great, it now has displays of the king's exquisite furniture. The Neuer Flügel and the upper floor can be visited independently.

The Orangery was originally used to protect rare plants during the winter, but in the summer months was used as a scene for festivities by the court. It has been rebuilt and is now a concert and events venuel.

The park surrounding the palace is one of the most picturesque places in Berlin. Among the many fine monuments dotted around the grounds are the charming Neoclassical **Neuer Pavillion** (New Pavilion), whose interior is furnished in period style, and the **Belvedere** (1788), housing a large collection of porcelain.

Central tower and 18th-century cupola of Schloss Charlottenburg

Restaurant in the Forsthaus Paulsborn in the Grunewald

⑳ Grunewald

Ⓢ Grunewald. 🚌 115. Jagdschloss Grunewald: **Tel** 030-813 3597. **Open** 10am–6pm Tue–Sun.

Just a short S-Bahn ride from central Berlin lie the vast forests of the Grunewald, bordering some of the city's most elegant suburbs. Once the haunt of politicians, wealthy industrialists, and renowned artists, some of the villas here now serve as the headquarters of Berlin's academic institutes.

On the shore of the picturesque Grunewaldsee is the **Jagdschloss Grunewald**, one of the oldest civic buildings in Berlin. Built by Elector Joachim II in 1542, it was reconstructed in the Baroque style around 1700. Inside the small palace is Berlin's only surviving Renaissance hall, which houses canvases by Rubens and van Dyck among others. Opposite the Jagdschloss, the **Jagdzeugmagazin** (Hunting Museum) holds displays of historic hunting equipment. Just 4 km (2 miles) away is the Waldmuseum, the only museum devoted to forest life in the Berlin area.

To the southwest of the Grunewaldsee is **Forsthaus Paulsborn**. This rather picturesque hunting lodge, which nowadays houses a very good restaurant, was constructed in 1905.

㉑ Dahlem

Ⓤ Dahlem Dorf. 🚌 101, 110, X11, X83. Museumszentrum: **Tel** 030-266 424242. **Open** Tue–Sun.

First mentioned in 1275, by the 19th century Dahlem had grown from a small village into an affluent, tranquil city suburb. At the beginning of the 20th century, a number of museums, designed by Bruno Paul, were built. They were extended considerably in the 1960s, when the **Museums-zentrum** was created to rival East Berlin's Museum Island (see pp504–6).

Highlights from this cluster of museums include bronzes from Benin in West Africa and gold Inca jewelry from South America at the Ethnologisches Museum (Museum of Ethnography). The other collections range from the Museum für Indische Kunst (Museum of Indian Art) and the Museum für Ostasiatische Kunst (Museum of Far Eastern Art), now known together as the Museum of Asian Art, to the Nordamerica Ausstellung (Exhibition of Native North American Cultures).

Not far from the Museums-zentrum, the **Museum Europäischer Kulturen** specializes in European folk art and culture. Among the exhibits you can expect to see are earthenware items, costumes, jewelry, toys, and tools.

Domäne Dahlem is a rare oasis of country life in the Berlin suburbs. This Baroque manor house (c.1680) boasts splendid period interiors, while the 19th-century farm buildings and courtyard host regular artisans' markets. There is also a petting zoo for children.

The elegant Functionalist building occupied by the **Brücke-Museum** was built by Werner Düttmann in 1966–7. Today, the museum houses German Expressionist paintings by members of the artistic group known as Die Brücke (The Bridge).

The combined museum and working farm of Domäne Dahlem

㉒ Potsdam and Park Sanssouci

An independent city close to Berlin, Potsdam has almost 160,000 inhabitants and is the capital of Brandenburg. The first documented reference to the town dates from AD 993; it was later granted municipal rights in 1317. The town blossomed in the 1600s, during the era of the Great Elector, and then again in the 18th century, when the splendid summer palace, Schloss Sanssouci, was built for Frederick the Great. Potsdam suffered badly in World War II, particularly on April 14 and 15, 1945, when the Allies bombed the town's center.

A Russian-style wooden house in the charming Alexandrowka district

Exploring Potsdam

Despite its wartime losses, today Potsdam is one of Germany's most attractive towns. Tourists flock to see the magnificent royal estate, Park Sanssouci *(see pp512–13)*, to stroll in the Neuer Garten, which boasts its own grand palaces, and to see the pretty Alexandrowka district and the historic Dutch quarter.

Marmorpalais

Am Ufer des Heiligen Sees (Neuer Garten). **Tel** 0331-969 4550. 692, 695. **Open** May–Oct 31: Tue–Sun; Nov 1–Apr: Sat & Sun.

The Marmorpalais (Marble Palace) is located on the edge of the lake in the Neuer Garten, a park northeast of Potsdam's center. Completed in 1791, the grand Neoclassical building owes its name to the Silesian marble that decorates its facade. The rooms in the main part of the palace contain Neoclassical furnishings from the late 18th century, including Wedgwood porcelain and furniture from the workshops of Roentgen. The concert hall in the right wing, whose interior dates from the 1840s, is particularly impressive.

Schloss Cecilienhof

Am Neuen Garten. **Tel** 0331-969 4244. 692, 695. **Open** Tue–Sun.

Schloss Cecilienhof was built for the Hohenzollern family between 1914 and 1917. In July 1945 the palace played an important role in history, when it served as the venue for the Potsdam Conference – an event that played a major part in establishing the political balance of power in Europe following the end of World War II. Today, it is a museum as well as a hotel.

Alexandrowka

Russische Kolonie Allee/ Puschkinallee. 604, 609, 638, 639. 92.

A trip to Alexandrowka, in the northeast of the city, takes the visitor into the world of Pushkin's fairy tales. Wooden log cabins, set in their own gardens, form a charming residential estate. The houses were built in 1826 for singers in a Russian choir established to entertain military troops. Peter Joseph Lenné was responsible for the overall appearance of the estate, named after the Tsarina, the Prussian Princess Charlotte.

VISITORS' CHECKLIST

Practical Information
Brandenburg. 160,000.
Brandenburger Straße 3
Tel 0331-27 55 80.
w potsdam.de

Transport
from Bahnhof Zoo, Berlin to Potsdam-Stadt.

Holländisches Viertel

Friedrich-Ebertstraße/Kurfürstenstr./ Hebbelstr./Gutenbergstr. 138, 601, 602, 603, 604 & many others.

The Dutch Quarter features stores, galleries, cafés, and beer cellars, especially along Mittelstraße. The area was built up in the early 1700s, when Dutch workers, invited by Friedrich Wilhelm I, began to settle in Potsdam. Today, you can still see the pretty red-brick, gabled houses that were built for them.

Filmpark Babelsberg

Großbeerenstraße. **Tel** 0331-721 2750. **Open** mid-Apr–Oct: daily **Closed** Mon in May & Sep.

This film park was laid out on the site of the film studios where Germany's first movies were made in 1912. From 1917, the studios belonged to Universum-Film-AG, which produced some of the most renowned movies of the silent era, such as Fritz Lang's futuristic *Metropolis* (1927). Later, Nazi propaganda films were also made here. The studio is still in operation today, but part of the complex is open to the public. Visitors can see old film sets, special effects demonstrations, and stuntmen in action.

Original film prop on display at the Filmpark Babelsberg

Park Sanssouci

The enormous Park Sanssouci, covering an area of 287 hectares (709 acres), is among the most beautiful palace complexes in Europe. The first building to be constructed, Frederick the Great's Schloss Sanssouci, was built on the site of an orchard in 1745–7. Its name – *sans souci* is French for "without a care" – gives an indication of the building's flamboyant character. Over the years, the park has been enriched by other palaces and pavilions. Today, the park is made up of small gardens dating from different eras, all maintained in their original style.

Communs (1766–9)
This house for the palace staff has an unusually elegant character, and is situated next to a pretty courtyard.

★ Neues Palais
The monumental New Palace, constructed in 1763–1769, is crowned by a massive dome. Bas-reliefs on the triangular tympanum depict figures from Greek mythology.

0 meters 200
0 yards 200

KEY

① **The Chinesisches Teehaus** (Chinese Teahouse) features an exhibition of exquisite Oriental porcelain..

② **The Römische Bäder** (Roman Baths) date from 1829 and include a mock-Renaissance villa and a suite of Roman-style rooms.

③ **The Lustgarten** (pleasure garden) has a symmetrical layout lined with rose beds.

④ **Neue Kammern**

⑤ **Bildergalerie** (art gallery)

Schloss Charlottenhof
The most interesting interior of this Neoclassical palace is the Humboldt Room, also called the Tent Room due to its resemblance to a marquee.

Practical Information
Chinesisches Teehaus:
Ökonomieweg (Rehgarten).
Tel 0331-969 4202. **Open** May–
Oct: Tue–Sun. Communs: Am
Neuen Palais. Römische Bäder:
Lenné-Strasse (Park Charlotten-
hof). **Tel** 0331-969 4202.
Open May–Oct: Tue–Sun.

Transport
Schopenhauerstraße/Zur
Historischen Mühle. 612, 614,
695. Chinesisches Teehaus: 606, 695. 94, 96. Communs:
605, 606, 695. Römische
Bäder: 605, 606. 91, 94.

Orangerie
This Neo-Renaissance palace,
the largest in the park, was
built in the mid-19th
century to house
foreign royalty
and guests.

Neues Palais
Am Neuen Palais. **Tel** 0331-969 4202.
605, 606, 695. **Open** Wed–Mon.

This imposing Baroque palace
was begun at the request of
Frederick the Great in 1763.
Decorated with hundreds of
sculptures, the vast two-story
building contains more than 200
richly adorned rooms. Especially
unusual is the Grottensaal
(Grotto Salon), where man-made
stalactites hang from the ceiling.

Schloss Sanssouci
Zur Historischen Mühle. **Tel** 0331-969
4202. 612, 614, 695. 94, 96.
Open Tue–Sun.

Schloss Sanssouci is an enchanting Rococo palace, built in
1745–7. Frederick the Great
made the original sketches for
the building. The walls of the
Konzertzimmer (Concert Hall)
are lined with paintings by
Antoine Pesne. The greatest
treasures are the paintings
of *fêtes galantes* by Antoine
Watteau (1684–1721), a favorite
artist of Frederick the Great.

Orangerie
Maulbeerallee (Nordischer Garten).
Tel 0331-969 4200. 695.
Open Apr: Sat & Sun; May–Oct:
Tue–Sun.

The highlight of this guest
house is the Raphael Hall,
which is decorated with copies
of works by the great Italian
Renaissance artist. The view
from the observation terrace
extends over Potsdam.

Schloss Charlottenhof
Geschwister-Scholl-Strasse.
Tel 0331- 969 4202. 606. 94,
96. **Open** May–Oct: Tue–Sun.

This small Neoclassical
palace was designed by

The elegant Baroque exterior of the Neue
Kammern

Friedrich Schinkel and Ludwig
Persius in 1829, in the style of
a Roman villa. The rear of the
palace has a portico that opens
out onto the garden terrace.
Some of the wall paintings,
produced by Schinkel, are still
in place.

Neue Kammern
Zur Historischen Mühle (Lustgarten).
Tel 0331-969 4202. 612, 614, 695.
Open Nov–Apr: Wed–Mon; May–Oct:
Tue–Sun.

Originally built as an orangery
for Schloss Sanssouci in 1747,
the Neue Kammern (New
Chambers) was remodeled as
guest accommodations in 1777.
The most impressive of the
building's four elegant Rococo
halls is the Ovidsaal, with its rich
reliefs and marble floors.

Bildergalerie
Zur Historischen Mühle. **Tel** 0331-969
4202. 612, 614, 695. **Open** May–
Oct: Tue–Sun.

Constructed between 1755
and 1764 to a design by J.G.
Buring, the Bildergalerie holds
an exhibition of paintings
once owned by Frederick
the Great. Highlights include
Caravaggio's *Doubting Thomas*
(1597), and Guido Reni's
Cleopatra's Death (1626), as
well as a number of works
by Rubens and van Dyck.

★ Schloss Sanssouci
The oldest building in
the complex, this palace
contains the imposing
Marmorsaal (Marble Hall),
decorated with pairs of
columns made from Carrara
marble. Frederick the Great
wanted the room to be
based on the Pantheon
in Rome (see p382).

Eastern Germany

Closed to the West for over 40 years of Communist rule, Eastern Germany is now fast rebuilding its reputation as an attractive tourist destination. The powerful duchy of Saxony, whose rulers were also Electors and, in the early 18th century, kings of Poland, has left behind a rich cultural heritage for visitors to explore. After Berlin, the area's main attractions are Dresden, the ancient capital of Saxony, the old university town of Leipzig, and the important cultural center of Weimar in Thuringia.

❷ Dresden

Saxony. 535,000. 15 km (9 miles) N. Schloßstr. 2 (0351-501 601 60). **dresden.de**

One of Germany's most beautiful cities, Dresden blossomed during the 18th century, when it became a cultural center and acquired many magnificent buildings. Almost all of these, however, were completely destroyed during World War II, when Allied air forces mounted vast carpet-bombing raids on the city. Today, meticulous restoration work is in progress to return the city to its former glory.

The most celebrated building in Dresden is the **Frauenkirche**. The landmark Church of Our Lady (1726–43) was left in ruins during the Communist era to serve as a reminder of World War II damage but reconstruction began after reunification. The church was finally reconsecrated in 2005, and now serves as a symbol of reconciliation between former warring nations.

Vermeer's *Girl Reading a Letter*, Gemäldegalerie Alte Meister

The **Zwinger** is an imposing Baroque building constructed in 1709–32 with a spacious courtyard surrounded on all sides by galleries housing several museums, including the **Gemäldegalerie Alte Meister**. This contains one of Europe's finest art collections, with works by Antoine Watteau, Rembrandt, van Eyck, Velázquez, Vermeer, Raphael, Titian, and Albrecht Dürer.

The 19th-century **Sächsische Staatsoper** (Saxon State Opera) has been the venue for many world premieres, including *The Flying Dutchman* and *Tannhäuser* by Wagner, as well as works by Richard Strauss.

Dresden's **Residenzschloss** was built in stages from the late 15th to the 17th centuries. The palace now houses some of the most beautiful art collections in Eastern Germany. The Verkehrsmuseum has been a museum of transportation since 1956. The Residenzschloss also houses the famous **Grünes Gewölbe**, a vast royal treasury.

Once part of the town's fortifications, the **Brühlsche**

The Baroque Wallpavilion, part of the Zwinger building in Dresden

Rebuilt from the Ashes

Once known as the "Florence of the north," Dresden was one of the most beautiful cities in Europe. Then, on the night of February 13, 1945, 800 British aircraft launched the first of five massive firebomb raids on the city made by Allied air forces. The raids completely destroyed the greater part of the city, killing over 35,000 people, many of whom were refugees. The rebuilding of Dresden began soon after the war, when it was decided to restore the Zwinger and other historic buildings, and create a new city of modern developments on the levelled land around the old city center. Much of Dresden has now been reconstructed, though some reminders of the city's destruction remain.

The center of Dresden after Allied carpet-bombing

For hotels and restaurants see pp546–8 and pp549–51

Terrasse was subsequently transformed into magnificent gardens by Heinrich von Brühl. Offering splendid views over the Elbe river, it is known as "the balcony of Europe." The **Albertinum** houses several magnificent collections, including the **Gemäldegalerie Neue Meister**, which holds paintings from the 19th and 20th centuries. These include landscapes by Caspar David Friedrich, canvases by the Nazarene group of painters, and works by Degas, van Gogh, Manet, and Monet.

On the banks of the Elbe stands **Schloss Pillnitz**, the charming summer residence of Augustus the Strong. The main attraction is the park, laid out in English and Chinese styles.

⛫ Gemäldegalerie Alte Meister
Theaterplatz 1. **Tel** 0351-4914 2000.
Open 10am–6pm Tue–Sun. 🖼

Environs
Meissen, 19 km (12 miles) northwest of Dresden, is famous for its porcelain manufacture. The **Albrechtsburg** is a vast fortified hilltop complex with a cathedral and a palace once used by the Electors. Europe's first porcelain factory was set up in the palace in 1710 but moved to premises in Talstrasse in 1865. Documents relating to the history of the factory and examples of its products are on display in the palace rooms.

🏠 Albrechtsburg
Domplatz 1. **Tel** 0351-811 58 21.
Open daily. 🖼

❸ Leipzig

Saxony. 🚇 539,000. 🚉 🚌 🚍
ℹ Katharinenstr. 8 (0341-710 42 60).
🌐 leipzig.de

Leipzig is not only one of Germany's leading commercial towns, but also a center of culture and learning. Most of the interesting sights can be found in the old town, including Europe's biggest train station, the **Hauptbahnhof**.

Lovers of Johann Sebastian Bach's music can visit the

The lofty Neoclassical interior of the Nikolaikirche, Leipzig

Thomaskirche (1482–96), where he was choirmaster from 1723. It now contains his tomb. The **Bacharchive und Bachmuseum** houses items relating to the composer.

The 16th-century **Nikolaikirche** (Church of St. Nicholas) was redecorated in Neoclassical style in 1784–97. The grand Renaissance **Altes Rathaus** (Old Town Hall), built in only nine months in 1556, is now the municipal museum. The **Museum der Bildenden Künste** has an excellent collection of German masters, including works by Caspar David Friedrich and Lucas Cranach the Elder, as well as van Eyck, Rubens, and Rodin.

The **Grassimuseum** complex houses three collections: a museum of ethnography, a museum of applied arts, and a large collection of musical instruments.

⛫ Museum der Bildenden Künste
Katharinenstr. 10. **Tel** 0341-216 99. **Open** Tue–Sun (Wed: noon–8pm).

❹ Weimar

Thuringia. 🚇 65,000. 🚉 🚌
ℹ Markt 10 (03643-7450).
🌐 weimar.de

Weimar rose to prominence due to the enlightened sponsorship of its rulers, particularly Duke Carl Augustus and his wife Anna Amalia in the 18th century. Former residents include Goethe, Schiller, and Nietzsche, as well as the designers of the Bauhaus School, founded here in 1919.

Weimar is fairly small, and most of its museums are in the town center. To the north stands the **Neues Museum**, which holds a large collection of modern art. The nearby **Stadtmuseum** is devoted to Weimar's history, while the **Goethe-Museum** displays items associated with the famous writer.

The Neoclassical **Deutsches Nationaltheater**, built in 1906–7, was the venue for the world premiere of Wagner's *Lohengrin*. In 1919 the National Congress sat here to pass the new constitution for the Weimar Republic.

The vast ducal castle, **Weimar Schloss**, has original interiors and fine paintings by Albrecht Dürer, Peter Paul Rubens, and Claude Monet. Also known as the Grünes Schloss (Green Castle), the **Herzogin-Anna-Amalia Bibliothek** was converted into the duchess' library in 1761–6. It has a splendid Rococo interior. Set in attractive Belvedere Park, the ducal summer residence of **Schloss Belvedere** (1761–6) has fine collections of Rococo decorative art and vintage vehicles.

🏠 Weimar Schloss
Burgplatz 4. **Tel** 03643-54 59 60. **Open** Tue–Sun. 🖼

Weimar Schloss with its tall Renaissance tower

Bavaria

Bavaria is the largest state in the Federal Republic of Germany. Ruled by the Wittelsbach dynasty from 1180, the duchy of Bavaria was elevated to the status of a kingdom in 1806. In addition to historic cities, fairy-tale castles, and exquisite Baroque and Renaissance palaces, the region has more than its fair share of glorious Alpine scenery, beer halls, and colorful festivals.

The auditorium of Bayreuth's Markgräfliches Opernhaus

❺ Bayreuth

🏙 71,000. 🚉 ℹ Luitpoldplatz 9 (0921-885 88). 🎭 Richard-Wagner-Festspiele (Jul–Aug). 🖥 **beyreuth-tourismus.de**

Music lovers associate this city with the German composer Richard Wagner (1813–83), who lived here from 1872. The **Villa Wahnfried** was built for Wagner by Carl Wölfel and today houses a museum dedicated to the famous musician. Nearby, the **Franz-Liszt-Museum** occupies the house where the Hungarian composer died in 1886.

Other sights of interest in Bayreuth include the **Markgräfliches Opernhaus**, the lavish Baroque opera house, dating from the mid-18th century, and the **Neues Schloss**. Built for Margravine Wilhelmine in the 1700s, the palace has splendid Baroque and Rococo interiors and English-style gardens.

❻ Bamberg

🏙 71,000. 🚉 ℹ Geyerswörth-straße 3 (0951-297 62 00). 🖥 **bamberg.info**

Bamberg's most interesting historical monuments are clustered around Domplatz, including the magnificent **Cathedral of St. Peter and St. George**. Begun around 1211, the cathedral combines the late Romanesque and early French-Gothic styles. The eastern choir contains the famous equestrian statue of the "Bamberg Rider" (1225–30), whose identity remains a mystery to this day.

The west side of Domplatz is flanked by the **Alte Hofhaltung**, the former bishop's residence. Built in the 15th and 16th centuries, it houses a museum of local history. The more recent Baroque **Bishop's Palace** (1763) stands behind the cathedral.

Also on Domplatz is the **Neue Residenz** (1695–1704), with its richly decorated apartments. Inside, the Staatsgalerie has a collection of old German masters.

On the east side of the town, the **Altes Rathaus**, originally Gothic in style, was remodeled in 1744–56 by Jakob Michael Küchel.

🏛 **Neue Residenz**
Domplatz 8. **Tel** 0951-519 390. **Open** daily. 🄿

Neumann's stunning Treppenhaus (staircase) at Würzburg's Residenz

❼ Würzburg

🏙 124,000. 🚉 ℹ Marktplatz, Am Falkenhaus (0931-37 23 35). 🖥 **wuerzburg.de**

Located on the bank of the Main river, Würzburg is an important cultural and commercial center, and home of the excellent Franconian wine.

The city's most impressive landmark is the **Residenz**, where Würzburg's prince-bishops lived from 1744. A highlight of this lavish Baroque palace is the huge Treppenhaus (staircase), by Balthasar Neumann (1687–1753). Above it is a glorious ceiling fresco by the Venetian artist, Giovanni Battista Tiepolo.

Before the Residenz was built, the city's prince-bishops resided in the fortress known as the **Festung Marienberg**, which has stood on a hill overlooking the river since 1210. The Mainfränkisches Museum, housed inside the fortress, illustrates the history of the town and holds a number of works by the renowned German sculptor Tilman Riemenschneider (1460–1531).

Bamberger Reiter (Bamberg Rider) in the city's cathedral

Würzburg's cathedral, the **Dom St. Kilian**, dates from 1045 and is one of Germany's largest Romanesque churches. North of it is the 11th-century basilica **Neumünster**. Its imposing Baroque dome and sandstone facade are 18th-century additions. Dating from the 13th century, the picturesque **Rathaus** (Town Hall) has a late-Renaissance tower, added 1660.

🏛 **Residenz**
Residenzplatz 2. **Tel** 0931-35 51 70. **Open** daily. 🄿

🏰 **Festung Marienberg**
🕐 Apr–Oct: 11am, 2pm, 3pm, 4pm Tue–Fri, 10am, 11am, 1pm, 2pm, 3pm, 4pm Sat & Sun. 🄿 Mainfränkisches Museum: **Tel** 0931-205 940. **Open** Tue–Sun. 🄿

❽ Rothenburg ob der Tauber

🏠 11,000. 🚉 ℹ️ Marktplatz 2 (09861-40 48 00). 🌐 **tourismus. rothenburg.de**

Encircled by ramparts, Rothenburg is a perfectly preserved medieval town in a picturesque setting on the banks of the Tauber river.

At the heart of the town is Marktplatz, whose focal point is the **Rathaus** (Town Hall), combining Renaissance and Gothic styles. Off the main square, **St. Jakobs Kirche** (1373–1464) and the **Franziskanerkirche** both contain many historical treasures.

Two museums of note are the **Reichsstadtmuseum**, devoted to the town's history, and the **Mittelalterliches Museum**, which contains a large collection of medieval instruments of torture.

Through the Burgtor, a gateway in the city walls, you arrive at the **Burggarten** – pretty gardens offering great views.

❾ Nuremberg

🏠 486,000. ✈️ 🚉 ℹ️ Königstraße 93 (0911-233 60). 🌐 **tourismus. nuernberg.de**

The largest town in Bavaria after Munich, Nuremberg (Nürnberg) flourished in the 15th and 16th centuries, when many prominent artists, craftsmen, and intellectuals worked here, making it a leading European cultural center. The city is divided in two by the Pegnitz river. In the southern half, the mighty **Frauentor** is one of several gateways in

Rothenburg's Rathaus (Town Hall), built in the 14th century

the massive 15th and 16th-century ramparts. A short walk away is the **Germanisches Nationalmuseum**. Founded in 1853, the museum houses a superb collection of antiquities from the German-speaking world, including masterworks by Tilman Riemenschneider, Lucas Cranach the Elder (1472–1553), and Albrecht Dürer (1471–1528).

Overlooking the bustling Lorenzer Platz, the Gothic **St. Lorenz-Kirche** is one of the city's most important churches. Begun in 1270, it boasts some glorious stained-glass windows.

As you cross over the Pegnitz to the north side of town, look out for the **Heilig-Geist-Spital** (Hospital of the Holy Spirit), which dates from 1332 and spans the river.

A major landmark north of the river is the **Frauenkirche**, commissioned by the Holy Roman Emperor Charles IV in the mid-14th century. Also of importance is the **Albrecht-Dürer-Haus**, where the

celebrated Renaissance painter lived in 1509–28. Copies of a wide selection of his works are on display here.

A climb up Burgstraße brings you to the **Kaiserburg**, the imperial castle complex. The oldest surviving part is a pentagonal tower, the **Fünfeckturm**, which dates from 1040. At its foot is the Kaiserstallung (Imperial Stables), now a youth hostel.

At the Christkindlmarkt, the lively Christmas fair held during Advent in the Hauptmarkt, you can warm yourself with a glass of hot red wine spiced with cloves and buy locally made crafts.

🏛️ **Germanisches Nationalmuseum**
Kartäusergasse 1. **Tel** 0911-13 310.
Open Tue–Sun. 🖼️

🏛️ **Albrecht-Dürer-Haus**
Albrecht–Dürer–Straße 39. **Tel** 0911-231 25 68. **Open** Tue–Sun (Jul–Sep: daily). 🖼️ 🎫

The half-timbered buildings of Nuremberg's Kaiserburg at the top of Burgstraße

⑩ Munich

Founded in 1158, Munich became the capital of Bavaria in the 16th century. The town rapidly overshadowed once powerful neighbors, such as Augsburg and Nuremberg, to become southern Germany's main metropolis. The period of greatest growth was in the 19th century, when the city was developed along Neoclassical lines. Many of the grand buildings around Königsplatz and along Ludwigstrasse date from this time. As well as historic monuments, Munich has first-class museums and excellent shopping. It also hosts the world-famous annual beer festival, the Oktoberfest.

Sights at a Glance

① *Residenz pp520–21*
② Frauenkirche
③ Marienplatz
④ Stadtmuseum
⑤ Asamkirche
⑥ Glyptothek
⑦ Alte Pinakothek
⑧ Neue Pinakothek
⑨ Pinakothek der Moderne
⑩ Deutsches Museum
⑪ Bayerisches Nationalmuseum
⑫ Englischer Garten

Greater Munich *(see inset map)*

⑬ Olympiapark
⑭ Schloss Nymphenburg

Key

 Sight / Place of interest
Pedestrian street

Getting Around

Most of the main sights of interest can be reached by Munich's efficient U- and S-Bahn train networks, including sights located farther afield, such as Olympiapark and Nymphenburg. Buses and trams also serve many of the main tourist spots. There is a large pedestrianized zone at the heart of the city making walking a pleasant alternative to public transportation.

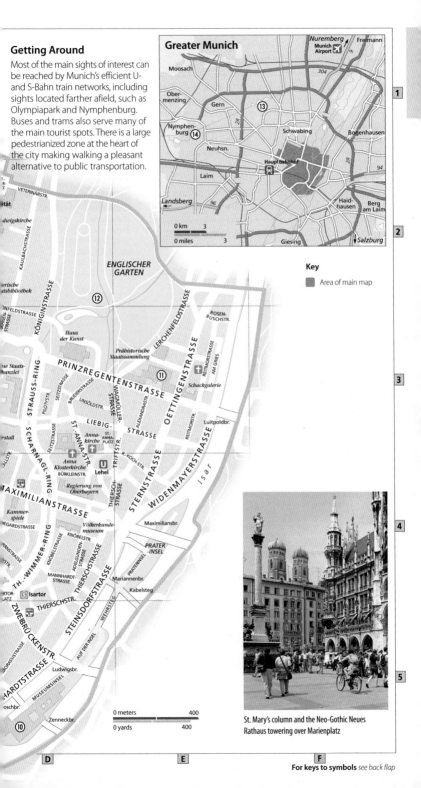

Greater Munich

Key

Area of main map

St. Mary's column and the Neo-Gothic Neues Rathaus towering over Marienplatz

❶ Residenz

The origins of Munich's grand Residenz – the former residence of Bavarian kings – go back to the 14th century, when a castle was built here for the Wittelsbach dynasty. In the following centuries, the fortress was replaced by a palace complex, which in turn was gradually modified and extended. Major work in the 17th century included the construction of two chapels, the Reiche Kapelle and the Hofkapelle. The Königsbau, containing the superb Nibelungensäle, was added by Leo von Klenze in the first half of the 19th century. Since 1920, the palace has been open to the public as a museum, displaying a wealth of magnificent treasures. In addition to the collections of the Residenzmuseum and the Schatzkammer (Treasury), there is an interesting museum of Egyptian art, the Staatliches Museum Ägyptischer Kunst.

Hofkapelle
This imposing chapel, which dates from the early 17th century, was modeled on nearby St. Michael's Church.

Patrona Boiariae
The Renaissance facade features two magnificent portals, and a statue of the Holy Virgin as Patroness of Bavaria (Patrona Boiariae).

★ Nibelungensäle
The Nibelungensäle (Halls of the Nibelungs), a series of five rooms in the Königsbau, take their name from the wall paintings depicting scenes from the great German epic, the *Nibelungenlied*.

KEY

① **Grottenhof (Grotto Court)**

② **The Reiche Kapelle**, built for Maximilian I, contains beautiful, lavish furnishings.

③ **Kaiser Hof** (Emperor's Court) is housed in this wing of the Residenz.

④ **The Brunnenhof** has as its centerpiece an elaborately decorated fountain dedicated to the Wittelsbachs.

★ Antiquarium
This magnificent vaulted chamber, with its stunning frescoes, was begun in the second half of the 16th century to house the royal collection of antiquities.

Cuvilliés-Theater
Designed in 1751–3 by François de Cuvilliés, this is Europe's finest surviving Rococo theater and is still in use today.

Main entrance

★ Schatzkammer
The rooms of the treasury hold many priceless artifacts, including liturgical objects, jewelry, and items of gold. The highlight of Room V is the Bavarian crown jewels.

② **Frauenkirche**

Frauenplatz 1. **U** or **S** Karlsplatz, Marienplatz. 🚊 19. Tower: **Open** Apr–Oct: Mon–Sat. 📷

The site of the Frauenkirche was originally occupied by a small chapel dedicated to the Virgin Mary, built in the 13th century. Some 200 years later, a new, much larger church was built here by the architects Jörg von Halspach and Lukas Rottaler. The new Frauenkirche (or Dom) was completed in 1488, although the distinctive copper onion domes were not added to its towers until 1525. The church is one of southern Germany's largest Gothic structures. Over 100 m (330 ft) long and 40 m (130 ft) wide, it can accommodate a congregation of about 2,000 people. The vast triple-naved hall has no transept. There are long rows of side chapels and a gallery surrounding the choir. For a good view of central Munich, you can take an elevator to the top of one of the towers.

Partly demolished in 1944–5, the church was rebuilt after World War II. Church treasures that escaped destruction include a painting of the Virgin by Jan Polack (c.1500), the altar of St. Andrew in the Chapel of St. Sebastian, and the huge monumental tomb of Ludwig IV the Bavarian, the first member of the house of Wittelsbach to be elected Holy Roman Emperor (c.1283–1347). The monument was the work of Hans Krumpper (1619–22).

Altes Rathaus and the Talbrucktor on Marienplatz

③ **Marienplatz**

U or **S** Marienplatz. Spielzeugmuseum: **Tel** 089-29 40 01. **Open** daily. 📷

In medieval times, Marienplatz was Munich's salt- and corn-market. In the center stands a column with a statue of the Virgin Mary dating from 1623. The square is dominated by the Neo-Gothic **Neues Rathaus** (New Town Hall), built in 1867–1909. Its walls are adorned with statues of Bavarian rulers, mythological figures, saints, and monstrous gargoyles. At 11am and 5pm, the center of attention is the clock tower. The bells ring out a carillon, while figures of knights fight a tournament and a crowd dances. The dance is the "Coopers' Dance," first performed in 1517 to raise citizens' morale during a plague epidemic. At the eastern end of the square stands the **Altes Rathaus** (Old Town Hall). Originally built in the late 15th century, it has been rebuilt many times since. The high tower, above the old city gate beside the town hall, was rebuilt in 1975 to a design based on pictures dating from 1493. Since 1983, the tower has been the home of the city's **Spielzeugmuseum** (Toy Museum).

④ **Stadtmuseum**

St. Jakobsplatz 1. **Tel** 089-23 32 23 70. **U** or **S** Marienplatz. **U** Sendlinger Tor. **Open** Tue–Sun. 📷

The collection of the city museum has been housed since 1880 in this former arsenal. Exhibits illustrate daily life in Munich throughout the ages. One of the greatest treasures is the "Dancing Moors" by Erasmus Grasser (1480). Originally, there were 18 highly expressive limewood carvings of dancing figures surrounding the figure of a woman, but only ten survive.

The Waffenhalle has a fine collection of arms and armor. There are also displays of furniture, paintings, prints, photographs, dolls, and musical instruments. The vast doll collection includes paper dolls from India and China, as well as automata and puppets.

Also located in the square is the Judisches Zentrum Jakobsplatz (the Jewish Center), housed in a cube-shaped, freestanding building. Three floors of exhibitions, a library, and a learning center offer extensive information on Jewish culture and history, and highlight important aspects of contemporary Jewish life.

⑤ **Asamkirche**

Sendlinger Straße 32. **U** Sendlinger Tor. 🚊 16, 17, 18, 27. 🚌 52, 152. **Open** daily.

This extraordinary Rococo church is dedicated to St. John Nepomuk, but is known as the Asamkirche after the brothers Cosmas Damian

The distinctive roof and towers of Munich's Frauenkirche, seen from the top of city hall

For hotels and restaurants see pp546–8 and pp549–51

and Egid Quirin Asam, who built it as a private family church. Completed in 1746, the tiny church is a riot of decoration with a dynamically shaped single nave, where no surface is left unembellished. The eye is drawn to the altar, and its sculptural group of the Holy Trinity. The house next door to the church was the residence of Egid Quirin Asam, who was a stuccoist and sculptor. From one of the windows of his house, he could see the altar.

The richly decorated altar of the Rococo Asamkirche

⑥ Glyptothek

Königsplatz 3. **Tel** 089-28 61 00.
Ⓤ Königsplatz. **Open** Tue–Sun.
🅿 Staatliche Antikensammlung:
Königsplatz 1. **Tel** 089-59 98 88 30.
Open Tue–Sun. 🅿

On the northern side of Königsplatz stands the Glyptothek, a collection of Greek and Roman sculpture, notably statues from the

Temple of Aphaia on the Greek island of Aegina. The museum's imposing facade, with the portico of an Ionic temple at the center, is part of a kind of Neoclassical forum created in the first half of the 19th century to house the archaeological finds acquired by King Ludwig I of Bavaria. On the opposite side of the square, the **Staatliche Antikensammlung** houses smaller treasures, in particular a vast array of Greek vases.

⑦ Alte Pinakothek

Barer Straße 27. **Tel** 089-23 80 52 16.
Ⓤ Königsplatz. 🚋 27. 🚌 100.
Open Tue–Sun. 🅿 ♿

This magnificent gallery is filled with masterpieces of European art from the Middle Ages to the mid-18th century. Many of the Wittelsbach rulers of Bavaria were great collectors, the first being Wilhelm IV the Steadfast, who ruled from 1508 to 1550. The Alte Pinakothek (Old Picture Gallery) was built for Ludwig I by Leo von Klenze in 1826–36 in the form of a Florentine Renaissance palazzo. The ground floor is devoted to the works of German and Flemish Old Masters from the 16th and 17th centuries. On the first floor are works by Dutch, Flemish, French, German, Italian, and Spanish artists.

Of the German works, pride of place goes to Albrecht Dürer's famous *Self-Portrait* (1500) and two panels of an altarpiece showing *Four Apostles*. Among the other German artists represented are Lucas Cranach the Elder and Grünewald. Early Flemish masterpieces include

Four Apostles (1526) by Albrecht Dürer, in the Alte Pinakothek

St. Luke Painting the Madonna by Rogier van der Weyden, and works by Hans Memling and Pieter Brueghel the Elder.

Of later artists, the one with most works on display is the prolific Rubens. There are also interesting works by El Greco, Rembrandt, Raphael, Titian, and Tintoretto.

⑧ Neue Pinakothek

Barer Straße 29. **Tel** 089-23 80 51 95.
Ⓤ Theresienstraße. 🚋 27. 🚌 100.
Open Wed–Mon. 🅿

Bavaria's collection of late 18th- and 19th-century European painting and sculpture occupies a purpose-built gallery completed in 1981. German painting of every artistic movement of the 19th century, including Romanticism, the "Nazarenes," German and Austrian Biedermeier, and Impressionism is well represented. There are also works by French Realists, Impressionists, and Symbolists purchased when the gallery's director was the art historian Hugo von Tschudi.

The open space between the Neue and Alte Pinakothek has been turned into a sculpture park.

Neoclassical facade of the Glyptothek, which houses a collection of Greek and Roman sculpture

⑨ Pinakothek der Moderne

Barer Straße 40. **Tel** 089-23 80 53 60.
Ⓤ Königsplatz. 🚋 27. 🚌 100.
Open 10am–6pm Tue–Sun (to 8pm
Thu). 🚭 except Sun. 🚻 🖥
🌐 pinakothek-der-moderne.de

Designed by the German
architect Stephan Braunfels,
this sleek contemporary
museum brings together the
worlds of art, design, graphics,
and architecture under one
roof. The collections of four
previously separate museums,
including the Staatliche
Graphische Sammlung, the
design collection of Die Neue
Sammlung, and the models,
drawings, and objects of the
Architekturmuseum, are now
housed here. As well as the
individual permanent displays,
there are also temporary and
mixed exhibitions.

⑩ Deutsches Museum

Museuminsel 1. **Tel** 089-217 91.
Ⓢ Isartor. 🚋 18. 🚌 52, 56. **Open**
daily. 🚭 🌐 deutsches-museum.de

Reputed to be the largest
science and technology
museum in the world, the
Deutsches Museum is also the
most popular museum in
Germany. Founded in 1904, the
vast collection features more
than 28,000 exhibits across a
wide range of subject areas,
from agriculture to
telecommunications.

In the basement and on the
ground floor are some of the
museum's largest
exhibits. The
aeronautics
section holds an

Neapolitan crib in the Bayerisches Nationalmuseum

aeroplane that belonged to
the Wright brothers and a 1936
Messerschmitt ME 109. A hall
charting the history of seafaring
houses a 14th-century cog, a
trading ship used by the
Hanseatic League, and a
19th-century fishing vessel.

The museum's superb
collection of automobiles and
other exhibits related to land
travel is now largely on display
in the Deutsches Museum
Verkehrszentrum at Am
Bavariapark 5, in the west
of the city.

Temporary exhibitions are
regularly held at the museum,
which also has an excellent
library archive and a range
of multimedia facilities.

⑪ Bayerisches Nationalmuseum

Prinzregentenstraße 3. **Tel** 089-211 24
01. 🚋 17. 🚌 100. **Open** Tue–Sun.

Founded in 1855 by King
Maximilian II, the Bavarian
National Museum holds a
superb collection of fine and
applied arts and historical
artifacts. Since 1900, the
museum has occupied
an impressive
building

on Prinzregentenstrasse,
designed by Gabriel von Seidl.
The ground floor contains works
from the Romanesque, Gothic,
Renaissance, Baroque, and
Neoclassical periods. Star
exhibits are German sculptor
Conrat Meit's *Judith* (1515)
and a beautiful sculpture of
the Madonna by Tilman
Riemenschneider (c.1460–1531).
The first-floor collections
include German porcelain,
clocks, glassware, ivory carvings,
textiles, and items of gold.

In the basement rooms, the
Christmas nativity scenes by
Bavarian and Italian artists are
especially worth seeing.

⑫ Englischer Garten

Ⓤ Giselastraße. 🚌 54.

The idea of creating a park in
the heart of the city open to all
Munich's citizens came from the
American-born Count von
Rumford, who lived in Bavaria
from 1784. In 1789, taking
advantage of his position as
Bavaria's Minister of War, he
persuaded Elector Karl Theodor
to put his plans into action.
Opened in 1808, the Karl-
Theodor-Park is today simply
known as the Englischer Garten
(English Garden). The park
covers an area of 3.7 sq km
(914 acres), and has become
a popular place for walking,
jogging, or simply relaxing.

Several interesting buildings
dotted about the gardens
include the Monopteros, a
Neoclassical temple (1837) by
Leo von Klenze, and the Chinese
Tower (1789–90), similar to the
pagoda in London's Kew

Benz's tricycle, the first petrol-driven vehicle,
on display at the Deutsches Museum

Gardens (see p.). In the delightful Japanese Teahouse, demonstrations on the art of tea brewing are held. Within the Englischer Garten are three beer gardens, where locals and tourists alike come to drink and listen to live music. Visitors can also take out rowing boats on the park's lake, the Kleinhesseloher See.

The late 18th-century Chinese Tower in the Englischer Garten

⑬ Olympiapark

Tel 089-30 670. Ⓤ Olympia-zentrum. 🚎 20, 21, 27. Pavilion: **Open** daily.

Built for the 1972 Olympic Games, the Olympiapark is visible from almost anywhere in Munich, identifiable by the 290 m (950 ft) high television tower, the Olympiaturm. The site has three main facilities: the Olympic stadium, which seats over 60,000 spectators, the Olympic Hall, and the Swimming Hall. All three are covered by a vast transparent canopy, stretched between several tall masts to form an irregular-shaped pavilion. Also within the complex are an indoor skating rink, a cycle racing track, and tennis courts.

As well as sporting occasions, the Olympiapark hosts many popular cultural events, such as fireworks displays and open-air rock and pop concerts during the summer months.

⑭ Schloss Nymphenburg

Tel 089-17 90 80. Ⓤ Rotkreuzplatz. 🚌 668. **Open** daily. 🌳 Botanischer Garten: **Open** daily. 🌳

Located northwest of the city center, the stunning Schloss Nymphenburg grew up around an Italianate villa, built in 1663–4 for Electress Henrietta-Adelaide. The Electress dedicated the palace, which became the summer residence of the Wittelsbachs, to the pastoral pleasures of the goddess Flora and her nymphs, hence the name. Several additions were made in the following century, including the construction of four pavilions, connected to the original villa by arcaded passageways.

The palace's interior boasts some magnificent examples of the Rococo style. One of the most impressive rooms is the **Festsaal** – a sumptuous ballroom, designed by father and son, Johann Baptiste and Franz Zimmermann. Equally impressive is the **Schönheitengalerie** (Gallery of Beauties). Hanging here are 38 portraits of beautiful women – favorites of King Ludwig I. The palace also houses a small natural history and science museum. The old stables are now home to the **Marstallmuseum**, a collection of wonderfully ornate carriages that once belonged to Bavarian rulers. The approach to the

Interior of the Amalienburg, in the grounds of Schloss Nymphenburg

palace is dominated by a broad canal, bordered by immaculately presented gardens. On the edge of the gardens is the Porcelain Factory, established in 1741, and one of the oldest factories of its type in Europe.

Behind the palace stretches the **Schlosspark**, an English-style country park dotted with lakes and various royal lodges. The most notable of these is François de Cuvilliés' **Amalienburg**, a hunting lodge with a lavish Rococo interior. Its highlight is the splendid Spiegelsaal (Hall of Mirrors). Joseph Effner, the principal architect of the palace's extensions, was also responsible for designing the **Pagodenburg**, used for entertaining, and the Baroque bathing house, the **Badenburg**. Also in the park is the **Magdalenenklause**, built as a hermitage for Maximilian Emmanuel, but not completed until after the Elector's death in 1725.

North of the palace, the **Botanischer Garten** (Botanical Garden) holds many rare and exotic species.

Facade of the splendid Schloss Nymphenburg, begun in the 17th century

The Beers of Germany

Although Germany produces many fine wines, it is for its beer that the country has won worldwide renown. Nowhere is the business of brewing and beer drinking taken so seriously as in Munich. Bavarians are probably the world's greatest consumers of beer, with an annual average intake of 240 liters per head. However, this figure is possibly inflated by the vast quantities downed at the annual Oktoberfest, during which some 7 million lovers of beer converge on Munich for 16 days of revelry lasting from late September to early October. When traveling in Germany, make a point of trying the specialties of the local brewery, in a *Bierkeller* (beer cellar) or *Bierstube* (pub) in winter, and in summer in a *Biergarten* (beer garden).

The tankard known as a *Mass* (measure) holds one liter, although German beer is always served with a considerable head on it. Waitresses at the Oktoberfest have no difficulty carrying eight or nine of these at once.

Pilsener

The most widely drunk beer in Germany is Pils (short for Pilsener), a light lager-style beer produced by bottom-fermentation. This method was perfected in Pilsen (Plzeň in the Czech Republic) in the 19th century. Fermentation occurs at low temperatures, so takes longer than with other beers. The essential ingredients are barley, hops, and crystal-clear water. Two of the main breweries producing this kind of beer in Munich are Löwenbräu and Paulaner.

Munich's Oktoberfest attracts so many visitors, a great tented village, with stalls, a funfair, and loud music, is set up on Theresienwiese, just to the west of the city center. This open space was where the marriage of King Ludwig was celebrated in 1810.

Other German Beers

Germany produces many varieties of beer, some of which are brewed only at certain times of year. Of these seasonal beers, it is worth trying spring beers such as the strong *Maibock*. Other interesting beers include dark styles – known as *Dunkelbier* or *Schwarzbier* – and *Weizenbier*, a beer made from wheat rather than barley. The Berlin version of the latter, *Berliner Weisse* (white beer), is served with fruit juice. Many local breweries have their own specialties. Bamberg is famous for its *Rauchbier*, which has a light smokiness. In the lower Rhine valley, *Altbier* is still produced; this is a top-fermented beer, prepared by traditional methods.

Berliner Weisse (wheat beer)

Dunkelbier

Oktoberfest beer

St. Stephans Dom, Passau's imposing Baroque cathedral

⓫ Passau

🏠 50,000. 🚇 🚌 **i** Rathausplatz 3 (0851-95 59 80).

Passau lies on a peninsula between the Danube and the Inn, near the Austrian border. In 739, the Irish monk St. Boniface founded a major bishopric here. After two destructive fires in 1662 and 1680, the town was rebuilt by Italian architects, who left many fine Baroque buildings, including the cathedral, **St. Stephans Dom**. However, the town retains a medieval feel in its narrow alleys and archways. The Gothic town hall dates from the 14th and 15th centuries. Opposite it is the **Passauer Glasmuseum**, which has a fine collection of Bohemian, Austrian, and Bavarian glass. High above the Inn stands a pretty Baroque pilgrimage church, the **Wallfahrtskirche Mariahilf**.

⓬ Neuschwanstein

🚌 to Schwangau. **Tel** 08362-93 98 80. **Open** Oct–Mar: 10am–4pm daily; Apr–Sep: 9am–6pm daily. 🎫 📷 ♿ (limited access).

Set amid magnificent mountain scenery on the shores of the Alpsee, this fairy-tale castle was built in 1869–86 for the eccentric Bavarian King Ludwig II, to a design by the theater designer Christian Jank. Its pinnacled turrets have provided the inspiration for countless models, book illustrations, and film sets.

The walls of the vestibule and other rooms in the castle are lavishly covered with paintings depicting scenes from German myths and legends. The gilded interior of the throne room is reminiscent of a Byzantine basilica, while the dining room has intricately carved panels and fabulous pictures and furniture. The pale grey granite castle, which draws on a variety of historical styles, is a 20-minute walk from the village of Schwangau.

Gilded apse of the throne room, Neuschwanstein

In the village itself is another castle, **Schloss Hohenschwangau**, built in 1832 by Maximilian, heir to the throne of Bavaria, over the ruins of a medieval castle. A tour of the Neo-Gothic castle gives a fascinating insight into the history of the Wittelsbach family, rulers of Bavaria from 1180 to 1918. There are also some fine 19th-century furnishings and the castle's terraced gardens afford magnificent views.

🏠 **Schloss Hohenschwangau**
Tel 08362-819 80. **Open** daily.
Closed Dec 24. 🎫 📷

⓭ Lake Constance

🚉 Konstanz. 🚌 **i** Bahnhofsplatz 13, Konstanz (07531-13 30 30).

Lake Constance (in German, the Bodensee) lies on the borders of Germany, Austria, and Switzerland. The area surrounding the lake is one of the most attractive in Germany, in terms of both natural beauty and cultural heritage. The best time to visit is summer, when local fishermen stage colorful festivals and there are plenty of opportunities for water sports and cruises on the lake.

Konstanz (Constance) is the largest town in the region, and its main attraction is the magnificent 11th-century Romanesque cathedral. The town is in two parts: the old town (Altstadt) is a German enclave in Switzerland on the southern shore, while the newer part stands on a peninsula between the two main arms of the lake.

The many romantic old towns and beautiful islands of Lake Constance attract hordes of visitors every summer. The exquisite little town of **Meersburg** opposite Konstanz is a very popular destination. So too is **Mainau**, the "Island of Flowers." The most beautiful gardens on the island are in the park of the Baroque palace, built in 1739–46. At the northeastern (Bavarian) end of the lake, the medieval island town of **Lindau** is the major draw.

Lake Constance, with the Swiss Alps rising above the southern shore

Baden-Württemberg

Baden-Württemberg, which includes territories of the former Grand Duchy of Baden, is one of Germany's most popular tourist destinations. Its magnificent castles, luxurious resorts, and the beautiful recreation areas of the Black Forest guarantee a memorable vacation, while the region's long and turbulent history has given it a rich cultural and religious diversity. Germany's oldest university, Heidelberg, is also located in the region.

The Kaufhaus, Freiburg's historic merchants' meeting hall

⓮ Freiburg im Breisgau

🏛 218,000. 🚆 🚌 **𝑖** Rotteckring 14 (0761-388 18 80). 🎭 Fasnet (end of carnival), Weintage (Jun). 🌐 **freiburg.de**

Freiburg is a natural gateway to the Black Forest. The counts von Zähringen first established the town in 1120, and since 1805 it has been part of Baden. From the Middle Ages, fast-flowing canals, or *bächle*, have run through the town, providing water to help extinguish the once frequent fires.

The **cathedral** was built in the 13th century in Gothic style. Münsterplatz, the picturesque cathedral square, is lined with houses from various architectural periods.

Completed in 1520, with ground-floor arcades and richly adorned gables, the **Kaufhaus** was used by merchants for meetings and conferences.

⓯ Black Forest

🚆 to Freiburg. 🚌 to all towns. **𝑖** Wehratalstraße 19, Todtmoos (07674- 906 00). 🌐 **todtmoos.de**

Densely planted with tall firs and spruces, the Black Forest (Schwarzwald) is one of Germany's most picturesque

regions. The area is famous for *Schwarzwälder Kirschtorte* (Black Forest gateau) and *Kirschwasser* (schnapps), as well as for its therapeutic spring waters.

Todtnau is a popular sports center and a base for hikers. Nearby, Hangloch-Wasserfall is one of the most magnificent waterfalls in the region.

The heart of the resort of **Todtmoos** is the Baroque pilgrimage church, which dates from the 17th–18th centuries. Popular dog-sled races are held annually in the town.

In the health resort of **St. Blasien** stands a Benedictine Abbey, founded in the 9th century. Its church (1783) is an excellent example of early Neoclassical style.

The main attraction of **Furtwangen** is its clock museum (Uhrenmuseum), which houses a collection of more than 4,000 chronometers.

In the open-air museum near the small town of **Gutach** visitors can see the Black Forest's oldest house – the 16th-century Vogtsbauernhof.

Rembrandt's *St. Paul in Prison* (1627), Staatsgalerie, Stuttgart

⓰ Stuttgart

🏛 598,000. ✈ 🚆 🚌 **𝑖** Königstraße 1A (0711-222 80). 🌐 **stuttgart-tourist.de**

Stuttgart grew from humble beginnings as a stud farm to become the ducal and royal capital of Württemberg. It is now one of the largest and most important towns of the Federal Republic. Beautifully situated among picturesque hills, the town is a major industrial and cultural center, with a world-famous ballet company, chamber orchestra, and splendid art collections.

When Württemberg Castle burned down in 1311, the family seat was moved to Stuttgart. The ducal residence, the **Altes Schloss**, was given its present square layout in 1553–78. The palace now houses the Württembergisches Landesmuseum, which holds vast collections of decorative art and jewelry. On the east side of Stuttgart's main square is a huge

The Vogtsbauernhof in Gutach, the oldest house in the Black Forest

palace complex, the **Neues Schloss**, built in 1746–1807. The palace gardens still have much of their original charm, with neat avenues and impressive sculptures.

The **Staatsgalerie** grew from a fine art museum containing King Wilhelm I of Württemberg's private collection. Among the Old Masters on display are Rembrandt and Bellini, while modern artists include Monet, Picasso, and Modigliani.

A building exhibition held in 1927 left behind a complete housing estate, the **Weißenhofsiedlung**, which contains houses by Mies van der Rohe, Le Corbusier, Peter Behrens, and Hans Scharoun. Another must for all lovers of modern architecture, the **Liederhalle** congress center is a successful synthesis of tradition and modernism.

The **Linden Museum** is one of Germany's finest ethnology museums, containing exhibits from all over the world. Figures from the Indonesian theater of shadows and a 6th–8th-century mask from Peru are among the eclectic items on display.

To the east of the center is the famous **Mercedes-Benz-Museum**. Its splendid collection illustrates the development of the automobile with over 70 historic vehicles, all in immaculate condition. Stuttgart's other famous car manufacturer has created the **Porsche-Museum**, which includes around 50 examples of these high-speed, expensive vehicles.

Once an independent health resort, **Bad Cannstatt** is now a district of Stuttgart. Set in a beautiful park, it has a late-Gothic church, a Neoclassical town hall, and a *kursaal* (spa-house). One of its main attractions is the magnificent Schloss Rosenstein (1824–9).

Ⅲ Staatsgalerie
Konrad-Adenauer-Straße 30–32.
Tel 0711-470 400. **Open** Tue–Sun.

Ⅲ Mercedes-Benz-Museum
Mercedesstraße 100. **Tel** 0711-173 00 00. **Open** Tue–Sun.

Classic cars on display in the Mercedes-Benz-Museum, Stuttgart

⑰ Heidelberg

150,000. 🚉 🚌 🛈 Willy-Brandt-Platz 1 (06221-584 44 44).
W heidelberg.de

Situated on the banks of the Neckar river, Heidelberg is one of Germany's most beautiful towns. For centuries, it was a center of political power, with a lively and influential cultural life. In 1386, Germany's first university was established here by the Elector Ruprecht I. The construction of the town's palace began during his reign, continuing until the mid-17th century. However,

French incursions in the late 17th century totally destroyed medieval Heidelberg. The town was subsequently rebuilt in the 18th-century in Baroque style.

Towering over the town, the **Heidelberger Schloss** is a vast residential complex that was built and repeatedly extended between the 13th and 17th centuries. Originally a supremely well-fortified Gothic castle, it is now mostly in ruins.

The **Universitätsbibliothek** (University Library), erected in 1901–5, has one of the largest book collections in Germany, with over two million volumes.

The French Count Charles de Graimberg built up an extensive collection of fine drawings, paintings, arms, and other curios. His collection forms the core of the **Kurpfälzisches Museum**, which also has a fascinating archaeology section.

The Baroque domes of the **Heiliggeistkirche** are city landmarks. Former canons of the college were university scholars, and the church aisle features extensive galleries of books.

Ⅲ Kurpfälzisches Museum
Hauptstraße 97. **Tel** 06221-583 40 20. **Open** Tue–Sun (Wed: 10am–6pm).

Heidelberger Schloss rising above Heidelberg's Alte Brücke (Old Bridge)

The Rhine and Mosel Valleys

The Rhine and Mosel Valleys offer a series of fairy-tale landscapes – spectacular gorges, rocky crags topped by romantic castles, and picturesque villages surrounded by vineyards producing excellent white wines. After flowing into Germany from France, the Mosel meanders between steep-sided banks to join the Rhine at Koblenz. South of Koblenz lies one of the most stunning stretches of the Rhine, which is also the birthplace of German myths such as the Lorelei and the *Nibelungenlied*, the great medieval epic poem of vengeance and honor.

The colorful portal of Trier's Kurfürstliches Schloss

⑱ Trier

Rhineland-Palatinate. 🏙 106,000.
🚆 🚌 **i** An der Porta Nigra (0651-97 80 80). **W** trier.de

Germany's oldest town, Trier was founded by the Emperor Augustus in 16 BC. Its monumental Roman gateway, the **Porta Nigra**, was built in the 3rd century AD. Among the city's other Roman relics are the **Aula Palatina**, a vast, austere building that served as the throne hall of Roman emperors and also as a church, the **Basilika und Kurfürstliches Schloss**. The basilica was built for Emperor Constantine around AD 305. In the 16th century, part of it was incorporated into a Renaissance castle, later transformed into a Baroque palace for the archbishop-electors of Trier. The 4th-century **Kaiserthermen** (Imperial Baths) are also in the same building. A superb collection of Roman

artifacts is held in the nearby **Rheinisches Landesmuseum**.

🏛 **Rheinisches Landesmuseum**
Weimarer Allee 1. **Tel** 0651-977 40.
Open 9:30am–5:30pm Tue–Sun. ♿

⑲ Mosel Valley

i Am Gestade 6, Bernkastel-Kues (06531-50 01 90). 🚌 Hans Michels (06531-8222); Gebrüder Kolb, Briedern (02673-1515).
W mosellandtouristik.de

On the stretch of the Mosel between Trier and Koblenz, romantic castles tower above vineyards. Between May and October, river trips are available all along the river – either short daytrips or longer cruises. However, progress can be slow because of the number of locks. A tour by car or bus is a pleasant alternative. Popular excursions include those from Trier to Bernkastel-Kues and from Koblenz to Cochem. Wine-tasting and eating play a big part in visitors' enjoyment of the region. Of the many castles that line the river, be sure to visit **Burg Eltz** – the core of which has survived more or less intact since it was built in the 12th century – a short walk from the town of Wierschem.

🏰 **Burg Eltz**
🚌 to Wierschem. **Open** Apr–Oct: daily. ♿

⑳ Mainz

Rhineland-Palatinate. 🏙 207,000. 🚆 🚌 **i** Im Brückenturm am Rathaus (06131-24 28 88). **W** touristik-mainz.de

Mainz enjoyed power and influence under the Holy Roman Empire, as the city's Archbishop was one of the Electors. The **Kaiserdom**, the Romanesque cathedral, dates back to the 11th century. Like others from this period, it has a choir at each

Burg Eltz, the most evocative castle in the Mosel Valley

The apse and towers at the east end of the Kaiserdom, Mainz

end – one for the emperor and one for the clergy. The nave is filled with the splendid tombs of the archbishops, ranging in date from the 13th to the 19th century. The **St. Gotthard-Kapelle** beside the cathedral was the private chapel of the archbishops. It has a fine 12th-century arcaded loggia.

Other attractions include the well-preserved old half-timbered houses of the **Kirschgarten** area and the Baroque **Kurfürstliches Schloss**, now a museum of Roman and other relics.

Mainz is also famous for the development in the 1440s by Johannes Gutenberg of printing with movable metal type. The **Gutenberg Museum** has a recreation of his studio and a copy of his famous 42-line Bible.

🏛 **Gutenberg Museum**
Liebfrauenplatz 5. **Tel** 06131-12 26 40. **Open** Tue–Sun. **Closed** public hols.

㉑ Rhine Valley

ℹ Bahnhofplatz 17, Koblenz (0261-194 33). 🚢 K-D Linie, Konrad-Adenauer-Ufer, Koblenz (0261-310 30).

Cruises on the Rhine are available along much of its length, but the most scenic and popular stretch is the Rhine Gorge between Mainz and Bonn. The gorge starts at Bingen, where the Nahe joins the Rhine on its 1,320-km-(825-mile) journey from Switzerland to the North Sea. Popular sights along the route include **Bacharach**, a pretty

town on the left bank, and the striking white-walled island castle of **Pfalzgrafenstein**, which levied tolls on passing ships until the mid-19th century. Past the town of Kaub on the right bank is the rock of the **Lorelei**, a legendary siren who lured sailors to their deaths with her song and her beauty. A modern statue marks the spot. Across the river is the town of **St. Goar**, dominated by the ruined Burg Rheinfels, blown up by French troops in 1797. **Burg Katz** offers one of the best-known views of the Rhine valley. At **Boppard**, the attractions include the 13th-century Church of St. Severus and more spectacular views. Just south of Koblenz stands **Schloss Stolzenfels**, created in the early 19th century for King Friedrich Wilhelm IV. There are no bridges on this stretch of the river, but if you are exploring by car, there are ferries at various points along the route. However, the best way to enjoy the Rhine's magnificent scenery is by boat.

㉒ Koblenz

Rhineland-Palatinate. 🗺 110,000. 🚉 🚌 ℹ Bahnhofplatz 17 (0261-194 33), Jesuitenplatz (0261-13 09 20). 🌐 **koblenz-touristik.de**

Koblenz stands at the confluence of the Mosel and Rhine rivers. On the **Deutsches Eck**, the spur of land between the two rivers, stands a huge equestrian statue of Emperor Wilhelm I.

Florinsmarkt takes its name from the Romanesque-Gothic **Church of St. Florin**, which dates from the 12th century. Nestling among the square's historic buildings is the **Mittelrheinisches Museum**, with medieval art and archaeological collections.

The present appearance of the **Alte Burg**, with its fine Renaissance facade, dates from the 17th century, but a fortress has stood on this site since the early Middle Ages.

Other sights of interest are the **Liebfrauenkirche**, which has a beautiful Gothic choir, the **Kurfürstliches Schloss** (the Electors' palace), and **Festung Ehrenbreitstein**, where the archbishops of Trier resided from 1648–1786.

Environs

Northwest of Koblenz, the Benedictine abbey of **Maria Laach** is a masterpiece of Romanesque architecture. It was begun in 1093 on the orders of Count Palatine Heinrich II, who lies buried here. The Paradise courtyard, meant to symbolize the Garden of Eden, resembles the Alhambra in Granada (*see pp32–13*).

Detail on tomb of Heinrich II, Maria Laach

🏰 **Maria Laach**
Off A61, 25 km (16 miles) NW of Koblenz. **Tel** 02652-590. 🚌 from Andernach or Niedermendig. **Open** daily.

Burg Katz above the town of St. Goarhausen in the Rhine Gorge

Frankfurt's skyscraper district, nicknamed "Mainhattan"

㉙ Frankfurt am Main

Hesse. 🅟 685,000. ✈ 🚉 🚌 🚢
ℹ Hauptbahnhof (069-21 23 88 00).
🌐 frankfurt-tourismus.de

Frankfurt am Main is one of the main economic and cultural centers of Europe. The headquarters of many major banks and newspaper publishers are based here, and the city's International Book Fair is the world's largest event of its kind.

Since 1878, the **Städelsches Kunstinstitut** has occupied a Neo-Renaissance building on Schaumainkai, the picturesque "museum embankment." The ground floor houses a collection of Dutch and German prints and drawings, the first floor is devoted to 19th- and 20th-century art, and the second

floor displays works by Old Masters such as Botticelli, van Eyck, Vermeer, and Rembrandt.

Another interesting museum in the Schaumainkai complex is the **Deutsches Architektur-museum**, which concentrates mainly on developments in 20th-century architecture.

Nearby is the **Deutsches Filmmuseum**, which holds documents and objects relating to the art of film-making and the development of film technology. The museum has its own cinema, which shows old and often long-forgotten films.

The great German poet, novelist, and dramatist Johann Wolfgang von Goethe was born at the **Goethehaus** in 1749. The house was totally destroyed in World War II, but later lovingly restored, its interior reconstructed in typical 18th-century style. The desk at which Goethe wrote his early works, such as *The Sorrows of Young Werther* (1774), remains.

Located in the center of the old town, the **Römer** is a collection of 15th- to 18th-century houses, including the Altes Rathaus (Old Town Hall), rebuilt after World War II. Opposite is a group of half-timbered houses, known as the **Ostzeile**.

On the banks of the Main stands **St. Leonhardkirche**, a fine example of Gothic and Romanesque architecture.

Portrait of a Woman (c.1480) by Botticelli, Städelsches Kunstinstitut

Built in stages in the 13th and 15th centuries, the church contains many treasures, including a copy of Leonardo da Vinci's *Last Supper* by Hans Holbein the Elder, from 1501.

The **Historisches Museum** has an interesting display of items relating to Frankfurt's history, including a fascinating model of the medieval town, a collection of local prehistoric finds, and several decorative fragments from buildings destroyed during World War II.

The twin-naved **Alte Nikolaikirche**, or Church of St. Nicholas, is popular for its fine statues of St. Nicholas and the 40-bell carillon, which plays German folk songs twice a day.

The **Kaiserdom**, an imperial cathedral, was built between the 13th and 15th centuries. It has several priceless masterpieces of Gothic artwork, including the 15th-century Maria-Schlaf-Altar.

The collection at the **Museum für Moderne Kunst** (Museum of Modern Art) represents all the major artistic trends from the 1960s until the present day, with works by Roy Lichtenstein and Andy Warhol.

The **Liebieghaus**, a museum of sculpture, has works ranging from antiquity through to Mannerism and Rococo. There are some superb examples of ancient Egyptian and Far Eastern art, as well as splendid works from the Middle Ages and the Renaissance.

🏛 Städelsches Kunstinstitut
Schaumainkai 63. **Tel** 069-605 09 80.
Open Tue–Sun. 🅿 ✓

🏛 Museum für Moderne Kunst
Domstraße 10. **Tel** 069-21 23 04 47.
Open Tue–Sun. 🅿

Environs
Hanau, 30 km (19 miles) east of Frankfurt, is the birthplace of the brothers Wilhelm and Jakob Grimm. There is an exhibition devoted to their lives and work at the local historical museum.

The Ostzeile on the Römerberg, one of the symbols of Frankfurt

For hotels and restaurants see pp546–8 and pp549–51

The Baroque Elector's palace, housing Bonn University

㉔ Bonn

North Rhine-Westphalia. 320,000. Windeckstraße 1 (0228-77 50 00). bonn.de

There has been a crossing over the Rhine at Bonn since pre-Roman times, but the settlement first rose to prominence under the Archbishops of Cologne in the 13th century. Bonn was the capital of the Federal Republic of Germany between 1949 and 1991.

The central market square is surrounded by a mixture of modern and Baroque architecture, including the late-Baroque **Rathaus** (Town Hall), built in 1737–8. Just north of the market square stands the 18th-century Baroque house where Beethoven was born. The **Beethovenhaus** is now a museum housing an impressive collection of memorabilia.

Bonn has many fine museums. The **Rheinisches Landes-museum** has a vast collection of archaeological exhibits dating back to Roman times, as well as medieval and modern art.

A Neanderthal skull is also exhibited here. The **Kunstmuseum Bonn**, a museum of modern art, has a superb display of Expressionist paintings.

㉕ Cologne

North Rhine-Westphalia. 1,045,000. Unter Fettenhennen 19 (0221-22 13 04 00). koelntourismus.de

Originally founded by the Romans, Cologne (Köln) is one of the oldest settlements in Germany. Present-day Cologne is an important ecclesiastical and cultural center, boasting 12 Romanesque churches and the famous cathedral (see pp534–5), as well as several excellent museums, historic buildings, and superb galleries.

The **Wallraf-Richartz-Museum** contains 14th- to 19th-century paintings organized by the schools of art they represent. Featured artists include Rubens, Dürer, Munch, and Max Liebermann. Housing archaeological finds from Cologne and the Rhine Valley, the modern **Römisch-Germanisches Museum** displays Roman weapons, tools, and decorative objects, as well as the superb Dionysus mosaic from around 250 BC.

The **Museum Ludwig** boasts one of Europe's best collections of modern art. German Expressionists, Surrealists, and American Pop Artists are all represented.

The Romans built a sports arena on the site now occupied by the 12th-century **Groß St. Martin**. Remains of the baths have been uncovered underneath the crypt.

Cologne's **Rathaus** (Town Hall) is an irregular-shaped building, the result of successive modifications after 1330. Under a glass pyramid at the front are the remains of 12th-century Jewish baths.

Highlights of the late-Gothic **Church of St. Peter**, built in 1515–39, are its stained-glass windows and the magnificent Crucifixion of St. Peter (c.1637) by Peter Paul Rubens.

The southern chamber of the **Church of St. Ursula** is lined with many shrines. According to legend, they hold the remains of St. Ursula and 11,000 virgins, reputedly killed by the Huns.

Wallraf-Richartz-Museum
Obenmarspforten. **Tel** 0221-22 12 11 19. **Open** Tue–Sun.

Skyline of Cologne, dominated by the spires of the Rathaus, Gross St. Martin, and the cathedral

Cologne Cathedral

The history of Germany's greatest Gothic cathedral is long and complicated. The foundation stone was laid on August 15, 1248, the chancel was consecrated in 1322, and building work continued until about 1520. The cathedral then stood unfinished until the 19th century, when the original Gothic designs were rediscovered. It was finally completed in 1842–80. Precious works of art include the fabulous Shrine of the Three Kings, the Altar of the Magi, and an early-Gothic carving of the Virgin Mary (c.1290) known as the Mailänder (Milanese) Madonna.

Cathedral Exterior
Built out of porous sandstone, the facade is susceptible to environmental impurities, such as traffic fumes.

Cathedral Interior
The chancel, the ambulatory, and the chapels retain a large number of Gothic, mainly early 14th-century, stained-glass windows.

KEY

① **The Petrusportal** is the only entrance built in the Middle Ages. Of the figures flanking the doorway, five were original Gothic statues, but these have been replaced by copies.

② **Buttresses** support the entire bulk of the cathedral.

③ **Elaborately decorated** pinnacles top the supporting pillars.

④ **The north tower**, at 157.38 m (516 ft), is slightly higher than the south tower.

Main entrance

Englebert Reliquary (c.1630)
The treasury on the north side of the cathedral is famous for its large collection of gold objects, vestments, and the beautifully decorated liturgical books.

★ **Choir**
The massive oak stalls were built in 1308–11. They are backed by beautiful painted walls.

★ **Shrine of the Three Kings**
This huge Romanesque reliquary was made by Nikolaus von Verdun in 1181–1220, to hold the relics of the Three Kings. These were brought to Cologne from Italy in 1164 by Emperor Friedrich I Barbarossa.

High Altar
The Gothic altar dates back to the consecration of the chancel. The frieze depicts the Coronation of the Virgin Mary, flanked by the twelve Apostles.

★ **Altar of the City Patrons**
This magnificent altarpiece (c.1442) by Stephan Lochner depicts *The Adoration of the Magi.* When the panels are closed, it shows *The Annunciation.*

Northern Germany

Three federal states – Lower Saxony and the city-states of Hamburg and Bremen – occupy a huge swathe of northern Germany. Lower Saxony's capital, Hanover, has splendid architecture and fine museums. Hamburg and Bremen were wealthy Hanseatic trading towns, and today their ports still play an important role in city life. The region's other main attractions are the well- preserved medieval towns of Münster, in North Rhine-Westphalia, and Lübeck in Schleswig-Holstein.

The beautifully restored facade of Münster's Gothic Rathaus

㉖ Münster

297,000. ✈ 🚉 ℹ️ Heinrich-Brüning-Straße 9 (0251-492 27 10).
🌐 **muenster.de**

Münster's main sights of interest are located in the Altstadt, the historic heart of the city. The imposing Gothic **Rathaus** (Town Hall), carefully restored following damage during World War II, dates from the late 12th century. In 1648, the Treaty of Westphalia was signed here, ending the Thirty Years' War.

Münster's great cathedral, the **Dom St. Paulus**, on Domplatz, was built in 1225–65. Its best-known treasure is the astronom-ical clock (1540). Also on the square is the **Westfälisches Landesmuseum**, specializing in Gothic art. Nearby, the **Lambertikirche** (1375–1450) is a fine example of the hall-churches typical of Westphalia.

West of the center stands the **Residenzschloss**. Built in 1767–87, the splendid Baroque palace, now the headquarters of Münster's university, overlooks pleasant gardens.

㉗ Hanover

519,000. 🚉 ℹ️ Ernst-August-Platz 8 (0511-12 34 51 11). 🎭 Schützenfest (Jun–Jul).

Hanover (Hannover) is the capital of Lower Saxony, and for more than a century, from 1714 to 1837, shared a succession of rulers with Britain. Heavily bombed during World War II, the city has been largely rebuilt.

Among the city's finest landmarks are the grand **Opernhaus** (Opera House), built in Neoclassical style in 1845–57, and, on Tramm-platz, the **Neues Rathaus** (Town Hall), which dates from 1901–13 and combines Neo-Gothic and Secessionist detail. The latter's massive central dome offers fine views of the city.

On Marktplatz, in the old town, are many restored, 15th-century, half-timbered houses, as well as the **Markt-kirche St. Georg und St. Jacobus** with its 14th-century nave and fine Gothic altar. One of Europe's best museums of modern art, the **Sprengel-Museum** holds works by Munch, Chagall, Picasso, and Christo. Also worth visiting is the **Niedersächsisches Landesmuseum**, whose picture gallery has German medieval and Renaissance paintings, Dutch and Flemish works by Rubens, Rembrandt, and van Dyck, and 19th- and 20th-century German art.

West of the city center, the **Herrenhäuser Gärten** are among the most beautiful Baroque gardens in Germany.

🏛 **Sprengel Museum**
Kurt-Schwitters-Platz. **Tel** 0511-16 84 38 75. **Open** Tue–Sun. ♿

🏛 **Niedersächsisches Landesmuseum**
Willy-Brandt-Allee 5. **Tel** 0511-980 7686. **Open** Tue–Sun.

㉘ Bremen

556,000. 🚢 🚉 ℹ️ Am Bahnhofplatz 15 (0421-308 000).
🌐 **bremen-tourism.de**

A member of the Hanseatic League from 1358, in the Middle Ages, Bremen was a thriving seaport, trading in grain, wine, and salt. Today, the independent city-state still prospers from its port, Germany's second-largest.

Bremen's **Rathaus** (Town Hall), on Marktplatz, was built in 1405–10 and boasts a fine Renaissance facade, added to the original Gothic structure 200 years later. Opposite is the 11th-century Romanesque **Dom**, which contains some

Hanover's medieval quarter, with the Church of St. George and St. Jacobus

Attractive gabled houses and the statue of Roland in Bremen's Marktplatz

fine bas-reliefs. In Marktplatz itself stand a tall statue of Charlemagne's knight Roland (1404) and a sculpture of the *Musicians of Bremen* (1953), recalling the Grimm fairy tale.

Two museums of note are the **Kunsthalle**, with European art dating from the Middle Ages to the 20th century, and the **Focke Museum**, a museum of local history and decorative arts.

Musicians of Bremen sculpture

🏛 **Rathaus**
Marktplatz. **Open** for guided tours only (11am, noon, 3pm, 4pm) book ahead 🛈 🖼 🖸

🏛 **Kunsthalle**
Am Wall 207. **Tel** 0421-32 90 80. **Open** 10am–9pm Tue, 10am–6pm Wed–Sun.

🌀 Hamburg

🗺 1,743,000. ✈ 🚢 🚉 🛈 Hauptbahnhof, Kirchenallee (040-30 05 12 00). 🌐 **hamburg-tourism.de**

For many years, Hamburg, Germany's second largest city, was a leading member of the Hanseatic League and an independent trading town. In 1945, it became a city-state of the Federal Republic.

Hamburg sustained considerable damage during World War II, and little of the old town remains. The ruined tower of the Neo-Gothic **Nikolaikirche**

serves as a monument to the tragic consequences of war. Nearby, the **Jakobikirche** (1340) has been rebuilt in its original style. Inside is a massive 17th-century Baroque organ by Arp Schnitger. Another fine church is the Baroque **Michaeliskirche**, whose 132-m- (433-ft-) tower gives splendid views of the city.

Hamburg's Neo-Renaissance town hall, on the Rathausmarkt, is the fifth in the city's history. Just north of it is a large recreational lake, the Binnenalster. Also nearby, the prestigious **Kunsthalle** traces the history of European art from medieval times to the 20th century. The section devoted to the 19th-century German Romantics is especially good.

The best-known example of the city's collection of Expressionist buildings is Fritz Höger's **Chilehaus** (1922–4) in Kontorhausviertel.

Hamburg is the second largest port in Europe after Rotterdam, and a tour is highly recommended. There are two museum ships moored here:

Triptych adorning the main altar in Hamburg's Jakobikirche

the freighter *Cap San Diego* and the sailing boat *Rickmer Rickmers* (1896).

🏛 **Kunsthalle**
Glockengießerwall. **Tel** 040-428 13 12 00. **Open** Tue–Sun.

⚓ **Port**
Ⓤ Baumwall or St-Pauli-Landungsbrücken. Cap San Diego: **Tel** 040-36 42 09. **Open** daily. Rickmer Rickmers: **Tel** 040-319 59 59. **Open** daily.

Lübeck's 15th-century Holstentor, on the western edge of the town

❸ Lübeck

🗺 214,000. 🚉 🛈 Holstentorplatz 1 (0451-409 1950). 🌐 **luebeck-tourism.de**

The most important town in the Baltic basin at the end of the Middle Ages, Lübeck is known for its wealth of superb medieval architecture.

The city's 13th-century **Marienkirche** (St. Mary's Church) boasts the highest vaulted brick nave in the world. A short walk away, the turreted **Rathaus** (Town Hall) dates from 1226 and is a fine example of Lübeck's distinctive Gothic brick architecture. The Gothic **Dom** (Cathedral) was begun in 1173. Nearby, the **St. Annen-Museum** has historical artifacts dating from the 13th to the 18th centuries. Another famous monument is the **Holstentor** (1466–78), the western gateway to the city.

The **Buddenbrookhaus** is a museum devoted to the great writers Thomas and Heinrich Mann, whose family lived here in 1841–91.

🏛 **Buddenbrookhaus**
Heinrich-und-Thomas-Mann-Zentrum, Mengstrasse 4. **Tel** 0451-122 4192. **Open** daily. **Closed** Dec 24, 25 & 31. 🖼

Practical Information

Germany is renowned as a safe, clean, and efficient country to visit. Travelers will find that every town has a helpful tourist information center offering advice on restaurants, attractions, and activities. Larger cities also have Internet websites which give up-to-the-minute information. Hotels are plentiful but may be busy during the festivals and fairs which occur throughout the year in different parts of the country.

When to Visit

The climate in Germany is pleasantly temperate. Cities and historic monuments are best visited in spring or early fall, particularly in the south of the country where it can be very warm. July and August are ideal months for a restful holiday by the sea, in the lake districts or in the mountains. In Bavaria during the second half of September and early October, the Oktoberfest takes place. This is an annual beer-drinking event which is open to all visitors. In December, everybody is pre-occupied with Christmas shopping, while during winter, skiing is a popular pursuit in the Black Forest, the Alps, and the Harz Mountains. The roads are busiest during the school holidays, dates of which vary from state to state, and during the "long weekends" at Easter, Whitsun, and other national public holidays.

Visa Requirements and Customs

Citizens of countries that are members of the EU, as well as citizens from the US, Canada, Australia, and New Zealand, do not need a visa to visit Germany, so long as their stay does not exceed three months. Visitors from South Africa must have a visa. Visitors from EU countries do not require a passport to enter Germany, as long as they have a national ID card.

Drugs, animals, animal products, such as cured meats, and exotic plants under special protection are totally prohibited from importation into Germany. Regulations also restrict the import of cigarettes and wine.

Personal Security

As in other countries, visitors are far safer in small towns and villages than in big cities, where extra care must be taken against street theft – particularly when traveling on public transport during the rush hour. Pickpockets tend to frequent popular tourist sights and any events where large groups of people gather. It is worth using a money belt to conceal your money and documents. Also keep cameras and audio equipment out of sight. Better still, leave valuable items in the hotel safe.

Police

German police uniforms and signs are mostly blue (they are green in Bavaria and the Saarland, but otherwise blue). Look out for motorized police units, the *Verkehrspolizei*, which are concerned with safety on the streets, roads, and highways, and are distinguished by their white caps. Certain town police have navy-blue uniforms and their job is to catch motorists for parking offences for which they can impose an on-the-spot fine. Remember that you should carry ID such as a passport, driving license or student card with you at all times.

Pharmacies

Look out for the stylized letter "A" (*Apotheke*), which indicates a pharmacy. They are usually open from 8am to 6pm; in small towns, they close between 1 and 3pm. In larger towns, there is always a rota and this is displayed in the window of each pharmacy with a note of addresses. Information on rota pharmacies may also be obtained from tourist offices.

Accidents and Emergencies

If you have an accident or a serious breakdown on the motorway, it is best to use one of the special telephones that are situated at regular intervals along the hard shoulder. Throughout the country, a special emergency number, 110, is answered by an operator who

The Climate of Germany

Germany lies in a temperate climatic zone. In the north, with marine influences predominating, summers tend to be quite cool and winters mild, with relatively high rainfall. In the eastern part of the country, however, the climate is more continental and this produces harsher winters and hotter summers. Germany's highest rainfall and lowest temperatures are recorded in the Alps.

BERLIN			
°C/°F			
	23/73		
13/56	12/54	14/57	
3/37		3/37	1/34 -5/23
6 hrs	8 hrs	4 hrs	2 hrs
24 mm	60 mm	41 mm	31 mm
month **Apr**	**Jul**	**Oct**	**Jan**

MUNICH			
°C/°F			
	23/73		
14/57	11/53	13/56	
3/37		3/37	2/36 -5/23
5 hrs	8 hrs	5 hrs	2 hrs
56 mm	99 mm	48 mm	46 mm
month **Apr**	**Jul**	**Oct**	**Jan**

will inform the appropriate emergency services. This number is free on all telephones, including mobiles. If you lose your passport, you should go to your consulate.

Tourist Information

A well-developed network of tourist information centers exists in Germany. These are usually run by the city or regional tourist authorities, *Verkehrsamt*. They provide advice on accommodations, addresses, and opening hours of monuments, museums, tours, and excursions, as well as brochures covering the most important tourist attractions. They may also be able to find and book you a hotel room.

Opening Hours

The opening hours of stores, offices, and most other businesses depend to a great extent on the size of the town. In larger cities, office hours are usually from 9am until 6pm, and larger shops are open from 9am to 8pm weekdays, and until 6pm

on Saturday. Banks operate shorter hours: 9am–3:30pm Monday–Friday, with a lunchbreak between noon and 1pm. They usually stay open later one evening a week until 6pm. Some new shopping malls are open on Sundays. In smaller towns, not much tends to open before 10am, and many businesses close from 1–2pm for lunch, on Saturday afternoons, Sundays and public holidays.

Disabled Travelers

There are ramps or lifts for people confined to wheelchairs at large museums and major historical sites. Banks are also accessible by wheelchair and there are lifts at railroad stations and larger underground stations. Some public transport is adapted to take wheelchairs. Most higher grade hotels have suitably equipped bedrooms. Public restroom facilities in parking lots, train stations, and airports usually have suitable cubicles. For information contact **Bundesverband Selbsthilfe Körperbehinderter (BSK)**.

Communications

As everywhere in Europe, the introduction of cell phones has brought about a revolution in telephone usage. Visitors wishing to use their cell phone in Germany should contact their service provider for information. The number of payphones taking coins is constantly dwindling, and a telephone card gives better value for money. They can be bought at post offices and most newsagents. Other phones are operated by credit card only. These phones have their own phone number, so you can arrange to be called back.

Post offices are usually open from 6am–8pm on weekdays and from 8am–noon on Saturdays. Stamps can be bought at post offices as well as stamp machines, and are sometimes sold along with postcards.

Banking and Currency

Germany has used the euro since 2002 *(see p23)*. Foreign currency can be changed at banks, most hotels, or bureau de change *(Wechselstube)*.

DIRECTORY

Tourist Information

German National Tourist Office
Tel 069-97 46 40.
w germany-tourism.de

Berlin
Am Karlsbad 11, 10785 Berlin.
Tel 030-25 00 23 33.
w visitberlin.de

Frankfurt am Main
Hauptbahnhof Empfangshalle, 60329 Frankfurt am Main.
Tel 069-21 23 88 00.
w frankfurt-tourismus.de

Munich
Marienplatz, Rathaus, 80331 Munich.
Tel 089-2339 6500.
w muenchen-tourist.de

Stuttgart
Königstraße 1a, 70173 Stuttgart.
Tel 0711-222 82 53.
w stuttgart-tourist.de

Embassies

Australia
Wallstraße 76–79, 10179 Berlin. Tel 030-880 08 80.
w australian-embassy.de

Canada
Leipziger Platz 17, 10117 Berlin. Tel 030-20 31 20.
w kanada-info.de

New Zealand
Friedrichstraße 60, 10117 Berlin. Tel 030-20 62 10.
w nzembassy.com/germany

South Africa
Tiergartenstraße 18, 12683 Berlin.
Tel 030-22 07 30.
w suedafrika.org

UK
Wilhelmstraße 70, 10117 Berlin.
Tel 030-20 45 70.
w britischebotschaft.de

US
Clayallee 170, 14195 Berlin. Tel 030-83050.
w usembassy.de

Consulates

UK
Neuer Jungfernstieg 20, 20354 Hamburg.
Tel 040-44 80 32 36.

US
Königinstraße 5, 80539 Munich.
Tel 089-288 80.

Emergency Numbers

Police and Fire services
Tel 110 or 112.

Ambulance
Tel 112.

Disabled Travelers

Mobility International
North America.
Tel 541-343 1284.

Bundesverband Selbsthilfe Körperbehinderter (BSK)
Postfach 20, 74238 Krautheim.
Tel 06294-42810.
w bsk-ev.org

Travel Information

Traveling to and around Germany is fast and easy. In every large city there is an airport, and most of these offer international connections. The whole of Germany is linked by a dense network of highways, while the main roads are of a high standard and well signposted. Train travel throughout the country is comfortable and reliable; for longer journeys, it is worth taking advantage of the fast connections offered by InterCityExpress (ICE). Buses are also comfortable and efficient and can be essential in rural areas that cannot be reached by train. Large cities have tram, bus, and sometimes subway services.

Arriving by Air

Germany's most important airports are Berlin, Frankfurt am Main, Munich and Düsseldorf. You can get connecting flights from these to other cities such as Hamburg and Stuttgart. The country's national airline is **Lufthansa**, which flies between Germany and most of the world's major destinations. From the UK, flights are operated by **BA** and **BMI**. **Ryanair**, **Air Berlin**, **easyJet**, and **Germanwings** all offer cheaper alternatives as well.

There are frequent flights from the US to Germany, mainly to Munich and Frankfurt, which is Germany's largest airport and one of the busiest in Europe. Direct flights are available from many major US cities.

Although Canada does not have many direct flights to Germany, **Air Canada** operates regular flights to Frankfurt from Toronto and Vancouver. **Qantas** connects to Frankfurt from many Australian cities.

Domestic Flights

In addition to Lufthansa, there are a number of smaller airlines in Germany including Air Berlin, which may offer cheaper fares than Lufthansa on internal routes, as well as providing air links with small airports, such as Augsburg, Dortmund, and Erfurt.

Border Crossing

There are many crossings into Germany and provided that you carry the necessary documents and your car does not look disreputable, you should experience a minimum of delay and formalities at the border. There are limits on the amount of duty-free items that can be brought in by non-EU citizens (see p21).

Traveling by Car

The fastest and most comfortable way to travel around the country is by road. Germany's excellent network of toll-free highway routes guarantees fast journeys over long distances, while a well-maintained system of good smaller roads means that many interesting places throughout the country are within easy reach. On smaller roads and in remote areas, filling stations may be few and far between.

The German *Autobahn* (highway) network is extensive. An *Autobahn* is indicated by the letter "A" followed by a number – some also have a letter "E" and a number, denoting that the road crosses the German border. They are all toll-free and have regularly spaced filling stations, as well as parking lots with restrooms, restaurants, and motels. A *Bundesstraße* (main road) has the letter "B" and a number.

In the event of an accident on an *Autobahn*, or if sudden traffic congestion means you have to brake hard, drivers should turn on their flashing emergency lights to warn drivers behind of the danger. Along the hard shoulder there are yellow poles with emergency buttons, which can be used to call for help if you have a breakdown or an accident. The two automobile associations **Allgemeiner Deutscher Automobil Club (ADAC)** and **Automobilclub von Deutschland (AvD)** offer roadside assistance.

Rules of the Road

In Germany, the same road traffic regulations apply as in most European countries. The car must carry a plate indicating country of origin, and be equipped with a red warning triangle for use in case of breakdown.

The wearing of seatbelts is compulsory and children under 12 must sit in the back, with babies and toddlers secured in child-seats.

Driving after drinking a small amount of alcohol is allowed, but if you have an accident, the consequences will be more severe if a breathalyzer shows alcohol in your blood.

In built-up areas, the speed limit is 50 km/h (31 mph); beyond this it is 100 km/h (62 mph), and on highways there is no limit, of which many drivers take full advantage. When traveling with a caravan or camping trailer outside built-up areas, drivers should not exceed 70 km/h (44 mph), and on highways 100 km/h (62 mph). Road traffic police are strict about imposing fines for speeding. Drivers can also be fined for driving too close to the vehicle in front and for parking in prohibited areas.

Parking in Towns

Finding a place to park is not easy; it is often best to use a multi-level parking lot, which is indicated by *"Parkhaus"*; a sign with the word *"Frei"* indicates that spaces are available. It is never worth leaving your car in a prohibited area. If you do risk it, a traffic warden may find your car, immediately impose a fine and arrange for the car to be towed away. Retrieving your car is then expensive and difficult.

Cars left in a parking zone must either display a parking ticket or be at a meter.

Traveling by Train

Traveling around Germany by train is not the cheapest form of transport, but it is undoubtedly one of the most efficient. Trains operated by **Deutsche Bahn**, the German rail company, are renowned for their punctuality, safety, and cleanliness. The fastest are InterCityExpress (ICE) trains; these are aerodynamically designed, painted white, with air-conditioning in the coaches and airline-style seats. Unfortunately, there is not much room for luggage. These trains can travel at more than 200 km/h (125 mph), which means that a journey from Hamburg to Munich takes just under six hours. ICE trains operate on just a few routes linking the largest cities. The InterCity (IC) trains, which stop only at certain stations, are cheaper but still offer an express service. For short distances, it is best to take the Regional Express (RE) trains. The *S-Bahn* (short for *Schnellbahn*) is a fast commuter rail network which operates in some of the major German cities.

Train Fares

Train fares in Germany are quite expensive and there is a compulsory surcharge *(Zuschlag)* for express train travel. It is not usually necessary to reserve seats, but in the high season this is a good idea and it does not cost a lot. If you are staying for some time and want to use trains frequently, one way to travel more cheaply is to buy a *BahnCard*. After an initial hefty outlay, this gives you a 50 per cent discount on rail tickets for a whole year.

City Transport

Several major cities in Germany, including Berlin, Hamburg, Munich, and Nuremberg, have a network of fast connections by subway (*U-Bahn*). U-Bahn stations are indicated by square signs with a white "U" on a dark blue background, while *S-Bahn* stations have round signs with a white "S" on a green background. The *U-Bahn* offers very frequent services – at peak hours, trains normally run every 3–5 minutes – and stations are only a short distance from each other. The *S-Bahn* trains are less frequent and the stations are farther apart.

In some cities (especially in eastern Germany), trams are the most common method of travel; in some cities, they also have underground sections. Trams are ideal urban transport because they do not get stuck in traffic jams. You can use the same tickets as on buses and the *S-Bahn*. When they are above ground, remember that trams have right of way.

Various types of ticket can be bought from machines located by the entrance to stations. Children under six travel free, while those under 14 get a reduced rate.

Traveling by Bus

There is a good network of inter-city bus services in Germany, though journeys are generally no cheaper than traveling by train. Most towns have a *Zentraler Omnibus Bahnhof* (ZOB) close to the train station. Most bus services originate here and you can also get timetables and buy your tickets here.

Cycling Tours

Cycling is a slow but environmentally friendly means of getting around. It also enables you to combine sightseeing with physical exercise. It is easy to rent bikes in some tourist areas, particularly at main train stations from April to October. Bikes can be taken on trains, on the *U-Bahn*, and the *S-Bahn*. For cycling routes, you will find that many newsstands, bookstores, and tourist offices have excellent maps.

DIRECTORY

Airlines

Air Berlin
W airberlin.com

Air Canada
Tel 069-27 11 51 11.
W aircanada.ca

American Airlines
Tel 069-5098 5070.
Tel 800-433 7300 (US).
W AA.com

BMI
W flybmi.com

British Airways
Tel 0421-557 57 58.
Tel 0844-493 0787 (UK).
W britishairways.com

easyJet
W easyjet.com

Germanwings
W germanwings.com

Lufthansa
Tel 069-86 79 97 99
Tel 800-645 3880(US).
W lufthansa.com

Qantas
Tel 069-299 571 421.
W qantas.com

Ryanair
W ryanair.com

United Airlines
Tel 069-86 79 97 99
Tel 800-864 8331 (US).
W united.com

Airport Information

Berlin Airports
Tel 030-60 91 11 50.

Frankfurt am Main
Tel 01806-372 46 36.

Munich
Tel 089-975 00.

Car Rental

Avis
Tel 01806-21 77 02.
W avis.com

Hertz
Tel 01806-33 35 35.
W hertz.com

Sixt Rent-a-Car
Tel 01806-25 25 25.
W sixt.com

Emergency Services

ADAC
Tel 01802-222 222.

AvD
Tel 069-660 63 00.

Train Travel

Deutsche Bahn
National Rail Inquiries:
Tel 01806-99 66 33.

Shopping

Stores in Germany are generally of high quality but many products are not cheap. In Berlin, almost anything can be bought, so long as you know where to look; outside Berlin, you'll discover that in many areas of the country, the tradition of producing handicrafts and various types of folk art continues. A visit to a local market could give you the chance to buy a regional specialty to take home as a souvenir. The vast shopping malls that are springing up in every large city offer a wide choice of stores and top-quality brands.

Markets

A weekly market, known as a *Wochenmarkt*, is held in many towns throughout Germany. In smaller towns, stalls are set up in the market square, while in larger towns and cities, markets may be held in specially designated squares in different neighborhoods. At these markets, you can buy fresh fruit and vegetables, cheeses, and many everyday items. Specialist fairs are often held at weekends – for example *Blumenmärkte*, where flowers are sold, or *Kunstmärkte*, where artists and craftsmen display their work for sale.

Every large town also has its *Flohmarkt* (fleamarket) where, among the masses of junk, pieces of amusing kitsch and genuine antiques can sometimes be found. In Berlin, the **Antik-und Trödelmarkt** is worth a visit.

In Munich, there is a famous market specializing in crafts, antiques, and hardware called **Auer Dult**. This is held during the last weeks of April, July, and October.

Regional Specialities

Almost every state in Germany produces its own regional specialty and although you might not be able to take certain fresh foods back home, you could try them while you are visiting. For example, Lübeck is known for marzipan, while Nuremberg is synonymous with gingerbread. The Spreewald region is known for its pickled cucumbers, while you'll find the cherry jam produced in the Black Forest region is excellent.

In Friesland and Schleswig in the north, marinated herrings and excellent cheeses are worth trying. The hams of Westphalia have a well-deserved reputation, as do sausages from Braunschweig (Brunswick).

Gifts and Souvenirs

Just about every region of Germany has something special to offer. You could buy a beer stein from a beer hall, or a cuckoo clock from the Black Forest, for instance. If you are keen on dressing up, traditional clothes such as lederhosen and dirndl skirts can be found in Bavaria. For children, handmade puppets and marionettes are good gifts, while in Nuremberg there is a wide selection of toys. Don't forget that German optical items such as cameras, binoculars, and lenses are top quality and may be cheaper than at home.

Alcoholic Drinks

Renowned German beers are best drunk straight from the barrel, but it is also worth looking out for the bottled beers that are rarely seen outside Germany.

There are a number of fine German wines, especially those from vineyards in the Mosel and Rhine valleys. Excellent wines are also produced in Bavaria and Baden-Württemberg.

Various types of spirits, as well as herbal and root-flavored liqueurs and bitters, are produced on a large scale. If you visit a monastery, you may be able to buy a bottle of a herbal infusion or a liqueur that is made to a centuries-old recipe.

Shopping in Berlin

Although German cities all boast shopping malls and every town has a shopping district popular with local residents, Berlin stands out with its choice and quality of shops. If it is luxury you want, you must head for the large stores on the Kurfürstendamm, Friedrichstraße, and Potsdamer Platz, where all the major fashion houses and perfume makers have their stores. Alternatively, if you want to explore the smaller boutiques of lesser-known designers, make your way to Berlin's Hackescher Markt in the Mitte district, or to Prenzlauer Berg.

Kaufhaus des Westens, better known as **KaDeWe** in Wittenbergplatz, is the biggest and the best department store in Berlin. Only products of the highest quality are sold in these luxurious halls, where virtually everything you need is on sale – from unusual perfumes and elegant underwear to haute couture, all sold in a system of stores-within-stores. The food hall on the sixth floor is legendary for its restaurant overlooking Tauentzienstrasse.

Galeries Lafayette on Friedrichstraße is nothing less than a slice of Paris placed in the heart of Berlin. Its perfumes, household items, and clothing attract an enormous clientele, many of whom also visit the food counter, which offers a wide range of French specialties. An extraordinary glass cone rises through the middle of the store, reflecting the interiors of the stores.

Another very popular store is **Karstadt** on the Kurfürsten-damm. Although its range of goods is not as broad as that at Galeries Lafayette, there is still an enormous choice and its top-floor restaurant offers excellent views over the city.

New shopping malls are being opened all the time, usually situated conveniently close to S-Bahn stations. *Passagen* (arcades) are massive three-level structures, resembling huge arcaded passageways, which contain an enormous number of stores, ranging from supermarkets and pharmacies to bars, fashion outlets, and bookstores. Like most of the stores in Berlin, they stay open until 8pm during the week and are open on Sundays.

One of the newest shopping malls is the **Potsdamer Platz Arkaden**. Built in October 1998, this is now very popular both as a shopping mall and a meeting place for Berliners and visitors.

A symbol of the old West's resurgence, the shapely **Bikini-Haus** is a reincarnation of a 1950s' shopping mall, with upmarket design and fashion retailers, restaurants, a boutique hotel, a movie theater, and a panoramic view over Berlin Zoo.

Shopping in Other Cities

Most shoppers in Munich make a beeline for the pedestrian precinct in the old town center between Karlsplatz and Marienplatz. Here, you will find many big department stores such as **Ludwig Beck am Rathauseck** and chain stores where you can buy fashion and shoes as well as jewelry, souvenirs, and music. For haute couture in Munich, the big-name stores are concentrated in these streets: Maximilianstrasse, Theatinerstrasse, Residenz-strasse, and Briennerstrasse.

The place to shop for food in Munich is the colorful **Viktualienmarkt** near Marien-platz. This has been the city's main food market for more than 200 years.

The largest and most interesting shopping area in Frankfurt is the Zeil, while in Hamburg it is the Alsterhaus. Hamburg also prides itself on its many fine shopping arcades, several of which are covered and heated, making them ideal for window shopping.

Ceramics and Glass

Porcelain made by Meissen is among the most sought-after in the world but it is expensive. Meissen porcelain can be found in the town itself at the **Staatliche Porzellan-Manufaktur** (see p515) or in several shops situated along the popular Kurfürstendamm in Berlin. Munich's **Porzellan Manufaktur Nymphenburg**, which has a factory and a shop in the grounds of Schloss Nymphenburg (see p525), produces china of similarly exquisite quality. Berlin's **KPM** (Königliche Porzellan-Manufaktur), which has been in operation for over 250 years, also makes excellent porcelain.

German glassware is renowned. Old glassworks in Saxony and Bavaria still make glassware by traditional techniques; for example, beautifully cut and polished crystal tableware and ruby-colored glassware.

Some porcelain and glassware factories operate retail outlets with showrooms. Visitors can arrange to have purchases sent to their home.

Bookstores

When you need a book in English or an American newspaper, **Dussmann English Bookshop** is the place to go in Berlin. In Munich, look for the **Words' Worth** and **Geobuch** for good maps and guides. In Frankfurt, try the **British Bookshop**.

The **Bücherbogen** chain offers a huge choice of books and has several outlets in Berlin and elsewhere; the one under the S-Bahn bridge near Savignyplatz in Berlin has the largest stock.

DIRECTORY

Markets

Antik-und Trödelmarkt
Ostbahnhof, Erich-Steinfurth-Straße, Berlin.
Open 9am–5pm Sun.

Auer Dult
Mariahilfplatz, Munich.
Open last weeks of Apr, Jul & Oct.

Shopping in Berlin

Bikini-Haus
Hardenbergplatz 2, Berlin.
🅦 bikiniberlin.de

Galeries Lafayette
Französische Straße 23, Berlin. **Tel** 030-20 94 80.

KaDeWe
Tauentzienstraße 21–24, Berlin. **Tel** 030-212 10.

Karstadt
Kurfürstendamm 231, Berlin.
Tel 030-88 00 30.

Potsdamer Platz Arkaden
Alte Potsdamer Straße 7, Berlin. **Tel** 030-255 92 70.

Shopping in Other Cities

Ludwig Beck am Rathauseck
Am Marienplatz 11, Munich. **Tel** 089-23 69 10.

Viktualienmarkt
Peterplatz–Frauenstraße, Munich. **Open** Mon–Sat.

Ceramics and Glass

KPM
Wegelystraße 1, Berlin.
Tel 030-39 00 90.

Porzellan Manufaktur Nymphenburg
Schloss Nymphenburg, N. Schloßrondell 8, Munich.
Tel 089-179 19 70.
Odeonsplatz 1, Munich.
Tel 089-28 24 28.

Staatliche Porzellan-Manufaktur
Talstraße 9, Meissen.
Showroom Open
9am–6pm (Nov–Apr: to 5pm). **Tel** 03521-46 82 08.

Bookstores

British Bookshop
Börsenstraße 17, Frankfurt am Main.
Tel 069-28 04 92.

Bücherbogen
Savignyplatz, Berlin.
Tel 030-31 86 95 11.

Dussmann English Bookshop
Friedrichstraße 90, Berlin.
Tel 030-20 25 11 11.

Geobuch
Rosental 6, Munich.
Tel 089-26 50 30.

Words' Worth
Schellingstraße 3, Munich.
Tel 089-280 9141.

Entertainment

With so much on offer in Germany, it is possible to indulge just about any taste, whether you are looking for avant-garde theater and performance art, atmospheric clubs, or prestigious music festivals. Outside Berlin, the larger cosmopolitan cities, such as Munich and Frankfurt, also offer a wide range of entertainment, from classical drama to eclectic nightclubs, from grand opera to discos.

Entertainment Listings

Tourist information centers offer basic information in every city and town, but the most comprehensive guides are in the local press and listings magazines. In Berlin, there are *Tip* and *Zitty*, which are published every other Wednesday. The daily *Berliner Morgenpost* publishes its supplement *bm Live* on Fridays, while *Ticket* comes out on Wednesdays, together with *Tagesspiegel*.

Useful listing magazines in Munich are *In München* and *Münchener Stadtmagazin*. There is also a monthly review in English called *Munich Found,* available from the Tourist Office. You can get a monthly jazz magazine called *Münchener Jazz- Zeitung* in music shops and at jazz cafés and clubs.

In Frankfurt, a magazine detailing events called *Prinz* is on sale from news kiosks. There are also free publications such as *Fritz*, while the *Frankfurter Woche* is available from the tourist office for a small sum.

Booking Tickets

Theater and concert tickets can usually be booked up to two weeks in advance, and you can buy directly at the box office or by telephone. Reserved tickets must be picked up and paid for at least half an hour before the performance. For many performances in Berlin, you can also pre-book tickets at **Ticket Online**.

One Berlin agency that specializes in last-minute ticket purchase is **Hektiket Theaterkassen** on Hardenbergstraße, where you can get tickets on the day, even

up to as little as an hour before a show. These tickets are usually sold at a 50 per cent discount.

Students, senior citizens, and the disabled are entitled to a 50 per cent discount on tickets, for which they must present proof of their status.

Theater

As you would expect in the land of Goethe and Schiller, theatrical traditions are very strong in Germany. Almost every large town has a good local theater. Berlin's most famous theater is the magnificent **Berliner Ensemble**, which was once managed by Bertold Brecht. The **Deutsches Theater** offers an ambitious program, while the **Volksbühne** stages works by young playwrights. Munich has many theaters, with most of the productions in German. A venerable venue is the **Cuvilliéstheater** in the Residenz (*see pp520–21*), while the **Deutsches Theater** offers some foreign plays. The **Kammerspiele** is dedicated to contemporary works.

Frankfurt has a theater that offers productions in English, aptly called the **English Theatre**. You will find a range of old and new plays put on at the city's main theater, the **Schauspiel Frankfurt**.

Classical Music and Dance

Berlin has one of the finest orchestras in the world – the Berlin Philharmonic Orchestra, whose home, the **Philharmonie**, is also one of the world's most beautiful concert halls. The city boasts three opera houses: the **Staatsoper Unter den Linden**

(being renovated until 2018) and the **Komische Oper** are in the eastern part of city, while the **Deutsche Oper Berlin** is in the west. The three opera houses have ballet programs built into their repertoires, and these are performed largely by resident dance companies.

Munich has two opera houses and several distinguished resident orchestras. A visit to the **Bayerische Staatsoper** is a must if you appreciate grand opera and ballet. The **Gasteig** is a modern complex offering a range of classical concerts, large and small. Munich's **Prinzregententheater** is the main venue for ballet and other musical performances.

Frankfurt has a wide choice of musical events. At the **Alte Oper**, there are three halls for orchestral and vocal performances, while the **Jahrhunderthalle** also offers classical recitals and concerts.

Jazz, Rock, and Pop

Berlin is always a popular destination for world-famous musicians, whose concerts are often held in the **Waldbühne**. Numerous music clubs offer daily opportunities to hear good music. Favorite venues are **Quasimodo** in the western part of the city center, **Schlot** in Mitte and **Junction Bar** in Kreuzberg. Good traditional jazz can be heard at Berlin's annual Jazzfest in the first week of November. The most popular rock and pop festival is Berlin Music Week, held every September in Templehof's old aircraft hangars and nightclubs around town.

In Munich in the late evening, you could drop into a small, hip club like **Atomic Café** or go to hear blues, rock, or jazz at **Feierwerk**. Dixieland jazz is played at the **Alabamahalle** and traditional jazz at **Jazzclub Unterfahrt**. There are often free rock concerts in Munich in summer at the Theatron in Olympiapark. Frankfurt has an enthusiastic jazz scene which is centered around *Jazzgasse* (Jazz Alley) or Kleine Bockenheimer Straße. Here, you will find the city's top jazz venue, **Jazzkeller**, in a cellar. If you like to listen to different kinds of live music such as African, Asian, and salsa, try **Brotfabrik**, which also has a café.

Discos in Munich and Frankfurt mainly cater, naturally enough, for a young crowd and play music of all kinds: from chart hits, funk, and techno to heavy metal. Some have a dress policy.

Festivals and Fairs

Germans love festivals and fairs and this country probably has more than most other European countries. The most famous is the Oktoberfest in Munich (see p526), which is a huge event that celebrates beer with two weeks of drinking, from the last week in September. Not to be outdone, wine-drinkers can enjoy a wine festival (Weinfest) in August in the Rhine-Mosel area and in October in the Rhineland. Germany has

produced many of the world's foremost musicians, so classical music festivals are popular and take place in many German towns. To give a few examples, there is a Bach Festival in May in Leipzig (see p515), while Bonn (see p533) is the venue for the International Beethoven Festival from late September. Beginning in late July, Bayreuth (see p512) hosts the annual Opernfest of Richard Wagner's Ring Cycle. However, be aware that you cannot just turn up for a performance here – you will have to book tickets at least a year in advance or else get them with a package holiday.

December brings a rush of fairs. Many towns and cities, including Berlin and Munich, stage a Christmas market (Christkindlmarkt), but the one in Nuremberg is considered to be the most impressive.

Outdoor Activities

Germany is the ideal destination for a range of outdoor activities, including hiking, cycling, fishing, and sailing. It also has a number of winter-sports resorts with first-class ski slopes, the best being in the Bavarian Alps, which lie only an hour's drive from Munich.

There is a tradition of great horsemanship in Germany. Keen riders will find excellent facilities in many areas, as well as the chance to attend international competitions.

Tennis is the second most popular sport (after soccer) and there are several annual professional tournaments. You can play on the many public courts, or find a hotel with its own facilities. Golfers with the appropriate handicap can play on most golf courses simply by paying a green fee.

DIRECTORY

Booking Tickets

Hekticket Theaterkassen
Hardenbergstraße 29d, Berlin. **Tel** 030-23 09 930.

Ticket Online
Tel 01806-447 00 00.
ticketonline.de

Theater

Berliner Ensemble
Bertolt-Brecht-Platz 1, Berlin. **Tel** 030-28 40 81 55.

Cuvilliéstheater
Residenzstraße 1, Munich. **Tel** 089-21 85 19 40.

Deutsches Theater
Schumannstraße 13a, Berlin.
Tel 030-28 44 12 25.

Deutsches Theater
Werner-Heisenberg-Allee 1, Munich.
Tel 089-55 23 44 44.

English Theatre
Kaiserstraße 34, Frankfurt. **Tel** 069-24 23 16 20.

Kammerspiele
Maximillianstraße 28, Munich.
Tel 089-233 966 00.

Schauspiel Frankfurt
Neue Mainzer Straße 17, Frankfurt.
Tel 069-212 494 94.

Volksbühne
Rosa-Luxemburg-Platz, Berlin. **Tel** 030-24 06 57 77.

Classical Music and Dance

Alte Oper
Opernplatz, Frankfurt.
Tel 069-134 04 00.

Bayerische Staatsoper
Max-Joseph-Platz 2, Munich.
Tel 089-21 85 19 20.

Deutsche Oper
Bismarckstraße 35, Berlin.
Tel 030-34 38 43 43.

Gasteig
Rosenheimer Straße 5, Munich. **Tel** 089-480 980.

Jahrhunderthalle
Pffafenwiese, Frankfurt.
Tel 069-360 12 36.

Komische Oper
Behrenstraße 55–57, Berlin.
Tel 030-47 99 74 00.

Philharmonie
Herbert-von-Karajan-Straße 1, Berlin.
Tel 030-25 48 89 99.

Prinzregenten-theater
Prinzregentenplatz 12, Munich. **Tel** 089-21 85 02.

Staatsoper
Unter den Linden 7, Berlin.
Tel 030-20 35 45 55.

Jazz, Rock, and Pop

Alabamahalle
Domagkstraße 33, Munich.
Tel 089-368 14 50.

Atomic Café
Neuturmstraße 5, Munich.
Tel 089-228 30 54.

Brotfabrik
Bachmannstraße 2–4, Frankfurt.
Tel 069-247 90 800.

Feierwerk
Hansastraße 39, Munich.
Tel 089-72 48 80.

Jazzclub Unterfahrt
Einsteinstraße 42, Munich.
Tel 089-448 2794.

Jazzkeller
Kleine Bockenheimer Straße 18a, Frankfurt.
Tel 069-28 85 37.

Junction Bar
Gneisenaustraße 18, Berlin. **Tel** 030-694 66 02.

Quasimodo
Kantstraße 12a, Berlin.
Tel 030-31 80 45 60.

Schlot
Invalidenstraße 117, Berlin. **Tel** 030-448 21 60.

Waldbühne
Am Glockenturm, Berlin.
Tel 030-23 09 93 33.

Where to Stay

Berlin

EAST OF CENTER: Three Little Pigs Hostel Berlin
€
Historic   **Map** E4
Stresemannstraße 66, 10963
Tel *030-263 958 80*
w three-little-pigs.de
Comfortable accommodation set in an old convent building in a vibrant, multicultural area.

EAST OF CENTER: Adlon Kempinski
€€€
Luxury   **Map** E3
Unter den Linden 77, 10117
Tel *030-226 115 55*
w kempinski.com
The Adlon offers exquisitely decorated bedrooms. Facilities include a Michelin-starred gourmet restaurant and a spa.

EAST OF CENTER: Hotel de Rome
€€€
Luxury   **Map** E3
Behrenstraße 37, 10117
Tel *030-460 60 90*
w roccofortecollection.com
A lavish hotel featuring classy furnishings and alfresco dining on a rooftop terrace.

WEST OF CENTER: Altberlin
€€
Modern   **Map** D4
Potsdamerstraße 67, 10785
Tel *030-260 670*
w altberlin-hotel.de
Enjoy great modern amenities in an enviable location. All 50 rooms at this hotel are furnished with exquisite antiques.

WEST OF CENTER: Sofitel Berlin Kurfürstendamm
€€€
Luxury   **Map** C4
Augsburgerstraße 41, 10789
Tel *030-800 99 90*
w sofitel.com
Sleek high-rise in a great location. Unwind at the wellness center, which has a sauna and solariums.

DK Choice

FARTHER AFIELD: Circus €€
Modern
Rosenthalerstraße 1, 10119
Tel *030-200 039 39*
w circus-berlin.de
This fun hotel close to the city's nightlife has high standards of service and is great value for money. Extras on offer range from bike rentals to rickshaw tours and babysitting. The Circus Café serves elaborate breakfasts and good coffee.

FARTHER AFIELD: Ackselhaus
€€€
Boutique
Belforterstraße 21, 10405
Tel *030-443 376 33*
w ackselhaus.de
A beautifully restored 19th-century property with individually designed rooms and suites.

FARTHER AFIELD: Riehmers Hofgarten
€€€
Historic
Yorckstraße 83, 10965
Tel *030-780 988 00*
w riehmers-hofgarten.de
A grand mansion set in an over 200-year-old courtyard. Elegant decor and modern amenities.

Eastern Germany

DRESDEN: Innside by Melia
€€
Modern
Salzgaße 4, 01067
Tel *0351-795 150*
w innside.com
Chic hotel in a central location. Rooms have avant-garde decor, and there is a rooftop bar.

DRESDEN: Schloss Eckberg
€€
Historic
Bautznerstraße 134, 01099
Tel *0351-809 90*
w schloss-eckberg.de
A 19th-century castle with stylish decor, elegant grounds, and a superb restaurant.

DRESDEN: Taschenbergpalais Kempinski
€€€
Luxury
Taschenberg 3, 01067
Tel *0351-491 20*
w kempinski.com
Located right next to the Royal Palace. Most of the luxury rooms have views of the river or the old market square.

DK Choice

LEIPZIG: Steigenberger Grandhotel Handelshof €€€
Luxury
Salzgäßchen 6, 04109
Tel *0341-350 58 10*
w steigenberger.com
The huge rooms at this hotel are decorated in an avant-garde style with lots of color. Superb dining options include two restaurants and a brasserie, while the basement has a large fitness complex with a sauna and Turkish bath. Free Wi-Fi.

DK Choice

WEIMAR: Villa Hentzel €€
Boutique
Bauhausstraße 12, 99423
Tel *03643-865 80*
w hotel-villa-hentzel.de
The 19th-century Villa Hentzel has been home to several writers; for a time, it also played host to the Chilean Embassy. Lovingly renovated, the large rooms are individually furnished and boast touches that are reminders of the building's past. Within walking distance of central Weimar, the hotel is wonderful value for money.

WEIMAR: Best Western Premier Grand Hotel Russischer Hof
€€€
Historic
Goetheplatz 2, 99423
Tel *03643-77 40*
w russischerhof-weimar.de
More than 200 years old, this luxurious hotel has a great café and bakery on site.

WEIMAR: Romantik Hotel Dorotheenhof Weimar
€€€
Luxury
Dorotheenhof 1, 99427
Tel *03643-45 90*
w dorotheenhof.com
This is the place for reasonably priced luxury in superb surroundings. Lovely rooms of various sizes.

Simple but smart decor at Circus, an affordable option in Berlin

Munich

Amalienburg €€
Boutique
Amalienburgstraße 24–26, 81247
Tel *089-891 15 50*
W amalienburg.de
Set in a tranquil corner of the city, the Amalienburg features artistic design touches in its attractive, modern rooms.

Hotel Laimer Hof €€
Historic
Laimerstraße 40, 80639
Tel *089-178 03 80*
W laimerhof.de
A Neo-Renaissance villa with classically furnished rooms. The Laimer Hof provides free bikes to explore the peaceful environs.

DK Choice

Motel One München Sendlinger Tor €€
Modern **Map** B4
Herzog-Wilhelm-Straße 28, 80331
Tel *089-517 772 50*
W motel-one.com
This reliable budget chain has really taken off in Germany, and with good reason. The Munich establishment offers excellent-value rooms with bright turquoise features that lend a certain minimalist elegance. There is also a great café-bar and lounge on site.

Charles Hotel €€€
Luxury
Sophienstraße 28, 80333
Tel *089-544 55 50*
W charleshotel.de
This sumptuous hotel has huge rooms with good views over the nearby botanical gardens.

Cortiina €€€
Boutique
Ledererstraße 8, 80331
Tel *089-242 24 90*
W designhotels.com
Elegant hotel whose individually decorated rooms and cocktail bar ooze creative opulence.

Southern Germany

BAMBERG: St Nepomuk €€€
Gasthöfe and Pensionen
Obere Mülbrücke 9, 96049
Tel *0951-984 20*
W hotel-nepomuk.de
Pleasant, airy rooms with modern facilities at this old timber-framed hotel with an exceptional location on the river.

Distinctive turquoise touches at Motel One München Sendlinger Tor, Munich

BAYREUTH: Ramada Hotel Residenzschloss Bayreuth €€
Modern
Erlangerstraße 37, 95444
Tel *0921-758 50*
W ramada.de
Fairly standard chain hotel with comfortable rooms, a sauna, and a good restaurant.

DK Choice

FREIBURG IM BREISGAU: Zum Roten Bären €€€
Historic
Oberlinden 12, 79098
Tel *0761-38 78 70*
W roter-baeren.de
Germany's oldest hotel, Zum Roten Bären opened in 1120 and became part of the city gate in 1250. The contemporary rooms feature the occasional antique item, providing a sense of history. First-class breakfasts.

HEIDELBERG: Der Europäischer Hof €€€
Luxury
Friedrich-Ebert-Anlage 1, 69117
Tel *06221-5150*
W europaeischerhof.com
Premier hotel with individually decorated rooms, several great restaurants, and a bar.

HEIDELBERG: Zum Ritter St Georg €€€
Historic
Hauptstraße 178, 69117
Tel *06221-1350*
W ritter-heidelberg.de
Housed in a magnificent late-Renaissance mansion in the city center. Not all rooms are en-suite.

NUREMBURG: Le Méridien Grand €€€
Boutique
Bahnhofstraße 1, 90402
Tel *0911-232 20*
W lemeridiennuernberg.com
Hotel with sleek Art Deco and Art Nouveau stylings. Sauna and an excellent regional brasserie.

PASSAU: Wilder Mann €€
Historic
Rathausplatz, 94032
Tel *0851-350 71*
W wilder-mann.com
A centrally located hotel with traditional furniture – including a royal wedding bed.

ROTHENBURG: Gerberhaus €€
Historic
Sptialgasse 25, 91541
Tel *09861-949 00*
W hotel-gerberhaus.de
Stay in an attractive room in this converted 16th-century tannery.

STUTTGART: Hotel Espenlaub €
Modern
Charlottenstraße 27, 70182
Tel *0711-210 910*
W stadthotels-erkurt.de
Basic hotel with bright rooms and a modest breakfast buffet.

STUTTGART: Der Zauberlehrling €€€
Boutique
Rosenstr. 38, 70182
Tel *0711-237 77 70*
W zauberlehrling.de
Located in a hip district, this hotel has tastefully themed rooms.

WÜRZBURG: Hotel Würzburger Hof €€
Modern
Barbarossaplatz 2, 97070
Tel *0931-538 14*
W hotel-wuerzburgerhof.de
Richly decorated rooms come in a range of styles and prices.

Western Germany

BONN: Schlosshotel Kommende Ramersdorf €€
Historic
Oberkasselerstraße 10, 53227
Tel *0228-440 734*
W schlosshotel-kommende-ramersdorf.de
A beautiful castle with antique-filled rooms and a good eatery.

A home away from home at the Fairmont Hotel Vier Jahreszeiten, Hamburg

DK Choice

COLOGNE: Excelsior Hotel Ernst
€€€

Luxury
Trankgaße 1–5, 50667
Tel *0221-2701*
W excelsiorhotelernst.com
A historical and truly grand hotel beside Cologne Cathedral, with rooms and suites that are contemporary but retain timeless, classical features. The several dining options here include the Michelin-starred gourmet restaurant Taku.

COLOGNE: Hotel im Wasserturm
€€€

Boutique
Kaygaße 2, 50676
Tel *0221-200 80*
W hotel-im-wasserturm.de
Housed in a former water tower. The oddly shaped rooms are fitted with all modern amenities.

FRANKFURT AM MAIN: Hamburger Hof
€€

Modern
Poststraße 10–12, 60329
Tel *069-271 396 90*
W hamburgerhof.com
A modern hotel with sleek design and a breakfast buffet.

FRANKFURT AM MAIN: Hessischer Hof
€€€

Luxury
Friedrich-Ebert-Anlage 40, 60325
Tel *069-754 00*
W hessischer-hof.de
Exquisitely styled, with well-equipped classic rooms, some furnished with antiques.

MAINZ: Hotel am Römerwall
€

Modern
Am Römerwall 51–55, 55131
Tel *06131-25 77*
W roemerwallhotel.de
A *Jugendstil* villa with simple but comfortable rooms in a quiet, leafy area near the Old Town.

MAINZ: Hof Ehrenfels
€€

Historic
Grebenstraße 5–7, 55116
Tel *06131-971 23 40*
W hof-ehrenfels.de
Housed in a 15th-century convent overlooking the cathedral, this smart, half-timbered hotel features a rustic wine bar.

MAINZ: Hyatt Regency Mainz
€€€

Luxury
Malakoff-Terraße 1, 55116
Tel *06131-731 234*
W mainz.regency.hyatt.com
This sophisticated five-star hotel, with a busy beer garden, is housed in a striking building overlooking the Rhine.

TRIER: Becker's
€€

Boutique
Olewigerstraße 206, 54295
Tel *0651-938 080*
W weinhaus-becker.de
Stylish vineyard guesthouse in a wine-producing suburb of Trier. The room decor is reminiscent of Japanese minimalism.

TRIER: Villa Hügel
€€€

Luxury
Bernhardstraße 14, 54295
Tel *0651-937 100*
W hotel-villa-huegel.de
This upscale Art Nouveau villa sports cheerful rooms and a sun terrace, with lovely valley views.

Northern Germany

BREMEN: Heldt
€

Gasthöfe and Pensionen
Friedhofstraße 41, 28213
Tel *0421-436 03 00*
W hotel-heldt.de
The Heldt is a contemporary small hotel with tasteful rooms, as well as apartments. Services include free bike rental.

BREMEN: Atlantic Grand Hotel
€€

Historic
Bredenstraße 2, 28195
Tel *0421-620 620*
W atlantic-hotels.de
Old-town hotel with stylish rooms. The rooftop lounge is great for city views.

HAMBURG: Gastwerk Hotel Hamburg
€€

Historic
Beim Alten Gaswerk 3, 22761
Tel *040-890 624 24*
W gastwerk.com
Housed in an impressively renovated gasworks plant. Industrial-style rooms and lofts feature all modern amenities, and there is an exceptional spa.

DK Choice

HAMBURG: Fairmont Hotel Vier Jahreszeiten
€€€

Historic
Neuer Jungfernstieg 9–14, 20354
Tel *040-349 40*
W fairmont-hvj.com
An elegant hotel with many rooms overlooking the Alster, and some with a private balcony. Subtle luxury, subdued design, superb service, and a great spa and fitness club are some of the features. Guests can also choose from several bars and restaurants, including the Haerlin, which has two Michelin stars.

HANNOVER: Central-Hotel Kaiserhof
€€€

Historic
Ernst-August-Platz 4, 30159
Tel *0511-368 30*
W centralhotel.de
Classically furnished guest rooms in a historic building. The acclaimed restaurant serves trout from the courtyard fountain.

LÜBECK: Kaiserhof
€€

Historic
Kronsforder Allee 11–13, 23560
Tel *0451-703 301*
W kaiserhof-luebeck.de
A grand old hotel with impressive classic rooms, and a seafood restaurant.

MÜNSTER: Romantik Hotel Hof zur Linde
€€€

Modern
Handorfer Werseufer 1, 48157
Tel *0251-327 50*
W hof-zur-linde.de
A lovely farm hotel with magnificent river views. Suites and cottages have their own fireplaces.

Key to Price Guide *see page 546*

Where to Eat and Drink

Berlin

EAST OF CENTER: Nante-Eck   €
Traditional German   **Map** E3
Unter den Linden 35, 10117
Tel *030-224 872 57*
Berlin-style cheap eats are on
offer at this casual pub. Fill up
on calf's liver with port sauce
or meatballs with mustard, and
wash them down with local beer.

**EAST OF CENTER: Zur
Letzten Instanz**   €€
Traditional German   **Map** F3
Waisenstraße 14–16, 10179
Tel *030-242 55 28*   **Closed** *Sun*
Berlin's oldest pub, dating from
1621. Classic fare including
eisbein (pork knuckle) and
rinderroulade (beef olive) is
served in a wood-paneled room.

EAST OF CENTER: Facil   €€€
Modern Fusion   **Map** D4
Potsdamerstraße 3, 10785
Tel *030-590 051 234*
A glass-roofed pavilion is the
backdrop for famed chef Michael
Kempf's inspired cuisine, which
uses the freshest market produce
and subtly exotic spices.

DK Choice

**EAST OF CENTER:
Fischers Fritz**   €€€
Modern French   **Map** E3
Charlottenstraße 49, 10117
Tel *030-203 363 63*
The creative flair of chef Christian
Lohse has won Fischers Fritz
two Michelin stars. The meat
dishes are tempting, but it is
the seafood dishes that get the
most accolades. Try the Breton
lobster roasted with salt, chili
and coriander, or the roast
scallops with caramelized
Hokkaido pumpkin and Jaipur
curry. The fixed-price lunches
are good value.

**WEST OF CENTER:
Café am Neuen See**   €
German/Mediterranean   **Map** C4
Lichtensteinallee 2, 10787
Tel *030-254 493 00*
This café has a lakeside terrace
and a menu offering Bavarian
snacks and draught beers, as well
as Italian mains such as pizzas.
Cozy seating in winter, plus boat
rentals and a sandpit for kids.

DK Choice

**WEST OF CENTER:
Esswein am Fasanenplatz**   €€
Modern German   **Map** B4
Fasanenstraße 40, 10719
Tel *030-889 292 88*   **Closed** *Mon*
Esswein is making waves on
Berlin's culinary scene thanks
to its contemporary German
cooking. The seasonal menu
may feature *Pfälzer Wurstsalat*
(Rhineland sausage with cheese
and bread), or *Ochsen Fetzen*
(ox slices baked in a ragout
of grapes, mushrooms, and
chestnuts). Choose from a
selection of more than 40 Mosel
wines to accompany the meal.

**FARTHER AFIELD:
Blockhaus Nikolskoe**   €€
German
Nikolskoer Weg 15, 14109
Tel *030-805 29 14*
This restaurant occupies a *dacha*
(country house) built for the heir
to the Russian throne in 1819.
The food, especially the fresh fish
and local game, suits the lovely
views and waterside setting.

FARTHER AFIELD: Pasternak   €€
Russian/Jewish
Knaackstraße 22/24, 10405
Tel *030-441 33 99*
A long-time favorite with Berlin's
sizeable Russian community,
Pasternak prides itself on its
authentic fare. The focus is on
a rich assortment of *zakuski*

Price Guide	
Prices are based on a three-course meal for one, with half a bottle of house wine, and all extra charges.	
€	under €40
€€	€40 to €80
€€€	over €80

(starters), but do not overlook the
blini (buckwheat pancakes filled
with spinach and cheese, salmon
and horseradish, or caviar).

Eastern Germany

DK Choice

DRESDEN: Schillergarten   €
German
Schillerplatz 9, 01309
Tel *0351-811 990*
Located in a historic building
next to the Blau Wunder
bridge, this fine pub and
restaurant is the perfect
place to eat well and at a
reasonable price in the city
center. Sample great local
food, including first-class
bratwurst, as well as an
extensive range of beers.
There is also a wonderful
summer terrace on the
embankment of the Elbe
River. Reserve ahead.

**DRESDEN: Sternerestaurant
Caroussel**   €€€
Fine Dining
Königstraße 14, 01097
Tel *0351-800 30*   **Closed** *Sun & Mon*
Expect only the finest
contemporary fare from this
Michelin-starred restaurant in the
magnificent Bulow Palace Hotel.

LEIPZIG: Auerbachs Keller   €€
German
Grimmaischestraße 2–4, 04109
Tel *0341-216 100*
One of Leipzig's oldest eateries,
with a great selection of beers to
wash down the superior German
cuisine that features lots of game.
Reservations are recommended.

LEIPZIG: Zest   €€
Modern Fusion
Bornaischestraße 54, 04277
Tel *0341-231 91 26*
A fresh and creative take on
modern European food. There
are plenty of vegetarian dishes
on the menu, and the great
prices make it worth the short
trip out of the city center.

Chandeliers and candlelight at the Michelin-starred Fischers Fritz, Berlin

WEIMAR:
Zum Schwarzen Bären €
German
Markt 20, 99423
Tel *03643-853 847*
One of Weimar's oldest restaurants, Zum Schwarzen Bären offers a Thuringian gastropub experience right in the center of town. Simple, tasty food, including great bratwurst.

DK Choice

WEIMAR:
Anna Amalia €€€
Fine Dining
Geleitstraße 8, 99423
Tel *03643-495 60*
Located in the Hotel Elephant, this Michelin-starred gourmet restaurant offers contemporary dining in a historic 17th-century building. The tasting menu is an eight-course extravaganza featuring outstanding food, as well as a range of fine wines. Visit the Anna bistro on the charming garden terrace for a simpler, cheaper option.

Munich

DK Choice

Wirtshaus in der Au €
Regional German
Lilienstraße 51, 81669
Tel *089-448 14 00*
Waitresses dart around in traditional *dirndl* dresses at this lovely Bavarian inn. The dumplings on offer include spinach and beetroot versions. They have also published a cookbook and run a dumpling restaurant – the Münchner Knödelei – on the Oktoberfest grounds during the festival.

The popular outdoor dining area at Wirtshaus in der Au, Munich

Café Glockenspiel €€
International **Map** C4
Marienplatz 28, 80331
Tel *089-26 42 56* **Closed** *Sun dinner*
Café-restaurant with magnificent rooftop views from its terrace. Menu highlights include sea bass with lemon hollandaise, and lamb saddle served on Parmesan polenta.

Tavernetta €€
Italian **Map** D4
Hildegardstraße 9, 80539
Tel *089-21 26 94 24* **Closed** *Sun*
Sample fine Italian fare, including seafood pastas and satisfying *antipasti* such as courgette and wild mushroom *carpaccio*. Save room for the tiramisu.

Weinhaus Neuner €€
International/Regional **Map** B4
Herzogspitalstraße 8, 80331
Tel *089-260 39 54* **Closed** *Sun*
Smart wine bar featuring a menu with strong Mediterranean influences. Diners can also enjoy a range of piquant Bavarian mustard sauces.

Restaurant Pfistermühle €€€
International **Map** C4
Pfisterstraße 4, 80331
Tel *089-237 038 65* **Closed** *Sun*
A small, seasonal and regionally inspired menu is served under elegant 16th-century arches. Reserve in advance.

Southern Germany

BAMBERG: Hoffmanns
Steak & Fish €€
International
Schillerplatz 7, 96047
Tel *0951-700 08 85* **Closed** *Sun*
Renowned for its perfect steaks, Hoffmanns is also credited with introducing nouvelle cuisine to the city. The menu has a range of innovative dishes.

FREIBURG IM BREISGAU:
Hausbrauerei Feierling €
German
Gerberau 46, 79098
Tel *0761-24 34 80*
Cheerful microbrewery with a wood-and-copper interior and Freiburg's best beer garden. First-class pub food, including giant schnitzels.

FREIBURG IM BREISGAU:
Englers Weinkrügle €€
Regional German
Konviktstraße 12, 79098
Tel *0761-383 115*
A wood-paneled *weinstube* (wine bar) with great regional food and an amazing Black Forest dessert: cherries in hot liqueur with vanilla ice cream.

HEIDELBERG:
Zum Roten Ochsen €€
German
Hauptstraße 217, 69117
Tel *06221-209 77*
The collectables and sepia photos on the walls of this atmospheric student haunt bear witness to its popularity since the early 19th century.

HEIDELBERG: Simplicissimus €€€
French
Ingrimstraße 16, 69117
Tel *06221-673 25 88* **Closed** *Sun*
Superb French cuisine, including imaginative beef, veal, and seafood concoctions. Sit in the intimate dining room or in the pretty, flower-filled courtyard.

NUREMBURG:
Bratwurstglöcklein €
Regional German
Waffenhof 5, 90402
Tel *0911-227 625* **Closed** *Sun*
Located in a historic inn dating back to 1313, Bratwurstglöcklein serves Franconian set meals consisting of dumpling soup, pork knuckle, and sausages simmered in onions and vinegar.

NUREMBURG: Essigbrätlein €€€
International
Weinmarkt 3, 90403
Tel *0911-225 131* **Closed** *Sun & Mon*
An intimate little restaurant with remarkable food, wine, and service. The daily menu often features fish and exquisite desserts. Reserve in advance.

PASSAU: Heilig Geist €€
Regional German
Heilig-Geist-Gaße 4, 94032
Tel *0851-26 07* **Closed** *Wed*
Rustic wine bar with tiled stoves. On the menu is Bavarian food – mostly local fish, pork, and beef. Ask for a table in the courtyard.

Elegant Art Nouveau decor at Hamburg's Café Paris

ROTHENBURG: Hotel-Restaurant Kloster-Stüble €€
Regional German
Herrngaße 21, 91541
Tel *09861-93 88 90*
Popular inn in a 1534 farmhouse. Relish delicacies such as pork roast with crackling, mushrooms, and bread dumplings. Fine town views from the terrace.

STUTTGART: Calwer-Eck-Bräu €€
Regional German
Calwerstraße 31, 70173
Tel *0711-22 24 94 40*
Stuttgart's oldest microbrewery features organically produced, seasonal beers. It also serves typical local food, including *maultaschen* (a type of ravioli).

STUTTGART: Délice €€€
International
Hauptstätterstraße 61, 70178
Tel *0711-640 32 22*
This intimate, seven-table restaurant offers inventive high-quality gourmet food and an award-winning wine list.

WÜRZBURG: Ratskeller €€
Regional German
Langgasse 1, 97070
Tel *0931-130 21*
Reliable regional food in the cellars of the city's former town hall. The cinnamon and Silvaner white-wine soup is a must-try.

Western Germany

BONN: Zur Lindenwirtin Aennchen €€
International
Aennchenplatz 2, 53173
Tel *0228-312 051*   **Closed** *Sun*
A romantic restaurant with impeccable service. The kitchen produces international dishes with a strong bias toward French fare. There is a carefully chosen wine list as well.

COLOGNE: Alcazar €
French/German
Bismarckstraße 39a, 50672
Tel *0221-515 733*
An institution in Cologne's nightlife quarter, this appealing little bar-restaurant fuses French and German cuisines. Lunch is the best bet for a table, since evenings are often packed.

COLOGNE: Il Carpaccio €€
Italian
Lindenstraße 5, 50674
Tel *0221-236 487*   **Closed** *Sun*
Relish fantastic pasta and other classic Italian dishes prepared with fresh, top-quality ingredients in a stylish setting. Remarkable wine selection. Live music at weekends.

COLOGNE: Maitre €€€
French
Olympiaweg 2, 50933
Tel *0221-485 360* **Closed** *Mon & Tue*
The gourmet restaurant of the Landhaus Kuckuck Hotel has a reputation for its fine cuisine, as well as its well-stocked wine cellar. The frequently changing menu uses plenty of seasonal produce.

DK Choice

FRANKFURT AM MAIN: Restaurant Villa Rothschild €€€
Gourmet French
Im Rothschildpark 1, 61462
Tel *06174-290 80*   **Closed** *Sun & Mon*
Situated in a castle-like mansion, this Michelin-starred restaurant is one of the best in Germany and a must-visit for gourmands. Chef Christian Eckhardt's team specializes in imaginative versions of French haute cuisine, complemented by the extensive selection of wines and champagnes. Book ahead.

Northern Germany

BREMEN: Ratskeller €€
German
Am Markt, 28195
Tel *0421-32 16 76*
Housed in Germany's oldest wine cellar, Ratskeller has an extensive wine selection and serves tasty food in a magnificent setting.

HAMBURG: Café Paris €€
French
Rathausstraße 4, 20095
Tel *040-325 277 77*
Enjoy delicious French food, coffee, and cakes in this gorgeous former butchery with Art Nouveau-tiled walls and ceiling. The bistro menu also has oysters and steak tartare.

DK Choice

HAMBURG: Die Bank €€€
International
Hohe Bleichen 17, 20354
Tel *040-238 00 30*   **Closed** *Sun*
Inside a magnificent historic bank building, this elegant dining hall is always buzzing. Chef Thomas Fischer creates unexpected variations of well-known local dishes, with an emphasis on fresh fish and vegetables. The wine list is equally impressive. Expect a business clientele for lunch and an arty crowd for dinner.

HANNOVER: Pier 51 €€
International
Rudolf-von-Bennigsen-Ufer 51, 30173
Tel *0511-807 18 00*
Built on a pier jutting over Lake Masch, this is a stylish, award-winning restaurant offering delicious light fish, meat, and pasta dishes. Enjoy a cocktail on the elegant terrace afterward.

HANNOVER: Clichy €€€
French
Weissekreuzstraße 31, 30161
Tel *0511-312 447*   **Closed** *Sun*
A beautiful restaurant serving modern interpretations of classic French cuisine with some German and Italian influences. Try one of their fish specialties.

MÜNSTER: Villa Medici €€
Italian
Goethestraße 96, 64839
Tel *0251-342 18* **Closed** *Sun & Mon*
Dine on well-balanced, imaginative, and wonderfully presented food in one of Germany's best Italian restaurants. The multi-course set menu changes monthly.

AUSTRIA

Austria has existed as a country for less than 100 years but, despite inauspicious beginnings, has thrived thanks to its position at the heart of Europe. Visitors are attracted by the glories of its Imperial Habsburg past, especially in the capital, Vienna. Austria also has a strong musical tradition and great natural beauty, especially in the Alps and the valley of the Danube.

Present-day Austria emerged in 1919, when the lands of its former empire were granted independence, as a curiously shaped, landlocked country. It is bordered by Switzerland and Germany to the west and north. Along the rest of its border lie the former lands of the old Habsburg Empire, the Czech Republic, Slovakia, Hungary, Slovenia, and the South Tyrol. The regions of the west, the Vorarlberg and the Tyrol, are mountainous, dominated by the eastern Alps. This is where you will find the most familiar images of Austria: well-appointed skiing resorts, snow-capped peaks, and beautiful valleys cloaked in forest.

The Alps are not the traditional heart of Austria – this lies in the regions of Upper and Lower Austria in the northeast, where the Danube (Donau) flows eastwards across the country for 360 km (225 miles). Vienna stands at a point just beyond where the great river emerges from the mountains to flow into the Hungarian plain. The east of the country is more populous, with more agriculture and industry.

History

In the 1st millennium BC, settlements in the region of present-day Austria prospered from mining iron and salt. One settlement, Hallstatt, has given its name to an important Iron Age culture that spread across Europe. It was iron that first drew the Romans to occupy the region, where they established the provinces of Rhaetia, Noricum, and Pannonia, making the Danube the frontier of their empire. When the Romans withdrew, the region was settled by Germanic tribes, such as the Alemanni and the Bavarians, and Slavs, but it was the German-speaking peoples who prevailed.

The geographical kernel of Austria (Österreich) was the Ostmark (eastern march or border county) established by Charlemagne in the 9th century to protect the frontier of his empire. In the 10th century, the Babenbergs acquired the county, which was elevated to a dukedom in 1156. Their dynasty died out in the 13th century and their lands were fought over until they came under the

Ruined castle of Aggstein overlooking the Danube in the Wachau region

◀ The magnificent interior of the Vienna State Opera House

control of Rudolf of Habsburg, who was elected Holy Roman Emperor in 1273.

Over the next three centuries, the Habsburg domains grew, occasionally by conquest, but usually by means of marriages and inheritances. In time, it became a matter of course that they were elected as Holy Roman Emperors.

From the 15th century, Turkish invasions threatened the Habsburg lands. In 1683, the Turks laid siege to Vienna, but they were dispersed by a relieving army. This marked the start of many successful campaigns in the Balkans. In the 18th century, Austria was a major power, although the rise of Prussia and Napoleon's occupation of Vienna in 1809 dented Habsburg pride. The Austrian empire was considerably weakened in the 19th century by the growth of nationalist movements, but Vienna enjoyed its heyday as a great cosmopolitan European capital.

After World War I, the defeated Austrian Empire was dismembered and countries such as Czechoslovakia and Hungary gained their independence. There

The Central, one of the grandest of Vienna's coffee houses

followed bitter struggles between Right and Left for control of the new Austrian republic. The country was annexed by Germany in 1938 and then, following Hitler's defeat in 1945, came under Allied control until 1955, when it became a sovereign state once more. As a keen member of the EU, Austria has flourished economically, but the old political divisions have arisen. The far-right FPÖ (then led by Jörg Haider) were part of government coalitions from 2000 – resulting in international outrage – until the Social Democratic party (SPÖ) took over in 2006. Elections in 2013 saw a

Exploring Austria

Austria's main attractions are the alpine resorts in the west of the country around Innsbruck and the capital, Vienna, in the east. In between, there are many other sights worth seeking out: ancient monasteries and castles, well-preserved medieval cities, such as Salzburg and Graz, the picturesque lakes of the Salzkammergut region, and the scenic stretch of the Danube known as the Wachau. Road and rail communications along the main axis of the country between Vienna, Linz, Salzburg, and Innsbruck are very good.

Sights at a Glance

1. *Vienna pp556–65*
2. Eisenstadt
3. Graz
4. Melk and the Wachau
5. Linz
6. Hallstatt
7. Salzburg
8. Innsbruck

Skiing at the fashionable resort of Kitzbühel in the Austrian Alps

For hotels and restaurants see p574 and p575

sharp rise in votes for the FPÖ, now led by H.C. Strache. In 2013, after lengthy negotiations, a coalition was formed between the SPÖ and the conservative People's Party (ÖVP).

Language and Culture

Austria is linguistically homogenous, with 98 percent of the population speaking German. There are, however, considerable differences in dialect between the various regions.

Culturally, Austria is synonymous with music, the long list of great Austrian composers including Mozart, Haydn, Schubert, and Mahler, not forgetting the Strausses, father and son, and their famous waltzes. Vienna's intellectual and artistic life enjoyed an extraordinary flowering in the late 19th and early 20th century with the Secession movement in painting, architecture, and design. It was also the period of Sigmund Freud's investigations, which laid the foundations of modern psychology.

KEY DATES IN AUSTRIAN HISTORY

c.800 BC Rise of Hallstatt culture

15 BC Noricum occupied by Romans

AD 976–1246 Babenberg dynasty rules Eastern March of the Holy Roman Empire

1276 Rudolf of Habsburg ruler of Austria

1519 Charles V is elected Holy Roman Emperor

1618–48 Thirty Years' War

1683 Siege of Vienna

1740–80 Reign of Maria Theresa

1805 Napoleon defeats Austrians at Austerlitz

1815 Congress of Vienna

1848 Revolutions throughout Habsburg Empire

1918 Defeat in World War I brings Habsburg rule to an end – Austria declared republic

1938 Anschluss – Austria absorbed by Germany

1945–55 Vienna occupied by Allies

1994 Austria joins EU

2004 Elfriede Jelinek receives Nobel Prize for Literature

2006 After FPÖ party splits in 2005, Social Democrats defeat conservatives in elections

2008 Jörg Haider dies

2009 200th anniversary of the death of composer Joseph Haydn

2010 Heinz Fischer of the SPÖ wins the presidential election with just under 80 percent of the vote

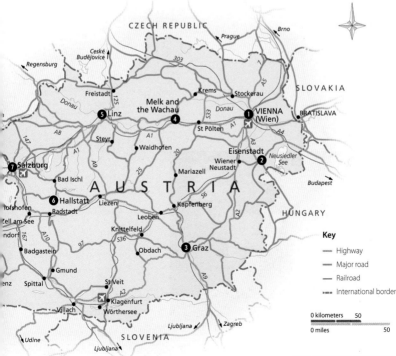

Key

— Highway

— Major road

— Railroad

▬▪▬ International border

0 kilometers 50

0 miles 50

For keys to symbols *see back flap*

❶ Vienna

Greater Vienna has a population of 1.6 million, but the Austrian capital is a compact city with many of the important sights, especially those that date from the Habsburg era, clustered around the Hofburg, the former imperial court. In the mid-19th century, the city's old defenses were pulled down and a wide circular boulevard, the Ringstrasse, was built linking new political and cultural institutions, such as Vienna's great art gallery, the Kunsthistorisches Museum. Completed in the 1880s, the Ringstrasse still defines the Innere Stadt, or heart of the city. The Danube (Donau) river flows through the east of the city, where it has been canalized to prevent flooding.

Sights at a Glance

① *Hofburg pp558–60*
② Burgtheater
③ Stephansdom
④ Staatsoper
⑤ Naturhistorisches Museum
⑥ Kunsthistorisches Museum
⑦ MuseumsQuartier Wien
⑧ Freud Museum
⑨ Museum of Applied Arts
⑩ Secession Building
⑪ Karlskirche
⑫ Albertina

Greater Vienna *(see inset map)*

⑬ Prater
⑭ Belvedere
⑮ Schönbrunn Palace and Gardens

Lipizzaner stallion at the Spanish Riding School in the Hofburg

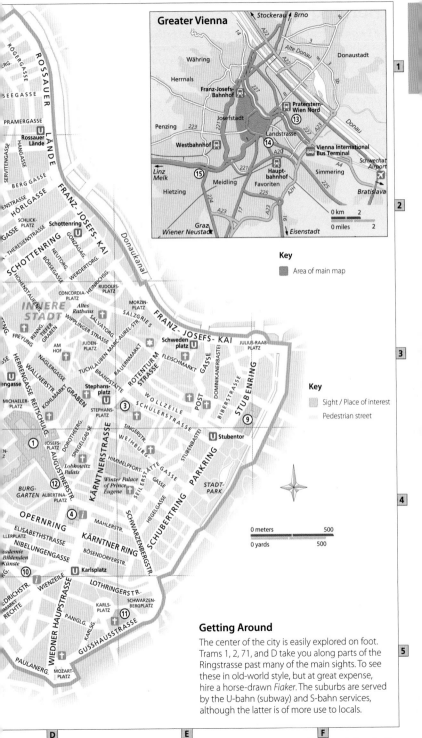

Greater Vienna

Key

Area of main map

Key

Sight / Place of interest

Pedestrian street

Getting Around

The center of the city is easily explored on foot. Trams 1, 2, 71, and D take you along parts of the Ringstrasse past many of the main sights. To see these in old-world style, but at great expense, hire a horse-drawn *Fiaker*. The suburbs are served by the U-bahn (subway) and S-bahn services, although the latter is of more use to locals.

① Hofburg

What began as a small fortress in 1275 grew over the centuries into a vast palace, the Hofburg. It was the seat of Austrian power for over six centuries, and successive rulers were all anxious to leave their mark. The various buildings range in style from Gothic to late 19th-century Neo-Renaissance. The complex was still expanding up until a few years before the Habsburgs fell from power in 1918. The presence of the imperial court had a profound effect on the surrounding area, with noble families competing to site their palaces as close as possible to the Hofburg.

★ **Augustinerkirche**
The former parish church of the Habsburgs houses the spectacular late 18th-century tomb of Maria Christina, Maria Theresa's favorite daughter, by Antonio Canova.

★ **Spanish Riding School**
The white Lipizzaner horses are stabled in the Stallburg opposite the Riding School itself, where they are trained and give performances.

KEY
Entrance

① **The Schatzkammer** (rooms containing the Hofburg's collection of treasure) are housed in the Alte Burg, the core of the old palace.

② **The Michaelertor** is the gate through which visitors reach the older parts of the palace.

③ **Stallburg**

④ **Statue of Joseph II** (1806) in Josefsplatz

⑤ **The Albertina** houses a collection of Old Master drawings and prints.

⑥ **Burggarten**

⑦ **The Burgtor** or outer gate was built to a design by Peter Nobile in 1821–4.

⑧ **Heldenplatz**

⑨ **The Burgkapelle**, the Hofburg's chapel, is where the famous Vienna Boys' Choir sings.

Prunksaal
The showpiece of the Austrian National Library (1722–35) is the grand, wood-paneled Prunksaal, or Hall of Honor.

For hotels and restaurants see p574 and p575

Mozart Memorial (1896)
Viktor Tilgner's statue of
the composer stands
just inside the
Ringstrasse entrance.

VISITORS' CHECKLIST

Practical Information
Michaelerplatz 1, A-1010.

Transport
Ⓤ Stephansplatz, Herrengasse,
Volkstheater. 🚌 48A, 57A. 🚊 D,
1, 2, 71. For details of museums,
see p560. Ⓦ **hofburg.wien.info**

Neue Burg
A monument to
the great general,
Eugene of Savoy
(1663–1736), stands in
front of the newest
wing of the palace,
completed in 1913.

Volksgarten

★ State Apartments
The table in the state
banqueting hall is laid as
it used to be in the latter
part of the reign of Franz
Joseph I (1848–1916).

Schweizertor
This 16th-century gateway leads
to the Schweizerhof, the oldest
part of the Hofburg, originally a
stronghold with four towers.

Exploring the Hofburg Complex

The vast Hofburg complex contains the former imperial apartments and treasuries (Schatzkammer) of the Habsburgs, several museums, a chapel, a church, the Austrian National Library, the Winter Riding School, and the President of Austria's offices. The entrance to the imperial apartments and the treasuries is through the Michaelertor on Michaelerplatz.

10th-century crown of the Holy Roman Empire, Schatzkammer

Portrait of the Empress Elisabeth by Winterhalter (1865)

Neue Burg

Heldenplatz. **Tel** 01-5252 4484. **Open** 10am–6pm Wed–Mon.

The massive curved Neue Burg on Heldenplatz was added to the Hofburg in 1881–1913. Archaeological finds from Ephesus are on display in the **Ephesos Museum**, while pianos that belonged to Beethoven, Schubert, and Haydn are housed in the musical instrument museum – the **Sammlung alter Musikinstrumente**. The weapons collection in the **Hofjagd und Rüstkammer** is one of the finest in Europe. There is also an excellent ethnological collection – the **Weltmuseum Wien**, as well as collections from the Kunsthistorisches Museum (see p562).

Augustinerkirche

Augustinerstraße 3. **Tel** 01-533 7099. **Open** daily. hochamt.at

The church has one of the best-preserved 14th-century Gothic interiors in Vienna. In the Loreto Chapel are a series of silver urns that contain the hearts of the Habsburg family. The church is also celebrated for its music, with masses by Schubert or Haydn performed here on Sundays and holidays.

State Apartments

Michaelerkuppel-Feststiege. **Tel** 01-533 7570. **Open** 9am–5pm daily. hofburg-wien.at

The State Apartments (Kaiserappartements) in the Reichskanzleitrakt (1726–30) and the Amalienburg (1575) include the rooms used by Franz Joseph from 1857 to 1916, Empress Elisabeth's apartments from 1854 to 1898, and those where Czar Alexander I lived during the Congress of Vienna in 1815.

Spanish Riding School

Tel 01-533 9031. **Open** for performances & morning training Tue–Sun (except Jul). **Closed** public hols. some areas. srs.at

The Spanish Riding School is believed to have been founded in 1572 to cultivate the classic skills of *haute école* horsemanship. By breeding and training horses from Spain, the Habsburgs formed the Spanische Reitschule. Today, 80-minute shows take place in the building known as the Winter Riding School, built in 1729–35 to a design by Josef Emanuel Fischer von Erlach.

Schatzkammer

Schweizerhof. **Tel** 01-525 240. **Open** 10am–6pm Wed–Mon. **Closed** Jan 1, May 1, Nov 1, Dec 25. khm.at

Treasures amassed during centuries of Habsburg rule are displayed in 21 rooms, known as the Schatzkammer or Treasury. They include relics of the Holy Roman Empire, the crown jewels, and liturgical objects of the imperial court. Admire the dazzling gold, silver, and porcelain once used at state banquets.

Burgkapelle

Schweizerhof. **Tel** 01-533 9927. **Open** 10am–2pm Mon–Thu, 11am–1pm Fri. **Closed** Jan 1, Nov 1, Dec 8, Jul & Aug. Vienna Boys' Choir: Jan–Jun & Sep–Dec: 9:15am Sun (book by phone). hofburgkapelle.at

From the Schweizerhof, steps lead up to the Burgkapelle, originally constructed in 1296. The interior has Gothic statues in canopied niches. On Sundays, visitors can hear the Wiener Sängerknaben, the Vienna Boys' Choir (see p573).

Burggarten and Volksgarten

Burgring/Opernring/Dr-Karl-Renner-Ring. **Open** daily.

Some of the space left around the Hofburg after Napoleon had razed part of the city walls was transformed by the Habsburgs into gardens.

The Volksgarten opened to the public in 1820, but the Burggarten was the palace's private garden until 1918.

Ornamental pond in the Volksgarten, with Burgtheater in the background

② Burgtheater

Universitätsring 2, A-1014. **Tel** 01-51444 4145. **U** Schottentor. 🚋 1, 71, D. **Open** for performances. **Closed** Good Fri, Dec 24; Jul & Aug (exc for guided tours). 🎭 🛗 📷 afternoons (call 01-5144 44140). **W** **burgtheater.at**

The Burgtheater is the most prestigious stage in the German-speaking world. The original theater, built in Maria Theresa's reign, was replaced in 1888 by today's Italian Renaissance-style building by Karl von Hasenauer and Gottfried Semper. It closed for refurbishment in 1897 after the discovery that several seats had no view of the stage. At the end of World War II, a bomb devastated the building, leaving only the side wings containing the Grand Staircases intact. The restoration was so successful that today it is hard to tell the new parts from the old.

Detail from the Wiener Neustädter Altar in the Stephansdom

③ Stephansdom

Stephansplatz 3, A-1010. **Tel** 01-51552 3526. **U** Stephansplatz. 🚌 1A, 2A. **Open** daily. 🛗 **W** **stephanskirche.at**

The Stephansdom, with its magnificent glazed-tile roof, is the heart and soul of Vienna. It is no mere coincidence that the urns containing the entrails of some of the Habsburgs lie in a vault beneath its main altar.

A church has stood on the site for over 800 years, but all that remains of the original 13th-century Romanesque church are the Giants' Doorway and Heathen Towers. The Gothic nave, the choir, and the side

Auditorium of the Staatsoper, the Vienna State Opera House

chapels are the result of rebuilding in the 14th and 15th centuries, while some of the outbuildings, such as the Lower Vestry, are Baroque additions.

The lofty vaulted interior contains an impressive collection of works of art. Masterpieces of Gothic sculpture include the fabulously intricate pulpit, several of the figures of saints adorning the piers, and the canopies over many of the side altars. To the left of the High Altar is the 15th-century winged Wiener Neustädter Altar bearing the painted images of 72 saints. The altar panels open out to reveal delicate sculpture groups. The most spectacular Renaissance work is the tomb of Friedrich III, while the High Altar adds a flamboyant Baroque note.

④ Staatsoper

Opernring 2, A-1010. **Tel** 01-51444 2250. **U** Karlsplatz. 🚋 1, 2, 71, D. **Open** for performances. 🎭 🛗 📷 by arrangement (call 51444-2613). **W** **wiener-staatsoper.at**

Vienna's opera house, the Staatsoper, was the first of the grand Ringstrasse buildings to be completed; it opened on May 25, 1869 to the strains of Mozart's *Don Giovanni*. Built in Neo-Renaissance style, it initially failed to impress the Viennese. Yet when it was hit by a bomb in 1945 and largely destroyed,

the event was seen as a symbolic blow to the city. With a brand new auditorium and stage, the Opera House reopened in November 1955 with a performance of Beethoven's *Fidelio*.

⑤ Naturhistorisches Museum

Burgring 7, A-1014. **Tel** 01-52177 217. **U** Volkstheater. 🚌 48A. 🚋 1, 2, 46, 49, 71. **Open** 9am–6:30pm Thu–Mon (to 9pm Wed). **Closed** Jan 1, May 1, Nov 1, Dec 25. 🎭 📷 Wed & Sun (rooftop). 🛗 **W** **nhm-wien.ac.at**

Almost the mirror image of the Kunsthistorisches Museum, the Natural History Museum was designed by the same architects, and opened in 1889. Its collections include archaeological, anthropological, mineralogical, zoological, and geological displays. There are casts of dinosaur skeletons, the world's largest display of skulls illustrating the history of man, one of Europe's most comprehensive collections of gems, prehistoric sculpture, Bronze Age items, and extinct birds and mammals. In the archaeological section, look out for the celebrated Venus of Willendorf, a 25,000-year-old Palaeolithic fertility figurine, and finds from the early Iron Age settlement at Hallstatt *(see p568)*.

Venus of Willendorf, Naturhistorisches Museum

Hunters in the Snow by Peter Brueghel the Elder (1565)

⑥ Kunsthistorisches Museum

Maria-Theresien-Platz. **Tel** 01-525 4025. Ⓤ MuseumsQuartier, Volkstheater. 🚌 57A. 🚋 D, 1, 2, 71. **Open** 10am–6pm Tue–Sun (Jun–Aug: 10am–6pm daily); picture gallery also 6–9pm Thu. **Closed** Jan 1, May 1, Nov 1, Dec 25. 🚻 ♿ 📷 🅿 w khm.at

The Museum of the History of Art attracts more than one and a half million visitors each year. Its collections are based largely on those built up over a number of centuries by the Habsburgs.

The picture gallery occupies the first floor. The collection focuses on Old Masters from the 15th to the 18th centuries. Because of the links between the Habsburgs and the Netherlands, Flemish painting is well represented. About half the surviving works of Peter Brueghel the Elder (c.1525–69) are held by the museum, including *The Tower of Babel* and most of the cycle of *The Seasons*.

The Dutch paintings range from genre scenes of great domestic charm to magnificent landscapes. All the Rembrandts on show are portraits, including the famous *Large Self-Portrait* of the artist in a plain smock (1652). The only Vermeer is the enigmatic allegorical painting, *The Artist's Studio* (1665). The Italian galleries have a strong

Blue ceramic hippopotamus from Egypt (around 2000 BC)

collection of 16th-century Venetian paintings, with a comprehensive range of Titians and great works by Giovanni Bellini and Tintoretto. Also on show are the bizarre vegetable portrait heads, representing the four seasons, made for Emperor Rudolf II by Giuseppe Arcimboldo (1527–93).

The German section is rich in 16th-century paintings. There are several works by Dürer, including his *Madonna with the Pear* (1512). The most interesting of the Spanish works are the portraits of the Spanish royal family by Diego Velázquez (1599–1660).

On the ground floor are the Greek, Roman, Egyptian, and Near Eastern collections, with new rooms devoted specifically to Greek and Roman antiquities. Among the Egyptian and Near Eastern antiquities is an entire 5th-Dynasty tomb chapel from Giza (c.2400 BC) and a splendid bust of King Tuthmosis III (c.1460 BC).

The sculpture and decorative arts collection (Kunstkammer Wien) houses some fine, late Gothic religious statues by artists such as Tilman Riemenschneider (c.1460–1531), and curiosities owned by various Habsburg monarchs, such as automata and scientific instruments, as well as the famous *saliera*, or salt cellar, by Benvenuto Cellini.

⑦ Museums-Quartier Wien

Museumsplatz 1. **Tel** 01-523 5881. Ⓤ MuseumsQuartier, Volkstheater. 🚌 48a to Volkstheater. 🚋 49 to Volkstheater. Visitor Centre: **Open** 10am–7pm daily. 📷 🎫 ♿ 🅿 💻 w mqw.at

This museum complex is one of the largest cultural centers in the world, housed in what was once the imperial stables and carriage houses. Here, you will find art museums, venues for film, theater, architecture, dance, new media, and a children's creativity center. The visitor center is a good starting point.

Among the attractions is the **Leopold Museum** which focuses on Austrian art, including many works by Egon Schiele and Gustav Klimt. The **Museum of Modern Art Ludwig Foundation Vienna** shows contemporary and modern art from around the world. **ZOOM Kinder-museum** offers a lively introduction to the world of the museum for children. **Architekturzentrum** is dedicated to 20th- and 21st-century architecture.

⑧ Freud Museum

Berggasse 19. **Tel** 01-319 1596. Ⓤ Schottentor. 🚌 40A. 🚋 D. **Open** 9am–5pm daily. 📷 w freud-museum.at

No. 19 Berggasse is very like any other 19th-century apartment in Vienna, yet it is now one of the city's most famous addresses. The father of psychoanalysis, Sigmund Freud, received patients here from 1891 to 1938. The flat housed Freud's family, too. Memorabilia on display

Beautifully restored patients' waiting room in the Freud Museum

include letters and books, furnishings, and photographs. Even his hat and cane are on show. The apartment was abandoned when the Nazis forced Freud to leave, but still preserves an intimate domestic atmosphere.

⑨ Museum of Applied Arts

Stubenring 5. **Tel** 01-711 360. 🇺 Stubentor, Landstraße. 🚃 74A. 🚊 1, 2. **Open** 10am–10pm Tue, 10am–6pm Wed–Sun. **Closed** Jan 1, May 1, Nov 1, Dec 25. 🖼 ⬇ ✏ 🎥 💳 🌐 **mak.at**

The MAK (Museum für angewandte Kunst) was founded in 1864 as a museum for art and industry. Over the years, it also acquired objects representing new artistic movements. The museum has a fine collection of furniture, including some classical works of the German cabinet-maker David Roentgen,

textiles, glass, Islamic and East Asian art, and fine Renaissance jewelry. There is also a whole room full of Biedermeier furniture. The most important Austrian artistic movement was the Secession, formed by artists who seceded from the Vienna academy in 1897. Their style, also known as *Jugendstil*, is represented through the many and varied productions of the Wiener Werkstätte (Viennese Workshops), a cooperative arts and crafts studio, founded in 1903.

Brass vase (1903) by Kolo Moser

⑩ Secession Building

Friedrichstraße 12. **Tel** 01-587 5307. 🇺 Karlsplatz. **Open** 10am–6pm Tue–Sun (to 8pm Thu). 🖼 ⬇ 🌐 **secession.at**

Joseph Maria Olbrich designed the unusual Secession Building

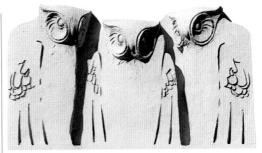

Group of stone owls decorating the Secession Building

in *Jugendstil* style as a showcase for the Secession movement's artists in 1898. The almost windowless building is a squat cube with four towers. The filigree globe of entwined laurel leaves on the roof gave rise to the building's nickname: "The Golden Cabbage."

Inside, Gustav Klimt's famous *Beethoven Frieze*, designed in 1902, covers three walls and is 34 m (110 ft) long.

⑪ Karlskirche

Karlsplatz. **Tel** 01-505 6294. 🇺 Karlsplatz. 🚃 4A. 🚊 D, 1, 2. **Open** daily. 🖼 🌐 **karlskirche.at**

During Vienna's plague epidemic of 1713, Karl VI vowed that, as soon as the city was delivered, he would build a church dedicated to St. Charles Borromeo (1538–84), a patron

Karlskirche, with column showing scenes from the life of St. Charles Borromeo

saint of the plague. Johann Bernhard Fischer von Erlach's eclectic Baroque masterpiece borrows from the architecture of ancient Greece and Rome. The interior was embellished with carvings and altarpieces by leading artists of the day.

Johann Michael Rottmayr's huge fresco in the cupola (1725–30) depicts St. Charles in heaven interceding for deliverance from the plague.

⑫ Albertina

Albertinaplatz 1. **Tel** 01-534 830. 🇺 Karlsplatz, Stephansplatz. 🚃 2A. 🚊 D, 1, 2, 71. **Open** 10am–6pm daily (to 9pm Wed). 🖼 ⬇ 💳 🎥 ✏ 🌐 **albertina.at**

Hidden away in a corner of the Hofburg is the Albertina, a palace named after Duke Albert of Sachsen-Teschen, Maria Theresa's son-in-law. Its collection includes one million prints, 65,000 watercolors and drawings, and over 70,000 photographs. The gems of the collection are by Dürer, with Michelangelo and Rubens also well represented. Picasso heads a fine 20th-century section. The Batliner Collection traces the progression from Impressionism to Modernism.

The palace has been restored to its former glory and now, for the first time in over 200 years, it is possible to visit the Habsburg State Rooms with their Neoclassical architecture and interior decoration.

Vienna: Farther Afield

For a city of 1.6 million inhabitants, Vienna is surprisingly compact. Nonetheless, some of the most interesting sights are away from the city center. At Belvedere, the palace and gardens of Prince Eugene impress with their scale and grandeur. Farther away at Schönbrunn sprawls the immense palace and gardens so loved by Empress Maria Theresa. There are also many parks and gardens around the city, the largest and most interesting of which is the Prater. A former hunting ground of the Habsburgs, it is now open to the public for numerous leisure activities.

The colorful Volksprater Funfair, Prater

⑬ Prater

Prater. Ⓤ Praterstern. 🚋 0, 5. Park: **Open** daily. Ferris Wheel: **Open** daily. 🚲 W prater.wien.info

Originally an imperial hunting ground, this huge area of woods and meadows between the Danube and the Danube Canal was opened to the public by Joseph II in 1766. The central avenue, or Hauptallee, stretches for 5 km (3 miles) through the center of the Prater, and was for a long time the preserve of the nobility and their footmen. During the 19th century, the northern end of the Prater became a massive funfair, dominated by a giant ferris wheel, one of Vienna's most

famous landmarks. There is also a planetarium, an exhibition center, and a trotting stadium nearby.

The southern side of the Prater contains extensive woodland – interlaced with cycle paths, a municipal golf course, and the Freud-enau Racetrack, where flat racing meetings are held from April to November.

⑭ Belvedere

Upper Belvedere: Prinz-Eugen-Straße 27. **Tel** 01-795 560. 🚌 13A, 69A. Ⓢ Quartier Belvedere. 🚋 0, 18, D. **Open** 10am–6pm daily. 🚲 ♿ 📷 Lower Belvedere: Rennweg 6. **Tel** 01-795 570. 🚋 71, D. **Open** 10am–6pm daily. 🚲 ♿ 📷 Gardens: **Open** daily. ♿ W belvedere.at

The Belvedere was built by Johann Lukas von Hildebrandt as the summer residence of Prince Eugene of Savoy, the brilliant military commander whose strategies helped vanquish the Turks in 1683. Situated on a gently sloping hill,

the Belvedere consists of two palaces linked by a formal garden laid out in the French style by Dominique Girard. The huge garden is sited on three levels, linked by two elaborate cascading waterfalls. Different areas of the garden are meant to convey a complicated series of Classical allusions: the lower part of the garden represents the domain of the Four Elements, the center is Parnassus, and the upper section is Olympus.

Standing at the highest point of the garden, the Upper Belvedere has a more elaborate facade than the Lower Belvedere, with lavish stone ornamentation, statues, and balustrades. The domed copper roofs of the end pavilions were designed to resemble Turkish tents – an allusion to Prince Eugene's many victories over the Turks. In fact, the whole palace was intended to be a symbolic reflection of the prince's power

Sphinx from Upper Belvedere garden

and glory, and was appropriate to the grand festive occasions for which it was originally used. The many impressive interiors include the Sala Terrena, with four Herculean figures supporting the ceiling, and a grand, sweeping staircase, the ornately decorated chapel, and the opulent Marble Hall.

The building also houses the collections of 19th- and

Imposing Baroque facade of Prince Eugene's Upper Belvedere palace

The Sala Terrena, the grand entrance hall of the Upper Belvedere

20th-century paintings belonging to the Austrian Gallery. Many of the works are by Austrian painters, including an excellent collection by Gustav Klimt. There are also works by Ferdinand Georg Waldmüller and Van Gogh.

The Lower Belvedere was used by Prince Eugene for day-to-day living, and the building itself is less elaborate than the Upper Belvedere. Many of the rooms are just as grand, however, for example the ornate, golden Hall of Mirrors. A museum here shows temporary exhibitions. Next door to the Lower Belvedere is the handsome Orangery, originally used to shelter tender plants in winter.

Masterpieces from the Baroque collection are exhibited on the first floor of the east wing in the Upper Belvedere. These include the character heads by Franz Xaver Messerschmidt and sculptures by Georg Raphael Donner, as well as paintings by J. M. Rottmayr, Martino Atomonte, Daniel Gran, and Paul Troger. The ground floor of the Upper Belvedere houses some masterpieces of Austrian Medieval Art. These include the Znaimer Altar, the seven panels painted by Rueland Frueauf the Elder (1490–94) which show the Passion taking place in an Austrian setting, and the 12th-century Romanesque Stammerberg Crucifix, one of the oldest surviving examples of Tyrolean woodcarving.

⑮ Schönbrunn Palace and Gardens

Schönbrunner Schloss Straße 147, Schönbrunn. **Tel** 01-811 13239.
Ⓤ Schönbrunn. 🚌 10A. 🚊 10, 58.
Open daily. 🅿 (gardens free). ♿ ▯
🄯 📷 🆆 schoenbrunn.at

This magnificent former summer residence of the imperial family takes its name from a "beautiful spring" that was found nearby. An earlier hunting lodge was destroyed by the Turks, so Leopold I asked Johann Bernhard Fischer von Erlach to design a grand Baroque residence here in 1695.

The project was finally completed by Nikolaus Pacassi in the mid-18th century, under Empress Maria Theresa. The strict symmetry of the

architecture is complemented by the extensive formal gardens, with their neat lawns and careful planting. An array of fountains and statues is framed by trees and alleyways. The gardens also contain a huge tropical Palm House with an interesting collection of exotic plants, a small zoo, a butterfly house, an orangery, and the Gloriette – a large Neoclassical arcade which crowns the hill behind the palace.

Inside the palace, the Rococo decorative schemes were devised by Nikolaus Pacassi. In the state rooms, the dominant features are white paneling, often adorned with gilded ornamental framework. The rooms vary from the extremely sumptuous – such as the Millionen-Zimmer, paneled with fig-wood inlaid with Persian miniatures – to the quite plain apartments of Franz Joseph and Empress Elisabeth.

The Memorial Room contains the portrait and effigy of the Duke of Reichstadt, the son of Napoleon and Princess Maria Louisa, daughter of Austrian Emperor Franz I. A virtual prisoner in the palace after Napoleon's fall from grace, the duke died here in 1832 aged 21. Alongside the palace is a museum of imperial coaches and sleighs.

The beautiful Schönbrunn Palace, as seen from the gardens

The historic center of Graz, overlooked by the thickly-wooded Schlossberg

❷ Eisenstadt

🏔 14,000. 🚍 🚌 ℹ️ Glorietteallee 1 (02682-673 90). 🌐 eisenstadt-tourismus.at

The main attraction of Eisenstadt is the grand residence of the Esterházy princes, the Hungarian aristocrats who claimed to be descendants of Attila. **Schloss Esterházy** was built for Prince Paul Esterházy in 1663–73. In the Haydnsaal, a huge hall of state decorated with 18th-century frescoes, the famous composer Joseph Haydn (1732–1809) conducted the family orchestra. Haydn lived on Haydngasse, and his house is now a museum. He is buried in the **Bergkirche**, west of the palace.

Until World War II, Eisenstadt had a large Jewish community, and there is a **Jewish Museum** near the palace.

Schloss Esterházy, a mix of Baroque and Neoclassical styles

🏛 **Schloss Esterházy**
Esterházyplatz. **Tel** 02682-719 3000.
Open Apr–mid-Nov: daily; mid-Nov–Mar: Fri–Sun. 📷

❸ Graz

🏔 254,000. ✈️ 9 km (6 miles) S. 🚍 🚌 ℹ️ Herrengasse 16 (0316-807 50).

Almost entirely surrounded by mountains, Graz is Austria's second largest city. During the Middle Ages, its importance rivaled that of Vienna. In the late 14th century, the Habsburg Duke Leopold III chose Graz as his base, and in the following century, the town played a vital strategic role in the war against the invading Turks.

The city is dominated by the Schlossberg, the huge hill on which the town's medieval defenses were built. During the Napoleonic Wars, Graz was occupied by French troops, who blew up most of the fortifications in 1809. Among the ruins visible today are a 28-m- (92-ft-) high clock tower, the **Uhrturm**, dating from 1561, and the **Glockenturm** (bell tower), from 1588. The former houses the **Schlossbergmuseum**, with exhibits illustrating the history of Graz. From the summit of the hill, there are splendid views.

At the foot of the Schlossberg lies the Old Town, a UNESCO World Heritage site. The medieval **Burg** (fortress) was built in several stages and

completed in 1500. To the south are the late-Gothic **Cathedral of St. Ägydius**, with its striking Baroque interior, and the **Mausoleum of Ferdinand II**, designed by the Italian Pietro de Pomis in the late 17th century.

The **Universalmuseum Joanneum** includes the Neue Galerie (New Gallery), previously housed in the Herberstein Palace, and the Natural History Museum. The **Alte Galerie** (Old Gallery) at Schloss Eggenberg (see below) houses the Archaeology Museum and a notable coin collection. Also of interest is the **Landeszeughaus**, with its impressive array of over 30,000 weapons and pieces of armor.

🏛 **Universalmuseum Joanneum**
Joanneumsviertel 5. **Tel** 0316-8017 9716. **Open** 10am–6pm Tue–Sun. 📷 🌐 museum-joanneum.at

Environs
A few kilometers west of the city, **Schloss Eggenberg** was built by Johann Ulrich von Eggenberg in 1625–35. Open daily, the Baroque palace houses the Alte Galerie (an archaeology museum), a collection of local prehistoric finds, coins, antiquities, and gemstones. Its rich collection of paintings includes works by Lucas Cranach the Elder (1472–1553) and Peter Brueghel the Younger (1564–1638). There are displays of stuffed animals in the Jagd-museum (Hunting Museum).

❹ Melk and the Wachau

Melk. Babenbergerstraße, Melk (02752-5230 7410). Benedictine abbey: **Open** May–Sep: 9am–5:30pm daily; Apr & Oct: 9am–4:30pm daily; winter: guided tours only (11am and 2pm daily). **stiftmelk.at**

Melk lies at the western end of one of the loveliest stretches of the River Danube, the Wachau, which extends some 40 km (25 miles) downstream to Krems.

Dotted with Renaissance houses and old towers, **Melk** itself is most famous for its Baroque Benedictine abbey, a treasure trove of paintings, sculptures, and decorative art. One of its most impressive rooms is the Marble Hall, with beautiful ceiling paintings depicting mythological scenes.

A boat trip is the best way to enjoy the Wachau, though for the energetic, there are cycle paths along the banks of the river. Landmarks to look for traveling downstream include the picturesque castle of **Schönbühel** and the ruined medieval fortress at **Aggstein**. Though not visible from the river, nearby **Willendorf** is the site of famous prehistoric finds.

At the eastern end of the Wachau are the well preserved medieval towns of **Dürnstein** and **Krems**. The latter's tiny hillside streets offer fine views across the Danube to the Baroque **Göttweig Abbey**.

The opulent interior of the 17th-century Church of St. Ignatius in Linz

❺ Linz

186,000. 10 km (6 miles) SW. Hauptplatz 1 (0732-7070 2009). **linz.at**

Austria's third city, Linz has been inhabited since Roman times, when it was a port called Lentia. In the early 16th century, it developed into an important trading center. Although, today, Linz is a busy industrial city, the Old Town contains many historic buildings and monuments.

The Hauptplatz, one of the largest medieval squares in Europe, is bordered by splendid Baroque facades. Among the finest buildings is the **Town Hall**, home to the Museum Linz Genesis, which tells the history of the city. The 20-m- (66-ft-) high marble Dreifaltigkeitssäule (Trinity Column) was completed in 1723.

In the southeast corner of the square is the **Church of St. Ignatius**. Also known as the Alter Dom, it was built in the 17th century in Baroque style and boasts a wonderfully ornate pulpit and altarpiece. Nearby, the **Landhaus** is well worth seeing for its three beautiful Renaissance courtyards and loggia.

The streets west of the Hauptplatz lead up to Linz's hilltop **castle**, built for Friedrich V (Holy Roman Emperor Friedrich III) in the 15th century. The castle houses the Schlossmuseum, with paintings, sculptures, and historical artifacts.

On the other side of the river, the **Ars Electronica Center** is a superb new museum that allows visitors to experiment with the latest technological innovations. Hidden away in the Lentia 2000 shopping mall is the **Lentos Kunstmuseum**, containing a fine collection of 19th- and 20th-century Austrian art, including works by Egon Schiele (1890–1918) and Gustav Klimt (1862–1918).

For splendid views of Linz, take a ride on the Pöstlingbergbahn train, which climbs to the top of Pöstlingberg Hill.

River cruises along the Danube west to Passau, in Germany, and east to Vienna depart from the quay at the Nibelungenbrücke. On-board entertainment includes themed events, such as a "Bavarian afternoon" or an "Italian night."

Ars Electronica Center
Ars-Electronica-Straße 1. **Tel** 0732-727 20. **Open** Tue–Sun. **aec.at**

Lentos Kunstmuseum
Ernst-Koref-Promenade 11. **Tel** 0732-7070 3600. **Open** Tue–Sun. **lentos.at**

Melk's massive Benedictine abbey on the banks of the Danube

Hallstatt, an attractive lakeside village in the Salzkammergut

❻ Hallstatt

🏔 1,000. 🚉 🚌 ⛴ ℹ️ Seestraße 169 (06134-8208).

This pretty village on the bank of the Hallstätter See lies in the Salzkammergut, a stunning region of lakes and mountains. The area takes its name from the rich deposits of salt *(salz)* that have been mined here since the 1st millennium BC. From Hallstatt, it is possible to visit a working mine, the **Salzbergwerk**, by taking the cable car from the southern end of the village up to the mine entrance on the Salzberg mountain. The **Rudolfsturm**, the tower that stands close to the station at the top, was completed in 1284 to defend the mine workings.

The **Museum Hallstatt** contains Celtic Iron Age artifacts discovered near the mines. Today, the name Hallstatt is used to refer to the Celtic culture that flourished from the 9th to the 5th centuries BC.

Behind the **Pfarrkirche**, the town's late-Gothic parish church, the **Beinhaus** (Charnel House) has been used to store human remains since 1600.

🏛 **Salzbergwerk Hallstatt**
Tel 06132-200 2400. **Open** end Apr–Oct: daily. 📷 🌐 salzwelten.at

🏛 **Museum Hallstatt**
Tel 06134-828 015. **Open** Apr–Oct: daily; Nov–Mar: Wed–Sun. 📷
🌐 museum-hallstatt.at

Environs
The mountains and the crystal clear waters of the Hallstätter See offer many opportunities for swimming, water sports, scuba diving, hiking, and cycling. There are also boat trips on the lake. At the southern end of the Hallstätter See, about 2 km (1 mile) from Hallstatt, are the **Dachstein limestone caves**, open daily from May to mid-October. A cable car from south of Obertraun climbs to the entrance of the caves, giving superb views of the lake and surrounding mountains.

❼ Salzburg

🏔 150,000. ✈ 3 km (2 miles) W. 🚉 🚌 ℹ️ Mozartplatz 5 (0662-8898 7330). 🎭 Salzburger Festspiele (late Jul–Aug). 🌐 salzburg.info

Salzburg rose to prominence in about AD 700, when a church and a monastery were established here. Until 1816, when it became part of the Habsburg empire, Salzburg was an independent city-state ruled by a succession of prince-archbishops. Best known as the birthplace of Wolfgang Amadeus Mozart, today the city has a thriving musical tradition. Each summer, large numbers of tourists arrive for the Salzburger Festspiele, a festival of opera, classical music, and theater.

Salzburg's medieval fortress, the **Festung Hohensalzburg**, looms over the city from its hilltop position. The castle dates from the 11th century, but the state apartments are an early 16th-century addition.

The **Residenz**, where Salzburg's prince-archbishops lived and held court, owes its early Baroque appearance to Archbishop Wolf Dietrich von Raiteneau, who resided here from 1587. The palace contains the Residenzgalerie, a collection of European art of the 16th to 19th centuries. Among the city's

Wolfgang Amadeus Mozart

Salzburg's most famous son, Wolfgang Amadeus Mozart, was born in 1756, the son of Leopold, a member of the Prince-Archbishop's chamber orchestra. He learnt to play the harpsichord at the age of 3, and by the age of 5 had already written his first compositions. From 1763, Mozart traveled widely, performing for the aristocracy across Europe. His mastery of all the musical genres of the day swiftly earned him renown at home and abroad. During his short life, his prodigious output included 56 symphonies, over 20 concertos, and 15 operas, among them *The Marriage of Figaro* and *Don Giovanni*. Mozart's aspirations to lead the kind of lifestyle enjoyed by his patrons, however, led him into financial difficulties. In his final years, the musician was continually debt-ridden and prone to depression. He died in 1791 and was buried in a common grave.

Wolfgang Amadeus Mozart (1756–91)

fine religious buildings are **St. Peter's Abbey** and **Benedictine monastery**, dating from c.AD 700, and the **Cathedral** (Dom), begun in 1614 to a design by Santino Solari. The **Franziskaner-kirche** boasts a splendid Baroque altarpiece (1709) by Johann Bernhard Fischer von Erlach.

A notable museum is the **Salzburg Museum**, with its historical and fine arts collections, and the **Haus der Natur**, a museum of natural history. The **Mozarts Geburtshaus** is Mozart's birthplace, while the **Mozart Wohnhaus** features audio-visual displays telling the story of his life.

On the right bank of the Salzach, **Schloss Mirabell**, with its Baroque garden, was built by Archbishop Wolf Dietrich for his Jewish mistress, Salome Alt. Only a 25-minute bus ride from the city center is the Renaissance palace of **Hellbrunn**, built for Salzburg's Prince-Archbishop Markus Sittikus.

🏰 **Festung Hohensalzburg**
Mönchsberg 34. **Tel** 0662-8424 3011.
Open daily. 🅿 📷

🏛 **Residenz**
Residenzplatz 1. **Tel** 0662-8042 2690.
Open daily. (Residenzgalerie Tue–Sun). **Closed** 1st 2 weeks Nov. 🅿 📷

🏛 **Salzburg Museum**
Mozartplatz 1. **Tel** 0662-6208 080.
Open 9am–5pm Tue–Sun. **Closed** Nov 1, Dec 25. 🅿 ⓦ salzburgmuseum.at

🏰 **Schloss Mirabell**
Mirabellplatz 2. **Tel** 0662-80720.

🏰 **Schloss Hellbrunn**
Fürstengasse 37. **Tel** 0662-8203 720.
Open daily. 🅿 📷 ⓦ salzburg.info

Innsbruck's Annasäule, crowned by a statue of the Virgin Mary

❽ Innsbruck

🏘 124,000. ✈ 4 km (2.5 miles) W.
🚈 🚌 ℹ Burggraben 3 (0512-59850). ⓦ innsbruck.info

Capital of the Tyrol region, Innsbruck grew up at the crossroads of the old trade routes between Germany and Italy, Vienna, and Switzerland.

One of the city's finest pieces of architecture is the **Goldenes Dachl** (Golden Roof), commissioned by Emperor Maximilian I, who chose Innsbruck as his imperial capital at the end of the 15th century. Made of gilded copper tiles, the roof was constructed in the 1490s to cover a balcony used by members of the court to observe events in the square below. Beneath the balcony is the **Museum Goldenes Dachl**, which focuses on the life of the Habsburg emperor, who ruled from 1493 to 1519.

Innsbruck's **Hofburg** (Imperial Palace) dates from the 15th century, but was rebuilt in Rococo style in the 18th century by Empress Maria Theresa (ruled 1740–80).

Built in 1555–65, the **Hofkirche** contains the impressive mausoleum of Maximilian I, which features 28 bronze statues. The highlight of the **Domkirche St. Jakob** (1717–22) is Lucas Cranach the Elder's painting of the *Madonna and Child*, which adorns the high altar.

Innsbruck's many museums include the **Tiroler Landesmuseum Ferdinandeum**, which has European art from the 15th to the 20th centuries, and the **Tiroler Volkskunstmuseum**, with exhibitions of local folk art and crafts.

🏛 **Museum Goldenes Dachl**
Herzog-Friedrichstraße 15. **Tel** 0512-5360 1441. **Open** Tue–Sun. 🅿

🏛 **Hofburg**
Rennweg 1. **Tel** 0512-587 186.
Open daily. 🅿 ⓦ hofburg-innsbruck.at

🏛 **Tiroler Landesmuseum Ferdinandeum**
Museumstraße 15. **Tel** 0512-59489.
Open Tue–Sun. 🅿 ⓦ tiroler-landesmuseen.at

🏛 **Tiroler Volkskunstmuseum**
Universitätsstraße 2. **Tel** 0512-594 89510. **Open** daily. 🅿

Salzburg's magnificent Baroque cathedral, dominating the skyline of the Old Town

Practical & Travel Information

Austria is well equipped for tourism in both winter and summer. The extensive winter-sports facilities mean that even in the mountainous west of the country, communications are good and most roads are kept open all year. Public transport, especially the train services between the main cities, is reliable, and banking and exchange facilities are widely available. The country is generally safe for visitors except for a few unsavory bits of Vienna. Hospitals are of a high standard and, for lesser ailments, pharmacists are highly respected.

Tourist Information

Austria has a wide network of local and regional tourist offices and the **Austrian National Tourist Office** has branches in many countries abroad. In the busier skiing resorts in winter, local offices often stay open as late as 9pm. In Vienna, **Wiener Tourismusverband** is a very helpful organization, especially with regard to forthcoming events and booking accommodations.

Visa Requirements

Citizens of the US, Canada, Australia, and New Zealand need just a passport to visit Austria. No visa is required for stays of up to three months. Most European Union (EU) visitors need only a valid identity card to enter the country.

Personal Security

Although crime in the cities is rare, there are a few parts of Vienna that are best avoided at night, especially around the Wien Nord station. Fights and pickpocketing are quite common at the Prater funfair at night.

In case of emergencies while on vacation, the appropriate services to call are listed in the Directory opposite.

Health Issues

It is best to take out full health insurance which also covers flights home for medical reasons. This is true even for visitors from EU countries such as Great Britain. There is a reciprocal arrangement with Austria whereby emergency hospital treatment is free upon presentation of a British passport, but obtaining free treatment can involve rather a lot of bureaucracy.

In the case of a medical emergency, call an ambulance (*Rettungsdienst*) or the local **Doctor on Call**. For minor ailments or injuries, visit an *Apotheke* (pharmacy). All pharmacies display a distinctive red "A" sign. When closed, they give the address of the nearest open pharmacy.

Facilities for the Disabled

Awareness of the needs of the disabled is growing in Austria. Wiener Tourismusverband has a good online information service with details of the ease of wheelchair access at tourist sights, hotels, and public restrooms.

Etiquette

Austrians are a conservative people and formal in their modes of address. Waiters are summoned with a deferential "Herr Ober," and greetings in the street are accompanied by the use of titles, such as "Herr Doktor," and much handshaking.

Banking and Currency

The euro became the unit of currency in Austria in January 2002 (*see p23*).

Banks are usually the best places to change money. Most are open Monday to Friday from 8am to 12:30pm and from 1:30pm to 3pm (5:30pm on Thursdays). Some banks, generally those at main train stations and at airports, stay open longer and do not close for lunch. Though major credit cards are accepted at most large stores, hotels, and restaurants, they are not used as frequently as, for instance, in the UK or France, so it is a good idea to carry some cash with you. Alternatively, payment by debit card is widely accepted.

Communications

The Austrian telecommunications network is run by Telekom Austria. Calls are among the most expensive in Europe. Public phones are slowly being phased out, since most people have cell phones, but you can make long-distance calls from most post offices. The cheapest way to use your cell phone is to buy a pay-as-you-go SIM card in Austria, thereby avoid high international roaming charges. Numbers starting in 05 can be dialled from anywhere in Austria at a local call rate. The postal service is reliable, verging on the pedantic, and posting a

The Climate of Austria

Altitude obviously plays an important role in the climate of Austria. The Alpine part of the country experiencing lower temperatures and receiving more rain and snow than Vienna and the east. Snow cover in the Alps lasts from November to May. Daytime temperatures in summer can be high, but the evenings are cool. There is a risk of thunderstorms from June to August.

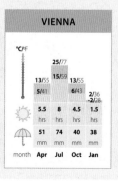

VIENNA			
°C/°F			
	25/77		
13/55	15/59	13/55	
5/41		6/43	2/36
			-2/28
5.5 hrs	8 hrs	4.5 hrs	1.5 hrs
51 mm	74 mm	40 mm	38 mm
month **Apr**	**Jul**	**Oct**	**Jan**

letter can take some time. Each letter is carefully weighed and every size and shape coded separately.

Most post offices are open between 8am and noon and 2pm and 6pm from Monday to Friday. You can also buy stamps at newsagents.

Flying to Austria

If you fly from the United States, there are direct flights with **Delta Air Lines** from New York and Orlando to Vienna's Schwechat airport. **Austrian Airlines** flies from New York, Washington, and Chicago and **Lauda Air** has flights from Miami. Direct flights from Australia are run by **Emirates Airlines** and **British Airways**, which both operate services from Sydney and Melbourne.

Connections to all of the major European cities are good. There are several flights a day from London's Gatwick and Heathrow airports. British Airways is the main British airline with regular flights to Vienna, and the main Austrian carrier is Austrian Airlines. **Ryanair** also offers regular services at low prices.

You can get APEX tickets if you book two weeks in advance, and charters are available at very competitive prices. Weekend package deals, including the price of two nights at a good Viennese hotel, can be excellent value, sometimes costing less than the economy-class ticket price.

Rail Travel

Austria's rail network is run by the state-owned Österreichische Bundesbahnen (ÖBB). Hauptbahnhof Wien station will handle all international routes by 2015 and is located at Südtirolerplatz, with connections to the U1 subway line and the Schnellbahn as well as several bus and tram routes. The Westbahnhof still handles trains from the west, with frequent services to Innsbruck and Salzburg, and is served by the U6 and U3 subway lines. Eventually, the Westbahnhof will run regional routes only. Trains to southern and eastern areas are temporarily served by Meidling Hauptbahnhof, which is linked to the U6 subway, Schnellbahn, and tram lines. Trains to Neusiedl/See, Marchegg, Bratislava, and Brno leave from Hauptbahnhof Wien, located at Südtirolerplatz. The Franz-Josefs-Bahnhof, which runs services from the north, is served by the U4 and U6 subway lines, the Schnellbahn, and the cross-city D tram, which goes directly to Ringstrasse.

The travel agency (Verkehrsverein) at Westbahnhof, open 8am to 9pm daily, provides rail information and helps book hotels. In Vienna, there is a phone number for obtaining railway information in English (see below).

Traveling by Bus

Austria's long-distance buses serve those parts of the country that are not reached by train. Bus and train timetables are well integrated. In most towns, buses leave from the train station or the post office.

Traveling by Car

Even in winter, Austrian road conditions are good and autobahns (highways) link all the major cities. There are also convenient routes into Austria from neighboring countries. Highways are subject to a toll, which is paid by buying a windshield sticker valid for a certain period of time. Stickers can be bought at the border or at post offices, gas stations, and tobacconists throughout the country. Tolls are also payable on certain mountain roads and tunnels. All drivers in Austria must carry their driver's license, car registration documents, and insurance documents.

DIRECTORY

Tourist Offices

Austrian National Tourist Office
W austria.info

Australia
36 Carrington Street, 1st floor, Sydney, NSW 2000.
Tel 02-9299 3621.

Canada
2 Bloor Street West, 400 Toronto, Ontario M4W. 3E2. **Tel** 416-967 4867.

UK
9–11 Richmond Bldgs, London W1D 3HF.
Tel 020-7440 3830.

US
120 West 45th St, 9th floor, New York, NY 10036.
Tel 212-944 6885.

Wiener Tourismusverband
Cnr of Albertinaplatz/ Tegethoffstraße/Meysedergaße, Vienna. **Tel** 01-24555. W wien.info

Embassies

Australia
Mattiellistraße 2–4, -1010 Vienna. **Tel** 01-506740.

Canada
Laurenzerberg 2, A-1010 Vienna. **Tel** 01-5313 83000.

UK
Jaurèsgasse 12, A-1030 Vienna. **Tel** 01-716130.

US
Boltzmanngasse 16, A-1090 Vienna. **Tel** 01-31339.

Emergency Numbers

Ambulance
Tel 144.

Doctor on Call
Tel 141.

Fire
Tel 122.

Police
Tel 133.

Airlines

Austrian Airlines
Tel 05-1766 1000.
Tel 800-843 0002 (US).
W aua.com

British Airways
Tel 0844 493 0787 (UK).
W britishairways.com

Delta Air Lines
Tel 01-79567 023.
Tel 800-221 1212 (US).
W delta.com

Emirates Airlines
Tel 01-532 6028.
Tel 800-777 3999 (US).
W emirates.com

Lauda Air
Tel 05-1766 73700.
Tel 800-588 8399 (US).

Ryanair
Tel 0871-246 0000 (UK).
W ryanair.com

Rail Information

ÖBB
Tel 05-1717. W oebb.at

Shopping and Entertainment

Shopping in Austria can be expensive, but it is a good place to buy certain high-quality traditional goods, such as Loden coats, porcelain, and glass. Famous for its coffee shops, Christmas markets, world-class opera, and orchestras, Vienna is the center of entertainment in Austria, although some important music festivals are held across the country. Outside the city, such rural pleasures as skiing and hiking are available in the west of the country, in the Tyrol, Salzburger Land, and Salzkammergut regions.

Opening Hours

Stores usually open at 8:30 or 9am and close at 6 or 7pm. Smaller ones may close for lunch. Most shops stay open all day on Saturday, especially in larger towns. In rural areas, however, they may close around noon on Saturday. Shops are closed on Sundays and public holidays, but you can buy items such as groceries, flowers, and newspapers at major train stations.

Food and Drink

Austria is justly famous for its cakes and pastries, and in Vienna and large towns a good *Café-Konditorei* (cake shop and café) will mail cakes back home for you. Buy a prettily-packaged *Sacher-torte*, the world-famous Viennese chocolate cake. In November and December, try the buttery Advent *Stollen*, stuffed with fruit and nuts and dusted with icing sugar, available from the **Meinl am Graben** delicatessen or any good baker. Specialist chocolate shops, such as **Altmann & Kühne**, are also worth a visit, both for the unusual packaging and the chocolates themselves.

Eiswein (so-called because the grapes are left on the vines until the first frosts) is a delicious white dessert wine. **Zum Schwarzen Kameel** in Vienna also sells the rarer red variety.

Luxury Goods

Desirable Austrian goods include clothes made of *Loden*, a felt-like woollen fabric, custom-made sheets, and high-quality down pillows and duvets. Petit point embroidery, which adorns handbags, powder compacts, and similar articles, is a Viennese specialty. A wide range is available at **Petit Point** and **Maria Stransky**.

Trachten (Austrian costume) shops are fun, selling a wide selection of hats, children's dresses, jackets, and blouses.

Glassware – including superb chandeliers – and Augarten porcelain come in highly original designs, but are very expensive. **Ostovics** is a good glass and porcelain shop for such items. The **Schloss Augarten** porcelain factory is open to visitors.

Booking Tickets

You can buy tickets direct from the appropriate box office or reserve them by phone. Agencies are reliable; try the **Reisebüro Mondial**. Vienna's four state theaters, the Burgtheater, Akademietheater, Opera House, and Volksoper have a central booking office, the **Bundestheaterkassen**. In most cases, tickets go on sale one month before the performance. Written applications for tickets must reach the Österreichische Bundestheater Verband (address as Bundestheaterkassen) at least three weeks in advance for opera tickets, and 10 days ahead for the theaters. Standing-room tickets (over 500 at the Opera House) are sold at the evening box office one hour before the start of the performance.

Theater

Viennese theater enjoys a high reputation and the Burgtheater (*see p561*) is the most prestigious venue. Classic and modern plays are performed here and at the associated Akademietheater.

The **Volkstheater** offers more modern plays as well as the occasional classic and some operetta performances.

The **Raimund Theater** and the **Ronacher** are part of the Vereinigte Bühnen Wien, the city's own theaters. Both specialize in lavish musicals.

The Wiener Festwochen, held in May and June, features theater, including musical theater, at various venues.

Vienna has a wide range of fringe theater from one-man shows to *Kabarett* – satirical shows not cabarets – but fairly fluent German is needed to appreciate them.

Opera and Operetta

The opera season runs from September to June. The historic **Theater an der Wien** is a full-time venue for opera and other forms of classical music. At the Staatsoper in Vienna, operas are usually performed in the original language. At the **Wiener Volksoper**, where the repertoire includes light opera by Mozart and Puccini and operettas by Strauss and Lehár, they are sung in German. The same singers often appear at the two venues. The New Year's Eve performance at the Opera House is always Johan Strauss the Younger's *Die Fledermaus*, and famous guests sometimes make surprise appearances during the second act.

A wonderful smaller opera house is the **Wiener Kammeroper**. Here, you can expect anything from Rossini and classic operetta to rock versions of familiar operas and opera parodies. July sees opera performances in the Kaiserhof courtyard of the palatial religious foundation at **Klosterneuburg**, a short way north of Vienna.

Classical Music

The principal venues for classical music concerts are the **Musikverein** (including the restored Brahms-Saal) and the concert halls of the **Konzerthaus**. Performances are also held in many other halls and historic palaces around Vienna.

The New Year's Concert is televised live from the Grosser Musikvereinsaal in the Musik-verein every year. You can apply for tickets by writing direct to the **Wiener Philharmoniker** or online. Applications must be received on January 2 (not before, not after) for the next year's concert.

The city supports two great orchestras, the Wiener Philharmoniker and the Wiener Symphoniker. There are also a number of chamber music ensembles and church music is often of concert quality. The world-famous Vienna Boys' Choir can be heard during mass at the Burgkapelle in the Hofburg complex *(see p560)* every Sunday and religious holiday at 9:15am except from July to about mid-September (the box office is open the Friday before). You can also hear them at the Konzerthaus every Friday at 3:30pm in May, June, September, and October. Tickets are available from hotel porters and from Reisebüro Mondial.

Music Festivals

Seasonal events in Vienna include the Vienna Festival in May and June, and **Wien Modern**, a festival of post-1945 and contemporary classical music, with an emphasis on the avant-garde.

Inaugurated in 1920, the **Salzburg Festival** of opera, drama, and music claims to be the largest of its kind in the world. It is held annually in late July and August, attracting the world's finest conductors, soloists, and opera and theater companies. The spectacular venues include the Felsenreitschule, the riding school of the prince-archbishops of Salzburg. There is always a strong emphasis on Mozart, the city's most famous son, but the festival has also won acclaim for its contemporary music and innovative productions of classic and modern drama.

Another smaller festival is the **Haydn Festspiele**, held at the magnificent Schloss Esterházy in Eisenstadt *(see p566)*. The festival itself is in September, but Haydn concerts are given in the palace throughout the summer.

Coffee Houses and Heurige

The Viennese coffee house is a throwback to a more leisured age, serving coffee in a bewildering range of styles and allowing patrons to sit and read newspapers at their leisure. The *Heuriger* is a uniquely Austrian establishment. Its literal meaning is "this year's," and it refers both to the youngest available local wine and to venues that sell it. The most famous are in villages to the north and west of Vienna, such as Heiligenstadt and Grinzing. A sign reading *Eigenbau* means that the wine is from the owner's vineyards.

Winter Sports

Austria's facilities for winter sports are second only to Switzerland's. Ski resorts vary from fashionable Kitzbühel and St. Anton to small family resorts with less demanding slopes. Package tours are available from many countries around the world. Information on 800 resorts can be found on the **Austria Tourism** website, along with snow reports and other useful information.

DIRECTORY

Food and Drink

Altmann & Kühne
Graben 30, Vienna.
Tel 01-533 0927.

Meinl am Graben
Graben 19, Vienna.
Tel 01-532 3334.

Zum Schwarzen Kameel
Bognergasse 5, Vienna.
Tel 01-533 8125.

Luxury Goods

Maria Stransky
Hofburg Passage 2,
Vienna. Tel 01-533 6098.

Ostovics
Stephansplatz 9, Vienna.
Tel 01-533 1411.

Petit Point
Kärntner Straße 16,
Vienna. Tel 01-512 4886.

Schloss Augarten
Obere Augartenstraße 1,
Vienna. Tel 01-2112 4201.

Booking Tickets

Bundestheater-kassen
Opernring 2, Vienna.
Tel 01-51444 7810.

Reisebüro Mondial
Operngasse 206, Vienna.
Tel 01-5880 4150.

Theater

Raimund Theater
Wallgasse 18, Vienna.
Tel 01-5883 0200.

Ronacher
Seilerstätte 9, Vienna.
Tel 01-514 110.

Volkstheater
Neustiftgasse 1, Vienna.
Tel 01-521 110.

Opera and Operetta

Oper Klosterneuburg
Kaiserhof Stift,
Klosterneuburg.
Tel 02243-444 424.

Theater an der Wien
Linke Wienzeile 6,
Vienna.
Tel 01-58885.

Wiener Kammeroper
Fleischmarkt 24, Vienna.
Tel 01-588 300.

Wiener Volksoper
Währinger Straße 78,
Vienna.
Tel 01-514 4430.

Classical Music

Konzerthaus
Lothringerstraße 20,
Vienna. Tel 01-242 002.

Musikverein
Bösendorferstraße 12,
Vienna. Tel 01-505 8190.

Wiener Philharmoniker
Bösendorferstraße 12,
Vienna. Tel 01-505 8190.

Music Festivals

Haydn Festspiele
Schloss Esterházy,
A-7000 Eisenstadt.
Tel 02682-618 66.

Salzburg Festival
Hofstallgasse 1, Postfach
140, A-5100 Salzburg.
Tel 0662-804 5579.

Winter Sports

Austria Tourism
W austria.info

Where to Stay

Four-poster beds and all modern conveniences at Hollmann Beletage, Vienna

Vienna

CENTRAL VIENNA:
Altstadt Vienna €
Modern   Map C4
Kirchengaße 41, 1010
Tel *01-522 66 66*
W altstadt.at
The Altstadt's exquisite rooms
and suites combine period
character and modernity.

CENTRAL VIENNA: Domizil €
Pension   Map E3
Schulerstraße 14, 1010
Tel *01-513 31 99*
W hoteldomizil.at
Comfy hotel featuring rooms with
homely touches. Internet access,
24-hour reception, and multi-
lingual staff who can help with
sightseeing recommendations.

DK Choice

CENTRAL VIENNA:
Hollmann Beletage €€
Boutique   Map E3
Köllnerhofgaße 6, 1010
Tel *01-961 19 60*
W hollmann-beletage.at
This great little establishment
has rooms that are
contemporary in style and
boast an eye-popping array of
gadgets. Mammoth breakfasts,
friendly staff, and a sauna are
just a few of the many benefits
of this family-run B&B – it also
has a library, pretty courtyard
garden, and bicycle storage.

CENTRAL VIENNA:
Hotel Am Stephansplatz €€
Modern   Map D3
Stephansplatz 9, 1010
Tel *01-534 05 0*
W hotelamstephansplatz.at
A popular, environmentally
friendly hotel with rooms and
suites that feature contrasting
warm colors, natural woods, and
paintings by contemporary artists.

CENTRAL VIENNA:
Palais Coburg €€€
Luxury   Map E4
Coburgbastei 4, 1010
Tel *01-518 18 0*
W coburg.at
Stay in a grand ceremonial room
built for an emperor, and enjoy
Vienna's most decadent culinary
indulgence and spa therapies.

CENTRAL VIENNA:
The Ring Hotel €€€
Boutique   Map D4
Kärntner Ring 8, 1010
Tel *01-221 22*
W theringhotel.com
Beyond The Ring's sober façade
is a warm interior with creative
touches. Rooms and suites blend
old with new, while the spa offers
city views and great service.

Rest of Austria

GRAZ: Hotel Daniel €
Boutique
Europaplatz 1, 8021
Tel *0316-71 10 80*
W hoteldaniel.com
A cool, minimalist design sets
the tone at the hip Hotel Daniel.
Rooms are compact but
efficiently laid out.

DK Choice

GRAZ: Augarten €€
Boutique
Schönaugaße 53, 8010
Tel *0316-20 80 0*
W augartenhotel.at
This smart design hotel beside
the Augarten park features
modern furnishings in the
rooms, and a wealth of art
from the private collection
of the owner. The building,
designed by Günther Domenig,
combines curvy surfaces and
lots of glass to ensure a feeling
of light and space.

Price Guide
Prices are based on one night's stay in
high season for a standard double room,
inclusive of service charges and taxes.

€	under €150
€€	€150 to €250
€€€	over €250

HALLSTATT:
Seehotel Grüner Baum €€
Pension
Marktplatz 104, 4830
Tel *06134-82 63*
W gruenerbaum.cc
This lakeside hotel dates back
to at least 1700. The rooms are
charmingly furnished with both
modern and antique pieces.

INNSBRUCK: Altpradl €
Pension
Pradlerstraße 8, 6020
Tel *0512-345 156*
W hotel-altpradl.at
A centrally located hotel with
simple but comfortable rooms.
Sauna and steam bath facilities.

INNSBRUCK:
Schlosshotel Igls €€€
Luxury
Viller Steig 2, 6080
Tel *0512-377 217*
W schloss-igls.com
Every guest is treated like royalty
at this discreet mountain castle
with superb views of the Alps.

LINZ: Austria Trend Hotel
Schillerpark €€
Modern
Schillerplatz, 4020
Tel *0732-69 50*
W austria-trend.at
This cube-like building offers
fully equipped modern rooms,
a restaurant, and several bars.

SALZBURG:
Schloss Mönchstein €€€
Historic
Mönchsberg 26, 5020
Tel *0662-84 85 55*
W monchstein.at
A 14th-century castle with its
own park, offering city views
and high standards of comfort.

ST. WOLFGANG IM
SALZKAMMERGUT:
Im Weissen Rössl €€€
Luxury
Markt 74, 5360
Tel *06138-23 06*
W weissesroessl.at
This famous lakeside hotel
boasts rooms decorated in a
romantic style. The impressive
pool is heated and appears to
float at the lake's edge.

Rathaus Keller
Demel

Where to Eat and Drink

Vienna

CENTRAL VIENNA:
Trzesniewski €
Austrian **Map** D3
Dorotheergaße 1, 1010
Tel *01-512 32 91* **Closed** *Sun*
This Viennese institution offers
a wide selection of appetizing
open sandwiches. Enjoy them
with a small beer *(pfiff)*.

CENTRAL VIENNA:
Café Sacher €€
Austrian **Map** D4
Philharmonikerstraße 4, 1010
Tel *01-514 56 0*
One of the city's swankiest venues
is the birthplace of the famous
Sachertorte. This café is also a
great place to enjoy great coffee.

CENTRAL VIENNA:
Lebenbauer €€
Vegetarian **Map** D3
Teinfaltstraße 3, 1010
Tel *01-533 55 56* **Closed** *Sat & Sun*
Lebenbauer boasts a creative,
meat-free menu. Highlights
include a flavor-packed pumpkin
risotto. The recipes use mainly
organic produce and are cooked
without fat, eggs, or flour.

CENTRAL VIENNA:
Kim Kocht €€€
Asian
Merkur Hoher Markt 12, 1010
Tel *01-319 02 42* **Closed** *Sun & Mon*
This is the eponymous restaurant
by one of the most popular
Asian chefs on Vienna's dining
scene. Book a table weeks in
advance to enjoy Kim's signature
"surprise dinner."

CENTRAL VIENNA:
Palmenhaus €€€
European **Map** D4
Burggarten 1, 1010
Tel *01-533 10 33*
A plush venue with a menu to
match, Palmenhaus also serves

a good-value Carpe Diem breakfast of fresh pineapple, mint,
honeycracker, bread, goat-cheese
omelette, and rolls with jams.

CENTRAL VIENNA: Procacci €€€
Italian **Map** D4
Göttweihergaße 2, 1010
Tel *01-512 22 11* **Closed** *Sun*
Located between Spiegelgaße
and Seilergaße, this elegant
Italian restaurant specializes in
Florentine food, with a special
emphasis on truffle dishes. Light
lunches are served at the bar.

DK Choice

FARTHER AFIELD:
Noir Vienna €
International
Neubaugaße 8/II, 1070
Tel *0800-101 99 9* **Closed** *Sun & Mon*
Those keen to connect with
food in an exciting new way
should try Noir. Dinner here
is a tantalizing exploration of
tastes, textures, and aromas, as
dishes are served and enjoyed
in complete darkness, which is
meant to heighten the senses.

Rest of Austria

GRAZ: Magnolia €€€
International
Schönaugaße 53, 8010
Tel *0316-82 38 38* **Closed** *Sat & Sun*
Located in the Augarten hotel,
Magnolia has a reputation for
creative cooking, although the
inexpensive business lunches
should not be overlooked.

INNSBRUCK: Goldener Adler €
Regional
Herzog-Friedrich-Straße 6, 6020
Tel *0512-57 11 11*
Located in one of the oldest inns
in Europe, this restaurant serves

Price Guide
Prices are for a three course meal
for one, including half a bottle of
house wine, and all extra charges.

€	under €35
€€	€35 to €65
€€€	over €65

traditional schnitzels, as well
as poultry and game dishes.
Mozart is rumored to have
eaten in these very rooms.

DK Choice

INNSBRUCK: Chez Nico €€
Vegetarian
Maria-Theresien-Straße 49, 6020
Tel *0650-45 10 62 4* **Closed** *Sun & Mon*
At Chez Nico, chef Nicolas Curtil
follows a molecular approach to
vegetarian cuisine. The menu
changes seasonally, and the
inventive dishes feature fresh,
seasonal produce. Opt for the
superb-value two-course
lunchtime menu, or the more
expensive seven-course evening
gourmet menu. Book in advance.

LINZ: Brandl €
Café
Bismarckstraße 6, 4020
Tel *0732-77 36 35* **Closed** *Sun*
This long-standing Linz bakery
has a sit-down section where
diners can munch on a range
of crusty-bread sandwiches,
croissants, and brioches.

LINZ: Cook €€
Fusion
Klammstraße 1, 4020
Tel *0732-78 13 05* **Closed** *Sun*
Wok-fried salmon and curried
herring are on offer at this
Scandinavian-Asian restaurant,
with a chic café-bistro interior.

SALZBURG: Triangel €€
Traditional Austrian
Wiener Philharmonikergaße 7, 5020
Tel *0662-84 22 29* **Closed** *Sun*
A classic Austrian culinary
repertoire is served here – with
added contemporary pizzazz. Try
the inexpensive daily specials,
chalked up beside the bar.

SALZBURG: Esszimmer €€€
Gourmet
Müllner Hauptstraße 33, 5020
Tel *0662-87 08 99* **Closed** *Sun & Mon*
Enjoy modern European fare in
this atmospherically lit restaurant.
Esszimmer also offers good-value
three-course lunch menus.

Diners enjoying the chef at work at Cook, Linz

SWITZERLAND

The stereotypical images of Switzerland – cozy wooden chalets, alpine meadows, and chic skiing resorts – are easy to find. But there are many other sides to this small, diverse country that are equally accessible, from picturesque medieval towns to world-class art and fine gastronomy. Switzerland's rural retreats offer wonderful opportunities for relaxing and recharging.

Switzerland lies at the very heart of Europe, landlocked between the Alps and the Jura mountains. It is bordered to the west by France, to the north by Germany, to the east by Austria and Liechtenstein, and to the south by Italy.

Mountains make up almost a third of Switzerland's 41,285 sq km (15,949 sq miles). The St. Gotthard Massif is the source of many lakes and two major rivers, the Rhine and the Rhône. Central Switzerland has the highest concentration of picturesque Alpine peaks, although the loftiest Alps are those of the Valais in the southwest. The valleys of Graubünden in the east provide the setting for many winter resorts. In the west, the cities lining the northern shore of Lake Geneva comprise the "Swiss Riviera," while a series of high passes provides overland access from German-speaking Switzerland to the Ticino, the Italian-speaking part of the country, and to Italy.

With almost a quarter of its area comprising high Alps, lakes, and barren rock, and with no seaboard and few natural resources other than water power, the country has managed to preserve a proud and united spirit of independence.

History

Switzerland's geography has presented both opportunities and disadvantages. Its story has been of a gradual coming together, not without bloodshed, of a population of diverse cultures, religions, and languages, making what is today viewed as a haven of peace and reason.

The Jura mountains provide the earliest evidence of Switzerland's habitation, which dates to over 50,000 years ago. By the start of the Christian era, Celtic peoples were living in western Switzerland and Germanic tribes in the north and east. Many of these communities were under the control of the expanding Roman Empire, whose influence spread after 58 BC.

The Germanic tribes to the north eventually broke through Roman

The snow-capped Jungfrau, one of the Alps' most famous peaks

◀ A traditional church in a small mountain village in the Dolomites region of the Swiss Alps

defenses; by the 5th century AD, the era of Roman rule had ended. During the so-called "Dark Ages," the Burgundian tribe controlled the west, the Alemanni the center and east. In the 5th century, both tribes came under the control of the Franks, and later the Holy Roman Empire. The 13th century saw the rise of powerful local families such as the Habsburgs and the Zähringen, who established feudal rule over the area.

In 1291, three forest cantons around Lake Lucerne – Uri, Schwyz, and Unterwalden – came together to swear an Oath of Allegiance, thus forming an independent Swiss state. Over the coming centuries, more cantons came to join the Confederation. These included lands south of the Alps known as the Ticino, and those to the west, where Charles of Burgundy was defeated by the Swiss in 1477. Switzerland was

Huldrych Zwingli (1484–1531), leader of the Swiss Reformation

famous at this period for producing skilled mercenaries, who were paid handsomely to fight battles well beyond Swiss frontiers.

Protestantism took root in Switzerland in the 16th century, spread by the teachings of Zwingli and Calvin. Swiss cities embraced the new doctrines, whereas rural cantons remained mostly Catholic. Tensions between the two communities erupted into violence from time to time, and apart from a brief period at the turn of the 19th century when Napoleon established the Helvetic Republic, these issues were not resolved until the adoption of a federal constitution in 1848.

With stability came development – railways were built, agriculture diversified, resorts developed. A tradition of humanitarianism began in the mid-19th century with the founding of the

Exploring Switzerland

Switzerland is a small country – only 350 km (220 miles) by 220 km (140 miles) at its greatest extent. The Alps run across the southern part of the country, and in the northwest, the Jura mountains stretch along the French border. Mediterranean influences can be felt and seen in mild winters and palm-lined esplanades south of the Alps. Traveling by car is the most flexible mode of transportation, but the reliable rail network makes sightseeing by train easy and surprisingly affordable.

Sights at a Glance

1. Geneva
2. Lake Geneva
3. Neuchâtel
4. Basel
5. Bern
6. Interlaken and the Jungfrau
7. Zermatt
8. Lucerne
9. Zürich
10. Chur
11. Swiss National Park
12. Ticino

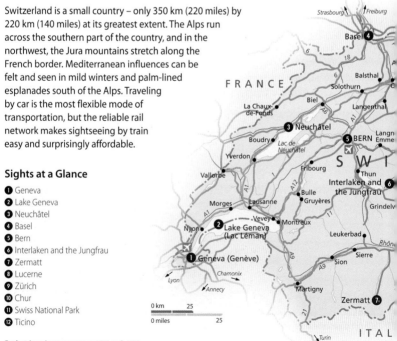

For hotels and restaurants see p594 and p595

International Red Cross. In the 20th century, Switzerland remained neutral during the two world wars, and concentrated on furthering its economic development, notably in the sectors of finance and pharmaceuticals.

Language and Culture

Switzerland is a quadrilingual nation. German, French, Italian, and Romansch (the language of a few valleys in the canton of Graubünden) are spoken in different parts of the country, though German is the language of the majority.

For many centuries, Swiss culture had a predominantly rural tradition, and wine festivals are still a feature of village life. Great pride is taken in traditional crafts and regional specialties, such as the famous Emmental cheese. Swiss chocolate is also renowned for its high quality. Switzerland is now an outward-looking country, keen to export its expertise in finance and watchmaking worldwide.

KEY DATES IN SWISS HISTORY

58 BC–AD 400 Roman occupation

AD 400–1100 Germanic peoples inhabit the area

12th century Holy Roman Empire extends feudal law over much of present-day Switzerland

1291 Oath of Allegiance marks beginning of the Swiss Confederation

1351 Zürich joins the Confederation

1477 Charles the Bold of Burgundy defeated by Swiss troops at Battle of Nancy

16th century Reformation; Protestantism takes firm hold in Swiss cities

1798 Napoleon creates the Helvetic Republic

1815 Power of cantons re-established

1830–48 Federal constitution drawn up

1864 International Red Cross set up

1914–18 & 1939–45 Switzerland remains neutral during two world wars

1946 UN offices established in Geneva

1990 Swiss women granted right to vote in every canton

2002 Switzerland declared member of the UN

2008 Switzerland joins EU Schengen Area, removing road and rail border checks

2014 Swiss government implements strict immigration quotas, which invalidates Schengen agreement

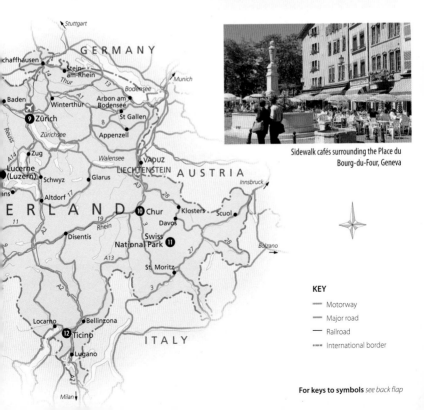

Sidewalk cafés surrounding the Place du Bourg-du-Four, Geneva

KEY

▬▬▬ Motorway

▬▬ Major road

▬ Railroad

▪▪▪ International border

For keys to symbols *see back flap*

Narrow, winding street in Geneva's historic old town

❶ Geneva

Geneva. 🚠 198,000. ✈ 🚆 🚌 🚢 𝒊
Rue du Mont-Blanc 18 (022-909 7000).
🎭 Fêtes de Genève (early Aug).
🌐 geneva-tourism.ch

Geneva is an ancient settlement with origins that go back to Roman times. The **old town**, situated on a craggy hill up above the western end of Lake Geneva, is the most attractive part of the city, with narrow, cobbled lanes and streets, fountain-filled squares, and an array of galleries, shops, and cafés.

In the heart of the old town stands the **Cathédrale St-Pierre**. Although the building dates from the 12th century, it was much altered in the 16th century – the plain facade and interiors are in keeping with its Reformist heritage. A splendid 14th-century town-house close by, the **Maison Tavel**, gives a good insight into life in the developing city of Geneva through the centuries. In Rue Jean-Calvin, the **Barbier-Müller Museum** displays artifacts and objects from traditional societies in Africa and the Asia-Pacific region. There is a mesmerizing array of beautiful carvings, jewelry, and textiles.

Geneva's grandest museum, however, is the **Musée d'Art et d'Histoire**, at the eastern end of the old town. The stately early 19th-century edifice houses a diverse array of Swiss and European art and artifacts, from prehistory to the modern age.

It also has a sizeable collection of Egyptian antiquities.

At the foot of the old town, Geneva's main shopping street – the Rue de Rive – runs parallel to the lake shore. The quays either side of the lake are pleasant places to stroll, with the Jardin Anglais and the **Jet d'Eau** (one of the world's largest fountains) on the Left Bank, and the Quai du Mont-Blanc on the right. It is from the latter that the ferries and paddlesteamers operate pleasure cruises and regular services to towns along the lake. Farther along the Right Bank are the city's **botanic gardens**, and if you take the road bordering them you will come to the international quarter of the city. Here, the **Palais des Nations** – European headquarters of the UN – runs frequent guided tours through the day (ID documents mandatory). Opposite, the **International Red Cross and Red Crescent Museum** offers a moving testimony to the need for such an organization.

🏛 **Musée d'Art et d'Histoire**
Rue Charles-Galland 2. **Tel** 022-418 2600. **Open** Tue–Sun. 🚻 ♿ for temporary exhibitions (free 1st Sun each month). 🌐 ville-ge.ch/mah

🏛 **Palais des Nations**
Avenue de la Paix 14. **Tel** 022-917 4896. **Open** Mon–Sat. 🎫 obligatory. **Closed** Sep–Mar: Sat. 📷 ♿
🌐 unog.ch

Jet d'Eau fountain, Geneva harbor

❷ Lake Geneva

Vaud. 🚆 🚌 🚢 𝒊 Avenue d'Ouchy 60, Lausanne (021-613 2626).
🎭 Nyon Paléo Music Festival (Jul).
🌐 region-du-leman.ch

The region skirting Lake Geneva offers a string of interesting settlements in a landscape replete with rolling hills, pretty stone-built villages, vine-clad slopes, and palm-fringed esplanades.

Coppet, 15 km (10 miles) north of Geneva, is a quaint medieval village. The 17th-century Château de Coppet was the home of Madame de Staël, whose literary soirées and opposition to Napoleon enhanced the popularity of the château in the 18th century.

Farther along the lake, **Nyon** is a charming lakeside town dating from Roman times, a heritage displayed at the excellent Roman Museum. With its fortress-like château and network of lanes, Nyon commands a fine hilltop view over the lake.

Lausanne, 60 km (38 miles) east of Geneva, is a bustling city with a fine old town, a beautiful Gothic cathedral, and excellent shopping. The city is also home to the international Olympic movement – at the lakeside district of Ouchy, the Musée Olympique (www.museum. olympic.org) is a must for all sports enthusiasts. The resort of

Wine château and vineyards near the town of Nyon

Montreux at the eastern end of the lake has a palm-lined promenade and a busy marina. As well as *belle-époque* hotels and health resorts, the town boasts one of Switzerland's top attractions – the **Château de Chillon**. This former bastion of the dukes of Savoy has all the accoutrements of a medieval castle – damp dungeons, weaponry, and huge banqueting halls.

About 25 km (15 miles) north of Montreux, the wonderfully preserved medieval hilltop town of **Gruyères** is also a major tourist attraction. The walled town is divided by a cobbled main street flanked by tempting restaurants. You can see the famous cheese being made in the traditional way in Moléson-sur-Gruyères.

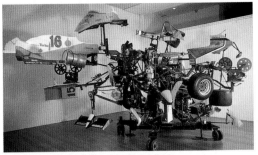
Pit Stop (1984), sculpture in the Museum Jean Tinguely, Basel

⊞ Château de Chillon
Avenue de Chillon 21, 1820 Veytaux.
Tel 021-966 8910. **Open** daily.
Closed Dec 25, Jan 1. ♿ 🔳 chillon.ch

❸ Neuchâtel

Neuchâtel. 🚏 33,000. 🚆 🚌
🛈 Hôtel des Postes (032-889 6890).
🍷 Wine Festival (late Sep).
🔳 neuchatel-tourisme.ch

Neuchâtel, an old religious center and university town, lies at the eastern end of Lake Neuchâtel at the base of the Jura mountains. It is a little off the beaten track, but has an extensive and attractive old town overlooked by the partly Romanesque **Collegiate Church**. Just below the church, the **Tour des Prisons** offers a stunning view of the lake and city. The market square – Place des Halles – is bounded by elegant 17th-century buildings, including the turreted **Maison des Halles**, now a restaurant. The area around Neuchâtel is known for its wines, including Perdrix Blanche.

Environs
20 km (12 miles) northwest of Neuchâtel lies **La Chaux-de-Fonds**, the largest of Switzerland's watchmaking towns. Located 992 m (3,255 ft) above sea level, it does not have the feel of a typical Swiss town. Its rigid grid

pattern was adopted when the town was rebuilt after a devastating fire in the 18th century. Le Corbusier and Louis Chevrolet are famous sons, though there is little evidence of the former in the town's architecture. The **Musée International d'Horlogerie** has a wonderful collection devoted to the watch industry, and is well worth a visit.

⊞ Musée International d'Horlogerie
Rue des Musées 29. **Tel** 032-967 6861.
Open Tue–Sun. **Closed** public hols.
♿ 🔳 mih.ch

Enameled watch (c.1665) in the Musée International d'Horlogerie

❹ Basel

Basel. 🚏 166,000. ✈ 🚆 🚌
🛈 Basel Tourismus, Stadt-Casino, Barfüsserplatz (061-268 6868).
🍷 Fair (Oct–Nov). 🔳 basel.com

Basel sits in the northernmost corner of Switzerland, straddling the Rhine at the farthest point that the river is navigable to sea-going vessels. This large commercial city is a world center for the chemical and

pharmaceutical industries. This is a legacy of its liberal past, when the city offered a home to Huguenots fleeing persecution. Their traditional silk-weaving skills eventually led to the development of synthetic dyes and pharmaceutical processes.

The **old town** remains the heart of the city and is a maze of fine streets and squares, including Marktplatz with its daily fruit and vegetable market. The striking red-painted **Rathaus** (city hall) stands here, on the southern bank of the Rhine.

The twin sandstone towers of the Gothic **cathedral** are major landmarks. This imposing 12th-century building stands in a grand square – site of the famous autumn fair that has been an annual event since the 15th century. Basel has a modern side too, with a vibrant cultural scene and a number of interesting museums, most notably the **Kunstmuseum**, which includes an impressive range of 20th-century artists such as Picasso, and the **Beyeler Foundation**, in Baselstrasse, a collection of around 200 paintings by modern masters.

Switzerland's most famous artist, Jean Tinguely (1925–91), has a museum devoted to his outlandish mechanical sculptures – **Museum Tinguely**.

⊞ Kunstmuseum
St. Alban-Graben 16. **Tel** 061-206 6262. **Open** Tue–Sun. ♿ 📷 ♿
🔳 kunstmuseumbasel.ch

⊞ Museum Tinguely
Paul Sacher Anlage 1. **Tel** 061-681 9320. **Open** Tue–Sun. ♿ ♿
🔳 tinguely.ch

The tall spire of Bern Cathedral rising above the city skyline

❺ Bern

Bern. 🚐 128,000. ✈ 🚍 🚊
ℹ Central Railway Station (031-328 1212). 🎭 Ziebelemaerit (Nov).
🌐 berninfo.com

Bern is the capital of Switzerland and its most attractive city – it has the best-preserved medieval town center in the country. It is located on raised land in a bend of the Aare River. From the city's terraces, there are spectacular views over the river and across to the peaks of the distant Alps.

The city was founded at the end of the 12th century by the Duke of Zähringen and allegedly named after the first animal – a bear – killed in the forests which previously covered the area. The bear has been the city's emblem ever since. Most of the center of Bern, with its many fine stone Renaissance houses and covered arcades, dates from the 16th and 17th centuries.

Since 1848, Bern has been the capital of the Confederation. The massive **Bundeshaus** (Parliament House) is the home of the Swiss Parliament, and the building is open to visitors when parliament is not in session. It is situated at the end of the city's main market squares – Bärenplatz and Bundesplatz. These linked squares are also the site of the annual onion market which takes place on the fourth Monday in November, when the local onion harvest is traditionally celebrated. The attractive **old town** at the heart

of Bern is a UNESCO World Heritage site, famous for its arcaded streets, which offer comprehensive protection in the event of bad weather. The main streets – Kramgasse, Spitalgasse, Marktgasse, and Gerechtigkeitsgasse – are all lined with tempting shops, galleries, and cafés.

The city's famous **clock tower** stands where Kramgasse meets Marktgasse. The clock dates from 1530, and on the hour a series of figures – including bears, a jester, and a rooster – plays out its performance. The old town is filled with magnificent fountains, each of which depicts a famous historical or legendary figure. A wander around the city center will reveal the likenesses of Moses, the Duke of Zähringen, and the gruesome child-eating ogre, the Kindlifresser.

The **cathedral** on Münstergasse was built in the 15th century and is a beautiful example of late Gothic architecture. The building's most magnificent element is the main portal –

The grotesque Kindlifresser or Ogre Fountain

a masterpiece of carved and painted stone, which depicts the Last Judgment. The tall spire was only added in the late 19th century. To the right of the cathedral is a delightful small park overlooking the Aare flowing far below. This makes a good picnic spot in summer.

A huge bear park is situated on the shore of the Aare just below the old **Bärengraben**, or bear pits. The park's caves, pools, and forest give the bears a more natural home than the 19th-century pits. The city's **Historical Museum** – located just south of the old town over the river across Kirchenfeldbrücke – provides a great introduction to the city's history. Among the notable exhibits are wonderful Flemish tapestries. There is also the brand-new **Paul Klee Centre**, on Monument in Fruchtland, which contains around 4,000 works by the renowned Expressionist artist, who lived in Bern for 33 years.

🏛 **Historical Museum**
Helvetiaplatz 5. **Tel** 031-350 7711.
Open Tue–Sun. **Closed** Nov 26, Dec 25. 🅿 ♿ 🅿 🌐 bhm.ch

Environs
To the southeast of Bern is the **Emmental Valley**. This verdant agricultural region, with its lush grazing, is famous for the cheese of the same name. A drive around the region can make an ideal half-day countryside tour. Take in some of the delightful towns and villages – Burgdorf, Affoltern, or Langnau im Emmental – and the gentle rolling hills dotted with covered wooden bridges and distinctive gabled wooden farmhouses of the area.

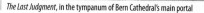

The Last Judgment, in the tympanum of Bern Cathedral's main portal

Interlaken cruise ship moored by the banks of the Thunersee

⑥ Interlaken and the Jungfrau

Bern. 🚩 5,700. 🚉 🚌 ℹ️ Höheweg 37 (033-826 5300). **w interlaken.ch**

Interlaken, as its name suggests, lies between two lakes – the Thunersee and the Brienzersee – in the foothills of the Alps. To the south is the classic landscape of the Jungfrau mountains – one of the first regions of Switzerland to be opened up to tourism in the middle of the 19th century. Tourism is virtually the only industry in town, which caters for skiers in winter and sightseers by the busload in summer. A **funicular**, built in 1906, takes visitors up to the summit of the Heimwehfluh (680 m/2,230 ft), a wonderful vantage point above Interlaken. From here, you can walk along woodland paths, visit an open-air model railway, or take the bob-run all the way down to the base station in Interlaken. There is also a restaurant and a children's play area.

Environs

One of the Alps' most famous peaks, the 4,158-m- (13,642-ft-) **Jungfrau** lies 20 km (12 miles) to the south of Interlaken. The almost equally high **Mönch** and **Eiger** mountains are neighbors and the stretch between Interlaken and the mountains is full of pretty alpine valleys and villages. From **Wengen** and **Grindelwald**, you can take a train up to Kleine Scheidegg,

and another to Jungfraujoch, at 3,454 m (11,332 ft), Europe's highest train station. Another popular viewpoint is the **Schilthorn** peak at the head of the Lauterbrunnen valley. This can be reached via **Mürren** and **Gimmelwald**, by cable car on the last stretch. The region is perfect skiing and hiking territory, with walking trails to suit all ability levels.

A few kilometers east of Brienz, the main town on Brienzersee, lies the Swiss Open Air Museum (known as the **Ballenberg**). Original buildings from all over the country have been brought to this living museum. A special bus runs from Brienz train station to the Ballenberg.

🏛 Ballenberg

Tel 033-952 1030. **Open** Apr–Oct: daily. 🚗 ♿ 📷 **w ballenberg.ch**

⑦ Zermatt

Valais. 🚩 6,000. 🚉 ℹ️ Bahnhofplatz (027-966 8100). **w zermatt.ch**

Switzerland's most famous resort, Zermatt sits directly below the **Matterhorn**, a peak of 4,478 m (14,688 ft), which has been a mountain-climbers' mecca for the best part of two centuries. In addition to mountaineering, Zermatt offers top-quality skiing and hiking. Skiing is possible all year round at this, the highest of Swiss resorts, and there are miles of well-marked trails accessible to all walkers.

The most scenic way to arrive in Zermatt is via the Glacier Express from St. Moritz, but most tourists arrive by train from Täsch, 5 km (3 miles) down the valley. Taxis from Täsch to car-free Zermatt cost about the same as the train.

Hinterdorf is the most historic part of town. The parish church and cemetery contain some poignant reminders of the dangers of the high mountains. The displays at **Zermatlantis**, an alpine museum near the church, reflect the importance of the region's mountaineering tradition.

Gornergrat is probably the best viewing point for the Matterhorn, and can be reached by taking a cog-wheel railroad. You can carry on by cable car to the **Stockhorn** peak for more mountain views.

Cog-wheel mountain railroad, with the Matterhorn peak rising behind

The Alps

The Alps are one of the oldest mountain ranges in the world, formed 65 million years ago when the Eurasian and African tectonic plates collided. They dominate Switzerland's landscape, covering more than half its surface area, and have shaped its history and economy. Switzerland is home to many well-known, distinctive peaks – such as the Matterhorn, Jungfrau, and Eiger – which were early tourist attractions in the 18th and 19th centuries. Trade and pilgrimage routes have crossed the Alps since Roman times, but it is only in the last century that this wild and beautiful landscape has become truly accessible, with the development of long road and rail tunnels, mountain railroads, and cable cars.

Peak of the Matterhorn and the Gornergrat mountain railroad

Lake Lucerne surrounded by peaks and alpine meadows

Alpine Flora

Deciduous trees are common on the lower slopes of the Alps, but these gradually give way to coniferous spruce and pine. Between the tree line and the snow line lie lush alpine meadows famous for their wildflowers.

The Alpine aster is one of many beautiful, brief-flowering, alpine plants found throughout the higher slopes and pastures. It blooms from July to August.

Androsace alpina, or rock jasmine, grows in mats which cling to alpine rockfaces. The shoots produce pinky-white flowers between July and August.

Edelweiss is the country's most famous flower, a symbol of purity and everlasting love. Increasingly rare, it is now a protected species.

Alpine Wildlife

Several national parks amid the Alps ensure the preservation of the unique native fauna. Although some animals have disappeared, a few species have adapted well to the higher altitudes, such as the marmot, chamois, ibex, mountain hare, and alpine chough.

Marmots are difficult to spot but quite easy to hear, and live in burrows high on the valley slopes. Found throughout the Alps, these mammals are particularly abundant in Graubünden and Ticino.

Chamois are goat-like antelopes which can be seen adeptly scaling the highest mountain ridges. In the past they were hunted for their hide, which makes a very soft leather, but hunting quotas are now imposed.

The alpine chough, a crow-like bird with a yellow bill, glossy blue-black plumage, and gregarious disposition, spends the summer above the tree line. They descend to the valleys and villages in winter, where they accept food from tourists.

The Alps in Summer

Long before skiing became popular, foreign visitors were coming to Switzerland's alpine areas for quiet, relaxing holidays full of fabulous vistas and fresh air. In general, alpine resorts are quieter in summer than during the ski season, but there are good outdoor activities provided in most areas. Some resorts, such as Verbier and Gstaad, host summer music festivals of some note. Most cable cars and mountain railroads operate throughout the summer, transporting hikers and sightseers.

Hikers and mountain bikers are very well-catered for in summer, as Switzerland has thousands of kilometers of designated footpaths. Trails are well-marked and maintained, with regular refreshment stops en route.

Désalpe, a traditional Swiss festival, celebrates the return of herds of cows from the high mountain pastures at the end of summer. In alpine valleys and the Jura, lines of groomed and festooned cattle are herded down the country roads, stopping off at village cattle troughs and fountains for refreshment, on their way back to the lowland farms.

The Alps in Winter

Switzerland has ski resorts to suit most tastes and budgets, from the chic, five-star hotels of St. Moritz, where celebrity spotting is almost as popular as skiing, to family-oriented resorts with facilities and slopes for all abilities such as Grindelwald. Some are predominantly modern – Verbier has grown from the unvisited hamlet of 50 years ago into one of the biggest ski resorts in Switzerland. Others, such as Zermatt – with its historic town center, alpine museum, and slow pace of life – are more traditional.

Davos is the largest resort in Switzerland, attracting visitors from all over the world. The twin towns of Davos Dorf and Davos Platz offer a wide choice of activities off piste, with an indoor sports center and many bars, nightclubs, and restaurants.

Edward Whymper

An illustrator by profession, the mountaineer Edward Whymper (1840–1911) was one of a long line of British climbers who came to the Swiss Alps in the 19th century to scale hitherto unconquered peaks. In 1865, he reached the peak of the Matterhorn at 4,478 m (14,688 ft), together with two Swiss guides. Today, despite remaining a difficult ascent, more than 2,000 climbers scale the Matterhorn in a good summer.

Winter snow is what draws most visitors to the Alps, whether for traditional skiing or snowboarding. More bizarre sports include horseboarding (like water-skiing with a horse) and "zorbing" (tumbling down the slopes strapped to the inside of a balloon).

Breathtaking Lake Lucerne and its surrounding mountain peaks

❽ Lucerne

Lucerne. 🚗 79,000. 🚉 🚌
ℹ️ Zentralstrasse 5 (041-227 1717).
🎭 Lucerne Festival Sommer (mid-Aug–mid-Sep). 🌐 **luzern.org**

The city of Lucerne makes a good base for touring most of central Switzerland. The surrounding countryside is possibly the most stereotypically Swiss – crystal-clear lakes ringed with snow-capped mountains, hemmed with lush pastures in summer, and criss-crossed with cog-wheel railroads. This is also the heartland of the Swiss Confederation – the three forest cantons of Uri, Schwyz, and Unterwalden, which swore the original Oath of Allegiance in 1291 (*see p578*), border the shores of Lake Lucerne. Today, the region remains one of the most conservative parts of Switzerland.

The town's historic center stands on the north bank of the Reuss river, which flows out of Lake Lucerne at its westernmost corner. Stretches of the ancient city wall and its watchtowers can be clearly seen bounding a ridge that marks the northern edge of the old town. The cobbled streets and shady squares are bustling both day and night.

The **Kapellbrücke** is the city's most famous symbol. Spanning the river at the lake end, this covered wooden bridge was

built in 1333, and formed part of the city's original boundary. Much of the bridge, including its decorative paintings, had to be renovated following a destructive fire in 1993. Also nearby is the **Rosengart Collection**, with over 200 works by various classic Modernist artists such as Klee, Picasso, and Cézanne.

The Rosengart now houses the collection of the former Picasso Museum. The works include photographs of Picasso, taken during the last 20 years of his life by British photographer David Douglas Duncan – images which further illuminate the artist's character.

🏛 Rosengart Collection
Pilatusstrasse 10. **Tel** 041-220 1660.
Open daily. **Closed** Feb 27, Mar 3 & 4.
📷 🎧 Sun am. 🌐 **rosengart.ch**

Environs
Ten minutes from the central train station along the lake to the east is Switzerland's most visited museum, the **Swiss Museum of Transport**. Highly interactive and fun for families, the museum has both plane and helicopter flight simulators, as well as trains, boats, and cable cars.

About 28 km (17 miles) east of Lucerne, **Schwyz** is the capital of one of the original three forest cantons, and has given the country its name. The charter detailing the 1291 Oath of Allegiance which marks the beginning of the Swiss Confederation is housed in the town's Bundesbrief-museum. More interesting is the **Ital Reding Hofstatt**, a fine 17th-century mansion on the northwest side of town, built on the proceeds of one of Switzerland's first exports – mercenaries. The fighting skills of the men of Schwyz were highly prized by warring European rulers until well into the 18th century.

Pilatus and **Rigi** mountains tower over the area and both are easily accessible. Mount Rigi has the distinction of being the first mountain in Europe to have a rail line constructed to the summit. This starts at Vitznau on the lake shore. Mount Pilatus to the south is higher and gives unrivaled views of the Alps. Its peak can be reached either by cable car from Kriens or cog-wheel railroad from Alpnachstad.

🏛 Swiss Museum of Transport
Lidostrasse 5. **Tel** 041-370 4444.
Open daily. 📷

The 17th-century mansion of Ital Reding Hofstatt in Schwyz

❾ Zürich

Zürich. 🏘 381,000. ✈ 10 km
(6 miles) N. 🚉 🚌 ℹ️ Hauptbahnhof
(044-215 4000). 🌐 **zuerich.com**

The dominant position of Zürich in the nation's economy has long been felt – in medieval times the guilds ruled the city and, boosted by the Reformation, Zürich and its inhabitants developed a talent for hard work and accumulating wealth. The stock exchange, which is the world's 13th largest, opened in 1877, and today Swiss bankers control the purse strings of many international companies and organizations.

Despite this tradition, the city also knows how to enjoy itself, and the medieval town center, which stretches either side of the Limmat river, is a hive of cafés, bars, and hip boutiques. On the east bank, the warren of streets and alleys lies close to the university, adding to the café culture of this district. Also on the east bank, the extremely austere **Grossmünster** dominates the city. This was the church from which Ulrich Zwingli launched the Reformation on the receptive burghers of Zürich in 1520. Along Limmat Quai, you can see the town hall (*rathaus*) built out on supports over the river, opposite one of Zürich's guildhalls.

On the other side of the river, there are a number of interesting sights. **Lindenhof**, a small hill, overlooks the city and was the site chosen by the Romans to

Grossmünster and Fraumünster in Zürich, separated by the Limmat river

build a customs post and thus found the city. **Fraumünster** and **St. Peter's** churches are nearby; the latter, with its Romanesque cloisters and stained-glass windows created by Marc Chagall, is well worth a visit.

Augustinergasse, which leads down from St. Peter's, is a delightful street with traces of medieval storefronts. It is a world away from Zürich's main shopping street, which it meets; Bahnhofstrasse is one of the world's most famous shopping areas – a wide, tree-lined avenue with trams running along its length. There are plenty of high-priced emporia, especially towards the southern lake end, but interesting and reasonably priced shops and department stores can be found here or in the streets nearby. At No. 70, **Orell Füssli** is Switzerland's largest English-language bookshop, and nearby on Löwenplatz, you will find one of 11 hard-to-resist outlets of the celebrated **Confiserie Sprüngli**.

Just behind the main train station at the top of Bahnhofstrasse, housed in a suitably Schloss-like building, the **Swiss National Museum** contains a comprehensive collection of art and artifacts detailing the history and cultural diversity of the country.

🏛 **Swiss National Museum**
Museumstrasse 2. **Tel** 044-218 6511.
Open Tue–Sun. 🅿 ♿
🌐 **nationalmuseum.ch**

Environs
Winterthur, 25 km (15 miles) northwest of Zürich, is an interesting and little visited Swiss town. Its history as an industrial center in the 19th century has left a legacy of old factory and mill architecture. It also boasts excellent museums; the best of these are the eclectic Oskar Reinhart Collection am Römerholz and the Fotomuseum.

The nucleus of medieval **Stein-am-Rhein**, 40 km (25 miles) northeast of Zürich, is unchanged since the 16th century. Rathausplatz and Understadt, at its heart, are lined with buildings covered in colorful frescoes, with oriel windows and window boxes.

Lively flea market at a lakeside park in Zürich's old town

Oriel window and frescoed facade of the Gasthaus zur Sonne, Stein-am-Rhein

⑩ Chur

Graubünden. 🗺 35,000. 🚊
ℹ Bahnhofplat 3 (081-252 1818).
🌐 churtourismus.ch

Chur, the capital of Switzerland's largest canton Graubünden, is a quiet, ancient town with origins that go back 2,000 years. It is located on the upper reaches of the Rhine, on an ancient route between northern Europe and Italy. It has long been a religious center – the bishop of Chur controls dioceses as far away as Zürich – as well as a commercial center, and is famous throughout the country for the Passugger mineral water which is bottled just outside the town.

The pedestrianized historic town center is a maze of cobbled streets and small squares, including Arcas Square with its sunny, café-filled corners in summer. At the southern tip of the old town, the late-Romanesque **cathedral**, set in a square, overlooks the rest of town. The highlight of the cathedral is its intricately carved and gilded 15th-century altarpiece, depicting Christ stumbling under the weight of the cross and scenes from the life of St. Catherine. Unfortunately, lighting levels are so low inside the building that its full glory is hard to discern. Next to the cathedral stands the **Bishop's Palace** (not open to

Elaborate 15th-century gilded altarpiece in Chur Cathedral

the public) and at the bottom of the small flight of steps leading up to the cathedral square is the **Rätisches Museum**, which focuses on the history and culture of the canton of Graubünden.

🏛 Rätisches Museum
Hofstrasse 1. **Tel** 081-254 1640.
Open Tue–Sun. 📷 🌐 rm.gr.ch

Environs
To the east of Chur, there are a number of world-class ski resorts. The two best-known, with very different characters, are **Klosters** and **Davos**. The former, famous as the favorite ski destination of British royalty, is a small traditional resort filled

with charming chalets. Davos, on the other hand, is a big, brash town with plenty of diversions away from the slopes. It has grown from a 19th-century mountain health resort to a major sporting center, renowned for skiing, snowboarding, paragliding, and tobogganing in the winter, and hiking, running, and cycling in the summer.

⑪ Swiss National Park

Graubünden. 🚊 Zernez, Scuol, S-Chanf. ℹ National Park House, Zernez (081-851 4141). **Open** Jun–Oct: daily. 📷 🌐 nationalpark.ch

Switzerland has many small nature reserves but only one national park. By international standards, it is small, covering only 170 sq km (66 sq miles), but it is an area where conservation measures have been strictly enforced since 1914, and people always take second place to the natural environment.

The Ofenpass road, linking Switzerland with Austria, cuts through the center of the park and affords good views of one of the park's valleys. Otherwise, the best way to see the park is to take some of the 80-km- (50-miles-) of marked trails – walkers are not allowed to deviate off the paths.

The landscape is one of wooded lower slopes and jagged scree-covered ridges, including the park's highest peak at 3,174 m (10,414 ft) – Piz Pisoc. Among the abundant wildlife, you may see are chamois, ibex, marmots, and the glorious bearded vultures, which are very rare in Europe and were reintroduced into the park in 1991. From June to August, with the retreat of the snows at higher altitudes, a carpet of beautiful alpine flowers, including edelweiss and Swiss androsace, appears.

The park has an interesting bear exhibition in the Schmelzra Museum, the former headquarters of a lead and silver mining company.

The lively winter-sports resort of Davos, in the mountains east of Chur

Hilltop sanctuary of Madonna del Sasso, Ticino, with its lakeside views

⑫ Ticino

✈ Agno. 🚉 Bellinzona, Locarno, Lugano. 🛈 Via Lugano 12, Bellinzona (091-825 7056). 🎬 Locarno International Film Festival (early Aug). 🌐 **ticino.ch**

The Ticino, Switzerland's most southerly canton, feels much more Italian than Swiss, with its mild climate and Italian cuisine and language. It lies south of the Alps, bordering the Italian lakes *(see p411)*, and is traversed by routes up the Alpine passes of St. Gotthard and San Bernadino. The three main towns of Bellinzona, Locarno, and Lugano all make attractive bases for exploring the area, with plenty of attractions, cafés and restaurants. Beyond, the valleys of the Ticino offer great sightseeing opportunities.

Bellinzona is the capital of the canton. Lying on the main north–south route between the Alps and Italy, it provides the first hint of Italian life with elegant piazzas, hilltop fortresses, and fine Renaissance churches. The

three castles of **Castelgrande**, in the town, **Montebello**, in the middle, and **Sasso Corbaro**, on top of the hill, feature on UNESCO's list of protected monuments. Castelgrande, with its imposing battlements, was the stronghold of the Visconti family in medieval times. Bellinzona is also appealing on Saturdays, when the streets of its old town are filled with tempting market stalls.

Locarno is located at the northern end of Lake Maggiore. The suitably named Piazza Grande is the heart of town, which, for two weeks in August, becomes a giant open-air cinema during the **International**

Film Festival. The festival aims to keep alive experimentation, discovery, eclecticism, and passion for auteur cinema. Moviegoers of all ages and nationalities gather in the square to watch a movie on one of the world's biggest screens.

Winding lanes filled with restaurants and boutiques radiate off the piazza. Above the town, easily accessible by a funicular railroad, the sanctuary of **Madonna del Sasso** is a major tourist and pilgrimage site. There has been a church here since 1480, when a vision of the Virgin Mary appeared to a local monk. The Baroque church is filled with marvelous frescoes and commands a fantastic view over the lake.

Probably the most charming of the three main centers of the region is **Lugano**, with its palm-lined lakeside location and attractive historic center of elegant piazzas. The arcaded streets are full of interesting old shops selling local produce.

Away from the main centers, there are plenty of quaint villages along the Maggiore and Lugano lakes, such as **Ascona** and **Gandria**. These are now filled with waterside restaurants and arts and crafts shops. The valleys to the north offer great hiking and beautiful, peaceful scenery. Val Verzasca, north of Locarno, is one such valley, with the photogenic stone hamlet of **Corippo** clinging to the steep sides, and the pretty villages of **Brione** and **Sonogno** towards the head of the valley.

🏰 **Castelgrande**
Monte San Michele, Bellinzona. **Tel** 091-825 8145. **Open** daily. ♿

🏛 **Madonna del Sasso**
Via Santuario 2, Orselina. **Tel** 091-743 6265. **Open** daily.

Crowd gathered for Locarno's annual International Film Festival

Practical & Travel Information

Thanks to the famous Swiss efficiency, traveling around Switzerland is generally a pleasant and hassle-free experience. The country prides itself on its excellent transportation systems, with an extensive national rail network and frequent tram and bus services in the big cities. There are abundant tourist information offices and banking and communication facilities are of a high standard. Switzerland has four national languages – German, French, Italian, and Romansh – but the use of English is widespread, especially in tourist destinations.

Tourist Information

Up-to-date information on many of Switzerland's towns and cities can be obtained from brochures and Internet sites. Most large cities have at least one centrally located tourist information office *Verkehrsverein*, *Tourismus*, or *Office du Tourisme*, offering a wide range of information and facilities. Even the smallest towns and resorts have tourist offices, but the opening hours of those in ski resorts may be limited in summer. Embassies are located in Bern, but many countries also have a consulate or diplomatic mission in Geneva.

Opening Hours

The 24-hour society has yet to reach Switzerland, and while large stores in cities may have late-night opening (usually on a Thursday), most shops, museums, and offices close at 5 or 6pm. Many museums are closed on Mondays and village restaurants often close one or two days a week.

Visa Requirements

Visitors to Switzerland must have a valid passport to enter the country. A visa is not required for visitors from the European Union, USA, Canada, Australia, and New Zealand for stays of up to 90 days. Border controls at road and rail frontiers have been abolished within the Schengen Area, which covers Switzerland and 24 other European countries.

Safety and Emergencies

Switzerland is one of the world's safest countries but you should still take all the usual precautions. Since Switzerland has no public health system, travel and health insurance are essential, especially considering the medical costs associated with skiing accidents. Hospitals have 24-hour emergency cover and in cities and towns there is always a pharmacy open. All pharmacies should post details of a 24-hour roster in their window. Emergency services, including **helicopter rescue**, are very efficient, and there is also an **avalanche bulletin** hotline. If skiing or hiking at altitude, remember that dehydration or sunburn can cause problems.

Banking and Currency

The unit of currency in Switzerland is the Swiss franc (CHF). Banking hours are generally 8:30am–4:30pm Monday to Friday, with some branches in tourist resorts also opening on Saturdays. Outside the big cities, some banks may close for lunch between noon and 2pm. Money can be changed at banks or at bureaux de change. The latter are found in hundreds of locations, including at major train stations. Swiss francs and euros can also be withdrawn from cash machines. Credit cards are widely accepted.

Communications

Switzerland's bright yellow mail boxes are easy to spot, though post offices are not as prevalent as they used to be. They usually open from 7:30am to noon and from 1:30 to 6:30pm Monday to Friday, and from 8 to 11am on Saturday. However, times can vary from region to region, and smaller post offices often have more restricted hours. Public telephones are plentiful, and take phonecards – available from post offices and newsagents – credit cards, and euro and Swiss franc coins. Internet facilities are found at airports and train stations, among other places.

The principal newspapers with nationwide circulation are the *Neue Zürcher Zeitung* from Zürich and *Le Temps* from Geneva. Most British newspapers are available in major centers from lunchtime.

Flying to Switzerland

Switzerland has international airports at Zürich, Geneva, Basel, Bern, Lugano, and Sion. Among the major airlines that fly to Switzerland are Swiss International Airlines (Swiss), Qantas, American Airlines, and British Airways. Low-cost airline easyJet (*see p25*) flies from

The Climate of Switzerland

Generally summers are sunny with temperatures frequently reaching 25° C (77° F), though thunderstorms can be a feature of summer evenings. Winters are cold with plenty of snow, but many places get a lot of winter sunshine, especially the ski resorts of the Valais. South of the Alps, in the Ticino, the climate is milder and much more Mediterranean in character.

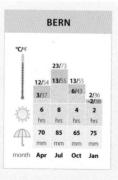

BERN			
°C/°F			
	23/73		
12/54	13/55	13/55	
3/37		6/43	2/36
			-2/38
6 hrs	8 hrs	4 hrs	2 hrs
70 mm	85 mm	65 mm	75 mm
month Apr	Jul	Oct	Jan

London Gatwick, London Luton, and other European cities to Zürich and Geneva.

Because of the many business travelers who fly to Switzerland on a weekly basis, Monday and Friday flights can be hard to obtain, especially during the skiing season.

Traveling by Train

Switzerland is at the heart of Europe and rail links to major European cities are fast and efficient. The journey time from Zürich to Paris is six hours; from Geneva to Paris it is three and a half hours.

Switzerland's rail network is operated by the state-owned **Swiss Federal Railways** and private companies. It reaches all major cities and towns and some of the smallest villages in the mountains. There is an integrated ticketing and fare system. When traveling to a major city, ask for a ticket that covers your destination's transportation network too – this usually costs only a small amount more. The Swiss Travel System (www.swisstravelsystem. com) offers a range of discount offers, which vary depending on how long you want to stay and

where you want to go. Most popular is the Swiss Pass, which allows unlimited travel on trains, lake ferries, and many mountain railways. Switzerland has a number of spectacular train routes. The best-known are those that pass through the Alps, such as the Glacier Express between St. Moritz and Zermatt. These services are included in the Swiss Passes and are reasonably priced.

Traveling by Car

The most direct route by car from Great Britain to Switzerland is via the Channel Tunnel and French motorways to western Switzerland. If you want to make use of the excellent motorway network, you will need to buy a motorway sticker *(vignette)*, available at border crossings, tourist offices, and gas stations.

Most of the international car rental firms have offices at airports and in the major towns. Many allow you to leave the car at a destination in France, Germany, or Italy.

As in the rest of continental Europe, the Swiss drive on the right. Since most freight is moved by rail in Switzerland, the majority of country routes, main roads, and motorways are generally free

of congestion. Driving around major cities, however, can be more difficult. Road signs are generally clear, with main roads in blue and freeways in green. Historic sights are usually signposted in brown. Speed limits are strictly enforced – 120 km/h (75 mph) on freeways, 80 km/h (50 mph) on main roads, and 50 km/h (30 mph) in built-up areas. Many mountain passes are closed from November to June. A sign at the foot of the pass will indicate whether the road is open or closed.

Getting around Cities and Towns

Buses and trams are found in the major cities and they provide frequent and reliable services. Tickets can be purchased from machines at bus and tram stops. Taxis are generally very expensive. Some cities such as Bern offer bicycle rental facilities, as do 80 of the major train stations. Many small villages that are not served by trains are on a "post bus" route, which usually originates at the train station of the nearest main town. Buses are timed to coincide with the arrival and departure of trains.

DIRECTORY

Tourist Information

UK
Switzerland Tourism,
30 Bedford Street,
London WC2E 9ED.
Tel 00800-100 200 30
(international toll free).

US & Canada
Swiss Center, 608 Fifth
Ave, New York, NY 10020.
Tel 00800-100 200 30
(international toll free).

Switzerland & all other countries
P.O. Box 695, 8027 Zürich.
Tel 00800-100 200 30
(international toll free).
🅦 **myswitzerland.com**

Embassies

Australia
Chemin des Fins 2,
Case Postale 172,
Geneva 1211.
Tel 012-799 9100.

Canada
Kirchenfeldstrasse 88,
3005 Bern.
Tel 031-357 3200.

Ireland
Kirchenfeldstrasse 68,
3005 Bern.
Tel 031-352 1442.

UK
Thunstrasse 50, 3000
Bern. **Tel** 031-359 7700.

US
Sulgeneckstrasse 19, 3007
Bern. **Tel** 031-357 7011.

Emergency Numbers

Ambulance
Tel 144.

Avalanche Bulletin
Tel 187.

Fire
Tel 118.

Helicopter Rescue
Tel 1414 / 1415.

Police
Tel 117.

Weather Forecast
Tel 162.

Swiss International Airlines

Australia
Tel 130-072 4666.

Ireland
Tel 01-890 200 515.

New Zealand
Tel 0800-945 220.

Switzerland
Tel 0848-700 700.

UK
Tel 0845-601 0956.

US & Canada
Tel 1-877 359 7947.
🅦 **swiss.com**

Traveling by Train

Swiss Federal Railways
Hochschulstrasse 6,
3000 Bern.
Tel 0900-300 300.
🅦 **sbb.ch**

Shopping & Entertainment

There are plenty of high-quality Swiss-made products to take away from your trip, including, of course, watches and chocolate. Porcelain, lace, wine, and cheese are also popular purchases. Apart from major events, such as the Montreux Jazz Festival, there is entertainment on a smaller scale throughout the country. Classical and jazz concerts abound in the large cities, which also have cinemas, opera halls, and dance venues. Most regions hold a number of seasonal local events, from wine festivals to antiques and bric-a-brac fairs. Switzerland's greatest attractions, however, are its landscape and outdoor sports. The mountains welcome skiers in winter and climbers, hikers, and cyclists in summer, with all levels of ability catered for.

Where to Shop

In the large cities, the old town areas usually have the most rewarding shopping – often you'll find narrow streets crammed with interesting, if often expensive, specialist stores and galleries. Bern's old town, with its arcaded streets, offers varied and sheltered shopping whatever the weather. The major department stores, such as Globus, offer a fairly standard international shopping experience. Competitively priced nationwide supermarket chains, including Migros, Coop, and Denner, now offer an interesting array of Swiss foodstuffs and wine.

What to Buy

After you have stocked up with Swiss chocolate, other items you might consider taking away with you as souvenirs and gifts are linen and lace. Switzerland has a long tradition of textile-working in the northeast of the country and the quality is generally very good.

Swiss army knives are popular and incredibly useful; keep an eye out for Victorinox, the only genuine manufacturer. Swiss porcelain and pottery can also be a good buy. Many of the designs favor strong colors and rural motifs.

Basketry and carved wooden items (such as toys) make ideal gifts, and these can sometimes be found on market stalls. A wide range of watches and jewelry is available, particularly at the top end of the market. Watches are one of Switzerland's most important exports, so the quality of Swiss watchmaking is very high.

Other places where you might find suitable gifts include any branch of **Schweizer Heimatwerk**, which is a national chain of Swiss handicraft stores. They have outlets in many large towns and cities, as well as at the airports if you leave your present-buying late.

Major museums, cheese showrooms and similar locations will often have a small store. In the major tourist destinations, such as Gruyères, there is no shortage of shops selling cheap tourist souvenirs, but you will also find knowledgeable retailers offering high-quality genuine Swiss-made items.

Markets

Outdoor produce and craft markets are common in Switzerland. Most towns and cities have a market on one or two mornings a week, and almost always on a Saturday morning. These are great places to try out local wines and cheeses, as well as simply to savor the lively atmosphere.

Food and Drink

Very little Swiss wine is exported, so it makes an unusual gift. Some of the Valais wines, such as *Fendant* (white) and *Dôle* (red), are among the best. Among more transportable food items are dried meats from the German parts of Switzerland, such as *Bündnerfleisch*, alpine cheeses such as Gruyère, and spicy *Leckerli* biscuits from Lucerne or Basel. Even packets of ready-made *rösti* mixture from supermarkets can make a fun gift.

Entertainment Listings and Tickets

A great variety of small town- and village-based concerts, festivals, and events takes place in Switzerland throughout the year. Local tourist offices can supply details of what's happening during your visit, while the Swiss Tourist Board offices abroad can provide comprehensive listings of all major sporting and cultural events taking place in Switzerland over the coming year.

Most major cities have a variety of venues dedicated to the arts, whether it be classical music, theater, cabaret, or jazz. Information about events can be found on the websites of the local tourist offices (for example, www.zuerich.com/events), on www.my switzerland.com or via the ticket office **Ticketcorner**.

Entertainment Venues

Many venues in Switzerland offer more than one type of entertainment. The **Reitschule** in Bern is used for live music, theater, film, and dance, while the **Théâtre de l'Usine** in Geneva hosts concerts, theater, film, and cabaret.

The Zürich Tonhalle Orchestra is based at the **Opernhaus**, a popular venue for opera and ballet. Zürich has a thriving club scene. **Rote Fabrik** by the lakeshore is inexpensive and plays alternative music. The **Widder Bar** has live jazz performances.

Cinemas in Switzerland often show films in their original language, with subtitles in French, German, Italian, or English. Zürich has more than

40 cinemas, almost all of which have regular showings of English-language films.

Festivals and Public Holidays

Across Switzerland, public holidays and religious events are celebrated in different ways. Lent and Easter are marked by masked parades, lantern processions, music concerts, and tree- and fountain-dressing in many parts of the country. Swiss National Day (August 1) commemorates the swearing of the Oath of Allegiance between the original forest cantons. Bonfires are lit and huge firework displays put on all over the country. Even the smallest village has a party with wine, food, and music.

Switzerland has many other annual festivals and themed events. Geneva's famous International Motor Show is held every year in the spring. The **Montreux International Jazz Festival** takes place in July, as does the **Paléo Music Festival**, a week-long open-air concert of world music at the town of Nyon on Lake Geneva. August brings the **Locarno International Film Festival** and Lucerne's International Music Festival. Other annual festivals

include the huge autumn fair in Basel, harvest festivals in the country's wine-growing regions, and the Combats de Reines, a form of cow fighting popular in some areas of the Valais. In spring, the animals are released from their often-cramped winter quarters. The cows butt heads in a natural fight for dominance, to see who is "Queen of the Herd." Injuries are rare.

Winter Sports

Skiing and snowboarding are just a couple of the many activities that Switzerland has to offer. Despite the country's reputation for high costs, it is possible to ski inexpensively. There is a wide range of options, from small, traditional villages to large modern resorts packed with lots of additional facilities such as swimming pools and ice-skating rinks. Advice on the range and suitability of different resorts can be sought from Switzerland Tourism *(see p590)* or the **Ski Club of Great Britain**, which provides information, advice, and holiday and tuition packages. Cross-country skiing is very popular – some of the best places to try this are the villages of the Jura and the Lower Engadine Valley.

Summer Sports

In the summer, mountaineering and hiking take over from skiing as the most popular draw, though skiing all year round is an option at one or two high-altitude resorts, such as Zermatt. There are 60,000 km (37,200 miles) of marked hiking trails all over the country, including some long-distance ancient trade and pilgrimage routes, such as the Grand St-Bernard trail. Yellow markers indicate standard hiking trails. Higher, rougher trails have red and white markers and the very high-altitude trails are marked in blue. These should only be attempted with an experienced guide. Mountain biking is also catered for, with trails clearly indicated. Maps and information are available from the **Swiss Alpine Club** or the **Swiss Hiking Federation**.

Other Outdoor Activites

Sailing and swimming are possible during summer at the country's clean lakes. River rafting is also a popular activity, especially along the Rhine. If slightly gentler sports – such as hot-air ballooning or horseback riding – are more your thing, tourist offices will be able to provide suggestions.

DIRECTORY

Handcrafts

Schweizer Heimatwerk
w heimatwerk.ch
Schneidergasse 2, Basel.
Tel 061-261 9178.
Airport, Geneva.
Tel 022-788 3300.
Bahnhofstrasse 2, Zürich.
Tel 044-221 0837.
Uraniastrasse 1, Zürich.
Tel 044-222 1955.

Entertainment Tickets

Ticketcorner
Tel 0900-800 800.
w ticketcorner.com

Entertainment Venues

Opernhaus
Falkenstrasse 1, Zürich.
Tel 044-268 6400.
Fax 044-268 6401.
w opernhaus.ch

Reitschule
Neubrückstrasse 8, Bern.
Tel 031-306 6969.
Fax 031-306 6967.
w reitschule.ch

Rote Fabrik
Seestrasse 395, Zürich.
Tel 044-485 5858.
w rotefabrik.ch

Théâtre de l'Usine
11 Rue de la
Coulouvrenière, Geneva.
Tel 022-328 0818.
w theatredelusine.ch

Widder Bar
Widdergasse 6, Zürich.
Tel 044-224 2411.
w widderhotel.ch

Festivals

Locarno International Film Festival
w pardo.ch

Montreux International Jazz Festival
w montreuxjazz.com

Paléo Music Festival
w paleo.ch

Outdoor Activities

Ski Club of Great Britain
57–63 Church Road,
London SW19.
Tel 020-8410 2000.
w skiclub.co.uk

Swiss Alpine Club & Swiss Hiking Federation
Monbijoustrasse 61, Bern.
Tel 031-370 1818.
w sac-cas.ch

Where to Stay

Lake Geneva

GENEVA: Hôtel de la Cloche Ⓕ
Budget
Rue de la Cloche 6, 1201
Tel *022-732 94 81*
🅆 geneva-hotel.ch/cloche
Popular hotel with the appeal of a 19th-century family home.

DK Choice

**GENEVA: Hôtel
Beau-Rivage** ⒻⒻⒻ
Luxury
Quai du Mont-Blanc 13, 1201
Tel *022-716 66 66*
🅆 beau-rivage.ch
Geneva's oldest hotel is poised on the edge of the lake, with views of the Jet d'Eau. It is an architectural gem, with crystal chandeliers, a four-story interior atrium, marble walls, and Grecian columns. In addition to exceptional concierge service and opulent rooms, there are also four apartments.

**GRUYERES: Hôtel de
Gruyères** ⒻⒻ
Family
Ruelle des Chevaliers, 1663
Tel *026-921 19 33*
🅆 chevaliers-gruyeres.ch
Peaceful hotel with comfy rooms. Cyclists are particularly welcome.

LAUSANNE: Hotel Bellerive Ⓕ
Budget
Avenue de Cour 99, 1007
Tel *021-614 90 00*
🅆 hotelbellerive.ch
Great-value central hotel with impeccable, modern rooms and splendid lake views.

Western Switzerland

BASEL: Hotel D ⒻⒻ
Boutique
Blumenrain 19, 4051
Tel *061-272 20 20*
🅆 hoteld.ch
Classy, modern rooms with sweeping views of the Old Town. Organic breakfasts. Great value.

BERN: Waldhorn Ⓕ
Budget
Waldhöheweg 2, 3013
Tel *031-332 23 43*
🅆 waldhorn.ch
A comfortable option with great service and spotless rooms, just a few minutes from the city center.

**GRINDELWALD:
Mountain Hostel** Ⓕ
Budget
Grundstrasse 58, 3818
Tel *033-854 38 38*
🅆 mountainhostel.ch
Clean double rooms and dorms amid spectacular scenery. Great place for biking, skiing, and golf.

DK Choice

**INTERLAKEN:
Victoria-Jungfrau** ⒻⒻⒻ
Luxury
Höheweg 41, 3800
Tel *033-828 28 28*
🅆 victoria-jungfrau.ch
This is one of Europe's most majestic grand old hotels. The public rooms are opulent, while bedrooms are generously sized and elegantly appointed. Convenient for lake excursions, the Victoria-Jungfrau also has an extensive, state-of-the-art spa, and fitness and beauty facilities.

ZERMATT: Riffelalp ⒻⒻⒻ
Luxury
Riffelalp, 3920
Tel *027-966 05 50*
🅆 riffelalp.com
This luxurious 19th-century hotel is perched high on a hill. Tranquillity is guaranteed, as it is accessible only by train.

Zürich and Lucerne

**LUCERN: Grand
Hotel National** ⒻⒻ
Luxury
Haldenstraße 4, 6006
Tel *041-419 09 09*
🅆 national-luzern.ch
Splendid 19th-century hotel with lake and city views from its lavishly furnished rooms.

ZÜRICH: Lady's First ⒻⒻ
Boutique
Mainaustraße 24, 8008
Tel *044-380 80 10*
🅆 ladysfirst.ch
This 19th-century hotel is aimed toward women, although men are welcome on the lower floors.

ZÜRICH: Widder ⒻⒻⒻ
Luxury
Rennweg 7, 8001
Tel *044-224 25 26*
🅆 widderhotel.ch
Individually furnished rooms at this hotel famous for its service.

Graubunden and Ticino

DAVOS: Waldhotel ⒻⒻ
Family
Buolstraße 3, 7270
Tel *081-415 15 15*
🅆 waldhotel-davos.ch
Rooms with mountain views, a gourmet restaurant, and a pool.

KLOSTERS: Rustico Ⓕ
Budget
Landstraße 194, 7250
Tel *081-410 22 88*
🅆 hotel-rustico.ch
Guesthouse with wood-paneled rooms and rustic furniture.

LOCARNO: Belvedere ⒻⒻ
Luxury
Via Monti della Trinità 44, 6600
Tel *091-751 03 63*
🅆 belvedere-locarno.com
Delightful hotel in a former 16th-century palazzo. Superb spa.

Streamlined elegance in a large room at the Victoria-Jungfrau, Interlaken

Where to Eat and Drink

The splendid frescoed vaulted ceiling at the Kornhauskeller, Bern

Lake Geneva

GENEVA: Café de Paris ⑤⑤
French
Rue de Mont-Blanc 26, 1201
Tel *022-732 84 50*
This is the original home of a famous butter-based sauce, which they also sell in small pots. The steak and chips is to die for.

GENEVA: Du Parc des Eaux-Vives ⑤⑤⑤
French
Quai Gustave-Ador 82, 1211
Tel *022-849 75 75* **Closed** *Sun & Mon*
Classic French cuisine is served in a superbly elegant room housed in a historic château. There is also a beautiful terrace for summer dining.

LAUSANNE:
La Croix d'Ouchy ⑤⑤
French/Italian
Avenue d'Ouchy 43, 1006
Tel *021-616 22 33* **Closed** *Jun*
This lakeside gourmet restaurant offers French and Italian cuisine with good vegetarian choices. Try the sublime risottos and the black truffle ravioli. Sunny terrace.

MONTREUX:
Le Pont de Brent ⑤⑤⑤
French
Le Pont de Brent, 1817
Tel *021-964 52 30* **Closed** *Sun & Mon*
A Michelin-starred restaurant serving exquisite French dishes in pleasant surroundings. It is very pricey, though the business lunch is quite reasonable.

Western Switzerland

BASEL: Cheval Blanc ⑤⑤⑤
Mediterranean
Grand Hotel Les Trois Rois, Blumenrain 8, 4001
Tel *061-260 50 07* **Closed** *Sun & Mon*
Regal restaurant with two Michelin stars, run by award-winning chef Peter Knogl. Lovely views of the Rhine from the summer terrace.

DK Choice

BERN: Kornhauskeller ⑤⑤
Mediterranean
Kornhausplatz 18, 3000
Tel *031-327 72 72*
A treat for the eyes as much as for the palate, the cellar dining room of the Kornhauskeller features dramatic vaulted arches painted with frescoes. It was once used as a grain storage facility, among other functions. Restored to its glory, the cellar is now very popular with visitors.

INTERLAKEN: Goldener Anker ⑤
International
Marktgaße 57, 3800
Tel *033-822 16 72*
Renowned for its large portions and reasonable prices. The fresh fish dishes and enormous pork chops are excellent. Book ahead.

ZERMATT: Zum See ⑤⑤
Mediterranean
Zum See, 3920
Tel *027-967 20 45* **Closed** *May & Nov*
This highly regarded mountain restaurant offers a seasonal menu – mountain berries and fresh vegetables in summer, and game in autumn.

Zürich and Lucerne

LUCERNE:
Old Swiss House ⑤⑤⑤
Swiss
Löwenplatz 4, 6004
Tel *041-410 61 71*
In a landmark half-timbered house with great decor, this eatery serves innovative fare – do not miss the Wienerschnitzel. Phenomenal wine list.

ZÜRICH: Haus zum Rüden ⑤⑤
French
Limmatquai 42, 8001
Tel *044-261 95 66* **Closed** *Sat & Sun*
This restaurant has a Gothic dining hall with a stunning wooden ceiling. The menu lays an emphasis on game and seasonal vegetables.

ZÜRICH: Kronenhalle ⑤⑤⑤
German/French
Rämistraße 4, 8001
Tel *044-262 99 00*
A Zürich institution, Kronenhalle is unmissable – for both its interiors and its cooking. Its walls feature original artworks by Picasso, Matisse, and Braque. It is popular with both locals and visitors for its generous portions.

Graubunden and Ticino

BELLINZONA: Castelgrande ⑤⑤
Swiss
Salita al Castello 18, 6500
Tel *091-814 87 81* **Closed** *Mon; Jul & Aug*
Outstanding restaurant with two dining options. The Grotto has a cavern-like feel where specialties such as risotto and gnocchi are on offer, while the gourmet dining room has a streamlined, modern decor.

KLOSTERS: Rustico ⑤⑤
Tapas Bar
Landstraße 195, 7250
Tel *081-410 22 88* **Closed** *Sun & Mon*
An inexpensive and lively dining option. Enjoy live music and hefty portions of comfort food like chicken wings and chili.

LOCARNO: Cittadella ⑤⑤
Italian
Via Cittadella 18, 6600
Tel *091-751 58 85*
Situated in the heart of the Old Town, Cittadella occupies two floors of a characterful building. Pizzas are baked in a wood-burning oven, and there is also a great selection of seafood dishes.

LUGANO: Al Portone ⑤⑤⑤
Mediterranean
Viale Cassarate 3, 6900
Tel *091-923 55 11*
A gourmet restaurant that serves refined and inventive dishes. Specialties include risotto and home-made pastas. Fine wines.

Price Guide
Prices are for a three-course meal for one, including a half-bottle of house wine, tax and service.

⑤	up to 40 CHF
⑤⑤	40 to 100 CHF
⑤⑤⑤	over 100 CHF

SCANDINAVIA

Scandinavia at a Glance

The Scandinavian countries – Denmark, Norway, Sweden, and Finland – are, arguably, among the least known countries in Europe. In Norway, Sweden, and Finland, the majority of the population lives in the south, in affluent, modern cities, which are also rich in history and tradition. Away from the main towns and cities lie vast expanses of unspoiled, often wild terrain, from the breathtaking Norwegian fjords to the dense pine forests and clear lakes of Finland. At just over seven hours by train from Helsinki, St. Petersburg, Russia's second city, is easily accessible from eastern Scandinavia.

Oslo *(see pp622–6)*, Norway's capital, is an attractive city of grand Neo-Classical buildings, wide boulevards, and green open spaces. In Frogner Park, one of the largest parks, is a collection of works by the eccentric Norwegian sculptor Gustav Vigeland (1869–1943).

Bergen *(see p628)* was the largest town and most important port in medieval Norway. Its streets are lined with fine historic monuments, including the 12th-century Mariakirken, the oldest building in the city.

Copenhagen *(see pp638–43)* is a cosmopolitan city with a relaxed and welcoming atmosphere. Among the Danish capital's most visited attractions is the theme park, Tivoli Gardens, with its famous Chinese Pagoda.

Mo i Rana

Storum

Trondheim

Ålesund

Sund

NORWAY
(see pp618–33)

G.

Bergen

Drammen

Oslo

Karlstad

Stavanger

SWEDEN
(see pp600–17)

Kristiansand

Jönköp

Gothenburg

Väx

Aalborg

Halmstad

DENMARK
(see pp634–49)

Århus

Esbjerg

Copenhagen

Malmö

Odense

◀ Brightly-painted buildings along Nyhavn, in Copenhagen, Denmark

omsø

0 km 100
0 miles 100

Locator Map

Kemijärvi

Luleå

Kemi

Oulu

Umeå

FINLAND
(see pp650–63)

Kuopio

Vaasa

Jyväskylä

Tampere

Lahti

Turku

Helsinki

St. Petersburg

Stockholm

Visby

Helsinki *(see pp654–8)*, the capital of Finland, boasts an impressive mix of Neo-Classical and modern 20th-century architecture. The city's hub of activity is Market Square on the waterfront, which in summer fills with crowds browsing the craft and food stalls.

St. Petersburg *(see pp658–9)*, Russia's "culture capital", is an easy side trip from Helsinki. The city's main artery, Nevskiy prospekt, is packed with shops, cafés, and monumental architecture.

Stockholm *(see pp604–9)* enjoys an unrivaled setting surrounded by water and unspoiled countryside that stretches right into the center. Overlooking the Riddarfjärden channel is the Stadshuset (City Hall), a symbol of the city.

SWEDEN

The Swedes are justly proud of the natural beauty of their country. From the snow-capped mountains of the north, through rolling countryside dotted with forests and lakes, to the tiny islands of the Baltic archipelagos around Stockholm, the country is a mecca for outdoor enthusiasts. Like its people, Sweden's cities are modern and dynamic, but also rich in tradition.

Sweden is Europe's fifth-largest country, with an area about the size of California. Roughly 1,600 km (1,000 miles) lie between its southernmost and northernmost points. About 15 percent of its area lies north of the Arctic Circle, where, for a few days each summer, the sun never sets, and never rises for a similar period in winter. The Swedish climate is not severe, thanks to the warming influence of the Gulf Stream.

Only 7 percent of Sweden's area is cultivated farmland; more than half the country is covered by timberlands, consisting mainly of coniferous forests. Mountains, fells, and wetlands occupy nearly a quarter of the country. Sweden has about 100,000 lakes, which include Vänern, the third-largest body of fresh water in Europe. Norrland, the northern three-fifths of the country, is rich in natural resources, including timber, ore deposits, and rivers, whose waterfalls contribute to the national energy supply. It is here that the Sami (formerly known as the Lapps) earn their traditional livelihood herding reindeer.

History

Although the Swedish Vikings were seafaring warriors like their Danish and Norwegian cousins, they were primarily known as Sweden's first traders, opening up routes along the Russian rivers to the east as far as the Black Sea. Ruthlessly exploiting the Slav population of the area, they dealt mainly in slaves and furs. The Viking reign ended with the successful Christianization of Sweden at the end of the 11th century.

The German traders of the Hanseatic League arrived in Sweden some time during the 13th century, and dominated Swedish life for the next hundred years. In 1397, the Germans were forced out by the Union of Kalmar, which brought Scandinavia under Danish rule. This state of affairs continued until Gustav Vasa, resenting Denmark's influence, succeeded in ousting the Danes in 1523, becoming king of an independent Sweden.

The 17th and early 18th centuries were dominated by two military giants, Gustav II Adolf and Karl XII, whose conquests made Sweden for the first time more powerful

Dancers in traditional folk costume in the village of Sundborn, Dalarna province

◀ Stockholm City in the summer sun

than Denmark. In the 18th century, the Swedes contributed to Europe's Age of Enlightenment with advances in science and major developments in the arts, especially under the patronage of Gustav III. He opened the magnificent Royal Opera House in 1782, and was responsible for the construction of the Royal Dramatic Theater in 1788.

By 1809, Sweden's military power had waned to such an extent that the country was forced to surrender Finland to Russia. A new constitution transferred power from the king to Parliament, marking the beginning of Sweden's democratic monarchy. In the early 19th century, Sweden was also a poor country, suffering from stagnation in agriculture and trade. In the course of the century,

Karl XII of Sweden (1697–1718), the "warrior king"

nearly one million Swedes migrated, mostly to America. Their departure was a sobering lesson to those that remained, inspiring the philosophy of cradle-to-grave care that was put into practice in 20th-century Sweden's welfare state.

In a single century, Sweden grew from a poor rural economy to a leading industrial nation. The 1990s saw many significant changes take place. Engineering expanded rapidly, particularly in the field of telecommunications, led by the Ericsson company. Sweden joined the EU, and the church severed its role with the state after more than 400 years. In the year 2000, Malmö in Sweden and the Danish capital of Copenhagen were connected by the completion of the Öresund Bridge, symbolic of the long-standing friendship that has replaced the animosity between these once warring nations.

Language and Culture

Swedish belongs to the northern group of Germanic languages, along with Norwegian, Danish, Icelandic, and Faeroese. Various dialects are spoken, most notably in Skåne, southern Sweden, where the accent is almost Danish.

A nation of nature lovers, the Swedes are apt to retreat to their country cottages in all seasons. Deeply traditional, they love their rituals, from maypole dances at midsummer to the St. Lucia procession in December. Beneath their reserve, the Swedes are a friendly people, their warmth readily unleashed with a *skål* (toast) and a round of schnapps.

Swedes are open-minded, trend-hungry, and tech-friendly. Stockholm offers the latest in design and architecture, and Sweden has become increasingly multicultural. While this new Sweden doesn't always blend easily with the old, most Swedes recognize that the country is richer for its diversity.

KEY DATES IN SWEDISH HISTORY

AD 800–1060 Era of the Swedish Vikings

13th century Hanseatic League of German merchants at height of its power in Sweden

1397 Kalmar Union links the Nordic countries

1523 Gustav Vasa becomes king of an independent Sweden

1611–32 Reign of Gustav II Adolf, whose campaigns turn Sweden into a great European power

1718 Death of Karl XII, Sweden's last great military king, at siege of Fredriksten in Norway

1721 Sweden cedes Baltic provinces to Russia

1772 Gustav III crowned and mounts *coup d'état* giving the monarchy absolute power

1809 Sweden loses Finland to Russia

1814 Sweden gains Norway from Denmark

1869 Emigration to North America increases due to crop failure

1905 Parliament dissolves union with Norway

1939 Sweden declares neutrality in World War II

1995 Sweden joins European Union

2000 Öresund Bridge opens, finally connecting Sweden and Denmark

2003 Single European currency rejected

2010 Crown Princess Victoria marries Daniel Westling

2012 Princess Estelle born to Crown Princess Victoria and Prince Daniel

Exploring Sweden

The natural starting point for exploring Sweden is the capital Stockholm, built on a cluster of Baltic Sea islands. From here, visitors can explore the castles of Lake Mälaren or head north to Uppsala, a thriving university town. On the way south to Malmö or west to Gothenburg lies the Glass Kingdom, where some of the world's best-known glassmakers ply their trade. Travel throughout Sweden can be conducted quite easily by high-speed trains or by car, though the long distances involved make travel quite expensive.

Sights at a Glance

1. Stockholm pp604–9
2. Lake Mälaren
3. Uppsala
4. Dalarna
5. Gotland and Visby
6. Gothenburg
7. Växjö
8. Malmö

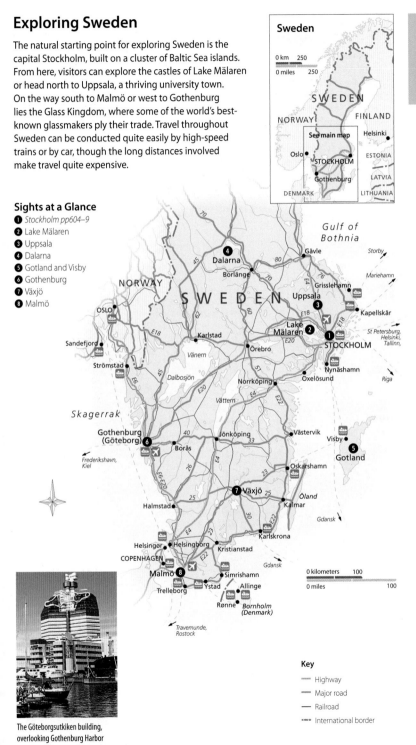

The Göteborgsutkiken building, overlooking Gothenburg Harbor

Key

— Highway
— Major road
— Railroad
--- International border

For keys to symbols *see back flap*

❶ Stockholm

Stockholm was founded around 1250 on a small island in the narrow Strömmen channel between the Baltic Sea and Lake Mälaren. Today, the Swedish capital stretches across 14 islands. As well as a stunning waterside location, Stockholm boasts a rich cultural heritage. Its 750-year history has produced a wealth of beautiful buildings, such as the Royal Palace and Drottningholm – symbols of Sweden's era as a great power in the 17th and early 18th centuries. Many other impressive treasures from the past can be discovered in the city's fine museums.

The Stadshuset, Stockholm's City Hall, on the island of Kungsholmen

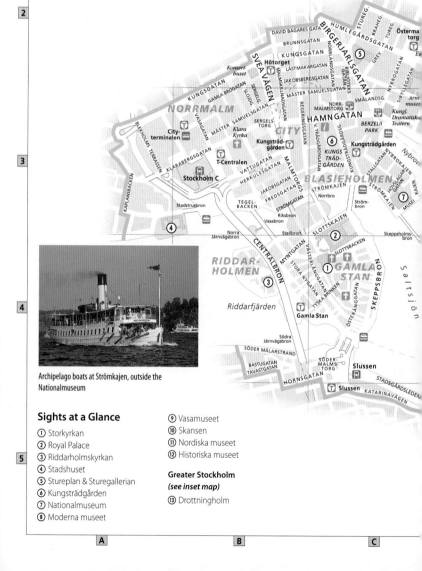

Archipelago boats at Strömkajen, outside the Nationalmuseum

Sights at a Glance

① Storkyrkan
② Royal Palace
③ Riddarholmskyrkan
④ Stadshuset
⑤ Stureplan & Sturegallerian
⑥ Kungsträdgården
⑦ Nationalmuseum
⑧ Moderna museet
⑨ Vasamuseet
⑩ Skansen
⑪ Nordiska museet
⑫ Historiska museet

Greater Stockholm
(see inset map)
⑬ Drottningholm

Greater Stockholm

Arlanda Airport
Lidingö
Sundbyberg
Solna
Bromma Airport
Ängby
Alvik
Lovön
Tappström
Hägersten
Bredäng
Norrköping, Södertälje
0 km   2
0 miles   2

Key

Area of main map

ERMALM
NARVAVÄGEN
GUMSHO RNSG.
STORGATAN
GREV MAGNIGATAN
TORSTENSSONG
BANERGATAN
ULRIKAGATAN
STORGATAN
STRANDVÄGEN
NOBEL-PARKEN
RANDVÄGEN
Ladugårdslandsviken
Djurgårdsbron
GALÄR-PARKEN
SKEPPS HOLMEN
SKSUNDSVÄGEN
A RADEN
AMIRALSVÄGEN
Kastellholms-bron
KASTELL-HOLMEN
DJURGÅRDSVÄGEN
FALKENBERGS GATAN
DJUR-GÅRDEN
Gröna Lund

0 meters   400
0 yards   400

Key

Sight / Place of interest
Pedestrian street

① Storkyrkan

Trångsund 1. **Tel** 08-723 30 16.
Gamla Stan. 2, 43, 55, 76.
Open 10am–4pm daily. in English: 10:15am Wed (Aug: daily).
storkyrkan.nu

Stockholm's 700-year-old cathedral, known as Storkyrkan (literally, "big church") is of great national religious importance. From here, the Swedish reformer Olaus Petri (1493–1552) spread his Lutheran message around the kingdom. The cathedral is also used for royal ceremonies.

A small church was built on this site in the 13th century, probably by the city's founder Birger Jarl. In 1306, it was replaced by a much bigger basilica, St. Nicholas.

The 15th-century Gothic interior was revealed in 1908 during restoration work. The late Baroque period provided the cathedral's so-called "royal chairs," the pews nearest the chancel, which were designed by Nicodemus Tessin the Younger (1654–1728) to be used by royal guests on special occasions. The 66-m- (216-ft-) high tower was added in 1743.

The cathedral houses some priceless artifacts, such as Bernt Notke's late-Gothic sculpture of *St. George and the Dragon* (1489), celebrating Sten Sture the Elder's 1471 victory over the Danes. Other prized treasures are the silver altar (1650s) and the *Parhelion Painting*, which depicts a light phenomenon observed over Stockholm in 1535. Research has proved the painting is not the original, but a copy from the 1630s.

The Italian Baroque-style facade of Stockholm's Storkyrkan

The grand facade of Stockholm's Kungliga Slottet (Royal Palace)

② Royal Palace

Kungliga Slottet. **Tel** 08-402 61 30.
Ⓣ Gamla Stan, Kungsträdgården. 🚌
2, 43, 55, 76. **Open** mid-May–mid-Sep:
10am–4pm daily; mid-Sep–mid-May:
noon–3pm Tue–Sun (except Royal
Chapel & Museum of Antiquities).
Closed during official functions of the
Court. 🅿 📷 👤 ♿ 🇼 kungahuset.se

Completed in the mid-13th
century, the Tre Kronor (Three
Crowns) fortress was turned
into a royal residence by
the Vasa kings during the
following century. In 1697, it
was destroyed by fire. In its
place, the architect Nicodemus
Tessin the Younger (1654–1728)
created a new palace with an
Italianate exterior and a French
interior that also shows
Swedish influences.

Though the palace is no
longer the king's residence,
the **State Apartments**
are still used for official
functions. Banquets for
visiting heads of state
are often held in the
magnificent Karl XI's
Gallery, which is
modeled on the Hall
of Mirrors at Versailles
outside Paris (see
pp168–9), and is a fine
example of Swedish
Late Baroque. Look out
for the exquisite ivory
and silver saltcellar,
designed by Flemish
painter Rubens. The
two-story Hall of State,
designed by Tessin
and Carl Hårleman,
combines Rococo and
Classical elements, and
contains one of the
palace's most valuable

treasures, the splendid silver
coronation throne of Queen
Kristina (reigned 1633–54).

Below the Hall of State is
the **Treasury**, where the State
regalia are kept, including King
Erik XIV's crown, scepter, and
orb. Other priceless artifacts,
such as two crystal crowns
belonging to the present
monarchs, King Carl XVI Gustaf
and Queen Silvia, are on view
in the **Royal Chapel**.

Within the palace are two
museums. **Gustav III's Museum
of Antiquities** opened in 1794
in memory of the murdered
king, and contains artifacts
collected during his journey
to Italy in 1783–4. The **Tre
Kronor Museum** illustrates the
palace's 1,000-year history, and
has relics rescued from the
burning palace in 1697. A very
popular tourist event, the daily

Tre Kronor (Three Crowns) symbol atop the 106-m
(348-ft) tower of the Stadshuset

changing of the guard, takes
place at midday in the palace's
Outer Courtyard.

③ Riddarholms-kyrkan

Birger Jarls Torg. **Tel** 08-402 61 30.
Ⓣ Gamla Stan. 🚌 3, 53. **Open** mid-
May–mid-Sep: 10am–5pm daily.
🅿 📷 (noon in English). ♿

Built on the site of the late
13th-century Greyfriars abbey,
founded by Magnus Ladulås,
this majestic brick church is best
known for its ornate burial
vaults. Dating back to the
17th century, the vaults hold
the remains of all the Swedish
sovereigns from Gustav II Adolf,
with two exceptions: Queen
Kristina, buried at St. Peter's in
Rome in 1689, and Gustav VI
Adolf, who was interred at
Haga, on the city outskirts,
in 1973. Especially moving are
the graves of royal children,
including the many small
tin coffins that surround the
tombs of Gustav II Adolf and
his queen, Maria Eleonora.

④ Stadshuset

Hantverkargatan 1. **Tel** 08-508 290 58.
Ⓣ Rådhuset. 🚌 3, 62. **Open** for
guided tours. **Closed** some public
holidays and for special activities. 🅿
📷 obligatory. ♿
🇼 stockholm.se/cityhall

Probably Sweden's biggest
architectural project of the 20th
century, the Stadshuset (City
Hall) was completed in 1923
and has become a symbol of
Stockholm. It was designed by
Ragnar Östberg (1866–1945)

and displays influences of both the Nordic Gothic and Northern Italian schools. Many leading Swedish artists contributed to the rich interior design, including Einar Forseth (1892–1988), who created the stunning Byzantine-inspired gold-leaf wall mosaics in the Golden Room.

The building contains the Council Chamber and 250 offices for administrative staff. As well as a work place for the city's councillors, the Stadshuset also provides a venue for special events, such as the annual Nobel Prize ceremony, which takes place in the lavish Blue Hall.

Stureplan, a popular meeting place for Stockholmers

⑤ Stureplan and Sturegallerian

ⓣ Östermalmstorg. 🚌 1, 2, 55, 56, 91. Sturegallerian: Stureplan 4. **Tel** 08-453 52 00. **Open** daily (Sun: pm only). Sturebadet: **Tel** 08-545 015 00. **Open** daily.

After a fire at the Sturebadet swimming pool in 1985, the Stureplan district was revamped and restored to its late 19th-century glory.

Part of the renovation of the area included building a stylish shopping mall, the Sture-gallerian, which boasts some 60 retail outlets. The Sturebadet public baths, within the mall, have been rebuilt according to their original late 19th-century Art Nouveau design.

Kungsträdgården, known as Stockholm's "open-air living room"

⑥ Kungsträdgården

ⓣ Kungsträdgården. 🚌 2, 43, 55, 62, 65, 71, 76. Kungliga Operan: **Tel** 08-791 44 00. Ticket office **Open** noon–6pm Mon–Fri, noon–3pm Sat. 🚪 by appt. 🚻 📷 📱 🖥 operan.se

The city's oldest park, the King's Garden takes its name from when it was a royal kitchen garden in the 15th century. During the summer, open-air theater, dancing, concerts, and food festivals take place here. In winter, the skating rink is a popular attraction. At the center of the park is a bronze fountain (1866) by J.P. Molin, who also designed the statue of Karl XII (1868) at the park's southern end. Overlooking this part of the park is the city's royal opera house, the **Kungliga Operan** (1898), whose ornate interior includes the Gold Foyer, with ceiling paintings by Carl Larsson.

In the 16th century, the kitchen garden was transformed into a Renaissance garden. The 17th-century summer house built for Queen Kristina still stands on the park's western flank.

⑦ Nationalmuseum

Södra Blasieholmshamnen. **Tel** 08-519 543 00. ⓣ Kungsträdgården. 🚌 2, 55, 59, 62, 65, 76. **Closed** for restoration until 2017. 🎨 📷 📱 🖥 nationalmuseum.se

The location of the National-museum, on the Strömmen channel, inspired the 19th-century German architect August Stüler to design a building in the Venetian and Florentine Renaissance styles.

Completed in 1866, the museum houses some 500,000 paintings, sculptures, prints, and drawings from the 15th to the early 20th centuries. The focus of the painting and sculpture section is Swedish 18th- to early 20th-century art, but the 17th-century Dutch and Flemish, and 18th-century French schools are also well represented. Highlights include Rembrandt's *The Conspiracy of the Batavians under Claudius Civilis* (1661–62) and *The Lady with the Veil* (1769) by Swedish portrait painter Alexander Roslin. The decorative arts department contains 30,000 works spanning the last five centuries. Among the wide range of exhibits on show is Scandinavia's largest display of porcelain, glass, silverware, and furniture. Another exhibit, Design 19002000, tracks the history of design to the present day. During renovations, part of the collection will be on display at Konstakademien (Fredsgatan 12).

The Venetian-style building housing Stockholm's Nationalmuseum

The Moderna museet's airy interior, designed by Catalan Rafael Moneo

⑧ Moderna museet

Exercisplan 4, Skeppsholmen. **Tel** 08-520 235 00. Ⓣ Kungsträdgården. 🚌 65. **Open** Tue–Sun. **Closed** Jan 1, Easter Mon, Whit Mon, midsummer eve, Dec 24, 25 & 31. 🏛 📷 🏬 🚻 💻 🏛 W **modernamuseet.se**

The Museum of Modern Art is an airy, contemporary building, designed by the Catalan architect Rafael Moneo in 1998. The light and spacious venue provides a perfect setting for the museum's world-class collection of international and Swedish modern art, photography, and film. Built partly underground, the museum includes a cinema and auditorium.

All the works on display date from between 1900 and the present day. Two of the star exhibits are *The Child's Brain* (1914) by Italian artist Giorgio de Chirico, widely considered a precursor to the Surrealists, and

Monogram (1955–59) by the late American painter and sculptor Robert Rauschenberg. Among the collection of Swedish works is Nils Dardel's Expressionistic painting, *The Dying Dandy* (1918).

⑨ Vasamuseet

Galärvarvsvägen 14, Djurgården. **Tel** 08-519 548 00. 🚌 44, 69. 🚊 7. 🚢 Djurgårdsfärja. **Open** daily. **Closed** Jan 1, Dec 23–25 & 31. 🏛 ♿ 📷 🚻 🏬 💻 🏛 Museifartygen: **Tel** 08-519 548 83. **Open** mid-Jun–Aug: 11am–6pm daily. 🏛 📷 W **vasamuseet.se**

The centerpiece of the city's most popular museum is the massive royal warship, *Vasa*, which capsized in Stockholm harbor on its maiden voyage in 1628. Rediscovered in 1956, the vessel has been painstakingly restored to 95 per cent of its original appearance.

The warship is decorated with around 700 sculpted figures and carved ornaments, designed as a type of war propaganda. King Gustav II Adolf, who commissioned *Vasa*, was known as the Lion of the North, so a springing lion was the obvious choice for the figurehead on the ship's prow. It is 4 m (13 ft) long and weighs 450 kg (990 lb).

Although visitors cannot board the ship, full-scale models of *Vasa*'s upper gun deck and the Admiral's cabin provide a glimpse of what life on board was like. There is also a

fascinating display of items retrieved in the salvage operation, including medical equipment, an officer's back-gammon set, and a chest still neatly packed with clothing and other personal belongings.

Moored in the dock alongside the museum are two other historic vessels, collectively referred to as the **Museifartygen**. The lightship *Finngrundet* was built in 1903 and worked for 60 years before becoming a museum. *Sankt Erik* was commissioned in 1915 and was Sweden's first seagoing icebreaker.

Midsummer celebrations at the open-air museum, Skansen

⑩ Skansen

Djurgårdsslätten 49–51. **Tel** 08- 442 80 00. 🚌 44. 🚊 7. 🚢 Djurgårdsfärja. **Open** daily. 🏛 📷 Jun–Aug (call in advance). ♿ 🚻 💻 🏬 W **skansen.se**

The world's first open-air museum opened in 1891 to show an increasingly industrialized society how people once lived. Around 150 buildings were assembled from all over Scandinavia, to portray the life of peasants and landed gentry, as well as Lapp *(Sami)* culture.

In the Town Quarter glass-blowers and other craftsmen demonstrate their skills. Two of Skansen's oldest "exhibits" are a 650-year-old wooden farm-house from Dalarna, and a 14th-century storehouse from Norway.

Nordic flora and fauna can be seen, with moose, bears, and wolves in natural habitat enclo-sures and marine animals in an aquarium. Gröna Lund theme park offers 30 attractions, includ-ing a love tunnel, haunted house, white knuckle roller coasters, and hosts many music concerts.

The restored 17th-century royal warship, *Vasa*, at the Vasamuseet

⑪ Nordiska museet

Djurgårdsvägen 6–16. **Tel** 08-519 546 00. Ⓣ Karlaplan. 🚌 44, 69, 76. 🚋 7. ⛴ Djurgårds-färja, Allmänna Gränd. **Open** 10am–5pm daily. **Closed** Jun 25, Dec 24, 25 & 31. 🚻 ♿ 🅿 🎁 🛍 📷 Ⓦ nordiskamuseet.se

Housed in a Renaissance-style building, the Nordiska museet's collection was started by Artur Hazelius (1833–1901), founder of the Skansen open-air museum, with the intention of reminding future generations of the old Nordic farming culture. Today, the museum has over 1.5 million exhibits portraying everyday life in Sweden from the 1520s to the present day. Items on display range from priceless jewelry, to furniture, dolls' houses, and replicas of period rooms, such as the splendid 17th-century state bed-chamber from Ulvsunda Castle. Highlights include the monumental gilded oak statue of King Gustav Vasa (1924), and 16 paintings by the Swedish author and dramatist August Strindberg (1849–1912).

Carl Milles' huge statue of King Gustav Vasa in the Nordiska museet

⑫ Historiska museet

Narvavägen 13–17. **Tel** 08-519 556 00. Ⓣ Karlaplan, Östermalmstorg. 🚌 44, 56. **Open** daily. **Closed** Mon (Oct–Apr); some major holidays. 🚻 ♿ 🎁

Sweden's National Historical Museum was opened in 1943. It originally made its name with

The magnificent Drottningholm palace, on the island of Lovön

relics from the Viking era, as well as its outstanding collections from the Middle Ages. The latter include one of the museum's star exhibits – a richly gilded wooden Madonna figure, from Sweden's early medieval period. In the prehistoric collection is the Alunda Elk, a ceremonial stone axe, discovered in 1920 at Alunda and thought to have been made around 2000 BC.

Since the early 1990s, the museum's priceless collection of gold and silver, dating from the Bronze Age to the Middle Ages, has been on show in the Guldrummet (Gold Room). Look out for the stunning Elisabeth Reliquary, an 11th-century goblet, with a silver cover made in 1230 to enclose the skull of St. Elisabeth.

Madonna figure in the Historiska museet

⑬ Drottningholm

10 km (6 miles) W of Stockholm. **Tel** 08-402 62 80. Ⓣ Brommaplan, then bus 301, 323. 🚢 May–Sep from Stadshusbron. **Open** May–Sep: daily; Oct–Apr: Sat & Sun. (Chinese Pavilion: May–Sep only; Theater Museum: May–Sep only.) **Closed** public hols. 📷 🎁 Ⓦ royalcourt.se

With its sumptuous palace, theater, park, and Chinese pavilion, the whole of the Drottningholm estate has been included in UNESCO's World Heritage list. Contemporary Italian and French architecture inspired Nicodemus Tessin the Elder (1615–81) in his design of the royal palace. Begun in the 1660s on the orders of King Karl X Gustav's widow, Queen Hedvig Eleonora, the building was completed by Tessin the Younger. Today, the present royal family still uses parts of the palace as a private residence. The most lavish rooms open to the public include Queen Lovisa Ulrika's library, designed by Jean Eric Rehn (1717–93), and Queen Hedvig Eleonora's state bedroom, decorated in Baroque style.

The Baroque and Rococo gardens and lush parkland surrounding the palace are dotted with monuments and splendid buildings. The blue and gold Chinese Pavilion (Kina Slott) was built for Queen Lovisa Ulrika in the latter half of the 18th century, and contains many interesting artifacts from China and Japan. The designer of the Chinese Pavilion, Carl Fredrik Adelcrantz, was also responsible for the Drottningholm Court Theater (Slottsteatern), which dates from 1766. This simple wooden building is the world's oldest theater still preserved in its original form. The scenery, with its wooden hand driven machinery, is still in working order. In summer, the theater hosts opera and ballet. There is also a museum, which focuses on 18th-century theater.

The Renaissance Gripsholms Slott, on the shore of Lake Mälaren

❷ Lake Mälaren

Birka 🚢 May–Sep daily from Stadshusbron, Stockholm. Mariefred: 🚢 in summer from Stadshusbron, Stockholm. 🚆 from Centralstationen, Stockholm to Läggesta, then bus or steam train.

To the west of Stockholm lies Lake Mälaren, a vast stretch of water, whose pretty shores and islands offer several day excursions from the city.

Sweden's first town, **Birka**, was founded on the island of Björkö in the 8th century, although archaeological finds indicate that trading activity took place here at least 1,500 years ago. In the 9th and 10th centuries, Birka grew into a busy Viking center. The **Birkamuseet** has displays of local archaeological finds and provides a fascinating insight into the daily lives of the town's early inhabitants. There are also guided tours of ongoing excavations.

The most striking feature of the pretty town of **Mariefred** is the majestic **Gripsholms Slott**, built for King Gustav Vasa in 1537, and later modified under Gustav III in the 18th century. The palace is known for its well-preserved interiors,

and also houses the National Portrait Gallery, with more than 4,000 paintings spanning some 500 years.

Mariefred itself has a lovely 17th-century church and an 18th-century timber Rådhus (law courts' building), as well as several specialist stores, galleries, and antique shops. In summer, one of the most enjoyable ways to travel there from Stockholm is aboard the *Mariefred*, a historic, coal-fired steamboat. The trip takes around three and a half hours and allows passengers to enjoy the spectacular scenery along the route.

🏛 **Birkamuseet**
Tel 08-560 514 45. **Open** May 1–Sep 26: daily. 🅿 📷

🏰 **Gripsholms Slott**
Tel 0159-101 94. **Open** mid-May–mid-Sep: daily; mid-Sep–mid-May: Sat & Sun. **Closed** Dec 18–Jan 2. 🅿 📷 📷

❸ Uppsala

🏙 200,000. ✈ 🚆 🚌
ℹ Fyris Torg 8 (018-727 48 00).
🌐 destinationuppsala.se

One of Sweden's oldest settlements, Uppsala, on the banks of the Fyrisån river, is also a lively university town. On the last day of April, crowds of students wearing white caps parade through the town for the traditional spring season celebrations.

Dominating the town's attractive medieval center is the **Domkyrkan**, Scandinavia's largest Gothic cathedral. Its chapel contains the relics of Sweden's patron saint, Saint Erik. The onion-domed **Gustavianum**, opposite the cathedral, dates from the 1620s and houses the Uppsala University Museum. The museum's exhibits include a 17th-century anatomical theater and Egyptian, Classical, and Nordic antiquities. Just a short walk away stands the **Carolina Rediviva**, the impressive university library.

Uppsala Slott, the town's hilltop fortress, was built in the 16th century by King Gustav Vasa, although it was later destroyed by fire. Now restored, it also houses the Uppsala Art

Aerial view of Uppsala, with its massive Gothic cathedral, the Domkyrkan

For hotels and restaurants see p616 and p617

Museum. A short bus ride north of the town center, Gamla Uppsala is the site of the Kungshögarna, royal burial mounds believed to date from the 6th century. The **Historiskt Centrum** acquaints visitors with the history, legends, and lore surrounding the burial mounds and contains displays of local archaeological finds.

🏛 Gustavianum
Akademigatan 3. **Tel** 018-471 75 71.
Open Tue–Sun.
w gustavianum.uu.se

🏰 Uppsala Slott
Slottet, entrance E. **Tel** 018-727 24 82.
Open Wed–Sun. Jun–Aug.

🏛 Historiskt Centrum
Disavägen. **Tel** 018-23 93 00. **Open** May–Aug: daily; at other times: call for information.

❹ Dalarna
🚉 Falun, Mora. 🚌 Falun, Mora.
ℹ️ Trotzgatan 10–12 (023-640 04); Strandvägen 14a, Mora (0250-59 20 20).

With its proud tradition of music, dance, and handicrafts, Dalarna is Sweden's folklore district. The charming rural landscape, dotted with red, wooden cottages, attracts many tourists seeking a quiet country retreat in the summer. In winter, the area's mountain resorts, Sälen and Idre, are packed with skiers.

The main sights of interest are located around Lake Siljan. **Mora**, the largest of the lakeside towns, was home to one of Sweden's best-known artists, Anders Zorn (1860–1920). Open daily, the Zorn Museum, at No. 36 Vasagatan, holds paintings by the artist, and you can also visit his former home and studio.

Dalarna is famous for its midsummer festivals. In **Leksand** and **Rättvik**, you may see traditionally dressed locals dancing and playing musical instruments or rowing on the lake in wooden

Musician at a midsummer festival in Dalarna

longboats during the towns' colorful celebrations.

Around 15 km (9 miles) from the provincial capital and largely industrial town of **Falun** is **Sundborn**, where Swedish painter Carl Larsson (1853–1919) and his wife, Karin, a textile artist, lived in the early 20th century. Their work still has a big influence on contemporary Swedish design. The couple's lakeside house is open to the public.

❺ Gotland and Visby
🏠 60,000. ✈ 🚌 to Visby.
ℹ️ Donnerska Huset, Donners Plats 1, Visby (0498-20 17 00). **w gotland.info**

The island of Gotland, Sweden's most popular holiday destination, boasts a stunning coastline, a rich cultural heritage, and a superb climate, enjoying more hours of sunshine than anywhere else in the country.

In the Viking Age, Gotland, the largest island in the Baltic Sea, was a major trading post and later its capital, Visby, became a prosperous Hanseatic port. Surrounded by one of the best-preserved city walls in the world, Visby is like a living museum, with pretty step-gabled houses and a web of narrow cobbled streets and small squares. The original Hanseatic harbor is now a park,

The Norderport, one of the gateways in Visby's medieval city walls

but the **Burmeisterska Huset** (Burmeister's House), dating from 1645, is a fine surviving example of the architecture of the Post-Hanseatic period. Strandgatan contains some of Visby's most attractive historic buildings, the former homes of wealthy merchants. In the same street is the excellent historical museum, **Gotlands Fornsal**, which holds a collection of artifacts spanning 8,000 years. The **Domkyrkan** (Cathedral of St. Maria) below Kyrkberget is the only medieval church still intact and in use in Visby.

Away from Visby, the rest of Gotland is dotted with many unspoilt farmhouses, old medieval churches, and secluded beaches. Among the most impressive sights are the subterranean limestone caves of **Lummelundagrottorna**, 13 km (8 miles) north of the city, and, off the northeastern tip of the island, **Fårö**. This island, known for its severe beauty, can be reached by a daily, half-hourly ferry from Fårösund. Besides old fishing hamlets such as Helgumannen, visitors can enjoy the long stretch of white sandy beach and the swimming at Sudersands. Look out for Fårö's spectacular *raukar*. These are huge limestone rock formations, rising out of the sea on the west side of the island.

🏛 Gotlands Fornsal
Strandgatan 14, Visby. **Tel** 0498-29 27 00. **Open** May–mid-Sep: daily; mid-Sep–Apr: pm Tue–Sun. in summer.

Poseidon fountain, at the end of Kungsportsavenyn in Gothenburg

❻ Gothenburg

🏠 550,000. ✈ 25 km (16 miles) E.
🚊 🚌 ⛴ 🛈 Kungsportsplatsen 2
(031-368 42 00).
🌐 gothenburg.com

Gothenburg (Göteborg), Sweden's second largest city, has a distinctive character, with beautiful architecture, pleasant café-lined boulevards, a bustling harbor, and a dynamic cultural life.

Scandinavia's largest seaport is dominated by the **Göteborgsutkiken**, a huge lookout tower providing stunning panoramic views of the city and its surroundings. A short walk west along the quayside are the daring, industrial-style **Göteborgsoperan** (Opera House), built in 1994, and the **Maritiman**, reputedly the world's largest floating ship museum. Moored in the dock are a dozen different types of vessel, all open to the public. They include a light ship, a destroyer, and a submarine.

The pulse of the city is Kungsportsavenyn, simply known as Avenyn, or "The Avenue." This 900-m- (2952-ft-) long boulevard is lined with restaurants, pubs, and cafés, and is a favorite haunt of street musicians and hawkers. On a side street off Avenyn, **Röhsska Museet** is Sweden's only museum devoted to arts, crafts, and industrial design. At the southern end of the avenue is Götaplatsen, whose focal point is the famous Poseidon fountain by the Swedish sculptor Carl Milles. The square is flanked by the fine **Konstmuseet** (Art Museum), which specializes in 19th- and 20th-century Scandinavian art.

Southeast of Götaplatsen is **Lisebergs Nöjespark**, the largest amusement park in Sweden.

🏛 **Maritiman**
Packhusplatsen 12. **Tel** 031-10 59 50.
Open May–Sep: daily. 🍴 🖥 📷

🏛 **Röhsska Museet**
Vasagatan 37–39. **Tel** 031-368 31 50.
Open pm Tue–Sun. 🍴 🖼 🖥 📷
🌐 designmuseum.se

🏛 **Konstmuseet**
Götaplatsen 6. **Tel** 031-368 35 00.
Open Tue–Sun. 🍴 🖼 ♿ 🖥 📷

❼ Växjö

🏠 83,000. 🚉 🚌 🛈 Residenset, Stortorget (0470-733 280).
🌐 turism.vaxjo.se

Located right at the heart of Småland, Växjö is an ideal base from which to explore the Glasriket, or "Kingdom of Glass," Sweden's world-famous region of glassworks. The town's main attraction is the **Smålands Museum**, which tells the story of 400 years of glassmaking, and provides a good introduction to a visit to any one of the many glassworks scattered throughout the surrounding forests.

The best-known glassworks are at **Orrefors** and **Kosta**, within 90 km (56 miles) of Växjö, but other factories worth visiting include **Åfors** and **Strömbergshyttan**. Most of the factories have excellent glass-blowing demonstrations, and all have a shop where you can choose from a wide selection of products. In the past, Småland's glassworks were more than just a place of work. Locals used to meet here in the evenings to bake herrings and potatoes in the furnace, while music was provided by a fiddler. Today the Orrefors and Kosta glassworks arrange similar forms of entertainment, known as *hyttsill* evenings. Visitors to Växjö should not miss the **Utvandrarnas Hus** (House of Emigrants). This interesting museum recounts the story of the one million Swedes who, in the face of famine in the late 19th and early 20th centuries, left Småland for a better life in America.

Swedish glassware from Småland

🏛 **Smålands Museum**
Södra Järnvägsgatan 2. **Tel** 0470-7042 00. **Open** Jun–Aug: daily; Sep–May: Tue–Sun. 🍴 🖼 🎨 ♿ 🖥

🏛 **Kosta Glassworks**
Stora vägen 96, Kosta, on route 28.
Tel 0478-345 00. **Open** daily.
Closed some public hols. 🎨 📷

🏛 **Utvandrarnas Hus**
Vilhelm Mobergsgatan 4.
Tel 0470-201 20. **Open** daily. 🍴

❽ Malmö

🏙 300,000. ✈ 🚢 🚌 🚋
ℹ Central Station (040-34 1200).

Malmö is the capital of the province of Skåne in southwestern Sweden. In the 16th century, it was a major fishing port, competing with Copenhagen as Scandinavia's most influential city. Today, the city is well-known for its busy harbor, as well as for its rich architectural heritage.

The imposing 16th-century Malmöhus was built by the Danish king Christian III, when Skåne formed part of Denmark. It contains the **Malmömuseer** (Malmö Museums), which include the Art Museum, the Museum of Natural History, the City Museum, the Science & Technology and Maritime Museum, and the Kommendants Hus (Commander's House).

The Dutch Renaissance style is evident in Malmö's impressive **Rådhuset** (Town Hall), which dates from 1546 and dominates the city's main square, Stortorget. Northeast of here is the 14th-century **St. Petri's Kyrka**, built in the Baltic Gothic style. The church's most beautiful features include the altarpiece

Malmö's main square, overlooked by the Renaissance Rådhuset

(1611), Scandinavia's largest, and a wonderfully ornate pulpit. Amid the city's maze of café-lined pedestrianized streets is Lilla torg (Little Square), with its cobblestones and charmingly restored houses. The square has a lively atmosphere and draws crowds of tourists and locals alike. At Möllevångstorget, you will find a part of town that reflects a diversity of cultures, especially around the square. There is a farmers' market and many small ethnic shops.

Located south of Lilla Torg is **Malmö Konsthall**, a vibrant museum of modern art which opened in 1975. Its vast contemporary exhibition space houses an excellent collection of avant-garde and experimental art and installations, as well as photography and sculpture.

🏛 **Malmömuseer**
Malmöhus, Malmöhusvägen 6.
Tel 040-34 44 00. **Open** 10am–5pm daily. **Closed** Dec 24, 25 & 31, Jan 1.
🅿 🔲 📷 🅦 **malmo.se/museer**

🏛 **Malmö Konsthall**
St. Johannesgatan 7. **Tel** 040-34 12 86.
Open 11am–5pm daily. **Closed** Dec 24, 25 & 31, Jan 1. 🅿 ♿ 🔲 📷

The Öresund Bridge

Despite a legacy of mutual warfare and rivalry, in May 2000 the close ties between Denmark and Sweden were strengthened with the inauguration of the Öresund Bridge.

A 16-km- (10-mile-) long combined suspension bridge and tunnel now connects the Danish capital, Copenhagen, with the Swedish provincial capital, Malmö, on either side of the channel of water known as the Öresund. The bridge is the strongest cable stay bridge in the world, designed to carry the combined weight of a motorway and a dual-track railway, while the tunnel is the world's largest immersed tunnel in terms of volume. The project has been hailed as a renaissance for southern Sweden, which now seems poised to become a prospering center of trade, science, industry, and culture at the heart of the cross-border Danish-Swedish Öresund region.

The majestic Öresund Bridge, connecting Sweden and Denmark

Practical & Travel Information

With Sweden growing rapidly as an important tourist destination, standards in the travel industry have improved greatly. Foreign visitors will enjoy a comfortable stay in Sweden, not least because most people speak English. Sweden's infrastructure is constantly being improved – there are many new highways and the rail system has been upgraded for high-speed trains. There is also a direct link to Denmark via the Öresund Bridge. In Stockholm, public transportation on buses, subway trains, ferries, and local trains is efficient, and covers the entire city and surrounding region.

Tourist Information

Tourist information offices are located throughout Sweden, and you can contact the **Swedish Travel & Tourism Council** for more information. Stockholm's official tourist information organization is the **Stockholm Visitors Board**. Most hotels in the capital, as well as many department stores and museums, stock the free monthly listings brochure *What's On Stockholm*.

Most museums in Sweden are open from 10 or 11am to 5 or 6pm all year round, and often have longer opening hours in the summer. They are usually closed on Monday.

Visa Requirements

Passports are not required for visitors from most EU countries, but visitors from the US, Canada, the UK, Ireland, Australia, and New Zealand still need a valid passport. Citizens of almost all countries can enter Sweden without a visa.

Personal Security

Violent crime is rare in Sweden, although pickpockets are known to frequent the busier pedestrian shopping streets and train stations in the main cities. Swedish emergency services are efficient and reliable. The police are extremely helpful and most speak good English.

Health Issues

No special vaccinations are necessary to visit Sweden. Hygiene standards are among the highest in the world, and the tap water is safe to drink. For prescription and non-prescription medicines, visit a pharmacy (*apotek*), open during normal store hours. A 24-hour *apotek* service is available in major cities.

Currency and Banking

The Swedish unit of currency is the krona, abbreviated to SEK or kr. Banking hours are generally 10am–3pm Monday to Friday, though some banks stay open until 6pm at least one day a week. Bureaux de change can be found in the main cities and airports, and normally provide a better exchange rate than banks.

All the well-known credit cards are widely accepted in Sweden. Withdrawals can be made from cash machines using all internationally accepted credit cards in conjunction with a PIN.

Communications

Public phone booths are owned by the state-run Telia company, and are usually operated by card only. Phonecards can be bought at tobacconists and newspaper kiosks, though normal credit cards or international telephone cards work just as well.

Post offices are open 10am–6pm on weekdays and 10am–1pm on Saturdays. Many of the post offices have been closed and postal services moved to some grocery stores instead. Stamps can be purchased at these locations as well as at post offices, Pressbyrån kiosks, and tourist information offices.

Flying to Sweden

Most major European cities have direct flights to Stockholm. Many of the world's leading airlines serve Arlanda Airport, located about 40 km (25 miles) north of the city center. International flights also serve Gothenburg and Malmö. Services from the UK are operated by **Finnair**, **SAS** (Scandinavian Airlines), British Airways, and low-cost airline **Ryanair**. Direct flights from North America are available from SAS and Finnair, and from the US airline American.

Traveling by Ferry

Ferries to Gothenburg from Fredrikshavn in Denmark (2–3 hours), and from Kiel in Germany (20–22 hours), are operated by **Stena Line**.

Large passenger and car ferries sail to Stockholm from Finland; both **Viking Line** and **Silja Line** operate daily services from Helsinki (with a crossing time of about 15 hours) and

The Climate of Sweden

Sweden's summers are usually fairly cool, although sometimes there can be heatwaves for several weeks at a time. Winter temperatures often fall below freezing, but it is rarely severely cold, except in the far north. The snow may lie until well after March in the north; however, in the rest of the country some recent winters have been virtually free of snow.

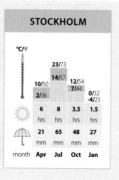

STOCKHOLM			
°C/°F	23/73		
	14/57	12/54	
10/50		7/44	0/32
2/36			-4/25
6 hrs	8 hrs	3.5 hrs	1.5 hrs
21 mm	65 mm	48 mm	27 mm
month Apr	Jul	Oct	Jan

Turku-Åbo (with a crossing time of about 11 hours).

Within Sweden, ferries to Visby in Gotland leave from Nynäshamn, about 75 km (47 miles) south of Stockholm. There are two crossings daily by catamaran (2 hours 50 mins) and one or two crossings daily by ferry (5 hours). Both services are run by **Destination Gotland**.

Traveling by Bus

Travel by long-distance bus is inexpensive and hassle-free. There is an excellent network of express services, such as those run by **Swebus**, between the larger towns and cities in south and central Sweden, and between Stockholm and towns in the north.

Rail Travel

Rail travel to Sweden from mainland Europe is fast and comfortable. Journey times have been cut considerably with the opening of the Öresund Bridge; traveling from Copenhagen to Malmö now takes less than 40 minutes.

Within Sweden, the state-owned rail company Statens Järnvägar (SJ) operates many of the long-distance trains. Some routes are run by private companies – Tågkompaniet runs trains from Stockholm to Narvik, Umeå, and Luleå in the far north of Sweden.

The journey time by high-speed train from Malmö to Stockholm is about 5 hours; the journey from Gothenburg to the capital takes about 3 hours.

Traveling by Car

Visitors driving from Denmark can use the Öresund toll bridge between Copenhagen and Malmö. On the Swedish side, the bridge connects with the E4, a 550-km- (340-mile-) highway to Stockholm.

Fines for speeding are high, and even if the limit is only slightly exceeded, you can lose your license. The maximum permitted blood alcohol level is so low that drinking is effectively banned for drivers. When driving in the Swedish countryside, be particularly cautious, as moose and deer may appear unexpectedly in the middle of the road.

Traveling in Stockholm

Most of Stockholm's sights and attractions can be reached by subway train or bus. Tunnelbana, the underground rail system, has 100 stations on three main routes. Travelcards are available for one-day, three-day, and monthly periods, and are also valid on bus and ferry services.

Traveling by bus is a pleasant and economical way to see the city. The best routes for sightseeing are 3, 4, 46, 62, and 69, which cover the central area and stop near many sights.

Boats and ferries provide a delightful way of getting to know the city and its environs. **Strömma Kanalbolaget** runs various hour-long excursions during the summer months.

A worthwhile purchase for any visitor is the Stockholm Card, which allows free travel on Tunnelbana trains, local buses and trains, free parking at official city parking areas, and free admission to over 80 sights.

DIRECTORY

Tourist Offices

Stockholm Visitors Board
Vasagatan 14, Stockholm.
Tel 08-50 82 85 00.
W **stockholmtown.com**

Swedish Travel & Tourism Council
Sveavägen 21, Stockholm.
Tel 08-789 10 00.
W **visitsweden.com**

UK
5 Upper Montague Street, London W1H 2AG.
Tel 020-7108 6168.

US
Grand Central Station, New York, NY 10017.
Tel 212-885 9700.

Embassies

Australia
Klarabergsviadukten 63, Stockholm. **Tel** 08-613 29 00.
W **sweden.embassy. gov.au**

Canada
Klarabergsgatan 23, 6th Floor, Stockholm.
Tel 08-453 30 00.
W **canada international.gc.ca**

Ireland
Hovslagargatan 5, Stockholm.
Tel 08-661 80 05.

UK
Skarpögatan 6-8, Stockholm.
Tel 08-671 30 00.
W **ukinsweden. fco.gov.uk**

US
Dag Hammarskjölds Väg 31, Stockholm.
Tel 08-783 53 00.
W **usemb.se**

Emergency Numbers

Ambulance, Police and Fire
Tel 112.

Airlines

Finnair
Tel 0771-78 11 00 (toll-free in Sweden).
Tel 0870-241 4411 (UK).
Tel 800-950 5000 (US).
W **finnair.com**

Malmö Aviation
Tel 0771-55 00 10.
W **malmoaviation.se**

Ryanair
Tel 0900-100 05 50.
W **ryanair.com**

SAS
Tel 0770-727 727 (toll-free in Sweden).
Tel 0870-1226 7760 (UK).
Tel 800-221 2350 (US).
W **scandinavian.net**

Ferry Services

Destination Gotland
Tel 0771-22 33 00.
W **destination gotland.se**

Stena Line
Tel 077-057 5700.
W **stenaline.se**

Tallink Silja Line
Tel 08-666 33 30.
W **tallink.com**

Viking Line
Tel 08-452 40 00.
W **vikingline.se**

Traveling in Stockholm

Strömma Kanalbolaget
Tel 08-120 04 000.
W **strommakanal bolaget.com**

Swebus
Tel 0771-218 218.
W **swebusexpress.se**

Where to Stay

Stockholm

CENTRAL STOCKHOLM:
Clarion Hotel Sign Ⓚ Ⓚ
Boutique **Map** A3
Östra Järnvägsgatan 35, 101 26
Tel *08-676 98 00*
Ⓦ clarionsign.com
The city's largest hotel has 558
rooms. Each floor is dedicated
to a Scandinavian designer.

CENTRAL STOCKHOLM:
First Hotel Reisen Ⓚ Ⓚ
Historic **Map** C4
Skeppsbron 12, 111 30
Tel *08-22 32 60*
Ⓦ firsthotels.com
In an 18th-century building
overlooking the waterfront. Some
rooms have sauna and Jacuzzi.

DK Choice

CENTRAL STOCKHOLM:
Hotel Sven Vintappare Ⓚ Ⓚ
Historic **Map** B4
Sven Vintappares Gränd 3, 117 27
Tel *08-22 41 40*
Ⓦ hotelsvenvintappare.se
A house whose centuries-old
façade masks a modern interior.
The wooden floors are a nod
to the past, while a number
of other original features –
including fireplaces and
ceramic heaters – have been
incorporated into the suites.
All have small kitchenettes.

CENTRAL STOCKHOLM:
Story Hotel Ⓚ Ⓚ
Boutique **Map** C3
Riddargatan 6, 114 35
Tel *08-54 50 39 40*
Ⓦ storyhotels.com
Bohemian-inspired design hotel
with free Wi-Fi, organic cotton
linen, and plenty of art.

CENTRAL STOCKHOLM:
Berns Hotel Ⓚ Ⓚ Ⓚ
Luxury **Map** C3
Näckströmsgatan 8, 111 47
Tel *08-566 32 00*
Ⓦ berns.se
This grand old dame of luxury
has hosted everyone from the
Dalai Lama to Marlene Dietrich.

EASTERN STOCKHOLM: Af
Chapman Hostel Ⓚ
Boutique **Map** D4
Flaggmansvägen 8, 111 49
Tel *08-463 22 66*
Ⓦ stfchapman.com
Stay in a well-known city landmark:
a renovated ship built in 1888.

EASTERN STOCKHOLM:
Hotel Lydmar Ⓚ Ⓚ Ⓚ
Luxury **Map** C3
Södra Blasieholmshamnen 2, 103 24
Tel *08-22 31 60*
Ⓦ lydmar.com
Classic luxury and comfort,
with complimentary Wi-Fi,
movies, and breakfast.

EASTERN STOCKHOLM:
Hotel Skeppsholmen Ⓚ Ⓚ Ⓚ
Boutique **Map** D4
Gröna Gången 1, 111 86
Tel *08-407 23 00*
Ⓦ hotelskeppsholmen.com
A design hotel in a historic
building, with modern and
stylish interiors.

Rest of Sweden

GOTHENBURG: Best
Western Hotel Eggers Ⓚ Ⓚ
Luxury
Drottningtorget, 411 03
Tel *031-333 44 40*
Ⓦ hoteleggers.se
Rugs, tapestries, chandeliers, and
old-world charm in this luxurious
hotel. The rooms are beautifully
decorated and staff are attentive.

DK Choice

GOTHENBURG: Clarion
Hotel Post Ⓚ Ⓚ
Boutique
Drottningtorget 10, 411 03
Tel *031-61 90 00*
Ⓦ clarionpost.com
A design hotel housed inside
a former post office building.
Hotel Post has all mod cons in
a historic setting – 500 modern
rooms, a sun terrace, a pool,
and a pool bar on the rooftop.
This is also Sweden's first hotel
with a health and beauty
center, including a spa.

GOTHENBURG: Hotell
Barken Viking Ⓚ Ⓚ
Boutique
Lilla Bommens Torg 10, 411 04
Tel *031-63 58 00*
Ⓦ barkenviking.com
Sleep aboard a three-star
ship moored in Gothenburg's
harbor. There are 29 superior
rooms and a restaurant.

MALMÖ:
Hotel Mäster Johan Ⓚ Ⓚ
Modern
Mäster Johansgatan 13, 211 21
Tel *040-664 64 00*
Ⓦ masterjohan.se
Mäster Johan offers standard,
business, and superior rooms
or suites. Gym and sauna in the
basement; bike hire available.

UPPSALA: Clarion
Hotel Gillet Ⓚ
Modern
Dragarbrunnsgatan 23, 753 20
Tel *018-68 18 00*
Ⓦ clarionhotelgillet.com
Hotel Gillet has modern rooms,
as well as a popular restaurant
and bar. The sauna, gym, and
pool are free for guests.

VÄXJÖ: Clarion Collection
Hotel Cardinal Ⓚ
Modern
Backgatan 10, 352 30
Tel *047-072 28 00*
Ⓦ clarionhotel.com
This Clarion hotel offers all
modern amenities, including
high-speed Internet. Guests
also enjoy a complimentary
full organic breakfast, with
tea, coffee, and fruit.

Colorful furnishings at the luxurious Berns Hotel, Stockholm

Where to Eat and Drink

Stockholm

CENTRAL STOCKHOLM:
Nalen
Traditional Swedish **Map** B2
Regeringsgatan 74, 111 39
Tel *08-50 52 92 00* **Closed** *Sun*
The menu at Nalen focuses on simple Swedish dishes, made using seasonal ingredients. A bar, nightclub, and concert hall are also on the premises.

CENTRAL STOCKHOLM:
Sturehof ⓚⓚ
Modern Swedish **Map** C2
Sturegallerian 42, Stureplan 2, 114 46
Tel *08-440 57 30*
Boasting an illustrious history as one of Stockholm's first seafood restaurants, Sturehof serves the freshest daily catch and other Swedish produce.

CENTRAL STOCKHOLM:
Fredsgatan 12 ⓚⓚⓚ
Fine Dining **Map** B3
Fredsgatan 12, 111 52
Tel *08-50 52 44 04* **Closed** *Sun*
This Michelin-starred restaurant offers dishes created from the finest ingredients. Try the pheasant, oysters, or clams.

DK Choice

CENTRAL STOCKHOLM:
Operakällaren ⓚⓚⓚ
Fine Dining **Map** C3
Operahuset, Karl XII's Torg, 111 86
Tel *08-676 58 00* **Closed** *Sun & Mon*
One of Sweden's historic culinary institutions, the Michelin-starred Operakällaren (meaning "Opera Cellar") got its name as early as 1787, when it was indeed the cellar underneath the Opera House. The magnificent surroundings complement the exquisite dining experience. Also on the premises are Café Opera, Opera Bar, and the Bakfickan Bar.

EASTERN STOCKHOLM: Mathias
Dahlgren Matsalen ⓚⓚⓚ
Fine Dining **Map** C3
Grand Hôtel Stockholm, Södra Blasieholmshamnen 6, 103 27
Tel *08-679 35 84* **Closed** *dinner; Sun & Mon*
Head here for a fine dining experience, complete with wine pairings. The Michelin-starred kitchen serves gourmet Swedish fare with a modern twist, and the bistro is also open for lunch.

Vintage posters and terracotta floors adorn the dining room at Salt & Brygga, Malmö

SOUTHERN STOCKHOLM:
Bistro & Grill Ruby ⓚⓚ
Bistro **Map** C4
Österlånggatan 14, 111 31
Tel *08-20 60 15* **Closed** *Sun (bistro only)*
This is the place to visit for delicious charcoal-grilled beef, pork, and lamb. Ruby also offers a weekend brunch at noon.

SOUTHERN STOCKHOLM:
Pontus! ⓚⓚ
Fine Dining **Map** C4
Brunnsgatan 1, 111 30
Tel *08-54 52 73 00* **Closed** *Sun*
Lunch and dinner menus at Pontus! are devised by Swedish master chef Pontus Frithiof. From burgers to *foie gras*, dishes here are a careful balance of rustic and sophisticated.

Rest of Sweden

GOTHENBURG:
Fiskekrogen ⓚⓚ
Fine Dining
Lilla Torget 1, 411 18
Tel *031-10 10 05* **Closed** *Sun*
One of the best seafood restaurants in Stockholm, Fiskekrogen has been serving the tastiest catch since 1977. There is a choice of set menus, a seafood buffet, and a variety of fish dishes.

GOTHENBURG:
Restaurang Trägår'n ⓚⓚ
Modern Swedish
Nya Allén 11, 411 36
Tel *031-10 20 80* **Closed** *Sun*
This large restaurant is a stone's throw away from Avenyn, the city's main thoroughfare. Events

Price Guide
Prices are for a three-course meal for one, half a bottle of house wine, and all extra charges.

ⓚ	under 450 SEK
ⓚⓚ	450 to 1,000 SEK
ⓚⓚⓚ	over 1,000 SEK

and shows are held in the evening, and there is also a nightclub on the premises.

GOTHENBURG: Smaka ⓚⓚ
Traditional Swedish
Vasaplatsen 3, 411 26
Tel *031-13 22 47*
Rustic home-cooking in a pleasant red-brick building. There is outdoor seating in summer and a good selection of beers.

GOTHENBURG:
Sjömagasinet ⓚⓚⓚ
Fine Dining
Adolf Edelsvärds Gata 5, 414 51
Tel *031-775 59 20* **Closed** *Sun*
This Michelin-starred restaurant serves classic and innovative seafood dishes in an atmospheric environment.

MALMÖ:
Bastard Restaurant ⓚⓚ
European
Mäster Johansgatan 11, 211 21
Tel *040-12 13 18* **Closed** *Sun & Mon*
One of the trendiest places in Malmö. The chefs at Bastard use local, organic ingredients in their dishes. Craft beers and organic wines also available.

DK Choice

MALMÖ: Salt & Brygga ⓚⓚ
Traditional
Sundspromenaden 7, 211 16
Tel *040-611 59 40* **Closed** *Sun*
Salt & Brygga is known for using local, organic produce and fish from sustainable sources, as well as Fair Trade coffee. Incorporating the finest ingredients from Skåne, this restaurant re-creates traditional Swedish cuisine with exciting innovative influences. Organic bread and a salad buffet are included in all lunchtime meals.

UPPSALA: Villa Anna ⓚⓚ
Modern Swedish
Odinslund 3, 753 10
Tel *018-580 20 00* **Closed** *Sun*
The award-winning chefs at Villa Anna concoct culinary delights from rustic Swedish fare. The emphasis is on local and organic ingredients whenever possible.

NORWAY

Norway's great attraction is the grandeur of its scenery. The landscape is one of dramatic contrasts: great mountain ranges, sheer river valleys, mighty glaciers, deep green forests, and the spectacular fjords that indent the western coast. In the far north, above the Arctic Circle, visitors can marvel at the Northern Lights and the long summer nights of the Land of the Midnight Sun.

The fjords that make the coastline of Norway one of the most jagged in the world were carved by glaciers during the last Ice Age. As the glaciers began to recede about 12,000 years ago, the sea level rose and seawater flooded back to fill the deep, eroded valleys. Norway's extraordinary geography has had a great influence on its people and development. In the past, scarcity of agricultural land led to economic dependence on the sea. In contrast, Norway today has abundant hydroelectric power as well as rich oil and gas deposits on its continental shelf.

The first settlers arrived 10,000 years ago as the Scandinavian icesheets retreated. They were hunters of reindeer, deer, bears, and fish. By the Bronze Age (1500–500 BC), rock carvings show that these early Norwegians had learnt to ski. Other inhabitants of the region were the Sami (formerly known as the Lapps), with origins in the northern regions of Russia, Finland, Sweden, and Norway, where they haved lived for thousands of years by fishing and herding reindeer. Some still follow the nomadic life of their forefathers but the majority now live and work in much the same way as Norwegians.

History

It is for the Viking Age (c.800–1050) that Norway is best known. As a result of overpopulation and clan warfare, the Norwegian Vikings traveled to find new lands. They mostly sailed west, their longships reaching the British Isles, Iceland, Greenland, and even America. The raiders soon became settlers and those who remained at home benefited both from the spoils of war and the fact that farmland was no longer in such short supply. The country was united by Harald the Fairhaired in the 9th century. This great age of expansion, however, effectively ended in 1066, when King Harald Hardråde was defeated at the battle of Stamford Bridge in England.

The 11th and 12th centuries were marked by dynastic conflicts and the rising influence of the church. In 1217, Haakon IV came to power, ushering in a

The harbor at Bergen, the main center for tours of Norway's fjords

◀ View over Lake Ringedalsvatnet, with the rock of Trolltunga (the troll's tongue) in the foreground

Norwegian explorer Roald Amundsen checking his position after reaching the South Pole in 1911

"Golden Age," when Norway flourished under strong centralized government. In 1262, both Iceland and Greenland came under Norwegian rule. However, in the following century, after suffering terrible losses in the Black Death, Norway was reduced to being the least important of the Scandinavian countries. From 1380 to 1905, it was under the rule first of Denmark and then of Sweden.

The 19th century saw the growth of a national identity and a blossoming of Norwegian culture. Most of Norway's most famous individuals were born in this century, among them the composer Edvard Grieg, dramatist Henrik Ibsen, Expressionist painter Edvard Munch, and polar explorer Roald Amundsen.

Following independence from Sweden in 1905, the government set about industrializing the country, expanding the merchant fleet, and establishing healthcare and education as the cornerstones of a welfare state.

Norway pursued a policy of neutrality in World War I and World War II. The price was high in World War I, since German submarines attacked shipping indiscriminately and Norway lost half its chartered tonnage. In World War II, Germany occupied the country, but encountered a massive resistance movement. Norway's part in the war helped it gain in status and it became one of the founding members of the UN in 1945 and entered NATO in 1949.

The biggest issue of the postwar years has been whether or not to join the EU. Twice Norway has refused, but the economy thrives regardless, thanks in large part to revenues from North Sea oil.

Language and Culture

There are two official Norwegian languages: *Bokmål* (book language), a modernization of old Dano-Norwegian used in the days of Danish rule, and *Nynorsk*, based on rural dialects, which was codified in the 19th century as part of the resurgence of nationalism. Despite the government's efforts to preserve the use of *Nynorsk*, it is in decline. As in other parts of Scandinavia, you don't need to speak Norwegian to get by, since most people speak English.

Perhaps because independence was so long in coming, most Norwegians are great patriots. National Independence Day (May 17) is celebrated the length and breadth of the country, with festive gatherings even at remote farms. Norwegians also have a great attachment to outdoor pursuits – fishing, hiking, walking, and skiing – and many families have a *hytte* (cottage or cabin) in the mountains or on the coast.

KEY DATES IN NORWEGIAN HISTORY

AD 800–1050 Viking Age

866 Vikings control most of England

900 Norway united under hereditary rule

1030 Christianity established

1217–63 Reign of Haakon IV

1380–1814 Norway in union with Denmark

1660 Modern boundaries of Norway established, through peace of Copenhagen

1814 Union with Sweden, but Norwegian parliament, the Storting, has extensive powers

1887 Norwegian Labour party is founded

1905 Norway established as a separate kingdom

1940–45 German occupation of Norway during World War II

1969 Discovery of oil and gas in North Sea

1972 Following a referendum, Norway declines membership of the EU

1994 Second referendum on membership of the EU; majority again votes "no"

2011 Seventy-seven people die in terror attacks

2013 Norway celebrates 100 years of women's suffrage

2014 Norway celebrates 200 years of its Constitution

Exploring Norway

Norway is so long and narrow that, if Oslo remained fixed and the rest were turned upside down, it would stretch all the way to Rome. There are two main areas of attraction: Oslo, a lively, open city, particularly in summer, and Bergen and the fjords in the west. Elsewhere, up to 95 percent of the country is forested or uncultivated. Transportation (which comprises trains, buses, and coastal ferries) is reliable, though services can be cut back severely in the winter months, especially in the north.

Cruise ships moored in the Geiranger Fjord between Bergen and Trondheim

Sights at a Glance

1. Oslo pp622–6
2. Stavanger
3. Bergen and the Fjords
4. Trondheim

See inset map

5. Tromsø

Key

— Highway
— Major road
— Railroad
••• International border

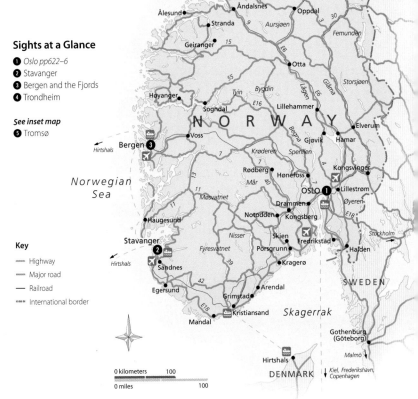

Norway

0 km   250
0 miles   250

See main map

Tromsø
Trondheim
SWEDEN
FINLAND
NORWAY
Helsinki
Bergen   OSLO   Tallinn   ESTONIA
Stockholm
LATVIA
DENMARK   Copenhagen   LITHUANIA

Tromsø
17
E6

Trondheim
Orkanger   Selbusjøen
65

Molde
Åndalsnes   Oppdal   30
Ålesund
Stranda   9   Aursjøen   3
Geiranger   15   Femunden

Otta
55   Storsjøen
Tvin   Byglin
Høyanger   E16
Sogndal   Lillehammer
N O R W A Y
Voss   Elverum
7   Gjøvik   Hamar
Hirtshals   Krøderen   Spenllen
Bergen   Rødberg   Hønefoss   Kongsvinger
Mår   40
3   OSLO   Lillestrøm
Norwegian   11   Møsvatriet   Drammen   Øyeren
Sea   Notodden   Kongsberg   E18
Nisser   Skien   Stockholm
Haugesund   Fyresvatnet   Porsgrunn   Fredrikstad
Stavanger   Kragerø   Halden
Hirtshals   Sandnes   39
42   Arendal   SWEDEN
Egersund   Grimstad
E18   Kristiansand
Mandal   Skagerrak

Gothenburg
(Göteborg)
Malmö
0 kilometers   100   Hirtshals   Kiel, Frederikshavn,
0 miles   100   DENMARK   Copenhagen

❶ Oslo

Founded around 1048 by Harald Hardråde, Oslo is the oldest of the Scandinavian capital cities and occupies an enormous area, with about 1 million inhabitants. The heart of the city is largely made up of late 19th- and early 20th-century Neoclassical buildings, wide avenues, and landscaped parks. The city center is compact and easy to explore on foot, and most of the city's sights are within walking distance of each other. The city is a cultural hotspot, with a large number of museums and art galleries. The Nordmarka area of forests to the north of the center gives a glimpse of the beautiful Norwegian countryside.

Sights at a Glance

① Akershus Slott and
   Hjemmefrontmuseet
② Opera House
③ Rådhus and
   Aker Brygge
④ Kongelige Slottet
⑤ Nationaltheatret
⑥ Nasjonalgalleriet
⑦ Munch-museet
⑧ Vigelandsparken
⑨ Frammuseet
⑩ Kon-Tiki Museum
⑪ Vikingskipshuset
⑫ Norsk Folkemuseum

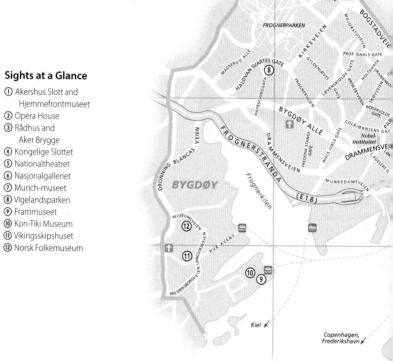

Boats moored along the quayside, in front of the Akershus Slott

Getting Around

Oslo has around 60 bus and tram routes. Most buses set out from the terminal a few hundred meters northwest of Oslo Sentralstasjon, the main train station. Route 30 goes to the museums on the Bygdøy Peninsula. From mid-March to mid-October, you can also reach the peninsula by ferry from the boarding point by the Rådhus. The Tunnelbanen is most useful for reaching the city suburbs, including Nordmarka.

Busy shopping street in Oslo's city center

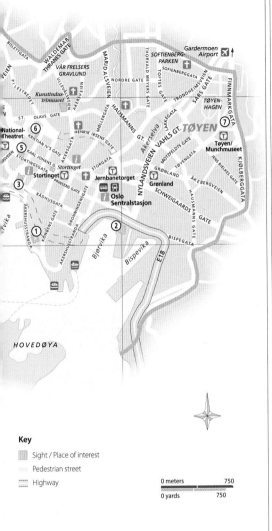

Key

▦ Sight / Place of interest

▭ Pedestrian street

▨ Highway

0 meters		750
0 yards		750

HOVEDØYA

① **Akershus Slott and Hjemmefront-museet**

Festningsplassen. 🚌 12 to Christiana Torv. **Akershus Slott** Ⓣ Stortinget. **Tel** 23 09 39 17. **Open** May–Aug: daily, Sep–Apr: Sat & Sun. **Closed** public hols. 🖼 📷 **Hjemmefrontmuseet Tel** 23 09 32 80. **Open** daily. **Closed** public hols. 🖼 📷

Located on a knoll overlooking the Oslofjorden, the Akershus Slott (Akershus Castle) is the city's most notable memorial to medieval times. Built around 1300, the castle was besieged several times before King Christian IV of Denmark transformed it into a lavish Renaissance residence in the 1620s. He also built a new fortress around the castle. Known as the Akershus Festning, it is still in use today. Little remains of the castle's former glory, most of the rooms being relatively bare, although the tapestries in the Romerike Hall are impressive. You can also visit the royal chapel and the royal mausoleum, where members of the present Norwegian dynasty lie buried.

The most somber period in the Akershus Slott's history was during World War II, when the occupying Nazis tortured and shot members of the Norwegian resistance here. Pictorial displays at the Hjemmefrontmuseet (Resistance Museum), located by the gates of the castle, provide a moving account of the war in Norway, from occupation through resistance to liberation.

Akershus Slott, Oslo's finest surviving medieval monument

② **Opera House**

Kirsten Flagstads Plass 1. **Tel** 21 42 21 21. ① Bjørvika. 🚌 32, 34, 70, 504. **Open** 10am–11pm Mon–Fri, 11am–11pm Sat & Sun. 🅰 🖶 daily (Sat & Sun in English). 🅆 **operaen.no**

The home of the Norwegian National Opera and Ballet is situated right on the waterfront at Bjovika, and much of this building is positioned in or under the sea. A defining feature of the design is its sloping roof, which is covered in white marble and granite. This creates the illusion of glistening ice, like a glacier rising from the edge of Oslofjord. There are three main performance spaces for opera, ballet, and concerts, and concerts are also held in the foyer or on the roof.

③ **Rådhus and Aker Brygge**

Rådhuset i Oslo, Fridtjof Nansens Plass. **Tel** 23 46 16 00. ① Nationaltheatret, Stortinget. 🚌 30, 31, 32, 45, 81, 83. 🚋 12, 13, 19. **Open** daily. **Closed** public hols. 🖼 (May–Sep). 🅰 🖶 🅆 **oslokommune.no**

Inaugurated in 1950 to commemorate Oslo's 900th year, the Rådhus (City Hall) is the city's most conspicuous landmark and has become a popular symbol of civic pride. Providing a complete contrast to the exterior, the colorful murals, sculptures, and frescoes inside the building celebrate Norwegian artistic and intellectual achievements, as well as those in exploration.

The Rådhus is famous as the place where the Nobel Peace Prize is presented. All the other prizes are awarded at the Stadshuset in Stockholm *(see p606)*. Past recipients have included the Red Cross, Martin Luther King, Mother Teresa and Barack Obama.

Close by is Aker Brygge. This old shipyard is now a glass-and-chrome leisure complex with shops, restaurants, bars,

cinemas, and a theater. It is a popular place in the city to go for a beer and a meal, especially during the long Scandinavian summer evenings, when you can sit outside and enjoy the scenery of the Oslo Fjord.

④ **Kongelige Slottet**

Drammensveien 1. **Tel** 22 04 87 00. ① Nationaltheatret. 🚌 30, 31, 32, 34, 45, 81, 83. 🚋 11, 13, 17, 18, 19. **Open** end Jun–mid-Aug: 6am–9pm daily. 🖼 🖶 compulsory. 🅰 🖶

The Neoclassical Royal Palace is a monument to openness, standing as it does in the freely accessible Palace gardens (Slottsparken). Without gates or walls, the gardens symbolize Norway's "open" monarchy. The palace itself was built in 1825–48 at the request of King Karl Johan. Every day at 1:30pm, the ceremony of the changing of the guard takes place. On Norway's National Day on May 17, the palace becomes the focal point of celebrations when the royal family stands on the balcony to greet the processions of school children.

Viking warrior detail from Rådhus main doors

Oslo's Nationaltheatret, overlooking its attractive, busy piazza

⑤ **Nationaltheatret**

Johanne Dybwads Plass 1. **Tel** 22 00 14 00. ① Nationaltheatret. 🚌 30, 31, 32, 34, 45, 81, 83. 🚋 11, 13, 17, 18, 19. **Open** Aug–mid-Jun: daily. 🖶 (call in advance). 🖼 🖶

Built in 1899, Norway's National Theater is Neoclassical in style, and flanked by imposing statues of the nation's two greatest 19th-century playwrights – Henrik Johan Ibsen and Bjørnstjerne Bjørnson, who is little known outside Scandinavia these days, but was a prolific writer of plays and poetry during the 19th century. The theater has four stages, and a varied program, with all performances given in Norwegian. Visitors can make special arrangements to have a guided tour of the interior.

Henrik Johan Ibsen (1828–1906)

Born in the southern town of Skien, the young Ibsen was brought up in poverty, after his timber merchant father suffered bankruptcy in 1836. Managing to escape, he lived first in Kristiania and then Bergen, where he began writing and producing his first dramas. In 1864, he left for Germany and Italy, where he spent the next 27 years. His most famous plays include *Peer Gynt* (1867), *A Doll's House* (1879), and *Hedda Gabler* (1890). Regarded as one of the founders of modern drama, Ibsen's legacy to the European stage was his introduction of themes such as the alienation of the individual from a morally bankrupt society, loss of religious faith, and women's desire to free themselves of their roles as wives and mothers – a clear departure from the unchallenging theater of the time. After returning to Norway, he died in 1906.

Playwright Henrik Johan Ibsen

Simple, red-brick facade of the Nasjonalgalleriet

⑥ Nasjonalgalleriet

Universitetsgaten 13. **Tel** 21 98 20 00.
Ⓣ Nationaltheatret. 🚌 11, 17, 18.
🚊 13, 19. **Open** Tue–Sun. **Closed**
public hols. 🎫 ♿
Ⓦ nasjonalmuseet.no

Norway's biggest collection of art is housed in this grand 19th-century building. It includes an impressive collection of works by the country's most famous painter, Edvard Munch, from the 1880s to 1916. The main part of the collection is housed on the second floor. There is a strong international collection including Impressionist paintings by Manet, Monet, and Degas, Post-Impressionist works

by Gauguin and Cézanne, and early 20th-century paintings by Picasso and Braque. The museum also holds an important collection of Norwegian art. Among the paintings on display are some spectacular fjord and country scenes from the 19th-century National Romantic period by leading Norwegian landscape painters, notably Johan Christian Dahl. There are also works by Realist artists such as Harriet Becker, Christian Krohg, and Erik Werenskiold, as well as sculptures by Gustav Vigeland. The Munch room contains such important works as *The Sick Child* (1885) and *The Scream* (1893), the swirling forms and colours of which were to greatly inspire the growing Expressionist movement.

⑦ Munch-museet

Tøyengata 53. **Tel** 23 49 35 00. Ⓣ
Tøyen. 🚌 20. **Open** Jun–Aug: daily;
Sep–May: Tue–Sun. **Closed** Jan 1, May
1, May 12, Dec 24–25. ♿ 🎥 🎫 🚫
Ⓦ munch.museum.no

One of Scandinavia's leading artists, Edvard Munch (1863–1944) left an amazing 1,100 paintings, 4,500 drawings, and 18,000 graphic works to the city of Oslo when he died. Most of these are housed at the Munch-museet, which opened in 1963.

Munch led a troubled life, plagued by melancholy and depression due, in part, to the untimely deaths of his favorite sister and younger brother. He nevertheless remained a highly prolific artist whose intensely psychological work remains one of the great cornerstones of early Expressionist art. Since the Munch-museet is a fairly small museum, only a fraction of his work can be shown at any one time, which prevents it from being

Young Woman on the Shore (1896) by Edvard Munch, at the Munch-museet

overwhelming and means that displays are frequently changed. The core of the collection is the series of outstanding paintings from the 1890s, although other periods of his life are well represented. Munch was also a prolific graphic artist, and the print room reveals his talents using etching, lithographic, and woodcut techniques. The basement houses a permanent display of Munch's life and times, and there is also a comprehensive library.

View back towards the city across Vigelandsparken sculpture park

⑧ Vigelandsparken

Kirkeveien. **Tel** 23 49 37 00.
Ⓣ Majorstuen. 🚌 20, 45. 🚊 12.
Open daily. 🚫 🖥

Vigelandsparken lies within the larger green expanse of Frognerparken. The park takes its name from the larger-than-life sculptures of Gustav Vigeland (1869–1943), which form extraordinary tableaux of fighting, play, and love. Work on display includes a series of 58 bronzes of men, women, and infants, flanking the footbridge over the river and leading up to his most famous creation, a 17-m- (56-ft-) granite obelisk of no fewer than 121 intertwined figures depicting the cycle of life. One of Oslo's most visited attractions, the park is a massive artistic creation that took Vigeland 40 years to complete. Some other examples of his work can be seen at Vigelandsmuseet near the park or at the Nasjonalgalleriet.

The Bygdøy Peninsula

No trip to Oslo is complete without a visit to the Bygdøy Peninsula, which lies off the western edge of the city. The area offers beaches, walking, numerous historic sites, and fascinating museums. These include a folk museum showing traditional ways of life, the Vikingsskipshuset, which traces Norway's maritime history, and others celebrating the famous Norwegian explorers Roald Amundsen and Thor Heyerdahl.

⑨ Frammuseet

Bygdøynesveien 36. **Tel** 23 28 29 50.
🚌 30. 🚢 **Open** daily. 🅿️ 🆆 **fram.
museum.no**

Designed in 1892 by Scottish-Norwegian shipbuilder Colin Archer, the *Fram* is best known as the ship that carried Norwegian explorer Roald Amundsen on his epic journey to the South Pole in 1911. The *Fram* was an ideal vessel for this undertaking. Its sides are perfectly smooth, making it impossible for ice to get a grip on the hull. Visitors can ease themselves between the remarkable array of beams in the ship's hull and marvel at the assortment of equipment – ranging from a piano to surgical instruments – that the crew managed to take with them. A series of fascinating displays around the ship relate the history of Arctic exploration.

⑩ Kon-Tiki Museum

Bygdøynesveien 36. **Tel** 23 08 67 67.
🚌 30. 🚢 **Open** daily. **Closed** public hols. 🆓 🅿️ 🆆 **kon-tiki.no**

On display at the superb Kon-Tiki Museum are the unbelievably fragile-looking vessels used by Thor Heyerdahl to make his legendary journeys across the Pacific and Atlantic Oceans. The aim of his voyages was to prove that trans-oceanic contact was possible between ancient civilisations. The balsawood *Kon-Tiki* raft carried Heyerdahl and a crew from Peru to Polynesia in 1947, confirming his theory that the first Polynesian settlers could have sailed from pre-Inca Peru. In 1970, he sailed a papyrus boat, *Ra II*, from Morocco to

Thor Heyerdahl's vessel, *Ra II*, at the Kon-Tiki Museum

the Caribbean to prove that the ancient peoples of Africa or Europe might have had contact with South America. These, and other eventful sagas, are outlined in the exhibition.

⑪ Vikingskipshuset

Huk Aveny 35. **Tel** 22 85 19 00. 🚌 30.
🚢 **Open** daily. **Closed** public hols.
🅿️ 🆓 🆆 **khm.uio.no**

Norway is best known for its Viking explorers, and this museum contains three beautifully preserved 9th-century longships. All three were unearthed from burial mounds in Norway, and funeral goods from each of the vessels are on display, including ceremonial sleighs, chests, and tapestries. Viewing platforms allow visitors to study the magnificent 22 m by 5 m (72 ft by 16 ft) Oseberg ship and the slightly larger Gokstad boat, both of which were discovered on the western side of the Oslofjord. Fragmented sections of a smaller boat, the Tune, remain much as they were when they were found on the eastern side of the fjord in 1867.

⑫ Norsk Folkemuseum

Museumsveien 10. **Tel** 22 12 37 00.
🚌 30. 🚢 **Open** daily. **Closed** Jan 1, May 17, Dec 24, 25 & 31. 🅿️ 🆓
🆆 **norskfolkemuseum.no**

Established in 1894, this excellent attraction is devoted largely to Norwegian rural life, and visitors should set aside half a day to view the many (over 150) restored buildings. These include barns, storehouses, and a splendid stave church (c.1200) with typical steep, shingle-covered roofs and dramatic dragon finials. The indoor collections consist of displays of folk art, toys, folk dress, the playwright Ibsen's study, and a pharmacy museum. On Sundays in the summer there are displays of folk dancing, and guides demonstrate skills such as weaving tapestries or baking traditional flatbread.

A reassembled grass-roofed house at the Norsk Folkemuseum

The Vikings

From the 8th to the 11th century, the Vikings, or Northmen, sailed from their overpopulated fjords in Scandinavia and made their way across Europe, plundering, looking for trade, and offering mercenary service. The Swedes (or Varangians) established themselves throughout the Baltic and controlled the overland route to the Black Sea, while the Danes invaded parts of England, Portugal, and France. The Norwegians, however, were unparalleled in their success, and their adventures became the stuff of Viking legend. After overrunning the Orkneys, the Shetlands, the Hebrides, and parts of Ireland, the Norwegians established colonies in the Faroes, Iceland, and Greenland. They even sailed to the coast of North America. The Vikings were undoubtedly the most feared Europeans of their day, and their impact on history was immense. Fear of the Viking raid unified many otherwise disparate tribes and kingdoms, and many new political states were created by the Vikings themselves. Despite profiting from the spoils of war, it was their success as settlers and traders that was the Vikings' greatest achievement.

Viking religion was dominated by the supreme gods Odin (god of war), Thor (thunder), and Frey (fertility). Valhalla was their equivalent of heaven. Warriors were buried with whatever it was thought the afterlife required, and the rich were entombed in ships, often with their servants. Most had converted to Christianity by the late 10th century, but Sweden remained pagan well into the 11th century.

Burial "ships" made of stone for warriors from poorer families, near Aalborg in Denmark

Frey, god of fertility

The longship was the main vessel of the Viking raid. Longer, slimmer, and faster than the usual Viking ship, it had a large rectangular sail and between 24 and 50 oars. The sail was used in open sea and navigation was achieved by taking bearings from the stars.

The prow, curled into a "shepherd's crook," formed a high defensive barrier.

The keel was characteristically shallow to allow for flat beach landings.

The beautifully restored Oseberg ship, unearthed in 1904, on display at the Vikingskipshuset in Oslo

Weapons and armor were the backbone of Viking culture, so the blacksmith's art was always in demand. Bronze and iron swords were endlessly produced, many of which followed their bearers to the grave. Arrows, axes, shields, helmets, and coats of mail were standard military gear, examples of which survive in pristine condition today.

Gold armlet

Jewelry design often showed Arab and eastern European influence, which illustrates the extent of the Viking trading network. Gold and silver were a sign of wealth and prestige, although many ornaments were made of bronze, pewter, colored glass, jet, and amber.

Picture stones were memorial blocks that celebrated the glory of dead relatives. They were carved with pictures and runic writing.

Viking helmet with noseguard

Picture stone from Gotland

View of the waterfront at Stavanger's attractive marina

❷ Stavanger

🏙 130,000. ✈ 🚢 🚌 🚆
ℹ️ Domkirkeplassen 3 (51 85 92 00).
🎭 Maijazz (May); Glamat Food Festival (Jul).

Stavanger is best known today as Norway's major oil town, with North Sea oil having provided its prosperity since the 1970s. Earlier in its history, in the mid-19th century, the town grew rich on herring exports.

Small enough to be seen on foot, much of the center of Stavanger is modern. One exception is the cathedral, the **Stavanger Domkirke**, which dates back to the 12th century but has been restored several times since. Later 17th-century additions include a flamboyant pulpit and a number of huge, richly carved memorial tablets hanging in the aisles.

Stavanger's main attraction is Gamle Stavanger (Old Stavanger), west of the harbor. Visitors can wander down the narrow cobble-stone streets of this old city quarter, amid the white-painted wooden houses, and imagine life here in the 19th century. An interesting museum in the town is the **Hermetikkmuseet** (Canning Museum) at No. 88 Øvre Strandgate, which tells the story of Stavanger's fisheries. Overlooking the harbor, the **Norsk Oljemuseum** (Norwegian Petroleum Museum) gives an insight into North Sea oil exploration.

❸ Bergen and the Fjords

🏙 255,000. ✈ 🚢 🚌 🚆
ℹ️ Strandkaien 3 (55 55 20 00).
🎭 Bergen International Festival (May–Jun).

Surrounded by no fewer than seven mountains, Norway's most westerly port offers the visitor plenty to do and see, although it rains relentlessly here. Founded in the 12th century, Bergen is one of Norway's prettiest cities, with a medieval quarter dating back to the days when the port was an important center of European trade for the all-powerful German Hanseatic League. Many of the surviving Hanseatic buildings are found on the **Bryggen** (quay), where brightly-painted old wooden warehouses – now museums,

shops, and restaurants – make up an attractive harborside. Close by the harbor is the busy Fisketorvet (Fish Market), where fresh fish, produce, and local crafts can be found. Also nearby are the 11th-century **Mariakirken** (St. Mary's Church) and the **Hanseatiske Museum** – an excellently preserved late Hansa house from the 18th century.

Around Lille Lungegårds-vann, the city's central lake, are a number of interesting art galleries. Finally, no visitor to Bergen should miss the chance to take a trip up Mount Ulriken for a panoramic view of the area. A cable car takes you from the edge of the city to the summit.

Elaborate Baroque pulpit in the Mariakirken, Bergen

Environs

Just outside the city is **Troldhaugen**, an enchanting villa filled with paintings, prints, and other memorabilia, where Norway's most famous composer Edvard Grieg (1843–1907) spent the later years of his life and composed much of his work. A short way beyond is **Fantoft Stavkirke**, a traditional, ancient wooden church, originally built in Sognefjord, but moved here.

Bergen also makes a good base for viewing the western fjord scenery, which extends from south of Bergen to distant Kristiansund in the north. Boat trips leave from Bergen throughout the summer (a few run year-round), visiting local fjords. One of the closest is **Osterfjord**, but **Hardangerfjord**, with its majestic waterfalls, is perhaps the most spectacular.

The stunning scenery of the Sognefjord, north of Bergen

To the north, **Sognefjord**, at 206 km (128 miles) long and 1,308 m (4,291 ft) deep, is the deepest and longest fjord in the world.

🎫 Troldhaugen

Troldhaugveien 65, Paradis. **Tel** 55 92 29 92. **Open** May–Sep: daily; Jan–Apr: Mon–Fri. 🅿️ ♿ 🎫 🖥️ 📷
w troldhaugen.com

❹ Trondheim

🏔️ 180,000. ✈️ 🚌 🚃 🚆 🚌 **i** Nordre Gate 11 (73 80 76 60). ⛷️ St. Olav Festival (Jul). **w** trondheim.com

Called Nidaros (which means the mouth of the River Nid) until the 16th century, Trondheim has benefited from having a good harbor and being situated in a wide and fertile valley. Founded in AD 997, the city was for many centuries the political and religious capital of Norway, with the earliest Parliament (or *Ting*) being held here. This period saw the construction of Trondheim's most beautiful building – and one of Norway's architectural highlights – the **Nidaros Cathedral**, begun around 1077. Until the Reformation in the 16th century, the cathedral attracted pilgrims from all over Scandinavia. Notable features of this colossal building include the Gothic-style great arched nave and a magnificent stained-glass rose window above the entrance – the work of Gabriel Kjelland in 1930. Since 1988, the cathedral

Detail from the facade of Nidaros Cathedral, Trondheim

has been home to the Norwegian Crown jewels and the modest but beautiful regalia of the King, Queen, and Crown Prince, which are on display in a side chapel.

Another reminder of Trondheim's medieval past is provided by the wharves alongside the harbor and the narrow streets that wind between brightly painted warehouses. Although the buildings you see today only date back to the 18th century, the layout of the area is much as it was in earlier times when fishing and timber were the main source of the town's wealth.

Other attractions of the city include Scandinavia's largest wooden building, the **Stiftsgården**, built between 1774 and 1778 as a private home. Today, it serves as the king's official residence in Trondheim. The **Nordenfjeldske Kunstindustrimuseum** (Decorative Arts Museum) houses an extensive collection of furniture, tapestries, ceramics, silver, and glassware from the 16th to the 20th century, including a fine collection of Art Nouveau pieces, plus contemporary arts, crafts, and design.

🏛️ Nordenfjeldske Kunstindustrimuseum

Munkegaten 5. **Tel** 73 80 89 50. **Open** Jun–Aug: daily; Sep–May: Tue–Sun. **Closed** some public hols. 🅿️ 📷 🎫 ♿

❺ Tromsø

🏔️ 74,000. ✈️ 🚌 🚌 **i** Kirkegata 2 (77 61 00 00). ⛷️ Northern Lights Festival (Jan).

Situated inside the Arctic circle, Tromsø, the so-called capital of North Norway, is a lively university town. There are not many specific sights and attractions in the town itself, but its fine mountain and fjord setting makes it well worth a visit. The most spectacular time to stay is in the summer, during the period of the "midnight sun."

Tromsø's modern concrete and glass Arctic Cathedral

Due to the high latitude, the sun remains above the horizon from May 21 to July 21, and the sky often glows red throughout the night. Tromsø is also a good place to view the Northern Lights.

Since Tromsø is a compact town, it is possible to stroll through the center, which sits upon a small hilly island reached by a bridge, in around 15 minutes. The major sight here is the striking white **Ishavskatedralen** (Arctic Cathedral). The cathedral is intended to represent the type of tent used by the *Sami*, the region's indigenous semi-nomadic people. Tromsø's **Polarmuseet** (Polar Museum) documents the history of the local economy – seal trapping played a big part until the 1950s – and polar expeditions, in particular the voyages undertaken by Norwegian explorer Roald Amundsen. Tromsø is a famous starting point for Arctic expeditions, and Amundsen made his last expedition from here to the Arctic ice cap, where he died in 1928. Visitors should not miss the opportunity to take the cable car (Fjellheisen) up the mountain behind the city to get a real sense of the setting of this polar town.

🏛️ Polarmuseet

Søndre Tollbugata 11. **Tel** 77 62 33 60. **Open** daily. **Closed** public hols. 🅿️
📷 **w** visitnorway.com

Practical & Travel Information

Norway has a reputation as an expensive destination, but the cost of traveling around the country is fairly reasonable. Norway's public transportation system is comprehensive and reliable, although visitors should expect a reduced service during winter. Once within the Arctic Circle, there is a period around midsummer during which the sun never sets (the "midnight sun"). Conversely, there is a "polar night" around midwinter, during which the sun never rises at all. These effects occur for longer periods the farther north you travel.

Tourist Information

Norway has around 350 local tourist offices, as well as almost 20 regional offices. Visitors to the capital can use **Oslo Promotion Tourist Information** in the center of town. For brochures and more general information on all parts of the country, contact the **Norwegian Tourist Board** before you leave home.

As well as providing information on hiking routes and guided mountain tours, **Den Norske Turistforening** (Norwegian Mountain Touring Association) sells maps and hiking gear, and maintains more than 300 mountain huts throughout the country.

Opening Hours

Many museums and attractions are open all year round, although a few have seasonal opening hours. Stores are generally open from 10am to 8pm Monday to Friday, and from 10am to 6pm on Saturday. Most stores are closed on Sundays.

Visa Requirements

Citizens of the EU, the US, Canada, Australia, and New Zealand do not require a visa for stays of less than three months. Citizens of most EU countries can use a national identity card instead of a passport for entry to Norway.

Safety and Emergency

Norway is a safe country, and crime against tourists is relatively rare. Standards of healthcare are excellent. Hotels and tourist offices have lists of local doctors, or you can look in the telephone directory under doctors (*leger*). You will have to pay a fee for a doctor's appointment and for prescriptions, but EU citizens with an E111 form will be reimbursed for part of the cost of any treatment.

Banking and Currency

The Norwegian unit of currency is the Norwegian krone, abbreviated to NOK. Cash and traveler's checks can be changed at banks and post offices for a small commission.

Outside banking hours, you can change money at hotels, some campsites, and (in Oslo) exchange booths. The greater the amount you exchange, the better rate you will get. Major credit and charge cards are accepted in most places.

Banks are open from 8:15am to 4pm Monday to Wednesday and Friday, and 8:15am to 5pm on Thursday. Between June and August, they close 30 minutes earlier.

Communications

Telecommunications and postal services in Norway are very efficient and reliable. Coin-operated phone booths are being phased out in favor of those that will only take phone-cards (Telekort). These cards can be purchased in news kiosks.

E-mail can be collected at the country's growing number of Internet cafés (all major cities have at least a couple) or at most public libraries.

Thanks to state subsidies and loans, there is a large number of newspapers in Norway. Most British and some American newspapers are sold in large towns from Narvesen newsstands.

Tax-Free Shopping

Visitors to Norway can benefit from the nation's decision not to join the EU by taking advantage of the tax-free shopping scheme. This means that if you purchase goods over a certain value from any one of the 3,000 outlets that participate in the scheme, you can have the VAT refunded. You will receive a tax-free voucher, which you must present upon your departure from the country. The goods must be unused for you to receive the refund.

Arriving by Air

Most international flights arrive at Oslo's airport, **Gardermoen**, 60 km (37 miles) north of the city, although some carriers also fly to Stavanger, Bergen, Tromsø, and Kristiansand. From Britain,

The Climate of Norway

The climate of Norway experiences intense seasonal changes. The short summer (roughly mid-June to mid-August) can be quite hot, though rain is regular and temperatures in the far north can plunge during the summer nights. Winter is long and dark, and the north is subject to sub-zero temperatures which can persist for months at a time.

OSLO			
°C/°F		21/70	
		12/54	
	9/48		9/48
	1/34		3/37	0/32
				-6/21
	5 hrs	7 hrs	3 hrs	2 hrs
	48 mm	79 mm	99 mm	58 mm
month	Apr	Jul	Oct	Jan

daily direct flights are operated by British Airways, **SAS** (Scandinavian Airline System), **Norwegian**, and Ryanair. SAS offers direct flights from other major European cities, such as Stockholm, Berlin, and Amsterdam.

Flying to Norway from North America may involve changing planes, although SAS, Norwegian and a few other airlines offer direct flights to Oslo from New York and other major cities.

Domestic flights can be useful if you are short on time – especially if you wish to visit the far north – and are operated by a variety of carriers, including SAS.

Traveling by Sea

Ferries from Germany, Denmark, and Sweden make daily crossings to Norway. It is also possible to travel directly from Newcastle in the UK, but the journey can take as long as 27 hours. Routes are operated by **Fjord Line** and **DFDS Seaways**.

Once in Norway, you are never very far from the sea and local ferries are an invaluable means of transportation across the fjords. Hurtigruten, the Norwegian Coastal Express

service, sails from Bergen to Kirkenes, far above the Arctic Circle, putting in at 35 ports en route.

It is a superb way to see Norway's dramatic coastline. Call ferry companies **OVDS** or **TFDS** to make a reservation.

Rail Travel

Many rail services link Norway with the rest of Scandinavia and mainland Europe. The major point of entry to Scandinavia from mainland Europe is Copenhagen, where trains cross the new Øresund Bridge before heading to Oslo. Within Norway, the **Norges Statsbaner** (Norwegian State Railroad) operates a more extensive network in the south than in the north, but there are routes to all the major towns.

A Norway rail pass allows unlimited travel on all trains in Norway for a specified number of days in a given period. The pass is available from rail ticket agents in Norway and abroad.

Oslo's Tunnelbanen (T-bane) consists of eight metro lines, which converge in the city center. The system runs from around 6am to 12:30am.

Buses and Taxis

Buses cover the length and breadth of Norway, and are useful for getting to places the train network does not reach. Bus journeys are also reasonably priced. Most long-distance buses are operated by the national company, **NOR-WAY Bussekspress**.

Taxis are extremely expensive in the cities and towns, but in Oslo, the excellent public transportation network generally means that you can avoid having to use taxis at all.

Traveling by Car

Car rental is fairly costly, although Norway's main roads are fast and extremely well maintained. All of the major international car rental companies are represented. Road regulations are strictly enforced, particularly those relating to drunken driving. Be aware that speeding in Norway can incur hefty fines, even if you are driving only a few miles above the limit. Most main roads have cameras.

Due to poor visibility and bad weather, many minor roads in Norway close during the dark winter months.

DIRECTORY

Tourist Information

Den Norske Turistforening
Tel 40 00 18 68.
🔲 turistforeningen.no

Oslo Turistinformasjon
Rådhuset, Fridtjof Nansens Plass 5, 0160 Oslo.
Tel 81 53 00 55.
🔲 visitoslo.com

Norwegian Tourist Board
🔲 visitnorway.com

Norway
Innovasjon Norge, Akersgata 13, Postboks 440 Sentrum, 0104 Oslo.
Tel 22 00 25 00.

UK
5th Floor, Charles House, 5 Regent Street, London SW1Y 4LR.
Tel 020-7839 2650.

US
655 Third Avenue, 10017 New York.
Tel 212-885 9700.

Embassies

Australian Consulate
Strandveien 20, Lysaker.
Tel 67 58 48 48.

Canada
Wergelandsveien 7, Oslo. Tel 22 99 53 00.

UK
Thomas Heftyes Gate 8, Oslo. Tel 23 13 27 00.

US
Henrik Ibsen Gate 48, Oslo. Tel 21 30 85 40.

Emergencies

Ambulance
Tel 113.

Fire
Tel 110.

Police
Tel 112.

Air Travel

Gardermoen Airport
Tel 815-502 50.

Norwegian
🔲 norwegian.no

SAS
Tel 815-20 400.
Tel 0845-60 727 727 (UK).
Tel 800-221 2350 (US).
🔲 scandinavian.net

Ferry Services

DFDS Seaways
Tel 22 41 90 90.
Tel 08702 520 524 (UK).
🔲 dfds.co.uk

Fjord Line
Tel 55 54 87 00.
Tel 0191-296 1313 (UK).
🔲 fjordline.co.uk

OVDS/TFDS
Tel 76 96 76 93 (OVDS).
Tel 77 64 82 00 (TFDS).

Rail Travel

Norges Statsbaner
Tel 81 50 08 88.

Buses

NOR-WAY Bussekspress
Karl Johans Gate 2, Oslo (Visitor Centre). Tel 815-444 44. 🔲 nor-way.no

Where to Stay

Oslo

CENTRAL OSLO EAST:
Rica G20 ⓚ
Modern **Map** D3
Grensen 20, 0159
Tel *22 01 64 00*
ⓦ rica.no
Rooms at this hotel close to
Oslo's main shopping street
feature floor-to-ceiling windows.

CENTRAL OSLO EAST: Clarion
Collection Hotel Bastion ⓚⓚ
Boutique **Map** D3
Skippergata 7, 0152
Tel *22 47 77 00*
ⓦ nordicchoicehotels.no
A trendy design hotel, with a
sauna and fitness center.

CENTRAL OSLO EAST: Comfort
Hotel Grand Central ⓚⓚ
Historic **Map** D3
Jernbanetorget 1, 0154
Tel *22 98 28 00*
ⓦ nordicchoicehotels.no
Individually designed rooms in
an original train station building
dating back to 1874.

CENTRAL OSLO EAST:
Grand Hotel ⓚⓚⓚ
Luxury **Map** D3
Karl Johans Gate 31, 0159
Tel *23 21 20 00*
ⓦ grand.no
Amenities at this 1874 hotel
include a gorgeous spa and pool.

CENTRAL OSLO WEST:
Frogner House Apartments ⓚ
Modern **Map** C2
Skovveien 8, 0257
Tel *93 01 00 09*
ⓦ frognerhouse.no
Elegant and airy apartments, with
the option of self-catering. Long-
and short-term rentals available.

CENTRAL OSLO WEST:
Carlton Hotel Guldsmeden ⓚⓚ
Boutique **Map** C3
Parkveien 78, 0254
Tel *23 27 40 00*
ⓦ hotelguldsmeden.dk
Rooms – some with four-poster
beds – have traditional
furnishings. Near the Royal Palace.

CENTRAL OSLO WEST:
Thon Hotel Cecil ⓚⓚ
Modern **Map** D3
Stortingsgata 8, 0161
Tel *23 31 48 00*
ⓦ thonhotels.com
Modestly sized yet comfy rooms.
A buffet breakfast and light
evening meals are served daily.

CENTRAL OSLO WEST:
Hotel Continental ⓚⓚⓚ
Luxury **Map** D3
Stortingsgata 24–26, 0117
Tel *22 82 40 00*
ⓦ hotelcontinental.no
Renowned luxury hotel set in a
building more than a century old.

DK Choice

CENTRAL OSLO WEST:
The Thief ⓚⓚⓚ
Boutique **Map** C3
Landgangen 1, 0252
Tel *24 00 40 00*
ⓦ thethief.com
This amazing hotel – located
next to the Astrup Fearnly
Museet – is packed with art.
Even the hotel's linen carries a
top designer's name. Magnificent
views of the Oslofjord.

Rest of Norway

BERGEN: Steens Hotel
Bed & Breakfast ⓚⓚ
Historic
Parkveien 22, 5007
Tel *55 30 88 88*
ⓦ steenshotel.no
This elegant, peaceful villa from
1890 retains a traditional style.

BERGEN:
Scandic Neptun ⓚⓚⓚ
Boutique
Valkendorfsgaten 8, 5012
Tel *55 30 68 00*
ⓦ scandichotels.com
A hotel that is synonymous with
good food, wine, and art.

STAVANGER: Thon Hotel
Maritim ⓚ
Modern
Kongsgata 32, 4005
Tel *51 85 05 00*
ⓦ thonhotels.com
Modern and functional in design,
the Maritim is a well-priced hotel.

STAVANGER: Victoria ⓚⓚ
Historic
Skansegata 1, 4006
Tel *51 86 70 00*
ⓦ victoria-hotel.no
Opened in 1990, the Victoria is
an elegant hotel, with a popular
on-site bar and restaurant.

TRONDHEIM: P Hotels
Trondheim ⓚ
Modern
Nordre Gate 24, 7010
Tel *73 80 23 50*
ⓦ p-hotels.no
A chic, pleasant hotel with family
rooms and indulgent breakfast in
bed option available.

DK Choice

TRONDHEIM: City Living
Schøller Hotel ⓚⓚ
Modern
Dronningens Gate 26, 7011
Tel *73 87 08 00*
ⓦ cityliving.no
Simple yet elegant rooms
and self-catering apartments,
some split over two levels,
in a superb location across
from the Stiftsgården royal
residence. The hotel offers room
service and is perfect for longer
stays, especially for families.

TRONDHEIM:
Britannia Hotel ⓚⓚⓚ
Historic
Dronningens Gate 5, 7011
Tel *73 80 08 00*
ⓦ britannia.no
A luxury hotel dating back to
1897, the Britannia offers all the
latest gadgets and facilities. There
is also a great spa with a pool.

Luxurious bed furnishings at The Thief hotel in Oslo

Where to Eat and Drink

The simple decor belies the inventive cuisine on offer at Maaemo, Oslo

Oslo

CENTRAL OSLO EAST:
Fiskeriet
Seafood **Map** D3
Youngstorget 2, 0181
Tel *22 42 45 40* **Closed** *Sun*
A must-visit for all seafood fans.
The delicious food at Fiskeriet
includes a Norwegian take on
fish 'n' chips. Bar seating.

CENTRAL OSLO EAST:
Kaffistova
Scandinavian **Map** D3
Rosenkrantz Gate 8, 0159
Tel *23 21 42 10*
Bright and airy, this is one of
Oslo's top lunch spots. It serves
big portions of classics such as
meatballs and reindeer burgers.

CENTRAL OSLO EAST:
Vega Fair Food
Vegetarian **Map** D3
Akersgata 74, 0180
Tel *47 92 12 14*
One of the very few vegetarian
eateries in Oslo, Vega has a
good hot and cold buffet
with plenty of variety.

CENTRAL OSLO EAST:
Brasserie France
French **Map** D3
Øvre Slottsgate 16, 0157
Tel *23 10 01 65* **Closed** *Sun*
Enjoy a fine selection of classic
French cuisine prepared by top
chefs at this unpretentious and
charming spot. Reserve ahead.

CENTRAL OSLO EAST:
Olympen
Bistro **Map** E3
Grønlandsleiret 15, 0190
Tel *24 10 19 99*
Olympen's amazing selection
of beer and food is a cut above
ordinary pub grub. If ordered a
day in advance, they even do a
whole suckling pig.

DK Choice

CENTRAL OSLO EAST:
Maaemo
Scandinavian **Map** D2
Schweigaards Gate 15, 0191
Tel *91 99 48 05*
With its two Michelin stars,
Maaemo is perhaps Norway's
best restaurant. It is possible
to spend an entire evening
enjoying a 25-course seasonal
menu, which comes paired
with fine wines. The dishes
take diners on an adventure
through the flavors of
Scandinavia, with twists from
around the world.

CENTRAL OSLO WEST:
D/S Louise
Scandinavian **Map** C3
Stranden 3, 0250
Tel *22 83 00 60*
Located over a number of floors,
this place has great views of the
harbor. It serves terrific food –
the fish soup is an Oslo legend.

CENTRAL OSLO WEST:
Ylajali
Scandinavian **Map** D3
St. Olavs Plass 2, 0165
Tel *22 20 64 86* **Closed** *Sun*
Enjoy sensational Nordic food in
a grand 19th-century building
with great ambience. Some
of the tasting menus are
seemingly endless.

Rest of Norway

BERGEN: To Kokker
Scandinavian
Enhjørningsgården 29, 5003
Tel *55 30 69 55*
The best spot in town for
steaming pots of mussels
and much more. A pub and
restaurant rolled into one.

BERGEN: Wesselstuen
Fine Dining
Øvre Ole Bulls Plass 6, 5012
Tel *55 55 49 54*
Dating back to 1957, Wesselstuen
is one of Bergen's legendary
dining rooms. The menu features
Norwegian food and includes
treats such as fillet of reindeer
served with pickled red onion.

STAVANGER: Café Sting
Bistro
Valbergjet 3, 4006
Tel *99 11 38 78*
Enjoy coffee, cakes, and a range
of light meals in a simple yet
charming café that has fast
become a Stavanger institution.
Good choice for a cheap lunch.

DK Choice

STAVANGER: Straen
Fiskerestaurant
Seafood
Nedre Strandgate 15, 4005
Tel *51 84 37 00* **Closed** *Sun*
Amusingly touted as being
"world-famous throughout
Norway," Straen Fiskerestaurant
is indeed one of the best
seafood eateries in the country.
The interior is straight out of
the 1950s, and the windows
offer fantastic views of the
harbor. In addition, there is
another restaurant downstairs
with a bistro-oriented menu,
and a hip nightclub upstairs.

TRONDHEIM: Bakgarden
Bar & Spiseri
Tapas
Kjøpmannsgata 40, 7011
Tel *45 22 24 88*
A terrific place for tapas and light
meals, and one of the best-value
eateries in Trondheim. It uses
locally sourced fresh produce.

TRONDHEIM:
Palmehaven
Brunch
Dronningens Gate 5, 7011
Tel *73 80 08 00* **Closed** *Sun lunch*
A large dining room with a
fantastic all-you-can-eat buffet
for breakfast and lunch that
always features a wide range
of of fish and meat dishes.

DENMARK

Denmark is a peaceful and pleasant place. Its landscape is largely green, flat, and rural – with a host of half-timbered villages reminiscent of a Hans Christian Andersen fairy tale. It is an easy country to visit – not only do the majority of Danes speak English, but they are friendly and extremely hospitable. Above all, the pace of life is not as frenetic as in some European mainland countries.

Denmark consists of no fewer than 405 islands and the Jutland peninsula, which extends north from Germany. Located as it is between Scandinavia proper and mainland Europe, Denmark not surprisingly shares characteristics with both. It has the least dramatic countryside of the Scandinavian countries, yet there are also a number of important Viking sites dotted throughout the land. Zealand, the largest island, is the focal point for Denmark's 5.5 million inhabitants, a quarter of whom live in Copenhagen. Funen and Bornholm are much more tranquil islands, popular for holiday retreats. The Jutland peninsula has the most varied scenery, with marshland and desolate moors alternating with agricultural land.

History

Although nomadic hunters inhabited Jutland some 25,000 years ago, the first mention of the Danes as a distinct people is in the chronicles of Bishop Gregor of Tours from 590. Their strategic position in the north made them a central power in the Viking expansion that followed.

Constant struggles for control of the North Sea with England and western Europe, for the Skagerrak – the straits between Denmark and Norway – with Norway and Sweden, and for the Baltic Sea with Germany, Poland, and Russia, ensued. But thanks to their fast ships and fearless warriors, by 1033 the Danes controlled much of England and Normandy, as well as most trading routes in the Baltic.

The next three hundred years were characterized by Denmark's attempts to maintain its power in the Baltic with the help of the German Hanseatic League. During the reign of Valdemar IV (1340–1375), Sweden, Norway, Iceland, Greenland, and the Faroe Isles came under Danish rule. Valdemar's daughter Margrethe presided over this first Scandinavian federation, known as the Kalmar Union.

The next period of Danish prosperity occurred in the 16th century, when Denmark profited from the Sound dues, a levy charged to ships traversing the Øresund, the narrow channel between Denmark and Sweden. Christian IV (reigned 1588–1648), the "builder king,"

Evening illuminations in Tivoli Gardens, Copenhagen

◄ Aerial view of Copenhagen, with the Rådhus in the background

instigated a huge program of construction that provided Denmark with a number of architectural masterpieces, such as the Rosenborg Slot in Copenhagen *(see p643)*.

By the 18th century, Denmark had discovered lucrative trading opportunities in the Far East, and consolidated its position in the Baltic. However, an alliance with the French in the Napoleonic Wars (1803–15) led to the bombardment of Copenhagen by Britain's Admiral Nelson, and King Frederik VI was forced to hand over Norway to Sweden in 1814.

Christian IV of Denmark (1588–1648)

The remainder of the 19th century witnessed the rise of the social democrats and the trade unions. The year 1901 saw the beginnings of parliamentary democracy and a number of social reforms, including income tax on a sliding scale and free schooling.

Denmark was neutral during both world wars, but during World War II the country was occupied by the Nazis, a move that heralded the development of a huge resistance movement. Social reforms continued after the war, and in the 1960s, laws were passed allowing abortion on demand and the abolition of all forms of censorship. In 1972, Denmark became the first Scandinavian country to join the European Community, and has developed a reputation for addressing environmental issues and supporting the economies of developing nations.

As the 21st century begins, Danish citizens have a high standard of living and state-funded education and health systems, although this has been achieved through high tax bills. Nevertheless, Denmark remains one of the cheaper Scandinavian countries.

Language and Culture

A North Germanic language, Danish is similar to Norwegian and Swedish, but there are some significant differences in word meaning ("frokost" for example, means "lunch" in Danish, but "breakfast" in Norwegian) and pronunciation. English and German are widely spoken, so visitors should have few problems in making themselves understood.

For such a small country, Denmark has produced a number of world-famous writers and philosophers, including Hans Christian Andersen *(see p645)* and the 19th-century philosopher Søren Kierkegaard, who is claimed to have laid the foundations of modern existentialism. However, it is best known for its 20th-century design and craftsmanship, which have given the country an international reputation. The works of companies such as Georg Jensen silversmiths and Royal Copenhagen porcelain, and the furniture of architect Arne Jacobsen, enjoy a worldwide reputation.

KEY DATES IN DANISH HISTORY

AD 590 First written account of the Danes in the chronicle of Bishop Gregor of Tours

960 Denmark becomes officially Christian with the baptism of King Harald "Bluetooth"

1033 Danes control much of England and Normandy and dominate trade in the Baltic

1282 Erik V forced to grant nobles a charter limiting his powers – first Danish constitution

1397 Queen Margrethe I unites Scandinavia under the Danish throne in the Kalmar Union

1814 Norway transferred from the Danish to the Swedish crown

1849 Under Frederik VII, Denmark becomes a constitutional monarchy

1890s Social reforms lay the foundations of the present welfare state

1914–18 Denmark neutral in World War I

1940–45 Despite declaring its neutrality, Denmark invaded and occupied by the Nazis

1945 Becomes a charter member of the UN

1972 Denmark joins the EC (now the EU)

2000 Danes reject euro as their currency

2002 EU presidency held by Denmark

2012 Same-sex marriage legalised

Exploring Denmark

Copenhagen is Denmark's main attraction, a small
yet lively capital with a considerable number of
sights concentrated in the center. Outside the capital,
the pace of life is slow, and the flat countryside is
punctuated by half-timbered villages and the
occasional manor house. Roads are of a high standard,
and the trains and buses extremely punctual and
efficient. Denmark's relative lack of hills makes it an
excellent place for cycling.

Tranquil park in Odense, the principal town of
the fertile island of Funen

Sights at a Glance

1 *Copenhagen pp638–43*
2 Helsingør
3 Frederiksborg Slot
4 Roskilde
5 Odense
6 Århus
7 Aalborg
8 Legoland

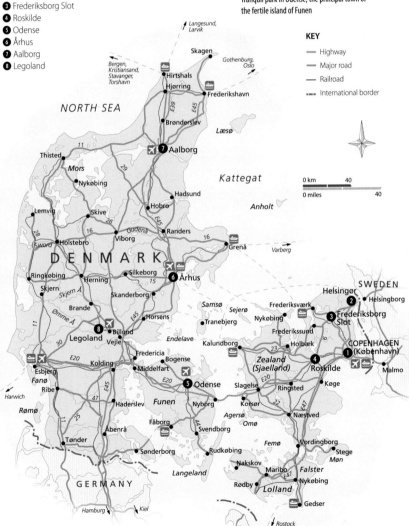

KEY

— Highway
— Major road
— Railroad
▪▪▪ International border

   For keys to symbols *see back flap*

❶ Copenhagen

Copenhagen is Denmark's largest city, with a population of around 1.2 million. Founded in 1167 by Bishop Absalon, who built a fortress on the island of Slotsholmen, the town grew quickly, prospering from trade in the Baltic. In 1461, it was declared the capital of Denmark. During the reign of Christian IV (1588–1648), the city was endowed with many fine Renaissance buildings, some of which still stand today, including the splendid Rosenborg Slot and Børsen. As a change from sightseeing, visitors can head for the lively, cosmopolitan shopping area of Strøget, Europe's longest pedestrian street, or simply relax in one of the many restaurants and cafés of bustling Nyhavn, with its charming, gabled townhouses.

Cannon in the grounds of the city's 16th-century fortress, Kastellet

Sights at a Glance

① Tivoli Gardens
② Ny Carlsberg Glyptotek
③ Rådhuset
④ National Museum
⑤ Christiansborg Palace
⑥ Børsen
⑦ Strøget
⑧ Nyhavn
⑨ Amalienborg
⑩ Little Mermaid
⑪ Kastellet and Frihedsmuseet
⑫ Statens Museum for Kunst
⑬ Rosenborg Slot
⑭ Christiania

Getting Around

All the city's attractions are in a small area, within walking distance of each other. Underground trains (S-trains) serve some of the main sights, while there are also numerous buses.

The main hub of the S-train network is København H, also known as Central Station. The city's metro opened in 2002, and now runs as far as the airport.

The Nimb building, with its domes and minarets, at Tivoli Gardens

① Tivoli Gardens

Vesterbrogade 3. **Tel** 33 15 10 01.
🚉 København H. 🚌 2A, 5A, 11A, 66,
2505. ◯ mid-Apr–late Sep, mid-Oct
(Halloween), & mid-Nov–late
Dec: daily. 🅆 **tivoli.dk**

One of Copenhagen's most famous tourist attractions, the Tivoli Gardens opened in 1843. This highly popular entertainment park combines all the fun of fairground rides with fountains and fireworks, concerts and ballets, top-quality restaurants and fast-food outlets. Based on the 18th-century ornamental gardens popular in Europe at the time, Tivoli features Chinese-style pagodas and Moorish pavilions, as well as modern additions, such as the Hanging Gardens.

Among the many fairground rides are a traditional roller coaster, a ferris wheel, a "freefall" tower, and the 80-m- (262-ft-) Star Flyer, which provides views over Copenhagen. There are also amusement arcades, shooting galleries, and children's rides.

The gardens are at their most enthralling after dusk, when thousands of tiny lights illuminate the park. At night, open-air theaters host all forms of entertainment, from big bands to Friday night rock concerts, and during the summer season, performances of the unique Danish pantomime.

A good time to visit Tivoli is between late November and Christmas, when the gardens are transformed into a bustling Christmas fair. You can sample traditional Danish seasonal fare, buy many specialty Christmas gifts, try the toboggan run, and generally get acquainted with Danish Christmas traditions.

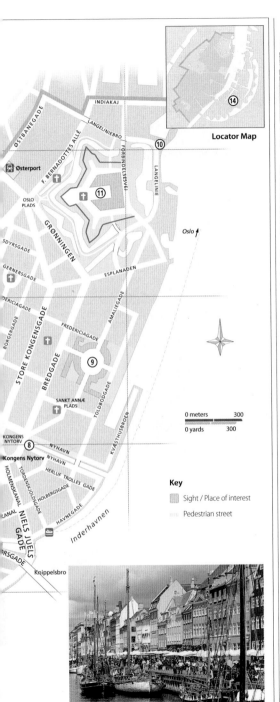

Locator Map

Oslo ↑

0 meters   300
0 yards   300

Key

🟦 Sight / Place of interest

▨ Pedestrian street

Copenhagen's Nyhavn canal, lined with brightly colored houses and busy sidewalk cafés

The richly decorated Neoclassical facade of Ny Carlsberg Glyptotek art gallery

② Ny Carlsberg Glyptotek

Dantes Plads 7. **Tel** 33 41 81 41. 🚇 København H. 🚌 1A, 2A, 11A. **Open** Tue–Sun. **Closed** Jan 1, Jun 5, Dec 24 & 25. 🎟 except Sun. ♿ partial. 🏠 📷 ✏ 🆆 glyptoteket.com

Copenhagen's most elegant art gallery was opened in 1897 by Carl Jacobsen, son of the founder of the Carlsberg Brewery, to give more people the chance to see classical art. Housed in a magnificent Neoclassical building, the Glyptotek is best-known for its exquisite antiquities, in particular its collections of Etruscan and Roman art.

The main building's collections are completed with Egyptian, Greek, Roman, and French sculpture and works from the "Golden Age" of Danish painting (1800–1850). A modern wing, designed by acclaimed Danish architect Henning Larsen, contains Impressionist paintings by Monet, Sisley, Pissarro, Gauguin, and works by David and Bonnard. The museum also has changing exhibitions.

③ Rådhuset

Rådhuspladsen. **Tel** 33 66 33 66. 🚇 København H. 🚌 2A, 5A, 6A, 14, 26 & many others. **Closed** Sun, public hols. 🎥 in English with 🎟 3pm Mon–Fri, 10am & 11am Sat. ♿ 📷

At the edge of the Indre By (city center), in the middle of a wide open square, is the Baroque-style Rådhuset or City Hall, built in the early 1900s. A statue of Copenhagen's 12th-century founder, Bishop Absalon, sits above the entrance. Climb the

300-step staircase to the top of the bell tower for a view of the city. On the way, check out the First World Clock, a super-accurate timepiece with a 570,000-year calendar designed by Jens Olsen. It took 27 years to design, and was completed in 1955.

The modern, central atrium of Denmark's National Museum

④ National Museum

Ny Vestergade 10. **Tel** 33 13 44 11. 🚇 København H. 🚌 1A, 2A, 11A, 14, 26. **Open** 10am–5pm Tue–Sun. **Closed** Dec 24, 25 & 31. ♿ 📷 ✏ 🆆 natmus.dk

Like so many of Denmark's museums, the National Museum contains beautifully presented exhibits. The extensive ethnographic and antiquities collections detail Danish history from prehistoric to modern times, and include some fascinating exhibits of Viking life.

Many of the items on display come from the Danish isles, such as items of jewelry, bones, and even several bodies found preserved in peat bogs, as well as imposing rune stones with inscriptions dating from

around AD 1000. There is also a children's museum and a host of educational activities, all housed in the restored 18th-century royal residence. Close by, and part of the museum, is a Danish home with authentic interiors from the 1890s, complete with decorated panels and elaborately carved furniture (view by guided tour at 2pm on Saturday in summer only; book in main museum).

⑤ Christiansborg Palace

Slotsholmen. **Tel** 33 92 64 92. 🚌 1A, 2A, 26. **Open** May–Sep: daily; Oct–Apr: Tue–Sun. 🎟 📷 🖥 📷 🆆 christiansborg.dk Teatermuseet: Christiansborg Ridebane 18. **Tel** 33 11 51 76. **Open** Tue–Thu, Sat & Sun. **Closed** Jan 1, Dec 24, 25 & 31. 🎟 Thorvaldsen's Museum: Bertil Thorvaldsens Plads 2. **Tel** 33 32 15 32. **Open** Tue–Sun. 🎟 🖥 📷

Situated on the island of Slotsholmen, the **Christiansborg Palace** has been the seat of the Danish Parliament since 1918, and also houses the Royal Reception Rooms, the Queen's Library, the Supreme Court, and the Prime Minister's Office. Built on the site of a fortress constructed in 1167 by Copenhagen's founder, Bishop Absalon, the palace has twice burnt down and been rebuilt, then altered and extended. Much of this work was carried out during the 18th century under Christian VI, whose elaborate visions were realized both in the architecture and in the lavish interiors. The current palace dates mostly from the early 20th century, and it is possible to visit the Royal Reception Rooms, the Harness Room, the Stables and Coach House, and some ruins from the original fortress.

Above the riding stables is the Royal Court Theater, built by Christian VI in 1767. Now a museum, much of it has been restored to its original 18th-century appearance. Exhibits illustrate the history of Danish theater up to the present day. The auditorium, with its plush, red furnishings and small, gold side boxes, houses a wealth of memorabilia – including costumes, old theater programs, wigs, and even old make-up boxes and a reconstructed dressing room. The whole theater is dominated, however, by the grand royal box, built for King Frederik VII in 1852. Situated at the back of the auditorium, it seems almost to upstage the stage itself. Unusually, the king's wife, the former ballet dancer Louise Rasmussen, had a private box to the right of the royal box, where she sat if she was alone.

Along the north side of the palace, the **Thorvaldsen's Museum** houses the work of the country's most celebrated sculptor, Bertel Thorvaldsen (1770–1844). After completing his education in Denmark, Thorvaldsen lived for nearly 40 years in Rome, where he gained a worldwide reputation. As well as his own impressive Neoclassical sculptures, the museum houses his collection of antiquities and 19th-century Danish art. There is also a detailed account of his life.

Børsen, Copenhagen's beautiful old stock exchange

⑥ Børsen

Børsgade. 🚌 2A, 66. **Closed** to public.

Built in 1619–40 by King Christian IV, Denmark's old stock exchange is an architectural masterpiece. The building combines tiny windows, steep roofs, and decorative gables, and is topped by a spire representing four intertwined dragon's tails. Originally a marketplace, it became a commodities and stock exchange in the 19th century. Today, the building is used as offices, since the modern stock exchange has long since moved to Strøget. It is not open to the public.

⑦ Strøget

Frederiksberggade to Østergade. 🚉 København H, Nørreport. 🚌 1A, 2A, 11A, 26.

Running between Rådhus-pladsen (City Hall Square) and Kongens Nytorv (King's New Square), Strøget (pronounced "Stroll") is Europe's longest pedestrian street. Located at the center of a large traffic-free zone in the heart of the city, Strøget consists of five streets – Frederiksberggade, Nygade, Vimmelskaftet, Amagertorv, and Østergade. The area is home to several exclusive stores, including top inter-national designers Burberry and Gucci. Other stores sell the best in Danish porcelain, modern design, glass, and furnishings – all areas in which Denmark has a world-class reputation.

The best selection can be found in the Royal Copenhagen shopping mall, facing Amagertorv, which includes Royal Copenhagen, Georg Jensen, and Illums Bolighus. There are also many bustling cafés and restaurants, street performers, and musicians, making it a lively place for walking or for relaxing with a coffee. The area is extremely popular with locals and visitors, particularly on a Saturday, but it is still possible to enjoy the atmosphere and admire the many surviving 18th-century buildings.

The impressive Christiansborg Palace, once a seat of royalty and now home to the Danish Parliament

⑧ Nyhavn

Kongens Nytorv. ▣ 1A, 11A, 26, 3505. ▣ 991, 992.

A narrow canal flanked by a wide promenade, Nyhavn (New Harbor) was originally built 300 years ago to attract trade. It leads up to Kongens Nytorv (King's New Square). For much of its history, the district was far from inviting, being mainly frequented by sailors, but after the 1970s, the area was transformed. The harbor is lined either side with brightly painted town houses, a number of which date from the 18th century. Author Hans Christian Andersen lived in three of them (numbers 18, 20, and 67). Shops, restaurants, and bars have replaced all but one of the tattoo parlors that used to be here.

The attractive buildings, as well as the dozens of old wooden sailing ships moored on the water, make Nyhavn a lively and picturesque place to spend an hour or two enjoying a meal or a beer, at least in the summer months. It is also a good starting point for seeing the city, as some boat tours of the canals leave from here.

Nyhavn, Copenhagen's picturesque and popular harborside promenade

Changing of Queen Margrethe's guard, Amalienborg

⑨ Amalienborg

Amaliegade. **Tel** 33 12 21 86. ▣ Østerport. ▣ 1A, 26. ▣ 991, 992. **Open** May–Oct: daily; Nov–Apr: Tue–Sun. ▣ for museum. ▣ call in advance. ▣ Changing of the guard: noon daily. ▣ slke.dk

The Amalienborg (Amalia's Castle) consists of four identical Rococo buildings arranged symmetrically around a large cobbled square with an imposing equestrian statue of Frederik V in the middle. Changing of the guard takes place every day at noon outside the palace of the present queen, Margrethe II. The buildings have housed the Danish royal family since 1874, and two of them are usually open to the public. However, Christian VII's Palace is currently closed for renovation. Part of Christian VIII's palace serves as the museum of the Danish monarchy. It is home to part of the Royal Collection, the bulk of which is housed at Rosenborg Slot, and some of the official and private rooms are open to the public. The highlights are the study by King Christian IX (1818–1906) and the drawing room of his wife, Queen Louise, which are filled with family presents, photographs, and the occasional Fabergé treasure.

There are two attractive but contrasting views from the square. On the harborside is Amaliehaven (Amalia's Garden), dating from 1983 and with a fountain in its center; in the opposite direction is Marmorkirken, a white marble church officially known as Frederikskirken, which has one of Europe's largest domes, inspired by St. Peter's in Rome. Its construction was begun in 1749 with expensive Norwegian marble, but was not completed until 150 years later (with less expensive Danish limestone) owing to the huge costs incurred. Inside, the church is decorated with many frescoes and statues.

⑩ Little Mermaid

Langelinie. ▣ Østerport. ▣ 1A, 26, then a short walk. ▣ 901, 902.

The subject of many Danish postcards, the Little Mermaid (Den Lille Havfrue) has become the emblem of Copenhagen and is much visited by tourists. Sitting on a stone by the promenade at Langelinie, and looking out over the Øresund, she is difficult to spot from the road and smaller than her pictures would have you believe. Sculpted by Edvard Erichsen and first unveiled in 1913, this bronze statue was inspired by the Hans Christian Andersen character, who left the sea after falling in love with a prince. The mermaid has suffered over the years at the hands of mischievous pranksters, even losing her head and an arm. Happily, she is currently in possession of all her "parts."

Copenhagen's emblem, the Little Mermaid

⑪ Kastellet and Frihedsmuseet

Churchillparken. **Tel** 33 13 77 14.
🚇 Østerport. 🚌 1A, 19, 26.
🚢 901, 902. Kastellet: **Open** daily.
Frihedsmuseet: **Closed** for restoration
until 2017. 📷 ♿

The grassy grounds of this
fortress, built by Christian IV in
the 16th century (and added to
by his successors), are good for
strolling around or sitting quietly
by the moat. Currently occupied
by the Danish army, its buildings
are closed to the public, but
near the south entrance is the
Danish Resistance Movement
Museum (Frihedsmuseet). This
charts the German occupation
of Denmark in World War II and
the growth of the organization
that saved more than 7,000 Jews
from the Nazis by hiding them
in "safe houses" and helping
them escape to neutral Sweden.

⑫ Statens Museum for Kunst

Sølvgade 48–50. **Tel** 33 74 84 94.
🚇 Nørreport, Østerport. 🚌 6A,
26, 184, 185, 150S. **Open** Tue–Sun.
Closed Jan 1, Dec 24, 25 & 31. 💰 (for
special exhibitions only). ♿ 📷
🌐 **smk.dk**

The extensive Statens Museum
for Kunst (State Art Museum)
holds Danish and European art
from the 14th century to the
present. Among its many
artworks are paintings by Titian,
Rubens, Rembrandt, El Greco,
Picasso, and Matisse. Danish
artists are particularly well
represented in the new modern
art wing. There is also a vast
collection of prints and drawings.

The enchanting Rosenborg Slot, set within magnificent parkland

⑬ Rosenborg Slot

Øster Voldgade 4A. **Tel** 33 15 32 86.
🚇 Nørreport. 🚌 6A, 11A. **Open** May–
Oct: daily; Nov–Apr: Tue–Sun. **Closed**
Jan 1, end Dec. 💰 📷 📷 📷
🌐 **dkks.dk**

Originally built by Christian IV as
a summer residence in 1606–7,
the Rosenborg Slot was inspired
by the Renaissance architecture
of the Netherlands. The "builder
king" continued to add to it over
the next 30 years until the castle
looked much as it does today –
a playful version of a fortress.
The interiors are particularly well
preserved and its sumptuous
chambers, halls, and ballrooms
are full of objects
including amber
chandeliers, life-
size silver lions,
tapestries, thrones,
portraits, and
gilded chairs.
Two of the 24
rooms open to
the public are
stacked from
floor to ceiling
with porcelain
and glass. The
Porcelain Cabinet
includes examples from the
famous *Flora Danica* dinner
service made for 100 guests,
created by the Royal
Copenhagen Porcelain factory
between 1790 and 1803. The
colorful Glass Cabinet houses
nearly 1,000 examples of old
Venetian glass as well as glass
from the Netherlands, Bohemia,
England, and most of the
German glassworks.

⑭ Christiania

Bådsmandsstræde 43. 🚇
Christianshavn. 🚌 66. **Open** daily.
📷 for pre-booked groups only.
🌐 **christiania.org**

Originally set up in 1971 on
the site of a former military
barracks, this "free town" is an
enclave of an alternative
lifestyle: colorful, anarchic,
and self-governing. However,
since 2004, there has been
no open selling of drugs
due to government pressure.
Attractions include shops (one
being the famous Christiania
Bikes), a gallery, cafés, a
restaurant, and a concert
venue, as well as a lake.

Modern art wing of the Statens Museum for Kunst

❷ Helsingør

Zealand. 🏠 46,300. 🚢 🚌 🚆
ℹ️ Havnepladsen 3 (49 21 13 33).
🅦 visitnorthsealand.com

Helsingør, or Elsinore, lies at the narrowest point of the Øresund, the waterway dividing Denmark and Sweden. Its attractive medieval quarter has many well-preserved merchants' and ferrymen's houses. On the waterfront stands the Maritime Museum of Denmark.

The town is dominated by **Kronborg Slot** (Kronborg Castle), which stands on a spit of land overlooking the sea. Famous as the setting of *Hamlet*, the fortress actually dates from the 1500s, much later than Shakespeare's character would have lived. Highlights include the 62-m- (210-ft-) banqueting hall. A statue of the Viking chief Holger Danske slumbers in the castle cellars – according to legend he will awaken to defend Denmark if needed.

🏠 **Kronborg Slot**
Kronborg. **Tel** 49 21 30 78. 🚆 840, 842. **Open** Apr–Oct: daily; Nov–Mar: Tue–Sun. 🅿️ 🅒 🅳 🅦 **kronborg.dk**

❸ Frederiksborg Slot

Hillerød, Zealand. **Tel** 48 26 04 39. 🚆 to Hillerød, then bus 301, 302, 324. **Open** daily. 🅿️ 🅰️ 🅳 🅒 🅦 **dnm.dk**

One of Scandinavia's most magnificent royal castles, the Frederiksborg Slot is built across three small islands surrounded

The spires and turrets of the Kronborg Slot, Helsingør

by an artificial lake. Created as a residence for Frederik II (1559–88), the castle was rebuilt in the Dutch Renaissance style by his son, Christian IV (1588–1648).

The vaulted black marble chapel, where monarchs were once crowned, sits directly below the Great Hall, with its fine tapestries, paintings, and reliefs. The castle also houses the National History Museum.

❹ Roskilde

Zealand. 🏠 47,000. 🚆 🚌
ℹ️ Stændertorvet 1 (46 31 65 65).
🅦 visitroskilde.com

The settlement of Roskilde first came to prominence in AD 980, when a Viking king, Harald Bluetooth, built Zealand's first Christian church here. Once the center of Danish Catholicism, the town declined after the Reformation. Today, it is a quiet town, except when it hosts northern Europe's largest annual music festival in the first weekend of July. **Roskilde Domkirke** stands on the site

of Harald Bluetooth's original church. Begun by Bishop Absalon in 1170, the building is now a mix of architectural styles. The cathedral also functions as Denmark's royal mausoleum – some 39 Danish kings and queens are buried here.

Overlooking Roskilde Fjord is the **Vikingeskibsmuseet**. This Viking ship museum contains five reconstructed Viking ships, first built around AD 1000, excavated from the bottom of the fjord in 1962. In the waterside workshops, Viking ship replicas are built using authentic period tools and traditional techniques.

🏛️ **Vikingeskibsmuseet**
Vindeboder 12. **Tel** 46 30 02 00.
Open daily. **Closed** Dec 24, 25 & 31.
🅿️ 🅒 in summer. 🅰️ call in advance.
🅳 🅗 🅦 **vikingeskibsmuseet.dk**

❺ Odense

Funen. 🏠 167,600. 🚆 🚌
ℹ️ Rådhus, Vestergade (63 75 75 20).
🅦 visitodense.com

Odense is Denmark's third-largest urban center. It lies at the heart of an area dubbed the "Garden of Denmark" for the variety of fruits and vegetables produced here. The town is most famous as the birthplace of Hans Christian Andersen.

Odense is easily explored on foot. Looking like a storybook village, the old town contains some fine museums, including three art museums, one of which, Brandts, is dedicated to photography. Odense's showpiece is the **Hans Christian Andersen Museum**, where the storyteller's life is detailed

View from the outer courtyard of Frederiksborg Slot

For hotels and restaurants see p648 and p649

through drawings, photographs, letters, and personal belongings. A library contains his works in more than 90 languages. The **H.C. Andersens Barndomshjem** (H.C. Andersen's Childhood Home) shows where the writer lived with his parents in a room measuring barely 2 m (6 ft) by 1.5 m (5 ft).

🏛 Hans Christian Andersen Museum

Bangs Boder 20. **Tel** 65 51 46 01. **Open** late Jun–Aug: daily; Sep–late Jun: Tue–Sun. 🎟 📷 by prior arrangement only. 🌐 **museum.odense.dk**

Half-timbered buildings at Den Gamle By outdoor museum, Århus

❻ Århus

Jutland. 🔼 250,000. ✈ 44 km (27 miles) NE. 🚌 🚃 🚢 ℹ Pakhus 13, Nordhavnsgade 4 (87 31 50 10). 🌐 visitaarhus.com

Denmark's second city and Jutland's main urban center, Århus has a thriving culture scene, with a major art museum, ARoS, and an annual summer arts festival, Aarhus Festuge.

Århus divides clearly into two parts. The old town is a cluster of medieval streets with several fine churches. **Den Gamle By**, the city's open-air museum, consists of 60 or so half-timbered houses and a watermill, transported from locations all over Jutland and carefully reconstructed.

In the modern part of the city, the controversial **Rådhus** (City Hall) was built by Arne Jakobsen and Erik Møller in 1941. Its coating of pale Norwegian marble still provokes differing opinions to this day.

🏛 Den Gamle By

Viborgvej. **Tel** 86 12 31 88. **Open** daily. **Closed** Jan 1, Dec 24, 25 & 31.
🎟 📷 📷

❼ Aalborg

Jutland. 🔼 122,000. ✈ 🚌 🚃 🚢 ℹ Kjellerups Torv 5, Kedelhallen (99 31 75 00). 🌐 **visitaalborg.com**

The port of Aalborg spreads across both sides of the Limfjord, which slices through the tip of the Jutland peninsula. Aalborg is the leading producer of the spirit aquavit, the fiery Danish national drink.

The well-preserved old town has several sights of interest, including the suitably dark and atmospheric dungeons of the town castle, the **Aalborghus Slot** (1539). The **Budolfi Domkirke**, a 16th-century Gothic cathedral, houses a collection of portraits depicting Aalborg merchants from the town's prosperous past.

Kunsten (Museum of Modern Art Aalborg) houses a collection of Danish modern art, as well as works by foreign artists such as Max Ernst and Chagall.

On the edge of Aalborg is the historical site of **Lindholm Høje**. Set on a hilltop overlooking the city, it contains more than 650 marked graves from the Iron Age and Viking Age (see p627). A museum depicting the history of the site stands nearby.

🏠 Lindholm Høje

Vendilavej, Nørresundby. **Tel** 99 31 74 40. **Open** daily. Museum: **Open** Apr–Oct: daily; Nov–Mar: Tue–Sun.
🎟 📷 📷 📷 📷

Legoland® transportation – the colorful Lego® train and monorail

❽ Legoland®

Billund, Jutland. **Tel** 75 33 13 33. ✈ 🚌 to Vejle, then bus. **Open** Apr–Oct: daily. 🎟 📷 📷 🌐 **legoland.dk**

The Legoland® Billund theme park celebrates the tiny plastic blocks that have become a household name worldwide. The park opened in 1968, and more than 45 million Lego® bricks were used in its construction.

Aimed primarily at 3–13 year olds, Legoland® is divided into different zones. As well as Lego® sculptures of animals, buildings, and landscapes, there are many rides and stage shows. Highlights include Miniland, a collection of miniature Lego® towns that represent places around the world, and a driving track where children can take a safety test in a Lego® car.

Hans Christian Andersen

Denmark's most internationally famous writer, Hans Christian Andersen (1805–75) was born in Odense, the son of a poor cobbler. Andersen was admitted to the University of Copenhagen in 1832, and the following year made his debut as an author with his first novel. Several plays and other novels followed, but he remains best known for his children's fairy tales, published between 1835 and 1872. Andersen used everyday language, thus breaking with the literary tradition of the time. Some of his tales, such as "The Little Mermaid" (see p642), are deeply pessimistic and unhappy. A strong autobiographical element runs through these sadder tales; throughout his life, Andersen saw himself as an outsider and he also suffered deeply in his closest relationships.

Statue of Hans Christian Andersen, Copenhagen

Practical & Travel Information

Visitors are always treated with courtesy and hospitality in Denmark; the Danes are one of the most tolerant nations in the world, and the Danish concept of *hygge* (coziness) makes the country a very comfortable place to stay. Denmark's travel facilities are plentiful, reliable, and easy to use. There is an extensive rail network and city public transportation services function efficiently. The capital, Copenhagen, is a compact city, which makes getting around by public transport quite straightforward. Since most Danes speak fluent English, you should have no problems with communication.

Tourist Information

General and location-specific information on all parts of Denmark can be obtained from the **Danish Tourist Board**, which has offices in many countries, including the US and the UK. Visitors to the capital can obtain brochures, maps, and other useful information at the **Copenhagen Visitor Centre**.

Opening Hours

Many tourist attractions close on Mondays, and a few have seasonal opening hours; several museums stay open late on Wednesdays. Stores are open 10am–5:30pm Monday to Thursday, 10am–7pm on Friday, and 9am–2pm on Saturday; Sunday openings are becoming more frequent, especially in Copenhagen. Office hours are 9am–4pm Monday to Friday.

Visa Requirements

Visitors who are not citizens of a Scandinavian country require a valid passport to enter Denmark. Citizens of the EU may use a national identity card in lieu of their passport. No visa is required for visitors from the US, Canada, the UK, Ireland, Australia, or New Zealand.

Safety and Emergencies

Denmark is a peaceful country and street crime is rare, although travelers are advised to take out comprehensive travel insurance. Danish tourist offices and health offices have lists of doctors and local hospitals. For prescriptions (obtainable at a pharmacy or *apotek*) or a doctor's consultation, you will have to pay the full cost on the spot, but EU citizens can obtain a refund by taking their passport and European Health Insurance Card (EHIC) to a local health office.

Banking and Currency

The Danish unit of currency is the krone (DKr), which is divided into 100 øre.

Danish banks usually open 9:30am–4pm Monday to Wednesday and Friday, and 9:30am–6pm on Thursday. For the most favorable exchange rates, change money and traveler's checks at a bank. Outside bank opening hours there are exchange booths at post offices, and most airports, main train stations, and ferry terminals. Major credit and charge cards are accepted in most places, and local currency can be obtained with credit or debit cards from cashpoint machines (ATMs).

Communications

Denmark still has some public phone booths, and phone cards can be purchased from all post offices and kiosks.

Most post offices open from 10am to 6pm Monday to Friday, and 10am to 1pm on Saturday, although smaller branches may have restricted opening times.

Wi-Fi Internet is available in most hotels, some cafés, and on some trains (included in the price of a first-class ticket).

English-language newspapers are usually available the day after publication at train stations and many of the larger newsagents.

Flying to Denmark

Most international flights arrive at **Copenhagen Airport, Kastrup**, 8 km (5 miles) from the city center. British Airways, easyJet, Norwegian, and **SAS** (Scandinavian Airline System) operate direct flights from Britain. SAS also offers direct flights from New York; most flights from North America, however, require a stopover.

Traveling by Sea

If you are considering traveling to Denmark by sea, **DFDS Seaways** operates a ferry service between Harwich in England and Esbjerg, on Denmark's west coast, three or four times a week. The crossing takes around 20 hours. Special midweek offers are often available, which can cut the cost of travel considerably.

The Climate of Denmark

The climate of Denmark is the least extreme of the Scandinavian countries, but the country's close proximity to the sea means that the weather can change very quickly. The summer months are generally sunny; temperatures in July can top 26° C (78° F). Winters are cold and rainy, although not severe, and there may be snow from December to March.

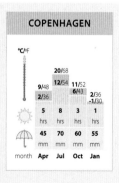

COPENHAGEN

°C/°F			
	20/68		
9/48	12/54	11/52	
2/36		6/43	2/36
			-1/30
5 hrs	8 hrs	3 hrs	1 hrs
45 mm	70 mm	60 mm	55 mm
month Apr	Jul	Oct	Jan

Norway and Sweden are also well connected to Denmark by sea. Ferries from Oslo call at Copenhagen, Hirtshals, and Frederikshavn; a ferry linking Frederikshavn and Gothenburg is operated by **Stena Line**.

Ferries also link all the Danish islands and range in size from the car- and bus-carrying catamarans and ferries of **Mols-Linien**, which travel between Zealand and Jutland, to tiny vessels serving small settlements off the mainland and major islands.

Rail Travel

Like the rest of the public transportation system in Denmark, the trains are clean and reliable, and are by far the best way to get around. **Danish State Railways** (DSB) operates an efficient network that covers most parts of the country, with the exception of south Funen and northeast Jutland.

In Copenhagen, a local train service, the **S-tog**, provides transportation between the city center and the surrounding areas, and as far as Hillerød and

Ishøj, while the underground Metro service runs from the Vanløse suburb in the west to the airport.

Traveling by Car

Car rental in Denmark is expensive. To rent a vehicle you must be at least 20 years of age, and hold an international driver's license.

Driving in central Copenhagen is not advisable due to the traffic and lack of parking.

The Danish authorities conduct random breath tests, and penalties for driving under the influence of alcohol are severe. The **Forenede Danske Motorejere (FDM)** offers a breakdown service to Automobile Association (AA) members.

Buses, Taxis, and Bicycles

Buses are cheaper than trains, if not as comfortable. However, they are useful for traveling to remote areas not covered by the train network. Copenhagen's **Movia Kundecenter** (customer services) has a bus information

hotline. Most taxi drivers speak English, but cabs are often expensive, especially at night and all day at weekends.

Cycling is an excellent way to enjoy Denmark's mostly flat landscape, since traffic is light on the country roads and most towns have cycle tracks. Bikes can be rented at most hotels, youth hostels, tourist offices, and bike stores, and at some train stations. In Copenhagen, **Kobenhavns Cykelbørs** is a reliable bike rental store. Contact the **Dansk Cyklist Forbund** (Danish Cycling Association) for more information.

Sightseeing in Copenhagen

If you plan to do a lot of sightseeing in the capital, it is worth investing in a Copenhagen Card (valid for one, two, or three days). The card gives unlimited use of public transportation in the metropolitan area (including North Zealand), free or cheaper admission to many museums, as well as price reductions with certain car rental companies and on ferry crossings to Sweden.

DIRECTORY

Tourist Offices

Copenhagen Visitor Centre
Vesterbrogade 4a,
Copenhagen V.
Tel 70 22 24 42.
w visitcopenhagen.dk

Danish Tourist Board
w visitdenmark.com

Denmark
Vesterbrogade 4a,
Copenhagen V.
Tel 70 22 24 42.

UK
55 Sloane Street,
London SW1X 9SY.
Tel 020-7201 5958.

US
655 Third Avenue,
Suite 1810, New York.
Tel 212-885 9700.

Embassies

Australia
Dampførgevej 26,

Copenhagen Ø. **Tel** 70 26 36 76. **w** denmark. embassy.gov.au

Canada
Kristen Bernikows Gade 1,
Copenhagen K. **Tel** 33 48 32 00. **w** canadainternational.gc.ca

Ireland
Østbanegade 21,
Copenhagen Ø.
Tel 35 47 32 00.
w embassyofireland.dk

UK
Kastelsvej 36–40,
Copenhagen Ø. **Tel** 35 44 52 00. **w** gov.uk/government/world/denmark

US
Dag Hammarskjölds Allè 24, Copenhagen Ø. **Tel** 33 41 71 00. **w** denmark. usembassy.gov

Emergency Numbers

Ambulance, Fire and Police
Tel 112.

Air Travel

Copenhagen Airport, Kastrup
Tel 32 31 32 31. **w** cph.dk

SAS
Tel 70 10 20 00.
w flysas.com

Ferry Services

DFDS Seaways
Tel 78 79 57 29.
w dfdseaways.com

Mols-Linien
Tel 70 10 14 18.
w mols-linien.dk

Stena Line
Tel 96 20 02 00.
w stenaline.dk

Rail Travel

Danish State Railways
Tel 70 13 14 15.
w dsb.dk

S-tog Information
Tel 70 13 14 15.

Road Travel

Dansk Cyklist Forbund
Tel 33 32 31 21.
w dcf.dk

Forenede Danske Motorejere (FDM)
Tel 70 13 30 40.

Kobenhavns Cykelbørs
Gothersgade 157,
Copenhagen K.
Tel 33 14 07 17.
w cykelboersen.dk

Where to Stay

Copenhagen

DK Choice

CENTRAL COPENHAGEN:
Danhostel Ⓚ
Budget **Map** C5
H.C. Andersens Blvd 50, 1553
Tel *33 11 85 85*
Ⓦ danhostelcopenhagencity.dk
Do not be deceived by
Danhostel's high-rise exterior:
the interiors and sleek rooms
would put most mid-level
hotels to shame. Many of the
rooms have superb views over
the city. Amenities include free
Internet, a pleasant TV lounge,
and laundry facilities.

CENTRAL COPENHAGEN:
Andersen Hotel ⓀⓀ
Boutique
Helgolandsgade 12, 1653
Tel *33 31 43 44*
Ⓦ andersen-hotel.dk
A design hotel with exceptional
standards of service and
comfortable rooms.

CENTRAL COPENHAGEN:
Generator Hostel ⓀⓀ
Budget **Map** C3
Adelgade 5–7, 1304
Tel *78 77 54 00*
Ⓦ generatorhostels.com
Stylish, spacious, and popular,
with doubles, triples, and dorms.

CENTRAL COPENHAGEN:
Hotel Amager ⓀⓀ
Budget
Amagerbrogade 29, 2300
Tel *32 54 40 08*
Ⓦ hotelamager.dk
Delightful rooms with antique
furniture, and a shared kitchen.

CENTRAL COPENHAGEN:
Hotel Tiffany ⓀⓀ
Family
Colbjørnsengade 28, 1652
Tel *33 21 80 50*
Ⓦ hoteltiffany.dk
Simple rooms with kitchenettes,
as well as free pastries and hot
drinks. Faultless service.

CENTRAL COPENHAGEN:
Savoy Hotel ⓀⓀ
Family
Vesterbrogade 34, 1620
Tel *33 26 75 00*
Ⓦ savoyhotel.dk
Smart, central hotel in a red-brick
building, with comfortable rooms
overlooking a quiet courtyard.

DK Choice

CENTRAL COPENHAGEN:
Hotel d'Angleterre ⓀⓀⓀ
Luxury **Map** D4
Kongens Nytorv 34, 1050
Tel *33 12 00 95*
Ⓦ dangleterre.com
One of the most respected
hotels in Copenhagen, the
Angleterre has been in business
for over 250 years and remains
the top choice for visiting
dignitaries. The rooms are large,
classically decorated, and filled
with amenities. Located close
to the Queen's residence.

CENTRAL COPENHAGEN:
Ibsens Hotel ⓀⓀⓀ
Boutique **Map** B3
Vendersgade 23, 1363
Tel *33 45 77 77*
Ⓦ arthurhotels.dk
This family-friendly hotel
comes with individually styled
rooms, ranging from modern
Scandinavian to classical English.

CENTRAL COPENHAGEN:
STAY Apartment Hotel ⓀⓀⓀ
Boutique
Islands Brygge 79a, 2300
Tel *72 44 44 34*
Ⓦ staycopenhagen.dk
Fully equipped apartments, some
with waterfront views. Free Wi-Fi
Internet access and cable TV.

Rest of Denmark

AALBORG: Helnan
Phønix Hotel Ⓚ
Family
Vesterbro 77, 9000
Tel *98 12 00 11*
Ⓦ helnan.info
This historic hotel built in 1783 is
still providing classic hospitality
in an elegant setting.

AALBORG: Hotel Chagall Ⓚ
Family
Vesterbro 36–38, 9000
Tel *98 12 69 33*
Ⓦ chagall.dk
Pleasant, centrally located hotel.
Rooms are bright and airy.

AALBORG: Radisson Blu
Limfjord Hotel ⓀⓀ
Business
Ved Stranden 14–16, 9000
Tel *98 16 43 33*
Ⓦ radissonblu.com
High standards and an excellent
location facing the river and near
famous Jomfru Ane Gade street.

ÅRHUS: Hotel Faber Ⓚ
Family
Eckersbergsgade 17, 8000
Tel *70 26 70 11*
Ⓦ hotel-faber.dk
This modern hotel offers its
guests soundproofed rooms
with private kitchen facilities.

ODENSE: Cabinn Odense Ⓚ
Budget
Østre Stationsvej 7, 5000
Tel *63 14 57 00*
Ⓦ cabinn.com
Stay in compact rooms inspired
by ships' cabins. Splendid views
from the top-floor breakfast bar.

ODENSE: Hotel Ansgar ⓀⓀ
Family
Østre Stationsvej 32, 5000
Tel *66 11 96 93*
Ⓦ millinghotels.dk
Refurbished in an Italian style,
this handsome red-brick hotel
is centrally located and has
excellent standards of service.

Simple rooms livened up by splashes of color at Copenhagen's Andersen Hotel

Where to Eat and Drink

Copenhagen

CENTRAL COPENHAGEN:
Slotskælderen hos Gitte Kik
Danish   Map C4
Fortunstræde 4, 1065
Tel *33 11 15 37*
An excellent lunch-only spot right off Strøget that specializes in *smørrebrød* (open sandwich). Diners make their selection from behind the glass counters, and the staff brings it over. Also good *sild* (herring) and *frikadeller* (meatballs).

CENTRAL COPENHAGEN:
Cap Horn   Ⓚ Ⓚ
Danish   Map D4
Nyhavn 21, 1051
Tel *33 12 85 04*
Weathered walls, wooden floors, and an open fireplace create the setting for Cap Horn's classic yet regularly changing menu, which focuses on seafood and organic dishes. Fast service.

CENTRAL COPENHAGEN:
Det Lille Apotek   Ⓚ Ⓚ
Danish   Map C4
Store Kannikestrade 15, 1169
Tel *33 12 56 06*
The city's oldest restaurant has a dark-wood interior. Classic Danish fare includes *apotekaregrytan* – a tasty stew of tenderloin pork in a paprika sauce.

CENTRAL COPENHAGEN:
Ida Davidsen   Ⓚ Ⓚ
Danish   Map D3
Store Kongensgade 70, 1264
Tel *33 91 36 55*   **Closed** *Sat & Sun*
Ida Davidsen's menu features more than 250 types of *smørrebrød* (open sandwich), all made with fresh ingredients. The family has been making open sandwiches since 1888. Open for lunch only.

CENTRAL COPENHAGEN:
Krebsegaarden   Ⓚ Ⓚ
Scandinavian   Map B4
Studiestræde 17, 1455
Tel *20 12 40 15*
Small yet enormously popular for its excellent service. Krebsegaarden has a cozy interior, and a changing menu inspired by the exhibitions in the adjacent gallery.

CENTRAL COPENHAGEN:
Oliver and the Black Circus   Ⓚ Ⓚ
Scandinavian   Map B4
Teglgårdsstræde 8A, 1452
Tel *74 56 88 88*   **Closed** *Sun & Mon*
This restaurant's mission to provide adventurous cuisine at affordable prices has gone

Bright and cozy dining room at Koefoed, Copenhagen

down well with both local and visiting diners. Try the chicken with rhubarb and asparagus, and the popcorn and cola dessert.

CENTRAL COPENHAGEN:
Tight   Ⓚ Ⓚ
International   Map C4
Hyskenstræde 10, 1207
Tel *33 11 09 00*
This busy, central eatery has a reputation for the best steak and burgers in town, but it also serves top-notch seafood and pasta dishes at reasonable prices. Book a table in advance.

DK Choice

CENTRAL COPENHAGEN:
Koefoed   Ⓚ Ⓚ Ⓚ
Scandinavian   Map D3
Landgreven 3, 1301
Tel *56 48 22 24*   **Closed** *Sun & Mon*
Located on a side street just off Store Kongensgade, Koefoed finds both inspiration and produce – including meat, beer, and wine – from the island of Bornholm. The menu changes seasonally. Book well in advance.

CENTRAL COPENHAGEN:
Noma   Ⓚ Ⓚ Ⓚ
Scandinavian
Strandgade 93, 1401
Tel *32 96 32 97*   **Closed** *Sun & Mon*
Located in an old warehouse on the waterfront, Noma has built a reputation on its strict use of seasonal, Nordic-sourced ingredients, resulting in a truly fascinating menu that changes monthly. Very popular, so reserve months in advance.

Rest of Denmark

AALBORG: Duus Vinkjælder   Ⓚ Ⓚ
Scandinavian
Østerågade 9, 9000
Tel *98 12 50 56*   **Closed** *Sun*
This atmospheric cellar restaurant and bar is renowned for its delicious *frikadeller* (meatballs) and its variety of Danish *smørrebrød* (open sandwich).

AALBORG:
Søgaards Bryghus   Ⓚ Ⓚ
Microbrewery
C.W. Obelsplads 1, 9000
Tel *98 16 11 14*
Søgaards Bryghus's modern Danish kitchen matches its seasonal brews with brunch, lunch, and dinner options, from hearty burgers to herring platters.

ÅRHUS: Miro   Ⓚ Ⓚ
Danish/French
Marstrandsgade 2, 8000
Tel *86 13 87 00*   **Closed** *Sun & Mon*
Meticulously prepared dishes are loosely based on artworks by the famous Catalan artist. Each dish is matched with a wine from an extensive range.

ÅRHUS: Navigator   Ⓚ Ⓚ
Danish/French
Marselisborg Havnevej 46D, 8000
Tel *86 20 20 58*
Head to this lively restaurant for well-cooked Danish-French staples in tune with the seasons. When the weather permits, there is an outdoor grill and salad bar.

ODENSE: Den Gamle Kro   Ⓚ Ⓚ
Scandinavian
Overgade 23, 5000
Tel *66 12 14 33*
Located in a 1683 building, Den Gamle Kro offers dishes such as smoked eel with scrambled eggs and strawberries soaked in champagne.

ODENSE: Sortebro Kro   Ⓚ Ⓚ Ⓚ
Scandinavian
Sejerskowej 20, 5260
Tel *66 13 28 26*
Set within the grounds of a historic farmhouse, this restaurant serves an excellent range of traditional Danish dishes.

FINLAND

Finland is perhaps the least known of the Nordic countries. Historically, geographically, and economically, the country straddles East and West, trading and maintaining links with both Western Europe and the former states of the Soviet Union. The Finnish have a strong sense of national identity, and are rightly proud of their beautiful unspoiled landscape of forest, lakes, coast, and islands.

About a third of Finland (*Suomi* in Finnish) is covered by native pine, spruce, and birch forests. Most of the rest is covered by water – an estimated 188,000 lakes, numerous rivers, and extensive areas of marshland. Finland's coastline is extremely indented and dotted with thousands of islands, most of which can be found in the archipelagos of the southwest. The land is generally flat, apart from mountainous areas in Lapland. About one third of the territory lies within the Arctic Circle, where the landscape is strikingly beautiful, if sometimes bleak.

Most of Finland's towns and cities are found in the southern coastal region, where they vie for space with extensive stretches of farmland. The lake district, at the heart of Finland, is not so populous, but industrialization of the area has been steadily increasing since the mid-20th century. Northern Finland is still fairly undeveloped, with small pockets of Finns inhabiting the south, while the Sami (the nomadic people of Lapland) are spread over the far north.

Although by nature modest and not very practised at marketing themselves, the Finns have achieved much economic success, excelling in the fields of technology and design. Nokia, the mobile phone giant, is Finland's best-known success story in global terms, although many people are unaware of the company's Finnish origins.

History

Little is known of early Finnish history, although it is believed that the ancestors of the Sami first arrived in Finland about 9,000 years ago. Another group, whose language evolved into modern Finnish, arrived some 3,000 years later. In the 1st millennium BC, the arrival of more groups, including the ancestors of the present-day Finns, forced the Sami to withdraw northwards to Lapland.

Even before the beginning of the Viking age (8th–11th century AD), Swedes had settled on the southwest coast of Finland, and in 1216, Finland became part of Sweden. Under Swedish sovereignty, the

A busy main street in central Helsinki

◀ A group of islands in the Baltic Sea, near Helsinki

Finnish tribes gradually developed a sense of unity, which would later form the basis for a proud national identity.

From the 13th to the 18th centuries, Finland was a battleground for power struggles between Sweden and Russia. In 1809, Sweden ceded Finland to Russia, and the territory became an autonomous Grand Duchy of Russia. Helsinki was decreed the Finnish capital in 1812, and by the 1830s, the transformation of this rocky fishing harbor into a major Baltic trading city was well underway.

When Czar Nicholas II unwisely removed Finland's autonomous status, a determination to achieve independence took root. This independence was finally won in 1917, aided by the maneuverings of General Carl Gustaf Emil Mannerheim (1867–1951). Mannerheim ousted the Russian soldiers still garrisoned in Finland and thus averted the immediate danger that the fledgling USSR might extend its Communist regime into the country. Finland's declaration of independence was finally recognized by the Soviet government on December 31, 1917.

Statue of General Mannerheim, architect of independence

Between the two world wars, Finland was dominated by a controversy over language. The Finns fought for the supremacy of their native tongue, and the use of Swedish declined sharply.

Despite its independent status, tensions between Finland and the Soviet Union remained throughout the early 20th century. Years of fear culminated in the 1939–40 Winter War against an invading Soviet army, swiftly followed by the "War of Continuation" (1941–44), in which Finland aided German troops against the Soviet Union. Deep suspicion of the Soviet Union continued for decades, but following the demise of the USSR in 1991, Finland reached a new agreement with Russia which pledged to end disputes between them peacefully.

In recent years, Finland has carved for itself a peace-brokering reputation, and has expanded economically through membership of the European Union and the efforts of its entrepreneurs.

Language and Culture

What began as a linguistic and cultural exploration of Finnishness in the 1800s has evolved into a confident, outward-looking sense of nationhood. At the heart of Finnishness lies the notion of *sisu*, a kind of courage against the odds, but it also embraces everything in which the Finns take pride, such as the freedom to harvest berries and mushrooms in the forests.

Outdoor pursuits have an important place in the national psyche, especially cross-country skiing, swimming, boating, and cycling. Finland is also successful in some competitive sports, such as long-distance running and rally driving.

In the arts, the music of composer Jean Sibelius remains Finland's best-known cultural export. Finnish architects and designers, in particular Alvar Aalto (1898–1976) and the Marimekko company, are renowned worldwide.

KEY DATES IN FINNISH HISTORY

1155 First Swedish crusade to Finland

1216 Finland becomes a duchy of Sweden

1550 New market town of Helsinki established

1714 & 1721 Russia and Finland are at war

1748 Island fortress of Suomenlinna under construction to defend Finland against Russians

1809 Finland is separated from Sweden and becomes an autonomous Grand Duchy of Russia

1812 Helsinki becomes capital of Grand Duchy

1917 Declaration of independence

1939–44 Russia and Finland at war

1995 Finland joins the European Union

2000 Helsinki is European City of Culture and celebrates its 450th anniversary

2002 Finnish mark replaced by Euro

2006 Finland assumes EU presidency

2012 Helsinki is World Design Capital

Exploring Finland

After many years in the tourism wilderness, Finns are working hard to put their country on the map of world travel destinations. Wonderful natural amenities, a manageable and attractive capital city, and excellent public transportation make Finland an easy country to promote. Trains are the most convenient way to get around the country, although long-distance buses are often faster on east–west journeys. Destinations in the populous south are all easy to reach, but in the far north, traveling takes more time and planning.

Sights at a Glance

1 *Helsinki pp654–7*
2 Turku
3 Savonlinna
4 *Side Trip to St. Petersburg pp658–9*

Lake Saimaa sightseeing cruise leaving Savonlinna

For hotels and restaurants see p662 and p663

For key to symbols *see back flap*

Key

— Highway
— Major road
— Railroad
▪▪▪ International border

❶ Helsinki

Finland's capital since 1812, Helsinki is called the "White City of the North," a reference to the gleaming white Neoclassical buildings commissioned by its Russian rulers in the 19th century. It also boasts impressive modern architecture, from the copper, glass, and rock Temppeliaukio Church to the futuristic Kiasma center. The city is at its best in summer, when long days and clear light lift the mood of Finns, and the parks and waterfront cafés fill with lively crowds.

Key

Sight / Place of interest

Pedestrian street

Sights at a Glance

① Market Square
② Uspenski Cathedral
③ Senate Square
④ Helsinki Cathedral
⑤ Ateneum Art Museum
⑥ Kiasma, Museum of Contemporary Art
⑦ Finlandia Hall
⑧ National Museum
⑨ Temppeliaukio Church

Greater Helsinki

⑩ Suomenlinna Sea Fortress

Getting Around

The center of Helsinki is easily explored on foot. The city's efficient transportation network consists of buses, trams, and a metro system, although the latter is of limited use to tourists. Virtually all bus and tram routes converge on the streets around Helsinki Central Station. Suomenlinna Sea Fortress can be reached by ferry only, from Market Square.

The National Museum of Finland, with its landmark tower

Stall holder moored alongside the quay at Helsinki's Market Square

① Market Square

Head of South Harbor. 🚌 16. 🚋 1, 1A, 2, 4, 4T. 🚢 6.30am–6pm Mon–Fri, 6:30am–4pm Sat, 9am–4pm Sun. **Closed** Sun in winter.

In summer, a short season that must sustain a nation through a long winter, the people of Helsinki sun themselves in the cobbled Market Square (Kauppatori).

Finnish craftsmen sell hand-made wares alongside fish, fruit, and vegetable stalls. Farmers will often travel for many miles by small wooden boat to sell fresh produce grown on their small holdings just like their forefathers did.

Among the fine buildings lining the square are the blue-painted **City Hall**, by Carl Ludwig Engel (1778–1840), and the 19th-century red- and yellow-brick **Old Market Hall**, containing several gourmet and specialist food shops.

Leading westward from Market Square is **Esplanadi** park, a favorite gathering place for Finns, who can be seen strolling down its wide boulevards. At the eastern end of the park is a bronze statue of a nude, *Havis Amanda* (1905) by Ville Vallgren, now a symbol of the city.

② Uspenski Cathedral

Kanavakatu 1. **Tel** 09-634 267. 🚋 4, 4T. **Open** Tue–Sun (Sun: pm only). ♿ ask for assistance.

With its dark red-brick exterior, this Russian Orthodox cathedral is a colorful landmark in the ubiquitous white of the historic city center. Its green copper roof and gold "onion" domes make it highly visible on Helsinki's skyline.

Designed in the Byzantine-Russian architectural style by A.M. Gornostayev of St. Petersburg, the cathedral was built between 1862 and 1868. Uspenski is the biggest Russian Orthodox church in Scandinavia, and its spacious interior is resplendent in gold, silver, red, and blue. The terrace gives magnificent views over the heart of Helsinki, and the immediate area has been improved by converting old warehouses into shops and restaurants. The sheer exuberance of the building forms a sharp contrast to the Lutheran austerity of Helsinki Cathedral.

The red-brick exterior and "onion" domes of Uspenski Cathedral

③ Senate Square

🚋 1, 1A, 2, 4, 4T, 7A, 7B. 🚌 16.

Senate Square (Senaatintori) is the masterpiece of Carl Ludwig Engel (1778–1840). It was built by Finland's Russian rulers in the early 1800s, and a statue of Czar Alexander II of Russia stands in the center.

The pleasing proportions of the square are best viewed from the top of the steps to Helsinki Cathedral. From here, the **Senate Building** lies to the left and the **University of Helsinki** to the right. Adjacent to the square is **Sederholm House** (1757), the oldest stone building in Helsinki.

The steep south-facing steps leading to the Neoclassical Helsinki Cathedral

④ Helsinki Cathedral

Unioninkatu 29, Senaatintori. **Tel** 09-234 06120. 🚋 1, 1A, 2, 4, 4T, 7A, 7B. 🚌 16. **Open** daily, except during services. ♿ call in advance. Crypt: **Open** Jun–Aug: daily. 🌐 **helsingin kirkot.fi/en/churches/cathedral**

The five green cupolas of the gleaming white Lutheran Cathedral are a landmark on Helsinki's skyline. Designed by C.L. Engel, the Neoclassical building sits at the top of a steep flight of steps.

White Corinthian columns decorate the splendid exterior, while the inside is rather spartan. There are, however, statues of the 16th-century Protestant reformers Martin Luther, Philipp Melanchthon, the great humanist scholar, and Mikael Agricola, translator of the Bible into Finnish. Beneath the cathedral is a crypt, now used for concerts and exhibitions.

⑤ Ateneum Art Museum

Kaivokatu 2. **Tel** 0294-500 401. 🚋 1A, 2, 3, 4, 4T, 6, 6T, 7B, 9. **Open** 10am–6pm Tue & Fri, 9am–8pm Wed & Thu, 10am–5pm Sat & Sun. 🎨 📷 ♿ 🖥 🌐 **ateneum.fi/en**

Located in the heart of the city, next to the main station, this museum is part of the Finnish National Gallery and houses the biggest collection of art in Finland. In addition to over 20,000 works of art spanning two centuries (1750s–1950s), there are interesting temporary exhibitions. The building was designed by Theodor Höijer and completed in 1887.

⑥ Kiasma, Museum of Contemporary Art

Mannerheiminaukio 2. **Tel** 09-945 00501. 🚌 🚋 4, 4T, 7A, 7B, 10 & many routes. **Open** Tue–Sun. **Closed** public hols. 🎨 📷 ♿ 🖥 📷 🌐 **kiasma.fi**

This glass and metal-paneled building, designed by American architect Steven Holl, was completed in 1998 at a cost of over 227 million Finnish markka. With its fluid lines and white interior, the museum is built in a curve to maximize natural light in the exhibition spaces.

Intended as an exhibition space for post-1960 art, Kiasma hosts mixed media shows, art installations, contemporary drama, and art workshops.

⑦ Finlandia Hall

Mannerheimintie 13E. **Tel** 09-40241. 🚋 4, 4T, 7A, 7B, 10. 🚌 40. 🎨 📷 by appt. ♿ 🌐 **finlandiatalo.fi/en**

Located in the tranquil setting of Hesperia Park, striking Finlandia Hall is one of architect Alvar Aalto's best-known works. Despite poor acoustics, the hall is a leading concert venue, hosting regular performances by the Helsinki Philharmonic.

⑧ National Museum

Mannerheimintie 34. **Tel** 040-1286 6469. 🚌 40. 🚋 4, 4T, 7A, 7B, 10. **Open** 11am–6pm Tue–Sun. **Closed** public hols. 🎨 ♿ 📷 by appt. 🖥 📷 🌐 **nba.fi/en/nationalmuseum**

Dating from the start of the 20th century, the National Museum is one of Helsinki's most notable examples of Finnish National-Romantic architecture. The museum illustrates the history of Finland, from prehistory to the present day through a variety of artifacts. One of the highlights is the throne of Czar Alexander I from 1809.

The striking wall painting by Akseli Gallen-Kallela (1865–1931) in the entrance hall depicts scenes from Finland's national epic, a poem known as the *Kalevala*.

⑨ Temppeliaukio Church

Lutherinkatu 3. **Tel** 09-234 06320. 🚋 2. 🚌 14, 18, 39, 39B, 41, 42, 45, 70T, 205. **Open** daily (Sun: pm only). ♿

Built into a granite outcrop with walls of stone, this circular "Church in the Rock" is an astonishing piece of modern architecture. Consecrated in 1969, it is the work of architects Timo and Tuomo Suomalainen. The ceiling is an enormous, domed, copper disk, separated from the rough-surfaced rock walls by a ribbed ring of glass, which allows light to filter in from outside. The austere interior is relatively free of iconography and religious symbolism.

As well as being a major visitor attraction – some half a million people come to admire the church each year –

Interior of Temppeliaukio Church, with its copper and glass dome

For hotels and restaurants see p662 and p663

this popular Lutheran place of worship is also used for organ concerts and choral music.

⑩ Suomenlinna Sea Fortress

🚢 from Market Square to residential area of island. **Tel** 09-684 1880. 📷 by appointment. ♿ limited. 🎫 📷
w suomenlinna.fi

Constructed by the Swedes between 1748 and 1772, this island fortress is the biggest in Scandinavia, and is now a UNESCO World Heritage Site. Designed to defend the Finnish coast, Suomenlinna offered security to Helsinki's burghers and merchants, enabling the city to flourish. The fortress contains about 200 buildings, most of which date from the 18th century. Until the early 19th century, the fortress had more residents than Helsinki.

Nine hundred people still live on the islands which receive around 700,000 visitors a year who come to enjoy the cobbled castle courtyards and marinas. There are many eateries, galleries, and museums, including a doll and toy museum.

❷ Turku

🏙 180,000. ✈ 🚌 🚍 🚢 🚢
ℹ️ Aurakatu 4 (02-262 7444). 🎭 Medieval Market (late Jun–Jul), Turku Music Festival (Aug). **w** visitturku.fi

Turku (Åbo in Swedish), a bustling port with a modern city center, was Finland's principal city during the sovereignty of Sweden, and

Exploring the courtyard of the late 13th-century Turku Castle

Suomenlinna Sea Fortress, the largest sea fortress in Scandinavia

remains the center of Finland's second language, Swedish.

Completed in 1300, **Turku Cathedral** is the principal place of worship for the Evangelical-Lutheran Church of Finland. The museum holds many ecclesiastical treasures.

Work on **Turku Castle** began in the late 13th century, but reached its prime in the mid-1500s with the addition of further rooms. The history of Turku and the castle are presented in the **Historical Museum of Turku**. A double museum comprising **Aboa Vetus** and **Ars Nova** focus on life in medieval Turku and 20th-century Finnish and international art respectively.

Other attractions include the west bank of the River Aura and the indoor market. Archipelago steamship cruises are also available.

🏰 Turku Castle
Linnankatu 80. **Tel** 02-262 0300. **Open** Tue–Sun. **Closed** public hols. 📷 in summer. 🎫 🎫 📷
w museumcentreturku.fi

🏛 Aboa Vetus and Ars Nova
Itäinen Rantakatu 4–7. **Tel** 02-250 0552. **Open** Apr–mid-Sep: daily; mid-Sep–Mar: Tue–Sun. **Closed** public hols. 🎫 📷 ♿ (limited).
w aboavetusarsnova.fi

Environs
Just west of Turku lies **Naantali**, a popular seaside resort with cruises available from the harbor. **Moominworld**, a childrens' theme park based on Tove Jansson's creations, is also here.

Moominworld
Naantali. 🚌 11, 110 from Turku. **Tel** 02-511 1111. **Open** Jun–Aug: daily; w/ends for rest of Aug. 🎫
w muumimaailma.fi

❸ Savonlinna

🏙 36,000. 🚍 🚌 🚢 in summer. ℹ️ Puistokatu 1 (015-517 510). 🎭 International Opera Festival (Jul). **w** savonlinna.travel

A good base from which to make excursions into the Saimaa Lakelands, Savonlinna also has charms of its own. Spread over several islands, the town boasts the castle of **Olavinlinna** (St. Olav's Castle), one of the best-preserved medieval castles in Scandinavia. The castle is home to the world-renowned Savonlinna International Opera Festival.

Founded in 1475, the castle consists of three towers and a bailey with an encircling wall reinforced by more towers. There are two museums: the **Castle Museum** illustrates the history of the castle, while the **Orthodox Museum** displays items of Russian Orthodox iconography from both Finland and Russia.

🏰 Olavinlinna
Tel 040-128 6043. **Open** daily. **Closed** some public hols. 🎫 🎫 (free for children under 7). 📷

Environs
From Savonlinna harbor, steamships make excursions on Haapavesi and Pihlajavesi lakes, widely considered Finland's most beautiful scenery.

❻ Side Trip to St. Petersburg

Russia's second city, St. Petersburg is situated at the meeting of the Neva river and the Gulf of Finland, and is easily accessible from Helsinki by air, train, and boat. Founded in 1703 by Peter the Great and dubbed the "Venice of the North", the city comprises a bewitching mix of grand Neoclassical and Baroque architecture, sparkling waterways, and majestic bridges. Nearby, the extravagant imperial palaces of Peterhof and Czarskoe Selo offer an insight into the excesses of Czarist days.

Exploring St. Petersburg

The southern bank of the Neva is lined with stately palaces, and opposite, over the Troitskiy Most, sits the Peter and Paul Fortress. To the west lies Sennaya Ploschad, an area of pretty tree-lined canals and to the east is the Gostinyy Dvor, where shops, bars, and cafés line Nevskiy prospekt. The center is easily explored by foot but a boat trip is one of the highlights of a visit.

① Nevskiy Prospekt

Ⓜ Nevskiy Prospekt, Gostinyy Dvor.

Russia's most famous street, Nevskiy prospekt, is also St. Petersburg's commercial hub. Laid out in the early days of the city, today the street teems with people late into the night.

The western stretch contains a wealth of fine buildings including the Baroque Stroganov Palace. Farther east, there are growing numbers of cafés and bars as well as three historic shopping arcades.

The Church on Spilled Blood, covered in colorful mosaics

② Russian Museum

Inzhenernaya ulitsa 4. **Tel** 595 4248. Ⓜ Nevskiy Prospekt, Gostinyy Dvor. 🚌 3, 7, 22, K-128, K-129, K-169. **Open** Wed–Mon. 🅰 ♿ phone for details. 📷 English (314 3448 to book). 🆆 **rusmuseum.ru**

One of Carlo Rossi's finest Neoclassical creations, the Mikhaylovskiy Palace is the splendid setting for a truly outstanding collection of Russian art, ranging from medieval icons to the latest painting, sculpture, and applied art. The palace was built in 1819–25 for Grand Duke Mikhail Pavlovich. Alexander III's plans to create a public museum were realized by his son Nicholas II when the Russian Museum opened here in 1898. The grand staircase and White Hall are original features.

③ Church on Spilled Blood

Naberezhnaya Griboyedova Kanala 26. **Tel** 315 1636. Ⓜ Nevskiy Prospekt, Gostinyy Dvor. **Open** Thu–Tue. 🅰 📷📷

Also known as the Resurrection Church of Our Savior, this church was built on the spot where on March 1, 1881 Czar Alexander II was assassinated. His successor, Alexander III, launched a competition for a permanent memorial. The winning design, in the Russian Revival style, was by Alfred Parland and Ignatiy Malyshev.

A riot of color, the overall effect of the church is created by the imaginative juxtaposition of materials that are lavished on the building, including 7,000 sq m (75,300 sq ft) of mosaics.

④ The Hermitage

Dvortsovaya ploshchad 2. **Tel** 710 9079. 🚌 7, 10, T-228, K-147, K-209. **Open** Tue–Sun. 🅰 ♿ 📷 English (571 8446 to book). 🆆 **hermitagemuseum.org**

Occupying a grand ensemble of imperial buildings including the impressive Winter Palace, the Hermitage houses one of the world's greatest collections of art and artifacts. Ranging from Egyptian mummies to a dazzling array of Old Master and Impressionist paintings, it is essential to be selective.

The golden dome of St Isaac's Cathedral, visible across the city

⑤ St. Isaac's Cathedral

Isaakievskaya ploshchad. **Tel** 315 9732. Ⓜ Nevskiy Prospekt, Sadovaya. 🚌 3, 10, 22, 27, K-169, K-180, K-190, K-252, K-289. **Open** Thu–Tue. 🅰 📷

St. Isaac's, one of the world's largest cathedrals, was designed in 1818 by the architect Auguste de Montferrand. The construction of the colossal building was a major feat of engineering. Thousands of wooden piles were sunk into the marshy ground to support its 300,000 tonnes. The cathedral opened in 1858 but was designated a museum of atheism during the Soviet era. Officially still a museum today, the church is filled with myriad impressive 19th-century works of art.

The Mariinskiy Theater, one of Russia's most important cultural institutions

⑥ Mariinskiy Theater

Teatralnaya ploshchad. **Tel** 346 4141.
3, 22, 27. **Open** daily; shows at 7pm. **W** mariinsky.ru/en

This theater has been home to the world-famous Mariinskiy (Kirov) Opera and Ballet Company since 1860. Hidden behind its imposing facade is the sumptuous auditorium where many of Russia's greatest dancers have performed. Named in honor of Czarina Maria Alexandrovna, wife of Alexander II, the building was erected in 1860 by the architect Albert Kavos who designed the Bolshoy Theatre in Moscow.

⑦ SS Peter and Paul Fortress

Petropavlovskaya krepost.
Gorkovskaya. Cathedral: **Tel** 230 6431. **Open** daily. English.
W spbmuseum.ru.

The founding of the Peter and Paul Fortress on May 27, 1703, on the orders of Peter the Great, is considered to mark the founding of the city. Its history is a gruesome one, since hundreds of forced laborers died while building the fortress, and its bastions were later used to guard and torture many political prisoners, including Peter's own son Aleksey. The cells where prisoners were kept are open to the public, alongside a couple of museums and the magnificent cathedral housing the tombs of the Romanovs.

Environs

Just a 45-minute trip by hydrofoil from the Hermitage, Peter the Great's sprawling Baroque residence, **Peterhof**, is a must-see when staying in the city for a few days. Designed by Jean Baptiste Le Blond, and built 1714–23, the palace lies at the center of a magnificent landscaped park complete with ornamental ponds and spurting fountains. Altogether, a perfect expression of imperial triumphalism.

Tsarskoe Selo, the lavish palace built for Czarina Elizabeth also lies within easy reach. Designed by Rasterelli in 1752, the 300-m- (980-ft-) long blue, gold, and white facade is a glitteringly striking sight.

Peterhof

Petrodvorets, 30 km (19 miles) W of St. Petersburg. **Tel** 450 5287. from Baltic Station to Novy Petergof then bus 348, 350, and others. board outside the Hermitage (May–Oct). **Open** Tue–Sun. **Closed** last Tue of month.
W peterhofmuseum.ru

Tsarskoe Selo

25 km (16 miles) S of St. Petersburg. **Tel** 465 2024 (Russian only). from Vitebsk Station to Detskoe Selo, then bus 371 or 382. **Open** hours vary; check website. **Closed** last Mon of month. **W** eng.tzar.ru

Central St Petersburg

① Nevskiy Prospekt
② Russian Museum
③ Church on Spilled Blood
④ The Hermitage
⑤ St. Isaac's Cathedral
⑥ Mariinskiy Theater
⑦ SS Peter and Paul Fortress

Practical & Travel Information

The Finnish are a practical people, and tourists can expect the local information services to be both accurate and helpful. Finland's main cities are all served by an efficient railroad system and regular, inexpensive internal flights. Finns take pride in their public transportation systems and promote environmentally friendly modes of travel. Cycling and walking in summer and cross-country skiing in winter are an in-built part of the national psyche. The capital, Helsinki, is easy to navigate on foot, by bicycle, or using public transportation.

Tourist Information

For general and location-specific information, get in touch with the **Finnish Tourist Board**, which has offices in major cities all over the world. The Finnish Tourist Board office in Helsinki has information about different parts of Finland in several languages. Helsinki, Turku, and Savonlinna all have a local tourist office.

The best time to visit Finland is between May and September, but winter in northern Finland has its own special, snow-laden charm. Many tourist attractions in Finland close on Mondays, and some have seasonal opening hours.

Visa Requirements

Visitors who are not citizens of Norway, Denmark, Sweden, or Iceland must have a passport to enter Finland. Members of most EU countries may use an official EU identity card in lieu of their passport. Visas are not required for visitors from the UK, Ireland, the United States, Canada, Australia, or New Zealand.

At Finnish customs, there is a blue channel for citizens of EU countries.

Safety and Emergencies

Finland has very low crime statistics, although drunks (largely harmless) have been a common sight in Finnish towns and cities for years. Mosquitoes are very active during the summer months near water (which is just about everywhere), but their bites do not carry disease. Tap water is safe to drink.

In case of emergencies, the appropriate number to call is listed in the Directory opposite.

Language

Finland has two official languages – Finnish, which is spoken by 94 per cent of the population, and Swedish, which is spoken by 6 per cent. Road signs and maps are often in both languages and there are different national newspapers for each language, too. Younger Finns invariably speak some English, and are very eager to practise it.

Banking and Currency

The Finnish currency unit is the euro (see p23). All euro notes and coins are exchangeable in each of the participating Eurozone countries.

Banks usually open from 10am to 4:30pm Monday to Friday. Most international credit cards are accepted in many places all over Finland.

Communications

Post offices in Finland usually open from 9am to 6pm Monday to Friday, although the main post office in Helsinki operates longer hours. You can buy stamps from kiosks and bookstores, as well as at post offices.

Public telephones are no longer available. Prepaid SIM cards for cell phones can be bought from kiosks and vending machines.

Saunas

Many hotels have a sauna, but they are usually electric ones. For a memorable sauna experience, seek out a wood-fired sauna – preferably close to a lake or the sea – or a traditional "smoke sauna" (savusauna). The sauna is a popular and family-friendly place in which to relax and unwind – there are over a million in Finland. Helsinki boasts the superb Kotiharjun wood-fired sauna (call 09-753 1535). The Finnish Sauna Society has two wood-fired saunas and three smoke saunas set beside the sea (call 09-686 0560 for more information).

The Climate of Finland

In northern Finland (beyond the Arctic Circle), the sun remains above the horizon for a month in summer. This gives Finland its sobriquet "Land of the Midnight Sun." Even in Helsinki, there are almost 20 hours of daylight in summer. In winter, the average temperature falls well below 0° C (32° F), but low humidity makes the extreme cold less raw.

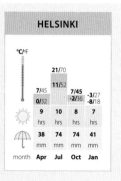

HELSINKI

°C/°F	Apr	Jul	Oct	Jan
		21/70		
		11/52		
	7/45		7/45	-3/27
	0/32		-2/36	-8/18
☀ hrs	9	10	8	7
☂ mm	38	74	74	41
month	Apr	Jul	Oct	Jan

Flying to Finland

Most international flights arrive at Helsinki's **Vantaa Airport**, which is 19 km (12 miles) north of Helsinki. **Finnair** and British Airways both operate daily scheduled services from London Heathrow to Helsinki. Some special "visit Father Christmas" winter flights fly direct from the UK to Rovaniemi on the Arctic Circle. KLM and SAS operate regular flights from Amsterdam and Copenhagen respectively to Helsinki. Travel from North America to Helsinki usually involves connecting flights (changing in Greenland or in Europe) but Finnair flies direct from New York to Helsinki.

Arriving by Sea

The luxury ferries that ply the waters between Stockholm in Sweden and the Finnish ports of Helsinki and Turku have a reputation for offering a state-of-the-art cruising experience. The superliners – operated by **Silja Line** and **Viking Line** – take about 17 hours to make the crossing, which allows plenty of time to enjoy shopping, entertainment, and the celebrated *smörgåsbord* buffets.

Rail Travel

Finland's national rail network is run by the State Railroads of Finland (Valtion Rautatiet or VR). Finnish trains are reliable and clean. Advance reservations are recommended for long-distance, intercity (IC), and some express (EP) trains. In Helsinki, tickets can be bought either at **Helsinki Central Station** or from **Strömma**, which is located at the Helsinki City Tourist Office.

Traveling by Bus

Buses in rural areas are infrequent (but reliable), while intercity buses are fast and efficient. Long-distance journeys are very time-consuming, so it is worth considering the relatively inexpensive domestic flights.

Traveling by Car

Car rental has come down in cost since Finland joined the EU. Even so, car hire using the main international agencies is still pricey. **Europcar** offers some of the more reasonable rates.

Laws about driving under the influence of alcohol are strict and rigidly enforced, as are speed restrictions. Elk and reindeer are a serious road danger, so do pay attention to animal hazard signs.

Getting around Helsinki

Helsinki is manageable on foot or by bicycle, but buses, trams, and the metro provide easy alternatives. The number 2 tram circles central Helsinki, stopping at several important sights. Bear in mind that this line changes its name to number 3 halfway through its route.

Cycle tours, city walks, and cruises are all available from the TourExpert office. Taxis are an expensive way of getting around; ask the driver for an idea of the cost before you embark on your journey.

Finland's island-hopping passenger motorcruisers are a fun form of transportation, giving a real taste of relaxed Finnish summer living.

If you plan to visit several attractions, it is worth investing in a Helsinki Card (available from the Helsinki City Tourist Office and from most hotels). Valid for one, two, or three days, the Card gives unlimited travel on public transportation and on some ferries, reductions on some theater, dance, and opera tickets, and free admission to all major Helsinki sights and nearly 50 museums. Other benefits include reductions on sightseeing tours and on goods in some shops.

Another option is the Helsinki City Transport tourist ticket, which entitles you to unlimited travel on all buses, trams, the metro, and local trains in Helsinki. The ticket is valid for one, three, or five days and is available at all Helsinki City Transport (HKL) points and tourist offices.

DIRECTORY

Where to Stay

Helsinki

CENTRAL HELSINKI:
Help Hostel €
Budget
Linnankatu 3, 00160
w helphostels.com
This convivial hostel in the central
Katajanokka island district has a
spacious lounge and dining area.

CENTRAL HELSINKI:
Hostel Domus Academica €€
Budget
Hietaniemenkatu 14, 00100
Tel *09-131 14334*
w hostelacademica.fi
Great option with a sauna and
decent facilities. Open Jun–Sep.

CENTRAL HELSINKI:
Hotel Klaus K €€
Luxury **Map** C4
Bulevardi 2–4, 00120
w klauskhotel.com
Tel *020-770 4700*
A family-owned design hotel
with soundproofed rooms, a
superb restaurant, and its own
nightclub. Great service.

CENTRAL HELSINKI:
Original Sokos Vaakuna €€
Modern **Map** C4
Assema-aukio 2, 00100
Tel *020-123 4610*
w sokoshotels.fi
One of Finland's most stylish
hotels, with great views of the
city from the top-floor restaurant.

CENTRAL HELSINKI:
Scandic Paasi €€
Boutique
Paasivuorenkatu 5b, 00530
Tel *09-231 1700*
w scandichotels.com
Ultra-modern design hotel by the
sea. Interiors are bold yet tasteful.

DK Choice

CENTRAL HELSINKI:
Kämp €€€
Luxury **Map** C4
Pohjoisesplanadi 29, 00100
Tel *09-576 111*
w hotelkamp.fi
Founded in 1887, this *belle-
époque* property is one of
Helsinki's most outstanding
hotels. Many of the rooms
have a 19th-century style
while featuring modern
amenities and opulent marble
bathrooms with a separate
bath and walk-in shower. The
breakfasts are divine.

Rest of Finland

SAVONLINNA: Family
Hotel Hospitz €€
Family
Linnankatu 20, 57130
Tel *015-515 661*
w hospitz.com
A serene hotel with restaurant on
the shore of Lake Saimaa, close to
Olavinlinna Castle. Open Apr–Dec.

SAVONLINNA:
Lossiranta Lodge €€
Family
Olavinkatu 8, 57130
Tel *044-5112 323*
w lossiranta.net
Charming lakeside hotel located
opposite Olavinlinna Castle.

SAVONLINNA: Seurahuone €€
Modern
Kauppatori 4–6, 57130
Tel *015-202 02*
w sokoshotels.fi
Panoramic lake views from most
rooms, as well as from the rooftop
restaurant and sixth-floor saunas.

TURKU: Omena €
Budget
Humalistonkatu 7, 20100
w omenahotels.com
Unique self-service establishment
without a receptionist. Book
online or at the hotel's kiosk.
Great value, modern rooms.

TURKU: Park Hotel €€
Boutique
Rauhankatu 1, 20100
Tel *022-732 555*
w parkhotelturku.fi
A lovely hotel in an Art Nouveau
building. Quirky features include
a parrot at the reception.

Atrium, featuring a speculator chandelier,
of the opulent Kämp hotel, Helsinki

TURKU: Scandic Julia €€
Modern
Eerikinkatu 4, 20100
Tel *02-336 000*
w scandichotels.com
This hotel has immaculate rooms,
free bike hire, sauna, gym, and an
indoor children's play area.

St. Petersburg

GOSTINYY DVOR: Polikoff $
Budget
26 Nevsky Prospekt 64/11
Tel *995 3488*
w polikoff.spb.ru
This smart hotel has good-sized
rooms and excellent breakfasts.

GOSTINYY DVOR: Pushka Inn $$
Boutique
Naberezhnaya Reki Moyki 14
Tel *644 7120*
w pushka-inn.com
Stay in fabulous rooms within a
restored 18th-century mansion
close to the Hermitage.

PALACE EMBANKMENT:
Casa Leto $$
Boutique
Bolshaya Morskaya 34
Tel *600 1096*
w casaleto.com
One of the city's best mini-hotels,
with just five classically styled
suites. Superb central location.

PALACE EMBANKMENT:
Comfort $$
Family
Bolshaya Morskaya 25
Tel *570 6700*
w comfort-hotel.ru
A simply furnished hotel within
walking distance of most of the
city's central sights. Tabletop
games and DVD players.

PALACE EMBANKMENT:
Astoria $$$
Luxury
Bolshaya Morskaya 39
Tel *494 5757*
w thehotelastoria.com
The opulent Astoria has a
distinctive historic charm. Rooms
at the front offer views over St.
Isaac's Cathedral and Square.

Where to Eat and Drink

A huge mural of the eponymous creatures decorates the Sea Horse, Helsinki

Price Guide

Prices are for a three-course meal for one, including a glass of house wine, tax, and service. Prices for St. Petersburg are in US dollars.

€	up to €15 (up to $30)
€€	€15 to €35 ($30 to $40)
€€€	over €35 (over $40)

Helsinki

CENTRAL HELSINKI:
Gran Delicato €
Mediterranean **Map** B4
Kalevankatu 34, 00180
Tel 09-694 0403
This popular, brightly decorated café in the center of town serves excellent sandwiches and salads, plus its own blends of coffee.

CENTRAL HELSINKI:
Strindberg €€
International **Map** C4
Pohjoisesplanadi 33, 00100
Tel 09-612 86900
One of the most loved and central eateries in the capital. Downstairs, the café offers tasty pastries for breakfast, while the menu at the upscale restaurant upstairs has reindeer, Rydberg steak, and Baltic fish dishes.

CENTRAL HELSINKI:
Kuu Kuu €€€
Finnish
Museokatu 17, 00100
Tel 09-270 90974
This laid-back restaurant serves modern interpretations of traditional Finnish cuisine. The menu features such dishes as wild boar, meatballs, and veal liver. There is a terrace to sit on during the summer.

CENTRAL HELSINKI: Saslik €€€
Russian
Neitsytpolku 12, 00140
Tel 09-742 55500
The lavish decor, period furnishings, and traditional folk singing in this Russian restaurant may be too much for some, but Saslik is still a great place to sample bear steak and Russian staples such as blini.

DK Choice

CENTRAL HELSINKI:
Sea Horse €€€
Finnish
Kapteeninkatu 11, 00140
Tel 09-628 169
In business since the 1930s, this legendary restaurant is as renowned for its dish of 16 fried herrings as it is for its reindeer steak. The owners' winning recipe of serving hearty Finnish food in simple, unpretentious surroundings has long attracted celebrity diners and consistently rave reviews.

CENTRAL HELSINKI: Zetor €€€
Finnish **Map** C4
Mannerheimintie 3–5, 00100
Tel 010-766 4450
Owned by the Kaurismäki brothers, who are Finnish icons, this quirky late-night restaurant offers a meat-and-potato-centric menu. The decor includes a rusty tractor and sawdust on the floor.

Rest of Finland

RANTASALMI: Järvisydän
Piikatyttö €€€
Finnish
Porosalmentie 313, 58900
Tel 020-729 1760 **Closed** Sep–mid-Jun
Feast on food inspired by 17th-century recipes at this inn 50 km (30 miles) from Savonlinna.

SAVONLINNA: Huvila €€€
Finnish
Puistokatu 4, 57100
Tel 015-555 0555 **Closed** Sun
Lakeside restaurant and brewery serving delectable local fish such

as Arctic char and pikeperch. A lovely spot to sample a few glasses of the local brew.

TURKU: Hus Lindman €€€
International
Piispankatu 15, 20500
Tel 040-044 6100 **Closed** Sat & Sun
Occupying an idyllic position on the bank of the River Aura, this reasonably priced lunchtime restaurant is located within an elegant 18th-century house.

TURKU:
Viikinkiravintola Harald €€€
Finnish
Aurakatu 3, 20100
Tel 044-766 8204
A Viking-themed restaurant with animal heads adorning the walls. The fixed-price menus of hearty meat dishes are named after the several Viking voyages.

St. Petersburg

GOSTINYY DVOR: Kavkaz-Bar $$
Caucasus
Karavannaya ulitsa 18
Tel 312 1665
Kavkaz-Bar has a superb location, close to Nevskiy prospekt, and an intimate atmosphere. It also serves the best vegetarian kebabs in town.

PALACE EMBANKMENT: 1913 $$
Russian
Voznesenskiy prospekt 13/2
Tel 315 5148
Named after the last year of Russian imperialism, 1913 prides itself on generous portions of outstanding regional dishes such as *draniki* (potato pancakes) with bacon and sorrel soup, as well as lobster dishes.

PALACE EMBANKMENT:
Via Dell'Oliva $$$
Mediterranean
Bolshaya Morskaya ulitsa 31
Tel 314 6563
This huge taverna, with its own bakery, offers a healthy and varied Greek menu, an extensive salad bar, and a good range of Mediterranean hors d'oeuvres.

CENTRAL AND EASTERN EUROPE

Central and Eastern Europe at a Glance

At the geographical heart of mainland Europe, Hungary, Poland, and the Czech Republic have witnessed a huge surge in visitor numbers since the end of Communism in the late 1980s and early 1990s. Despite the widespread destruction caused by two world wars, their towns and cities retain a wealth of historic monuments, many of which have been painstakingly restored to their former glory. Fortunately, tourism has not destroyed the unique cultural identity of these once little-known countries.

Prague *(see pp672–83)*, the capital of the Czech Republic, is a vibrant city with a rich architectural and cultural heritage. The hilltop castle complex is dominated by the magnificent St. Vitus's Cathedral, whose treasures include many royal tombs.

Bohemia *(see pp684–5)* holds the greatest appeal for most foreign visitors to the Czech Republic. The region boasts elegant spas, fairy-tale castles perched high on thickly wooded hillsides, and many perfectly preserved medieval towns, such as Český Krumlov in the far south.

Lake Balaton *(see p700)*, a huge freshwater lake in western Hungary, is the country's most popular summer vacation destination. Bordered by dozens of resorts, it offers beaches, safe bathing, and water sports, and also provides a habitat for a wide variety of flora and fauna.

Koszalin
Szczecin
Bydgosz
Poznań
Wrocław
Ústí nad Labem
Liberec
Karlovy Vary
Prague
Plzeň
CZECH REPUBLIC *(see pp668–89)*
Olomouc
Brno
České Budějovice
Győr
Szombathe
Kaposvár

◀ View of Old Town from Charles Bridge in Prague, Czech Republic

Locator Map

Warsaw *(see pp710–15)* was largely rebuilt during the Communist era following complete destruction in World War II. Many of its grandest buildings date from the Baroque period, including the splendid Royal Castle.

Cracow *(see pp716–19)*, in southern Poland, has historic monuments spanning hundreds of years, and has been declared a UNESCO World Heritage Site. Its skyline is dominated by dozens of churches, the most important being the Gothic St. Mary's Church in Market Square.

Budapest *(see pp694–9)* is rich in historical treasures, from medieval ruins to late 19th- and early 20th-century Secessionist buildings. Mátyás Church preserves some of its original Gothic features, such as the glorious stone carving on the Mary Portal.

POLAND
see pp706–23)

Gdańsk

Toruń

Białystok

Warsaw

Łódź

Radom

Lublin

Częstochowa

Katowice

Cracow

trava

Miskolc

Eger

Budapest

Debrecen

HUNGARY
(see pp690–705)

Kecskemét

Szeged

cs

0 km   75

0 miles   75

CZECH REPUBLIC

The Czech Republic is one of Europe's youngest states. In the years after World War II, foreign visitors to what was then Czechoslovakia rarely ventured farther than the capital, Prague. Today, the country's beautifully preserved medieval towns and castles are attracting an ever-increasing number of tourists.

The Czech Republic is divided into two regions, Bohemia and Moravia. Rolling plains and lush, pine-clad mountains, dotted with medieval chateaux and 19th-century spa resorts, characterize the landscape of southern and western Bohemia. In spite of the recent influx of tourists, life here still proceeds at a gentle, relaxed pace. In contrast, much of northern Bohemia has been given over to mining and other heavy industry, with devastating effects on the local environment. Moravia has orchards and vineyards in the south, and a broad industrial belt in the north of the region.

Bohemia's largest city and the capital of the Czech Republic, Prague is a thriving cultural and commercial center that bears little relation to most people's expectations of an "Eastern" European city. Its wealth of magnificent architecture, spanning over a thousand years, has withstood two world wars in the last century.

Since the early 1990s, the Czech Republic has emerged as a relatively healthy democratic state. Its economy has been boosted by tourism. The country is a member of NATO and it held presidency of the EU in 2009.

History

From 500 BC, the area now known as the Czech Republic was settled by Celtic tribes, who were later joined by Germanic peoples. The first Slavs, the forefathers of the Czechs, came to the region around 500 AD. Struggles for supremacy led to the emergence of a ruling dynasty, the Přemyslids, at the start of the 9th century. The Přemyslids were involved in many bloody family feuds. In 935, Prince Wenceslas was murdered by his brother, Boleslav. Later canonized, Wenceslas became Bohemia's best-known patron saint.

The reign of Holy Roman Emperor Charles IV in the 14th century heralded a Golden Age for Bohemia. Charles chose Prague as his imperial residence and founded many prestigious institutions there, including central Europe's first university.

Rooftops of Prague's Malá Strana (Little Quarter), covered in snow

◀ The splendid medieval castle overlooking the village of Karlstein, Bohemia

In the early 15th century, central Europe shook in fear of an incredible fighting force – the Hussites, followers of the reformer Jan Hus, who preached in Prague and attacked the corrupt practices of the Catholic Church. His execution for heresy in 1415 led to the Hussite wars. The radical wing of the Hussites, the Taborites, were finally defeated at the Battle of Lipany in 1434.

Engraving showing the radical cleric Jan Hus being burned at the stake

At the start of the 16th century, the Austrian Habsburgs took over, beginning a period of rule that would last for almost 400 years. Religious turmoil led, in 1618, to the Protestant revolt and the 30 Years' War. The end of the war ushered in a period of persecution of all non-Catholics and a systematic Germanization of the country's institutions.

KEY DATES IN CZECH HISTORY

500 BC Celts in Bohemia and Moravia. Joined by Germanic tribes in 1st century AD

AD 500–600 Slavs settle in the region

867 Dynasty of Přemyslids founded

880 Přemyslids build Prague Castle

1333 Charles IV makes Prague his home, marking the start of the city's Golden Age

1415 Jan Hus burned at the stake for heresy; start of the Hussite Wars

1526 Habsburg rule begins with Ferdinand I

1576 Accession of Habsburg Emperor Rudolf II

1618 Protestant revolt leads to the 30 Years' War

1627 Beginning of Counter-Reformation committee in Prague

19th century Czech National Revival

1918 Foundation of Czechoslovakia

1948 Communist Party assumes power

1989 Year of the "Velvet Revolution"; Communist regime finally overthrown

1993 Czechoslovakia ceases to exist; creation of the new Czech Republic

2004 Czech Republic joins the EU

2009 Presidency of the EU

The 19th century saw a period of Czech national revival and the burgeoning of civic pride. But, a foreign power still ruled, and it was not until 1918 and the collapse of the Habsburg Empire that the independent republic of Czechoslovakia was declared. World War II brought German occupation, followed by four decades of Communism.

In 1968, a program of liberal reforms was introduced, known as the "Prague Spring"; the reforms were swiftly quashed by Soviet leaders, who sent in troops to occupy the country. The overthrow of Communism did not come until 20 years later: in November 1989, a protest rally in Prague against police brutality led to the "Velvet Revolution" – a series of mass demonstrations and strikes that resulted in the resignation of the existing regime. The most recent chapter in Czech history was closed in 1993 with the peaceful division of Czechoslovakia into two independent states – Slovakia and the Czech Republic.

Language and Culture

Under the Habsburgs, Czech identity was largely suppressed and the Czech language became little more than a dialect, mainly spoken among the peasant population. In the 19th century, however, Austrian rule relaxed, and the Czechs began rediscovering their own culture. The first history of the Czech nation was written by the Moravian František Palacký, and Czech was re-established as an official language.

Since the Golden Age of the 14th century, Prague has prided itself on its reputation as a flourishing cultural center. In the early 20th century, the city had a Cubist movement to rival that of Paris. The Czech Republic has produced writers, artists, and musicians of world renown including Franz Kafka, Alfons Mucha, and Antonín Dvořák.

Exploring the Czech Republic

One of Europe's most beautiful capital cities, Prague is undoubtedly the highlight of a visit to the Czech Republic. Away from this bustling, cosmopolitan city, however, the tranquil Bohemian countryside is home to dozens of castles and historic towns, whose appearance has remained virtually unchanged for hundreds of years. Most of the main sights of interest can be visited on a day trip from Prague, and are easily reached from the capital by good public transportation and road networks. Slightly farther afield, Český Krumlov merits at least a couple of days' exploration.

Prague's Charles Bridge and the buildings of the Old Town

Sights at a Glance

1. *Prague pp672–83*
2. Karlstein
3. Kutná Hora
4. Karlsbad
5. Český Krumlov

0 km 45
0 miles 45

Czech Republic

0 km 100
0 miles 100

GERMANY
POLAND
Liberec
PRAGUE (Praha)
Katowice
Ostrava
CZECH REPUBLIC
Olomouc
Brno
Vienna (Wien)
SLOVAKIA
AUSTRIA
Bratislava

Berlin, Leipzig

GERMANY
Děčín
Liberec
Teplice
Terezín
Turnov
Chomutov
Žatec
Mladá Boleslav
Karlsbad (Karlovy Vary)
Kladno
PRAGUE (Praha)
Poděbrady
Hradec Králové
Marienbad (Mariánské Lázně)
Karlstein (Karlštejn)
Kutná Hora
CZECH REPUBLIC
Pilsen (Plzeň)
Moravia
Nuremberg
Bohemia
Humpolec
Klatovy
Tabor
Jihlava
Strakonice
Písek
Brno
Jindřichův Hradec
Munich
Budweis (České Budějovice)
Znojmo
Key
Český Krumlov

═══ Highway
──── Major road
──── Railroad
▪▪▪▪ International border

AUSTRIA
Vienna
Linz

For keys to symbols *see back flap*

❶ Prague

Prague, capital of the Czech Republic, has a population of just over one million. In the late Middle Ages, during the reign of Charles IV, Prague's position as the crossroads of Europe aided its growth into a magnificent city, larger than Paris or London. In the 16th century the Austrian Habsburgs took over and built many of the Baroque palaces and gardens that delight visitors today. Some of these palaces now house important museums and galleries. Prague's Jewish Quarter has a handful of synagogues and a cemetery, which remarkably survived the Nazi occupation. Despite neglect under Communist rule, the historic center of the city has been preserved.

The Three Fiddles, an old house sign in Nerudova Street

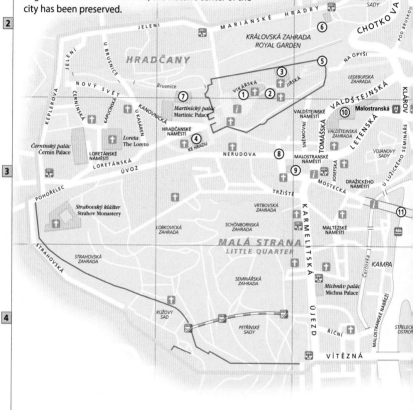

Sights at a Glance

① St. Vitus's Cathedral
② Royal Palace
③ St. George's Convent
④ Schwarzenberg Palace
⑤ Golden Lane
⑥ Royal Garden and Belvedere
⑦ Sternberg Palace
⑧ Nerudova Street
⑨ Church of St. Nicholas
⑩ Wallenstein Palace
⑪ Charles Bridge
⑫ Old-New Synagogue
⑬ Old Jewish Cemetery
⑭ Old Town Square
⑮ Old Town Hall
⑯ Municipal House
⑰ Wenceslas Square
⑱ National Theater

Key

▨ Sight / Place of interest
⋯ Pedestrian street
⌁ City walls
⌁ Funicular railway

Getting Around

Prague's subway, known as the metro, is the fastest way of getting around the city. It has three lines, A, B, and C, and 62 stations. Line A covers all the main areas of the city center. Trams are the city's oldest method of public transport. There are also a number of night trams. Routes 14, 17, 18, and 22 pass many major sights on both banks of the Vltava.

Corner of Old Town Square, with the Church of St. Nicholas

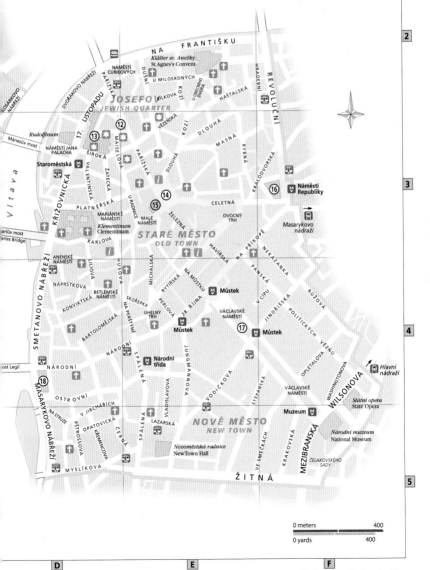

STARÉ MĚSTO
OLD TOWN

NOVÉ MĚSTO
NEW TOWN

JOSEFOV
JEWISH QUARTER

NA FRANTIŠKU

Klášter sv. Anežky
St. Agnes's Convent

U MILOSRDNÝCH

Rudolfinum

NÁMĚSTÍ JANA
PALACHA

Staroměstská

Mariánské
NÁMĚSTÍ

Klementinum

Karlův most
Charles Bridge

Anenské
NÁMĚSTÍ

Betlémské
NÁMĚSTÍ

Národní
třída

Národní muzeum
National Museum

Státní opera
State Opera

Muzeum

Náměstí
Republiky

Masarykovo
nádraží

Hlavní
nádraží

Václavské
NÁMĚSTÍ

Můstek

Novoměstská radnice
New Town Hall

ŽITNÁ

0 meters   400
0 yards   400

Street-by-Street: Prague Castle

The history of Prague begins with the castle, founded by Prince Bořivoj in the 9th century. Despite periodic fires and invasions, it has retained churches, chapels, halls, and towers from every period of its history, from the Gothic splendor of St. Vitus's Cathedral to the Renaissance additions of Rudolph II, the last Habsburg to use the castle as his principal residence. The courtyards date from 1753–75, when the whole area was rebuilt in Late Baroque and Neoclassical styles. The castle became the seat of the Czechoslovak president in 1918, and the current president of the Czech Republic has an office here.

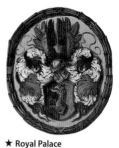

★ Royal Palace
The uniform exterior of the palace (*see p676*) conceals many fine Gothic and Renaissance halls. Coats of arms cover the walls and ceiling of the Room of the New Land Rolls.

The Powder Tower was used in the past for storing gunpowder and as a bell foundry. It is now a museum.

To Royal Garden

★ St. Vitus's Cathedral
This stained-glass window by Alfons Mucha is one of many 20th-century works of art added to the cathedral.

The Picture Gallery of Prague Castle, in the restored stables of the castle, has a good collection of Renaissance and Baroque paintings.

President's office

To Hradčanské náměstí (Castle Square) and Schwarzenberg Palace

Matthias Gate (1614)

Church of the Holy Rood

Steps down to Little Quarter

0 meters   60
0 yards   60

Key

— Suggested route

South Gardens
Various gardens have been laid out along the old ramparts overlooking the Little Quarter. These statues date from the 18th century.

Dalibor Tower
This grim 15th-century tower takes its name from the first man imprisoned in it, a young knight sentenced to death for harboring outlawed serfs.

Golden Lane (see p676) is lined with picturesque artisans' cottages, built in the late 16th century for the Castle's guards and gunners.

White Tower

JIŘSKÁ

Steps down to Malostranská metro

The Lobkowicz Palace dates from 1570. Some original *sgraffito* has been preserved on the façade.

Rosenberg Palace

St. George's Convent

★ **St. George's Basilica**
The vaulted chapel of the royal Bohemian martyr St. Ludmilla is decorated with 16th-century paintings.

The Defenestration of 1618

On May 23, 1618, more than 100 Protestant nobles stormed the Royal Palace to protest against the succession of the Habsburg Archduke Ferdinand. The two Catholic Governors, Jaroslav Martinic and Vilém Slavata, were confronted and thrown out of the eastern window along with their secretary, Philipp Fabricius. Falling some 15 m (50 ft), they landed in a dung heap. This event signaled the beginning of the Thirty Years' War. The Catholics attributed the survival of the Governors to the intervention of angels.

① St. Vitus's Cathedral

Prague Castle, third courtyard. Ⓜ Malostranská. 🚋 22 to Prague Castle (Pražský hrad). **Open** daily (except during services). ♿ Steeple: **Open** daily. **Closed** in bad weather. 🖼️ 📷

Work began on the city's most distinctive landmark in 1344 on the orders of John of Luxemburg. The Gothic cathedral replaced an earlier Romanesque basilica that stood on the site of a small rotunda dating back to the time of St. Wenceslas (c.925). The first architect of the new Gothic structure was the Frenchman Matthew of Arras. After his death, the Swabian Peter Parler took over. The eastern end of the cathedral dates from this period. The original entrance was the Golden Portal on the south side of the building. The present entrance, the western end of the nave, and the façade with its twin spires were added in 1873–1929.

The chapels house many saintly relics, the Bohemian crown jewels, and a number of royal tombs. The tomb of "Good King" Wenceslas stands in the St. Wenceslas Chapel, which is decorated with Gothic frescoes. Another spectacular memorial is the huge silver tomb (1736) of St. John Nepomuk, whose cult was encouraged during the Counter-Reformation.

The spectacularly vaulted chancel of St. Vitus's Cathedral

② Royal Palace

Prague Castle, third courtyard. **Tel** 22
43 73 102. Ⓜ Malostranská. 🚋 22.
Open daily. 🖼 📷 ♿ Ⓦ **hrad.cz**

From the time Prague Castle
was first fortified in stone in the
11th century, the Royal Palace
was the seat of a long line of
Bohemian kings.

The building consists of three
different architectural layers.
A Romanesque palace, built
around 1135, forms the
basement of the present
structure. Over the next 200
years, two further palaces were
built above this – the first by
Přemysl Otakar II in 1253, and
the second by Charles IV in
1340. On the top floor is the
massive Gothic Vladislav Hall,
with its splendid rib vaulting.
Designed for King Vladislav
Jagiello, it was completed in
1502. The Riders' Staircase, just
off the hall, is a flight of steps
with a magnificent Gothic rib-
vaulted ceiling. It was used
by knights on horseback to
get to jousting contests.

Under Habsburg rule, the
palace housed government
offices, courts, and the old
Bohemian parliament. The
Bohemian Chancellery, the
former royal offices of the
Habsburgs, is the site of the
famous 1618 defenestration
(see p675). In 1619, the Bohemian
nobles deposed Emperor
Ferdinand II as King of Bohemia,
electing in his place Frederick
of the Palatinate. This led to
the first major battle of the
Thirty Years' War.

The Riders' Staircase leading to the
Vladislav Hall, Royal Palace

The distinctive red facade of St. George's Basilica

③ St. George's Convent

Prague Castle, Jiřské náměstí. **Tel** 25
75 31 644. Ⓜ Malostranská. 🚋 22.
Open daily. 🖼 📷 Ⓦ **ngprague.cz**

Bohemia's first convent was
founded here in 974 by
Prince Boleslav II. Rebuilt over
the centuries, it was finally
abolished in 1782 and converted
into barracks.

Adjoining the convent, **St.
George's Basilica** was founded
by Prince Vratislav in 920.
Enlarged in 973 and rebuilt
following a fire in 1142, it is the
best-preserved Romanesque
church in Prague. The huge twin
towers and austere interior have
been restored to give an idea of
the church's original appearance.
However, the rusty red facade is
a 17th-century Baroque
addition. Buried in the church
is St Ludmila, who became
Bohemia's first female Christian
martyr when she was strangled
as she knelt at prayer. Throughout the Middle Ages, the
convent and the basilica formed
the heart of the castle complex.

④ Schwarzenberg Palace

Prague Castle, Hradčanské náměstí 2.
Tel 22 48 10 758. Ⓜ Malostranská. 🚋
22. **Open** daily. 🖼 Ⓦ **ngprague.cz**

Built in the 16th century for the
Count of Lobcowicz, the noble
Schwarzenberg family acquired
the palace in 1719 by marriage.
It is considered to be one of the

best preserved Renaissance
buildings in Prague. Its facades
are decorated with black and
white *scraffitto* dating back to
1580; inside, preserved ceilings
have valuable examples of
Renaissance figurative painting.

The palace houses the National
Gallery permanent exhibition,
Baroque Art in Bohemia.
Sculpture and paintings from the
late Renaissance and Baroque
periods include Petr Brandl's
Simeon and the Infant Jesus (1725)
and works by Matyáš Bernard
Braun, Ferdinand Maximilián
Brokof, and Karel Škréta.

⑤ Golden Lane

Ⓜ Malostranská. 🚋 22. **Open** daily.
🖼 Ⓦ **hrad.cz**

Named after the goldsmiths
who lived here in the 17th
century, this is one of the most
picturesque streets in Prague.
The tiny, brightly painted
houses that line one side of it
were built in the late 1500s for
Rudolph II's castle guards. A
century later, the goldsmiths
moved in. By the 19th century,
the area had degenerated
into a slum, populated by
Prague's poor and the criminal
community. In the 1950s, the
area was restored to something
like its original state, and most
of the houses were converted
into shops selling books,
Bohemian glass, and other
souvenirs for the tourists who
flock here. Golden Lane has
been home to a number of

well-known writers, including Franz Kafka (1883–1924), who stayed at No. 22 for a few months between 1916 and 1917.

⑥ Royal Garden and Belvedere

Prague Castle, Královský Letohrádek. Ⓜ Hradčanská, Malostranská. 🚋 22. Garden: **Open** May–Oct: daily. ♿ Belvedere: **Open** only for exhibitions. 📷 ♿ 🌐 **hrad.cz**

Prague's well-kept Royal Garden was created in 1535 for Ferdinand I. The garden contains some fine examples of 16th-century architecture, including the Belvedere, a beautiful arcaded summerhouse with slender Ionic columns and a blue-green copper roof. Also known as the Royal Summer Palace (Královský letohrádek), the Italian Renaissance building was commissioned in the mid-16th century for Ferdinand's wife. It is now used as an art gallery. In front of it is the Singing Fountain, which owes its name to the musical sound the water makes as it hits the bronze bowl.

Also in the garden is the Ball Game Hall (Míčovna), built in 1569, and used primarily for playing a form of real tennis.

At the entrance to the garden, the Lion Court was where Rudolph II had his zoo (now a restaurant).

Artisans' cottages on Golden Lane, Prague Castle

⑦ Sternberg Palace

Hradčanské náměstí 15. **Tel** 23 30 90 570. Ⓜ Hradčanská, Malostranská. 🚋 22 to Brusnice or Prague Castle. **Open** Tue–Sun. 📷 📹 🌐 **ngprague.cz**

Franz Josef Sternberg founded the Society of Patriotic Friends of the Arts in Bohemia in 1796. Fellow noblemen would lend their finest pictures and sculpture to the society, which had its headquarters in the early 18th-century Sternberg Palace. Since 1949, the fine Baroque building has been used to house the National Gallery's collection of European art.

The palace has an impressive array of exhibits, including some particularly fine examples of Italian medieval art, Neapolitan works of the 17th and 18th centuries, Dutch and Flemish masterpieces, and Austrian and German art of the 15th to 17th centuries. The 19th- and 20th-century exhibits, including works by Klimt, Picasso, and Miró, were moved to the Veletržní Palace, northeast of the city center, in 1996.

The palace boasts many masterpieces; among the highlights are Albrecht Dürer's *The Feast of the Rosary* (1506), *Head of Christ*, painted by El Greco in the 1590s, and Rembrandt's *Scholar in his Study* (1634).

Visitors can also see art from ancient Greece and Rome, a collection of Renaissance bronzes, as well as the fascinating Chinese Cabinet, a richly decorated chamber, which combines the Baroque style with Far Eastern motifs.

The Belvedere, Emperor Ferdinand I's summer palace in the Royal Garden beside Prague Castle

Malá Strana

Malá Strana (the Little Quarter) is the part of Prague that has been least affected by recent history. Hardly any new building has taken place here since the 18th century, and the quarter is rich in splendid Baroque palaces and churches, and old houses with attractive signs. Founded as a town in 1257, the area is built on the slopes below the castle, enjoying magnificent views across the river to the Old Town. The center of Malá Strana is Little Quarter Square, dominated by the impressive Church of St. Nicholas.

Cupola and bell tower of the Church of St. Nicholas

Sign of Jan Neruda's house, At the Two Suns, 47 Nerudova Street

⑧ Nerudova Street

Ⓜ Malostranská. 🚋 12, 20, 22.

This narrow picturesque street is named after the 19th-century writer Jan Neruda, who wrote many short stories set in this part of Prague. He lived in the house known as At the Two Suns (No. 47) between 1845 and 1857.

Before the introduction of house numbers in 1770, the city's houses were distinguished by signs. Nerudova's houses have a splendid selection of heraldic beasts and emblems. Ones to look for in particular are the Red Eagle (No. 6), the Three

Fiddles (No. 12), the Golden Horseshoe (No. 34), the Green Lobster (No. 43), and the White Swan (No. 49).

Nerudova Street also has a number of grand Baroque buildings, including the Thun-Hohenstein Palace (No. 20) – now the Italian embassy – and the Morzin Palace (No. 5) – home of the Romanian embassy. The latter has an interesting facade featuring two massive statues of Moors.

⑨ Church of St. Nicholas

Malostranské náměstí. **Tel** 25 75 34 215. Ⓜ Malostranská. 🚋 12, 20, 22. **Open** daily. 🎨 🎫 Ⓦ **stnicholas.cz**

Dominating Little Quarter Square, at the heart of Malá Strana, is the Church of St. Nicholas. Begun in 1702, it is the acknowledged masterpiece of architects Christoph

and Kilian Ignaz Dientzenhofer, who were responsible for the greatest examples of Jesuit-influenced Baroque architecture in Prague. Neither lived to see the completion of the church – their work was finished in 1761 by Kilian's son-in-law, Anselmo Lurago.

Among the many works of art inside the church is Franz Palko's magnificent fresco, *The Celebration of the Holy Trinity*, which fills the 50-m- (165-ft-) high dome. A fresco of St. Cecilia, patron saint of music, watches over the church's splendid Baroque organ. Built in 1746, it was played by Mozart in 1787. Another star feature is the ornate 18th-century pulpit, lavishly adorned with golden cherubs. The impressive statues of the Church Fathers, which stand at the four corners of the crossing, are the work of Ignaz Platzer, as is the statue of St. Nicholas that graces the high altar.

⑩ Wallenstein Palace

Valdštejnský Palác, Valdštejnské náměstí 4. **Tel** 25 70 75 707. Ⓜ Malostranská. 🚋 12, 18, 20, 22. State Rooms: **Open** 10am–5pm Sat–Sun. Riding school: **Open** for exhibitions. ♿ Garden: **Open** Apr–Oct: daily. Ⓦ **senat.cz**

The first large secular building of the Baroque era in Prague, this palace was commissioned by the imperial military commander Albrecht von Wallenstein (1581–1634).

The superbly ornamented Baroque organ in the Church of St. Nicholas

His victories in the Thirty Years' War made him vital to Emperor Ferdinand II. Already showered with titles, Wallenstein started to covet the crown of Bohemia. He began to negotiate independently with the enemy, and in 1634 was killed on the Emperor's orders by mercenaries.

Wallenstein's intention was to overshadow even Prague Castle with his vast palace, built between 1624 and 1630. The magnificent main hall has a ceiling fresco of the commander portrayed as Mars, riding in a triumphal chariot. The palace is now used by the Czech Senate, but the State Rooms are open to the public.

Dotted with bronze statues and fountains, the gardens are laid out as they were when Wallenstein resided here. The Grotesquery is an unusual feature – an imitation of the walls of a cave, covered in stalactites. There is also a fine frescoed pavilion. The old Riding School is today used for National Gallery exhibitions.

Charles Bridge and the Little Quarter Bridge Tower

⑪ Charles Bridge

Ⓜ Staroměstská (for Old Town side). 🚋 12, 20, 22 to Malostranské náměstí (for Little Quarter side); 17, 18 to Staroměstská (for Old Town side). Little Quarter Bridge Tower: **Open** daily. Old Town Bridge Tower: **Open** daily.

One of the most familiar sights in Prague, the Charles Bridge (Karlův Most) connects the Old Town with the Little Quarter. Although it is now pedestrianized, at one time it took four carriages abreast. The bridge was commissioned by Charles IV in 1357 after the Judith Bridge was destroyed by floods.

The bridge's original decoration consisted of a simple wooden cross. In 1683, a statue of St. John Nepomuk – the first of the many Baroque statues that today line the bridge – was added. The vicar general Jan Nepomucký was arrested in 1393 by Wenceslas IV for having displeased the king.

He died under torture and his body was thrown from the bridge. A number of finely worked reliefs depict the martyrdom of this saint, who was revered by the Jesuits as a rival to Jan Hus.

Between 1683 and the latter half of the 19th century, several more statues were erected. Sculpted by Matthias Braun at the age of 26, the statue of St. Luitgard is regarded as one of the most artistically remarkable.

Another splendid piece of decoration, the 17th-century Crucifixion bears the Hebrew inscription "Holy, Holy, Holy Lord," paid for by a Jew as punishment for blasphemy.

At the Little Quarter end of the bridge stand two bridge towers. The shorter of these is the remains of the Judith Bridge and dates from the early 12th century. The taller pinnacled tower was built in 1464. It offers a magnificent view of the city, as does the late 14th-century Gothic tower at the Old Town end.

The vast 17th-century Wallenstein Palace and its gardens

⑫ Old-New Synagogue

Built around 1270, this is the oldest synagogue in Europe, and one of the earliest Gothic buildings in Prague. The synagogue has survived fires, the slum clearances of the 19th century, and many Jewish pogroms. Residents of the Jewish Quarter have often had to seek refuge within its walls, and today it is still the religious center for Prague's Jews. It was originally called the New Synagogue, until another synagogue was built nearby – this was later destroyed.

Right-hand Nave
The glow from the bronze chandeliers provides light for worshippers using the seats lining the walls.

★ Jewish Standard
The historic banner of Prague's Jews is decorated with a Star of David, within which is depicted the hat that had to be worn by Jews in the 14th century.

★ Five-rib Vaulting
Two massive octagonal pillars inside the main hall support the five-rib vaults.

KEY

① **The cantor's platform** and its lectern are surrounded by a wrought-iron Gothic grille.

② **These windows** formed part of the 18th-century extension, built to allow women a view of the service.

③ **Candlestick holder**

④ **14th-century stepped brick gable**

⑤ **The Ark** is the holiest place in the synagogue and holds the sacred scrolls of the Torah. The tympanum above it is decorated with 13th-century leaf carvings.

Entrance to the synagogue from Červená Street

Entrance Portal
The tympanum above the door in the south vestibule is carved with a vine, which bears 12 bunches of grapes, symbolizing the tribes of Israel.

View across the Old Jewish Cemetery towards the Klausen Synagogue

⑬ Old Jewish Cemetery

Široká 3 (main entrance). **Tel** 22 23 17 191 (reservations); 22 48 19 456 (Jewish museum). **M** Staroměstská. 17, 18. **Open** Sun–Fri. includes entry to all Jewish sites except Old-New Synagogue.

Founded in 1478, for over 300 years this was the only burial ground permitted to Jews. Because of the lack of space, people had to be buried on top of each other, up to 12 layers deep. Today you can see over 12,000 gravestones, but around 100,000 people are thought to have been buried here – the last person, Moses Beck, in 1787. The most visited grave in the cemetery is that of Rabbi Löw (1520–1609). Visitors place hundreds of pebbles and wishes on his grave as a mark of respect. On the northern edge of the cemetery, the **Klausen Synagogue** (1694) stands on the site of a number of small Jewish schools and prayer houses, known as *klausen*. Today, it is home to the **Jewish Museum**, whose exhibits trace the history of the Jews in Central Europe back to the Middle Ages. Next to the synagogue is the former ceremonial hall of the Jewish Burial Society, built in 1906. It now houses a permanent exhibition of childrens' drawings from the Terezín concentration camp.

Also bordering the cemetery, the **Pinkas Synagogue** was founded in 1479, and now serves as a memorial to all the Jewish Czechoslovak citizens who were imprisoned at Terezín. Excavations at the synagogue have turned up fascinating relics of life in the medieval ghetto, including a *mikva*, or ritual bath.

Prague's Jewish Quarter

In the Middle Ages, Prague's Jewish community was confined in an enclosed ghetto. For centuries, the Jews suffered from oppressive laws – in the 16th century, they had to wear a yellow circle as a mark of shame. Discrimination was partially relaxed in 1784 by Joseph II, and the Jewish Quarter was named Josefov after him. In 1850, the area was officially incorporated as part of Prague. A few years later, the city authorities razed the ghetto slums, but many synagogues, the Town Hall, and the Old Jewish Cemetery were saved.

Ten Commandments motif on the Spanish Synagogue

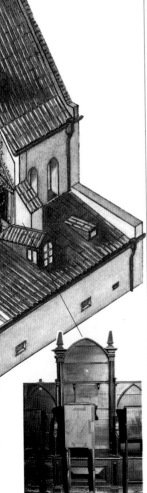
★ **Rabbi Löw's Chair**
A Star of David marks the chair of the Chief Rabbi, placed where the 16th-century scholar, Rabbi Löw, used to sit.

The Old and New Towns

The heart of the city is the Old Town (Staré Město) and its central square. In the 11th century, the settlements around the castle spread to the right bank of the Vltava. A marketplace in what is now Old Town Square was first mentioned in 1091, and houses and churches quickly sprang up around it. Founded in 1348 by Charles IV, the New Town (Nové Město) was mainly inhabited by tradesmen and craftsmen. In the late 19th century, much of it was demolished and completely redeveloped, giving it the appearance it has today.

Church of Our Lady before Týn in the Old Town Square

⑭ Old Town Square

Ⓜ Staroměstská, Můstek. 🚋 17, 18.

Free of traffic, except for a handful of horse-drawn carriages, and ringed with historic buildings, Prague's enormous Old Town Square (Staroměstské náměstí) ranks among the finest public spaces of any European city.

Dominating the east side of the square is the **Church of Our Lady before Týn**, with its magnificent Gothic steeples. Begun in 1365, from the early 15th century until 1620 it was the main Hussite church in Prague.

Also on the east side of the square, the **House at the Stone Bell** has been restored to its former appearance as a Gothic town palace. The splendid 18th-century Rococo **Kinský Palace**, with its pretty pink and white stucco facade,

was designed by Kilian Ignaz Dientzenhofer. Today, it houses art exhibitions by the National Gallery.

At the northern end of the square, the **Church of St. Nicholas** stands on the site of a former church dating from the 12th century. The present building, completed by Kilian Ignaz Dientzenhofer in 1735, has a dramatic white façade, studded with statues by Antonín Braun. In summer, evening concerts are held here.

A colorful array of arcaded buildings of Romanesque or Gothic origin, with fascinating house signs, graces the south side of the square. Among the most attractive are the house called **At the Stone Ram** and the Neo-Renaissance **Štorch House**, also known as At the Stone Madonna.

At one end of the square stands the huge monument dedicated to the reformist Jan Hus, who was burnt at the stake for heresy in 1415.

In addition to historic buildings, there are also many shops, as well as restaurants and cafés, whose tables and chairs spill out onto the pavements of the square in summer.

⑮ Old Town Hall

Staroměstské náměstí 1. **Tel** 23 60 02 629. Ⓜ Staroměstská, Můstek. 🚋 17, 18. **Open** daily. ♿ 🛗 📷

Standing at the southwest corner of the Old Town Square, the Old Town Hall is one of the most striking buildings in Prague.

Established in 1338 after King John of Luxemburg agreed to set up a town

council, the Town Hall grew in the course of the next few centuries, and today consists of a row of colorful Gothic and Renaissance buildings.

The Old Town Hall Tower is one of the building's star features and dates from 1364. The gallery at the top provides a magnificent view of the city. Located on the first floor is the 14th-century Oriel Chapel, with its ornate restored ceiling.

Another famous sight is the Astronomical Clock, built by the clockmaker Hanuš in 1490. The mechanism of the clock we see today was perfected by Jan Táborský between 1552 and 1572. The clock records three different kinds of time, Old Bohemian time, time as we know it, and so-called Babylonian time. It also shows the movement of the sun and moon through the 12 signs of the zodiac. Every time the clock strikes the hour, mechanical figures perform above the zodiac signs, drawing crowds of spectators. The lower section of the clock consists of the Calendar.

Astronomical Clock and Calendar on the Old Town Hall Tower

This beautifully decorated revolving dial, designed by celebrated artist Josef Mánes, dates from 1866.

⑯ Municipal House

Náměstí Republiky 5. **Tel** 22 20 02 101. Ⓜ Náměstí Republiky. 🚊 5, 8, 24, 26. Gallery: **Open** daily. 📷 ♿
🌐 **obecnidum.cz**

Prague's most prominent Art Nouveau building occupies the site of the former Royal Court palace, the king's residence between 1383 and 1484. The exterior is embellished with allegorical statuary, and above the main entrance there is a mosaic entitled *Homage to Prague* by Karel Špillar.

Inside is Prague's principal concert venue, the Smetana Hall, which is also used as a ballroom. The interior is decorated with works by leading Czech artists of the early 20th century, including Alfons Mucha, one of the most successful exponents of the Art Nouveau style.

On October 28, 1918, Prague's Municipal House was the scene of the momentous proclamation of the new independent state of Czechoslovakia.

⑰ Wenceslas Square

Ⓜ Můstek, Muzeum.
🚊 3, 9, 14, 24.

Originally a medieval horse market, today Wenceslas Square remains an important commercial center, with shops, hotels, restaurants, and clubs.

At one end of the square is the **National Museum**. This grand building, with its monumental staircase and rich marbled interior, was completed in 1890 as a symbol of national prestige. The museum's collections are devoted mainly to mineralogy, archaeology, anthropology, and natural history. The huge equestrian statue of St. Wenceslas that stands

View across the Vltava River to the National Theater

in front of the National Museum was erected in 1912, the work of the 19th-century sculptor Josef Myslbek. At the foot of the pedestal there are smaller statues of Czech patron saints.

Also worth seeing are the Art Nouveau-style **Hotel Europa** (1906) and the **Church of Our Lady of the Snows**. This towering Gothic building is only part of a vast church planned in the 14th century but never completed.

Wenceslas Square has witnessed many important events in Czech history. In November 1989, a protest rally against police brutality took place here, leading to the Velvet Revolution and the overthrow of Communism.

Statue of St. Wenceslas flanked by Czech patron saints in St. Wenceslas Square

⑱ National Theater

Národní divadlo, Národní 2. **Tel** 22 49 01 448. Ⓜ Národní třída. 🚊 6, 9, 17, 18, 22 to Národní divadlo.
Open for performances only or by arrangement (22 17 14 152). ♿
🌐 **narodni-divadlo.cz**

The National Theater has always been an important symbol of the Czech cultural revival. Work began on the building in 1868. The original Neo-Renaissance design was by the Czech architect Josef Zítek. After it was completely destroyed by fire – just days before the official opening – Josef Schulz was given the job of rebuilding the theater, and all the best Czech artists of the period contributed toward its lavish decoration. During the late 1970s and early 80s, the theater underwent restoration work and the New Stage was built.

The theater's auditorium has an elaborately painted ceiling adorned with allegorical figures representing the arts. Equally impressive are the sumptuous gold and red stage curtain, and the ceiling fresco in the theater's lobby. The fresco is the final part of a triptych, painted by František Ženíšek in 1878, depicting the *Golden Age of Czech Art*.

The theater's vivid sky-blue roof, covered with stars, is said to symbolize the summit all artists should aim for.

Excursions in Bohemia

The sights that attract most visitors away from the capital are Bohemia's picturesque towns and castles, and its famous spa resorts. The castle at Karlstein, for example, stands in splendid isolation above wooded valleys that have changed little since Charles IV hunted here in the 14th century. Further south, the historic town of Český Krumlov retains a medieval atmosphere. Still popular as a therapeutic retreat, the spa town of Karlsbad is located in the leafy Teplá valley and offers a welcome respite from Prague's crowds.

Karlstein Castle, built by Emperor Charles IV in the 14th century

❷ Karlstein

Karlštejn, 25 km (16 miles) SW of Prague. **Tel** 311 68 16 17. 🚆 to Karlštejn (1.5 km/1 mile from castle). **Open** Mar–Nov: Tue–Sun. 🎨 🎫 obligatory. Chapel of the Holy Rood: **Open** Jun–Oct: Tue–Sun. 🎨 🎫 obligatory and by advance reservation only. 🌐 hradkarlstejn.cz

Karlstein Castle was founded by Charles IV as a country retreat and a treasury for the imperial crown jewels. The present structure is largely a 19th-century reconstruction by Josef Mocker. The original building work took place between 1348 and 1365, supervised by the French master mason Matthew of Arras, and after him by Peter Parler. You can still see the audience hall and the bedchamber of Charles IV in the Royal Palace.

The central tower houses the Church of Our Lady, with its faded 14th-century wall paintings. A passage leads to the Chapel of St. Catherine, whose walls are adorned with semi-precious stones. The Chapel of the Holy Rood in the Great Tower, where the crown jewels were once kept, has gilded vaulting studded with glass stars. At one time, the chapel held 129 panels painted by Master Theodoric (1359–67), one of the greatest painters of Charles IV's reign. Some panels have been restored and can now be seen in Prague's St. Agnes's Convent, along with other medieval art.

❸ Kutná Hora

70 km (45 miles) east of Prague. 🏛 21,000 🚆 🚌 ℹ Palackého náměstí 377 (327 51 23 78). 🌐 kutnahora.cz

After deposits of silver were found here in the 13th century, Kutná Hora evolved from a small mining community into the second most important town in Bohemia after Prague. The Prague *groschen*, a silver coin that was in circulation all over Europe, was minted at the **Italian Court** (Vlašský dvůr), so-called because Florentine experts were employed to set up the mint. Strongly fortified, the Italian Court was also the ruler's seat in the town. In the late 14th century, a palace was built, containing reception halls and the Chapel of St. Wenceslas and St. Ladislav. They can be visited by guided tour.

Kutná Hora's **Mining Museum**, housed in a former fort called the Hrádek, and the splendid 14th-century Gothic **Cathedral of St. Barbara** are also worth visiting.

❹ Karlsbad

Karlovy Vary, 140 km (85 miles) west of Prague. 🏛 54,000 🚆 🚌 ℹ Lázeňská 14 (355 32 11 71). 🌐 karlovyvary.cz

Legend has it that Charles IV discovered one of the sources of mineral water that would make Karlsbad's fortune when one of his staghounds fell into

The three steeples of Kutná Hora's great Cathedral of St. Barbara

For hotels and restaurants see p688 and p689

The spa town of Karlsbad with its 19th-century Mill Colonnade

Czech Beers

Czech beer-bottle cap

The best-known Czech beer is Pilsner, which is made by the lager method: top fermented and matured at low temperatures. The word "Pilsner" (now used as a generic name for similar lagers brewed all over the world) derives from Plzeň, a town 88 km (55 miles) southwest of Prague, where this type of beer was first brewed in 1842.

The brewery that developed the beer still makes Plzeňský prazdroj (original source), better known by its name Pilsner Urquell, as well as the very popular Gambrinus. Guided tours of the brewery include a tasting. České Budějovice is Bohemia's other famous brewing town – home to the Czech Republic's biggest selling export beer, Budweiser Budvar.

Selection of Czech beers

a hot spring. By the end of the 16th century, more than 200 spa buildings had been built in the town. Today, there are 13 hot mineral springs. The best-known is the Vřídlo (Sprudel), which, at 72°C (162°F), is also the hottest.

Among the town's historic monuments are the 18th-century Baroque parish **church of Mary Magdalene**. The elegant 19th-century **Mill Colonnade** (Mlýnská kolonáda) is by Josef Zítek, architect of the National Theater (see p683) in Prague.

Karlsbad is also known for its Karlovy Vary china and Moser glass, and for summer concerts and cultural events.

Environs
Around 60 km (38 miles) southwest of Karlsbad is another of Bohemia's spa towns, **Marienbad** (Mariánské Lázně). Here, the cast-iron colonnade, with frescoes by Josef Vyleťal, is an impressive sight. There are also many pleasant walks in the local countryside, especially in the protected Slavkov Forest.

❺ Český Krumlov

180 km (112 miles) south of Prague. 🚐 14,000 🚉 🚌 ℹ náměstí Svornosti 2 (380 70 46 22). 🌐 ckrumlov.info

Of all the Czech Republic's medieval towns, Český Krumlov must rank as the finest. Almost entirely enclosed by a bend in the River Vltava, the beautifully preserved Inner Town (Vnitřní Město) appears to have changed very little in the last few hundred years, although some buildings suffered severe flood damage in 2002. A maze of narrow cobbled streets radiates out from the main square (Náměstí Svornosti), which is lined with elegant arcaded Renaissance buildings including the former town hall. On one of these streets – Horní – is the magnificent 16th-century sgraffitoed **Jesuit College** (now a hotel) and, opposite, a **museum** explaining the town's history. **Schiele Centrum** is housed in a 15th-century former brewery. The museum has an excellent collection of works by the Austrian painter Egon Schiele.

Český Krumlov's most famous sight is its 13th-century castle – the **Krumlovský Zámek** – in the Latrán quarter. In the older, lower part of the castle complex, the splendidly restored castle tower can be climbed for superb views of the whole town. Other highlights of the castle include a Rococo chapel, a lavishly decorated ballroom – the Maškarní sál – and the ornate 18th-century Rococo theater. The castle gardens provide a tranquil spot to sit and relax, while performances of opera and ballet take place in the gardens' open-air theater in July and August.

In summer, renting a canoe from one of a number of outlets in the town is a good way to enjoy the fine views of Český Krumlov from the river.

🏛 **Krumlovský Zámek**
Latrán. **Open** Apr–Oct: Tue–Sun.
📷 🎫

Český Krumlov's castle tower rising above the medieval Inner Town

Practical & Travel Information

The Czech Republic saw a vast increase in tourism following the overthrow of Communist rule in 1989. Since then, the country has responded well to the huge influx of visitors, and facilities such as banks and information centers have improved considerably. The best way to explore Prague is on foot; if you are traveling to places of interest outside the capital, buses and trains are reliable and inexpensive.

When to Visit

The busiest months are August and September, although Prague can be very crowded in June and at Easter also. The main sights are always packed at these times, but the crowds lend a carnival atmosphere, which can make a visit all the more enjoyable. Many sights are closed between October and April.

Tourist Information

Tourist information offices in the Czech Republic are run by several different agencies, including formerly state-owned **Čedok**. Many employ English speakers and offer a variety of English-language publications, maps, and guides. The efficient **Prague Information Service (PIS)** is the best source of tourist information for visitors to the capital. It has three offices in the city center, providing information in several languages, including English.

Visa Requirements

Citizens of the US, EU, Australia, New Zealand, and countries of the European Free Trade Association need a valid passport to enter the Czech Republic, and can stay for up to 90 days without needing a visa.

Safety and Emergencies

Violent crime against tourists is rare in the Czech Republic. The main problem, especially in Prague, is petty theft from cars, hotel rooms, and pockets. At night, lone women are advised to avoid Prague's Wenceslas Square, which used to be a hangout for prostitutes.

It is an unwritten law that you should have your passport with you at all times in the Czech Republic. Although you are unlikely to be asked to produce it, having it could save a lot of problems.

In case of an emergency, the numbers to call are listed in the directory opposite.

Health Issues

No inoculations are required for the Czech Republic. Visitors should take note that in winter, sulphur dioxide levels in Prague often exceed the World Health Organization's safety levels. For prescription and non-prescription medicines, visit a pharmacy (*lékárna*).

Facilities for the Disabled

Disabled travelers seeking advice on transportation, accommodations, and sight-seeing tours should contact the **Czech Association of Persons with Disabilities**, the **Prague Wheelchair Association**, or **Accessible Prague**. Other useful websites with information on disabled travel on public transportation are www.dpp.cz/en/barrier-free-travel (buses, trams, and metro) and www.cd.cz/en/vnitrostatni-cestovani/ (trains).

Banking and Currency

The Czech unit of currency is the Czech crown (Kč). Banking hours are generally 8am to 5pm Monday to Friday, with some branches closing at lunch. Bureaux de change in tourist spots are open every day, and some offer a 24-hour service. Although they give much better exchange rates than the banks, their commission charges are huge, often as high as 12 per cent. Traveler's checks can only be changed in banks. Credit cards are becoming more widely accepted in the Czech Republic, but never assume that you can pay with them.

Communications

Card-operated public phone booths are found all over the Czech Republic. You can buy phonecards (*telefonní karta*) from most tobacconists and newsstands. It is possible to make international calls from a public phone, a post office or a hotel, although the latter option is usually highly expensive.

Most post offices are open 8am–6pm Monday to Friday, and on Saturday mornings. Stamps (*známky*) are sold at most tobacconists and news-stands, as well as post offices.

Flying to the Czech Republic

Czech Airlines (ČSA) is the only airline that offers direct flights from the United States

The Climate of Czech Republic

The Czech Republic enjoys long, warm days in summer, the hottest months being June, July, and August. The winter months can get bitterly cold; temperatures often drop below freezing and heavy snowfall is not uncommon. The wettest months are October and November but frequent light showers can occur in the summer months as well.

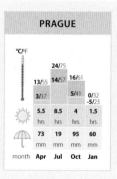

PRAGUE			
°C/°F			
	24/75		
13/55	14/57	16/61	
3/37		5/41	0/32
			-5/23
5.5 hrs	8.5 hrs	4 hrs	1.5 hrs
73 mm	19 mm	95 mm	60 mm
month Apr	Jul	Oct	Jan

to Prague. Other carriers, including **Delta Air Lines**, **KLM**, and **Lufthansa**, operate flights from the US and Canada to the Czech Republic, via another European city.

Carriers operating direct scheduled flights daily from the UK to Prague include **British Airways** and Czech Airlines (ČSA). Low-cost **easyJet** and **Jet2.com** have flights to Prague from several UK airports.

Among a number of airlines flying from Australia and New Zealand to Prague are Lufthansa and KLM. Flights from Australasia require a stopover in Europe or Asia.

Čedaz runs an inexpensive and efficient minibus service from Prague's Ruzyně airport to the city center.

Rail Travel

Prague is connected by rail to all the major capitals of Europe, although it can be a rather slow way of getting to the Czech Republic. For example, the journey time from London to Prague is 19 hours. Many international trains arrive at and depart from Hlavní nádraží, the city's biggest and busiest station.

The Czech Republic's state-run rail company, České Dráhy (ČD), operates several types of domestic routes. Supercity trains (SC) are the fastest trains and you pay a premium to travel on them. Express trains (*rychlík*) stop only at the major towns and cities. The slow trains, or *osobní*, stop at every station.

For help with timetables and advice on fares in Prague, visit the local PIS or Information at Hlavní nádraží station.

Traveling by Bus

Traveling by bus to Prague from other major European cities can be slow, but it is significantly less expensive than rail or air travel. Seats get booked up very quickly, especially in summer, so reserve well in advance. **Eurolines** is one of the main operators of international bus routes to Prague. Within the Czech Republic, long-distance buses are run by **Student Agency** and local companies. There is an extensive route network, and buses are often a less expensive way of traveling between towns than the trains. For popular routes, buy your ticket in advance from the bus station.

The main bus terminal in Prague is Florenc, which serves all international and long-distance domestic routes.

Traveling by Car

There are several highways in the Czech Republic, but to travel on them you must buy a tax disc (*dálniční známka*), valid for 10 days, one month, or a year and available at the border or from post offices and gas stations.

Most of the major car rental firms have offices in Prague and at Ruzyně airport, but renting is relatively expensive.

DIRECTORY

Czech Tourist Offices Abroad

UK
Czech Centre,
13 Harley Street,
London W1G 9QG.
Tel 020-7307 5180.
W czechcentres.cz
Czech Tourism
W czechtourism.com

US
321 East 73rd Street,
New York, NY 10021.
Tel 646-422 3399.
W new-york.czech
centres.cz

Tourist Offices in Prague

Čedok
Na příkopě 18, Prague.
Tel 800 112 112 (toll-free).
W cedok.cz

Prague Information Service
Tel 22 17 14 714
(walking tours).
W praguewelcome.cz

Embassies and Consulates

Australian Consulate
Klimentská 10, Prague.
Tel 22 17 29 260.

Canadian Embassy
Ve Struhách 2, Prague.
Tel 27 21 01 800.
W canada.cz

UK Embassy
Thunovská 14, Prague.
Tel 25 74 02 111.
W ukinczechrepublic.
fco.gov.uk

US Embassy
Tržiště 15, Prague.
Tel 25 70 22 000.
W czech.prague.
usembassy.gov

Emergency Numbers

Ambulance, Fire, Police
Tel 112 (English).

Facilities for the Disabled

Accessible Prague
W accessibleprague.
com

Czech Association of Persons with Disabilities
Tel 22 23 17 489.

Prague Wheelchair Association
Benediktská 6, Prague.
Tel 22 48 27 210.

Airlines

British Airways
Tel 23 90 00 299.
Tel 0870-850 9850 (UK).
Tel 1-800-AIRWAYS (US).
W britishairways.com

Czech Airlines
Tel 23 90 07 007.
Tel 207-365 9189 (UK).
W csa.cz

Delta Air Lines
Tel 23 30 90 933.
Tel 800-241 4141 (US).
W delta.com

easyJet
W easyjet.com

Jet2.com
W jet2.com

KLM
Tel 23 30 90 933.
Tel 800-618 0104 (US).
W klm.com

Lufthansa
Tel 23 40 08 234.
Tel 1800-645 3880 (US).
W lufthansa.com

Bus Companies

Eurolines
Tel 24 50 05 245.
Tel 08717-818 181 (UK).
W eurolines.co.uk

Student Agency
W studentagency.cz

Where to Stay

Prague

LITTLE QUARTER:
Design Hotel Sax   ⓚ
Modern   **Map** B3
Jánský vršek 328/3, Praha 1
Tel *25 75 31 268*
Ⓦ hotelsax.cz
Comfortable and charming hotel
decked out in vintage furnishings.

LITTLE QUARTER:
Domus Henrici   ⓚⓚ
Boutique   **Map** A3
Loretánská 11, Praha 1
Tel *22 05 11 369*
Ⓦ domus-henrici.cz
Housed in a historical building
equipped with modern amenities.

NEW TOWN: Alton   ⓚ
Budget
Legerova 62, Praha 2
Tel *22 25 24 066*
Ⓦ altonhotel.cz
A neat, simple, and friendly hotel
with affordable en-suite rooms.

NEW TOWN: Anna   ⓚ
Budget
Budečská 17, Praha 2
Tel *22 25 13 111*
Ⓦ hotelanna.cz
Stay in Art Nouveau rooms at this
hotel with a lovely breakfast
room and a quiet location.

NEW TOWN: Icon   ⓚⓚ
Modern
U Jámé 6, Praha 1
Tel *22 16 34 100*
Ⓦ iconhotel.eu
Hip hotel with wonderful rooms,
all-day breakfasts, and efficient
staff. Spa and lounge bar, too.

NEW TOWN: Le Palais   ⓚⓚ
Luxury
U Zvonarky 1, Praha 2
Tel *23 46 34 111*
Ⓦ palaishotel.cz
A *belle époque* hotel with plush,
bright rooms, attentive staff, and
a great wellness center.

NEW TOWN: Carlo IV   ⓚⓚⓚ
Luxury
Senovážné náměstí 13, Praha 1
Tel *22 45 93 111*
Ⓦ prague.boscolohotels.com
This hotel boasts Italian opulence
and impressive spa facilities.

OLD TOWN: Fusion   ⓚⓚ
Boutique   **Map** F4
Panská 9, Praha 1
Tel *22 62 22 800*
Ⓦ fusionhotels.com
A quirky hotel with industrial-
chic rooms and a rooftop terrace.

DK Choice

OLD TOWN: Josef   ⓚⓚ
Boutique   **Map** E3
Rybná 20, Praha 1
Tel *22 17 00 111*
Ⓦ hoteljosef.com
A beautiful modern hotel, the
Josef features lots of white
surfaces and lovely, color-
coordinated rooms, with
interiors designed by Eva Jiřičná.
Other perks include a truly
outstanding breakfast, a small
but well-equipped gym on the
top floor, and multilingual staff.

OLD TOWN:
Maximilian   ⓚⓚ
Modern   **Map** E2
Haštalská 14, Praha 1
Tel *22 53 03 118*
Ⓦ maximilianhotel.com
This comfortable establishment
is more popularly known as the
"Goldfish Hotel" due to the
optional pets offered to guests.
All rooms have DVD/CD players.

OLD TOWN: Kempinski
Hotel Hybernska   ⓚⓚⓚ
Luxury
Hybernská 12, Praha 1
Tel *22 62 26 111*
Ⓦ kempinski-prague.com
A beautifully reconstructed hotel
with large rooms, abundant
amenities, and a lovely garden.

OLD TOWN: Paříž   ⓚⓚⓚ
Luxury   **Map** F3
U Obecního domu 1, Praha 1
Tel *420 222 195 195*
Ⓦ hotel-pariz.cz
The beautiful rooms and *fin-de-
siècle* decor at Paříž contribute to
the creation of a luxurious vibe.

Rest of the Czech Republic

BRNO: Holiday Inn   ⓚⓚ
Luxury
Křížkovského 20, 603 00
Tel *54 31 22 111*
Ⓦ hibrno.cz
The Holiday Inn offers large
rooms in warm colors and high
standards of service. Located
near the city's trade-fair grounds.

ČESKY KRUMLOV: Leonardo   ⓚ
Boutique
Soukenická 33, 381 01
Tel *38 07 25 911*
Ⓦ hotel-leonardo.cz
Situated in a 16th-century
building, the Leonardo features
lovely wooden ceilings and
a Baroque staircase.

KARLSBAD (KARLOVY VARY):
Grandhotel Pupp   ⓚⓚ
Luxury
Mírové náměstí 2, 360 91
Tel *35 31 09 111*
Ⓦ pupp.cz
The 18th-century Pupp offers
luxurious rooms with mod cons,
and a Neo-Baroque concert hall.

KUTNÁ HORA:
U Vlašského Dvora   ⓚ
Budget
28 října 511, 284 01
Tel *32 75 14 618*
Ⓦ vlasskydvur.cz
In a 15th-century building, with
well-appointed rooms that have
views over the Old Town.

OLOMOUC: Arigone   ⓚ
Boutique
Univerzitní 20, 779 00
Tel *58 52 32 351*
Ⓦ arigone.cz
This stylish hotel in the historic
center boasts Romanesque
stonework and en-suite rooms.

Step back to the funky 1970s at Design Hotel Sax, Prague

Where to Eat and Drink

The rainforest-inspired decor at Lehká Hlava, Prague's premier vegetarian restaurant

Prague

LITTLE QUARTER:
Café Lounge   Ⓚ
Café
Plaská 615/8, Praha 1
Tel *25 74 04 020*
A beautiful café with a secret courtyard. The great coffee and creative menu make this a go-to place from morning till night.

LITTLE QUARTER:
La Terrassa   ⓀⓀ
Spanish
Janáčkovo nábřeží – Dětský ostrov, Praha 5
Tel *72 51 61 616*
Enjoy tapas and other Spanish fare on a beautifully renovated boat. Attentive staff and a good wine list ensure a stream of regular customers.

DK Choice

LITTLE QUARTER:
Lehká Hlava   ⓀⓀ
Vegetarian   **Map** D4
Boršov 2/280, Praha 1
Tel *22 22 20 665*
One of the best vegetarian restaurants in Prague, with a creative take on its extensive menu – ranging from Asian to Mexican to Lebanese. The Thai red curry with tofu is a real treat, and the burrito will probably force diners to skip dessert. Hip ambience and cool interiors.

LITTLE QUARTER: SaSaZu   ⓀⓀ
Asian
Bubenské nábřeží 13, Praha 7
Tel *28 40 97 455*
Classic Indonesian, Thai, and Vietnamese dishes are prepared with flair and served in Oriental-palace surroundings. There is also a popular nightclub in the same building, so stay after dinner for a fun night out.

LITTLE QUARTER:
Kampa Park   ⓀⓀⓀ
Fusion   **Map** C3
Na Kampě 8b, Praha 1
Tel *29 68 26 102*
The place for modern fusion cuisine with a focus on seafood, served up in extravagantly decorated rooms on Kampa Island, on the Vltava river.

NEW TOWN: Nota Bene   ⓀⓀ
Czech
Mikovcova 4, Praha 2
Tel *72 12 99 131*   **Closed** *Sun*
A rotating beer list and authentic Czech fare make Nota Bene one of the hottest places around. Head to the basement beer hall for beer and snacks.

OLD TOWN: Lokál   Ⓚ
Czech   **Map** E3
Dlouhá 33, Praha 1
Tel *22 23 16 265*
This old-style pub serves Czech classics and lots of refreshing Pilsner Urquell beer. Modern lighting and long wooden tables create a cozy but cool ambience.

OLD TOWN: Sansho   ⓀⓀ
Fusion
Petrská 25, Praha 1
Tel *22 23 17 425*   **Closed** *Sun & Mon*
Quality Asian-influenced fusion cuisine in a casual living-room space. The menu depends on what is fresh at the local market.

OLD TOWN:
Grosseto Marina   ⓀⓀⓀ
Italian   **Map** D3
Alšovo nábřeží, Praha 1
Tel *60 54 54 020*
Enjoy superb service, beautiful river views, and excellent Italian food – pasta dishes, pizzas, and fabulous desserts – on a boat. The top deck is a great place to have a drink.

OLD TOWN:
La Degustation   ⓀⓀⓀ
International   **Map** E2
Haštalská 18, Praha 1
Tel *22 23 11 234*
Step into La Degustation for the ultimate Prague dining experience. Expect several courses of imaginative dishes prepared with skill and verve.

OLD TOWN: Plzeňská   ⓀⓀⓀ
Czech
Náměstí republiky 5, Praha 1
Tel *22 20 02 770*
An enjoyable evening is in store at this restaurant with fabulous Art Nouveau interiors, friendly staff, and authentic Czech dishes.

Rest of the Czech Republic

ČESKY KRUMLOV:
Pivovar Eggenberg   ⓀⓀ
Czech
Latrán 27, 381 01
Tel *38 07 11 917*
Beer sets the tone at this eatery, located in the cooling rooms of a former brewery. It is a good place to enjoy hearty Czech fare that can be washed down with local light and dark beers.

KARLSBAD (KARLOVY VARY):
Lázně 5   ⓀⓀⓀ
Czech/Mediterranean
Smetanovy sady 1145/1, 360 01
Tel *60 22 66 088*
Located in a historic spa building, this elegant restaurant offers traditional Czech fare as well as Mediterranean cuisine. Lázně 5 is justly famous for its steaks.

OLOMOUC:
Svatováclavský Pivovar   ⓀⓀ
Czech
Mariánská 4, 779 00
Tel *58 52 07 517*
A centrally located restaurant with a huge range of own-brewed beers, daily specials, and a long menu of meat and dumplings.

HUNGARY

Uniquely in central Europe, Hungary is peopled by descendants of the Magyars, a race from central Asia who settled here at the end of the 9th century. In more recent times, the country has fought against Turkish, German, Austrian, and Russian occupiers, yet its rich indigenous culture remains intact. In 1989, Hungary became the first Soviet Bloc country to embrace Western-style democracy.

Hungary has an extremely varied landscape, with forests and mountains dominating the north and a vast plain covering the rest of the country. The Tisza river and its tributaries shape the eastern regions, while the west has Lake Balaton, one of the largest lakes in Europe. The Danube flows through the heart of the country, bisecting the capital, Budapest, where one-fifth of the population lives. Ethnically the country is 92 percent Magyar, 3 percent Roma, and the rest divided between Germans, Slovaks, Slovens, and others. About one percent of the population is of Jewish origin.

History

In AD 100, the Romans established the town of Aquincum near modern-day Budapest, and ruled the area corresponding roughly to Hungary (then called Pannonia) for three centuries. The arrival of the Huns in the early 5th century led to the complete withdrawal of the Romans. After the death of Attila the Hun in 453, the area was ruled by the Goths, the Longobards, and the Avars. The ancestors of the modern Hungarians, the Magyars, migrated from the Urals in 896, under the leadership of Prince Árpád, whose dynasty ruled until 1301, when King András III died without leaving an heir.

The throne then passed to a series of foreign kings, including the French Angevins and the Lithuanian Jagiellos, but the country flourished, and during the reign of Mátyás Corvinus (1458–90), it became the greatest monarchy in Middle Europe. Mátyás's marriage to Beatrice, a Neapolitan princess, saw the Renaissance blossom throughout Hungary, but all was soon eclipsed by a series of Turkish invasions. The Turks won a major victory at the Battle of Mohács in 1526, then they returned in 1541 to take Buda, which became the capital of Ottoman Hungary. To quell the Turkish advance, the Austrians, under Ferdinand of Habsburg, occupied western (or "Royal") Hungary, while the central plains stayed under Ottoman

The Gellért monument in Budapest, dedicated to a martyred 11th-century bishop

◄ The dramatic interior of Dohany Street Great Synagogue in Budapest control; the eastern region, including Transylvania (now in Romania), became a semi-autonomous land, feudally tied to the Turks.

Christian armies led by the Habsburgs fought to recapture Buda, and finally defeated the Turks in 1686. Economic prosperity came with Austrian rule, but nationalism was cruelly suppressed, culminating in a major uprising in 1848. After crushing the rebellion, Emperor Franz Joseph I sought to unite the two nations, and so created the Dual Monarchy of Austro-Hungary in 1867.

Following World War I, the Habsburg Empire was dismantled, and Hungary lost two-thirds of its territory to the "successor states" of Yugoslavia, Czechoslovakia, and Romania. It was to regain these territories that Hungary backed Germany in World War II, but in 1945, Budapest was

Mátyás Corvinus, King of Hungary (1458–90)

taken by the Russians. The subsequent Communist rule was ruthlessly upheld, most visibly in 1956 when an attempted revolution was crushed by Soviet tanks. Nevertheless, free elections finally took place in 1989, resulting in victory for the democratic opposition. Since then, the country has invested heavily in tourism, which is now a major source of income.

Language and Culture

Modern Hungarian, like Finnish, derives from a language originally spoken by the Finno-Ugric tribes of the Urals. It differs greatly from most other European languages, although Slavic, German, Caucasian, Latin, and Turkic words have been incorporated.

Traditional peasant culture was all but destroyed in the 20th century, but folk songs and dances still survive; Christmas and Easter are the best times

Exploring Hungary

Budapest has a pivotal location at the heart of central Europe, and it is also the perfect base for exploring Hungary itself. Szentendre, with its Serbian religious art, and Esztergom, where Hungary's first Christian king was crowned, are both only a short drive north, while Lake Balaton lies only a little further west. Pécs, a treasure trove of European history, lies to the south, while Eger and Tokaj stand in the wine-producing area to the east; the former, with its castle and Turkish minaret, is one of Hungary's most popular towns.

Sights at a Glance

1. Budapest pp694–9
2. Szentendre
3. Esztergom
4. Lake Balaton
5. Pécs
6. Eger
7. Tokaj

0 kilometers 50

0 miles 50

Chess-players in a bathhouse in Budapest

to witness these, particularly in the countryside. Musically, the country has always had much to be proud of, including composers Franz Liszt and Béla Bartók, while in literature, the Communist years produced some very powerful voices, among them Tibor Déry and István Örkény. Otherwise, the country is best known for its cuisine, which incorporates a wide range of wines and meat-based dishes (such as goulash), the latter invariably spiced with paprika, the country's most famous export.

KEY DATES IN HUNGARIAN HISTORY

c.AD 100 Romans establish Aquincum

c.410 Huns overrun the region

896 Magyar tribes arrive

1001 Coronation of István I, Hungary's first king

1300s Angevin rule begins

1458–90 Reign of Mátyás Corvinus

1526 Turks win the Battle of Mohács

1526–41 Turks conquer Buda on three occasions

1541 The start of Ottoman rule

1686 Christian troops enter Buda, ending Turkish rule in Hungary

1848 Hungarian Nationalist uprising

1867 Compromise with Austria gives Hungary independence in internal affairs

1873 Buda and Pest become Budapest

1918 With the break-up of the Austro-Hungarian Empire, Hungary gains independence after nearly 400 years of foreign rule

1941 Hungary enters World War II

1945 Russian army takes Budapest

1956 Russia suppresses a nationalist uprising

1989 Hungary proclaimed a democratic republic

2003 Hungary becomes a member of EU

2014 Viktor Orban wins a second consecutive term as prime minister

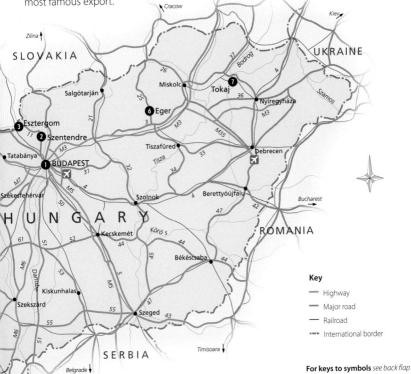

Key

— Highway

— Major road

— Railroad

--- International border

For keys to symbols see back flap

❶ Budapest

Budapest was founded in 1873 after the unification of three separate towns, Buda and Óbuda on the west bank of the Danube and Pest on the east. The city dates largely from the late 19th and early 20th centuries and is very much the creation of the nationalist enthusiasm of that era. All three towns had originally grown up in the second half of the twelfth century and Buda was the seat of Hungary's rulers from 1247. Turkish rule from 1541 to 1686, when it was recaptured by the Habsburgs, left little mark, except for the city's wonderful bathhouses.

Sights at a Glance

① Royal Palace
② Mátyás Church
③ Gellért Hotel and Bath Complex
④ Inner City Parish Church
⑤ Hungarian National Museum
⑥ State Opera
⑦ St. Stephen's Basilica
⑧ Parliament
⑨ Museum of Fine Arts
⑩ Vajdahunyad Castle

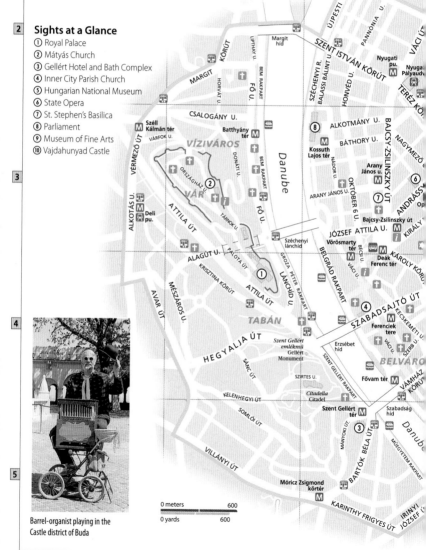

Barrel-organist playing in the Castle district of Buda

0 meters 600
0 yards 600

Getting Around

Trams are a convenient means of transportation for tourists, especially the 18, 19, and 61 on the Buda side and the 2, 4, and 6 in Pest. There are also some 200 bus routes. The four metro lines and the HÉV rail lines link the center with the suburbs.

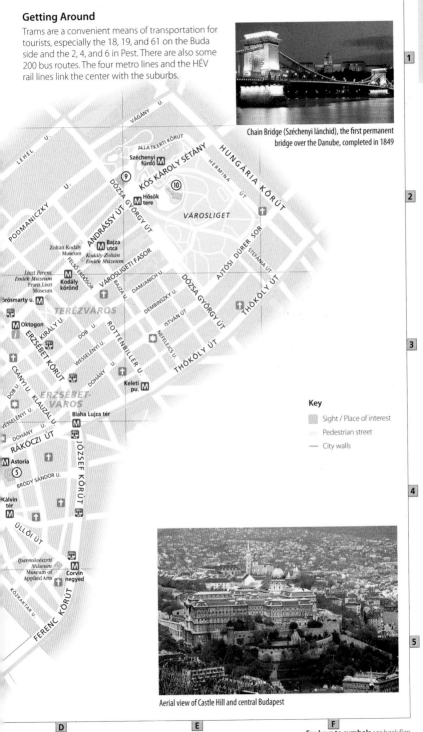

Chain Bridge (Széchenyi lánchid), the first permanent bridge over the Danube, completed in 1849

VÁGÁNY U.

LEHEL U.

U.

ALLATKERTI KÖRÚT

Széchenyi fürdő Ⓜ

KÓS KÁROLY SÉTÁNY

⑨

HUNGÁRIA KÖRÚT

HERMINA U.

PODMANICZKY U.

DÓZSA GYÖRGY ÚT

Ⓜ Hősök tere

⑩

VÁROSLIGET

✝

ANDRÁSSY ÚT

Zoltán Kodály Museum

Ⓜ Bajza utca

Kodály Zoltán Emlék Múzeum

AJTÓSI DÜRER SOR

STEFÁNIA ÚT

Liszt Ferenc Emlék Múzeum Franz Liszt Museum

FELSŐERDŐSOR

Ⓜ Kodály körönd

VÁROSLIGETI FASOR

BAJZA U.

DAMJANICH U.

DÓZSA GYÖRGY ÚT

THÖKÖLY ÚT

Vörösmarty u. Ⓜ

TERÉZVÁROS

✝

DEMBINSZKY U.

✝

Ⓜ Oktogon

KIRÁLY U.

DOB U.

ROTTENBILLER U.

ISTVÁN U.

NEFELEJCS U.

ℹ

ERZSÉBET KÖRÚT

WESSELÉNYI U.

THÖKÖLY ÚT

✝

CSÁNYI U.

DOHÁNY U.

✝ Keleti pu. Ⓜ

DOB U. KLAUZÁL U.

ERZSÉBET- VÁROS

WESSELÉNYI U.

Blaha Lujza tér

DOHÁNY U.

RÁKÓCZI ÚT

JÓZSEF KÖRÚT

Ⓜ Astoria ✝

⑤

BRÓDY SÁNDOR U.

Kálvin tér

Ⓜ ✝

ÜLLŐI ÚT

Iparművészeti Múzeum Museum of Applied Arts

Ⓜ Corvin negyed

KÖZRAKTÁR U.

FERENC KÖRÚT

Key

░░ Sight / Place of interest

░░ Pedestrian street

— City walls

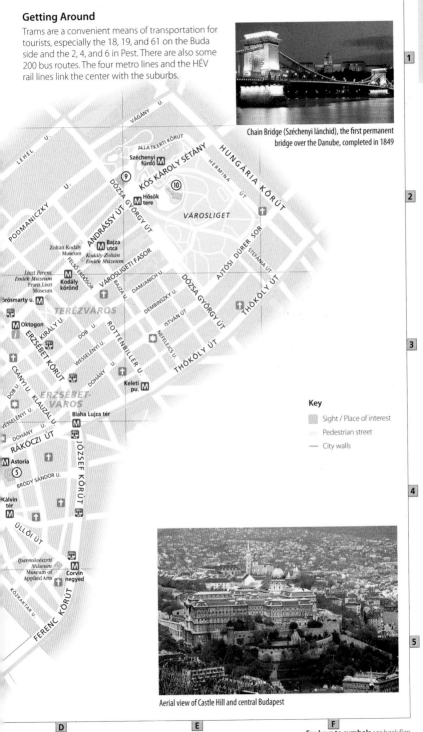

Aerial view of Castle Hill and central Budapest

Buda

In 1247, Béla IV chose Buda, on the Danube's west bank, as his capital city. Its position, at 60 m (197 ft) above the river, made it a strategic choice. Buda expanded during Angevin rule, reaching a zenith under Mátyás Corvinus (1458–90), although further development was hindered by the Turkish occupation of 1541–1686. The Habsburgs' attempts to recover the city were devastating and by the time of its liberation, the city had been largely destroyed. In the 18th and 19th centuries, the Habsburgs set about rebuilding the palace and the old town, adding some magnificent buildings, but most had to be rebuilt again after the siege of 1945.

altarpieces, some Renaissance and Baroque art, and a wonderful selection of 19th- and 20th-century Hungarian works.

Notable early works include *The Madonna of Bártfa* (1465–70), and the folding St. Anne Altarpiece (1510–20).

Among the 19th-century works, look out for the historical scenes by Bertalan Székely and the landscapes of Mihály Munkácsy (1844–1900), widely held to be Hungary's greatest artist. The 20th-century works by Tivadar Kosztka Csontváry give a unique, idiosyncratic vision of the world.

St. Anne Altarpiece, National Gallery

The rebuilt Royal Palace with a grand statue of the heroic Eugene of Savoy

① Royal Palace

Színház utca. 5, 16, Várbusz.

King Béla IV (1235–70) built a royal castle in Buda, but its exact location is unknown. Around 1400, it was replaced by a Gothic palace, subsequently remodeled in Renaissance style by King Mátyás in 1458. Under Turkish rule, the palace was used to stable horses and store gunpowder, leading to its destruction in 1686 during the reconquest. A new palace, begun in 1719 by the Habsburgs, grew in size and grandeur under Maria Teresa, but this too was destroyed in the uprising of 1849 and had to be rebuilt in the second half of the 19th century.

When the Habsburg palace was again razed to the ground in February 1945, remains of the 15th-century Gothic palace were uncovered. These were incorporated into the restored palace that visitors see today.

Various statues, gateways, and fountains have survived from the 19th-century palace. In the northwest courtyard stands the Mátyás Fountain (1904), depicting Mátyás Corvinus (1458–90) and his legendary love, the peasant girl, Ilonka. In front of the palace's rebuilt dome stands an equestrian statue (1900) of Prince Eugene of Savoy, victor of the Battle of Zenta against the Turks in 1697.

Today, the palace houses a series of important national collections, including the Széchenyi National Library, with over five million books and manuscripts, the National Gallery, the Budapest History Museum, and the Museum of Contemporary History.

🏛 Hungarian National Gallery

Royal Palace A-B-C-D Wings, Szent György tér 2. **Tel** (1) 201 90 82. 5, 16, Várbusz. **Open** Tue–Sun.
w mng.hu

Established in 1957, the National Gallery has a superb collection of Hungarian art from medieval times to the 20th century. The permanent exhibits include a section of sculpture and stonework – the Lapidarium. There are also regular temporary exhibitions.

Highlights include a carved stone head of King Béla III, from c.1200, religious artifacts spanning several centuries, including many fine Gothic

🏛 Budapest History Museum

Royal Palace E Wing, Szent György tér 2. **Tel** (1) 487 8800. 5, 16, 116A, Várbusz. **Open** Tue–Sun.
w btm.hu

The city's history museum (*Budapesti Történeti Múzeum*), also known as the Castle Museum, illustrates the city's evolution from its origins under the Romans.

Damage to the palace in World War II led to chambers dating from the Middle Ages being uncovered in the south wing. These were recreated in the basement.

The ground floor exhibits cover the period from Roman times to the 15th century and include some Gothic statues, unearthed here in 1974. The first floor traces the history of the city from 1686 (the end of Turkish rule) to the present.

15th-century majolica floor in the Budapest History Museum

West front of the Mátyás Church, with the tiled Béla Tower on the left

② Mátyás Church

Szentháromság tér 2. **Tel** (1) 489 07 16.
🚌 5, 16, 16A, 116, Várbusz. **Open** daily.
Closed Sat pm, Sun am. 🖼 🎦 ♿
🌐 matyas-templom.hu

This church is mainly a Neo-Gothic reconstruction dating from 1874–96. Most of the original church (13th–15th centuries) was lost when the Turks turned it into their Great Mosque in 1541. The building had to be restored again after damage in World War II. The great rose window has been faithfully reproduced in its original Gothic style.

The tombs of King Béla III (13th century) and his wife can be seen in the Trinity Chapel, while the Mary Portal (near the main altar) is considered the finest example of Gothic stone carving in Hungary. Also fascinating is a Baroque statue of the Madonna; according to legend, the original was set into a wall during the Turkish occupation. When the church was virtually destroyed in 1686, the Madonna made a miraculous reappearance, which the Turks took as an omen of defeat.

Mátyás church stands in the heart of Buda's old town, which developed to the north of the Royal Palace from the 1200s onward.

In front of the church is Holy Trinity Square, with a memorial column to those who died in the plague of 1691. On the square stands the Old Town Hall, an elegant Baroque building with an onion-domed clock tower.

Baroque Madonna, Mátyás Church

③ Gellért Hotel and Bath Complex

Kelenhegyi út 4. **Tel** (1) 466 61 66.
🚌 7, 86. 🚋 18, 19, 47, 49. **Open** daily.
🖼 ♿ 🌐 gellertbath.com

The earliest reference to the presence of healing waters at this site is found in the 13th century. In the later Middle Ages, a hospital stood here and then, during the Turkish occupation, baths were built. The area takes its name from Bishop Gellért, whose monument on the hill is visible from many parts of the city. He was supposedly martyred here in 1046 by a group opposed to the introduction of Christianity. From the top of the hill, one can admire a beautiful view of the whole of Budapest.

The Gellért Hotel, with its famous spa, was built between 1912 and 1918 in the Secession style, at the foot of the hill. It boasts elaborate mosaics, stained-glass windows, statues, and fanciful balconies fronting the rooms. Its eastern-style towers and turrets offer superb views.

The complex houses an institute of water therapy. The baths are separated into different areas for men and women. Each has plunge pools, a sauna, and a steam bath. The facilities have been modernized, but the glorious Secession interiors remain.

There is also an outdoor swimming pool with a wave machine, installed in 1927 and still in operation. The baths and health spa, with their sun terraces, restaurants, and cafés, are open to the public as well as to hotel guests.

Other Museums in Budapest

Practical Information

Franz Liszt Museum:
Vörösmarty utca 35. **Tel** (1) 322 98 04. **Open** Mon–Sat. 🖼
🌐 lisztmuseum.hu
Museum in a house built in 1877 for Liszt (1811–86).
Kodály Memorial Museum:
Andrássy út 89. **Tel** (1) 352 7106.
Open Wed–Sun. 🖼
🌐 kodaly-inst.hu
The house in which the composer Kodály (1882–1967) lived and worked.
Museum of Applied Arts:
Üllői út 33–37. **Tel** (1) 352 71 06.
Open Tue–Sun. 🖼 ♿
🌐 imm.hu
Fine collection of decorative arts, especially Art Nouveau artifacts.
Museum of Contemporary Art and Ludwig Museum:
Komor Marcell utca 1.
Tel (1) 456 51 07.
Open Tue–Sun. 🖼 ♿
🌐 ludwigmuseum.hu
A contemporary art museum with works by Warhol and Hockney.

Transport

Franz Liszt Museum:
Ⓜ Vörösmarty utca.
Kodály Memorial Museum:
Ⓜ Kodály Körönd
Museum of Applied Arts:
Ⓜ Ferenc körút.
Museum of Contemporary Art and Ludwig Museum:
🚌 15, Csepeli HÉV. 🚋 1, 2, 4, 6.

The men's section at the Gellért Baths

Pest

At the end of the 17th century, much of the walled city of Pest, on the east bank of the Danube, was in ruins and few residents remained. Gradually, new residential districts began to be developed, extending beyond the medieval walls, and people started to return.

After a flood in 1838, which destroyed most of the rural dwellings in the areas around Pest, redevelopment schemes introduced grand houses and apartment blocks. The area of Városliget (City Park), once an expanse of marshland, was also developed in the 19th century.

The first bridge linking Pest and Buda was built in 1766. The two cities were united as Budapest in 1873.

The predominantly Baroque nave of the Inner City Parish Church

④ Inner City Parish Church

Március 15 tér 2. **Tel** (1) 318 3108. Ⓜ Ferenciek tere. **Open** daily.

During the reign of István I (AD 1001–38), a small church stood on this site. St. Gellért was buried here after his martyrdom in 1046.

Work began on the Inner City Parish Church (Belvárosi Plébánia templom), adding to the existing building, in the 12th century. It is the oldest building in Pest. In the 14th century, it was remodeled in Gothic style, and later used as a mosque by the Turks. After the fire of 1723, it was partly rebuilt in the Baroque style.

On the south side of the church is a Renaissance tabernacle bearing the Crest of Pest, created in the 16th century. Close to the main altar is a reminder of Turkish occupation: a mihrab, or prayer niche, indicating the direction of Mecca.

⑤ Hungarian National Museum

Múzeum körút 14–16. **Tel** (1) 338 21 22. **Open** Tue–Sun. Ⓜ Kálvin tér, Astoria. 🚌 7, 9, 15, 173. 🚋 47, 49. 📷 ♿ 🅆 hnm.hu

The Hungarian National Museum was founded in 1802, when Count Ferenc Széchényi gave his personal collection to the nation. It is housed in an impressive Neoclassical edifice (1837–47).

In 1848, on the steps of the museum, poet Sándor Petőfi first read his National Song, which sparked the uprising against Habsburg rule. A re-enactment is staged each year on March 15.

The museum's eclectic exhibits span the 11th century to the present day. Items on display include an 18th-century campaign chest, decorative weapons of Transylvanian princes, and a printing press used to print nationalist propaganda in 1848.

The museum is home to the Coronation Mantle donated by St. Stephen in 1031. It is made of Byzantine silks and is one of the oldest and best-preserved textile masterpieces in Europe.

Baroque campaign chest in the National Museum

Lavish interior of the 19th-century State Opera House

⑥ State Opera

Andrássy út 22. **Tel** (1) 814 71 00. Ⓜ Opera. **Open** daily. 📷 ♿ 3pm & 4pm obligatory. ♿ 📷 🅆 opera.hu

The State Opera (Magyar Állami Operaház), opened in 1884, was the life's work of architect Miklós Ybl. The facade expresses musical themes, with statues of two of Hungary's most prominent composers, Ferenc Erkel and Franz Liszt. The opulence of the foyer, with its chandeliers, murals, and vaulted ceiling, is echoed in the grandeur of the sweeping main staircase and of the three-story auditorium.

⑦ St. Stephen's Basilica

Szent István tér 1. **Tel** (1) 388 21 51. Ⓜ Deák Ferenc tér. Treasury: **Open** daily. 📷 ♿ ✝ daily. 🅆 bazilika.biz

This Neoclassical church, dedicated to St. Stephen, or István, Hungary's first Christian king (1001–38), was built in 1851–1905 on a Greek cross floor plan. The church received the title Basilica Minor in 1938, the 900th anniversary of the king's death. On the main altar is a marble statue of the saint; scenes from his life are depicted behind the altar. A painting to the right of the main entrance shows István dedicating Hungary to the Virgin Mary. His mummified forearm is kept in the Chapel of the Holy Right Hand.

The main entrance to the basilica is a massive door, decorated with carved heads of the 12 apostles. The dome reaches 96 m (315 ft) and is visible all over Budapest. Its interior is decorated with mosaics by Károly Lotz.

The basilica also has two distinctive towers. The one to the left of the main door houses a bell weighing 9 tons. This was funded by German Catholics to compensate for the loss of the original bell, which was looted by the Nazis in 1944.

⑧ Parliament

Kossuth Lajos tér 1–3. **Tel** (1) 441 40 00. **M** Kossuth tér. 70, 78. 2, 2A. **Open** daily. **Closed** during ceremonies. (free for EU citizens). **parlament.hu**

The Parliament (Országház) is Hungary's largest building – 268 m (880 ft) long, 96 m (315 ft) high, with 691 rooms. Built between 1884 and 1902, it was based on London's Houses of Parliament (see p53). Although the facade is Neo-Gothic, the ground plan follows Baroque conventions, with a magnificent dome at the center. Beneath it is the Domed Hall, off which is the Gobelin Hall, with a Gobelin tapestry of Árpád (see p691) and fellow Magyar chiefs

Tapestry of Árpád and Magyar chiefs in the Parliament building

taking a blood oath. The greatest artists of the day decorated the interior of the building, and there are some spectacular ceiling frescoes by Károly Lotz and György Kiss.

Between the Domed Hall and the south wing is the National Assembly Hall. On the opposite side is the Congress Hall, a virtual mirror image of the National Assembly Hall. Both have public galleries.

Since 2000, the royal insignia have been displayed here.

⑨ Museum of Fine Arts

Hősök tere. **Tel** (1) 469 71 00. **M** Hősök tere. 20, 20E, 30, 30A 105. 72, 75, 79. **Open** Tue–Sun. **w szepmuveszeti.hu**

In 1870, the state bought a magnificent collection of paintings from the Esterházy family. Enriched by donations and acquisitions, the collection moved to its present location in 1906. As well as great European

paintings from every era from the Middle Ages to the 20th century, there are Egyptian, Greek, and Roman antiquities. Renaissance pieces include a wonderful unfinished Raphael known as the *Esterházy Madonna* and a small bronze by Leonardo da Vinci of François I of France. There are also paintings by Holbein and Dürer, seven works by El Greco, and a fabulous collection of old master drawings.

French 19th-century art is also very well represented, with works by Manet, Gauguin, and Toulouse-Lautrec.

⑩ Vajdahunyad Castle

Városliget. **Tel** (1) 422 07 65. **M** Széchenyi Fürdő. **Open** Tue–Sun. **w mmgm.hu**

This fantastical castle stands among trees at the edge of the lake in Városliget. It is in fact a complex of pavilions illustrating the evolution of Hungarian architecture. Created for the 1896 Millennium Celebrations as a temporary exhibit, it proved so popular that it was rebuilt permanently, in brick.

The pavilions are grouped in chronological order of style: Romanesque is followed by Gothic, Renaissance, Baroque, and so on, but the elements are linked to suggest a single, cohesive design. Details from more than 20 of Hungary's best-loved buildings are reproduced.

The greatest emphasis is given to the medieval period, which is thought to be the most glorious in the country's history.

View across the lake of the Gothic (left) and Renaissance (right) sections of the Vajdahunyad Castle

❷ Szentendre

20,000. from Budapest. Dumtsa Jenő utca 22 **Tel** (26) 312 657. **szentendreprogram.hu**

Szentendre was settled by Serbian refugees, who first came here in the 14th century. After the Turkish occupation of Belgrade in 1690, more Serbs arrived, ushering in a period of great prosperity.

The Slavic interiors of the town's many churches are filled with incense, icons, and candlelight. **Blagovestenska Church** on Fő tér, the main square, has a magnificent iconostasis, while other sites worth visiting are **Belgrade Cathedral**, for Sunday Mass, and the bishop's palace. Next door, the **Museum of Serbian Art** contains displays of icons and other religious artifacts.

Many artists have made their home in Szentendre, including the Hungarian ceramic artist, Margit Kovács (1902–77). Her work can be seen at the **Margit Kovács Museum**.

Margit Kovács Museum
Vastag György utca 1. **Tel** (26) 310 244.
Open Mon–Sun.

❸ Esztergom

30,000. from Budapest.

St. István, Hungary's first Christian king, was baptized in Esztergom and later crowned here on Christmas Day in AD 1000. Dominating the city's skyline is the huge **Catholic Cathedral**, built in the early 19th century on the site of a 12th-century church. In the treasury are religious artifacts from the original church. The 16th-century marble Bakócz burial chapel, next to the southern entrance, was built by Florentine craftsmen. South of the cathedral, the remains of Esztergom's **Castle** date from the 10th century.

In the picturesque old town, Esztergom's central square is bordered by many lively pavement cafés.

Castle
Szent István tér 1. **Tel** (33) 415 986.
Open Tue–Sun.

The Tihany Peninsula, jutting out into Lake Balaton

Esztergom's vast cathedral, on the banks of the Danube River

❹ Lake Balaton

Siófok: to/from Balatonfüred. Viztorony, Pf: 75 **Tel** (84) 310 117. Balatonfüred: to/from Siófok and Tihany. Kisfaludy u. 1 (87) 580 480.

Every summer Lake Balaton, Europe's largest fresh-water lake, attracts thousands of vacationers. The southern shore is the more developed, with sandy beaches and a wide choice of tourist accommodations. The largest resort is **Siófok**, characterized by high-rise buildings, lively bars, and noisy nightlife. By day, windsurfing, sailing, and pleasure cruises are available.

Those in search of a more peaceful atmosphere should head for **Balatonvilágos**, set atop attractive wooded cliffs, or **Balatonberény**, which has a nudist beach. Southwest of Balatonberény, the tiny lake known as **Kis-Balaton** (Little Balaton) is a protected nature reserve, home to over 80 species of birds.

One of the most popular destinations on Balaton's northern shore is the spa town of **Balatonfüred**, whose mineral springs have been used for curative purposes since Roman times. From here, you can visit the **Tihany Peninsula**, which became Hungary's first national park in 1957, and boasts some of the most beautiful scenery in the area.

At the far northwestern tip of the lake, the university town of **Keszthely** has three beaches, as well as a number of other attractions, including the Balaton Museum, which covers the history and natural history of the region, and the imposing Festetics Palace. A 15-minute drive from Keszthely brings you to **Hévíz**, an old 19th-century spa resort, where you can bathe in the world's second largest thermal lake.

For hotels and restaurants see p704 and p705

⑤ Pécs

🏙 180,000. 🚉 🚌 ℹ️ Széchenyi
tér 9 **Tel** (72) 213 315.

First a Celtic, then a Roman
settlement, Pécs was later
ruled by the Turks from 1543
until 1686. Several monuments
testify to these different periods
of Pécs' history.

The city's main square,
Széchenyi tér, is overlooked by
the **Catholic Church**, formerly
the Mosque of Gazi Kassim
Pasha, built under Turkish
occupation. Inside, a delicately
decorated *mihrab* (prayer niche)
serves as a reminder of the
building's origins. Behind the
church is the **Archaeological
Museum**, whose exhibits date
from prehistoric times to the
Magyar conquest.

On Dom tér are Pécs' four-
towered, Neo-Romanesque
Cathedral, which stands on
the foundations of an 11th-
century basilica, and the Neo-
Renaissance **Bishop's Palace**
(1770). South of here, on Szent
István tér, a stairway leads to
the ruins of a 4th-century
underground **chapel**, which
contains a wonderful collection
of frescoes. On nearby Apáca
utca, recent excavations have
unearthed a collection of
Roman tombs.

Remains of the city's **medieval
walls**, erected
after an invasion
by the Mongols
in the 13th
century, include
a 15th-century
barbican. Pécs'

Impressive candlelit interior of Pécs'
Neo-Romanesque cathedral

museums include the
Csontváry Museum, showing
works by the artist Kosztka
Tivadar Csontváry (1853–1919),
and the **Vasarely Museum**,
dedicated to Hungarian Op
artist Victor Vasarely (1908–97).

🏛 **Archaeological Museum**
Janus Pannonius utca 1. **Tel** (72) 310
544. **Open** Tue–Sat. 📷

🏛 **Vasarely Museum**
Káptalan utca 3. **Tel** (30) 873 81 29.
Open Tue–Sun. 📷

⑥ Eger

🏙 60,000. 🚉 🚌 ℹ️ Bajcsy Zsilinsky
u 9 **Tel** (36) 517 715.

One of the most popular
tourist destinations in Hungary,
Eger is famous for its world-
class wines.

At the heart of the town, on
Eszterházy tér, are the Neoclassical **Cathedral** (1830s) and
the **Lyceum**. A highlight of the
latter is the observatory, which

affords stunning views of the
town and surrounding vineyards.
Eger's 40-m- (130-ft-) **minaret**
is a relic of 16th-century
Turkish occupation, while the
splendid Baroque **Minorite
Church** on Dobó István tér
dates from the 1770s.

Eger Castle was built in the
13th century following the
Mongol invasion. The castle
complex includes the Bishop's
Palace (1470), which houses a
museum of historical artifacts,
and underground casemates.

🏰 **Eger Castle**
Egri Vár. **Tel** (36) 312 744.
Open daily. 📷

Environs
Just west of the town, in the
Szépasszony Valley, you can
sample the region's wines,
including the famous dry red,
Egri Bikavér, or Bull's Blood.

⑦ Tokaj

🏙 20,000. 🚉 🚌 ℹ️ Serház utca 1
Tel (47) 352 259. 🌐 tokaj-turizmus.hu

Tokaj is located at the center
of one of Hungary's
most important wine-
growing areas. Tokaji
dessert wines owe
their distinctive full-
bodied flavor to the
volcanic soil in
which the vines
grow, and a type of
mold peculiar to
the region. The
best cellars to visit
for a tasting are
the **Rákóczi Cellar**,
run by a foreign
company, and the
privately owned
Hímesudvar at No. 2 Bem utca.
Tokaj has a **synagogue** and
a **Jewish cemetery**, relics of
the period before World War II,
when the town had a large
Jewish population. The **Tokaj
Museum** gives an interesting
insight into the history of the
town and its environs.

Hungarian
dessert wine
Tokaji Aszú

🍷 **Rákóczi Cellar**
Kossuth tér 15. **Tel** (47) 352 408.
Open Apr–Oct: daily (call in
advance). 📷

Eger's Baroque Minorite church, towering over Dobó István tér

Practical & Travel Information

Tourism is an important part of the Hungarian economy, and as a result, there have been vast improvements in communications, banking facilities, and public transportation. The biggest problem tourists face is the formidable language barrier. However, staff at many tourist offices, hotels, and other attractions, usually speak English or German.

When to Visit

The most popular times to visit Hungary are between April and the end of June, and from the middle of August until October. July and August can be extremely hot, and it is almost unbearable to stay in Budapest, although away from the capital, the heat is less severe. From November until March, many museums have shorter opening hours or may close altogether.

Tourist Information

Before leaving for Hungary, you can obtain various information leaflets and maps from the Hungarian National Tourist Office, which has branches worldwide.

Within Hungary, there are tourist information offices in most large towns. In Budapest, advice on sightseeing, accommodation, and cultural events is given by the offices of **Tourinform Budapest**.

Visitors to the capital may wish to invest in the Budapest Card, which entitles cardholders, along with one child under 14, to unlimited use of the city's public transport system, discounts on entry to museums, the zoo and funfair, and on selected guided tours, and 10 to 20 percent discount on selected cultural events and at certain restaurants.

A modern addition to the city's public transport system is a metro line that runs between southwest Buda and northeast Pest.

Visa Requirements

Citizens of the US, Canada, Australia, and New Zealand need only a valid passport to visit Hungary for up to 90 days. EU citizens need only an identity card.

For more information about visas and extended visits, see the Hungarian Ministry of Foreign Affairs' website (www. mfa.gov.hu).

Personal Security

Hungary is on the whole a safe country to travel in. As in most cities that attract large numbers of tourists, pickpockets operate in Budapest, targeting crowded metro stations, buses, and shopping malls. Rákóczi tér and Mátyás tér, in district VIII, are traditional hangouts for prostitutes; lone women should avoid these areas at night. In the case of an emergency while on vacation, the relevant numbers to call are listed in the directory opposite.

Health Issues

No special vaccinations are required. Allergy sufferers and people with breathing difficulties who intend to visit Budapest should take account of the summer smog conditions, which are particulary acute in Pest. Those susceptible might consider staying in the castle district, where cars are banned, or retreating to the wooded Buda hills.

For treatments for minor ailments, visit a pharmacy (Gyógyszertár or Patika). If your nearest store is closed, it should display a list of 24-hour emergency pharmacies.

People with heart conditions who wish to use Hungary's thermal baths should seek a physician's advice beforehand.

Facilities for the Disabled

Hungary's public transportation systems, museums, and other attractions are gradually being renovated to make them wheelchair-friendly, but people with disabilities may still encounter accessibility problems. For more detailed information contact the **Hungarian Disabled Association**.

Banking and Currency

The Hungarian currency is the forint (HUF or Ft). If you need to change money, the best rates of exchange are offered by banks and bureaux de change. Banks are generally open from 8am to 5pm Monday to Friday, with a few opening on Saturday mornings, too. Credit cards are more widely accepted now than before; however, their use is still not as widespread as elsewhere in Europe and you shouldn't expect to be able to use them everywhere. It's wise to carry a little extra cash.

The Climate of Hungary

Hungary enjoys some of the sunniest weather in Europe, with an average of eight hours of sunshine a day in summer. June, July, and August are the hottest months. In winter, temperatures can fall well below freezing and there may also be snowfall. Hungary has comparatively low rainfall. June usually gets the most rain, while the fall is the driest season.

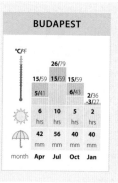

BUDAPEST			
°C/°F			
	26/79		
15/59	15/59	15/59	
5/41		6/43	2/36
			-3/27
6 hrs	10 hrs	5 hrs	2 hrs
42 mm	56 mm	40 mm	40 mm
month Apr	Jul	Oct	Jan

Communications

The Hungarian telephone system used to be notoriously bad, but improvements are now slowly being made. Phonecards, which are available from tobacconists, post offices, petrol stations, and some newspaper kiosks, are the best option when using public phones, although some booths still accept coins.

Post offices open from 8am to 6pm, Monday to Friday, and on Saturday mornings. Service can be slow and there are often long lines, so be prepared to wait.

Flying to Hungary

Direct scheduled flights between New York's JFK airport and Budapest's **Liszt Ferenc** international airport are operated by many airlines. Major airlines flying from the US and Canada to Hungary include **Air France**, **British Airways**, **KLM**, and **Lufthansa**, although services usually entail a transfer or touch-down in another European city. British Airways and Air France each operate

three daily scheduled flights from London. Many low-cost airlines, such as **Ryanair**, **easyJet** and **Wizz Air**, also operate daily flights from London.

Budapest airport is located 16 km (10 miles) from the center of Budapest. The efficient **Airport Minibus Shuttle** will take passengers from the airport to any address in the capital. Taxis are a quick and comfortable way of getting into the city.

Rail Travel

The Hungarian national rail network is very efficient, with trains invariably departing and arriving on time. Budapest has direct international rail links with 25 other capital cities, Keleti pu station handling the majority of the international traffic. High-speed trains to Vienna, the main communications hub for western Europe, depart approximately every three hours and take around 2 hours 25 minutes. There are also car-train services from Keleti pu to

Thessaloníki in Greece. Within Hungary, local trains are categorized according to speed: "slow" (személy), "speedy" (sebes), or "fast" (gyors). There are also modern intercity services between Budapest and the larger cities. A number of concessionary fares are available for those planning on doing a lot of rail travel in Hungary.

Traveling by Bus

International buses to all European destinations depart from Népliget station. Nationally, buses are run by Volánbusz, which operates routes to most cities and towns in Hungary.

Traveling by Car

To rent a car in Hungary you must be aged 21 years or over, and have held a full driver's license for at least a year. An international driver's license helps also. Most of the big, international firms have offices at the airport in Budapest, or you can arrange rental at hotels and travel agencies throughout the country.

DIRECTORY

Hungarian National Tourist Offices

Hungary
W gotohungary.com

UK
46 Eaton Place,
London SW1X 8AL.
Tel 020-7823 1032.
W gotohungary.co.uk

US
450 7th Avenue, Suite 2601, New York, NY 10123. **Tel** 212-695 1221.
W gotohungary.com

Tourist Information

Tourinform Hotline (24 hrs)
Tel 06 80 630 800. **Tel** +36 30 30 30 600 (abroad).

Tourinform Budapest
Sütö utca 2, Budapest V.
Tel (1) 438 80 80.

Embassies

Canada
1027 Budapest, Ganz ú. 12–14. **Tel** (1) 392 33 60.
W canada.hu

Ireland
1054 Szabadság tér 7, Bank Center, Platina Tower, 6th Floor, Budapest.
Tel (1) 301 49 60.
W embassyof ireland.hu

UK
1051 Harmincad utca 6, Budapest.
Tel (1) 266 28 88.
W britishembassy.hu

US
1054 Szabadság tér 12, Budapest. **Tel** (1) 475 44 00. W usembassy.hu

Emergency Numbers

Ambulance
Tel 104.

Fire
Tel 105.

Police
Tel 107.

Facilities for the Disabled

Hungarian Disabled Association
1032 San Marco utca 76, Budapest. **Tel** (1) 388 23 87. W meosz.hu

Air Travel

Liszt Ferenc Airport
Tel (1) 296 70 00.

Air France
Tel (1) 483 88 00.
Tel 0871-663 3777 (UK).
Tel 800-237 2747 (US).
W airfrance.hu

British Airways
Tel (1) 777 47 47.
Tel 0844-493 0787 (UK).
Tel 800-247 9297 (US).
W britishairways.com

easyJet
Tel (1) 255 07 91.
Tel 0843-104 5000 (UK).
W easyjet.com

KLM
Tel (1) 373 77 37.
Tel 800-374 7747 (US).
W klm.hu

Lufthansa
Tel (1) 411 99 00.
Tel 800-645 3880 (US).
W lufthansa.com

Ryanair
W ryanair.com

Wizz Air
Tel 06 90 181 181.
W wizzair.com

Where to Stay

Budapest

BUDA: Abel Panzió   ⓤ
Budget   **Map** B5
Ábel Jenö utca 9, 1113
Tel *(1) 209 25 37*
W abelpanzio.hu
This restored family villa in a leafy
street in Buda offers charming
rooms and good service.

BUDA: BI & BI Guesthouse   ⓤ
Budget
Retek utca 16, 1024
Tel *(1) 786 09 55*
W bibipanzio.hu
Stay in neat rooms and enjoy
a decent breakfast at this
friendly guesthouse close to
the Castle District.

BUDA: Burg   ⓤⓤ
Modern   **Map** B3
Szantháromság tér 7, 1014
Tel *(1) 212 02 69*
W burghotelbudapest.com
The Burg provides small but
comfortable en-suite rooms,
several of which boast fabulous
views of the Mátyás Church.

DK Choice

BUDA: Gellert   ⓤⓤⓤ
Luxury   **Map** C4
Szent Gellért tér 1, 1111
Tel *(1) 889 55 00*
W danubiushotels.com
Home to Hungarian high
society since World War I, this
legendary spa hotel has both
indoor and outdoor pools fed
by healing spring waters. The
rooms are opulently decorated,
and the social areas feature Art
Nouveau decor. Massages and
other wellness treatments are
available. Wonderful views
across the Danube.

PEST: Hipster Hostel   ⓤ
Budget   **Map** D4
Baross utca 3, 1082
Tel *(1) 788 94 41*
W hipsterhostel.com
A welcoming hostel on the rim
of central Pest, the Hipster has a
good mixture of different-sized
rooms, all attractively decorated.

PEST: Leo Panzió   ⓤ
Modern   **Map** C4
Kossuth Lajos utca 21a, 1053
Tel *(1) 266 90 41*
W leopanzio.hu
A superb pension in the heart of
Pest, Leo Panzió offers exemplary
service and good value for money.

PEST: Astoria   ⓤⓤ
Boutique   **Map** D4
Kossuth Lajos utca 19–21, 1053
Tel *(1) 889 60 00*
W danubiushotels.com
In a predominantly Art Nouveau
building, the Astoria has spacious
rooms, an elegant café, and a lovely
Neo-Baroque breakfast room.

PEST: Bohem Art Hotel   ⓤⓤ
Boutique   **Map** C4
Molnar út 35, 1056
Tel *(1) 327 90 20*
W bohemarthotel.hu
A superbly central design hotel
that incorporates minimalist
interiors with artworks and kitschy
details. Good buffet breakfast.

PEST: Cotton House   ⓤⓤ
Boutique   **Map** C3
Jókai út 26, 1066
Tel *(1) 354 26 00*
W cottonhouse.hu
This atmospheric hotel has some
of the best-decorated rooms in
Hungary, each themed on a
famous stage or screen star.

PEST: K & K Opera   ⓤⓤⓤ
Modern   **Map** C3
Révay utca 24, 1065
Tel *(1) 269 02 22*
W kkhotels.com
Located close to the Opera House,
this hotel boasts a splendid
façade and offers comfy rooms.

PEST: Kempinski Corvinus   ⓤⓤⓤ
Luxury   **Map** C4
Erzsébet tér 7, 1051
Tel *(1) 429 37 77*
W kempinski.com
An exclusive hotel popular
with visiting heads of state, the
Corvinus has luxurious rooms
and a host of excellent facilities.

Colorful artworks decorate the walls at the
Bohem Art Hotel, Budapest

**PEST: Mamaison
Hotel Andrassy**   ⓤⓤⓤ
Boutique   **Map** D2
Andrassy út 111, 1063
Tel *(1) 462 21 00*
W mamaison.com
Situated in a Bauhaus-style
building, the Andrassy offers
elegance, intimacy, superb
service, and a touch of romance.

Rest of Hungary

EGER: Senator-ház   ⓤⓤ
Modern
Dobó tér 11, 3300
Tel *(36) 411 711*
W senatorhaz.hu
In an atmospheric building from
1753, this hotel enjoys a main-
square location and boasts cozy
rooms, many with castle views.

KESTHELY: Helikon   ⓤⓤ
Room with a view
Balaton-part 5, 8360
Tel *(83) 889 600*
W hotelhelikon.hu
The modern high-rise Helikon
offers plush rooms, many with
superb views across the water.

PECS: Palatinus   ⓤⓤ
Boutique
Király utca 5, 7621
Tel *(72) 889 400*
W danubiushotels.com
The Palatinus is decorated with a
mixture of Art Nouveau and Art
Deco styles. Sumptuous rooms
and a basement spa center.

PECS: Patria   ⓤⓤⓤ
Boutique
Rákóczi utca 3, 7621
Tel *(72) 889 500*
W danubiushotels.com
The wonderfully designed Patria
is a modernist masterpiece. The
rooms are bright and colorful.

**SIÓFOK: Janus
Boutique Hotel & Spa**   ⓤⓤⓤ
Boutique
Fö ut 93–95, 8600
Tel *(84) 312 516*
W janushotel.hu
Individually designed rooms at
this hotel have themes ranging
from Japanese to Gothic.

Where to Eat and Drink

Budapest

BUDA: Régi Sipos 🔵
Seafood
Lajos utca 46, 1036
Tel *(1) 250 80 82*
Set apart from the tourist trail, Régi Sipos serves up fish specialties such as *pontypörkölt* (carp goulash) and *harcsapaprikás* (catfish stew), with cheesy lasagne-like noodle sheets.

BUDA: Alabárdos Etterem 🔵🔵🔵
Hungarian **Map** B3
Országház út 2, 1014
Tel *(1) 356 08 51* **Closed** *Sun*
Set in an outstanding Gothic building, Alabárdos serves classic cuisine from days gone by. Everything, from the service to the presentation, exudes elegance.

BUDA: Búsuló Juhász Etterem 🔵🔵🔵
Hungarian **Map** B4
Kelenhegyi út 58, 1118
Tel *(1) 209 16 49*
There are spectacular views from this restaurant on the slopes of Gellért Hill. Expect traditional Hungarian specialties and live gypsy music.

BUDA: Fekete Holló 🔵🔵🔵
Hungarian **Map** B3
Országház út 10, 1014
Tel *(1) 356 23 67*
Located on Buda Hill, this is a gem of a traditional restaurant, where the kitsch medieval decor fails to detract from the excellent food. It can get very busy.

PEST: Bohémtanya 🔵
Hungarian **Map** C3
Paulay Ede út 6, 1061
Tel *(1) 267 35 04*
Savor hearty Hungarian food in pleasant surroundings. Diners are seated in wooden alcoves large enough for eight, and that might mean sharing a table with others.

PEST: Café Kör 🔵
European **Map** C3
Sas út 17, 1051
Tel *(1) 311 00 53*
A popular, good-value bistro that serves Hungarian and European mains, as well as fine salads and a handful of vegetarian dishes. Originally a wine bar, Kör is also a good place to drink wine, liquers, spirits, and more.

PEST: Vakvarjú 🔵
International **Map** C3
Paulay Ede út 7, 1061
Tel *(1) 268 08 88*
Providing excellent views of one of Budapest's busiest streets, this lively restaurant offers an extensive menu of inexpensive international fare.

PEST: Károlyi Etterem 🔵🔵
Hungarian **Map** C4
Kárlyi Mihály utca 16, 1053
Tel *(1) 328 02 40*
Enjoy elegant, sophisticated dining in the courtyard of the Károlyi Palace, with a traditional menu of Hungarian classics. Popular with wedding parties at weekends.

PEST: Kárpátia 🔵🔵
Hungarian **Map** C4
Ferenciek tere 7–8, 1053
Tel *(1) 317 35 96*
Ostentatiously decorated with Transylvanian folk motifs, the 19th-century Kárpátia is a long-established favorite. The goulashes remain of unimpeachably high quality.

PEST: Soul Café 🔵🔵
Hungarian **Map** D5
Ráday út 11–13, 1092
Tel *(1) 297 69 86*
An intimate restaurant on a thriving street, Soul Café offers diners well-prepared international and Hungarian cuisine. There is plenty of choice for vegetarians.

Price Guide

Prices are for an average three-course meal for one, including half a bottle of house wine, and all extra charges.

🔵 under 3,000 HUF
🔵🔵 3,000 to 5,000 HUF
🔵🔵🔵 over 5,000 HUF

DK Choice

PEST: Bock Bisztró 🔵🔵🔵
Hungarian **Map** D3
Erzsébet körút 43–49, 1073
Tel *(1) 321 03 40* **Closed** *Sun*
With an interior that is lined with cookery books and wine magazines, Bock Bisztró has made old-school Hungarian cooking sexy again. Traditional mains such as *borjúpaprikás* and veal *paprikash* are served alongside European and East–West fusion dishes. Bock is also a wine shop, so diners get good advice on wine pairings.

PEST: Menza 🔵🔵🔵
Hungarian **Map** D3
Liszt Ferenc tér 2, 1061
Tel *(1) 413 14 82*
Classic Hungarian dishes are made with fresh produce and a postmodern twist. The 1960s decor provides a fitting backdrop.

Rest of Hungary

EGER: Fehérszarvas Vadásztanya 🔵🔵
European
Klapka út 8, 3300
Tel *(36) 411 129*
Eger's silver-service restaurant is a little way from the center but well worth the trek. Feast on game and freshwater fish in a cellar filled with hunting trophies.

KECSKEMÉT: Kecskeméti Csárda és Borház 🔵🔵
Hungarian
Kölcsey 7, 6000
Tel *(76) 488 686*
One of the best-regarded eateries in the country, this place specializes in the paprika-rich cuisine of the great plain.

PECS: Cellarium 🔵🔵
International
Hunyadi János út 2, 7621
Tel *(76) 314 596*
Housed in catacombs that once provided shelter from attacking Ottomans, Cellarium offers delicious local specialties and classic international dishes.

Diners enjoying traditional Hungarian cuisine at Bock Bisztró, Budapest

POLAND

Located between Russia and Germany, Poland has always been a fiercely contested land. Released from the eastern bloc in 1989, the country is now developing rapidly, especially in the cities of Warsaw, Cracow, Gdańsk, and Wrocław. Monuments attest to a stormy history, but Poland is famed for its virtues, especially the generosity of its people and the excellence of its vodka.

Although situated on the plains of central Europe, Poland has an extremely varied landscape. Alpine scenery predominates in the Tatra Mountains to the south, while the north is dominated by lakes. Mountain lovers can make use of the well-developed infrastructure of hostels and shelters, such as those found in the Tatras. The countless lakes of Warmia and Mazuria, collectively known as the Land of a Thousand Lakes, are a haven for watersports enthusiasts.

Poland's inhabitants, who number almost 39 million, all but constitute a single ethnic group, with minorities accounting for less than 4 percent of the population. The largest minorities are Belorussians and Ukrainians, who inhabit the east of the country, and Germans, who are concentrated mainly around the city of Opole in Silesia. The majority of Poles are Catholic, but large regions of the country, such as Cieszyn Silesia, have a substantial Protestant population. In the east, there are also many Orthodox Christians. Religious denomination does not necessarily coincide with ethnic identity, although Belorussians tend to be Orthodox, while Ukrainians belong to the Greek Catholic (Uniate) Church.

History

Poland's borders have changed continually with the course of history. The origins of the Polish nation go back to the 10th century, when Slav tribes living in the area of Gniezno united under the Piast dynasty, which ruled Poland until 1370. Mieszko I converted to Christianity in 966, thus bringing his kingdom into Christian Europe, and made Poznań the seat of Poland's first bishop. The Piast dynasty ruled Poland with variable fortune and embroiled the nation in domestic quarrels for 150 years. After this dynasty died out, the great Lithuanian prince Jagiełło took the Polish throne and founded a new dynasty. The treaty with Lithuania signed in 1385 initiated the long

Statue of the great 19th-century poet and patriot Adam Mickiewicz in Market Square, Cracow

◀ Altarpiece depicting the Assumption in St. Mary's Church, Cracow, carved by Veit Stoss (1447–1533)

Solidarity demonstrators staging a mass rally during a papal visit to Poland in 1987

process of consolidation between these nations, culminating in 1569 with the signing of the Union of Lublin. Nevertheless, the so-called Republic of Two Nations *(Rzeczpospolita Obojga Narodów)* lasted until 1795. In 1572, the Jagiellonian dynasty died out, after which the Polish authorities introduced elective kings, with the nobility having the right to vote.

The 17th century was dominated by wars with Sweden, Russia, and the Ottoman Empire, and although the country survived, it was considerably weakened, and its time of dominance was over. In 1795, it was partitioned by Russia, Prussia, and Austria, and was wiped off the map for more than 100 years. Attempts to wrest independence by insurrection were unsuccessful, and Poland did not regain its sovereignty until 1918. The arduous process of rebuilding and uniting the nation was still incomplete when, at the outbreak of World War II, a six-year period of German and Soviet occupation began. The price that Poland paid was very high: millions were murdered, including virtually its entire Jewish population. The country suffered devastation and there were huge territorial losses, which were only partly compensated by the Allies' decision to move the border westwards. After the war, Poland was subjugated by the Soviet Union, but the socialist economy proved ineffective. The formation of Solidarity *(Solidarność)* in 1980 accelerated the pace of change, which was completed when Poland regained its freedom after the June 1989 elections.

In 1999, Poland became a member of NATO, and in 2004, it joined the European Union.

Language and Culture

The legacy of more than 100 years of partition rule is still visible in Poland's cultural landscape. Russian, Prussian, and Austrian administrations left their mark not only on rural and urban architecture, but also on the customs and mentality of the people.

The Poles have a deep reverence for religious symbols and rituals, and the presence of the church can be seen everywhere, either in the form of lavish Baroque buildings or images of the Black Madonna. Wayside shrines are also a regular feature.

Polish is a West Slavic language closely related to Slovak and Czech. Many of its words (such as *Solidarność*) are borrowed from Latin, although German, Italian, and English words are also common.

KEY DATES IN POLISH HISTORY

966 Adoption of Christianity under Mieszko I

1025 Coronation of Bolesław the Brave, first king of Poland

1320 The unification of the Polish state

1385 Poland and Lithuania unite under the Treaty of Krewo

1569 The Union of Lublin creates the Polish-Lithuanian Republic of Two Nations

1596 The capital moves from Cracow to Warsaw

1655 Beginning of the "Deluge" (the Swedish occupation), ending in 1660

1772–1918 Poland divided three times between Russia, Prussia, and Austria. The final partition (1795) is made after a Polish uprising led by Tadeusz Kościuszko

1918 Poland regains independence

1939 Soviet and German forces invade

1940 Auschwitz-Birkenau established; 1.5 million Poles and Jews are gassed during the war

1945 Communist government takes control

1980 Solidarity formed, led by Lech Wałęsa

1989 First free post-war elections are held. Lech Wałęsa wins the presidency by a landslide

1999 Poland joins NATO

2004 Poland joins EU

2011 Poland holds EU rotating presidency for the first time

Exploring Poland

Bordering the Baltic Sea, Poland is one of the largest countries of Central Europe, with a population of around 39 million. Warsaw, the capital, is located at the center of Poland, on the banks of the River Vistula (Wisła). Its location makes it an ideal base for visiting other cities, such as Cracow, the ancient royal capital; Gdańsk, the Hanseatic city whose shipyards gave birth to Solidarity; and Poznań, one of the oldest Polish cities. Cracow is one of the country's greatest treasures, offering excursions to the Polish mountains and the Cracow-Częstochowa Valley.

Children in traditional dress on a Polish public holiday, Cracow

Sights at a Glance

1 *Warsaw pp710–15*
2 *Cracow pp716–19*

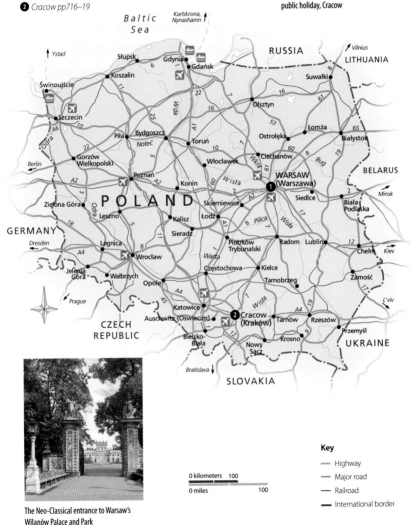

The Neo-Classical entrance to Warsaw's Wilanów Palace and Park

0 kilometers 100

0 miles 100

Key

— Highway
— Major road
— Railroad
— International border

For hotels and restaurants see p722 and p723

For keys to symbols *see back flap*

❶ Warsaw

Warsaw is believed to have been founded in the late 13th century, when Duke Bolesław built a castle here overlooking the Vistula. It became capital of Poland in 1596, making it one of Europe's youngest capital cities. The present castle and other grand buildings of the Old Town date largely from the Renaissance and Baroque periods. By the end of World War II, some 80 per cent of the buildings had been reduced to rubble. What you see today is the product of meticulous reconstruction undertaken during the Communist era. Warsaw is rich in museums and sights and the Varsovians are immensely proud of their history of resistance to oppression. The center has been declared a UNESCO World Heritage Site.

Wilanów Palace, a 17th-century royal retreat, which stands in a magnificent park on the outskirts of the city

Sights at a Glance

① Old Town Market Square
② St. John's Cathedral
③ Royal Castle
④ St. Anna's Church
⑤ Royal Route
⑥ Grand Theater
⑦ Monument to the Ghetto Heroes
⑧ Monument to those Fallen and Murdered in the East
⑨ Palace of Culture and Science
⑩ National Museum

Greater Warsaw (see inset map)

⑪ Łazienki Park
⑫ Wilanów Palace and Park

0 meters 350
0 yards 350

Getting Around

The sights in the Old and New Town areas are easily visited on foot, since most of the streets are pedestrianized. Trams are best for short trips across the center. There is also an extensive bus service, and two metro lines meeting at Świętokrzyska station. Taxis are reasonably priced, but use a reputable firm. Driving is getting more problematic, but the streets are still less crowded than in most European cities.

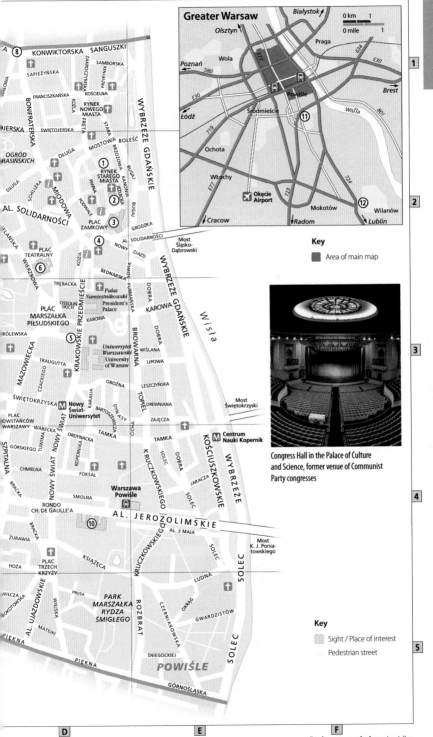

Greater Warsaw

Białystok

Olsztyn

Praga

Poznań

Wola

Brest

Powiśle

Łódź

Śródmieście

WisŁa

Ochota

Włochy

Okęcie Airport

Cracow

Mokotów

Wilanów

Radom

Lublin

0 km 1
0 mile 1

Key

Area of main map

KONWIKTORSKA SANGUSZKI

SAPIEŻYŃSKA

SAMBORSKA

PRZYRYNEK

FRANCISZKAŃSKA

KOŚCIELNA

RYNEK NOWEGO MIASTA

FRETA

STARA

KOZŁA

WYBRZEŻE GDAŃSKIE

BONIFRATERSKA

ŚWIĘTOJERSKA

OGRÓD RASIŃSKICH

DŁUGA

MOSTOWA BOLEŚĆ

BRZOZOWA

BUGAJ

KANONIA

MIODOWA

PIWNA

RYNEK STAREGO MIASTA

JEZUICKA

AL. SOLIDARNOŚCI

PODWALE

PLAC ZAMKOWY

GRODZKA

BUGAJ

PLAC TEATRALNY

NOWY ZJAZD

AL. SOLIDARNOŚCI

Most Śląsko-Dąbrowski

WIERZBOWA

TRĘBACKA

BEDNARSKA

WYBRZEŻE GDAŃSKIE

Palac Namiestnikowski
President's Palace

PLAC MARSZAŁKA PIŁSUDSKIEGO

OSSOLIŃSKICH

KAROWA

KAROWA

KRAKOWSKIE PRZEDMIEŚCIE

WISŁA

KRÓLEWSKA

Uniwersytet Warszawski
University of Warsaw

BROWARNA

DOBRA

WIŚLANA

MAZOWIECKA

TRAUGUTTA

CZACKIEGO

KARASIA

OBOŻNA

LIPOWA

LESZCZYŃSKA

ŚWIĘTOKRZYSKA

Nowy Świat-Uniwersytet

DYNASY

BARTOSZEWICZA

TOPIEL

DREWNIANA

Most Świętokrzyski

PLAC POWSTAŃCÓW WARSZAWY

WARECKA

TAMKA

ZAJĘCZA

GÓRSKIEGO

TUWIMA

ORDYNACKA

TAMKA

Centrum Nauki Kopernik

SZPITALNA

CHMIELNA

NOWY ŚWIAT

KOPERNIKA

FOKSAL

KRUCZKOWSKIEGO

SOLEC

DOBRA

JARACZA

KOŚCIUSZKOWSKIE

BRACKA

SMOLNA

Warszawa Powiśle

SOLEC

RONDO CH. DE GAULLE'A

AL. JEROZOLIMSKIE

ŻURAWIA

BRACKA

AL. 3 MAJA

Most K. J. Ponia-towskiego

HOŻA

PLAC TRZECH KRZYŻY

KSIĄŻĘCA

KRUCZKOWSKIEGO

SOLEC

LUDNA

WILCZA

MOKOTOWSKA

AL. UJAZDOWSKIE

PRUSA

WIEJSKA

PARK MARSZAŁKA RYDZA ŚMIGŁEGO

ROZBRAT

CZERNIAKOWSKA

OKRĄG

GWARDZISTÓW

SOLEC

PIĘKNA

MATEJKI

PIĘKNA

ŚNIEGOCKIEJ

POWIŚLE

GÓRNOŚLĄSKA

Congress Hall in the Palace of Culture and Science, former venue of Communist Party congresses

Key

Sight / Place of interest

Pedestrian street

For keys to symbols *see back flap*

D | E | F

Horse-drawn carriages in Warsaw's Old Town Market Square

① Old Town Market Square

Rynek Starego Miasta. ▦ 116, 175, 180, 195, 503. History Museum: **Tel** 022-635 16 25. **Open** Tue–Sun.

Painstakingly restored after World War II, the Old Town Market Square was the center of Warsaw public life until the 19th century, when the focus of the growing, modern city moved. The tall, ornate, and colorful houses, which lend the square its unique character, were built by wealthy merchants in the 17th century.

The houses on one side form the **Warsaw History Museum** (Muzeum Historyczne m st Warszawy). This displays the city's history through paintings, photographs, sculpture, and archaeological finds. There is also a film show, with footage of the Nazis' systematic destruction of Warsaw in 1944. Today, café tables and stalls line the square, and horse-drawn carriages offer tours of the Old Town.

② St. John's Cathedral

Świętojańska 8. **Tel** 022-831 02 89. ▦ 116, 175, 178, 180, 195, 503. **Open** daily (Sun: pm only).

Completed in the early 15th century, St. John's Cathedral (katedra św Jana) was originally a parish church. Gaining collegiate status in 1406, it was not until 1798 that St. John's became a cathedral. The coronation of Poland's last king, Stanisław August Poniatowski, in 1764, and the swearing of an oath by the deputies of the *Sejm* (Parliament) to uphold the 1791 Constitution took place here.

After World War II, various elaborate 19th-century additions were removed from the facade, and the cathedral was restored to its original Mazovian Gothic style. The interior features religious art, richly carved wooden stalls, and ornate tombs, including those of Gabriel Narutowicz (1865–1922), Poland's first president, assassinated two days after taking office, and Nobel prize-winning novelist Henryk Sienkiewicz (1846–1916). In a chapel founded by the Baryczka family hangs a 16th-century crucifix, which is credited with several miracles.

③ Royal Castle

Plac Zamkowy 4. **Tel** 022-355 51 70. ▦ 116, 175, 178, 180, 195, 503. **Open** daily (separate tickets for Royal Apartments and Parliament). **Closed** Oct–Apr: Mon; some public hols. 🖼 (free Sun). ▣ ⓦ **zamek-krolewski.pl**

Warsaw's Royal Castle (Zamek Królewski) stands on the site of an original castle built here by the Mazovian dukes in the 14th century. It was transformed between 1598 and 1619 by King Zygmunt III Waza, who asked Italian architects to restyle the castle into a polygon. The king chose this castle as his royal residence in 1596, after the *Sejm* (Parliament) had moved here from Cracow in 1569. In the 18th century, King Augustus III remodeled the east wing in Baroque style and King Stanisław August Poniatowski added a library.

In 1939, the castle was burned, and then blown up by the Nazis in 1944. Reconstruction, which was funded by public donations, took from 1971 to 1988.

The castle's fascinating interiors are the result of its dual role: being a royal residence as well as the seat of parliament. Meticulously reconstructed, the castle has royal apartments, as well as the Chamber of Deputies and the Senate. Some of the woodwork and stucco is original, as are many of the furnishings and much of the art. Among the paintings are 18th-century works by Bellotto and Bacciarelli.

The opulent interior of the Marble Room in the Royal Castle

The magnificent Rococo organ loft of St. Anna's Church

④ St. Anna's Church

Krakowskie Przedmieście 68. 🚌 116, 175, 178, 180, 195, 503. **Open** daily.

This imposing church on the Royal Route was founded by Anna, the widow of Duke Bolesław III, and built in the late 15th century, along with a Bernardine monastery. Extended between 1518 and 1533, the church was destroyed during the Swedish invasion of 1655, but later rebuilt in Baroque style. The Neoclassical facade was a subsequent addition, as was the free-standing bell tower, which dates from the 1820s.

The church has a magnificent interior, with several Rococo altars, a splendid organ, and frescoes by Walenty Żebrowski. A side chapel contains the relics of St. Władysław of Gielniów, Warsaw's patron saint. St. Anna's is a popular choice for weddings, partly due to the superstition that any marriage celebrated here will be a happy one.

Next to the church are the remains of the 16th-century Bernardine monastery, which was closed in 1864. The old cloisters in the monastery's east wing, however, have retained their original vaulted ceilings. Behind St. Anna's there is an attractive Neoclassical colonnade, known as Odwach. This is the city's best location for second-hand booksellers, and good for browsing.

⑤ Royal Route

Krakowskie Przedmieście and Nowy Świat. 🚌 116, 180, 195, 503.

The Royal Route (Trakt Królewski) is one of Warsaw's most historic and beautiful streets. Starting by Castle Square (Plac Zamkowy), and continuing all the way to the royal palace at Wilanów, the most interesting part of the route is along Krakowskie Przedmieście and Nowy Świat. These thoroughfares developed in the late Middle Ages, with their rural setting, by the banks of the Vistula river, attracting Warsaw's aristocracy and wealthy merchant class.

This social elite built grand summer residences and town houses here, while religious orders established lavish churches and monasteries. Krakowskie Przedmieście features many buildings from the 17th and 18th centuries, with several imposing palaces standing back from the road behind tree-lined squares and courtyards. Alongside, there are impressive town houses and some of the city's most interesting churches, including **St. Anna's**, **St. Joseph's**, and the **Church of the Assumption**. **Warsaw University** and the **Fine Arts Academy** are also located here, while various monuments pay tribute to eminent Poles.

Nowy Świat is lined with long rows of 18th- and 19th-century town houses. It is also one of the busiest shopping streets in the world, and full of large stores, fashionable boutiques, colorful sidewalk cafés, and a wide choice of restaurants.

Imposing Neoclassical facade of the Grand Theater

⑥ Grand Theater

Plac Teatralny. **Tel** 022-692 02 00. 🚌 111, 128, 175. Ticket office: **Open** daily.

One of the city's largest buildings before World War II, the Grand Theater was built in 1825–33, to a design by Antonio Corazzi and Ludwik Kozubowski. Many renowned craftsmen also contributed to the sublime, palatial interiors. Initially, the building was to be named the National Theater, but the defeat of the 1830 November Uprising forced a change of name. The two statues that stand in front of the building are of the 19th-century composer Stanisław Moniuszko, known as the father of Polish opera, and of Wojciech Bogusławski, the man who instigated the construction of the theater.

The theater currently houses the National Opera and Ballet and a small theater museum. Severely damaged during World War II, the theater retained only its impressive Neoclassical facade and a few of its rooms. Greatly enlarged in the course of reconstruction, it acquired many modern interiors and far more extensive backstage facilities.

Statue of Poland's most famous astronomer, Nicholas Copernicus (1473–1543), on the Royal Route

⑦ Monument to the Ghetto Heroes

Pomnik Bohaterów Getta, Zamenhofa. 🚌 111, 180.

The Nazis created the Jewish ghetto in 1940 by driving the Jewish inhabitants of Warsaw and nearby villages into an area in the northwest of the city. The ghetto initially housed around 450,000 people, but by 1942, over 300,000 had been transported to death camps, and 100,000 others had died or been killed in the ghetto. The Ghetto Uprising of 1943 was an action of heroic defiance against the Nazis, planned not as a bid for liberty, but as an honorable way to die. Built to commemorate this action, the Monument to the Ghetto Heroes stands in the center of the former ghetto. It depicts men, women, and children struggling to flee the burning ghetto, together with a procession of Jews being driven to Nazi death camps.

A **Path of Remembrance**, lined with a series of granite blocks dedicated to events or heroes of the ghetto, links the ghetto memorial to the nearby Bunker Monument – on the site from where the uprising was co-ordinated – and the Umschlagplatz Monument. Engraved with hundreds of names, it marks the place from where many Jews were deported to the death camps, and represents the cattle trucks used for transportation.

Detail from the Monument to the Ghetto Heroes

⑧ Monument to Those Fallen and Murdered in the East

ul. Muranowska. 🚌 116, 178, 503. 🚊 18, 35.

This emotionally stirring monument, designed by Mirosław Biskupski and unveiled in 1995, takes the form of a typical railway wagon in which Poles were deported into the depths of the Soviet Union. It is filled with a pile of crosses symbolizing the hundreds of thousands of Poles carted off to the East in cattle vans and subsequently murdered in Soviet prison camps.

⑨ Palace of Culture and Science

Plac Defilad 1. **Tel** 022-656 76 00. Viewing Terrace: **Open** daily. 🚗

This monolithic building was a "gift" from Soviet Russia to the people of Warsaw, and intended as a monument to "the inventive spirit and social progress." Built in 1952–5 by the Russian architect, Lev Rudniev, it resembles Moscow's Socialist Realist tower blocks.

The palace still inspires extreme emotions among Varsovians, ranging from admiration to demands for its demolition. Since the end of Soviet domination, the building's role has changed. The tower itself now provides office space, and the Congress Hall, which once held Communist Party congresses, is now a venue for concerts and festivals. The palace remains a cultural center in other ways, with the Theater of Dramatic Art, a cinema, puppet theater, technology museum, and a sports complex.

The imposing Socialist Realist Palace of Culture and Science

⑩ National Museum

Aleje Jerozolimskie 3. **Tel** 022-629 30 93. 🚌 111, 117, 158, 507, 517, 521. 🚊 7, 8, 9, 22, 24, 25. **Open** 10am–6pm Tue–Sun (to 9pm Thu). **Closed** public hols. 🚗 (free Tue). Military Museum: **Tel** 022-629 52 71. **Open** 10am–5pm Wed, 10am–4pm Thu–Sun. **Closed** some public hols. 🚗 (free Sun). 🚗 Ⓦ mnw.art.pl

Originally established in 1862 as the Fine Art Museum, the National Museum (Muzeum Narodowe) was created in 1916. Its vast collection was started in 1862 with the purchase of 36 paintings. Subsequent acquisitions have turned the museum into one of the city's finest. Collections include ancient Greek, Roman, and Egyptian art, archaeological finds from Faras in present-day Sudan, and medieval Polish religious paintings, altarpieces, and sculptures.

The foreign art collection features Italian, French, Dutch, and Flemish works. There is a fine *Madonna and Child* by Sandro Botticelli. In the vast Polish art collection are works by Bernardo Bellotto (1720–80), nephew of Canaletto, who settled in Warsaw and painted fine views of the city. Of native Polish artists, Jan Matejko (1838–93) is one of the finest on display. He painted historical subjects such as *The Battle of Grunwald*. In an east wing, the **Military Museum** illustrates the history of Polish firearms and armor.

For hotels and restaurants see p722 and p723

The impressive Neoclassical facade of Wilanów Palace, designed for King Jan III Sobieski

⑪ Łazienki Park

Łazienki Królewskie, Agrykola 1. **Tel** 022-506 00 24. 116, 166, 180, 195. Park: **Open** daily until dusk. Palace on the Water: **Open** mid-Apr–mid-Oct: 11am–6pm Mon, 9am–6pm Tue–Sun (mid-Apr–mid-Oct: to 8pm Thu–Sat). **Closed** days after public hols. **W** lazienki-krolewskie.pl

This huge park, studded with monuments, palaces, and temples, dates from the Middle Ages, when it belonged to the Mazovian dukes. By the early 17th century, it was owned by the Polish crown, and housed a royal menagerie. In 1674, the Grand Crown Marshal Stanisław Herakliusz Lubomirski acquired the park, and Tylman of Gameren designed its hermitage and bathing pavilion. The pavilion gave the park its name, as *łazienki* means "baths."

In the 1700s, the park was owned by King Stanisław August Poniatowski, who commissioned Karol Agrykola, Karol Schultz, and Jan Schuch to lay it out as a formal garden. A number of buildings were added during this time, and the pavilion was redesigned, by Dominik Merlini, as a royal summer residence. Known as the **Palace on the Water**, this is one of the finest examples of Neoclassical

architecture in Poland. It now houses an architecture museum. The king enjoyed the palace only for a few years: after the Third Partition of Poland, he was forced to abdicate, and left Warsaw on January 7, 1795. Upon their withdrawal, the Nazis set fire to the palace. It was rebuilt by 1965.

Solomon's Hall in the Palace on the Water, Łazienki Park

⑫ Wilanów Palace and Park

S.K. Potockiego 10–16. **Tel** 022-842 25 09. E2, 116, 163, 180, 317, 519. Palace: **Open** daily. **Closed** Jan, Tue (in winter). Park: **Open** 9:30am–dusk daily. (free Sun).

Although it was a royal residence, Wilanów Palace, which is set within parkland and beautiful formal gardens, was

actually designed as a private retreat for King Jan III Sobieski, who valued family life above material splendor. The original property, known as Villa Nova, was purchased in 1677 and within two years had been rebuilt as a mansion, designed by royal architect Augustyn Locci. The elaborate facades were adorned with sculptures and murals, while the interiors were decorated by Europe's finest craftsmen.

Enlarged over subsequent years by its many different owners, the palace gained two large wings, a pair of towers, and a first-floor banqueting hall. The north wing comprises 19th-century rooms, formerly used as living quarters and as a gallery. The largest room, the Great Crimson Room, is used as a venue for entertaining VIPs. The south wing includes the late Baroque Great Dining Room, designed for King August II Mocny, as well as Princess Izabela Lubomirska's apartments, which feature a bathroom dating from 1775.

The most interesting rooms in the main part of the palace are the Neoclassical Great Hall, with marble detailing and allegorical friezes, and the ornate King's Bedchamber, with its 17th-century Turkish bed canopy. There are also apartments once occupied by King Jan III Sobieski and his wife Marysieńka, which retain many of their original 17th-century features, as well as an old nursery, governesses' rooms, and a fascinating portrait gallery. Outside the palace, in the old riding school building, there is an interesting poster museum.

The enchanting Palace on the Water, Łazienki Park

❷ Cracow

For nearly six centuries, Cracow was the capital of Poland and the country's largest city. Polish rulers resided at Wawel Castle until the court and parliament moved to Warsaw in 1596. Even then, Cracow continued to be regarded as the official capital and rulers were still crowned and buried in the cathedral on Wawel Hill. The city still plays an important role in preserving the national identity. The prestigious Jagiellonian University is the oldest in the country and the city is full of memorials to illustrious Poles. Perhaps Cracow's greatest attraction lies in the fact that, unlike so many Polish cities, it was scarcely damaged in World War II. In recent years, many buildings and monuments have been restored to their former glory.

Royal Castle
The Birds Hall, with its gilded coffered ceiling and marble fireplace, is one of the later 17th-century rooms in the castle's Royal Apartments.

Wawel Hill

In about 1038, Kazimierz the Restorer made the citadel on Wawel Hill the seat of Polish political power. In the 16th century, the Jagiellonian rulers transformed the Gothic castle into a magnificent Renaissance palace and endowed the cathedral with new chapels and works of art.

Statue of Tadeusz Kościuszko

Cathedral Museum

Lost Wawel Exhibition

Fortified walls

Dragon's Lair

Cracow Cathedral
The Zygmunt Chapel with its striking gilded dome was one of many additions to the cathedral made in the early 16th century.

The foundations of medieval houses that stood within the castle walls have been excavated here. The houses were razed by the Austrians in 1805–6 to create a parade ground.

🏛 Royal Castle

Wawel 5. **Tel** 012-422 51 55.
🚋 3, 6, 8, 10, 18. Royal Apartments:
Open daily. **Closed** Mon; public hols.
🎫 (Nov–Mar: free Sun).
Orient in the Wawel: **Open** Tue–Sun.
Closed Mon; public hols. 🎫 📷
Ⓦ wawel.krakow.pl

The present Renaissance castle was built in the first half of the 16th century. After the royal court moved from Cracow to Warsaw in 1596, the castle fell into decay. At the start of the 20th century, it was given to the city of Cracow and work began to restore it to its former glory.

The richly decorated Royal Apartments are the main reason for visiting the castle. Most of the rooms reflect the tastes of the last Jagiellonian kings. They contain Italian paintings and furniture, painted friezes around the walls, and a fine collection of Flemish tapestries. The Hall of Deputies was where the lower house of the Polish parliament, the *Sejm*, met for debates. It is also known as the Hall of Heads because the ceiling is decorated with carved heads. On the top floor, there is a suite of rooms from the 17th century, with portraits of the Waza kings, including one of Prince Władysław (later Władysław IV) by Rubens. The Crown Treasury and Armory are situated on the ground floor. The treasury's collection of royal jewels and regalia includes the coronation sword of the Polish kings.

The "Orient in the Wawel" collection on the first and second floors features Turkish tents and banners seized by the victorious Christian troops at the Siege of Vienna in 1683.

Turkish tent in the "Orient in the Wawel" exhibition in the castle

Royal Castle with the so-called Hen's Claw Wing on the right

🏛 Lost Wawel Exhibition

Wawel Hill. **Tel** 012-422 51 55.
Open daily. **Closed** Nov–Mar: Mon, public hols. 🎫 (free Sun in winter, Mon in summer).

An exhibition in the basement includes the remains of an early church, thought to date from the 11th century. Computer models illustrate the development of Wawel Hill.

Baroque silver reliquary of St. Stanisław by Peter von der Rennen (1669–71), Cracow Cathedral

🏛 Cracow Cathedral

Wawel 3. **Tel** 012-429 33 27. 🚋 8, 18.
Open daily (Sun: pm only). **Cathedral Museum Tel** 012-429 33 21.
Open Mon–Sat. 🎫

Originally founded in 1020, the present cathedral is the third to stand on this site. It was completed in 1364 during the reign of Kazimierz the Great. The resting place of many Polish kings, the cathedral has always held great symbolic significance for the nation. It is dedicated to St. Stanisław, whose relics are housed in an ornate reliquary in the shape of a coffin beneath an eye-catching Baroque altar canopy in the center of the nave.

The original Gothic cathedral has seen many later additions, notably the Baroque spire built in the early 1700s and the side chapels, which have been remodeled many times. There are many fine tombs of Polish rulers. The Renaissance Zygmunt Chapel was built in 1519–33 by the Italian Bartolomeo Berrecci. It contains an impressive double monument in red marble to Zygmunt the Old (reigned 1506–48) and his son Zygmunt August (reigned 1548–72). Look out too for the late Gothic canopied sarcophagus of Kazimierz Jagiellończyk carved by Veit Stoss (1492) in the Chapel of the Holy Cross. The marble tomb of Stefan Batory (reigned 1576–86), created by Santi Gucci in 1595, stands behind the altar.

The crypt is divided into sections containing the tombs and sarcophagi of other Polish rulers, leading poets, and national heroes, including Tadeusz Kościuszko, leader of the failed insurrection of 1794.

The Cathedral Museum houses a collection of sacred art and a selection of Polish royal regalia, including the coronation robe of the last Polish king, Stanisław August Poniatowski (reigned 1764–95).

🏛 Dragon's Lair

Wawel Hill. **Open** Apr–Oct: daily.

Beneath Wawel Hill is a series of caves associated with the legend of a dragon. In summer, part of the cave system can be reached by a set of spiral steps. Children take delight in the bronze, fire-breathing statue of a dragon at the entrance.

Cracow: the Old Quarter

In 1257, Cracow was granted a charter by Duke Bolesław the Chaste. This was of key importance to the city, ensuring local government and trade privileges and stimulating the city's future development. The charter stipulated certain conditions: a large centrally located square, surrounded by a regular grid of streets, was to become the city center. The size of each plot determined the size of the houses. Although the architecture became ever more opulent over the centuries, this urban scheme has survived almost intact. To this day, the Old Quarter remains the heart of modern Cracow. Many of the streets are pedestrianized, allowing visitors to enjoy the great concentration of historic sights.

The Slacker Crucifix (1496) by Veit Stoss in St. Mary's Church

The City Hall Tower in the western corner of Market Square

🏛 Market Square

Rynek Główny.

The Market Square is said to be the largest town square in Europe. In summer, nearly 30 street cafés remain open here until the early hours. Flower stalls, street musicians, and artists selling their works all contribute to the lively atmosphere. The ornate Cloth Hall virtually divides the square in two. Two other buildings stand in the square: the small green-domed Church of St. Adalbert, below which is a museum of the history of the square, and the City Hall Tower, a relic of the original Gothic town hall. There is also a monumental statue of the great Polish poet Adam Mickiewicz (1798–1855).

Buildings around the square retain elements from every era in the history of the city. Many are decorated with an emblem that gives the house its name, for example the Palace of the Rams on the west side of the square, home of a famous cabaret since 1956. Christopher Palace takes its name from a 14th-century statue of St. Christopher. The house was remodeled in 1682–5 around a beautiful arcaded courtyard. It is home to the Museum of Cracow, where paintings, gold artifacts from local workshops, documents, and memorabilia are displayed in a series of grand stuccoed rooms.

🏛 Cloth Hall

Market Square 1/3. **Tel** 012-433 54 00. **Open** Tue–Sun. 🏛 🏛

The Cloth Hall (Sukiennice) in the middle of Market Square originated in medieval times as a covered market. It was rebuilt after a fire in 1555 and then remodeled entirely in 1875 with arcades along the exterior that give it a Venetian look. Most of the stalls today sell souvenirs of various kinds and there is a gallery of 19th-century Polish painting on the upper floor. The Cloth

Hall also contains a number of cafés – the Noworolski Café is one of the best in Cracow.

🏛 St. Mary's Church

Mariacki Square 5. **Tel** 012-422 05 21. **Open** daily (pm only Sun). 🏛 🏛

St. Mary's facade with its two impressive Gothic towers is set at an angle on the east side of Market Square. The left-hand tower is topped by a spire added in 1478. It served as the city's watch tower and still today a bugle call is played every hour. It is even broadcast on Polish radio at noon. The projecting porch between the towers was added in the Baroque period.

The church's greatest treasure is the huge altarpiece, 12 m (39 ft) high, by Veit Stoss, who lived in Cracow from 1477 to 1496. The outer panels show scenes from the lives of Christ and the Virgin. The middle shutters are opened each day at noon to reveal the huge carved centerpiece, *The*

Horse-drawn cabs lined up in front of the Cloth Hall in Market Square

Assumption of the Virgin. There is also a fine crucifix by Veit Stoss, known as the Slacker Crucifix.

🏛 Czartoryski Museum

Św. Jana 19. **Tel** 012-422 55 66.
🚌 152, 304, 502. 🚊 2, 3, 4, 14, 19, 24.
Open Tue–Sun. 🎫 📷 (Sun).

The core of the museum is the art collection assembled by Princess Isabella Czartoryska in the late 18th century. It contains some magnificent paintings, notably Leonardo da Vinci's *Lady with an Ermine* and Rembrandt's *Landscape with the Good Samaritan*. The museum also has a collection of decorative arts from all over Europe and a section on Polish history.

Leonardo's *Lady with an Ermine* in the Czartoryski Museum

🏛 Collegium Maius

Jagiellońska 15. **Tel** 012-422 05 49.
🚌 152, 304, 502. 🚊 13, 18. **Open**
Mon–Sat. 🎫 📷 obligatory (call to book visit).

This is the oldest building of the Jagiellonian University. In the 15th century, a number of houses were amalgamated to create lecture rooms and housing for professors. It was extensively remodeled in the mid-19th century. At the heart of the building is an attractive Gothic cloister. The University Museum moved here after World War II. Visitors can see the 16th-century Libraria and Great Hall, rooms still used by the Senate of the university, and the Treasury. There is also a Copernicus Room dedicated to the great astronomer, who studied here in 1491–5.

🏛 Planty

Open daily.
The Planty green belt follows the outline of Cracow's medieval walls, which were demolished in the early 19th century. A circuit through the park of about 5 km (3 miles) starting from Wawel leads along tree-lined paths and avenues, past fountains and statues. Only a small stretch of the city walls survives beside St. Florian's Gate at the north end of the Old Town. Nearby stands a well-preserved round barbican built in 1498–9, when Turkish incursions were a serious threat to the city.

🏛 Old Synagogue

Szeroka 24. **Tel** 012-422 09 62.
🚊 11, 13, 19, 24, 52. **Open** daily.
📷 (free Mon).

In the late 15th century, Cracow's Jewish quarter was established in the Kazimierz district, east of Wawel Hill. At the outbreak of World War II, there was a community of some 70,000 Jews. The Nazis moved them all to a ghetto across the river, from where they were eventually deported to concentration camps.

Amazingly, a number of Jewish sites have survived. The Old Synagogue, carefully restored after the war, is not used for worship, but houses the Jewish Museum. The **Remu'h Synagogue** (c.1553), also on Szeroka Street, still functions. It is named after Rabbi Moses Remu'h, a 16th-century philosopher, whose tomb in

Hall of Prayers in Cracow's Old Synagogue

Entrance gate to the Auschwitz extermination camp

the **Remu'h Cemetery** attracts pilgrims from all over the world. Most of the graves were destroyed by the Nazis, but fragments from them have been piled up to form a "wailing wall."

Environs

Although the name Oświęcim means little to most foreigners, its German form **Auschwitz** evokes fear and horror in people all round the world. It was here near the little town of Oświęcim, about 55 km (35 miles) west of Cracow, that the Nazis established their largest complex of concentration and extermination camps. The Auschwitz camp opened in June 1940, and in March 1941, a much larger camp was set up at nearby Birkenau (Brzezinka in Polish). In all, over 1,500,000 Jews and others were murdered here. The gas chambers, capable of killing thousands daily, were in use from 1942 to January 1945, when the camps were liberated by Soviet troops.

The area has been declared a UNESCO World Heritage Site and the two camps are preserved as the **Muzeum Oświęcim-Brzezinka** – a grim warning to future generations of mankind's capacity for inhumanity. Many structures were destroyed as the Nazis left, but the gate, with the chilling words "Arbeit macht frei" ("Work makes free") written above it, still stands.

🏛 Muzeum Oświęcim-Brzezinka

ul. Więźniów Oświęcimia 20. 🚉 🚌
Tel 033-844 80 99. **Open** daily (closing time varies between 3pm in winter and 7pm in summer).
🌐 auschwitz.org.pl

Practical & Travel Information

Since the fall of Communism in 1989, tourism has greatly increased in Poland. New shops and hotels have sprung up, and the quality of service has improved, especially in banks and post offices. Nevertheless, much of Poland's economy has yet to adjust to the post-Communist era; the health service has been reformed, but it lags behind the country's many developing sectors. In general, goods in Poland are much cheaper than in Western Europe.

Visas and Customs Information

A valid passport is required for admittance to Poland, but you may not need a visa; contact the Polish embassy in your country for details. Personal items may be brought into the country, but limits are imposed on the import and export of alcohol, tobacco, and cigarettes. Antiques exported from the country require a special permit. Gifts worth up to €300 may be imported duty free.

Personal Security

Polish cities suffer from the same crime and security problems as most European capitals, so vigilance and care are needed. Security is provided by the state police, the highway police, and a number of private security organizations. The latter are often hired to protect public buildings and private houses, and to keep order at various events. In the city of Warsaw, it is advisable to avoid the Praga district after dusk, and in particular Ulica Brzeska.

Medical Emergencies

Citizens of the following countries are entitled to free medical treatment in Poland: EU members, Belarus, Tunisia, Ukraine, Mongolia, China, and the countries of the former Yugoslavia.

For visitors from other countries, first aid is provided free of charge at hospitals, but other types of treatment may incur a charge. Nevertheless, all visitors are advised to take out full medical insurance before arriving in Poland. Keep your policy documents with you at all times, as well as a passport for identifying yourself to hospital staff. An ambulance service is available 24 hours a day.

Tourist Information

Information centers are generally found at train stations; these provide general regional information. For specific enquiries about accommodations, tickets, and trains, the **Polish National Tourist Office** is preferable. Hotel employees are also a good source of information.

Currency and Banking

The official Polish currency is the złoty, each of which is divided into 100 grosze. In January 1995, four zeros were knocked off the złoty, so that 10,000 złoty became one Polish New Złoty (PLN). The old banknotes were withdrawn and replaced with new notes. Money can also be changed at bureaux de change, many of which offer better rates than banks. Most banks are open from 8am to 6pm.

Disabled Travelers

Poland has a poor record for providing for disabled people, but things are rapidly changing. All renovated or new public buildings have ramps or lifts built into them, and there are also special taxis available. However, many traditional sites of interest may prove difficult to enter. For general advice or for information about specific sites, contact the **Disabled People's National Council**.

Communications

Widespread use of cell phones means there are fewer payphones than before, but phonecard-operated telephones can still be found, especially around railway stations, post offices, and the city center. Phonecards can be bought at post offices and newsagents. Charges for long-distance national calls vary according to the time of day. The highest charges are for calls made between 8am and 6pm. Local calls are cheaper from 10pm to 6am. The charges for international calls do not vary with time of day. Poland has four cell telephone networks, which operate on two wavelengths, 900 MHz and 1,800 MHz, and cover almost all of the country.

Poczta Polska, the Polish postal service, provides a wide range of services, and its offices are open from 8am to 8pm on weekdays; the main post office in Warsaw is open 24 hours a day, seven days a week. Letters to destinations

The Climate of Poland

Poland's climate is influenced by cold polar air from Scandinavia, and sub-tropical air from the south. Polar-continental fronts dominate in winter, bringing crisp, frosty weather, while late summer and autumn (the most popular times to visit) enjoy plenty of warm sunny days. Winters, which always bring snow, can be very cold in the north.

WARSAW			
°C/°F			
		21/70	
	7/45	11/52	7/45
	0/32		2/36	-3/27
				-8/18
5 hrs	7.5 hrs	3 hrs	1.5 hrs
42 mm	56 mm	40 mm	40 mm
month	Apr	Jul	Oct	Jan

within Poland usually arrive within three or four days of posting, while international mail may take up to a week; intercontinental mail can take up to three weeks. Post boxes are red and easily identifiable. For urgent mail, Poczta Polska provides both an express service and a courier service. The international DHL and UPS courier agencies also operate in Poland.

Traveling by Plane

Poland is well connected with the rest of the world. International flights from some 90 cities in 40 countries arrive in Warsaw. The airports at Gdańsk, Katowice, Szczecin, Poznań, Wrocław, and Cracow also have international flights, linking Poland with much of Western Europe, as well as Prague, Budapest, Bucharest, Sofia, and the capitals of the former Soviet Union. Some 30 airlines, including British Airways, Air France, SAS (Scandinavia), and Lufthansa (Germany), operate from **Warsaw Chopin** airport, which has direct connections with Canada, the US, Israel, and Thailand. **Cracow John Paul II**, the second largest airport in

Poland, offers a substantial number of domestic and international flights.

Traveling by Bus

Most long-distance routes within Poland are served by Polish Motor Transport, Polska Komunikaja Samochodowa (PKS). A competitor is Polski Bus, which offers cheaper fares, air-conditioned coaches, and wireless Internet access, but they connect only the major cities.

Local buses are sometimes the only means of getting to minor towns and villages. The services are generally punctual, although before 8am and in the afternoon they may be crowded. Tickets for these are always bought from the driver.

Traveling by Train

International train services run between all major European and Polish cities. The journeys by fast train from Warsaw to Prague and Berlin take just six and nine hours respectively. The main rail route runs across Poland from east to west, connecting Russia with western Europe.

Express lines connect almost all the big cities, and the trains

are fast and usually arrive on time. The most comfortable, and most expensive, are the InterCity trains, which also give passengers a snack. InterCity trains provide compartments for mothers with children and for disabled people. Fares for ordinary and fast trains are very reasonable; express trains and sleeping cars are expensive, although not by the standards of the rest of Europe.

Suburban routes are served by electric trains, which sometimes consist of open-plan, double-decker cars.

Traveling by Car

Poland has few highways, but new routes are added each year to build a network of highways spanning the entire country. While this work is being carried out, drivers might be affected by delays.

Wherever you drive in Poland, always carry your passport, car insurance, license, green card, and rental contract with you, and if you are driving a foreign car, display the international symbol of its country of origin.

All the major international car rental companies operate in Warsaw and Cracow.

DIRECTORY

Tourist Offices in Poland

Cracow
Rynek Główny 1–3.
Tel 012-433 73 10.

Warsaw
ul. Krakowskie Przedmieście 65.
Tel 022-635 18 81.

Tourist Offices Outside Poland

UK
Level 3, Westgate House, West Gate, London W5 1YY. **Tel** 030-0303 1812.
w **poland.travel/en-gb**

US
5 Marine View Plaza, Suite 303B, Hoboken, New Jersey 07030. **Tel** 201-420 9910.
w **poland.travel/en-us**

Emergency Numbers

Ambulance
Tel 999.

Fire Brigade
Tel 998.

Medical Advice
Tel 94 39.

Police
Tel 997.

Embassies

Australia
ul. Nowogrodzka 11, Warsaw.
Tel 022-521 34 44.

Canada
ul. Matejki 1/5, Warsaw.
Tel 022-584 31 00.
w **canada.pl**

UK
ul. Kawalerii 12.
Tel 022-311 00 00.
w **ukinpoland.fco. gov.uk**

US
Al Ujazdowskie 29/31, Warsaw.
Tel 022-504 20 00.
w **poland. usembassy. gov**

Facilities for the Disabled

Disabled People's National Council
ul. Andersa 13, Warsaw.
Tel 022-530 65 70.

Train Stations

Warsaw Central
Jerozolimskie 54.
Tel 022-94 36.

Airports

Cracow John Paul II
Tel 012-295 58 00.

Warsaw Chopin
Tel 022-650 42 20.

Car Rental

AVIS Poland
Cracow, ul. Lubicz 23.
Tel 012-639 32 89.
Warsaw Airport.
Tel 022-650 48 72.
w **avis.pl**

Hertz Rent-a-Car
Cracow, al. Focha 1.
Tel 012-429 62 62.
Warsaw Chopin Airport.
Tel 022-650 28 96.
Warsaw Modlin Airport.
Tel 022-650 28 96.
w **hertz.com.pl**

Where to Stay

Warsaw

CITY CENTER:
Chmielna Guesthouse ②
Boutique **Map** C4
ul. Chmielna 13, 00-021
Tel *022-828 12 82*
🆆 chmielnabb.pl
Stay in charming small rooms –
some with en-suite bathrooms
and some with shared facilities.
Accommodations have a travel
theme and are grouped around
a common lounge/dining room.

CITY CENTER:
SleepWell Apartments ②
Boutique **Map** D4
ul. Nowy Świat 62, 00-357
Tel *022-828 12 82*
🆆 sleepwell-warsaw.pl
Each of these centrally located
studio apartments boasts a
bold interior design ranging
from modern to kitsch.

DK Choice

CITY CENTER: Rialto ②②
Boutique
ul. Wilcza 73, 00-670
Tel *022-584 87 00*
🆆 rialto.pl
An Art Deco vibe runs through
this characterful and elegant
hotel. Every detail, from the
furniture to the light fittings, is
a faithful reproduction of the
Roaring Twenties style, and
many of the bathrooms have
beautiful period tiling. The
stylish rooms are comfortable
and have contemporary
amenities including flat-screen
TVs and espresso machines.
Helpful and attentive staff.

CITY CENTER:
Sofitel Victoria ②②
Modern **Map** D3
ul. Królewska 11, 00-065
Tel *022-657 80 11*
🆆 sofitel.com
Located opposite Warsaw's
lush Saxon Gardens, the Sofitel
Victoria offers well-furnished
rooms with all the amenities.

CITY CENTER:
Hotel Bristol ②②②
Luxury **Map** D3
*Krakowskie Przedmieście 42/44,
00-325*
Tel *022-551 10 00*
🆆 hotelbristolwarsaw.pl
Housed in a sumptuous building,
the Bristol has a guest list that
includes presidents and rock

stars. The rooms combine
old-school luxury with all
modern conveniences.

CITY CENTER:
InterContinental ②②②
Luxury **Map** C3
ul. Emilii Plater 49, 00-125
Tel *022-328 88 88*
🆆 warsaw.intercontinental.com
Large rooms and great facilities at
this hotel in one of the city's tallest
and most luxurious buildings.

CITY CENTER: Residence
St. Andrews Place ②②②
Luxury **Map** D4
ul. Chmielna 30, 00-100
Tel *022-826 46 40*
🆆 residence standrews.com.pl
The St. Andrews offers luxury
apartments in a renovated pre-
World War I building. Short- or
long-term stays.

FARTHER AFIELD:
Premiere Classe ②
Budget
ul. Towarowa 2, 00-811
Tel *022-624 08 00*
🆆 premiereclasse.com.pl
Budget travelers can stay in
basic but clean and neat rooms
in a modern building with
helpful staff.

Cracow

OLD QUARTER: Abel ②
Boutique
ul. Józefa 30, 31-056
Tel *012-411 87 36*
🆆 hotelabel.pl
Small but characterful rooms,
each individually furnished, in
the heart of the bohemian
district of Kazimierz.

Art Deco design touches and neutral tones
at the Rialto hotel, Warsaw

Price Guide
Prices are based on one night's stay in
high season for a standard double room,
inclusive of service charges and taxes.

②	up to 300 złoty
②②	300 to 600 złoty
②②②	over 600 złoty

OLD QUARTER: Batory ②
Budget
ul Sołtyka 19, 31-529
Tel *012-294 30 30*
🆆 hotelbatory.pl
Within walking distance of both
the Old Town and Kazimierz, this
family-run hotel has warmly
decorated rooms.

OLD QUARTER: Francuski ②②
Boutique
ul. Pijarska 13, 31-015
Tel *666-195 831*
🆆 hotel-francuski.com
A classic Cracow hotel with
antique furnishings, exemplary
service, a good restaurant, and
a superb Old Town location.

OLD QUARTER: Hotel Royal ②②
Boutique
ul. Św. Gertrudy 26/29, 31-048
Tel *012-421 35 00*
🆆 hotelewam.pl
Housed in a 19th-century
building with Art Nouveau
features, the Royal has simple
en-suite rooms.

OLD QUARTER:
Wit Stwosz ②②
Modern
ul. Mikołajska 28, 31-207
Tel *012-429 60 26*
🆆 wit-stwosz.com.pl
Close to the main square, this
hotel in a historic building offers
spacious rooms, the coziest of
which are on the attic floor.

OLD QUARTER: Grand
Hotel Cracow ②②②
Historic
ul. Sławkowska 5/7, 31-014
Tel *012-424 08 00*
🆆 grand.pl
Offering the best in comfort
and service for over a century,
the Grand has regally furnished
rooms in a former palace.

OLD QUARTER:
Sheraton ②②②
Luxury
ul. Powiśle 7, 31-101
Tel *012-662 10 00*
🆆 sheraton.pl
The Sheraton has comfortable
rooms, a full range of facilities,
and smooth service. Located on
the banks of the Vistula river.

Where to Eat and Drink

Elegantly laid-out tables in the dining room at Wentzl, Cracow

Price Guide
Prices are based on a three-course meal for one, with half a bottle of house wine, and all extra charges.
ⓩ up to 50 złoty
ⓩⓩ 50 to 75 złoty
ⓩⓩⓩ over 75 złoty

Warsaw

CITY CENTER: Cafe 6/12 ⓩ
Café **Map** D4
ul. Żurawia 6/12, 00-503
Tel *022-622 53 33*
Versatile café with a broad choice of light and main meals, ranging from breakfast to salads and mains with an Oriental twist.

**CITY CENTER:
Kompania Piwna** ⓩ
Polish **Map** D2
ul. Podwale 25, 00-261
Tel *022-635 63 14*
An Old Town gem with a courtyard designed to resemble a town square. Savor heaps of meat and potatoes, served on wooden boards.

CITY CENTER: Adler ⓩⓩ
German **Map** D5
ul. Mokotowska 69, 00-530
Tel *022-628 73 84*
Adler embodies the atmosphere of a Bavarian beer hall, with staff rushing around delivering gigantic portions of pork knuckle and schnitzel.

CITY CENTER: Papaya ⓩⓩⓩ
Asian **Map** D4
ul. Foksal 16, 00-372
Tel *022-826 48 51*
This upscale fusion restaurant on a popular bar-and-restaurant strip serves imaginative Oriental meat and seafood dishes in über-cool surroundings.

**FARTHER AFIELD:
India Curry** ⓩⓩ
Indian
ul. Żurawia 22, 00-515
Tel *022-438 93 50*
An Indian restaurant that gets everything right, with a varied menu of truly spicy food, plenty of choices for vegetarians, and a tasteful, relaxing interior.

**FARTHER AFIELD:
Sakana Sushi Bar** ⓩⓩ
Japanese
ul. Moliera 4/6, 00-076
Tel *022-826 59 58*
One of the best sushi restaurants in town, Sakana serves a range of Japanese classics to a fashion-conscious crowd.

**FARTHER AFIELD:
Dom Polski** ⓩⓩⓩ
Polish
ul. Francuska 11, 03-906
Tel *022-616 24 32*
This restaurant serves some of the classiest fare in Poland. The menu is seasonal and often features superb game dishes.

**FARTHER AFIELD:
Warszawa Wschodnia** ⓩⓩⓩ
Polish/European
ul. Mińska 25, 01-999
Tel *022-870 29 18*
Modern Polish-European cuisine served up in chic surroundings, in a former factory in the Praga suburb. The menu changes daily according to what is fresh.

Cracow

OLD QUARTER: Chimera ⓩ
Polish/Mediterranean
ul. Św. Anny 3, 31-008
Tel *012-292 12 12*
Self-service restaurant offering a pick-and-mix selection of mains and salads. Vegetarians are well catered for.

OLD QUARTER: Klezmer Hois ⓩ
Jewish
ul. Szeroka 6, 31-053
Tel *012-411 12 45*
Dine at this characterful restaurant in the former Jewish quarter. On the menu is a range of Jewish-influenced dishes featuring meat, fish, and fowl.

**OLD QUARTER: Zapiecek
Pierogarnia** ⓩ
Polish
ul. Sławkowska 32, 31-014
Tel *012-422 74 95*
This inexpensive restaurant specializes in *pierogi*, the typically Polish pastry parcels stuffed with a variety of savory and sweet fillings.

OLD QUARTER: Marmolada ⓩⓩ
Italian/Polish
ul. Grodzka 5, 31-006
Tel *012-396 49 46*
A winning blend of Polish classics and Italian-themed dishes is served in a candlelit interior bedecked with flowers.

**OLD QUARTER: Cyrano
de Bergerac** ⓩⓩⓩ
French
ul. Sławkowska 26, 31-014
Tel *012-411 72 88*
A world-class French restaurant occupying elegant rooms, Cyrano offers exquisite food and a huge list of wines. The set lunches are excellent value.

OLD QUARTER: Farina ⓩⓩⓩ
Mediterranean
ul. Św. Marka 16, 31-018
Tel *012-422 16 80*
Farina is one of the best seafood restaurants in town, with Mediterranean-themed dishes served up in a homely room with wooden tables.

DK Choice

OLD QUARTER: Wentzl ⓩⓩⓩ
European
Rynek Główny 19, 31-008
Tel *012-429 52 99*
Opened by local merchant John Wentzl in 1792, this has been one of the best restaurants in the city ever since. The high ceilings, polished oak floors, and outstanding service provide a classy environment in which to feast on a well-chosen blend of French and Central-European fare. The wine list is extensive and the next-door Wentzl café serves superb cakes as well as ice cream.

General Index

Acknowledgments

Dorling Kindersley would like to thank the following people whose contributions and assistance have made the preparation of this book possible.

Main Contributors Amy Brown, Nina Hathway, Vivien Stone, Kristina Woolnough.

Additional Contributors John Ardagh, Rosemary Bailey, David Baird, Josie Barnard, Rosemary Barron, Gretel Beer, Ros Belford, Marc Bennetts, Willem de Blaauw, Kathleen Blankenship Sauret, Susie Boulton, Gerhard Bruschke, Caroline Bugler, Paula Canal, Chloe Carleton, Christopher Catling, Robin Clapp, Anthony Clark, Juliet Clough, Deidre Coffey, Dan Colwell, Marc Dubin, Paul Duncan, Sylvia Earley, Joanna Egert-Romanowska, Olivia Ercoli, Judith Fayard, Jane Foster, Stephanie Ferguson, Lisa Gerard-Sharp, Mike Gerrard, Jane Graham, Andrew Gumbel, Mark Harding, Andy Harris, Vicky Hayward, Zöe Hewetson, Sally Hogset, Adam Hopkins, Lindsay Hunt, Nick Inman, Tim Jepson, Colin Jones, Emma Jones, Marion Kaplan, Ciara Kenny, Alister Kershaw, Piotr Kozlowski, Wojciech Kozlowski, Sarah Lane, Michael Leapman, Philip Lee, Alec Lobrano, Sarah McAlister, Jerzy S. Majewski, Fred Mawer, Lynette Mitchell, Colin Nicholson, Melanie Nicholson-Hartzell, Roger Norum, Tadeusz Olsański, Małgorzata Omilanowska, Agnes Ördög, Robin Osborne, Lyn Parry, Robin Pascoe, Alice Peebles, Tim Perry, Polly Phillimore, Filip Polonski, Paul Richardson, Anthony Roberts, Barnaby Rogerson, Zöe Ross, Doug Sager, Kaj Sandell, Jürgen Scheunemann, Jane Shaw, Barbara Sobeck-Miller, Vladimír Soukup, Solveig Steinhardt, Robert Strauss, Martin Symington, Allan Tillier, Nigel Tisdall, Roger Thomas, Tanya Tsikas, Annika Tuominen, Alison Vagen, Gerard van Vuuren, Roger Williams, Timothy Wright, Scott Alexander Young.

Illustrators Acanto Arquitectura y Urbanismo S.L., Stephen Conlin, Gary Cross, Richard Draper, Nick Gibbard, Paul Guest, Stephen Gyapay, Studio Illibill, Kevin Jones Associates, Paweł Marczak, Maltings Partnership, Chris Orr and Associates, Otakar Pok, Robbie Polley, Jaroslav Staněk, Paul Weston, Andrzej Wielgosz, Ann Winterbotham, John Woodcock, Martin Woodward, Piotr Zubrzycki.

Revisions Team Ashwin Adimari, Douglas Amrine, Emma Anacootee, Claire Baranowski, Sonal Bhatt, Julie Bond, Surya Deogan, Mariana Evmolpidou, Emer FitzGerald, Ansgar Frankenberg, Fay Franklin, Rhiannon Furbear, Jeremy Gray, Lucinda Hawksley, Matthew Ibbotson, Jacky Jackson, Laura Jones, Zafar ul Islam Khan, Priya Kukadia, Michelle de Larrabeiti, Delphine Lawrance, Jude Ledger, Darren Longley, Hayley Maher, Catherine Palmi, Helen Partington, Helen Peters, Dave Pugh, Pete Quinlan, Marisa Renzullo, Lucy Richards, Simon Ryder, Sands Publishing Solutions, Surya Sankash Sarangi, Kathleen Sauret, Sadie Smith, Leah Tether, Hugh Thompson, Conrad van Dyk, Karen Villabona, Simon Wilder, Dora Whitaker, Alex Whittleton.

Factchecker Jessica Hughes.
Proofreader Stewart J. Wild.
Index Hilary Bird.

Additional Picture Research Marta Bescos, Nicole Kaczynski.
Additional DTP Vinod Harish, Vincent Kurien, Azeem Siddiqui.
Additional Cartography Uma Bhattacharya, Mohammad Hassan, Jasneet Kaur.
Production Joanna Bull, Sarah Dodd, Marie Ingledew.
Publishing Manager Helen Townsend.
Managing Art Editor Jane Ewart.
Director of Publishing Gilllian Allan.
Additional Photography Max Alexander, Peter Anderson, Gabor Barka, Steve Bere, Clive Bournsnell, Maciej Bronarski, Demetrio Carrasco, Andrzej Chec, Krzysztof Chojnacki, Stephen Conlin, Joe Cornish, Andy Crawford, Michael Crocket, Wojciech Czerniewicz, Tim Daly, Jiří Doležal, Philip Dowell, Mike Dunning, Philip Enticknap, Jane Ewart, Foto Carfagna Associati, Philip Gatward, Steve Gorton, Barry Hayden, A. Hayder, Heidi Grassley, John Heseltine, Gabriel Hilderbrandt, Roger Hilton, Rupert Horrox, Ed Ironside, Dorota Jarymowicz, Mariusz Jarymowicz, Piotr Jamski, Colin Keates, Paul Kenward, Alan Keohand, Dave King, Jiří Kopřiva, Mariusz Kowalewski, Vladimír Kozlík, Adrian Lascom, Cyril Laubscher, Neil Lukas, Eric Meacher, Wojciech Mędrzak, Neil Mersh, Jo hn Miller, John Moss, Roger Moss, David Murray, Hanna Musiał, Maciej Musiał, Tomasz Myśluk, Stephen Oliver, John Parker, Agencja "Piękna," Milan Posselt, František Přeučil, Rob Reichenfeld, Tim Ridley, Kim Sayer, Jules Selmes, Helena Smith, Anthony Souter, Clive Streeter, Stanislav Tereba, Matthew Ward, Alan Williams, Peter Wilson, Jeremy Whitaker, Linda Whitwam, Stephen Whitehorn, Paweł Wójcik, Stephen Wooster, Francesca Yorke, Jan Zych.

Photography Permissions
Dorling Kindersley would like to thank all the churches, museums, galleries, and other sights that kindly gave their permission for us to photograph their establishments and works of art.

Picture Credits
a = above; b = below/bottom; c = center; f = far; l = left; r = right; t = top.

Works of art have been reproduced with the permission of the following copyright holders: Guernica Pablo Picasso © Succession Picasso/DACS, London 2011 39bc; *Maman* (1999) by Louise Bourgeois © DACS, London/VAGA, New York 2011 67tl; Pit Stop (1984) Jean Tinguely © ADAGP, Paris and DACS, London 2011 581tr; Young Woman on the Shore Edvard Munch © Munch Museum/Munch – Ellingsen Group, BONO, Oslo/DACS, London 2011, 625bl.

The publisher would like to thank the following individuals, companies, and picture libraries for permission to reproduce their photographs:

4Corners: Günter Gräfenhain 144, SIME / Paolo Giocoso 368 **AISA - Archivo Iconográfico S. A., Barcelona:** Museo del Prado, *The Triumph of Bachus* by Velasquez 278cla; Prado, Madrid 32bl. **Akg-images:** Vatican Museums, Rome, Emporer Augustus 1c, 35tl; San Francesco, Assisi, Stefan Diller, *St Francis Appears to the Monks at Arles* by Giotto 36br; Staatliche Kunstsammlungen, Kassel, *William I of Orange* by Anthonis Mor (1556) 238tc; Rijksmuseum, *Winter Landscape with Skaters* by Hendrick Avercamp 248ca; Museum Boymans-van Beuningen,

Rotterdam, *The Tower of Babel* by Peter Brueghel the Elder 255br; *Cosimo de Medici* 402bc; *St Augustine* by Carpaccio 403crb; *Niccolo Macchiavelli* 403br, *Farnese Hercules* 426c; Collection Archiv fur Kunst und Geschichte, Berlin 446tr, 680cla; Naturhistorisches Museum, Eric Lessing 561bc; Niederschisisches Landesmuseum, Hannover, *Frederick II* by Antoine Pesne 496tc. **Alan Copson Photography:** 222cl. **Alamy Images:** hemis.fr/Ludovic Maisant 440br; Louise Heusinkveld 676tr; Brendan Hoffman 658bl; LOOK Die Bildagentur der Fotografen GmbH 332br; RGB Ventures 668; Ken Welsh 349tl; Westend61 GmbH 23ca. **Alvey and Towers:** 147br. **Amsterdams Historisch Museum:** 245cl. **The Ancient Egypt Picture Library:** 1978 The Trustees of The British Museum 32cla. **Andersen Hotel:** 648br. **Angelo Hornak Library:** 86cl. **Apex Photo Agency:** 47t. **Arenas Fotografia Artistica:** 315c. **The Art Archive:** The Imperial War Museum 225br; British Library 127bl. **Art Directors & TRIP:** C. Rennie 601b, 603bl, 611bc. **Artothek SpecialArchiv Fur Gemaelefotografie, Peissenberg:** *Four Apostles* (1526), by Albrecht Durer 523tr. **James Austin:** 152br. **Austrian National Tourist Office:** 558clb, 567tc. **Avignon Tourisme:** 191cr. **Basílica De La Sagrada Família:** Pep Daudé 303crb. **Bayerische Schlösserverwaltung, München, www. schloesser.bayern.de:** 516b, 521t, 527c. **Bayerisches Nationalmuseum, Munich:** 524tr. **Berliner Dom:** Karola Buhn 506br. **Bethnal Green Museum, V&A, London:** 65bc. **Belga Queen:** 235br. **Berns Hotel:** 616br. **Bibendum Restaurant Ltd:** 107tl. **Bildarchiv Preußischer Kulturbesitz, Berlin:** 504bl, Kunstgewerbemuseum 503c; Pergamon Museum 33tl. **Bock Bisztró:** 705bl. **Bohem Art Hotel:** 704bc. **Gerard Boullay:** 155cr, 155bl. **The Bridgeman Art Library:** *Equestrian Portrait of Louis XIV* (1638-1715) Crowned by Victory, c.1692 (oil on canvas), Mignard, Pierre (1612-95) / Chateau de Versailles, France / Giraudon 37tr; *Madonna of the Rocks*, c.1478 (oil on panel transferred to canvas) by Vinci, Leonardo da (1452-1519) / Louvre, Paris, France 37bl; Reduced model of a guillotine (wood & metal), French School, (18th century) / Musee de la Ville de Paris, Musee Carnavalet, Paris, France / Giraudon 38cla; *The Oath of Horatii*, 1784 (oil on canvas), David, Jacques Louis (1748-1825) / Louvre, Paris, France / Giraudon 38clb; *Guernica*, 1937 (oil on canvas), Picasso, Pablo (1881-1973) / Museo Nacional Centro de Arte Reina Sofia, Madrid, Spain 39cb; *Portrait of Queen Elizabeth I* (1533-1603) (oil on panel), Gheeraerts, Marcus, the Younger (c.1561-1635) / Private Collection / 46tc; British Museum / Sutton Hoo helmet 60c; British Museum / *Festival of Sekhtet* 60br; British Museum / Portland vase 61tl; British Museum / The young Prince with his parents, from the 'Akbarnama' (vellum), Persian School, (16th century) 61c; Princes Edward and Richard in the Tower by Sir John Everett Millais / Royal Holloway & Bedford New College 69bc; Many fall in battle and King Harold is killed, detail from the Bayeux Tapestry, before 1082 (wool embroidery on linen)/ Musee de la Tapisserie, Bayeux, France 173tl; Field Marshall King Leopold I of Belgium, Pieneman, Nicholas, The Crown Estate, Institute of Directors, London 214tc; *The Martyrdom of St. Philip*, 1639 (oil on canvas), Ribera, Jusepe de (lo Spagnoletto) (c.1590-1652) / Prado, Madrid, Spain / Giraudon / Museo del Prado / 278c; The Clothed Maja by Goya / Museo del Prado / 279cr; *The Three Graces* by Rubens / Museo del Prado 279crb; *The Naked Maja* by Goya, Museo del Prado 279br, The Annunciation by Fra Angelico, Museo del Prado 280cr; *The Adoration of the Shepherds* by El Greco, Museo del Prado 280bl; *The Ecstasy of St. Francis* by Giotto di Bondone, San Francesco, Upper Church, Assisi, Italy, Giraudon 388clb; *The Venus of Urbino* by Titan / Galleria degli Uffizi 404bc, *Duke of Urbino* by Piero della Francesca / Galleria degli Uffizi 405tl, *Duchess of Urbino* by Piero della Francesca / Galleria degli Uffizi / 405tc, *Madonna of the Goldfinch* by Raphael / Galleria degli Uffizi 406bl; Matthias I, Hunyadi (1440-90) / Kunsthistorisches Museum, Vienna 692c, *Young woman on the Shore* by Edward Munch / Munch-Museet, Oslo 625bl. **The Trustees of the British Museum:** Bust of Perikles 34tr, 61br, 455bl.**Britstock-ifa:** F. Aberham 583br; AP&F / Thomas Ulrich 585bc; Erich Bach 587br, 588bl; S. Bohnacker 566t; Bernd Ducke 566bl; Torsten fleer 229br; Gunter Graefenhain 229cla, 567bl, 613tr, 645cl; P. Graf 612tl; S. Grafenwhain 553b, 584cla, 586tl; B. Moller 610br. **Budapesti Torteneti Muzeum:** 696br. **Budapesti Turisztikai Hivatal:** 697bl. **Cafe du Palais:** 210tr. **Café Fábulas:** 363br. **Café Paradiso:** 139br. **Café Paris:** 551tl. **Camera Press:** Cecil Beaton

54bc. **CH Bastin & J Evrard:** 226bc. **Chur Tourismus:** 588tc. **Circus Hotel, Berlin:** 546br. **Collections du musée international d'horlogerie, La Chaux-de-Fonds, Suisse:** Photo Institut l'homme et le Temps 581c. **Cologne Cathedral Metropolitabkapital Dombauarchiv:** 534cl, 534br, 535tl, 535cra, 535crb, 535bl. **Cook:** 575bl. **Corbis:** Archivo Iconografico, SA, *An Old Woman Cooking Eggs* by Velazquez 93bl; Arte & Immagini srl, *The Annunciation* by Fra Angelico 397tr; Yann Arthus-Bertrand 294tl; Bettman Archive 497bl, 620tl; For Picture / Stephane Reix 371bl; Historical Picture Archive 38br; Hulton-Deutsch Collection 321cr; JAI / Alan Copson 355t; Bob Krist 554tr; Macduff Everton 612c; Dennis Marsico 389tc; National Gallery / Bathers at Asnieres 57br; Richard T. Nowitz 587tr; Jose F. Poblete 589tl; Gregor Schmid 495b; SOPA RF / Sandra Raccanello 2-3/ Maurizio Rellini 8-9; Ted Spiegel 627cl; Michael St. Maur Sheil 719tr; Peter Turnley 708tl; Adam Woolfitt 143crb. **Joe Cornish:** 157tc, 290tr. **COVER:** Ilenas Quim 294br. **Crown: Historic Royal Palaces:** 71tr. **Da Paolino restaurant:** 443br. **Daimler AG:** 529tc. **De Jopenkerk:** 261tl. **Dean and Chapter of Westminster:** 524tl. **Delic:** 333tl. **Design Hotel Sax:** 688bl. **Deutsches Museum:** 524bl. **CM Dixon:** Vatican Museums, Rome 33bl. **Domaine des Hauts de Loire:** 207tr. **Dorling Kindersley:** Max Alexander / TAP Service Archaeological Receipts Fund Hellenic Republic Ministry of Culture 34cl; The British Museum 34br; Mike Dunning / Capitoline Museums 35bl; Matthew Ward / Bethnal Green V&A 65bc; The Provost and Fellows of King's College, Cambridge 81tr; National Museum of Ireland 117crb; Eric Meacher / Musee Rodin 162crb; Max Alexander / Musee des Beaux Arts Dijon 182br; Max Alexander / Palais des Papes 191cr; Linda Whitwam / Museu Nacional do Azulejo 342c; Marques de Pombal / Museu da Cidade, Lisboa 345tc; John Heseltine / Triumph of Faith over Heresy by Pierre Legros / Gesu 383cl; Mike Dunning / Musei Capitolini 383bc; John Heseltine / Museo Borghese 387tc; John Heseltine / Portrait of a Young Man in a Red Hat by Carpaccio / Museo Correr 420tl; John Heseltine / Flight into Egypt by Tintoretto / Scuola Grande di San Rocco 420br; TAP Service Archeological Receipts Fund Hellenic Republic Ministry of Culture 454clb, 455tl, 455cb; Peter Wilson / TAP Service Archeological Receipts Fund Hellenic Republic Ministry of Culture 454cla; John Heseltine / TAP Service Archaeological Receipts Fund Hellenic Republic Ministry of Culture: Thessaloniki Archaeological Museum 464bc; Joe Cornish / TAP Service Archaeological Receipts Fund Hellenic Republic Ministry of Culture 467tl; Erik Svensson / Jeppe Wikstrom 605br; Peter Anderson / Danish National Museum 627cb; Peter Anderson / Statens Historiska Museum 627cr. Dreamstime.com: Steve Allen 706; Daria Angelova 634; Antartis 13tr; Anyaivanova 494; Bagaroll 690; David Bailey 17r; Michal Bednarek 140-141; Dan Breckwoldt 576; Coplandj 336; Mikael Damkier 600; Dennis Dolkens 12br; Adam Dufek 15tl; Sergii Figurnyi 28-29; Frenta 266; Fverheij 613b; Hel080808 16bl; Inkwelldodo 14br; Javarman 618; Jakub Jirsák 490-491; Leonardoboss 212; Marcin Ciesielski / Sylwia Cisek 40-41; Marsana 16tr; Mpanch 110; Panagiotis Karapanagiotis 444; Pavel068 552; Prostoguss 17bl; Rudi1976 664-665; Sborisov 236, 262-263; Scanrail 596-597; Diamantis Seitanidis 12tl; Henry Soesanto 11tr; Stevanzz 364-365; Straga 344t; Victor Torres 14tl; Tupungato 44, 522bl; Oleg Zhukov 650; Zoom-zoom 15br. Duchas, The Heritage Service: 124br. **El Celler de Can Roca:** 334tc. **El Correo Cocina Argentina:** 488tc. **European Commission:** 23. **Eye Ubiquitous / Hutchison:** James Davis 306br. **Fairmont Hotel Vier Jahreszeiten:** 548tl. **Fischers Fritz, Berlin:** 549bl. **FMGB Guggenheim Bilbao Museoa, London 1999:** Erica Barahona Ede. 39crb. **Funky Gourmet:** 487tc. **Getty Images:** Panoramic Images 502t; Hugh Sitton 73r; James Strachan 666clb. **Giuseppe Carfagna & Associati:** 409bc. **Godo-foto:** 308br. **Grand Hotel de la Minerve:** 438bl. **Grand Hotel Karel V:** 260br. **Michael Grychowski:** 716tr. **Guiness Ireland Ltd:** 123c. **Gordon Henderson:** 89tl. **Hera Hotel:** 484bc. **Het Scheepvaartmuseum:** 247bl. **Hollmann Beletage, Vienna:** 574tl. **Hôtel Bristol:** 208tl. **Hotel Kämp:** 662bc. **Hotel Pelops:** 485tl. **Hulton Archive/Getty Images:** 37tc, 146br, 222br, 245c, 447c, 624br; Hulton Deutsch 670tc; Imperial War Museum 39tl. **Hungarian National Gallery:** 696tr. **Hungarian National Tourist Office:** 666cr, 701tc. **Ideal Photo A.E:** T. Passios 465tl. **Il Dagherrotipo:** Riccardo D'Errico 425tc. **Imagestate:** 283ca, 283cl. **Impact Photos:** Brian Harris 369b. **Index Fototeca:** 313cr.

Institute e Museo di Storia della Scienza di Firenze: 401br. Instituto Portugues de Museus: Museu Grao Vasco 346cr. International Bulbflower Centre: 253tc. Stanisawa Jabonska: 717bl. Jarold Colour Publications: 2001 His Grace Duke of marlborough & Jarold Publishing 83tc. Jewish Historical Museum, Amsterdam: Liselore Kamping 243tr. JORVIK: 87tl. Oldrich Karasek: 684cl, 684br, 685tl, 685br. Koefoed: 649tc. Koninklijk Museum voor Schone Kunsten: As the Old Sang, The Young Play Pipes by Jacob Jordaen 224bl. Kornhauskeller: 595tl. Kunsthistorisches Museum, Vienna: 33cr, 560tr, 562c; Empress Elisabeth by Winterhalter 560cl; Hunters in the Snow by Peter Brueghel the Elder 562tl. Maria Laach Kunstverlag: 531c. L'Arpège: 209bl. La Belle Aurore: 193br. La Marquière: 211bl. La Paloma: 335b. Le Pavillon de la Reine: 206bl. Le Place d'Armes Hotel: 234tl. Lehka hlava, Prague: 689tl. Locarno Film Festival: 589br. Luxembourg Tourist Office: 215bl. Maaemo: Bandar Abdul-Jauwad 633tl. Madame Tussaud's, London: 62clb. Magyar Nemzeti Muzeum: 698bc. MAK-Osterreichisches Museum fur ange wandte Kunst: 563cl. Markgrafliches Opernhaus: 516tl. Mary Evans Picture Library: 36tr, 38tr, 83bl, 89br, 112tl, 268cr, 568cb, 602tc, 636tc; Napoleon Bonaparte by David by 146tc. The Merrion Hotel: 138tc. Michael Jenner Photography: 126bc. Middlethorpe Hall: 106b. Motel One: 547tr. Musees Royeaux Des Beaux-arts De Belgique: 220bc. Museo Nacional del Prado (Spain): The Garden of Delights by Bosch 278bl. Museo Thyssen Bornemisza: Our Lady of the Dry Tree 276bl. Museu de Marinha: Manuel I by Alberto Cutileiro 338c; Portrait of Vasco da Gama 347br. Museum Amstelkring: 242tr. Museum Huis Lambert van Meerten, RBK: 255cl. Museum Jean Tinguely Basel: Christian Baur Basel 581tr. The National Museum of Ireland: 119c; Jonathan Swift 120ca. National Museums of Scotland: 36cla. National Gallery of Ireland: 119bc. The National Gallery, London: Paul Jackson 57tl. The National Trust Photo Library ©NTPL: 132br; Nick Meers 85c. Nicholas P Goulandris Foundation Museum of Cycladic and Ancient Greek Art: 450bl. Nippon Television Network Corporation: Original Sin by Michelangelo 380br. Nobu: Mark O'Flaherty 108br. Nordiska Museet: 609clb. Oronoz Archivo Fotográfico: 283cla, 289tc; J. A. Fernandez 294tr. Osteria da Rioba: 442tl. PA Photos: DPA, Germany 39tr, 514br, 526cla; EPA 497tr. Palac Kultury I Nauki: 711cr. Palais Het Loos: E Boeijinga 253bl. Palazzo Abadessa: 439tl. The Peat Inn: 109tr. Photoshot / World Pictures: 554bl, 693tl. Pilsner Urquell/ SABMiller: 685fcra. Robbie Polley: 226clb. Portixol: 332tl. Powerstock Photolibrary: 712tl; Mauritius Gallery 564b. Princes Czartoryski Museum and Library: Lady with an Ermine by Leonardo da Vinci 719cl. Prisma, Barcelona: The Fall of Granada 268tl. Hotel Rector: 331tr. Rex Features: Denis Cameron 315tr, PAID 74c, 75cr, 79c; Sipa Press 196tr. Rialto: 722bc. Richmond House: Blue Cloud Photography / Mark Bowditch 104bl. Rijksmuseum Amsterdam: The Wedding Portrait, c.1622 by Frans Hals 32tr; The Kitchen Maid by Vermer 248cl; St Elizabeths Day Flood 248cb; The Night Watch by Rembrandt 249tc; sculpture of St Catherine 249c; Woman at her Toilet by Jan Steen 249br; The Jewish Bride by Rembrandt 250br. Ritz: 330bl. RMN: Gilles or Pierrot c.1717 by Watteau, Louvre, Paris 32clb; Venus de Milo / The Louvre / Herve Lewandowski 160c; La Jaconde by

Leonardo Da Vinci / The Louvre / Lewandowski / LeMage 160cl. Robert Harding Picture Library: 31tr, 31cr, 35tr, 159bl, 171t, 269tr, 377br, 569tc, 584tr, 585tr, 585cla, 585clb, 587bl, 599br, 611tr, 644tr, 651b; K. Gillam 653bl; Simon Harris 568tl; Gavin Heller 701bl; G. Hellier 569b; Roy Rainford 493bl; Adina Tovy 46br; Adam Woolfitt 598cla, 637tr, 645tr. Rocabella Art Hotel: 486bl. The Royal Collection © Her Majesty Queen Elizabeth II: 69tl, 74tr, 75c, 75bl; Christ by Michelangelo 75tl; Her Majesty Queen Elizabeth II 68br, 68br. The Royal Crescent: 105tr. SABMiller: 526c. Salt & Brygga Restaurant: 617tc. Photo Scala, Florence: 403ca, 405cb, 425cl; After the Bath by Degas, Edgar 33ca; Galleria degli Uffizi, Florence 33crb; Cassone Adimari by Lo Scheggia / Galleria dell'Accademia 397b; Photo Scala, Florence - courtesy of the Ministero Beni e Att. Culturali 376clb, 376br, 378bc; Death of St. Martin by Martini / 388tr; The Deposition by Lorenzetti 388cl; David by Donatello / Bargello, Florence 400cl; Pope Leo X 402clb; The Procession of the Magi by Gozzoli 402-403c; Quattro Prigioni by Michelangelo 403tl; The Ognissanti Madonna / Galleria degli Uffizi 404c; The Birth of Venus by Botticelli / Galleria degli Uffizi 405cr; The Holy Family by Michelangelo / Galleria degli Uffizi 405br; Madonna of the Long Neck by Parmigianino / Galleria degli Uffizi 406tr; The Feast in the House of Levi by Veronese / Academia Venizia 423b. Herman Scholten: 237b. Science Museum: 64tl, 64bl. Scope: 186tr, 187c, 187br. Sea Horse: 663tl. Solar do Castelo: 362tl. Sonia Halliday Photographs: 43ca. Staatliche Kunstsammlungen, Dresden: Girl Reading a Letter by Vermeer 514tr. Staatsgalerie, Stuttgart: St. Paul in Prison, 1627, by Rembrandt 528tr. Stad Brugge Stedelijke Musea: Moreel Triptych by Hans Memling 228tc. Stadelsches Kunstinstitut und Stadlisches Galerie: Portrait of a Girl by Botticelli 532c. Statens Historiska Museum: 609c. Stiftung Preußisch Schlösser Und Gärten Berlin-Brandenburg: 513br. Stockphotos: David Hornback 267b. SuperStock: Johner 607br. Swiss National Museum, Zurich: 578c. Swiss National Park: 584clb, 584cb, 584bl. Swiss Tourist Board: 586br. Tate, London 2001: Marcus Lee 67tl. The Thief: Jason Strong & Mattias Hamren 632br. TopFoto.co.uk: 585cr. Toros Magazine: 283cr. The Travel Library: Galleria dell'Accademia 394bl. Travel Pictures: 644bl, 700tr. Courtesy Of The Board Of Trinity College, Dublin: Portrait of St Matthew from the Book of Kells 118c, 127tc. Van Gogh Museum, Amsterdam: The Bedroom at Arles by van Gogh / Courtesy of the Vincent van Gogh Foundation 251tl, 251c. Vasa Museum, Stockholm: Hans Hammarskiold 608bl. Victoria-Jungfrau Grand Hotel & Spa: 594br. Volcano Blue: 489bl. Wentzl: 723tl. Jeremy Whitaker: 83clb. Jeppe Wikstrom: 604cl, 606bc, 607tr. Christopher Wilson: 86bl. Wirtshaus in der Au: 550bl. Wonderful Copenhagen: 635b, 641tr, 643bl, 683tr. York Castle Museum: 87c. Zefa: 492cla, 527br, 528br, 533b.

Jacket: Front – 4Corners: Reinhard Schmid Main; DorlingKindersley: Demetrio Carrasco bl; Spine – 4Corners: Reinhard Schmid

All other images © Dorling Kindersley. See www.dkimages.com for more information.

Special Editions of DK Travel Guides

DK Travel Guides can be purchased in bulk quantities at discounted prices for use in promotions or as premiums. We are also able to offer special editions and personalized jackets, corporate imprints, and excerpts from all of our books, tailored specifically to meet your own needs.

To find out more, please contact:
in the United States SpecialSales@dk.com
in the UK travelspecialsales@uk.dk.com
in Canada DK Special Sales at general@tourmaline.ca
in Australia business.development@pearson.com.au

Europe's Rail Network

It was in Britain that railroads were first developed in the second quarter of the 19th century, and Europe is still crisscrossed by tens of thousands of kilometers of track. Only the main routes are shown on this map. Although many lines are badly in need of modernization, the main intercity routes use high-speed, comfortable trains, making this a quick and convenient form of transportation for many journeys both within and between countries (see p26). London to Paris, for example, takes just over two hours, and you can travel from Paris to Marseille in the same time. Prices vary considerably from country to country. In Great Britain, for example, standard tickets are almost three times the price for equivalent journeys in Italy. Details on the train services of individual countries are given in the *Travel Information* sections of the appropriate chapters.